Illustrations by
Jerry A. Vanderlinde

THE ART OF WAR
IN THE WESTERN WORLD

THE ART
OF WAR
IN THE
WESTERN
WORLD

ARCHER JONES

UNIVERSITY OF ILLINOIS PRESS
Urbana and Chicago

Library of Congress Cataloging-in-Publication Data

Jones, Archer, 1926–
 The art of war in the Western world.

 Includes index.
 1. Military art and science—History. 2. Military
history. I. Title.
U27.J65 1987   355'.099   86-25017
ISBN 0-252-01380-8 (alk. paper)

For
Helen Johnston Skinner
and
Joanne Leach Jones

CONTENTS

LIST OF SCHEMATICS

LIST OF TABLES

LIST OF DIAGRAMS

LIST OF ILLUSTRATIONS

LIST OF MAPS

INTRODUCTION

The Art of War in the Western World is not a traditional history of war. Its purpose is to trace and explain, at an introductory and somewhat advanced level, the changes in certain operational variables over most of the span of Western warfare for which we have a record. These constitute the themes of the work, which thus contains more emphasis on explication than is usual in a narrative history. Nevertheless, most important campaigns and battles receive the attention they merit, though with economy of phrase and accent on aspects that support and illustrate the interpretations presented. Although continuity provides a major motif, the story necessarily stresses change. This inevitably leads to some distortions in emphasis when compared to a work that has narrative history as its primary goal. For example, the treatment of the Roman art of war receives brief attention, only enough to show how it differed from the Greek and Alexandrian models that preceded it and that are described in greater detail.

This book has a narrow focus: it considers only selected operational variables, omitting all noncognitive aspects of such history and leaving virtually all of the affective domain of warfare, such as morale and motivation, to such experts as John Keegan in history and Morris Janowitz in sociology. It ignores not only most political factors but also the new military history of the environment of armed forces. It defines strategy narrowly, deleting most grand strategy and the integration of political, economic, military, and naval ends and means. This results in understating the strategic role of seapower, leaving most of its treatment separate and to an approach analogous to that used for presenting warfare on land. By not including much of both the traditional and new content of military history, I do not mean to derogate them. On the contrary, all receive competent attention from others. But today operational history seems to suffer from neglect, and I hope that this work, in restating and trying to give shape to much of what we know about this field, is an assertion that the new military history should also revive and improve analytical operational history.

One of the implicit themes of this book is that military factors suffice to explain most military events. The exposition of this thesis does not intend to disparage the significance of other causes nor to deny multiple causation. Rather, it wishes to give more, and deserved, prominence to endogenous causes of military events. In the process I have exaggerated my case in making this point as well as in giving so much salience and certainty to my themes. Sometimes I did this by design, and often, I am sure, by too much zeal for an interpretation. The cases of intentional overemphasis overstate and repeat the point to insure that it is fully understood. I ask your indulgence at these times.

In offering the rational and logical in military behavior, I do not mean to deny the importance of the influence of the quality of military leadership, good and bad, and of the only occasionally mentioned considerations that reduced military efficiency without contributing to the attainment of political or other objectives. But just as the aggregate of all economic behavior tends toward the rational satisfaction of needs, so also have most military methods and organization over time tended to forward military goals. In part, this presentation stresses the reasonableness of the conduct of war, to counter quick judgments sometimes made about the past in the light of present knowledge and conditions that are not wholly applicable to conditions and constraints existing earlier.

This book has much in common with those of Carl von Clausewitz and Antoine Henri Jomini, who offered powerful interpretations of the warfare of the Napoleonic era and the period immediately preceding. It differs, however, in a number of respects, most conspicuously in its presentation of the history upon which I base my generalizations, rather than, as in *On War* and *Summary of the Art of War*, a mere reference to the campaigns and battles and a reliance on a reader's familiarity with them. Although I do not know the specific source of many of the themes in this book, most I owe to these masters and to others of more recent vintage. For example, for my understanding of the difficulty of forcing battle in warfare before Napoleon and for the significance of the new system of deployment, I am indebted to Jean Lambert Alphonse Colin. I am obligated to J. F. C. Fuller for the concept of logistic strategy and to B. H. Liddell Hart for the primacy of the defense, though, I suspect, I first learned this indirectly through his influence as expressed in the popular press just before World War II. Mao Tse-tung contributed significantly to my ideas on guerrilla warfare. Clausewitz and Jomini are so much a part of the culture of military writers that I can attribute nothing to them directly, other than Jomini's interior lines and Clausewitz's characterization of simultaneous advances on exterior lines as a concentration in time.

Although I intend for this book to be understood by readers with little or no knowledge of European warfare or the fundamentals of operations, by combining the insights of so many acknowledged masters, I hope also to appeal to the more sophisticated. But in striving to reach such a broad audience, I elaborate and recapitulate ideas familiar to such experts. These readers might consider reading the last chapter first and then using the contents, expository schematics, and the index to read the parts that then seem most relevant to their needs. Do remember, however, that the narrative explains the history that gave rise to the generalizations as well as illustrates their applicability, and for that reason alone should interest all readers.

This account of Western warfare, which makes no pretense at originality, came from the standard secondary works. It has no notes, other than references to the source of quotations, and has no bibliography other than the works of the masters of this kind of history already mentioned. For those who wish to pursue the subject of European warfare, William H. McNeill's *The Pursuit of Power* addresses the subject at the highest level of generalization. Richard A. Preston and Sydney F. Wise's *Men in Arms* places this work in context, and Theodore Ropp's *War in the Modern World* offers a wise and comprehensive treatment of the modern period. All of these provide good bibliographical references as does John E. Jessup, Jr., and Robert W. Coakley's valuable *Guide to the Study and Use of Military History*.

I dedicate this book to my mother, who encouraged my interests, in spite of her dismay at their military bent, and sustained me through an overlong period as a student. The dedication to my wife reflects my gratitude for her encouragement and her important help with my writing, both as editor and teacher. I am indebted to North Dakota State University for a development leave in 1982–83 to do the bulk of the writing and to the U.S. Army Command and General Staff College for the stimulating opportunities presented when I served as Morrison Professor in 1976–77.

My friend and colleague Andrew Keogh has over many years provided indispensable criticism and encouragement as I gradually evolved the interpretations presented here. I am also indebted to others who read and critiqued the manuscript: Robert A. Doughty, Jeffery A. Gunsburg, Malcolm Muir, Theodore Ropp, and T. R. Young. I owe much to the faculty of the History Committee of the Command and General Staff College in 1976–77 for teaching me a great deal about war as well as military history. Among these, in addition to Colonel Doughty, Theodore Crackel, L. D. F. Frasché, and Harold W. Nelson each gave me particularly valuable help. I am grateful to Susan L. Patterson for her superb editing. Others to whom I am indebted include John W. Aljets, D. K. Cliff, Owen S. Connelly, E. W. Gale, John Helgeland, Gail Hokenson, and Michael Lyons. The help of all of these, and many others, reduced greatly the errors of interpretation as well as of fact; what remain are, of course, my own responsibility.

1

ANCIENT
WARFARE

A study of the conduct of Western military operations most easily begins with the ancient Greeks as scholars have learned a good deal concerning how the Greeks fought 2,500 years ago. The Greeks also present a good starting point because operational methods much like those they developed long dominated the Mediterranean basin. The Greeks also lend themselves well to introducing the art of war because their military system evolved from the simple to the complex. Initially they relied almost exclusively on shock action, fighting hand-to-hand with clubs, swords, or spears. Only gradually did they adopt missile weapons such as the bow and arrow, and they proved equally slow in employing these two modes of combat, shock and missile, when mounted on horses. Since their methods of supply and strategy also progressed slowly from the elementary to the sophisticated, they provide, in these branches of the military art as well, a model that facilitates the study of the subject.

Although an analytical approach has obvious disadvantages, including obscuring a great deal about the course of ancient military history itself, this type of scrutiny facilitates attention to fundamental variables, clarifies the process of change, and, by making causation in warfare more comprehensible, lays a better foundation for understanding subsequent eras.

An analytical approach to military operations permits one to divide the topic according to the three major components of the art of war: tactics, logistics, and strategy. Tactics deals with combat and with the weapons, methods, and maneuvers on the battlefield. Logistics concerns providing the men themselves and the support of military operations, including the movement of armies and navies and the supply of weapons, food, clothing, and shelter for the soldiers and sailors. Strategy integrates tactics and logisitics to determine the military objectives and the means of carrying them out. Naval warfare lends itself best to a separate treatment.

TACTICS

Hand-to-Hand Combat on Foot

The early tactics of the ancient Greeks exemplify the most basic form of combat. The Greeks fought on foot, hand-to-hand, with spear and sword, in a form of fighting known as shock action. The Greek soldiers, called hoplites, naturally protected themselves with shields, helmets, and breastplates and covered other parts of their body as well. This usually metal armor, together with sword and spear, constituted a substantial burden, which made running difficult, and gave these soldiers their name, heavy infantry.

The completeness and quality of their equipment made up the only professional attributes of the Greek hoplites. Militiamen, they had full-time occupations as farmers, artisans, and tradesmen, furnished their own armor, had engaged in some training, and tried to keep in good physical condition. Though this constituted the extent of their preparation for war, coming from the same community and having participated in group exercises provided the men with some cohesion, feelings of mutual interdependence, and group esprit. Albeit armed with a short sword, the hoplites relied mainly on a spear about seven feet long. The tactical formation adopted by the Greeks supported their morale in the frightening experience of combat, the spearmen standing shoulder to shoulder at least four and usually eight or even more ranks deep.

Such a formation, called a phalanx, admirably suited the militia. The civilian soldiers, who had little training, could fight with courage behind a wall of shields bristling with spears. The presence of others, often friends from civilian life, gave confidence to all, and the deep array meant that the men in the front felt well supported. The combatants thus sustained their morale with the feeling of safety in numbers. Their physical condition, practice with weapons, and, for some, the experience of a previous combat buttressed their bravery in battle, the outcome of which usually decided the campaign. But before the combat, the hoplite commander usually addressed them to raise their confidence and courage. The men shouted as they charged to embolden one another.

Only the front rank fought; the second rank waited to fill the places of the fallen or fatigued. Because of the depth of the formation, those in the rear did not have much involvement and felt little hesitation in leading a retreat if the front ranks showed signs of giving way. Although they often fought with skill and valor, the Greek militiamen had no compunction about acknowledging defeat and trying to live to carry on their civilian occupations, if not to fight another day.

That the small city-states of Greece normally fought wars for limited objectives made it easy for them to admit defeat; the loss of a battle had only limited consequences and, though the casualties of the vanquished usually exceeded those of the victor, rarely did either side suffer heavily.

The comparative value of a deep formation as contrasted with a shallower array is not clear. Four ranks may have sufficed for veterans and eight seemed ample for green militia; but on occasion the troops formed twelve, sixteen, thirty-two, and even fifty ranks deep. One school of thought believes that the deeper the group, the more power it possessed, the extra men in the rear ranks supplying an impetus that enabled the deep array to overwhelm a similarly armed but shallower formation. The opponents of this view insist that only the front rank fought. The second rank constituted an immediate reserve to take the place of the men in the front when they were killed, wounded, or exhausted by the hard work of hand-to-hand fighting. Additional ranks served only as reserves for the second, and proponents of a thin line see a depth of more than four ranks as redundant. The opponents of the deep order also argue that the men in the rear could merely stand and wait: any pushing from behind would only jostle the men in the front, hardly a good way to help.

Proponents argue that the large numbers behind probably strengthened the morale of those in front, intimidated the enemy, and provided ample replacements to feed the frontal fight. A deeper array also had an advantage if there was any thinning of the ranks, for example, to fill in gaps created in marching the line forward in the advance to combat. Since the men could have difficulty maintaining a uniform depth of the line before and during the combat, the additional ranks provided insurance against a line too thin at some locations and the consequent potentially disastrous break in the continuous front. The deeper formation could also provide a physical impetus, especially when picked men constituted the last rank. These rear-rank men would not only prevent straggling and keep the middle ranks in their places but also supply an impulse that could be transmitted to the front ranks by causing all men to push. If, as sometimes happened with the Greeks, the front ranks faced each other shield-to-shield, shoving, this push from the rear could enable one side to force back the other and precipitate a retreat.

Still, the soldier and historian Xenophon once asked: "When a phalanx is too deep for the men to reach the enemy with their weapons, what harm do you think they do to the enemy or good to their friends?" Nevertheless, the Greeks, on at least some occasions, found use for the rear ranks in deep array. Perhaps the possibility of a pushing contest alone warranted the extra depth, in spite of its cost in terms of the breadth of the line.[1]

In mountainous Greece the opposing spearmen sought level ground for their battles. Normally the defender could hope to enjoy a significant benefit by, for example, choosing a site on a slope so that the attackers would have to advance and fight uphill. But the uphill position had so great an advantage that attackers usually declined to engage, avoided the enemy's army, and destroyed his crops instead. Thus defenders rarely enjoyed any dominance, battles being fought by mutual consent on open, level ground.

The deep, compact formation had virtually no power to maneuver; it could only advance to the front or flee to the rear. The early phalanx of hoplites had no subdivision that would have helped to carry out elementary movements by permitting men on a flank, for example, to respond to an order to face in a different direction. Such deficiency in articulation inhered in the nature of the formation and in the essentially amateur character of the militia. Subdivision and practice by subunits in exercises useful in battle required groups that constantly drilled together under subordinate officers. Greek citizen-soldiers lacked this practice.

The hoplite force of the city-state Sparta did have a capacity for maneuver based on subdivision of its phalanx. As Greece's only professional army, the Spartans marched to music and developed a battlefield drill based on the tendency of all phalanxes to drift to the right as they advanced. This proclivity stemmed from the large shield carried on the left arm, which, because it safeguarded his neighbor's unshielded right side, caused each soldier unconsciously to move toward his right. This meant that the right wing of each phalanx usually overlapped the opposing left and won the battle on that side. The Spartans exploited this by turning their right side to the left and completing the defeat of the enemy by attacking the opposing phalanx's unprotected flank.

The Spartans thus used their limited, but superior, articulation to carry out the most basic tactical movement in war, capitalizing on the weakness of the flank. This exploitation could take the form used by the Spartans, assailing the enemy soldier's vulnerable side, or it could rely on going around the flank to reach and assault the enemy's rear, a movement called an envelopment. Either of these maneuvers conferred an overwhelming advantage on the attacker because, although he could not expect the defender lamely to present his side or back to his assailant, the defender beset in flank or rear obviously had a serious hindrance in combat, since he had arrayed himself to fight in one direction and must suddenly fight in another. This disadvantage might not be the greatest drawback that the flanked or enveloped enemy faced; his confidence and morale received what may have proved a more serious blow, and he might not stay to fight in his new position. Of course, disciplined and experienced troops did better, as did a well-articulated force that had subdivision enough to turn and face a threat to flank or rear.

But the phalangeal formation had only limited capability for flank attacks and none to maneuver to reach the enemy's rear. Thus the tactics of the day left little scope for generalship, and because the leader had no role once the battle had begun, the general usually fought in the ranks to encourage his men. Innovations in tactics consisted of strengthening the usually overlapped left of an army while holding back the then-weakened right. But this response did not require much ability to maneuver because the tactical innovation rested on the battle plan made in advance, one reflected in the initial array of the army. The phalanx, an admirable formation to defend against a frontal assault, lacked any capacity for offensive action other than to engage in a frontal fight.

As the art of war became more sophisticated and professional soldiers began to replace milita, the phalanx became better drilled and more able to maneuver. The Spartans matured a technique that systemized the tendency of the right to overlap the hostile left. Before the battle began, but after the combatants had formed their lines, the right-hand segment of the well-drilled Spartan line would face to the right and march forward, thus detaching itself from the main force but remaining an extension of the line of battle. After a short march to the right as a column, the portion would turn left toward the enemy and continue until they had reached the line along which the enemy had arrayed its army. The Spartans' separated detachment then halted, faced to the left, and advanced in line of battle to attack the enemy's flank (schematic 1.1).

Spartans

Schematic 1.1. Spartans' Flanking Maneuver

In this geometrically correct flanking position, the segment then moved forward and defeated the enemy's less well-disciplined phalanx, fully retrieving any reverse suffered by their own overlapped left flank. Meanwhile, the often-defeated Thebans had evolved their own tactic of strengthening their left wing by increasing its depth. The Spartan system had won two significant battles against less-disciplined and sophisticated opponents, and the Thebans had enjoyed one modest success. Meanwhile, the Thebans embellished their new tactics by creating the Sacred Band, a picked force of 300 men who could maneuver separately from their phalanx.

The Theban and Spartan systems met in combat at the Battle of Leuctra in 371 B.C. Each knew the other's method, the Spartans expecting the deep Theban formation and the Thebans anticipating the Spartan's flank-attack march. The Spartans relied on their standard maneuver, but Epaminondas, the brilliant Theban commander, had the plans and the skill to counter it. He had formed most of his hoplites fifty deep, creating a solid mass with a depth half its breadth. With these he faced the Spartan right, his right and the Spartan left both hanging back and having little participation in the battle. In reserve, behind his main hoplite force, he kept the elite Sacred Band. In preparing so well for the daunting task of fighting the awesome Spartans, Epaminondas early displayed that "particular combination of prudence and daring" that the historian Xenophon thought characterized his later campaigns.[2]

When the Spartans began the execution of their march to the right and formation at right angles to the Theban line, Epaminondas realized what they were doing. He then led his deep hoplite array diagonally across the field to attack the extreme right of the Spartan line, and, from the Sacred Band's position in the rear of his phalanx, Epaminondas sent these picked men on a separate maneuver on the field. The Sacred Band carried out its preplanned, independent action to assail the Spartan detachment lining up to prepare its attack on the flank of the Theban hoplites. The combined effect of these maneuvers overwhelmed much of the Spartan right, inflicting great casualties and winning the battle in which the Spartan king died.

This contest between these two hoplite armies demonstrates that the Greeks had grasped the value of concentration, the Thebans seeking this through depth in their formation. Similarly the Greeks saw the value of attacking weakness, the Spartans using their maneuver to place part of their phalanx at right angles to the enemy's line to assault the enemy's vulnerable flank. But the movements on the battlefield also clearly exhibit the intrinsic difficulty of maneuvering infantry even on the level, treeless plain where the Thebans and Spartans fought.

Without an array, infantry became a mob that could neither move nor fight in an organized way. But to maneuver groups of men, especially lines, presented enormous difficulties. Even a line advancing on a level plain had great trouble keeping alignment and preventing gaps. With their line extending farther to the right than the Thebans', the Spartans could have easily carried out their envelopment by wheeling the end of their line to the left until it formed the bar of a T with the Theban line—if a line of infantry could carry out a wheeling movement. But such a movement required the soldiers on the circumference of the wheel to march farther and faster than those closer to the pivot. It is almost impossible to carry this out and have the troops arrive properly aligned and formed for battle. Gaps in a line of spearmen could have meant defeat because they exposed the men's vulnerable sides to an adversary's unbroken line. Even a diagonal move across a battlefield was hard, the Thebans executing it without difficulty because their great depth meant that they had a very narrow front. The Theban Sacred Band could carry out their separate maneuver because they used only 300 well-drilled, picked men for an essentially preplanned, perhaps rehearsed, task.

The preplanned, stilted character of the Spartan enveloping movement also dramatizes the difficulty of maneuvering infantry in line on a battlefield. Leaders could desire envelopments and might wish to change dispositions or maneuver during a battle, but infantry in phalanx lacked the capacity to execute the needed movements. Even Epaminondas fought in the ranks to encourage his men; he had no better task, since he could not influence the course of the battle after it had begun.

Combat on Foot with Missiles

The combat of heavy infantry arrayed in small compact formations admirably fit the terrain of Greece, a mountainous country without many large level spaces. Missile fighting required more room. Nevertheless, the Greeks did use men armed with missiles, most often as auxiliaries to their heavy infantry.

The Greeks evolved three kinds of missile infantry. The archer, the most effective of these, could shoot his complement of fifteen to twenty arrows eighty to a hundred yards. The arrow lacked penetrating power against a hoplite's shield or breastplate, but the number of arrows available and the nasty wounds they could inflict on an unarmored portion of a hoplite's body made the archer a potentially formidable weapon system.

Although a good bow and handmade arrows represented a significant investment, the archer's equipment cost much less than the hoplite's armor, spear, and sword. But the man himself was more expensive, if only because of the longer training needed to acquire the skill needed to shoot an arrow quickly and accurately. In addition, the archer had to fight as an individual rather than as a member of a group, a feat demanding more skill, initiative, and morale than that needed by the hoplite, fighting shoulder-to-shoulder with his fellow hoplites.

The Greek economy of the sixth century B.C., barely above the subsistence level, made time a scarce resource. For the same reason that they could afford few regular soldiers, the Greeks did not have as many citizens who had the leisure to keep up the constant practice necessary to become good archers. These effective but relatively expensive weapons remained comparatively rare in Greece, except in combat at sea, where the range of the arrow gave it prominence.

The archer fought individually because he could not use the heavy infantry's tactical formation. Had archers armored themselves and formed a dense array, the hoplites could easily have rendered the bows useless by coming to close quarters and quite literally slaughtering the archers. The bowmen wore no armor, enabling them easily to run away from the heavily burdened hoplites. By keeping their distance, archers could avoid shock action and use their missile weapons. But since running and shooting is easier as an individual than in a formation, Greek archers did not usually fight as a coordinated, mutually dependent group. Because they lacked the weight of armor, they were called light infantry, and they had greater speed on the march as well as in tactical situations. Their method of depending on missiles and more on individual than group action has ever since been called light infantry tactics.

Another form of light infantry armed themselves with slings. Even with the small outlay for the sling and the frequent use of rocks for ammunition, the immense difficulty in accurately using a sling resulted in a scarcity of competent slingers. Releasing the missile at the precise moment to insure propelling it in the proper direction required, quite literally, a lifetime of practice. Most slingers came from the island of Rhodes, where inhabitants traditionally relied on the sling as a weapon, even teaching children its use. The sling had yet another drawback: slingers required plenty of space between each other, and it was difficult to have many in one place and thus to develop much firepower. The sling had a slight advantage over the bow in range, and if the slingers used lead slugs instead of rocks, they could carry fifty of these, double or triple the number of arrows archers carried.

The third kind of light infantry consisted of the man equipped with a javelin. Throwing a spear required far less skill than using a bow or sling, and several javelins cost less than a bow and a quiver of arrows. Still, the javelin had the

Illustration 1.1. Light Infantry

drawbacks of its short effective range, rarely more than twenty yards, and the small number a man could carry. But it was possible for a soldier to reuse his javelin, the large, durable weapon being more easily retrieved than the small, fragile arrow or the tiny shot of the sling. Because of its inexpensive cost, the relative ease of learning to use it, and its suitability in cramped fighting areas, men armed with the javelin became the predominant light infantry weapon system in Greece.

In spite of its inflexibility and the vulnerability of its flanks, the hoplite phalanx, adapted to Greece's terrain and social organization, proved to be an efficient weapon system. The expensive equipment protected the soldier in close combat, an essential requirement against the thrust of spear and sword and the cutting of a sword. The costly equipment, a durable, long-term investment, combined with the tactical system made possible the use of an inexpensive militiaman. The well-equipped amateur could fight effectively in an array eight or even sixteen deep, which suited his weapons, sustained his morale, and required a minimum of skill.

Mounted Combat

Greeks also fought on horseback, but mounted warfare did not initially divide into the two distinct methods of fighting characteristic of the infantry—shock and missile action—in part because mounted combat suffered the serious handicap of horsemen riding without the aid of stirrups. None of the ancient civilizations, Chinese, Indian, Egyptian, Mesopotamian, Greek, or Roman, had invented stirrups, and without them a rider had to depend on the pressure of his knees to hold himself on his horse. This feeble seat made it awkward for a soldier, especially an unpracticed rider, to fight mounted. Even to throw a javelin could prove trying, and to strike with a cutting sword and miss might even cause the rider to lose his seat. Nevertheless, Greek cavalry fought in a variety of ways: at a distance with javelins; at close quarters with spears; or even dismounting and fighting on foot. Often the rider wore armor and sometimes the horse had protection.

The men mounted in this way made a weapon system distinctly inferior to infantry. They could not expect to charge heavy infantry successfully because the men on foot had better weapons for shock action and a more secure fighting platform, the ground. Equally, the mounted men had a disadvantage in engaging light infantry with missiles. The foot soldiers' superior fighting platform gave them a distinct advantage. Men on foot could outfight those mounted because they had only one task—to fight. The men on horseback had to control their mounts as well as fight.

But the cavalry's superior mobility gave it one formidable advantage over the infantry. Though a group of cavalry might lack subdivision and any articulation, it could use its mobility to attack the flank or rear of a phalanx. The weakness of the stirrupless cavalry should mean that such an attack with shock action presented little real threat to heavy infantry in battle, provided the men on foot could face their assailants. Even though the heavy infantry could not reply to an attack with javelins thrown from horseback, the battle of the heavy infantry would very likely end before the javelin attack on the rear could have much opportunity to affect the outcome.

But this calculation offered small consolation to soldiers who risked being struck by a horseman's javelin. Such a flank or rear attack would have a tremendous psychological effect, coming as it did from an unexpected direction against troops not arrayed to meet it. The horses themselves would add another cause of demoralization, for they would look large and menacing. A Greek general sought to dispel this fearful aspect of cavalry by telling his infantry that "no man ever perished in battle from being bitten or kicked by a horse. The foot soldier can strike harder and with truer aim than the horseman, who is precariously poised on his steed, and is as much afraid of falling off as he is afraid of the enemy."[3]

Because of their superior mobility and their ability to go into action without dismounting, cavalry, compared with the slow-moving infantry, might well be called offensive troops, assailing the enemy's vulnerable flank and rear. But because the cost of horses made mounted men an expensive weapon system and since skill in riding required much practice, the Greeks had little cavalry. Also

Greece offered few pastures, and cavalry had difficulty operating in much of Greece's rugged terrain.

Fortification and Siegecraft

The Greeks protected their cities with walls, fortified hills, and defiles. Frequently building with stone and taking advantage of inequalities in the terrain, they made fortifications difficult to assail. Further, militia armies often lacked both the skill needed to attack fortifications and soldiers who could stay away from their civilian occupations to conduct a long blockade. The empires of Asia, however, with their professional armies, developed sophisticated siege methods against their often more vulnerable walls and towers, many times built on level terrain with mud bricks.

Fortifications effectively took the place of many soldiers on the defense and were in a sense a substitution of capital for labor, a good replacement because of their efficiency. Unlike the soldiers they supplanted, fortifications required neither food nor fodder, vastly simplifying the defenders' supply problems. In addition, they efficiently combined the defensive merits of light and heavy infantry. Walls and ditches presented a more formidable barrier than a shield wall, the defenders of the wall usually having an advantage in hand-to-hand fighting with the attackers. Also, the defenders, functioning as light infantry in directing missiles at the attackers, enjoyed the protection against missiles provided by the wall as well as the advantage of range and velocity the height of the wall gave to their missiles.

Fortifications, however, were by their nature immobile, and an equal investment in soldiers offered more versatility if less power on the defense. Of course, fortifications could aid the offense by so economizing soldiers defending one place as to allow a superior concentration for offensive action elsewhere. Because walls were easy to defend, the use of fortifications to protect cities was widespread and sensible, and the inhabitants of the cities provided an immediately available reservoir of unskilled but useful defenders.

Fortifications have existed from primitive times, and early on had the two essential characteristics that they have retained until the present. (1) They should present an obstacle to attackers, the simplest barrier being a thorn hedge. (2) Fortifications should also offer protection for defenders, such as an earthen bank or bulwark behind a ditch. A palisade in the ditch or on the bank strengthened the obstacle. Since the earth from the ditch furnished the material for the bank, soldiers or laborers could construct such a fortifiction quickly, and because soldiers could erect them speedily, they were called field fortifications, to distinguish them from carefully engineered, permanent fortifications, usually constructed of masonry.

The ancients had developed permanent fortifications in the form of the stone or brick wall. In addition to height, a wall needed enough thickness to resist battering and to provide a fighting platform for the defenders on top. To reduce costs, builders erected inner and outer walls of masonry, which they filled in with stones or earth; they paved the top to provide the fighting platform. They built the outer wall higher than the fighting platform and crenelated it to provide the defenders with protected positions for fighting, shooting arrows, or throwing other missiles at attackers.

Military engineers supplemented the wall with a ditch, the excavation of which supplied filler for the wall. The ditch also increased the effective height of the wall and helped to form a barrier to efforts to batter it down. Builders soon strengthened the wall by building in towers at intervals, which furnished a significant addition to the defensive power: jutting out beyond the face of the wall, the towers provided a fighting platform from which the defenders could direct enfilade fire against attackers, and assaults on the tower would face the same enfilade fire from the defenders of the wall. Because of the higher effectiveness of shooting at a soldier's flank and the often greater ease and safety of discharging missiles at soldiers attacking an adjacent tower or wall than throwing projectiles downward at one's own attackers, this principle of mutual support has remained fundamental in the design and defense of fortifications since ancient times.

Asians developed elaborate fortification long before the Greeks. As far back as 2000 B.C., Nineveh on the Tigris River is said, doubtless with much exaggeration, to have had a defended perimeter fifty miles long with walls 120 feet high and 30 feet thick supported by 1,500 towers. Such a stress on fortification naturally called forth a sophisticated system of attack, which Asiatic armies had also developed to a high state of perfection.

Among their siege methods, the Asiatics employed two ways of coping with walls. The first, avoiding the wall, consisted of going over the wall with ladders or movable towers, which worked well on level terrain. Far more effective than ladders, movable towers had to be higher than the wall attacked. The largest such towers required solid wood wheels as much as 12 feet in diameter and 4 feet thick. To protect against efforts to set them on fire, towers had rawhides as coverings and even had their own fire-fighting water supply. Shooting down upon the defenders, archers at the top of the tower cleared the wall and lowered a drawbridge in the tower; the attackers rushed onto the wall to take possession. In reality, the attackers had accomplished little: they controlled only the top of the wall between the adjacent towers whose defenders shot at them with arrows from the crenelated defenses that commanded the wall. The attackers also lacked stairways to the ground, for only the defenders' towers had stairs. Movable towers had greater utility for dominating the defenders of the wall, so that other means of attack could proceed more readily.

Tunneling under the wall, the second method of avoiding the wall, also undermined it, one of the two basic methods of destroying a wall. This technique involved excavating galleries under the wall, which the attackers supported with wooden props. When the gallery or mine had reached the proper size, the attackers destroyed the wall by burning the props and the fall of the mine caused

Illustration 1.2. Siege Tower

the wall to collapse. Defenders countermined, either to cave in the attackers' unfinished galleries or to enter their tunnels and drive out the workmen.

The battering ram offered the other method of destroying the wall. The attackers placed the battering ram under a strong movable shed and brought it up to the wall by filling in the ditch. Then, using slings or rollers to move the ram, men worked it to knock down the wall, a technique more effective against brick than stone. This activity, like opening a mine entrance close to the wall, required that the attackers have cover furnished by trenches, ramparts, and overhead protection. Domination of the adjacent wall by a movable tower facilitated the work of battering or opening a mine. A less effective and demanding form of attack consisted of picking at a wall to dislodge stones or bricks rather than battering to shake down the whole structure.

Both attackers and defenders had artillery whose missiles depended on the thrust provided by counterweights, tension on animal sinew, or torsion on twisted ropes or animal sinew. Because of its range and power, artillery found many uses in a siege. Some machines could hurl missiles as far as 600 yards and literally batter down a wall with projectiles as heavy as 600 pounds. Attackers and defenders could also use artillery to throw burning substances or noxious objects such as dead animals or people.

These are only some of the great variety of equipment and methods used in the attack and defense of fortified places. Clearly, in a siege the defenders obviously enjoyed an advantage even against sophisticated and well-equipped attackers. But, given enough time, a sufficient superiority in men and materiel, and adequate means to supply the besiegers, the attack would prevail.

Besiegers sometimes built their own walls, usually earthen field fortifications, around the city. Called lines of contravallation, these helped besiegers resist the sorties of the besieged as well as fully interdicting the city's communication with the outside. Often besiegers had to contend with an army trying to rescue the city and sometimes protected themselves with fortified camps or even lines of circumvallation, a second ring of field fortification facing outward to ward off the relieving army.

If the besiegers could completely blockade the city, they could eventually starve it out if they could supply their own army long enough. Even for armies with sophisticated siege methods, a successful siege required a great superiority, one adequate to overcome the defenders, ensure an adequate flow of supplies, and defeat or keep at bay any relieving army.

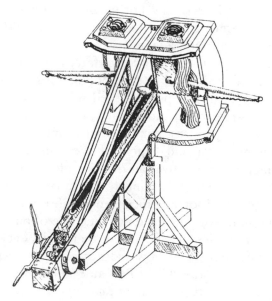

Illustration 1.3. Siege Artillery

Greek Heavy Infantry against Persian Light Infantry and Cavalry

When the Greeks met the vast Persian Empire, they faced not only experts in fortification but also masters of a well-developed military system that had evolved over several thousand years. Originally relying on spears, axes, and maces because of a lack of ferrous metals to fashion good swords, the armies of Egypt and western Asia developed differently from those of the Greeks. For instance, they created a composite bow of such power that it could shoot effectively to a distance of several hundred yards. This weapon came to dominate much of their warfare, giving an advantage to states that had the technical knowledge to produce it and the resources to make large numbers and to provide men with the skill and strength to use it.

Having much level terrain, particularly in Mesopotamia, the Asians stressed mobility because they could harness asses to chariots and use them as fighting platforms, first for a man with a javelin and later for a bowman. Chariots carried a driver and at least one bowman. Because the driver usually had a spear and the chariot could carry at least one spearman in addition to the bowman, the chariot could also engage in combat at close quarters with its spearmen fighting either in the chariot or dismounted.

As they completed the protracted task of mastering the horse, the Asians not only harnessed two of them to their chariots but also began to fight mounted on the horse itself. Eventually, with the development of the saddle, a skilled rider learned the difficult lesson of controlling his horse while using both hands to shoot a bow. In part because a horseman cost far less than a chariot and could negotiate terrain impassable for a wheeled vehicle, the cavalryman gradually superseded the charioteer. The horseman also fought at close quarters, usually with a spear. Bowmen continued to dominate among the infantry, though heavy infantry had an important role in sieges.

Long engaged in almost continuous warfare, the Asiatic monarchies had permanent armies. Small in relation to their populations, these armies consisted of expert professionals, proficient parts of their weapon systems, who practiced sophisticated and well-integrated modes of warfare. These full-time soldiers provided a foundation for the vast empires that characterized the region.

In establishing the latest and largest of these immense monarchies, the Persians had extended their rule over all of the region from India to the Mediterranean, including Egypt and Asia Minor. They also maintained a professional army composed largely of foot bowmen and cavalry and combined these by deploying their light infantry in the center of their line of battle and their cavalry on each flank. Persian tactics depended less than did Greek on coordination within the group since shooting a bow did not require the help of others. In fighting other light infantry, the skilled Persian regular bowmen arrayed themselves several ranks deep and relied on their rapid and accurate barrage of arrows to halt attackers at bow distance. Here depth of formation conferred an advantage not found in shock action. When phalanx fought phalanx, the rear ranks could not participate; for the most part they provided moral support to the front rank and replacements for the fallen. But with overhead fire by arrows, the second ranks of the Persians could fire effectively and at a distance: with a high trajectory for the arrows, additional ranks could shoot over the heads of the ranks ahead and direct their arrows down upon the enemy beyond the front rank. So the Persians grouped their light infantry in a shallow line, the men equipped with a large wicker shield for protection against hostile arrows and sometimes with an assistant to carry and hold the shield. They wore no armor and, often armed only with a dagger, had no real equipment for close combat.

Standing at bow distance, the Persian infantry disorganized the enemy's infantry with arrows. The Persian cavalry, armed with short spears, daggers, and bows or javelins, then left its position, poised on the flanks, and charged the enemy's flank, completing its defeat. The antithesis of the Greek way of war, the Persian tactical system relied on a combination of two weapon systems, the Greek on only one. The Persians depended on cavalry and light infantry, both auxiliaries in the Greek system, and made little use of the Greek mainstay, heavy infantry.

In fighting heavy infantry the Persians did not rely on the tactic of keeping their distance and destroying the enemy with their missiles while using the superior speed of their light infantry archers to evade any charge by the heavy infantry. Instead, the Persians depended on a flank attack by their professional cavalry to halt the heavy infantry. Charged by cavalry, the flanks of the heavy infantry formation would halt to fend off the attack, thus bringing the entire charge to a standstill within range of the Persian bows. The hail of missiles from the Persian infantry line and the cavalry on the flanks would then defeat the motionless heavy infantry.

The first clash between these two radically distinct tactical systems occurred at Marathon in 490 B.C., under circumstances that placed the Persians at a considerable disadvantage. Having come to Greece by sea, the Persian army lacked many of their decisive offensive arm, the horsemen. The conflict, which took place on a plain beside the sea, pitted the virtually unaided Persian light infantry against the Greek heavy infantry, the Greek militia having protected their flanks by hills and artificial obstacles against the small number of Persian cavalry at hand.

When the two lines of infantry came within bowshot and the Persians began their arrow barrage, the Greeks charged at a slow run. Their armor did not prevent their running a short distance while it offered protection against Persian arrows. They ran through the zone in which the arrows fell and engaged the stationary Persian archers in hand-to-hand combat.

Having strengthened the flanks of their phalanx, the men on the ends of the Greek line reached the Persians and engaged them hand-to-hand; the charge of the thinner center ranks did not weather the hail of arrows and could not reach the Persian line. But once in close combat on the flanks, the armored Greeks with spear and sword defeated the Persians, unequipped and untrained

Map 1.1. Greece

for shock action. The Persians fled, the Greeks pursuing for a mile. By the time the victorious Greeks could reorganize themselves and march the two additional miles to the Persian ships, the Persians had embarked most of their men, and the Greeks captured only seven ships. The Battle of Marathon well exhibited the easily anticipated inability of light infantry to hold its ground in a battle against heavy infantry. Hit-and-run tactics seemed the only effective method for the bowmen in the absence of cavalry to halt the charge of the hoplites.

The subsequent Graeco-Persian war provided a better test between the two systems. A decade after the Battle of Marathon, the Persians came to Greece with a powerful army of infantry and cavalry, a force of regular troops that accurately reflected the military capability of the huge empire. In addition to cavalry and large numbers of foot archers, the Persians had some hoplites of their Greek allies. But the distinctive strength of the Persian army lay in its numerous cavalry equipped with bows, javelins, and spears. The Greeks, lacking any cavalry, depended on heavy infantry and some light infantry.

At Plataea the two forces met in a fair trial of strength. In the initial disposition of the two well-commanded armies, the typically Greek rough ground protected the flanks of the Greeks from the Persian cavalry. But as each army waited for the other to attack, one exposed detachment of hoplites suffered from the missiles of Persian cavalry, which like light infantry could stand off at a distance and use bows and javelins. Since the Greek spearmen could not hope to charge the cavalry successfully, they could offer no defense. So the Greeks then posted in this exposed position 300 Athenian hoplites supported by some archers, a type of light infantry favored by the seafaring Athenians. Against this combination of two Greek weapon systems, the Persian cavalry used hit-and-run tactics, their horsemen riding up in groups and shooting their arrows or hurling their javelins. One group then withdrew and another took its place in rotation, each conducting its missile attack. The hoplites held their ground against the cavalry that did not charge, while the arrows of the Greek bowmen seriously harmed the Persians. The foot archers had the advantage over the mounted bowmen, because, able to concentrate wholly on their bows, they had superiority in the accuracy and number of their arrows.

The experience of a Persian cavalry leader also showed the vulnerability of the horse. In front of the other cavalry, his horse, in the words of a historian of the time, "received an arrow in his flank, the pain of which caused him to rear and throw his rider." The hoplites then rushed forward and killed the Persian commander. His men, "with loud cheers," then charged with shock action to recover the body of their leader, but, in spite of their inferiority in numbers, the foot soldiers demonstrated their superiority to the mounted men by successfully resisting the determined hand-to-hand attack of the stirrupless Persian regulars. With the approach of hoplite reinforcements, the Persian cavalry abandoned the contest.[4]

The Greeks then moved forward until they faced the Persians across a small stream. Each army arrayed its infantry opposite the other, but both refused to risk an attack when crossing the stream would disrupt their formation. Pausanias, the sagacious and circumspect Spartan king who commanded the Greeks, had difficulty restraining his allies, who displayed great impatience to attack. Mardonius, the shrewd and experienced commander of the Persian regulars, had less difficulty in awaiting a more favorable moment to assume the offensive.

Even after they moved forward, most of the Greek hoplites still had the protection the terrain offered against a direct attack by the missles of the Persian cavalry. Nevertheless, in some positions cavalry "with their javelins and their arrows—for though horsemen they used the bow—sorely distressed the Greek troops which could not bring them to close combat."[5]

Soon after their forward move, the Greeks decided to withdraw to a position that had access to water and from which they could more effectively cover their lines of communication. They did this at night to avoid harassment by the enemy cavalry, but one Greek commander delayed because he thought it dishonorable to retreat, and some forces lost their way. This had the result that in the morning the Greeks found their army's deployment badly disarranged. The Persian cavalry promptly took advantage of the situation to harry the Spartan contingent as it withdrew, causing the Greeks to halt to defend themselves. The success of the Persian commander's cavalry convinced him that the Greeks were fleeing, and he sought to exploit the enemy's disorder by sending his infantry forward across the stream. But the Spartans were neither retreating nor disordered, and Persian light infantry faced Greek hoplites.

Coming within bowshot, the Persians, led by Mardonius on a white horse, "made a rampart of their wicker shields, and shot from behind them such a cloud of arrows, that the Spartans were sorely distressed." As the Persians drew closer, the Spartans charged. As at Marathon, the terrain protected the flanks of the hoplites from attack by the Persian cavalry, and, without the cavalry attack to halt their charge, the Spartans promptly closed with the Persians. The light infantry had superior mobility, but the mass of the Persians, though strong in firepower, could not fall back quickly: their own numbers hemmed them in, other troops having come up in their rear. They had no choice but to engage the Spartans, and "first the combat was at the wicker shields. Afterwards, when these were swept away," there ensued a "hand-to-hand struggle" in which the Persians "many times seized hold of the Greeks spears and broke them, for in boldness and warlike spirit the Persians were not a bit inferior to the Greeks; but they were without bucklers, untrained, and far below the enemy in respect to skill" in the shock combat for which the Greeks had instruction, arms, and armor. With the gallant and skillful Mardonius killed in combat, the Persian infantry retreated. This defeat at Plataea ended their invasion of Greece.[6]

Although the Greeks won and the Persians thereafter incorporated heavy infantry in their army, the Greek tactical system had not displayed any intrinsic superiority. In spite of the failure of the Persian bowmen, clearly light infantry could defeat heavy infantry if it could fully exploit its natural advantages, by avoiding shock combat, keeping its distance, and using its missiles. But two attempts, at Marathon and Plataea, to use light infantry in a frontal fight with heavy infantry had exhibited the vulnerability of light infantry when it lacked the aid of cavalry and could not use its superior mobility to avoid the charge of the heavy infantry.

The Persian cavalry had exhibited its ability to use its greater mobility to keep away from the heavy infantry and effectively employ missile weapons. To the degree that the cavalry had tried shock action against the heavy infantry, the infantry had shown its superiority. The man on foot in formation had the advantage over the stirrupless mounted man in hand-to-hand combat because the ground provided a better fighting platform and he could give his undivided attention to combat. The success of the Greek foot archers against the mounted Persian bowmen also gave a strong indication that the light infantryman had a distinct ascendency over a mounted man using the same tactics.

Greek Light Infantry in Combat with Greek Heavy Infantry

For more than a century following the war with Persia, the Greek system of war continued essentially unchanged. The heavy infantry phalanx remained the predominant weapon system, even though on several occasions light and heavy infantry exhibited their relative merits. In one instance Athenian heavy infantry invaded the rugged country of the Aetolians, whose militia normally armed itself with javelins. Because the Aetolian javelin men, called peltasts, wore no armor, they could outrun the Athenian heavy infantry and use their faster speed to avoid a contest. Instead of fighting a battle as had the Persian archers, the Aetolians attacked with their javelins and then promptly retreated to avoid contact with the heavy infantry, which naturally charged the javelin throwers.

At first the Athenians, accompanied by a contingent of archers, easily held the Aetolians at bay. But the vulnerable, unarmored Aetolian javelin men kept their distance from the longer range bows until the archers had exhausted their arrows. A Greek historian described how the Aetolians then carried out their javelin attack: "when the Athenian army advanced they retired, and when the Athenians retired they pressed upon them. The battle, which lasted long, was nothing but a series of pursuits and retreats, and in both the Athenians were at a disadvantage." Finally the Athenians "grew weary of the long and tedious struggle. The Aetolians came closer and closer, never ceased hurling darts at them. At last they turned and fled. . . . The Aetolians, who were light armed and swift of foot, followed at their heels, hurling darts, and caught and slew many in their flight."[7]

Another historian explained the effectiveness of light infantry against heavy infantry, commenting that "the heavy infantry of the Arcadians positively refused to face them in the field, so profound was the terror in which they held these light troops. In compensation, the light troops themselves entertained a wholesome dread of the Lacedaemonians and did not venture to approach within javelin-range of their heavy infantry. They had been taught a lesson when, within that distance, some of the younger hoplites had made a dash at them, catching and putting some of them to the sword." The Lacedaemonians, convinced of their ability to deal with the light infantry peltasts, disparaged those who feared them as standing "in as much awe of these peltasts as children of the hobgoblins of their nurses."[8]

These confident Lacedaemonians soon met javelin-armed peltasts who planned to catch the Lacedaemonians on the march where they "would be cut up by showers of javelins," and, if the Lacedaemonians "were tempted to take the offensive, they with their peltasts, the nimblest of all light troops, would easily slip out of their grasp." When the peltasts carried out their attack, "here a man was wounded, and there another killed." Then the Spartan commander, called a polemarch, "ordered the younger men to charge and drive off their assailants. Charge, however, as they might, they took nothing by their pains— not a man could they come at within javelin range. Being heavy infantry opposed to light troops, before they could get at close quarters the enemy's word of command sounded, 'Retire!' " Failing to catch any peltasts, the Lacedaemonian heavy infantry would fall back, scattered because of their charge at full speed "where each man's individual speed had told." The peltasts then "turned right about and renewed the javelin attack." In their initial attack the peltasts "had shot down nine or ten, and, encouraged by this success, pressed on with increasing audacity. These attacks told so severely that the polemarch a second time gave the order (and this time for more of the younger men) to charge. The order was promptly obeyed, but on retiring they lost more men than on the first occasion.... Again and again the monotonous tale of doing and suffering repeated itself, except as their own ranks grew thinner and their courage ebbed, the courage of their assailants grew bolder and their numbers increased."[9]

Light infantrymen, if they can keep out of the way, have an obvious superiority over heavy infantrymen. On billiard table terrain of infinite extent, light infantry could defeat heavy infantry if it had enough missiles and patience and adhered to its light infantry tactics of avoiding shock combat in which the heavy infantry specialized. Most Greek states continued to rely primarily on heavy infantry, but successes such as those recounted above caused the heavy infantry to acknowledge the presence of the light infantry by substituting leather or stiffened cloth for metal armor and sometimes using felt instead metal for their helmets. In this way the heavy infantry reduced the advantage in speed enjoyed by the light infantry while still remaining well enough armored to fight other heavy infantry and, of course, amply protected to defeat light infantry in close combat.

The Greeks also developed some cavalry, though this weapon system, expensive and limited by the terrain, never became predominant and remained essentially an auxiliary system. In battle the main hoplite forces tended to fight each other, and the auxiliary light infantry and cavalry each engaged the other in their own separate battles. But when Epaminondas defeated the Spartans at the Battle of Leuctra, he combined the action of his better cavalry force with his deep array of infantry and the flank assault by his Sacred Band. The cavalry did not prove the decisive element, but, after defeating the inferior Spartan cavalry, its attack helped disrupt the Spartan flank maneuver and the action of the cavalry helped the Sacred Band's flank attack against the Spartan flanking segment.

Alexander's Conquests with a Complete Combined-Arms Army

The Greeks did not develop further either the infantry maneuvers or the role of cavalry exemplified at Leuctra. Others did, creating a method of combining arms that had theoretical as well as practical superiority over the old Greck as well as the initial Persian way of war. King Philip of the northern Greek kingdom of Macedon perfected this system, and his son, Alexander the Great, used it to conquer Greece and the Persian Empire. Conceptually the Macedonian tactical method blended the Greek and Persian systems by depending heavily on cavalry but substituting in the line Greek heavy infantry for Persian light infantry. The reliance on cavalry had its origin not only in the Persian practice but also in the traditional importance Macedonians had attached to cavalry in a country more suited to the horse.

Philip bequeathed to Alexander a force of heavy cavalry. Whereas Greek and Persian cavalry used the javelin or the bow and were prepared to thrust with a javelin or light spear, some Macedonian cavalry relied primarily on shock action. Like the heavy infantry, these men wore armor and carried shields and a short lance, a cavalry spear. About nine feet long and weighing four pounds, the lance had an iron point on each end. Though the horseman lacked a stirrup, training and practice enabled him to keep his seat reasonably well in combat at close quarters. When he thrust with his lance, he released it at or just before the moment of impact to avoid transmitting to himself the shock of the blow. He thus escaped the danger of losing his seat on his mount.

Macedonian horsemen also differed from Greek cavalry in that they were thoroughly disciplined and trained to work together in groups and to respond to commands. They thus had better articulation, training, and skill in addition to their primary reliance on shock action. Over cavalry relying on javelins and rarely closing with the enemy, this doctrine enabled them to enjoy the same advantage as Greek heavy infantry held over light infantry in shock combat. Cavalry unprepared for determined shock action could not resist their charge. Heavy cavalry had the same dominance over light infantry as did heavy infantry, with an important difference—light infantry could not escape by running away. Only the heavy infantry, a formation of armored hoplites with their spears, could resist the charge and best them in hand-to-hand combat.

This Macedonian heavy cavalry, a small elite group, was called Companions of the King. The Macedonian army also had far more of the traditional, hybrid, or general-purpose cavalry, which largely relied on missile action, principally the

Illustration 1.4. Heavy Cavalryman

javelin. And the bulk of the Macedonian army remained infantry. Light infantry had an important role: in battle it deployed in front of the heavy infantry where it could use its traditional tactics of slinging missiles, shooting arrows, or hurling javelins while keeping away from its heavy infantry opponents. Before the lines of hoplites clashed, the light infantry withdrew out of harm's way, its usefulness ended. Thus the tactics involved an initial reliance on the intrinsic ascendency of the light over the heavy infantry.

The Macedonians changed the heavy infantry by doubling the length of the spear, at least for the ranks behind the first two. The longer spear enabled those of several ranks to project beyond the front, utilizing more rear-rank men and making an advance by this phalanx formidable indeed. If the front ranks used the short spear and rear ranks progressively longer spears, a simultaneous push by several ranks almost always drove back the opponents. The longer spears also made body armor less important, the rear ranks requiring none at all, a substantial saving in equipment costs. Relying more on the action of the group, individual soldiers needed less skill. Still the Macedonians made a virtue of the tactical innovation of the long spear and drilled their phalanx of professional soldiers so that it could function as a unit. In addition, they subdivided their troops, giving some articulation and maneuverability to an inherently unwieldy formation. But the longer spear reflected a subtle change, placing greater reliance on the advance of a wall of spears and less on the individual effort by the men in the front rank.

The creators of this army, the astute Philip and his son, Alexander, integrated these four weapon systems into a mutually supporting combat team. Heavy and light infantry each had its role as did the light and heavy cavalry, with the shock action of the elite Companions of the King held for a decisive blow. No weapon system had primacy, and none a merely auxiliary role; all had a significant part to play.

With an essentially professional army organized on the new Macedonian model, the Greeks under Alexander invaded Asia. They had a well-developed tactical doctrine and in Alexander a leader of unsurpassed genius. To his high native ability the young king added, through counsel, the wisdom of the talented and seasoned soldiers who had served under his gifted father. In bringing his balanced, combined arms against the Persians, Alexander faced an improved Persian tactical system. To their combination of cavalry and light infantry the Persians had added heavy infantry, mostly Greek mercenaries. Although they too used the method of deploying light infantry in advance of a solid line of hoplites, their use of this stronger infantry base did not alter their traditional reliance on a cavalry attack to decide the battle.

But the Persians lacked any heavy cavalry comparable to Alexander's Companions. Although Persian cavalry wore mailed shirts and carried swords, it continued to rely primarily on bows and javelins and had not prepared for the shock action of Alexander's spear-wielding Companions. In the first battle, at the Granicus River, the decisive young king, undaunted by the enemy's formidable position, ordered his Companions to charge across the river against the defending Persian cavalry, which met them "with a terrible discharge of darts; but the Macedonians fought with spears. . . . Though they fought on horseback, it seemed more like an infantry than a cavalry battle; for they struggled for the mastery, horses being jammed with horses and men with men. . . . At last Alexander's men began to gain the advantage, both through superior strength and military discipline and because they fought with spears whose shafts were made of cornel wood, whereas the Persians used only" javelins as lances.[10]

Ill-equipped and untrained for shock action, the Persian cavalry could not hold its ground against the charge of the Macedonians. The "hurling of javelins or the dextrous deploying of horses," which had been "the common practice in cavalry battles," availed little against shock tactics. Since Alexander's heavy cavalry could rout the enemy's cavalry, he could count on using it to decide the battle. At the Battle of the Granicus, Alexander promptly led his victorious Companions to the assistance of his phalanx, which had attacked the Persian heavy infantry. Having ordered "the cavalry to fall upon them from all sides," Alexander had the satisfaction of seeing that his horsemen had "soon completely surrounded them and cut them up, so that none of them escaped except such as might have concealed themselves among the dead bodies." Though heavy infantry could have resisted the charge of heavy cavalry directed at its front, an attack on its unprotected flanks and rear produced a slaughter as the mailed companion cavalry closed in for hand-to-hand combat with their spears.[11]

The splendid victory showed the value of Alexander's and his father's preparation for the kingship and for war. Tutoring in his youth by the great philosopher Aristotle had sharpened the king's intellect as well as fostered his scientific and literary interests. In addition to his mental attributes and kingly bearing, this handsome, athletic young man had displayed at the Battle of the Granicus keen judgment and physical and moral courage. Equally important, his combined-arms army and his heavy cavalry Companions had clearly exhibited that they provided the right instrument to execute his ambitious plans of conquest.

At Issus, Alexander faced the Persians commanded by their capable king, Darius III. The Persians stood on the defensive in a strong position behind a shallow river where it emptied into the sea. With its cavalry deployed on each flank, the Macedonian phalanx went forward "in close array with measured step," moving slowly toward the enemy, "lest by a too hasty march any part of the phalanx should fluctuate from the line and get separated from the rest."[12] On reaching the Persian line, the phalanx attacked across the shallow river against a bank held by Greek hoplites employed by the Persians. As one would expect in a contest between similar weapon systems, the defenders, in their well-chosen position, prevailed. "Finding many parts of the bank steep and precipitous" or defended by a Persian stockade, the Macedonians "were unable to preserve the front of the phalanx in the same line. Here the struggle was desperate," and the disorganized attackers failed. But on the inland—or left—flank of the Persian army Alexander had already led his heavy cavalry across the same river and, having charged and routed the light infantry holding the bank, "wheeled round towards the Grecian Mercenaries of Darius." Macedonian heavy infantry, called hypaspists, probably armed with a spear of the traditional length and wearing light armor, followed the cavalry and soon joined it in an attack on the flank and rear of Darius's hoplites, who had successfully held the river bank. The Persian hoplites retreated and, seeing the battle lost, so also did the king of Persia.[13]

The mobility and articulation of his elite cavalry and the excellent training and good articulation of the hypaspists enabled Alexander at Issus to carry out an envelopment without having to rely on a preplanned parade ground maneuver like that used by the Spartans. Envelopment required overwhelming or going around an enemy's flank and attacking the remainder of his line in flank and rear. Difficult to accomplish, it demanded either a successful frontal attack to break the line or a detour around the enemy's flank. Alexander's envelopment involved both means, as he pierced a weakly held extension of the Persian left. Unless accomplished by cavalry, a detour around a flank could consume so much time that the battle could be decided before the enveloping force arrived. The cavalry's superior speed made it ideal for such movements.

Envelopments also required the ability to deploy rapidly from march to combat formation. Cavalry could do this easily because, no matter how well organized, cavalrymen still fought as individuals and relied less on the actions of their fellows than did formed infantry. With its greater speed, cavalry could deploy rapidly from column of march to line of battle, a task made easier as its combat formation was less organized and integrated than was infantry's. By its higher mobility and its capacity for rapid deployment, cavalry came very close to fighting as it marched and so exemplifed offensive troops, who found their best employment in carrying out envelopments.

Alexander's hypaspists represent a successful effort to adapt heavy infantry to the role of an enveloping force. Lighter equipment speeded up their march, and with a high degree of individual skill these well-trained regulars had less dependence on their formation. Doubtless also, they had subdivision into groups, which were more responsive to orders and easier to deploy. By diminishing their need for a carefully drawn up formation and improving their articulation and hence their ability to maneuver, the Macedonians had a type of heavy infantry well suited to battlefield maneuver and to executing envelopments. The art of war had already come a long way since the Greek phalanx and Epaminondas' clumsy array of fifty ranks on one flank, for Alexander's hypaspists could envelop a Greek phalanx and, closing with shock action, help the cavalry guarantee the enemy's defeat.

At Arbela, Alexander's third major battle against the Persians, he again met Darius, who had assembled a large, heterogeneous army which even included chariots and a few elephants. To save his crumbling empire, Darius waited to receive the Greek invaders in battle, having wisely chosen level ground suitable for his cavalry and chariots. Since his army, though powerful, lacked much heavy infantry, he had placed his mounted troops in the forefront of his array. Alexander moved his army forward to attack the Persian army, leading the right flank himself. He could clearly see Darius in the center, "conspicious in the midst of his life-guard, a tall and fine-looking man, drawn in a lofty chariot, defended by an abundance of the best horse, who stood in close order about it, ready to receive the enemy."[14]

As the armies became closely engaged, Alexander led his Companions and heavy infantry phalanx against the enemy center, the Companions defeating the Persian cavalry by "thrusting themselves against the Persians and striking their faces with their spears" and routing their center. Darius saw that "all was lost, that those who were placed in front to defend him were broken and beat back upon him, that he could not turn or disengage his chariot without great difficulty, the wheels being clogged and entangled among the dead bodies, which lay in such heaps as not only stopped, but almost covered the horses, and made them rear and grow so unruly, that the frightened charioteer could govern them no longer." The defeated Persian monarch did escape, mounted on a horse. Alexander turned away with his men to rescue his hard-pressed left and win a decisive victory.[15]

Without Alexander's genius the Greeks could not have conquered the Persian Empire, but Alexander's masterful use of shock cavalry contributed importantly, perhaps decisively, to the tactical successes upon which the conquest depended. By a brillant use of the four basic weapon systems, Alexander defeated the formidable Persians whose otherwise sophisticated tactical system did not include heavy cavalry. This significant Macedonian innovation completed the development of a basic tactical system that endured for many centuries. Alexander also advanced the art of war by his flexibility: he did not rely on a single disposition of his army for battle nor on a set-piece plan but adapted both plans and dispositions to the circumstances. Also, in his employment of battering rams and movable towers and in his mastery and effective use of siegecraft, he brought the Greek art of war to the level of the Asians in this essential respect.

But in combat Alexander still followed the practice of personal participation, leading his cavalry in battle to command at the critical point. This decision virtually precluded his control of the fight once it began. Although Alexander carried out a move from the right to left by his cavalry at Arbela, the initial dispositions usually governed the overall strategy of the battle. Responses to the changing situation in an Alexandrian battle depended, therefore, on the initiative of subordinates rather than on Alexander's overall direction. Thus, a commander who could direct the battle and redeploy forces during the combat had yet to emerge. Even with the flexibility of four weapon systems and a far less stereotyped battle, the difficulties of control still prevented even as skilled a leader as Alexander from commanding the whole battle.

Commanders also lacked the concept of holding back or subtracting a part of the army for use later in the battle to meet emergencies or to exploit opportunities. Troops not so fully engaged that they can be redeployed during a battle also constitute a reserve. A commander, however, cannot know when, where, or whether he will have troops sufficiently unengaged to meet an emergency or exploit an opportunity. But a subtracted reserve, that is, one established before the battle and held back for an unspecified commitment during the battle provides a sure resource to enable a commander to influence the outcome. Alexander the Great had not fully realized the value of such a force nor been able to implement, or perhaps even completely recognize, the idea of a commander who did not personally involve himself in combat.

The Roman Art of War

While the Macedonians were perfecting the art of war in their fashion, the army of Rome, a small Italian city-state, evolved in a different direction. Like the Greeks, the Romans fought with a phalanx of hoplites assisted by light infantry and a general-purpose cavalry. But the Romans abandoned the spear as their principal weapon fairly early and adopted versatile offensive arms. For defense, they placed heavy reliance on a large convex shield, two and a half feet wide and four feet high. This wooden shield, covered with cloth and then with calf skin and reinforced in the center with iron, could turn "aside the more formidable blows of stones, pikes, and heavy missiles in general." A contemporary explained that "its upper and lower rims are strengthened by an iron edging which protects it from descending blows and from injury when resting on the ground." Since the Romans engaged in many sieges, faced the long pikes or spears of the Greeks, and fought the Celts who wielded a two-handed cutting sword, they eventually devised a shield effective against all opponents. They completed their protection with a helmet and a brass breastplate or, for the wealthier, a coat of chain-mail.[16]

For attack the Romans depended for shock combat on a short sword, "excellent for thrusting, and both of its edges cut effectually, as the blade is very strong and firm." Such a sword would prove its worth at close quarters with an opponent whose two-handed sword or long pike could be turned aside by the shield. The bulk of the infantry also carried two of a javelin called a pilum. This had a point that bent or broke if it struck a hard object so that "the enemy is unable to return it. If this were not so, the missile would be available to both sides." This suited Roman tactics, which consisted of throwing the javelin and then closing quickly to fight with sword and shield.[17]

The distinctive organization matured by the Romans proved more funda-mental than their use of the sword. Arraying their army in three successive lines, each six ranks deep, they subdivided these lines into maniples, each maniple having two centuries of sixty men each. This subdivision provided rudimentary articulation and promised some maneuverability. The Romans exploited this organization by leaving gaps between each maniple in each line; the maniples of the second line were staggered so that they covered the gaps in the first. The third line differed from the first two as its maniples had only half the front, with sixty rather than 120 men. The men of the third line were the older citizens and still used the spear as their principal weapon. The maniples of the third line positioned themselves behind the holes in the second line, making the whole formation somewhat like a checkerboard. This was the basic formation in which the Romans advanced to the fight. Since gaps would almost certainly form in any line of battle as it advanced, the Romans anticipated this by providing the intervals systematically. Before the Roman line closed with the enemy in combat, the second line filled the breaks in the first with either a century or a full maniple pushing into the spaces in the front line. The third line moved up into the vacant positions in the second line and, with the remainder of the second line, con-stituted a reserve if not needed to help fill a large gap in the first line. This organization gave the Roman line of battle a flexibility and responsiveness that the phalanx lacked.

The administrative organization provided another element of strength in the Roman system. Ten of the first- and second-line maniples of 120 men each and ten of the sixty-man third-line maniples comprised an administrative or-ganization called a legion. With a proportion of orderlies, clerks, porters, etc., some of whom doubled as light infantry, and a small amount of cavalry, the legion numbered over 4,000 men. When the Romans expanded their army, they added legions, thus providing good administration and organization for any large field army.

Another significant attribute of the Romans' military practice was their passion for entrenchment. No Roman field force on the march ever camped without first entrenching according to a standard plan. Every night the troops dug a trench and piled up a rampart, protected with a palisade. Accustomed to this labor because of its regularity, Roman armies took for granted what would have been a demoralizing imposition in any other military organization. This entrenchment meant that Roman armies were prepared against surprise and had a fortified place of refuge in case of defeat in battle.

The Romans had learned about entrenchment from the Macedonians, who had, in turn, derived their practice from the Greeks, who fortified their camps only when they remained in place for a time, and the Asians, who more consistently entrenched their camps. The Persians, for example, fell back to an elaborately fortified camp after their defeat at Plataea. The Roman innovation consisted of entrenching their camps with relentless regularity and in having a standard plan that insured that every soldier and unit always had the same relative position in the camp.

The Roman soldier had to be a seasoned marcher, for, in addition to his armor, sword, and javelin, he carried shovels, axes, and stakes to make the palisade for the camp. But each day's march ended early to provide time to entrench the camp.

Like their marching and camping, the Romans practiced a slow but sure strategy, and gradually Rome dominated much of Italy. Since political astuteness complemented military skill, they bound to themselves as firm and willing allies the areas they controlled and extended to these allies the Roman organization and style of warfare. By the time of Alexander the Great, Rome had become a formidable power, ready to come into military contact with others in the Mediterranean.

The Romans in Confrontation with the Alexandrian System of Pyrrhus and Hannibal

The Macedonian system as used by Alexander became the standard for the eastern Mediterranean and much of the old Persian Empire. The difference between the Macedonian and Roman systems lay not primarily in the Roman use of swords and the Macedonian reliance on the spear; the difference was more subtle. The Roman army depended on their sword-wielding, partially articulated heavy infantry with their light infantry and cavalry filling the roles of auxiliaries. In their evolution from the phalanx to the manipular array, they had improved the infantry but had not developed in the direction of the Macedonian system of Alexander, which relied on the combined effect of all arms, including a cavalry force trained for real shock combat.

In the first major Roman combat with the Macedonian or Alexandrian system the combined-arms force won. The particulars of these battles with King Pyrrhus of the Greek Kingdom of Epirus are obscure, but, in Pyrrhus, the Romans faced not only a relative and disciple of Alexander the Great but also a general whose many campaigns had earned for him a most exalted reputation. The

Romans attributed much of Pyrrhus's success to his use of elephants, which Alexander's successors had incorporated into the Macedonian system after Alexander faced them in India. Often unreliable, occasionally stampeding through their own infantry when attacked by javelins and other missiles, elephants proved most effective against cavalry because they frightened the enemy's horses. Pyrrhus based his successful battles with the Romans not on his elephants but on the success of his cavalry, presumbly aided by elephants, in defeating the Roman cavalry and attacking the Roman infantry in flank and rear. But in defeat the Romans inflicted such severe casualties on Pyrrhus that he remarked that more such victories would force him to return to Greece alone.

In its first contest with the Romans, the African power Carthage copied the Macedonian system of war, even retaining a Greek general to command the army in the campaign to drive back the Roman invasion of Africa. Stationed, as usual, on the flanks, the more powerful heavy cavalry of the Carthaginians defeated the Roman cavalry on the flanks and attacked the Roman infantry in the rear. The articulation inherent in the Roman three-line system meant that the rear maniples could turn about to fend off this assault, but this effective defensive tactic did not save the Romans: the Carthaginians won the Battle of Tunis and captured the Roman commander.

In their second war with Carthage the Romans faced Hannibal, one of the greatest military geniuses of all time. In invading Italy, the youthful Hannibal, barely thirty years of age, relied on the Macedonian system; the defending Romans continued to give their infantry primacy in their combined-arms army. In his first battle, at Trebia in 218 B.C., Hannibal inflicted a disastrous defeat on the Romans. In numbers, the armies differed little, but Hannibal had a cavalry superiority of five to two, a victorous force that swept around the flanks of the Roman army and, aided by the light infantry, attacked the Roman infantry in the rear. Even though the rear maniples turned to confront this assault, Hannibal defeated the surrounded and immobilized Roman army.

The Battle of Cannae in 216 B.C., in addition to its fame as a military classic, exhibits the final development of the Macedonian art of war in the hands of a master. Wary of Hannibal, the Romans fought with over 80,000 men to Hannibal's 50,000. But Hannibal had 10,000 cavalry to 6,000 for the Romans. The Cathaginians had another advantage: the Roman commander, Tarentius Varro, not only lacked military experience and skill but also had too much self-confidence and pugnacity. Varro planned to exploit his great numerical preponderance by increasing the depth of his formation. He retained the deployment in three lines but had each maniple narrow its front until each line had three or four times its usual depth, intending thus to overwhelm the Carthaginian infantry.

Equally anxious for a battle, Hannibal supported his own assurance and aggressiveness by his mastery of the use of the sophisticated Macedonian combined-arms tactical system to which he had added significant improvements. In addition to the usual array of heavy infantry in the center and cavalry on the flanks, he held back part of his heavy infantry, which he then placed in columns at the flank of his line of heavy infantry. Here these forces, subtracted from the thin line of heavy infantry opposing the deep Roman formation, could reinforce the center should it falter.

Hannibal thus had at his disposal a true reserve. But if his infantry line held, he intended to use these two columns of his best infantry for an envelopment. He reinforced his weak infantry line by stationing himself with the men who had to meet the onset of the deep Roman formation. But, unlike Alexander the Great, the perceptive Hannibal did not lead his troops in battle; his presence strengthened the confidence of this thin infantry line, but from his position he could also observe the battle and control his reserve.

As in his previous battles, his light infantry had a role beyond skirmishing in front of the heavy infantry before the lines met. Hannibal planned for his light infantry to withdraw to the flanks where it would remain available to participate in his planned envelopment. He guaranteed success for his heavy cavalry by concentrating all of it on one flank.

When the armies joined battle, all went according to Hannibal's plan. Though the Roman heavy infantry pressed back the shallow Carthaginian array of swords-men, Hannibal's heavy cavalry enjoyed an immediate, decisive success and, promptly riding around the Roman army, charged the rear of the Roman cavalry on the opposite flank. Then, joined by the light infantry from the flanks, the Carthaginian light and heavy cavalry attacked the rear of the Roman infantry. Meanwhile, according to the plan, Hannibal committed his reserve infantry to complete the envelopment of the Roman army. In a column on each end of his line, the reserve marched past the Roman flank and then, facing the enemy, assaulted the Roman's flanks. His method had some resemblance to that of the Spartans in bringing a column perpendicular to the enemy's line and then facing and attacking.

Beset on all sides and pressed together where their numbers availed them nothing except to assure that every Carthaginian missile found a target, the Roman army suffered one of the greatest military disasters of all time—three-fourths of the force were killed or captured. Forty percent of the Carthaginian army was killed or wounded: inflicting a crushing defeat on a Roman army did not come cheap.

The Romans avoided battle with Hannibal for fourteen years. When they again met him, they had in their commander, Scipio, a brilliant general who, though in his early thirties, had ample experience. Having fought at Trebia and Cannae, he took command in Spain and by victories in battle and gaining the allegiance of many Spanish chiefs, conquered Spain from the Carthaginians in four years. Scipio then commanded in Sicily where he built up a fine army. In spite of his taste for luxury and his Greek culture, Scipio easily instilled confidence in his troops. He then led his army into Africa while the steadfast Hannibal still remained in southern Italy. By this time the Romans no longer fielded militia, and Scipio commanded and inspired the devotion of an army largely composed of well-trained and disciplined veterans of many campaigns. Scipio and Hannibal met in Africa in 202 B.C. at the Battle of Zama, where each exhibited his genius. The contest between these two masters advanced the art of war.

With their allies, the Numidians, the Roman army had decisive superiority in cavalry, an advantage that usually belonged to Hannibal. But Scipio did not rely exclusively on his cavalry for success. He deployed his infantry in a manner that he had developed in Spain. Instead of having the maniples of the second and third lines close to and covering the intervals in the first line, he kept them back a distance of probably several hundred feet. He correctly believed that when the six-deep first line engaged the enemy infantry, the veterans would manage well without additional ranks behind them. The rear ranks constituted Scipio's reserve, which in Spain he had used to envelop the flanks of the enemy infantry.

But Scipio also had to cope with the Carthaginian army's eighty elephants. For this reason he abandoned the usual Roman initial array in a checkerboard formation and stationed the second and third lines of maniples directly behind those of the first. The intervals of the first he filled with the light infantry, "ordering them to open the action, and if they were forced back by the charge of the elephants to retire, those who had time to do so by the straight passages as far to the rear of the whole army, and those who were overtaken to right or left along the intervals between the lines."[18]

Hannibal, realizing that he could not rely on his cavalry for victory, also had in a rear line of infantry a reserve that he could deploy. As at Cannae his best troops made up this reserve, but he altered his disposition of them. At Cannae he had placed the reserve in a column on each flank of his infantry line, ready to advance, face, and attack the Romans in their flank. But, since such a disposition was too obvious against Scipio, he kept this reserve in line, behind and parallel to his main infantry line. Superior in infantry, Hannibal counted on winning by using his reserve to envelop the Roman infantry line.

When the battle opened and as the light cavalry skirmished between the lines, "Hannibal ordered the drivers of the elephants to charge the enemy. When the trumpets and bugles sounded shrilly from all sides, some of the animals took fright and at once turned tail and rushed back" upon the Carthaginians. But some of the unpredictable and dangerous beasts did go forward against the Roman line, faced the javelins of the courageous Roman light infantry, "and finally in their terror escaped through the gaps in the Roman line which Scipio's foresight had provided." Others fled to the flanks, clearing the field for the serious engagement of the infantry and cavalry.[19]

Then the imposing lines of the Roman and Carthaginian heavy infantry joined battle. Meanwhile, the Roman and Numidian cavalry had driven Hannibal's cavalry from the field and, as Hannibal doubtless had anticipated, instead of attacking the Carthaginian infantry, had pursued the fleeing enemy cavalry far from the field of battle. This often happened in battle, commanders being unable to control their cavalrymen who naturally sought to follow their beaten foes. At Cannae Hannibal's well-disciplined and well-led professional cavalry had immediately turned against the rear of the Roman infantry, but at Zama the Roman and allied cavalry lacked the discipline, restraint, and leadership to enable them to make this critical maneuver.

With all cavalry off the field of battle, Hannibal had an infantry battle alone and moved promptly to exploit his numerical superiority and the articulation provided by his reserve of veterans. He moved out his rear infantry formation, extending its line preparatory to enveloping the flanks of the Roman infantry. But Scipio saw the maneuver in time to commit his rear-line reserve, extending his line equally, and the infantry of the two armies remained locked in a frontal battle of doubtful outcome. Then, before the infantry battle reached a decision, the Roman and allied cavalry returned to the battlefield and carried out their mission of attacking the rear of the relatively thin, fully committed line of Carthaginian infantry. This decided the battle, the Romans and Numidians virtually annihilating the Carthaginian army, leaving a field covered with "slippery corpses which were still soaked in blood and had fallen in heaps."[20]

The role of the cavalry in the Roman victory at Zama revealed that the Romans had adopted the Macedonian system. But the use of a reserve by both combatants and the superior articulation that made this possible shows that the art of war had surpassed that of Alexander's era. Neither Hannibal nor Scipio had participated in the battle, both remaining where they could manage the contest and commit their reserves at the critical time and place. This represented a major advance over Alexander's preplanned battles, as did the concept of the subtracted or uncommitted reserve and the improved articulation of the infantry that enabled the reserves to maneuver on the battlefield. The excellent articulation of the Roman army had done much to permit Scipio to command all of the army in battle rather than, as had Alexander, only a part.

Years later, when Scipio visited the court of an Asiatic monarch where Hannibal lived in exile, Scipio asked Hannibal to rank the great generals. Hannibal placed Alexander first, Pyrrhus second, and himself third. To Scipio's question about the rating if Hannibal had won at Zama, the Carthaginian said he would then rank himself above Alexander. Hannibal's and Scipio's greatness and their contributions to improved articulation, their use of a subtracted reserve, and their positioning themselves to manage the battle entitle both to the positions assigned by Hannibal either expressly or by implication.

The Roman Victories with the Alexandrian System

When the Romans fought in Greece and Asia, they again confronted the Macedonian system of war. Although the Romans also used this combined-arms method, they still stressed their heavy infantry and never raised their cavalry to the quality or the importance that it had with Alexander. But they also never had to make war with the united forces of Alexander's by-then divided empire, and they almost always fought with the aid of local allies. The Romans had critical help from an ally in their major battle against their most-imposing opponent, Antiochus the Great, ruler of Syria and much of Asia to the east. In the conflict in 190 B.C. at Magnesia in Asia Minor, they faced a formidable army under Antiochus himself with the exiled Hannibal as his advisor. The details of the battle are vague, but clearly the powerful cavalry of the Roman ally, the king of Pergamum, played an important role in the Roman victory. Increasingly the Romans relied on their allies to provide cavalry.

The apparent challenge to the dominance of the Romans' tactical system came not from the possibility that their opponents might have superior cavalry but from a further development of the Macedonian phalanx. When in 197 B.C. the Romans faced an army of the Macedonian kingdom, they found that the phalanx had lengthened at least some of its spears to twenty-one feet. Apparently the front ranks had shorter spears, probably nine feet, which they held in one hand; the fifth rank used both hands to carry twenty-one-foot spears that projected beyond the front rank; the intermediate ranks seem to have had spears of varying lengths so that all the spear points projected about the same distance beyond the front rank. The front ranks carried shields; the rear rank, using both hands to hold their long spear, had either no shields or very small ones slung on a strap across their chests. Behind the first five ranks the phalanx had an additional eleven ranks, the men holding their spears elevated until needed.

This formation marched shoulder-to-shoulder and for its effectiveness relied on the combined effect of the spears; the individual had no role except to hold his spear and keep his formation. Since the Romans fought with swords and so needed more space between them than the men in the phalanx, the phalanx had two men in front for every Roman. Each Roman thus faced ten spears. According to the historian Polybius, "It is both impossible for a single man to cut through them all in time once they are at close quarters and by no means easy to force their points away." It seemed, therefore, that this new phalanx could bear down all opposition, giving the Macedonians victory because of their better infantry.[21]

But the articulated Roman infantry easily defeated this apparently invincible tactical innovation. In connection with their success at the Battle of Zama, Polybius had pointed out that the subdivided Roman tactical organization enabled "every man individually and in common with his fellows to present a front in any direction, the maniples which are nearest to the danger turning themselves by a single movement to face it. Their arms also give the men both protection and confidence owing to the size of the shield and owing to the sword being strong enough to endure repeated blows." Thus the Roman could maneuver, and if he could get past the hoplite's spear, he had overwhelming superiority at close quarters, especially against the shieldless men with the two-handed spears.[22]

In the first conflict the Romans won the infantry combat because they caught the phalanx before it had formed and while some of its members were still marching to the place of battle. But even under favorable conditions the phalanx depended so much upon keeping its formation that it could never have succeeded against the Roman infantry. Polybius pointed out, "The phalanx requires level and clear ground with no obstacles such as ditches, clefts, clumps of trees, ridges and water courses, all of which are sufficient to impede and break up such a formation." Of course, gaps in a phalanx would enable the Roman swordsmen to come to close quarters with disastrous consequence for the hoplites in the phalanx.[23]

Even on level ground the phalanx proved vulnerable, for, Polybius wrote, "the Romans do not make their line equal in force to the enemy and expose all of the legions to a frontal attack by the phalanx, but part of their forces remain in reserve and the rest engaged the enemy. Afterwards whether the phalanx drives back by its charge the force opposed to it or is repulsed by this force," the phalanx exposes itself either "in following up a retreating foe or in flying before an attacking foe." When this happens, the phalanx then leaves "behind the other parts of their own army, upon which" the Roman "reserve have room enough in the space formerly held by the phalanx to attack no longer in front" but appear "by a lateral movement on the flank and rear of the phalanx" and so with sword and shield at close quarters on the flank slaughter the hoplites whose formation and weapons made them almost defenseless.[24]

Thus the improved infantry of the Romans helped Rome establish its mastery over the Mediterranean basin. The Romans had incorporated all of the features of the Macedonian system and had learned from Hannibal the value of an infantry reserve and the concept of a general who kept out of combat so that he could control the reserve and direct the battle.

The Roman Legion Perfected

The Romans soon perfected their infantry by abolishing the vestiges of the old phalangeal organization and introducing a completely rational plan of articulation. They eliminated the distinction between the traditional three lines, abolishing the spears and the smaller formations of the third line. They could deploy the legion's homogeneous heavy infantry into as many or as few lines as the circumstances warranted. They divided the legion into ten heavy infantry cohorts of 600 men each; a cohort consisted of three maniples of 200 men; each maniple contained two centuries. Every unit had a commander with full authority over his subordinates. This arrangement is substantially similar to the composition of the modern division with the cohorts corresponding to battalions and the maniples to companies. The chain of command is also similar, with an army composed of separate legions and the commander of each subordinate unit, down to the century, firmly under the authority of the commander above him.

The Romans thus created a fully articulated army capable of maneuvering and responding promptly to the orders of its leaders. Yet it remained very difficult for commanders to understand what was transpiring on the battlefield and even harder to transmit messages to subordinates. Messengers, horns, and drums provided uncertain means of communication. Still, the Romans had improved the situation considerably, not only by subdividing their army but also by equipping their units with standards that permitted the soldiers to recognize their places and gave commanders a better opportunity to know the location of their units. Until the portable radio in the twentieth century, tactical command remained fundamentally as difficult as the Romans found it and so mitigated the benefits of articulation.

Roman subdivision and subordination did have another advantage: it gave real scope for the initiative of subordinates in a battle. And the change to a professional army made this organization function in practice as well as it could in theory, and firm discipline, good training, and constant experience in war assured that the Roman army could always perform as intended.

The legion also possessed some light infantry, archers and slingers, and a small proportion of cavalry. But the skill and structure of the infantry reduced its vulnerability to cavalry because excellent articulation enabled parts of an army, either legion or cohort, to maneuver to protect a flank, and the good subdivision permitted the commander to assign a unit or units to guard the flanks. Since formed heavy infantry could stop the charge of formed heavy cavalry, Roman commanders felt little anxiety about their flanks.

The regularity of procedure that caused Roman forces to entrench at every halt carried over to providing good arrangements for supply and payment of their troops. The Romans, who campaigned methodically and persistently, completely supported this kind of warfare with their professional army and its thorough, unimpetuous way of war.

The Romans against the Mounted Parthians

This perfected Roman army readily triumphed over the Gauls, the inhabitants of present-day France. Called barbarians by the Romans, the Gauls, like the Romans, fought with heavy infantry and cavalry but lacked the Romans' disciplined and carefully articulated infantry. Nor did the Gauls have the Romans' addiction to, much less their mastery of, fortification and siegecraft; further, Gallic armies lacked the finances and the supply organization provided by the fully developed Roman state. In spite of the Gauls' persistent and capable resistance, the Romans, having a great commander in Julius Caesar, conquered Gaul in seven years.

But the Romans failed dramatically against the Parthians who ruled Mesopotamia and the region eastward to India. The Parthians only fought mounted, a method amply suited to the level, treeless terrain of Mesopotamia. They clearly distinguished between heavy and light cavalry, the aristocracy providing the former while training and equipping their retainers as horse archers. The heavy cavalry wore armor, as did their horses, and equipped themselves with a lance so long and heavy that the Romans nicknamed it "the barge-pole." Since the armor and the heavy lance seriously aggravated the problem of fighting on horseback without stirrups, the Parthian aristocracy seemed to have undertaken an almost impossible task. But they mastered it, and the Parthian heavy cavalry proved formidable indeed. The inertia of the heavy lance not only contributed to the power of its blow but also diminished the shock to the rider who, presumably, held it loosely. Though shooting a bow expertly requires very great skill and is even more difficult when mounted on horseback without stirrups, the light cavalry had a comparatively easy task in combat, for their tactics kept them at a distance from the enemy while they shot their arrows.

While Caesar conquered Gaul, his wealthy and ambitious colleague Crassus invaded Parthia with a large Roman army, perhaps numbering 36,000 men, including 4,000 cavalry and 4,000 light infantry. The confident Crassus already knew something of the Parthian art of war but thought that his military problem "consisted only in the tediousness of the march and the trouble of chasing men who durst not come to blows." He ignored the implication of reports that "by flight it is impossible to escape" the Parthians "and as impossible to overtake them when they" flee, just as he had naturally discounted reports of their impenetrable armor and of their arrows, "a new and strange sort of darts, as swift as sight." With arrogance and even less wisdom, Crassus, according to the historian Plutarch, declined the invitation of the king of Armenia who, knowing firsthand the Parthian way of war, suggested the Romans march through his kingdom whose hills and mountains made it "almost impassable to horse."[25]

The Parthians waited to engage the Romans until Crassus had marched far out on the level, sandy terrain of Mesopotamia. When they met the Parthian army near Carrhae, the Romans deployed in a square, full of confidence if only because the Parthian army drawn up before them seemed smaller than they expected. They did outnumber the Parthians three to one, but since the Parthian commander had hidden some of his force behind a rise in the ground, the Romans at first saw only part of the armored Parthian array. But then the Parthians, seeking to demoralize the Romans, made "a hideous noise and terrible clamor. For the Parthians do not encourage themselves to war with cornets and trumpets but with a kind of kettle-drum, which they strike all at once in various quarters. With these they make a dead hollow noise like the bellowing of beasts mixed with sounds resembling thunder. . . . When they had sufficiently terrified the Romans with their noise," they brought their whole army into view and "threw off the covering of their armor, and shone like lightning in their breastplates and helmets of polished Margianian steel, and with their horses covered with brass and steel trappings."

Not only did the Romans face a trained and elaborately equipped host but also a formidable and prudently prepared opponent in Surena, the Parthian commander. "He was the tallest and finest looking man himself, but the delicacy of his looks and the effeminacy of his dress did not promise so much manhood as he really was master of; for his face was painted, and his hair parted . . . whereas the other Parthians made a terrible appearance, with their shaggy hair gathered in a mass upon their foreheads."

Seeing the depth and strength of the ranks of the Roman heavy infantry, Surena wisely did not order his heavy cavalry to charge. Instead, he spread out his light cavalry, which "began to shoot from all sides, not aiming at any particular mark (for, indeed, the order of the Romans was so close, that they could not miss if they would) but simply sent their arrows with great force out of strong bent bows, the strokes from which came with extreme violence. The position of the Romans was a very bad one from the first; for if they kept their ranks, they were wounded, and if they tried to charge, they hurt the enemy none the more, and themselves suffered none the less. For the Parthians threw their darts as they fled."

Since his light infantry, lacking many archers or slingers, failed to be of much use against the light cavalry, Crassus waited for the enemy to exhaust his arrows. But when he learned that the enemy had "numerous camels loaded with arrows," Crassus sent his son, Publius, with a force of almost 5,000 heavy infantry, 1,300 cavalry, and 500 archers to attack the enemy. The Parthians fell back before this force until it had advanced far from the main body. Though outnumbered, the Roman archers in Publius' command should have played a significant role because on foot they could shoot with greater speed and accuracy than the mounted Parthians. But pitted against more numerous horse archers with doubtless more powerful bows, they do not seem to have affected the outcome at all.[26]

Publius' cavalry, largely recruited in Gaul, suffered the fate of the Persian general-purpose cavalry nearly 200 years before, which had fought the heavy cavalry of Alexander's Companions of the King. The Parthians met the charging Gallic cavalry with their heavy cavalry, meeting the "weak and little javelins" of Publius' Gauls with body armor and shields "of tough raw hides and iron, whereas the lightly clad bodies of his Gaulish horsemen were exposed to the strong spears of the enemy." But the courageous Gallic cavalrymen gave a good account of themselves; they "would catch hold of the great spears, and close upon the enemy and so pull them from their horses, where they could scarce stir by reason of the heaviness of their armor, and many of the Gauls quitting their own horses, would creep under those of the enemy, and stick them in the belly."[27]

The unhorsed survivors of the Gallic cavalry joined the Roman heavy infantry, beset on every side by the enemy light cavalry whose vaunted darts rained upon the close-packed Romans who were "hit and killed, dying, not by a quick and easy death, but with miserable pains and convulsions; for writhing upon the darts in their bodies, they broke them in their wounds, and when they would by force pluck out the barbed points, they caught the nerves and veins, so that they tore and tortured themselves. Many of them died thus, and those that survived were disabled for any service, and when Publius exhorted them to charge the cuirassiers, they showed him their hands nailed to their shields, and their feet stuck to the ground." Having defeated Publius' detachment with their missiles, the Parthians closed in on the remnant "with their lances, killed them fighting, nor were above five hundred taken prisoners. Cutting off the head of Publius, they rode off directly towards Crassus."[28]

Crassus' predicament differed little from his son's, for "the missiles falling thick and fast upon them from all sides at once struck down many by a mortal blow, rendering many useless for battle, and caused distress to all. They flew into their eyes and pierced their hands." Thus Crassus' men found that "it was impracticable to move and impracticable to remain at rest."[29]

Though the missiles of the light cavalry carried the burden of the Parthian victory, the heavy cavalry did its part when the men "with their spears drove the Romans close together, except those who rushed upon them. . . . Neither did these do much execution, being quickly dispatched; for the strong thick spears made large and mortal wounds, and often run [sic] through two men at once." Not only did the heavy cavalry keep the Romans bunched together so every arrow found its mark, but if the Romans crowded upon one another too close to use their weapons but able to cover each other with locked shields, they made themselves vulnerable to the heavy cavalry, which were "upon them with a rush, striking down some and at least scattering the others; and if they extended their ranks to avoid this, they would be struck with the arrows."[30]

It took longer than a single day to complete the destruction of Crassus' army on the open plain near Carrhae. At the end of the day, some of the Parthians' lances "were bent and others were broken, while the bowstring snapped under the constant shooting, the missiles were exhausted, the swords all blunted and, most of all, . . . the men themselves grew weary of the slaughter." The struggle continued the following day, and ultimately the Parthians killed Crassus and many others as well as capturing a large portion of his army.[31]

The Parthians attempted to follow their success by invading Syria. But though "almost invincible in their own country and in any that" had "similar characteristics," they lacked the means of besieging the cities and, in one case, even of approaching one because "the neighborhood of this city was overgrown with timber." Since "they did not dare, nay they were not even able to penetrate this with cavalry, they formed a plan to cut down the trees and lay bare the whole place, so that they might approach the town with confidence and safety. But finding themselves unable to do this, because the task was a great one," they changed their objective to another town. Meanwhile, the Romans had "harassed those of them who had scattered abroad," and, soon after losing men in an ambush, the Parthians abandoned their campaign in the uncongenial environment of Syria.[32]

Crassus' disastrous experience clearly demonstrated the superiority of the light cavalry weapon system over heavy infantry when campaigning on terrain suitable for horses. The heavy cavalry aided the Parthian victory; but with sufficient arrows, which their commander had carefully provided, their light cavalry could have won the battle unaided. Greek heavy infantry had sometimes found the Persian mounted bowmen dangerous, but the rugged terrain of Greece had saved the Greeks from disaster. But in the Parthians' own country, Roman heavy infantry met annihilating defeat.

Summary of the Capabilities of the Four Weapon Systems

The four basic weapon systems of the ancients are summarized in schematic 1.2. Each of these has its own special capability and relative dominance. The Parthians dramatically demonstrated the power of light cavalry against heavy infantry on terrain suitable for cavalry. They also exhibited what Alexander had already shown, that neither light cavalry nor general-purpose cavalry not specifically trained and equipped for shock action can resist heavy cavalry. But the Parthian heavy cavalry did not charge the infantry when the Romans had formed a square to meet them. Alexander, too, never used his heavy cavalry against the front of a phalanx, because properly formed heavy infantry can resist the charge of heavy cavalry.

	Foot	*Mounted*
Shock	Heavy Infantry	Heavy Cavalry
Missile	Light Infantry	Light Cavalry

Schematic 1.2. Weapon Systems Matrix

In close combat with a man on foot, a man on horseback enjoyed a number of advantages, including a higher position and a consequent ability to strike down at his opponent. The horse itself was often a valuable ally. These advantages, coupled with the initiative provided by the cavalryman's greater mobility, could make him an excellent shock weapon system if the cavalryman were well enough trained to overcome the precariousness of his seat.

To resist the shock cavalry, the heavy infantry had to form a group. Against skillful Roman soldiers, thoroughly armored, protected by large, strong shields, and formed six ranks deep, even the armored Parthian heavy cavalry with their long lances could not prevail. Depth, the better fighting platform of the earth, and the ability to give undivided attention to the combat, together with a square formation that left no side vulnerable, meant that cavalry could not match the coordinated group action of the foot soldiers. Though formed as a group and working together under a leader, cavalrymen still had to fight as individuals. This attribute made it easy for them to go into action promptly—because they could fight adequately without having to order their array—but this characteristic of individual action reduced their effectiveness in frontal combat with a formed group of foot soldiers. The cavalry was, however, the ideal weapon system for the offensive mission of reaching and promptly attacking the infantry's weak flanks and rear.

The horse archer had a much more pronounced disadvantage in combat against the foot archer. By giving his undivided attention to his shooting, the foot archer had a greater rate of fire and, even independent of the benefits of his steady platform, greater accuracy. The foot archer could, as did the Persian archers who faced the Greeks, protect himself with a large, lightweight shield.

Illustration 1.5. Heavy Cavalryman Defeats Light Infantryman

The horseman could not defend himself that way and still use his bow and manage his horse. In addition, as the Persian cavalry saw in its attack on the Greek archers at Plataea, the horse presented a large and vulnerable target. But the foot archer would have no chance against heavy cavalry. Just as the Greek heavy infantry defeated the Persian foot archers at Marathon and Plataea, so could heavy cavalry close quickly through the zone where the arrows fell and, protected by armor, use lance and sword to defeat the light infantry. The lightness of the bowmen's equipment would not even avail them of the opportunity to run away because the cavalry could easily overtake them.

So it is clear that if Crassus could have organized a Roman army of half heavy infantry and half old-model Persian archers, he could have readily resisted the Parthian attack. The heavy infantry could have protected the archers from the Parthian lancers and the bowmen could have kept at bay the Parthian horse archers. Such a Roman army would, however, have had only a defensive capability: it could have controlled only the ground upon which it stood.

But the terrain severely restrained the apparent predominance of the mounted way of war. Cavalry could not function in forests, and in dense woods even foot bowmen had a disadvantage because of limitations to their visibility and mobility. This formidable restriction inspired the Parthians to consider cutting down a forest. Mountainous country inhibited cavalry less but usually confined its action to the valleys. Thus the Parthians remained invincible in their own country but never were able to conquer the Roman provinces in Syria or Asia Minor.

Geography had much to do with the development of regional or national models of warfare, as seen with the Greeks, the Persians, and the Parthians. Alexander and the Carthaginians and Romans amalgamated these methods, but their terrain caused the Parthians to recreate a national system that they could use successfully against the Romans.

Another disadvantage of the cavalry was its cost. In ancient times a horse cost as much as a man; equipping the horse with a protective covering added to the expense; and carrying its armor in addition to an armored man required a robust steed. Breeding war horses strong enough for these tasks raised the price of the horse, and even a lighter, faster animal for the light cavalry required a particular breed. In addition, the mounted men themselves cost more, for they required more training than the foot archer to learn to shoot well from horseback and more skill to fight at close quarters from horseback than from the ground. Thus, though Crassus's Roman army had triple the number of their Parthian opponents, it cost very little more. Although the outcome of the campaign amply justified this variance in price per man for the Parthian forces, the difference in expense also forcefully argued that the terrain and the tactical situation should clearly warrant the use of mounted troops before governments or commanders should decide to give up two or three foot soldiers to have one mounted man.

The mounted way of war was irrelevant for sieges. Because horses were useless against ditches and walls, infantry conducted sieges. Of course, the cavalrymen could dismount, but serving as infantrymen wasted their training, and they may have lacked some of the skills needed for fighting on foot. Their background as cavalrymen might even predispose them against the digging and artisan work inseparable from sieges.

So, in open country a just combination of heavy and light infantry could resist a mixture of light and heavy cavalry. In mountainous, forested, or broken terrain the cavalry could not function effectively, and here the relatively inexpensive infantry reigned supreme and infantry had to fight infantry. On the defense, infantry had the advantage against the opponent's infantry similarly armed. With arrows or slings the motionless man could shoot more accurately and could provide himself either with natural cover or with artificial protection such as the Persian's shield. An uphill position would give any of the defender's missiles superior velocity and range.

Heavy infantry, on the other hand, obtained little special facility from the defense in a conflict with other heavy infantry, and, in fact, the ancients thought it poor tactics to receive a charge and a benefit to rush the opposing line just before contact. But they did value the uphill position for fighting at close quarters. Defenders early improvised field fortifications because of the power they conferred on the defense. Darius III employed these at Issus, and the successsors of Alexander used them also; but in a sense the Romans started any operation with the defensive when they entrenched their camp every night. If they fought a battle the next day, they had already prepared a place of retreat should they lose. Whenever they occupied a position, they dug in if they had the time. Though heavy infantry did most of the digging, the light infantry benefited from the field fortifications as well.

Cavalry enjoyed few of infantry's advantages on the defensive. The light cavalry could not take cover, though it might find the halt helpful in using the bow. For the heavy cavalry defense was a distinct liability, and heavy cavalry on the defense had to retreat or charge.

This different behavior was necessary because the cavalryman, though functioning as an individual combatant, had two brains instead of one, and the strongest component—the horse—usually had the least trainable brain. When the horse's brain sensed a threat greater than the rider, it said: "run, stay with the herd," and did not stop until the threat became the rider again. No matter what the rider directed, the halted, frightened horse would make agitated movements, preventing the rider from using any weapons he carried, until it could run again. Once it ran, it provided a fairly steady, short-range weapon platform, increased the velocity of hand-held weapons, became a fleeting target, and, in the offense, became a weapon itself, to which any about-to-be-trampled defender would have agreed.[33]

Warfare among the Greeks exhibited the factors controlling combat between the two types of infantry. The success of javelin-throwing peltasts against hoplites forecast the victory of the Parthian horse archers over Crassus's legions. But, because of the only slight difference in mobility between light and heavy infantry, peltasts ran great hazards in applying this throw-and-run tactic. The defeats of the Persian foot archers at Marathon and Plataea show the difficulty of using light infantry against heavy infantry in a battle; the immobile mass created by the large numbers of the Persian bowmen destroyed their light infantry's slender margin of mobility. But lessening the weight of the hoplite's armor, with a consequent increase in mobility, doubtless had much to do with preventing the flowering of a full-fledged tactic based on the superior mobility of the javelin-throwing light infantryman.

In the combat of heavy infantry with heavy infantry at the Battle of Leuctra, Epaminondas applied both the ideas of concentration and envelopment. At Cannae Hannibal's two reserve forces of heavy infantry advanced this notion as did his and Scipio's use of their infantry at Zama. In articulation lay the key to applying with infantry the concepts of a reserve, concentration, and envelopment. The disciplined professional infantry of the Romans, divided into legions, cohorts, maniples, and centuries, provided an army that had the articulation and responsiveness to establish a reserve that the commander could maneuver on the battlefield and use to envelop the enemy by striking at the flank, a point of weakness.

Alexander's introduction of a combined-arms army overshadowed the utility of this articulation in a battle of heavy infantry against heavy infantry. In using each of the four weapon systems, Alexander relied on his heavy cavalry to defeat the enemy's cavalry and attack the enemy's infantry in the rear while first his skirmishing light infantry, and then his heavy infantry, engaged the enemy's infantry in front and his light cavalry engaged some of the enemy's cavalry. Even if Alexander had not introduced heavy cavalry, which had no trouble driving through the Persian general-purpose cavalry, he would have had an advantage because in shock action, defense conferred no benefit on cavalry. Against the enemy's unarticulated heavy infantry, the cavalry attack in the flank and rear usually decided the battle. One exception to this occurred at the Battle of Arbela, where Alexander's cavalry broke through the weak Persian center. But the heavy infantry center of Greek armies usually proved impervious to penetration.

In the Alexandrian system victory on unobstructed and unfortified terrain seemed to go to the army that had better cavalry either in quality, quantity, or a combination of these factors. Cannae and Zama support this generalization, in spite of the decisive role of Hannibal's infantry at Cannae and the role of excellent articulation of the infantry on both sides at Zama. The Romans never fully adopted the Alexandrian reliance on cavalry but won their key victories over Alexandrian armies because their allies provided critical supremacy in cavalry. Against the Gauls their own cavalry and the ability of their articulated infantry to cover its flanks proved adequate to deal with the enemy's cavalry. But they based their Gallic victories on the predominance of their infantry and their reliance on the defensive power of entrenchments.

On one major occasion in a traditional Alexandrian battle a preponderance in cavalry failed to ensure victory. This occurred in a Civil War battle between two famous antagonists, Julius Caesar, the military and political genius who came to rule Rome, and Pompey, a soldier who had won renowned victories on three continents but who showed less aptitude for politics. The armies of these two superb leaders met in 48 B.C. at the Battle of Pharsalus. As they faced one another, each had one flank reaching the bank of a river. Pompey logically concentrated his stronger cavalry on the open flank along with all of his slingers and archers. Seeing this, Caesar, an experienced and resourceful commander, not only placed all of his cavalry there but also formed as a reserve a fourth line of about 10 percent of his heavy infantry. He placed this reserve behind his open flank, facing outward at right angles to his line.

As both Caesar and Pompey expected, Pompey's cavalry drove back Caesar's and, displaying good discipline, turned then against Caesar's flank. Caesar then ordered forward his reserve cohorts who "advanced rapidly with colours flying" and "attacked Pompey's horse with such fury that not one of them stood their ground." Having driven off the cavalry, the cohorts of Caesar's heavy infantry reserve met the archers and slingers who, "defenceless, without support, were slain." Pushing on and supported by Caesar's cavalry, which had returned to the field of battle, the reserve attacked the flank of Pompey's legions. Either lacking a reserve or unable to deploy it in time, Pompey, a great general, went down in defeat in spite of his splendid cavalry. But against a less articulated infantry than Roman legions, the cavalry almost surely must have succeeded in winning the battle by reaching the flank and rear of Caesar's army.[34]

Although the Alexandrian battle pitted light infantry skirmishers against light infantry skirmishers, one line of heavy infantry against another, and the cavalry on the flanks against the enemy's cavalry, the ideal remained that of bringing a stronger weapon system against an inferior one. The triumph of Greek heavy infantry against immobilized Persian light infantry, the victory of javelin-throwing peltasts over slower-moving hoplites, and the success of the Parthians against the Romans remained the model for attaining tactical mastery with the least effort. But when opponents placed their light infantry ahead as skirmishers to use their missiles against the heavy infantry, identical weapon systems fought, just as cavalry fought cavalry because each general placed it on the wings where it could reach the heavy infantry's vulnerable flank and rear. At Pharsalus Caesar enjoyed a rare combined-arms battle success in pitting one better weapon system against another when his heavy infantry defeated first Pompey's cavalry and then his light infantry, opening the way for his own light infantry and cavalry, as well as his heavy infantry flank force, to attack the enemy's flank and rear. To put the stronger weapon system against the weaker remained the goal, but one difficult to achieve when armies had essentially the same combination of weapon systems.

Caesar's rapid success, like those of the victors at Cannae and Zama, exhibits how much quicker a battle with shock action may end when compared with the slow work of the peltasts' javelins or the Parthian arrows against Crassus at Carrhae. But, unlike Caesar's at Pharsalus, the Parthians' victory was inevitable, founded as it was on the employment of tactics and weapon systems that had an invincible, intrinsic advantage on the terrain of the battle.

The certainty of success for a dominant weapon system made it the choice of the ancients whenever they had the opportunity. The hope that elephants would constitute a superior weapon system doubtless does much to explain their persistent, but usually futile, employment in battle. The paramount weapon system abolishes any distinction between attack and defense. Alexander's heavy cavalry won for him on the offensive, but Parthian cavalry, and the peltasts who defeated hoplites, attacked to make use of their supremacy, even though they had only defensive objectives.

Fortifications almost always provided one sure resource for the defenders. Cavalry was useless against walls and ditches, and against infantry the defenders of fortifications combined the benefits of both light and heavy infantry. Sophisticated siege warfare redressed much of the imbalance between the two, but not enough to deprive the defense of an advantage.

The commander on the offensive who faced a predominant weapon system should, if he had learned anything from Crassus's disaster, abandon his aggressive designs. If both attackers and defenders had essentially the same weapon systems, and the defender did not take refuge behind fortifications, the ancients sought another means of assailing their opponent's weakness. Heavy infantry, formidable against a frontal assault of their own kind and nearly invincible against such a charge by the heavy cavalry, proved to have vulnerable flanks and rear, even to the weaker heavy cavalry weapon system. In the enveloping attack the ancients found another means of striking at their opponent's weakness. With phalanxes that drifted to the right, such envelopments occurred naturally, the modest degree of articulation possessed by the Spartans giving them the ability to exploit this more effectively than their opponents. Epaminondas at Leuctra carried out an envelopment not based on an initial overlapping of the enemy line. He also had the aid of cavalry that screened his movements and prevented the Spartans from seeing the Sacred Band, facilitating his envelopment.

The phalanx's lack of articulation made its use for envelopment difficult, and Alexander showed that the cavalry's mobility and modest requirement for a careful array made it best suited for the offensive tactic of the enveloping movement. This ability to move more rapidly than the infantry and to go into combat in essentially the same formation in which they moved to battle made horsemen ideal offensive troops who had as their most decisive mission the attack on the enemy's flanks and rear. Weaker than the heavy infantry in frontal combat, the cavalry had formidable powers when it struck the enemy's unprotected flank and rear.

Whether involving one or more weapon systems, combat between armies with essentially the same composition revolved around envelopment. From this fundamental tactic developed both the concept of the reserve and the practice of generals who commanded, rather than fought in, the battle. The Roman improvement in articulation made easier the creation of a reserve as well as provided protection to the flank and rear and enabled them to use infantry for envelopments.

LOGISTICS

The Provision of Soldiers and Supplies

Logistics embraces the methods of supplying armies and moving them from place to place; broadly construed, it can even include their initial creation. Often war has supported war, and victorious armies have maintained themselves at an enemy's expense. In the absence of this opportunity, the size of a nation's armed forces depends on its population and its productivity. In ancient times most people engaged in farming, sustaining themselves and producing an excess sufficient to feed only quite small populations of merchants, artisans, priests, and officials. A society of such low economic productivity could keep under arms only a small proportion of its populace. Even when nations had a well-developed money economy, primitive systems of taxation, finance, and banking made raising money difficult. Only in comparatively modern times have states had available income taxes, fractional reserve banking, and debt monetization to divert a large portion of national output to support war. In ancient times even these devices would have produced little because so many of the people, living at subsistence level, had no surplus for war. The Roman Empire, though amply developed politically and economically, still kept less than 1 percent of its population in the armed forces.

Lack of both real and financial resources made the militia a popular manpower system. Under the militia system some or all free males had an obligation to serve in the armed forces in time of need. Usually they had to equip themselves at their own expense, though in consideration of this the state might excuse them from certain taxes. Some militias trained, often spending significant amounts of time practicing essential skills. Others, however, lacked combat skills and even specialized arms, coming to fight with agricultural tools as weapons, for example. Though militias sometimes supplemented professional soldiers, they also often constituted the whole armed forces of a state.

The militia had an obvious advantage: it cost very little in peacetime. Offsetting its lower cost was its lower effectiveness. The Greeks long relied on a militia and thus were able to field as many soldiers as the professional army of their huge Persian opponent. The Romans, too, initially relied on militia but, like the Greeks, found that continuous warfare made the specialist not only more effective but also essential. Further, a militia could not fight a long war or even a long campaign; its members had to return to civilian occupations. Stated another way, a state could afford a large militia but could only mobilize it for a brief period. For protracted warfare, professionals, kept under arms for an extended time, had obvious advantages. States not engaged in continuous warfare could prefer a professional army, a choice that burdened its citizens with taxes rather than the expense, inconvenience, and potential danger of military service. A force composed of expensive career professionals had the disadvantage of smaller size but the benefit of soldiers with a higher level of proficiency as compared with the amateurs of a militia.

Supplying an army presented no particular difficulties in peacetime. The militia forces provided for themselves through their normal civilian pursuits of agriculture, commerce, or industry. The state easily met the needs of the professional soldiers because they were usually distributed throughout the country and could readily obtain their most basic need—food—through the established civilian market organization.

Only the concentration of an army, whether militia or professional, created the problem of food supply. An army gathered together for a campaign was comparable to a town: it had a dense population and did not produce its own provisions. But, unlike a town, it had neither a preexisting transportation network nor any established pattern of local suppliers for its various needs.

The ability of an army to be furnished with food in a given vicinity depended in part on the season of the year. If a region was self-sufficient in food, an army could acquire by purchase or force what it needed from the stored food supplies. Immediately after a harvest, the army would have access to a year's supply; just before a harvest, the army would find the granaries empty; in the winter, halfway between harvests, the granaries would contain a six months' supply.

The ratio of the size of the army to the population of its area of concentration also affected the army's ability to feed itself. If the ratio were one soldier per civilian, then the soldiers could subsist as long as the civilians, assuming the soldiers deprived the civilians of everything. If there were ten soldiers per civilian, the soldiers could exist one-tenth as long as the civilians. For example, if the army reached a region 180 days prior to harvest and it outnumbered the civilians 10 to 1, it could remain for 18 days before it must move, assuming it found all of the available food, denied any of it to the civilians, and left them destitute upon departure. An army that could spread over a wider area would, of course, effectively reduce the ratio of soldiers to civilians and so could subsist longer.

For a substantial army to remain long in one place, it usually had to have access to water transportation. Sailing vessels were usually small, though lengths of up to 180 feet were not uncommon during the Roman Empire; their breadth was one-fourth to one-third their overall length; larger ones also had deep, decked-over holes. These vessels moved slowly, due to their stubby design and the use of only a single mast. Primitive rigging limited their ability to sail against the wind, and the lack of navigational aids meant that mariners preferred to remain within sight of land and to seek sheltered places on shore to spend the night. At the same time, even a small vessel could carry 60,000 pounds of provisions, a day's rations for 20,000 men. The alternative—land transportation—meant either a slow-moving ox cart, with an average speed of two miles per hour, or a donkey carrying a load of up to 100 pounds. The lack of suitable roads limited the use of carts, and even after surfaced roads improved arterial transportation, the best land transportation cost at least thirty times that by water.

So armies found great difficulty drawing supplies any distance from their immediate area of concentration. For a substantial force to remain long in one place, it usually had to have access to water transportation. An army large in relation to the population and resources of the region where it quartered itself would thus have to move constantly to new areas unless it had convenient water transportation and had abundant supplies available for the ships to carry to it. This logistic requirement to move might well conflict with its need to resist or advance against an enemy.

The cavalry presented another major supply problem, twenty pounds a day constituting a fair allowance for a horse on campaign. If the number of horses in the army bore the same ratio to the number of horses in the region of concentration as did the number of soldiers to civilians, then local supplies could feed the horses as well as the soldiers. If, however, the army had a larger proportion of horses, the amount of fodder would control how long an army could remain in one place. An army composed entirely of cavalry would have to move far more frequently than an army composed only of infantry. If the army concentrated at some some distance from the enemy, it could spread out and draw its supplies from a greater area. If it had cavalry, the cavalry could spread itself even farther, as its better mobility would permit it to regroup more quickly than an equally dispersed infantry. In this way the greater mobility of cavalry could often permit it to keep its need for fodder from forcing an army to move before the infantry had exhausted the food resources of the region.

Most of the army's other needs did not require replenishment during a campaigning year. Clothing would last a season, though shoes, if the army had them, might need replacement. Since battles occurred infrequently, the initial supply of missiles would usually suffice. Artisans in an army could repair and even fabricate needed items.

Climate also affected military operations. Cold weather and the often con-comitant lack of grass for animals seriously impeded, though rarely prevented, winter campaigning.

The quality of the roads controlled the army's movement by dictating its rate of marching and its use of pack animals or wheeled transport. Mountainous terrain implied poor roads except in the valleys. The number of roads were important, particularly if an army were large in relation to the population of the area through which it marched. Such an army could find it necessary to spread out and march on several roads to find enough for the men and horses to eat.

Thus the movement of armies depended on a number of variables. Small armies with few horses would find themselves little trammeled by logistical considerations and could operate fairly well concentrated, remaining in one place for a substantial length of time. A large force, strong in cavalry, had to disperse as much as possible and move frequently.

The Greek militiaman provided his own arms, as did mercenaries. In the brief campaigns typical of the warfare between Greek city-states, the soldiers carried on their backs the wheat needed to make flour and bake bread, the staple of their diet. They brought wheat, and handmills to grind it, because it kept better than flour. The many servants and slaves accompanying a hoplite army helped with the carrying, ground the flour, and baked the bread. The soldiers supplemented their bread diet with meat, cheese, and vegetables such as onions.

Before the beginning of the short campaign, the state provided the soldiers with money to buy supplies, specifying how many days the campaign would last. But otherwise the government rarely made any provision for supplying the sol-diers. On long campaigns the soldiers were expected to purchase food and drink from their pay. With wages comparable to those of skilled craftsmen, the soldiers could readily meet their needs unless a shortage forced up prices. The government rarely furnished a supply depot even for long campaigns, anticipating that its armies would live on the country.

In a campaign in the territory of allies, soldiers were expected to purchase supplies, but they often followed this practice even in enemy territory, where the invaders could live at the enemy's expense and use loot for pay. In both instances the armies depended on the merchants who accompanied the army to offer their goods for purchase by the soldiers. Thus, for its commissary, the Greeks trusted to private enterprise, even in enemy territory. In a hostile country, the uncertain ability of the soldiers to find supplies and the dispersal necessary while they looked made commanders rely on native merchants, who were more likely to know the location of the supplies that enemy territory offered.

Though depending on the activities of private entrepreneurs, the Greek armies really had a primitive, centralized commissary system. When, for example, one Greek commander captured enemy ships laden with food supplies, he sold the food and used the proceeds to pay the men who, in turn, purchased their food from the merchants. This system also assured that profits made in the enemy's country inured to the state or the general.

Logisitics Illustrated by Alexander's Persian Campaign

The Persian campaign of Alexander the Great presents a ready illustration of an excellent ancient supply organization at work. Unlike the Greeks, Alexander and his father did not trust the initiative of private entrepreneurs for what they needed but had an army organization that provided the supplies for the huge force assembled for the Persian campaign. In addition, Alexander's father had minimized the logistical requirements of the army by reducing the number of servants supporting the soldiers. Since, unlike the Greek hoplite, the Macedonian had to carry his own armor and weapons, Alexander's army had only about one servant to every four soldiers. Because a man can march for long distances bearing eighty pounds, the army moved much of its own baggage but, with fewer servants, could carry less of its own food.

For the remainder of its transport the army depended on pack horses and mules, each having a capacity of about 200 pounds. In spite of the truth of the aphorism that an animal can pull more than it can bear on its back, the Macedonian army preferred pack animals to wagons or carts. Not only could these beasts more easily follow the army over difficult terrain, but also the inefficient harness used in ancient times gave carts and wagons only a small margin of advantage over pack animals. Yoked much like an ox, the horse or mule could not exert his maximum strength pulling because the harness pressed on his windpipe. The ox had more strength than a horse and could pull effectively with his neck, but its temperament was unreliable, it had less endurance than the horse, and it moved at two miles per hour compared with the horse's four. The ox could not even keep up with the infantry's average marching rate of two and one half miles an hour.

The army also needed pack animals to transport such equipment as tents, siege apparatus, assorted tools, medical supplies, and other items, at least one pack animal for every fifty men in the force. Thus, when Alexander crossed into Asia, his army, its servants, and other personnel probably numbered 65,000; he would have needed 1,300 pack animals for the equipment not borne by human beings.

Map 1.2. Persian Empire (dotted line indicates Alexander's march)

CASPIAN SEA

ARAL SEA

SOGDIANA

BACTRIA

SALT DESERT

PERSIAN GULF

Indus R.

Alexander timed this campaign to begin just before the harvest. An earlier start would have found him in a country of exhausted granaries with some of the population on the verge of starvation as they awaited the ripening of the crops. Starting at this time also protected his supply vessels from the stronger Persian navy with its thousands of oarsmen and sailors, which could not take the sea until the new crop had furnished the necessary stock to provision the fleet. On entering Asia, Alexander had a ten-day store of grain, three pounds per day per man and ten pounds per day for the animals. He kept most of this on ships because for each day's supplies the army carried he would have needed more than 1,100 additional pack animals to move the 269,000 pounds of grain for 65,000 people, 6,100 cavalry horses, and 1,300 pack animals. But such an initial inventory gave him some freedom from foraging while he met the Persian army on the Granicus and established his control of northwestern Anatolia.

Having defeated the Persian army, Alexander, following in part the dictates of logistics, advanced along a coastal route where he found productive agriculture and towns with a sufficient transportation network for gathering in food. He thus supplied his army by requisitioning or buying from towns where food would be abundant at harvest. The thickly settled coastal route also offered good roads for marching, so the army could move as much as fifteen miles per day with a day of rest each week both to refresh the men and to allow the pack animals a day without their loads as well as time for grazing to supplement their grain diet. The route also had major rivers, fundamental to the army's daily require-ment of over 90,000 gallons of water to furnish a half gallon a day for each human and eight gallons for each animal. Alexander could depend on ships for carrying supplies from point to point along the coast and even for bringing water when he besieged a town on a waterless peninsula. A large merchant ship of the day could carry 400 tons, the same load as 4,000 pack animals.

The Persians commanded the sea, but Alexander could rely on his cargo ships maintaining his communications along the Anatolian shore because ancient warships could remain at sea for only a limited time. A small, light warship carried 200 sailors and oarsmen to provide the fighting power as well as for propulsion independent of the wind. But the 200 men required 600 pounds of food and 100 gallons (800 pounds) of water a day. The ship in which the design had dedicated everything to minimizing weight and bulk to enhance its speed could carry only a circumscribed amount of food and water. The fleet lacked the ability to cruise far and counted on staying close to land for frequent re-plenishment of supplies. On one occasion, Macedonian troops drove off the Persian fleet by patrolling the shores of a river mouth and preventing a landing to restore the fleet's water supplies. A fleet so tethered by logistics had great difficulty maintaining a tight blockade.

Alexander reached southwestern Anatolia by fall, subduing the country as he advanced. He divided his huge army during the winter, which both facilitated supply and brought more of the country under his control. The following year he began his march in late July, in accord with the later harvest of the higher elevations of central Anatolia. But he had to make preparations ahead of time to pass through desolate terrain that had very little water. Since the pack animals alone drank eight gallons of water daily, he could not contemplate carrying water.

After first securing the submission of the people of the area and probably taking hostages to ensure their continued loyalty, he sent out advance parties along his projected route. These brought supplies with them and also bought or requisitioned more locally to create depots. In addition, by damming up the small streams they tripled their yield of water, because two-thirds of the water in a flowing stream runs away from soldiers trying to quench their thirst. Because of these preparations, which depended on the cooperation of the local government, Alexander could march eighty-two miles through a region initially without food or water.

For his march along the eastern coast of the Mediterranean to Egypt, sea transport proved indispensable. During the seven-month siege of the fortified port city of Tyre, a river near the city provided Alexander's army with an adequate supply of water but the adjacent agricultural area produced less than a tenth of the army's grain needs. Though pack animals could haul in grain from a sixty-mile radius, even within this radius the area lacked sufficient productivity to sustain the besiegers. Transport by water made possible the siege. In its harvest-time march south from Tyre toward Egypt the army found abundant grain supplies but had to depend on water transport for the army's drinking water. Conquering Egypt in the late fall, Alexander spent the winter in the fertile Nile Valley.

In this long war to conquer the vast Persian Empire and invade India, Alexander encountered logistical obstacles greater than those he met in his march from the Hellespont to Egypt, but even this part of the campaign shows the importance of supply and the constraints logistics imposed not only on the movement of armies but also on their remaining in place.

Alexander's return from India exhibited the extreme of the hazards that marches could present. Alexander planned to march through the Gedrosian Desert on the north coast of the Arabian Sea by following the coast and drawing supplies from the fleet. The army would control the coast and furnish the fleet with water from the intermittently flowing rivers in the region, which the summer monsoon rains would fill. But the very monsoon winds that brought the moisture kept the fleet from sailing and forced Alexander and his army, unable to retrace its steps over a territory already both foraged and devasted to bring the local rulers to terms, to march 150 miles through desert with little to eat and long distances between the rivers. And, according to the historian of Alexander's conquests, on its march the army "met with lofty ridges of deep sand, not closely pressed and hardened, but such as received those who stepped upon it just as if they were stepping into mud, or rather into untrodden snow." Only Alexander's charismatic leadership carried the army through such an ordeal.[35]

That the soldiers "slaughtered most of the horses and mules" for food meant the army had little means of carrying their disabled. "Thus some were left behind along the roads on account of sickness, others from fatigue or the effects of the heat, or from not being able to bear up against the drought." To avoid the heat, the army "generally made the marches by night, some of the men were overcome by sleep on the road; afterwards rousing up again, those who still had strength followed upon the tracks of the army; but only a few out of many overtook the main body in safety. Most of them perished in the sand, like men getting out of their course at sea."[36]

Even the rain, which filled the rivers and kept the survivors from dying of thirst, also could prove a dangerous enemy. "On one occasion, when the army bivouacked, for the sake of water, near a small brook which was a winter torrent, about the second watch of the night the brook which flowed there was suddenly swelled by the rains in the mountains which had fallen unperceived by the soldiers. The torrent advanced with so great a flood as to destroy most of the wives and children of the men who followed the army, and to sweep away all of the royal baggage as well as all the beasts of burden still remaining. The soldiers, after great exertions, were hardly able to save themselves." Truly Alexander accomplished a great feat to bring a quarter of his army through this march.[37]

This experience most dramatically demonstrates why ancient armies had to plan their marches to pass through regions of adequate food and water at a time to avoid the period before the harvest. They needed the good will of the local inhabitants but could rely on coercion; but force produced less food than cooperation. Dispersing an army in small groups and marching over different routes greatly facilitated the provisioning of larger forces, and scattering an army during the winter enabled it to draw on a more ample area of agricultural production.

Supply from a depot in the rear depended on transport by sea or river because pack animals could carry useful amounts only from within a radius of sixty miles. The use of water transport from a distance implied, of course, a logistic organization and the money or power to have supplies available for the water transport to convey to the distant army. Alexander's Persian campaign showed that his competently organized kingdom had all of these logistic requisites; except for the one near-disaster in the desert, Alexander and his army remained adequately provided for throughout his long Persian campaign.

Alexander's efficient system also clearly exemplifies the logistic organization and methods with which the Roman state maintained its armies. The excellence of Roman logistics always furnished them with parity and usually superiority over their enemies in this respect and so formed a fundamental support for the successful strategy of their conquest and conservation of their empire.

STRATEGY

Persisting and Raiding Strategies Distinguished

Military strategy combines tactics and logistics to shape the conduct of operations. As traditionally defined, strategy has three parts. Grand strategy integrates political objectives with military means to determine the broad outlines of the plan for the conduct of war. Strategy proper has to do with the concentration and movement of armies and navies. Grand tactics, the lowest branch of strategy, concerns the maneuver of armies, usually the activities that create the conditions for battle. This book uses the term strategy to designate strategy proper and grand tactics. This has been the traditional province of the term strategy. Throughout this work the term will have a purely military connotation, and will not deal with politics or economics or other such factors affecting the relations between powers, considerations more properly confined to the concept of grand strategy. This definition differs little, if at all, from that branch of the art of war that the U.S. army currently calls operations.

Just as ancient warfare exhibits most of the variables that have concerned tacticians in modern times, so also does it offer examples of almost every dimension of strategy. The great masters of the art of war in ancient times displayed a perceptiveness and sophistication in their strategy that their successors have rarely surpassed.

Warfare in the ancient world made much use of raids, which were temporary intrusions into a hostile country, as well as invasions, which were temporary or permanent occupations of the territory invaded. Though a form of military action, raids often had objectives that were not solely military. A foray into foreign territory, for example, might have had the purely economic goal of carrying off booty, the raiders seeking to avoid any military conflict. Such an incursion might also have had a political purpose, and destruction of what the raiders did or could not carry off added to its effectiveness. Such an inroad—or the threat of such an inroad—sought to extract political concessions from the raided country. If the raiders had cavalry and their opponents did not, they might carry out the foray without serious risk of combat. With a weapon system similar to that of the defender, a raider ran a higher risk of conflict but could still depend on the primacy of retreat over pursuit.

Regardless of the objective—economic, political, or military—raids presented similar problems for the executants and defenders. And the transitoriness of presence did not necessarily mean conflict was to be avoided: a superior army might actually seek battle in enemy territory without intending to remain to control the country invaded.

One may thus distinguish between raids and a persisting strategy of invasion. Whereas the former used a temporary presence in hostile territory, a persisting offensive strategy envisioned a longer, even permanent, occupation of the territory of the adversary or his allies. A persisting defensive strategy sought to prevent such an occupation. On both the defensive and the offensive, the persisting strategy envisioned the possibility of conflict between the principal hostile forces; raiders, on the other hand, often could attain their objective without significant military conflict and frequently sought to do so.

The ancient Greeks often used a raiding strategy. They had limited political goals and rarely sought the overthrow of their enemy. Their method involved making a foray into the neighboring city-state just before harvest and destroying the crops by marching through the fields. They could accomplish more serious destruction by burning buildings and cutting down olive trees and grape vines. The invaded state had a choice: to yield, to lose its agricultural resources, or to call out its hoplite militia and fight.

If the invaded state resisted, the battle usually took place by mutual consent on level ground. If the defenders had taken up a strong position on a hill, the raider could "refuse to meet us on such ground but go around," explained the historian Polybius, "devastating the territory." This would not just force the defender from his strong position but tempt him to strike the intruders, dispersed to carry out the work of destruction. If the invader had invited attack from a strong position, the defender could wait him out because he could easily supply himself while the attacker, immobile in a hostile country, would have to leave his position to find food. Even if the intruder could manage to wait in his strong position, he would lose much of the leverage of his raid because the defender would be gathering in his harvest.[38]

The stronger contestant had to rely on these devastating raids because he could not compel the inferior belligerent to face him in circumstances that did not nullify his greater strength. The weaker army could take refuge behind city walls, offer battle in a strong position, or simply take advantage of its ability to retreat faster than the more powerful force could pursue. In fact, the weaker could simply move about erratically, feeding off the country in which it maneuvered, and fairly easily elude the stronger. Commanders in ancient warfare had to contend with their inability to induce an unwilling opponent to fight a battle. Destructive raids provided both a substitute for a victory in the field and a means of coercing the inferior army into fighting.

Against agricultural economies the raiding strategy forced an enemy either to make the desired political concessions or to fight to protect the crops. If the defender perceived the chances of defeat were greater than the burden of political concessions, he would yield; if not, he would fight. But there was a third alternative: if the defender thought the raiders' political demands too burdensome and the chance of victory in battle too slight, he might bear the cost of the raid and keep his army in its strong position or within the walls of his city.

The Greeks used a raid to pursue simultaneously military and political objectives. If the destruction of the enemy's crops caused the concession, the foray would have attained its political aim directly. If it provoked the weaker enemy army to fight, the incursion would have attained a military goal, and the victory in the resulting battle could lead to the desired political result. This dual-purpose raid represented only one type of raid and was fairly distinctive in its combination of military and political objectives.

The victor in the hoplite battle usually won the short war, even though the battle might not be very bloody nor the losses of the defeated very severe. But in view of such a very limited political objective as the annexation of a small piece of territory, a single military action of moderate consequences sufficed to attain or defeat the purposes of the war. Usually the energy expended in a war was proportional to the political goal, modest aims eliciting a small effort, great objectives major and persevering exertions. If the issue of the war meant more to one side than to another, the contender that saw the greater stake in the war would make proportionately greater endeavors. The best of ancient soldiers and statesmen saw no reason to make unlimited military efforts for limited objectives.

The Greeks' raiding strategy was a direct result of the Greeks' dependence on militia forces: standing armies might have fortified strong points and contested the raiders at the border. The use of militia also had much to do with the brevity of wars. Neither combatant could afford to keep his forces mobilized for very long and so away from civilian occupations in a society close to the margin of existence. The raiding strategy also relied on the small geographical size of the contenders and the relatively large size of their militia in relation to the space and crops to be defended. A king of Sparta at war with Persia used raids to devastate part of Asia Minor, an area vastly larger than all of Greece. His use of this strategy against a small part of a distant province completely failed to coerce the king of Persia residing far away in Mesopotamia.

Alexander's Campaign: An Exemplification of Combat, Logistic, and Persisting Strategies

Alexander the Great's invasion of the Persian Empire of Darius III presents an excellent example of the persisting strategy of aiming at occupation of the enemy's territory. Alexander's political objectives were too ambitious to attain even by the very extensive and destructive raids his huge army could have carried out in Persian territory.

With as many as 35,000 and perhaps nearly 50,000 infantry and cavalry, Alexander had a larger army than the Persians forces in Anatolia and a formidable weapon system essentially unknown to the enemy in his Companion heavy cavalry. Although the Persian army had a strong force of hired Greek hoplites, it recognized Alexander's preponderance in infantry. In the absence of the king, this provoked a debate among the Persian generals as to whether their strategy should embrace combat against Alexander's men or whether they should direct their efforts toward defeating his army by destroying its logistic base.

The leader of the Greek infantry advised the council of generals and governors "not to risk a conflict with the Macedonians, since they were far superior to themselves in infantry, and Alexander was there in person; whereas Darius was not with them. He advised them to advance and destroy the fodder, by trampling it under their horses' hoofs, to burn the crops in the country, and not even to spare the very cities. 'For then Alexander,' said he, 'will not be able to stay in the land from lack of provisions.' " Such a logistic strategy, if rigorously applied, would surely have defeated Alexander's invasion in a country that had only intermittent areas of intensive cultivation. And Persian command of the sea would have prevented Alexander from carrying food from Greece across the Aegean to supply his army.

In addition, the Persians had used such a logistic strategy earlier during the Plataea campaign. Instead of assaulting the enemy's army to defeat a Greek advance, Mardonius, the shrewd Persian commander, had used his superb cavalry to raid the Greek army's supply lines to compel a retreat from its strong position at Plataea. The cavalry had intercepted some supplies, but then a detachment of cavalry sent to the Greek rear "came upon a body of 500 pack animals which were just entering the plain, bringing provisions to the Greek camp. . . . Seeing this prey in their power, the Persians set upon them and slaughtered them, sparing none, neither man nor beast; till at last, when they had had enough of slaying, they secured such as were left and bore them off" to the Persian camp. This augmented an already plentiful Persian supply, for in nearby Thebes the Persians had "abundant stores of corn for themselves, and of fodder for their beasts of burden."[39] Able to interdict the supply line of the stationary Greek army, the Persian cavalry also gained temporary control of the spring that furnished water to much of the Greek army, leaving it "choked up and spoiled." The Greek army found their supply situation desperate, for, in addition to a lack of water, "all the provisions they had brought with them were gone; and the attendants who had been sent to fetch supplies . . . were prevented from returning to camp by the Persian horse, which now closed the passage."[40]

Yet even with this background and the advice of the leader of the Greek infantry, the Persian conference rejected a logistic strategy, the governor of the area closest to Alexander's army asserting that "he would not allow a single house belonging to the people placed under his rule to be burned."[41]

So the Persian conference chose the combat strategy, their army contesting Alexander's advance soon after he crossed into Asia. They lost their defensive battle on the Granicus River when the Companion cavalry defeated the Persian general-purpose cavalry and then attacked their Greek heavy infantry in the flank and rear; the conflict cost the Persians heavily, in both killed and prisoners among their infantry. This attrition together with the psychological impact of the defeat meant that no Persian field army contested Alexander's advance through Anatolia. Meanwhile, in Mesopotamia, Darius III began creating a new army.

In carrying out his invasion, Alexander had no choice but combat strategy, for he had no means of attacking the logistics of the Persian army. But he did have an alternative in dealing with the splendid Persian fleet that effectively interdicted most Macedonian trans-Aegean sea traffic. "Notwithstanding their superiority," Alexander's principal subordinate, the wise and experienced Parmenio, "advised Alexander to fight a sea-battle, expecting the Greeks to be victorious with their fleet. . . . He also urged that if they won the battle, they would reap a great advantage from it in regard to their main object in the war; and if they were beaten, their defeat would not be of any great moment; for even as it was, the Persians held the sovereignty of the sea." Alexander argued that he did not want to give up on so "unstable an element" as the sea "the advantage which the Macedonians derived from their skill and courage." But he stressed the political consequences of defeat in a naval battle that would do "no small damage to their first prestige in the war, both for other reasons, and especially because the Greeks, being animated with courage at the news of the naval defeat, would attempt to effect a revolution" against Macedonian dominance of Greece.[42]

But Alexander had a logistic alternative to combat; he could "get the mastery over the Persian fleet by defeating their army on land." Alexander explained that he would be able to break up the Persian fleet "if he captured their maritime cities; since they would neither have any ports from which they could recruit their crews, nor any harbor in Asia to which they could bring their ships." Initially, this strategy fitted his own logistic need to follow the fertile Anatolian coast and to keep in touch with his supply ships moving along the coast.[43]

This line of advance also had an important political advantage, for the coast had a mostly Greek population, one often in revolt against Persian authority. Since Alexander represented a federation of Greek states, the Greek cities of Anatolia found it easy to yield to him. Alexander had counted on finding such a substantial political base for his conquest, knowing that this was fundamental to his success. Had Alexander faced the united political opposition of the subjects of the Persian king, his military victory on the Granicus would have availed him nothing, for, in spite of the substantial size of his army, he could not possibly have dominated so large a hostile country. But the Greek cities surrendered to him as he advanced, and he, acting as their liberator from Persian rule, appointed politically acceptable governors, usually from the cities and regions that surrendered to him.

Alexander's invasion shows the importance of two variables in implementing the persisting strategy of territorial conquest. If Alexander had brought his huge army into a small state, such as one of those in Greece, he would have had such a high ratio of force to space as to render a popular resistance impossible. But even in the Anatolian provinces of the Persian Empire, he would have lacked the men to subdue and hold in subjection such a large country had he faced real political opposition. He succeeded because of the political support he found there and that he cultivated carefully and shrewdly.

Alexander's accomplishment illustrates the important role of political attitudes and of fostering them, but the experience of Antiochus VII of Syria exhibits this factor even more graphically. In 130 B.C. Antiochus marched into Mesopotamia to recover territory recently conquered by Parthian invaders from the East. Having defeated the Parthians in the field and receiving a welcome from the cities Greek in culture and by many others dissatisfied with Parthian rule, Antiochus conquered Mesopotamia in a single campaign and drove the Parthian monarch back into his own domains. To secure his conquest, Antiochus wintered in his conquered territories, distributing his army and quartering it in a number of cities. But the burden of supporting the troops and their repellent behavior alienated these cities from Antiochus, and they began to yearn for a return of Parthian rule. Meanwhile, King Antiochus apparently spent the winter very convivially rather than attending to his duties as commander. Parthian agents managed to arrange for the people of the cities where Antiochus had quartered his troops to make a simultaneous attack on the soldiers, and at the same time the Parthian army took the field early, finding supplies and support in a land that had recently welcomed Antiochus. The Parthians killed Antiochus, and they and the inhabitants of the cities captured most of his surprised army.

Most of the non-Greek areas of the Persian Empire also yielded to the firm but magnanimous Alexander. But because of the moderation and politicial astuteness of Alexander's rule, they did not turn against him as did Antiochus' supporters. The Macedonian king could take advantage of a favorable political situation in that for more than half a century the Persian empire had displayed marked centripetal tendencies with frequent revolts led by the local rulers, called satraps. Only with difficulty and frequent conflict had the kings maintained their authority over the whole of the empire. Darius III had ruled for only two years and as yet lacked established authority and prestige, if only because he came from a distant branch of the royal family and had come to the throne by the assassination of his two predecessors. Alexander exploited this political situation and usually secured the submission of most satrapies even before he crossed their borders. Wisely, he then carefully conserved vested interests, often confirming in power the Persian satrap who had yielded to him.

Even without this political weakness of the central government, local authorities would have found it difficult to make a strong resistance after Alexander had defeated the Persian army. Unlike the Greeks, Persian cities and provinces lacked a militia. Most of the non-Greek citizens of the empire had no tradition of or training for military service, having long relied on the professional forces of the king and the satrap. If local authorities had strongly opposed Alexander, lacking a militia to defend their walled cities they would have had to abandon a defensive persisting strategy of seeking to keep Alexander out of their domains. Instead, they would have had to resort to a defensive raiding strategy of harrying Alexander's army. Alexander would face this kind of opposition later in the course of his long conquest.

After Alexander had conquered western and central Anatolia, he advanced along the coast toward Syria. Here in early fall Darius III, a capable soldier, marched to meet him and, arriving from Babylon with his army, took up a position in northwestern Syria on the flank of Alexander's advance down the Syrian coast. The Persian army occupied a well-watered position in a fertile plain where the king could easily supply his army and where, if a battle developed, he would have ample space for employing his numerically dominant cavalry. Darius's army occupied a flank position, one where he could reach the enemy's rear if Alexander marched past him down the Syrian coast.

But instead of attacking, Alexander waited, moving his army back and forth to find food and relying also on supply by ship. As Alexander anticipated, Darius's large army rapidly consumed the provisions in his vicinity, forcing him either to advance or retreat. But just as Alexander's delay had exhausted Darius's supplies and the king moved his army forward to the coast, Alexander held a council of war and, not knowing of Darius's move, decided to advance with his army down the coast. Thus it worked out that in spite of Alexander's astute delay, Darius's army reached the coast in Alexander's rear where the Persian army had a line of retreat into Syria while blocking the withdrawal of the Macedonians.

Darius's army had occupied what is called a flank position, in which an army blocks an enemy's advance by its ability to move into the rear of the enemy army should it march past. Alexander did not attack the Persian force in its flank position, disposed on a plain that provided admirable terrain for the action of the numerous and excellent Persian cavalry. Instead, he resorted to the logistic strategy of delay, so that a shortage of supplies would force Darius out of his flank position. Though Alexander did not realize it, his logistic strategy worked when Darius had to move his army forward. Preferring, apparently, to fight Darius on the coast rather than the plain, Alexander marched past while Darius's move forward executed the threat implicit in the flank position by moving into Alexander's rear, blocking his route back to Anatolia.

Since Alexander's army lived on the country and relied on coastal shipping for some supplies, Darius's position in its rear did not cut its communications. But this location did open Anatolia to the Persians, threatening the Macedonian conquests already made and presenting the possibility of turning Alexander's invasion into a raid in which he passed through the country but did not control it. So Alexander could not readily ignore Darius and continue his march south, and he could accomplish nothing by seeking to march around the Persians back into Anatolia. Thus, Alexander had to face Darius's army, a confrontation he hardly dreaded. But the Persian move to Alexander's rear had given Darius the advantage of the tactical defensive in the battle he must fight to save his crumbling empire.

To attempt to deal with the enemy army by a logistic strategy would work against Alexander's large force in the narrow valley just as effectively as it would against the Persian's. So Alexander immediately chose the combat alternative and marched north to attack Darius on constricted terrain that provided less scope for the action of the formidable Persian cavalry. But Darius made the most of the advantages of the tactical defensive given him by his move from his flank position into Alexander's rear. The Persian king placed his army behind a stream, strengthening his front with some field fortifications, and concentrated his cavalry near the coast on the only open ground. But the tactical ascendancy of Alexander's heavy cavalry and his sophisticated combination of the four weapon systems decided the battle. The Macedonian victory in the Battle of Issus, inflicting heavy losses on the Persians in both manpower and prestige, opened to Alexander the remaining Mediterranean provinces of the empire, including Egypt. These Alexander proceeded to occupy.

In choosing to conquer Persian territory instead of conducting a strategic pursuit of Darius into Mesopotamia, Alexander remained true to his logistic strategy of defeating the Persian fleet by depriving it of its bases. For this reason he spent seven months of the winter and spring of the following year besieging and finally capturing the important city and naval base of Tyre, thus striking successfully at the Phoenician coast and the heart of Persian seapower. By delaying until the following summer his invasion of Mesopotamia, Alexander had fully conquered and organized his rear before he moved forward on the next stage of his conquest during the best campaigning season. And this campaign followed the model of its predecessors, Alexander winning another major tactical victory at the Battle of Arbela, conquering Mesopotamia, and sending Darius fleeing into the easternmost portion of his empire.

The night before the Battle of Arbela, the confident Alexander slept so well that when his generals had trouble awakening him in the morning, one "asked him how it was possible, when he was to fight the most important battle of all, he could sleep as if he were already victorious. 'And are we not so indeed,' replied Alexander, smiling, 'since we are at last relieved from the trouble of wandering in pursuit of Darius through a wide and wasted country, hoping in vain that he would fight us?' " Of course, the king overestimated Darius's political strength and so the alternatives open to the Persian, but easily saw the problems presented by his comparatively small force in the immense space still remaining in the Persian empire and the consequent difficulty of forcing battle on an unwilling opponent.[44]

After defeating Darius at Arbela, Alexander again pushed eastward, receiving the submission of most of the Persian provincial satraps. Alexander claimed, by his defeat of Darius, the crown of the Persian Empire for himself, treated the defeated Persians with mercy and respect, and even began wearing clothing of the Persian style. These measures helped reconcile Persian officials to his rule as did the murder of the fleeing Darius by Bessus, one of his own subordinates, who then proclaimed himself king. Alexander's advance brought the country under his control, and he usually continued in office the satraps who surrendered to him. His conquest had paid for his war and had provided ample resources to continue it by the capture of the Persian treasury, 7,290 tons of gold and silver.

Alexander's Encounter with a Raiding Strategy

The pattern of surrender by satraps did not apply in mountainous Bactria or the near-desert Sogdiana (presently northern Afghanistan and the adjacent regions of Soviet Russia). Led by local leaders, the warlike inhabitants of these two regions resisted Alexander's rule. Alexander, having marched through both provinces, occupied the major cities, and captured Bessus, believed that he had brought the country under his rule. But almost immediately rebels attacked and captured eight of his fortified posts in Sogdiana. Alexander sent a relief expedition to the most distant one, Maracanda, and personally directed the forces that besieged and captured the seven other posts. He killed all of the inhabitants of the garrisons, but, instead of intimidating the rebels, this application of terror intensified resistance to his rule. Terror can be an effective weapon only if its victims, as Clausewitz pointed out, believe that the terrorism can continue indefinitely.[45]

Apparently the rebels did not believe that Alexander could prevail, and the fate of the Maracanda relief expedition must have bolstered that idea. Upon the approach of the Macedonian force of about 800 light cavalry and 1,500 heavy infantry, the rebels besieging Maracanda retreated. The relief expedition pursued them, and the rebels, who had many light cavalry with bows, made a stand in a level place near the desert. When the Macedonian infantry attacked, the historian Arrian recounts that the rebel cavalry "rode around and discharged arrows at the phalanx of infantry," and the Macedonian cavalry, "exhausted by the incessant marching, as well as by a lack of fodder," made no contribution to what had become a defensive battle. The horse archers pressed upon the Macedonians "whether they halted or retreated. Many of them were wounded by the arrows, and some were killed. The leaders therefore arranged the soldiers into the form of a square and retreated to the river," where, after some confusion, they ended up on an island in the shallow river. Here "they were entirely surrounded by" the cavalry, "and all killed with arrows, except a few of them whom they reduced to slavery." This demonstration of the tactical power of light cavalry, a forecast of what would later befall Crassus at the hands of the Parthians, doubtless heartened the rebels and helped make Alexander's terrorism ineffective in suppressing political opposition.[46]

Alexander, of course, marched to avenge this defeat, but even with fresh light cavalry could not overtake the mounted rebels. This was a representative situation upon which ancient strategists had to base their strategy. Between similar weapon systems, retreat was faster than pursuit. Heavy infantry could retreat faster than heavy infantry could pursue; light infantry could withdraw faster than light infantry could follow; the same rule applies to the mounted weapon systems. This was a strategic truth, though in tactics the situation could differ and terrain obstacles such as rivers may modify this for strategy. But forces in retreat could obstruct the way by cutting down trees, burning bridges, sinking boats, and leaving a rear guard to delay the pursuers while the main body of the retreating force continued its march. The tactical and strategic advantage of retreat over pursuit meant that Alexander's use of light cavalry to pursue rebel light cavalry failed.

Alexander faced a situation in which numerous parties of armed and mounted rebels disputed his rule and controlled points not occupied by his forces. His opponents essentially followed a raiding strategy, attacking his outposts and, except for their strong points, avoiding contact with large contingents of his army. Alexander reacted by dividing his army into five parts, marching through the rebellious country, and subduing enemy strongholds. He had nothing to fear from the enemy's light cavalry, for he had great preponderance in the numbers and the quality of his army and an ample force of light cavalry as well of foot archers and slingers. He also increased his own light cavalry by local enlistment.

His opponents met Alexander's persisting strategy with raids. Relying on the primacy of retreat over pursuit, they sought to avoid strong Macedonian forces, concentrating on overwhelming weak detachments and then withdrawing before Alexander's men could force battle. These raids, carried out by the weaker side, differed markedly from those employed by the Greeks, who, as the stronger side, used raids to destroy crops to compel political concessions or bring the weaker to battle. The Greek city-states, unable to fight their elusive enemy, attacked their resources; the Bactrians and Sogdianians, on the other hand, pursued a combat strategy while evading the main hostile force. This type of raid had an analogy in tactics when peltasts approached hoplites to hurl their javelins and then fled to avoid shock combat. This use of raids, which depended on the ambiguity of the raiders' objective and their ability to keep away from their pursuers, constituted the fundamental basis of guerrilla warfare.

Having overcome the enemy strongholds, Alexander then moved to deprive the guerrillas of one of their requisities, the untrammeled mobility needed to avoid pursuers. He established and garrisoned a large number of fortified military posts throughout the settled part of the country. These reduced the vulnerability of his forces to the attacks of the raiders and impeded their movements. These posts controlled the communication routes, so that at one point Arrian says that the rebel leader "saw that every place was occupied by the Macedonians with garrisons, and that there was no way of flight open to him." Geography facilitated this task of interdicting rebel movements and so making their raids difficult and hazardous, because the mountains in Bactria confined the roads to the settled valleys, and the arid nature of Sogdiana restricted most settlement to the irrigated areas near the rivers.[47]

Each of Alexander's fortified posts had mounted forces available to pursue raiders. Arrian recounts how the rebel leader, Spitamenes, and Scythians from the Steppes captured one of the forts in Bactria, but finding another one too strong, the rebels "marched away after collecting a great quantity of booty." The garrison of this second fort contained sixty members of the Companion cavalry, recuperating from illness, and "these men, hearing of the incursion of the Scythians, and having now recovered from their illness, took their arms and mounted their horses. Then, collecting eighty mercenary Grecian horsemen" from the garrison and "some of the royal pages, they sallied forth." Attacking "the Scythians, who had no suspicion of such an event, they deprived them of all the booty at the first onset, and killed many of those who were driving it off. But as no one was in command, they returned without any regard to order: and being drawn into ambush by Spitamenes and other Scythians, they lost seven of the Companions and sixty of the mercenary cavalry."[48]

Such double surprises certainly must have been typical of the guerrilla war that occupied Alexander for two years. Although the measures taken by the Macedonians strengthened the defense against attack and inhibited the enemy's movements, they failed to prevent the guerrillas' raids. The invaders had too few soldiers to stop the raids in a large country in which the guerrillas had political support among the population.

So Alexander added a new political approach: he abandoned terror and turned to conciliation. The key to placating the opposition lay in his marriage to Roxana, daughter of Oxyartes, one of the principal magnates of Bactria. Alexander could not have found this political gesture too painful, for he was said to love Roxana, whom the men in Alexander's army thought "the most beautiful of all the Asiatic women whom they had seen, with the single exception of the wife of Darius." This reconciled Oxyartes to Alexander's rule and in this "way could shame be taken from the conquered and haughtiness from the victors." Through other comparable political acts Alexander built a political base that complemented his effective military measures and finally overcame popular resistance to his rule.[49]

In Bactria and Sogdiana, as in his conquest of the remainder of the Persian Empire, Alexander needed an adequate political base to support his military success; otherwise, with such a small force in relation to the vast size of the dominions of Darius, he would surely have failed, just as the effects of Antiochus VII's later military success evaporated in the face of popular political opposition.

Military Victories without Political Support: Hannibal's Experience with the Fabian Strategy

Hannibal and his Macedonian system of combat possessed the same tactical predominance over the Romans as did Alexander over the Persians and, like Alexander, the Carthaginian leader enjoyed a succession of tactical triumphs. But he faced a completely different political situation. Though Italy was minute compared to the vast Persian Empire, it still had too large an area and population for Hannibal to dominate it with an army that initially could not have exceeded 50,000 men. Even after Hannibal's overwhelming victory at Cannae, most of the cities of Italy remained loyal to Rome, "such was the awe and respect that the allies felt for the Roman state." Further, the Romans themselves, plus their allies, all had militias, which meant that every city could defend itself and the Romans could create and replace, if destroyed, larger armies than could the king of Persia. Although the mobilized militia infantry lacked the combat effectiveness of Hannibal's regular army and could not duplicate his Macedonian combined-arms tactics, it had the qualities necessary to build and defend fortifications. Hannibal thus faced what in the twentieth century would be called national resistance in a country large and populous enough to prevent his army from controlling very much of it at one time.[50]

Even before the Battle of Cannae, Hannibal's initial victories in entering Italy had induced the Romans, under the leadership of Fabius, to adopt a more circumspect strategy. On taking command, the perceptive and prudent Fabius moved toward Hannibal who, "having possessed himself of so large an amount of booty that his army could not drive or carry it all off," had halted "near the Adriatic in a country abounding in all kinds of produce," where he "paid great attention to recruiting the health of his men as well as of his horses." Fabius

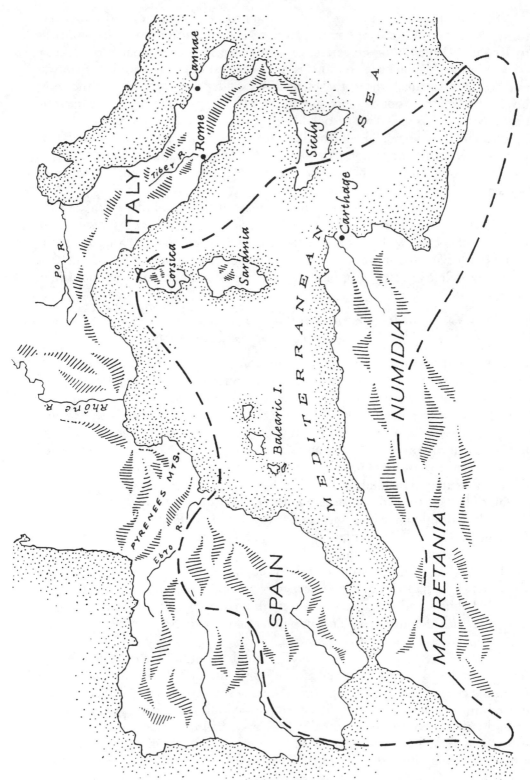

Map 1.3. Carthaginian Area of Influence

camped six miles from Hannibal, who "wishing to strike such a blow as would effectually cow the enemy, led his forces out and drew them up in order of battle at a short distance from the Roman camp, but after waiting some time, as nobody came out to meet him, he retired again to his own camp. For the astute Fabius, having determined not to expose himself to any risk or to venture on a battle, but to make the safety of the army under his command his first and chief aim, adhered steadfastly to this purpose."[51]

Hannibal, the greatest soldier of his age, had naturally declined to attack Fabius' Roman army in its fortified camp where its defensive power would have readily overmastered the tactical skill of the Carthaginian veterans. But Fabius' strategy involved more than merely avoiding defeat. Whenever the Carthaginians moved their army, "the Romans continued to hang on their rear at a distance of one or two days' march, refusing to approach nearer and engage the enemy." On other occasions Fabius would "move parallel to the enemy, always occupying in advance the positions which his knowledge of the country told him were the most advantageous." In so tracking Hannibal's army, the wily Fabius complicated his enemy's logistics and won some skirmishes because, when Hannibal had to spread out his army to find food and some of his men would "stray far from their own camp in foraging," the Romans could "take or kill numbers of the enemy." In this way Fabius could "keep on reducing the strictly limited numbers of the enemy" and, through raids against foragers, also restore "by partial successes the spirits of his own troops."[52]

Fabius based his strategy on his ability to refuse battle, on the tactical power of the defense, on his control of the walled cities, and on his excellent logistics. In pouncing on foragers and stragglers he used small raids to concentrate against weakness; in his dominance of the country and willingness to accept battle behind entrenchments he employed a defensive persisting strategy; and in his frequent reliance on retreat he also depended on a raiding strategy. He could do this because, between similarly constituted armies, the pursuing cannot overtake the retreating. Fabius could always keep away from Hannibal as long as he could avoid trapping himself against some obstacle like a river, and his knowledge of the terrain protected him against this blunder. Of course, Fabius would have been delighted to have a battle on his own terms, entrenched in a fortified camp, but Hannibal never became so exasperated by the enemy's Fabian strategy as to make the mistake of fighting where Fabius wished.

Hannibal did devastate a pacticularly fertile area, hoping to "compel the enemy to fight," but Fabius had too much wisdom to engage in battle on the enemy's terms where he believed he faced almost certain defeat at the hands of a great general using the dominant Alexandrian tactical system. Instead, Fabius exploited the strategic power of the defense to retreat or its tactical capacity to defend a strong position against a frontal attack and took advantage of the ease with which he could obtain supplies in his own country. With the resources of the granaries of the cities readily available to him, Fabius "never allowed his soldiers to forage or to straggle from the camp on any pretext, but keeping them continually massed together watched for such opportunities as time and place afforded" to catch Carthaginian foragers or stragglers and then promptly to avoid conflict with a large Carthaginian force. Although Fabius's method of operation had some of the elements of a logistic strategy, its main offensive element consisted of concentration against weakness in implementing a cautious raiding combat strategy.[53]

Just as in offensive tactics, commanders like Epaminondas sought to attack their enemy's weak flank or rear or to bring greater numbers to bear on part of the enemy's line, so in strategy did Fabius do the same when he concentrated larger numbers against Carthaginian foraging parties. Concentration against weakness in raids proved as effective in strategy as it did in tactics, and, as in tactics, the defender's weakness was only relative to the attacker's ability to concentrate more men. But unlike tactics, where the enemy had already committed himself to combat, the side on the strategic offensive that had superior numbers must still force battle on the weaker. This Fabius did by surprising and blocking the retreat of Carthaginian foragers.

Hannibal's strategy eventually succeeded. Devastating the countryside did not force Fabius into battle, but it finally compelled a change in Roman commanders and strategy. This led to the disaster of Cannae, which in turn caused the Romans to return to Fabius's strategy and not again to swerve from it. Hannibal established a base area for himself in southern Italy, still able to move at will throughout the peninsula. His strategy depended on the Romans' modifying their war aims and negotiating a peace acceptable to the Carthaginians. But if the Romans sometimes displayed ineptitude, they always persevered, even though Hannibal and his army remained in Italy for thirteen years after Cannae.

In addition to those elements exploited by Fabius, Roman military power lay in their large forces, based on a trained militia in every town. Roman power also resided in control of the urban centers and in the defensive strength of the fortifications of these towns. Since the roads went through the population centers, these obstacles hampered Hannibal's movements as well as assured continued Roman control of the dependent countryside and its supplies. Because his preeminence depended on cavalry, against fortified cities Hannibal had no tactical advantage over the Romans, who had equal skill in siege warfare. Almost insuperable logistical problems confronted Hannibal in any sustained attack on fortifications. Nor could he count on supplying any such prolonged operation by water, for the powerful Roman navy ruled the sea. To the usual difficulties of supplying a large army by pack mule, Hannibal would have had to cope with a Roman army circumscribing his supply area and killing and capturing his foragers. So Hannibal attempted no sieges.

The defeat at Cannae struck a severe blow at Roman political strength: a number of Rome's allies defected and others became lukewarm. The Romans proceeded vigorously against the disloyal cities, able to act because Roman forces dominated any area in the absence of Hannibal's army. Hannibal could not relieve a besieged city because the Romans built lines of contravallation to enclose the defenders and constructed a well-supplied fortified camp for their army. Sometimes, such as in the siege of the very important city of Capua, they constructed a second line of fortifications, lines of circumvallation, around their siegeworks, which protected the besieging army from Hannibal's army. One by one the Romans subdued the defecting allies and progressively reduced the area of Italy friendly to Hannibal. The Carthaginian general had never succeeded in becoming more than a raider, and the Romans were employing an almost exclusively persisting strategy against him, gradually limiting the region in which he could move freely. Hannibal failed to wear the Romans down; instead, Roman perseverance gradually destroyed his strategy, for the Roman armies were not only succeeding in Italy but also slowly and surely subduing Carthaginian Spain.

Hannibal's success in maintaining himself for so long in a hostile country reflects not only his tactical genius but also his ability as an organizer. For example, he had to recruit local troops and train them in his methods of combat. But this he did, and by his leadership continued to bind this heterogeneous force to him and his cause.

In the end Hannibal proved to be never much more than a raider, lacking either of the requisites for controlling Italy: an adequate ratio of force to space or enough of the political support that Alexander found and fostered in the Persian Empire. The Carthaginian's long campaign fell into five phases, divided largely by the Roman strategy employed against him. Initially the Romans played into his hands with a defensive persisting strategy of offering battle, which Hannibal, confident of his tactical dominance, gladly accepted.

Fabius introduced the second phase by basing his defensive persisting strategy on the fortified character of the country and his ability to refuse battle except in an entrenched position of his own choice. Still Fabius's strategy included a raiding element when he followed the Carthaginian army and pounced on its foragers. But because Fabius remained in the field, willing to fight on his own terms, the Romans did not wage guerrilla warfare, as did the Bactrians and Sogdianians, who had lost control of their country and could not face Alexander in battle.

In the third phase, when the Romans made a brief return to a persisting strategy based on battles, the defeat at Cannae so aggravated the problem of defection of their allies that they were compelled to take the persisting offensive in the fourth phase to subdue the defecting cities by sieges. Simultaneously, they resumed Fabius's persisting defense against the Carthaginians. In the last phase Hannibal, largely baffled by the Roman strategy of fortified defense, relied on his base area in southern Italy. At the same time the Romans, still unable to meet Hannibal in an offensive battle, could not effectively pursue an offensive persisting strategy against the Carthaginian base area. Instead, they waged successful campaigns outside of Italy, conquering Spain and, finally, invading Africa.

Hannibal's failure against political opposition invites comparison with Alexander's success in Bactria and Sogdiana. In each case the great captains faced formidable political opposition but had military predominance. Alexander, however, held sway over what formal authority then existed and had a certain legitimacy as the conquerer of Darius. On the other hand, the Romans retained the powerful governmental machinery that they had created over several centuries. Whereas the Romans controlled the cities and the focal points of communications, these had belonged to Alexander in Bactria and Sogdiana. Finally, Alexander was able to buttress his already strong constitutional situation, but Hannibal's political strength, dependent solely on his initial military victories, withered away. Without such local support and with his tactical supremacy in the field circumscribed by the tactical advantage of city walls and Roman field fortifications, Hannibal failed. His chance of victory lay in Rome's willingness to make a compromise peace to rid itself of Hannibal's army, but the Romans proved too devoted to their goal of complete destruction of Carthaginian power. Hannibal's failure clearly exemplified the limits that political factors may place on military success.

A Rare Instance of the Use of Interior Lines of Operations in Ancient Times

One victorious campaign of the Romans against Hannibal's forces exhibits the value of strategic concentration of force. The Romans triumphed not over Hannibal but over his brother, Hasdrubal, who in 207 B.C. marched from Spain to join Hannibal in Italy. The Romans had posted one army in north Italy to guard against this while another, under Consul Nero, faced Hannibal's near the old battlefield of Cannae. Capturing the messengers sent by Hasdrubal to Hannibal to ask that Hannibal move north to join him, the Romans knew of the threat presented by Hasdrubal while Hannibal remained ignorant of the arrival of his reinforcement.

Nero responded promptly by secretly marching 250 miles north with 7,000 picked men to join the army opposing Hasdrubal. Realizing his opponent had received reinforcements and not wishing to fight without Hannibal, Hasdrubal declined battle. But in the night retreat his forces lost their way, failed to find their crossing over the Metaurus River, and had to fight the next day. The Romans won a complete victory, killing Hasdrubal, inflicting serious casualities, and scattering the remainder of his men. Nero then marched his contingent south again, rejoining his army watching Hannibal's. Hannibal had remained ignorant of Hasdrubal's arrival in Italy and Nero's temporary departure from his front until the Romans threw Hasdrubal's head over the rampart into Hannibal's camp.

Nero's march presents an excellent example of strategic concentration, made possible by exploiting his position between the two Carthaginian armies. In this situation, one of interior lines of operations, the Roman legions facing Hasdrubal and Hannibal, though 250 miles apart, had their backs to one another and stood between the Carthaginians. Each Roman contingent had a line of operations, its line of advance or retreat against the opponents, and each Carthaginian army

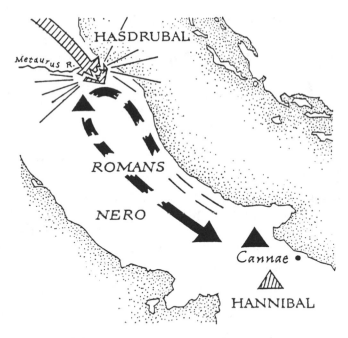

Diagram 1.1. Roman Interior Lines

also had its line of operations against the opposing Roman enemy. The Romans had the interior lines of operations, the Carthaginian the exterior. This meant that one Roman contingent could dispatch reinforcements directly to the other, but the two Carthaginian forces could send reserves to each other only if they could in fact pass around the opposing Roman legions.

Such employment of interior lines provided one of the principal strategic means of concentrating against weakness. The use of interior lines to concentrate a superior force exploited the enemy's weakness because weakness inheres in circumstances where one side can concentrate and the other cannot. The full realization of the potential of this situation depended on bringing the enemy to battle. Had Hasdrubal not lost his way and trapped himself against the river, the Romans, unable to bring him to battle, would probably have made their concentration in vain. Concentration on interior lines had only occasional use when the stronger could not compel the weaker to fight.

Interior lines of operations usually conferred an advantage on the forces that possessed them because of the opportunities that they presented for concentrating against first one hostile force and then the other. This situation contrasted with that in tactics where a position between two opponents, called envelopment, had serious disadvantages. Instead of having the choice of concentrating against one or the other, an enclosed army had to fight all enemy troops simultaneously. The envelopers, front, flank, and rear, pressed their mutually supporting attacks against an opponent deprived of the power of maneuver and rarely oriented to fight on all sides equally well. The difference between this tactical circumstance and the strategic situation of interior and exterior lines of operations lay in the distance and whether the exterior forces were close enough to one another to afford each other mutual support.

Caesar's Strategy in the Conquest of Gaul

The Roman politician and soldier Julius Caesar devoted seven years to the conquest of Gaul, roughly the same area as present-day France. He conquered such a large territory so rapidly because of his consummate mastery of the Roman art of war. He combined thorough preparation, patient and perceptive strategy, and a high standard for engineering and logistics with superlative tactical skill. Nor did he overlook the political conciliation of his opponents, a task for which his magnanimous disposition as well as his political experience and talents perfectly fitted him. Though an epileptic of unimposing physique, he exposed himself to danger and shared his men's hardships, reinforcing his brilliant leadership of hardened soldiers who responded to his magnetism and his almost extravagant recognition of their acts of courage and skill. The historian Plutarch noted that he inspired in his soldiers a "passion for distinction." They must also have had an appreciation of his use of the defense whenever possible, a strategy made more formidable by the Romans' skill in entrenching themselves and the regularity with which they carried it out.[54]

Caesar's campaign continued centuries of conflict between the Gauls and the Romans, which had resulted in the Romans conquering the Gallic portion of north Italy and extending their control as far as the Rhone River. Though Caesar faced a national resistance, the Gauls lacked political unity both among the various tribes and perhaps between the aristocracy and the peasants who Caesar said were bound to the nobility virtually as slaves. In addition, some Gallic tribes had friendly relations with the Romans, Caesar largely relying on the Gauls for his cavalry. Thus Caesar had elements of significant strength in the political situation.

Although initially Caesar could engage one Gallic tribe at a time, he finally faced a winter rising of all of the tribes, which under the leadership of the perceptive Vercingetorix pursued a logistic strategy. According to Caesar, the Gauls had as their "prime objective" to "interdict the Romans from forage and supplies," an easy task given their strength in cavalry and the season of the year. Since "in the winter there was no grass to cut," the Romans "must necessarily scatter to find fodder in barns in small parties, which could be picked off by the cavalry day by day." Not only did the Gauls use the raiding aspect of Fabius' strategy, but they relied on the method that the Persians had refused to use against Alexander. The determined Vercingetorix specified that "private interests must be sacrificed to the common cause. To either side of the road as far as foragers could reach, steadings and barns must be burned down. They would themselves be adequately supplied, for they would draw on the resources of the peoples in the theatre of operations. The Romans must either starve or go far afield from their camp at great risk; and it made no difference whether they killed them or took their baggage, for without it they could not make war." Ruthless in his application of his logistic strategy, Vercingetorix even planned to burn the towns that he could not defend in order to eliminate "ready stocks" of provisions "for the Romans to pillage and carry off."[55]

Vercingetorix did not originate the use of logistic strategy in the Gallic War. A chieftain had earlier employed it against Caesar, and Caesar had used it with effect himself. When one tribe, the Belgae, had concentrated all of their forces to fight him, Caesar declined battle except on the ramparts of his fortified camp. As he expected, the Belgae proved wise enough not to attack him in such a strong position. Instead they waited for Caesar to come out of his amply provisioned camp; Caesar, in turn, waited for the Belgae to consume their supplies just as, during the Issus campaign, Alexander had waited for Darius to exhaust the provisions in his flank position. Caesar had more success than Alexander: the Belgae, finding, as Caesar explained, that "their own commissary was beginning to fail," decided to disperse their large concentration so it could return to their "home-grown supplies." Caesar then left his fortifications to campaign against the separated groups of the Belgae.[56]

The subtle and resourceful Vercingetorix, applying his strategy rigorously and effectively, avoided battle when Caesar marched against him. Keeping his distance and avoiding the temptation to fight, Vercingetorix stuck with his logistic strategy not to "tempt Fortune in a pitched battle but keep the enemy from grain and forage." Caesar then countered with a strategy "either of enticing him out of his marshes and forests or of blockading him into submission." His initial effort involved simultaneously besieging two cities, a difficult task with a Gallic army nearby. At the siege of Bourges, Caesar described Vercingetorix's army lurking nearby "on the watch for our foraging and grain-gatherer parties, and when necessarily scattered far afield he attacked them and inflicted serious losses." This "imposed such scarcity upon the army that for several days they were without grain and staved off starvation only by driving in cattle from remote villages."[57]

Although he managed to keep his army provisioned, Caesar realized that he could no longer maintain his forces in central Gaul. Not only could he not continue to feed his army, but in eastern Gaul Vercingetorix carried out raids against the territory of tribes friendly to the Romans. Caesar marched east, followed by Vercingetorix with a large force. But realizing that the "Romans would return when they had enlarged their army and would never put an end to the war," the desperate Vercingetorix, perhaps overconfident or pressed to action by his followers, turned to a combat persisting strategy and risked battle. Defeated, the Gallic leader fell back to the town of Alesia, where Caesar besieged him while fending off a large relieving army.

Supply for the Roman army presented the usual difficulty, but the Roman commissary overcame the obstacles and kept the army provisioned, probably by bringing food and fodder from a navigable river forty-five miles away. The siege clearly exhibits the thoroughness and effectiveness of Roman engineering. To enclose the besiegers, Caesar built a line of entrenchments ten miles long. These consisted of a trench that the troops dug 600 paces from the main fortification. The primary line of defense included, Caesar explained, "two trenches fifteen feet wide and of the same height," the inner one filled, "where it crossed the plain or depressions, with water drawn from the river." Behind the ditches rose a "rampart and palisade twelve feet high" and around the "entire circuit" the engineers "erected towers at intervals of eighty feet."[58]

To render the fortifications "defensible by a smaller number of soldiers," Caesar cut down trees and, with the trunks and branches "stripped and sharpened at the end," placed these in front of the rampart and ditches, digging them five feet into the ground where they were "firmly anchored so that they could not be torn loose, with the boughs projecting above" ground. "These were woven together and interlaced in rows of five, and anyone that stepped in would impale himself on very sharp stakes. These the men called gravestones. In front of these, pits three feet deep were dug, gradually tapering to the bottom." Into these pits "smooth logs of the thickness of a thigh, with the tops tapering and hardened in fire, were let down so that no more than four inches projected above ground. To fix the stumps and make them steady the earth was tramped down for a foot from the bottom; the rest of the pit was covered over with twigs and brush to hide the trap." Named by the men lilies, "there were eight rows of this kind, at intervals of three feet." In front of these traps the men placed "foot-long blocks into which iron hooks had been sunk." These spurs "were wholly buried in the ground, thickly scattered over the whole field."[59]

Caesar's army then reproduced this whole line of fortifications as a line of circumvallation to resist the relieving army. Coordinated attacks by the besiegers and the relieving army failed against such thoroughly prepared positions, and the valiant Vercingetorix finally surrendered. This defeat gave military control of Gaul to Caesar, and wise Roman administration ultimately not only reconciled the Gauls to Roman rule but also eventually made them Roman in language, culture, and feeling.

But before the defeat at Alesia, Vercingetorix's strategy had driven Ceasar from central Gaul. In addition to their defensive logistic strategy of scorching the earth, the Gauls had relied on raids rather than on meeting the Roman army in battle to keep it from their territory. In this way they practiced a guerrilla war comparable to that waged by the Bactrians and Sogdianians.

In applying their guerrilla warfare of raids they could avoid combat because their forces, having an essentially similar group of weapon systems as the Romans, could exploit their ability to retreat and avoid battle. Vercingetorix would have failed had they attempted to wage this campaign on the plains and the Romans had armed themselves in the manner of the Parthians. In finding and over-whelming Roman foragers as Fabius had done to Hannibal's men, the Gauls concentrated against weakness to win many small victories. Their strength in cavalry helped them concentrate rapidly, facilitating the application of the combat element in their strategy, though attacking foragers and grain-gatherers was also intrinsic to the logistic aspect of their campaign. Caesar summed up the problems of dealing with such a strategy: "If Caesar chose to finish the business and extirpate the whole scoundrelly crew he would have to break up his units and send out numerous small detachments; if he chose to keep his formations together, as required by the established practice of the Roman army, the natives would have the advantage of terrain, and they were bold enough to ambush scattered parties and cut them off. In this difficult situation every possible care was taken, on the principle that it was better to sacrifice an opportunity to injure the enemy if the injury would involve a loss on our part."[60]

Such guerrilla warfare and the defensive logistic strategy applied concomitantly had one other requirement: it needed enough political strength to keep the population committed to the war and the costly, slow method of waging it. The Gallic resistance may have lacked enough such motivation to persevere; certainly the Gauls did not have an abundance of the political unity and support needed to defeat the Romans. The Gauls fought on their own territory, devastating their own fields and burning their own farmsteads; the Romans fought far from home with a regular army. The tolerance and quality of Roman rule, demonstrated in Rome's adjacent Gallic province, may not have made the state of independence worth the effort for enough Gauls.

Caesar's Ilerda Campaign: An Unusual Occurrence of the Turning Movement

The Roman civil war that followed Caesar's conquest of Gaul pitted Caesar against Pompey, able as a politician and outstanding as a general. In his fine army in now-pacific Gaul, Caesar had the stronger land forces. But Pompey controlled the sea and all of the land except Gaul. Caesar, situated between Spain and Italy and having interior lines of operations, struck first at the virtually defenseless Italian peninsula. Popular in Italy and soon in control there, Caesar then marched against Spain while Pompey fled to Greece and began to organize and concentrate the troops there and in Rome's eastern Mediterranean provinces.

When Caesar turned against Spain, he found a substantial army loyal to Pompey garrisoning that province, which the Romans had conquered from Carthage a century and a half before. Caesar's lieutenant advanced westward along the Mediterranean coast of France and in early spring crossed the Pyrenees without meeting resistance from the inferior forces of Pompey's men. Caesar's numerical preponderance may have been on the order of 35,000 to 25,000 for his opponents in Spain; his army also had far greater strength in cavalry; and his men, unlike the Spanish garrisons of Pompey's supporters, had recent combat experience. Afranius and Petreius, Pompey's capable and loyal generals in Spain, wisely standing on the defensive, took up a position at Ilerda on the Sicoris River in northern Spain, about twenty-five miles north of the place where the Sicoris empties into the Ebro. On a hill west of Ilerda and the river the Pompeians built a fortified camp, which protected their army and covered the stone bridge that connected the two sides of the river. Though they occupied a strong position, they viewed it only as an outpost, for they planned to make their main resistance on the Ebro. When they were ready, they could easily retreat across the Ebro by means of a bridge of boats that they planned to construct near the mouth of the Sicoris.

The Ilerda campaign illustrates the power of the defense with both armies similarly constituted, as were these opposing Roman armies each of which relied primarily on its heavy legionary infantry. Thus the shrewd defenders of Spain, careful to make the most of their position, succeeded in making their inferior force too strong for Caesar's army to attack, even after Caesar himself took command. Nor could Caesar's invading troops bypass the position, for, though this move would open Spain to invasion, the Pompeian army could then march toward Italy where they could potentially do more damage to Caesar's cause than Caesar could inflict on Pompey's by moving about at will in Spain.

The key to the strength of the Pompeian position lay in the ample store of supplies in Ilerda and in the Pompeians' control of the stone bridge, which gave them secure and reliable communication over the Sicoris, a river liable to sudden rises in the spring just when Caesar invaded Spain. The bridge enabled Caesar's opponents easily to concentrate their troops on either side of the river and gave them access to the foraging area east of the river.

Caesar built a fortified camp near that of the Pompeians and sought to gain access to the east bank of the Sicoris by building two bridges upstream, which he used to send troops and foragers to the east bank of the Sicoris. But floods promptly swept away one bridge; as soon as he rebuilt it, Caesar explained, unprecedented rainfall "washed down the snow from all the mountains, over-topped the banks of the river, and in one day broke down both the bridges." This flood also detained a supply convoy from Gaul and deprived Caesar's army of provisions during late spring, logistically "the most difficult season of the year, when there was no corn in the winter stores and the crops were not far from being ripe while the communities were exhausted" because the Pompeians had removed all remaining supplies in creating their reserve. Eventually Caesar bridged the Sicoris far upstream from Ilerda, received his supply convoy, and relieved his logistical emergency. But he still could do nothing to dislodge his opponent.[61]

Thus supply difficulties, combined with the defensive power of a fortified army in a position astride a key communications link, enabled an expertly com-manded but inferior army to baffle a greater force, notwithstanding Caesar's brilliant and determined leadership. But in mid-June, with the end of the spring floods, Caesar erected a bridge eighteen miles upstream and succeeded in creating a ford in the river near the city. These provided more secure communication with the east bank and enabled his stronger cavalry to dominate the foraging zones on which the enemy depended. This menace and the possibility Caesar might now be able to begin a siege caused Pompey's generals to fall back to the Ebro, their next line of defense. The knowledge that in their rear some natives of Spain had gone over to Caesar reinforced their decision. Using the east bank of the Sicoris in their retreat to the Ebro, twenty-five miles distant, they moved out well before dawn, getting a good start on Caesar who, delayed by the difficulty of crossing rapidly by the ford, followed several hours behind his retreating opponents.

But, as Caesar explained, he used his battle-seasoned light cavalry to "annoy and harass the enemy's line of march," forcing the Pompeian forces to retreat very slowly because the cavalry impeded "their march by pouring a great number of men around their flanks." At times, "the end of the column was being held up and even being cut off from the rest, while at other times their colours were pushed forward" and Caesar's cavalry "were driven back by a charge of the cohorts in a body, and then again wheeled around and pursed the foe."[62]

The enemy's necessarily slow pace enabled a forced march by Caesar's veterans to bring his army upon the rear of the retreating Pompeians, who promptly drew up their line of battle on high ground. The location gave the legions such a defensive advantage that Caesar did not consider an attack with his fatigued troops. The Pompeians, however, wished to reach and cross the Ebro if only because they could not long find food for their men and forage for their horses in the rugged, mountainous country, which they had reached in their retreat. But, "worn out by a whole day's fighting and the toil of their march, they" did not resume their withdrawal the next day, spending the time reconnoitering the country in their rear and the nine miles that separated them from their bridge across the Ebro. Their observations revealed that behind them stretched "five miles of level route, then follows rugged and hilly ground, that there is no difficulty in the enemy being stopped by whosoever first occupies these defiles." They planned "to set out next day at early dawn."[63]

Caesar had also examined the route, and at dawn the next day he began a march in which he executed a turning movement, one of the most difficult and potentially decisive maneuvers in warfare. When Caesar moved his army "at early dawn," on a route that initially led back toward Ilerda, the enemy "soldiers joyfully ran out of their camp to see the spectacle," believing Caesar's army was "fleeing under the stress of lack of necessary food, and were on their way back to Ilerda." But soon they saw that Caesar's plan took his men around them in a "wide circuit," overcoming "large and difficult valleys, steep rocks," and a lack of roads or paths.

Belatedly realizing Caesar's objective, the enemy promptly set out for the passes five miles in their rear, and "the whole contest turned on speed—which of the two would first seize the defiles and the hills." Caesar would surely have lost the race had his cavalry not operated on the level ground of the enemy's march to delay them. "Caesar completed the distance first" and, with his army arrayed for battle on level ground, blocked the enemy's retreat.[64]

Realizing that the advantage of fighting on the tactical defensive now belonged to Caesar, the astute Afranius and Petreius had no intention of making a frontal attack on Caesar's larger and qualitatively better army. The Pompeians

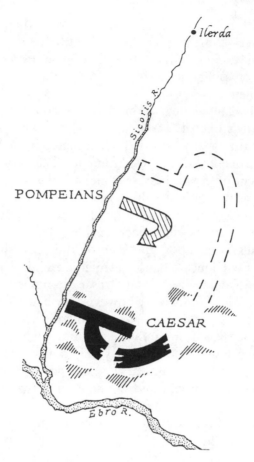

Diagram 1.2. Turning Movement

attempted to move south by another way, but Caesar had little difficulty cutting off all routes of escape to the south because the rugged terrain limited the number of lines of march for the enemy. In addition to the topography, Caesar enjoyed the advantage that in relation to the small size of the area in which the two armies by then operated, he had a very large army. With such a large ratio of force to space, Caesar could readily station troops to contest all possible routes and still have the main body close enough to these detachments so that the whole army could promptly aid any of the detachments should the enemy move in full force against one of them. In a larger space with more level terrain, the Pompeians would have had a good chance of getting around Caesar's army.

Effectively blocked, and unwilling to make a frontal attack on Caesar, the Pompeians could only attempt the logistic strategy of trying to starve out Caesar's army and compel it to move out of its blocking position in search of food. Caesar, however, had the advantage, for not only had his men brought several days' rations with them but also his excellent cavalry dominated all of the level ground, the only place where the enemy foragers could find food or fodder. So effective was Caesar's cavalry that his opponents even had difficulty in securing water and their soldiers began to desert to Caesar's army.

Blocked and starved out, the Pompeians then began to retreat north toward Ilerda with Caesar's army and cavalry following. On the march to Ilerda the Pompeian force found itself crippled because their baggage animals, "without fodder for four days," broke down. Without "water, firewood, and forage" for their army, Afranius and Petreius asked for a conference, then surrendered their army when Caesar, the veteran politican, offered to discharge all of their men rather than use them against Pompey.[65]

Without a battle Caesar destroyed an entire enemy army. His strategic offensive turning movement gave him the advantage of the tactical defensive. It had accomplished for Caesar what the flank position had achieved for Darius before the Battle of Issus. Darius's flank position, a defensive maneuver, had given Alexander the choice of halting his advance, attacking Darius to drive him from his flank position, or marching forward, with the risk of having Darius in his rear. After using a logistic strategy to try to drive Darius from his position, Alexander chose the third option and soon found Darius behind him. Alexander then selected the combat alternative and attacked the Persian army. The turning movement, an offensive maneuver, gave Caesar the same advantage, that of placing his army in the enemy's rear with the benefit of the tactical defensive if the enemy chose to attack.

The tactical defensive had more value for Caesar than for Darius, because both Roman armies had basically the same constitution and both had as their primary weapon system the heavy infantry legion. The defensive provided a major tactical advantage and the turning movement had conferred this on Caesar's army. The terrain and the high ratio of force to space enabled Caesar to keep Afranius and Petreius from moving around him to resume their retreat to their supplies, the security of their bridge, and the Ebro barrier. Caesar's excellent cavalry assured his foraging and interdicted the enemy's, and his blocking the Pompeians withdrawal also cut off their supplies, forcing them to retreat northward into country still dominated by his cavalry. Finally, Caesar's politically wise offer to discharge the prisoners completed the campaign by making it easy for the enemy commanders to surrender instead of continuing their retreat to Ilerda, which they still controlled and where they still had a small supply of food and fodder.

Caesar's success in reaching the enemy's rear had obviated a battle. A similar success by Darius III against Alexander had enabled the Persians to fight a defensive battle, which the superiority of the Macedonians and their leadership had won. Before the Battle of Plataea, the Persian commander had avoided a similar situation, withdrawing when he observed the Spartan army advancing toward a point where it could block his retreat from the Attica peninsula. The Persian commander had not wanted to fight, knowing that "Attica was not a country where cavalry could act with advantage; and further, that if he suffered defeat in a battle," with the enemy blocking his withdrawal route, "no way of escape was open to him, except through defiles, where a handful of troops might stop all his army."[66]

Caesar's campaign also shows the significant strategic utility of light cavalry. As the most mobile of the four basic weapon systems, light cavalry had great power off the battlefield if it could function in reasonably level, unwooded terrain suitable for cavalry. The preeminent tactical mobility of this cavalry permitted it to avoid any other type of weapon system and its ability to march at double the rate of infantry enabled it to operate at a distance from the main force of the army. Commanders could employ the better strategic mobility of light cavalry to attack enemy communications and use it, as had Caesar, to dominate areas from which both armies drew supplies. In the Plataea campaign the Persians had made similarly effective strategic use of their cavalry to interdict Greek supplies.

Though tactically the light cavalry could not attack a force composed of light and heavy infantry, it could easily evade the foot soldiers and control all of an area except where the infantry stood. Its greater mobility enabled it to reconnoiter better than the enemy and concentrate rapidly against an objective such as a foraging party or a pack train. Even if light infantry protected the foragers or train, the light cavalry could use its mobility to concentrate a force far too strong for the few light infantry guards.

Successful use of light cavalry in this important strategic role depended on suitable terrain: woods or mountains would nullify this capability. But in terrain unsuitable for cavalry, light infantry could employ its relatively better mobility to carry out the same function, controlling foraging areas and attacking enemy supply trains. Of course any kind of soldier could carry out this mission but the greater mobility of cavalry particularly adapted it to this task. If the contesting armies had lacked cavalry, light infantry could have used its very modest but real degree of superior strategic mobility to carry out the light cavalry's functions as the instrument for the application of a strategy aimed at crippling the enemy's logistics.

Caesar's Campaign against Pompey

Having conquered Spain, Caesar marched east into southern Italy where he planned to embark his army to attack Pompey in Greece. He dared attempt the crossing of the Adriatic in the face of his formidable opponent's more powerful fleet because heavily manned warships could not remain long at sea. Nevertheless, taking a serious risk, Caesar crossed the waters with as many men as he could find ships for and landed on the Adriatic coast of Greece, where a stalemate resulted as Caesar faced Pompey while waiting for the remainder of his army to cross. The blockading squadron, taking possession of a small island near the Italian port where Caesar's transports waited, kept a more consistent blockade, even though the island could not supply all of the water needed by the men on the ships. Since patrols from the army waiting to cross kept the fleet from landing on the Italian coast to find water, the transports finally slipped through, bringing Caesar's force to full strength.

As an indecisive war of position, the ensuing campaign had much in common with that around Ilerda in that neither of the experienced and prudent generals would attack the other in their strong positions. Pompey, a famous general with ability not incomparable to Caesar's, waited for logistic difficulties to force Caesar away, while Caesar pinned Pompey's stronger army against the coast to make it appear he had the upper hand and to keep Pompey's more numerous cavalry from interfering with his supplies. Since Pompey controlled the sea, Caesar could not embarrass Pompey for food when he had his back to the coast.

Finally, the resourceful Pompey concentrated against one end of Caesar's fifteen-mile fortified perimeter, used his fleet to land a force in Caesar's rear at that point, and forced him to retreat. Caesar then marched inland, the shrewd Pompey following, but, "afraid to hazard a battle on which so much depended, and being himself provided with all of the necessaries for any length of time, thought to tire out and waste the vigor of Caesar's army, which could not last long." Besides the fatigue of many campaigns, an infectious disease was present in Caesar's army, and, in territory friendly to Pompey, the invaders, Pompey believed, would have to yield since they had neither "money nor provisions."[67]

Yet finally at Pharsalus, by mutual consent, they met in battle. Though Caesar had an army inferior in both infantry and cavalry, he fought because he could see no other opportunity to fight Pompey. With his control of the sea, Pompey had many strategic alternatives in addition to his logistic strategy, but, under pressure from his partisans, he yielded to the temptation to settle the war by a battle. He lost at Pharsalus when Caesar counterbalanced his inferiority in cavalry by using a heavy infantry detachment on his flank to defeat Pompey's victorious cavalry and light infantry. Pompey's heavy losses gave Caesar mastery in the east, and the provinces there immediately switched their allegiance from Pompey to Caesar.

SUMMARY OF WARFARE ON LAND

These generalizations from ancient warfare rely more on the best models—Alexander, Hannibal, and Caesar—than they do on the representative. The best are more available, as they have attracted the attention of ancient and modern historians, and they are more valuable for understanding the development of sophistication in the art of war. At the same time, however, tactical systems result from adaptations to geographical, political, social, economic, and technological conditions and only rarely reflect the genius of one man.

In tactics the ancients sought to attack the enemy's weakness. If they could do this with a more powerful weapon system, as employing javelin-throwing light infantry against heavy infantry, they availed themselves of the opportunity. But usually they had to rely on moving against the enemy's flank or rear, depending on the inappropriateness of the opposing disposition, rather than having a better weapon system. The difficulty of maneuvering heavy infantry made its use for flank or rear assaults an almost insuperable task. The slowness with which the ancients developed even poorly articulated formations shows not that they lacked intellect but rather the difficulty of originating such simple but important ideas. Alexander, for example, who mastered very sophisticated tactics, strategy, and logistics, could neither articulate his army to a sufficient degree nor communicate with its parts well enough to function as an overall commander. In part for this reason, he only dimly saw that a subtracted reserve could give him a choice during battle of concentrating force either to exploit an enemy's vulnerability or to counter an enemy's strength.

Cavalry, weak in shock action, proved to be valuable as an offensive weapon that could attack an enemy's flank or rear. Its greater mobility and the modest requirements for fighting in carefully drawn up formations made it ideal for this task, in spite of its far higher cost as compared to infantry.

Better mobility decided most battles, but Caesar defeated mobility at Pharsalus by bringing his heavy infantry into an unexpected head-on collision with the enemy's cavalry and light infantry, an instance of bringing a superior weapon system against an inferior in a battle with a mixture of weapon systems.

In strategy the same principle applied, concisely stated by the soldier and historian Xenophon: "Wise generalship consists in attacking where the enemy is weakest, even if the point be some way distant." The underlying assumption—win with minimum effort—Xenophon only seemed to qualify when he wrote: "If you attack expecting to prevail, do it in full strength, because a surplus of victory never caused any conqueror one pang of remorse." In strategy the most basic application of this principle of least effort was found in a choice between logistic and combat strategy. Caesar, who said he preferred logistic strategy—"conquering the foe by hunger rather than by steel"—implicitly assumed the availability of a choice between the two strategies and decided that hunger involved the least effort. Neither of these assumptions was always true.[68]

Before the Battle of Issus, Alexander, for example, faced with Darius's army in a flank position on a plain, chose the logistic strategy of hunger to force Darius from his position. He selected this method because it involved minimum effort and the greatest chance of success when compared with combat, which he would have had to employ on terrain that favored the Persian predominance in cavalry. Later, facing Darius on the coast, he had no logistic strategy available to him and used combat strategy on terrain less favorable for Persian cavalry.

Further, military strategy was the servant of the political objective. The Parthians could have driven Crassus back by depriving his army of food and water, a logistic strategy, and doubtless this bloodless victory would have involved less effort in terms of men, horses, and weapons. They would have used their cavalry strategically, as did Caesar in the Ilerda campaign, to cut off the Romans' access to food and water. Instead, the Parthians used their cavalry tactically, pursuing a combat strategy, for a victory through hunger would have had significantly less political impact than the virtual annihilation of a Roman army by the use of their mounted weapon systems. In choosing the most politically effective strategy, the Parthians found themselves in the relatively rare situation of not risking defeat with either military strategy.

Political factors also give significance to military success. Nothing better demonstrates this truth than the contrast between the results of the victories of Alexander against Darius and those of Hannibal against the Romans. The quick and impressive success of Antiochus VII in conquering Mesopotamia, followed almost immediately by his disastrous failure, illustrates how much importance the sentiments of the population may have even in the absence of formal political organization. Antiochus's experience also shows how the behavior of soldiers can affect the attitude of the population, an alienation in this case that led to catastrophic consequences.

In the absence of a Parthian combat strategy based on possession of a superior weapon system on terrain suitable for its use, strategy had to cope with the tactical primacy of the defense. With armies composed of essentially the same weapon system or having the same mixture of weapon systems, the defender could usually take up a topographically strong position, even buttressing it, as the Romans almost uniformly did, with entrenchments. The defender had the equally effective alternative of retreat, confident that a similarly constituted army could not overtake him. Though the strategic use of light cavalry to delay the enemy's march modified this generalization, Caesar's stalemated campaigns at Ilerda and against Pompey amply illustrated the power of the defense and its capability either to resist frontal attacks from strong positions or to exploit the ascendancy of retreat over pursuit. A battle could only occur when each contestant considered it beneficial. Caesar showed the efficacy of the turning movement in overcoming the power of the strategic defense by giving himself the advantage of the tactical defense. But successful turning movements were necessarily rare, requiring a high ratio of force to space, which the ancients usually lacked, as well as constraints such as those imposed by terrain or supply that inhibited the movement of the turned force.

The ability of similarly constituted armies to avoid battle seriously limited the efficacy of using interior lines of operations to concentrate greater forces. This the Consul Nero had accomplished when he led 7,000 men from his army facing Hannibal 250 miles north to attack Hasdrubal's Carthaginians, who had just entered Italy. "Thus," said the historian Livy, "a single consul in defense of both regions of Italy had confronted two armies and two generals, here with his strategy and there in person." But the concentration would have availed Nero nothing had Hasdrubal not blundered by backing his army against a river and having to accept battle when, wisely, he had sought retreat.[69]

Significant outcomes also depended on the relation of the success to the political goal. After his defeat at Issus, Darius offered Alexander the western part of his empire; Alexander, relentlessly determined to conquer and aiming at control of the entire Persian empire, declined. The importance of the victory also depended on the ratio of the force of the victors to the size of the potential theater of operations. A victorious army that was small in relation to the space could usually only dominate a relatively small area, even in the absence of a hostile army contesting its movements.

A defender might use a persisting strategy, as did Darius, meeting the enemy in battle. If the defender felt too weak to meet the hostile army, he might, like the Greeks, avoid combat by retreating or taking refuge in a walled city or fortress. But this defensive strategy would not succeed against an opponent who could apply a persisting strategy of territorial occupation. Against an invader like Alexander who could command political support in the invaded land, the strategy of avoiding battle, unless in pursuit of a logistic strategy, would fail.

But if the defending regime had adequate political strength, the people as well as the space constituted obstacles. A nation with a military tradition, such as the Roman, walled cities, and rugged terrain made a formidable opposition for a victorious force small in relation to the number of people, the obstacles, and the area. The political and military strength of the Romans in their country enabled them, with a Fabian strategy, to avoid the comparatively small Carthaginian army yet pursue with success a persisting strategy of defense that reduced Hannibal to conducting a raiding rather than a persisting offensive strategy. Ultimately Hannibal found himself almost imprisoned in a small enclave in southern Italy.

Defenders, lacking the Roman strength in fortifications, space, and people, still resisted without battle, but they had to resort to a raiding rather than a persisting strategy and accepted the occupation of their country. Then, like the Bactrians, Sogdianians, and Gauls, they conducted raids against isolated detachments of the invading force and their supplies. They concentrated against weakness by picking small enemy forces and, when they attacked supply convoys or foragers, they pursued a logistic as well as a combat strategy. This kind of raiding strategy employed the tactical offensive in pursuit of the strategic defensive and is usually called guerrilla warfare.

Defenders too weak to employ a persisting strategy on the defense found a raiding strategy effective because a raiding offensive was stronger than a defensive persisting strategy. Whereas a persisting defense dominated a persisting offensive, it was weaker than a raiding offense because a raider used retreat, normally the strategic resource of the defender. Because raiders had no settled line of operations and no territorial objective, they might choose their objective almost at random; and, because retreat predominated over pursuit, they could usually avoid the persisting defender's strong forces and use their inherent ambiguity of objective to surprise weakly defended combat or logistic objectives. Thus, raiders have admirable opportunities to concentrate against weakness and, though on the offensive, have almost exclusive possession of the source of the defense's strategic primacy, retreat. Without this intrinsic superiority of the raiding offensive over the persisting defensive, the Bactrians and Sogdianians could not possibly have had so much success against Alexander the Great or Vercingetorix against Caesar.

Thus strategy falls into the four categories defined by the matrix in schematic 1.3. This matrix should have three dimensions to allow for a division into offensive and defensive, because the measures often differ somewhat depending on the objective.

	Persisting	Raiding
Combat		
Logistic		

Schematic 1.3. Strategy Matrix

Alexander's invasion and Darius's defense exemplify persisting combat strategy. Territorial conquest that deprived the defender of revenues and recruits also implemented an offensive, logistic, persisting strategy as did Alexander's successful campaign to deprive the Persian navy of its bases. In destroying crops and even villages, Vercingetorix employed a defensive logistic strategy of the same scorched-earth kind the Persian command contemplated, but rejected, to halt Alexander.

The raid by Persian cavalry, which killed or captured Greek pack mules during the Plataea campaign, illustrates a raiding logistic strategy equally applicable to defense and offense. The Romans against Hannibal and Vercingetorix against Caesar also applied such logistic raids. The Greeks used the raid to implement a combat strategy when they destroyed crops in an effort to induce the defender to fight, and Hannibal adopted the same method against the Romans. The Bactrians, Sogdianians, and Gauls also used these raids in their guerrilla resistance.

Although these guerrilla combat raids employed the tactical offensive, they relied equally on the defensive's capability of retreat. Because a raider aimed at only a transitory presence in the raided territory, withdrawal was an essential element. This raiding strategy proved an effective means of defense, prolonging wars when the defenders had adequate political support.

The Romans' experience in expanding their empire shows the difficulty of overcoming such a guerrilla resistance. When they invaded Britain in 43 A.D., they found the lowland southeast already somewhat Romanized by its proximity to Gaul. Nevertheless, the Romans required four years to subdue this receptive, level, thinly populated country in which they initially established their rule partly through dependent native princes. Expanding northward toward the Scotch border and into Wales required another thirty years. Two hundred years after the occupation of southeastern England, the conquerors had Romanized its aristocracy in language and culture and secured full popular acquiescence to their rule. Yet the fringe area in the north and also in Wales to the west, with its uneven and in places mountainous terrain, remained partially hostile. In these regions the Romans maintained about seventy fortified posts that controlled the roads they had built. These overawed the inhabitants and inhibited raiders. Continued opposition, favored by the terrain, which offered refuge to the guerrillas, made these measures essential, and the legions had to maintain constant vigilance against raiders from areas still not dominated by the forts. It took the tactical supremacy of the Roman regular army and its powerful combination of four weapon systems, the Roman practice of building forts and roads, Roman patience and perseverance, and Roman culture and political skill and institutions to achieve conquest here and in other fringe areas of the European empire.

NAVAL WARFARE

Naval warfare relied largely on two forms of shock action. (1) When opposing ships touched each other, soldiers on one attempted to board the other and fight with spear, sword, and shield. The use of bows, javelins, and slings could precede and supplement this action, but at such close quarters shock action itself predominated. (2) Shock action between the ships themselves constituted the first reliance of the rival forces, and it was this consideration that dominated the design of the ships. Since a quick victory with negligible losses would reward the sinking of an opposing vessel, the design of warships aimed at facilitating the ramming of the opposing ship below the waterline and opening a large hole to flood the rammed ship.

For this reason warships differed markedly from merchant ships. Instead of stubby, sturdy ships relying on sail, navies had narrow, lightly built ships depending primarily on oars. These had relatively high speed because of their many oarsmen, light weight, and great length in relation to breadth. In contrast to merchant ships, naval ships had a ratio as high as ten to one: other things being equal, a narrower ship moves through the water more readily and can attain a higher speed before it encounters a sharp increase in the resistance offered by the water. This speed made the ram at the bow even more menacing.

By the time of warfare between the Greeks and Persians, warships had reached almost full development. A representative vessel might have had a length of eighty feet and a breadth of eight to ten feet. By seating oarsmen partially above as well as behind one another, the ship could accommodate twenty-five oars on each side. This many oarsmen gave the ship high speed and its design provided for considerable strength in resisting a blow against the bow; but the light weight precluded any other elements of structural strength. The ships, built with planks on wooden ribs attached to a keel, differed little in design from wooden warships built ever since.

An oar-propelled warship could easily defeat a merchant ship, even though the merchant ship might carry many more soldiers. Able to move largely independent of the wind and having higher speed and the greater maneuverability provided by its disciplined oarsmen rowing under command, the warship could overtake and ram the merchant vessel. Piercing the ship under water, the strong ram, attached to a ship designed to withstand the shock, would open a large hole that would promptly sink the merchant ship.

But when warships fought each other, neither had an advantage. Tactics involved ships advancing in line abreast, thus placing opposing ships bow to bow, ram to ram. In spite of the similarity between the phalanx of spearmen and the line of ships, the oars kept the ships apart and allowed some maneuvering and attempts to reach the opposing ships' flanks to ram their sides. The skill of individual captains and the quality of the oarsmen had much to do with success in these endeavors. But when the ships came together, often using hooks to maintain their position, it was soldiers who frequently settled the action between ships.

Sea battles involved elements similar to land battles, including concentration of force, flanking or enveloping attacks, and the employment of a reserve. For example, when the Persians invaded Greece in 480 B.C., they first met the Greek fleet near Cape Artemesium on the coast, close to where the Persian army was advancing southward and seeking to enter Greece through the pass of Thermopylae. The Greeks took up a position in a narrow strait between the mainland and the large island of Euboea, so that their commander could protect the flanks of his fleet against the larger number of Persian ships.

The Persians at first sought to reach the rear of the Greek position by sending some of their ships around the island of Euboea. But when a storm arose and destroyed the fragile Persian warships on their short voyage, the Persians launched a frontal attack and the fleets met bow to bow. Some ships broke through the Greek line and prepared to use their superiority in force to take Greek ships in the rear and to use two Persian vessels against one Greek. But as they passed through the gap in the Greek line, the momentarily victorious Persians received a counterattack from a second line of Greek ships held in reserve. As the Persians came through the first line of Greek ships, the Greek reserve attacked the sides of the hostile ships and sank several. Discouraged by these repulses, by the storm, and by the skill of the smaller Greek fleet, the Persians withdrew.

Later, when the Greek fleet made another stand between the shore and an island, the Persians, having blocked both exits of the strait between the island of Salamis and the shore, attacked the Greek vessels holding the eastern end of the strait. The Persians expected an easy victory because they knew that the Greeks were divided over whether to fight or retreat. A small island in the strait divided the advancing Persian battle array and the narrow channel may even have forced some of their ships to enter the strait in line ahead instead of abreast.

The Greeks exploited the ensuing Persian disarray and enveloped the right flank of the Persian fleet. Able to ram the vulnerable sides of the enemy vessels, the Greeks pushed the Persian right wing back upon its center, causing additional confusion, which the Greeks again exploited, driving back the Persian ships with heavy loss. The Persian fleet, having suffered psychologically and materially in two defeats, withdrew to Asia Minor to protect the army's communications there, and the Persian king reduced the size of his army in Greece to one small enough to live on the area of Greece it had conquered. Thus the tactical success of the Greek fleet halted the Persian advance and deprived the Persian army of the secure water communications necessary to supply its full strength. The next year, at Plataea, the Greek armies defeated this diminished Persian force.

Sea warfare clearly exhibited many elements in common with combat on land. The vulnerability of the flank, compared with the front, and the consequent importance of a flank attack stand out as does the value of a reserve. With a thin line of ships rather than a deep line of heavy infantrymen, numerical superiority and concentration of force at one point in a line had greater significance, even when fleets had their flanks protected by land masses.

Ships at sea displayed many of the qualities of mounted warfare on land. Like the cavalry, the ships could go into action rapidly, and their often relatively small numbers, compared to the horsemen of the armies, made it easy for the ships to maintain their array, something more decisive for ships than for cavalry. But in their reliance on a well-aligned formation, the ships had more in common with infantry than with cavalry formations. Yet this similarity with infantry did not dominate warfare between ships, because their few numbers, the greater discipline of the ship captains compared with individual cavalrymen, and the maneuverability conferred by oars sufficiently offset the need to maintain formation to make the tactical attributes of fleets more like that of cavalry than infantry.

In spite of the fleets' placing little or no reliance on an impetuous charge, warfare at sea shared another trait with mounted shock action on land. Defense had no superiority over attack, even when the ships on both sides had identical features, unless the weather, like the terrain, favored one adversary over the other. Without any predominance conferred by topography and neither contestant enjoying an advantage from remaining motionless, neither offense nor defense had any primacy in naval combat. Of course, the outline of the land did give benefits, as the Greeks skillfully exhibited when they protected their flanks in the battle at Artemesium, but it conferred none in frontal attack. Nor could defenders at sea emulate the Romans in entrenching themselves, though beached fleets did fortify their landing areas. So, tactically, the warfare of sailors in ships to a large degree resembled that of soldiers mounted on horses who engaged in shock, rather than missile, combat.

But naval logistics differed markedly from that of land armies in that navies could not live on the country the way armies could. On the sea, however, they had the most efficient means of communication and so could, and found it necessary to, depend on bases for supply, a method nearly impossible for any armies divorced from water communication. Although merchant ships could take advantage of their efficiency as carriers to supply themselves for long voyages, warships could not do this. Light and narrow of beam, they lacked the carrying capacity of merchant ships and their large complements of oarsmen and soldiers required huge quantities of food and water.

The fragility of warships made them, even more than merchant ships, dependent on the safety of staying close to shore, and their shallow draft and flat bottoms made it easy for warships to beach themselves for the night. Moving along the coastline facilitated foraging for food and water. But, unlike an army on the move, the vessels lacked alternative routes, and even when they found a promising area to forage, the sailors could search in only half the circumference available to an army and lacked pack animals or carts to bring in supplies. In addition, with sailors and so many oarsmen, a fleet had a small military capability in relation to their demand for human food. Only the absence of animals made their subsistance problem simpler than an army's. For these reasons, navies could not consistently rely on foraging along the shore, and they remained dependent on bases that offered ample water and from which they could draw food supplies.

Fundamentally, naval strategy had a logistic objective. It sought to control the sea to secure its own commerce, to deny the use of the sea to the enemy's traders, to move and provision its own armies, and to prevent the movement and support of enemy forces. The success of the Greek fleets in interdicting the supply lines of the Persian forces and so diminishing their numbers exemplified the crucial role that the navy's logistic strategy could play.

But to obtain this dominance of the sea, the hostile fleets had to aim at one another. The victory at Salamis, an application of combat strategy, gave the Greeks the control necessary to employ the navy's logistic strategy against the communications of the Persian armies. Alexander's strategy of using his army to capture the bases of the Persian fleet exhibits the use of a logistic strategy to defeat the enemy fleet.

But much naval warfare took place without a decisive command of the sea on either side. Weaker fleets avoided battle by remaining secure in their base ports. The persisting strategy of a blockade of the inferior fleet in its port would accomplish the same objective as a victory, but this task proved especially difficult for the warships of ancient times. Unable to keep at sea for long, ships could not blockade consistently. Even foraging on a hostile shore had its dangers because armies found beached ships a vulnerable and important objective. The success of the supply ships of Alexander the Great in transporting provisions along the coast of Asia Minor amply demonstrates the difficulty of warships in interdicting hostile commerce, particularly along friendly shores. But even Alexander used this commerce only as a supplement. The inability of Pompey's fleet, even with an island to provide much of its needed water, to prevent the passage of Caesar's army across the Adriatic illustrates the hindrances to a blockade with oar-driven ships. But blockade, in which a stronger fleet used the threat of combat action to obtain the same results given by a victory in battle, nevertheless remained an essential part of the strategy of aiming at the enemy fleet. A blockade also functioned as a means of interdicting commerce as well as troop movements or the activity of an enemy fleet. But, unlike the siege on land, the intermittent blockade had difficulty forestalling the hostile force, and the blockaders had all of the land besiegers' supply problems.

In the absence of blockade, hostile navies convoyed troop transports and even merchant vessels. In the absence of convoys, raiding ships, individually or in small flotillas, preyed on ships carrying men or commodities. Thus the strategy of raids, important in land warfare, had a role on the sea. In raids against supply, merchant, or troop ships, the raiders, rather than relying on the combat action of battle or its threat through a blockade, applied directly the navy's logistic strategy of attacking the enemy's supplies.

The Persian command of the sea in the Marathon campaign showed that the navy could deliver to the army something more than the most efficient means for moving and supplying troops. By transporting and escorting the invading army, the navy's collaboration enabled the Persian commander to pursue a combat strategy. The Persian fleet protected the shipborne soldiers from Greek warships during the voyage to Marathon while making it too dangerous for Greek land forces to venture a crossing of the Aegean Sea to attack Persian territory. Further, the Persian army could land at any of many different places in Greece, a capability enhanced by the ability of ancient mariners to beach their ships and not have to rely solely on ports.

Thus, for the Persians the sea constituted both a moat to protect their own country and a highway over which to advance to attack the Greeks. This situation conferred on the Persians, to an unparalleled degree, the power to initiate action. The initiative gave them an opportunity for strategic surprise, without which the Persians would have found themselves at a distinct tactical disadvantage had they disembarked on a defended beach. So the command of the sea assured the invaders the ability that surprise implies—to concentrate against weakness.

In any case, the stronger Persian army could have taken the offensive, and this would have given it the choice of objectives and routes of advance. But command of the sea magnified the Persian advantage: because the commander had to make no strategic dispersal of his troops since he had no apprehension that the Greeks would attack his territory.

The Persians used their initiative, which, like surprise, is not a theme of this work, to distract the Greeks. Aiming at Athens, where he expected to find political support, the Persian commander did not land on the west coast of the peninsula, near Athens; rather he landed twenty-six miles away at Marathon on the peninsula's east shore. This distraction drew the Athenian army to Marathon at the same time that the Persians reembarked half of their army and sailed around the peninsula, intending to land near Athens and capture the city while the Athenian hoplites fought the enemy at the original landing place.

After their victory over the Persians at Marathon, the Greeks sent a messenger on the now-famous run to Athens with the news while the army marched back, arriving before the Persian army had disembarked from their ships to assail Athens. Thwarted by the successful Athenian use of its interior line of operations between the two hostile armies, the Persian fleet and army withdrew. Nevertheless, a delayed Greek attack at Marathon might have caused the victorious army to return only to find the Persians occupying Athens. The command of the sea had given the Persian general the opportunity to distract his opponent and create a weakness at Athens that he very nearly had the opportunity to exploit.

The navy's contribution to the army's operations as well as its warfare at sea displayed many parallels with that on land. It had its great effect on land warfare by its influence on strategy through logistics, the sea providing the most efficient and often the only reasonable communication between two points on land. The effect of the Greek command of the sea in weakening the Persian army prior to the Battle of Plataea offers an illustration of the navy's most typical strategic significance for land warfare just as the Marathon campaign demonstrated the strategic benefits sea power could give an invading army.

2

THE DIVERSITY OF THE MEDIEVAL WAYS OF WAR, 200–1200

The Dissolution of the Roman Empire

Ancient warfare slowly blended into medieval warfare, in part by way of the alterations that took place as the Roman army faced the onslaught of barbarians on Rome's European frontiers and fought its traditional enemies in the East. The gradual changes in the Roman army primarily centered on a strengthening of the cavalry. These units, recruited among the German barbarians, reflected both the important role heavy cavalry had among the German tribes who supplied so many Roman soldiers and the utility of cavalry in defending the frontiers against raiders. In addition, Roman infantry, having lost much of its preeminence as barbarian heavy infantry acquired armor and better weapons, needed the aid of cavalry in attacking the enemy's flank and rear. By 300 A.D. the Roman art of war had evolved into an almost exact replica of the Macedonian/Alexandrian system, a necessary change in fighting barbarian armies, some of which relied both on heavy infantry and heavy cavalry.

At the Battle of Strasbourg in 357 A.D. superior Roman forces caught a barbarian army crossing the Rhine and forced a battle. Though inferior in numbers and discipline, the barbarians possessed remarkable courage, even ferocity, and an adequate grasp of tactics. Both armies rested one flank against a terrain obstacle and concentrated their cavalry on the open flank. The infantry engaged and, in the words of a contemporary historian, the barbarian cavalry charged, "extending their weapons in their right hands and monstrously gnashing their teeth" while "the flowing hair of these extraordinary maniacs was bristling and a frenzy shown from their eyes." This charge, if not just the intimidating appearance of these horsemen, routed the Roman cavalry. The barbarian cavalry, displaying good leadership and discipline, did not pursue but turned, in the Alexandrian manner, against the flank and rear of the Roman infantry.[1]

But the Romans' splendid articulation saved them, the Roman commander, Julian, later emperor and, as a convert to paganism, known as Julian the Apostate, promptly covering his flank with a reserve force of heavy infantry. Since the cultured Julian had undoubtedly read Caesar and knew the Battle of Pharsalus, it is likely that in advance of the beginning of the conflict, he had placed a detachment where it could carry out this movement. Though not able to execute the remainder of the Pharsalus maneuver by enveloping the enemy, the Roman commander made decisive use of his numerical advantage to win the contest. The Romans captured the barbarian commander, and a substantial part of his force drowned in the Rhine while trying to escape.

Twenty-one years later the Romans suffered, at the Battle of Adrianople, a catastrophe approximating Cannae. When the numerous cavalry of the barbarians routed the Roman cavalry and enveloped one flank of the Roman army, the horsemen held the infantry virtually imprisoned in a dense mass. Here they killed a large proportion of them, including the emperor commanding the Roman army. Even the legions could not count on protecting their flanks against the fierce and determined charge of barbarian cavalry. The lack of training and discipline did not handicap the effectiveness of the barbarian cavalry, since heavy cavalrymen generally fought as individuals, depending on cohesion and mutual cooperation, as did heavy infantry.

But this return to a more faithful replica of the Macedonian role for cavalry and to a battle characteristic of Alexander and Hannibal proved a transitory development. During the fifth century the western portion of the empire succumbed to the German barbarians, though for the most part, it remained theoretically in existence. Although the causes of the Roman failure in the West are complex, two familiar elements contributed. Relying on their professional army, the Romans no longer had any local military tradition or a militia. Nor had they much local patriotism, the allegiance of most of the people going to the distant emperor and the concept of the empire. Since most barbarian invaders acknowledged the emperor and often received grants of land and authority from him, they had an adequate political base for a conquest, the process of which spanned a century.

This division of the empire into what became, in fact, barbarian kingdoms in Italy, France, Spain, and north Africa helped to create a diversity in tactics, especially as the empire continued in the East. From the homogeniety of the Macedonian-Roman method, which characterized the battles of Strasbourg and Adrianople, the ancient world came again to have regional or national systems of war that reflected local geographical, economic, social, and political conditions.

Changes in Military Organization and Tactical Emphasis

Warfare in the West reflected the disappearance of the Roman professional army, which had remained concentrated in camps under discipline and engaged in drill as well as weapons practice. The dominant military system of the barbarians relied on a militia that had many, but not all, of the attributes of a professional force. The men, hunters and herdsmen, had regarded themselves as warriors and had been pleased to enter Roman service and devote full time to what many considered their primary calling. In infantry combat they relied on heavy infantry alone, frequently arrayed in formations with as many ranks as files. They rushed the enemy, counting on their impetuosity and then on their courage and devotion to overwhelm their opponents. They lacked training in fighting together and substituted for discipline their long association as a family group under a leader.

When the barbarians established themselves in the Roman western provinces, they often dispersed in small groups among the Roman population. This settlement pattern often deprived them of the cohesion provided by their old family group, and their small numbers meant that they had no opportunity to practice Roman methods of formation and drill. Not enough warriors found themselves together to permit the development of groups with the unit training of the Greek and Roman militia. Although this generalization oversimplifies, it is fair to say that as the Roman Empire lacked any militia, so initially did the barbarian kingdoms. They relied on professionals but scattered theirs and quartered them on the countryside, rather than concentrating them, supported by taxes and provided with the occasion to learn to work together in disciplined, cohesive groups. Gradually the barbarian professionals evolved into a rural militia in which some had good equipment and training and many had little of either. Ultimately this became a system of military obligation based on holding land, feudalism, in which a hierarchical pattern developed with military service owed to smaller landholders who in turn had duties to a higher lord; the pyramid ended with the king.

This change elevated individual prowess, and an infantryman's strength, skill, and courage meant more than the organization and the level of training of his group. But heavy infantry's strength lay in the group, and the barbarians typically relied on heavy infantry. Thus the new, dispersed arrangement of the professionals significantly diminished the value of the heavy in the barbarian kingdoms of the West.

The reduction in the quality of heavy infantry increased the relative merit of heavy cavalry. Both heavy and light cavalry together had composed less than 20 percent of Roman armies, Alexander the Great having employed no higher proportion. The cost of cavalry—at least double that of infantry—depended not only on the expense of the horse but also on the cost of training to achieve the greater skill required to fight mounted. The ineffectiveness of heavy cavalry in frontal attacks against heavy infantry limited its value in the Macedonian system, a drawback accentuated by the better articulation of Roman infantry, which could often defend its own flanks and envelop the flanks of the opposing infantry.

The decline in the West of not only well-articulated Roman infantry but also of heavy infantry trained to work together in a phalanx elevated the comparative effectiveness of cavalry without raising its cost. Further, the dispersal of the professional soldiers and the loss of the opportunity to train together affected cavalry less because heavy cavalry combat had never relied on group action in the way heavy infantry had. Moreover, the new stress on individual prowess and the dispersed professional's opportunity for individual training emphasized the qualities needed in the heavy cavalry.

The cavalryman also had the skill and inclination to fight on foot as well as mounted. Where the terrain or the besieging of fortifications, for example, made infantry essential, the Western professional soldier displayed a readiness and willingness to fight skillfully on foot, but he fought in the same way, as an individual rather than as part of a formation. The revaluation of cavalry meant that the proportion of cavalry rose in the armies in the western kingdoms of the Roman Empire. But this increase represents only an average; individual kingdoms displayed great variations: the Vandals who conquered Africa, for example, fought almost exclusively mounted and the Franks in Gaul preferred for the most part to fight on foot.

So armies in the West continued as small professional forces supplemented by untrained and ill-armed militia. They stressed shock action, with neither light cavalry nor light infantry playing much role. In this sense the barbarians followed the Greek and Roman tradition. In the eastern Roman or Byzantine Empire, the art of war also changed, but for other reasons.

Least Effort Exemplified: Byzantine Tactics and Strategy

The army of the Byzantine Empire differed significantly from the old Roman army and from previous models in Europe and the Near East. Roman in its sophisticated engineering and logistic organization, the Byzantine army relied on cavalry and light infantry to a most un-Roman degree. In part this reflected the triumph of cavalry at the Battle of Adrianople—to a degree the later Roman system for frontier defense—and also the diversity of Byzantium's enemies, which included the successors of the Parthians. After initially relying on buffer states and diplomacy, the Romans had gradually adopted a frontier garrisoned by their own forces. The Rhine and Danube rivers marked these borders as did walls of earth and stone where no rivers flowed. The army could not, of course, man these long defensive lines in strength, nor could it prevent raiders or invading armies from piercing them.

But the defenses did provide a line of posts that warned of a crossing of the barrier and triggered a concentration of defenders to repel and, if possible, capture the marauders. The line of defense provided a valuable obstacle to the retreat of an enemy making a foray. In this way the Romans organized a persisting defense, both to cope with the offensively stronger raiding strategy of the economically motivated barbarians and to resist or expel those who persisted by trying to conquer Roman territory.

Even though the physical obstacle of the barrier often compelled the raiders to leave their horses behind, the Roman concentration necessary to deal with such a raid required a speed in marching beyond the capability of the heavy infantry. The Roman cavalry met the requirement, as did light infantry, which could march faster than booty-laden raiders on foot. Since most raiders wished to avoid combat and the defenders had the objective of trapping the retreating intruders against the frontier obstacle, the speed of the cavalry and light infantry gave them precedence over the slow-moving legions' predominance in combat. Only in resisting a persisting invasion did the legions come into play. Thus, the proportion of light infantry and cavalry gradually increased in the Roman army. Forces defending the boundaries became a sort of militia when the government gave the men an allotment of farm land in lieu of pay.

In the fourth century the Romans abandoned their efforts to keep their frontier inviolate and adopted a defense in depth to resist the constant major incursions along their borders. This strategy involved a reliance behind the empire's boundaries on fortifications ranging from farmhouses to walled cities. The fortified points served as supply depots, blocked major routes of ingress, obstructed the raiders' movements, denied them facility in retreat, and presented serious obstacles to the advance of invaders intending to persist. Further, these strong points provided places of refuge for the defenders and the area's inhabitants, their animals and portable possessions. Any force that bypassed these strong points faced the threat of a rear attack by the fort's garrisons. But fortified positions in depth constituted only part of the defense; the defenders needed a mobile field army to take advantage of the difficulties that the fortifications and obstructed communications imposed on the enemy. The requirement for speed in reaching an invaded area as well as ease in concentrating or in refusing battle made a force stressing cavalry and light infantry ideal for the mobile field army.

But the most formidable threat to the eastern part of the empire came from the successors of the Parthians, the Persians, who fought, like their predecessors, almost exclusively with light and heavy cavalry. The fate of Crassus at Carrhae dramatically demonstrated the inadequacy of the Roman tactical system for dealing with Parthian cavalry on its own terrain. For this reason the Byzantine heavy cavalry carried bows. Although it is difficult to train and expensive to equip a soldier to fight with both weapon systems and it is likely that, with his heavy equipment, the Byzantine horseman had his greatest competence in shock action, the bows and the knowledge of their use gave the Byzantine cavalry a valuable versatility. For shock combat and protection against enemy arrows each wore a steel cap, a long mail shirt that reached to his thighs, and steel shoes. Some horses wore armor also. In addition to a bow, the cavalryman carried a sword, dagger, and a long lance, though he must have put aside the lance to use the bow. Although the Byzantine armies had some light cavalry, these dual-purpose but essentially heavy cavalry constituted the bulk of the mounted forces and as much as half of an army.

The Byzantine light infantryman carried a bow with a quiver of forty arrows, a small shield, and a weapon, such as an axe, for close combat. A few who lacked skill with the bow armed themselves with javelins. Some wore a light mail shirt. Combat experience had demonstrated the predominance of these foot bowmen over enemy horse archers. The Byzantines, facing Persian and other mounted bowmen and, according to a contemporary authority, knowing these enemies had a "special dread" of the foot archer, made the light infantry the most numerous branch of their foot soldiers. In addition to shield and body armor the Byzantine heavy infantry carried a spear, a sword, and an axe. The spear was consistent with late Roman practice when a decline in training and discipline and the strength of the enemy's cavalry charges impelled the legions to strengthen their javelin enough so that they could also use it as a spear. Heavy infantry, a relatively small part of the army, played the same role as heavy infantry in the Macedonian and Roman armies.[2]

The high cost of so many mounted Byzantine soldiers contributed to keeping Byzantine armies small, but they displayed great effectiveness against the variety of national tactical systems that surrounded the empire. Well adapted to fight the mounted Persian horse archers, the Byzantine forces proved equally adept in combat against the barbarian armies of both the Goths and Franks in the Byzantine campaign to reconquer Italy during the sixth century.

The same factors that enabled the barbarians to seize the western Roman provinces made them vulnerable to Byzantine reconquest. The Gothic kingdom of Italy had such small forces that to concentrate a field army to resist the Byzantine invasion, it had to give up garrisoning the cities. The Goths, recognizing that the inhabitants of these cities had no loyalty to them, destroyed the town walls to deprive the citizens of the power to resist reoccupation. Compelled by political necessity to adopt a persisting strategy, they then risked all in a battle against the invading Byzantines. Both armies had mercenaries. The Byzantines employed Huns, Armenians, Persians, Arabs, and Slavs as well as many German barbarians. The Gothic forces included many who had previousy served in the armies of the Byzantine Emperor and the Goths had not considered it absurd to offer their elective kingship to Belisarius, a brilliant Byzantine general who had defeated them in an earlier campaign.

In 552 the Byzantine Emperor Justinian the Great sent a fine army to reconquer Italy. He appointed Narses to command, rather than the often-victorious Belisarius. The short, thin Narses, a septuagenarian eunuch with little more than two years of active military service, apparently had little to recommend him beyond the trust Justinian had in him. Yet the abilities that had brought him to high positions at court and the courage and resourcefulness he had displayed in crises proved good gauges for his military talents.

The two armies met at Taginae, in central Italy, Narses's 15,000 Byzantines slightly outnumbering the Goths, commanded by the capable King Totila. Both commanders desired battle and formed their forces across a narrow, level valley and waited. Narses, anxious to protect his flank, sent fifty picked heavy infantry to occupy a small hill on the left of his line, where they took up a position in a path, "standing shoulder to shoulder and arrayed in the form of a phalanx." When Totila dispatched a body of heavy cavalry to take the hill, the fifty blocked the way, "making a barrier with their shields and thrusting forward their spears." The attackers, trying to manage excited horses "that did not in the least obey their urging," failed against "men packed so closely together and not giving an inch of ground."[3]

This skirmish proved an accurate forecast of the outcome of the battle. The Goths relied on their heavy cavalry, and Narses, arraying his army on this supposition, took advantage of the defensive primacy of the soldier on foot over the horseman. To strengthen his heavy infantry, the inexperienced Byzantine general, displaying a clear comprehension of the comparative merits of each weapon system, had much of his heavy cavalry dismount and join the infantry, and athwart the valley the men on foot formed a phalanx with spears and lances. On each flank Narses placed 4,000 archers with heavy cavalry behind. He was eager to receive the enemy's attack.

The following morning the Goths, formed their heavy cavalry in front of their infantry, only two bow shots from the Byzantine front. After a delay, the Gothic cavalry made its famous, impetuous charge. But it failed to overwhelm the phalanx, and, halted before the infantry, the flanks of the Gothic cavalry had to receive a rain of arrows from the Byzantine bowmen. Seeing the cavalry halted, unable to overthrow the infantry, and the arrows wounding horses and men, Narses ordered his heavy cavalry to attack the flank as the infantry moved forward. The Gothic cavalry fled, becoming entangled in their own infantry in the process, and King Totila received a mortal wound during his flight from the field.

This battle overthrew Gothic rule in Italy and returned Italy to the empire. It is not clear why Totila had his cavalry charge the Byzantine center rather than ride over the vulnerable archers on the wings. Since such ineptitude did not ordinarlily characterize him, perhaps terrain obstacles—or even ditches—that the Byzantines had used in earlier battles—may have forced the attack into the center. The battle again exhibited the ability of heavy infantry to resist the charge of heavy cavalry. Even though the mercenary foot soldiers probably had had little drill together, their spears and lances, their depth, and their skill as professionals were ample to defeat the frontal charge of the formidable Gothic cavalry.

Having conquered Italy from the Goths, Narses faced a force of Franks raiding from the north. In spite of a lack of any armor but shield and helmet, the Frank made a formidable heavy infantryman. Armed with a short sword and an eighteen-inch dagger, he also carried an axe and at least one light spear. He used both the axe and spear for throwing as well as in close combat, and, as a contemporary explained, a Frank throwing his spear, "if they strike an enemy the barbs are so firmly fixed in his body that it is impossible to draw the weapon out. If it strikes a shield, it is impossible for the enemy to get rid of it by cutting off its head, for the iron runs too far down the shaft. At this moment the Frank rushes in, places his foot on the butt as it trails on the ground, and so, pulling the shield downwards, cleaves his uncovered adversary through the head, or pierces his breast with a second spear." The Franks fought in a huge column or square from which they could fight in any direction. They lacked drill or articulation but had great bravery and cohesiveness.[4]

In 554 at Casilinum, blocking its route of retreat, the astute Narses met this redoubtable body of heavy infantry by again dismounting some heavy cavalry to strengthen his own heavy infantry. He could have some confidence that on the defensive his armored professionals could resist the Franks. He may also have had some natural or artificial strength for their defensive position. On his flanks he posted the bulk of his cavalry, primarily armored lancers also equipped with bows. The charge of the Franks broke the first two lines of Byzantine infantry and engaged the third and last line when Narses ordered forward his bow-armed heavy cavalry on the flanks. Threatened by this double attack, the Frankish infantry in their dense formation had to halt to resist the charge of the cavalry. But the cavalary did not charge; instead they began to shower the Franks with arrows. If the Franks had broken their formation, they would not have made so easy a target for the mounted bowmen; but they kept their close square together, for they realized that breaking it made them vulnerable to the charge of the armored Byzantine cavalry, who would immediately put aside their bows and use their lances and swords. After a time, immobilized under a shower of arrows, the Franks began to withdraw to the rear. In their retreat the formation began to lose some of its integrity, and Narses's cavalry finally charged and broke into the formation, inflicting hideous casualties.

These two battles exhibit the versatility of the Byzantine army. Its variety of weapon systems enabled a skillful general to confront his enemy's weakness. At Taginae Narses used heavy infantry to stop heavy cavalry; two years later at Casilinum he resisted heavy infantry with heavy infantry until he brought missile weapons into play against a vulnerable heavy infantry, unable to flee.

In spite of defeats that deprived it of all of its Asiatic possessions except Asia Minor, the Byzantine Empire maintained itself for centuries as a formidable Eastern power. Its survival depended on its excellent army, one animated by professionalism and religious zeal. The Byzantines codified their tactics and strategy into what today one would call doctrine, which stressed the defensive and winning at the minimum cost. Viewing their expensively equipped and well-trained professional soldiers as a capital asset, they preferred winning without a battle and always carefully measured the benefits of victory against the costs of defeat. Thus, in arguing against following a retreating enemy, the famous general Belisarius said: "So if we compel them against their will to abandon their purpose of withdrawing and come to battle with us, we shall win no advantage whatsoever if we are victorious—for why should one rout a fugitive?—while if we are unfortunate, as may happen, we shall both be deprived of the victory we now have, . . . and also we shall abandon the land of the Emperor to lie open to the attacks of the enemy without defenders."[5]

Such a strategy assumed the status quo as the only reasonable political and military objective and implicitly presumed that the Byzantines occupied a more fragile position than the enemy. For 300 years the conservative, careful strategy of limited military aims succeeded admirably in preserving the empire intact. Because they faced the same difficulty as the Romans in protecting their domains from raiders, the Byzantines adhered to a doctrine that continued the Roman system of defense in depth. When employed against Arab raiders from Syria, for example, this system first provided for early warning of the movement of the mounted men through a pass. The local cavalry force tracked the raiders, keeping the military district headquarters informed of their own route and location while harrying the raiders, picking off stragglers, and retarding their advance. Meanwhile, local infantry, militia and regular, moved to the passes in the mountains. At the same time the cities and fortresses closed their gates after citizens had taken refuge within the walls. As the raiders moved forward, the commander of the local military district, reinforced from adjacent districts if he faced a large raid, marched out with a purely cavalry force. He aimed at a battle, an ambush of the raiders on their return, or, best of all, trapping the raiders in a pass closed by infantry that already occupied the likely routes of egress. Thus the Byzantines dealt with raiders by inhibiting their movements and denying them their most fundamental requisite, retreat.

Perhaps the Battle of Manzikert in eastern Asia Minor in 1071 confirmed the wisdom of the conservatism of Byzantine strategy. This defeat cost the Byzantines the control of most of Asia Minor, the recruiting area for their army and source of much of their wealth. Few battles in history have had such a significant result as the loss of much of the Byzantine professional army. Emperor Romanus IV was determined to punish the Seljuk Turks, who had raided his territory and captured several important cities. Wanting a decisive campaign, Romanus, an able general who had come to the throne by marrying the empress and who had already fought the Turks with success, assembled a huge army. The Turks, horse archers from the steppes, had already conquered the Moslem states in what had been the Persian and Parthian empires and had continued the tradition of raids into and warfare with the Byzantine Empire.

The Byzantines had long coped with the skillful tactics of the steppe light cavalry. Without body armor and carrying only a sword and sometimes a javelin, the Turk relied on his bow, a quiver of thirty to fifty arrows, and the mobility provided by his horse; on campaign he brought at least one spare horse. In their battle tactics, according to a European observer, the horse archers "never mix with the enemy, but keep hovering about him, discharging their arrows first from one side and then from the other, occasionally pretending to fly, and during their flight shooting arrows backward at their pursuers, killing men and horse, as if they were combatting face to face." To cope with these tactics, so like the Parthian, Byzantine doctrine prescribed always keeping the foot bowmen near the cavalry, never fighting with uncovered flanks or rear, and never permitting the army to disperse. At the Battle of Manzikert the Emperor Romanus had committed all of his infantry to a siege elsewhere; he also violated other canons derived from his army's long experience with light cavalry.[6]

The Byzantines faced in the Turkish sultan a sagacious and determined opponent, whose name, Alp Arslan, meant valiant lion. But he, having three times suffered defeat at the hands of the Byzantines, twice from Romanus, and having a well-informed respect for Byzantine military prowess, also displayed the attributes of the fox.

After a parley between the two rulers, the aggressive Romanus advanced against the Turks with his armored and mounted army arrayed in a single line on a broad front and backed by a strong rear guard. The Turks retreated, easily keeping their distance on their more lightly burdened horses. But they attacked on the flanks, showering the Byzantine cavalry with arrows. These missiles doubtless killed few of the armored riders, but the horses suffered and many riders certainly lost their mounts. Some of the Byzantine heavy cavalry still had bows, but the soldiers no longer had the skill of earlier centuries. So the Turks had no difficulty in overmastering them. The mass of the Byzantines made a good target; the moving Turks did not. The soldiers on the flanks, "having been harassed by the Turks, were obliged to pursue [the enemy archers] because otherwise they would shoot from afar and kill their horses. But in pursuing them thoughtlessly, they fell into an ambush." Meanwhile, the emperor continued to move the army forward against constantly receding opponents until "the twilight took him by surprise."[7]

As the emperor attempted to return his army to camp in the darkness, the wings did not understand the signals and the army fell into disorder. Romanus, in the center and separated from the wings, compounded the confusion when he moved forward again as the rear guard continued toward the camp. The Turks attacked and enclosed the separated parts of the army in a whirl of galloping archers, showering arrows on the disorganized host of armored horsemen. "It was like an earthquake with howling, sweat, a swift rush of fear, clouds of dust, and, not least, hordes of Turks riding all around us. Depending on his speed, resolution and strength, each man sought safety in flight. The enemy chased them, killing some, capturing some and trampling others under the horses' hooves. It was a terribly sad sight, beyond any lamenting or mourning." The Turks killed or captured virtually all of the troops except those in the rear guard and destroyed the flower of the Byzantine professional army.[8]

The battle demonstrated what the Byzantines had long known, that heavy cavalry could not cope with light cavalry. This knowledge underlay their doctrine of keeping light infantry with the cavalry. The light cavalry did not have a great margin of superiority in mobility, but its modest advantage enabled it to refuse battle while still using its bows. Just as Greek light infantry peltasts with javelins had avoided shock combat with heavy infantry hoplites while wounding and killing them with missiles, so the Turkish horse archers had defeated the Byzantine heavy cavalry.

The capture of the emperor at Manzikert had much to do with the Byzantine civil war, which began immediately and which exacerbated the sudden military debility of the empire. So, from raiders in Asia Minor, the Turks suddenly became conquerers. But how could the Mohammedan Turks occupy a populous and well-organized Christian territory over twice the size of Italy and one that presented an essentially national resistance to rule by infidels?

Without realizing it, the Turks had already provided the means of securing the acquiescence of the Christians of Asia Minor. An eyewitness described the events as one Byzantine city fell to Turkish raiders: "The army entered the city, massacred the inhabitants, pillaged and burned it, leaving it in ruins, making prisoners of those who escaped the massacre." The observer continued: "I wanted to enter the city and see it with my own eyes. I tried to find a street without having to walk over corpses. But that was impossible." More hostile, a Christian characterized the Turks' capture of another city thusly: "Like famished dogs, bands of infidels hurled themselves on our city, surrounded it and pushed inside, massacring the men and mowing everything down like reapers in the fields, making the city a desert. Without mercy they incinerated those who had hidden themselves in houses and churches." The same author wrote: "Lift your eyes and your looks to your sons taken into slavery, your infants smashed without pity against stones, your youths given to the flames, your venerable ancients thrown down in public places, your virgins, raised gently and in comfort, dishonored and marched off on foot into slavery." If the Turks had wished to terrorize the remaining inhabitants of Asia Minor, this author furnished good propaganda.[9]

If continued without any prospect of remission, such a ruthless and thorough reign of terror could substitute for a political program. The cost in devastation and depopulation proved immense, but the Turks acquired most of Asia Minor in the ensuing decade, having crushed by terror all popular resistance. Though the Byzantine Empire continued for almost another four centuries, its military power declined and it ceased really to exemplify the Greek and Roman art of war. Meanwhile, Western Europe was undergoing a substantial change in its tactical outlook and strategic requirements.

The Stirrup's Enhancement of the Effectiveness of Cavalry

Early in the eighth century Mohammedans from Africa overthrew the weak Gothic kingdom of Spain, beginning a long period of Moslem dominance of the Iberian peninsula. Pushing across the Pyrenees into the kingdom of the Franks, the Mohammedans failed to expand their domain, suffering defeat at Tours in 732 when their shock cavalry failed against the combined forces of the Frankish infantry, and the dismounted Frankish cavalry. This battle was the major event of a series of raids that lasted past the middle of the century. The eclipse of Christian Spain, together with an increase in strength and size of the kingdom of the Franks, made the Franks the dominant power in the Christian Roman West. By 800 the pope had crowned their king, Charles the Great, emperor in the West, and his domain included in addition to France much of present-day Germany, Czechoslovakia, Italy, Austria, and Yugoslavia. Thus Frankish military developments of this period had a profound and long-lasting influence on Western Europe.

The Franks reorganized the system of decentralized professional soldiers, basing the new military force on feudalism, which decentralized political power and placed it in the hands of essentially hereditary magnates who governed and who owed the king military service. In practice, this service involved a high proportion of essentially untrained and ill-armed militia and a number of properly equipped and, in many cases, skilled infantry and cavalry. For distant campaigns the king called only the well-equipped and competent fighters, the professionals, using the militia solely to resist invasion.

The Franks, both on foot and horse, increasingly protected themselves with a steel helmet and mail shirt. The foot soldiers carried a six-foot spear and a sword. The king's regulations required that all infantry and all mailed cavalry also have a bow and twelve arrows and specified that even the most ill-armed man should have a bow, even if he lacked shield or sword. This stress on the bow, a weapon traditionally foreign to the Franks, reflected the king's campaigns against the Avars of present-day Hungary who fought as mounted horse archers. The king's regulations, which actually failed to make many competent archers among the Franks, exhibit the same response to the identical tactical problem faced by the Byzantines.

Far more effective was the stress that successive Frankish rulers placed on cavalry. Traditionally infantry from a forested country, the Franks had begun to mount even though initially they dismounted to fight. But combat against mounted Avars from the East and the Moslems from Spain made cavalry essential. Just as the Romans strengthened and the Byzantines had stressed cavalry to combat raiders, so the Franks also followed the same adaptation in their mix of weapon systems. But a major technological innovation made it easier for the Franks to become a nation preeminent in heavy cavalry in less than a century.

Early in the eighth century the stirrup became available in Western Europe. Of uncertain origin, the stirrup spread rapidly over the Western world, its obvious utility guaranteeing rapid acceptance: with stirrups a rider lost most of the hazard of falling from his horse. In combat he could, in a charge with his lance, transmit the full force of his horse's motion to his target, secure in his unity with the horse provided by saddle and stirrups. In combat with his sword he had little reason to fear that a missed stroke might bring him off his horse. He could even increase his height above an opponent on foot by standing in his stirrups. In addition, this innovation made it possible for mediocre riders to perform well and greatly enchanced the effectiveness of the best heavy cavalry.

The stirrup, so simple in concept, produced one of technology's most fundamental modifications in land warfare since the introduction of the four basic weapon systems and the development of fortification and siegecraft. The riding of horses had superseded chariots, and elephants had ultimately proven ineffective. Steel replaced iron as iron had supplanted bronze, both conferring advantages on the possessors of the improved weapons. These changes, like improved bows, affected warfare in an important, if not fundamental, way. And the increase in effectiveness that the stirrup conferred on the heavy cavalry amounted to a difference as crucial as any of these, for it altered the balance among the four weapon systems. This change proved to be especially marked because it came when Western Europe no longer had any professional heavy infantry or even any urban militia of the Greek and Roman type. Shock cavalry had greater opportunities against undrilled heavy infantry, and the stirrup markedly enhanced these.

The Franks became famous for the irresistible charge of their stirrup-stablized heavy cavalry, and their method spread to Christian Western Europe. After meeting such cavalry, the Byzantines concluded: "So formidable is the charge of the Frankish chivalry with their broadsword, lance, and shield, that it is best to decline a pitched battle with them till you have put all the chances on your side." But, the Byzantine manual continued, the best strategy would be "to protract the campaign, and lead them into the hills and desolate tracts, for they take no care about their commissariat, and when their stores run low their vigour melts away. They are impatient of hunger and thirst, and after a few days of privation desert their standards and steal away home as best they can." After comparing the logistic weakness of a Frankish army with the tactical strength of its fearsome cavalry, the Byzantines concluded that a logistic rather than a combat strategy offered the easiest route to victory. "On the whole, therefore, it is easier and less costly to wear out a Frankish army by skirmishes, protracted operations in desolate districts, and the cutting off of supplies, than to attempt to destroy it at a single blow."[10]

The improvement in Frankish cavalry, largely completed by the beginning of the ninth century, proved fortunate indeed because this empire and its successors faced a far more serious challenge than that offered by the Avars and Moslems.

Western Europe's Struggle against Raiders

Just as the Romans had to cope with barbarians, so also did the kingdoms into which the Frankish empire soon dissolved. In the ninth century the Vikings, coming by ship from present-day Denmark and Norway, raided the coasts of Europe, including those of England. Like many of the raiders faced by the Romans and Byzantines, these had an essentially economic motivation. In the tenth century similar motives led the Magyars, inhabitants of what is now Hungary, to raid Germany and Italy.

Talented sailors, the Vikings came in small undecked vessels, usually with a single large sail, but these ships relied primarily on the oars of their crew of forty to 100 fighting men. The profits were so great that these raids became the principal occupation of the Viking communities. Their command of the sea and their ability to beach their boats gave the Vikings wide latitude in their choice of landing places. Therefore they had unequaled facility for avoiding their opponents' strength and concentrating against weakness, readily implementing their raiding strategy and search for weakly defended booty. And they proved far from vulnerable when they left their ships and marched inland.

Though initially without armor, the Vikings made fierce heavy infantry. Famous for their heavy axes with six-foot handles, using two hands they could cut through an opponent's shield and helmet with a single blow. They also carried a shield, a short sword, and a javelin, and, though they usually fought at close quarters, they had great skill with a bow. Formidable as soldiers and skillful as sailors, they looted coastal cities and soon moved up rivers, plundering interiors. Among other booty, these predatory bands soon provided themselves with helmets and mailed shirts, completing their heavy infantry outfit and fully equipping themselves to deal with the still feeble resistance of local authorities and the weak and warring monarchies of Western Europe.

So successful that some bands stayed to winter on islands off the coast, the Vikings soon left their ships and began to carry out raids by marching inland from the coasts or rivers. Extremely vulnerable to having their ships burned in their absence, they protected them by building and garrisoning a stockade where they beached their ships. For their inland raids they appropriated horses found near their landing points and so could move mounted on their looting forays. But they fought on foot when they met resistance. They thus became mounted infantry and had the strategic mobility of cavalry but the advantages, and disadvantages, of heavy infantry in combat. By the middle of the ninth century Viking raids had devastated much of the coast of Germany and France. Local levies of untrained, ill-armed, and often unarmored shock infantry had little chance in combat against Vikings, who by now had become well-armed and skilled professional soldiers and raiders.

Combating raiders presented an extraordinarily difficult strategic problem if only because they were not necessarily oriented to any specific objective and so could use the defender's power of retreat and evasion whenever they found it convenient. The ambiguity of their objective gave the raiders unrivaled opportunities to concentrate against weakness and to minimize the defense's strength on the tactical defensive. Further, because raiders relied on retreat, they had appropriated for their own use the strategy capability normally an attribute of the defense. Thus a raiding strategy on the offensive was stronger against a persisting strategy on the defensive.

Since in meeting this powerful threat there could be no question of protecting every possible landing point, the defense in depth provided the only reasonable strategy. The heavy cavalry, fostered by the Franks and whose effectiveness the stirrup had enhanced, already existed. Though the mounted Vikings had strategic mobility comparable to the heavy cavalry, their stolen rural nags lacked the speed and endurance of the Frankish cavalry's picked horses, and often their booty slowed the Viking movement even more. But the defenders faced a tactical as much as a strategic problem, for when the cavalry caught the raiders, the Vikings dismounted.

Even if they had competence as cavalrymen, the Vikings might well have dismounted to fight. Cavalry was weak on the defensive and had to resort to a countercharge only to equal the attacker's power. But dismounted, the heavy cavalry became heavy infantry. Earlier Narses had thus strengthened his heavy infantry on two occasions, and the Franks had used this disposition against the Mohammedans at Tours. So leaving their horses the Viking mounted infantry became heavy infantry, which still had a defensive supremacy over heavy cavalry. When defending themselves, the Vikings always chose a strong position, a hill or behind a stream, or even in a village or a church. The Franks could not use archery because they had failed to develop adequately their bowmen, and in any case the Vikings were good archers, too. When the cavalry caught the raiders, the battles thus often consisted of heavy infantry resisting the charge of the heavy cavalry. Though the Vikings had not drilled, they usually won because they were professional fighters accustomed to campaigning together.

Yet the Vikings occasionally suffered disconcerting reverses, as at Louvain in 891. Here they had established an impregnable camp in a bend in a river, which they had sealed off with a ditch and an embankment topped by a stockade. But when the German king, Arnulf, arrived, he dismounted his cavalry and attacked on foot. Leading his men against the fortifications, the warrior king with his knights cut through the wooden palisade with their swords and drove the Vikings into the river where many drowned.

So foot combat could often have given better offensive capabilities than remaining mounted. Still the Vikings had come to loot, not to win battles. Not only did a battle defeat their primary objective, but even a small force of cavalry tracking their march presented a serious menace by restricting looting, picking off stragglers, and impeding their advance at such points as bridges and fords.

But greater success rewarded a program of fortification, the other element of the defense in depth. His control of the fortified towns had provided one element in Alexander's success in Bactria and Sogdiana and to that of the Romans not only against Hannibal but also in consolidating their empire. In France and Germany near the coast even small towns erected fortifications that the militia, though useless in the field, could defend. In addition, the local magnates fortified defensible points in the country and provided enclosures as refuges for the people in the region and their movable possessions. Although these early examples of the castles, like the new walls of the towns, consisted of a ditch and an earthen bank with a wooden palisade, they provided an efficacious defense. Though adept at most things, Vikings originally knew nothing of siegecraft and, in any case, had not come to conduct sieges. Denied access to the cities, the raiders found little in the often-plundered countryside, especially when the people with their animals and other valuables had taken refuge in the castle.

Thus, raiding ceased to pay well and the constant conflicts with the cavalry made it hazardous indeed. Further, in wintering and then establishing settlements on the coast, the Vikings had created the basis for a new restraint on their raids. When the settled Vikings raided for booty, the Franks retaliated with counter-raids, which had the political objective of deterring future Viking raids. Finally, in 911, a Viking chief accepted a part of France—Normandy—from the king in exchange for giving feudal allegiance to the king and a promise to abstain from future raids. This political settlement worked, and eventually the Viking settlers of Normandy became French in language and culture—and added heavy cavalry to their weapon systems.

In resisting the Vikings the English adopted essentially the same defense. Fortifying with equally good results, they often used large earth and timber enclosures, which could shelter many people and animals. As a nation of heavy infantry and lacking the heavy cavalry of the Vikings' Continental opponents, they depended on the Viking expedient of mounting their best men to pursue and harry the raiders but fighting them on foot. But soon the English faced more than raiders, for the Vikings, chiefly from Denmark, came in large numbers and adopted the persisting strategy of conquest.

The English did not stem the tide of the Danish advance until they had lost half of England, the invaders controlling local government and settling many people in the occupied region. But the English, united by King Alfred the Great, who built a navy that threatened the Vikings at sea, halted the advance of the Danes. The English immediately went over to the offensive under Alfred's son, the patient and perspicacious King Edward the Elder who, with the aid of his equally capable sister, Ethelfleda, conducted a sustained, twenty-year campaign against his disunited opponents.

Continuing to rely on his father's large earth and timber fortifications enclosing areas of as much as twenty acres or more, Edward used the larger of these offensively, somewhat in the Roman manner, as shelters for his advancing army. Following a persisting strategy and fortifying the country he subdued, he steadily overcame Danish England until he had secured the submission of all of the former conquerors. King Edward made this an easier task by his political program of neither disturbing the land holdings of the Danish settlers nor taking control of local government from their leaders. This sustained counteroffensive brought the English more than had the analogous political settlement of the king of France in making Normandy a feudal dependency because it brought the Danes firmly under the rule of the comparatively centralized English monarchy.

For the inhabitants of what is now Germany the Magyars presented a different problem because, like the Avars they had supplanted in Hungary, they were light cavalrymen from the steppe. Though as early as 910 they had demonstrated their ability to defeat the German heavy cavalry, they made no effort to conquer, dispersing widely to plunder better, and relied on their superior speed to avoid contact with the Germans. A contemporary described them thus: "They went not in one mass but in small bands, because there was no Christian army in the field, spoiling the farms and villages and setting fire to them when they had spoiled them: they always caught the inhabitants unprepared by the swiftness of their appearance. Often a hundred of them or less would come suddenly galloping out of a wood on the prey: only the smoke and the nightly sky red with flames showed where each of their troops had been." Their largest raid, in 954, exhibited the characteristics of a raid as well as the scale of Magyar operations. Entering Bavaria in south Germany, they pillaged their way west until, crossing the Rhine near its mouth, they cut across France into Italy, through north Italy, and back to Hungary. Lacking any base, raiders could move in any direction and had no need to return the way they came. This ambiguity, both as to objective and route of retreat, as well as the primacy of retreat over pursuit gave raiders their offensive superiority over the persisting defense.[11]

If the German heavy cavalry could have overtaken the Magyar horse archers, the Germans would have faced the same tactical problem as the Byzantines later met at Manzikert and analogous to that encountered in forcing the Vikings to fight—the heavy cavalry was a less effective weapon system when compared with either heavy infantry or light cavalry. But the superlative Magyar mobility meant that conflict rarely occurred, even though carrying booty on pack animals rather than in carts slowed the Magyar raiders.

Only the small numbers of the Magyars prevented their raids from having the seriousness of the Viking menace. The Germans applied the defense-in-depth strategy by pursuing with heavy cavalry and by fortifying thoroughly, one emperor earning the title "the builder." By walling towns and fortifying and garrisoning places of refuge, the Germans reduced the yield from raids and induced the Magyars to come less frequently but in larger numbers. In 955 a huge Magyar raiding force besieged Augsburg in Bavaria when the Emperor Otto with 8,000 heavy cavalry approached them from the east. The Magyars crossed the Lech River to fight, placing themselves between the imperial army and the river. Fighting in the manner of the Turks a century later at Manzikert, they retreated in front while showering the emperor's heavy cavalry with arrows from the flank and rear. But instead of dispersing, the Germans held, and a sudden charge by some of their cavalry on the flank drove the Magyars on the flank back toward their main body in front of Otto's line. The emperor then ordered a charge of his whole line, which drove the Magyars back to the river, where the heavy cavalry slew many and more drowned trying to cross the river. This dramatic and costly defeat ended the Magyar raids, already seriously circumscribed by the fortifications. When backed against an obstacle, light cavalry had no more chance against heavy cavalry than, under similar circumstances, the Persian light infantry had against Greek heavy infantry at the Battle of Marathon.

The strategy employed against raiders by the Franks, Germans, and English varied little from that employed by the Romans and Byzantines. Nor did all of these differ significantly from those used by Fabius and other Romans in their long struggle against Hannibal. All relied on fortifying the population centers and controlling the routes of communication while harrying the raiders to catch stragglers and limit their activity, whether it was the Vikings' search for booty or foraging by Hannibal's men. Nor, essentially, did the strategy differ from that Alexander employed in his struggle against the rebels in Bactria and Sogdiana or the Romans in consolidating their new European conquests, exemplified by their numerous forts in Britain. Raiders or guerrillas relied on their ability to avoid action, even though, in the case of the Magyars and the Vikings, they could count on having a much better than an even chance of winning a battle. These raiders, though acting from the economic motive of securing booty rather than pursuing political or military objectives, behaved just as they would were they following a logistic strategy, one that avoided combat and aimed at the enemy's army by attacking its logistic base.

Although the Roman campaign against Hannibal differed from those against the Vikings, the strategies were alike and essentially symmetrical. Fabius and the employers of his strategy used their ability to avoid battle, something the Western European heavy cavalry, which so often lost to the Vikings, might well have considered. But, except for this divergence, the Roman strategy for defeating Hannibal was the same as that used against Viking, Magyar, barbarian, and Arab raiders as well as against guerrillas in Bactria and Sogdiana. To essentially the same strategic problem both ancient and medieval soldiers applied an almost identical solution.

William's Combined-Arms Army in the Conquest of England

Although the decentralized medieval armies lacked both the logistic organization of Macedonian and Roman armies and the benefits of training and articulation conferrred by remaining concentrated in one place, the battle and campaign of Hastings exhibits the high level of strategic and tactical sophistication of a skillfully conducted medieval campaign. Without ready access to the military experience and methods of the ancient world, these medieval soldiers exhibited their firm grasp of the same essentials that animated the best commanders of antiquity.

The conquest of England came only a few years after the country had escaped a period of Danish rule, which had followed by a century Alfred the Great and Edward the Elder's defeat of the initial invaders. The death of King Edward the Confessor in early 1066 precipitated a crisis in the succession: two foreigners, the king of Norway, asserting the Danish claim to the crown, and the late king's cousin, Duke William of Normandy, both sought the throne. The English themselves chose not King Edward the Confessor's nearest relative—a child—but his brother-in-law, the powerful Earl Harold who like his father had dominated the pious king and virtually ruled the land. Determined and competent, Harold seemed best able to deal with the foreign claimants, of whom Duke William, supported by the pope, seemed the more menacing. King Harold's military and political experience well complemented his intelligence and courage, but in Duke William of Normandy he faced a formidable antagonist. The portly but robust duke, less than forty years of age, had already gained deserved fame as a warrior in several campaigns, including two against the king of France.

Ambitious and thorough, William promptly prepared a campaign to assert his claim to the throne. He collected a powerful force, not so much by virtue of his control of the military resources of his duchy or his hiring of a number of mercenaries but because he promised to his vassals and many others large rewards if he should succeed in gaining the crown of England. Many men of substance joined him with soldiers to gamble on the possible rewards. In effect, William was a hirer of some of his mercenaries on a contingent-fee basis, and many of those who accompanied him were men of means making a speculative investment. William spent the spring and early summer concentrating his forces and readying his fleet of transports on the French coast near England.

King Harold sent his powerful English fleet to sea in June and concentrated his 2,000 housecarles or regulars in the south of England. He had warned the country to be prepared to mobilze at a moment's notice. Like the Greeks facing the sea invasion of the Persians in the Marathon campaign, Harold could not know where William would land, but, with his fleet at sea, he imposed on Duke William the serious peril of exposing his transports to an attack by the English war fleet.

But bad weather prevented William's force from sailing in early August. At this time Harold had to face another menace, an invasion of the north by the king of Norway, just as his ships had to put into port to replenish supplies and make repairs. Long aware of this threat, the decisive Harold immediately decided to risk the possibility of a Norman landing and take advantage of his interior lines of operation to march north with his housecarles to resist the Norwegian invasion. Displaying commendable energy, Harold left London on September 16, 1066, and marched 200 miles north to York, arriving there on the 24th, an excellent march, even for a mounted force on an old Roman road. The next day he joined his housecarles with the mobilized northern forces and and, making a surprise attack, defeated the Norwegian host at Stamford Bridge, killing their king in battle and compelling them to return to Norway.

While Harold campaigned in the north, the weather cleared, and in the absence of the English fleet William had no difficulty in landing his army on the southeast coast of England on September 28, three days after Harold's victory and while the king rested his forces in York and celebrated his triumph. Since the antidote to the strategic advantage of interior lines is simultaneous advances, the fortuitous coordination of the Norwegian invasion with good weather gave William time to take the initiative.

But William did not advance the fifty miles to try to seize London or otherwise to capitalize on Harold's absence. Doubtless the sagacious duke felt more comfortable fighting near the coast where he had expected a battle, and he certainly limited his risk of serious losses by staying near his ships and the fortifications that he had erected to protect his landing site. He could well have made the implicit calculation that the chances of high casualties and his possible capture more than balanced any increase in the chance of gaining the crown by an immediate advance. Near the coast he was much surer of keeping his duchy, though, perhaps, a little less likely to become king.

When Harold learned of William's landing, he ordered a general mobilization and marched south, reaching London in nine days. He doubtless would have preferred to move against William after all of his forces from the north and west had joined him, but William's systematic devastaton of the country in southeastern England forced him to act. Recently elevated to the throne and his title shaky, Harold could not afford tardy action in protecting his subjects. Since a strategy for forcing battle in ancient Greece worked just as well in medieval England, Harold marched toward William's landing place with only his housecarles and the heavy infantry from the south. On the evening of October 13 he concentrated his army on a hill eight miles from William's landing place.

Harold arrayed his force of heavy infantry in a strong defensive position along the hill with his flanks protected by the steepness of the ascent. A dense forest in the rear offered shelter in case of retreat. His men probably numbered between 5,000 and 11,000. The housecarles, originally 2,000 strong, had suffered casualities in the battle with the Norwegians but still provided a significant proportion of Harold's strength. His other troops consisted of thegns, recently mobilized professionals who owed military service to the king. In addition to the thegns with helmets and mailed shirts, Harold had untrained militia, variously equipped, some without any armor and a few armed only with agricultural implements. Doubtless the most capable and best armored men stood in the front ranks; the king took a position on the highest point on the hill, where he could survey his battle line.

Duke William had to attack promptly, for Harold's force would increase daily, adding not just militia but more of the formidable thegns who rode to join Harold but fought on foot. William marched to the enemy position in the morning and arrayed his army, which was probably about the same strength as Harold's, in three similar divisions, each composed of three linear formations, one behind the other. In the first line the experienced duke placed his archers; in the second, well-armored heavy infantry equipped with spear and sword; and in the third, his heavy cavalry, famous for the power of its charge. The duke planned for his light and heavy infantry to open gaps in the English infantry line into which the cavalry could penetrate. All of William's men were professional warriors. But the duke's army had to make a frontal attack on a very strong position.

William opened the battle by advancing his archers, who could shoot relatively unmolested by the few archers in Harold's army. Pelted with a hail of arrows, the English line remained immovable. Under similar circumstances, Spartans had charged the peltasts, who threw the javelins at them. But with William's powerful heavy cavalry close at hand, Harold's men realized that they should not break ranks. Then, when the archers approached closer to the motionless English shield wall, Harold's men showered them with a miscellany of missiles, including javelins, throwing axes, and throwing hammers made of stones with sticks attached. The duke's bowmen then fell back, having inflicted some damage on the English, even though they had to shoot up hill against shielded men. The heavy infantry attacked next but, predictably, failed to make an impression on the advantageously situated and thick English line. Then the heavy cavalry charged, and a struggle ensued as the cavalry tried to break in among the infantry. The

Normans were shocked to find that the English still used the old-fashioned heavy Viking two-handed axe with the six-foot handle; a single blow from this axe could knock down a horse. When the infantry defeated the cavalry, the horsemen and heavy infantry in the Norman left division fell back in demoralized confusion, apparently fleeing the field. Perhaps without orders, the English infantry surged down the hill in pursuit and quickly the alert and resourceful Duke William, from his position in the center, led the middle division of cavalry against the flank of the English who had left the hill. The redoubtable Norman cavalry quickly and easily cut down the infantry that after leaving their position lacked any formation. Only a few escaped to their post on the hill. Though Harold had lost some men to the arrows and far more to the effort to pursue an unbeaten enemy, the king's army still remained an immovable object atop the hill near Hastings.

William's cavalry attacked again—and retreated again, either accidentally or by the duke's desire to simulate flight. The English infantry again made the mistake of pursuing the retreating men, and William again directed another cavalry charge in the flank that cut them down. The English suffered heavy casualties, but Harold's army still remained on the hill. William then sent his archers to shower the English with arrows and followed this with an assault of his entire force. He alternated the missile and shock attacks, inflicting casualties and demoralizing a force that had to receive both forms of assault passively. A contemporary historian described this phase of the battle as one "where one side works by constant motion and ceaseless charges, while the other can but endure passively as it stands fixed to the sod. The Norman arrow and sword worked on: in the English ranks the only movement was the dropping of the dead: the living stood motionless." Finally an arrow mortally wounded King Harold in the eye, and the remainder of the physically and morally exhausted English army gave way at the next charge, retreating into the forest in the dusk.[12]

Duke William set about systematically reaping the fruits of his victory. First he moved down the coast to capture the important port of Dover, to secure better his communications with Normandy. Then, not receiving the expected submission of the leaders of the kingdom, he marched to London, spreading his army out on two or three routes to find adequate supplies in the sparsely populated medieval countryside. Yet London still refused to surrender to the conqueror of Harold.

Rather than attacking or trying to besiege the large fortified city, William carried out an ostentatious raid, scattering his army and marching around the capital in a broad circuit, destroying supplies as well as feeding his men and horses. Thus, he again exerted political pressure and demonstrated his mastery, including capturing Canterbury, the ecclesiastical center of the kingdom, and receiving the submission of Winchester, a city of traditional political importance.

The capitulation of cities and castles and the destructive march of the victor of Hastings demonstrated to the English leaders gathered in London the futility of a resistance in the south of England, especially when the death of Harold had deprived them of any strong leader. By the time Duke William had completed two-thirds of his unopposed circuit of the country's leading economic center, a delegation from London surrendered the city and the crown to him.

As a soldier William deserved his throne. In the battle, where three horses had fallen under him, he had successfully combined the qualities of his light infantry and heavy cavalry. He used his bowmen to attack the English heavy infantry without fear that the English would charge and drive them from the field. When the English did break ranks, the result exhibited the decisive predominance of stirrup-stabilized heavy cavalry over unformed infantry. By wisely using the different capabilities of these weapon systems, the duke won a completely merited tactical victory, which had good support from his ability to organize his command and logistics, his wise strategy, and his political claims to a throne. He completed the subjection of the country, ruled England effectively, and paid off handsomely the participants in his military venture. Displaying a strategic mastery on a par with his tactical skill, he triumphantly applied a persisting combat strategy, just as had Alexander against Darius.

In carrying out what was an essentially military occupation of England, William the Conqueror had to contend with some opposition to his rule, even though he had taken over the central administration of the country, had the legitimacy of his kinship to the late King Edward, and had the backing of the pope. But opposition to the French-speaking foreigners, exacerbated by the looting of his soldiers, helped cause revolts over the next three years.

William suppressed each of these and steadily built fortifications throughout the country, as had Alexander in Bactria and Sogdiana and the Romans in Britain and elsewhere. He introduced the French castle, similar to the earth and timber enclosures of Alfred and Edward the Elder but much smaller. Sited to dominate cities, road junctions, and river crossings, these consisted of a small pile of earth surrounded by a ditch from which the earth for the mound had come. Upon such a low eminence the builder erected a wooden stockade or tower, and to this he often attached an oval wooden palisade, which usually did not surround the mound but formed an attached enclosure, the stockade standing on a low bank behind a ditch. The palisaded area provided a living place for the garrison and their horses, but the whole structure required a relatively small garrison. Capable of quick construction of plentiful materials by largely unskilled labor, it offered a powerful defense against attackers who had little experience in siegecraft. Thus the rude castles provided a base for operations, dominated the country around them, and provided a place of refuge for the conquerors in time of trouble.

Although William ruled by conserving English institutions and generally sought to conciliate the conquered, in suppressing the third rebellion in 1069 he devastated thousands of square miles in the North. This application of both a logistic strategy and a program of political terror caused many to die of starvation and more to flee. The land was so depopulated that fifteen years later the area still contained much wasteland.

This last of the rebellions having ended William's effort to depend on the native aristocracy, he gave English lands and jurisdiction to foreigners, largely from Normandy, in exchange for providing a specified number of fighting men on call. The backbone of this military force consisted of at least 4,000 armored knights, who usually fought mounted as heavy cavalry but could perform as effectively on foot as the English housecarles and thegns who fought at Hastings. These men, with their castles, defended the country from invaders and also enabled William to control the land and gradually reconcile the English to his rule. Thus the new king followed a successful combination of measures used in the past: political conciliation, controlling communications, fortifying and garrisoning the country, and patience and determination.

Attack and Defense of Fortifications

William's French castle was similar to the model used throughout Europe. Because attackers might well first assail the weaker palisade, whose fall would not effect the defensive strength of the structure on the mound, this elementary castle embodied, to a modest degree, the principle of successive lines of defense. But the simple design provided no opportunities for flanking fire. The stone castle, which in the eleventh century began to supersede the wooden, included these two fundamental principles while adhering to the basic model developed for the wooden castle. A powerful stone tower with a walled stone enclosure, which embodied smaller towers for flanking fire and in more elaborate castles two complete concentric lines of walls, meant a structure with as many as three lines of resistance—outer walls, inner walls, and main tower. Town fortifications that began as wood also progressed to stone, incorporating the same principles as ancient town walls. Usually towns had a castle or citadel, which served as a place of final defense and as a stronghold from which the ruler could dominate the town.

But the early Norman castle concentrated almost all of its strength in a single enormous tower known as a donjon or keep. An outer wall enclosed a courtyard, but it had for flanking fire only little turrets, not much more than sentry boxes, and they were only a subordinate feature.

Norman military engineers preferred to put most of their money into a single tower that combined height and a maximum of space inside with only a narrow perimeter to defend. Defenders needed only men enough to man the battlements and to drop things down on anyone trying to sap the base of the wall. Increased height made it harder for the sappers to resist the fall of whatever dropped, and it also gave a more extensive view.

Sometimes the castle had a shell keep—a round structure with an open space in the center. Such a work developed naturally from the original palisaded ring on a mound and often replaced it, especially as the artificial mounds might not be firm enough to stand the weight of a solid tower. The typical Norman keep was solid and square, with a square turret at each corner and often a flat-strip buttress up the middle of each side. Designers usually placed the entrance one story above ground, up a stairway inside an oblong lower building resting against one side of the main structure. The masonry was crude, the stones small and separated by broad mortar joints. In William the Conqueror's keep, the White Tower in the Tower of London, the joints are so broad that the wall contains more mortar than stone. The walls are no less than fifteen feet thick at the ground level and ten feet even at the top. When builders expanded a keep into a castle, the keep remained the strongest part and the last line of defense in the castle.

Medieval soldiers used all the ancient siege devices except the Roman agger. An agger was a huge mound high enough to command the defenses that besiegers established out of effective range and gradually extended toward the walls. Once they had completed it, the defenders had to resist storming columns advancing with a fairly broad front on a level, or even a downward, slope. No medieval army could command or feed the labor necessary to make it.

Until the beginning of the twelfth century, the only known kinds of artillery were catapults worked by torsion and tension. A torsion catapult used a heavy timber frame with a mass of twisted rope strung across near the front. In this twisted rope the builder secured one end of a movable beam having a spoon-shaped hollow in its other end. Operators pulled this free end backward and down by a large winch at the rear of the frame, against the resistance of the twisted ropes, and placed the stone to be thrown in the spoon-shaped cavity. They then released the free end of the movable beam by releasing a catch. The force of the twisted ropes then made the beam describe an upward and forward curve, moving fast enough to flip off the stone at a high angle of elevation. Such a catapult was known as a mangon, mangonel, or sling. Of course the projectiles were seldom uniform in weight, and weather affected the ropes. Accordingly, the shots of this type of machine dispersed so widely that it was generally used for bombarding large objectives, such as towns or castles.

A tension catapult, usually known as a ballista, consisted of an exaggerated bow wound up by winches. It shot bolts or enormous arrows with great force, flat trajectory, and considerable accuracy. Although they could not penetrate walls, they were used by besiegers and besieged against small, fairly distant objectives, such as men out of range of infantry weapons.

In making good their approach, besiegers protected themselves against the plunging fire of the defenders behind mantlets, screens strong enough to resist arrows but light enough to move easily. Besiegers might roll up movable towers, as high as or higher than the defenses, until the towers could drop drawbridges on the battlements. Attackers might then deliver an assault by moving up the towers and across the drawbridges. Meanwhile, archers or crossbowmen posted on the tower top tried to pick off the defenders.

The defects of the movable tower are obvious. It was not only heavy but top-heavy. Accordingly, it could move forward only over ground that was smooth, level, and particularly firm. It needed protection against combustibles; rawhides

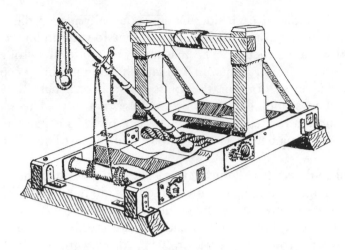

Illustration 2.1. Catapult

were generally used in front and to some extent upon its sides. Defenders shot at it with arrows carrying balls of burning tow. Most effective were the huge arrows from the tension type of catapult.

It was a little easier to move forward some sort of low shelter that would protect men working against the base of the defenders' walls. These shelters were fairly long, so that their occupants might come and go by the rear end (which could not be too close under the wall), and narrow and steep-roofed in proportion to their length so that they could resist stones and heavy weights dropped from above. For greater strength, the roof had a steep point and was protected against fire by rawhides.

Either the shelter was brought within a few feet of the wall, which workmen then attacked with ram or borer, or its head was pushed up against a wall to give cover for men attacking the masonry with pickaxes, hammers, and crowbars. The ram and borer both consisted of great beams, the largest that the besiegers could find, swung by chains from the ridgepole of the shelter. The ram had a broad solid head (like the forehead and horns of a true ram), which it butted against the wall; the borer had a pointed head, intended to break down the opposing masonry stone by stone. If the wall were not too thick or well built, the ram could shake, crack, and finally break it by repeated blows in the same spot. The borer had a slower and more localized effect.

It is hard to see what any ram could have accomplished against walls fifteen feet thick, like those of William's Tower of London. Nor can one estimate the time necessary for a borer (which was used less often than the ram) to make any sort of impression on such walls. Meanwhile, the defenders, even if they failed to smash or burn the shelter from above, might grip the head of the ram or borer with large pincers to prevent the crew from pulling it back for a forward stroke or might try to deaden its blows by means of rope pads or sacks thickly stuffed with soft material with which they would cover the face of the wall at

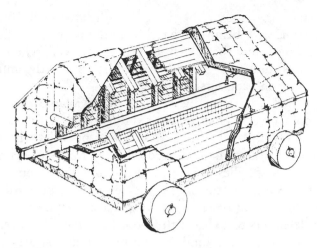

Illustration 2.2. Ram

the point where the blows were falling. If pincers or padding succeeded, the attackers had no alternative but to advance the shelter and sap the base of the wall with hand tools.

The mine provided attackers with another resource. Starting from a sheltered position near the wall, the besiegers dug deep and then under the wall. As the mine gallery advanced under the wall, the miners shored it up with lumber. When they judged they had dug enough, they burned the timber, collapsing their mine; if they had made a large enough hole, a section of the wall would come down, leaving a breach.

Fortresses were seldom taken by regular sieges as no one had the resources to sustain the necessary men. On the merits of the case in military engineering alone, the attackers would have won in the end, even if the defenders' provisions and water held. The military axiom still held that any fortress, however strong, must fall if besieged by numbers sufficient to blockade it and carry on an active regular siege at the same time. A garrison persistently attacked must decline in strength through casualties and fatigue. But in practice medieval fortifications rarely fell in this way.[13]

The long siege of the island city of Paris by the Vikings in 885–886 illustrates the use of virtually every technique known to early medieval siegecraft. After failing to scale the walls of a fortified bridgehead with ladders, the Vikings tried to break through the stonework with a lightweight pick. But boiling oil and burning pitch from the walls burned the shelter and the men, enough to cause them to jump into the river. Then facing a narrow breach made with a mine, the besieged defended this gap so well with missiles that the Vikings failed to carry it and, overwhelmed by the defenders' artillery, temporarily withdrew until they had three battering rams ready. They delayed their attack, apparently because the two men pierced by the same javelin thrown by a defender's ballista were the Vikings' siege engineers. Resuming their attack, they filled the ditch, moved up the battering rams, and began to demolish the walls. But the Parisians caught the huge rams with beams lowered from the walls and held them so that the Vikings could not draw them back to pound the wall. The defenders completed the attackers' defeat by smashing the shelter for the rams with heavy projectiles from torsion catapults.

The Vikings had used virtually every device available to besiegers except aggers and movable towers. Their failure exhibits the defensive strength of even primitive fortifications in medieval times. Hunger provided the surest method for besiegers, but the Vikings had allowed relieving forces to get provisions into Paris. The problem of supplies, however, also limited besiegers. It proved to be a difficult task to sustain an attacking force and, often, because of the limited term that feudal forces had to serve, to keep the besieging army together long enough for the defenders to exhaust their food reserve. The strength of castles and fortified towns remained a fundamental tactical and strategic factor in medieval warfare.

Medieval Tactics

The strengthening of fortifications in the eleventh and twelfth centuries had followed improvements in the armor of the heavy cavalrymen, who had lengthened the mailed shirt until it reached the knees and attached to the conical helmet chain mail that protected the back and sides of the head and the neck. Joined to the skirt, it became one piece of mail armor that weighed at least thirty pounds. Under the mail, the cavalryman wore a padded cover to absorb the shock of blows. Additional changes included a nose piece for the helmet, a longer sword for cutting only, and a long, kite-shaped shield of wood and leather that gave good protection mounted or on foot. The complete outfit cost as much as a small farm.

Just as twelfth-century armies had essentially similar equipment, so also did they have the same weapon systems. The fully equipped heavy cavalryman with complete armor, the knight, had an especially robust horse for carrying the additional weight of the man's armor and weapons. A heavy cavalryman who lacked full equipment, having, for example, only a mail shirt and helmet, was called a sergeant. Having the same heavy cavalry role as a knight, a sergeant was less effective but cost less to employ.

Practically no twelfth-century Western European army had any light cavalry. Bowmen might have horses, but these archers functioned as mounted infantry, using their mounts to march but fighting on foot. The light cavalry that did develop, largely on the fringes of Europe, played more of a strategic role and did not usually exploit the latent tactical capability so dramatically demonstrated at the battles of Carrhae and Manzikert.

Most light infantry used a bow; only a few relied on javelins. In place of the traditional bow, many had a crossbow, a Roman invention, forgotten by the Byzantines, which may have survived in Gaul and flourished in the eleventh and twelfth centuries. Really a miniature ballista, the crossbow consisted of a short, strong bow affixed to a stock that had a groove for an arrow, a catch to hold the bowstring, and a trigger to release the catch. The bowman cocked his crossbow by placing it on the ground with his feet on it and pulling the string with both hands. He then inserted a short, heavy arrow or bolt, aimed, and released the trigger. Compared to the ordinary bow, the crossbow had a lower rate of fire and higher cost. The advantages, which led to its widespread adoption, lay in its great power and the lower level of skill required of the bowman. An example of substituting capital for labor, the machine, in this case the crossbow, required less skill to aim and less strength to pull. Proficiency with an ordinary bow required practice to acquire the necessary mastery of aiming and the muscle development to make repeated, consecutive full pulls of the bowstring.

Twelfth-century heavy infantry lacked the uniformity of equipment found among the light infantry and heavy cavalry. The best, most often mercenaries and civic militia, came equipped with helmet, mail shirt, shield, sword, and pike (a long spear). These heavy infantry, like the bowmen, had great value as castle garrisons and in the attack and defense of towns and castles. For this reason they often were mercenaries, full-time professionals serving for pay. This made them always available, rather than on call, as were feudal vassals with a military obligation. In addition to the mercenaries, the feudal or decentralized system produced a few properly armored and armed heavy infantry. Further, the military system could call on a larger number of men with inadequate equipment, many coming without mail shirts, and with little skill with weapons. A full mobilization could produce a totally untrained and unorganized infantry militia armed only with agricultural implements.

The similarities to the Byzantine forces are more striking than the differences. The emphasis on heavy cavalry reflected like responses to the same strategic problems; the greater prominence of the bow among the Byzantines responded to their continuous conflict with formidable light cavalry. Like that of the Byzantines, Western European heavy cavalry, ineffective on the defensive, could dismount to fight, thus converting itself into heavy infantry. Though not trained or drilled to work together on foot, the heavy cavalrymen, armored and possessing great skill with their excellent arms, made such effective heavy infantry that they could resist the charge of heavy cavalry that used saddles with stirrups. But like the medieval heavy infantryman, they had no power of maneuver and, without the system and drill of Greek or Roman infantry, had difficulty doing more than standing fast on the battlefield. At the Battle of Bouvines in 1214 Emperor Otto's excellent, pike-armed infantry advanced and, in a frontal fight, easily defeated the much inferior French infantry. After the French infantry fled, the French cavalry charged the victorious pikemen and, because movement had disordered the foot soldiers' ranks, penetrated their formation and drove them from the field with heavy casualties. The infantry's simple act of defeating the enemy's infantry and moving forward had created enough gaps in the unarticulated mass of pikemen to enable the cavalry to break into the array and attack with their heavy swords.

The great contrast betwen the Byzantine and Western European armies lay not in the mix of their weapons systems but in organization and doctrine. Some of the differences stemmed from the variety of national systems of war with which the Byzantines had to contend, but more had their origin in the even more decentralized and part-time nature of the medieval military organization. Lacking the permanent, regular army of the Byzantines, most Western armies formed themselves only for a particular campaign. A Western commander usually would not have in advance a clear idea of the forces he would have, even if many of them were mercenaries whose employment he had arranged. He would not know the total numbers, the proportions of light and heavy infantry and of cavalry, or the quality of his heavy infantry. When the commander had concentrated his army, he rarely had time to train it as a unit but had to embark immediately upon the campaign, if only because supply difficulties compelled him to move promptly and the limited time for which medieval vassals served or restricted funds to pay mercenaries meant he had to use them when available.

Commanders did know the total size of an army would be small. The expensively armed and armored and splendidly mounted knight cost as much as several Greek hoplites or Persian bowmen. The higher proportion of particularly expensive cavalry in a medieval army meant that it emphasized quality over quantity. In addition, Western Europe had a smaller population than in Roman times, and trade, regional economic specialization, and the divison of labor had probably declined since then. These factors, together with a less effective governmental system, meant that large medieval armies numbered 5,000 to 10,000. The maximum effort of the French king in the year 1214 put less than 30,000 men in the field.

The consequences of this system is illustrated at the Battle of Lewes in 1264, when the experienced commander, Simon de Montfort, spent a day and a night marshaling his forces. He had to assign groups of unequal size and uneven composition and quality to places in the battle line and, consequently, in the line of march to the battle field. Though he could not impose articulation, he had at least to provide an orderly array of the forces. He found this a formidable task in the absence of an established chain of command in an army without units of uniform size, any drill, or a common experience in combat. The infrequency of battles aggravated this condition by depriving both commanders and men of experience, and it meant that medieval battles displayed an incredible diversity in the composition and array of the forces. Sometimes the armies had no infantry at all; sometimes cavalry dismounted; sometimes the armies had a linear deployment and at others as many as three divisions, one behind the other. So commanders had no doctrine beyond dividing an army into three parts.

At the Battle of Steppes in 1213, when the count of Loos and the courageous and combative bishop of Liége brought the shifty duke of Brabant to bay, both sides had armored, pike-armed, heavy infantry that they placed in the center, flanked by heavy cavalry. The infantry struggled against one another as did the cavalry. When the bishop and the count's cavalry on one wing successfully routed the horsemen, it turned against the flank and rear of the enemy's unarticulated heavy infantry. This attack helped to defeat the duke's infantry and win the battle. In this contest, the deployment of the forces and the roles of the infantry and cavalry followed fairly closely the Alexandrian model.

But this battle is not representative. Often commanders placed their cavalry in front of their heavy infantry, as at Legnano in 1176 when the Emperor Frederick I, a brave and broadly experienced soldier, advanced rapidly, charged with his cavalry, and, dispersing the cavalry facing him, attacked the Italian pikemen. While he struggled in vain against infantry "with shields set close and pikes held firm," the Italian cavalry rallied, charged the emperor's cavalry in flank, and won the battle. Frederick, who should not have attacked a superior enemy, never brought his infantry into action at all.[14]

In two later fights in southern Italy, Benevento in 1266 and Tagliacozzo in 1268, both armies had cavalry only, each side arraying itself in three divisions, one behind the other. King Charles I of Naples, a capable and ruthless soldier and monarch, won both battles, in each case by committing his third division last. But at Tagliacozzo Charles concealed his third division and waited, either by design or because the combat did not go as he had anticipated, until the enemy had driven his first two divisions from the field before surprising the enemy, who had dispersed to pursue and loot his camp.

Rather than take a position where they could control the battle, medieval commanders usually fought in the ranks where they could have little influence beyond their own division. At the Battle of Bouvines both the king of France and the emperor were knocked from their horses in combat and barely escaped capture. But with inadequate chains of command and little articulation, medieval commanders would have lacked those opportunities to influence the battle that were available to Hannibal or Scipio. Even with so much heavy cavalry that relied little on articulation, few displayed a real grasp of the role of a commander or of the concept of a reserve. Because of the knight's emphasis on individual skill and performance with lance and sword, perfected in jousting matches and tournaments, commanders of this school frequently thought of battles as an aggregate of such frontal combats, and often cavalry battles turned out much like this. Such a culture meant that medieval commanders ignored Xenophon's principle that "wise generalship consists in attacking where the enemy is weak." With hearts of oak, such leaders often acted as if their heads were of the same substance. Two small actions show this attribute of medieval command as well as further exhibiting the diversity of medieval tactics.

In 1119 the portly King Louis VI of France invaded Normandy with 400 knights, devoting himself to plundering the countryside rather than besieging cities or castles. When King Henry I of England rode out with 500 knights to meet him, King Louis, though a capable and seasoned soldier, unwisely decided to attack. Henry, displaying the military talent befitting a son of William the Conqueror, dismounted 400 of his knights and placed the remaining 100 in front of the knights that he had converted to heavy infantry. The first of the three French divisions dispersed the cavalry and broke in among the far more numerous dismounted knights, who succeeded in pulling them from their horses and taking them prisoner. After the second French division had charged and suffered the same fate, the third, under King Louis, fled, closely pursued by Henry's remounted knights.

Count Waleran, a rebel against King Henry, also displayed similar main-strength-and-awkwardness generalship when the king's men intercepted him and blocked his road. Part of the king's heavy cavalry dismounted and set up a defensive position across the road. The king's commander also possessed forty bowmen, also on horseback, whom he dismounted and placed along the road on his left where they could shoot at the unshielded, sword side of any force attacking on the road. Count Waleran, who was only engaged in raiding, could easily have turned back, but he determined to charge the "mercenaries and rustics" who had the temerity to block his path. When his knights charged, the line of dismounted knights stopped them while the archers shot their horses. The king's men then captured Count Waleran and eighty fallen knights, the bulk of the forces that made the foolhardy charge.[15]

The skirmish against Count Waleran displays the heavy casualties of the defeated, an attribute of medieval as well as ancient battles. But the casualties among the knights were largely in the form of being taken prisoner. Though bruised by blows and falls from horses and often wounded, medieval knights rarely died in battle because of their complete suits of chain mail. The heavy infantry, losing its cohesion in defeat, provided the bulk of the men killed, as the cavalry of the victor often slaughtered them mercilessly. Armored mounted men frequently suffered heavily when they fled to avoid capture: on many occasions fleeing mailed men drowned in crossing rivers. After the Battle of Lewes, for example, where Simon de Montfort had defeated King Henry III of England, some of the king's men tried to swim their horses over a marshy river at high tide. The next day, at low tide, observers on the bank could see many of them on mud flats, drowned and still astride their drowned horses, which were deeply mired in the mud.

But the heavy casualties of the defeated did not deter commanders whose incompetence took the form of too-precipate engagements or failure to try to find the path of least resistance to victory. Often, however, they felt constrained to reach a decision early, before the term of service of their men expired or the money to pay mercenaries gave out. If many medieval commanders proved prone to frontal attacks and to gallantry rather than circumspection, it is fair to assume that they may have displayed less of the kind of incapacity that overestimates difficulties, exaggerates the enemy's strength, or finds other excuses for delay or inaction. Although the art of war has long offered good models to emulate, most medieval generals lacked access to records of the campaigns of Alexander, Hannibal, and Caesar and had to rediscover much for themselves. And in an era of few battles but constant warfare, they had more practice with strategy and developed settled practices that accorded with the principles of the ancients.

Medieval Strategy: The Evesham and Bouvines Campaigns

Twelfth-century strategists exploited the overwhelming advantage conferred on the defense by the superb stone walls of cities and castles. Though devastating the countryside could sometimes force a foe to come out of his fortifications, attackers usually could not harm the defender so strong were the defenses against the available means of attack. An invader could raid an area but could not dominate it without taking the fortifications. A siege tied up the besieging army for a whole campaigning season, even if it could supply itself so long in one place, often in the face of interference from the defender's army of relief. The strategic situation and the methods had much in common with the defense against raiders, not because experience against raiders had ingrained these methods into medieval strategic thinking but because fortifications supported by a field army provided the best means of defense and effectively prevented the conquest of territory. Small armies in large spaces, confronted by formidable fortifications, faced almost insuperable obstacles in implementing a persisting strategy.

Often campaigns centered around control of communications. The campaign of Evesham of 1265 distinctly illustrates the importance of communications in the strategy of medieval campaigns. In an English civil war this campaign pitted the king's son, the gifted young Prince, Lord Edward, against the far older politician and former crusader, Earl Simon de Montfort. On the border of Wales, the astute and worldly-wise de Montfort found that the tall, athletic Prince Edward had raised a powerful army east of his and that the prince's troops separated de Montfort's from London and the main forces of his dominant faction. Before the earl realized the seriousness of the situation, Prince Edward's men had seized the towns on the Severn River, broken their bridges, taken possession of the boats on the river, and deepened the river's fords. But de Montfort had difficulty even in reaching the Severn, for in trying to cross the Wye, though he captured the castle, he found the enemy force entrenched, facing the bridge. Rather than fight under such unfavorable circumstances, the earl marched south, seized Newport, and prepared to march east by ferrying his army across the Bristol channel. But the prince's men descended the Severn from Gloucester in three galleys captured there and entered Newport harbor where they sank or captured the earl's transports.

The earl then marched north, his soldiers suffering from lack of provisions in the thinly populated Welsh countryside. Further, men used to bread found it very distasteful to subsist on a Welsh diet of mutton and milk. But the earl inspired his men, and while he then rested them preparatory to another effort to march east, he knew that his son was marching west from the London area, gathering a large army as he came. When de Montfort moved toward the upper Severn, he found Prince Edward there, again thwarting his effort to cross. But Simon had acquired some sizable boats, which he prepared to launch at an unguarded spot. Meanwhile, his son's army, after a too leisurely march, had

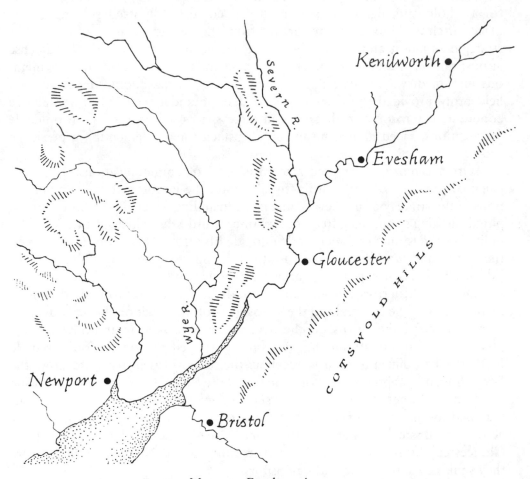

Map 2.1. Evesham Area

reached Kenilworth, only thirty miles from his father. But the perceptive Prince Edward, moving promptly to exploit his interior lines, marched against young Simon. The young prince, gracious in manner and attractive in his person, could inspire his men as well as the earl. So Edward marched his men all night, and at dawn he swept into the town of Kenilworth where the enemy army slept, believing that distance made them secure. Killing the few sleepy men who offered resistance, Prince Edward captured most of young Simon's army, only those in the town's castle saving themselves.

Ignoring the castle but securing his prisoners, the prince, displaying an energy that matched the prescience of his strategy, turned immediately toward the earl who had at last crossed the Severn and was marching to join his son. Ignorant of the surprise at Kenilworth, the earl rested his hungry army in the little town of Evesham, situated on a bend in a river so that it had water on three sides. Edward, learning of Simon's presence in Evesham, made another night march and again achieved surprise. In early morning the earl, finding the town's sole bridge blocked by a strong hostile force and realizing the trap he was in, exclaimed: "Now may God have mercy on our souls, for our bodies are in the power of our enemies." He then took the only alternative to surrender and led his small force out to engage most of the prince's army, which blocked the only land exit from the town. Outnumbered more than three to one, the earl died in battle, on foot with sword in hand and surrounded by foes, as did most of his men, many drowning in the river in their attempt to flee.[16]

Except that battle and death resulted instead of surrender, young Prince Edward had achieved the same success as had Caesar in the Ilerda campaign. Such a trap, sprung by the prince's perspicacity and vigor in making another night march, provided the only means available to a medieval general to catch an enemy army. To carry out the always difficult turning movement, Caesar had had favorable terrain, cavalry superiority, which enabled him to cripple the enemy's logistics, a high ratio of force to space, and a large force of particularly well-articulated heavy infantry which could march and maneuver quickly and easily take up strong defensive positions. Practically never did a medieval army have the numbers in relation to the land area to block an enemy retreat without the aid of such an obstacle as the river bend at Evesham.

Medieval and ancient war actually differed little in the difficulty of the turning movement. In most circumstances no army, ancient or medieval, could block any force similarly constituted and having the same mobility. Bridges, fords, or other narrow places could not long delay the armies that were small in relation not just to these obstacles, but to the space in which they campaigned. With many alternative routes available and with supplies usually equally available wherever they marched, one army could as easily avoid another as would be the case if two opposing kings had exclusive possession of a checkerboard of greatly expanded size. To contain an opposing army within a given space presented the same problems encountered in coping with Viking raids: a small force in a large space could not prevent another from moving confusingly to and fro, ultimately reaching its destination.

By his skillful use of the river, Prince Edward contained the wily earl, just as the Pompeians long stymied Caesar from their position at Ilerda. Prince Edward's achievement kept the earl from joining his son and prevented him from affecting the uncertain political situation in England. This success in blocking the earl also provided Prince Edward with the interior lines that he exploited so brilliantly to bring on two battles with his divided opponents. If, however, containing an opponent presented almost insuperable difficulties, forcing battle on an unwilling foe usually proved impossible. Exploiting interior lines would have availed the prince nothing had his surprise night marches not caught one opponent asleep and trapped the other against the river.

In the campaign of Evesham both sides exhibited a thorough grasp of strategy and the whole course of events shows the importance of controlling routes of communication. This kind of warfare had also characterized campaigning in thickly settled, quite urban northern Italy. King John of England, a man notable for his complex mixture of talent and defects of character, showed equal strategic grasp in an operation on a grander scale in a plan for war against France in which he and his nephew and ally, the young Emperor Otto, deliberately operated on exterior lines. For his part of the campaign King John landed on the southwest coast of France in February of 1214 and marched north to gain control of territories to which he had claim. King Philip II Augustus of France, a determined organizer and gifted statesman, had mobilized and moved south to cut off King John's retreat. But John, having consolidated his position in the southwest and drawn the king of France southward, fell back toward his coastal base. At this the cautious and crafty King Philip, judging Otto's threat from the north more serious, detached his son, Louis, a warrior prince and future king, with a force to resist John while he marched his main army north of Paris to resist Otto.

Leading a coalition of Low Country princes, Otto had faced so many of the delays that habitually plague coalitions that he had time during the campaign to marry the daughter of one of the allied princes. Thus King Philip returned north before Otto could march to Paris. Upon Philip's march northward, John renewed his own advance north but, failing to deter the French king from concentrating his forces against Otto and facing strong opposition from Louis, fell back just before Philip met and defeated Otto in the Battle of Bouvines in July 1214.

John's campaign failed in that the emperor did not take advantage of his distraction in the south to advance on Paris in the north; yet it succeeded in that Philip still deployed some troops in the south instead of leading them on the field at Bouvines. In planning a campaign on exterior lines, King John aimed to distract King Philip, to induce him to concentrate in the opposite direction from the main attack. King John could operate on exterior lines without fear of having to fight a stronger adversary in battle because he knew how to exploit the ability of his army to retreat and refuse battle. During the campaign King John exercised great care that the French should not catch him unaware or force him against an obstacle.

Examples of an Offensive Persisting Strategy against Raiders

Medieval soldiers had successfully coped with the problem of Viking and Magyar raids by using fortifications that, perfected into elaborate and well-designed structures, gave the defense primacy over the offense. Medieval strategists also used castles to conquer areas held by hostile and warlike people. The English penetration of Ireland exhibited this means of implementing a persisting strategy. The Irish, unconquered by the Romans, had defended themselves against the Vikings by utilizing the defensive qualities of the extensive bogs and forests in their thinly populated country. In bogs they dug a trench across the road and fortified it. On such a narrow, entrenched front, which the attacker could not avoid, the Irish readily held their own, even though they lacked body armor or any skill with the bow. In the thick forests they built extensive abatis of branches that lined the road as well as blocked it, again giving the otherwise inadequately equipped defenders supremacy. These defenses limited the inroads of the Viking, but in 1169, when the heavy cavalry of the English arrived, the Irish made the mistake of meeting them in the open field. Without body armor or pikes and with no conception of a tight cohesive formation, the Irish infantry had no chance. Soon the knights drove the Irish back to their bogs and forests, and the invaders built castles to control the open country. Thus each had fortified his share of the country and neither could dominate the other. This stalemate lasted 400 years.

In Wales the advance of the Anglo-Normans took a different course against the determined opposition of a people who had yielded to the Romans but successfully resisted the Saxon barbarians. Mountainous, rugged, and often heavily forested terrain protected Wales as did the damp climate, which, with rainfall frequently exceeding eighty inches a year, could bog down invaders. Nor did the largely pastoral economy offer much logistical support, for the Welsh, in retreat, would take their flocks and herds with them, leaving little to subsist an enemy army.

The Welsh relied little on cavalry, depending on infantry with a shield, helmet, and often a mail shirt. In the south the infantry used a long strong bow, and in the north most had only spears. This almost total dependence on infantry suited the terrain far better than the heavy cavalry that had played such an important part in the English system of warfare after William's Norman conquest.

But against the fiercely independent and warlike Welsh, the English had the advantage of their sophisticated combined-arms army, which had light and heavy infantry as well as heavy cavalry to pit against the Welsh infantry. In addition, the English could exploit the political disunity of the Welsh, which not only precluded a united effort against a foreign invasion but also saw the Welsh fighting each other as well as, or instead of, their aggressive enemy on the eastern frontier.

As its first task the new Norman government of England had to protect the frontier against the incursions of the Welsh seeking booty. The English not only studded the frontier with castles but also, as had the Romans in resisting

Map 2.2. Wales

barbarians, provided a number of smaller fortified points, sometimes only a few hundred yards apart. Thus the English sealed their border against small forays; against a major raid the defenders usually had enough warning to concentrate a large force to contest its advance, one necessarily circumscribed by English control of the fortified road junctions and river crossings.

On the border of southern Wales, soon after William's conquest, the capable William, earl of Hereford, showed the applicability to the offensive of this method of defense. Exploiting the political disunity of his opponents and giving authority to local chiefs too weak to resist him, during his brief rule he gained command of a region of about 400 square miles. The earl erected castles to control this area and its communications, the castles dominating the conquered country much as they had helped to protect the English frontier against Welsh raiders. English tactical predominance enabled them to master the lowlands, which forced the Welsh into less fertile regions and added a logistic element to the invader's combat persisting strategy.

Once the English controlled a region and erected their castles, the castles, in turn, often became the sites of towns and the means of extending English economic and cultural as well as military and political influence—generally effective because the Welsh found the towns' markets so attractive.

The castles, which substituted the capital of the fortifications for the labor of additional soldiers, utilized the power of the defense in its most effective form by throwing upon the Welsh, on the strategic defensive, the burden of the tactical offensive if they were to prevent the permanent loss of the territory that the earl had occupied and garrisoned. An effective offensive persisting strategy based on these castles, coupled with political shrewdness in taking advantage of the disunity of his opponents and in co-opting many of their leaders, enabled William to complete his conquest of this small region in less than three years and to build an enduring addition to the area of Anglo-Norman rule.

The earl of Hereford's success exemplified the methods the English would use to conquer Wales. In a local, rather than a national, effort, William's successors eventually pushed forward into additional territory in the south, the earl of Shrewsbury following a similar policy along the middle of the frontier. On the northern border, Chester had as its earl, Hugh the Fat, whose girth, which prevented his mounting a horse, belied the vigor with which he expanded into northern Wales. Within twenty years of the Battle of Hastings the English had added as much territory in central Wales and also in the north as the earl of Herford had conquered in the south. In these areas the earls of Shrewsbury and Chester had built castles to consolidate their rule in the same manner as had the earl of Hereford in the south.

But then the English pushed forward rapidly and by 1094 had reached the Irish sea and more than tripled their area of domination. The Welsh responded with many successful assaults upon the now far-flung English castles and even with raids into England. Seeing his extensive domain thus threatened, the portly, red-faced King William II, inheritor of some of his conqueror father's military talent, intervened, leading a powerful invading army into Wales. Knowing that the Welsh avoided battle with the English but had great talent for ambushes, the English army moved slowly, preceded by woodcutters who penetrated into thickets that might conceal the enemy. But their adversaries had, in the words of a contemporary, gone with their animals "into mountains and moors, so it was impossible to come at them," leaving the king to make a futile march until he abandoned a campaign made unpleasant by "the meanness of the country and the badness of the weather."[17]

Welsh efforts to expel the English largely succeeded in the area of the invader's most recent triumphs but failed completely in the regions slowly subdued and carefully consolidated in the twenty years following the Norman conquest. The insurgents could not take these longer established castles. And, after William II's failure, the English persevered and gradually began reestablishing their castles, particularly in the south. In the next four decades the invaders situated themselves along the Irish sea in southern Wales so thoroughly that they had an average of one major castle for each 100 square miles of newly acquired territory, approximately the same ratio that prevailed in their area of the earliest domination and double the average for all England.

So the pertinacity of the English border earls and the political disunity of the Welsh permitted a continuation in the south of the pattern of incremental conquest in which control of a small region and the building of a castle initially and then permanently raised the ratio of force to space, giving the invader the power to pursue a persisting strategy. As the English organized their new dominions, they harnessed the revenues and military manpower to the task of expansion while their systematic advance relentlessly diminished the number of their adversaries. Thus their persisting combat strategy incorporated another logistic element that strengthened them and weakened their opponents.

Another widespread Welsh counterattack in 1134 interrupted this gradual English conquest. In addition to improved political unity, the Welsh had some heavy cavalry and much more sophisticated military methods. They met 3,000 English troops in battle. The Welsh victory turned into a battle of annihilation when a bridge collapsed under the fleeing English, drowning many. When the Welsh burned a town and many of the survivors who had taken refuge there, this completed the virtual destruction of the English force. Castles fell to the Welsh, who by then were equipped with siege engines, and at least one English relief expedition turned back when faced by roads obstructed with fallen trees and the threat of ambushes along the route of advance. The Welsh had great success in the recently conquered areas; in one region with at least nine English castles, for example, only one remained untaken.

As Welsh political unity gradually improved, that of the English declined as a dispute over the succession to the throne brought in a decade of intermittent civil war. When in 1154 England was again united under that relentlessly energetic statesman, King Henry II, the king, a competent soldier, mounted several major campaigns into Wales. None had any military significance. One penetrated forests and crossed moors only to find the Welsh offering battle in an impregnable position; another, led by Henry himself and employing troops not only from England but also from the king's French dominions, moved slowly, clearing thickets and timber as it advanced to avoid ambushes and keep at bay small Welsh bands, which preyed on foragers and stragglers. Having ascended to an elevation of 2,000 feet into more open country, the invading English host encountered no enemy but steady rain, which ruined the roads and bogged down the king's army. Immobilized by the mud, the huge force with its excessive amount of cavalry could not supply itself and soon retreated, again adhering to the pattern of failure established in the earlier campaign.

Lacking the patience and leisure to seek victory by the slow, incremental methods used by the border earls, Henry, an accomplished diplomat, showed a readiness to compromise. Intimidated by the great power of the English and the huge army representing the great extent of the Anglo-Norman empire, Lord Rhys, the popular and respected chieftain in southern Wales, had the same view. Rhys acknowledged Henry's supremacy, helped him suppress a revolt, and even sent Welshmen to aid him in his war with the king of France. King Henry made the chief lord of the parts of south Wales he controlled, but English lords and English castles dominated much of the region. In the north, however, the Welsh leader Owain, as adept in war as in politics, had too much strength for the king to exercise much sway over the considerable unconquered portions of that land. So Owain gave nominal allegiance to the king, but remained virtually independent.

A century of campaigning by the English validated the gradual method pioneered by the earls of Hereford and Chester. Based on patience and perseverance and relying on castle building and the imperialism of the English medieval economy and culture, it differed little in principle from that used by the Romans to conquer Britain and other barbarian lands. King Henry's invasions, like that of William II before, failed, at least in part, because the Welsh had skillfully exploited the strategic defense's ability to retreat and also because the English lacked the ratio of force to space to implement a quick persisting strategy against an enemy who, though lacking in political unity, was determined to resist foreign domination. Only a slow, incremental persisting strategy could, through successive concentrations and then the construction of castles, have the requisite force to space, and the political strength to overcome the Welsh resistance.

There followed almost a century of relative stability in which, in spite of intermittent war, English influence dominated in the south while a Welsh prince, in theory the vassal of the English king, ruled in the north. As the English consolidated their rule in the south, the Welsh in the north developed a centralized authority and a princely government that enjoyed powers comparable to the monarchies and principalities then common in Europe.

The English experience in conquering part of Wales, in spite of its slow progress, compared favorably with the Western European defense against Viking and other raiders with logistic objectives. A comparison of these two protracted wars shows that an offensive raiding strategy was stronger than the defense against it, exactly the opposite of the case of the primacy of the defense against a persisting strategy. This is true because a raiding strategy nullified the defense's two major attributes—the tactical supremacy of the defense against frontal attack by a similar or weaker weapon system and the defender's strategic ability to use retreat's superiority over pursuit. Since raiders sought to avoid combat with strong forces and relied on retreat, the defense's two premier advantages became immaterial.

Defenders against raiders tried to make themselves strong everywhere by the use of fortifications and militia and to facilitate a combat strategy of pursuit by impeding raiders' communications through fortifying bridges and garrisoning road junctions. The Romans and Byzantines had also sought to trap loot-burdened raiders against the obstacle of a river, wall, or mountain pass. But even with the huge forces used, the less numerous raiders were still victorious on the offensive.

But the English, on the offensive against raiders employing guerrilla warfare, rendered irrelevant the raiders' distinctive qualities. The raiders' avoidance of battle and the dependence on retreat had no utility against an offensive persisting strategy; in fact, such approaches facilitated the methodical advance of the English. In giving up territory to the enemy, the Welsh yielded their base area to the English, who promptly converted it to their own use and even recruited native Welshmen into their armed forces. Thus an offensive, logistic, persisting strategy had primacy over a defensive raiding strategy. That the sporadic English advance rarely used more than the forces of the border areas to make substantial conquests shows at least the parity of the persisting offensive against the Welsh who relied on guerrilla warfare. The English also owed their success to the successive concentrations of force in the small areas they occupied. Of course, the Welsh had adopted guerrilla warfare because they lacked the military strength to follow a persisting, combat, defensive strategy of meeting the English in battle.

In the two cases, defending against Vikings and other raiders and assuming the offensive into Wales, the method of fortification and inhibiting communication did not differ. That the English penetrated the Welsh base area distinguished their offensive campaign from that of the earlier defenders against the incursions of Vikings and others. Against such raiders, defense with a combat strategy enabled the Vikings to use retreat and even resistance against frontal attack; the conquerors of Wales used a persisting logistic strategy that showed an ascendency over the raiding defensive. Whereas intruders into settled areas in search of booty pursued a logistic strategy, which strengthened the attackers and weakened the defender, the persisting conquerers of Wales employed a logistic strategy, which weakened their opponent and augmented their strength by more than the booty of raids.

This gradual method of carrying out a persisting strategy also proved effective in Spain as the native Christian Spaniards gradually constricted the area of Moslem domination. Here each expansion of territory definitely increased the military and political strength of the Christians as it diminished their opponents' power base. In conquering a country inhabited by a sympathetic population, the Spaniards added willing subjects to their domain, which exaggerated the benefits of the conquest. Nevertheless, this example trenchantly illustrates that a persisting strategy of territorial conquest incorporates a logistic strategy.

The effectiveness of this method of fortification and its logistic importance is also vividly demonstrated in the otherwise insignificant case of Geoffrey de Mandeville who, rebelling against King Stephen, took refuge in the extensive marshes of eastern England. From this base he and his many followers plundered and terrorized the adjacent country, Geoffrey, in the words of a chronicler, devoting "himself with insatiable greed to the plundering of flocks and herds; everything belonging to adherents of the king's party he took away, used up, and destroyed." He even surprised, captured, looted, and then burned the town of Cambridge. Aided by the difficult terrain, Geoffrey easily avoided a powerful force that King Stephen himself led against him.[18]

But his elusiveness availed him nothing when the king switched to a logistic strategy. Confined to the marshy terrain by a line of fortified posts that Stephen erected, Geoffrey soon could not feed his followers. His raids had not only harassed the king and enriched him and his followers, but also the provisions he carried off had been fundamental to his logistic base. So Geoffrey and his men had to turn against their own supporters. "Many thousands they killed with hunger," according to a contemporary. "They laid imposts on the towns continually," and "when the wretched men had no more to give, they robbed and burned all the towns. . . . Then was grain dear, and meat, and cheese, and butter; for there was none in the land. Wretched men died of hunger; some went seeking alms who at one time were rich men." Not only did the logistic requirements of his force markedly exceed the output of the region, but Geoffrey, by taking the oxen that drew the plows, also destroyed its productivity. Soon forced by hunger from his denuded region, Geoffrey fell, mortally wounded, during an unsuccessful attack on one of Stephen's castles. Without his leadership, Geoffrey's followers soon succumbed to the king's forces.[19]

King Stephen's successful campaign exhibits the strategic sophistication of the age as well as the prominent role of fortifications in medieval warfare. Practiced in strategy and in the attack and defense of fortifications, soldiers in the Middle Ages frequently displayed less skill in the field. Often inept tactically and lacking the opportunities to develop a settled doctrine for the battlefield as had the Macedonians, Romans, and Parthians, medieval soldiers probably had the best heavy cavalry the world had ever seen, adequate light infantry, and, at their best, steady, if unarticulated, heavy infantry. If their strategy produced a stalemate, this resulted as much from the strategic sagacity of the defenders as from the supremacy of fortifications over siegecraft. Medieval strategists also displayed perceptiveness in using the castle for offensive purposes, and the necessarily patient and thorough work in Spain produced a major political change while in Wales and Ireland comparable methods laid foundations for rapid conquests later. The Crusades, a campaign into the East to conquer Palestine inspired in part by religious zeal, clearly demonstrated the real elements of excellence in the medieval art of war.

Combined-Arms Combat in the Crusades

Initially the Crusaders displayed great ineptitude as they approached Palestine on marches from Constantinople through Anatolia to Syria. Much of this land the Moslem Turks had held since the Battle of Manzikert, twenty-six years before the Christians began their first march. Not only did the Crusaders lack any knowledge of the Turkish light cavalry way of war, but also they had supreme confidence that their heavy cavalry could vanquish any opponent. Their first surprise came in 1097, when the first Christian army marched from Constantinople into the territory of the Turkish sultan, advancing in two columns about six or seven miles apart, in order to find supplies more readily. The Turks, concentrating against the left division, appeared before the Crusaders' army early one morning. Halting, camping, and leaving its large force of infantry to guard the camp, the Christian army arrayed its heavy cavalry against the mounted Turkish horse archers.

The Turks, of course, did not close but rode along the Christian array shooting their arrows and presenting no mass against which the knights could charge. Small groups did charge, but the Turks fell back, continuing their shower of arrows. The mail armor of the Crusaders adequately protected the men, but the arrows killed many horses and the charging parties suffered heavily as, separated from the main body, the Turks completely surrounded them. After several hours the Crusaders drew close together and moved back toward their camp, already penetrated by the Turks against the ineffectual resistance of the disorganized infantry. A contemporary described the scene: the knights were "crushed one against another like sheep penned up in a fold, hopeless and panic-stricken, we were shut in by the Turks on every side."[20]

It seemed to be another Manzikert when suddenly the cavalry from the right-hand Crusader division appeared and charged the Turks in flank and rear. Seeing this, the dispirited knights of the beleaguered left division also charged. The panicked Turks fled, some riding their horses to death miles from the battlefield even though no Christians pursued. But because of their mobility, the Turks had suffered relatively few casualties; the armored Crusaders actually lost more men. The Christians had avoided another Manzikert because the men of the right-hand column, responding to a messenger sent early in the battle, had arrived from their position seven miles to the south after the battle had gone on for nearly five hours. Apparently the Turkish sultan either had failed to locate the right-hand column or had, in the heat of his successful battle, forgotten about it. By surprise and an attack from two sides the heavy cavalry had routed the Turkish light cavalry.

The defeat so shook the Turks that they did not molest the Christian columns for several weeks and did not harm them seriously on the remainder of their march. Still, this respite did not relieve the army of its other problem—supply. The Crusaders could easily have reached the Holy Land by water because the Byzantine navy and the fleets of the Italian maritime cities controlled the sea. But the sea made the leaders uneasy, and they chose the land route through the same country in which Alexander the Great had opened his campaign against the Persian Empire. Yet the Christian leaders lacked not only Alexander's genius but also his capacity for planning and his logistical organization. In addition to effective Turkish opposition, they faced other difficulties unknown to the Macedonian conqueror. Unlike Alexander, they burdened their force with hordes of noncombatants, many of whom were on pilgrimage to the Holy Land. Moreover, they lacked geographical knowledge because the Crusaders did not always heed Byzantine advice and often claimed their information was defective since things had changed. As a contemporary explained, "A land once rich and excellent in all the fruits of the earth, had been so cruelly ravaged by the Turks, that there were only small patches of cultivation to be seen at long intervals."[21]

The Crusaders found diminished supply sources on their route, and the Turks combined a logistic strategy with combat strategy in defense against the marches of successive Christian armies. They drove off the cattle on the Crusaders' route and burned the grass, crops, and even the villages, an effective strategy that the Persians had declined to use against Alexander.

The Turkish combination of the two strategies proved disastrous for many marchers. The Turks destroyed one column that moved east from Constantinople, a few survivors finding refuge at a Byzantine port on the Black Sea. Another had 700 survivors, dismounted knights, who hid in the mountains where Turkish cavalry had difficulty pursuing. A third saved itself by turning back, and one reached its destination on foot, the Turks having shot its horses. A very large army also fell victim to logistic difficulties, its men almost dying of thirst by the time they reached a river. Breaking ranks at the sight of water, the whole army was drinking at the river when the Turks attacked; few survivors reached nearby mountains. Another column avoided starvation by eating its horses, reaching its destination on foot.

Crusading armies that included light infantry had little tactical difficulty with the Turks. But this weapon system could do nothing to alleviate the supply difficulties. Since the Turks preferred to avoid the mounted men at the head of a marching column, they concentrated their attacks on the rear. Here the Crusaders placed their bowmen, crossbowmen, and dismounted knights. The bowmen, having the advantage of shooting on foot and having the Turk and his horse for a target, mastered the horsebowmen, and the knights on foot protected the crossbowmen from charges by the sword-carrying Turkish horse archers. The armies, which heeded the advice of those who had made the march, found this combination of superior weapon systems more than adequate to deal with the Moslem light cavalry.

Fortunately the Crusaders in Syria learned this tactical lesson quickly and applied it in combating the Moslem masters of that former Byzantine province. But in their first encounter with horse archers, the Christians, lacking bowmen, successfully substituted boldness. After learning that the enemy had assembled a huge army to raise the siege of Antioch, the Crusaders resolved to meet it. Because they had lost so many horses on the march to Syria, they could field only 700 knights to attack a force of at least 12,000 Moslem soldiers. Nevertheless, the Crusaders picked a place seven miles east of Antioch where they could conceal their small force in rolling ground and through which the Moslem host would have to advance through a mile-wide gap, between a river and a lake. As the enemy army passed at dawn through this gap, the Crusaders suddenly charged. Driving the screening force back among the equally surprised main body, still in march order, the Crusaders inflicted terrible casualties on the un-armored light cavalry who, jammed together and hemmed in by water on two sides, had difficulty in fleeing. As many as 2,000 may have died by the sword or drowning before the Moslem army retreated from a cramped position where their numbers prevented use of their horse-archer tactics. Again surprise, combined with an obstacle in the rear, enabled the heavy cavalry to overcome the intrinsically more powerful light cavalry.

In the next encounter the Crusaders arrayed their larger, balanced force near the recently captured Antioch. Fearful of meeting their adversaries outside the city, but compelled to do so because of a lack of food, the Christians took pains to organize their infantry advantageously and stiffen them with dismounted knights. In placing their heavy cavalry behind the infantry, they showed that they had grasped the importance of light infantry in dealing with light cavalry. Forming their line of battle so one flank rested on a river and the other on hills, they protected their flanks and compelled the Turkish horse archers to attack in front. Here the long line of infantry, fronted by bowmen, advanced slowly against the Turks, shooting as they moved forward. Though the mounted Turks doubtless had more skill as bowmen, the infantry were shooting on foot, and the crossbowmen's powerful machines more than compensated for their lack of skill.

Steadily pressed back by a continuous hail of arrows, the Turkish cavalry eventually fled, joined by another group that had earlier worked its way into the rear of the Christian army and that had defeated the Crusader reserve. Part of the reason for that Moslem victory stemmed from their realization of the primacy of the foot bowmen over those mounted. To counter this advantage, the Moslems had changed to shock tactics: their light cavalry charged and attacked the infantry with swords. But in spite of this achievement, the force had retreated when they saw the main body leave the field.

In both parts of this battle the Moslem cavalry had suffered negligible losses, but when the main body abandoned the camp and its attendants to the Christian army, the men on foot had no way to escape or defend themselves against the heavy cavalry. The foot bowmen had won the main frontal battle; the Crusader cavalry dominated the action only toward the end.

Within a year of reaching Syria the Western European soldiers had found the best method of defeating the Turks, employing the inherently dominant foot bowman against the horse archer. Fortuitously, they had also developed the proper combination to deal with the Moslem Arabs from Egypt, who used an entirely different tactical system.

In advancing into Palestine in 1099 and besieging and taking Jerusalem, the Crusaders had invaded territory belonging to Egypt, the Moslem power that controlled Palestine and had frequently engaged in war with the Moslem states of Syria and Mesopotamia. The Egyptians organized their army differently from their light cavalry opponents to the north and east: they continued to rely on the original Arab heavy cavalry tradition, modified by conflict with the Byzantines. Now having also adapted their tactical system to deal with their horse archer opponents, they deployed first a large number of both light and heavy infantrymen, some armed with bows and some with maces. Behind these, they posted their Byzantine-inspired mailed heavy cavalry, and on the wings, a small proportion of unarmored spear-armed cavalry. In adopting this balance of weapon systems and placing the archers in front with heavy infantry to protect them and the heavy cavalry in reserve, the Egyptians clearly had an array splendidly suited to deal with horse archers. But just as Turkish light cavalry tactics had taken the Crusaders unaware, so the Crusaders' tactics surprised the Egyptians.

When the Christians met the Egyptians at Ascalon in 1099, each had a flank on the coast. The Christians, also organizing their army to combat the light cavalry tactical system, placed in front nine divisions of mixed light and heavy infantry with a division of heavy cavalry behind each of these. The battle opened with an attempt by the unarmored Egyptian cavalry to turn the Crusaders' open flank, but a flank division of Christian heavy cavalry easily dispersed them. Meanwhile, the infantry lines made contact at bowshot and began to exchange fire. At this point the Crusaders' heavy cavalry charged through the gaps between the infantry divisions, riding down the Egyptian archers and their heavy infantry. Armed with maces rather than pikes and unprepared for such a charge, the Moslem heavy infantry could make no effective resistance. The cavalry charge then reached the Egyptian heavy cavalry, catching many of them at the halt. But even with a countercharge the Egyptians would probably have had the worst of it against the matchless élan of the more heavily armored and more skillful knights of France. The completely disrupted Egyptian army suffered very heavy casualties among the infantry and in cavalry. The sea on one flank caused many to drown, though some fugitives successfully swam to Egyptian warships off the coast. The town behind offered a refuge, but the narrow gate meant that many were slaughtered waiting to get through and others were crushed to death in the panicked crowd at the gate.

The Crusaders did not always exhibit the high competence revealed in these early battles. On two occasions the same leader, displaying absurd overconfidence, charged with a few hundred knights into an entire Moslem army, losing most of his men in the second attempt. A century later Crusaders met the horse archers, defeated them near a city with the ominous name of Carrhae, and pursued them for twelve miles with only the heavy cavalry. But the Moslems were not defeated; they were drawing the Crusaders on. Their light cavalry opponents having disappeared over the horizon, the Christians decided to camp for the night rather than try to ride their weary horses back to Carrhae. After they had dismounted and many had taken off their armor, the Moslems charged with sword as well as bow. Their assailants destroyed about a third of the force before the Christians found refuge on a hill. Most made good their escape in the night, largely because the Moslems quarreled over the division of the plunder from the Crusaders' camp. The disaster, caused by a reckless pursuit, occurred at almost the same place where Parthian cavalry had killed Crassus's son and his men, including Gallic cavalry.

At the Battle of Hab in 1119 the Christians followed their now-settled doctrine against horse archers of placing infantry and cavalry together "that the two arms might give each other the proper support, the knights protected by the arrows of the foot and the foot by the lances of the knights." But the Moslems had grasped the Christian practice, too, and their light cavalry charged with sword and lance. Though these unarmored bowmen made very poor heavy cavalry, they were too much for the Christian archers, unorganized and ill equipped for shock action. Only the effective use by the Crusaders' commander of a heavy cavalry reserve staved off defeat and secured a drawn battle in which both sides claimed victory.[22]

Toward the end of the twelfth century the small Christian state in Palestine faced the formidable power of a revived Egyptian empire under the leadership of the brilliant soldier and statesman, Saladin. Having conquered Syria, Saladin advanced into Palestine with an army strong in light cavalry in addition to the usual Egyptian heavy cavalry and infantry. Besieging Tiberias on the Sea of Galilee, he captured it easily, but the citadel still held out. To resist this powerful invasion, the Christians concentrated all of the forces of their kingdom, virtually denuding their garrisons in their cities and the castles with which they had dotted the land. Concentrated at the village of Saffaria, sixteen miles west of Tiberias, the leaders debated what to do. Between their force and Saladin's at Tiberias lay a thinly populated region in which Saladin's army had scoured the land of supplies and spoiled the wells. In the heat of summer a waterless march presented a serious obstacle.

One side in the debate advocated a logistic strategy, arguing that lack of supplies must soon force Saladin away. If the Moslem ruler wished to fight, let him try the march west and face the Crusader army if he succeeded in making a hot, waterless march through desolate country. If the Christians had to risk in a battle the whole military force of the kingdom, they should make the odds as favorable as possible. But the advocates of a combat strategy won the debate, arguing that their honor compelled them to relieve the garrison of the citadel and that a victory could be decisive because Saladin's back would be to the Sea of Galilee.

The Moslem horse archers harassed and slowed the army's march toward Tiberias. In the afternoon, six miles from Tiberias, the Crusaders faced the low hills on which they saw Saladin's main force. The attacks of the enemy light cavalry had compelled the rear guard to halt to fight them, and the fatigued army had exhausted its water during the hot march. The commander decided to camp for the night, a night spent without water under the fire of arrows constantly landing in their camps. Saladin's men also set fire to the grass up wind of the camp, blanketing the Crusaders with smoke, which accentuated their need for water. The next morning exhausted, thirsty men and parched, hungry horses had to contend with Saladin's whole army. But before the armies closed, the Christian infantry fled to the top of a hill, saying they were dying of thirst and were too weary to fight. The Moslem horse archers attacked the cavalry, and the remainder of the army charged the demoralized Christian infantry, which promptly gave up. After a longer stand under the hail of arrows, the knights also surrendered. The arrows had wounded many, only a few severely, and killed even fewer; their armor had protected them well.

Neglect of logistics contributed to the defeat. But—and this is typical of a medieval force—the Crusader army lacked experience working together. In particular, the infantry from the castle garrisons lacked subdivisions, a chain of command, unit esprit or cohesion, and any articulation to enable them to maneuver. Lack of water and food helped the collapse of morale, and without any organization the infantry became a demoralized as well as disorganized mob. Deprived of their foot archers, the heavy cavalry had no chance against the horse archers. Saladin's brilliant management made the most of his advantages, avoiding a battle until arrows, hunger, and thirst had physically and morally weakened the enemy's men and horses. Saladin, an experienced monarch and soldier, also arranged his supplies well.

Having destroyed the bulk of the Christian army and with it the larger part of the fortress and town garrisons, Saladin promptly captured Jerusalem and most of the fortified places in the interior of Palestine. The Christians had left only a few ports where the fortifications and the support of the Italian fleets still gave them a toehold. But Saladin faced a serious menace in the formidable force of a new Crusade, which had arrived by sea in the summer of 1191 and had established itself on the coast. Under the leadership of King Philip II Augustus of France and King Richard I of England, the Christian army planned to march south along the coast before striking inland in an attempt to recover Jerusalem. Saladin intended to strike an army on the march again. Following the model of his earlier victory, he planned to use his horse archers to harass and wear down this army until he attacked his weakened adversary with his main force.

But in King Richard the determined Saladin faced a formidable antagonist. In spite of the implication of his "Lion-Hearted" nickname, Richard, who showed more talent and enthusiasm for military than civil pursuits, proved to be a shrewd and careful commander. The young king had already exhibited his grasp of the tactical realities in Palestine when he had organized a small force to defend against a horse archer attack. In the front line he placed a pikeman on one knee with his pike butt in the sand and the point at the level of a horse's chest. In the intervals he placed a crossbowman, standing, with another crossbowman behind who cocked and placed the arrow in the crossbow passed back by the man in front, passing him the cocked and loaded one in exchange. There was hardly a battle, the enemy horse archers falling back before the hail of crossbow arrows, unwilling to close and use their swords because of the line of pikes. Richard did sortie with a few knights, but his imaginative tactical combination of two weapon systems settled the day.

When King Richard prepared his campaign, he made use of his tactical sophistication as well as the lessons taught by the disastrous march to Tiberias. For his own move south he divided his cavalry and infantry each into twelve groups, pairing the two arms. Then to provide a higher level of articulation, he formed the twelve groups of pairs into five unequal divisions. Since his army had landed in early June and he did not begin his operation until the latter part of August, his men had time to get used to one another and the organization. Planning to march close to the shore, he could count on supplies from the sea, securely controlled by Italian navies. Saladin's men had already denuded his route of food and fodder. He intended to move by easy stages, with none longer than twelve miles and alternate days devoted to rest. Saladin would face an amply supplied, thoroughly rested, and at least reasonably organized army. King Richard's order for the movement placed the supply column next to the shore, then the twelve groups of cavalry, and, on the outside, the groups of infantry distributed so as to make a continuous column. The bowmen wore light and inexpensive protection in the form of the quilted jackets that knights customarily wore under their mail.

As soon as the advance began, the enemy horse archers attacked. A contemporary described them as "not weighed down with heavy armor like our knights, but always able to outstrip them in pace." The king, who behaved like a commander in his constant riding back and forth along the column to supervise, interdicted any charges because, the contemporary explained, "when charged they are wont to fly, and their horses are more nimble than any others in the world; one may liken them to swallows for swiftness. When they see that you have ceased to pursue them, they no longer fly but return upon you; they are like tiresome flies which you can flap away for a moment, but which come back the instant you have stopped hitting at them."[23]

Since the rear presented the army's most vulnerable point, exposed to attack on the back as well as the side, Saladin concentrated his efforts there, hoping to cause those elements to halt and so open a gap, dividing Richard's army. But the well-supervised veteran soldiers in the last formation kept up the march, even though some of the bowmen walked backward so they could shoot while on the move. A Moslem contemporary explained: "The enemy moved in order of battle: their infantry marched between us and their cavalry, keeping as level and firm as a wall. Each foot soldier had a thick cassock of felt," the quilted undergarment for mail, which was "so strong that our arrows made no impression on them." The Moslem observer saw "men who had from one to ten shafts sticking in their backs, yet trudged on at their ordinary pace and did not fall out of ranks." But the horse archers aimed at the cavalry beyond, "endeavoring to irritate the knights and to worry them into leaving their rampart of infantry. But it was all in vain: they kept their temper admirably."[24]

Still this persistent attack began to disable more and more horses and the Crusader cavalry did become increasingly impatient with their passive and dependent role. Yet Saladin's army suffered serious losses, the shooting from the crossbows striking "down horse and man among the Moslems." Finally Richard's army neared the end of its march where it passed a forest only three miles from the beach. Here, as he had planned, Saladin concealed his army. But King Richard, ready for battle at this likely spot, had his well-organized and still fresh army completely in hand when Saladin's whole force emerged from the woods, foot archers as well as horse, in advance of their heavy cavalry. Saladin planned to fight all along the line but push his main attack on the rear; King Richard intended to wait until Saladin had fully committed his forces before making a charge with his heavy cavalry. Though the knights of the rear guard passed through their infantry and charged before the king gave the order, the battle went much according to Richard's plan. In a series of three successive charges, the Christian knights drove Saladin's army into the forest. The Moslem infantry and cavalry on the field got in each other's way, and the cavalry suffered as well as the infantry. Realizing Richard's tactical mastery, the brave but sagacious Saladin did not renew the contest when the Christian army resumed its march.[25]

But Richard's victory did not give him Jerusalem. On his march inland to the city he found that Saladin had destroyed the crops, burned the grass, and poisoned or filled in the wells. Successful in combat but unable to overcome Saladin's logistic strategy, King Richard withdrew his hungry and thirsty army, abandoning the quest for Jerusalem.

Since all medieval military leadership came from the ranks of the knights, commanders tended to discount infantry, not understanding its employment except in sieges. Nevertheless, the successful combination of light infantry and heavy cavalry during the Crusades shows that commanders could overcome their bias and solve a problem upon which victory depended. But since they were accustomed by their own training and the nature of cavalry action to individual rather than group action, medieval commanders allowed their infantry to remain comparatively disorganized. Dispersal as professional garrisons in castles or as a rural militia precluded much unit training, in any case; yet medieval military leadership lacked any vision of the importance of the drill of Greek civic militia much less Roman professionals. Still the Crusaders' understanding of the proper integration of weapon systems would have been essential had Western Europe experienced more than a brief encounter with Mongol cavalry.

Jenghiz Khan and Mongol Warfare

The Mongols had a mounted force much like the Parthians, about three-fifths light cavalry and two-fifths heavy cavalry. Their light cavalry carried spare bows, three quivers of arrows, and at least one additional horse. Most of the heavy cavalry, protected by leather armor, could keep up with the light cavalry. The Mongols organized their competently disciplined and thoroughly articulated army on the decimal system, a basic unit of nine men and a leader combined into a larger unit of 100, ten of these into a unit of 1,000, and finally ten of these into a unit of 10,000. Their generals commanded battles, keeping out of the fight and posting themselves with the reserve. They had a thoroughly organized commissariat and had learned sophisticated siegecraft from the Chinese whose empires they had conquered. Under Jenghiz Khan, a minor prince whose ability had brought him rule over the mounted herdsmen of the steppes of Asia, the Mongols had overrun all of the areas bordering their homeland on the northeast Asian plain.

Their conquest of the Khwarizmian empire amply illustrates an essential feature of their method. Within a year they overthrew this monarchy, which stretched from Mesopotamia to the Indus and included Bactria and Sogdiana which had given Alexander the Great so much trouble. And as soon as they had completed their occupation and installed their administration, the Mongols had the same experience as Alexander. The devout Moslem population rose against their conquerers, displaying a hostility intensified by the behavior of the occupying troops. Towns revolted, and the natives assassinated Mongol officials and massacred the garrisons of small posts.

The Mongols retaliated by sending a huge army on a campaign of extermination. The army proceeded systematically to reconquer the country, besieging and taking each city with remarkable speed. The Mongols possessed a sophisticated knowledge of siegecraft and ample equipment, having for one siege 4,000 scaling ladders and 4,000 siege engines, including some adapted to throwing pots of burning naphtha over the walls into the besieged city.

The Mongols overcame their inadequate ratio of force needed to subdue the space and population of the huge country because they never left garrisons in captured towns: they killed or drove away all of the population, leaving "neither a cat nor a dog." The prisoners, artisans and men of military age, which they took away with them, increased the strength of the Mongol army in the next siege by doing the needed digging and building and assisting in carrying out assaults. These unwilling conscripts cooperated, though they faced serious danger assailing the fortifications, because they knew that certain death awaited them if they failed to fight. These prisoners supplied most of the casualties in the combats and few of them survived.[26]

The Mongols did spare the inhabitants of the large city of Herat. But no sooner had the army departed than the inhabitants revolted and killed the Mongol governor. Critical of the misguided mercy extended to this city, Jenghiz Khan asked the army's commander: "Why did this rising take place? How has it come about that the sword has failed of its effect so far as these people of Herat are concerned?" He then directed the commander to return: "Since dead men have come to life again I command you to strike their heads from their bodies." This the commander did, taking the city and killing its several hundred thousand people. A final inspection revealed forty people left alive.[27]

Talking to a captured Khwarizmian prince, Jenghiz Khan, wishing to know whether his campaign of terror would permanently subdue the people of the Khwarizmian empire, asked: "Do you think that this bloodshed will remain for ever in the people's memories?" The prince replied: "If Jenghiz Khan continues this campaign of murder, no one will be left alive to harbour a memory of the bloodshed."[28]

This exchange clearly exhibits both elements in the Mongolian method: the political strategy of terror and the ultimate logistic strategy of killing civilians, the potential soldiers as well as the producers who supported them. The political program worked, so intimidating the people that when a single Mongol soldier rode into a village, he so overawed the population that he could take what he desired and kill whom he wished without the slightest resistance. Thus, Jenghiz Khan quickly subdued a large Mohammedan nation united to resist domination by heathens.

Eastern Europe lacked forces to face such an invincible military machine, the Russians relying on heavy cavalry and heavy infantry, the Poles on heavy cavalry only, and neither having enough foot archers to resist the Mongol light cavalry. Destroying the Russians' armies in 1238 and burning their wooden-walled cities and castles, the Mongols turned away from Novgorod, a city in forested and swampy terrain. Like the Parthians' cavalry, that of the Mongols could not function in forests. Defeating the Poles, the Mongols concentrated against the Hungarians, who had marshaled a great host, including many horse archers. Though lacking a dominant weapon system, the Mongols defeated the Hungarians because of their generalship and the tactical skill of their well-articulated army of veteran regulars. Mongol detachments then penetrated south and west until they reached the Adriatic. This did not prove an easy task because the natives ambushed them in the mountains and cut off their supplies, mounted forces having as much difficulty in mountains as in forests.

As pope and emperor sought to mobilize Europe to resist this invasion of heathen barbarians, the Mongols disappeared more quickly than they came. The death of the Khan far away in Asia provided the occasion for the ending of a four-year campaign. Mountains, forests, and masonry-fortified cities and castles ahead must have provided additional incentives to leave, as did the logistical obstacles presented by forested country that had few pastures and little grain compared with the enormous requirements of the all-mounted Mongol armies. So the booty-laden invaders returned home to their steppes, leaving desolation behind them. This withdrawal may not have saved all of Western Europe from the fate of Russia—domination by the Mongols—but it certainly spared them much loss of life and property.

Summary of Medieval Tactics and Strategy

Medieval warfare accentuated the different functions among the four weapon systems and emphasized the relative advantage each had compared to the others. The stirrup strengthened the shock cavalry and made more pronounced the specialization that, despite the Byzantine horsemen with lance and bow, largely abolished dual- or general-purpose cavalry. Although dismounted knights, skilled fighters on foot as well as horseback, could resist the assault of heavy cavalry, most infantry required pikes and a dense, immobile formation to stand fast against a cavalry charge. The menace of the stronger cavalry would have eliminated the open, sword-wielding Roman formation in any case, but the decentralization of medieval armies aggravated the situation. Undrilled, unarticulated infantry, when formed shield to shield, could only defend. Medieval heavy infantry did not even have the maneuverability of a Macedonian phalanx. Further, the soldiers often lacked the morale and cohesion that training and living together brings and usually did not have the responsiveness that comes from service under familiar leaders.

Since both mounted and missile troops functioned more as individuals than groups, medieval armies suffered little, if any, erosion in the quality of these weapon systems. In fact, their heavy cavalry was probably the best the world had ever seen. In archery the substitution of the crossbow compensated for the lack of an archery tradition in much of Europe. In spite of the availability of a few mounted crossbowmen, Europeans had displayed little interest in light cavalry.

With heavy infantry specialized to resist heavy cavalry and light infantry indispensable in sieges and finding its most effective employment in the field against light cavalry, the art of war about the year 1200 had these clearly distinguishable capabilities: using the symbol $>$ to mean was superior to, heavy infantry $>$ heavy cavalry, heavy cavalry $>$ light infantry, light infantry $>$ light cavalry, and light cavalry $>$ both heavy infantry and heavy cavalry. These relationships are conveniently summarized in schematic 2.1, in which A means ability to attack successfully in the direction of the arrow and D means ability to defend successfully in the direction of the arrow. Attack includes the capability

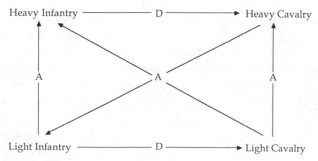

Schematic 2.1. Tactical Capabilities of Weapon Systems

to compel the attacked to fight; defend implies only the capacity for successful resistance but no ability to force action. The schematic assumes a flat surface.

The ability of the cavalry to dismount modifies this diagram. When the heavy cavalry dismounted, it became heavy infantry and confirmed the generalizations that the man on foot is superior to the mounted man and the defensive is stronger when the same weapon systems confront one another. Light cavalry could gain comparable advantages by dismounting, and in each case the dismounted cavalry in the defense could easily take advantage of terrain or artificial obstacles, something more difficult to do mounted. Medieval soldiers grasped and often exploited the value of dismounting heavy cavalry but, lacking light cavalry, could never make use of this transformation. They did occasionally mount bowmen, giving them the strategic mobility of the light cavalry. They more rarely resorted to a similar mounting of heavy infantry, probaby because of their ample supply of heavy cavalry. Yet to have mounted heavy infantry on nags would have been a far more economical solution had knights customarily fought on foot. It would have saved the considerable cost of a robust war horse and the expensive, but unused, skill in fighting mounted.

Medieval warfare with its heterogeniety of tactical arrays contributed little else to tactics than this firmer differentiation of roles. In strategy, the defense dominated, in spite of the improvement of the offensive capabilities of heavy cavalry. Wood and masonry castles and city walls overpowered the offense. Medieval strategy again showed that forcing the enemy to fight on favorable, or at least equal, terms continued one of the most intractable strategic problems if armies had similar composition. If either had better mobility on suitable terrain, the decision to fight belonged to the army with the better mobility. Thus the Mongols could force or refuse battle with any European army. But within Europe a commander could not compel a reasonably alert enemy to fight unless, as did the Emperor Frederick at Legnano, he left his infantry behind and attacked with his cavalry; in this case, the emperor suffered defeat when he could not overcome the Italian infantry. But instead of retreat, medieval defenders frequently used defense's other recourse—defending in a strong position—and for this purpose their walled cities and castles provided the best means. The attacker, faced with the alternative of raids or usually unsuccessful sieges, could rarely carry out a decisive, persisting campaign.

Magyar and Viking raiders made the principal use of the retreat alternative, and the persisting strategy of defense in depth employed against them combined pursuit with fortification of cities and key communication points, which also served as refuges for civilians and barriers to movement. The strong point system proved more efficacious than pursuit in dealing with these raiders, especially as the Magyars had greater mobility and the Vikings the tactically dominant heavy infantry facing the heavy cavalry that had overtaken them. Medieval conquerors also used fortification systems for an offensive persisting strategy, the Frankish ruler Charles the Great building forts to control the Saxons he had defeated. By having among their new subjects forts that controlled communication routes, the Franks exercised a certain measure of influence over the country, especially since the forts had great defensive strength and their garrisons could take the offensive. In Spain and Wales the invaders overran enemy territory piece by piece, consolidating each conquest by erecting castles. The fortification approach, whether on the offensive or the defensive, constituted an application of persisting strategy.

Fortification also meant an employment of combat strategy, an extreme case of taking up a strong position and exploiting the power of the defense to resist a frontal attack. Further, since fortifications embodied the attributes of both heavy and light infantry, they comprised the ultimately superior weapon system on the defense and assured the primacy of the strategic defensive. A late medieval military writer emphasized reliance on fortifications to resist invasion as an alternative to meeting the enemy in battle when he recommended that a ruler "repair and supply with foodstuffs, artillery and men the principal places of the frontier" and "to demolish those which were not defensible." The number of castles in many areas made such a strategy quite formidable. One region in the eastern part of present-day France had seventy castles in an area of less than 3,000 square miles, a castle for about every forty square miles.

Such powerful defenses often reduced invaders to raiding to seek to secure political concessions by making the war expensive through their depredations. The destructiveness of such raids encouraged defenders to add to their formidable combat defense in depth of the castles a defensive logistic strategy. Thus the same authority urged the defenders "to withdraw all livestock from the frontier and a broad swathe into the interior of his country and to place all food supplies from the countryside in strong places so that the enemy might not find anything when they come to lay siege and ride about in strength." No wonder the medieval strategic defense had such paramountcy.[29]

The use of fortifications for offensive purposes—making possible a gradual encroachment into hostile territory—could also implement an offensive logistic strategy. Over several centuries the persistent Christian conquest and fortification of successive pieces of Moslem Spain had just such a logistic effect. Each new piece of Christian territory added military manpower to the states. But these acquisitions also subtracted an equal amount from the military resources of the Moslem monarchs. Since almost any logistic method in strategy also required combat to carry it out, the Christian strategy in Spain could be characterized as basically logistic in effect if not in immediate purpose. Thus, a persisting strategy could win gradually and attain its success as a logistic strategy. It might, of course, secure victory more quickly, as an application of combat strategy, if the aggressor had sufficiently limited goals or the defender had a weak enough motive for resistance.

With frontiers against the Celts in England, the Moors in Spain, and the Slavs in the East, medieval soldiers and governments learned thoroughly the means of vanquishing hostile peoples. Of course, the Turkish and Mongolian systems accomplished the objective more quickly. To have killed off the military manpower of the Celts and Slavs would have subdued their resistance by terror and deprived them of the manpower resources to resist. On one occasion the Romans, who sometimes resorted to such measures, had carried this policy to its logical conclusion. When a small tribe in Africa, the Nasamones, revolted, the Roman commander "attacked them and annihilated them, even destroying all the non-combatants." The Emperor "Domitian was elated at this success and said to the Senate: 'I have forbidden the Nasamones to exist.' " But the Christian rulers of Europe usually used the more humane, if less rapid, means of gradual conquest and pacification through fortification.[30] This policy, which continued unchanged through the close of the Middle Ages and involved specialized warfare against different opponents on varying terrain, had much to do with the re-emergence of regional and national tactical systems.

3

THE EMERGENCE OF A NEW COMBINED-ARMS TACTICAL SYNTHESIS, 1200–1600

The French Version of Medieval Warfare

The armed forces of France, where the Franks had done so much to establish the heavy cavalry tradition, best exemplified the medieval methods and concepts of warfare. Bounded by Spain, Italy, Germany, and, across the Channel, England, France occupied such a central position in medieval Europe that the experience of frontier warfare had little effect on the French way of war. In France the medieval emphasis on heavy cavalry and on the offensive in battle reached its highest development. Because mounted men have a disadvantage on the defensive, French commanders, almost invariably drawn from the heavy cavalry nobility, naturally thought in terms of the offensive. Without good archers, with the crossbow difficult to use mounted, and with little tradition of light cavalry, the charge of the heavy cavalry dominated the concept of cavalry in French military thought.

While they largely overlooked the key role infantry could play in battle, the French had strong tactical reasons for thus neglecting the deployment of light infantry on the battlefield. Valuable in sieges and indispensable for dealing with Turkish horse archers, light infantry proved too vulnerable to heavy cavalry to have a place on a battlefield where mailed horsemen prevailed. Heavy infantry, also of high value in sieges, too found little place in the French idea of the battlefield because the mercenaries who helped garrison and attack castles had no tradition or organization for forming to resist the charge of the heavy cavalry. Rural militia might array themselves in close order, but, ill-armed and untrained, they could not resist the cavalry either. Believing the offensive the strongest mode of combat and thinking in terms of cavalry as the premier weapon system, French leaders never considered trying to develop a heavy infantry that could resist the cavalry. Their own tactical training centered on the joust and the battle-like mounted tournament in which they perfected the techniques of mounted combat.

The neglect of the infantry also had a foundation in aristocratic contempt for the social inferiors who fought on foot. On one occasion, when French infantry seemed to be winning a battle without the aid of the cavalry, a historian of the time saw jealousy as a motive for the charge of the cavalry; he had one of the French leaders say: "Forward great lords and little lords, look to it that we have the honor and the victory in this battle." Social bias reinforced the perspective of the leaders. And the real difficulties in providing suitable heavy infantry also convinced French commanders not to alter their usual practice of relying primarily on their heavy cavalry.[1]

These same factors had much to do with the tendency to think of combat in terms of the frontal attack. The culture of chivalry and the concept of honor made the French think of accepting challenges and fair fights on even terms, thus buttressing the fixation on the frontal fight experienced in the joust. Moreover, limited battle experience further inhibited the development of the tactics of envelopment, a maneuver difficult in any case for cavalry to execute against cavalry. Unlike infantry, cavalry can change its front fairly readily because its combat, involving more individual than group action, depends less on formation and drill. The assumption of the superiority of the offensive also contributed to the culture of the frontal attack. Of course, the assumption had truth when heavy cavalry faced heavy cavalry, light infantry, or inadequately equipped or prepared heavy infantry. In 1229 the young king of Aragon, for example, with only 400 knights charged 2,000 Moslem pikemen as they moved toward him. His charge succeeded—as he had foreseen—because the pikemen's advance had opened gaps in their line into which the Aragonese knights charged with devastating effect.

Thus the French as exemplars of medieval military methods failed to understand many of the insights of the soldiers of the ancient world. Notions of envelopment, concentration against weakness, and winning with the least effort had little or no place among their operational ideas. They had only a modest notion of a subtracted reserve and even less of a commander who managed the battle rather than led his troops. Because of the infrequency of battles and the ad hoc character of most feudal armies, the French lacked adequately organized and articulated armies as well as any command structure. In fact, a French army, composed of many men important for their wealth, social prestige, and political power, had much more in common with a collection of prima donnas than an army organized on the Macedonian or Roman model. Many of these same factors kept them from developing an adequate logistical organization. Only the Byzantine and Mongol armies of the East equaled the ancient models.

But French soldiers did comprehend the signficance of fortifications; they built increasingly strong and complex castles and town walls and astutely founded their strategy on the primacy of the permanently fortified defense. Medieval leaders could display sophistication in their strategy, as did King John in other operations besides his campaign with the Emperor Otto against King Philip of France. Nor were the French, who played the most important role in the Crusades, incapable of grasping principles clearly understood by the ancients. Their use of crossbowmen to defeat horse archers and Richard the Lion-Hearted's perceptive mixing of crossbowmen and pikemen showed they could understand the relative advantages of the different weapon systems. The French Crusaders also used the tactics of surprise and of flank attacks. In Europe, however, except for their fortifications, the Crusaders made little effort to use the lessons of the East to modify their tactical methods. It took the experience of war on frontiers nearer than Syria and Palestine to affect late medieval warfare, and these occurred against a backdrop of changes in military technology and logistics.

Changes in Logistics

Late medieval warfare saw significant logistical changes as the expansion of commerce and regional specialization and division of labor increased productivity and the use of money. Improved agricultural methods and implements also augmented wealth, enabling rulers to support larger armies. More and more such rulers relied on professionals, relegating militias to service in sieges and to resisting raids or invasions. But the professional soldiers were not of the Roman type, recruited and organized by monarchs and kept constantly under arms and in training. Instead, they were mercenaries, soldiers who hired themselves out for a period rarely exceeding a year. William the Conquerer, for example, had depended heavily on such men in his conquest of England. Usually the ruler worked through military contractors, who undertook to provide a certain number and type of troops for a given campaign. The growth in the circulation of money and increased tax revenues enabled monarchs and princes to employ professionals rather than to rely on a military tax in kind paid through obligatory military service.

This substitution of professional soldiers meant more competent armies and enabled campaigns to continue as long as a ruler's funds lasted. But even though many soldiers, as individuals or groups, worked for the same contractor year after year, the armies lacked the professionalism of the Roman and later Byzantine standing forces because the composition of the armies did change from year to year. This fluctuation in personnel meant that mercenary armies, lacking settled organization, had no established unit size, chain of command, or experience in training together. Without these, they lacked articulation and had little unit cohesiveness or esprit de corps. As a consequence, the heavy infantry composed of such mercenaries, though skilled in sieges, lacked ability to maneuver on the battlefield. This kind of private enterprise in the creation and operation of armies proved less effective than the socialistic Roman model of state ownership of armies.

An expansion of agricultural production and, until the plague that began in the middle of the fourteenth century, a growth in population enhanced the ability of armies to provide for themselves and to carry out sustained campaigns. The greater availability of money facilitated the purchase of food, lodging, and fodder while campaigning and encouraged the use of private contractors to supply the army's needs. But technological progress also profoundly affected logistics: the introduction of the horseshoe and the perfection of the horse collar permitted horses to pull harder, using their shoulders rather than their necks. The spread of an effective tandem harness enabled better-designed wagons to have as many pairs of horses as the load warranted. The faster horse with greater endurance gradually superseded the ox. Where adequate roads existed, the wagon drawn by horses replaced the oxcart and the pack animal. These innovations brought about such a dramatic growth in efficiency that the costs of road transport fell by two-thirds. In Roman times the expense of hauling grain 100 miles had equaled the value of the grain; in the thirteenth century the transport charge for 100 miles fell to only 30 percent of the price of the grain. Such a change profoundly affected military supply, enabling stationary armies to draw from a far-larger radius and, if necessary, to carry with them a much greater amount of food.

Shipping also underwent a major transformation during the later Middle Ages, one essentially complete by the year 1600. Merchant ships grew in size and sailing ability. Single masts gave way to two, three, and even four masts, and with as many as three sails on a given mast, ships could sail faster and closer to the direction from which the wind came. At first, the larger ships had deep drafts, high freeboards, and stubby dimensions, a breadth of half the length of the keel and a third of the overall length. These vessels proved resistant to bad weather but slow and difficult to maneuver. In the sixteenth century appeared lower ships with a beam a third of the length of the keel. These had higher speed, better sailing characteristics, and greater facility for maneuvering.

But the more significant advance for water transport came with progress in navigation. The introduction of the compass made it far easier for ships to sail out of sight of land. By using the time a ship required to pass an object in the water, a mariner could estimate the speed of his ship and thus the distance traveled. Although difficulties in determining latitude at sea and the inability to know longitude still made navigation approximate rather than exact, these advances enormously augmented the capabilities of ships. Mariners became competent and confident in sailing out of sight of land.

Changes in Weapons

In the thirteenth century armored men began to use plates to strengthen their mail armor at particularly vulnerable points, such as the shin and knee. Gradually heavy cavalry added more and more plate to the mail until a complete suit of plate armor, which protected the wearer from the shock of blows and deflected both hand weapons and crossbow bolts, became common. A helmet that completely covered the face had already been adopted. A suit of the new armor could weigh seventy pounds, and, together with its own armor, the horse had to carry over 100 pounds of metal alone. With a horse protected from lance wounds in the chest and the rider virtually proof against harm, the knight became far more formidable. However, this alteration both raised the cost of the mounted man and seriously reduced his mobility. The heavily burdened horse found it harder to gallop and the rider had difficulty in executing any maneuver but the straight-ahead charge. Dismounted, the rider could walk only with difficulty and had trouble in climbing onto his horse and in rising if he fell.

The invention of gunpowder took a long time to affect land warfare. Its significant use proved to be not in rockets or in bombs thrown by siege engines but in propelling missiles from a tube. By the middle of the fourteenth century cannon had become common, but 100 years elapsed before the cannon had enough power to batter down walls easily enough to bring about a revolution in the art of war. Then, when existing castles and city walls became obsolete, military engineers developed a new approach, and defenders erected new fortifications.

Because of its much greater effectiveness the siege artillery powered by gunpowder replaced the siege engines then in use. Some of the new cannon were large enough to fire a stone cannonball weighing 400 or more pounds, but most

Illustration 3.1. Plate Armor

were so difficult to move and took so much time to emplace that they were considered fixed. But just as the Romans had carried small ballista on wheeled carriages into the field and had evolved the hand ballista in the form of the crossbow, so did mobile and portable guns develop. The fifteenth century saw both small cannon on wheels and small cannon carried by individual soldiers. The mobile artillery, on very primitive carriages, proved hard to move and aim and had little influence on battles for a long time. Lacking the mobility of the light cavalry's and light infantry's portable missile systems, the mobile artillery also shared these systems' inability to resist the charge of either of the heavy weapon systems. Unlike the light infantry and light cavalry, the guns lacked the mobility to escape the heavy infantry.

The gun found its major tactical employment in the relatively immobile version in sieges and in the portable handgun. Early handguns made little impression because of difficulty in aiming and shooting. Firing a handgun—a miniature cannon attached to a stick—involved bringing a burning substance into contact with a small touchhole in the rear of the muzzle-loaded barrel, causing the charge to ignite and the gun to shoot. Usually a smoldering cord, called a match, supplied the ignition. To hold the gun in one hand and touch the match to the hole with the other made aiming virtually impossible. Lacking greater power and with a slow rate of fire, the handgun could not compete with the precision of the crossbow, the high rate of fire of the bow, or the accuracy of either in skilled hands.

In the middle of the fifteenth century the matchlock improved the ability to aim the handgun. By attaching the burning end of the match to a trigger-operated hook, the operator could use the trigger to move the match into contact with the touchhole while simultaneously holding the gun with both hands and aiming. But shooting a matchlock remained slow work. In order to load, the gunner had to measure out powder, put it in the barrel, insert the lead ball, and place a wad in to hold in the bullet and powder. Beside the touchhole was a small pan that when filled with powder and ignited with the match would flare to ignite the powder charge in the barrel. The gunner completed loading by closing a cover on the pan to keep the powder from falling out until he was ready to shoot. While he loaded, he had both to keep his match away from the powder and also to keep it alight. This he did after loading by blowing on it or by grasping it some distance from the burning end and whirling it around in the air. When ready to shoot he fixed his match to his hook, opened his pan, took aim, and pulled the trigger. About half the time the gun shot, sending out a lead ball about three-quarters of an inch in diameter. The other half of the time his match went out, the powder fell from his pan, the powder flashed in the pan without igniting the charge, or some other accident prevented a shot. If the gun shot, the gunner had about a fifty-fifty chance of hitting a line of men shoulder to shoulder 100 yards away.

In spite of increases in power, this matchlock, called an arquebus, could not have competed with the crossbow had it not been for its low cost. A simple

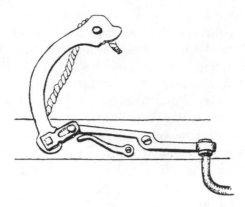

Illustration 3.2. Matchlock

iron or brass tube on a wooden stock with an uncomplicated hook and trigger, the weapon cost far less than a crossbow that had a windlass or reduction gears for cocking to augment its power. Making a crossbow required a week of skilled labor and the windlass took another week. It could take as little as a day's labor to make a gun. Making a crossbow bolt required a half hour of skilled labor; handgun balls could be cast in batches. With power equal or greater than the crossbow and with about the same rate of fire, the arquebus began to supplant the crossbow by the end of the fifteenth century.

Comparable in rate of fire to the crossbow, the arquebus was not as reliable or accurate. The flaw was in the weapon itself (the ball fitted only loosely in the barrel), so skill in aiming did not constitute a factor in handgun training— although an experienced man who knew his ammunition and the idiosyncrasies of his weapon could shoot far better than a novice. So rather than accuracy soldiers stressed speed and reliability in loading movements so as to increase their rate of fire, a more dependable combat variable than precise aiming. As the less costly weapon system, the arquebus rapidly displaced bows in the sixteenth century. But arquebuses merely replaced bows without adding much to the effectiveness of soldiers armed with missile weapons. And though siege artillery did develop so much power as to render existing fortifications obsolete, this change did not occur until about the middle of the fifteenth century. So gunpowder contributed nothing to the regional tactical specialization that had emerged by the later Middle Ages and that gave a different flavor to European warfare in the thirteenth century and after.

Persisting Strategy and the Completion of the English Conquest of Wales

After another century of intermittent warfare between the Welsh and the English, a significant conflict between them broke out in 1276. The Welsh in the north had, in Prince Llywelen, a shrewd and experienced leader with the title Prince of Wales and a power base that extended well into the south. Llywelen had already expanded his domain at the expense of the English, but in the new king, Edward I, he faced an accomplished soldier and master strategist who, as Prince Edward, had displayed his brilliance against the de Montforts in the Evesham campaign. In 1276 the king assembled a large force of paid troops, with little cavalry but many bowmen, spearmen, carpenters, and diggers. Rather than the impressive but ephemeral and ineffective invasions of his regal predecessors, he planned a persisting campaign of occupation. He avoided serious logistic difficulties by the use of little cavalry and had a force that could fight the Welsh on their own terms on moors and in mountains and forests.

King Edward's initial campaign quickly conquered the peripheral and lukewarm subjects of Prince Llywelen. Then, faced in the winter with a compact, rugged, and hostile area in northwestern Wales, he continued campaigning, beginning a systematic but rapid pursuit of the implicit strategy of the previous two centuries. Not neglecting a logistic strategy, potent against such a barren area, he interdicted the movement of supplies into Llywelen's domain. His winter campaign proved so effective that in less than a year the Prince of Wales made peace, accepting markedly diminished territories and influence. Certainly in concluding peace Llywelen must have taken into account King Edward's further application of logistic strategy in September 1277, when he captured the large, fertile island of Anglesey, just off the coast of northern Wales. The king's men harvested the crops that would normally have gone to the mainland to supply Edward's adversaries.

King Edward, a thorough builder, then pushed the repair of castles and started to construct new ones. That the Welsh had built their own meant that the English found ready many that they needed to dominate their new conquests. Five years later, in another war lasting a year, the king's forces, well over 90 percent infantry and large in relation to the area and the number of the hostile population, occupied the remaining area of north Wales and took all of its castles.

This persisting campaign, which spanned the winter, completed the conquest of Wales. The English faced a less difficult task than they expected because Llywelen, as he hurried to join a detachment of his men, met an English soldier who, not recognizing the Prince of Wales, ran him through with his spear. The loss of his leadership and the morale of his followers made Edward's task easier. And the king moved quickly to consolidate his rule by repairing castles. In seven years the king had constructed or rebuilt nine castles of enlarged size and in accord with an improved design.

In the next eleven years the English faced two rebellions but dealt quickly and effectively with each. Throughout Edward's campaigns, Welshmen had composed the majority of his forces. Wales then, in spite of a brief, fierce rebellion a century later, remained a peaceful and a gradually more English part of the king's domains. Edward conciliated many of the Welsh when he made his son Edward, who had been born in Wales, Prince of Wales, thus continuing but appropriating the title of the local ruler. But the gradual penetration of Wales over the previous two centuries provided the primary political component of the conquest.

The military means for subduing Wales consisted of a persisting strategy, essentially combat but with a logistical element important over the long run. The English would not have needed two centuries for the task had they used more of their kingdom's resources and if they could have pursued the effort in a continuous rather than intermittent way. Nevertheless, the method required patience. The conquest of an area, such as a valley, and the building of a castle to control communication and to dominate the area took time. Once the English had established their control and had begun to harness the resources of the vanquished region to their own uses, they could, had they made an unremitting effort at conquest, have promptly moved on to repeat in another area the process of invasion and dominance through fortification.

The castles exploited the power of the defense in its most telling form, throwing upon the defenders the burden of a particularly difficult tactical offensive if they were to prevent the loss of another parcel of territory. Concentration of the initial occupation and pacification effort in a small area also enabled the invaders to increase the ratio of force to space and their castles not only prevented Welsh reconquest of areas already taken but also inhibited raids into these territories. Thus the English could gradually reconcile the defeated to their rule, acculturizing them until holding the district required less force and freeing men for the invasion and control of the next segment of territory. The growth of towns and cultivation of the soil accelerated this process of propagating the English outlook, institutions, and, eventually, language in Wales.

The English Combined-Arms Tactical System in Scotland

Although the campaigns in Wales involved a number of sieges, the adversaries engaged in few battles, as the Welsh depended largely on the raids and ambushes of guerrilla warfare. When the Welsh in the north did face the English in battle, they employed their characteristic phalanx of pikemen. A country like Wales with limited commerce and agricultural productivity could not afford the expensive, armored horseman. It adopted inexpensive infantry and, like the Macedonians, used the long pike that kept the enemy at a distance, making costly body armor less important. In combating this powerful defensive formation the English used the same tactics employed by William the Conqueror at Hastings. Instead of a futile cavalry charge against the serried ranks of Welsh pikemen, the English first sent forward their bowmen and crossbowmen whose missiles so weakened the passively defending Welsh that a cavalry charge could succeed.

In southern Wales the English had encountered Welshmen armed with the longbow, which is far more formidable than the ordinary bow. Very strong and as long as a man's height, this weapon had power comparable to a cross or composite bow. In one instance the point of an arrow shot at a wooden door four inches thick actually protruded slightly on the other side of the door. But the essential feature of the longbow lay in the man rather than in the bow: it required years of practice to develop the strength to pull it and to acquire the mastery for accurate shooting. The crossbow substituted a machine for the strength and facility of the man; the longbow relied on a superlatively well-trained man. The superior skill of the man raised the cost of the weapon system, but not so much in a poor country like Wales. Depending on a miltia to resist first Saxon, then Viking, and finally English invaders, a Welsh shepherd could make an avocation of skill with the longbow because the bow itself was inexpensive. A skillful bowman could make use of his weapon's versatility and use the game shot to supplement his diet. The Welsh specialization in this particularly labor-intensive bow produced a far more powerful weapon system than the crossbow. Because the longbow shot at three or four times the crossbow's rate, a very skillful archer at long range could shoot rapidly enough to keep two arrows in the air simultaneously. The English incorporated Welsh longbowmen in their armies and had so much success increasing the popularity of the longbow in England that it virtually displaced the crossbow.

But the longbow remained largely a Welsh and English weapon, efforts to popularize it in France failing because of the long training required to master it. The arquebus ultimately replaced both bows, though its slower rate of fire and poor accuracy delayed the substitution in England. But the strength and skill necessary to shoot the longbow raised the cost of that weapon system far above that of the arquebus, a factor that eventually guaranteed the adoption of the arquebus.

But for two centuries the English and Welsh had a virtual monopoly of the longbow and so had the best light infantry in the Western world. In turning from Wales to Scotland, the English learned how to use their better light-infantry weapon system. In 1298 King Edward I met the Scots in battle at Falkirk. Like Wales, Scotland was a rugged country of low agricultural productivity; like the Welsh, the Scots specialized in heavy infantry, a less expensive and better adapted system to most of their terrain than heavy cavalry. They did have some heavy cavalry, but their few archers lacked the effectiveness of the Welsh and English longbowmen.

At Falkirk, knowing their heavy infantry functioned best on the defensive, the Scots awaited attack. William Wallace, the competent Scots commander, had learned this when he had beaten the English earlier by standing on the defensive behind a swamp. For this battle he chose a similar position, on a hill behind soft ground.

Nevertheless King Edward, an expert tactician, resolved to attack. The Scottish heavy infantry had twelve-foot pikes and used a very deep formation in which, on the defensive, the front rank knelt holding their pikes with the butts in the ground while the remaining ranks leveled theirs. The Scots arrayed their heavy infantry in four large formations capable of all-around defense and placed their bowmen between these and on their flanks and positioned their few heavy cavalry behind the infantry. To pass the swampy ground the English heavy cavalry divided, approached the Scots on each flank, and, without orders, executed an impetuous charge against the motionless enemy. The onset dispersed the Scottish light infantry but made no impression on the four deep formations of pikemen. Just as the English knights were about to repeat their assault against the heavy infantry, the king arrived. Seeing that the spontaneous first charge had been productive by riding down the Scottish light infantry, the experienced and perceptive Edward also realized the futility of another charge against the pikemen. Forbidding another cavalry attack, he applied the tactics effective against Welsh pikemen by bringing up his longbowmen and directing them to concentrate their fire against a few places in the Scottish line. When the deluge of arrows had inflicted serious casualties and created some gaps, the king ordered a charge against the openings. The cavalry penetrated, defeated, and pursued the Scottish infantry, whose casualities, though severe, were limited by the proximity of a forest. The Scottish commander had selected a spot near a woods, to provide a refuge from the cavalry in case of defeat.

The battle, which had tactical similarities to William's victory at Hastings, again demonstrated that as in ancient times light infantry, though at the mercy of heavy cavalry, could stand off and seriously hurt heavy infantry. The battle showed that even elaborately armored elite men, mounted with stirrups on picked horses, could not prevail against densely formed heavy infantry with long pikes. This last lesson, the basis of Narses's victory at Tagenae, the English knights had shown difficulty in learning.

King Edward's victory at Falkirk reversed English fortunes against the Scots. In 1297, in the absence of the king, English forces had felt such assurance that they crossed a narrow bridge, even though the Scots had drawn up their army just beyond it. This overconfidence received its just reward when the Scottish heavy infantry charged after part of the English army had crossed. Most of the English force on the far bank were killed, captured, or drowned trying to escape.

Yet Edward's example at Falkirk did not immediately change English tactical doctrine. A few years later an English commander who knew Edward's method at Falkirk faced Robert Bruce's Scottish heavy infantry, which was blocking the narrow space between two patches of swampy land. Instead of bringing up his longbowmen, the English commander charged the pikes. After the second charge and 100 fatalities, the English commander retreated. Many medieval soldiers had trouble disabusing themselves of the idea that nothing on foot could resist the charge of the heavy cavalry. An aristocratic disdain for plebeians who fought on foot reinforced their arrogant conviction of the supremacy of the heavy cavalry.

The Scots had so much success in driving the English from their initial conquests that Edward II, Edward I's incompetent son and successor, at last stirred himself to action and invaded Scotland in 1314, bringing a huge army to relieve an important castle besieged by the Scots under Robert Bruce, their king. The king, a champion of Scottish independence who displayed equal brilliance in civil and military affairs, had learned much about war from William Wallace's example and his own campaigns with Edward I. Prepared for the English advance, he arrayed his army behind a marsh on a hill near the castle and the town where the English must attack him to raise the siege. Robert posted himself on a high point where he could see the whole battlefield. Lacking many bowmen, the Scots relied on their pikemen, stiffened by some of their heavy cavalry dismounted. Keeping 500 heavy cavalry mounted as a reserve, King Robert marshaled his infantry in four separate, deep formations.

To attack the Scots, the English had to bring their far-larger army across the marshy area, dotted with pools of water. When morning came, the English had completed this task but had not yet fully arrayed their cavalry and had hardly begun to deploy the infantry behind it. Instead of awaiting the English attack as he had planned, King Robert changed his mind, deciding to attack them before they could form. He then ordered forward his formations of pikemen, executing that rarity in war, an infantry attack on cavalry.

Just as Epaminondas at Leuctra could more readily move a block rather than a line of hoplites, the large, dense formations of Scottish pikemen could keep their order and avoid gaps in their front as they advanced steadily over the mile separating them from the English cavalry, still forming up in front of their infantry. One group of English cavalry promptly met the first Scottish formation with a countercharge, and, in the words of a contemporary historian: "The two hosts so came together, and the great steeds of the knights dashed into the Scottish pikes as into a thick wood; there arose a great and horrible crash from rending lances and dying horses, and they stood locked together for a space." The cavalry at the halt, outside of the line of pikes, had little chance to effect anything.[2]

Meanwhile, as the other Scottish formations came up to engage, the English succeeded in deploying some of their longbowmen on one flank and these "shot so fast that, if only their shooting had lasted, it would have been hard for the Scots." But King Robert, who had served at Falkirk and "well knew that archers were dangerous and their shot hard and right grievous," committed his reserve of 500 heavy cavalry. These charged and easily dispersed the English archers, the king now committing the only weapon system that could attack and defeat the light infantry. With no archers to menace them, all Scottish pikemen joined battle, pressing the English cavalry together and back on their immobile infantry who were hemmed in by the marsh pools they had crossed to reach the attack position. With rear ranks useless, the English finally began to retreat, taking their cue from King Edward's departure from the field. The huge English army suffered severe casualities, many drowning in crossing the water obstacles in the rear. At Bannockburn the English had bungled by placing themselves in such a dangerous predicament, but in the past the Scots had made it a practice to stand on the defensive. In the next major battle the Scots had their turn to suffer both from overconfidence and a refinement in English tactics.

In 1332 at Dupplin a small force invading Scotland took up a defensive position, and the Scottish army, all heavy infantry, advanced uphill in one large central mass and two smaller formations, one on each flank of the largest. The English wisely dismounted their cavalry, converting it into heavy infantry, and dispersed their numerous longbowmen on their flanks. Ignoring the bowmen, the Scottish central mass struck the stationary, dismounted cavalry but failed to overwhelm it. While the two forces of shock foot soldiers struggled against one another, the English archers moved forward and began rapid shooting from the right and left against the small flank formations, causing them to fall back against the main body. As the front ranks could make no forward movement and those on the flanks pushed inward as they flinched before the shower of arrows, the Scots were, according to a medieval historian, "thrust so close that they were crushed to death one by another, so that more fell by suffocation than by the sword." Assailed on three sides, the Scottish situation resembled the Romans' at Cannae, but "a marvel never seen or heard of before in any battle of the past was observed, for the heap of dead stood as high from the ground as the full length of a spear." When the Scots finally commenced a disorderly retreat, many of the English remounted and inflicted additional heavy casaulties. The English suffered relatively little, the Scots killing no bowmen at all.[3]

The following year at Halidon Hill the Scots again attacked an English formation. The energetic and talented young English king, Edward III, took a position on a steep hill and followed the new tactics of dismounting his cavalry and dispersing his archers both on the flank and in gaps between the cavalrymen. Shooting downhill against the Scottish advance, the longbowmen, unaided by the heavy cavalry converted into heavy infantry, came close to halting the pikemen. The Scots soon left the field, leaving victory to Edward, who at age twenty thus began an almost invariably successful military career.

From these Welsh and Scottish wars the English had developed a distinctive tactical system based on standing on the defensive, dismounting their cavalry to create heavy infantry, and using their formidable light infantry to harm the attackers in a way beyond the capability of heavy infantry by merely making a successful defense. The mixture of heavy and light infantry can prevail against a frontal attack by any combination of weapon systems except all light infantry. But against an all light infantry attack, the English cavalry would have been able to remount and ride down the bowmen. Against the same combination, light and heavy infantry, the defenders would have the advantage of the defensive when fighting against like weapon systems. Thus the English had, from an offensive-oriented heavy-cavalry background, created the perfect defensive system, one that not only mastered the Scots but that also could have defeated the Parthians.

After their defeats at Dupplin and Halidon Hill, the Scots fell back on the wise and effective strategy prescribed by King Robert. He had enjoined avoiding battle, relying on hills, swamps, and forests for protection rather than on castles and confining offensive action to ambushes and surprises. He also prescribed a defensive logistic strategy of destroying crops when the invader came because "then shall they pass away in haste when that they find nothing but waste." Such a logistic strategy cost much less than the destruction involved, for the English invaders themselves would have destroyed most that they did not consume. And the Scots reimbursed themselves through frequent plundering raids into adjacent England. In 250 years of intermittent warfare the tactics, the strategy, and the general situation changed little, the Scots never successfully fostering an archery equal to the Anglo-Welsh and the English never subduing the Scots nor containing their raids. But soon after his victory at Halidon Hill, Edward III turned his attention to a war with France.[4]

The Beginning of the Hundred Years' War and the Crécy Campaign

When England's King Edward III began his first campaign against France in 1339, he planned to depend on the dismounted heavy cavalryman and the longbowmen in the defensive array that he had used so successfully at Halidon Hill in 1333. Landing in the friendly territory of the Netherlands (now Holland, Belgium, and the adjacent part of France), he met a large force of allies and invaded France, then a country dotted with strong masonry castles. To cope with such an advantage for the defense and to use his defensive tactics, he employed a raid to devastate the countryside, hoping to compel King Philip VI to attack.

When King Philip, a ruthless man and an adequate soldier, at length approached with a large army, King Edward had drawn up his forces in three lines, with his front line heavy cavalry dismounted and his archers on the flanks. But instead of advancing to the attack, the French king arrayed his army some distance away and awaited an English assault. Even if the English tactics had provided for taking the offensive, King Edward would have hesitated, for he explained, Philip "made trenches all around him and cut down large trees in order to prevent us approaching him." Soon exhausting their food supplies, the two armies moved away from each other. Although King Philip neither fully grasped the defensive strength of the dismounted English cavalry nor understood the deadly menace presented by the longbowmen, his ordinary prudence prevented him from offering an attack against a large army well organized to receive it.[5]

In 1340 Edward III returned to the same theater and began his campaign by besieging the city of Tournai, using a river to keep the relieving army at bay for nearly two months. Then short of money to keep his forces in the field, the English king yielded to his allies' desires for a truce and concluded the campaign without capturing Tournai or fighting a battle.

In 1341 King Edward, having won control of the sea between England and France, shifted the theater of war to the Duchy of Brittany, the westernmost province of France, where he supported a pro-English claimant to the dukedom. There followed a typically medieval seesaw struggle of sieges that went on for many years. Meanwhile, the French advanced steadily in Guyenne, the long-held English possession in southeastern France. In this six-year campaign the French had pushed to within twenty-five miles of Bordeaux when King Edward's very competent cousin, Henry, earl of Lancaster, landed with a small army in 1345. His ability enabled him to reverse English fortunes.

Lancaster quickly advanced against the main French force, which held the town of Bergerac, and immediately began what proved to be a very brief siege. With the aid of ships in the river and the rapid fire of his archers, he quickly captured the town, the French forces escaping. The earl continued his advance and, avoiding the strong city of Périgueux, captured the town of Auberoche, nearly 100 miles from Bordeaux. But when the English commander returned to the coast, the French took the offensive by besieging Auberoche. Lancaster, leading a minute force of heavy cavalry and bowmen, promptly marched to relieve Auberoche, doing so by a late afternoon surprise attack that routed the besiegers. Lancaster then captured three towns, including La Réole, which he took by using movable towers and securing the surrender of the castle by convincing the garrison that he had undermined the walls and was ready to fire the props. These successes, which reconquered lost territory and threatened areas long French, led to the arrival of a huge French army under the command of the king's son. This army began the siege of Aiguillon, the much smaller English forces limiting their relief activities to replenishing the city's supplies.

Such medieval operations, which centered on sieges, also characterized the campaigning in Brittany. After seven years of warfare, no operation had resulted in a well-remembered battle. But in the summer of 1346, as the French army pursued the siege of Aiguillon, King Edward III prepared in England a large army, proclaiming Guyenne as his objective. Since the king had intended this announcement to mislead the French, after the fleet sailed, Edward utilized the initiative given him by control of the sea to have it land in Normany, to pursue a campaign in northeastern France.

Edward, whose strategic grasp fell short of his ability as a tactician, seemed to want to cooperate with his allies from the Netherlands, yet he landed 200 miles from them, and the two forces had to act on exterior lines with the French army between. He did relieve the pressure on English forces in Guyenne, for King Philip ordered the French army away, but not in time to reach him for his battle with Edward. If Edward wished to provoke a battle in which he could use his Halidon Hill defensive tactics, he succeeded but only at substantial risk.

Landing near the western tip of Normandy, King Edward mounted his infantry to give them a strategic mobility comparable to his cavalry. He began a march east and then north to meet his allies near the present border of France. When Edward had passed through Normandy, turned east, and approached the Seine near the large city of Rouen, he found that the French had broken the bridges and guarded the fords over the Seine. His opponent of six years before, King Philip VI of France, had reached Rouen with a large army. Marching east toward Paris—with the French army following on the opposite bank—King Edward did not find a bridge that he could capture and repair quickly until he had reached a point perilously close to the French capital. But turning his proximity to Paris to his advantage, he sent a force to threaten the city while his engineers spent three days repairing the bridge. Distracted by the menace to his capital, King Philip protected Paris instead of preventing Edward's passage of the river. Crossing with his army and getting a good start on the French, the English king marched fifteen miles a day toward the last obstacle between him and his allies, the Somme River. The force from the Netherlands had advanced as promised, and a crossing of the Somme would place the two armies in a position either to unite and fight the French or to find refuge in friendly territory.

But crossing the Somme presented another threat, for, King Philip had also moved quickly and again blocked Edward's passage from behind an unspanned river with guarded fords. King Philip was now close to attaining his objective to trap the far-smaller English army against a river and to force it to fight. While mobilization of the militia added to the size of the already much-larger French army, the English had worn out many horses on their march and had difficulty finding food. As the French army crossed to the south side of the Somme to fight him while he was pinned against the river, King Edward led his men to the tidal estuary of Somme, where he found a place over a mile wide where the army could cross at low tide in knee-deep water. Marching his army across the ford in spite of a French blocking force of crossbowmen and cavalry, Edward barely escaped the French army closing behind him, his wagons just passing as the incoming tide prevented French pursuit.

When he had crossed the last barrier between himself and his allies, Edward found that the allied army, having met determined opposition, had retreated. Nevertheless, now with a secure line of retreat and confidence in his tactical system, the English king, a consummate tactician, decided to fight the over-whelmingly more numerous French forces. Accordingly, he drew up his army near the village of Crécy on a low hill facing the road over which the French would approach. He divided his men into three divisions, two in front and one in reserve behind. Each consisted of dismounted cavalry with longbowmen on the flanks. which meant that archers composed both the center and the flanks of the front line. The bowmen constituted about two-thirds of the 10,000 men in the English army, the dismounted heavy cavalry having the aid of a few Welsh pikemen. The English flanks were protected by Crécy on their right and Wad-icourt on their left.

Before resuming his pursuit, King Philip, determined to attack the English raiders, had marshaled his army into a number of divisions and assigned them their places where he would later form the line of battle. Having drawn 6,000 crossbowmen from his fleet and assigned them to the front rank in battle, the king had these archers march near the front of his pursuing host. But the French, expecting a long chase, were surprised in late afternoon when they came upon the English army arrayed for battle. Since it was late in the day, the prudent King Philip gave orders that he would defer action until the next morning. But the knights in his disorganized and undisciplined army insisted on an attack, even though much of the cavalry was still arriving and no infantry had come up except the crossbowmen. Unable to control the situation, King Philip assented to an attack.

The only part of the attack that conformed to the king's plan was the initial advance of the light infantry, which used their bows against the dismounted English cavalry. The leaders of the crossbowmen, skilled professionals used to serving together in the fleet, formed their men in lines for an advance toward the slope upon which the English army awaited the French attack. In spite of the loose formation characteristic of light infantry, the crossbowmen halted twice to correct their alignment. Stopping at extreme range, they shot a volley of crossbow bolts that fell just short of the forward English longbowmen. Then the English began a rapid fire with their longbows whose arrows, going downhill, fell among the crossbowmen and inflicted such serious casualties that the French bowmen began to retreat. At this, the leading French knights charged, shouting, "Away with these faint-hearted rabble! They do but block our advance." The resulting rush into the retreating infantry entangled them all, halting them under a rain of English arrows. A charge by a second group of cavalry got past the debris of the first but lost so many horses to the English arrows that they too failed to reach the English line. Through twilight and into night the French delivered perhaps a dozen more onslaughts as different groups reached the front of their unorganized mass of cavalry. They avoided the longbowmen, directing all their attacks against the dismounted cavalry, ranged six to eight ranks deep. Although some charges reached them, and the mounted men engaged in severe shock combat with those on foot, the result conformed to past experience when heavy cavalry carried out frontal attacks against well-formed, good-quality heavy infantry. In spite of the French numerical advantage of three to one, Edward, who like Hannibal or Scipio directed the battle from his vantage point atop a windmill, never used his reserve.[6]

The French suffered severe casualties in spite of the security afforded by their plate armor. The armor of the horses proved completely inadequate to protect them, and the arrows wounded or killed many horses, and falls injured many riders. But the English formation was not invulnerable. If King Philip had been able to control his ad hoc feudal army and had proved as shrewd a tactician as King Edward, he could have fought the next day and, like a Macedonian commander, used his mounted men to turn the English position by sending a large force around the village on the English left to attack the immobile enemy in the rear. In any attack, whether against front, flank, or rear, the French should have first dispersed the longbowmen. The blundering courage that carried French knights through a hail of arrows to the line of English dismounted cavalry should have put them among the bowmen whom they could have ridden down as the English cavalry had the Scottish bowmen at Falkirk or the Scottish cavalry the longbowmen at Bannockburn. Then King Philip could have brought up his crossbowmen to shoot at the dismounted English until they were vulnerable to a charge.

Since Falkirk had exhibited the vulnerability of the light infantry, the English position undoubtedly offered the longbowmen the shelter of some terrain obstacle such as the terraces now on the battlefield but not mentioned in accounts of the battle. In Palestine Richard the Lion-Hearted had alternated bowmen and pikemen, which precluded a charge by Turkish light cavalry without armor and only with swords. But since a few pikes could not have resisted an attack by the heavily armed and armored French knights, the bowmen must have had some protection from the terrain, though it might not have presented a serious barrier, since the French would preferred to capture the wealthy knights whom they could then ransom. Doubtless the spirit of the joust and tournament and the conception of battles as decided by a charge of the heavy cavalry had helped lead the undisciplined French feudal army to conduct a disastrous frontal attack instead of exploiting their greater numbers and mobility to attack the English in flank or rear.

Of course, the French could have avoided battle and used their control of the country and formidable mounted strength to exploit English weariness and their incipient logistical troubles. To devastate the country ahead of them, block their path, kill their foragers, and harry their rear would have inflicted as many casualties as a major defeat, even if they had failed to fight the English advantageously before they escaped by sea or into friendly territory. But such a Fabian strategy was too foreign for the French leaders to adopt at this stage in the war.

King Edward harvested the fruits of his victory by beginning a siege of the channel port of Calais, which his control of the land and sea enabled him to take after a year during which his outer lines of circumvallation thwarted an attempt to relieve the city. If the results of so important a victory seem disproportionately small, there was no other impression that the small English army could make on such a large, thickly populated, and competently fortified country as France. For decisive results the English had far too small a ratio of force to space and population, as long as the French king and his people continued to resist the invaders.

The Hundred Years' War: English Raids and French Persisting Strategy

Following the fall of Calais the war next consisted of eight years of fighting in Brittany and Guyenne intermingled with truces and peace negotiations. But in the fall of 1355 the English began vigorous operations, King Edward advancing inland from Calais on a brief expedition in an effort to induce the new French king, John II, to attack him. But King John, though frivolous, avaricious, and stubborn, displayed the wisdom to stay within the strong city of Amiens and confined his efforts to ravaging the country ahead of the English march, this logisitic strategy costing the French little because the English customarily laid waste the countryside themselves.

Simultaneously King Edward's son, Edward, Prince of Wales, embarked on a gigantic eastward raid from Guyenne. The young prince had first learned war nine years earlier when he accompanied his father on the Crécy campaign and, barely sixteen years of age, had commanded a wing of the English army in the battle. Though the talented prince hoped to draw the French into battle, he also planned a thorough devastation of the country. A logistic strategy aimed at diminishing the French king's resources, the raid had the political object of making the war so costly to the French that they would agree to peace. Nor did the prince overlook the economic goal of subsisting his army at French expense and bringing back substantial booty. The young prince marched from the Atlantic to the Mediterranean and back, covering 675 miles in less than two and a half months. The French armies avoided him, but he accomplished his objective of thorough desolation along his march route.

The following summer the capable Lancaster, now elevated to duke, took a small force on a raid through Normandy, replenishing the supplies of the friends of England in their besieged castles. Covering 330 miles in twenty-two days, he eluded the French king's large army and came back with considerable booty, including 2,000 horses. Soon after the duke of Lancaster's return, the Prince of Wales began a second great raid from Guyenne, this time northward toward Paris. And King John of France moved south, determined to catch and fight this destructive raider.

The French had pondered the English tactics at Crécy and had applied, on at least two occasions, their remedy of dismounting most of their heavy cavalry so as to attack the English on foot. Though heavy infantry had little if any advantage over heavy cavalry in attacking defending heavy infantry, dismounting did keep vulnerable horses from the reach of the arrows of the English long-bowmen. Since the knights' plate armor usually turned aside most arrows, they could successfully close with the English dismounted infantry. For the second feature of their new tactics they relied on their heavy cavalry, some of which remained mounted to attack the bowmen.

The French had tried these new ideas in several small battles but with mixed results. At Mauron in 1352 the mounted force had driven the archers on one flank into a wood, but since they had limited the attack on the archers to one flank only, they had lost the battle by the defeat of their center and other flank. But the new tactics, which would receive another trial against the Prince of Wales, still envisioned a frontal attack. Understanding light infantry's vulnerability to heavy cavalry, the French failed to grasp the role given heavy cavalry by the ancients; they could understand the comparative merits of different weapon systems but could not sufficiently divest themselves of the idea of a frontal attack to comprehend the exploitation of cavalry's mobility and ease of deployment to attack the enemy's weakness, the flanks and rear. Instead, they reduced their vulnerability to arrows by dismounting most of the heavy cavalry and sought to use the remaining mounted portion to attack the longbowmen.

When the Prince of Wales made his raid as far north as Tours on the Loire River, King John, having assembled a huge army, overtook the slow-moving, booty-laden raiders at Poitiers as they marched back to Guyenne. With a vastly stronger army the inept king had determined to attack the English army, even though it had taken up a strong position. Following the now-settled English doctrine, the Prince of Wales dismounted his cavalry and deployed his archers on the flanks and in gaps in his line. A depression covered his left flank, some carts and a ditch his right. The front of his position had good protection from a strong hedge pierced only by two roads, one of which the English blocked. The archers used this hedge as a sheltered position from which to shoot at attackers.

King John divided his army into four divisions, ranged one behind the other. The first remained mounted and, together with an advanced party of 300 knights, was to attack the longbowmen. The king planned for the dismounted cavalry to follow and attack the English.

But the battle proved to be a fiasco for the French. The initial mounted attack lost its horses to arrows, for it could not get past the archer-lined hedge. The attack of the first foot division, aided by infantry and crossbowmen, failed to defeat the English dismounted cavalry, though the combat exhausted the English. A historian of the time described the English after the attack: "Some were carrying the wounded to the rear and laying them under the shelter of trees and thickets, others were replacing their broken swords and lances from the spoils of the slain; the archers were trying to replenish their stock of arrows even pulling them out of the bodies of the dead and wounded. There was no one who was not either hurt or utterly worn out with the battle, save only the reserve of four hundred men whom Edward still kept about his standard."[7]

When the next French division fled without attacking, Prince Edward determined to take the offensive against the last French detachment, commanded by King John himself. After a struggle at close quarters in which the bowmen participated as heavy infantry, the French gave way when a very small force, sent by Edward on a wide turning circuit, came in on the French flank and rear. The French lost 2,000 of their heavy cavalry, including their king taken prisoner. The foot attack had proven more effective than a mounted one, but the plate armor, which gave protection from arrows, made walking difficult and running impossible. It eliminated every trace of agility for a man already cumbersome when mounted.

Following his victory, Prince Edward resumed his march to Guyenne, returning with the booty of his raid. Though the battle had no military impact on the course of the war, the capture of the French king did prove a valuable prize and a two-year truce followed while the English negotiated with the captive king.

When the government, under John's astute son, the future King Charles V, as regent, refused a treaty agreed to by King John, King Edward of England made one last raid. In the fall of 1359, when he marched into France with a large army, Edward refrained from devasting the country in an attempt to win the French over to accepting him as their king. Following Charles's strategy, the French armies stayed in their cities, and Edward had no plans for long sieges. When Rheims refused to surrender to him, he abandoned his efforts to win over the French and resumed his devastations on a winter raid that carried him east of Paris and back to that city, where he remained only a short while, perhaps because the determined Charles had ruined the country in advance of the English. But soon Edward and Charles agreed on a peace that gave the English Calais and adjacent territory in northwestern France as well as greatly expanded English dominions in the Guyenne region. Yet war soon resumed with the French led by a new king, the patient, shrewd Charles. Edward continued to direct the English war effort.

In a war with so large a country as France, the English strategy basically had relied on raids to extract political concessions. The alternative, persisting strategy to occupy the country, would have taken years of sieges. French pursuit of and attacks on raiding armies had led to the great English victories of Crécy and Poitiers, but these, though inflicting heavy casualties on the French, had not taken any castles or walled towns nor prevented the French from assembling new armies. The thousands of square miles and the millions of people of France swallowed up English armies of 10,000 and even 20,000 men. The English had an inadequate ratio of force to French space and population and had no solution to the defensive strength of fortifications.

The renewed war centered in the south, where the population of the newly English areas, including the nobility, were hostile. King Charles exploited this in a strategy reminiscent of Fabius' against Hannibal. Like the Romans in dealing with Hannibal, Charles's French commander, du Guesclin, avoided battles, an easy task since the English doctrine depended entirely on the enemy's making a frontal attack on a strong defensive array. Du Guesclin, unprepossessing in appearance but experienced and brave, capably executed the sophisticated strategy of his crafty and persevering king. Instead of seeking battle with the English, du Guesclin strengthened the towns and castles and relied on these fortifications while taking the offensive and besieging isolated English posts or English-held towns where the population favored the French. But since the French lacked the Roman proficiency in engineering and siegecraft, they had to raise many sieges on the approach of the English. The more numerous French, however, displayed persistence with sieges and in harrying English forces on the march and so gradually encroached on English territory in Guyenne.

Like Hannibal, the English wanted more victorious battles and fell back on their raiding strategy to provoke the French into a fight and to diminish their resources and put pressure on the French for political concessions. The greatest of these raids went from Calais on the northern coast to the port of Bordeaux in the south. The English marched 1,000 miles in five months, laying waste the countryside but losing half their army. Though humiliated as well as harmed, the French avoided battle. In this raid and four others, the French, like the Romans shadowing Hannibal, followed the raiders, catching foragers, stragglers, and looters. After a decade of renewed war, the French regained mastery of the sea and their strategy not only recovered the lost territory in the south but also seriously encroached on territory in Guyenne that had been English for two centuries. Operations then ended in peace between countries exhausted by war and the plague.

English Persisting Strategy in the Last Phase of the Hundred Years' War

When war resumed in 1415, the situation favored England. France was distracted by factions during the long rule of an insane king, while in King Henry V the English had an important soldier who surpassed in abilities his great-grandfathers, Edward III and the duke of Lancaster. This cultured, devout, and temperate soldier and statesman strengthened the navy and regained supremacy at sea. He had a comprehensive strategy for the conquest of France, which he began in August 1415 when he landed a large army at the mouth of the Seine and besieged the strongly fortified port of Harfleur, his artillery helping him capture the town in five weeks. Though this siege constituted the first step in King Henry's plan of systematic conquest, he undertook to conduct a raid by marching his small army through northwestern France to return to England from the port of Calais. As a part of his new strategy the king instructed his men to commit no depredations, so as not to alienate his potential subjects. The principal purposes of the raid must have been to humiliate the French and end the campaign with some éclat. King Henry, with only 1,000 heavy cavalry and 5,000 light infantry, seemed anxious to avoid battle with the much larger French force in the field against him. His march would repeat that of Edward III before the Battle of Crécy, in that the French army sought to catch the English army against a river.

Consciously aiming to repeat the successful part of Edward's Crécy march, Henry planned to cross the Somme by the tidal ford in the estuary. Finding it defended by the French, he marched upstream looking for a passage, just as his great-grandfather had had to do when he sought to cross the Seine in his march to Crécy. Having exhausted their rations and experiencing difficulty finding anything in the country, his men had to eat unground wheat. They were continually soaked from rain and suffered from dysentery. The French must have tried to denude the country of supplies, and if du Guesclin's strategy could have controlled French operations, only a few of Henry's men would have reached Calais. The English had to march far up the Somme before they found an inadequately defended crossing. But a few days later, at the village of Agincourt, the French army blocked the English route to Calais.

Henry had few heavy cavalry to dismount, so he drew up his army in a defensive position with archers holding much of the 700-yard front. Woods protected each flank, and the archers covered themselves with a line of long wooden stakes pointed toward the enemy. In spite of his weakness in heavy cavalry, Henry had a strong defensive position. The French meanwhile had a chance to apply logistic strategy by allowing the English to sit in their position until hunger forced them to forage, attack, or try to resume their march.

But the French commander, the representative of the insane king, lacked the authority to restrain his army's numerous powerful feudal lords, who insisted that they could not allow themselves to be defied by the minute English army, largely composed of socially inferior bowmen. So the French arrayed themselves for attack, using two lines of dismounted cavalry, with a third, in the rear, still on horseback. In front, on each flank of the French army, the commander posted a small mounted group to charge the longbowmen on the English flanks. Even though King Henry moved his line forward some distance toward the French, inviting their attack, two factors presented almost insuperable complications for the French in carrying out an advance: the heavy cavalrymen had great difficulty functioning as heavy infantry because of the weight of their plate armor, and the heavy rain had created ankle-deep mud on the approach to the English position.

While the French dismounted men finally moved forward, the initial cavalry attack against the archers collapsed completely. The small number of men who took part, probably about 150 on each flank, and their slow advance because of the mud enabled the longbowmen to halt the horsemen: in the words of a contemporary historian, "[The French] horses were so wounded by the arrows that they were unmanageable." By the time the cavalry attack failed, the first line of French dismounted cavalry had approached the English line, hindered by their armor, the mud, and the hail of arrows. Though the longbowmen occupied part of the English line, the French knights concentrated their assault upon their social equals—and ransom prospects—the English dismounted cavalry. But King Henry ordered his muscular and agile archers into the fight, who "quitted their stakes, threw their bows and arrows on the ground and seizing their swords, axes, and other weapons, sallied out upon" the armored Frenchmen, and, entering breaks in their line, "killed and disabled the French . . . and met with little or no resistance" from fatigued and overweighted knights virtually mired in the mud.[8]

The success in shock combat of the English light infantry did not depend only on the French cavalry's poor performance as heavy infantry. Though lacking shields and without much training with their swords and axes, the English bowmen had a steel cap and a breastplate or a quilted garment for torso protection. Thus they readily proved a match for the dismounted cavalry who, even if unwounded, once they fell could not rise without assistance. The English defeated the attack of the first two French lines, killing many and acquiring large numbers of prisoners immobilized on the ground. And the French suffered particularly heavy casualties because their dismounted knights could not flee from the nimble English bowmen. The third French line, which had remained mounted, did not attempt to attack, though many lingered at a distance while the English sorted the fallen French into the living and the dead. But the combination of a raid on the English camp by some local militia and the impression that the remains of the third line were about to attack caused the English to kill many of their prisoners. The king ordered this action, fearing that the French might attack, recapture the fallen knights, and returning many of them to action well rested from their time prone in the mud. But no attack materialized, and the next day the king, twenty-eight years of age, marched toward Calais with 2,000 prisoners.

Other than raise English morale and enthusiasm for the war, the victory did nothing immediately to facilitate King Henry's strategy of systematic conquest of French territory, but the following year he began in Normandy, taking towns and castles one by one. Rival factions in a country with an insane king on the throne kept the French from intervening even when Henry besieged Rouen, the capital of Normandy. This large city, defended by strong walls five miles in circumference, succumbed to starvation when supplies conveyed by water from England enabled the king to keep his army in position for five months while paying his troops and restraining their looting. By 1419 Henry had completed the conquest of Normandy, collected large sums from cities, like Rouen, which had resisted him, and sought to reconcile the Normans to his rule by conserving their institutions. Political support within France soon allowed the English to dominate more territory, including the city of Paris, but then they had extended themselves as far as their means and French opposition would permit. The great space of France compared with British resources precluded more extensive conquests as long as so many Frenchmen so strongly resisted the English king's claim to the throne of France.

Then, inspired by Joan of Arc, the French counterattacked and gradually won back northern France. The new king, Charles VII, lacked intellectual vigor and physical prowess, but, finally served by wise advisors and influenced by a capable mistress, he provided good guidance to the sustained French counteroffensive. This involved a process of sieges, one accelerated by improvements in artillery. The French learned to avoid frontal assaults, waiting to attack the English on the march, in camp, or when they could not protect their flanks. As the besiegers, the French had opportunities to exploit the power of the defense, and the English had to assume the offensive.

The English owed their successes in the long war with France to their essentially professional army. Though not a standing army, continuity in personnel and frequent campaigning had given it many of the characteristics of a permanent force. Adequate funds to pay the troops, a good understanding of logisitics, and water communications from their bases also contributed to English victories. For most of the century-long conflict the English had able and experienced leaders who grasped the significance of a reserve, understood the power of the defense, acted on the principle of winning with the least effort, and usually comprehended that a commander must direct the battle rather than lead his troops.

Although the rapid, powerful, and accurate shooting of the longbowmen constituted almost a secret weapon, English success did not depend on this especially effective light-infantry weapon system. The joint use of light and heavy infantry provides the best combination for the defense, the heavy infantry withstanding heavy cavalry and the light infantry outshooting the light cavalry. Against an attack by a force of similar composition, these two weapon systems have the advantage of the defensive, including choice of ground and the ability to erect hasty defenses or, with enough time, field fortifications. In their three big battles with the French, the English always chose uphill positions with covered flanks and protected their bowmen with natural or artifical obstacles. Except at Crécy, enough dismounted cavalry could have withstood the French attacks if they had made the most of the advantages of the defense. At Crécy the longbowmen, who defeated the French crossbowmen, seemed essential. Yet even there, had the English lacked their superior light infantry, a charge by a few of their re-mounted heavy cavalry would have dispersed the slow-shooting crossbowmen.

As Henry V's risky march to Agincourt reveals, both English tactics and strategy counted on the French exemplifying the weaknesses of the unorganized feudal army and the flaws in French medieval operational concepts. The Agin-court campaign clearly shows that the English tactical system depended on the enemy's making the blunder of attacking in front. If the enemy failed to oblige, English doctrine had no offensive formula. In their own civil wars the English had no better idea than for the archers to shoot at each other and the dismounted cavalry to close in a frontal attack. Clearly their tactical methods would have failed against the ancient masters of the art of war. In spite of their emphasis on light infantry, even the English were in one way still prisoners of the medieval concept of the primacy of the heavy cavalryman. They had pikemen mounted on nags for strategic mobility, and they could readily have substituted them for dismounted heavy cavalrymen. Since a mounted pikeman cost less than half a heavy cavalryman and less than a quarter of an elite knight, the English could easily have used mounted pikemen for half of their heavy cavalry. But, though present on at least one occasion, they did not use their pikemen in the front line of battle.

In their strategy of extracting concessions by raids and then persisting by slow, systematic conquest, the English followed the ideas of the time and did as well as could be expected as long as the French remained loyal to their monarch and institutions. The English did not have large armies because they had a small population and, like all medieval economies, had only an insignificant surplus production to devote to war. In the vast area of France and among the millions of Frenchmen, the English armies lacked an adequate ratio of force to space. Had they used their tactical advantage and the protection offered by their insular position to apply a thoroughly Turkish-Mongolian strategy of destruction, massacre, and terrorism, they might have won, but such a strategy was unthink-able against fellow Christians.

In the tactical and strategic supremacy of fortified towns the Hundred Years' War showed the primacy of the defensive in medieval warfare. The enormous space of France constituted a powerful element in the strategic defensive, as illustrated by the failure of the English raids to do more than extract territorial concessions and the inability of the English, when they resorted to the persisting strategy of territorial conquest, to have adequate men to garrison very much of France. The success of the French use of Fabian strategy to repel the English in Guyenne and their ability to drive the English from the north without offensive battles also exhibited the strength of a defensive based on popular support. The virtually inconsequential strategic results that followed from the major English victories further confirm the strength of the strategic defense when supported by castles and fortified cities, a huge country, and an adequately determined political opposition. Crécy, Poitiers, and Agincourt had only tactical importance—the attrition that resulted—and could have no more value unless the English had only modest political objectives. For battles to have more of a result, either the losers must have the political weakness of Darius III when defeated by Alexander or the victor must destroy the bulk of a country's army in the battle, as at the Byzantine defeat at Manzikert. Of course, a lesser victory than Manzikert could lead to a momentous retreat and thus help implement a persisting strategy. And the attrition of such a lesser victory could change the balance of forces and facilitate subsequent successes by the victor.

But the lack of decisiveness of battles, the power of the fortified tactical defense, and the effectiveness of the Fabian strategy, all of which provided components of the strength of the strategic defense, did not distinguish medieval from ancient warfare. The length of time consumed in the systematic conquests of the Romans reflected patient efforts to overcome the power of the defense when the defenders had available ample space and a measure of political unity. Even the resilience of the Roman Empire shows this strategic defensive strength, illustrated in its successful defense after Hannibal's overwhelming tactical victories and attrition and the long time that barbarian invaders required to conquer territory from unwarlike inhabitants whose professional armies often engaged in civil wars.

The Experience of the English Tactical System in Spain

The English tactics, developed in fighting on their Welsh and Scottish frontiers, differed markedly from those evolved as the Christians gradually drove the Moslems from Spain. Though the medieval heavy cavalry had a premier place in the Spanish military system, the terrain gave a more significant role to the infantry. Most armed themselves with pikes, but some had sword and shield and, though lacking the Roman organization, fought as individuals rather than in a serried mass. The strategy of raids and constant irregular combat also affected cavalry, causing the development of a light cavalry called genetours. Proteced by a steel cap and mail shirt, the genetour carried two javelins and his sword. Though he had versatility and could fight at close quarters, the genetour usually chose to keep his distance and rely on his javelin.

In 1367 the veteran campaigner, Edward, Prince of Wales, invaded Spain from southern France to intervene in support of a claimant to the Spanish throne. When King Henry II of Spain blocked the invasion route, the Prince of Wales found another one and, by marching quickly, forced back the Spanish forces and admitted the prince's army to Spain. Insecure on his throne, King Henry felt obliged to fight and, strong in cavalry, resolved to take the offensive when he had moved to face the prince's army.

For the Spaniards to attack suited the prince, and near Navarette he used English tactics by dividing his dismounted cavalry into three successive lines and distributing his longbowmen among all three of these lines. King Henry, with French support and following a version of French tactics, composed his first line of dismounted heavy cavalry and a few crossbowmen, following it with a line of mounted cavalry and genetours aided by a few crossbowmen. The third line consisted of militia infantry. Henry opened his attack with the advance of his dismounted cavalry, which became locked in combat with the prince's first line. Then, taking advantage of Prince Edward's open flank, he advanced with his genetours to assault Edward's rear lines. But the English bowmen drove off the javelin-armed light cavalry more easily than Crusader crossbowmen had beaten off horse archers. Edward then advanced his second and third lines and surrounded King Henry's first line, still locked in dismounted combat with the prince's first line. The charge of King Henry's remaining heavy cavalry failed to break Prince Edward's dismounted knights, save his own first line from defeat, or prevent the rout of the Spanish army. King Henry's mounted forces suffered few casualties, but he lost heavily in infantry, including many drowned in the river behind the battlefield.

An even simpler example of the success of light infantry against light cavalry occurred at Aljubarotta in 1385 when the Portugese, with English assistance and advice, resisted a Spanish invasion. The Portugese dismounted their heavy cavalry and stationed their crossbowmen and English longbowmen behind hastily erected barriers on the flanks. This array stopped both dismounted and mounted Spanish attacks, the genetours suffering heavily from the light infantry's arrows. Other cavalry sent to turn the flanks became lost in the ravines of the rugged country and never accomplished their mission. As in the cases of the French against the English, more emphasis on the flanks and less on a frontal attack could have given the superior Spanish army victory.

The Wagenburg

In the early fifteenth century a Russian tactical innovation made a brief appearance in Europe. To combat the Mongolian light cavalry on the steppes, the Russians used wagons that drew together in a circle upon the approach of the enemy, thus making a fort to resist a cavalry charge and to provide cover for their bowmen to shoot at the Mongols. Called a wagenburg when the Czechs used it in their early fifteenth century rebellion against their king, it proved an admirable device for resisting the charge of heavy cavalry and an excellent platform for the use of a small cannon. Limited by terrain and its severely defensive mission, the wagenburg had only two decades of use but did help to interest the Germans in the use of handguns.

The Swiss Heavy Infantry

Neither the wagenburg nor the genetours had lasting influence in Europe, even though Europeans had begun to see the strategic value of light cavalry. The French king had no more success than the Scots in fostering the longbow; the long practice required to attain the necessary strength and skill helped preclude its spread beyond southern Wales and England. Only the English and French revival of the old practice of heavy cavalry's fighting dismounted received attention and emulation elsewhere. But the Swiss evolved a heavy infantry that rivaled the best of the ancients and had a profound effect on European warfare.

Fighting on foot came naturally to the impoverished mountaineers, suiting both their terrain and resources. Separated by mountains into small valley communities, the Swiss had rural and civic militias much like the small city-states of Greece and Italy. Without body armor or shields, they fought with a halberd, an axe with an eight-foot handle that had a point for use as a short pike and a spike opposite the axe blade, which also served as a hook to snag a horseman's reins or to pull down the rider.

As early as 1315 at Morgarten they demonstrated that their militias could defend their valleys against the heavy cavalry of their Austrian neighbors. Blocking with a wall the road between a forested mountain slope and a lake, the Swiss commander hid most of his men on the wooded slope until Duke Leopold's mounted column of Austrian heavy cavalry, stopped by the wall, halted along the road. Then the Swiss, springing their ambush, charged from the woods with their halberds, forcing the mounted cavalrymen to fight on the defensive with the lake at their backs. The heavy cavalry on the defensive against heavy infantry quickly lost the combat, the unassailed rear of the mounted column fleeing as the Swiss defeated the leading elements.

Aided by terrain, tactical surprise, and the preponderance of their heavy-infantry weapon system, the Swiss could have won with very little organization. But like the Greeks and Romans they had developed a simple, distinctive heavy-infantry doctrine and drilled themselves thoroughly in its application. Unlike the linear systems of the ancients, the Swiss adopted a formation similar to a solid square. If a formation had fifty ranks and fifty files, its front on the ground had twice its depth, because men require about three feet side by side but only a foot and a half back to front. Such a fifty-by-fifty formation contained 2,500 men and occupied a front of fifty yards and a depth of twenty-five. To cover a square of ground, a formation required twice as many ranks as files. A front of thirty-five men and a depth of seventy contained almost 2,500 men and formed a square of about thirty-five yards. Swiss formations probably did not deviate far from the range represented by these squares.

Even 2,500 heavy infantrymen, thus formed, could keep their formation and respond to orders because the Swiss subdivided their squares into files. The file leaders formed the front rank, and with no more than fifty men abreast these leaders could usually keep shoulder to shoulder with one another, maintain their short front in alignment, and avoid any gaps in their line. The men in the files, simply following the men ahead, could keep the square together without great difficulty. Just as a small Roman maniple could avoid gaps, so also could a well-drilled Swiss square maintain the integrity of its formation.

But, unlike the Romans, the Swiss did not form a line, usually arraying in three squares. They dealt with the problem of flank protection by drilling their square to resist attacks in flank or rear by halting and leveling their pikes in all directions. Lacking a line, the Swiss needed no flank protection because their squares had an all-around defense when halted. But, unlike usually immobile medieval heavy infantry, the Swiss stressed the offensive, their communities drilling their squares until they could move quickly in formation. Rapid movement with large formations required discipline and drill, but the marching of squares presented a task far easier than moving a line with its irresistible tendency to develop gaps and lose its alignment.

In 1339 at Laupen the Swiss militia demonstrated that it could win on an open field. Resisting the advance of heavy cavalry supported by feudal militia, the Swiss formed in two squares and took a position on a hill. The attacking cavalry picked the gentler slope, assigning the infantry the steeper advance. As the two bodies moved uphill against the Swiss, their two squares charged their separate opponents. The classic downhill charge routed the infantry, but the skilled regulars of the cavalry fell back, divided, and charged the Swiss square in flank and rear as well as in front. The Swiss, prepared for this eventuality, halted and faced their formation in all four directions. As the cavalry attacked the immobile square on all four sides, the other Swiss square, having defeated the infantry, kept its formation, marched to the rescue of the square beset by the cavalry, and quickly routed the enemy. The action clearly exhibited the mobility and the capacity for all-around defense of the Swiss square. But an all-around defense required a halt, as the Persians knew when their doctrine called for cavalry attacks on the flanks to keep Greek heavy infantry from closing with their light infantry.

Though the unarmored Swiss with their halberds had succeeded against heavy cavalry, they had difficulty in subsequent struggles, narrowly defeating Austrian heavy cavalry that had dismounted some of their men to fight. Later, the Swiss were glad to retreat when they fought an Italian force that used crossbowmen and dismounted its whole force of heavy cavalry. In spite of their bravery, discipline, and morale, the unarmored Swiss had trouble with halberds against their armored opponents.

The Swiss responded to the need to meet heavy cavalry in the open by adopting, gradually, a steel cap and breastplate and, more quickly and importantly, a pike with a long steel head. Even a short pike was a hard weapon to handle because once pikemen have leveled their pikes, they could not easily change direction. They held leveled pikes with two hands at shoulder level pointing slightly downward. But, even with the pike, the Swiss managed to retain the mobility on the field that characterized their halberd-armed formations. Part of their success came from the adoption of the pike as a national weapon, even children practicing with miniature pikes. But they retained in their squares some men armed with halberds. They stationed these more versatile soldiers in the center of the square, where they could combat any cavalry or infantry that breached the pike wall and from which the halberdiers could sally to attack an opponent's flank or rear.

In addition to the drill, which gave mobility to their square, the Swiss had a coherence lacking in most other units of the day. Since each group came from the same valley, town, or guild, the members knew one another and had drilled together often. Though still militia, they had some of the cohesion of the professional armies of ancient times, a unit spirit, and drill that the decentralized feudal military system lacked, even in many mercenary units. Before a campaign began, the Swiss marshaled their forces in the same order for marching and for battle, and so they moved rapidly and could go into action quickly. Usually they formed for battle in three squares, using an echelon arrangement of keeping the center square ahead of those on the flank. Though this made a virtue of the difficulty of keeping the formations aligned, the method protected at least one flank of the foremost unit and provided an attack composed of successive shocks. And, unlike most medieval pikemen, the Swiss believed in the offensive. Rarely did they receive an attack, preferring to advance against their opponent with a celerity always startling for such apparently unwieldy formations.

As the Swiss expanded the number of communities belonging to their federation, they began to have an importance beyond the confines of their mountain sphere. In 1444 they made a profound impression when outnumbered by as much as fifteen to one, they attacked a French army. French cavalry assaults on the flanks halted the Swiss, just as had Narses's threat of a cavalry charge stopped the Franks at Casalinum in 554. Then the French used their crossbowmen against the immobile Swiss mass. But the disciplined and confident Swiss stood their ground against alternating charges and showers of crossbow bolts until, at great cost, the French killed them all.

The Swiss, however, established their prestige by defeating Charles the Rash, duke of Burgundy, in three battles in less than a year, killing the duke in the third, his head split by a halberd stroke. In fact, the Swiss provided the military opposition that defeated the duke's ambitious plans to expand his dominions. Charles, a man of some culture and not lacking in ability, had assembled a large army to which in 1476 the town of Granson capitulated. But Charles showed his ruthless nature when he killed the garrison by hanging and drowning.

A few days later the brave duke faced the Swiss in a battle in which he, with his heterogeneous and unarticulated army of mercenaries from every nation, could neither match the discipline of the Swiss nor cope with the élan of their assault. After repulsing two cavalry charges, the Swiss advanced, and Charles's army, instead of responding to his orders to envelop the enemy, panicked and fled. Three months later, having formed his army into eight divisions and exercised them together, Charles met the Swiss at Morat, where he dug himself into a powerful defensive position. But the impetuous and well-coordinated attack of the three Swiss squares broke through Charles's defenses when the duke, thinking the Swiss would not attack, had allowed the bulk of his men to return to their camp. The Swiss defeated Charles's men, who entered the battle piecemeal, and captured the duke's artillery and much valuable booty. The following winter at Nancy two Swiss columns attacked in front while the third, having made a round-about movement through a wood, attacked the flank, routing Charles's army.

The Swiss thus acquired a reputation for invincibility, a conviction they shared, making them even more confident, determined, and formidable. But, unlike the English longbow, the Swiss heavy infantry system did not remain a monopoly of the originators. The Swiss willingly hired themselves as mercenaries and enrolled in the French and other European armies. But spending time as mercenaries did not at all dilute their essentially Swiss character; they continued to represent the same communities and to serve in their own way under their own leaders, thus losing none of their significant elements of morale, cohesion, and practice in drilling together.

The Swiss had created heavy infantry that could do more than engage in sieges or in an immobile formation passively resist a cavalry attack. Disciplined and moderately articulated, a heavy infantry capable of offensive maneuvers had returned to the battlefield. But the Swiss would not be the only source of such infantry because other nations developed their own pikemen, modeled on the Swiss. The Germans had the most success, with their formidable Landsknechts who also fought abroad as mercenaries. But without the community militia background and rarely kept together under arms for a long period, foreign infantry, even the Landsknechts, never achieved the morale, cohesion, or drill and mobility of the Swiss.

The Least Effort Warfare of the Italian Condottieri

Although they had occasional clashes with the Swiss, the Italians, with no major land frontier with any people who had a different military system, fought among themselves: the principal cities of the north contended with each other, with the papal states centered at Rome, and with the southern Italian kingdom whose capital became Naples. Having developed commerce, industry, and a flourishing money economy, the northern cities found it easier to pay soldiers than trust to obligated service. Just as the Greeks and Romans abandoned their militias as they engaged in essentially continuous warfare, the Italians came to employ professionals almost exclusively. But, instead of a state-owned army on the Roman model, the Italians used mercenary leaders with whom they made a

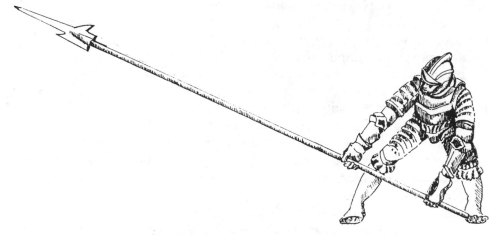

Illustration 3.3. Heavy Infantryman

contract (*condotta* in Italian) to supply and command a certain number of troops. Called *condottieri*, these professionals initially had contracts for a year or less and often would fight on different sides in different years. A desire for dependability led to the emergence of longer term contracts until by the middle of the fifteenth century the principal *condottieri* had become essentially permanent employees of a single state.

But part of the forces continued to follow the mercenary model of employing a *condottiere* captain and his company. Not a tactical unit, a company could be as small as a dozen or as large as a thousand. The captain, both a tactical leader and a business entrepreneur, raised men and secured contracts based on his reputation as a commander, his ability to manage his company, and his capital. Like other businessmen, captains often inherited companies from their fathers or fathers-in-law. For a long time they competed in a market in which they sold their skills as commanders and the quality of their troops. Naturally their employers often suspected, sometimes correctly, that their mercenary leaders deliberately avoided battles and casualties and that they prolonged a war to continue their employment. Cities also often attempted, sometimes successfully, to engage their enemy's commander as the leader of their own forces.

The desire for greater loyalty, which had induced the states to offer continuous service, involved creating peacetime armed forces. Rather than waiting until war broke out to hire an army, by the mid-fifteenth century Italian states not only had permanent commanders but also the nucleus of a force that they could expand by hiring more companies. The same motives that had inspired the cities to create long-term contracts and essentially permanent mercenary forces also led the Italians to establish gradually separate state forces headed by their own officials and composed of soldiers employed as individuals rather than as *condottieri*. By the late fifteenth century about half of the peacetime forces consisted of state employees. In addition, governments had created civilian military administrations to make contracts, disperse money, provide for supplies, and see to most of the noncombat aspects of the armed forces. The Italians were not innovators in respect to their increasingly state-owned and bureaucratic army organization, but their methods and their level of sophistication were representative of the best Europe had developed out of the feudal and mercenary military system characteristic of the Middle Ages.

In tactics the Italians remained essentially medieval in their reliance on heavy cavalry. Since, by the mid-fifteenth century, their excellent armorers made complete suits of plate armor that weighed only fifty pounds, the Italians had brought the heavy-cavalry weapon system to a high state of perfection. Though the *condottieri* had added some light cavalry for scouting and foraging, they had none that could function tactically. Their infantry consisted of equal proportions of crossbowmen, pikemen, and shield bearers, men who carried a very large shield that rested on the ground and provided protection for the other infantry. Properly mingled together behind the wall of big shields, the Italian infantry could resist any attack. But since such an array had even less mobility than most medieval infantry and since the professional soldiers of Italy refused to charge such a formation, an infantry without any capability for maneuver could play only a small role except for sieges. On the battlefield this formation largely constituted a position behind which the cavalry could rally, preparatory to a renewed effort.

By the mid-fifteenth century logistics had improved so that armies did not have to move every few days to a new source of supplies. This change enabled commanders to adopt field fortifications, devalued the shield bearer, and gave rise to the occasional use of some heavy infantry armed with swords and shields.

Italian warfare had reached a sophisticated level. The strategy of Italian warfare was typically medieval in its trust in the defensive power of fortifications, and it also employed sieges and devastation of enemy territory. Yet in spite of a high ratio of force to space, Italian wars lacked decisiveness, the protracted operations clearly exhibiting the preponderance of the defense that results when both sides have the same mixture of weapon systems. Implicitly grasping this, commanders avoided frontal attacks and concentrated on surprise attacks, ambushes, or the use of rapid marches to catch another at a disadvantage or backed against an obstacle. The use of a multitude of spies and the development of intelligence procedures resulted from the conditions also caused generals to bank on strong positions, field fortifications, and the elaboration of logistic strategy, such as poisoning wells. Armies became thoroughly organized, with squadrons of 75 to 150 cavalry often incorporated into units of eight to ten squadrons called columns. Commanders stressed the maneuverability of their cavalry on the battlefield and always provided a reserve.

Such competence and sophistication meant that battles happened rarely and often only after careful calculation of the probabilities of success and the costs of defeat. A good example occurred in 1448 when the crafty, ambitious, and skillful Francesco Sforza, leading the forces of Milan, besieged the Venetian town of Caravaggio. He faced another noted *condottiere*, the equally capable Michele Attendolo, called Micheletto because of his small size. When Attendolo arrived with the Venetian army to raise the siege, he halted nearby to assess the situation. Sforza's army covered the siege from a strongly fortified camp, and the little town could not long hold out against the artillery of the attackers. On the other hand, the town itself had little importance, and saving it could not justify the risk of defeat and the serious casualties that accompanied the loss of a battle. In addition, Attendolo's loss could seriously damage his own company, harm his personal business, and probably not only deprive him of his contract with Venice but also cause him difficulty in finding another.

But since the campaigning season had almost ended, Attendolo realized that his employers expected action and that a decisive victory could have a significant political result: the overthrow of the republican regime in Milan. He decided to attack when two competent subordinates reported that careful reconnaissance had shown that cavalry could get through the marshy forest that Sforza relied to protect one side of his camp. This changed the odds of winning and constituted the decisive factor in the shrewd and calculating Attendolo's decision to fight. The attack through the forest went well, but Sforza's forces made a determined resistance, including a cavalry attack on the Venetian rear. The battle ended in the capture of most of Attendolo's army and his discharge by the Venetians. In any event, such careful tactical appraisal and estimate of benefits set Italian warfare apart from much of that conducted elsewhere in Europe—as did the propensity of the Italian mercenary soldier to surrender when his situation looked hopeless.

Victors usually released rank-and-file prisoners after taking their weapons and horses, which saved the cost of guarding and maintaining the captured soldiers, who would be useless until they had found new equipment. This attitude, like the soldier's preference for becoming a prisoner rather than fighting against great odds, led to criticism of the whole system, including the "scientific" strategy of maneuvers, marches, entrenched camps, and battles in which prisoners predominated among the defeated's casualties. But when both sides had the identical culture and thus followed similar rules, essentially the same stalemate resulted whether or not the combatants had observed a more or less sanguinary mode of warfare. It matters little to the outcome of the conflict, for example, whether both sides release, imprison, or kill prisoners, but, to some contemporary critics, the Italian methods seemed unmartial. Other commentators alleged that there was one battle in which only a single man lost his life and that not to enemy action, but by drowning in a swamp. These characterizations lacked much foundation in fact other than the least effort strategy and a preference for taking prisoners and for surrender to death.

Perhaps the most significant aspect of Italian warfare lay in the professionalism of its leaders and in their thorough grasp of the ideas of envelopment, concentration against weaknesses, and winning with the least effort as well as their realization that frontal attacks usually failed, that reserves had a fundamental role to play, and that commanders should direct, not participate in, the battle.

Regional Tactical Systems in Conflict: The French Invasion of Italy

By the end of the fifteenth century European tactical systems had become quite diverse. Cultural factors hindered the adoption of weapons that flourished in another country. The king of France, for example, failed to induce his subjects to take up the English longbow, in part because of the reluctance of the French nobility to put such a formidable weapon in the hands of the lower classes. Therefore, much of the adoption of other weapon systems consisted of hiring foreigners, such as Swiss heavy infantry and Balkan light cavalry.

Nevertheless, all regional systems had much in common. The plate-armored heavy cavalryman remained fundamental, as did the tactic of frequently converting him into a heavy infantryman for combat. The English had demonstrated the value of light infantry on the battlefield, and though only the English had effective longbowmen, all armies had arquebusiers or crossbowmen. Heavy infantry pikemen who, usually standing immobile, could defend themselves against cavalry dominated this weapon system, but the Spanish and the Italians had heavy infantry with swords and shields, and the formidably mobile Swiss squares had spread from the mountains as the Swiss hired themselves out and imitators created infantry modeled on the Swiss system. Even light cavalry for tactical as well as strategic purposes existed in the form of the Spanish genetours, mounted crossbowmen, and arquebusiers who clumsily attempted to shoot while mounted. Along with this tactical variety existed the development of professional armies and leaders that had emancipated themselves from the hindrance of some aspects of medieval perspectives and sought to develop a scientific art of war. The French then initiated a long international war in Italy, which mixed these regional weapon systems and tactical perspectives. By the end of the sixteenth century a new combined-arms synthesis had emerged.

The source of the French-Italian wars lay in the ambitions of King Charles VIII of France. Unlike his crafty father, Louis XI, who had done so much to encompass the ruin of Charles the Rash, the young king lacked ability and judgment. Yet his imagination conceived vast projects, such as the capture of Constantinople, to which the conquest of Italy would provide a steppingstone. In 1494, when he invaded Italy, King Charles led an army far different from the feudal arrays that had met defeat at the hands of the English early in the century. Part of the troops were French regulars, formed in the last years of the Hundred Years' War; mercenaries composed most of the remainder of this formidable force. To their traditional excellence in heavy cavalry, the French had added the best artillery in Europe. Also a creation of the last years of the Hundred Years' War, French artillery, with high-quality gunners serving superlative bronze guns on wheeled carriages, had sufficient mobility to keep up with the army's march and function on the battlefield as well as in sieges. To an infantry force including large numbers of French crossbowmen, the king had added many Swiss mercenary heavy infantry. He entered Italy with 25,000 men, a huge number for that time. This army, formed in the latter years of the Hundred Years' War, represented the lessons of that war and French adaptation to the changes of the fifteenth century.

The size and excellence of the French army impressed the Italians and made it easy for King Charles to march south to his objective, Naples. With Venice neutral and the Duchy of Milan his ally, Charles moved onward and, overawing Florence and the pope, secured free passage through their territories to invade the southern Italian and Sicilian domain of the king of Naples. Unpopular with his subjects and with many of his nobility pro-French, the Neapolitan king offered only token resistance. King Charles conquered Naples, hardly having to strike a blow. Yet Charles's success frightened Milan, Venice, and the pope and also King Ferdinand and Queen Isabella of Spain and the Holy Roman Emperor, whose loosely knit empire had by then become essentially confined to Germany, Austria, and some adjacent lands. In 1495, when Charles, leaving half his army to garrison Naples, wished to return to France, he found the armies of Milan and Venice blocking his way through the Apennine Mountains. A splendid French army, but led by a king inexperienced in war, had to face a larger force of seasoned Italian soldiers under well-tested professional leadership.

The marquis of Mantua commanded the allied host. Instead of impeding or even blocking the French in the passes of the Apennines, he decided to use his numerical advantage to attack the French after they had descended from the mountains onto terrain suitable for the Italian cavalry to operate. The marquis wanted the glory of conquering the French, and the allies desired the military and political effect resulting from a serious defeat of the French. Since the French route north lay on a road running between a river and a line of hills, the marquis chose this place to attack the French on their march because he could count on the French to see that the river and the hills protected their flank and prepare for a battle in front. But the marquis, knowing that the river was so shallow that his men could easily charge across it, planned one attack on the French vanguard to halt their column while his main forces assaulted the flank of the center and rear of the French column. With perhaps 20,000 men, he outnumbered the French two to one.

But everything went wrong with the Italian plan. The French, despite King Charles's inadequacies, displayed foresight in their arrangements. Knowing that they had to fight their way through, the French had placed their formidable Swiss infantry in the vanguard and had formed their line of march so that by facing left or right they would already have formed their line of battle. They had ample time to position their line because heavy rains delayed the Italian attack across the river and forced the Italians to cross at the wrong place. The Swiss routed the forces assailing the head of the column, since the Italian light cavalry, which should have attacked the Swiss, looted the French camp instead, the belated main assault failed because the reserves remained inactive for the whole battle: the Italian plan had kept half the army in reserve, and the marquis's uncle, the only officer who could commit the reserves, was killed in the fighting. Nevertheless, the brevity of the battle—a mere quarter hour—also militated against the use of the reserve. In spite of the limited time, the Italians suffered heavy casualties, French servants killing fallen Italian heavy cavalrymen. The French continued their march after this brief battle at Fornovo.

This travesty of scientific generalship resulted from the rise in the river, the marquis's lack of experience in commanding so large an army, his leading one attack himself rather than commanding the battle, and from a plan that had too many complications for the size of force. The battle enhanced French prestige and diminished that of the Italian *condottieri*. But, except to confirm the offensive value of Swiss infantry, the battle revealed nothing about the proper use or combination of the weapon systems available to commanders at the beginning of the sixteenth century.

The Battle of Fornovo did not, however, secure the French title to Naples. The French lost the city to a sophisticated campaign by a Spanish expeditionary force led by a great soldier, Gonzalo of Córdoba, who landed on the toe of the Italian boot with 100 heavy cavalry, 500 javelin-armed genetours, and 1,500 infantry composed of a few arquebusiers and crossbowmen, men with swords and shields predominating. In their first battle the French heavy cavalry scattered Gonzalo's genetours and some of his swordsmen; the Swiss pikemen of the French force charged over his remaining Spanish swordsmen and light infantry.

The handsome and always gorgeously appareled Gonzalo had seen a decade of service in the final campaign for the conquest of Spain from the Moslems. Queen Isabella of Castile, discerning his latent capacity, had exerted her influence to secure the Italian command for a junior officer who had some of the attributes of an extravagant and apparently effete courtier. The queen made a wise decision, for Gonzalo became a renowned warrior and peerless leader of men.

After his defeat Gonzalo avoided battles, used his genetours to attack the enemy's convoys and foragers, and relied on entrenchments in his successful siege against the French forces. With the help of Spanish naval supremacy and the sympathy of the population, whom the French rule had soon alienated, Gonzalo retook Naples and compelled the French to withdraw in 1498. Though a Fabian strategy had made tactical success unnecessary, Gonzalo worked at reforming the Spanish army's combat methods. To assist his swordsmen in holding fortifications, he rapidly increased the number of arquebusiers while training men to use the pike in the Swiss manner so that, for combat in the open, he could combine his swordsmen and pikemen.

When hostilities resumed in 1503, Gonzalo, outnumbered, resisted the French in an entrenched camp with his back to the sea while his genetours attacked French supply convoys. When the French had dispersed much of their army in search of supplies, he took the offensive, seized their base at Cerignola, and prepared to meet the attack of the reconcentrated French in the open by digging a trench and heaping up a parapet. Unaware of the entrenchment because the genetours prevented reconnaissance and eager to catch Gonzalo in the open, the French promptly carried out a frontal attack. But the charging French cavalry could not pass the ditch, and the fire of the Spanish arquebusiers from the parapet stopped the infantry and killed the mounted French commander. When the attackers had halted in confusion, Gonzalo counterassaulted all along the line, with his small force of heavy cavalry coming around his flanks to join in. As the enemy retreated, his genetours inflicted additional casualties on the Swiss infantry.

When a very large French force came south to retrieve the situation, Gonzalo raided their wagons and blocked them in the inland passes until the French had exhausted the food and forage in the area and had to use the coast road to draw supplies from their fleet. But Gonzalo blocked them there also, for six rainy weeks, by fortifying the crossing of the Garigliano River. The armies suffered heavily from showers of sleet, living on ground covered with water, and a shortage of food. In the marquis of Saluzzo the French had a seasoned, knowledgeable, and vigorous commander, but he lacked the ability to maintain the morale of his men under such trying conditions.

After weeks of this grueling stalemate, Gonzalo, substituting daring for his usual circumspection, exploited the exceptional morale of his army to carry out a surprise attack against the equally cold and wet but demoralized French army. Preparing in advance the materials for a bridge, two days after Christmas Gonzalo quickly erected his bridge on the French flank, crossed his army, and routed the astonished enemy, inflicting heavy casualties and soon securing the agreement of the French commander to evacuate.

Gonzalo—Roman in his Fabian strategy, patience, reliance on fortification, use of his light cavalry genetours to implement the logistic element in his strategy, and attention to winning with the least effort—showed that the English and Italians did not have a monopoly of these qualities. He displayed brilliant generalship, sustaining the morale of his own troops and correctly assessing and exploiting the demoralization of his enemy.

Gonzalo made his lasting contribution in laying the foundation for the greatness of the Spanish army's tactical system. After his initial, and only, defeat, he largely confined his genetours to the strategic roles of reconnaissance, screening, and raiding enemy communications, though he did use them effectively in a tactical role when, in the pursuit after Cerignola, they employed to the greatest possible extent the traditional preponderance of light cavalry over heavy infantry. Realizing the need for pikemen to resist cavalry, he created his own as well as hired some Swiss. He also combined his swordsmen with the pikemen so that when the Spanish infantry later met pikemen, the swordsmen won the battle by getting under the pikes, often by raising them on their shields and closing with the pikemen with sword and shield. By increasing the number of arquebusiers, he complemented his tactic of entrenchment and created an effective light infantry. The Spaniards built upon this pike and arquebusier legacy.

Gonzalo's fairly clear perception of the interrelation of the various weapon systems placed him ahead of his time. Over thirty years of French campaigning in Italy resulted in an unprecedented number of battles in which the commanders experienced great difficulty in learning how best to use and combine the variety of weapon systems at their disposal.

The Search for a Combined-Arms Synthesis: Italian Battles, 1512–25

Italy provided the setting for the war that pitted the French against an alliance of the Spaniards and the Holy Roman Emperor; the Italian powers themselves were usually divided between the two sides. The mercenary forces included Greeks, Albanians, Africans, Swiss, Germans, Italians, and French. Italians had major command roles, and strategy owed much to *condottieri* practice and to the example of Gonzalo of Córdoba, the Italian wars enabling Europeans to assimilate the sophistication of Italian strategy. Though the English had realized the tactical primacy of the defense, they had no means of exploiting it other than to take up a strong position and count on the enemy's making the blunder of attacking in front. But fifteenth-century Italian generals, also grasping the power of the defense, especially when strengthened by field fortifications, did not rely on their equally perceptive opponents to make frontal attacks. Their strategy forced an enemy to attack by blocking his route of retreat or by besieging an important city, compelling the enemy to strike to raise the siege. Four of the five principal battles between 1512 and 1525 resulted from efforts to raise sieges: the French even began two sieges for virtually the sole purpose of bringing their elusive opponents to battle. In most instances the defender planned to exploit the advantages of entrenchments, but otherwise the battles lacked tactical consistency as the commanders sought to find the best role for the variety of tactical systems that were used in the international war for control of Italy.

At Ravenna in 1512 the Spanish army, seeking to raise a siege, dug itself in near the city to interfere with French siege operations without having to risk an offensive battle. Realizing that to act against the Spaniards he must make a frontal attack on a ditch and parapet, Gaston de Foix, the able young French commander, trusted to his excellent artillery to force the Spaniards to leave their entrenchments and attack. For two hours the hostile artilleries fired at each other, the Spaniards protecting their infantry by having them lie prone and their artillery inflicting serious casualities on the French infantry, massed in front of the Spanish field fortifications. But the enfilading fire of the French artillery finally goaded the unprotected Spanish cavalry into charging the French through a gap left in their parapet and ditch. The mobile artillery deployed on the field of battle had successfully functioned as light infantry, except that the range and power of the cannon had accomplished far more than even longbows. The cannonballs had a devastating effect on the cavalry formations, a single ball knocking down thirty-three men or horses.

When the shaken and diminished Spanish heavy cavalry charged through a narrow gap over uneven terrain, it met not stationary artillery but a countercharge of fresh French cavalry, the best in Europe. As the French horsemen drove off the Spanish, Gaston called forward his crossbowmen, supported by pikemen, with orders to shoot at a high angle over the parapet down upon the prone Spanish infantry. But the Spaniards quickly manned their parapet and drove back the French with their arquebus fire. An attack by the French army's German Landsknecht pikemen also failed, even though they crossed through the arquebus fire and enough of them scaled the parapet to give the Spanish swordsmen an opportunity to demonstrate the close-quarter advantage of sword and shield over an eighteen-foot pike. But the fortified defense demonstrated its preeminence, and the triumphant French cavalry passed thorough the gaps in the entrenched line, attacked the defending infantry in the rear, and completed the victory. The French cavalry played here the same role that the cavalry had played in Alexander's and Hannibal's battles. But much of the disciplined Spanish heavy infantry made good their retreat, defying the pursuing heavy cavalry by using the tight formations that they had learned from the Swiss.

During the retreat the brilliant but impetuous French commander, Gaston de Foix, spotted a group of Spanish pikeman marching along a raised path beside the river. When he recklessly led his staff in a charge against these men, every French soldier died in combat, Gaston of his wounds and several of his compatriots by drowning in their armor. When this same group of Spanish infantry later met a detachment of French cavalry, the Spanish leader called out—"Why meddle with us—you are not strong enough to break us—you know that you have won the battle and slaughtered our army—be content with your honour, and leave us alone." The French commander thought well of this reasoning, so reminiscent of Belisarius' advice about fighting a retreating foe, and the two parties passed without combat.[9]

At Novara in 1513 the French fought the Swiss. The victory belonged to the Swiss, with their by-then traditional methods. Realizing that the Swiss would attack to relieve the forces besieged in Novara, the French commander moved out to choose a good position in which to receive the Swiss assault. But the Swiss came at dawn, not giving the French commander time even to erect his portable wooden palisades, much less to entrench. The French did get their artillery into action and directed it against the main onslaught by a Swiss square of 6,000 men. In three minutes under artillery fire, the French cannonballs inflicted 700 casualties on the densely packed Swiss. But when the infantry reached the guns, the artillery's role ended. The Swiss quickly overcame the ill-formed and unready French pikemen and even turned against them their own artillery as they retreated. Since the Swiss defeated the infantry before the French cavalry could intervene, the cavalry retreated, knowing better than to charge Swiss pikemen. The artillery's role resembled that of Persian archers at Marathon and Plataea in that the guns did good work until the heavy infantry closed. As a missile weapon system, artillery could function as a more effective light infantry, but even the mobile guns used in the field did not begin to approach light infantry's other key attribute, mobility.

At Marignano in 1515 the French stumbled on the Persian doctrine for protecting the light infantry from the charge of the heavy infantry. In meeting an attacking line of hoplites with a motionless array of archers, the Persians had relied on cavalry charges on the flanks to make the heavy infantry halt to defend its flanks and so allow the bowmen to shower their immobilized opponents with arrows. In a two-day battle in which the promptness of the Swiss assault again precluded entrenchment, charges by French cavalry forced the Swiss formations to halt and form for all-around defense. This gave the French artillery an opportunity for prolonged fire as the cavalry and artillery alternated in attacks that defeated the Swiss. But this doctrine had limited utility because the Swiss fought alone, without cavalry or a significant force of light infantry. So simple a solution could not work against a combined-arms army.

Thwarted for a year by the adept and Fabian maneuvering of their acute adversary Prosper Colonna, the *condottiere* commander of the Spanish-Imperial forces, the French began a siege of the city of Pavia in 1522 to compel him to fight. Colonna then advanced within ten miles of Pavia, where he dug himself in at Bicocca. Lautrec, the commander of the more powerful French army, planned to cut off Colonna's supplies to force him out of his position so that they could attack him on the march, but the always belligerent and confident Swiss troops in the French army delivered an ultimatum to Lautrec. Unpaid, they demanded an immediate advance on Colonna so they could have the booty of victory they were sure would be theirs, or they threatened to return to Switzerland. Faced with the loss of most of his heavy infantry and the abandonment of the campaign, Lautrec, whose reputation probably exceeded his ability, agreed to the frontal attack on the entrenched enemy position.

The Swiss carried the main burden of the assault, dividing themselves into two squares of 4,000 each. Colonna's position consisted of a parapet behind a sunken road on which he had erected earthworks, including bastions from which his artillery could sweep both his front and the road. Four lines of arquebusiers manned the parapet, with pikemen behind them. In spite of the sogginess of the ground in front of the position, Lautrec wished to bring up his artillery and see whether he could damage the defense. But the supremely confident Swiss, impatient to launch their irresistible attack, refused to wait and promptly marched their squares against the parapet and artillery. Losing 1,000 men to the cannonballs, they reached the road, where they immediately received four volleys from the lines of arquebusiers. Stopped in the road, they continued under cannon and arquebus fire to try to scale the parapet.

The defending pikemen drove back the Swiss who got over the parapet; the Swiss fell back, with 3,000 dead. The remainder of the Swiss promptly returned home, leaving the French commander with a defeat and his army crippled by the loss of most of his heavy infantry. The exponents of field fortifications had the satisfaction of shattering the myth of Swiss invincibility. The battle also illustrated effectiveness of artillery and arquebuses when coupled with entrenchments.

The French invaded Italy again, under the leadership of their young king, Francis I. Brave, regal in bearing, a witty and affable patron of arts and letters, but frivolous and lacking in wisdom and constancy, Francis found hunting and tennis more important than the duties of a monarch.

In the winter of 1525 the French once more besieged Pavia, and the Spanish army again drew near in an attempt to raise the siege. The French, already protected by a line of contravallation, also fortified themselves on the side of the approaching Spanish army. The Spaniards dug in, too, and the two forces faced each other with entrenchments as close as forty yards apart. The departure of some mercenaries weakened the French army, and the Spanish, running out of money to pay their army, decided to attack. In a move reminiscent of Gonzalo's crossing of the Garigliano, the Spaniards broke through an unguarded wall and made a predawn march with most of their army, passed around the extreme flank of the French entrenched line, and at sunrise faced their men toward the French, converting their march formation into a line of battle at right angles to the French army. They then stood on the defensive, knowing that the French must attack to prevent them from marching past and getting astride the French line of communication with their base at Milan. Surprised and apprehensive of an attack against his dispersed and unformed army, King Francis wisely attacked immediately with his cavalry to cover the assembly and forming up of the remainder of his men. This decision resulted in a battle of successive attacks by different elements of the French army.

The Spanish army arrayed itself with its arquebusiers on the flanks and formations of heavy cavalry and Landsknecht heavy infantry in the center. King Francis himself led one of the successful charges of the French heavy cavalry against the Spanish heavy cavalry. But when he charged the two deep formations of Landsknechts, the serried wall of long pikes held off the determined French attack. The French army's Swiss pikemen made the next advance, directing their assault against the arquebusiers on the flank. Instead of running over the light infantry, the Swiss faltered before the steady fire of the arquebusiers, their attack failing, even though only a few Spanish pikemen aided the light infantry. The role of firearms and the parapet in the Swiss defeat at Bicocca explain the feebleness of the attack by the Swiss. A historian of the time wrote that after Bicocca the Swiss had gone "back to their mountains diminished in numbers, but much more diminished in audacity; for it is certain that the losses which they suffered at Bicocca so affected them that in the coming years they no longer displayed their wonted vigor."[10]

The last French effort consisted of an attack by their Landsknechts against the Spanish Landsknechts. As the two groups struggled against one another, Spanish light infantry shot at the French pikemen, and a second formation of Spanish Landsknechts struck the French in the flank. Overwhelming the French Landsknechts, the Spanish heavy infantry then dispersed the remaining French infantry, which made the last French assault of the day. The Spanish army then surrounded the courageous French king and a body of his cavalry, overwhelming them and capturing the king.

The battle increased the prestige of the arquebusiers, but not because they had resisted the charge of the Swiss. If the Swiss had displayed their usual determination or that shown by the Landsknecht pikemen on both sides, the heavy infantry would have scattered the light. But many of the Spanish arquebusiers used the traditional skirmishing tactics of the light infantry and, evading the French cavalry by seeking refuge in hedges and among the trees, kept up a steady, if slow, fire on the French cavalry and heavy infantry. The light infantry had demonstrated its effectiveness in the open as well as in entrenchments. A contemporary testified to their effectiveness, even against cavalry: "Often the most famous commanders and knights . . . were prostrated here and there in unavenged slaughter by the ignoble and common infantry."[11]

The artillery had little role in the improvised battle. The French had no plan to use guns, and the Spaniards had left most of theirs in entrenchments to keep up a distracting cannonade. The heavy infantry displayed its traditional ability to resist heavy cavalry, and the French heavy cavalry, in defeating the Spanish, again exhibited its superiority to other European cavalry. But the overthrow of their cavalry did not defeat the Spanish army; their excellent light infantry and their immovable heavy infantry held the field. The all-around defense of the blocks of pikemen enabled them to resist the victorious French cavalry, and this formation exhibited enough battlefield mobility to attack the French heavy infantry in flank.

The contest at Pavia ended a series of battles in which generals tried various mixes of new and old versions of heavy infantry, heavy cavalry, and light infantry. Although the defeat of the French and the heavy casualties in the battles from Fornovo to Pavia convinced generals to reduce sharply the number of battles in the subsequent periodic renewal of the French wars against the Spaniards and Germans, the combatants did digest the tactical lessons of the wars in Italy and developed their doctrine and organization accordingly. The Spaniards made the most successful integration of the weapon systems, and theirs had the greatest influence in Europe because their King Charles, also the Holy Roman Emperor, controlled Italy and ruled the Netherlands and the Habsburg dominions in Germany. He used Spanish, German, and Italian armies interchangeably with Spanish and Italian commanders prevailing, Spanish tactical doctrine thus virtually dominating Western Europe.

The Spanish Combined-Arms Tactics

Although the Italian wars confirmed Spain's traditional belief in the importance of infantry, they altered its weapons significantly. Having adopted the pike in southern Italy, the Spanish soon used it to replace the sword and shield entirely. They modeled their formation on the Swiss, using rectangles of pikemen numbering from 1,000 to 3,000 men. Their method of drill and organization resembled that of the Swiss, even though their squares may have lacked the mobility and verve long characteristic of the original. Instead of a consistent commitment to offensive action, the Spanish army often used its pikes as a defensive formation to resist the heavy cavalry and provide a rallying point for their own horsemen. But they did not rule out offensive action, their pikemen, like the Swiss and the German Landsknechts, having the ability to move on the battlefield and charge other infantry.

The Spaniards early abandoned the crossbow in favor of the arquebus and increased the proportion of light infantry in their army. Pavia had impressed the Spaniards with what arquebusiers could do as skirmishers. On that battlefield, which had trees, shrubs, and rough as well as smooth ground, the light infantry had displayed the individual initiative often characteristic of the light infantry of the ancients and had used the terrain to keep out of reach of the French heavy cavalry and to maintain a steady fire against the enemy's heavy cavalry and heavy infantry. The Spaniards, realizing that the sum of so many individually negligible efforts had had a major impact on the outcome of the battle, made this a salient role for their numerous arquebusiers. Whereas the English had used their longbowmen in the line of battle, the Spanish, confident of the defensive power of their pike squares, assigned their light infantry an independent role.

Yet the arquebusiers, belonging to the same unit as the pikemen, did not operate completely independently: the Spanish saw that each needed the other. In the absence of obstructed terrain, the square of pikemen provided the only place of safety where the light infantry might take refuge from the enemy's heavy cavalry. They could take a position on the flank of or behind the square, or, should the cavalry attack in flank and rear, many could find safety in the front ranks where the wall of pikes would protect them. In turn, the arquebusiers' fire could support the pikemen's defense, and the masses of the enemy's heavy infantry or the horses and men of the attacking heavy cavalry would provide fine targets for arquebus balls. The Spaniards gradually increased the proportion of arquebusiers to pikemen until, by the end of the sixteenth century, their regiments approached equal numbers of light and heavy infantry.

Soldiers and military authors gave much thought to the proper array for an army. In theory, an army formed itself before a battle by first surveying the ground and marking out locations for infantry formations that best reconciled the terrain and the available force. An officer known as the sergeant major general then calculated the size and composition of squares by using a formula or a set of tables. Knowing in advance, for example, the number of pikemen with and without body armor and the number of infantry with halberds, he could plan a square with, to illustrate, four outer ranks of pikemen with body armor, eight inner ranks of unarmored pikemen (who had cost less to hire or equip), and a core of halberdiers. To this square he could assign some arquebusiers to the front as skirmishers and others to each side, where they would form themselves in a long, loose column of four files of twelve men each. During the battle, the front ranks of the four files of arquebusiers on the sides would fire, then march to the rear to reload while the next rank moved forward to fire. In executing this drill, called a countermarch, the arquebusiers could keep up a steady, if limited, fire against any target within range.

Such ideas for the arrangement of the infantry had become universal in Europe by the latter part of the sixteenth century. This careful order of battle probably happened rarely in practice, and national and other unit distinctiveness inhibited the creation of the number and size of infantry formations that the commanders and the sergeants major general may have thought ideal under particular circumstances. But the theory of marshaling an army adequately exhibits the problems tacticians faced and the way they approached them.

The location of cavalry in this infantry array had no settled solution. But the role of the cavalry had declined in the Spanish army because the Spaniards had increased their infantry partly at the expense of it. Since a properly armored heavy cavalryman could cost four times as much as a pikeman or arquebusier, a small decrease in heavy cavalry could finance a huge addition to the infantry and bring about a dramatic alteration in the proportions between infantry and cavalry. Though a large part of their cavalry consisted of traditional full-armored lancers, the Spanish did have cavalry that performed a light cavalry's strategic duties of reconnaissance and attack on the enemy's stragglers, foragers, convoys, and logistic installations. Usually mounted arquebusiers filled this role. Because of the difficulties involved in using the arquebus while mounted, these horse arquebusiers were really mounted infantry—they usually dismounted to use their weapon. But on at least one occasion, after the Battle of Ceresole in 1544, mounted arquebusiers pursued retreating heavy infantry and, by dismounting to shoot and remounting to continue the pursuit, managed effectively to simulate the traditional Parthian or Turkish tactics of the light cavalry.

The rudiments of the new system received a trial at the Battle of Ceresole when a French army, under the young, vigorous Enghien and containing Swiss, Italian, and French mercenaries, met the emperor's Spanish-German-Italian force, commanded by Del Vasto, a solid, careful soldier. Each side had four blocks of infantry, pikemen with associated arquebusiers, which they placed in line with some of their small force of cavalry in the center and the remainder on the flanks. After four hours of skirmishing by the arquebusiers, the pattern that the battle assumed involved each force's engaging its opposite. This pitted cavalry against cavalry and infantry against infantry.

This action began when the French cavalry on the south flank charged and routed the opposing imperial cavalry and then unsuccessfully charged the adjacent infantry square. But this assault so shook the infantry that they stood fast rather than joining their adjacent Landsknechts in an attack. So, when the block of 7,000 Imperial Landsknechts advanced, they faced two squares of French infantry, one of which moved forward and attacked the Landsknechts in flank. The Imperial Landsknechts then displayed their excellent discipline and drill,

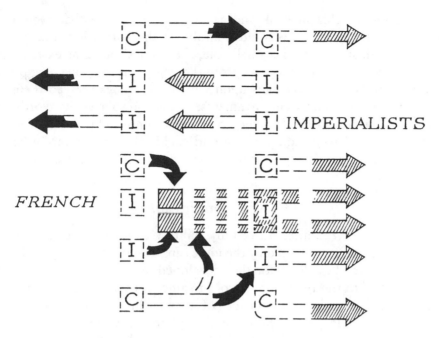

Diagram 3.1. Battle of Ceresole

dividing their formation into two parts, one for each antagonist. By the time the Landsknechts met the onslaught in flank, the French had placed arquebusiers in their second line, behind the pikemen of the first line, who, firing, shot down the first row of enemy pikemen with a volley just before contact, only to expose a line of German gunners who promptly shot the French front line of pikemen. After a severe struggle between the groups of pikemen, the Landsknechts gave way and had begun to retreat when a few French cavalry from the south flank and the center struck them on their unengaged sides.

Meanwhile, the other imperial infantry formation, immobile during this contest, began retreating, the cavalry in the center having left the field without participating in the contest and the French cavalry on the north flank having defeated the opposing imperial cavalry. When, however, on the north side of the battle, the squares of imperial infantry attacked the two opposing French formations, both fled, leaving the French infantry victorious in the south and the emperor's foot soldiers winners on the north. But the uniform successes of the French cavalry decided the day, the triumphant imperial infantry withdrawing rather than face an attack of both infantry and cavalry. The imperial force suffered so heavily among its Landsknechts that its casualties amounted to 25 or 30 percent of its force, double the proportion the French army lost.

The battle lacked much planning and had little direction, the wounded imperial commander leaving the field and the young French commander spending part of the battle leading cavalry charges. The French cavalry, greater in numbers and better in quality, proved its value by its ability to maneuver quickly and strike the Landsknechts in flank and again to demonstrate that even a futile charge against heavy infantry could immobilize the formation attacked. The artillery on both sides played a small role, the armies' being at extreme range and the soldiers' having protection before the engagement by keeping prone or beyond the crests of the low hills upon which the armies arrayed themselves. If attacked when placed in entrenchments, artillery displayed its worth as the best form of missile action. Still the comparative immobility of even wheeled field artillery limited its usefulness on the battlefield and its temporary ascendency in sieges ended quickly because of improvements in fortifications.

The New Fortifications

Since the middle of the fifteenth century military engineers had devoted their attention to the problem created by the increasing ability of artillery to demolish the walls of cities and castles. Soon they developed the essentials of a new system that they applied to the renovation of old fortifications and the construction of new. To implement their most basic idea of safeguarding the walls from artillery, they widened and deepened the ditch, completely covering its interior with masonry to prevent its filling by a collapse of the sides. The masonry wall of the ditch became a new barrier to the attackers, one well defended from artillery fire. A cross-section of the new method shows the protection offered by a wall sunk in a ditch. Artillery on the parapet could still fire at the enemy, but the parapet and wall received shelter from the earthen bank beyond the ditch.

The defense continued to rely on flanking fire in which low, broad bastions took the place of the towers. Not higher than the parapet, the bastions jutted out into the ditch so that artillery could both sweep the ditch and fire at the besiegers and their guns.

Illustration 3.4. Cross-Section of
New Fortifications

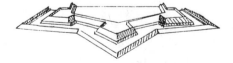

Illustration 3.5. Flanking Fire
in a Ditch

Illustration 3.6. Outline of
New Fortifications

The new fortifications conserved every element of strength of a castle and kept its stone walls from the fire of the besiegers' artillery. If anything, the advent of gunpowder missile weapons had strengthened the defensive because the defenders' artillery kept the besiegers under fire at a greater distance and gave the flanking fire more range and effectiveness. The sixteenth century witnessed the rebuilding of the defenses of important towns to incorporate the system of bastioned defense. Sieges again became as hopeless as in the Middle Ages, and starving out the defenders became the only certain method. In their three-year siege of the Dutch seaport of Ostend, for example, the Spaniards finally captured the town, even though the Dutch could supply it by sea. The siege cost the Spaniards 60,000 casualties; the Dutch lost 30,000.

Another Influence of Technology on Tactics

Since artillery did not permanently enhance the power of besiegers, it would have had a negligible tactical effect had it not augmented the strength of the tactical defensive entrenched in field fortifications. It also gained an added impact in field operations by the successful effort of the Spaniards to give artillery the mobility that had traditionally characterized missile weapons. In the early sixteenth century the Spaniards developed the musket. Essentially a very large arquebus, it could weigh as much as twenty pounds, over twice the weight of an arquebus, and, with a bore of at least 20 millimeters, fired a two-ounce ball, twice the weight of an arquebus shot. One man could operate this small cannon by use of a separate, forked rest to support the barrel. Its portability, great power, and 400-yard range made it so useful that in spite of its inaccuracy musketeers gradually replaced half the arquebusiers in Spanish infantry units and most European armies took up the musket. Its success also discouraged efforts to improve the mobility of field artillery, which remained formidable only in prepared positions.

Meanwhile, in the early sixteenth century an advance in the development of the gun, the wheel lock, wrought a revolution in tactics. The wheel lock included a steel wheel attached to a spring that the gunner could wind with a wrench and cock. Then, working on the principle of the cigarette lighter, when the gunner released the spring, the turning wheel struck pyrites or flint, sending sparks into the pan, igniting the powder, and thus firing the gun. But a wheel lock arquebus cost about $600 in 1980 dollars compared with about $225 for a matchlock. In addition, its delicate mechanism required frequent repair by highly-paid gunsmiths; but the simple, rugged matchlock hardly ever needed attention. The wheel lock, therefore, in spite of its better reliability and greater safety, never replaced the matchlock for military arquebuses or muskets.

Nevertheless, the wheel lock had an obvious advantage in that it required neither a lighted match nor any precautions to keep it smouldering. The one-handed gun, the pistol, had little utility as long as the user had to cope with the match. But the user could wind up a wheel lock pistol and keep it in a holster until ready for use. Armed with a wheel lock pistol, a cavalryman could have one hand free to hold the reins, thus vastly simplifying the task of shooting from horseback.

With such diminished skill requirements for light cavalry action, by the middle of the sixteenth century most cavalrymen had armed themselves with two or three pistols and revolutionized their tactics accordingly. Abandoning the lance, which required a hand to carry it, and using the saber, a cavalry sword, that could be sheathed when they used their pistols, these cavalrymen, called reiters, developed a tactic—the caracole—that used a deep formation in which the front ranks fired their pistols and then rode to the rear to perform the slow work of reloading while successive ranks fired and followed each other to the rear to reload and to fire again. In this way a cavalry battle could be a contest between the missiles of light cavalry tactics until one side lost heart and retreated.

But the reiter tactics of the caracole did not dominate mounted combat. At the Battle of Moorkerhyde in 1574 the Dutch reiters, having already fired all their pistols, met a body of old-fashioned Spanish cavalry armed with lances. Charging as the reiters were reloading their pistols, the Spaniards routed the Dutch with almost the same ease as heavy cavalry traditionally would have dispersed light cavalry. At the Battle of Ivry in 1590 during the French civil wars, many of the dashing King Henry IV's reiter cavalry, dispensing with pistol fire, charged and routed opponents who expected to caracole instead of fight at close quarters with sabers, again displaying the primacy of shock tactics at close quarters. The tactics of cavalry against cavalry remained eclectic and often involved both pistol fire and shock action. Meanwhile, the new cavalry, faced with the powerful musket, reduced the weight of its plate armor: cavalrymen kept the pistol-proof breastplate, but many dispensed with leg armor and relied on high heavy boots that could turn a pistol bullet. This change diminished the cost of a horseman, the greater numbers of these versatile cavalrymen apparently more than offsetting their reduced quality.

The caracole required drill, and units accustomed to its use developed a discipline, responsiveness to command, and cohesion that made them far more effective on the battlefield than the knights of old, who had fought more as an aggregate of individuals. Since units often found that they could not use the

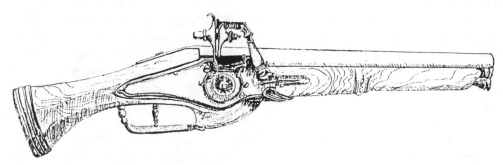

Illustration 3.7. Wheel Lock Handgun

caracole and since cavalry battles frequently involved a melee in which the men used both their pistols and swords, the better discipline and articulation of the new cavalry carried over into combat with the undrilled lancers and gave them an advantage. In addition, the men armed with sword and pistol cost less than lancers, due to the lower level of skill required to use the new weapons. In the latter years of the sixteenth century the better controlled men with pistol and saber gradually supplanted the lancers.

Yet the use of the pistol did not deprive cavalry of its capability for shock action. With its still liberal allowance of armor and its sword, the cavalry retained the characteristics of heavy cavalry and remained fully capable of earnest shock action. Dutch reiters fully exhibited this capability at the Battle of Nieuport in 1600 when they triumphantly charged and defeated the always redoubtable Spanish infantry. This battle involved a long, confused, infantry battle in which the Spanish pikemen, leaving their formation, had joined and mingled with the arquebusiers in the difficult but eventually successful task of driving back the Dutch infantry. At this point the Dutch reiters behaved as shock cavalry, charging with their swords the unformed and disorganized mixture of light and heavy infantry, routing them with ease.

But the reiter, having much in common with the old Byzantine heavy cavalryman who also carried a bow, had an authentic dual-purpose tactical capability. Dutch reiters ably exhibited this at Tournout in 1597 when they used their pistols against a formed body of Spanish pikemen until their fire had created gaps in Spanish ranks. The Dutch then charged into the openings with their swords and defeated the heavy infantry. By the end of the century only the Spaniards retained any lancers, most other Western European heavy cavalry having become reiters in weapons, tactics, drill, and versatility.

During the Crusades warfare employed four basic weapon systems, though only the Egyptians used all four. Combat thoroughly demonstrated the varying weapon capabilities and their respective superiorities as shown in Schematic 3.1, drawn from Chapter 2, in which A means the ability to attack successfully in the direction of the arrow and D means ability to defend successfully in the direction of the arrow.

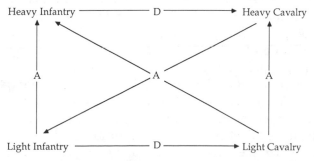

Schematic 3.1. Tactical Capabilities of Weapon Systems without Reiters

But the invention of the wheel lock pistol and the armored, sword-and-pistol-armed dual-purpose cavalryman changed this basic relationship to the one shown in Schematic 3.2.

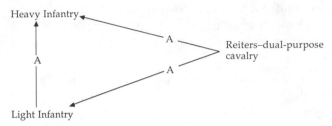

Schematic 3.2. Tactical Capabilities of Weapon Systems with Reiters

The reiter cavalry could attack heavy infantry with pistols, keeping its distance as did the Parthian horse archers against Crassus's Roman heavy infantry. It would not use shock action until and unless pistol fire had so disordered the ranks of the pikemen that they were vulnerable to a charge with the sword. The reiter cavalry could attack the light infantry but not by pitting their pistols against the greater power and range and the better accuracy of the arquebuses and muskets; the light infantry still had supremacy over the light cavalry. Rather, the reiter would charge, the speed of the horses quickly carrying the armored men through the danger space of the slow-firing handguns and promptly placing the mounted, armored swordsmen among the ranks of the light infantry, traditionally at a serious disadvantage in shock combat.

Yet the adoption of the pistol and the saber, which conferred the offensive capabilities of both light and heavy cavalry, deprived the horseman of much of his value on the defense. With no lance to serve as a pike when dismounted, the cavalryman became a swordsman, and one without the sword's traditional partner, the shield. Thus, unlike the medieval heavy cavalrymen who strengthened their defensive power against heavy cavalry and infantry by dismounting, the new dual-purpose cavalrymen, when dismounted, had less strength on the defensive than if they had remained mounted and used a countercharge to meet their mounted assailants on equal terms or relied on their mobility to avoid infantry. On foot the inferiority of their pistols to arquebuses or muskets made them at best an inferior type of light infantry. Thus cavalry had purchased its versatility and enhanced offensive capacity at the cost of the ability to resist effectively on foot, the efficacy of which the English had so dramatically demonstrated at the Battle of Crécy.

The new danger presented to infantry by this dual-purpose cavalry placed a premium upon cooperation between light and heavy infantry. The plan of keeping files of arquebusiers on either side of the pike square to maintain a continuous fire dominated tactical thought, but commanders also developed formations that arrayed the light infantry in four ranks all around the pike square with a routine in which the front rank fired and knelt, followed by the successive firing and kneeling of the next two ranks and the firing of the rear rank. Since this formation essentially blanketed the pikes, commanders devised a drill in which the pike square could open up, allow the gunners to march inside, and reform their phalanx of pikes. But this drill to provide a refuge for the light infantry not only thinned the ranks of the pikemen but also presented great difficulties in execution. Since the formation would be doomed if the cavalry caught the infantry while executing the movement, it found little favor in practice. The light infantry usually relied on its initiative and the shelter offered by trees, shubbery, buildings, and the inequalities of the ground to escape the reiters' swords; but it could not desert the pikemen and leave them at the mercy of the reiters' pistols. Commanders discovered no perfect antidote to cope with resolutely and skillfully handled dual-purpose reiter cavalry.

By 1600 European tactics had become essentially as sophisticated and complex as those of the ancients. The pistol had changed cavalry tactics and the basic tactical matrix of ancient and medieval warfare. Though the Western European use of squares of heavy infantry differed from the Greek and Roman linear practice, the resulting tactics had the same essential outlook as the ancients.

The Manpower System in 1600

At the end of the sixteenth century logistics remained much as it had in ancient times. The greater efficiency of the horse had improved road transport but had not altered fundamentally the supply of armies nor had the larger, better-rigged, compass-directed ships wrought any fundamental change in the nature or comparative advantage of water transport. The lack of good roads prevented full exploitation of the capabilities of the horse-drawn, four-wheel wagon. The heavily populated areas had a thick network of roads, but few had an adequate surface, and most were little more than tracks that rain usually rendered nearly impassable.

Most Western European armies, employing the manpower system evolved by the French and Italians, maintained small, permanent regular forces and utilized mercenaries to increase their forces in wartime. Often lacking ready credit and without large bureaucracies, rulers resorted for this expansion to independent contractors, either captains who raised companies of 250 to 300 men or colonels who raised regiments of ten or twelve companies, usually by subcontracting with captains. Often these entrepreneurs provided their own capital, delivering complete units before the government paid anything, but sometimes they depended on advances by the prince for whom the forces were raised. To be prepared for combat, governments often paid contractors a retainer to be ready in case of war. This enabled the contractor to keep his organization intact and assured the government that he would work for its prince rather than his enemy. The contractors provided the men, often lent much money, and, as captains of the companies or colonels of the regiments, commanded the troops that they had raised. Princes also often chose their generals from the ranks of these soldier-entrepreneurs.

At the beginning of the revolt of the Netherlands the Spanish showed the ability of this system to create a huge army in an amazingly short time. In the Netherlands the Spaniards maintained a regular force of 13,000 men, a substantial number for the time. On April 1, 1572, they called on their contractors; by August 31 they had an army of 67,000 men, including the original 13,000 peacetime force. The ability to raise so many men so quickly meant that few governments could resist the temptation to hire more men than they could afford to pay. Apprehension that the enemy would have more, together with the belief that victory would somehow provide the funds for wages, supplied a rationale for the excessive recruiting as did the belief that in the event of defeat many of the soldiers would not be present to collect their money.

Inability to compensate the troops, who depended on their stipend to provide their food, inevitably produced mutinies by Spanish and other unpaid soldiers. These strikes for back pay often crippled the Spanish armies as the men elected representatives who negotiated with the impecunious authorities and insisted that the soldiers would not campaign until paid. On rare occasions, as in 1576, the soldiers took their earnings by force. That year unpaid Spanish soldiers looted the prosperous commercial city of Antwerp, killing 6,000 civilians and burning 800 houses. In this "Spanish Fury" the soldiers destroyed much more than they took in lieu of their wages.

Chronic inability to compensate their men regularly induced the Spanish to begin paying their soldiers in part by issuing them food and reducing their wages accordingly. This measure kept the men from becoming desperate because they lacked money to buy food. The Spanish army customarily owed its troops part of their cash pay and even saw in this a virtue: preventing desertion. One of their commanders remarked: "To keep the soldiers together it is a good thing to owe them something." A contemporary agreed: "It is good to keep them short of money sometimes, in order to make them more obedient and to feed them with hope." Thus money became the only sinew of war, commanding all of the rest. Another contemporary expressed it well when he said, "He who has the most money wins." And to more than one commander of this era has been attributed the view that there were three things needed in war: money, money, and more money.[12]

Contractors could usually recruit in neutral as well as friendly territory, bringing in permanent or intermittent professional fighting men as well as the unemployed and those who hoped for riches through loot or who wished to try the adventure of a soldier's life. Sometimes captains used trickery as when a lady, having enticed "poor ruffians with food," then gave the captain help when "she shut them up by surprise in a cellar and left them there without food until they enlisted and accepted their wages."[13]

An enlistment had no set term; most governments, however, adhered to the custom of disbanding the army at the end of the fall campaign and hiring anew in the spring. But continuous campaigning year after year by the Spanish and Dutch led to their keeping men under arms all year round, these soldiers' having the obligation to serve until discharged. When contractors recruited professionals, the infantry came equipped with arquebus, musket, or pike and the cavalry with horse and suitable weapons. The rate of pay depended on equipment, cavalry receiving at least twice the infantry's wage and the footmen with armor for the torso receiving a premium for having that expensive piece of equipment. The contractor or the government outfitted the unequipped men, deducting the cost from their wages.

The soldiers received little formal training and had negligible experience with drill. Even though the permanent forces of Spain also neglected drill, the prominent Spanish commander, the duke of Alba, insisted that fighting men needed a year or two of peacetime service before they were fit for combat. On the march soldiers stayed in towns, moving in with families to spend the night. In enemy territory the troops took their food and lodging but were supposed to pay for them in friendly territory. Even so, civilians dreaded the approach of friendly soldiers who, even when sober, usually proved destructive, maliciously burning barns and requiring tips from their involuntary hosts for refraining from destroying property.

In the Spanish service the soldiers were usually foreign, for as a matter of policy the Spanish kept troops far from home to reduce desertion and preclude soldiers having conflicting allegiance. A Spanish official, stressing the use of men raised one place for campaigning in another, pointed out that "troops native to the country where the war is being fought disband very rapidly and *there is no surer strength than that of foreign soldiers*." Though the Spaniards largely kept their recruiting within their own large domains or in the empire of their Habsburg cousins, foreign-recruited troops continued to be as important for other countries as they had been in the Middle Ages and the sixteenth century. A French commander later summed up the advantage of foreign recruiting: "A German in the army serves us as three soldiers; he spares France one, he deprives our enemy of one and he serves us as one."[14]

Without much drill or training and often without any national or local loyalty to their cause, armies lacked many of the bases for cohesion in combat. But permanent regiments that remained in existence year after year did have a kinship that provided an esprit de corps and supplied a basis for morale that sustained them in battle. Part of this community included the informal but integral nonmilitary personnel of a regiment, such as officers' servants, sutlers, wives, washerwomen, and prostitutes. On one occasion on a long march, a Spanish force of 8,646 infantry and 965 cavalry had a total of 16,000 people and 3,000 horses. A contemporary remarked, with some exaggeration, of another Spanish force that "such a long tail on such a small body never was seen," because it was "such a small army with so many carts, baggage horses, nags, sutlers, lackeys, women, children and a rabble which numbered far more than the Army itself." Nevertheless, such a heavily burdened army could march twelve miles a day, a distance standard in ancient and medieval times for seasoned troops who could count on access to supplies along the route. But the number of supernumeraries, important as they were in making a home and a community for the soldiers, complicated supply and increased the burden on the civilians who had to provide quarters on the march.[15]

Sixteenth-Century Battles, Campaigns, and Strategy

With logistics essentially unchanged since ancient times and a tactical system that placed few demands on the poorly articulated and inadequately drilled mercenary heavy infantry, the strategy of commanders also displayed a high degree of continuity with the past. As in earlier times commanders concerned themselves with bringing on battle under favorable circumstances and avoiding it when conditions seemed likely to cause defeat. Particularly did they concentrate on the situation, hard to bring about, in which one army had its back to an obstacle and had to make a frontal attack to extricate itself. In addition, sixteenth-century commanders had two other dangers to avoid or opportunities to exploit. One arose from the difficulties of the transition from march to battle formation. No infantry or cavalry combat formation corresponded to the column, often four abreast, used for marching on a road. Arraying an army for battle involved having a plan, forming the squares of heavy infantry, posting the associated light infantry to act as skirmishers or to provide fire support, positioning the heavy cavalry units six or eight ranks deep, and placing any horse arquebusiers or unarmored cavalry according to the plan. Armies could do this on the field where they expected to fight or near the enemy's position. The attacking army would then march across country in battle formation to engage an already formed opponent, ready to give battle. Even with a simple battle formation of a few large masses of infantry and cavalry, the transition from columns for march to battle array always involved a slow and cumbersome process.

One instance in which the transition involved peril occurred when armies were face to face. Often forces confronted one another for days at a time, and the first to leave, often constrained to do so by lack of food, had to get into march formation with a battle-arrayed enemy close by. The Greeks encountered this situation at the Battle of Plataea after the Persian cavalry captured their pack train with food and spoiled the spring from which the Greeks drew their water. The disorder in the Greek formation created by a night withdrawal had precipitated the Persian attack. A similar instance occurred in Italy in 1553, when a French army, overtaking a force of the emperor and finding it entrenched before them, dug in 150 yards opposite. Neither force attacked, and after a week the French, getting the worst of the sniping and losing men when the enemy artillery bombarded their water supplies, resolved to retreat. Fearing the confusion of a night withdrawal, the competent French commander, Strozzi, attempted to extricate his troops at noon. But the enemy, immediately seeing the move, attacked and inflicted 4,000 to 5,000 casualties on a French force of 12,000 men. In the words of a contemporary, "The cavalry got mixed up with the baggage train, the infantry had been cut up on the roads," in part because "there was no attempt to do the only possible thing—to sacrifice a rearguard—300 or 400 arquebusiers, perhaps, and the cavalry—in order to get the main body off." Though a serious defeat rarely occurred in attempting such a movement, the maneuver was risky, and commanders had to plan it carefully and carry it out expeditiously if they were to avoid disaster.[16]

The mobility of cavalry and their ability to change quickly from march to battle array caused other problems for march formations. Although a pursuing army can move no faster than one retreating, a cavalry force by itself can overtake any army with infantry. This happened to the Dutch when, at Gemblours in 1578, screened by their cavalry, they fell back to a new position. Spanish cavalry promptly attacked when they detected the move, but the Dutch cavalry held them until the son of the duke of Parma, later a renowned general, led a force of Spanish cavalry around the Dutch and charged them in flank and rear. Routing the Dutch cavalry, the Spanish cavalry then assaulted the Dutch infantry as it marched along the road. Catching the men unformed for combat, the aggressive Spanish lancers defeated one formation of Dutch infantry after another. At negligible cost the Spanish cavalry, by its better mobility and its capacity for changing rapidly from march to combat formation, inflicted 5,000 to 6,000 casualities on the Dutch army.

Over twenty years later, at Tournout, 800 Dutch cavalry overtook a marching column of 5,000 Spanish infantry and 500 cavalry. Dispersing the Spanish cavalry, which made little effective resistance, the Dutch cavalry charged both ends of the Spanish column, defeating successive marching groups of crack Spanish infantry. With the aid of a few Dutch arquebusiers who helped attack the rear of the column, 800 Dutch cavalry killed 2,000 Spanish infantry and took 500 prisoners from the infantry.

The cavalry owed its success not only to its higher mobility but to its ability to move quickly and easily from march to battle array, a proficiency derived from the cavalry's homogeneity and the horsemen's greater reliance on individual action and consequent small need for the infantry's integrated formation. These offensive attributes not only made cavalry ideal for assailing forces on the march but also conferred the battlefield capacity of carrying out attacks against the enemy's flank and rear. So in spite of the predominance of field fortifications, which naturally stymied cavalry, and infantry formations, which united the defensive capabilities of light and heavy infantry, cavalry retained its tactical relevance. But even had it lost its tactical power on the battlefield, the triumph of the Dutch cavalry at Tournout against the Spanish marching column showed that better marching mobility gave it a strategically offensive capacity to overtake infantry and then exploit its tactically offensive characteristics in attacking the unready enemy infantry.

So in pursuing their strategy of avoiding battles except under very favorable circumstances, late sixteenth-century generals also had to be aware of the dangers and opportunities presented by withdrawal when both armies faced each other arrayed for battle. Commanders faced a more common hazard on marches, when the strategic mobility of cavalry eliminated the apparent security provided by distance from the enemy. Though the possibility and prospect of conflict conditioned military operations, battles proved to be relatively rare occurrences because generals still had no sure method of forcing a fight on an unwilling and alert opponent.

Of the better-known battles in Western Europe from 1495 until 1600, eleven occurred by mutual consent, each side either believing it could win a frontal engagement or preferring combat to retreat. In one case logistical difficulties, particularly the exhaustion of the army's supply of beer, presented the attacker with the choice of a frontal encounter or retreat. Seven of the engagements came about primarily from efforts to raise a siege, two might be attributed to this and another cause, and three occurred as a result of a surprise crossing of a river and the envelopment or overwhelming of the defender. Cavalry fought and largely won single-handedly two others when it caught armies on the march. Five of the eleven frontal battles by mutual consent took place between the amateurish forces of the French civil wars, and four others involved the relatively unseasoned English, Scots, and Dutch. Greater circumspection—or pessimism— apparently marked the conduct of the more experienced soldiers who tended to agree with each other as to the odds of winning and losing and sought to avoid offensive frontal battles.

Data on casualities are less reliable than those on the number engaged and are usually limited to the number dead and taken prisoner, omitting the wounded. In twenty battles between 1495 and 1600 the defeated lost 38 percent of their men, the victors only 6 percent. This great disparity reflected the disorganization of the losing force, a situation made worse by the primitive degree of articulation of the troops, the ad hoc character of the armies, and the lack of cohesion and esprit de corps in many formations. Without subdivision and a command hierarchy, it proved difficult to rally defeated units, to organize rearguard actions, and to impart purposeful movement and direction to retreats. Men with little experience serving together lacked confidence in their fellows and knew not what to expect of them in adversity. Often bodies of troops surrendered readily or easily panicked. This situation aggravated the unfavorable conditions produced by poor articulation. In addition, infantry suffered disproportionately heavy casualties, though these men usually had a better chance than the armored heavy cavalry if a water barrier obstructed the retreat. Not only could the infantry not move as fast as the cavalry, but also withdrawal often provided opportunities, denied on the battlefield, to use a more powerful weapon system against its inferior. Disorganization among the heavy infantry, for example, made it vulnerable to the heavy cavalry, thus adding danger to its traditional defenselessness against light infantry, mounted arquebusiers, or reiters. Light infantry in flight provided an easy mark for pursuing heavy cavalry.

This great disproportion in losses between victor and vanquished occurred in spite of the successful army's disorganization, an almost invariable consequence of winning and one exacerbated by the same lack of articulation that plagued the defeated. Triumphant armies were usually nearly as exhausted and confused, if not as depleted, by victory as the losers by their defeat and, lacking the incentive of self-preservation, usually displayed less vigor in pursuit than the vanquished in retreat. Often victors, elated at winning and relieved to have avoided defeat, made little organized effort to follow the losers.

Nevertheless, the average victory produced impressive tactical consequences. A more vigorous tactical pursuit doubtless would have improved the attrition ratio. Battles also had a strategic impact. This began with the retreat of the defeated army, an outcome that the victor might have augmented by strategic pursuit, pressing the enemy to prolong the retreat or compel another fight. The attrition of battle would have altered the balance of forces in favor of the winner, giving a preponderance of strength absent before combat. If both armies had 10,000 men before an average sixteenth-century battle, after the engagement the victors would have 9,400 and the vanquished 6,200, each including some wounded, a one and one half to one advantage in numbers.

Battles also had psychological effects. The losers' depression might cause an exaggerated reaction leading to a longer retreat than the new balance of forces would have warranted. The psychological impact might affect the political situation, causing an extravagant response to the changed strategic situation.

The actual effects of battles proved quite diverse. After one victory in the French civil war the brave and aggressive King Henry IV advanced against Paris; after another he took advantage of the lull to visit his mistress. After one triumph in Italy, the French took Milan; after another they retreated because their opponent received substantial reinforcements. After defeating a Spanish army that sought to prevent a siege of Nieuport, the Dutch commander used the reputation gained by his impressive victory to march home rather than begin the siege of which he disapproved. But none of the victories fundamentally altered the strategic situation. After losing at Novara in 1513, the French abandoned their invasion of Italy. But the French desire to conquer Italy, a large and relatively inaccessible peninsula, was unrealistic in the face of weak political claims and the opposition of the armies of the empire and the fleet and army of Spain. Victories proved equally ineffectual in acquiring such a territory. In saying that a battle "isn't a victory unless it ends the war," a sixteenth-century French essayist set a standard that virtually excluded all sixteenth-century battles and most of those in other eras as well.[17]

On one occasion the powerful Emperor Charles V used his military supremacy to cross the Alps and invade southern France just as the harvest was ripening. But the king of France, using a logistic strategy, drove off the livestock, burned crops in the field, and destroyed flour mills. Embarrassed by a lack of supplies and facing a strong French force standing on the defensive, the emperor retreated. In another instance the armies of the emperor and the king confronted each other for three weeks, with neither believing that the odds of victory counterbalanced the hideous costs of defeat. Finally, each monarch having depleted the money to pay his men, both armies retreated.

A small margin of production above subsistence, a situation aggravated by ineffective tax systems and credit mechanisms, prevented either contestant from raising forces adequate to overcome the size of the hostile space, the number of the opposing population, and the strength of the enemy's fortifications. Recalling the English efforts at the conquest of France in the fifteenth century, the French Marshal de Montluc wrote: "France if united cannot be conquered even by a dozen battles, considering the patriotism of its noblesse and the number of its fortresses. I hold those to be in error who said that if Paris fell, France was lost." To the fortified country and its loyal, warlike gentry, he added that besides Paris, "there are so many other cities and fortresses in this realm, that it would take thirty armies to capture and garrison them all. To hold down what he had won, the conqueror would have to unpeople his whole kingdom, which is obviously impossible. While the invader was taking one place, he would be losing another, for want of garrisons which he could not provide."[18]

Marshal de Montluc saw clearly why the English had to employ a raiding strategy early in the Hundred Years' War and why without more political support than King Henry V possessed his later introduction of a persisting strategy failed. In the smaller area of urbanized north Italy and the Netherlands, the invaders had an adequate ratio of force to space to pursue a persisting strategy, but in the Netherlands they met more enemy troops than they could overcome. In addition to soldiers, the invaders encountered a multitude of fortified towns and strong points.

This high ratio of force to space defeated the offensive in regions with the wealth to resist, town militias to aid in the defense, and cities protected with modernized fortifications. These factors enabled the provinces of present-day Holland to withstand conquest by the relatively large and efficient armies of Spain. After a major Spanish victory, an English observer pointed out the strategic irrelevance of battles in such a well-fortified country. To take advantage of his success the Spanish commander had to "expugne one towne after another, the least of a number wherof cannot cost him less than half a yeres siege with an infinite charge, loss of men and hazard of his fortune and reputation bycause (as men of warr are wont to say) one good towne well defended sufficeth to ruyn a mightie army." In the Netherlands the Spanish ultimately used more than 33,000 men to provide 208 places with garrisons as small as ten soldiers and one as large as 1,000; the average post numbered 160. The Dutch fortified and garrisoned as well, and most warfare consisted, in the words of a contemporary, of "fights, encounters, skirmishes, ambushes, an occasional battle, minor sieges, assaults, escalades, captures and surprises of towns." As the Romans did earlier, the Dutch used a continuous earthen breastwork to protect part of their area.[19]

In heavily fortified regions battles could hardly have any strategic significance and often lacked importance elsewhere. In view of the high attrition defeat inflicted on the vanquished, it is not surprising that the more able professional soldiers avoided combat unless the odds overwhelmingly favored victory. Further, since battles rarely had a major strategic impact, strategic considerations had no cogency in overruling tactical caution. In 1568 and again in 1572 the able duke of Alba, the Spanish commander in the Netherlands, defeated a Dutch invasion by avoiding a fight until winter came on, and, their money and supplies running low, the Dutch retreated. But though he could win in the field with or without combat, Alba could not overcome the multitude of Dutch fortresses. His talented successors did no better. Western European battles thus resembled those of Hannibal in Italy rather than those of Alexander in Asia. Confronted with strong fortifications, firm political opposition, and usually large spaces to control, victories that imposed high attrition on the defeated failed to yield proportionate strategic results.

The campaigns from 1590 to 1592 in northern France clearly exhibited the kind of sophisticated generalship that had developed in Italy under the *con dottieri* and matured as the sixteenth century found its new tactical synthesis. The duke of Parma, a Spanish-educated Italian duke and a grandson of Emperor Charles V, led Spanish forces from the Netherlands in support of the Catholics in a French civil war that by 1590 had pitted Protestant King Henry IV against Catholic insurgents who controlled Paris. The king's reckless courage overshadowed the tactical skill he had developed in the French civil wars, and his battlefield proficiency obscured his understanding of strategy. He proved an exemplary monarch, his sympathy for the common people becoming a legend and his gracious, accessible manner ensuring him a glowing reputation. In statecraft as well as war he remained firmly in command. The duke of Parma, a daring cavalry leader in his twenties, had embraced the least-effort school of warfare of the *condottieri* and had earned the reputation as the best general of his time. Although King Henry could never resist leading a cavalry charge in person, his successful command experience made him an opponent worthy of Parma.

The first conflict between the two came in the summer of 1590, when Henry's blockade of Paris had so reduced the city's food supplies that Parma and his Spanish army left the Netherlands with the objective of enabling Paris to resupply itself. Concentrating as many men as possible, King Henry met his advance east of Paris where Parma had halted, inviting Henry to attack him. Schooled in the amateurish French civil wars, Henry faced a new type of opposition when he reconnoitered Parma's heavily entrenched position. Disinclined to attack fortifications, Henry moved to threaten Parma, who promptly occupied and entrenched a new position. While Henry searched in vain for Parma's weakness, a Spanish detachment captured a bridge, opening a road into Paris through which supplies quickly flowed. Having opened Paris to provisions but himself finding little to eat near the city—where Henry's army had spent four months consuming everything available—and without money to pay his troops, Parma promptly marched back to the Netherlands, losing stragglers killed by the hostile French population. He sustained negligible losses, and his minimal intervention had saved Paris, the objective of his nearly bloodless campaign.

In 1591 Henry sought to strengthen his hold on northern France and in the fall began the siege of Rouen, a town near the mouth of the Seine. Again the king of Spain sent Parma to raise a siege. Beginning his advance in mid-January 1592 but reluctant to leave the Netherlands, where renewed fighting loomed, Parma, like all generals, disliked winter campaigns because the weather could hurt an army almost as much as a lost battle. In a December campaign in their civil war, for example, both French armies had lost a third of their men to illness and desertion caused by intense cold and continual sleet.

Familiar with Parma's Roman methods of warfare, Henry dismissed any idea of facing the entrenched Spanish general in the field. Instead he led 7,000 cavalry in an effort to catch the Spaniards on the march. But Henry, not expecting any significant tactical success, aimed primarily to harass the Spanish army by taking stragglers and cutting off detachments and foraging parties and so prevent the duke from reaching Rouen. Though Henry had mostly heavy cavalry, he took with him 1,000 horse arquebusiers. The king's strategy and the presence of the arquebusiers showed that he understood the strategic significance of light cavalry: like Caesar in the Ilerda campaign and Gonzalo in southern Italy, he planned to use his cavalry to carry out a strategy comparable to Fabius' against Hannibal.

Because of the excellence of French cavalry and the well-demonstrated vulnerability of an army on the march, the accomplished and careful duke took the not-unusual precaution of marching in a version of his battle array. Forming his infantry so that its squares made an oblong rectangle, he kept his heavy cavalry within the formation and used his light cavalry as scouts. Since the army had to move off the roads, it marched slowly. But, as a contemporary explained, "with the army always in order of battle, never moving unless the weather was favorable, and all the ground in front well reconnoitred, and halting each afternoon in time to allow of his camping ground being well entrenched," Parma's army proved invulnerable to the French cavalry and his Roman methods defeated the king's Fabian strategy.[20]

But the relentless Spanish advance never reached Rouen. While King Henry faced Parma, the Catholic commander in Rouen successfully sallied from the city and blew up the besieger's powder magazine, filled in their trenches, and opened his communications with the countryside. With no need to advance farther and the Catholics not anxious to have their cause too closely identified with foreign troops, the relieved duke of Parma halted, expecting Henry to do likewise.

When in mid-April Henry moved all of his forces to Rouen and reestablished the siege before the town could adequately resupply itself, Parma moved rapidly to Rouen, and Henry, not feeling strong enough to oppose him, raised the siege. Parma then turned aside from Rouen and besieged a small town to the west. But the always-prudent duke had underestimated Henry's energy and resources. Calling in forces from afar and bringing back to the colors nobility that had left to avoid winter campaigning, the king quickly concentrated a larger force that cut the Spaniards off from Rouen and penned them against the Seine, giving them the alternative of a frontal attack against French entrenchments or a retreat to Le Havre, a port blockaded by the ships of Henry's English and Dutch allies.

By his energy and skill Henry had achieved the goal of every sixteenth-century general—confronting an enemy with the choice of a hopeless battle or ultimate capitulation. But the resourceful Parma moved to a fortified position on the Seine River, where he met a secretly prepared bridge of boats assembled during the night and got his whole army across the river before the French could interfere. Then, displaying the energy always latent in his circumspect campaigning, he marched to the vicinity of Paris at the rapid rate of eighteen miles a day, strengthened the garrison, and marched back to the Netherlands to cope with a renewed Dutch offensive.

This skillfully conducted campaign exhibited the strategic maturity of late sixteenth-century generals. They fought no battles because they each perceived the same likely outcome. The combative king could easily have attacked the entrenched duke before he reached Paris or during his march to Rouen with only a negligible likelihood of affecting the outcome of the campaign, and the wily Parma could have attacked Henry before escaping over the river with little chance that he would have had anything but a diminished army to show for his selection of the battle alternative. As practitioners of the principle of least effort, neither the king nor the duke risked a fight when so sure of the outcome.

With warfare usually in progress somewhere in Europe at any time and with relatively young men receiving responsible commands and holding them for a long time, sophisticated soldiers, well tried in war, would command combat-seasoned veterans in the opening phases of the Thirty Years' War. They would have the strategic outlook and tactical method of the Spanish army and would readily dominate the first decade of military operations.

Revolution in Naval Tactics and Logistics

Medieval naval warfare in the Mediterranean Sea differed little from that in ancient times, galleys still constituting the war fleets. But on the Atlantic coast and in northern Europe larger waves and stormier weather made the fragile, narrow galleys more difficult to use, resulting in a considerable reliance on sailing ships. As the techniques of sailing improved and mariners learned to maintain a course much nearer to the direction from which the wind blew, the galleys lost some of their advantage as ships that could move independently of the wind. So they gradually assumed a smaller role in the north, especially as the medieval governments in that region often lacked the resources to maintain substantial fleets of vessels specialized for war. Warships increasingly depended primarily on sail, with oars as an auxiliary, and naval vessels more and more were merchant ships pressed into military service.

This difference meant that navies could not count on ramming. Sea fighting, usually a confused and disorganized melee, consisted entirely of boarding and the combat of soldiers. Tactics did not hinge on sailing in formation, something difficult for primitive sailing vessels in any case. The ships carried infantry, shock action predominating with bowmen providing support. Ships protected themselves from boarding with rope nets, which made the soldiers attempting to cut their way through vulnerable to both missile and shock weapons. High structures, called castles, on the bows and sterns of ships provided defensive positions and posts for the bowmen to shoot at enemy ships and boarders and for the heavy and light infantry to defend the ends of the ship should boarders gain control of the deck between the castles. They also provided positions to support with missiles their own boarders of hostile vessels.

Although the use of clumsy sailing vessels, which, unlike galleys, could maneuver only with difficulty and not ram effectively, removed much of the advantage of a flank attack and made it hard to count on committing a reserve at the right time and place, dependence on the wind did not eliminate concentration as an element of tactics. A fleet to the windward of another could either refuse or delay battle or initiate it by sailing down wind upon its opponent. Because of the difficulty of sailing ships against the direction of the wind, the leeward fleet could not readily take the initiative against one to the windward. Naval commanders thus sought the windward positions and often attempted to bring their whole fleet against a portion of the hostile fleet, planning to overwhelm it before the remainder could come upwind to its rescue. In general, though, fleets usually fought in unorganized masses, coming alongside their antagonists for the boarding combat.

On one occasion an English fleet intercepted an invading force, and the English captain made double use of his windward position. As he sailed down wind and came close to the heavily manned hostile flagship, the English captain had his men throw lime into the wind, which then blew onto the enemy ship, blinding the soldiers and sailors and making it easy for the English to come alongside and capture the ship and its crew.

Thus two kinds of sea warfare coexisted in medieval times, the largely galley warfare in the Mediterranean and the predominantly sailing warfare in the Atlantic and north. The advent of cannon, which wrought no permanent change in land warfare, profoundly influenced sea warfare and favored the sailing ship over the galley. Initially sea fighters merely substituted gunpowder weapons for bows, as did warriors on land. The castles of merchant ships and the few specially built warships carried numbers of small cannon as antipersonnel weapons. These provided better support for the heavy infantry and, because they did not need to be portable, usually had greater power than arquebuses and Spanish muskets.

Yet these changes, analogous to those on land, altered sea warfare no more than the substitution of the matchlock for the crossbow had modified land warfare. But carrying to sea cannon comparable to some of those used in sieges did bring about a revolution in sea warfare. These large guns could attack and seriously damage the structure of ships just as they harmed the masonry walls of medieval fortifications and provided a weapon system in some ways analogous to the ram of the galleys. Not only did guns attack the buoyancy of ships and damage the rigging, but when a cannonball pierced the side of a wooden vessel, it showered the interior of the ship with splinters that wounded the sailors and soldiers aboard the ship.

A ship could carry twenty, thirty, or even more cannon on each side, all firing a ball weighing nine pounds or more. This necessary arrangement of the guns changed ship-to-ship combat from the bow-to-bow of galleys to a broadside-to-broadside array. In spite of the vulnerability of the side of a slowly sailing ship to the ram of the galley, the new cannon-armed ships could vanquish the galleys of the Mediterranean. A salvo of twenty to thirty heavy cannonballs usually inflicted so much damage on a fragile, lightly built galley that one broadside disabled it.

But this new naval warfare did more than doom galleys. It also largely abolished the infantry combat of the soldiers and sailors on ships locked together for this purpose. A major naval campaign signaled the transition to artillery warfare at sea when the Spanish sent a large armada of ships against England.

In the summer of 1588 more than 100 Spanish ships entered the English Channel with the purpose of covering an invasion of England by the army in the Spanish part of the Netherlands, a force led by the redoubtable duke of Parma. Because a cooperating Dutch fleet blockaded the duke's army, the diversion provided by the Spanish armada availed Parma nothing. The English, with a somewhat larger fleet, waited to engage the Spaniards.

The Spanish naval commander, the duke of Medina Sidonia, did not resemble Parma. His principal qualification to lead the armada—that he was one of the richest men in Europe—meant he could help defray the costs of the expedition, and King Philip II appointed him in spite of Medina Sidonia's accurate protestations of ignorance of sea warfare and his excuse that he was always seasick.

Baron Howard of Effingham commanded the English fleet. A capable politician, diplomat, cavalry commander, and seasoned sailor, he planned to avoid a pitched battle with the Spanish armada. Howard had experienced seamen as subordinates, among them Sir Francis Drake, the brilliant privateer, Martin Frobisher, an explorer, and John Hawkins, a former privateer and a proficient naval administrator.

The Spanish armada, which carried 18,000 soldiers, had larger ships, half of them displacing more than 500 tons. The English fleet, with about 5,000 soldiers aboard, had much smaller ships, almost all of them displacing less than 500 tons. These differences, which reflected the Spanish reliance on the traditional boarding tactics and the English doctrine of depending on cannon fire, meant that the English ships possessed greater maneuverability than the taller, larger Spanish vessels.

The English vessels carried 1,972 guns, compared with only 1,124 on the Spanish armada. Almost all of the English cannon consisted of culverin, a long gun firing a 17-pound metal ball. The Spaniards had larger guns, many firing a less effective 25-pound stone shot. Spanish predominance in guns depended on their 163 heavy cannon to only 55 mounted in the English fleet. Firing a 50-pound metal ball, these powerful guns, with a shorter range than the culverin, could easily smash through ships at short range. Nevertheless, Spanish naval tactics relied primarily on boarding by the greater numbers of their excellent infantry, supported by over 1,000 small, antipersonnel guns mounted largely in the bow and stern castles of their ships.

When the fleets met, the English had the windward position and exploited it when groups of English ships approached the armada in line ahead and, as they passed, fired their broadsides at the Spanish ships. The Spanish ships, which still used the line abreast formation characteristic of galley fighting, could make only an inadequate reply. But the English did little damage because, wary of the heavy Spanish cannon, they kept their range long, which rendered their fire inaccurate and the impact velocity of the culverin shot low. Nevertheless, the English secured far more hits and inflicted on the Spaniards losses in personnel and morale.

The more maneuverable English ships easily followed Howard's strategy of avoiding Spanish efforts to close and use their boarding tactics and the shock action of their larger numbers of fine infantry. The engagement had much in common with the successful attack of the nimble, javelin-armed peltasts on the heavier hoplites who could never close for shock action.

This combat continued for over a week as the Spaniards moved through the channel. Both fleets had exhausted most of their ammunition, but when the English had partially replenished theirs from shore and realized the Spaniards no longer had any 50-pound balls for their big guns, the English closed the range. Without fear of the Spaniards' boarding their more agile vessels, the English ships came close to the Spaniards and, with the higher velocity of the diminished distance, repeatedly pierced the Spanish ships. During this combat at short range, the Spaniards suffered 600 killed, 800 wounded, and the impairment of the seaworthiness of many of their vessels.

Thwarted in his effort to open the way for Parma and unwilling to face headwinds or again to brave the English fleet in the channel, the duke of Medina Sidonia led the Spanish armada and its damaged ships back to Spain on a stormy and ill-supplied voyage around Scotland and Ireland during which the duke lost over half of his ships. The stress of this naval campaign and the arduous return voyage grayed Medina Sidonia's hair at the age of thirty-eight.

The success of the English in relying on the missiles of their powerful shipborne artillery signaled the full emergence of a new type of naval warfare, which had developed slowly during the century. The missiles of the artillery had replaced the shock action of ships and men in sea combat.

The transition from the narrow, shallow-draft galley to the broad and deep sailing ship also had a major effect on the logistics of naval operations. Since command of the sea depended on bases from which the ships could receive supplies and obtain repairs, the adoption of the sturdy, large-capacity sailing ship had a marked effect on the range of naval operations, the new ships' greater cargo-carrying capacity vastly increasing the distance from their bases at which they could operate. For example, a large sailing warship could remain at sea for three to five months without needing to replenish food and water. This greater endurance and consequent independence of ports increased the ratio of naval force to space.

Nevertheless, the slow and the uncertain rate at which wind-propelled warships sailed meant that they still required bases adjacent to their zone of operations because of the time needed to return to a port for supply and maintenance and again resume their stations. Since bases relatively distant from the theater of operations meant proportionately fewer ships available to control a given area of the sea, ships comparatively near a source of supply would permit a smaller number of ships to maintain the same size squadron on the station in the combat zone.

So navies still needed friendly ports capable of supplying food and water and carrying out repairs close to their zone of operations. When conducted against an opponent inferior in force but anxious to leave his base, operations by the stronger navy at too great a distance from its own base could render it the weaker or compel it to exercise only an intermittent command of that part of the sea. Yet, compared with galley fleets, the new sailing ships revolutionized the logistic capabilities and strategic range of navies.

4

THE NEW TACTICAL SYNTHESIS
IN TRANSITION,
1600–1700

The Logistics of the Thirty Years' War

The Thirty Years' War, which occurred in Germany between 1618 and 1648, provided ample scope for the exercise of the new tactical methods and served as a theater in which a new linear system exhibited its worth. It also showed in bold relief the particular logistical techniques characteristic of European warfare during the preceding centuries and that had, to a greater or lesser degree, provided the basis for war since the earliest times.

In this war political factors, which had at least as much importance as military, defy succinct summary. Nevertheless, a brief paragraph will help explain the few political factors mentioned. Protestant and Catholic principalities fought a civil war in a Germany divided among many autonomous states. The Calvinist and Lutheran Protestants had difficulty agreeing and Catholic princes easily became apprehensive at any aggrandizement by the Holy Roman Emperor, the leader of the Catholic forces. Foreign powers intervened early when the emperor's Spanish Habsburg relatives aided him, and eventually Denmark, Sweden, and France fought in the war for which Germany supplied the same kind of European battlefield that Italy had provided more than a century before. The experience gained in the war influenced logistics and strategy as well as tactics markedly.

The war began in 1618 in Bohemia, where the Protestants, rebelling against their Catholic Habsburg rulers, elected as their king a Protestant prince, the Count Palatine of the Rhine. The army of the league of Catholic princes and Spanish forces then intervened. These armies all used the Spanish system and had seasoned and competent commanders whose names—Tilly, Spinola, Bucquoi, and Dampierre—amply illustrate the international character of the military profession at the time. Facing more skillful leadership and more professional forces, the Bohemians soon suffered defeat and shortly the Habsburg-Imperial and Catholic forces also overcame the Count Palatine and overran his domains.

When the king of Denmark intervened for the Protestant cause, the armies of the emperor and the Catholic princes defeated him, overran much of his country, and drove him from the war. In 1629, after a decade of fighting, the belligerents paused. This period thoroughly exemplified the logistics used in the war and provided an opportunity to bring the system of using military contractors to its zenith.

The Catholic powers had enjoyed so much success because they had large forces in relation to the small area of the Palatinate, had limited objectives in dealing with the king of Denmark, and possessed much political support in the larger area of the kingdom of Bohemia in their campaign against opponents who had only just come to power.

Traditionally, armies had enemy property as an objective. Even when they did not have as a specific aim forcing battle, crippling enemy supply, or compelling political concessions, they sought to campaign in their adversaries' territory to find logistic support so that they might live at their enemies' expense. In the Thirty Years' War armies far too large for their governments to pay also had to make neutral and friendly territory the object of loot.

The career of Count Mansfeld, a particularly proficient and resourceful soldier and entrepreneur, dramatically exhibits the dependence of armies on extracting support from civilians in the area in which they operated. A Protestant military contractor and commander in Bohemia, Count Mansfeld left that kingdom with his troops when the Protestant Count Palatine suffered defeat. Mansfeld marched toward the Rhine and the principality of his employer, the Count Palatine. Without a logistic base, Mansfeld improvised brilliantly, acquiring from various sources money, food, and fodder to maintain his soldiers and horses. The towns of Heilbronn, Nuremberg, and Wimpfen paid him to avoid their territory or to keep his men from looting as they marched through. But he collected much more from four other towns in the form of contributions. Part of these payments had their origin in a ransom to avoid destruction, such as Heilbronn and the other towns had already offered, and part came from a special tax levied to sustain a war. During and after the Thirty Years' War commanders levied contributions on friendly, neutral, and enemy territory and, under the threat of looting and destruction, collected the payment in the form of food for the troops and money for their pay and the purchase of supplies. Commanders raked off as much as a third of the payment; on occasion military contractors lent the cities some of the money to pay the contributions they had levied.

Using these payments, together with funds freely offered by a city that he had delivered from a siege by the Spanish, Mansfeld kept his army supplied and partially compensated as he marched across Germany and then operated near the Rhine. Meanwhile, he unsuccessfully negotiated with the duke of Bavaria, the leader of the Catholic princes, about changing sides, asking for money to pay his troops and a substantial bonus for himself. Then, when the Count Palatine, his exiled employer, discharged him, Mansfeld became the commander of an army without an employer.

Again he negotiated with the enemy as well as with the king of France, a French duke who planned a campaign against his king, the Spanish ruler of the Netherlands, and the Dutch who were fighting the Spaniards. Receiving a Dutch contract for three months, he marched there, defeating en route a Spanish army, and assisted the Dutch in raising the Spanish siege of a town. His contract with the Dutch having expired, he proceeded to Ostfriesland on the German coast near the Dutch frontier. He looted this country, taking, among other booty, eighteen barrels of gold ready for shipment to Vienna to provide the dowry of a well-to-do father for his daughter. Finally, when the government of Ostfriesland paid him a substantial sum to leave the country, he paid off and disbanded his army, temporarily going out of business. Back wages presented no problem because he had only 5,000 men left of the 19,000 with which he had entered Ostfriesland. His forces had diminished so drastically because looting gave soldiers ample opportunity and motive to desert. A soldier who took a valuable gold or silver artifact often ignored the back pay due him and rode away on a stolen horse, heading home to buy a farm. Mansfeld himself soon disappeared from view. Raising a new army and using it to prosecute a campaign against the emperor's Austrian dominions, he marched into Hungary, where opposition forced him to disband his forces. He then went into Venetian territory where he died on the Dalmatian coast in 1626.

The short career of Mansfeld's army demonstrates the technique for supporting armies that came so signally to characterize the logistics of the Thirty Years' War, and Mansfeld's ability to continue his army and his logistical forays without any official backing or sanction exhibits the power and independence of the military contractors. The method of supply depended not only on contributions but also on looting by the unpaid soldiers. The undesirable conditions in and counterproductive activity by armies, always characteristic of warfare in varying degrees, reached proportions in the Thirty Years' War that almost caricatured the unattractive and destructive behavior of soldiers in most previous wars in Europe. The conduct of this war also very dramatically illustrates, in an exaggerated way, the defects from which the existing contractual system of raising armies had always suffered.

Soldiers visiting a village often gorged themselves on the available food and stole the horses and much of the remaining food, including chickens, hogs, and cattle. They also looted the houses, taking bed linen to make bags to carry booty and such items as a copper kettle, flattened to make it more portable (soldiers appreciated the sale value of the copper rather than the utility of the kettle). Frequently they tortured civilians to compel them to reveal the location of hidden valuables. This violence often led to wanton destructiveness of property, such as smashing household effects and burning buildings. Officers made little effort to restrain unpaid soldiers, realizing the loyalty that this indulgence could buy.

A Scottish officer serving in the Thirty Years' War described soldiers after they had looted a virgin area as all having "some thing to ballast their lightness." The pillaging enriched the troops and destroyed discipline: "The fury [of looting] past, the whole street being full of coaches and rusty waggons richly furnished with all sorts of riches, as Plate, Iewells, Gold, Money, Clothes, Mulets and horses for saddle, coach and waggons, whereof all men that were careless of their duties, were too careful in making of booty, that I did never see Officers lesse obeyed, and respected than here for a time, till the hight of the market was past: and well I know some Regiments had no man with their colours, till the fury was past and some colours were lost the whole night till they were restored the next day, such disorder amongst us all occasioned by covetousness."[1]

Straggling, which constantly diminished armies, also created a class of soldiers that lived on loot. "If a trooper loses his horse or a musketeer his health, or his wife and child fall ill and must stay behind," they become, a contemporary explained, stragglers whom he likened to gypsies. He wrote of "the many villages that, by chance or by malice, have been burned down by them." With some exaggeration he continued: "They plunder all they can find before, besides, and behind the army: and what they cannot comsume that they spoil so that the regiments, when they come to their quarters or into camp, do often find not even a good draught of water."[2]

With the land alive with marching or straggling soldiers, contributions covered only part of the cost of their support. In addition to loot and gratuitous or malicious destruction, soldiers committed many crimes. Rape occurred frequently, and on a peaceful, well-disciplined march a Spanish company of no more than 250 men accumulated accusations of forty-three crimes in a stay of one or two days. The sergeant alone accounted for six of these, all acts of violence. With crime accentuated by the presence of soldiers and armies, marching to and fro, often through neutral as well as friendly and enemy territory, civil-military relations frequently degenerated into continuous warfare between soldiers and villagers, often with neither discriminating between friend and foe.

Coincident with the beginning of the war, Protestant villagers in Catholic Austria engaged in a series of rebellions. Their Catholic ruler had suppressed these ruthlessly, first burning villages and later killing all peasants the soldiers could find. Applied against heretics, these Turko-Mongolian methods effectively crushed the revolts. But the tension between peasants and their rulers illustrated here and in an earlier peasant uprising added to the hostility, as did rulers who summoned their subjects to kill invading forces. In 1625, for example, on the call of their prince, peasants battled Tilly's formidable Catholic army, surprising camps and killing not only the soldiers but also the women and children following the army. The soldiers naturally took their revenge mercilessly, burning villages and killing every peasant they could find.

Throughout the war peasants, retaliating against looting and violence, engaged in sporadic but widespread ambushes of stragglers and surprise attacks on small bodies of soldiers. The Scottish officer who commented on looting above also experienced the hostility of the peasants. Using the old terms *boor* for peasant and *dorpe* for village, he wrote that on a march "Captaine Boswell comming after the Regiment was killed by a number of villanous Boores, ever enemies to souldiers ... no reparation [was] had for his death. But the Boores being fled, the Dorpe was burnt off." On another occasion he remarked how "the Boores on the march cruelly used our souldiers (that went aside to plunder) in cutting off their noses and ears, hands and feete, pulling out their eyes, with sundry other cruelties which they used, being justly repayed by our soldiers, in burning many Dorpes on the march, leaving also the Boores dead, where they were found." He even told of the massacre of a garrison. When the garrison had surrendered and marched out without any arms, "the Country Boores (ever crueil to Soldiers), remembering the hard usage of the soldiers to them in the winter time, seeing them come forth unarmed, raune violently upon the Souldiers, knocking them pittyfully downe." This "killing the poor Souldiers" continued until his superior ordered the Scottish officer to intervene to "supresse the Boores" and protect the soldiers. This his soldiers did and in the process "againe robbed the Boores of that they had taken from the enemy, and withall were well knockt."[3]

Inevitably the soldiers won most of the conflicts with the often-desperate peasants. But as the war wore on, the soldiers had difficulty finding enough to eat for gradually the conflict depleted Germany of much of the loot and contributions and the destructiveness of armies consumed the produce and damaged the productivity of many areas. In a region that had 1,717 houses at the beginning of the war in 1618, only 627 still existed in 1649. Only 316 families remained, all 4,616 sheep had disappeared, and but 244 of the original 1,402 oxen survived. Such areas could no longer support armies and their numerous followers. For example, an infantry unit of 480 soldiers had, in addition, 74 servants, 3 sutlers, 314 women and children, and 160 horses. In 1635 the alcoholic imperial general, Count Gallas, led his army into an exhausted area to spend the winter. The troops looted diligently, but with little left to take the soldiers died so rapidly that the army burnt the corpses every day to avoid the odor of the dead. Only the dying horses and oxen kept the army going. Finally, with winter coming on, Gallas moved his troops to an area where he could still find supplies. Ten to twelve thousand men perished in the snowy march, and women threw away their babies so as not to see them die of starvation. It is not surprising that there were stories of cannibalism during the war.

Campaigning could wear out an army also, the duke of Bavaria describing his troops in the fall thus: "The largest part of the cavalry marches on foot, the unfortunate soldiers are destitute, ragged, naked, worn out, starving and in such shape that we must in fairness commiserate them. A period of recovery is urgently needed if it is planned to use the troops next spring." Garrison life often offered little more to the soldiers than campaigning, because governments could not pay the soldiers. One of Mansfeld's colonels actually sold his fortress to the enemy for money to pay his soldiers. Mansfeld confirmed the colonel's judgment by giving him another command.

Though this was not an isolated incident, most commanders held their fortresses and subsisted on what the garrisoned region could supply through contributions. But frequently the exhausted countryside could not deliver enough to provide the food portion of the soldier's pay. A fictional garrison soldier wrote of his rations: "I was terrified every morning when I received mine: for I knew I must make that suffice for the whole day which I could have made away with at a meal without trouble." Some soldiers supplemented their pay by gambling when "they were better sharpers and could get their comrades' money from them with false dice." Some knew a trade that they practiced in the town, and many "took to themselves wives (yea, the most vile women at need) for no other cause than to be kept by the said women's work, either with sewing, washing, and spinning, or with selling of old clothes, higgling, or even with stealing." One married a midwife and lived well; the unskilled wife of another "gained a livelihood from the fields only; in winter she gathered snails, in the spring salad-herbs, in summer she took birds'-nests, and in autumn she would gather fruit of all kinds."[4]

Much of the enmity between soldiers and civilians resulted from conflict engendered by the unpaid soldiers' taking rations and pay from civilians. Unpaid soldiers also carried out much of the destruction that reduced agricultural output and contributed to the supply shortage that half starved a garrison and virtually destroyed Count Gallas's army. The looting as well as stealing food and artifacts resulted from a ruler recruiting more men than he could pay. Inability to remunerate the soldiers led to an inefficient and often counterproductive logistic system, and the looting caused straggling and desertion, steadily reducing the size of the unpaid army in spite of the pay owed the troops. The lack of wages eliminated the control that should have restrained looting and affected the discipline that the commanders believed essential in tactical situations.

In addition, looting aroused the hostility of civilians, inhibiting the movement of soldiers and engendering a small but steady drain on army manpower and causing peasants to hide or to fight to protect goods that often they would have willingly sold. Rulers, in spite of their inability to resist the temptation to raise too many men, yearned to rid themselves of a logistic system that harmed the armies themselves, reduced the value of their own as well as the hostile domains they coveted, and increased their armies' opponents. Rather than supporting war, these logistic methods seemed to subvert it.

Early in the war Albert von Wallenstein, a Bohemian military contractor, saw the baneful logistical and tactical effects of the existing ways and introduced more systematic and better-managed logistics. In the process of trying to save logistic and combat efficiency from the debilitating effects of the methods employed in the first decade of the war, Wallenstein helped to lead the way back to public enterprise and government ownership of armies, which the Romans and the other more effective military organizations of ancient times had found beneficial.

Wallenstein, an insignificant Bohemian nobleman who became wealthy by marrying an elderly but rich widow, had served the emperor in a competent manner as a military contractor and financier during the early stages of the war.

When the emperor repaid him with estates taken from rebellious Protestants in Bohemia, Wallenstein became a general contractor, offering in 1626 to raise an entire army for the emperor and to use his own money and credit to finance it. From the emperor he received the right to appoint his own subordinate officers and to raise contributions to support the army and to recover his start-up expenses.

When he had formed his army, Wallenstein, a vigorous and wise administrator of his own dominions, made an expanded and systematic use of contributions the foundation of his effective logistics. Earlier, Mansfeld had pointed out that he could not hold soldiers "under Discipline if their wages be not paid them. Neither they nor their horses can live by ayre, all that they have whether it be Armes or apparell, weareth, wasteth, breaketh. If they must buy more, they must have money. And if men have it not to give them, they will take it, where they find it, not as a part of that which is due unto them, but without weighing and telling it."[5]

Agreeing that unpaid soldiers destroyed everything and would not respond to discipline, Wallenstein raised the money and food to pay his men promptly through contributions. His contributions were large, his collections exacting and ruthless, but his method had the merit of efficiency. Because his regularly paid troops looted relatively little, his system reduced waste, fed and equipped his army sufficiently, and improved the discipline and combat effectiveness of his forces. As much a businessman as a soldier, Wallenstein stressed that his soldiers must not disturb civilians but took care that they protected the villages and their inhabitants so that planting and harvesting could go on. He also provided for his armies by buying and shipping in food. Much of this business he did with himself, buying grain and even baked bread from his Bohemian estates, which also furnished clothing and cannonballs for the army.

The success of his and Tilly's Catholic League armies against the Danes resulted in the conquest of a large part of Denmark and the occupation of much of Germany along the Baltic coast. Contributions in this area supplied the army well, even keeping it without significant cost to the emperor's always empty treasury. And Wallenstein's flourishing military entrepreneurship repaid his investment and managerial skills handsomely, his achievement encouraging his visionary schemes for reorganizing the empire. Wallenstein, showing off his prosperity by incredible ostentation, traveled, for example, with 50 six-horse carriages for himself and his attendants, 10 more for his personal servants, 50 four-horse carriages for the kitchen staff and supplies, followed by 50 grooms leading 100 horses for his personal use. His accomplishments, including the defeat of the Danish forces and the elimination of opposition, made him too powerful for the comfort of his Catholic employers, who reduced his army and dismissed him in 1630. He returned to Bohemia, where he lived in a regal style befitting an ambitious multimillionaire. But 1630 proved a bad time for the emperor to deprive himself of Wallenstein's services.

Gustavus Adolphus's Development of the Dutch Tactical System

Wallenstein's power and independence as well as his defeat of the Danes had much to do with the pressure from the princes of the empire to which the emperor yielded when he dismissed Wallenstein in 1630. But the war was far from over. The emperor's Edict of Restitution had decreed that Protestants must return all Catholic lands acquired since 1552. By appropriating these vested interests and by implication disturbing others, the emperor raised the political stakes in the war and consequently increased the measure of military success needed to achieve his now more ambitious goals. Many German Protestants displayed a readiness to fight again when the occasion would offer itself. The intervention of Protestant Sweden presented just that opportunity. Even without so much latent support, the Swedes would have been formidable foes of the emperor because of the military brilliance of their soldier-king, Gustavus Adolphus, and the new tactical organization upon which he had built his army.

Tested in war with the Poles and Russians, Gustavus's tactics came from the innovations the Dutch adopted in the last years of the sixteenth century during their war with the Spaniards. Soon after the introduction of the new tactics, a Dutch soldier went to Sweden to help reorganize their army. The Dutch system depended on a fundamental alteration in the structure of the infantry, a study of what ancient authors had written about the Roman legion helping to inspire this change. Maurice of Nassau, the perceptive Dutch leader, realized that the Roman model of well-articulated infantry, with three lines to incorporate the concept of a reserve within the array and a linear deployment, had the promise of helping defeat the existing system of large blocks of men that the Spanish army so brilliantly employed. Instead of a few solid masses of as many as 3,000 men, Maurice created far smaller units, deploying them in line. Originally using a formation ten-men deep, he finally arranged his pikemen five deep with a front of fifty men. On each side he stationed three groups of arquebusiers, four abreast and ten deep. In addition, he provided another sixty arquebusiers to act as skirmishers. He arrayed these battalions of about 500 men in three lines, enabling the commander to have reserves of balanced infantry units that he could commit to the place and in the numbers that the circumstances warranted. A number of smaller units also provided more opportunities for initiative on the part of lower commanders. To take advantage of this system and to furnish the leaders needed to realize the potential for maneuverability, Maurice provided for a high proportion of officers and noncommissioned officers.

With its shallow array, more Dutch pikemen could face the enemy, and none found themselves out of the action at the center of a square. The greater depth of the arquebusiers reflected the system of continuous fire accomplished by the front rank's firing and marching to the rear of the ten ranks to reload while the next rank stepped forward to fire and then march to the rear in its turn. The shallow arrangement of the pikemen and the fixed relationship between the pikes and the arquebusiers compelled the pikemen to practice extensively if the new battalion was to remain steady in shallow deployment as well as to exploit the promise of mobility and maneuver implicit in the smaller unit. To cope with the problem of mobility for a linear formation, Maurice took over the drill and even the words of command from the Roman legion and, for the first time since ancient days, created a drilled infantry in linear array. To subject his soldiers to the necessary discipline and training required regular pay, an innovation that the usually solvent Dutch government made. Maurice's infantry, regularly paid and serving year after year, had a proficiency, discipline, cohesion, and maneuverability unknown in the West since Roman times.

The new deployment purchased its advantages at a higher cost than drill and regular pay. The linear arrangement of pikemen of fifty files and five ranks had a vulnerable flank and rear, which the conventional block, based on the Swiss model, lacked. A cavalry charge against the flank or rear of a square would compel it to halt to adopt an all-around defense, but such a charge against a Dutch pike array would strike its vulnerable flank or rear. In addition, the large number of small formations, so useful in marching on the battlefield to concentrate against an attacker's strength or exploit an enemy weakness, made the army harder to maneuver. Although a battalion of 500 men moved more readily than a single unit of 3,000, a linear formation had to advance carefully to avoid disarray, and a commander with equal forces had six times as many units to control. This meant not only transmitting six times as many orders but also framing the orders for movement so as to retain the appropriate relationship among the various battalions. A commander could move several blocks of 3,000 men into a new array far more easily than he could accomplish the same task with a score or more of 500 in linear arrangement. Their non-linear deployment had held much of the secret of the mobility of the Swiss, just as Epaminondas's deep formation at Leuctra had a mobility impossible for a line that had to keep its alignment and avoid gaps in its ranks. But more officers leading promptly paid, carefully drilled soldiers could compensate for the difficulties and exploit the advantages of the new system.

Though the scarcity of battles in the wars in the Netherlands prevented a thorough test of Maurice's system against the established method practiced by the Spanish, young King Gustavus embraced the Dutch tactics. An accomplished linguist with a firm grounding in the classics as well as a mastery of German, Italian, and Dutch, the well-educated young prince read both Roman and Dutch authors on drilled, articulated linear infantry. But he made significant changes when he arranged not only his pikemen in an array six deep and thirty-six across but also the ninety-six arquebusiers on each side in six ranks. This shallower deployment reflected his hope for an increased rate of fire, which his adoption of paper cartridges containing an already measured amount of powder would make possible. He also substituted for the arquebus a lighter and handier musket, thus giving his light infantry a uniform and, in the aggregate, more powerful armament.

Giving stress to the enhanced firepower potential, he also adopted a volley-firing technique for his musketeers, made possible by the thinner line in which he could maintain a continuous fire by separate ranks. When all men had loaded their muskets, they could reduce the six ranks to three by filling the intervals between the men ahead. Even a close initial formation of musketeers provided adequate space for this maneuver because men with matchlocks needed elbow room to keep their matches alight and wished to keep other matches away as they worked with gunpowder loading their weapons. When the musketeers had completed the shoulder-to-shoulder rearrangement into three ranks, the front rank knelt, the second rank stooped, and all three ranks simultaneously fired a volley. In Gustavus's tactical thinking, such a volley provided an admirable preparation for a charge by his well-drilled pikemen because, according to an English expert, such a salvo not only would do the enemy "more mischief" but also would "quail, daunt, and astonish them three times more, for one long and continued crack of thunder is more terrible and dreadful to mortals than ten interrupted and severall ones."[6]

But Gustavus's reforms went far beyond adopting and improving the Dutch infantry system. He also increased firepower by giving to his battalions a small cannon, which shot a three-pound cannonball or, more usually, grape or cannister shot. These differed little from musketballs, except that a three-pounder cannon could shoot more than two dozen balls with each discharge. One horse could pull this cannon, and two or three men could move it on the battlefield.

Gustavus did not change the weapons of the cavalry, but he altered their doctrine. He had learned much in the 1620s when he tested his new tactical system in a war with the Poles and saw their old-fashioned heavy-cavalry lancers ride down his cavalry, who tried to function as light cavalry with their pistols, and then cut down his infantry, which then consisted largely of light infantry arquebusiers. Rather than adopting the lance, he arranged his cavalry in the old linear formation for charging and instructed the front rank to fire only one pistol and then charge for shock action with swords. Cavalry had come so much to rely on firing their pistols and falling back to reload that horsemen, particularly in Germany, had gotten out of the habit of charging either infantry or other cavalry with their swords. Gustavus's new cavalry doctrine, which would have the effect of pitting heavy against light cavalry in shock combat, would surprise German cavalry, just as Polish lancers had the Swedes or as Alexander's Companions had stunned the Persian cavalry that planned to hurl javelins and avoid serious shock action. Gustavus catered to his cavalry's belief that they needed missiles in battle by assigning some musketeers to work with the horsemen.

Gustavus's Persisting Strategy and Employment of Distraction

With 13,000 men of this new-model army Gustavus Adolphus landed on the north German coast on July 4, 1630. A decade of war had made the portly Swedish king, only thirty-three years of age, a seasoned commander who, though he had a propensity to lead reconnaissances and even charges himself, had a thorough grasp of all branches of the art of war and the ability to make brilliant application of his carefully acquired skill. Becoming king just before his seventeenth birthday, he had found himself prepared for his duties because of his good education and his father's associating him in the work of governing since he was thirteen. As capable at statecraft as war, Gustavus had the affection of his subjects and the services of an extraordinarily able chancellor to conduct the affairs of the kingdom in his absence.

Disembarking in north Germany, he promptly fortified his landing place just as William the Conqueror had. In immediately resorting to field fortifications, Gustavus practiced what had ruled as orthodoxy since the *condottieri* in Italy two centuries ago. Several years before, Gustavus's less-sophisticated Polish adversary had complained of the Swedish king that he could not fight an opponent "who like a mole fights under ground, and who being weaker in cavalry protects himself against it by trenches and bastions."[7]

An initial lack of cavalry constrained the Swedish army's operations, as did the determination of the thorough Gustavus to establish a firm base area before advancing. The Poles had defeated him two years earlier by avoiding battle and by devastating the country before him as he advanced, thus causing him to lose one-third of his army to the enemy's successful logistic strategy. This time Gustavus planned to pursue a persisting strategy and assure his own supplies as well as diminish those available to the enemy.

Initially occupying a small area already completely scoured by Wallenstein, Gustavus fed his army with supplies brought by sea from Sweden. But gradually he expanded along the coast and provided enough depth to his bridgehead that he could find sufficient grass to begin to bring in cavalry. His imperial opponents proved too weak to contest actively his gradual occupation of territory, and the duke of Pomerania, though still trying to maintain his neutrality, surrendered to the Swedes the city of Stettin near the mouth of the Oder, a major artery of commerce.

While he occupied the summer and fall in consolidating his position in Pomerania, Gustavus received no support from the Protestant leaders, many of whom viewed him with suspicion. The exception, the revolt against imperial rule of the city of Magdeburg, proved more of an embarrassment than a help because Gustavus believed he could not yet venture so far inland. He dared not risk an advance, when his invasion had received such a skeptical reception, nor could he carry out a march deep into territory dominated by the enemy.

Even if he had wished a march to relieve Magdeburg, he would have had to cross the neutral territory of the electors of Brandenburg and Saxony. Always politically alert, Gustavus, trying to make friends in Germany, did not wish thus to offend either the elector or other Protestant princes whom such a march would threaten and alienate. But since the emperor had only a very small force engaged in the siege of Magdeburg, Gustavus could expect the city to hold out indefinitely unless the formidable Count Tilly marched his powerful Catholic

Map 4.1. Germany

army east to join the siege. As the winter of 1630–31 approached, Tilly remained inert, and Gustavus faced equally quiescent opponents along the coast east and west of him and from a well-fortified enemy force at Gartz, up the Oder from Stettin.

Logistics continued to give him difficulty because the contributions he levied in Pomerania and the money from Sweden did not suffice to pay his troops. The resulting ravaging of the country by the soldiers, "worse," one of his men said, "than if we were in an enemy country," harmed discipline and alienated the Protestant Pomeranians. Sadly he wrote, "Popular feeling in the country has undergone a great alteration." But he managed to keep his army fed and clothed and carried out an operation that exploited the enemy's inability to do the same. Concentrating a force of 14,000 men, Gustavus moved by foot and in a flotilla on the unfrozen Oder on December 24 to attack the starving and undisciplined imperial force at Gartz. Reduced to 4,000 effective infantry with most of its cavalry in search of forage, the garrison of Gartz made only a token defense before their commander led them on a rapid march south. The commander slowed his retreat enough to burn every village on his route to leave a logistic barrier against Swedish pursuit. Instead of following, Gustavus, with the aid of his river supply route and having pushed up the Oder far enough to threaten Frankfort, built a fortified camp near the river.[8]

This move resulted in eliminating any immediate danger to Magdeburg. The threat that the Swedish king might advance against Frankfort and into the emperor's dominion of Silesia brought Tilly's main imperial army on a winter march east and carried him past Magdeburg, besieged by inadequate imperial forces, and on to Frankfort. Tilly intended to prevent Gustavus's invasion of Silesia, which would enrich the Swedes with contributions and impoverish the emperor's subjects, even if it did not annex the province to the Swedish sphere of influence. Though he did not discount the power of this threat nor the benefits of an invasion of Silesia or of even a move beyond into Bohemia and toward Vienna, Gustavus did not base his strategy on raids. Instead he persistently and methodically conquered the country, subduing and garrisoning the cities. Thus he brought Protestant territory securely under his sway and protected it by garrisons and improvements in the fortifications of the cities. In this way he created a secure base of at least potentially loyal territory, which could help supply his growing army. Also, as did Henry V of England when he adopted a persisting strategy and started to conquer France piece by piece after his victory at Agincourt, Gustavus aimed at the permanent acquisition of the land and its resources, a secure and valuable support for Protestantism and Sweden. The Protestantism of the country he occupied provided a political base for this intrusion of the foreign king.

The fall of Gartz had the desired result by causing Tilly to implement a decision already taken to strengthen Frankfort and, when he, with characteristic energy, made the 200-mile march in ten days, to do it with the exceptional celerity the situation merited. Now Gustavus faced a first-class imperial army

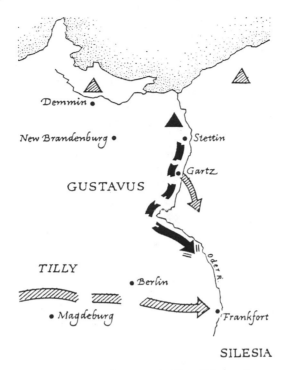

Diagram 4.1. Gustavus's First Distraction

commanded by a distinguished general. Having entered the army at age fifteen as a pikeman, the short, thin, long-nosed Tilly had almost sixty years of active service, twenty-seven of it as a general. He had fought under the command of the duke of Parma and against the Turks and had many years as an almost uniformly successful commander. But the young king had won the first round when his attack on Gartz had distracted Tilly, thus creating a weakness elsewhere. Even though Tilly had not intended to move his army to press the siege of Magdeburg, Gustavus, having drawn him to the east side of his perimeter, could take advantage of this for offensive, rather than his originally intended defensive, purposes. And the king had the strategic position to make the most of this distraction because he could utilize his interior lines to strike toward the west to broaden his base and so expand the area subject to his contributions and from which he could draw supplies.

In moving westward toward the Mecklenburg city of Demmin and capturing several towns as he did so, Gustavus opened the second round of a contest that extended over more than a year and a half and pitted him against two masters of the seventeenth-century art of war. These skillfully conducted campaigns ably exemplify strategy under conditions in which fortifications and terrain obstacles, though important, did not dominate combatants operating with a relatively low ratio of force to space. As had always been the case under these circumstances with similarly constituted armies, neither contestant could compel an unwilling opponent to fight.

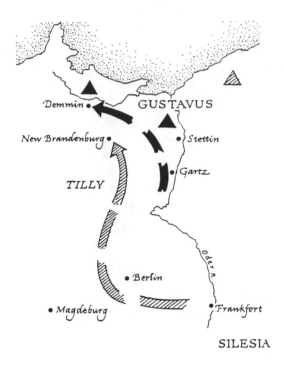

Diagram 4.2. Gustavus Exploits Interior Lines

Starting on January 29, 1631, Gustavus advanced toward Demmin and in less than three weeks captured six towns, including the powerfully fortified and strongly garrisoned Demmin itself, which the inept imperial commander readily surrendered. Although Tilly moved promptly to save the situation, Swedish control of the intervening towns and river crossings forced him to march west, to the south of Berlin, and then north, by which time Gustavus had completed his campaign to expand his base area. Having secured his objective and again foiled Tilly, Gustavus went into winter quarters.

But Tilly sought to redeem the campaign and perhaps have a battle with Gustavus by advancing with 13,000 men against the nearby Swedish-held town of Neu-Brandenburg, whose garrison of 750 lacked artillery or modern fortifications. Gustavus responded by concentrating 19,000 men to relieve the city. But apprehensive of a battle with the redoubtable Tilly when his cavalry, largely unpaid German mercenaries, might prove unreliable, Gustavus again tried to save Neu-Brandenburg by using the hitherto successful strategy of distraction. He again moved to threaten Frankfort and also interfered with Tilly's communications with the Magdeburg besieging force. But the operation failed. Tilly had not learned of the Swedish movements before he had stormed Neu-Brandenburg, killed a third of the garrison, and sacked the town.

Tilly then moved to Magdeburg, intent now on pushing the siege with vigor. Heretofore the besieging army, too small to do more, had maintained only a partially effective blockade of the city. Augmented by Tilly's force and with the shrewd old soldier in personal command, Madgeburg's besiegers could maintain a close blockade, attack the fortifications with artillery, mines, and all the other resources of siegecraft, and carry out an assault if a favorable opportunity presented itself.

On March 27 Gustavus, acting to create a new distraction sufficient to draw Tilly from Magdeburg, moved south on the Oder with a flotilla, 14,000 men and 200 guns, to attack Frankfort. Since the 6,000 defenders had capable commanders, a long siege seemed inevitable, but the navigation of the Oder would permit Gustavus to maintain it successfully. Hearing of Gustavus's move on March 31, Tilly promptly left Magdeburg and began a march to relieve Frankfurt. But, on April 3, the day after the king's army had reached Frankfort, the Swedish army stormed the city, massacred the garrison, and sacked the Protestant town. In this case, however, success meant failure for the distraction, since with the town lost Tilly turned back to resume the siege of Magdeburg.

Gustavus, having awaited Tilly's arrival at Frankfort in vain, turned to try to relieve the city directly, and to do this he had to negotiate passage for his army through the neutral electorates of Saxony and Brandenburg. On April 20, before Gustavus succeeded in gaining permission to march through this territory of the neutrals, Tilly carried out a victorious surprise assault against the city, after which his unpaid and badly fed soldiers burned the city and killed 20,000

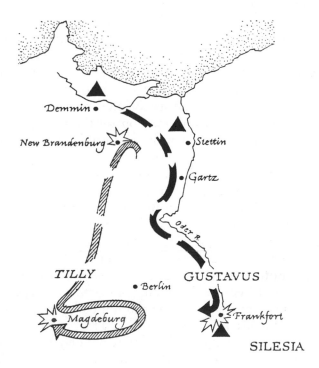

Diagram 4.3. Second Distraction Fails

civilians, two-thirds of the town's inhabitants. For two weeks after the sack of the city, bodies of the slain clogged the river that ran through Magdeburg.

In this campaign both Gustavus and Tilly had fought defensive campaigns: Gustavus sought to protect Magdeburg and Tilly needed to contain the Swedish bridgehead and cover the emperor's Silesian province. But each also had offensive goals: Tilly, the capture of the rebellious city of Magdeburg, and Gustavus, a need to expand his base area. Both failed in their defensive missions but attained their offensive objectives.

Swedish strategy relied on distractions, made easier to execute by the interior lines of operation provided by the semicircular bridgehead area of garrisoned and fortified cities. After his taking of Gartz had drawn Tilly to the Oder, Gustavus concentrated on the opposite side of the theater, overwhelmed a half-dozen towns, and significantly expanded his bridgehead. Gustavus thus ably applied Xenophon's aphorism: "Wise generalship consists in attacking where the enemy is weakest, even if the point be some way distant." But because competent opponents do not usually offer weak points to attack, the diversion provided by the Gartz operation proved essential in creating the weakness at Demmin against which Gustavus concentrated by utilizing his interior lines. Thus Gustavus showed his mastery of a technique basic to concentration against weakness, a distraction to lure an opponent into creating a weak point.

Gustavus also used this threat as a defensive strategy because political as well as military considerations made him reluctant to march through neutral territory deep into an enemy-held area and there risk defeat in a battle to relieve Magdeburg directly. The capture of Gartz proved effective in confirming Tilly's preexisting anxiety about the Oder line and thus distracting him from the Swedish weak point, Magdeburg. The effort to divert the imperial general from Neu-Brandenburg miscarried because Tilly captured the city before he learned of the Swedish menace elsewhere, and the attack on Frankfort failed because Gustavus captured the city before the threat persisted long enough to draw Tilly to its relief. Yet clearly the function of a distraction on the defense was quite symmetrical with its use on the offense. On the offensive a distraction or diversion created a weakness by drawing enemy forces away from the proposed point of attack; on the defensive, in causing the enemy to concentrate in the wrong place, it protected the defender's weak point from attack.

Except for Tilly's advance on Neu-Brandenburg when both commanders had a fight in mind, the expectation of combat had no role in these maneuvers. Since neither army could count on forcing battle on the other, a battle itself was unrealistic as an objective, and this condition provided a considerable measure of security for both armies. To turn an enemy, as had Caesar at Ilerda, usually proved impossible because the small, compact armies easily moved away from each other in the comparatively large and unobstructed spaces of northern Germany. A terrain obstacle could trap an army and force a battle or capitulation, but the Swedish and imperial commanders had too much ability and experience to compromise themselves. A siege, by threatening something vital, could often induce a battle, but Gustavus declined the opportunity before Magdeburg.

The use of distraction, which played so large a role in Gustavus's operations, typified the warfare of the period. Gustavus's menaces took two forms. In capturing Gartz and then Frankfort he expanded his base area, an objective in harmony with his persisting strategy. In presenting a danger to Silesia, however, he threatened a raid into one of the imperial base areas. Yet this involved no inconsistency for Gustavus because, with such small armies, raids had constituted a staple of strategy since the beginning of the Thirty Years' War as well as for thousands of years before.

Actually raids, rather than the persisting strategy followed by Gustavus and Tilly, typified these distracting operations, which often took the form of counter raids to induce an opponent to abandon his own. A Spanish minister characterized such strategy well: "If we put an army of 40,000 men in the field they bring out as many and more. With them they prevent us from doing anything. If we want to cross a river with all of our main army, they cross another with theirs. If we lay siege to one place, they lay siege to another of ours. In this situation, Sir, in order to get anywhere in this war it is necessary to have two armies."[9]

In their campaigns Gustavus pursued an essentially offensive persisting strategy and Tilly, in spite of the ultimately successful siege of Magdeburg, a defensive persisting strategy to contain Gustavus's offensive into Germany. And though neither had a primary objective of battle with the other, both pursued a combat strategy in that they focused their efforts not on their opponent's supplies but on the attack and defense of fortified cities.

Yet in the contest between these two fine generals, the weakness that, on the offensive, distractions aimed to create and, on the defensive, to protect, had a political and logistic character; so each sought to exploit the other's or protect his own political or supply vulnerabilities. In expanding his base in Mecklenburg, Gustavus deprived the enemy of supplies and contributions and expanded his resources by the same amount. Tilly posed more of a political than a military menace by his threat to take Magdeburg, because the fall of the city would confer significant political advantages on his cause through intimidating opposition by suppressing a rebellion against the emperor. An advance by Gustavus into Silesia and perhaps into Bohemia could amount to little more than a raid, but the supplies he could find and the large contributions he would collect would strengthen him and correspondingly weaken the emperor; such a raid could only hurt the imperial cause politically. So logistical and political aims often coincided.

An offensive persisting combat strategy, simply by the acquisition of a significant portion of hostile land area, could win the war if the attacking power had sufficiently modest political objectives. But with aims too ambitious to attain by the acquisition of such a piece of territory, the persisting strategy would embrace the logistic strategy of depriving the enemy of resources and, if political and other conditions permitted, also of aggrandizing the strength of the successful aggressor. Thus Gustavus's systematic conquest and fortification of Protestant territory slowly but surely built his resources in supplies and money. The Catholic forces, on the defensive against the Swedes, sought to retain territory both because lost land area stood for impaired political objectives and because retaining control of their domain implemented their defense against a persisting logistic strategy.

In other words, until a persisting strategy had taken enough land and cities from the enemy to constitute a big enough prize to extract from the defeated the concession of the goal of the war, territorial acquisition counted as a logistic strategy. Since political objectives defined the measure of military success needed for their attainment, modest aims required only limited victories and great expectations demanded important military achievements. Since Gustavus sought to reverse the tide of more than a decade of war, his impressive gains in north Germany did not suffice to carry him very far toward the kind of peace he desired.

Gustavus's Exploitation of the Triumph of His Linear System at Breitenfeld

Soon after the fall of Madgeburg Gustavus secured the cooperation of Brandenburg, including contributions and the right to recruit soldiers in Brandenburg territory. Using these resources, Gustavus resumed the expansion of his base area, extending west along the Baltic coast and southwest into the fertile, untouched country east of the Havel River, where he began to fortify towns to hold the line of that river. Meanwhile, Tilly had left the Magdeburg area, unable to sustain his army in the denuded country around the burned city. Leaving a small force in the vicinity of Magdeburg, he marched south to find supplies for his army and to meet reinforcements from Italy. But when he learned that Gustavus had crossed the Havel, had reached the Elbe, and had occupied the productive region between the rivers, the now-reinforced Tilly turned north, ready to fight this new Swedish expansion.

As Tilly's strong army moved north in late July 1631, Gustavus began to fortify a position at Werben in a bend in the Elbe. With his rear and both flanks protected by the river, he began erecting an elaborate line of field fortifications across the neck of land. With his back to the river Gustavus had ample water for his men, access to river-borne supplies, and protection for his flanks. Yet with only one bridge over the river, the king displayed the confidence which seventeenth-century generals typically had in their fortifications; if the enemy should attack and carry the fortifications, Gustavus, with only a single bridge as a route of retreat, would lose virtually his entire army. As anxious to fight as Tilly, the king made certain he had all of the advantages the defense offered. Digging rapidly, he finished his entrenchments before Tilly arrived; as a Scottish officer in Swedish service remarked, where Tilly "did but march with his army in the day time, we with spades and shovells, wrought our selves night and day in the ground, so that, before his coming, we had put ourselves out of danger of his Cannon." Having reached Werben with his army, the wise Tilly, daunted by the formidable fortifications, skirmished, fired his cannon, and withdrew twenty miles to the south.[10]

In late August Tilly himself seized the initiative: he marched south into Protestant Saxony to supply his troops and to lay waste the elector's territory in an effort to force the Saxon ruler to abandon the alliance he proposed to conclude with the Swedes. Gustavus marched quickly to unite his army with the elector's and fight Tilly or at least force him from Saxony. With additional reinforcements, Tilly had no aversion to accepting the offer of battle, which his application of the old strategy of devastating the country had provoked, and took up a position on level terrain at Breitenfeld, north of Leipzig. Gustavus's and the elector's armies moved to meet him.

The Scottish officer quoted above contrasted the appearance of the Swedish veterans with the Saxon army, fresh from garrisons or newly recruited, which "for pleasing the eye, was the most complete little Armie, for personages of man, comely statures, well armed, and well arraide, that ever mine eyes did looke on, whose officers did all looke, as if they were going in their best apparell and Armes to be painted." But the Swedes, "having lyen over-night on a parcell of plowd ground, they were so dusty, they looked out like Kitchen-servants, with their uncleanly rags." A Swedish observer made a similar observation about the Swedes and the imperial soldiers, the latter opulently attired in the loot of many campaigns: "Ragged, tattered and dirty were our men (from the continual labours of this last year) besides the glittering, gilded and plume-decked imperialists. Our Swedish and Finnish nags looked but puny, next their great German chargers. Our peasant lads made no brave show upon the field when set against the hawk-nosed and mustachio'd veterans of Tilly." And so the armies would fight as each commander, confident of the outcome, believed that the time and the field suited battle.[11]

Gustavus arrayed his army the evening before the battle, his men sleeping in the order in which, on the morning of September 17, they marched to combat near the little village of Breitenfeld. He formed his 500-man infantry units in two lines, with a reserve of infantry and cavalry between the two and a reserve of cavalry behind the second line. His linear system, with a depth of five for his pike and six for his musketeers, enabled him to make a front that equaled Tilly's and still provide ample reserves. The Swedish array did not differ in substance from that employed by the Romans. The seasoned Tilly, adopting the traditional doctrine, used formations with a fifty-man front and a depth of thirty, which he arranged in groups of three, the center rectangle a little ahead of the other two. Essentially in one line and with no reserve beyond some cavalry behind his infantry, Tilly's men assumed deep shapes, which had one significant attribute—the capacity for all-around defense—that Gustavus's shallow arrangement lacked. On their flanks each commander placed the bulk of his cavalry, Gustavus's with a reserve and groups of musketeers intermingled with his first line. To the Swedish left the elector of Saxony arrayed his army, with infantry in the orthodox large squares and cavalry on each flank. The allied Swedish and Saxon forces thus deployed as two separate armies, which divided their infantry by the wings of Swedish and Saxon horse. Thus the combined armies had cavalry in the center as well as on the wings.

In the morning the Swedish host marched cross country in battle array toward Tilly's already formed army. The opposing forces had essentially the same level of excellence, Gustavus's well-drilled Swedes and Tilly's veterans, each diluted, the Swedes by the green Saxon army and the imperialists by the indifferent quality of Tilly's reinforcements. In the emperor's aged field marshal the experienced young king met a worthy antagonist and proficient exponent of the sixteenth-century tactical methods that had dominated the first decade of the war.

With drums beating, trumpets blaring, and artillery booming, the action began with the charge of the cavalry on Tilly's left. The Swedish cavalry stood its ground and received the pistol attacks of the imperial cavalry with volleys from their musketeers and short charges with the saber. With the superior weapon systems of light infantry arquebusiers and shock action by mounted men fighting as heavy cavalry, the Swedes bested Tilly's horsemen who, like light cavalry, relied on their pistols. In this protracted struggle Tilly's cavalry, led by the impetuous but courageous and competent Count Pappenheim, advanced seven times. The Swedes defeated each attack as light cavalry tactics with the pistol failed against the muskets of the Swedish light infantry mingled with the cavalry and the Swedish shock-action charge with sabers, which then drove back the imperial pistoleers. The Swedish reserve cavalry extended the front and used countercharge with sabers to vanquish Pappenheim's effort to turn their flank. After the defeat of its seventh assault, Pappenheim's cavalry withdrew from the field.

While Tilly's cavalry made these charges on his left and the infantry stood immobile as each army's artillery sent cannonballs through the opposing ranks, the imperial cavalry on the right charged and routed the Saxon cavalry. Though the Swedish cavalry protected its infantry, the perceptive Tilly saw and immediately availed himself of the opportunity to exploit the weakness of the Saxons by sending the majority of his infantry against them.

Even though they lacked the drill of the Swiss, Tilly's advancing blocks of pikemen with their attached arquebusiers and musketeers moved easily on the level ground, crossed the field obliquely to their right, and attacked the already demoralized Saxon infantry, which promptly fled, pausing only to loot the Swedish camp as it left the scene of battle. With the rout of the Saxons, Tilly had defeated 40 percent of the enemy army and exposed the Swedish forces to a blow in the flank by his infantry formations. But as Tilly reordered his infantry into an array to roll up the Swedish flank, Gustavus and General Horn, his skillful subordinate on his left flank, formed the well-drilled Swedish infantry of the second line into a battle array at right angles to its front. In the nick of time, having barely fifteen minutes to complete this redeployment, the Swedish line faced Tilly's infantry.

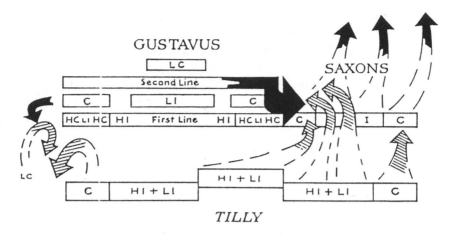

Diagram 4.4. Diagram of Positions and Movements at Breitenfeld

The course of the remainder of the battle is not clear, but the charge of Swedish cavalry on the king's left drove off Tilly's cavalry, and with its aid the Swedish infantry gained the upper hand. Part of this supremacy lay in the fire-power that their six-rank formation of musketeers could deliver in a short space of time. The imperial arquebusiers and musketeers, thirty ranks deep, used the countermarch to maintain a steady fire on a narrow front as each rank filed to the rear to reload. But the Swedish method permitted a concentration of fire in time, which proved more effective in supporting the charges of the Swedish cavalry and pikemen. And the light infantry fought one another also, a participant in the Swedish army describing the advance of his company thus: "First I had three of the smaller cannon I had in front of me fire, and I did not allow my musketeers to fire a salvo until we were within pistol range of the enemy. Then I had the first three ranks fire a salvo, followed by the other three ranks; then we drove in on them and struck away at them with our muskets or sabres." This same captain also witnessed a successful attack of imperial cavalry on pikemen unsupported by musketeers. "They moved up close to them and fired their pistol salvos once or twice, killing all of the Scottish color bearers, so that suddenly many colors fell simultaneously to the ground."[12]

In the closing phase of the battle, Tilly's infantry, deserted by its defeated cavalry from both flanks and faced with the fire of the excellent Swedish guns as well as its own artillery, which the Swedes had captured and turned against the enemy, held out gallantly. But with its commander wounded and its losses hideous, it abandoned the field, leaving 7,600 dead. Swedish cavalry or peasants seeking revenge on soldiers killed many more during the retreat, and the Swedes took 6,000 prisoners on the field and more later, many of these eventually enlisting in the Swedish forces. The Swedish dead numbered 1,500, the Saxon, 3,000.

The battle proved a dramatic endorsement of the linear system and cavalry, which relied more on the shock action of its sabers than on the fire of its pistols.

The Swedish employment of a formation in two lines to make a reserve enabled Gustavus to protect his army's flanks and differed in no essential respect from the use made of their second lines by Scipio and Caesar. Classical models had produced classical results.

Tilly retreated west, crossing the Weser with 13,000 men, the remains of the 34,000 he had deployed on the battlefield at Breitenfeld. Having inflicted more than 60 percent casualties on his opponent and more than made up his own losses by recruiting prisoners, Gustavus had achieved an exemplary tactical success. It had a major political effect, bringing in as allies many Protestant princes attracted by his victory or intimidated by his power. Gustavus harnessed them all to his military effort, occupying their territory and exacting contributions to maintain his now rapidly expanding army. To exploit his tactical achievement he immediately set out to enlarge his base, the area he garrisoned and that supported his forces by contributions. In this way he could augment his forces while diminishing the base from which the emperor could recruit and sustain his armies. This persisting strategy of systematic conquest had political objectives as well as a military foundation in the logistic strategy of using territorial conquest to deprive the enemy of the resources to supply his army. Gustavus's strategy up to this point differed little, except in the scale and speed of execution, from that which the English employed to conquer Wales or that used by Henry V in the last phase of the Hundred Years' War.

If Gustavus had remained consistent with his conservative policy of the previous twelve months, he would have used his victory to push west along the coast and to complete the conquest of the territory between the Weser River and the Dutch frontier. Such an objective would have constituted a fair strategic recompense for the tactical success of the high attrition gained at Breitenfeld and would have followed his earlier strategy of not advancing into more territory than he could quickly subdue, fortify, and garrison. His methodical progress had thus far proportioned the space conquered to the force then available to dominate it.

But the king's victory induced him to aim higher, and, leaving the conquest of the area to the west to subordinates, he marched south until he reached the Main River, levying contributions, organizing the conquered lands, and raising troops as he advanced. Meanwhile, the Saxon army invaded Silesia and pushed into Bohemia while Gustavus planned to move westward, down the Main to the Rhine. In addition to the control of this region, Gustavus hoped that his advance toward the Rhine would distract Tilly, drawing him out of the area west of the Weser where he had retreated, thus enabling the Swedish forces to make progress subduing that country.

Yet by recruiting and taking garrisons from some fortresses, Tilly had soon rebuilt his army to 25,000 men, and when he responded to Gustavus's distraction, he joined with another Imperial force and reached the Main with at least 40,000 men. The prudent Gustavus, intimidated by Tilly's numerically greater army, kept away from him, and Tilly, conscious of the low morale and deficient supply and equipment of his army, moved eastward in an attempt to divert Gustavus from his march down the Main by menacing Nuremberg, a city that proved too strong for him. But the threat presented by Tilly's Phoenix-like army clearly showed that the optimistic Gustavus, in going south to the Main rather than west of the Weser, had attempted more than the attrition of his victory at Breitenfeld had warranted. He had departed from his policy of consolidating his conquests before advancing again and of advancing no farther than he could readily control by garrisons and fortifications. This change had reduced the ratio of his force to the space it sought to dominate to a level that made it difficult for him to secure his new position in the large region along and south of the Main River. The king still pursued a persisting strategy but had, by moving too rapidly, so attenuated his control that he verged on a raiding strategy, if he had not actually crossed that line.

But with Tilly's move east toward Nuremberg, the king resumed his march down the Main, taking wealthy cities and supplying his army bountifully, "being in a fat land, as this was, abounding in all things except peace: they had plenty of corne, wine, fruite, gold, silver, Iewells, and of all sort of riches could be thought of." Having reached the Rhine, Gustavus consolidated his hold on the rich banks of the river and wintered his forces as he made plans to recruit 210,000 men for the campaign of 1632, enough to support an advance eastward into Bavaria and toward Vienna and to keep six other armies in the field. He would not raise more than 140,000, having overestimated the resources of the area under his control. But he did succeed in making war support war, for Swedes constituted only 13,000 of the 140,000 men; most of the money for the non-Swedish forces came from German contributions; but even though he had raised many less than he planned, Gustavus had recruited far more men than he could pay.[13]

Gustavus against Wallenstein: Logistic and Combat Strategies

In addition to Gustavus's search for men, Wallenstein's renewed activities helped exhaust the German supply of soldiers. The suddenly very dangerous Swedish threat had prompted the emperor to call back his most successful military contractor, and Wallenstein was raising an army in Bohemia in early 1632. He kept his recruiting efforts clear of Prague and the Saxon army that, having captured the city, enjoyed spending the winter at the enemy's expense. Aware that the elector of Saxony might again become neutral, Wallenstein sought to foster this development by his policy of carefully avoiding conflict with the Saxon troops occupying the Bohemian capital. Though apprehensive about Wallenstein enlisting a new army and what effect he might have on the Saxons, Gustavus began his spring campaign with an ambitious effort to enlarge his southern German base to include the Danube and even Bavaria. In late March the king reached the Danube and soon controlled the river from Ulm to Donauworth, which placed him at the border of staunchly Catholic Bavaria. The river Lech, deep, swift-flowing when the snows melted in the spring, marked this border.

Gustavus's victory at Breitenfeld brought him new allies and created new theaters of operation. He had success when the Saxon army penetrated Bohemia as far as its capital, Prague. But the efforts of his subordinates to extend his original base area westward to the Dutch frontier failed against the effective opposition of the talented and combative imperial commander, Count Pappenheim. Although Gustavus had command of many cities on the Main and Danube, his advance into eastern and southern Germany had yet to give him the same solid control and reliable base area that he had earlier established in the north. And without further attempts to consolidate his position, he prepared to invade Bavaria, which could only be considered a raid in such hostile country. Further, Wallenstein's new army in Bohemia inevitably cast a shadow over future operations. But Gustavus pushed on with his Bavarian campaign and, in the process, exhibited his mastery of combining distraction and concentration against weakness to cross a difficult and well-defended river line.

Although Tilly had broken all the bridges and had removed all of the boats, Gustavus attempted a crossing of the Lech in the face of a force of equal strength. Skillfully distracting Tilly with an artillery barrage at one place along the river and obscuring the point of their real crossing attempt with the smoke of gunpowder and burning straw, the Swedes crossed the river on a prefabricated floating bridge and, covered by their powerful artillery, established a firm bridgehead. The forest increased the effectiveness of the Swedish artillery because splinters from trees hit by cannonballs inflicted many injuries on Tilly's troops defending the crossing point. Gustavus's tactical diversion enabled him to cross the carefully defended river and overcome the weak defenders with his superior strength at the place he had selected.

Across the river, with the enemy army in retreat and Tilly mortally wounded, Gustavus began the systematic devastation of Bavaria in an effort to try political intimidation and to implement a logistic strategy of depriving the enemy of the resources of this rich land, hitherto untouched by war. The Bavarian elector ordered his subjects to kill the invaders, intensifying the usual bloody conflict between peasants and soldiers. But the capital, Munich, opened its gates to the Swedes to avoid a siege and a possible sack by paying a huge contribution. Gustavus's invasion of Bavaria had enriched his army with loot and depleted the resources of the elector but had not worked as a distraction to keep Wallenstein from marching his army to Saxony and possibly driving its often-indecisive elector from his alliance with Sweden.

The politically astute Wallenstein, however, still treated the elector's domain carefully and, having at last formed his army, confined his operations to retaking Prague and expelling the Saxons from Bohemia. But Wallenstein, preeminently the organizer and manager, had seen active military service early in the century and intermittently ever since and would prove his brilliance as tactician and strategist against Gustavus. Tall, thin, and red-headed, Wallenstein had an aloof and imperious manner that dominated all around him yet enabled him to inspire his soldiers with confidence and enthusiasm. The emperor's new commander would prove a worthy opponent for the great king of Sweden.

So just as Gustavus sought to safeguard Saxony by trying to draw Wallenstein to the south to protect Bavaria against his raid, Wallenstein aimed to draw Gustavus from Bavaria by his threat to the Saxons. Wallenstein's distraction worked when Gustavus at last decided to march to Saxony with half of his army. But the sagacious Wallenstein immediately moved south to prevent a junction of the Swedish and Saxon forces. When Gustavus reached Nuremberg, he learned that the formidable Wallenstein was marching south, presumably seeking battle. Emulating the earlier effectiveness of entrenchments in stopping Tilly at Werben, the careful Gustavus began to dig in at Nuremberg while calling for reinforcements from the Swedish forces beyond the Weser and from the Rhine and Danube. In late June, united with Tilly's old army, Wallenstein, with 48,000 men of very uneven quality, approached Nuremberg, eager for battle, only to find Gustavus's 20,000 men well dug in outside of the city.

Gustavus, the victor of Breitenfeld, suddenly found himself on the defensive at Nuremberg, his Saxon allies expelled from Bohemia, the campaign west of the Weser stymied by Pappenheim, and his efforts to consolidate a base area in southern and eastern Germany faltering while he dealt with Wallenstein. If Wallenstein had thrown his vastly stronger army against Gustavus's impregnable entrenchments at Nuremberg, the resulting Swedish victory would have again given the initiative to the king. But just as had Tilly at Werben, the cautious Wallenstein declined to attack the Swedish field fortifications.

In rejecting a combat strategy the resourceful imperial commander chose the logistic strategy of starving out Gustavus's army. With his greater numbers and his control of the nearby towns, Wallenstein dominated the territory north, east, and south of Nuremberg. Fortifying himself in a position on a river seven miles from the Swedish army, he believed that by depriving the Swedes of supplies, he could force Gustavus either to attack his fortified position or to undergo the loss of prestige attendant on a retreat. Meanwhile, Gustavus called for additional troops from his other armies and in the two months before they arrived each army sought to starve the other out by waiting, foraging, and interfering with the other's foragers. Neither succeeded, but Wallenstein's larger force foraged farther and fared better than Gustavus's. Meanwhile, as the Swedish reinforcements gathered at a distance, the king directed them to devastate the country as they marched to join him, destroying more of Wallenstein's supplies. In mid-August his reinforcements marched in, nearly 30,000 strong, bringing his army to 45,000 men.

Yet with the larger army, the situation for Gustavus changed little; instead of the Swedes' defying Wallenstein's formidable army from behind their entrenchments, Wallenstein now sought an assault on his well-entrenched position. The king must retreat, starve out Wallenstein, or attack. When Wallenstein moved his forces out on the west side of his position to invite attack in a strong

position, an inept Swedish scout reported that the imperial army was withdrawing. Gustavus moved to exploit this situation by assaulting the northeast side of
Wallenstein's position near an old fortification called the Alte Feste. With Wal-
enstein's army not in retreat but back manning its fortifications, the imperial
soldiers stopped the Swedish onslaught, losing only 600 men to 2,400 Swedish
casualties.

The defeat of this small attack at the end of August marked the time but
not the cause of the Swedish withdrawal. With the king's forces more than
doubled, Wallenstein's logistic strategy at last worked and worked well. By early
September 10,000 Swedish soldiers had deserted, and 6,000 horses had died.
On September 8 Gustavus began his departure, his cavalry reduced from 16,000
to 4,000 and the average size of his infantry companies cut from 150 to 57.
Wallenstein's logistic strategy had inflicted the attrition comparable to a major
combat defeat. The businessman-soldier had arranged his own supplies so well
that his own force had suffered much less.

As the two armies marched away from each other, neither commander knew
what to do next, other than respond to the logistical imperative to leave the
denuded Nuremberg area. Gustavus, moving south, finally decided to march
back to the Danube to complete the consolidation of his base for the 1633
campaign and to protect Saxony by launching another diversion into Bavaria
and toward Vienna. After vacillation, Wallenstein finally moved on Saxony, a
good place to winter his army and, by uniting with the successful Pappenheim,
to menace both Saxony and Gustavus's base area, a double diversion to draw
Gustavus from Bavaria. So each planned to exploit the offensive predominance
of the raid, make a foray into the other's base area, and so put his adversary on
the defensive. Between the competing distractions of threats to north Germany
and Saxony, on the one hand, to Bavaria, on the other, Wallenstein had the
better position. The Swedish king felt great solicitude for his carefully developed
northern base area, knowing that Saxony might leave the war if devastated while
Bavaria, the pillar of the Catholic league, would stay loyal to its cause.

So with his characteristic energy, the king marched north to protect Saxony
and secure his whole position in north Germany from Wallenstein and his capable
and tireless subordinate, Pappenheim, who had prevented Swedish generals from
subduing the region between the Weser and the Dutch frontier. Fearful that the
enemy might block the mountain passes leading to Saxony, the king marched
through the passes to Saxony, covering 380 miles in seventeen days, an average
of twenty-two miles per day. It says much for the discipline, morale, and har-
diness of his veterans that he made this remarkable march without seriously
diminishing his army.

Reaching Naumburg on the Saale at the end of October, Gustavus captured
this weakly defended town and crossed the river before Wallenstein's reinforcements arrived. Ignorant of the whereabouts of the armies of either Wallenstein
or his own Saxon allies, Gustavus dug in thoroughly at Naumburg, just as he
had at Werben and Nuremberg. Reconnoitering Gustavus's typically strong po-

sition, Wallenstein not only ruled out an attack but erroneously concluded in the inclement early November weather that Gustavus intended to spend the winter at Naumburg. Wallenstein himself had also planned to winter in Saxony and envisioned the application of a logistic strategy, a winter repetition of the Nuremberg struggle for control of the country and its supplies. So he began to disperse his army preparatory to this logistic contest and, remaining himself at Lützen, south of Leipzig, sent Pappenheim with a substantial force to Halle, twenty miles away.

But Wallenstein misjudged Gustavus's intent, and when the king learned of Wallenstein's dispersal, he promptly moved toward Wallenstein's position at Lützen. Realizing that a retreat would enable the king to unite with the Saxon army and reluctant to abandon his position between the two enemy armies or his communication with Austria and Pappenheim, Wallenstein resolved to fight the defensive battle that he was confident Gustavus would grant him.

Making the best use of the flat terrain, Wallenstein, afflicted by gout and carried in a chair, placed his right flank on a village, posting artillery nearby on a rise where it could enfilade the front, and covered his left flank with the very inadequate obstacle of a small stream. Here he arrayed all of his cavalry. In front of his army he made the most of a road flanked by two shallow ditches. The one on the side of the Swedish army he deepened, throwing up the dirt toward the enemy so that his musketeers could stand in the ditch and fire over a parapet. The ditch on the other side of the road he deepened more, throwing up the dirt on the side away from the Swedes. This created a second parapet, one protected by a ditch and sufficiently elevated so that the musketeers behind it could fire over the heads of those in the other ditch. In addition to these conventional preparations, Wallenstein demonstrated his flexibility by adopting smaller formations, no more than ten ranks deep, and arraying them in two lines. For his cavalry he employed a shallower arrangement and instructed them to emulate the Swedish tactic of shock action. Also in the Swedish fashion, he supported his cavalry with some musketeers and his infantry with a few light guns. Thus prepared, he awaited the Swedes and, more anxiously, the arrival of the redoubtable Pappenheim who was riding from Halle with his 3,000 cavalry to support his chief in the battle.

Reaching Wallenstein's position in the late afternoon, Gustavus placed his army in battle array, preparatory to an early morning advance to decide the battle before the arrival of Pappenheim. Without Pappenheim's cavalry, Wallenstein's imperial force had about 16,000 men, half cavalry, and the Swedes about 19,000, one-third cavalry. The Swedes adopted their traditional formation, with cavalry on both flanks, the best cavalry occupying the right, for the king planned to charge the imperial army's open left flank and then attack the infantry in flank and rear.

But a mist delayed the Swedish assault until eleven o'clock, and, just as the Swedish cavalry on the right had defeated the opposing imperial horsemen and was ready to turn against the infantry, Pappenheim arrived and turned the tide of the crucial cavalry battle. Meanwhile, the infantry had advanced, led by its king who received a musketball in the arm but continued at the head of his men, defeated the musketeers holding the ditches and, with the cavalry on its left, engaged in an indecisive struggle with the main imperial line. The tide of the cavalry battle on the Swedish right turned again when Pappenheim, mortally wounded by a cannonball, could no longer supply his incomparable leadership. But just as the Swedish cavalry again triumphed and once more began to attack Wallenstein's infantry, the mist returned and virtually halted the battle. Wallenstein made the most of the lull to send a brave and expert leader, Ottavio Piccolomini, and his remaining cavalry to his left where, when the mist lifted, his horsemen, inspired by the news of Gustavus's death and Piccolomini's vigorous and courageous leadership, restored the situation on Wallenstein's weak left. Piccolomini, who had five horses shot from under him, survived six bullet wounds to become the emperor's commander in chief and a prince of the Holy Roman Empire.

It looked as if Wallenstein had won the battle by successfully defending his position. But a strong attack by Swedish soldiers, anxious to avenge the death of the king, finally won on their left, carrying the village of Lützen, the rise in the ground, and the guns, together constituting the strongest part of the imperial position. Though the sun had set and his line still remained intact, the discour-

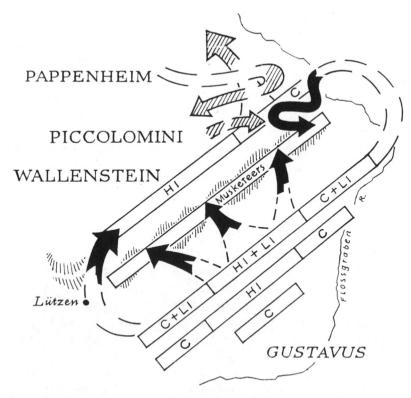

Diagram 4.5. Diagram of Dispositions and Actions at Lützen

aged Wallenstein resolved to retreat and, covered by his cavalry and supported by the arrival of Pappenheim's infantry, withdrew without difficulty. A more determined general might have retained his position and claimed victory at the Battle of Lützen. The Swedes, having lost a third of their army, proved too debilitated to pursue, even though the Imperialists had suffered in at least the same proportion. If the battle had an essentially neutral tactical impact, it produced valuable strategic results when Wallenstein decided to withdraw to Bohemia, leaving Saxony to the Swedes and removing the threat to the Swedish position in northern Germany. Wallenstein, too, soon passed from the scene, the victim of assassins who rid the emperor of his too powerful and independent subordinate.

The Impact of Gustavus's Tactics

Gustavus's death in battle did not end his tactical innovations. On the contrary, as Wallenstein's adoption of most of their fundamental concepts foreshadowed, they spread throughout Western Europe. Gustavus's modification of cavalry doctrine, with its stress on shock action in combat with other cavalry, became standard, even though most European cavalry made more extensive use of their pistols than Gustavus would have approved. But this amendment only restored to existing cavalry its real versatility that French cavalry well exemplified in the latter part of the sixteenth century. The most enduring legacy of Gustavus's changes was moving the infantry one more step in its evolution as the major force on the battlefield.

The Swiss pike-armed square had introduced an infantry that could dependably resist a cavalry charge from any direction, and Swiss drill and aggressiveness gave their squares the ability to attack. Originally light infantry had played no role in the Swiss infantry system, but the presence of an impregnable square gave light infantry an opportunity to perform on a battlefield dominated by heavy cavalry. Earlier light infantry had had a strictly defensive role in a defensive battle, as in the English system, which placed their longbowmen behind a physical obstacle. Since drilled and organized Swiss heavy infantry, unlike the dismounted English cavalry, could move about the battlefield, so also could light infantry which, finding security with the pikemen, could participate in any kind of battle and not have to rely on obstacles for defense.

The Swiss infantry thus became a universal model. At the same time the crossbowmen and arquebusiers gradually assumed more importance because the pikemen, usually lacking the drill, cohesion, and aggressiveness of the genuine Swiss product, did not have the mobility of the Swiss formations. The light infantry provided an offensive element: deployed as skirmishers, its men could shoot at the enemy's pikemen and, if they could find cover, even injure the cavalry. The increasing power of the arquebus, and especially the musket, made infantrymen dangerous to fully armored men and their horses. The development of reiter cavalry and its pistol attack against pikemen increased the importance of musketeers, now regarded as indispensable for protecting the heavy infantry from cavalrymen's pistols. Arquebusiers and musketeers came to play the same role as the crossbowmen in the Crusaders' wars with Turkish light cavalry.

The manpower system of the sixteenth century accentuated the offensive value of light infantry. The formal disbandment of mercenary armies after each campaign often prevented the pikemen from having the drill and acquiring the cohesion that the Swiss community system had given to its forces. But this same manpower system did not militate against the value of the light infantry, which traditionally fought as individuals, relying for its efficacy to a large degree on the skill and initiative of each arquebusier and musketeer, except when they joined the pike formation to find refuge from and help resist a cavalry attack. In any case, when musketeers fired, they performed an individual act, requiring a loose formation at best. Through several campaigns veteran professionals would have acquired the skills of skirmishing and firing. But equally experienced pikemen, who often served with unfamiliar compatriots, could not display the same effectiveness with tactics that depended on cooperation.

So the proportion of light infantry rose, in part because the manpower system retarded its skill development less than it did the heavy infantry's. At the same time it deprived the poorly drilled pikemen of much of their offensive potential. The advent of the reiter cavalryman increased the importance of the light infantryman, not just because of his role in protecting the pikeman from the horseman's pistol but because the reiter, in order to use his pistol, had discarded the lance and adopted the saber as his shock weapon. No longer faced with the charge of a medieval lancer, the pikeman lost some of his significance because reiter cavalry lacked the same power in shock action against pike-armed, heavy infantry. The development of pistol tactics for combat between cavalry also reduced the cavalry's capability and inclination to execute a vigorous and dangerous charge against a line of pikemen. So not only had the light infantry become essential to protect the heavy infantry from pistol fire, but the weaker cavalry attack required proportionately fewer pikemen to withstand it. By the seventeenth century the two arms had become full partners, equal in the prominence of their roles and in their numbers. Gustavus, through drill and doctrine, tried to restore to the pikemen their old offensive capability; but as his armies soon came to consist largely of German mercenaries, this part of his new tactical doctrine failed to persist, vitiated by the prevailing system and attitudes.

The change in the wages paid the two weapon systems reflected the modification in the comparative tactical value and quality of performance of the light and heavy infantry. At the beginning of the Thirty Years' War the pikeman received slightly better pay than the arquebusier or musketeer, but by the end of the war the gunner received nearly twice the pay of the pikeman. Wallenstein had already complained that the worst recruits received pikes, and the pay and tactical expectations reflected this development.

Thus the alterations of Maurice and Gustavus fitted into a process that had been going on for more than a century. Gustavus's changes further accentuated the role of the light infantry by giving it a major role in resisting a cavalry attack. By arming all handgunners with the more formidable musket and providing for volley firing, which enabled them to concentrate their fire at the critical moment, the musketeers, instead of taking refuge behind the pike, could become partners in repelling a cavalry charge. By adopting a linear formation Maurice and Gustavus fully recognized the modifications that had occurred since the introduction of the Swiss square. If pikemen had originally needed a square of fifty ranks and fifty files to resist the determined and skillfull attack of lance-armed, fully armored medieval cavalry, they hardly needed such depth to defeat the charge of partially armored men attacking with sabers. The linear formation, only five or six deep, could resist such an onslaught equally well. Even the pike became shorter, if only because it no longer needed to outreach the lance. The economy in men made possible by the thin formations facilitated the use of two lines, thus building a reserve into the army's array.

Most of these changes had started in the Spanish system, including the smaller formations and the improved coordination between the light and heavy infantry. For this reason also Gustavus's innovations spread rapidly, and they worked well, in spite of the increased shock power engendered by Gustavus's new cavalry doctrine of vigorous charges. The thinner formations of pike, assisted by volleys from the musketeers, had ample defensive power to resist a determined charge of not just saber-armed heavy cavalry but even of the Polish lancers that Gustavus's infantry had faced successfully. Gustavus had created a tactical system like the Roman one, with its two lines and its drill, necessary for the musketeers to fire their volleys and for the second line to move in good order if it were to fulfill its function as a reserve. But the new arrangement had greater versatility than the Roman because with 50 percent light infantry it could resist a Parthian attack by pistoleers as well as a charge by Gothic cavalry.

Gustavus's Roman scheme had one important drawback: its lack of all-around protection provided by formations modeled on the Swiss square. A line five ranks deep that could face only one direction meant vulnerable flanks and an assailable rear. In this respect such formations differed not at all from the Roman and, like the Romans, had the resources of a second line to support the first. And discipline, drill, and articulation comparable to that of the Romans provided another resource for the safeguarding of flank and rear. A second disadvantage of the new tactical formation lay in the loss of mobility inherent in the adoption of the linear formation of the Greeks and Romans. Whereas Swiss squares could move forward in a mutually supporting relationship without concern to keep their front aligned because each covered its own flanks, a linear formation had to keep each formation on the same line as the others. In addition, each unit, six deep with a front of a hundred or more, had trouble in keeping its own formation in line, a problem that a square with half the front never encountered. Further, good alignment had particular importance for the musketeers, who could shoot one another if they did not stand shoulder to shoulder when they fired their volley.

The deficient mobility of a line had shown itself in the experience of the ancients. Epaminondas at Leuctra had demonstrated the superior mobility of a square as he attacked the Spartan line by diagonal movement across the battle-field. Later the Scots and Swiss had often shown the battlefield mobility of their solid formations. But the loss in mobility remained largely in theory because the undrilled pikemen of the Thirty Years' War could not exploit the mobility inherent in the solid formations. Even Tilly's veterans had moved ponderously at Breitenfeld, the well-drilled Swedish lines equaling them in mobility.

Gustavus had markedly increased firepower by giving every light infantryman a musket, but his efforts to augment the role of artillery had less impact. His light artillery piece, which men could move in battle, still lacked enough mobility to provide much assistance in the offensive. More mobility for the guns made it easier for artillery to keep up with the army on the march and gave it greater assurance of a part in the battle. Yet that role remained largely defensive, and improvements in artillery continued to favor the defense because the defending line had the added firepower of artillery and the attacking line usually did not. The adoption of the linear system did diminish the vulnerability of infantry to long-range artillery fire because a cannonball could go through only six ranks. But this raised the value of enfilade fire and commanders like Wallenstein at Lützen sought to place their artillery on a flank where it could fire down an enemy's line or direct its balls on a diagonal path through an opposing linear formation. Cavalry, arrayed in a linear formation for shock action rather than in depth for the caracole with pistols, gained some protection from the destruc-tiveness of long-range artillery fire but remained vulnerable to enfilade fire.

Artillery acquired greater effectiveness from an improvement in its tech-nique. On level terrain a cannonball that struck the ground at a shallow angle would ricochet and skip along the ground, the way a flat rock will often skip on water. Ricochet fire intensified the danger of cannonballs to troops because they usually stayed below the height of a man's head and, in spite of the decreased velocity from contact with the ground, remained dangerous to human beings and horses. Ricochet fire mitigated artillery's ineffectiveness on the offensive; it provided a more potent method of attacking enemy formations prior to an onslaught. But once friendly troops began their assault, artillery, unless accom-panying the attacking troops, usually had to cease firing for fear of hitting its own men.

Artillery remained essentially powerful, but tactically immobile, light in-fantry. Movable enough to take the field and participate in battle, it still lacked the mobility characteristic of light infantry with its portable missile weapons. Its role in battle resembled that of the English longbowmen in their limitation to the defensive. But in sieges, it played the premier role in both attack and defense, and its range and power with either round or grape shot gave the guns an awesome versatility and deadliness. The tradition of the weaker blow of the missile weapon had disappeared with the musket, but the artillery's strength dwarfed musket, lance, and sword.

Though in their spread throughout Europe Gustavus's changes suffered dilution in letter and spirit, all armies eventually adopted the two-line battle array and the lines for pikemen that sacrificed all-around defense. But the linear formations enabled the two lines to make an essentially continuous front over a distance as great as previously covered by a single line of the old deep formations. An all-around defense through depth in the pike formation would have required either a shorter line, one easily overlapped and outflanked by an enemy with shallow linear formations, or a line that left such large gaps between the units that it could hardly interdict the passage of cavalry or even of enemy infantry formations. Thus the use of smaller formations arrayed in two lines to provide a reserve also carried with it the linear concept of deployment.

As the system evolved throughout the remainder of the seventeenth century, a subtle shift took place, and the musketeer took even greater precedence over the pikeman. The widespread use of slower-burning gunpowder enabled the explosive charge to give the ball a more sustained impetus and by making the most of the musket's long barrel increasing the velocity of the heavy bullet. Though the matchlock musket remained unreliable and difficult to fire more often than once a minute, its great power and its danger at a range of 250 yards meant that musketeers needed less help from the pikemen in protecting themselves against cavalry. The enhancement of the importance of firepower also argued for a linear formation in which every musketeer could use his weapon.

Even if generals tended to remain content with an essentially defensive role for pikemen, Gustavus's tactical method had made a fundamental innovation in its requirement that light infantry have the unified and cooperative action that only drill could provide. Instead of their usual role as skirmishers and their traditional reliance on individual initiative, the light infantrymen using the new plan of volley firing in ranks found it necessary to march together and maintain their interval and distance as well as to load at the same rate and fire on command. Even if commanders had contented themselves with a defensive role for the light infantry, as many did with their pikemen, the reliance on volleys for defense made drill imperative. The new tactics would place undrilled troops at a serious tactical disadvantage when they faced an adequately drilled opponent.

As the century wore on, tactics increasingly stressed the improvement of the firepower of the infantry. Neglecting Gustavus's idea of restoring the pikemen's offensive mobility, armies sought offensive as well as defensive strength through more numerous and better drilled musketeers. The proportion of pikemen thus declined until it fell as low as one-fourth of the whole of the infantry. Combats between infantry tended to become contests of light infantry using their missile weapons but arrayed in lines, much as Persian bowmen would have fought each other.

The standard infantry unit had become the battalion, usually about 600 or 700 strong, which arrayed itself with its pikemen grouped in the center and musketeers on either flank, both five ranks deep. If a cavalry charge should seem so menacing that it imperiled the battalion's musketeers, the pikemen formed a square within which some musketeers took refuge while the remainder placed themselves between the pikes to use their fire to help the pikemen defend against the cavalry. The solidity of the formation and the fire of the musketeers enabled the thin line of pikemen to turn back the charge of cavalry armed with sabers.

But the battalion's usual formation was far from compact, since the loading of the matchlock with its burning match required at least one yard between musketeers. To engage the hostile infantry, the battalion, five ranks deep with as many as 150 men abreast, moved slowly forward, carefully keeping its alignment, until less than 100 yards from the enemy. Then the opposing musketeers began to fire at one another, either each rank firing a volley and moving to the rear to reload, or all ranks from different portions of the line moving forward, spreading out to fire, and then falling back to their original positions to reload while another group moved out to fire. Since soldiers could only carry out their complicated reloading procedures while standing erect, both forces presented excellent targets for the inaccurate but powerful musket unless, as Wallenstein had provided at Lützen, one had the advantage of a parapet. The contest terminated when one side fled, the small number of pikemen having no role except as insurance against a cavalry charge. With combat limited to the light infantry's missiles, never in theory and not too often in practice did battles involve much shock action between hostile infantry, even though musketeers often carried swords.

In spite of its smaller and presumably more mobile units, the linear system did not give the infantry more mobility. Generals had no remedy for the need to move slowly and carefully to keep the long front in alignment. The Greek phalanx and the Roman legion had similar problems in their advances and had a particular concern to prevent gaps in the lines. The Romans eventually left openings that the second-line maniples filled before the first line made contact with the enemy. Gaps in a line of spearmen or swordsmen created flanks and permitted the enemy heavy infantry to penetrate and attack. The formation of the late seventeenth-century line followed Roman practice in its use of separate battalions with intervals as part of the formation of each of the lines. But unlike the Romans with their heavy infantry line, the seventeenth-century generals made no effort to fill the spaces. Because their predominantly light infantry force did not expect to close with the enemy, the generals did not fear the internal flanks that the openings created. In any case, the musketeers could cover these with their fire.

But the late seventeenth-century light infantry line had its own problems. The march forward could not unduly enlarge the interval between any two battalions because a wide hole would create a weak spot where the enemy could concentrate the fire of three of his battalions against the two that had lost their proper interval during the advance. Another difficulty, one special to the light infantry, had its root in the organization of the line. In addition to its five ranks, shallow compared to the deeper Greek and Roman formation, the line, with its drills to deliver fire, not only depended on each man keeping his proper place in his rank and file but also required that he keep the proper spacing and distance due to the complexity and danger of loading and firing a matchlock. So the musketeers needed to maintain their formation precisely to execute their shooting and reloading and as a necessary precaution against the matches lighting the powder each man carried and against the very real danger of the musketeers' shooting each other while firing on a smokey battlefield from a compressed, distorted, or disarranged formation.

In spite of the good discipline and drill to which commanders subjected their musketeers, an army lacked much articulation beyond that provided by its division into permanently constituted battalions. Though the battalions had subdivision into about a dozen companies commanded by captains, these never maneuvered independently. The requirements of fire discipline and the proper alignment of the battalion on itself and with the others gave the companies no tactical role in battle except when separate groups in the battalion carried out the firing. In a sense, the battalion came under a tyranny of the requirements of fire discipline. Whereas the Romans had needed separately maneuverable maniples and centuries for the second line to fill the gaps in the first, the late seventeenth-century line lacked any incentive to develop such subdivision and effective articulation since separately maneuvering companies on the battlefield would break the continuity of the front, diminish the line's firepower and could easily mask the fire of part of the line or cause friendly formations to fire at each other. Similarly, no permanent higher unit than the battalion existed, though commanders often formed ad hoc brigades. A linear system that treated the entire army's front as a unit had no tactical place for permanent groupings of battalions, any more than it could make much use of the capabilities for maneuver implicit in the existence of companies. Without an obvious need for independent action by the battalion's companies or to supply a permanent organization of brigades, the new armies, though linear like the Roman, lacked the Roman army's articulation and therefore its power to maneuver and its resilience when it lost its order.

With a more complex and easily disturbed formation and many more men to coordinate, infantry lacked the power of offensive action that the Swiss squares had displayed two centuries earlier. Though essentially substituting light for heavy infantry, the Europeans had at last reached the identical tactical situation as the Alexandrian and Roman armies had. Cavalry would have to play the same decisive role that it had in ancient times. The linear system and the battalion's lack of an all-around defense capability made the infantry particularly vulnerable to cavalry attacks on its flanks. And, unlike Roman heavy infantry, the musketeers could not protect themselves against shock action by saber-armed cavalry. By comparison with the Romans, they lacked the level of articulation that had often enabled Roman heavy infantry to maneuver so as to present a front to heavy cavalry and even, at Pharsalus, to take the offensive against the heavy cavalry attempting to attack the infantry's flank. Thus, to its intrinsic weapon-system advantage over infantry because it could use pistols against pikemen and sabers against musketeers, cavalry, through its better mobility, could exploit infantry's increased vulnerability in a linear array. With an infantry more exposed to cavalry and less able to take the offensive against enemy infantry, late seventeenth-century armies not surprisingly possessed a far-higher proportion of cavalry to infantry than did Roman armies.

The new system gave the mounted men the exact role they had had under Alexander the Great. Customarily deployed on the flanks as in ancient times, the cavalry had as its first objective the defeat of the enemy's cavalry; this mission completed, the horsemen, like Hannibal's at Cannae, aimed to attack the flank and rear of the enemy infantry. For this task the cavalry had the appropriate attributes of greater mobility and minimum requirements for careful array prior to executing its attack. If offensive troops may be defined as those that have mobility superior to that of their immediate opponents and the ability to go into action without delay, cavalry fully met these criteria on the battlefield created by Gustavus's reforms. Moving at a trot, well-trained horsemen could keep their formation in three lines and execute alterations in direction that, after the defeat of the opposing cavalry, enabled them immediately to charge with their sabers the flank or rear of the lines of enemy musketeers. Any effort to conduct such an attack with slow-moving, difficult-to-deploy infantry would have the handicap of such a sluggish advance and time-consuming and awkward deviation in direction that the enemy infantry would have ample time to change its front to meet the attack. Cavalry's greater mobility and ease of going into action made it ideal for the offensive, that is, for carrying out a movement to attack the enemy's weakness, the flank or rear.

In combat of cavalry against cavalry, the Swedish tactic of relying on the shock action of the charge with saber, though it affected all European cavalry, did not totally displace reliance on the pistol, many cavalry firing a pistol volley prior to charging the enemy cavalry. Cavalry usually used shock action exclusively against musketeers because a delay to fire pistols might expose the cavalry to another volley from the infantry's far more formidable muskets. So most cavalry adopted the shallow formation in three lines, which facilitated shock action, but continued to employ their pistols in cavalry engagements as well as to rely on them to prepare a charge against pikemen unprotected by musketeers.

Generals recognized the role of cavalry as the weapon system that had the necessary offensive capabilities to decide the battle. As in ancient battles, infantry fought infantry, often indecisively, with the defender having the benefit of choosing his ground, taking advantage of natural obstacles, and the freedom from the disturbance to his formation caused by a march to attack; and cavalry fought cavalry, each assuming the offensive because the nature of the horse made it unsuitable for receiving charges at the halt. Without a lance to use as a pike and with ample infantry forces on the battlefield, no cavalry dismounted to fight except the dragoons who, in addition to acting as cavalry, had received the weapon and training to fight as musketeers.

The Battle of Rocroi in 1643 well illustrates the decisive role of cavalry. The French, under the brilliant young son of the prince of Condé, advanced to relieve the fortress of Rocroi, besieged by a Spanish army. Confident of his veterans in a defensive battle, the Spanish commander arrayed his army to defend his siege. The French, willing to fight to raise the siege, moved up, the Spaniards cannonaded them at long range as they devoted much of the day to forming their army into line of battle. Each force had two lines of infantry with the cavalry on the wings, but the French had, behind their second line, an additional reserve of infantry and cavalry. A veteran of three campaigns, the future prince of Condé, aged twenty-two on this day, displayed all of the attributes that would make him one of the premier generals of the age. His eagerness to fight, his power of quick and firm decision, and his dauntless behavior in adversity all contributed to his first victory. Personally commanding the cavalry on his right, Condé opened the battle with a skillful and impetuous attack in which the traditionally excellent French cavalry defeated the mounted Spaniards opposing him. With part of his cavalry pursuing the defeated enemy horsemen, Condé had turned the remainder of his mounted force against the Spanish infantry when he learned of disaster on his left.

On the French left their cavalry had started its charge at too rapid a gait and met the enemy's vigorous countercharge with horses winded and ranks disordered. Having defeated the French cavalry, the Spanish horsemen, aided by the infantry on their right, attacked the French infantry and defeated both lines. Only the prompt action of the French reserve prevented total disaster on the French left; but their position remained desperate. Condé immediately grasped the situation and promptly led his cavalry around behind the Spanish infantry to the left of his line where he attacked the victorious Spanish horsemen in their rear, driving them from the field in panicky flight.

Having defeated all of the Spanish horsemen, Condé turned against the Spanish infantry, which had taken up a dense formation to resist cavalry. After first dashing his horsemen in vain against steady Spanish veterans, Condé then used his artillery and musketeers to create gaps in the Spanish ranks that his cavalry then exploited with a charge. Many Spaniards were killed when the French continued their attack, not realizing that the Spaniards were trying to surrender. The Spanish suffered immense losses in killed and prisoners among their infantry. After the battle a Frenchman asked a Spanish officer, "How many are you?" The Spaniard replied: "Count the dead and the prisoners—they are all." The French lost about 10 percent of their forces. At Rocroi the cavalry won the battle, and the infantry supplied the casualties. This overstates the case, but the battle does illustrate the crucial role of the cavalry in providing the offensive capability of the army, its mobility and ease of deployment enabling it to attack the weak flank and rear of the infantry.[14]

But cavalry did not play a new role at Rocroi or in the thinking of late seventeenth-century generals. Cavalry had usually had the decisive offensive mission in ancient, Byzantine, and medieval armies as well as in the sixteenth century. Only a failure to capitalize on its offensive capability of attacking the enemy's weak flank and rear had devalued it in French combats with the English; and the invulnerability of the Swiss square had shown again that heavy cavalry alone could not defeat heavy infantry, just as the Spanish infantry had shown again at Rocroi that no cavalry could defeat an effectively cooperating group of pikemen and musketeers. So the decisive role of cavalry at Rocroi represented no change in the traditional exploitation of cavalry's distinctive offensive attributes.

The Logistics of the Late Seventeenth Century

The Thirty Years' War marked a watershed in logistics, for in the ensuing years the practices advocated by Gustavus and Wallenstein came to prevail in most armies. Each had sought to make war support war, not by soldiers' looting but by commanders' levying contributions. Wallenstein had good success with this, but Gustavus, aiming to raise over 200,000 men, finally fell into the error of recruiting more men than he could pay. In 1632, when his contributions brought in less than one-fourth of his payroll, the Swedish army mutinied. Raising more men than an entrepreneur or government could afford brought about pillaging by the soldiers, a consequence both Gustavus and Wallenstein abhorred, for they knew that looting soldiers destroyed twice as much as they took. Such destruction and inefficient use of resources not only reduced the size of the armies that a region could immediately supply but also often ruined its productive capacities for the support of armies in the future.

Soldiers who had such a vivid experience of the logistics of the Thirty Years' War did not fail to note its defects. One writer commented that a region could maintain an army effectively if it "could be saved from the wanton spoile of the soldier." Gustavus wrote of the evil that ensued when his unpaid and unfed troops fended for themselves: "It has been impossible to restrain the horsemen . . . who live simply from wild plunder. Everything has been ruined thereby, so that nothing more can be found for the soldiers in towns or villages." Wallenstein also reflected this view on entering Saxony in 1632 when he gave the following orders: "Let nothing be destroyed or taken from the peasantry, for we must live during the winter on the supplies we can find here." These understandings animated the changes in logistics that marked the second half of the seventeenth century.[15]

Thus governments began to keep the size of their armies within the numbers that they could pay with reasonable regularity. Since they could thus feed and pay their own men, they could enforce a ban against looting. By taking from subject areas exclusively by contributions usually collected through the local government, they maximized the efficiency of converting the resources of the country to the support of the invading army. This procedure also minimized the enmity of local authorities and avoided arousing the active hostility of the peasants and their consequent punitive actions and guerrilla warfare against the soldiers. Armies also largely abandoned the practice, common amid the chaos and logistical calamities of the Thirty Years' War, of levying contributions on neutral or friendly territory, a practice that had also increased an army's enemies.

This policy of preventing soldier deprivations fostered an attitude of respect for civilian property that in the eighteenth century became a rule for the conduct of war. This had the result of divorcing civilians from war by insulating them from most of its harmful effects—other than taxes and government debt. The new approach conserved civilian productivity in both the rulers' own domains and in the provinces they coveted, which also reduced civilian hostility to invaders.

The new way of supply and its often scrupulous care for civilian property did reduce the needless costs of war and in this respect limited it. Sometimes armies carried the circumscriptions on the conduct of the soldiers to ridiculous extremes. For example, a small French force, fleeing from pursuing Austrians, crossed a river on a ferry, duly paying the civilian ferryman for his services. When the Austrians reached the ferry, they abandoned their pursuit because they lacked the money to pay the ferryman. Of course, in this instance, the limitation on the conduct of the soldiers did not alter the outcome; if the retreating French had disregarded the sanctity of civilian property and sunk the ferry, the Austrians still could not have crossed regardless of whether they were willing to seize the ferry.

The new tactics placed a premium on soldiers adequately fed and paid with reasonable regularity because only such an army could have proper discipline. The wealthy and businesslike Dutch had long recompensed their men promptly and had a sufficiently disciplined army that could implement Maurice's tactical concepts. The new shallow formations and the emphasis on volleys on command required a level of training that only this type of army could attain.

The need for better drilled troops also changed the method of recruiting armies. Instead of disbanding soldiers after each campaign, governments kept the forces in garrison during peace. Much of the saving in wages had been illusory anyway; employers saved winter wages but had to pay higher wage rates to their seasonal employees during the period of active campaigning. Keeping soldiers all year around cost little more and brought immense dividends in military effectiveness. The training accomplished during winter service constituted one of the smaller benefits of a standing army; the continued existence of the unit from year to year developed a community that provided cohesion and esprit de corps and accustomed soldiers to continuous service under the same officers and noncommissioned officers, further strengthening discipline, morale, and the resilience of the unit when it faced the hardships of campaigning. Even the practice of the drill needed for battlefield effectiveness contributed to unit cohesion and morale, creating a sense of unity and confidence among the men as well as strengthening the habit of obedience.

The existence of permanent regiments made possible the introduction of uniformity in drill and tactical doctrine in place of the variety of different regimental methods. In the French army Jean Martinet, inspector-general of infantry, enforced this consistency with such rigor and effect that his name has ever since denoted a punctiliousness in matters of discipline and drill, the depreciatory connotation suggesting the strictness with which Martinet enforced the new regulations.

The persistence of warfare in the latter half of the seventeenth century meant that keeping battalions on the payroll during the limited periods of peace did not constitute a very great additional burden, and even this cost governments diminished by keeping companies at reduced numbers during peacetime. When war broke out, rulers recruited the companies to full strength, adding the new men to a long-established, thoroughly trained unit in which they could expect to learn their duties promptly and easily acquire the morale of the veteran unit.

The practice of maintaining peacetime armies created another argument for prompt pay and supply during wartime. Looting encouraged desertion by presenting the opportunity for the dispersed soldiers to leave and encouraging soldiers to depart in the belief that since they had acquired a piece of valuable loot, they should leave their unit and their arrears of pay. Such losses had long constituted a serious drain on armies, but the desertion of a soldier, disciplined and trained during peacetime, constituted an even greater waste. The loss of such soldiers and their replacement by raw recruits caused a much greater reduction in efficiency than those borne from companies of poorly drilled mercenaries in units that might be dissolved at the end of each campaigning season. Armies were able to increase their precautions against desertion because food and pay permitted them to keep their men disciplined and concentrated under the supervision of their officers and non commissioned officers.

Maintaining formations in existence during peacetime, even at reduced strength, eliminated much of the role of the military entrepreneur. With few new regiments or companies needed for war, the soldier-businessman gradually disappeared, and government ownership of armies developed. Though proprietorship of companies and regiments continued, state control and management soon became a fact, and, except for private contractors' drawing the artillery and providing supplies, armies became entirely staffed by civilian administrators or soldiers paid by rulers.

Armies continued to recruit by voluntary enlistment, which often included chicanery and coercion. The public increasingly came to see armies as places for society's undesirables, and avoided enlisting productively employed citizens. Foreigners continued to appeal as recruits because they withdrew no one from the native work force. Such soldiers sometimes showed an alarming tendency to desert, and commanders had to give much attention to preventing desertion, even avoiding military movements through territory that favored desertion. The king of Prussia, for example, directed his officers "to familiarize themselves with the terrain around their garrison" station, not with the idea of preparing for combat but because it was "of the greatest necessity for all officers to know when they are looking for deserters."[16]

Such soldiers required discipline so thorough and severe that it completely acculturated them to unthinking obedience. The Prussian army, which had as many as two-thirds foreigners and relied on coercion in recruiting natives, had a particularly brutal discipline that involved not just formal corporal punishment but also in the course of drill. The same king of Prussia, Frederick the Great, prescribed that "at drill nobody must be struck or pushed or scolded. A man learns to drill with patience and method, not with blows." He also pointed out that "everything must be taught to a new recruit by kind explanations, without scolding and shaming, so that he is not at the very start made to feel depressed and fearful but will develop pleasure and love for his service." But the officers continued to rely on blows, intimidation, and fear as the basis of their discipline. Even the king had the ideal that soldiers must fear their officers more than the enemy.[17]

The officers increasingly became a separate and exclusive class in all European armies. Most of them came from the aristocracy, and few commissions went to commoners. They were distinct from the men in social differentiation as well as in organizational duties and privileges. This created a separation between officers and enlisted men greater than that which existed in the units raised by the military entrepreneurs. This alteration also reinforced the subordination to the hierarchy by adding distinction based on social class but augmenting the hostility between the two categories of soldiers.

Nobility serving exclusively as officers and largely monopolizing these positions supplied the only feudal or medieval attribute of the system. Every other aspect had changed. From private possession of governmental and military power, Western Europe had moved to a socialization first of political institutions and finally of the armed forces. The result differed little from the methods used by Rome. In a sense Roman tactics had fostered a Roman organization of the permanently established professional army, which belonged to the state and which remained concentrated where unit training could take place and group esprit develop. Changes in Western European kingdoms and principalities helped to make possible these modifications. The development of financial resources, both in taxation and credit, enabled rulers to create bureaucracies large and effective enough to manage sizeable permanent military establishments that their expanded resources could adequately finance.

The change in logistics responded to the needs of strategy. As the Thirty Years' War had worn on, logistics had increasingly fettered strategy. Campaigns conducted in exhausted territory inevitably failed for want of supplies, and armies even virtually perished in this way. Count Gallas, imperial commander-in-chief, became notorious for losing his emperor's armies as he marched into devastated areas where they could not subsist. Wiser generals allowed logistics to dictate strategy, but by the end of the war campaigning often consisted of ignoring the enemy in the search for areas that could supply the army. The French minister Richelieu properly summarized what the Thirty Years' War had taught about logistics: "History knows many more armies ruined by want and disorder than by the efforts of their enemies; and I have witnessed how all the enterprises which were embarked on in my day were lacking for that reason alone."[18]

Substituting contributions and businesslike supply methods for looting by unpaid troops increased the yield of supplies that any region could provide an army. But generals required other alternatives to become independent of the need to have their movements dictated by necessity to find food for their men and fodder for their horses. Though, as in ancient times, supply considerations would always condition strategy, the Roman logistical organization, like Alexander's, had given armies a maximum amount of liberty to pursue strategic aims. Late seventeenth-century armies followed this tradition when they developed magazines to collect and store wheat for bread and even oats and hay for the horses. By having an initial inventory with which to start the campaign and a reserve on which to draw later, armies gained a substantial amount of strategic liberty. They still placed primary reliance on living off the country through contributions or requisitions, and one major strategic aim remained: to try to invade the enemy's land and to support one's own army at his expense. But governments now had the money and armies the logistical organization to supply when necessary their men and, to a much smaller degree, their horses.

But even if governments had wished to provide all of their armies' needs from their own magazines and assuming their physical and financial resources would have permitted it, limitations on transportation would usually have made this impossible. Only waterways had the efficiency to transport enough food for the horses, and bad roads made it difficult and often impossible to supply men over a very great distance. Though a horse could pull twice as much as it could carry and roads had improved, wagon transportation still could not furnish the wants of troops over long distances. Nevertheless, improved logistics gave late seventeenth-century armies capabilities that earlier European armies had lacked. But the increased revenues of governments meant that armies grew in size, and their very numbers continued to tax severely the resources of the regions in which they operated and the ingenuity of their commissaries and quartermasters.

Representative Late Seventeenth-Century Campaigns and Battles

With expanded capabilities for supporting their armies, soldiers increasingly pursued a persisting strategy exemplified by Gustavus's conquest of northern Germany. And the new logistics facilitated this by diminishing the hostility that civilians felt toward invaders. So soldiers thought less in terms of raids that would temporarily support their force and extract political concessions and more in terms of solid territorial acquisitions that could provide a continuing flow of supplies and a conquest that their ruler might exchange for political goals. Yet such a strategic objective required many sieges and a slow campaign to make and consolidate gains. But the larger armies of the second half of the seventeenth century facilitated this change by increasing the ratio of force to space.

Yet this shift to a persisting strategy could affect operations very little, as a notable campaign in Germany graphically illustrates. In 1673 the great French marshal, Turenne, had to defend the Rhine while French armies pushed their campaign against the Dutch. The principal general of warlike King Louis XIV, Turenne, the marshal general of the armies of the king, had begun military service nearly fifty years before. After serving under capable commanders, Turenne had become a general at twenty-three and constantly improved his generalship in the years that followed. In an era of constant warfare he served in many campaigns and participated in a number of battles and sieges. One of these, the siege of Turin in 1640, illustrates the diversity of his experience. While the Italians in Turin besieged a French garrison in the citadel, a French army laid siege to the city but, in turn, had to cope with encirclement by a hostile army. From this long service Turenne learned strategy and tactics equally well and also how to win the affection of his soldiers.

Turenne expected an offensive by the emperor's brilliant and experienced commander, Raimondo Montecuccoli, whose army had yet to appear in western Germany. A military scholar and a veteran of the battles of Breitenfeld and Lützen, the imperial field marshal had already seen as much service as Turenne, and it had likewise earned him a deserved reputation as one of the premier soldiers of the day. For his offensive campaign against Turenne, Montecuccoli had the advantage of alternative strategic objectives. He could either proceed toward the north to reinforce the Dutch or go farther south to cross the Rhine and invade Alsace. The possession of the initiative and a choice of goals gave Montecuccoli an opportunity to bewilder his opponent by apparently aiming at one target, to draw Turenne away, and then striking out for the other, his real objective.

Since the imperial commander planned to aid the Dutch, he intended to distract Turenne by threatening to cross the Rhine and advance into Alsace. He thus moved his army westward south of the Main River rather than toward Bonn, where he planned to unite with the Dutch, take the city, and drive France's ally, the elector of Cologne, from the war. When Montecuccoli reached Nuremberg, Turenne, aware of the direction of his opponent's march, had gone south of the Main and negotiated with the elector of Mainz for the use of his bridge at Aschaffenburg. Crossing the bridge, he veered south to occupy the line of the Tauber River, planning to use it as an obstacle to prevent Montecuccoli from reaching the Rhine in pursuit of his apparent mission to cross it and advance into Alsace.

As Montecuccoli next marched westward from Nuremberg, the French marshal pushed eastward to meet him. A British soldier serving in the French army recorded: if Turenne could catch "the Imperialists at an advantage we shall certainly fight them, and doubtless they have the same intentions; so nowe two of the greatest generalls in Christendom employ all that their long experience has taught them . . . knowing the great consequence the loss of a Battle would be to each side." Turenne wished for a battle, but Montecuccoli had no intention of engaging Turenne, if merely because a fight would delay the completion of the allied concentration at Bonn. But when he began to deploy his army for battle at Windsheim, the imperial commander used the prospect of combat to help complete his distraction and aid him in carrying out his move north toward Bonn. As Turenne reached Windsheim and began the slow process of marshaling his army for the contest, the imperial forces slipped away, their baggage and one line of battle leading on the road to the bridge over the Main at Marktbreit. Turenne, hastily getting his men back in march order, pursued the imperial troops, and, reaching Marktbreit before his enemy could cross the river, took up a strong position nearby, ready to attack when Montecuccoli should have to divide his troops during the slow process of crossing the river. The armies faced each there for a week.[19]

In spite of his failure to cross before Turenne came up with him and his consequent inability to use the bridge immediately, Montecuccoli had placed his army in an advantageous position. As a German general campaigning in Germany, he operated in essentially friendly territory in spite of the neutrality of some of the rulers in the region. This meant that he controlled all of the bridges over the Main except that at Aschaffenburg, which Turenne had used to cross and at which he had left only a small garrison. Once over the river the imperial commander could cross and recross at will to take a direct line of march to reach the Aschaffenburg bridge before Turenne who would have to march south of the river. Then, having enclosed the French army south of the Main by taking the Aschaffenburg bridge, he could advance to Bonn. Montecuccoli had astutely used his control of the river to make it an obstruction for the defender; as a rule, defenders enjoyed an advantage of employing river obstacles.

Logistics helped Montecuccoli complete his crossing. The hostility of the country to the French made gathering supplies for their army difficult. As he watched Montecuccoli's army, Turenne wrote his minister of war that he needed more cavalry because "with the entire countryside opposed to me more troops will be needed to procure food." After a week of supply difficulties, Turenne fell back toward the Tauber, acutely conscious that even if Montecuccoli then crossed to the north side of the Main, the threat to Alsace remained because the imperial commander's control of the bridges would enable him to recross and again threaten the French province. For this reason Turenne did not make forced marches to try to cross at Aschaffenburg; he remained in genuine doubt as to his enemy's ultimate objective and somewhat trammeled by firm instructions from his government to protect Alsace.[20]

In the additional maneuvering that followed his crossing of the Main, Montecuccoli continued to exploit the ambiguity created by his two potential objectives. Ultimately controlling all bridges on the Main, he marched north to Bonn, which he and his allies soon captured, overrunning the adjacent territory and driving the elector of Cologne from the French alliance. Meanwhile Turenne, lacking control of a bridge, had to march south to cross at Philippsbourg, where he encountered a further delay because he had to forage for supplies. The campaigning year ended before Turenne's army could again take part in operations.

Montecuccoli had skillfully used the initiative conferred on him by his two potential goals to keep Turenne constantly in doubt as to his real objective. He had combined distraction with use of his control of the bridges over the Main to enable him not just to avoid the opposing army but to keep it from following him in time to intervene when he joined his allies. In addition, he had imposed on his opponent much hurried marching with its consequent straggling, desertion, and loss of equipment. The conduct and objectives of the campaign differed in no significant essentials from those of Gustavus nor, fundamentally, from that of four centuries before when Prince Edward and de Montfort maneuvered to deceive and to exploit or overcome a river obstacle, and when King Phillip thwarted Edward III on his march to Crécy.

The opening phases of the War of the Grand Alliance (1689–97) clearly exhibit military operations at the end of the seventeenth century. In 1688 French forces had raided in Germany almost as far as Munich, but, instead of intimidating the Germans, this raid contributed to the formation of a Grand Alliance against France consisting of Spain, Holland, the United Kingdom, the Holy Roman Emperor, and a number of German states including Brandenburg. Although unity of command and the great size and high level of excellence of the French army counterbalanced the apparent superiority of the allies, France stood on the defensive with armies guarding its Spanish, Italian, Rhine, and Netherlands frontiers.

Weakest along the Rhine frontier, the French used a logistic strategy when their cavalry devastated the Palatinate region to render it incapable of subsisting hostile armies. The technique did seal that part of the frontier, but, though Turenne had used the method in Germany fifteen years earlier, the thoroughness of the French cavalry in their work of destruction made the operation counterproductive. The hostility that it aroused in Germany added impetus to the war against France, while the effect on its own forces clearly showed why generals had abandoned looting as a means of supply and a source of pay and reward for soldiers. In spite of the absence of opposition, the French lost 4,000 cavalrymen, largely through desertion. They lost even more horses because in the orgy of plundering the soldiers neglected to feed their mounts and then overburdened them with loot. The French minister of war echoed the conclusion of one commander that "nothing is more dangerous for soldiers than excessive pillaging" when the minister bemoaned the "wasting away of the cavalry." Heavy troop casualties and intensified political opposition hardly made this application of a logistic strategy pay, especially when the allied army advanced north of the devastated region to besiege and capture the Rhine cities of Mainz and Bonn. Elsewhere the campaign of 1689 proved uneventful.[21]

In 1690 the allies again had difficulty mobilizing their strength for determined campaigns against the French. But in the Netherlands the successful operations of a gifted and aggressive French marshal, the duke of Luxembourg, clearly illustrate the persisting strategy characteristic of much campaigning in a thoroughly fortified region where, since the French alone fielded 100,000 men, the combatants operated with a very high ratio of force to space. Then the ablest of the marshals of King Louis XIV, the humpbacked Luxembourg had learned much as a disciple of his friend, the prince of Condé. The marshal's fame rested equally on his tactical mastery on the battlefield and his skill in marching and camping.

The marshal, commanding the center army of the three the French sent to the Netherlands, opened the campaign by moving toward the Spanish forces that held Ghent and occupying the adjacent country for a month, supplying his men and horses at the enemy's expense. But on June 12, when he learned that an allied army under the prince of Waldeck, an imperial field marshal, was advancing with the apparent purpose of besieging Dinant, the marshal began to move south and then east to intercept Waldeck. He conducted the latter stages of this march in the manner in which he planned both to camp and fight, following the duke of Parma's practice in France and Montecuccoli's maxim: "The secret of success is to have a solid body so firm and impenetrable that wherever it is or wherever it may go, it shall bring the enemy to a stand like a mobile bastion, and shall be capable of defending itself." To do this, the armies marched across country usually in at least five columns, the cavalry on each flank, the infantry next, and the baggage and artillery in the center. In this way the army protected itself against any enemy cavalry attack and could marshal its battle array quickly if it met an enemy force unexpectedly.[22]

When he learned of the approach of the French, Waldeck halted at Fleurus and placed his army where his flanks rested on villages and his front was obstructed by a marshy stream. The allied commander's willingness to fight under such circumstances would normally have meant that his opponent would not. But the pugnacious Marshal Luxembourg had called in reinforcements from the French troops on his right and, having reconnoitered the position, moved his men up to attack. While part of his force made an unsuccessful frontal assault, the marshal led the other around Waldeck's flank, undetected because woods and crops concealed his marching infantry and cavalry. Three hours after the contest began, Luxembourg's turning force began to array for battle in the allied rear. Though Waldeck used his reserve and second line to create a front to face the French marshal and protect his rear, he found himself waging a losing battle. Yet the allied army continued the fight, unsuccessfully, and finally the infantry retreated to adjacent broken ground by forming a huge square that resisted French cavalry by alternately marching and halting until it found refuge in a terrain unsuitable for cavalry.

This battle at Fleurus vividly exhibits the tactical and strategic limitations of the armies of the day. Luxembourg's marching formation provided security against the cavalry's mobility and advantage over musketeers. It made movement very slow, however, though Luxembourg, famous for his marching skill, managed to progress at eleven miles a day when carrying about 30,000 men cross country. His successful tactical turning maneuver, in which he reached the enemy's rear, failed to secure the benefits of surprise because of the time which it took to get his infantry into battle array. Infantry battalions normally made such marches across country in solid formations with a front ranging from eight to twenty files. On reaching the combat ground the battalions had to find their places in

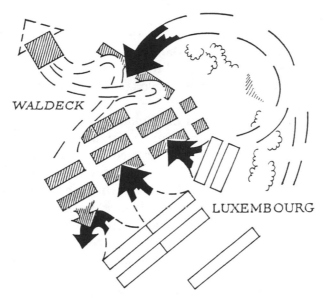

Diagram 4.6. Action at Fleurus

line and reform themselves five ranks deep with their pikemen concentrated in the center. By the time Luxembourg had completed the formation of his men for battle, Waldeck had redeployed his second line and reserve to make a front against them. Nevertheless, Luxembourg's maneuver contributed much to his victory, for his turning force defeated the opposing cavalry and infantry. It would have yielded really spectacular results if his infantry had had the ability to fight in the same formation as they marched. But by distracting the enemy with his frontal attack and carrying out an unobserved turning movement of a strong position, Luxembourg won the battle, attacking the allied army where it was weakest. The allies suffered 18,000 casualties, nearly half their force, the French 6,000, about 15 percent of theirs. Waldeck fell back to the vicinity of the fortified city of Brussels.

Though operations continued in the Netherlands for several more years and Marshal Luxembourg won two more substantial victories, the antagonists had too much equality and the country too many well-fortified points interdicting its communications for either side to make much progress or for the attrition of a victory in battle to change the balance of strength sufficiently for Luxembourg's triumphs to give the French enough superiority to do more than try to encroach on the enemy's territory by besieging and capturing an important city.

These operations differed significantly from those fifteen years earlier, when Turenne and Montecuccoli had faced one another along the Main with forces of less than 30,000 men. The armies were small in relation to space and the region had few enough fortified points to prevent their troops moving at will unless constrained by major rivers such as the Main and Rhine. Neither side could expect to exclude the other, but an invader could do no more than raid unless, as had Gustavus in the same region, he could systematically besiege, capture, and garrison the cities. In the Netherlands the high ratio of force to space produced a stalemate; in the Main country Turenne would have faced a different sort of stalemate had he tried to use his small army to subdue such a large territory; his troops could never have controlled more than a little of the area.

On the other fronts, the War of the Grand Alliance dragged on indecisively, with the allies unable to exploit their superiority on the Rhine. A French army did enter Spain where it remained and besieged Barcelona, conducting an ideal defensive campaign by maintaining itself in enemy territory and providing for its needs through contributions levied on the enemy. The seesaw struggle in Italy brought an allied invasion of southeastern France. But the active hostility of the French peasants led by their nobility made it so difficult for the invading army to obtain supplies that it soon fell back into Italy.

The seventeenth century had brought substantial changes to tactics with the linear method of deployment in which the firepower of light infantry in formation supplanted blocks of pikeman as the infantry's primary weapon system. Except for the role of light infantry in line, the organization resembled that of the Romans with its built-in reserve of a second line. But because the infantry had less offensive power than the Roman heavy infantry and the predominant musketeer had greater vulnerability to mounted shock action, cavalry had far more importance in late seventeenth-century battle tactics than it had had for the Romans in the heyday of the legion.

Logistics had become distinctively Roman in its reliance on a well-organized commissariat to supply troops, organize transportation, and accumulate reserves in magazines to assure supply and give armies greater liberty to pursue their strategic objectives. The new system of permanent peacetime armies, with continuity in units and stability of personnel, also emulated the Romans as did keeping the forces together for training and drill.

So strategy changed little. Still, no commander could force battle on an unwilling opponent. At Fleurus Marshal Luxembourg's failure to attack promptly Waldeck's rear stemmed from the infantry's inability to form quickly its delicate line from its compact marching formations. This same relative impotence of the infantry inhibited any army from forcing battle on another. While the would-be attacker formed his line of battle, the reluctant opponent marched away. But these insuperable difficulties did not first arise in the seventeenth century; they inhered in the nature of infantry formations. Greek and Roman infantry had suffered from the same limitations, and medieval heavy infantry had displayed virtual immobility. Only the simple Swiss formation with its drill and morale had been able to advance to combat in the formation in which it intended to fight. But its undrilled successors lost this mobility, and the linear system increased the difference between infantry's march and combat formations and added to the difficulty of the deployment problem. Only cavalry possessed the offensive attributes of better mobility and the capacity to deploy so rapidly that they could almost fight as they marched. But even so, a cavalry could not force battle on cavalry and could compel an army with infantry to fight only at the cost of facing the defensive predominance of the infantry. The defeat of the cavalry of the Emperor Frederick at Legnano by the opposing foot soldiers shows why cavalry rarely attempted this against formed infantry.

The eighteenth century would witness a change in the capabilities of infantry and an accentuation of some of the trends of the seventeenth century at the same time that military intellectuals sought to give improved offensive capabilities to the new linear array of light infantry.

The Development of Missile Warfare at Sea

The seventeeth century saw the working out of the consequences of the sixteenth century's big-gun revolution in naval warfare, which the defeat of the Spanish Armada had signaled. Naval architects designed warships to fight broadside to broadside and mount only heavy guns, placing them on the strong decks low in the ships where they fired through gun ports. The largest ships, ships of the line, had two and even three decks of long, heavy guns firing balls weighing from twelve to over thirty pounds. These ships of the line, mounting as many as ninety guns and intended for fighting other such ships, gradually became lower and larger. They possessed stout planking, especially around the waterline, and had far more power than merchant ships, which also continued to carry guns. Warships, designed to carry the largest number of heavy guns, had definitely become a distinct class in the Atlantic Ocean and the northern waters, just as they always had been in the Mediterranean.

Smaller and faster warships of various types, mounting fewer and smaller guns, completed the complement of any navy. These ships, fast and powerful compared even to larger merchant ships but less expensive to build and man than ships of the line, patrolled the trade routes and provided scouts for a fleet. The most powerful of these, the frigates, mounted thirty to forty guns of a size equivalent to the smaller guns of the big ships. Boarding and fighting by sailors and marines remained important, but rapid fire at close range usually decided battles. Badly battered ships often surrendered or, having sustained heavy personnel casualties, proved vulnerable to boarding by the crews and marines of enemy ships.

Tactics, as evolved by the latter part of the seventeenth century, involved ships moving in line ahead with an interval of about 100 yards between them. Because the ships fought with their sides rather than bows, the head or stern of the line constituted the potentially vulnerable part of the formation, not the flank as in galley and land warfare. To lead a line past the head or rear of an enemy column constituted the naval analog of the flank attack on land, because it enabled the whole attacking sequence of ships to deliver their broadsides in succession at ships unable to reply because their unarmed ends faced the enemy.

But the rear of a line actually presented little vulnerability because the attackers usually found it moving away from them.

And to attack the head of a line exposed the attacking fleet to having its own line cut. Because of the short range, little more than a mile, and deficient accuracy of the guns, a disadvantage accentuated by the motion of the waves, a ship breaking an enemy's line had only limited exposure to hostile shot. Even at close range only a few ships could fire at those breaking their line because guns firing through ports in the sides of ships, having little variation in the azimuth of their fire, could not be trained to shoot at targets oblique to their sides; aiming guns through larger arcs required aiming the ship. With an interval of three to five minutes, or more, between broadsides, a ship moving at no more than five or six miles an hour might receive no more than two broadsides at a dangerous range.

When one line of ships pierced another, its guns could return the fire it received during its approach by firing a single, short-range broadside in each direction as it passed between the enemy vessels. Further, the fleet that had broken the enemy's line also divided the hostile fleet and had the opportunity to concentrate against only a portion of the enemy force.

Thus a fleet lacked the kind of vulnerability found in an army. The peculiarity of having the combat front of the formation at right angles to its line of advance made maneuvering difficult. With fleets on parallel courses, admirals could attain concentration by reducing the intervals between their ships, but the enemy could respond by doing likewise. Another form of concentration involved breaking through the enemy's line with part of a squadron or otherwise positioning ships on each side of a portion of the enemy's line. Ships had an equal number of guns on each side but carried only enough crew to man fully the guns on one side of the ship. To work the guns on both sides simultaneously for more than one broadside seriously reduced the rate of fire, virtually nullifying the advantage of being able to use all guns.

These maneuvers proved difficult to execute, and concentration at one place created a weakness at another, which the enemy could detect and exploit by attack or by reinforcing the part of the fleet that opposed larger numbers. At the Battle of Beachy Head in 1690, for instance, the earl of Torrington, under pressure from his superiors, used his windward position to lay his Anglo-Dutch fleet alongside a stronger French fleet. When Torrington's fleet engaged, it had gaps between its divisions and, as the foremost and rearmost ships of the weaker Anglo-Dutch line closely engaged the French head and rear, the British center remained at long range. This enabled Admiral Tourville, one of France's most notable admirals, to direct ships from his center to come up on the far side of the lead ships of the Anglo-Dutch fleet while unengaged ships at the head of the French line turned back to do likewise. Assailed on two sides, the leading allied ships suffered heavily and, before the fleet could make good its withdrawal, lost ten of its fifty-seven ships of the line.

Although defenders afloat had no tactical advantage in resisting attack, they retained that other traditional advantage of the defense—the ability to retreat.

In principle, fleets of similar speed could not overtake one another, though in practice the flukiness of the wind, differences in seamanship, and cleanliness of the bottoms of ships did make successful pursuit possible. Yet opposing admirals always had essentially homogeneous forces, all with the same weapon system. Although the smaller vessels had greater speed than the ships of the line, their vulnerability and weak gun power made them almost useless against the big ships. Even in pursuit, the faster ships had little value except in attacking ships of the line disabled by the loss of masts. They could not, therefore, use their better mobility to play the role of cavalry in attack or pursuit.

So with no useful preponderance in speed and no differentiation in weapon systems at sea, the offensive enjoyed very little advantage. Even though the retreating fleet could not obstruct or delay the progress of pursuers, the equality in speed between opposing fleets prevented a fleet on the offensive from forcing battle on an inferior. Sea fighters lacked even the device of the siege for forcing battle; its analog, the blockade of a fleet in a fortified harbor, could neither take the port nor starve it out. The blockade could, however, play the land warfare role of devastating the countryside to force battle because the blockade interdicted the commerce of the port. By challenging the blockade, the blockaded fleet could open the port to trade if it could defeat and drive away the blockading squadron. Inferior fleets rarely attempted this.

A nearby shore often presented an obstacle against which to trap an inferior fleet. Protected anchorages and even well-fortified harbors sometimes provided inadequate shelter against an enterprising foe. But such successes were rare compared with the prolonged periods of security enjoyed by inferior fleets in fortified anchorages. Big guns in fortified land emplacements easily overmatched ships in any artillery combat.

Of course, sometimes fleets fought for command of the sea with no other issue than to precipitate the battle. But, as on land, battles occurred by mutual consent when a difference of opinion about the likely outcome or the stakes made admirals and governments willing to risk a contest.

But revolutions in tactics and logistics had little influence on the basic logistic character of naval strategy. Transporting and supplying troops remained an important objective, and interdicting commerce became easier as warships developed the sea endurance to engage in blockades to implement the persisting strategy at sea. The improvements of the sea-keeping qualities of warships extended the effectiveness of the strategy of raids against commerce.

A stronger sea power kept an inferior fleet in port either by a blockade or the latter's fear of meeting the hostile fleet or having itself cut off from its base. The blockade gave the smaller ships of the stronger fleet the liberty to interdict the commerce of the weaker. Though never complete, a commercial blockade often crippled the commerce of the inferior sea power and enabled the superior to capture many of the enemy's merchant vessels. But the weaker could resort to raids upon the enemy's commerce. Small, fast, armed ships could outrun warships and readily cruise the seas extensively, capturing the merchant ships of the stronger power. On these they could place crews and attempt to slip them back into friendly ports.

This kind of war appealed to private enterprise because of the huge profit in capturing a ship and its cargo. Many of the weaker power's subjects engaged in this kind of warfare; it became a speciality of the French, who had tempting targets in the large merchant marines of their British and Dutch opponents. In the War of the Grand Alliance, for example, the British gained command of the sea and ruined French overseas commerce by blockading its ports. On the other hand, the effective French policy of raids during the war took 4,000 of the enemies' merchant ships, a dangerous but not fatal blow at their adversaries' commerce.

Thus both sides used a logistic strategy in a warfare that resembled Roman and Byzantine protection of their frontiers and the Western European efforts to cope with Viking raiders. Naval warfare differed, however, in that the stronger power's defensive stance against raiders included its persisting blockade of enemy commerce, a more effective application of a logistic strategy than raids.

The number of sea battles sometimes exceeded the frequency of land battles. Often the protection of trade precipitated naval action. British, Dutch, or French fleets sought to defend or attack convoys of merchant ships. The stakes were large: on one occasion the French fleet attacked a British convoy of 140 ships and captured eighty. A seaborne invasion could also cause a battle, as when the inferior Dutch fleet fought the combined French and British fleets and, later, a French fleet attacked a much larger British-Dutch fleet at La Hogue in 1692 in a vain effort to open the way for a French army to land in England.

5

THE PRIMACY OF THE LINE OF BAYONETED MUSKETS, 1700–1791

The Bayonet, the Flintlock, and Further Changes in Tactics

At the beginning of the eighteenth century technological innovations significantly strengthened the tactical trend that had placed the light infantryman in line and relied on his firepower as the main offensive and defensive power of the infantry. The successful attempts to convert the musket into a short pike probably had as great tactical import for warfare on land as any change in weapons since the development of the four basic weapon systems. The first efforts involved a knife with a foot-long blade that plugged into the barrel of the musket. As early as the middle of the seventeenth century such weapons, called bayonets, began to appear, first in the French and then in other armies. A contemporary described it as "a broad dagger without any guard, generally made with a round taper handle to stick in the mussle of a musket, in which manner it serves instead of a pike to receive the charge of the Horse, all the men first having the advantage of their Shot" before inserting the plug bayonet into the muzzles of their muskets, thus converting all of the musketeers into pikemen.[1]

The disadvantage of the system lay not in the shortness of the pike, even though the musket and bayonet together measured only about six to seven feet. In fact, in combat with cavalry infantrymen would not hold their muskets as did a phalanx of men with long pikes but, instead, use them as stabbing weapons like short spears or stabbing swords. These could not, however, have proven effective against cavalrymen with lances, which demanded that the defenders have a bristling wall of long pikes. Yet with all men equipped with even inferior pike substitutes, the cavalry, armed only with sabers rather than long lances, faced too formidable a replacement for the traditional heavy infantry array to break through the ranks. But the musketeers, reluctant to forego their volleys, always ran the risk of receiving a charge before they had time to insert their bayonets.

By the 1690s the socket bayonet replaced the plug bayonet and made the pikeman completely obsolete. The socket bayonet consisted of a blade attached to the side of a metal sleeve that fitted over the barrel, leaving the musket free to fire with the bayonet attached. Now all infantrymen could simultaneously function as heavy and light infantry. By 1700, when the socket bayonet became universal, a successful frontal cavalry charge against formed infantry had become impossible. The cavalry had to face volleys from a formation made up completely of musketeers and, if they still could close with the infantry, then confronted a formation entirely composed of pikemen.

The pistol, when combined with the saber, had made horsemen into a truly dual-purpose weapon system, both heavy and light cavlary simultaneously. This development had strengthened the offensive capabilities of the mounted weapon system against the infantry, making it supreme on open ground unless light and heavy infantry cooperated closely. The bayonet tipped the scales all the way in the opposite direction. The cavalry lacked offensive power against any infantry, its pistols outclassed by muskets and its sabers ineffective against a wall of bayonets.

A prescription for the proper training of infantry illustrates the ascendency that formed infantry had over cavalry. In 1730 a Spanish general recommended that in front of his infantry an officer "should mount a strong and sturdy horse" and show the defensive power of infantry by then trying "to ride down a foot soldier, who will stand firm armed only with a pole; they will see that by pointing the stick at the horses's eyes or tapping its head with it, the horse will shy and refuse to advance." The officer would then take the "opportunity to point out to the soldiers that if a horse will not ride down a man armed only with a pole how much less will cavalry prosper against formed battalions, whose bayonets, bullets and din of arms . . . are even more capable of scaring the horses."[2]

But the cavalry retained its distinctive offensive advantages of greater mobility and the capacity to go into action without elaborate and time-consuming deployment. The linear system of infantry formation provided amply vulnerable flanks and rear against which cavalry could use its still formidable attributes. Since a three-rank array of bayonet-armed musketeers could resist a cavalry charge, infantry provided itself with all-around defense by forming into a hollow square, three ranks deep. But it took time to form into a square and cavalry attacks were often too rapid and, on a smoke-obscured battlefield, too unexpected for infantry always to have time to adopt its powerful defensive formation. Since, however, the bayonet did circumscribe cavalry's role and diminish its effectiveness, the proportion of cavalry in Western European armies declined, though gradually, throughout the eighteenth century.

The introduction of the bayonet made armies more homogeneous and simplified the tacticians' task. In ancient armies, with four weapon systems, tacticians had to achieve the optimum combination and sought to bring the superior weapon system to bear against the inferior. The Byzantines had based much of their success on employing their variety of weapon systems against various foes—

stopping Gothic heavy cavalry at Taginae with heavy infantry and dismounted cavalry and using their light infantry against Frankish heavy infantry at Casilinum. Crusaders also had based their tactics on employing the stronger weapon system against the weaker.

Since Western Europeans had never made significant use of light cavalry, the advent of the reiter with saber and pistol had not simplified their tactical problem; there remained cavalry and two kinds of infantry, each vulnerable to cavalry if unaided by the other. But the bayonet-armed musketeer not only reduced armies to two weapon systems but gave the infantry distinct primacy. With D meaning the power to defend against an attack, the two weapons had a simple relationship (schematic 5.1). Compared to the four weapon systems of earlier warfare, tactics had undergone a fundamental transformation.

The tactician no longer had the problem of defending against a better weapon system nor the opportunity of exploiting one. His analogous opportunity lay in using cavalry's shock action against disordered infantry or against the flanks or rear of infantry formed in line. Generalship lost some of its creative opportunities for talented commanders and some of its chances for inept tacticians to blunder. With greater homogeneity in the armies, battles should become less decisive and the casualties of the defeated smaller.

Important improvements in the musket also increased its firepower and strengthened the infantry's reliance on missiles. After over a half century in development and perfection, the flintlock reached the armies in quantity in the 1690s. The weapon ignited the powder in its pan with sparks from a flint hitting a steel. The flint, held by the spring-loaded hammer, struck a blow against a plate attached to the cover of the pan, opening the pan as it simultaneously caused sparks which ignited the powder and fired the musket. The mechanism proved much more reliable than the matchlock, initially firing two-thirds of the time as against the matchlock's 50 percent rate. Subsequent improvements enabled the musket to fire 85 percent of the time.

The flintlock greatly increased the rate of fire, a process speeded up by the use of an oblong paper cartridge that contained the ball and the proper amount of powder. With the old matchlock, a musketeer first filled his pan from a powderhorn; opened a small wooden cartridge and emptied its powder into the barrel; took a ball from its pouch and put it in the barrel along with a piece of cloth from his hat; took his ramrod and rammed the cloth and ball down upon the powder; and, finally, took the burning match attached to his wrist, blew on it, and fastened it to the lock, ready to fire at last. With a flintlock the musketeer bit off the end of the cartridge with his teeth, retaining the ball in his mouth; used some powder from the cartridge to fill the pan and poured the remainder down the barrel, following it with the ball from his mouth and the paper of

infantry ——————— D ——————▸ cavalry

Schematic 5.1. Musketeers with Bayonets versus Cavalry

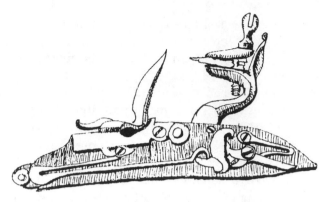

Illustration 5.1. Flintlock Mechanism

the cartridge; he then used his ramrod to drive paper and ball down on the powder, and he was ready to fire. Instead of one round a minute, the soldier with a flintlock with paper cartridge could fire two or three or even more rounds in a minute.

Another change involved better metal for the barrel, which permitted larger powder charges and resulted in a muzzle velocity of 1,000 feet per second with a one-ounce ball. Although armies had adopted shorter, lighter muskets with bores of no more than three-fourths of an inch, these flintlocks had a range and power nearly comparable to the older Spanish musket, which required a forked rest under the barrel. Further, they had triple the old weapon's rate of fire and a much greater percentage of shots fired for each pull of the trigger.

With its simpler loading procedure and no need to guard against accidents with a lighted match, the flintlock allowed a meaningful change in infantry formations. Whereas matchlock-equipped musketeers required at least a yard between them to load, infantrymen with flintlocks could load and form up shoulder to shoulder with as little as twenty-two inches per man. This could more than double the number of soldiers in each rank. Such a formation not only increased the number of weapons firing for each yard of front but presented the cavalry with a thicker wall of bayonets. Commanders could employ the closer spacing of men without any sacrifice in the width of the front because the more-rapid loading of the flintlock made possible a reduction in the ranks from six to three as well as the maintenance, if they used firing by rank, of a third of their men with loaded weapons.

But armies were slow to practice the tactical changes implied by the introduction of the flintlock, formation in four rather than three ranks lasting in many armies until nearly the middle of the century. Gradually they adopted three ranks that could fire together, the first rank kneeling, the second stooping, and the third standing. In an alternative method, the second rank stood and the third moved enough to the side to fire between the files of the second. Since the first method often involved broken collarbones among the men in the second rank, and the second method often inflicted arm and hand wounds on the men of the second rank, simultaneous fire by all three ranks never proved completely satisfactory. Ultimately, armies abandoned consistent use of the third rank but did not abolish it officially until the nineteenth century.

The smoothbore musket remained inaccurate. The burning of the black powder caused the barrel to foul and, to avoid having to clean the barrel during battle, the ball had a very loose fit, usually one-twentieth of an inch smaller than the bore. This sacrificed muzzle velocity and accuracy but speeded up loading and deferred the need to ream out barrels. For these reasons armies did not use rifles that required a tight fit for the ball going down the barrel if the ball were to engage the rifling coming out. The few military riflemen had mallets to hammer on their ramrods to drive the ball into the barrel.

With all men armed with muskets, firing received even more attention. When men stood shoulder to shoulder to fire, even uniforms had to change, the late seventeenth-century's broad-brimmed hats and coats with full skirts giving way to narrow-brimmed or brimless headgear and tight-fitting clothes suitable for men in close array. The best method of exploiting the enhanced firepower occupied tacticians, who sought better alternatives to the procedures used with the matchlock. The French, slow to change to make the most of the flintlock, clung to a deeper formation and controlled fire by ranks. When still arrayed in five ranks, the French would have the first four ranks kneel, the fifth fire, the fourth rise and fire, and so on until each rank had stood and fired. They could apportion or reserve their fire by having only one or more ranks fire.

But it proved difficult to control the fire of an entire battalion in this way, and other armies subdivided the battalion into as many as eighteen platoons for firing. If they organized platoons drawn from each part of the battalion line into three groups for firing purposes, each group could fire separately on command. Since the platoons firing at any one time were distributed over the whole front of the battalion, the entire front delivered and reserved fire each time one of the three groups of platoons fired. Simultaneous firing by all three lines of a platoon gave officers better opportunities to supervise and so took advantage of the battalion's subdivision and subordinate command structure to improve control and performance. In addition, it both simplified reloading when all ranks performed that task concurrently and, at the same time, assured that all parts of the line fired at one time while retaining some men with their muskets reloaded and ready to fire.

Drill helped battalions keep their alignment in battle, but on the battlefield a contemporary knew that the aligned marches and other "splendid evolutions" practiced in peacetime met difficulties in war. "A ploughed field or a churned up meadow are enough to reduce the harmony to dissonance. Some of the soldiers lose step, and in trying to regain it they make a couple of hops and fall behind. When they fall back into step the others promptly lose it. The advance hesitates and the whole line falters." The drill also gave soldiers skill in loading and firing rapidly, but when lines fired at each other at a hundred yards, the fire at command soon gave way to individual firing because officers could no longer control their men. "During long and hot actions, when many troops had been killed, they could not prevent their soldiers from firing at will." Another contemporary described such combats with muskets thus: "You begin by firing by platoons, and perhaps two or three would get off orderly volleys. But then would follow a general blazing away—the usual rolling fire when everybody blasted off as soon as he had loaded, when the ranks and files became intermingled, when the first rank was incapable of kneeling, even if it wanted to. The commanders, from subalterns to generals, would be incapable of getting the mass to perform anything else: they just had to wait until it finally set itself in motion forwards or backwards."[3]

In addition to devoting much drill to the perfection of firing, commanders trained their men to form squares to resist cavalry and to form into line of battle. Through drill they sought to produce soldiers who had such discipline and familiarity with their firing, marching, and tactical evolutions that they could function as smoothly and responsively as possible amid the smoke, din, and bloodshed of the battlefield. On the whole, they had a remarkable degree of success, even though the aristocratic officers tended to rely too much on driving the men and not enough on eliciting their loyalty and leading them.

Eighteenth-Century Logistics

Land transportation had undergone no major changes since the introduction of the horse, but small qualitative enhancements did increase its efficiency. The four-wheel wagon, which could carry more than a ton, could take best advantage of the rapid increase in the mileage of surfaced roads, the development of which characterized the late seventeenth and the eighteenth centuries. The growth in the number of canals also enhanced the economy of land transportation. The increase in the availability and accuracy of maps aided the planning and execution of campaigns, and the telescope made a similar contribution to the conduct of battles. Steady improvements in ships and their sailing qualities marked a similar gradual progress in sea transportation. The development of the chronometer permitted calculation of longitude, and better instruments augmented the accuracy of the determination of latitude and longitude.

Advances in commerce, agriculture, and manufacturing fostered economic productivity and went hand in hand with the marked population growth, also occasioned by the decline in the virulence of epidemic disease. The introduction of the potato not only helped food production but also put at the disposal of armies a crop that could substitute for bread but that did not require any elaborate processing. Soldiers could dig potatoes and cook them themselves.

But these changes did not change the logistical methods of supply established in the latter half of the preceding century. Reserves accumulated in magazines continued to play a role, but largely to support the initiation of a campaign or to sustain a siege. And even then magazines could only supply flour for bread; a magazine could not possibly meet the vastly greater requirements of forage for the armies' numerous horses. A typical army had two-thirds as many horses as men, and horses on campaign consumed twenty pounds of food a day compared to the one and a half pounds of flour needed to bake two pounds of bread for a man and another pound for meat, cheese, and other food. Ammunition, even in sieges, amounted to an insignificant item compared to the weight of the food and fodder needed by a besieging army.

Thus armies continued to live on the country, a process organized and regularized by contributions but still fully dependent on the exploitation of local sources of food and, especially, fodder. The great size of armies meant that they had difficulty remaining long in one place, even if good roads and an ample number of wagons widely extended the area from which they drew supplies. Stationary armies usually had to organize the resources of the region for themselves, establishing ovens to bake bread and harvesting hay for the horses and even wheat for the men's bread. These latter operations often had the attributes of a major military operation. Dispersal for such productive activities furnished excellent opportunities for soldiers to desert and for enemy cavalry or even infantry to catch the army at a disadvantage. A large force often accompanied the foraging parties. Since enemy cavalry raiders always found supply wagons tempting targets, the wagons usually moved in heavily guarded convoys, and the need to safeguard a large convoy often put the entire army on the alert.

Though more ample tax revenues and loan resources and better and more businesslike logistical arrangements tethered armies less to supply considerations than in any but ancient times, the ability to provide for armies still fundamentally conditioned strategy, as it had in Alexander's time. The frequency of sieges increased the importance of logistics, and the ability of the besiegers' supplies to outlast those of the garrison assumed fundamental importance in any operation against a large, well-fortified place. Thus, attackers offered liberal terms for an early surrender and threatened extermination for resistance to the end—which would never come if the besiegers exhausted the resources of the adjacent country before the garrison's supplies gave out.

Like the Greeks', but unlike Alexander's, eighteenth-century armies still had many noncombatants with them, including women and children. The baggage of the many well-to-do officers also was a major source of the large train that accompanied eighteenth-century armies. Many officers brought along a bed, chairs, a mobile kitchen, writing stand, and even brass candlesticks as well as large wardrobes, including nightcaps, slippers, and clothes brushes. The imperial army of the Austrian Habsburgs limited officers to one private wagon for their baggage, colonels to two, generals from two to four, and field marshals, of which the army had many, to five. In all armies very wealthy officers circumvented such regulations where they existed and brought into the field with them a very sumptuous lifestyle. Such officers brought valets, extensive wardrobes, and chefs and carried into the field elaborate silver services and one, a troupe of actors. Though not representative because it occurred on a maneuver and when the king was present with the army, the scale of entertaining by a French marshal, the duke of Boufflers, illustrates this problem. The marshal "had more than 72 cooks and at least 340 domestics, of whom 120 wore livery. There were 400 dozen napkins, 80 dozen plates of silver and six dozen of enamel besides plates and silver bowls for fruit, and everything else in proportion. On an ordinary day they consumed 50 dozen bottles and when the King and the Princes came to eat, 80. In one day 2,000 pounds of coffee were consumed and 268 litres of liqueurs." Even Wallenstein would have found it difficult to surpass the profuse magnificence of this style of living.[4]

The Strategy and Tactics of Marlborough's Campaigns

Tactical conditions basically precluded the realistic pursuit of a combat strategy that did not involve sieges. Though commanders who had confidence in the excellence of their armies and their own skill sought battles, they still lacked the power to compel the enemy to fight. Faced with the defensive strength of the bayonet-armed, dual-purpose infantry, the tactical offensive had lost power since commanders could no longer pit a superior weapon system against an inferior. So the greater homogeneity of armies strengthened the defense, already predominant between similarly constituted forces. Thus with Roman logistics, Roman linear tactics, and Roman skill in field and permanent fortifications, strategy exhibited the same indecisiveness that had characterized Roman operations when the Pompeians stymied Caesar at Ilerda and Caesar and Pompey each baffled the other until both decided they could profit from a battle at Pharsalus.

This condition of stalemate did not differentiate eighteenth-century warfare from preceding centuries, for even when heavy cavalry dominated the battlefield, the castle and fortified cities gave primacy to the strategic defense. Strategists continued to aim at logisitic objectives but had largely abandoned raids to supply the raiding army, deny resources to the enemy, and exert pressure on their opponent for political concessions. Instead, they sought to occupy enemy territory, to subsist there more permanently and efficiently than they could as raiders, deny more conclusively the resources to the enemy, and thus exert a more effective political pressure with a method that promised to arouse less active antipathy to soldiers or political opposition among the inhabitants and authorities. The French experience in devastating the Palatinate had shown that wanton raids could intensify opposition as well as intimidate.

The War of the Spanish Succession clearly exhibits military operations of the early eighteenth century and how much they had in common with those of the late seventeenth before the introduction of the bayonet. In this war France and Spain fought the United Kingdom, Holland, the Holy Roman Emperor, and the majority of the German principalities. But Bavaria sided with the French, and, reinforced by a powerful French army under Marshal Marsin, in 1704, the Franco-Bavarian forces posed a menace to the emperor's heartland, Austria. On the Rhine, imperial forces under the margrave of Baden faced a French army under Marshal Tallard and in the Netherlands Marshal Villeroi opposed allied forces, largely English and Dutch, under the duke of Marlborough. Although they fell far below the standard of Turenne and Luxembourg, Marsin and Tallard gave adequate performances as commanders. Marshal Villeroi, however, a polished courtier who received his command because of the friendship of King Louis XIV, proved hopelessly incompetent. On the other hand, the duke of Marlborough, who had also risen high by his connections at court, would become one of the greatest of British generals. His exceptional concern for the sensibilities of others and the charm of his manner made him excel in the diplomacy necessary in a coalition war and helped him bind his soldiers to him by his constant consideration of their needs. His strategy, characterized by careful planning, matched his tactical skill, founded in large measure on his invariable coolness on the battlefield.

Concerned about the Franco-Bavarian threat to the emperor, the duke of Marlborough determined to move there with part of the forces from the Netherlands. Beginning in early May, the duke marched south along the east bank of the Rhine, his intentions quite obscure to the enemy, a confusion he fostered by making preparations to cross the Rhine just as he left the river to march eastward to the Danube to strengthen the imperial armies facing the French and their Bavarian ally. But Marshal Villeroi had moved south, and the French plan called for him to face the margrave of Baden's imperial troops while Marshal Tallard's men crossed the Rhine farther south in a tentative advance eastward. Meanwhile, the emperor's ablest general, Prince Eugene of Savoy, had taken the command from Baden, who had joined Marlborough with a small reinforcement. Eugene had the task of keeping back the French on the Rhine while the duke of Marlborough sought to drive Bavaria from the war.

The duke had reached the Danube with his army in fine condition and with its full strength in spite of traveling perhaps 350 miles. He had marched only in the morning, given rest days, and still averaged more than nine miles a day. Knowing his itinerary before his departure, he had made advance logistic preparations along the route, even receiving new boots for the men. He minimized desertion because he usually kept his force concentrated, subsisting through his quartermasters. The friendly or neutral local authorities provided the supplies, responding to the promise of payment and a genteel form of pressure exemplified by his letter to the elector of Mainz: "It would please your highness . . . to see to it that we may find provisions on our way, pending prompt repayment. It would be very advantageous for the troops and also for the country in preventing disorders" in which, presumably, unfed, turbulent troops took loot as well as food.[5]

Arriving on the north bank of the Danube, the duke found the elector of Bavaria and Marshal Marsin in possession of all of the bridges over the river and with their forces disposed to keep him north of the Danube. Moving east along the river, Marlborough captured the fortified bridgehead at Donauwörth. He lost 5,000 men in an assault on the strongest part of the fortifications, one which so distracted the defenders that the main attack easily succeeded. The overwhelmed defenders lost 10,000 of their 14,000 men, and the duke had a bridgehead across the Danube, which he rapidly exploited to enter Bavaria, confining the Franco-Bavarian forces to the area west of the Lech.

With control of the bridge and an ability to cross and recross the Danube, Marlborough could pursue his logistic strategy of occupying the enemy's resource areas. Since he could not occupy them all simultaneously, he must, as Prince Eugene explained it, devastate Bavaria: "Thus I see in the final analysis that there is no other means but that entire Bavaria, together with the surrounding districts, must be totally destroyed and laid waste in order to deny the enemies the opportunity of continuing the war any longer either from Bavaria or any surrounding area."[6]

So Marlborough ravaged Bavaria, burning 300 villages preparatory to returning north of the river to control the enemy's remaining potential supply regions there. Since the enemy could find nothing to eat in Bavaria, this strategy would leave them dependent for food and fodder on the small area between the Lech and the Danube to subsist an army reinforced by the arrival of Marshal Marsin's army from the Rhine. And to carry it out Marlborough also had more men, Prince Eugene having slipped away from Villeroi and followed Tallard eastward. The prince awaited Marlborough north of the Danube.

But the Franco-Bavarian force had crossed the river at Hochstett and occupied a strong position from which they guarded their supply area and interdicted the allies' access to the supplies in the region northward toward Nuremberg. Since southward the allies had access only to devastated Bavaria, this new position of the Franco-Bavarian army would compel Marlborough and Eugene to retreat or attack to drive the Franco-Bavarian army from its source of rations for men and horses. Although Tallard invited a battle, he had confidence that Marlborough and Eugene would not assault him, posted as he was with flanks protected and his front obstructed by villages and a stream; rather, he thought they would fall back, leaving him in control of the Danube region. But the British and imperial commanders resolved to attack.

In Prince Eugene the duke had a worthy compatriot. From Savoy, a region on the border between France and Italy, the physically unprepossessing prince thirsted for military fame, serving the emperor because he could not obtain a commision from the king of France. The prince, seasoned in wars with the Turks as well as against the French in Italy, had already emerged as one of the premier soldiers of the age. Equally a master of strategy and tactics, in battle he displayed almost reckless courage and expected the same of his men. He and Marlborough, equally aggressive often commanded in the same theater, worked harmoniously together, and became fast friends.

As did Gustavus at Breitenfeld, Tallard commanded two armies, his own and the Franco-Bavarian of Marsin and the elector of Bavaria. Since he deployed them side by side, he, like Gustavus, had a high proportion of his cavalry in his center. Tallard protected his left by woods and his right by the village of Blenheim, which touched the Danube. Here he had a strong garrison of infantry. Shortly after noon Marlborough on the allied left and Eugene on the right began their assault. While Eugene attracted the attention of the enemy on his part of the front, Marlborough assailed the village of Blenheim with twenty battalions of infantry. When the first British infantry in line approached the French, 2,400 Englishmen received a volley at less than thirty yards from 4,000 Frenchmen, immediately losing 800 killed or wounded; but the British persisted and the alarmed French defender of Blenheim put in all of his infantry reserves, ultimately cramming 18,000 men into the little village, far more men than could employ with effect. An observer noted that "the men were so crowded in among one another that they couldn't even fire—let alone carry out any orders. Not a single shot of the enemy missed its mark, whilst only these few of our men at the front could return the fire."[7]

While he so successfully distracted the enemy on either end of the line, Marlborough moved infantry and cavalry to attack over the creek in the center of the enemy line of battle. Though both armies had about the same strength, he had 50 percent more cavalry in the center and twenty-three battalions of infantry to only nine for the French. Since the French had so few infantry and no reserves available from their right, their weakness was greater than their numbers indicated. Because their strength lay in cavalry, which had no predominance on the defense, they opposed the allied onslaught on their center with forces ill-adapted to the defense. Of infantry that could stand firm behind their bayonets and volleys they had barely 5,000, having to rely instead on cavalry whose only defense lay in the countercharge.

Small wonder that Marlborough's combined infantry and cavalry assault broke the French center and that many of the French cavalry fled to the Danube in a hasty retreat. "So tight was the press," wrote one participant in that panicky flight, "that my horse was carried along some three hundred paces without putting hoof to ground—right to the edge of a deep ravine: down we plunged a good twenty feet into a swampy meadow; my horse stumbled and fell. A moment later several more men and horses fell on top of me as the remains of my cavalry swept by all intermingled with the hotly pursuing foes. I spent several minutes trapped beneath my horse." Three thousand French cavalry drowned trying to swim the Danube, and the allies took a huge number of prisoners from the men who had crowded into Blenheim. The French suffered 35,000 casualties, including 14,000 prisoners. This amounted to two-thirds of their force, compared to an allied loss of 23 percent.[8]

The Battle of Blenheim inflicted the greatest attrition of any major Western European battle in the eighteenth century. It had the strategic result of removing the Franco-Bavarian threat to Austria, the allies occupying Bavaria and the French falling back to the Rhine.

The remainder of Marlborough's campaigns during the war occurred in the Netherlands. The French had occupied this Spanish province when the grandson of their king ascended the throne of Spain and the two countries became allied.

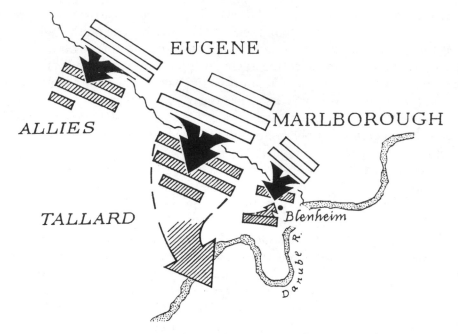

Diagram 5.1. Blenheim: Distraction and Concentration

The British and Dutch both had a keen interest in ousting the French, and Marlborough led Anglo-Dutch armies in this effort for the succeeding seven years. He faced a formidable task because fortified towns studded a country that had baffled the Spaniards in the sixteenth century and would tax Marlborough's genius. Like the Spaniards, he faced a defense in depth such as the Romans had organized to protect their frontiers. The fortifed cities provided supply depots and places of refuge for armies, as well as blocking all of the main roads and principal river crossings. For this reason armies found it not only difficult to by-pass them but hazardous also, as the garrisons sallied out to capture supply convoys and attack foragers and small forces within striking distance.

Siegecraft and logistical organization had developed so well and the Netherlands had such a dense population and abundant crops that an army could count on maintaining itself outside of a city for the month and a half to two months needed to take a strongly fortified city. But the besiegers required enormous numbers of men to surround a city and man its lines of circumvallation, sometimes as many as ten times those in the garrison. In addition, an army had to protect itself against the army of relief, which inevitably threatened to interfere, even if it never assumed the tactical offensive. This condition meant that a single siege could sometimes consume an entire campaigning season, usually limited to the period May through October.

But in 1706 Marlborough had the good fortune to face the inept Marshal Villeroi. In May Villeroi advanced, eager for a battle with the duke of Marlborough's allied army. Confident of his ability, he planned to give Louis XIV revenge for the defeat at Blenheim. The French drew up 60,000 men in a concave position, with the village of Ramillies in the center. Marlborough, far more justifiably confident of his ability to defeat Villeroi, deployed and began a frontal battle in the early afternoon. Both armies had the conventional deployment of infantry in the center and cavalry and some infantry on the wings. Marlborough began his offensive battle with probing attacks on either flank. On his left the duke's cavalry inflicted heavy casualties on some dismounted French cavalry, and his infantry captured two villages. On the duke's right an attack by twelve battalions of redcoated British infantry caused Marshal Villeroi to move infantry from his center, replacing them with infantry from his already weakened right.

When an assault in the center failed and French cavalry drove his back, exposing the infantry's flank, Marlborough acted. Perceiving that cavalry could not cross the marshy creek on his right and so knowing that the ground gave protection from a counterattack by the French cavalry, he called off his attack there, pulled back his cavalry, and marched them to his left, unobserved by Marshal Villeroi because of the smoke and the uneven terrain. These cavalry the duke used first to drive back the French cavalry and then, with nearly a two-to-one superiority in cavalry, to assault the French in a charge aided by the advance of the infantry in the center. These attacks succeeded and when, too late, the marshal realized that the danger lay on his right and center, his movement to the right of the unused cavalry of his left found his right and center in full retreat. The French lost 13,000 men, over 20 percent of their strength; Marlborough's army suffered less than 5 percent casualties. Just as at Blenheim, Marlborough's infantry attacks had distracted the enemy, causing him to weaken a part of his line against which the duke concentrated his cavalry.

But this victory, tactically inconsequential when compared with Blenheim, yielded major strategic results when Marlborough pushed forward against demoralized enemy resistance. "Towns that we thought would have endured a long siege are yielding without a stroke," commented one contemporary as the disheartened Villeroi fell back and his subordinates surrendered one fortified point after another.[9]

Lack of hostility from local inhabitants aided the allied advance. Since the Habsburgs had long ruled the Netherlands, the new Bourbon dynasty had less hold on the people, especially since the invader acted on behalf of an alliance which included the Holy Roman Emperor, a Habsburg cousin of the late king of Spain. Marlborough exploited this and the emperor's brother's claim to the throne of Spain as Charles III when he promised to guarantee to Charles III's Netherland subjects "the full and perfect enjoyment of all their estates, goods, and effects. We do hereby," Marlborough's proclamation read, "strictly forbid all the officers and soldiers of our army to offer the least injury to ye said inhabitants." This lack of indigenous resistance helped Marlborough capture Brussels, the capital of the Netherlands, and Antwerp, where the Spanish governor gave up his forces and part of the French garrison as well. Ultimately the allies controlled much of the Netherlands before the end of the campaigning season and the vigor of Marshal Vendôme, Villeroi's able replacement, halted the easy fall of formidably fortified places.[10]

In Vendôme, a great-grandson of King Henry IV, Marlborough faced an opponent of an entirely different caliber from Villeroi. Having entered the army at age eighteen and seen more than thirty years of active service, the marshal had demonstrated skill, courage, imagination, and an exceptional ability to influence men. Yet the following year proved uneventful, as the adroit marshal stayed on the defensive while making potentially menacing movements, and Marlborough, too, pursued the defensive with an army diminished to support other theaters. The next year the French took advantage of the Netherlanders' dissatisfaction with allied rule to use very small forces to recapture two major cities and so regain control of much of the Netherlands. But the divided French command, shared by the experienced Vendôme and the king's young grandson, contributed to Marlborough's ability to bring on a battle.

The two armies faced each other while small French forces seized the disaffected towns. Marlborough, marching fifty miles in two and a half days, reached a river at Oudenarde, only six miles from the point where the French army was crossing in the same direction. Marshal Vendôme learned of the presence of the allied army when some of the duke's cavalry routed his foragers. Having his men already across the river, the marshal determined to fight; Marlborough, knowing the French handicap of dual command, likewise believed he could win. Since each side pushed men into the contest as they became available, neither ever formed a regular line of battle. With a larger number of soldiers at hand, Vendôme could easily have driven back the allies had the king's grandson not misunderstood the marshal's plan and failed to add his wing of the army to support the attack. When Marlborough brought infantry and cavalry around Vendôme's flank, this assault won the Battle of Oudenarde and the French army successfully retreated as night fell. The allies suffered 3 percent casualties, the French 15. Thus the armies encountered each other, neither ready to fight nor occupying chosen ground, and both attacking as well as defending. With the French in retreat, Marlborough then confused the enemy as to whether he intended to besiege Tournai, Ypres, Mons, or Lille. He settled on Lille, moving forward in early August.

Lille, a major French city, had such symbolic and material significance that the French had garrisoned it with 16,000 men commanded by a senior marshal, the talented Boufflers. An allied force of 100,000 carried out the siege. Prince Eugene, the emperor's principal field marshal, supervised the besieging forces; Marlborough, the captain general of the British army, commanded the covering troops. Since artillery could not reach walls sunk in a ditch behind a sloping glacis of earth, the attackers slowly dug their way forward in trenches that ran parallel to the fortifications with zigzag trenches connecting them. They moved up artillery to continue bombardment of the fortifications, cannonballs aiming at the tops of the redoubts and mortar bombs falling within. The assailants needed this firepower as well as strong garrisons for the trenches they dug, to resist sorties by the besieged and to cope with any trench lines the defenders might build out from the fortifications to bring the trenches of the attackers under enfilade fire.

While this application of the fairly standard methods of siegecraft went on slowly against a determined defense and the superb fortifications of Lille, Marlborough had to protect the operation from a French army of 110,000 men that warily circled the town. Raising sieges had long occasioned battles, but Marlborough's strong position and his great reputation as a combat commander made the French give up the idea of battle, first in early September and again in October when Vendôme appeared with a second relieving force.

The French did succeed in bringing the garrison some gunpowder when 2,000 cavalrymen, each carrying a 100-pound bag of powder, suddenly tried to ride through the besieger's defenses. Half made it, but the others met disaster when, as a contemporary described it, bullets from the besiegers "made several sparks to set fire to some of the enemy's powder bags; in an instant several hundred of them were hurled into the air amidst a terrifying explosion." As the survivors then hastily retreated, some of their powder bags "sprang leaks, leaving a trail of powder along the road behind them. As they rode their horse-shoes made the sparks fly up which set fire to the powder trail and this in turn ignited the sacks, blowing up a number of men and horses with an infernal din. It was a horrible spectacle to see the remains of men and horses, whose legs, arms and torsoes even had been flung into the trees."[11]

But the fortress continued to hold out as the French succeeded in interrupting the besiegers' communications with their base at Brussels. Meanwhile, Marlborough established a new line of communications from Ostend on the coast, beat off French raids on the supply convoys, and, when the French let in sea water and flooded the country, used boats for part of the supply route from Ostend. The French made their last effort to raise the siege by employing the classic strategy of a diversion when they advanced to Brussels to threaten the city. But their bombardment neither intimidated the garrison of the city nor distracted Marlborough, who moved to menace their line of retreat, ending the possible peril for Brussels.

After four months Lille surrendered, a major triumph in view of the resources the combatants had lavished on the campaign. The capture of Lille resulted from the victory of Oudenarde, and the significance both sides attached to Lille indicates the real difficulties of rapid advance against competent and confident leadership supported by the defense in depth provided by the heavily fortified country.

In 1709 the allies besieged Tournai without serious interference from the weakened French under their best commander, the brilliant Marshal Villars. Having served under Condé, Turenne, and Luxembourg, the boastful and ambitious Villars proved a pupil worthy of his teachers. When Tournai fell and the allies began the siege of Mons, Villars felt bound to intervene. Counting on Marlborough's willingness to take the offensive in battle, the marshal advanced his army so close to Mons that he interfered with the siege and took up a position at the village of Malplaquet where he had his flanks adquately protected by woods. As Marlborough moved up and deployed his army, the French had a day and a night to fortify their front with redoubts separated by gaps to allow their cavalry to pass through.

As the astute Marshal Villars had anticipated, Marlborough and Prince Eugene, the harmonious pair of great generals, planned to attack the French flanks until they had compelled the French to withdraw so many men from their center that, as at Blenheim, the allied cavalry could sweep through to charge the rear of the French on the flanks and win the battle. The initial assaults failed when, on the allied right, successive volleys at fifty paces from French infantry four ranks deep repulsed the allied troops; on the right the attacking Dutch infantry suffered 5,000 casualties in half an hour when enfilading fire from a concealed battery of twenty guns supported the volleys of French infantry. With Marshal Villars commanding the French left and Marshal Boufflers the right, the French held firmly and avoided the mistakes of Blenheim.

But allied troops had gotten possession of the woods on the French left, and Villars had to withdraw infantry from his redoubts in center to counterattack the woods. In assembling 15,000 infantry to deal with this threat, he virtually denuded the center redoubts that the allied infantry captured, leaving the French cavalry behind as the only force holding the French center. Thirty thousand allied cavalry began passing through the gaps as a bullet wounded Marshal Villars, causing him to faint. Marshal Boufflers assumed command, ordered vigorous but unsuccessful attacks against the allied cavalry, and began to withdraw his wing from the field when he saw the French left begin to retreat.

Although the French withdrew, their army and leaders maintained their morale, and the depleted allied force could do no more than continue the siege of Mons to its successful conclusion. Marlborough had hoped for a signal victory that would enable him to advance into France. Instead, he lost 25,000 killed and wounded, 22 percent of his 110,000; the French had suffered only 12,000 killed, wounded, and prisoners, only 15 percent of their 80,000. After his costly triumphs over the Romans, Pyrrhus had remarked that more such victories would force him to return to Greece without an army. After his defeat at Malplaquet Marshal Villars wrote King Louis XIV, "If it please God to give your majesty's enemies another such victory, they are ruined." If attrition measured victory, the French had won the contest.

At Malplaquet Marlborough's distractions on the flanks had proved so costly that even victory could not redeem the price paid. But Marlborough's battles showed him to be a tactical master who successfully applied the principle of assaulting vigorously at one point to draw there the enemy's reserves and by this distraction creating a weak point elsewhere, which he exploited with the battle-winning attack. Marlborough always used cavalry for the final main attack because of its mobility and ease of deployment.

Persisting Strategy in North Italy

The campaigns in north Italy took place in a region comparable in size to the Netherlands, about 150 miles from east to west and about 70 miles from north to south. Although this area had a large number of cities and had often provided a theater for war between the French and Germans, it had fewer heavily fortified cities than the Netherlands. The tributaries to the Po River were the site of most cities and constituted the principal barriers to movement east and west. Once an army passed one of these rivers, it could march fairly freely until it reached the next river barrier. Operations in north Italy also involved fewer stalemates because of the lower ratio of force to space, both contestants in the War of the Spanish Succession fielding smaller armies there than they did in the Spanish Netherlands, so close and important to France, Britain, and Holland.

The French alliance with the Duchy of Savoy, situated on the French border, and with Spain, which still had control of much of north Italy, meant that at the outbreak of war in 1701 French armies and the forces of the duke of Savoy held all of north Italy up to the Adige River, the frontier of the neutral state of Venice. Standing on the defensive, the French commander, the capable Marshal Catinat, had had ample and successful experience commanding in Italy. He garrisoned a number of cities and kept his main force at Rivoli to block the emperor's invasion route between the Adige and Lake Garda. Rather than face Catinat and his army, Prince Eugene, the imperial commander, decided to violate the territory of neutral Venice and march south through the difficult terrain east of the Adige. Distracting Catinat with ostentatious preparations to advance from the north and hidden by the river and the rugged country, Eugene and his army reached Verona before the curiously negligent French marshal discovered Eugene's movement. A superb general, Eugene then threatened to cross the Adige at several points and, having convinced Catinat that he would cross north of Verona, built a bridge and passed over the Adige on July 9, far to the south at Castelbaldo.

With most of the imperial force on the other side of the river and his own troops dispersed, Marshal Catinat, uncertain as to Eugene's objective, fell back to the Mincio, only to find that Eugene had marched far to the northwest and, on July 28, had passed north of Catinat's army and bridged the Mincio a few miles south of Peschiera. Facing Eugene's continuing westward march to the Chiese, the scattered French resumed their retreat until they finally took a position behind the Oglio. By distracting the enemy and then exploiting their dispersion to guard the rivers, Eugene had driven them back over three river barriers and taken a third of their north Italian holdings.

In his advance Eugene did not conduct a raid. Rather, he dominated the area around his army, used it as a base of supplies, and essentially followed Gustavus's persisting strategy of systematic conquest. Save for one notable exception, both combatants in north Italy followed this strategy of trying to acquire, dominate, and exploit the resources of the fertile north Italian region.

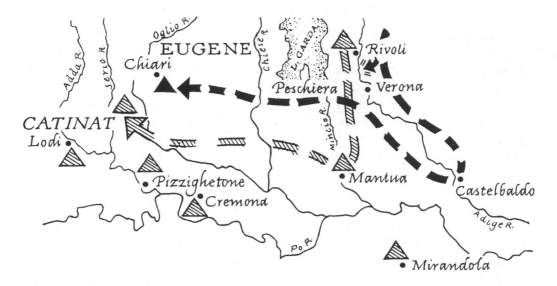

Diagram 5.2. Eugene Distracts Catinat

Concerned with the defeat in Italy, King Louis XIV of France replaced Catinat with the incapable Marshal Villeroi who, reinforced until he had 45,000 men to Eugene's 30,000, crossed the Oglio in late August and attacked Eugene's army in its strong position at Chiari. But since Villeroi did not push his unsuccessful attempt very hard, the French lost only 2,500, Eugene's force suffered only negligible losses. For the remainder of the fall the opposing armies tried to disrupt each other's foraging until they went into winter quarters. During this period Eugene blockaded the fortified city of Mantua, still held by the French.

In a winter raid Eugene's men captured Marshal Villeroi, but this proved a liability when Louis XIV replaced him with the keen and resourceful Marshal Vendôme. The marshal promptly turned the tables on Eugene: on May 12, 1702, he unexpectedly marched north from Cremona, crossed the Oglio at Pontevico, the Mella at Manerbio, the Chiese at Medote, and appeared at Goito on May 23, where he disrupted Eugene's blockade of Mantua. With this action Marshal Vendôme took control of the territory north and west of Mantua and occupied a position between Eugene and Austria, compelling the emperor's field marshal to concentrate his forces, dig in south of Mantua, and supply himself from the country south of the Po, where he had earlier established magazines.

Receiving additional reinforcements, Vendôme left 23,000 men fortified at Rivalto to face Eugene, moved west to the Po, crossed well upstream from the imperial forces, and advanced rapidly eastward, taking several cities in Eugene's base area south of the Po. The French commander then proceeded north to Luzzara, aiming to take the bridges over the Po and so force Eugene to enter Venetian territory and retreat back toward Austria. But without the knowledge of the French commander at Rivalto, Eugene had brought most of his army south across the Po and marched on Luzzara, determined to retrieve his situation by attacking half of Vendôme's divided army, which was no stronger than the imperial force.

Eugene took advantage of the canals, dikes, and woods in the Luzzara region to conceal his troops, hoping to surprise the French as they made camp. But while he still had his men in the usual precautionary five columns, Vendôme discovered the enemy army in ambush and deployed his own before the imperial commander could get his into line of battle. Nevertheless, Eugene attacked at 5:00 P.M. and the resulting frontal battle raged until midnight but without the imperial forces' driving the French from the field. The armies continued to face each other the following day but limited their combat to cannonading each other.

In fact, the armies faced each other for another fifty-five days, while the French used detachments to try to dominate Eugene's supply region and Eugene employed the same means to protect himself. In the end the French pushed Eugene eastward beyond the Secchia where he wintered his troops. With total forces nearly double those of Eugene, the skillful Vendôme had driven his more capable opponent from most of his conquests of the previous year, confining him to an area south of the Po. But he had not driven Eugene from Italy, and the brillant imperial field marshal had maintained himself at the enemy's expense and compelled the French and their ally, the duke of Savoy, to commit twice his numbers in their campaign to force him out.

As usual, battles only occurred by mutual consent, as when Vendôme was willing to stand on the defensive and Eugene took the risk of attacking in an

Diagram 5.3. Eugene's Interior Lines

effort to protect his base area from French occupation. Vendôme, by his sudden advance in May, had recovered much of the lost territory, and when he left half of his army near Mantua at Rivalto, he distracted Eugene while he crossed the Po to the west and invaded Eugene's base area. But by this division of his forces the French marshal had given the alert Eugene interior lines that he exploited to fight the stronger French with equal numbers at Luzzara.

In 1703 the duke of Savoy changed sides, joining the emperor in the war against the French. This created a double front in north Italy with the French facing the emperor's forces in the east in the region of Mantua and Lake Garda and those of the duke of Savoy in the west in the region around the duke's capital, Turin. In 1703, with Eugene absent from Italy, little occurred except that an imperial army slipped past the French to reinforce the duke. In 1704 the French forces, continuing under Vendôme and with Eugene still away, made headway against the duke of Savoy, capturing some of his important cities. In 1705 Eugene returned to Italy with instructions to reinforce the seriously beleaguered duke.

Advancing west of Lake Garda, Eugene faced Vendôme for a month while awaiting reinforcements. When the marshal left his indolent younger brother in command and took personal charge of the French forces facing the duke of Savoy near Turin, the prince passed through the mountains around the left of the younger Vendôme and had crossed the Oglio by the time the marshal had returned to take command. When Eugene then sought to cross the Adda by marching far north to cross at Paradiso, Vendôme learned of it in time to forestall him. Eugene then moved south with his 24,000 men to seize the fortified bridge-head at Cassano, only to find the marshal himself commanding the garrison of 10,000 men. Failing to distract the wiley French leader and get past him to reinforce the duke, Eugene determined to attack the much inferior French force in its strong situation at Cassano.

Vendôme had his back to the Adda in a position protected by a canal twenty feet wide and four or five feet deep. The French easily defeated the first imperial attackers who waded the canal because the neck-deep water had dampened the soldiers' powder. The main contest thus revolved around Eugene's efforts to capture a stone bridge over the canal. Twice his men seized it, but each time French counterattacks pushed them back. When the courageous Eugene at last led his troops in person, he drove back the French for a third time and seemed about to reach the river, cutting the French in half and driving them into the water. But Vendôme, in the manner of his ancestor Henry IV, led his men in a counterattack, and, when bullets wounded Eugene in the neck and the knee, the French prevailed. The imperial army fell back, losing over 4,000 casualties, about a sixth of their force; the determined French resistance had, however, cost them more than half of their 10,000 men. With respect to the tactical result of attrition, Eugene won the battle, but the marshal, still holding Adda, had the strategic victory. Outnumbered two and a half to one, the French had succeeded, again exhibiting the power of the tactical defense. The victory explained the unwillingness of the generals of the era to attack even such seemingly vulnerable detachments as that led by Vendôme, with its back to a river, and the readiness of commanders to take such seemingly hazardous positions.

After one more futile effort to pass around the French army, Eugene fell back to occupy winter quarters near Mantua. But as he marched eastward, the marshal followed and, by moving parallel and to the south, forced him to winter in the less attractive area on the west shore of Lake Garda while the French occupied the more abundant region north of Mantua. Vendôme had prevailed in keeping Eugene's army from reinforcing the duke, but the prince's effort had so occupied the marshal that he could not spare the men to begin the siege of Turin. Eugene properly characerized the Italian campaigns as "not a war of conquest nor of establishing winter quarters, but a war of diversion. This diversion involves a heavy expenditure for the French in men and money. They have to keep 80,000 men in Italy . . . whereas the Allies only have 40,000 there." But he also knew the traditional French interest in Italy and believed that France would not make peace as long as she controlled north Italy.[12]

In the fall of 1705 the situation in Italy looked bleak to Eugene. With his army unpaid, he wrote the emperor that "the soldiers resist punishment with force. I have to choose between the extremes of leniency and severity." As winter began, he reported: "My army is ruined, the horses worn out with past fatigues, no sure footing in the country, and the enemy reassembling their forces in my front. Besides the Venetians threatened to declare war against us, if we do not quit their territory." While Prince Eugene absented himself from Italy in April 1706, the marshal surprised the imperial army in winter quarters, driving it back into the mountains with a loss, including deserters, of 10,000 men. In mid-May the French began the siege of Turin, and 150 miles to the east Vendôme built fortifications to protect the crossings of the Adige and so preclude the possibility of Eugene's interfering with the siege. If the French could capture Turin, they would drive the duke of Savoy from the war and consolidate their grip on north Italy.[13]

In mid-May Eugene moved forward with 38,000 men against Vendôme and the 40,000 with which he guarded the Adige. In Venetian territory, as he awaited reinforcements before advancing, Eugene took pains to avoid arousing the hostility of his unwilling hosts. He wrote the emperor: "I have been so insistent on the strictest discipline that there have been no excesses; orchards have been quite untouched, harvest gathered without loss or hindrance, whilst where the French have been there has been wholesale spoliation." The Venetians took no action against the imperial army, appreciating the contrast between its careful behavior and French depredations. The French had gained a reputaton for their occupations, some of their contributions in Germany being so heavy that populations had emigrated, unable to pay the exhorbitant exactions.[14]

In early July, having left a force at Verona and successfully convincing the French he planned to cross the upper Adige, Eugene secretly marched south along the river until, far to the south and east, he crossed the Adige without opposition from the French. Instead of then turning west, he moved farther southward with his 27,000 men and crossed the Po. Since Louis XIV had called Marshal Vendôme to go to the Netherlands to retrieve the situation after the French defeat at Ramillies, the king's young cousin, the competent but inexperienced duke of Orleans, now commanded the French. He reacted promptly to Eugene's surprise movements, calling reinforcements from the besiegers of Turin and falling back to the Mincio. This river barrier he guarded with 30,000 men while he sent another 30,000 to block the prince's westward advance south of the Po. But when the advance of the force Eugene had left at Verona caused the duke of Orleans to fear losing the line of the Mincio and so to concentrate all of his forces north of the Po, Eugene proceeded to go forward rapidly, still south of the Po. As a result, the young duke failed even to hold the Mincio. The imperial field marshal could not so easily have distracted the seasoned and sagacious Vendôme.

The duke of Orleans saw that his only hope of blocking the enemy's route to Turin lay at Stradella, where the Apennine Mountains almost reached the banks of the Po. To block the pass he sent ahead a force of 7,000 infantry and cavalry, the infantry riding in wagons to increase their speed of movement in the summer heat of north Italy. When Eugene, who had maintained a modest pace and marched often at night because of the heat, learned of this, he, too, hurried forward 7,000 men, which he followed with another similar detachment and all of the cavalry under his personal command. The imperial lead detachment beat the French to Stradella, and Eugene marched his whole army past Stradella and pushed it rapidly forward, bypassing French-held fortresses, until he joined his cousin, the duke of Savoy, near Turin, the duke of Orleans following with much of his French army.

But Eugene's advance differed signally from those that had characterized the earlier seesaw campaigning in Italy. Like a raider, Eugene had merely passed through north Italy, leaving most of the territory still garrisoned and controlled by the French. His campaign, though skillful and brilliant, had amounted only to a march to reinforce the besieged garrison of Turin. Without success at Turin, he would have only conducted a raid that had disconcerted the French but accomplished little else.

Eugene's successful distractions and speedy, well-conducted march had brought both armies to Turin. But the French had 80,000 men, and the allies, who had 15,000 in the garrison and 42,000 in the relieving army, faced the usual problem in raising a siege: the besiegers would hold the outward-facing fortified lines of circumvallation. This defensive advantage of the besiegers would have much to do with the failure of larger French relieving forces to raise the siege of Lille two years later; before Turin, the prince, with inferior numbers, faced an even more difficult problem. Since the French stayed in their lines of circumvallation and only an attack could save Turin, Eugene reconnoitered and found on the west side of the city that the French had failed to construct thoroughly or adequately garrison a part of their lines that they regarded as relatively inaccessible. Leaving men on the east side to distract the enemy, an effort supported by the garrison that sent out militia to threaten the besiegers, the prince assembled most of his forces at the weak point in the enemy's fortified lines.

Concentrating 30,000 against 8,000 to 10,000 defenders, Eugene made a vigorous attack with infantry in two lines, followed by his cavalry also in two lines. Aided by an additional distraction in the French rear by the regular troops of the garrison, Eugene broke through the unreinforced French lines. When reinforcements did arrive, Eugene's men beat these in detail as they came up, routing the whole French army. The French lost nearly 10,000 men, the allies only a few more than 3,000. In retreat the French made a serious blunder: they fell back toward France rather than to Milan and the large area of north Italy that they still controlled through garrisons. Eugene then began to attack and take these Italian garrisons. In March 1707 Louis XIV and the emperor concluded an agreement for the evacuation of the remaining French forces, about 20,000 men.

Eugene's triumphant march had defied Vendôme's belief that the French had "too many positions to stop him for his ever dreaming of bringing relief" to Turin. In spite of the heat, the difficulty in finding water, and the lack of an advance provision for supplies, he had covered the 240 miles of his march at a rate of fifteen miles a day. But the march alone did not raise the siege. The French force had ample strength to control enough of the country around Turin to supply itself, as did Eugene's relieving army. And the French also had a large base area east of Turin in which to continue their occupation of much of Italy. Victory at Turin, impossible without the march, had an essential role in raising the siege. The French mistake of retreating west to France instead of east to their garrisons made the campaign decisive for gaining allied control of north Italy. Blunders in trying to block Eugene's advance and in the dispositions and entrenchments around Turin made possible Eugene's achievement. But Eugene displayed brilliance in defeating his numerically stronger opponents. His strategic method, distraction to create a weak point through which to march past his opponents, he repeated at the tactical level when, like Marlborough, he coupled diversions east of Turin with concentration against the weak point in the enemy's lines to the west of the city. His skillful conduct of the battle and his personal leadership completed the victory made possible by his excellent plan.[15]

The Evolution of the Linear System

In the years after the end of the War of the Spanish Succession in 1714, military study flourished, and soldiers and theorists gave much thought to the linear tactical system that had blossomed into fullest flower with the advent of the bayonet. One group of scholars and soldiers advocated a return to shock action. In 1724 Folard, a French soldier and veteran of many campaigns, proposed restoring shock action through the use of a column with about twice as many ranks as files. Inspired by his belief that Epaminondas had won at Leuctra because his block of hoplites had overwhelmed the Spartan line, Folard was convinced that a charge by such a column would easily break through a line of musketeers three-deep, at which time it would divide in half and, the parts advancing in opposite directions, roll up the flanks it had created. He proposed to arm the men in the outermost ranks of the column with short pikes. Although his ideas created much controversy and he acquired disciples as well as critics, Folard failed to convince many that his column could in fact brave the musket volleys and breach the line. Nevertheless, his theories remained influential in military thought throughout the remainder of the eighteenth century, causing the French army in particular to provide in its regulations for forming troops in column.

Another French soldier, Marshal Saxe, though disparaging columns, also thought in terms of shock action, advocating arming some troops with pikes and even shields. More significantly, as it turned out, he did see that formations with greater depth and less width would possess more mobility than the thin lines necessary to develop maximum firepower.

But the advocates of fighting at a distance with muskets remained unconvinced, and another line of military thought led to the revival of light infantry tactics. Traditionally Greek and Roman light infantry, whether armed with javelins, slings, or bows, had fought as individuals, avoiding formation so that they could use their missiles against the opposing heavy infantry while avoiding close combat with either the heavy infantry or the heavy cavalry. Many sixteenth-century arquebusiers employed the same tactics, though the pike square provided a place of refuge on the battlefield. When Gustavus Adolphus equipped all light infantry with muskets and placed them in line with the pikemen, the musketeers abandoned almost entirely the tactics traditional with light infantry. The introduction of the bayonet, which made the light infantry into heavy or shock infantry as well, completed the transition by forming the completely homogeneous infantry in the customary heavy infantry formation.

But this change and the consequent drill required of all infantry to fight in line as a group omitted the contribution that infantry could make by employing the traditional light infantry tactics. On a battlefield infantry adopting such tactics could hide in the terrain and in buildings and still fire at the line infantry without exposing itself to volleys. Troops using this approach also excelled at reconnaissance and in raids on enemy convoys and supply installations.

The realization of the neglect of this role for infantry led to an eighteenth-century distinction between light infantry and line infantry. The separation between the two lay not in a difference in weapon systems or in the action each used; both relied primarily on muskets. The line infantry utilized the disciplined and drilled group and formed itself to resist cavalry and deliver the maximum rate of fire. The light infantry depended primarily on an individual's performance in tactics, called skirmishing. It made use of cover and concealment to avoid the cavalry and the volleys of the line and concentrated on shooting at the target presented by the formed line infantry.

This training for skirmishing on the battlefield meant that light infantry excelled at outpost duty, reconnoitering, and raiding. Cavalry had already developed horsemen who specialized in the same functions for the mounted forces. Light cavalry, armed with saber and pistol, specialized in the strategic duties in which light cavalry had traditionally excelled while other similarly armed cavalry, often on larger horses and still protected by breastplates, trained for the shock action of the battlefield charge. Dragoons, armed also with a light musket and capable of fighting as infantry, also performed the strategic services of reconnaissance and raiding.

Although technological change had combined the missile and shock weapon systems for the infantry as well as for the cavalry, a higher level of mobility and, for the infantry, less dependence on a formation in which the soldiers filled interdependent roles fitted light infantry and light cavalry for separate functions. Differences in training and tactical and strategic roles rather than body armor or weapon systems henceforth distinguished the light and line branches of the infantry and cavalry. Variations in uniforms and equipment often served to differentiate the two types of troops. Some light infantry received the slow-loading but more accurate rifles as the best weapon for the battlefield and, since they did not have to resist cavalry charges, had no bayonets.

The third line of development in the first half of the eighteenth century concerned the improved handling of the formations of homogeneous infantry. Without both pikemen and musketeers, the task of forming an army for battle should have become simpler. The fullest realization of this in practice, largely through very thorough drill, occurred in Prussia.

Illustration 5.2. Light Cavalryman

Unlike many European armies in the 1720s and 1730s, the Prussian army had a uniform system of drill for all of the army's regiments. All units practiced loading and firing until a Prussian battalion could fire five rounds per minute, each of the battalion's eight platoons constituting a separate fire unit. Because the wooden ramrod tended to break under the stress of such rapid loading and firing, the Prussian army substituted a ramrod of iron. The Prussians also devoted much attention to constant training and great precision in marching in step, so that the battalion learned to keep its front aligned, and when the army brought together large numbers of troops, the routine included keeping a whole battle array even while marching forward in line of battle. To facilitate maintaining the battalions in line abreast, the regulations kept the rate of advance slow, seventy-five paces per minute.

The Prussian units, in which the men stood shoulder to shoulder with five feet between ranks, marched in step and repeatedly carried out such drills as forming a square to resist cavalry. They expected to use this cumbersome procedure rarely since, for cavalry in their rear, an about-face by the rear ranks provided an immediate response. But Prussian training did lead to an improved method of forming the army for battle. With homogeneous soldiers and the same drill for every regiment, the Prussians formed their infantry in two columns to march to the battlefield. Each column composed one of the standard two lines of battle and the battalions marched one behind the other. This meant that the army already stood in its combat formation and needed no sorting or rearrangement prior to forming the line of battle. The only problems consisted of converting the battalions from march to battle order and aligning the line of battle parallel with the enemy when, presumably, they had directed their march perpendicular to the enemy's deployment.

The Prussians used a march order in which the battalion's platoons moved forward, one behind the other, just as they would in line, three ranks deep and twenty-four musketeers abreast with an officer and noncommissioned officer on each flank. This formation had a front of less than twenty yards and a depth of four. The battalion's eight platoons marched one behind the other in an open order that left twenty yards, the width of the front of a platoon, between each platoon. When the battalion halted, it could have each platoon make a ninety-degree turn and the battalion would be in line of battle, since the distance between each platoon in the march column equaled the space of its front in line of battle (schematic 5.2).

A battalion in march thus had a length of about 150 yards, the same distance it would occupy on a front, and an army with, say, forty battalions of infantry would march in two parallel columns of battalions, each about two miles long. To form a line of battle the columns had only to halt and the platoons all make a ninety-degree turn.

To have the army face the enemy after this turn, the Prussians could have made the processional march in which the two parallel columns marched up to

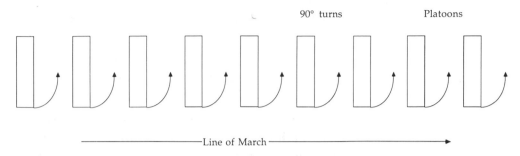

Schematic 5.2. Prussian Approach March

the left side of the expected battlefield, and when the lead battalion reached the planned left end of the line of battle, the column turned ninety degrees to the right, its platoons each turning one by one as the column marched parallel to the enemy and filled the space planned for the line of battle. The second line would have made a similar right turn several hundred yards in the rear and would continue its march parallel with the other. When the lead battalion reached the right-hand end of the proposed line of battle, all battalions halted and all the platoons turned left ninety degrees. The army then faced the enemy. (See schematic 5.3.)

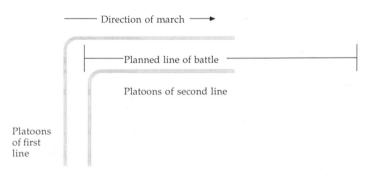

Schematic 5.3. Processional March

Excellent mastery of platoon and battalion drill enabled the Prussian army to perform this maneuver and have the army in order in the place that the commander had planned for it. Precision and rapidity of execution could bring the army to the enemy's front before he expected, or was ready for, the swiftly deploying Prussians. But the army could have much more rapid deloyment if it could march on the field of battle in a column of march parallel to the enemy's line of battle. If the commander could manage this, each platoon need only execute its ninety-degree turn when the column of march fronted the enemy's position. Such a procedure involved no deployment process except the halt and the quick turn of the platoons. If a Prussian commander could contrive to make this line of march parallel to the enemy's line of battle, the well-drilled Prussian army might easily arrive and deploy before the opposing force expected or had prepared to fight it.

Tactics and Strategy as Exemplified in the Silesian Wars of Frederick the Great

In 1740 Frederick the Great came to the throne of Prussia and promptly put into use the excellent army that he had inherited from his father. The cultured young king lacked military experience, but his performance would demonstrate a natural genius for war and government. Along with a superb army, he had inherited a well-organized and frugally governed state. He soon inspired great loyalty among his subjects and his soldiers. In immediately plunging into a war, he proved to have an unequaled grasp of this unfamiliar task, and Prussian military methods and success imposed on Europe new standards of military efficiency and gave an impetus to the search for improvements in the art of war.

Frederick's opportunity to use his army came in 1740, when the emperor died leaving his Habsburg estates to Maria Theresa, his twenty-three-year-old daughter. When the French and Bavarians displayed an interest in taking parts of Maria Theresa's inheritance, Frederick invaded Maria Theresa's province of Silesia at the head of an army of 27,000 men in the fall of 1740. With delapidated fortifications and only 6,000 men in the whole province, Maria Theresa's small force fell back into the mountains of Moravia. Frederick acquired a population of over a million, nearly half of that of all of the young king's other possessions.

But he aroused the enmity of a formidable opponent, whose domains included the Netherlands, Moravia, and part of north Italy as well as the Archduchy of Austria and the kingdoms of Hungary and Bohemia. Appealing in appearance and with great warmth and charm of manner, Maria Theresa had ability, judgment, and determination, which in many respects came close to matching Frederick's. Other menaces, however, distracted her attention, and even if Frederick had received the undivided attention of the Austrian army, his very solvent treasury and well-drilled army of 90,000 would have matched Austria's army of 108,000 scattered men and usually embarrassed exchequer. In spite of periodic warfare with the Turks, the Austrian army displayed all of the weaknesses that a long period of peace can bring to any military force. It lacked a uniform drill, each regiment having its own methods and not adequately practicing the drills which it had, its generals saying that their soldiers learned in combat, not on the parade ground.

In the early spring of 1741 Austria counterattacked. Field Marshal Neipperg led 18,000 men into Silesia to try to recover the province. The field marshal had a reputation as a witty conversationalist and for serious bungling in the last war with the Turks. He camped his army, his infantry mostly consisting of raw recruits, in a threatening position near the village of Mollwitz where the inexperienced Frederick, with energy that would typify his later campaigning, marched to attack him. Since the Prussian approach came toward the center of Neipperg's hastily formed line, it took the Prussian infantry a long time to form their line, giving the unready Austrians an opportunity to form for battle. While the infantry took up its array, the Austrian cavalry charged and routed the Prussian horsemen, the campaigning experience against the Turks proving a guarantee of victory against Frederick's cavalry, a neglected branch of the Prussian service. But the excellently drilled Prussian infantry began to advance and soon brought the Austrian battalions under fire. Untrained Austrian infantry still equipped with wooden ramrods could not compete; an observer noted: "The battalions sank into disorder, and it was pathetic to see how the poor recruits tried to hide behind one another, so that the battalions ended up thirty or forty deep, and the intervals became so great that whole regiments of cavalry could have penetrated between, even though the whole second line had been brought forward into the first."[16]

When the failure of the infantry so discouraged the Austrian cavalry that they refused to exploit their ability to attack the flank and rear of the Prussian infantry, Neipperg lost the battle. He withdrew in good order, losing a quarter of his men, the same proportion as the victorious Prussians of an army of the same size. But Neipperg remained in southern Silesia, and the twenty-nine-year-old Frederick, who had left the scene of his first battle when the Austrian cavalry won its initial success, was content to leave the Austrians alone throughout the campaigning season while he trained his cavalry and improved his army in the light of its first serious battle experience in nearly three decades. Frederick, who began inspection tours at 4:00 A.M., imposed a rigorous training schedule. A French observer witnessed the king drilling a battalion in person: "The weather was frightful and the snow was falling in large flakes, which did not prevent the battalion exercising as if it had been a fine day. I had some inkling before I came of the army's discipline, obedience and exactitude, but I must say that they were driven to such a degree that I was ill-prepared for the reality."[17]

In February 1742 Frederick moved into Moravia to winter at the enemy's expense, but the hostility of the peasants and other factors caused him to move to Bohemia, where an Austrian army found him in camp at Chotusitz the following May, partially surprised because of inadequate warning from the Prussian light cavalry. The battle at Chotusitz repeated Mollwitz in that the Austrian cavalry still proved its superiority over the Prussian but failed to exploit its advantage, and the excellent performance of the Prussian infantry again caused the Austrians to withdraw after sustaining casualties comparable to those of the Prussians. After this tactically indecisive battle, peace followed, and the Austrians, sorely beset on other fronts, ceded Silesia to Frederick.

But Frederick, made apprehensive by Austrian successes against France, resumed the war. In 1744 he invaded Bohemia and on September 16 captured Prague and its small garrison after only a brief siege. The Austrians promptly moved to oppose Frederick with a large army under the inept Prince Charles of Lorraine, who had secured important commands by his confident manner, his marriage to Maria Theresa's sister, and his brother's to Maria Theresa herself.

But, unfortunately for Frederick, Field Marshal Traun, a veteran of fifty years of variegated service, exercised the effective Austrian command, and this cunning old master of the defense avoided Frederick's army while using his predominance in light infantry and light cavalry to hamper Frederick's foraging. The Austrians had many of these particularly adept light troops drawn from the regions of their frontiers with the Turks.

And this force of 20,000 to 30,000 largely light infantry, was the key to Austrian success. They foraged for their own army, accumulating a large depot of supplies while denying resources to Frederick's forces. They kept close to the king, forcing him to entrench his camp, as they cut off his foraging detachments, captured his supply columns, and preempted his efforts to find food. When a Prussian detachment entered a Bohemian village, they found that the Austrians had taken away the inhabitants and the supplies. Just as in the Ilerda campaign Caesar's cavalry had crippled the Pompeians by controlling the countryside, so did the Austrian forces compel Frederick's withdrawal, in spite of Prussian tactical superiority. But Frederick could never force battle on his wily opponent, and even when he could get close to the elusive Field Marshal Traun, he found him thoroughly entrenched in a formidable position.

So Frederick, having entered Bohemia with 80,000 men, departed with 40,000, the remainder, including his heavy artillery and many wagons, casualties to starvation, sickness, desertion, and combat with the Austrian light forces. The king, recognizing the skill of his Fabian opponent in inflicting so severe a defeat, complimented Traun thus: "The conduct of the Marshal was a perfect model which every general who delights in his profession ought to study if he has the abilities to imitate." Field Marshal Traun's logistic strategy had inflicted on Frederick more casualties than the king had suffered in his two battles with the Austrians, and the experience strongly impressed on Frederick the hazards of a deep penetration into enemy territory.[18]

The following spring the young Prince Charles, having arrogated to himself credit for Traun's campaign, had sole command of the huge Austrian army that in May 1745 advanced into Silesia from the west. Frederick, his troops dispersed in winter quarters, concentrated and planned to attack the Austrians after they had passed through the mountains into Silesia. Prince Charles, assuming a Prussian retreat because he supposed that Frederick's men still suffered from the demoralization of their retreat from Bohemia, advanced slowly, confidently, and carelessly. After the Austrians and their Saxon allies camped their 70,000 men near Hohenfriedburg on June 3, Frederick began a night march toward them with his entire 65,000 men in open columns, ready to deploy. Frederick expected much of his cavalry, having instructed them as follows: "The cavalry must impetuously charge the enemy, sword in hand, and must make no prisoners during the heat of action; its blows must be directed at the head; after overthrowing and dispersing the cavalry it shall assail . . . the infantry of the enemy, and take it in flank or rear, according as the occasion shall require."[19]

The resulting battle at Hohenfriedburg occurred in two parts, the first when the Prussian right wing defeated the Saxons whose camp occupied the Austrian left. In a battle over by 7:00 A.M., the Prussian cavalry displayed the fruits of Frederick's rigorous training by defeating the Saxon cavalry, and the Prussian infantry, overcoming the obstacles of a marsh and a village, drove the Saxon infantry back in full retreat. Meanwhile, as Prince Charles discussed the noise of the battle as evidence of unimportant skirmishing, Frederick's left had deployed, his cavalry decisively defeating the vaunted Austrian cavalry but his infantry encountering difficulty and some battalions suffering 40 percent casualties in a frontal attack against Austrian veterans equipped with their new iron ramrods. But just as the Austrian infantry began to feel discouraged because of the defeat of the cavalry on both wings and the retreat of the Saxon infantry, 1,500 Prussian cavalry charged and overwhelmed twenty battalions of Austrian infantry, taking 2,500 prisoners.

Frederick had surprised an incautious enemy and, with the aid of the rapid deployment of his well-drilled army, defeated him in a frontal battle, inflicting over 10,000 casualties compared to less than 5,000 in his Prussian army. After his soldiers' night march and difficult victory, Frederick made no effort to follow Prince Charles back to Bohemia where he remained all summer. In September Prince Charles attempted to surprise an apparently negligent Frederick in his camp at Soor. But by the time the Austrians completed their bungling approach march and emerged from the woods, Frederick had learned of their arrival, formed his troops, and successfully attacked with both infantry and cavalry. Peace between Austria and Prussia followed soon after, reconfirming Frederick's possession of Silesia.

After the war both Austria and Prussia set to work refining their armies. The Austrians introduced uniform drill throughout all of their regiments, improved their artillery significantly, and conducted annual maneuvers in which officers and men became accustomed to working in large formations. Frederick continued training his cavalry and sought to perfect rapid infantry deployment, the value of which the unexpected battles of the war had dramatically demonstrated. He saw clearly the advantages of quick deployment made possible by an open-order approach march parallel to the enemy's line in which turns by each platoon would almost instantly convert the army from march formation to line of battle. The war had made Frederick an experienced general and his army a battle-seasoned organization. In peace he had perfected his army and had a thorough grasp of how to use it in the next war, which Maria Theresa's determination to recover Silesia made inevitable. But Maria Theresa's army, having farther to go, had made more progress during the years of peace, a fact Frederick did not fully appreciate.

The Seven Years' War: Tactics and Strategy in Defense against the Logistic Effects of a Persisting Strategy

Frederick took the initiative in the Seven Years' War because he wished to preempt the action of Austria, France, and Russia, a potential coalition that skillful Austrian diplomacy had done much to create by 1756. He occupied Saxony in the fall of 1756 and advanced far enough into Bohemia to get his nose bloodied when he blundered into an Austrian army at Lobositz, thinking he faced an outpost. But the Austrians withdrew, and Frederick completed the conquest of Saxony when he secured the capitulation of the small Saxon army. In taking Saxony Frederick had acquired a prosperous country that could contribute much to the support of his armies. Like Silesia, it also made an excellent theater of war because its population density—about two-thirds of that of the Netherlands—provided a large agricultural output that would maintain the armies well.

In 1757 Frederick faced France as well as Austria and could expect a French army to move eastward toward Saxony sometime during the year. To deal with this problem, he aimed to drive the Austrians away from Saxony and Silesia to give him the opportunity to deal with the French when they arrived. So in the spring he advanced into Bohemia by several routes, arriving before Prague in early May. Drawn up on a plateau, facing north outside of Prague, he found the army of the sluggish Prince Charles of Lorraine. When Frederick marched his columns south so that, as the platoons turned right, they faced the Austrian right flank, one of Prince Charles's able subordinates not only moved the Austrian second line to its right but also formed it and counterattacked the Prussians while they passed over difficult ground. But the Prussian maneuver had left the Austrian first line facing north with no Prussians deployed against it. The whole Prussian army attacked, and though the Austrians held, part broke through at the right angle where the two Austrian lines joined and forced a withdrawal of the bulk of the Austrian army into Prague. Both forces suffered about 22 percent casualties.

A few of Prince Charles's men joined the army of Field Marshal Daun, which headed toward Prague from the east. The capable and circumspect Daun, an experienced soldier who had much to do with the recent improvements in the Austrian army, moved to relieve the beleaguered Prince Charles, approaching close to Prague and threatening Frederick's supplies. Frederick then marched to meet Daun and resolved to attack when he found him at Kolin, facing north in battle array on a line of low hills. Frederick planned again to march past the Austrians and attack their right flank, but when Daun perceived the Prussian maneuver, he deployed his army to the right. In their frontal assaults the Prussians suffered heavily from the sniping of the formidable Austrian light infantry, the fire of its excellent artillery, and the rapid volleys of its thoroughly trained troops. At the close of the day Frederick fell back, having lost nearly 14,000 men, 43 percent of his force, compared to 9,000 for the Austrians, 20 percent of their force.

In these defensive battles the improved Austrian artillery had a devastating effect, as one Prussian participant testified: "A storm of shot and howitzer shells passed clear over our heads, but more than enough fell in the ranks to smash a large number of our men . . . I glanced aside just once and I saw an NCO torn apart by a shell nearby: the sight was frightful enough to take away my curiosity." Later, he continued, the men advanced "through long corn, which reached as far as our necks, and as we came nearer we were greeted with a hail of canister that stretched whole clumps of our troops on the ground. We still had our muskets on our shoulders and I could hear how the canister balls clattered against our bayonets."[20]

In the first two battles of the war Frederick had lost slightly more men than the enemy; in the third he had lost significantly more. Since the total Austrian army had a greater number of men than his and he had to face other opponents also, it seemed that he could not long continue to attack his enemies in their chosen positions. His deployment from a march parallel to the enemy's line had brought victory at Prague, but against the alert and cautious Daun at Kolin it had failed to do more than bring the army into a frontal battle in substantially the position in which Daun wished to fight it. The expertly drilled Austrian army had proven formidable in combat and resilient in defeat.

Prince Charles's strategy had made the Battle of Kolin necessary. After his defeat at the Battle of Prague the Austrian commander, instead of retreating into southern Bohemia as Frederick expected, had shut himelf up in Prague. In this way he had frustrated Frederick's strategic objective of driving him away from Saxony and Silesia and thus giving the king the opportunity to withdraw the bulk of his forces to deal with the French while the slow-moving Austrians sought to recover Bohemia rather than invade either of those provinces. Frederick's defeat at Kolin thwarted his entire strategy by forcing him to terminate the blockade of Prague and evacuate Bohemia, leaving Charles and Daun united and ready to advance just as the French took the field.

When Frederick withdrew into Saxony, Prince Charles moved at a dilatory pace, directing his forces into Silesia. As Frederick held his army in Saxony, the sedate Austrian advance besieged the fortress of Schweidnitz, the fall of which would enable the huge Austrian army to threaten Breslau, the principal city of Silesia. Meanwhile, Frederick had moved westward to deal with the French.

The army Frederick faced in the West consisted of ill-disciplined French troops under the command of the prince of Soubise, a general primarily noted for his lavish style of living in the field. But he amply exemplified French officers of the period, as the booty of the camp illustrated. Prussian cavalry captured not only valets but also actors and other evidences of the aristocratic lifestyle, including "whole chests full of perfumes and scented powders, and great quantities of dressing gowns, hair nets, sun shades, nightgowns, and parrots." In addition to Soubise's French force the Austrian Field Marshal Hildburghausen commanded a German army that, when joined with the French, proved an equally undisciplined force composed of German contingents, many supplied by princely military contractors. Both armies subsisted themselves by looting the countryside in the manner of the Thirty Years' War. When Frederick advanced against them with 22,000 men, half their force, Soubise and Hildburghausen wisely fell back. But when Frederick turned and moved back eastward toward threatened Silesia, the two commanders again advanced, which caused Frederick to turn and once more march westward after their again-retreating army. Frederick came up with them facing east in a strong position near Rossbach.[21]

After Frederick deployed opposite them, Hildburghausen and Soubise resolved to move their army into a line of battle south of the Prussian to take a position that would restrict Frederick's communications. The allied commanders did not have full agreement as to their purpose, Hildburghausen desiring a battle and Soubise wishing to avoid a full-scale conflict. Having observed this move, Frederick pulled back his army. The allied commanders then erroneously concluded that the Prussians had begun to retreat and changed their plan into one of pursuit. But Frederick, using the concealment provided by two hills, redeployed his army across the allied line of march. After his cavalry had charged and routed the surprised allied cavalry, a few battalions of his infantry advanced in line against the ill-drilled allied infantry, most of it still in march formation and disorganized by its movement. A cooperating charge by the Prussian cavalry compeleted the rout of the French and German infantry. In this Battle of Rossbach the Prussians lost less than 600 men, the allies over 10,000.

But immediately after his victory Frederick hurried east because Prince Charles had captured Schweidnitz, defeated the small army protecting Breslau, and captured that city. The Prussian king was losing a third of his dominions. In early December Frederick, having traveled in twelve days the 170 miles of his interior lines of operations and joined the force that had covered Breslau, had 33,00 men when he approached Prince Charles's 65,000 in battle array near the village of Leuthen.

Frederick marched directly toward the Austrians, made menacing movements toward the Austrian right, turned his own columns to his right, and marched parallel with the Austrian army, out of sight behind a line of low hills. Prince Charles, though in the tower of the church at Leuthen, could see nothing and responded to Frederick's distraction by moving his reserve to his right flank. But when the heads of the two superbly drilled Prussian columns, the distances between the marching platoons remaining exactly the width of each platoon's front, had passed the Austrian left flank, the columns veered left toward the

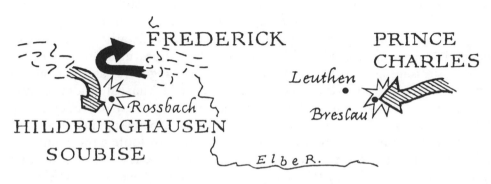

Diagram 5.4. Frederick's Interior Lines

enemy and continued their march until the heads of the two columns had passed beyond the Austrian flank. Then, on command, the platoons of the columns turned left, and the whole Prussian army lay in line of battle at nearly a right angle to the left flank of the Austrian position. The Prussians had carried out with their whole army a maneuver analogous to that used by the Spartans to attack their enemy in flank.

The Prussian infantry, arrayed in the conventional two lines of battle, then advanced and rolled up the Austrian flank. Prince Charles rushed troops from his right to his left, but they piled up in helpless masses as many as 100 men deep; the cavalry from the Austrian right came to attack, but Prussian cavalry, held back for the purpose, charged them in the flank. The Austrians retreated in confusion, losing 22,000 to less than 12,000 Prussian casualties. Breslau surrendered shortly after, adding 17,000 demoralized prisoners to Fredrick's bag.

Frederick had conserved his hold on Saxony and Silesia by energetic exploitation of his interior lines, but he owed debts to Soubise, Hildburghausen, and Prince Charles for offering him the battles that enabled him to exploit to the fullest the advantage of his strategic position. The Austrians fell back into Bohemia, Maria Theresa providing the only positive result of the battle by requiring the resignation of Prince Charles, her inept double brother-in-law.

Frederick had employed his interior lines to halt the French and recover Silesia, a move that had necessarily involved the battle that Soubise and Hildburghausen had initially denied him. As the two commanders fell back before Frederick and then advanced again when he fell back, Prince Charles systematically used his overwhelmingly superior force to conquer Silesia from Frederick's subordinate. Whereas Frederick exploited his interior lines to concentrate in space, his opponents had made simultaneous advances, concentrating in time, and secured the fall of Breslau as the reward of their cooperation. Had Soubise and Prince Charles managed their meetings with Frederick's army as well as they did their strategic cooperation, they would have attained significant success.

When the Roman general Nero exploited his interior lines to march against Hannibal's brother Hasdrubal, he had the good fortune to catch Hasdrubal's army with its back to a river and force battle on the unready Carthaginian general. When Prince Edward exploited his interior lines between the de Montfort father and son, he had surprised one and trapped the other's inferior force. But until Soubise and Haldburghausen left their strong position and blundered into disaster at Rossbach, they had either given Frederick no opportunity for battle or for one very much on their terms. Prince Charles, too, could have avoided battle but chose instead to offer it in a position without great natural strength. Nevertheless, he had compelled Frederick to attack double his numbers to reap the harvest of his interior lines and save Silesia, one of the fundamental bases of this military power. Yet in offering battle Charles did what the Byzantine Belisarius had disparaged, given his enemy a second chance at victory; he should have been content with the victory concentration in time had given him over Frederick's concentration in space.

Exploiting interior lines, his aggressiveness and confidence in the superiority of his army, and his tactic of deploying his whole army against one flank of the enemy caused Frederick to fight a remarkably large number of battles. The ineptitude of his opponents had helped to give him victories against them on their chosen ground. Unlike the earlier battles of 1757, Frederick could afford to fight more Rossbachs and Leuthens.

For the campaign of 1758 Frederick had little to fear from the French: his British ally had an army in the field that successfully occupied the attention of the French for the remainder of the war. But he could expect the Russians, who had already conquered East Prussia, to advance westward toward the Oder and the heart of his states. To deal with this menace, comparable to that presented by the French the previous year, Frederick resorted to the same strategy: push back the Austrians in Bohemia before his other foe arrived. Avoiding the Austrians, who guarded the routes into Bohemia, he invaded Moravia in the spring of 1758 and besieged the thoroughly fortified and strongly garrisoned town of Olmütz. He could also look forward to the enemy's coming to him in his chosen location because a seige always put the besiegers on the defensive against the relieving army.

But his opponent, the prudent Field Marshal Daun, though he approached very close and his light cavalry disrupted Frederick's foraging, carefully avoided obliging Frederick by an attack and relied instead on a logistical strategy while he remained in a virtually impregnable position. When the field marshal learned that an ammunition convoy of 4,000 wagons was coming to Frederick from Silesia, his subordinates, aided by their splendid light infantry, attacked, inflicted over 2,000 casualties on the convoy guard of 9,000 men, and destroyed the wagons and horses. Frederick, defeated by Daun's imitation of the logistic strategy of Traun, one reminiscent also of Fabius and du Guesclin, abandoned his siege and marched into Silesia, continuing northward to resist a Russian advance toward the Oder.

Although the Prussians had fought the Russians the year before and learned to respect the solidity of their infantry and the quantity and quality of their artillery, Frederick continued to regard them with some contempt. Lacking a siege train, the Russian army engaged in an ineffectual blockade of the Oder city of Custrin, which they raised when Frederick arrived with 14,000 men and united with his subordinate who had observed the Russians. Frederick determined to attack to induce the Russians to keep their distance.

When the Russian commander, General Fermor, placed his men in a rather poor situation behind a stream near Zorndorf, Frederick marched his army all the way around the Russian position, to take it in the rear. But when Fermor skillfully reversed his front, Frederick still had to fight a frontal battle. An observer in the Russian lines described the Prussians as they marched toward him: "Their weapons flashed in the sun and the spectacle was frightening. . . . Never shall I forget the silent majestic approach of the Prussian army," followed by "that splendid but alarming moment when the Prussian army suddenly deployed into a thin, staggered line of battle. . . . Then the menacing beat of the Prussian drums carried to our ears." But the Russians proved equal to the occasion, another observer commenting that, "the extraordinary steadiness and intrepidity of the Russians on this occasion is not to be described; it surpassed everything that one has heard of in the bravest troops. Although the Prussian balls mowed down whole ranks, yet not a man discovered any symptoms of unsteadiness, or inclination to give way, and the openings in the first line were instantly filled up from the second or the reserve."[22]

After a prolonged bloody fight, the Russians fell back a short distance and, encountering supply difficulties, withdrew completely two days later. After the battle a Prussian officer viewed some of the Prussian wounded "crawling on hands and feet, others were limping on muskets with the butts tucked under the armpit to serve as crutches." He also saw "the remains of blown-up ammunition waggons and powder carts, and nearby a multitude of half roasted gunners who were giving off an unpleasant smell of burning" flesh. Animals suffered, too, for he described "a whole train of two-wheeled Russian carts, with the horses shot in the traces, and around the whole battlefield ran wounded horses, with their intestines dragging the ground or hopping about on three legs." The Prussians lost 35 percent of their army, the Russians 53 percent.[23]

With the Russians driven back, Frederick then used his interior lines to hurry with part of his army, marching at twenty-two miles a day, to Saxony where Daun at last threatened the Saxon capital, Dresden. On Frederick's approach Daun withdrew, and each army had observed the other for more than a month when the overconfident and too casual Frederick came carelessly near the Austrians in an exposed position at Hochkirch. In an uncharacteristic effusion of the offensive spirit, Daun made a night march and surprised Frederick's camp in a dawn attack, the Austrians pouring in from all sides. The superbly disciplined Prussians escaped with a loss of 9,000 men to 7,000 for the Austrians. But Frederick, learning that another Austrian army threatened Silesia, marched there, raised the siege of Neisse, and marched back to Saxony quickly enough to prevent Daun from molesting Dresden. In 1758 concentration in time, languidly pursued, had failed to overmatch Frederick's vigorous concentration in space.

Frederick had once more used his interior lines effectively, but at Zorndorf and Hochkirch he had again lost more of the men whom he had thoroughly trained in the prewar period. Replacements kept his army up to strength, but its quality declined while that of the Austrian army steadily improved as it gained battle experience, winnowed out the less effective senior officers, and learned how better to employ its more powerful artillery in the defense. The Austrians had also created a staff corps that successfully helped commanders plan and supervise movements, supply arrangements, and even campaigns and battles.

In 1759 Frederick faced a renewed Russian advance with which the Austrians planned to coordinate a march by their main army into Silesia while continuing to menace Saxony in cooperation with the remains of the force Hildburghausen had led at Rossbach. Frederick disposed 30,000 men to face the 60,000 the Russians intended to bring and fielded another 30,000 to guard Saxony. In addition, he had 50,000 men in Silesia to cover that province and to use along his interior lines to reinforce Saxony or the army opposing the Russians. His British allies continued to hold the French at bay in the western part of Germany. This year Frederick remained on the defensive, waiting to counter his opponents rather than trying to press them back.

The Russians, moving eastward under the talented General Saltykov, marched around the opposing Prussian force and, entrenching at Kay facing eastward, bloodily repulsed the attack of the combative but simple-minded Prussian commander. Resuming his march east, Saltykov reached the Oder River, captured Frankfurt, and united with 24,000 Austrians sent by Daun under the command of the skillful General Loudon. But in early August Frederick marched away from Silesia, and Daun, after his display of dash at Hochkirch, reverted to his usual slow and unenterprising mode of operations.

With Daun's large army only fifty miles away, Frederick, with 50,000 men, attacked Saltykov and Loudoun's 60,000 Russians and Austrians at Kunersdorf. Starting his men at 2:00 A.M., he marched entirely around the allied flank, concentrating his entire force against the rear and flank of one wing of the allied position. But he found his alert opponents so thoroughly entrenched and well equipped with artillery that, in spite of driving back the attacked wing, the Prussian assaults ended in ghastly failure. Frederick lost 37 percent of his men, the allies 26 percent. Frederick's greater mobility had availed him nothing but a bloody repulse, which, however, gave the allies no strategic benefit. Combined with Daun's army, the allies could have marched to Berlin and, by collecting contributions and wintering in Brandenburg, crippled Prussian power by depriving the king of supplies, revenues, and recruits for his armies. But since the Russians were reluctant to undertake such an ambitious enterprise and Daun at first doubted that Brandenburg offered enough supplies for the winter, the Austro-Russian commanders vacillated and at one point resolved to wait until another army had occupied Saxony and then to seek to exploit their victory by wintering in Silesia.

But the two allies ended in disagreement, the Russians later marching to the east to winter, as usual, on the Vistula.

The Austrians had captured Dresden by the time Daun, followed shortly by Frederick, reached Saxony. A stalemate resulted, with Daun in too formidable a position for Frederick, who still controlled much of Saxony, to venture an attack. The deadlock lasted the year and was broken only by a successful surprise attack against a Prussian force that netted the Austrians over 13,000 prisoners.

Although the king recovered from his defeat at Kunersdorf, he thereafter sought to avoid having to fight a battle, reflecting that there were "situations in which one must fight; one should, however, allow himself to be drawn into battle only when the enemy, either in camping or on the march, is careless or when one can force him to accept peace by a decisive blow." Considering Daun's caution, the hardihood of the Russians in battle, and the vast size of his adversaries, he had little chance of meeting these conditions. Meditating on the history of the combative King Charles XII of Sweden, he continued: "Furthermore, it is certain that most generals who resort easily to a battle rely on this expedient only because they do not know what else to do. Far from being considered to their credit, one regards this rather as an indication of a lack of genius."[24]

In July 1760 Frederick, followed by Daun, moved to Silesia where his army faced the Russians advancing from the north and Loudon coming from the south. Daun and Loudon with 90,000 men moved to attack Frederick's 30,000. But Frederick changed his position, and at Liegnitz Loudon lost over a third of his troops in a vain, unsupported assault against Frederick's somewhat stronger force. In his first traditional defensive battle of the war Frederick forfeited only 11 percent of his men.

After a raid on Berlin, which exacted contributions from the city, Daun advanced to Saxony, digging himself in at Torgau in the center of the electorate. Since Frederick could not afford to lose the contributions and resources of Saxony, he decided to attack Daun's mightier force, thoroughly entrenched with 275 artillery pieces. He sent General Zieten with a third of the army toward the Austrian front; he marched with the remainder to assail the Austrian rear. But the imperturbable and vigilant field marshal observed Frederick's movement, formed a front to his rear, and administered bloody rebuffs to the assaults Frederick launched in the mistaken belief that the inert Zieten had his men in action. A contemporary noted of the last Prussian attacks that "even before the Prussians caught sight of the enemy the tree tops were severed by the enemy shot and fell on their heads, and the thunder of the cannon reverberated fearfully through the forest." When the Prussians left the trees to advance over the ground of previous attacks, they saw "a slaughter ground, full of corpses and mutilated bodies, panting and swimming in their blood." But when at last Zieten's troops acted and found a route to the Austrian flank and Frederick's men mustered one more attack, the Prussians turned the Austrian flank and compelled them to withdraw to Dresden. Saving his valuable hold on Saxony cost Frederick dearly: he lost 33 percent of his army compared to 29 percent for the Austrians.[25]

In 1761, when Frederick opposed the Austrians and Russians in Silesia, he took a leaf from Daun's book and dug in advantageously in a strong position. The armies faced one another for three weeks, each suffering supply difficulties. But Frederick's better logistic preparations enabled him to outlast his opponents, and when the Russians withdrew in September, the campaign ended for the year. In 1762 the Russians not only left the war but also changed sides, ending any real menace to Frederick's survival until he made peace with Austria in 1763. He retained Silesia, the political objective of his defensive war and Maria Theresa's goal in her third conflict with Frederick.

During the war the Prussians lost 180,000 dead but finished with more in the treasury than at the beginning. Frederick paid for the conflict in part from coinage debasement, which had substantially the same effect as inflation. But this means and loans formed a relatively small portion of the cost. Table 5.1

TABLE 5.1. Sources of Prussian Income
in the Seven Years' War

Coinage debasement	17 percent
Loans	10 percent
Taxes	26 percent
British subsidy	16 percent
Contributions (largely Saxon)	31 percent

shows the contribution of the various revenue sources. Since the balance on hand at the end exceeded that at the beginning by approximately the amount of the loans, Frederick had financed the war on an essentially pay-as-you-go basis.[26]

Frederick took the offensive in seven of his ten battles in the Seven Years' War. Except at Lobositz, he attacked his opponents in the positions they had chosen to receive him. He did so also at Rossbach, but since the enemy made the initial movement, on this occasion he defended. In these conflicts his casualties approximated 104,000 men (27 percent) compared with 123,000 (24 percent) for his opponents. Even though Frederick could not afford such losses as well as his imposing group of enemies, such contests on the foes' terms reflected a reasonable solution to Frederick's serious strategic problem and constituted a better alternative to the usual strategy of defending obstacles to deny the opponent access to his territory.

Frederick's bloody battles did impose caution on his adversaries. A French observer could say of Daun, who had defeated Frederick in two of their three engagements: "If only the field-marshal was a little less timid: but this is a vain hope. There is such a narrow margin between a timorousness of this kind, and the prudence you must always show when you are facing the King of Prussia, that a naturally cautious man is inclined to confuse the two." Frederick's skill and combativeness, combined with the psychological impact, losses, and disorganization of even a victory over his army, meant that his battles always served at least to halt the hostile advance. Upon this fundamental result of his fights Frederick implicitly founded his strategy. He could not survive if his adversaries occupied Saxony or his own extremely vulnerable territory.[27]

From Bohemia the Austrians had ready access to Saxony and Silesia. Since the Saxons had sided with Austria and Silesia had long belonged to the Habsburgs, Frederick could expect these areas to offer no local resistance, especially against the essentially German armies of Maria Theresa's husband, the emperor. The natural axis of the Russian advance took them to Brandenburg and western Prussia, major parts of Frederick's domains. Though the Russians had no claims to the territory, their care of civilian sensibilities had helped reconcile the East Prussians to their occupation. These areas had neither the defense in depth provided by the numerous fortresses of the Netherlands nor the obstacles presented by the sequence of river lines in north Italy. All of the provinces were sufficiently small in relation to the Austrian and Russian armies that the invaders could readily occupy and control them.

When the French and the emperor struggled for control of northern Italy and France and her enemies fought over the Netherlands, none of the combatants depended on the disputed region for much of their resources for keeping their armies in the field. But the situation differed markedly for Frederick; he relied on Saxony, Silesia, Brandenburg, and western Prussia for money and recruits. To lose even one would significantly reduce his forces the following year, increasing the danger to his remaining territory. For his enemies, a conquest of Frederick's provinces would constitute a war-winning logistic strategy.

To combat this strategy and to protect his vital logistic bases, Frederick could hardly employ the strategy of diversions used by Gustavus and Montecuccoli, for the enemy threatened objectives far more vital to him then any of those presented by the exposed Austrian holdings of Bohemia or Moravia. Likewise, he could not rely on protecting obstacles, for the seesaw campaigns in Italy had demonstrated that invaders could pass the rivers and base themselves in the country beyond. If the Austrians slipped into Silesia, for example, not only would they have an area to support their armies and force Frederick to forage elsewhere, but also they would have conquered nearly a third of the king's subjects. Thus Frederick sought to fight the war in Bohemia and so keep the enemy far from Saxony and Silesia. His vulnerability led him to accept a fight on the enemy's terms because battles kept the foe at bay.

Frederick's strategic vulnerability explains his battle at Torgau, where he attempted to attack Daun, dug in with the almost extravagant provision of five artillery pieces per 1,000 men. But however dim were the prospects of victory, Frederick had to make the assault because Daun controlled the bulk of Saxony. If Frederick could recover Saxony, he could hire new soldiers to replace his casualties; without Saxony he would have lost nearly a third of his revenues and could not have maintained his army at its existing strength. Frederick's attacks on Daun and on other opponents make eminently good strategic sense when viewed as a means to defeat his enemies' implicit but potentially deadly logistic strategy. Frederick survived because he did not face an opponent with the talent and enterprise of Marshal Vendôme, to say nothing of the quick defeat to a logistic strategy his weak situation could well have brought had he opposed men of the caliber of Marlborough and Eugene or of Marshals Luxembourg and Villars.

Later, when Frederick planned how he would conduct yet another war with the Austrians, he gave an explicit statement of the logistic bases of his strategy: "I would first conquer enough land to enable me to procure provisions, to live at the expense of the enemy, and to select as the theatre of operations terrain that is most favorable to me; I would hasten to fortify my defensive line before the enemy could appear in the vicinity."[28]

Frederick, based his reliance on battles not only on strategic necessity but also on his distinctive tactical approach. His victory at Leuthen best exemplified his objective. Here he placed his army obliquely to the Austrians and not only concentrated all of his force against one wing of the enemy but also attacked their flank, always a weak point. This oblique attack held back one flank, keeping it and the opposing enemy forces unengaged. Since Frederick intended that his unengaged flank always have a proportionately much weaker force than the unengaged portion of the enemy's army, this oblique attack simplified and accentuated the concentration of his troops. By advancing his battalions in echelon with each of them fifty to 100 yards behind that adjacent, he accelerated the engagement of the stronger part of his army and delayed that of the weaker. He could employ such an echelon formation because the firepower of the battalions amply covered the gaps between them.

Thus by the disposition of his army Frederick accomplished a concentration of force against weakness, the enemy's flank. At Leuthen he facilitated this maneuver by distracting Prince Charles and convincing him that the Prussian attack aimed at the opposite flank. In his other offensive battles he had less success than at Leuthen, but in every one he attempted to assail the enemy from an unexpected direction where he could anticipate finding the foe weaker than in front.

Frederick's method thus differed fundamentally from that of Marlborough, who fought the traditional frontal battle, using infantry assaults to attract the enemy's reserves and charges by cavalry to exploit the weakness created by the distractions. Frederick's approach relied on concentrating against weakness. Though his excellent cavalry continued to play a key role, his oblique attack gave infantry a much more basic offensive character. Frederick's method had something in common with Epaminondas' use of his Sacred Band at Leuctra as well as with the Spartan drill for a flank attack.

Changes in Attrition in Relation to the Composition of Armies

In spite of the devastating losses from the rapidly delivered volleys at close range, the armies of Frederick and his opponents suffered fewer casualties than one might expect. This reflected a trend of two centuries. Casualties of the victors during the Thirty Years' War amounted to 12.5 percent of their forces, those of the defeated, 37.4 percent. These percentages differ from those of a hundred years earlier but warrant no conclusion because the data lack comparability.

But comparable data for the period 1649 through 1701 indicate a marked change. Victor's casualties, 12.6 percent, did not change, but the losses of the defeated dropped to 27.6 percent. Although the linear system became universal and many soldiers had plug bayonets during the latter part of this period, permanent regiments and drilled standing armies seem the best hypothesis for explaining most of this dramatic decline. Disciplined, permanently established armies could better withstand the disorganization of defeat than could the often poorly trained mercenary infantry of the Thirty Years' War.

The era of the socket bayonet, 1702–63, witnessed, at 12.5 percent, no change in the victor's losses and a smaller drop, to 21.9 percent, in those of the defeated. Since homogeneous, bayonet-armed musketeers, superior as a weapon system to cavalry, suffered less in defeat than pikemen and musketeers without bayonets, this change in weapon systems seems the most likely explanation for the bulk of this decline. That armies fought less concentrated, spread in lines rather than assembled in blocks, may also have contributed to the drop in casualties, if only because the victors had to search farther to discover demoralized and vulnerable groups of defeated and often might find them in smaller numbers when they had the opportunity to assail them.[29]

Standing armies containing well-trained, bayonet-armed musketeers had apparently markedly reduced the casualties of the defeated in battle. This decrease in attrition diminished the tactical significance of a given battle and should have increased the number of battles. Field Marshal Daun succinctly expressed the attitude toward combat held by commanders since the *condottieri*: "My opinion is that you should offer battle when you find that the advantage you gain from a victory will be greater, in proportion, than the damage you will sustain if you retreat or are beaten." If the field marshal had added his estimate of the probability of victory, he would have fully stated the factors governing the decision to engage in a battle.[30]

If the costs of defeat fall, a commander should display a greater willingness to risk a contest even though, if a winner, the same factor lessens the tactical magnitude of victory, because many bettors will make smaller wagers more often than they will large ones, even when the odds are the same.

In the Seven Years' War Frederick fought often when compared with commanders in the Thirty Years' War, and, unlike Marlborough who fought less frequently, he suffered some defeats. But he gathered important strategic fruits from his battles when he successfully guarded his vital base territories and defended himself against his enemies' implicit logistic strategy.

Significant Developments in French Military Thought

While Frederick used his superbly drilled troops to make brilliant applications of the oblique attack to concentrate against weakness, the French army followed another line of development. Impressed, as was Frederick momentarily, by Folard's ideas about shock action, the French used columns in the Seven Years' War. But the columns had their principal utility as formations in which to hold reserves or move troops readily on or near the battlefield. The French also made systematic use of skirmishers ahead of the line, also a characteristic Austrian practice but one initially neglected by Frederick. Yet the distinctive French practice consisted in using a number of columns to increase speed of deployment against better-drilled opponents.

This tactical innovation helped to lead the French to separate their army into permanent divisions composed of both infantry and artillery. A division had no more than sixteen battalions—or less than 10,000 infantry. With battle a possibility, the army approached the enemy in four divisions, with each of these formed into two columns, both of four battalions for the first line and four for the second line. In this way the French sought to equal the speed of deployment of their opponent's better trained infantry. In the campaign of 1760 the perceptive and innovative Marshal Broglie made effective use of columns to maneuver his army, demonstrating the practicality of this approach.

An army separated into divisions could move faster than a concentrated force because it could make use of more roads. By abandoning the approach march with the army concentrated to ward off a cavalry attack, the French recognized that an infantry equipped with muskets and bayonets and divided into well-drilled battalions did not have enough to fear from cavalry to warrant the continued use of the self-defensive march formation used so skillfully by Parma and recommended by Montecuccoli. To guard against an unexpected confrontation with the enemy, Marshal Broglie screened his army with light infantry as well as light cavalry. By separating his army, the marshal could move it more rapidly when it was near the enemy, but it remained conceptually a unit, responsive to his orders and ready to concentrate immediately.

After the war the French continued their pursuit of tactical innovations. In 1766 they introduced a method of deploying a closed column into a line facing the direction of the column's line of march. Though such methods already existed, they were slow, ungainly, and usually involved an open column. The only quick deployment from line to column, that used by Frederick the Great, had relied on the simultaneous turn of all platoons from an open-order column. This had necessarily faced the resulting line at right angles to the column's line of march. The new French drill enabled a compact column quickly and easily to deploy into a three-deep line facing in the direction of march simply by having the column halt and the separate units within the column march diagonally to their places in the line. This deployment could even take place while the lead element continued to march by having the others run to their places in the line.

This ability to form line from column had the potential for a revolutionary impact on tactics. Troops in linear formation moved slowly to keep alignment. This remained true even after Frederick introduced the echeloning of battalions and tacticians realized that the fire of the flintlock could cover substantial gaps between battalions. But the battalions themselves had to maintain their own alignment to have their full firepower and to avoid the danger of the men's shooting each other. A three-deep formation with a front of 200 men had to move slowly to sustain its alignment, even on smooth terrain, but formed into a closed-up column of eight companies one behind the other, for example, it could move as a rectangle with twenty-five files and twenty-four ranks that had a front of fifty feet and a depth of perhaps 150. In this formation battalions could move with comparative ease to the battlefield and then deploy into line to utilize their firepower. Because their fire could cover the gaps between the battalions, they did not need precise alignment on each other.

At the same time that the French adopted divisions for their armies and groped their way toward the concept of maneuvering their troops on the battlefield in column but deploying them in line for actual combat, they made a number of important technical improvements in their artillery. When research revealed that smaller powder charges with shorter barrels and a tighter fitting ball, could produce the same range as formerly, cannon foundries could make the barrels thinner as well as shorter, halving the weight of some guns. Lighter carriages and improved harnesses also augmented mobility, and a better elevating mechanism, a significantly more effective sight, and an increased rate of fire enhanced performance. The advance in the mobility of the artillery made French soldiers confident of the ability of the artillery to keep up with the army in almost any march and made them believe that the artillery would have enough battlefield mobility to play a more consequential role in offensive battles, one comparable to its prominence on the defense. Since small balls packed in cannisters outranged the musket, artillery could be a powerful aid in the attack if the artillerymen could bring it into action on the battlefield at the time and place of the infantry's assault.

Much theorizing and controversy accompanied the changes in the French infantry and artillery, and many military philosophers influenced modifications in the drill and formation of French armies and on the education and thinking of officers. In the infantry these variations constituted as fundamental an alteration as when the Swiss suddenly exercised a profound influence on the battlefields of Europe. The Swiss infantry in their solid-block formation had displayed not only considerable battlefield mobility but also the capacity to march to the battlefield in their combat formation and go into action immediately. Their

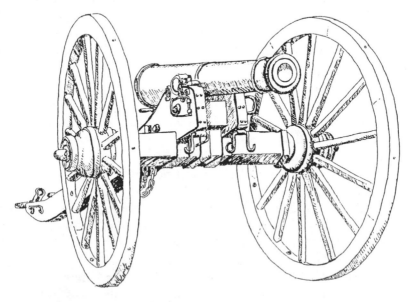

Illustration 5.3. Cannon Firing Twelve-pound Ball

mobile formation might well have dominated battlefields longer if they had not depended so much on drill and morale, if the square did not have to halt to defend its flanks against cavalry, and had the solid formation not been so vulnerable to missile fire and so ill adapted to returning it.

So the infantry that came to play a major role on sixteenth-century battlefields consisted of both pikemen and arquebusiers and required a careful battle array to insure that it provided mutual support against lance- or saber-armed cavalry as well as protection for the pikemen from musketeers and mounted pistoleers. Since this complex array had two interdependent types of infantry and had to adapt itself to the ground on which it fought, it could neither march to the battlefield in combat formation nor display much mobility on the field of battle. It lacked, therefore, two fundamental characteristics of the essentially homogeneous Swiss infantry formation.

The concept of offensive troops, helpful in understanding why cavalry retained its tactical importance after the bayonet-armed musketeer had rendered it an inferior weapon system, has some utility in understanding the significance of the differences between the Swiss infantry and its successors. The Swiss could fight in the same formation as they marched. To this attribute the Swiss owed their victory at Morat over the entrenched Burgundians.

Because of the threat of cavalry's using its greater mobility and capacity for attacking an army on the march without deployment and then employing sabers against musketeers and pistols against pikemen, armies within reach of the enemy's cavalry marched in a quasi-battle formation, a slow movement across country in the self-defensive formation prescribed by Montecuccoli. Whereas the Swiss could startle their opponents by marching rapidly to the field of battle and going into action promptly, the sixteenth-century heterogeneous infantry force moved slowly to the battle area and faced a seemingly interminable delay in forming for combat. It is hardly surprising that no commander thought in terms of forcing a battle on unwilling opponents other than by trapping them against obstacles or compelling attack to raise a seige.

The advent of Gustavus's linear system did not change this situation. The infantry remained heterogeneous, requiring a mutually supporting array, and except for their better subdivision and articulation, linear formations had even less battlefield mobility than the pike squares with their associated musketeers.

The bayonet made the army's infantry homogeneous, and the problems of marching near the enemy and of deployment potentially decreased significantly. Any group of bayonet-armed infantry could defend against cavalry if it could form itself at all. March columns lent themselves not only to the formation of a square but also to facing a line to the approaching cavalry. In battlefield deployment, with every infantryman and every foot unit a perfect substitute for the other, arraying for battle could become far simpler. In the drill that armies evolved to control their linear formations and develop safely their maximum firepower, commanders had the means at hand to realize this potential of the new infantry.

But it proved difficult for eighteenth-century soldiers to see the possibilities presented by homogeneous infantry, which could constitute a dominant weapon system over the cavalry. The linear formation, necessary to utilize all of the muskets, so crippled the infantry's battlefield mobility that soldiers continued to think of cavalry as the only weapon system with real offensive capabilities. The problem of battlefield mobility gave rise to the idea of columns, as did thoughts of the shock action of the previous century. But the logic of this line of thinking foundered on the power, reliability, and rate of fire of the flintlock musket, a weapon that seemed to doom both shock action and any formation that could not make best use of its firepower.

Soldiers had difficulty thinking in terms of offensive troops, which had the ability to fight in marching formation and the greater mobility to reach an enemy's rear. This action remained the prerogative of the cavalry, and the traditional limitations on combat between similarly constiuted armies, found long ago in Greek and Roman times, had endured so long that few soldiers could think of anything but frontal battles by mutual consent. A Prussian general, for example, on finding his army accidentally facing the enemy's flank, laboriously marched his army around to the enemy's front so that he could attack in the traditional way.

Frederick approached the joint problems of battlefield mobility, quick deployment, and flank attacks through his oblique order of battle, which increased the speed of deployment as well as made possible concentration against the weakness of a flank. But he only exploited the possibilities inherent in the existing system; he had created nothing new.

The French adopted the column—actually still a formation with greater breadth than depth. A battalion column often formed itself twelve deep with at least four times as many files as ranks. This column gave them a solid block of men, which had the same battlefield mobility as a Swiss square. But the drill that enabled the battalion to deploy quickly into a three-rank line meant that the mobile column could very nearly fight as it marched. Though French doctrine envisioned not only an advance in line but also a column attack with primary reliance on shock action, in practice tactics used columns to move troops on the battlefield and toward the enemy but usually deployed them into lines for actual combat.

This system could impart to French foot soldiers more celerity than that of the infantry opposing them in a linear formation and the ability to fight almost as they marched, qualities that had long made cavalry offensive troops. To exploit these attributes, the infantry could either concentrate great strength at one point on the battlefield or attack the flank and rear of the enemy infantry by moving with a speed impossible for deployed lines, since they had no alignment to conserve and could march around obstacles because they had no continuous front to maintain. When the columns reached the enemy's vulnerable flank or rear, they could quickly deploy into a line, an irregular one, to be sure, but one in which the firepower of three ranks of flintlocks covered the gaps between battalions. French organization facilitated control of the troops conducting such tactical enveloping or turning movements by combining battalions into regiments and regiments into brigades. Subdivision of battalions into nine companies completed the rather full articulation of the French infantry.

Improvements in the mobility of artillery enabled artillerymen to envisage collecting artillery together and focusing the fire of the guns in a way comparable to the capacity to use the mobility of columns to gather infantry at one point the way Marlborough had assembled his cavalry. The French artilleryman, the Chevalier du Teil, wrote that "it is necessary to multiply the artillery on the points of attack which ought to decide the victory." Believing in the concentration of the artillery to secure "decisive results," du Teil expounded this concept when he wrote that "it is necessary to assemble the greatest number of troops, and a great quantity of artillery, on the points where one wishes to force the enemy" and assure that this is a weak point by distraction elsewhere when "one threatens attacks upon the others. One will impose upon him by movements and false attacks."[31]

The new tactics, which provided the potential for tactical enveloping and turning movements as well as for artillery-reinforced battlefield concentrations, harmonized completely with the subdivision of French armies into permanently constituted divisions. In employing this separation of forces, the French could march near the enemy without adopting a quasi-battle formation as the infantry had less to fear from the cavalry now that it had the bayonet. A closed-up battalion marching on a road eight or twelve abreast presented a daunting target for cavalry, even if the infantry lacked the time to form a hollow square. Marching by battalions and making full use of the roads increased an army's strategic mobility. Separated into divisions and able to deploy rapidly from columns into lines of battle, the infantry might be able to maintain its maximum mobility until it reached the enemy and then be able to deploy so rapidly that, in a strategic sense, it could fight as it marched. The result was that infantry could have a strategic offensive competency similar to, though not as great as, that always enjoyed by the cavalry.

An army separated into divisions had the potential for forcing battle on an adversary. Once near an enemy, such an army could make an opponent's retreat more hazardous. It had long proven difficult to withdraw from an enemy when both armies had formed for combat; now it was harder to march away from a foe that wished to fight.

The separation of an army into divisions also presented another strategically offensive opportunity. The homogeneity and versatility of cavalry, a result of the development of the pistol in the sixteenth century, and the newer homogeneity of the infantry, made possible by the bayonet, created an army much less complex. Because infantry now had superiority as a weapon system, the army no longer needed a just mixture of weapon systems and a careful interrelation of its parts. This situation, new in the eighteenth century, made it easier to envision an army composed of separate, self-contained, interchangeable parts.

The idea of subdividing an army into divisions represented a major conceptual breakthrough. An army originally separated only to embark on different campaigns or to distribute detachments to guard cities, forts, bridges, or other strategic points. But the method of division through distributing detachments with specific missions—called the cordon system—weakened the army because commanders usually did not conceive of these detachments as still part of their army. By subdividing an army into divisions and viewing these separate units as still part of the army, as acting together and as capable of quickly reuniting— French soldiers introduced an idea and practice with major implications.

Divisions separated by as much as a day's march could move more rapidly; they had access to more roads and could cover a wider territory for supplies.

An army separated into divisions that marched over a front of twenty-five miles had a greater potential for making contact with an opponent. Contact with the enemy, combined with the strategically offensive attributes of more rapid movement when near the enemy and the facility of quick deployment into battle array, could easily involve the enemy in an encounter battle such as Marlborough and Vendôme had at Oudenarde. Of course, an encounter battle, in which only one of an army's four divisions engaged the entire enemy force, must almost invariably end disastrously for the division.

But the decline in the casualties of the defeated significantly mitigated the consequences of defeat. Better drilled and disciplined troops suffered, on the average, less than double the percentage casualties of the victor. The improved articulation of the French army mitigated the disorganization of and so diminished the casualties of defeat. Moreover, the division did not need to commit itself to a full-scale battle. If it could fight a day without heavy casualties or if it could engage the enemy without committing all of its troops, the result could delay an adversary reluctant to fight while the other divisions of the army marched to its aid; and these divisions could come from directions that might prove awkward for the concentrated enemy army facing a single division. Arriving on a flank, for example, and deploying rapidly, the divisions uniting on the battlefield could have distinct advantages of position. The resulting conflict could differ markedly from the traditional frontal battle by mutual consent.

Such encounter battles like Oudenarde had occurred in the past, but they had hardly typified combat and, usually happening by accident, had not figured much in military thinking except for precautions to avoid them. Separation of armies into divisions made encounter battles more likely and made them a possible objective of strategy. Such contests could confer an advantage not only on the army deliberately precipitating them but also on the army permanently separated into divisions. Fighting with such divisions would give the commander a predominance because the army had organized in advance for the impromptu battle through a preexisting command organization and its resulting improved articulation.

A French army, arranged in divisions and marching without special precautions, could move more rapidly than a unitary army and, when it united its divisions on the battlefield, could use its column formation to go into battle promptly. Prior to deploying all columns into line, the French commander could use their mobility to concentrate at a point of enemy weakness or to outflank the foe's line to attack it in the flank and rear with infantry. Thus, when compared with opponents using the methods of the Seven Years' War, a French army's infantry would have, on both the strategic and tactical level, the capabilities of offensive troops, attributes that infantry had lacked since the brief ascendency of the Swiss.

For such an army combat became a realistic objective of strategy. Previously battles had essentially depended on mutual consent, the more anxious contestant usually having to accept the disadvantage of the offensive against an enemy in a well-selected and sometimes entrenched position. Unless an unwilling opponent retreated directly to the rear, a commander of an army dispersed into divisions could count on the possibility of compelling the enemy to fight and of doing so in an encounter battle rather than by engaging an opponent defending a carefully selected position. With the maneuverability provided by the well-articulated French army, with its excellent chain of command from battalion to army commander, even contests in chosen positions could differ because the French army could more readily concentrate its infantry on the battlefield and more easily maneuver to attack the flanks and rear of strong positions.

This change could increase momentously the combat element in strategy, which had long been necessarily dominated by logistic goals. Although French military thinkers did not analyze the strategic and tactical possibilities in terms of the notion of offensive troops, some realized the potential of the changes in the French army. Bourcet saw that the dispersal of an army separated into divisions automatically created an ambiguity about the army's objective, which distracted the enemy as effectively as a successful feint by a concentrated army. Bourcet advocated that a general's plan of campaign should have several alternatives so that the commander could take advantage of the distraction that dispersal produced to concentrate where the enemy left himself weak. He saw the possibilities of turning the opponent's position and also believed in marching and countermarching to confuse the enemy as a preparation for concentrating the army against the enemy's weakest detachment.

Bourcet thus echoed Xenophon's maxim that "wise generalship consists in attacking where the enemy is weak, even if the point be some way distant" and gave full emphasis to the means of distacting the enemy so as to lead him to create a weakness to exploit by an offensive concentration. He explained how a divisional organization created an opportunity for a strategy for winning with the least effort.

Guibert, a precocious young man who had served with Marshal Broglie and devised the method of deploying a column into a line facing the direction of the march, embraced both tactics and strategy in his eloquently expressed vision of the possibilities offered by the kind of army he desired, one which, in part due to his efforts, the French army increasingly resembled as the century ended. He envisaged the commander of a traditional army in a strong position facing the kind of army he foresaw, one "able to move itself, to pounce rapidly on the weak part of a disposition, to pass in a moment from the order of march to the order of combat" and ready "to attack the flank or rear of his position." This new force would take away from the commander of the traditional army "the advantage of the ground on which he had relied, and he will be compelled to accept battle where he can." The mobility of the new model army should be such that "just as the lightning has already struck when one sees the flash, so when the enemy sees the head of the army appear, the whole of it should be there, allowing him no time to counteract the dispositions it takes."[32]

Guibert's model army, composed of troops "accustomed to the execution of grand maneuvers, who have methods of rapid deployment," could deploy and attack "before the enemy has had the time to discern where one wishes to strike him, or if he has discerned it, before he has had the necessary time to change his disposition in order to parry it." If, however, "arrived in sight of the enemy, and finding him not to be in a disadvantageous situation," the commander of Guibert's army "maneuvers opposite him, he seeks to deceive him, he makes use of all of the resources of the ground and of tactics in order to delude him concerning his project, he feints an offensive movement on his left in order to form his real attack on his right" until, if "he swallows the bait, abandons or occupies a post that lays himself open, or else weakens himself at a point, either in leaving too few troops there or in leaving too few of the army proper for its defense there, or in leaving the poorest troops of his army there, and then that fault is seized upon, the able and maneuverable general directs all his efforts upon the weakened part." If the distractions fail and the "enemy lays himself open, however, neither by his position nor by his disposition, then the general has committed nothing; he withdraws, takes a position and awaits a more favorable opportunity," having avoided a costly and unsuccessful offensive battle.[33]

So Guibert prescribed combat methods that relied on distraction to facilitate concentration against weakness and that were animated by the concept of winning with the least effort. Guibert saw, as the strategic consequences of this action by his new army, that his commander "will embarrass his enemy, will astonish him, will leave him no place to rest, will force him to fight or retreat continuously before him."[34]

In 1791 the French army adopted new regulations destined to endure for forty years, that embodied the tactical ideas of Guibert. Some of the leaders of the army had read the works of Bourcet and Guibert, and if they lacked their vision and competence, they and their army at least had a grasp of the new methods and some of their possibilities. And the rapid advance in population and wealth had multiplied the number of roads, facilitating the dispersion of an army into divisions because adjacent roads led in the same direction and lateral roads facilitated courier communication among the separately marching divisions. Advances in cartography and the greater availability of maps enabled commanders to plan and coordinate the movements of the different parts of the dispersed armies envisioned by Guibert.

Warfare in the Western Hemisphere

Europeans transplanted to the Western Hemisphere their weapons and military methods, but the different geography modified their operations. In heavily forested North America, for example, cavalry could play only a small part in combat. Without a serious threat from the cavalry charge, heavy infantry formations had little utility. So the predominant infantry consisted first of arquebusiers and musketeers suited to the defense of fortifications as well as fighting in forests. With the introduction of the bayonet, light infantry tactics still dominated, the rigidity of the linear system having little applicability in wooded terrain and in the absence of heavy cavalry.

In South and Central America the Europeans conquered most of the natives with relative ease, in major part because they decimated them with diseases of the Eastern Hemisphere to which the Europeans had become largely inured. In thinly settled North America the numerous European immigrants gradually drove back the natives, overwhelming them by their numbers as they saturated successive pieces of territory with agricultural settlements. The numerous armed settlers proved able to cope with the comparatively small numbers of their opponents with little aid from regular military forces.

In the American Revolution between 1775 and 1783 North America witnessed battles like those fought in Europe. But the vast expanse of the colonies made it impossible for the small armies of the British to dominate the country. With armies little larger than those used in the Hundred Years' War with France, the British had to cope with at least as much space.

In spite of a large number of sympathizers among the colonies, many of them armed, the Americans controlled the country, and, well organized politically and, as militia, militarily, they usually dominated the country in the absence of substantial British regular forces. Victories in battles and campaigns yielded to the British no more than Hannibal had long before attained in his invasion of Italy. In fact, the British had an even more difficult task than Hannibal because, unlike the Carthaginian, they aimed at the political subjugation of the enemy. With such an ambitious political objective, they lacked the military means to defeat such a determined opponent, especially when the Americans had the aid of two formidable military and naval powers, France and Spain.

Warfare at Sea

The eighteenth century saw a continuation of the trends in naval warfare established in the seventeenth century. Ships became increasingly standardized and classified by the number of guns they carried. Ships of the line had from seventy to 100 or more guns with two or three decks for heavy guns. For example, the 100–gun, three-decked British ship *Victory* carried on its lowest deck thirty guns firing 32–pound balls, on its next deck twenty-eight guns firing 24–pound balls, and on its upper deck and the truncated fore and stern castles forty-two guns firing 12–pound balls. The smaller ships of the line weighed 2,000 tons, the larger somewhat more, with a few weighing as much as 3,000 tons. Frigates had grown to displace as much as 700 tons and some even more. As with the musket, the flintlock had replaced the burning match as the means of firing cannon, and this change exemplified many small improvements in ship and rigging design and the working of the guns, all of which marked the gradual improvement in navies during the century.

Tactics remained that of combat between lines of ships on parallel courses. The attackers still sought the windward position. Britain and France were the premier naval powers, and contests between them established the norms of naval warfare. Indecisiveness characterized the naval battles in which the French usually had the smaller fleet. Realistic about their inferiority in battle, the French did not try to destroy the British fleet. The French fought to protect a convoy or to allow an overseas expedition to make good its departure. Consequently, they followed a conservative tactical doctrine, always choosing the downwind position to facilitate withdrawal from battle. Often they shot at the rigging of the British ships, aiming to damage their sailing ability rather than killing men, disabling guns, or impairing buoyancy. This tactic helped insure their retreat and could even force the British ships back to port to repair rigging. If this happened, the French fleet could exploit a brief period of command of the sea.

Toward the end of the century, at the Battle of the Saints in 1782, the British Admiral Sir George Rodney made a significant tactical innovation. Rodney, who had fifty years of service and ample command experience, faced in the Comte de Grasse an opponent of equal experience and ability who had larger ships with better sailing qualities. As Rodney's thirty-six ships passed the French fleet of thirty-one on the opposite course, Rodney took advantage of some gaps in the French line. The admiral and the leader of his rear turned into two different gaps in the French line, thus dividing the enemy fleet into three separate segments. The rearmost of the three segments comprised only twelve ships, against which the center and rear of the British line turned and toward which the head of the British line turned round to attack. This concentration of force against the rear of the French line resulted in heavy damage to many French ships and their withdrawal. The British captured five French ships, including the flagship on which they found the Admiral de Grasse and 400 dead. This battle exhibited the potential for concentration of superior force offered by the tactic of breaking the enemy's line.

The strategy for the exercise of sea power remained the same, the British following a persisting one in seeking to close French ports to trade and the French raiders preying on British commerce. In the War of the Austrian Succession from 1740 to 1748 each lost 3,300 merchant ships. But the French suffered greater damage because the British crippled French overseas commerce with blockades and seizures. In the Seven Years' War the British instituted such a close blockade of French ports that they almost completely paralyzed French commerce. In this war command of the sea enabled the British to send out and supply overseas expeditions and to score significant gains, particularly in driving the French from Canada and India. Britain's stranglehold on French commerce and its debilitating effect on the French economy indirectly aided her continental ally, Prussia, which maintained an army opposing the French in Germany, as did her direct financial support, based in part on the prosperity engendered by her commerce.

6

TACTICAL AND STRATEGIC TRANSFORMATION IN THE ERA OF THE FRENCH REVOLUTION AND NAPOLEON, 1791–1815

The Tactics and Strategy of the Opening Campaigns in the North

In 1789 the calling of the long-unused legislature of the French monarchy provided the means by which a revolution first limited the power of King Louis XVI and then eventually deposed and executed him. Successive elected assemblies provided the executive as well as the legislative leadership of a revolutionary government and gave reality to the ideals of political liberty and equality. This radical alteration in the traditional, noble-dominated French society not only aroused the hostility of monarchical Europe but also separated France from its European neighbors when the revolutionary government announced its intention of spreading its political gospel over Europe. When war came, both sides had far more ambitious and threatening aims than had animated European warfare for a long time. But though France and its enemies ostensibly aimed at the overthrow of what each saw as a hostile regime, conventional political objectives and more limited goals played an increasing role in guiding the course of military operations.

The revolution seriously affected the French army in which hostility to the privileges of the nobility had divided officers and men. Political agitation, extensive desertion, and the ultimate departure of two-thirds of the officers had reduced the size and effectiveness of the army as war with the emperor and Prussia seemed likely. The government asked for volunteers in the fall of 1791 and the 110,000-man army was augmented by one-third. The volunteers had separate units, wore blue rather than the king's white uniforms, and elected their own officers. They also began training with the new 1791 regulations, and with this force France went to war in 1792 against the formidable armies of Austria and Prussia.

Concerned about conditions in Eastern Europe, Austria and Prussia did not commit all of their troops in a campaign that French exiles assured them would receive the welcome of popular support for King Louis XVI and the foreign soldiers intervening to restore his power. The allies fielded armies along the Rhine and in the Netherlands, where the French conducted an offensive campaign with forces consisting of volunteers and disorganized regulars. These soldiers fled when they faced disciplined Austrian professionals and, blaming their officers, even shot one general for treason. The Austrians then took the offensive, besieging Lille and moving south to unite with the Austro-Prussian army of the duke of Brunswick, which moved steadily ahead, took the French fortress of Longwy in late August, and in early September joined the Austrian force from the Netherlands that had taken Verdun. The duke, a relative of Frederick the Great and brother-in-law of King George III of England, had displayed ability in responsible commands in the Seven Years' War. In commanding his army he exhibited the same competence and care that he showed in ruling his duchy.

On entering France, Brunswick's army encountered no welcome from the French population and suffered from dysentery and the heavy rains. Under these conditions a long march to Paris, deep in the heart of a hostile country, would have been unrealistic, even if the capable French politican-soldier General Dumouriez had not marched from the Netherlands to oppose them and unite his army with that from Metz under General Kellerman, a seasoned regular officer and proponent of the revolution. Dumouriez had already succeeded in imparting some training and discipline to his volunteers, and Kellerman's force had a higher proportion of regulars. With this combined army Dumouriez, taking up a position at Valmy on the flank of Brunswick's route to Paris, offered battle.

Unwilling to ignore even an army presumably rendered ineffective by revolutionary conditions, Brunswick moved to confront Dumouriez and Kellerman. The battle began with an Austro-Prussian cannonade, but when the French infantry remained steady and their artillery, which had lost only a third of its well-trained regular officers, proved equal to the best performance of the traditionally excellent French artillery, the duke did not carry out an infantry attack against the apparently firm French troops.

After the two armies faced each other for ten days, the allied forces withdrew toward the Rhine, ending whatever menace 50,000 soldiers presented to a country of 25 million people. In the absence of substantial and overt political support by partisans of the king, these troops could not have represented a serious threat, particularly in view of the political and military vigor of the revolutionary government.

Leaving Kellerman to watch Brunswick's withdrawal, Dumouriez moved his army back to the Netherlands theater where in early November, in six divisions marching over two separate routes, he surprised the Austrians in their well-fortified winter quarters and, with a numerical preponderance of at least two to one, defeated them at the Battle of Jemappes, drove them back, and captured Brussels. The French soldiers exhibited good morale and steadiness under fire and showed that they like their general had learned to use the simple, effective drill of the new 1791 regulations. At Jemappes most troops had moved up in columns, deployed into line, and conducted their attack in linear fashion; others also followed the manual when they used columns of attack in a successful assault on a village.

With the outbreak of war the French government resorted to compulsion to strengthen the army, again forming separate units in blue uniforms under elected officers. The men of the new units tended to select experienced soldiers for their leaders and displayed enough judgment to elect nine future marshals of France. But when one former sergeant became an officer, he learned that the spirit of the army militated against discipline as he tried to drill his battalion. His men denounced their new drill master's despotic hostility to liberty and equality and tried to hang him. Nevertheless, the enthusiasm of the volunteers and conscripts for their nation and its revolutionary ideas made the men willing learners and provided the foundation for a more democratic discipline under nonaristocratic officers of the same social background as their men. Three months of training enabled infantrymen to join a battalion and execute the new drill adequately.

To supply discipline and to watch the senior officers, the government sent to each army civilian political representatives called deputies on mission. These deputies had considerable success in imbuing the soldiers with revolutionary and patriotic feeling as well as watching and occasionally directing the army commanders whom they had the power of relieving. But zealous soldiers without discipline and training did not provide the best material with which to realize the military potential of the new tactical regulations and the ideas of Bourcet and Guibert. The government, faced with rebellion within France and war with Britain, Holland, and Spain as well as Austria and Prussia, lacked adequate military resources even though it had drafted hundreds of thousands of men in 1793. Since many of these new troops had little military value, the French were fortunate that the awesome coalition against them, still preoccupied with other political questions, did not exert its full military force or pursue its campaigns with much vigor.

In February, when Dumouriez tried to invade Holland, the imperial commander, the orthodox Prince Josias of Saxe Coburg, who had the aid of a good, even innovative, staff, advanced briskly against him. With 45,000 men Dumouriez immediately took the offensive, meeting the 40,000 men of the allies on March 18, 1793, at Neerwinden. But Coburg had spread his army enough to cover his flanks against Dumouriez's eight, widely spaced attacking forces, and with skillful subordinates in Clerfayt, who had distinguished himself as a subordinate in the Seven Years' War, and the young Archduke Charles, the Austrian commander resisted the French assaults. With the archduke's vigorous counterattack Coburg finally drove Dumouriez's men from the field. The defeat, together with the subsequent retreat, so demoralized the French that half of the army soon deserted. Dumouriez, after failing to persuade his men to march on to Paris and restore the monarchy, went over to the allies. And Coburg, pursuing a persisting strategy of capturing important places to keep or to use for diplomatic bargaining, promptly reoccupied the Netherlands and began the siege of the French town of Condé.

A new French commander rallied the army but lost his life in a battle to relieve Condé. The next two commanders who also failed to relieve Condé were executed for treason. Apprehensive because of rebellions within a country beset on every side, the republican leaders in Paris and the deputies on mission with the armies could not understand why their large but ill-trained forces could not make headway against the smaller, adequately commanded, professional forces of the allies.

When the siege and fall of the city of Valenciennes followed the surrender of Condé, the British contingent began the siege of Dunkirk, a base for French commerce raiders. The new French commander, Houchard, an inept, old cavalry officer guided by an able staff, assembled a huge force and directed it in a bumbling attack at Hondschoote against the Austrian army covering the siege of Lille. The troops sent to turn the enemy became lost, and Houchard, waiting in rain with his men under artillery fire, considered retreat when his well-disciplined enemy advanced, firing volleys as they came. Delbrel, the deputy on mission, persuaded Houchard not to retreat and, when Houchard went to get the right wing to attack, actually assumed command when he ordered the commander in the center, the young general Jourdan, to move against the enemy.

Having ordered the assault, Delbrel then returned the command to Jourdan and served him as an aide while Jourdan carried out the attack. Delbrel and another deputy, wearing red, white, and blue sashes and plumes in their hats, helped lead the charge, a contemporary believing that "the brilliant courage of these Deputies, the sight of the plumes and tri-coloured scarves which floated from their hats, produced, as always, an electrical effect" on the men. Jourdan's successful assault contributed significantly to the victory at Hondschoote.[1]

Houchard and his 40,000 Frenchmen, having pressed back less than half their numbers and opened communications with Dunkirk, then marched to the east and attacked and drove back an allied force at Menin. But when he pushed on, he met defeat at the hands of allied forces concentrated against him and withdrew.

Meanwhile, farther east, Coburg had taken still another city and had began the siege of Maubeuge. The government promptly brought Houchard to Paris, tried, then guillotined him. Doubtless with trepidation, the able young Jourdan accepted the command of the army and continued the strategy originated under Houchard. This consisted of exploiting the allied dispersal along a front of almost 100 miles. In September Houchard had attacked both the Dunkirk covering force and that at Menin; in October Jourdan led 100,000 men to the relief of Maubeuge, Coburg's last siege of the year. In a two-day battle at Wattignies, Jourdan's two-to-one numerical preponderance over his unreinforced opponent enabled him to drive back Coburg's force and raise the siege. To some degree the patriotism and revolutionary zeal of many of the soldiers had substituted for discipline and drill when large numbers fought effectively as skirmishers. Jourdan, holding back men in columns out of range until the skirmishers had unsettled the enemy, then moved in with his formed troops with a rush. Success in relieving Maubeuge permitted the government to send troops southeastward to the Rhine, where they helped push back allied forces in November and December.

In 1793, though they had lost the Netherlands and some important frontier towns, the French had survived, and their success in the field gave their new army some confidence as well as experience. Although their victories had inflicted only minor losses on their opponents and had cost them more casualties than the allies, they had saved Dunkirk and Maubeuge. The campaign exhibited the strategic merits of concentrations against successive points against opponents lacking adequate unity of command and the point of view to apply the same methods on the offensive or to use them to respond adequately with defensive concentrations. Although the essentially frontal battles did little more than press back hostile forces, the operations showed the strategic potential of dispersed armies in the hands of young generals who, stimulated by the deputies on mission and the shadow of the guillotine, took the risk of battle.

Along the Rhine and other frontiers the allies had some success, but the revolutionary armies gained experience and, in part by the execution of seventeen generals in 1793, found competent officers for the higher commands. Talent and luck hastened generals to the top, Jourdan, for example, rising from lieutenant to army commander in the first four years of the revolution. But the next year, when the government executed sixty-seven generals, it found officers declining promotion, and even privates, who had a very dangerous place in the line of battle, said that they would not become generals.

The French had used the conscripts of 1793 to bring up to strength the battalions of old regulars and those of the volunteers of 1791 and 1792. Having increased the old units and used the veterans to instruct and season the new men, for the 1794 campaign the French amalgamated their different volunteer and conscript units and then combined two battalions of these with one battalion of old regulars into a unit called a demi-brigade. They further blended the old and the new by moving around the constituent companies until they had created three new, thoroughly integrated battalions. A brigade consisted of two demi-brigades and a division of two or more brigades. This organization distributed the veterans throughout the armies, and provided them with excellent articulation from the battalion level upward. Primarily infantry units, divisions nevertheless had their own artillery and cavalry. Although still no match for their opponents, the French armies in 1794 surpassed those that had managed to defend the revolution in 1793.

The French revolutionary soldiers had many sources of morale and motivation to help substitute for discipline and training. The conditions of service reinforced the soldiers' belief and willingness to fight for the principles of liberty and equality for which the revolution stood. With the disappearance of aristocratic officers, the men had far less distance from and more attachment to their officers who tended to treat their men with the consideration due citizens of the republic. The soldiers' patriotism, self-respect, and allegiance to an ideal, which they saw working in practice in the army, also motivated them.

The organization of the soldiers also contributed to their morale. Many volunteers and conscripts, for example, came from the same locality, which, as a soldier's petition put it, meant that "citizens who fight alongside their friends and relatives" would display "more zeal." When the army broke up his small unit, another soldier alluded to the same source of motivation when he said, "little satisfied to serve with men whom they had never seen before, many comrades went back to Paris, and several returned to our department."[2]

The organization of the army into small groups that often lived and ate together, which the improved subdivision and articulation tended to foster, provided for better cooperation among individuals and sustained each soldier's motivation and performance. Such an army bore defeat in battle far better than many earlier ones, which disintegrated into an aggregation of individuals who lacked both the maneuverability of the better articulated force and the cohesion supplied by such groups.

Thus the newly formed armies had many sources of morale and motivation, some characteristic of long-established professional units and others at least somewhat unique to the French armies. The simplicity of the new regulations and the reduced dependence on the exact drill necessary to make a long advance in precise linear formation also aided in the quick conversion of citizens into effective soldiers. Three months of training sufficed to provide adequate maneuvering skill and to supply the basis upon which, combined with dedication, soldiers could give a good combat performance with their new tactics.

In strategy—by spreading their forces out in divisions that had a facility for and willingness to attack—the inexperienced generals of the armies of revolutionary France had already begun to impose new methods on their opponents. Distributed in a cordon to cover sieges or secure territory, the allied armies lacked the conceptual unity of one army scattered in divisions, a unity that the French generals as yet only dimly perceived and still exploited ineptly. Nevertheless, the revolutionary generals had in 1793 concentrated significantly greater numbers successively against their scattered opponents and, through this strategy, had contributed to keeping their enemies at bay.

In May 1794 the advance eastward of the northernmost French army in the Netherlands precipitated a conflict that exhibited the changes taking place in warfare. When the French army reached Lille and Courtrai, it found itself between Coburg at Tournai and Clerfayt north of the Lys River. Souham, the young French temporary commander who had enlisted as a private in the royal army, immediately planned to use his interior lines to hold Coburg and concentrate against Clerfayt. But Coburg had forestalled this, adopting the imaginative plan of Colonel Mack, a staff officer, to make a simultaneous converging attack against Souham. The plan called for the main army to move northwest from Tournai in three groups, on a six-mile front; two more detachments would advance from the south and, after defeating the French troops near Lille, form a link between the main army and Clerfayt, who would make his attack by crossing the Lys at Werwick.

If Coburg's men had moved rapidly enough and Souham had failed to act, the allied forces would have enveloped the French, enclosing 80,000 French within mutually supporting attacks by 70,000 allied soldiers. But Souham, grasping his enemy's purpose, promptly changed his plan and concentrated against Coburg. On May 17 the three main allied columns met Souham's men, and two of them succeeded in driving back the French; but Clerfayt, meeting opposition, could not cross the Lys until his pontoons arrived. Meanwhile, the other two forces farther south moved slowly; the southernmost column, under Archduke Charles, late starting and moving across country in the traditional defensive formation, had not even approached Lille. The coordinated allied attack had failed to reach its first-day objectives.

On May 18 Souham concentrated against the two main detachments, which had advanced the farthest, while a subordinate kept Clerfayt out of the action by attacking his flank as he moved forward; Coburg's two southern detachments dawdled, the archduke failing to respond to an urgent call from Coburg because his staff declined to disturb his sleep when the message arrived. With a two-to-one numerical superiority at this point, the French assailed their nearest adversaries on front and flank at Tourcoing and drove back the two allied northern columns almost to the Scheldt. The French fought well, an opponent describing their skirmishers as "sharp-sighted as ferrets, and as active as squirrels." And the men had mastered the new deployment, one soldier testifying that when his column came under fire, "we marched at the charge pace, or rather we ran, to put ourselves into line."[3]

The French had conspicuous success, not only repelling their opponent but also capturing fifty-six artillery pieces in line on a road as the enemy retreated. When French infantry overtook allied cavalry, its withdrawal blocked by the guns on the road, the infantry volleys shot down the cavalry, and the advancing French even brought their own artillery into action., Not only did they shoot the cavalry but also the civilians following the army, a British soldier reporting that he "saw a soldiers wife take a baby from her breast and, giving it a kiss, fling it into the stream or ditch, when she frantically rushed forwards and before she had got ten yards, was rent in pieces by a discharge of grape that entered her back, sounding like a sack of coals being emptied." But the attackers suffered, too, finding the enemy artillery powerful on the defensive. The soldier who had deployed on the run had a place in the second rank behind a soldier named Le Blond when a small cannister ball, he said, "struck the unfortunate Le Blond who covered me in the first rank. I saw him cross hands, fall to his knees, and then roll on his belly, with a total expression of pain. I deeply wanted to help him, but seized by fear . . . I drew back just like my company, which broke to find cover from the battery."[4]

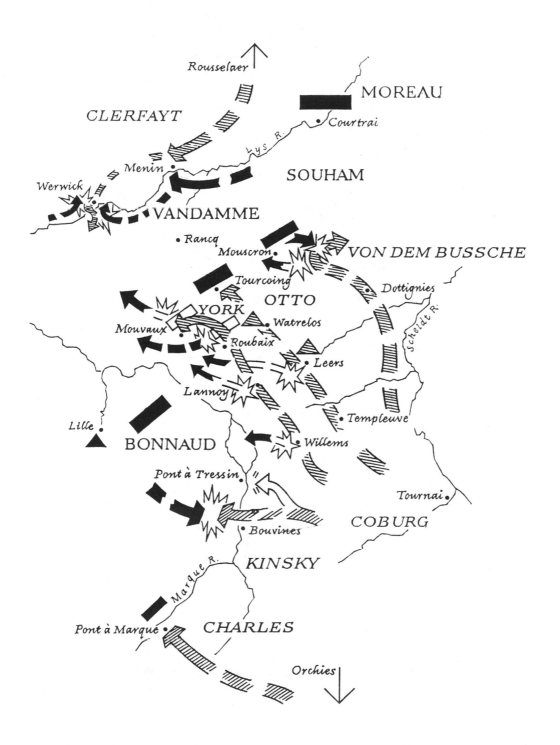

Diagram 6.1. Coburg's Attempted Envelopment

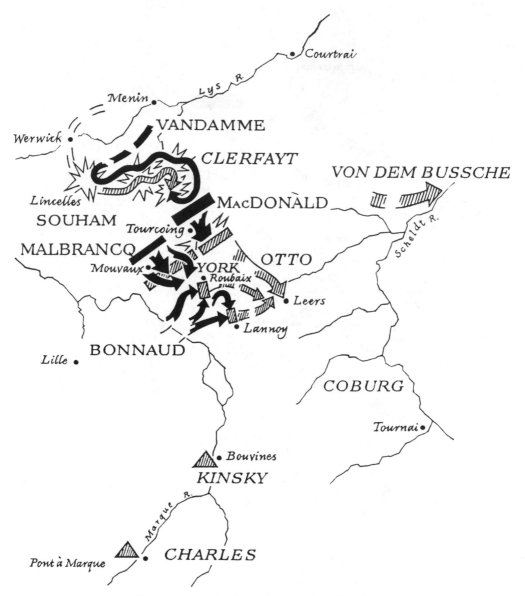

Diagram 6.2. Souham Acts on Interior Lines

Success in driving back Coburg's northern columns and the tardiness of the southern forces enabled Souham to concentrate against Clerfayt on May 19, only to find that Clerfayt had anticipated his coming by falling back well behind the Lys. By his energy and vigorous exploitation of his central position, Souham had saved his army from a well-conceived and menacing envelopment. But the disposition of the forces, the French between hostile concentrations a dozen miles apart, presented a situation on the border between envelopment and interior lines. Had the allies less distance between them, they could readily have enveloped and seriously hurt the French; if more distance had separated them, the French could have easily exploited their interior position. But Souham's energy and the allied difficulty of coordinating sometimes sluggishly moving forces on an outer ring rendered the circumstances one of interior lines and gave victory to the French.

In applying the new tactical regulations, which envisioned maneuvers in column and quick deployment into line for combat with musketry, the French displayed eclecticism and improvisation. They used columns for attack as well as for maneuver, finding opportunities when a column could overwhelm an unready enemy, even using combat with the bayonet against the opposing infantry. A column could effectively penetrate a gap in the hostile line as well as advance against an opposing line not ready to receive it with the orderly series of volleys, which could usually halt the assault of a column. The French also made much use of skirmishing by light infantry and by line infantry deployed ahead to use cover and concealment to keep up a fire at the adversary's line. This skirmishing could create an opportunity for a column attack, unsteady an opponent before a French line advanced, or diminish the vigor of an enemy's own attack.

The French skirmishers, dispersed for missile combat like the slingers, archers, and javelin men of old, could injure their adversaries, even though both sides had the same weapons. The French skirmishers could do this because the enemy infantry had a line formation both to use their bayonets in shock action and to develop the full firepower potential of their muskets. Taking advantage of ditches, ground cover, buildings, trees, crops, and hedges, the skirmishers could harm heavy infantry and artillery gunners without the risk of serious injury. But they could not resist the charges either of heavy infantry or heavy cavalry. A minority of the French infantry, the skirmishers, who were specially trained men or line infantry detailed for light infantry duties, deployed between the lines to a degree seldom practiced earlier in the century and did their work before the lines of infantry met. A German general of the Seven Years' War had written that light infantry "are always hidden behind trees like thieves and robbers and never show themselves in the open field, as is proper for brave soldiers." The French soldier, with his motivation to fight and his lack of reliance on automatonlike drill, proved admirable at this kind of combat. And the role of skirmishers could have much significance if they disorganized and weakened the enemy's line before the clash of formed infantry. They also functioned well in reconnaissance, supplementing and replacing the initially meager and poorly skilled French cavalry.[5]

So French infantry had skirmishers as well as linear formations and columns for assault and maneuver. Having also proficient mobile artillery with excellent materiel, the French army possessed an extremely versatile and effective tactical system that could adapt itself to almost any physical or tactical circumstance and perform well in defense, attack, retreat, and advance.

In strategy these operations have distinction because of the wide dispersal of the forces. In guarding towns and crossing points, the allies had customarily distributed their men in a thin cordon; in spreading their armies in divisions, the revolutionary generals had made an equal dispersion. In 1793 the French had used the conceptual unity of their forces to make successive concentrations, attacking the allies at Hondschoote, Menin, and then Wattignies. But, on the advice of Mack, Coburg had concentrated to make a converging attack in which, in addition to Clerfayt's separate advance, he distributed 50,000 men over an eighteen-mile front. Thus the allies as well as the French exhibited the flexibility inherent in armies in which the bayonet-equipped musketeer had become the primary weapon system. The casualties for one day of the battle—May 18— when the French had won at Tourcoing but Clerfayt had counterattacked and defeated the force that attacked him amounted to 8 percent of the well-disciplined allied forces; the poorly trained but better articulated French had suffered about the same percentage of casualties. The operations here showed, as had others, that commanders took little risk in widely dispersing such resilient formations.

Such dispersion contributed to the increased frequency of battles and changed their character. No longer did they necessarily occur between compactly arrayed unitary armies on a field selected by the defender. As with Frederick, infantry played a major offensive role, but the significance of cavalry had decreased still further and infantry displayed more versatility in the offense. The strategy of dispersed forces corresponded fully to that envisioned by Bourcet and Guibert, and Mack as well as Souham had seen some of the potential presented by the new situation. But since Souham had only a temporary command and Mack merely a staff position, it remained for a general who understood war to exploit the potentialities of the situation.

The Advent of General Bonaparte

In early 1796 good political connections enabled General Napoleon Bonaparte, then twenty-six, to receive command of the main French army facing Italy. The government gave him the mission of driving the kingdom of Sardinia and its strategically located Duchy of Savoy from the war and pushing back the Austrians. In addition to a genius for warfare and the will to dominate any situation, General Bonaparte had thoroughly learned the doctrine of the French army in which he had served as a young officer in the 1780s. Austrian intelligence correctly described him as a "profound theorist" for he knew well the ideas of Bourcet and carried on his campaign a copy of Guibert's work. He had an unequaled grasp of how to realize the potentialities of the French army.[6]

Bonaparte had at his disposal seasoned, if not particularly well-disciplined, infantry. Of cavalry he had little, most horses having failed to survive winter supply shortages, which also had deprived the soldiers of sufficient rations and adequate clothing. The army only received its barely sufficient supplies because ships could move along the coast, availing themselves of defended points of refuge and the negligence of the British navy in not using their preponderance to interdict this commerce. Beginning an offensive in early April, the magnetic Bonaparte had already inspirited his men and pointed out that the prosperous land of northern Italy could provide ample supplies.

Facing cooperating allies but not a unified command, the French planned to separate them and, by defeating Colli's Sardinian army, force Sardinia from the war; they expected that the Austrian commander, Beaulieu, would devote his attention to protecting the Austrian possession of Milan. When Beaulieu opened the campaign by concentrating to pounce on the exposed French force at Voltri, the Austrian commander himself provided the distraction that Bonaparte needed to enable him to drive north to Dego and separate the Sardinian and Austrian armies. On April 12, two days after Beaulieu's successful attack on Voltri, the French army began a night march from the coast toward Dego, while near Montenotte a French force of 7,500 assaulted 4,500 Austrians in front as 3,500 French completed a turning movement and attacked the Austrian rear. The Austrians fled, and their main forces did not participate further in the action. Beaulieu, a soldier past seventy years old, had initially failed to grasp what was happening and then made no real effort to reunite his forces; the Sardinians were commanded by the equally elderly and somewhat infirm Colli.

After difficulties capturing Dego and its subsequent loss to an enterprising Austrian commander while its garrison slept and its general lay in bed with a lady from the town, Bonaparte easily held the inert Beaulieu at bay and, through constant threats to turn his position, forced Colli back. Vigorous frontal attacks also played a role. A future marshal of France participated in an attack in which Serurier, an older general and a veteran of the Seven Years' War, displayed exemplary leadership. "To form his men in three columns, put himself at the head of the central one, throw out a cloud of skirmishers, and march at the double, sword in hand, ten paces in front of his column; that is what he did. A fine spectacle, that of an old general, resolute and decided, whose vigor was revived by the presence of the enemy." Escaping the hostile bullets, the general led his men to victory. When such vehement and efficacious actions had, along with the turning of his positions, forced Colli back until he drew near Turin, the king of Sardina asked for an armistice. On April 28, a little over two weeks after the beginning of the French advance, Sardinia had left the war.[7]

Fortunately this phase of the campaign ended promptly because the French army could find little to eat in the mountains and had scant reserves to send supplies from the coast on too few pack mules. Control of the foraging region on the coast had caused both the French occupation of Voltri and Beaulieu's capture of it. Lack of supplies had delayed operations an entire day in one case while the soldiers scoured the countryside to find food.

The armies fought widely dispersed, with as much as thirty miles separating the extremes of the French forces. But Bonaparte treated them as a unit and directed the movements of all parts of his army toward his strategic aim. Although no classical battle occurred between the opposing forces, fighting was almost continuous, as the two armies nearly always had contact. Small battles and tiny sieges punctuated and made possible the maneuvers that divided the Austrians and Sardinians.

Bonaparte had not only deliberately placed his army between his enemies' but also had to fight to create a gap into which to move. In a situation like Souham's between Coburg and Clerfayt, Bonaparte took advantage of his opponents' disunity to exploit his central position to drive back the Austrians and then concentrate against the Sardinians. Though outnumbered 50,000 to 40,000, because of his central position he enjoyed numerical superiority on almost every occasion, culminating in the ratio of two to one with which he drove Colli toward Turin. He and his subordinates knew how to bring the army into battle promptly, to use its numerical advantage, and to exploit its mobility and articulation, consistently employing turning and enveloping movements to defeat or force back the enemy.

French successes gave them access to the fertile regions of Savoy and adequate food supplies for the men, which with the exhilaration of victory raised the morale of the army of Italy and its confidence in its general. Bonaparte moved promptly to attempt to cross the Po River and move into the fertile and populous Duchy of Milan, where he could find a base ample for supplying his army, making him independent of communication with France. To cross the Po he had already provided a distraction by including in the Sardinian armistice permission to cross at Valenza, a fact that Beaulieu knew. Concentrating his army near Valenza, Bonaparte had two plans, one to march part of his army east and cross at Piacenza if Beaulieu should concentrate to resist his ostentatious preparations at Valenza, the other to cross at Valenza if Beaulieu should counter his plan for an eastern crossing.

Beaulieu, experienced in defending river lines, concentrated the bulk of his forces between the Po and the Ticino, and on May 4 he sent a detachment east to guard the Po as far as Piacenza. But the next day the French started, picked men marching rapidly in advance of the main force, reached Piacenza, and crossed the Po on captured boats before the Austrians could interfere. When the commander of the Austrian detachment took up a defensive position instead of attacking, all the French forces crossed, and Beaulieu, seeing his defense of the Po and Ticino compromised, fell back over the Adda. When a combination of luck and energetic exploitation of opportunities enabled a French force, under Bonaparte's personal command, to seize at Lodi a bridge over the Adda, the discouraged Beaulieau retreated to the Mincio. The capture of this bridge sealed the devotion of Bonaparte's men to their young general, whose small stature detracted not at all from his magnetism and ability to command.

Within two weeks after the Sardinian armistice Bonaparte had secured the Duchy of Milan and driven his enemy back 100 miles. Just as in 1702, when Marshal Vendôme had utilized his numerical preponderance to fix Eugene's attention while marching part of his army to turn the prince's position on the Po, so Bonaparte had used his greater numbers in the same way. Unlike Eugene, who sought to retrieve the situation by a battle with all his forces against half of the French, Beaulieu retreated; and, unlike Vendôme, Bonaparte quickly united all his forces, ready should Beaulieu attack. Beaulieu probably displayed wisdom in retreating before the French, who had marched rapidly eastward and had made another crossing; his dispersed army would doubtless have suffered heavily in a conflict with French divisions coordinated by the brilliant General Bonaparte.

The Austrian retreat enabled the French to occupy Milan and levy huge contributions on the duchy. In spite of initial revolts against them, the French enjoyed considerable political support. Bonaparte had tried, without complete success, to maintain the discipline of his soldiers and prevent the looting that usually characterized republican armies. The French revolutionary program of political liberty and equality appealed to the Italian middle class, creating a significant base of support for Napoleon. The population of Milan had cheered the arrival of the French, but, in part due to the behavior of the French soldiers, the city revolted against the French eight days later. Similar political support in Holland, together with an unprecedented winter that froze the water barriers, had already enabled the French to conquer that country, a feat that long before had baffled the best commanders and soldiers of the Spaniards and of Louis XIV.

With his troops paid as well as fed, his army refitted, rebellions but not all peasant guerrilla activity crushed, Bonaparte moved eastward at the end of May. Concentrating quickly from a march in three divisions, he forced a crossing of the Mincio at Borghetto and divided Beaulieu's army. While half the Austrian troops remained to garrison the powerful fortifications of Mantua, the remainder retreated with Beaulieu north along the Adige. With neutral Venice to the east, Bonaparte drove the Austrians from Italy in less than two months.

Having received reinforcements from France, for the next two months Bonaparte devoted himself to organizing his conquests, levying contributions, suppressing opposition to French rule, and sending forces south to impose peace and levies on the remainder of Italy. Bonaparte's success enabled him to send to France not only money but also valuable paintings for museums. He kept his army in the vicinity of Mantua, first blockading the garrision of over 12,000 men and then, when his seige artillery arrived, in mid-July beginning to dig the trenches that would bring the besiegers under cover to the fortress ditch and provide the opportunity to breach the defenses. To support the army, the French brought supplies by road from Milan via Brescia along an established, guarded route.

The Austrian counteroffensive naturally took the form of a move to relieve Mantua by driving away the besieging forces to resupply the garrison and fill in the siege trenches. To reach Mantua the Austrians divided their forces, expecting that if even one could get through, that would suffice to replenish supplies and demolish the siegeworks. Eighteen thousand men under Quasdonovich marched south on the west side of Lake Garda; on the east Field Marshal Count Würmser, the overall commander, led 24,000 men south along the Adige. Bonaparte had distributed his approximately equal forces so as to protect the siege, two detachments covering the Adige from Verona to Legnano, one under the capable General Masséna blocking Würmser's route, one conducting the siege, and only 4,500 men around Salo in Quasdonovich's path. The French had no central reserve when on July 28 the Austrians, having marched rapidly, suddenly appeared at all points.

Field Marshal Würmser, over seventy and quite deaf, proved a vigorous opponent and one capable of inspiring his men. As Würmser pushed back Masséna, Quasdonovich drove ahead and captured Brescia, cutting the French line of communications. On the evening of July 30, when he fully grasped the situation and realized that he faced envelopment, Bonaparte resolved to abandon the seige of Mantua and concentrate most of his forces against Quasdonovich and drive him back. If he succeeded, the French commander could then use his interior lines to turn against the field marshal; if he failed, he would have to retreat, either through Brescia or on a more southerly route.

But his rapid concentraton against Quasdonovich repelled the Austrians and recovered Brescia. Meanwhile at Mantua, the French having withdrawn eastward to cover their line of communciations and retreat, Würmser's forces entered the city, and the field marshal then planned to cross the Mincio and catch the French between his army and Quasdonovich's. But before Würmser acted, the French defeated Quasdonovich, and the Austrian general, concluding the French had beaten the field marshal also, began a retreat north. Thus Bonaparte could turn his whole force against Würmser, who had crossed the Mincio and deployed

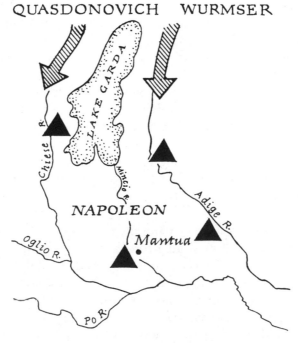

Diagram 6.3. Napoleon's Dispersion

for battle at Castiglione on terrain that did not favor the use of his numerous cavalry.

Having called in all his forces, the French commander delayed his main attack until the original besieging force from Mantua arrived and, as directed, took up its position on the Austrian left rear. Würmser turned his second line to meet this menace, but the movement disordered his men, and the French assault in front and flank drove the Austrians from the field and soon across the Mincio. The field marshal, who had narrowly escaped capture by French cavalry, then ordered a retreat north along the Adige. This proved an orderly and unmolested march because, as Bonaparte reported, "our troops, worn out by fatigue, could only keep up the pursuit for three hours."[8]

At Torgau Frederick the Great had attacked Daun in the front and rear simultaneously, but his deployment within sight of the enemy allowed the Austrian commander ample time to change his battle dispositions. Bonaparte, by not concentrating his army until it reached the field of battle, did not give Würmser the same notice.

The French claimed victory in the Battle of Castiglione and success in saving their army from defeat at the hands of Würmser and Quasdonovich. But the field marshal had accomplished his objective of strengthening Mantua's garrision, replenishing its supplies, demolishing the siegeworks, and capturing 179 French siege guns and 4 million pounds of lead. Henceforth, without artillery, the French could only blockade Mantua.

Diagram 6.4. Concentration on Interior Lines

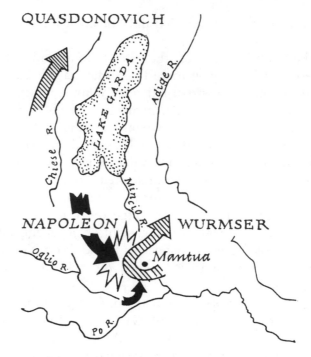

Diagram 6.5. Interior Lines Exploited

The battle at Castiglione had exhibited the strength of the French divisional system when a subordinate joined Bonaparte on the battlefield to attack the enemy's rear. This ability to disperse but act as a unit played a key role in the whole French response to what proved threatening concentric advances. In a situation much like Souham's, when he found himself betweeen Clerfayt and Coburg, Bonaparte used his interior lines to concentrate first against one and then the other. Also, like Souham, Bonaparte faced envelopment, the forces of the Austrians having a real opportunity to attack the French front and rear simultaneously.

Although the victory in the Battle of Castiglione gave a gloss of triumph to the French operations, Bonaparte failed conspicuously to cover the siege of Mantua, and the Austrians had very nearly defeated or driven him back. Although Bonaparte's abilties had much to do with avoiding these two consequences, the French owed much of their success to two principles implicit in the new French system of warfare. Bonaparte had apparently disposed his forces in the traditional cordon covering each route of advance and had provided no central reserve to reinforce a threatened point. He did not seem to apply to his strategic dispositions what the ancients had learned in tactics—always subtract part of the forces to act as a reserve to commit in a critical offensive or defensive situation. But the effectiveness and rapidity with which Bonaparte moved and ultimately concentrated his men showed that the dispersed French forces did not consist of detachments in a cordon, tied to the mission of guarding specific routes. Instead, they remained part of a single army, responsive to the will of the commander. Further, this responsiveness showed that Bonaparte had a reserve in that he could move any forces not irrevocably engaged with an enemy and that these forces thus constituted a reserve just as much as if they had been subtracted and held back in a central position. In tactics generals found it difficult to disengage troops fighting an enemy, but in strategy this presented a far simpler problem. Thus his dispersed army acted as a unit and all forces not resisting a major enemy thrust constituted a reserve at the disposal of the commander. The spirit of Bourcet and Guibert had truly animated Bonaparte's defense, and the army, effectively articulated in divisions and subordinate units, had an admirable organization to execute a strategy conceived by men who had so much influenced Bonaparte.

All of these attributes, so clear in the operations of Bonaparte, had already emerged in the earlier years of the revolution when Houchard and Jourdan had concentrated successively against points of the allied cordon in the Netherlands. But whereas Souham had blundered into a central positon before the Battle of Tourcoing, Bonaparte had deliberately created this situation when he forced himself between Beaulieu and the Sardinians. Just as interior lines revealed themselves as a pattern in Bonaparte's campaigns, so also did the use of the strategic and tactical mobility of the French army to turn or envelop an enemy position. In Bonaparte's first traditional battle, Castiglione, the prompt rear attack by a force called from twenty miles away constituted the decisive element in bringing about the victory. Throughout, operations exhibited the safety of dispersal when small forces delayed the movements of far larger while well-articulated veteran units suffered comparatively few casualties when fighting vastly superior numbers.

In resisting three additional Austrian efforts to relieve Mantua, Bonaparte continued to rely on rapid concentration of forces and the ability of the French infantry to move quickly from march to combat formation; he again exploited the enemy's division of its army by concentrating against first one and then the other of the opposing forces; and he and his subordinates usually made the most of their ability to turn or envelop the opponent's flank. Although the Austrians began to adapt to this new form of warfare, the fundamental organization, tactical doctrine, and strategic spirit remained essentially French. In the end Mantua fell and General Bonaparte's advance toward Austria led to an armistice in which the French acquired, among other gains, control of most of northern Italy, a triumph for the persisting strategy that both belligerents pursued.

In spite of constant fighting, Bonaparte's victory cost little. In his successful major engagements with the Austrians he had lost an average of less than 9 percent of his engaged forces compared to 26 percent for the Austrians, a ratio more favorable than that of eighteenth-century battles.

The Strategic Turning Movement of the Marengo Campaign

By 1800 General Bonaparte, after an invasion of Egypt, had made himself dictator. He then took personal command of the campaign to recover Italy, which the French had lost to the Austrians during his absence. An Austrian army of over 100,000 men, under the experienced and competent Melas, controlled north Italy, besieged Masséna's Frenchmen in Genoa, and pushed forward toward France along the Riviera against the resistance of only 14,000 French soldiers; Austrian forces garrisoned Italian cities and guarded the passes in the Alps. Against this strong enemy Bonaparte employed a new army, less than 40,000 largely green troops and 12,000 men ordered from south Germany.

Using five different passes through the Alps, the French army began to march into Italy in early May, the largest number coming through the great St. Bernard pass. Snow presented a serious obstacle for the artillery, but the soldiers improvised sledges to bring them over the pass. On the down slope the French encountered Fort Bard, "a small fortress perched on top of a preciptious rock at the point where the valley is narrowest." When the fort, which commanded the road and the village, successfully resisted assault, the French found a path around it for the infantry but could not use it for artillery. Finally, they took the few guns past the fort at night, the gunners "drawing their cannon in the dark through the town, close under the guns of the fort, by spreading straw and dung on the streets, and wrapping the wheels so as to prevent the slightest sound."[9]

So Bonaparte's main force and a few of its guns began to concentrate at Ivrea on May 23. Faced with the alternative of marching south to fight Melas and trying to relieve the determined and resourceful Masséna besieged in Genoa or heading east to Milan, Bonaparte chose Milan. Sending his advanced guard toward Turin to deceive the enemy as to his objective, he proceeded to Milan, where he expected to unite with the force from Germany that was coming through the Simplon and St. Gothard passes.

Melas misjudged the French action. His attention was fixed on the siege of Genoa and the Riviera campaign, and the small force that moved through the Mont Cenis pass also distracted him. He believed that he had to deal only with it and Bonaparte's advanced guard that, after its demonstration, had moved east to join the concentration on Milan. While Melas was beginning to comprehend the extent of the French movement, Bonaparte took Milan on June 2, occupied the duchy, captured large quantities of Austrian supplies, and acquired a base area ample to support his army. He relied on the St. Gothard pass for a line of communications and a route of retreat.

As Melas called back his force on the Riviera and began to concentrate his army to deal with the French, Bonaparte pushed south of the Po River, to block the Austrian route of withdrawal eastward. Overcoming the resistance of Austrian garrisons, his men crossed the river and held the defile at Stradella before an Austrian detachment reached it. In his 1706 march to raise the siege of Turin, Prince Eugene had beaten the French in a race to control this narrow passage between the Po and the Apennine Mountains. Now the French blocked it and interdicted not the advance but the escape of the enemy.

General Bonaparte had carried out on a very large scale the same turning movement that Caesar had executed at Ilerda against Pompey's forces in Spain.

When Caesar had placed his numerically larger army on the Pompeians' line of retreat, he had gained the advantage of the tactical defensive. Caesar could readily block his opponent's withdrawal because he could hold the passes in the mountainous terrain; with perhaps 25,000 men to cover a front of ten miles, he had a very high ratio of force to space. In addition, his opponents lacked food, and with his preponderance in cavalry Caesar could control the countryside, thus providing for his men and denying resources to the enemy.

But Bonaparte had a far different and more difficult problem. Not only had the Austrians supplies in magazines and access to a considerable fertile territory, but also Masséna had at last surrendered Genoa. Through this port they could count on obtaining supplies, since their British ally controlled the Mediterranean. In addition, the French did not significantly outnumber the Austrians, and they lay between Bonaparte's turning force and the small French army on the Riviera. Still the advantages of the tactical defensive would have outweighed any superiority of numbers if Bonaparte had possessed a ratio of force to space comparable to Caesar's. Nevertheless, with twice as many men as Caesar, the French commander had to block an Austrian advance through the gap fifty miles wide between the Alps and the Apennines. Bonaparte had the age-old problem of trying to prevent an enemy from passing him.

This same dilemma had faced Beaulieu four years earlier when he had tried to keep Bonaparte out of the Duchy of Milan. On the north side of the gap between the mountains, three rivers, the Po, the Ticino, and the Adda, would provide successive obstacles, but no rivers barred the route south of the Po that Bonaparte had used against Beaulieu in 1796. The Po also handicapped the defender because, by dividing the area between the mountains, it created an obstruction to rapid concentration of troops to the north or south. Unlike Beaulieu four years earlier, Bonaparte took the risk of dividing his forces, keeping over half with him south of the river. In addition he worried about Melas's falling back to Genoa where, with the British fleet at his back, he could either hold out forever or remove his army by sea.

Bonaparte, thinking that Melas would try to escape south of the Po but apprehensive that he might fall back to Genoa, was also concerned about Austrian bridge building over the Po at Casale. So he advanced eastward toward Alessandria, where he believed Melas had concentrated a smaller force than the 28,000 French available south of the Po. On approaching Alessandria and seeing no obvious signs of the Austrian army, Bonaparte sent 5,000 men south, to reconnoiter and delay any enemy movement toward Genoa, and distributed other forces for action should Melas attempt to head north.

Thus, on the morning of June 14 Bonaparte had only 14,000 men outside of Alessandria at the little village of Marengo when Melas moved rapidly out of the fortress and attacked with almost 31,000 men in an effort to open the way east along the south side of the Po. The bulk of the Austrian army deployed and, helped by their more powerful artillery, engaged in a long, severe struggle to wrest the town of Marengo from the French who found the many ditches and farmhouses a valuable aid in the defense. Just as determined Austrian attacks were about to push the French from Marengo, a second Austrian force came around the north flank of the French line. The French then began a retreat, and the seventy-one-year-old Melas, bothered by the heat and slightly injured when enemy fire killed two of the horses he had ridden, returned to Alessandria, leaving to subordinates the task of completing the victory.

The Austrians were slow in pursing the French, who late in the afternoon formed a new line three miles east of Marengo. When the lead Austrian units deployed about 5 P.M., they attacked the 5,000 French troops that Bonaparte had sent south but recalled in time to get in line for this second phase of the battle. The brief, desperate struggle reached a climax as some French brigades advanced when four French artillery pieces moved up to fire at the Austrians at short range, an ammunition wagon exploded, and 400 French cavalry charged the Austrian flank. The Austrians began a panicky flight, their cavalry rushing to the rear over its own men on the road in march column, and the whole Austrian army turned and made for Alessandria.

Successful in their defensive engagement, the French suffered less than 6,000 casualties compared to over 9,000 for the Austrians. Although the Battle of Marengo had stopped the Austrian effort to escape to the east, its army remained powerful and so well supplied that Melas had issued extra rations and new uniforms before the battle. So Bonaparte and Melas agreed to forego the un-

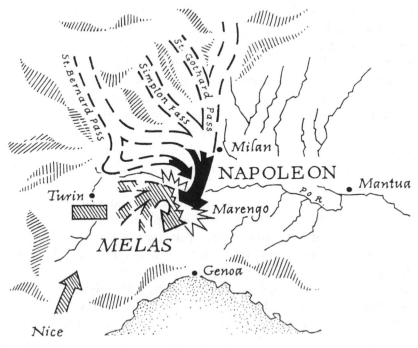

Diagram 6.6. Napoleon's Strategic Turning Movement

certainties of further operations when they negotiated an Austrian withdrawal to the Mantua area. Unlike Caesar's, Bonaparte's turning movement had failed to eliminate the opposing army, but it had, with modest casualties, quickly forced the enemy back 200 miles, recovering the bulk of north Italy and attaining the objective of the French persisting strategy.

His two campaigns in Italy demonstrated the potential of the new tactical doctrine of the French army and the strategic possibilities that it implied. The French ability to deploy rapidly from column to line had multiplied the amount of fighting, which the Austrian armies could not avoid without constant retreats. But the increase in combat did not primarily occur in the traditional battles of armies deployed with equal fronts on terrain suitable for combat. Rather, the hostile forces, both dispersed, had frequent contacts, and the French were eager to assume the offensive because the tactical mobility of their columns enabled them to concentrate more readily and to envelop and turn their opponents. Under many of the tactical circumstances that arose, the maneuverable, well-articulated French infantry had primacy on the offensive against an Austrian defensive conducted by disciplined, trained veterans fighting in the old way.

The strategic exploitation of these tactical capabilities and the strategic dispersal of forces increased the points of contact between opposing forces and permitted a brilliant but inexperienced commander like Bonaparte to use a dispersed yet still unified army to concentrate and fight at first one point and then another. Bonaparte exhibited his control of the separated army when he recombined its parts on the battlefields of Castiglione and Marengo. Against Colli's Sardinians and Beaulieu's Austrians and again against Würmser and Quasdonovich he used interior lines to engage a higher proportion of his forces than the enemy's, to fight without his opponent's consent and not even necessarily at his enemy's convenience, and to concentrate on successive interior lines of operations in an area much smaller than the theater in which Frederick the Great had earlier exploited interior lines. Because battles took place on fields not carefully chosen for flank protection, the French could often capitalize on their greater numbers to envelop or turn their opponents.

Although his methods varied somewhat, Bonaparte's strategy in his two brilliant conquests of north Italy had not differed much from some of his predecessors'. In each case the commanders had the objective of conquering territory that would provide political, financial, and logistical advantages. Instead of an essentially logistical strategy of avoiding the enemy to pass a river barrier and then dominating the invaded territory from tactically and strategically strong positions, Bonaparte relied extensively on combat, meeting the enemy in small battles to push it back; much of his success rested on his ability to engage the enemy, and not always on the enemy's terms. This combat strategy and the offensive strength of the infantry and its new deployment made the French army effective in gaining victory with unprecedented speed. Yet the result—acquisition of north Italy and the desirable logistical and political consequences of this—differed little from that of the campaigns of Vendôme and Eugene.

Napoleonic Operations on a Larger Scale: The Strategic Turning Movement of Ulm and Distraction and Concentration at Austerlitz

In 1805 Bonaparte, by then Napoleon I, emperor of the French, applied these methods in Germany and secured unique results. Though he faced the armies of Austria and Russia in south Germany and the Austrians in Italy, he had no opposition elsewhere in Germany nor in the Netherlands. With Bavaria as an ally and armies comparable in size and quality to those of Louis XIV, Napoleon had 165,000 men at his disposal for a campaign aimed at forcing peace on Austria. With forces the size of those of Louis XIV and without his more numerous opponents, Napoleon could attempt a campaign which lay beyond both the strength and vision of the French king. A century of economic progress also aided Napoleon, as improved roads, expanded populations, and increased agricultural productivity helped supply his huge army. Further, French armies had far less baggage than their opponents, not having, for example, to carry the belongings of wealthy, aristocratic officers. In a later campaign against the Prussians, the French had only one-eighth as much baggage as their opponents. Thus the French had fewer horses to feed and also the ability to move faster because they cluttered the roads less. In this respect French supply resembled that of Alexander the Great.

Napoleon divided his field army, three times as large as he had managed before, into a number of small armies called corps. His theater of operations, from the Main to south of the Danube, had double the width of the Italian theater and, if he marched the 400 miles to Vienna, nearly triple the depth. In spite of planning to make his initial march though the productive and friendly parts of Germany, Napoleon also made careful, if incomplete, preparations to supply his huge force in territory unfamiliar to him. By moving in early fall he had the assurance of ample stocks from the recent harvest. One region of 15,000 to 16,000 people, for example, furnished his army with 127,500 pounds of bread, 24,000 pounds of salt, 3,600 bushels of hay, 6,000 sacks of oats, 5,000 pints of wine, 8,000 bushels of straw, and 100 four-horse wagons. The supply officers used a method for contributions called requisitions, in which they required deliveries but gave receipts, for which, in friendly territory, the French government paid; in hostile territory owners of the receipts could try to collect from their own government. With a country full of food and fodder to march through, a thoroughly overhauled supply organization, and plans for a wagon route of communications to bring ammunition and clothing from France, Napoleon had made as much provision for the support of his army as he could under the existing technology of transportation.[10]

The Austrians took the offensive in early September, when Archduke Ferdinand marched into Bavaria with 70,000 men, the Bavarian army avoiding combat by moving north to join the French. When the Austrians reached Ulm, they halted to await the arrival of their Russian ally, General Kutusov and his army; meanwhile they had provisioned their army from the resources of Bavaria. The Austrian command really belonged not to the archduke but to General Mack, who had guided the Prince of Coburg in his operations over a decade earlier. Mack, an able man who had risen from the ranks, underestimated by half the number of men Napoleon would have and also assumed that the French would march directly on Ulm.

Napoleon came with more men than this part of Germany had ever seen, a fact that alone altered the character of operations. In 1673, when Turenne and Montecuccoli had maneuvered along the Main, each commanded armies of less than 30,000 men, hardly more than geometrical points in the large area in which they campaigned. Although Marlborough and Eugene had 60,000 men and their opponents had the same number, their concentrated forces had difficulty dominating much of the territory in which they campaigned. On September 25 Napoleon advanced on a 100-mile front with seven corps, each comparable in size to the entire army of Turenne or Montecuccoli. All directed their marches north of Ulm.

As the French corps advanced, they drew closer together, aiming for the Danube east of Ulm, which placed them between the Austrians and their slowly advancing Russian allies as well as in the rear of Ferdinand and Mack's army at Ulm. By October 6 the French approached the river, and Mack had concentrated his men at his fortified position at Ulm. Well could Napoleon announce that his "unexpected and novel" moves had carried the army "several days march

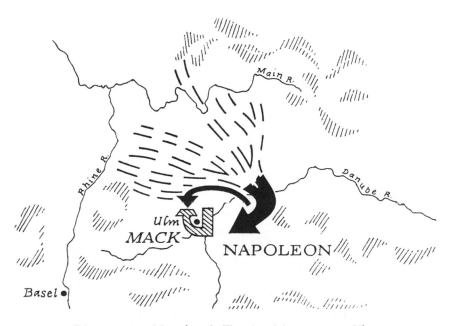

Diagram 6.7. Napoleon's Turning Movement at Ulm

into the rear of the enemy who has no time to lose if he is to avoid a complete disaster." When the French crossed to the south bank of the river at and east of Donauworth, Mack, at last clearly grasping his situation, planned to retreat by marching northeast from Ulm. But Napoleon assumed that Mack would emulate Melas and drive eastward, either directly or by veering southward. So the French emperor prepared for a battle east of Ulm and rushed virtually all of his troops south of the Danube, either to fight a battle or to try to prevent an Austrian retreat due south.[11]

The Austrians deliberated, delayed, and, encountering roads flooded by the Danube, only extricated one detachment by the northern route before Napoleon understood the situation and sent forces north of the Danube to block that exit. On October 20 Mack, the Archduke Ferdinand having fled, surrendered 27,000 men in Ulm; the French had a large number of prisoners already, and the Austrians had lost many men to desertion. The French army's official announcement of the victory claimed 60,000 prisoners for the campaign and concluded: "Never have victories been so complete and less costly." The young emperor, through his vast strategic turning movement, had inaugurated his empire auspiciously by essentially destroying the huge Austrian army. Yet Napoleon's execution did not match his brilliant conception when he acted on unfounded assumptions about what the enemy would do. Mack, too, performed badly, for at one point, when he learned the French troops were marching westward toward Ulm, he jumped to the conclusion that the French were retreating because they could not subsist in territory already foraged and denuded by the Austrians. But both men dealt with a situation virtually unique in war, its only modern precedent being Napoleon's Marengo campaign of 1800.[12]

Napoleon succeeded in a measure far greater than in the Marengo campaign because he had a numerical predominance of two to one and a ratio of force to space far higher than that in his comparable operation in Italy. These two factors very nearly assured his ability to prevent the retreat of the Austrians in any direction but westward, toward the French frontier, and made almost inevitable the Austrian defeat.

After organizing his supplies and dispatching detachments to control the region and deal with Austrians in the Alps, Napoleon began advancing eastward toward Vienna, his way barred by 40,000 Russians under Kutusov, a general whose excellent abilities had enabled him to profit from his more than forty years of experience. The Russians retreated rapidly, however, and soon the French occupied Vienna, finding the magazines of the Austrian capital bulging with weapons and food. The Russians continued their withdrawal northward into Moravia, where they met reinforcements and another Austrian force. The allies concentrated at Olmütz in Moravia, and Napoleon halted forty miles to the southwest at Brünn, where he again found fully stocked Austrian magazines.

Unable to feed 85,000 men for long around Olmütz, the allies advanced against Napoleon, trying to turn his right to cut him off from Vienna. In his dispositions west of the village of Austerlitz, Napoleon sought to reinforce the obvious allied intention to attack his right, adding to Russian overconfidence. To complete his distraction, he made his right look weak, the enemy being unaware of the planned presence well in the rear of the corps of the capable Marshal Davout, then making a hasty march to join the emperor. Even so, Napoleon had already concentrated his forces, the southern half of his line having far fewer men than the northern. Napoleon had prepared prudently to fight his first classical battle, and, standing on the defensive, he planned to make the most of his opponents' ineptitude and their obvious intention to overwhelm his right. He intended to use a powerful, preplanned counterattack against their center to inflict a crushing defeat. He succeeded in distracting them by tempting them to attack his right and had his men already concentrated in his center and on his left to assault their weak center. All depended on the ability of the skillful Davout to hold the right.

The combined allied army, under the command of the tsar of Russia, did not function well as a unit. The overconfident Russians patronized the recently defeated Austrians, and the tsar tended to ignore the advice of General Kutusov, the senior Russian general. The council of senior officers before the battle exemplified the state of the allied army: when an Austrian officer explained the tsar's plan, many officers present paid little attention, and Kutusov slept soundly. The allied command thus provided the perfect foil for Napoleon's maturing military genius. Even for a general like Napoleon to shine his brightest, inept opposition, of the kind the Romans supplied for Hannibal at Cannae, was essential.

The battle followed Napoleon's plan. Davout moved his corps up to resist the Russo-Austrian assault against the French right which began in a halting manner because of the difficulty of getting so many men moved forward and deployed on muddy, somewhat obstructed ground. As soon as the allies had thoroughly committed themselves in this effort and Davout began his successful resistance, Napoleon ordered his attack in the center. After overcoming stiff opposition, the French broke through and divided the allied army into three parts: the retreating center; their right, engaged in an inconclusive struggle with an equal number of French troops; and the large force attacking on their left. Napoleon then directed the bulk of his center against the flank and rear of the allied left just as Davout launched a vigorous thrust in front. Two large frozen ponds obstructed the flight of the disorganized allied troops, and the ice on one gave way under the weight of the fugitives and the fire of French artillery.

The Battle of Austerlitz, which occurred on December 2, 1805, the first anniversary of Napoleon's empire, proved both satisfactory and disappointing from a tactical standpoint. Of their 73,000 men the French lost about 9,000, the 12 percent long traditional for victors. The allies lost about 15,000 killed and wounded from their larger army, which, when added to 11,000 prisoners, equaled 30 percent of their forces. In spite of a disastrous defeat at the hands of a tactically superior army with a higher proportion of battle-seasoned troops and officers, the allies' 30 percent compared fairly favorably with the 22 percent

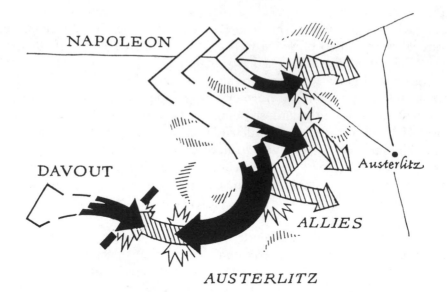

Diagram 6.8. Action at Austerlitz

for the losers of battles in the period 1702–63. Compared to Blenheim's over 60 percent loss, those at Austerlitz seem quite small. Better training, discipline, and articulation had made even the old-fashioned forces of Austria and Russia far more resilient in defeat than the bayonet-armed musketeers of a century before.

Nevertheless, the victory at Austerlitz had gratifying political results: the Austrian emperor promptly sued for peace. The tactical outcome of the battle had extended far beyond mere attrition, for the Russian and Austrian forces were now seriously disorganized and demoralized. The psychological impact of this serious defeat, which occured deep in the heart of his dominions, made the Austrian emperor pessimistic enough to concede defeat and make the territorial concessions that constituted Napoleon's price of peace. The tsar of Russia, vanquished in a foreign land and at some distance from his own borders, was in a situation quite different from his Austrian colleague and did not sue for peace.

The Austrians could have continued their resistance. Napoleon, having marched about 500 miles from the Rhine, had at Austerlitz less than half the force with which he had begun the campaign. The rest garrisoned the territory that he had captured and occupied positions to resist the other Austrian armies that still remained in the field. Now independent of the Russians, the Austrians remained a formidable opponent, if only because of the sheer expanse of their territory. Bohemia, Austrian Poland, and the vast domains of the Hungarian crown far exceeded the territory the French had subjugated. The French armies, though large in relation to southwestern Germany, were so small in comparison to the vast Austrian dominions that they could not dominate that much space in the absence of a political program appealing to the subjects of the Austrian emperor.

Unlike Darius III, the Emperor Francis commanded great loyalty from the subjects of his diverse empire, and the French program of political liberty and equality lacked appeal to a largely rural population. In addition, the French reputation for antipathy to religion created additional hostility against French rule. The Austrian emperor had too much political strength for Austerlitz to have the significance of Alexander's victory at Issus or Arbela. But Napoleon's comparatively modest political goals facilitated peace, and the enormous costs of a continued Austrian resistance far overbalanced the concessions that Napoleon demanded. As in the past, political leaders proportioned military means and political ends.

Some Characteristics of Napoleon's Campaigns

Napoleon's three victories over Austria reveal a tremendous variety of new and old operational characteristics. His approach to logistics differed little from that perfected in the eighteenth century, and he usually sought supplies through contributions, seeking to avoid the looting reminiscent of the Thirty Years' War and the early days of the republic. He depended less on magazines and supply from the rear because he had conducted few sieges. Not having to fight in the Netherlands relieved him of many sieges, and his willingness to bypass fortified points in Italy and Germany made them negligible there, too. Enough men to leave behind in garrisons facilitated this, and his ability to force battle on his opponents removed one of the traditional attractions of a seige—the opportunity to give a relieving army a strong incentive to fight on the besieger's terms.

The tactics of the battles continued the French revolutionary tradition of relying, with many variations, on the regulations of 1791. Maneuvering in a column twelve deep and fifty or sixty files broad, French battalions could rapidly deploy into reasonably well-aligned formations three deep. The battalions did not constitute a continuous line, but the firepower of the musket covered the gaps. Usually some battalions deployed in line while others remained in column ready to exploit weakness, reinforce success, or take advantage of a hole in the enemy's line by marching through, still in column formation. Variety characterized his tactics, but Napoleon preferred this and its spirit usually animated the dispositions of his subordinates.

Although the Austrians began gradually to adopt some of the French ideas, the tactics inspired by the regulations of 1791 gave the French better tactical mobility and the ability to make use of it by rapid deployment. In a sense they had a better weapon system. Just as Alexander's use of shock cavalry had given him a battle supremacy, so did the French tactical system give them a consistent advantage. They enjoyed this ascendency in spite of the preponderance of the excellent Austrian cavalry until Napoleon, like Frederick the Great earlier, improved the French horsemen after 1800.

The most striking feature of Napoleon's campaigns is the frequency of battles. Although the reduction of casualties in defeat should have made all commanders more willing to risk combat, this had done little to augment the numbers of battles in the eighteenth century. And no further reduction in casualties occurred during Napoleonic times to spur his increase in battles. The French possession of a better weapon system introduced a new factor that not only made them justifiably confident of the result of combat but also decreased the cost of replacing soldiers: their tactics reduced requirements for training. Although the French used an essentially linear system, only battalions needed proper alignment, musket fire covering gaps in the line. This smaller requirement for an exact linear array, together with much movement taking place in column, meant that soldiers needed less training in the drill necessary to enable many men to advance in linear deployment. In addition, since the French did not fight the traditional battle with continuous opposing fronts but used their mobility to concentrate against weakness or to envelop an enemy position, they did not depend so much on a more rapid rate of fire in a frontal fight with an opposing line. This meant that they could dispense with much musketry training. Replacements soon became fairly effective soldiers, especially if the new men did not greatly outnumber veterans in any battalion. Although as a proportion of population French armies under Napoleon did not exceed in size those of Louis XIV, conscription assured a continuous flow of men who needed comparatively little training. Further, French armies displayed more willingness than most of their opponents to draw on this source of manpower and could generally count on more patriotism and motivation from their conscripts than could their enemies.

But these factors explain only a small part of the change. Most important was the ability of an army dispersed in divisions to force combat. A dispersed army could turn strong positions, a maneuver long baffling to a well-concentrated force that had to fight as a unit. The French infantry's offensive attributes—marching rapidly and going into action quickly—compelled an opponent either to resist or to retreat to the rear. It was no longer possible to retreat sideways or, as Montecuccoli had done to Turenne, to march away past a flank. Now such a retreating army had to meet a division, which would soon be reinforced by the rest of its army.

Napoleon fought so many battles for a variety of reasons. With his genius and ability to inspire his men and his well-justified confidence in victory, he sought battle because he understood the value of the attrition inflicted by a victory and the political and psychological impact of a dramatic triumph in battle. Yet his battles always invariably had a significant strategic context.

In his initial campaign against the Sardinians and Austrians, he fought no major battle but used combat to place his army between his opponents and drive back first one and then the other. In his subsequent crossing of the Po and the Mincio rivers, he used the traditional method of distraction and crossing at the unexpected point that had long typified operations against the Italian river lines.

But his defense of his Mantua siege did not follow the usual pattern of the besieger's covering army standing ready on chosen ground to receive the attack of the relieving force. Instead, the Austrian system of advancing with two main columns in the expectation that one would get through threatened Bonaparte's rear but also presented Napoleon with the opportunity as well as the need to concentrate against each opponent in turn. This resulted in Würmser's receiving battle at Castiglione and Bonaparte's winning by attacking the Austrian left rear with a turning force. In each of the three succeeding Austrian efforts to relieve Mantua the pattern repeated itself, the divided Austrians always presenting an opportunity to exploit interior lines and, on one occasion, to attempt envelopment. In each instance Bonaparte drove back the enemy, finally securing the capitulation of Mantua and a garrison augmented by Field Marshal Würmser and part of his second relieving force.

On the strategic defensive covering his siege, Bonaparte had assumed the tactical offensive to counter the Austrians' method of relief and to exploit their division. The result of these operations, which extended over more than six months, proved very expensive for the Austrians. Their losses in battle and at Mantua far exceeded those of the French. Concentration on interior lines had as its objective the battles and the smaller conflicts not recorded as major battles. The French system of deployment from column to line and the divisional structure and articulation of French armies gave a major new importance to interior lines, forcing the enemy to fight or to retreat directly to the rear.

Napoleon's concentrations and successful combats had the strategic outcome of forcing the retreat of the relieving forces and the tactical result of attrition, which contributed a major share to the crippling cost of the relief efforts to the Austrians. By March 1797, with Mantua and its garrison in French hands, Bonaparte had the strength to assume the offensive into Austrian territory.

In the Marengo campaign battle also had an important part, and again Bonaparte reversed the usual correspondence between strategy and tactics. Whereas the strategic defense usually led to the tactical defense in battle, in defending his Mantua siege Bonaparte fought offensive battles. On the strategic offensive in Italy, he fought on the tactical defensive at Marengo: the Austrians had to fight their way back to their primary base area and line of communications with their homeland. The Battle of Marengo played a key role in blocking the Austrian retreat, and, though it did not result in capitulation, it did lead Austria to abandon most of northern Italy.

The same outcome occurred at Ulm, where most of the concentrated Austrian forces surrendered without a battle. The smaller battles from Napoleon's initial entry into Italy in 1796 to those around Ulm, like the battles from Castiglione to Marengo, all implemented and completed the strategic maneuvers that led to them. The fights, big and small, made the maneuvers possible, and the maneuvers gave strategic significance to these combats, many of which plucked the fruit made ripe by the marching which concentrated on interior lines or turned the enemy. The use of interior lines made battlefield success likely, and the subsequent victory forced the enemy back. The strategic turning movement forced the enemy to capitulate by cutting off its line of retreat; but the maneuver required a defensive battle if the enemy sought to retreat, as Melas did at Marengo. Without the strategic turning movement no battle would have occurred; without the battle, or the willingness to fight it in a position to block the enemy's retreat, the turning movement would have lost much of its import.

The ability to force battle, together with a better tactical system, which enhanced the likelihood of a French victory, gave an importance to interior lines and the strategic turning movement that they had lacked earlier. Used by Consul Nero against Hannibal and Hasdrubal, by Caesar against Pompey, by Prince Edward against the de Montforts, and Frederick against his encircling enemies, they had remained of little importance in warfare until the dispersed army and the ability to entangle an enemy in battle had suddenly made them important.

But Napoleon did not alter the fundamental strategic goals that had emerged from Gustavus's use of a persisting strategy. He aimed to capture enemy territory to support his army, to weaken his adversary, and to gain the leverage necessary to attain the political objectives of war. Although in the Ulm campaign he basically destroyed a major Austrian army, he could not have founded a strategy on consistently achieving such marked combat success. He had substituted a combat strategy based on maneuvers and battle for the logistic methods of his predecessors. He replaced the slow work of sieges with his new form of combat strategy. He superseded the distracton and bypassing of an enemy army, as exemplified by Vendôme and Eugene, to carry out the essentially logistic strategy of forcing back the foe by getting into and controlling an opponent's base area.

This earlier strategy did forecast the strategic turning movement used in the Marengo and Ulm campaigns. Marshal Vendôme had accomplished this maneuver against Prince Eugene, and the imperial commander had attacked to recover his base area. But the Ulm campaign most dramatically illustrated the difference, for Napoleon blocked the retreat and captured the Austrian army, something beyond the ability of Vendôme and his concentrated army. The old logistic strategy of bypassing the enemy could only force the enemy back by depriving him of supplies; the new combat strategy could capture his army since a broadly dispersed army could block the routes of withdrawal when the commander had a favorable ratio of force to space.

Napoleon, having brilliantly exhibited the potentialities of the new armies to implement the persisting strategy by a fundamentally new combat strategy, defeated Austria for the third time in a traditional battle at Austerlitz. He proved as brilliant at the conventional battle as he had in strategy, and the deep penetration of enemy territory resulting from his victory at Ulm made Austerlitz decisive for ending the war.

In some ways Napoleon's operations reflected a peculiar stage in the transformation of warfare. In contests between armies with the same weapon systems, the tactical defense always had had the advantage. Consequently, generals since the early sixteenth century were reluctant to fight offensive battles and had sought to exploit the primacy of the defense by attempting to trap an enemy against an obstacle, as Henry IV had almost succeeded in doing to Parma, or by forcing the enemy to attack to raise a siege. In strategy they often used logistics rather than combat to conquer an enemy's territory, avoiding an engagement under unfavorable tactical conditions.

Napoleon's use of the strategic turning movement at Marengo and Ulm introduced a novel method of forcing the enemy to assume the tactical offensive. Further, his offensive strategy, which employed the tactical defense, endowed the battle with a strategic importance that most contests could not have: the the enemy's retreat was blocked, just as the Seine had apparently foreclosed Parma's withdrawal. Victory on the tactical defense at Marengo thus had great strategic significance. The army, distributed in divisions but unified in action, had made this strategic turning movement possible, and the tactical strength of bayonet-armed musketeers had made commanders comfortable with a dispersion that invited attack by a cavalry excelling in mobility but weaker as a weapon system.

But Napoleon also effectively used the tactical offensive when he employed his interior lines to concentrate and attack an opponent who had often, as had Würmser at Castiglione, deployed himself for battle on his chosen ground. Napoleon could assume the tactical offensive because his army had a better ability to concentrate on the battlefield, and, with greater tactical mobility, French infantry could move and deploy rapidly enough to attack the enemy's flank or rear, the traditional preserve of cavalry.

Like Frederick the Great, Napoleon could afford to assume the tactical offensive. Frederick's and Napoleon's exploitation of interior lines augmented their numbers for a battle; to capitalize on it required an offensive battle unless the enemy obliged by attacking these augmented forces.

The Augmented Significance of Numerical Superiority

The size of armies was assuming greater importance in combat. In battles between Greek hoplites of equal strength, skill counted more than numbers. Only if both sides fought to the finish would the quantity of men tell. For example, a force of 10,000 would have at least 5,000 men remaining after killing or wounding all members of a force of 5,000. Through the sixteenth century and for some time after, skill continued to have more significance than quantity: fronts remained equal as generals carefully anchored their flanks on obstacles.

But the use of the musket and artillery gradually involved more men than the front rank alone, and when turning and enveloping movements extended battle lines, numbers became increasingly important. Not only could a larger army lengthen its front more readily, but it could easily bring more men into action. Thus on a discontinuous front or as a result of a movement against the flank, the greater force might engage two battalions against one.

A commander using his numerical superiority in this way attained an advantage that was more than proportional to his greater numbers. If all men of two forces, equal in skill but unequal in size, could fire at one another, each combatant would suffer losses proportional to the quantity of bullets received. Thus if force A had double the men of force B, B's would receive twice the bullets and have twice the casualties of A. If A had 2,000 and B 1,000 men and, in the first moment of the combat, A had lost 1 soldier, B would have lost 2. The ratio between the two forces would no longer be 2 to 1: A would have 1,999 and B 998, a ratio of 2 to 0.9985. A now would have relatively greater strength than at the beginning. As the battle progressed, A would gain relative strength until A annihilated B. If one followed this idea of F. W. Lanchester and used his differential equation to solve for the casualties, A would have losses not of 1,000 men, as in conventional shock action, but of only 268 men while at least one bullet would have hit all of B's soldiers.

Thus, when all men on both sides can fight with missiles, numerical superiority confers a disproportionate advantage, providing commanders can bring into action all men on each side. In fact, under these conditions, the fighting strength of forces is in proportion to the square of their strength: a force of 2,000 men is 4 times as powerful as the force of 1,000. This rule, which its originator, F. W. Lanchester, called the N-square law, assumes the same fighting value of the soldiers on both sides. If the fighting value differed, one would have to modify combat power by multiplying the squared strength by the combat value of the soldiers on each side. For example, if the soldiers in force B had twice the combat effectiveness of those in force A, their ratios would be 2 to 1, rather than 4 to 1 ($2,000^2$ or, 4,000,000, to $1,000^2$, or 1,000,000, x 2, or 2,000,000).

The same qualification applies with respect to combat between different weapon systems. Assume, for example, that force A consisted of Moslem horse archers and force B was Crusader crossbowmen, each equally brave and as skillful with their weapons. But since the men on foot, without the instability and distraction of managing mounts, had an advantage over mounted men, assume the crossbowmen had twice the effectiveness of the horse archers. Then force A would have only 2, rather than 4, times the combat value of force B ($2,000^2$, or 4,000,000, to $1,000^2$, or 1,000,000, x 2, or 2,000,000).

The N-square law also assumes that both forces are on the offensive. But between musketeers, for example, the men on the defensive have the advantage of maintaining continuous volleys without the interruption of the advance or concern with alignment. In addition, they may have cover, such as ditches and banks. Again one would have to modify the results of the N-square law by the augmented combat effectiveness conferred by fighting on the defensive under particular circumstances.[13]

In spite of the benefit of the defensive, the possession of more men had a magnified effect if a commander could fight so as to bring the additional men into action. Thus concentration of greater numbers, however achieved, could confer significant advantages. When combined with the unique tactical capabilities of French infantry and the benefits conferred by dispersal in divisions, Napoleon had opportunties on the tactical offensive unavailable to his opponents, even though French soldiers lacked the Austrian skill in volley firing. But since the Austrians enjoyed no such added strength on the tactical offensive, the French could exploit the traditional predominance of the defensive at Marengo while making the most of their offensive excellence at Castiglione and elsewhere. The French had the best of both worlds, and Napoleon's strategy made the most of it. The success that he enjoyed and his small losses indicate that he had not overlooked any easier path to victory. But his opponents began to adopt the French system, and by 1813 the French no longer had any advantage from their tactical methods, articulation, and dispersion in divisions.

Some Later Napoleonic Campaigns

Napoleon's later operations were consistent with his earlier campaigns. In 1806 he fought Prussia, pitting his well-led combat veterans against a force that had had no major battle experience in more than forty years and whose peacetime training had continued to stress the methods of Frederick the Great. He made the most of this advantage by a turning movement that placed his army on the Prussian flank and rear, and promptly attacked the enemy. Although the Prussians faced their attackers, French tactical primacy easily overwhelmed them. Napoleon followed up these twin victories at Jena and Auerstädt by a vigorous and unremitting strategic pursuit that overran a large part of Prussian territory and secured the capitulation of most of the demoralized Prussians' fortified points as well as their army. The huge French force soon dominated most of the small country's level terrain, including its most important and productive territory. Only the fortifications of Silesia and the troops in the distant provinces of Poland and East Prussia held out.

Napoleon then marched east against the Russians and the remains of the Prussian army. In a winter campaign in sparsely populated, nearly roadless Poland and East Prussia, Napoleon, sometimes confused by erratic Russian moves, pushed the elusive enemy back 150 miles until its commander chose a defensive battle over retreat and deployed for combat at Eylau. Here Napoleon, with inferior numbers, attempted to unite his forces on the battlefield to attack the Russian flank and rear. He failed to reach the Russian rear but won instead an essentially frontal battle with the traditionally obstinate Russians; each side lost about 30 percent of their forces. After a four-month interlude for winter quarters, rest, and resupply, Napoleon resumed the campaign. When again the Russians decided to fight rather than retreat, he had more success at Friedland, where in another fundamentally frontal battle his formidable army inflicted over 30 percent casualties on the ineptly commanded and badly positioned Russian army at a cost of less than 14 percent casualties in the French army.

As a result of these victories Napoleon overran the remainder of Prussian territory, but more than 1,000 miles from the Rhine, he had just reached the Russian frontier. The tsar, however, made peace, its modest cost only forcing him to sacrifice his goal of succoring the Prussians.

In April 1809 Napoleon faced war with a formidable Austrian army, part of whose strength lay in its sagacious commander, the Archduke Charles. The archduke, an epileptic, had by age thirty-seven demonstrated a profound mastery of strategy and tactics and garnered much prestige by his victories over French generals. But he had yet to meet Napoleon. He could approach this daunting task with confidence born of his accomplishments, his more than a decade of service in high commands, and the reformation, though yet incomplete, of the Austrian army, which he had guided.

Conscious that the Austrians might advance at any time, Napoleon remained in Paris, keeping in touch with his army headquarters in Germany through a significant innovation, the Chappe telegraph, installed in France fifteen years earlier. The Chappe telegraph consisted of a line of signal stations within sight of each other, the stations able to relay a message on a clear day at a top speed of 600 miles an hour. When the Archduke Charles suddenly advanced with 200,000 Austrians, Napoleon learned about it promptly, the message traveling the 700 miles from Ratisbon to Paris in twenty-four hours. Until he arrived to take personal command, Napoleon used the telegraph to direct his dispositions, though a storm so impaired visibility that it delayed a crucial telegraphic order.

When the Austrian army advanced along the Danube with six corps south of the river and two on the north bank, the Archduke Charles looked for opportunities to exploit the dispersion in winter quarters of the French army of 170,000 men. He saw his chance and directed one corps on the north of the river and five on the south against the incomparable Marshal Davout, whose corps occupied a forward position at Ratisbon. With two Austrian corps to the west to delay the movement of the French on both sides of the river, the archduke planned to use his five corps south of the river quickly to crush Davout and his one corps north of the river to prevent the French retreat. But Napoleon moved forward rapidly, split the Austrian forces in half, and drove part south and part over the Danube into Bohemia. Again Napoleon had divided his opponent and driven his wings in opposite directions.

As this operation drew to a close, the buoyant emperor, on passing a regiment of infantry, stopped and asked the colonel if he could see the bravest soldier in the unit. When the colonel introduced the man, a bandsman, the Emperor said to him: "I hear that you are the bravest man in this regiment. I appoint you a knight of the Legion of Honor, Baron of the Empire, and award you a pension of 4,000 francs." Such a gesture, including the raising of an enlisted man to a peerage, had, as the story traveled around the army, a profoundly favorable effect on the morale of the rank and file.[14]

Napoleon pursued the retreating Austrians, but when he reached Vienna, he had a protracted struggle marked by two battles before he succeeded in driving the Archduke Charles from the north bank of the river. He again imposed peace on Austria, subtracting 30,000 square miles from the shrinking Austrian Empire.

In 1812 Napoleon invaded Russia. He advanced with over 400,000 French and allied troops and made elaborate supply arrangements to cope with his large force in a thinly populated country. In three months he marched 600 miles from Poland to Moscow, the Russians retreating before him and to his flanks. The Russians fought twice, losing two frontal battles. Occupying the traditionally important Russian city of Moscow in mid-September, the French emperor then made peace overtures to the tsar of Russia.

The tsar displayed no more interest in peace than had French kings harassed by English raids during the Hundred Years' War. Though Napoleon had larger forces in proportion to the size of European Russia than the English in proportion to France, French forces in Russia still could do little more than garrison points on the route over which they advanced. The huge French army had no more effect on most of Russia than the English had in France, and it and its less systematic depredations made the soldiers just as unpopular in Russia as English looting had been in France. Though Napoleon's raid provoked Russian resistance in battle just as had English raids, the tsar displayed the same determination not to concede anything to a raiding strategy as had the French kings of the fourteenth century.

Napoleon, failing to grasp that he had made a raid that had failed, lingered a month in Moscow before beginning to march his army back to Poland in the third week of October. Like the Prince of Wales's raiders marching back toward Poitiers in 1356, Napoleon's army, also heavily laden with booty, moved slowly, the Russians harassing their march. Unlike the Prince of Wales, Napoleon lacked a balmy September climate and the fertile and well-populated French countryside upon which to forage. In addition, on much of the withdrawal the French armies marched over territory they had foraged on their advance. The management and the contents of the supply depots on their retreat also disappointed the French. Just as the French king caught the Prince of Wales at Poitiers, so the Russians caught the retreating French, almost preventing their crossing of the Beresina River.

Such raids as Napoleon's and those of the Hundred Years' War usually cost the raiders many stragglers. In their biggest raid in France, the English marched 1,000 miles in five months and lost half of their army; in Russia the French marched over twice as far, faced better organized opposition, and had to contend with cold weather and the barren Russian countryside. Their losses, variously estimated, far exceeded half of those involved in the campaign, including many French veterans.

This defeat brought Russia and Prussia into the war against France in 1813. With a new army of green troops, Napoleon displayed his usual abilities when he maneuvered a dispersed force of over 100,000 men between Dresden and Magdeburg. He drove back the Russians and Prussians from the Elbe into Silesia, winning two major battles in the process.

After a truce in June and July 1813 the allies, now joined by Austria, disposed three large armies under talented commanders. In the north around Berlin the capable Bernadotte, former French marshal and Crown Prince of Sweden, commanded about 100,000 men. To the east in Silesia the elderly Prussian Field Marshal Blücher had almost as many. The old cavalryman's mind had weakened: he sometimes walked on tiptoe because he thought French spies had heated the floor, and often he imagined himself pregnant with an elephant. But he possessed the invaluable assets of unremitting energy, physical and moral courage, the power of making firm decisions, and a harmonious relation with Gneisenau, his extraordinarily competent chief of staff.

To the south in Bohemia, Archduke Charles having retired, the Austrian command went to the astute young soldier-diplomat, Field Marshal Prince Schwarzenberg. Ironically, Schwarzenberg, who led 240,000 men, partly owed his elevation to the favorable impression he had made on Napoleon while on a mission to Paris. The Austrian commander also exercised control over all allied forces. But the tsar of Russia, the emperor of Austria, the king of Prussia, and two famous military experts accompanied Schwarzenberg, and the monarchs determined his decisions. Weaknesses in his own staff and the cluster of rulers and favorites caused even the diplomatic Schwarzenberg to lament, "It really is inhuman what I must tolerate and bear, surrounded as I am by feeble-minded people, eccentric projectors, intriguers, asses, babblers, and niggling critics."[15]

The allies did, however, make a plan designed to deal with Napoleon's use of interior lines. If Napoleon concentrated against any of the three armies, that force would retreat and avoid battle while the other two advanced. Thus in the area where Frederick had made the most of his interior lines in 1758, the allies would avoid combat and wear out the French with marching while they concentrated in time by gradually closing in until their three armies came near enough to each other to provide mutual support. Though the commanders properly stood in awe of Napoleon's military genius, many of their rank and file had better training and more combat experience than Napoleon's raw troops, and all allied armies had adopted French tactical and strategic doctrine, the Austrian and Prussian units having the tactical capabilities that had long distinguished the French armies. Against the formidable force of 450,000 men Napoleon had about 300,000.

When Field Marshal Blücher began the campaign by marching west, Napoleon, seeing that the forces in Bohemia would concentrate slowly, advanced to drive back Blücher before turning against Schwarzenberg. On the approach of Napoleon with augmented forces, Blücher followed the allied plan, avoided battle, and withdrew hastily to the east while Schwarzenberg emerged from Bohemia and threatened Dresden. Napoleon quickly moved troops westward toward Dresden, one body of men marching 120 miles in four days. He concentrated 100,000 men in the defense of Dresden in time to repel the attack of 200,000 allied troops and to defeat them in battle, inflicting 30,000 casualties to 10,000 for his forces. But in his pursuit of the retreating allies, he lost 19,000 men to only 11,000 for the allies on their march back into Bohemia. And this small victory at the end of defeat at the hands of the dreaded Napoleon raised the spirits of the allied leaders, changing, according to a Russian officer, into "a cry of joy the despair which was spreading through the valleys of Bohemia."[16]

Meanwhile, Blücher had invaded Silesia again, defeating the weakened French in engagements fought in such a continuous downpour of rain that many muskets would not fire. Yet since Bernadotte's tentative advance in the north presented an opportunity, Napoleon planned to concentrate against the northern army, drive it back, and take Berlin. But Blücher continued his advance, and Napoleon personally moved reinforcements against him while the exceptionally brave but frequently inept Marshal Ney marched north against Bernadotte. In a badly bungled battle, Ney suffered defeat against Bernadotte, and Blücher promptly retreated before Napoleon while the allied army of Bohemia again threatened Dresden. When Napoleon returned to Dresden, the allies withdrew again through the mountains into Bohemia.

After over a month of marching back and forth, Napoleon decided to withdraw westward to Leipzig, which would provide him with a better central position, if only because it lay farther from the refuge that the Bohemian mountains gave the allied army. At this time the allies received a reinforcement of 50,000 Russians who moved to Bohemia while Blücher marched northwest to reinforce Bernadotte. The allies now had only two forces on exterior lines, 180 degrees apart.

As he fell back to Leipzig, Napoleon sent reinforcements to Ney, directing them toward the eastern flank and rear of Bernadotte's and Blücher's forces. To counteract this menace, Bernadotte and Blücher retreated west instead of east, and by early October Blücher had begun to advance south on a line directed somewhat west of Leipzig. With French forces in their rear, Blücher and Bernadotte moved so that they threatened to place themselves in the French rear. In spite of the great size of the armies, the recent harvest provided ample supplies, though the incredibly active campaign allowed little leisure for gathering food or baking bread.

While Napoleon had directed his attention north, Schwarzenberg had emerged from Bohemia, advanced northward and had begun to threaten Leipzig from the south. But when Napoleon turned south to drive back the army of Bohemia, Blücher, followed by Bernadotte, pushed toward Leipzig. By October 16 Blücher and Schwarzenberg, though north and south of Leipzig, had drawn close enough together to support one another. In the Battle of Leipzig that followed, the allies defeated Napoleon, losing 80,000 of their 325,000; he, 60,000 of his 175,000.

The allied plan had worked because their armies in the north and east had ample space in which to retreat directly to their rear and the Bohemian mountains had provided an effective refuge for Schwarzenberg's army. Under these conditions the allies could avoid battle while gradually closing a ring around Napoleon. Except at Dresden, where they fought on the defensive with a two to one numerical superiority, they had avoided fighting Napoleon himself and had won the battles in which, with greater strength, they had met his subordinates. The exploitation of interior lines had depended on the ability to compel an unwilling enemy to fight, something not possible when the reluctant enemy had ample space directly in their rear and the other forces on exterior lines moved promptly and effectively against the diminished forces opposed to them. By coordinating their movements the allies had concentrated in time and effectively counterbalanced Napoleon's concentrations in space, simultaneous or cooperating movements counteracting concentrations on interior lines.

Operations in Spain: The French Encounter the Raiding Strategy of Guerrilla Warfare

Except for conducting a raid into Russia, Napoleon had used only a persisting strategy as had all of his opponents except the Spanish. Napoleon conquered Portugal in 1807 and in 1808 had deposed the Spanish king and placed his brother Joseph Bonaparte on the throne of Spain. But Napoleon had not reckoned on hostility in Spain, which had few urban merchants to whom liberty and equality appealed, many devout Catholics who detested the French reputation for atheisim, and a people attached to its monarchy and institutions. Looting by the undisciplined French conscripts completed the alienation of the Spanish.

The French situation resembled that of Hannibal's in Italy. The French could beat Spanish regulars almost as easily as they could the untrained and undisciplined forces raised by local Spanish authorities. Initially with 100,000 men, the French had perhaps quadruple Hannibal's force, but the Iberian Pennisula had at least four times the area of the part of Italy that Hannibal had sought to control. Though the Spaniards lacked effectively fortified cities and a well-drilled militia, much of their country had rugged mountains and agricultural productivity was very low. The French had difficulty feeding their troops, and instead of meeting a fortified urban defiance, they met an elusive rural resistance in which their opponents waged a guerrilla war of raids.

The Spanish, whether on foot or mounted, had the same fundamental weapon systems as the French and could thus rely in their raids on the primacy of retreat over pursuit when both combatants had the same weapon systems. Whereas against Hannibal the Romans, though they had used withdrawal to avoid battle, had made extensive use of the defense's preponderance against frontal attack, especially when aided by fortifications, the Spaniards, overmatched by the French even when on the defensive, relied almost exclusively on retreat.

The French applied a combat strategy when they pursued Spanish raiders but found them too elusive. With the sympathy of the inhabitants, the Spanish soldiers had good intelligence of French movements and could readily avoid the French troops sent against them. If necessary, Spanish guerrillas could amplify their power of withdrawal by dispersal or even by becoming indistinguishable from the civilian population. A French general described his frustration with such elusive opponents: "Hardly forty-eight hours after the enemy has been driven away he reappears and seeks to maintain a small war without result for us, but, on the contrary, of enormous advantage for him by enhancing the hopes of the blind mountain inhabitants."[17]

The same people, "blind" to the advantages of French rule, provided the warning of the coming of the French, supplied the intelligence that enabled the partisans to concentrate against small French detachments and posts and weakly guarded convoys and magazines. The French, on the other hand, followed a persisting strategy, garrisoning cities and communication focal points. But they lacked the strength to interdict the movements of the Spanish raiders, having far too low a ratio of force to space to dominate the country.

The French aggravated their problems not only by living on the country but often by allowing their men to forage for themselves, as soldiers had done in the Thirty Years' War. A French general complained that an "operation that was to exterminate" a band of partisans had failed, leaving the guerrillas "strengthened by the infuriated inhabitants who have had to leave their homes owing to the pillage which the troops have committed." So French waste, destructiveness, and brutality further alienated the peasantry and engendered more support for the guerrillas, who also had to live at the expense of the countryside. With methods often as irregular and sometimes as brutal as those of the French, the Spanish partisans would have sacrificed much more of their support had the French not first begun this method of dealing with the people. Moreover, the French artocities of rape, murder, and burning villages in retaliation for aid to the rebels alienated more Spaniards than did the guerrillas' more systematic and reasoned retribution against individual collaborators with the French. Still this unhappy position between the adversaries drove many peasants to desperation and violence against both oppressors.[18]

The war had a savage character as each combatant retaliated against the other. The French, facing opponents without uniforms, often treated guerrillas as beyond the application of the laws of war, killing their prisoners. The Spaniards replied in kind, one partisan chieftain, for instance, routinely cutting off one ear of a French prisoner prior to interrogating him.

Through many hard lessons of defeat in skirmishes with the French, the guerrillas learned the strategy appropriate to the kind of war they waged. Operating in small bands, they preyed upon messengers, small detachments, supply wagons, and lightly guarded towns and supply convoys. Taking advantage of their knowledge of the terrain, they had learned how to avoid the pursuing forces aroused by their raids. They compelled the invaders to erect field fortifications at all the unfortified points they held and eventually to provide escorts as large as 300 men, infantry as well as cavalry, for messengers carrying important dispatches or official mail. Their activities proved such a menace that at one point the French devoted as many as 90,000 of the approximately 230,000 troops then in the country to guarding against raids.

In addition to their mastery of the raiding strategy of guerrilla warfare, the Spanish received support from the British intervention in Portugal and Spain. A well-appointed, adequately supplied, and brilliantly led British army augmented the Portuguese and Spanish armies and compelled the French to increase their forces in Spain and devote a high proportion of them to a combat persisting campaign against the Anglo-Portuguese-Spanish armies. Further, the British assisted the partisans with weapons, supplies, and money, invaluable supports for their morale as well as their operations.

When a British force campaigned with guerrillas early in the war, a British officer had a lesson in their strategy after he witnessed sixteen French cavalrymen charge 400 mounted partisans and saw the Spaniards flee so precipitously that in their rush to the rear they drove a small British detachment off the road. The British cavalry having driven off the French, the Spanish commander explained his kind of warfare to the amazed and angry British officer. Spanish strategy, the guerrilla leader explained, did not contemplate making countercharges against French cavalry, trained and prepared for such combat; rather, his men had the mission of harrying the French and interrupting their supplies. Thus the Spaniards had learned the appropriate strategy but remained pathetically but quite wisely wary of meeting the French in combat. In time their tactical skill would match their mastery of strategy.[19]

The British had at first disparaged the heterogeniety of the weapons and clothing of their allies as well as their lack of the drill and discipline appropriate for the line infantry and cavalry of the British army. But at length they discerned that the Spaniards had developed a discipline and organization exactly adapted to their frequent use of light infantry and light cavalry tactics and their strategy that required quick advances on raids and elusiveness in retreat.

The French enjoyed their greatest success in dealing with guerrilla resistance in the northeastern Spanish province of Aragon. Here the defeat of the conventional forces in a prolonged siege and then a battle so discouraged the people of the province that the French commander, the astute General Suchet, could secure the cooperation of many of the aristocracy in ruling the country. Disheartened opposition and inept guerrillas, few in number, enabled Suchet to pacify the country by the beginning of 1810, though he still faced a passively hostile people.

Suchet had suppressed the guerrillas in his command by relentless activity. He began one sequence of movements in July 1809 by sending two regiments against the base of 3,000 partisans. After they retreated, the French burned their supplies and then fanned out to dominate the country. When a regiment reached the town of Calatayud, it found that the guerrillas had captured the officials the French had installed there in April. Yet, as soon as the French again left the city, the Spaniards returned and removed the newly appointed French officials. In early August the French came back to take Calatayud again, after a combat in which they inflicted over 100 casualties on the guerrillas. Subsequently Suchet's soldiers once more departed and the partisan chief returned, overwhelmed a small post nearby, and began to recruit his force. This prompted the French to send two columns from different directions, which failed to trap the Spaniards as they evacuated. The French then decided to garrison this town.

Such constant marching, sometimes at a rapid pace in an effort to surprise their opponents, caused significant French casualties from stragglers, probably more than from combat with their evasive, tactically inadept, and usually numerically inferior opponents. But the guerrillas suffered equally, and, deprived of a secure base area by the sweeps of the French columns, most withdrew to an area beyond Suchet's jurisdiction.

In December 1809 the commander in neighboring Navarre cooperated with Suchet in a campaign to send three converging columns, amounting to three battalions, to trap a guerrilla band. One column scattered 150 partisans en route, but the main hostile force eluded the concentric advances, leaving behind recriminations between the French commanders. In the next month, however, a new effort, with triple the force and using six columns to comb one area, eradicated the guerrillas. This high ratio of force to space had not achieved the capture of many Spaniards but did compel the guerrillas to disperse completely. It would require a long time before they could reorganize and again threaten the French occupation.

Thus French strength and energy subdued most of the guerrilla opposition. Suchet garrisoned the country, holding cities or fortified convents, usually with a force of 100 men or less. This plan provided the French with a post for every 500 square miles of Aragon, compared with one English castle for each 100 square miles in a newly conquered region of Wales. Nevertheless, this system worked well, even though it did not block many of the routes of communication; the posts controlled the adjacent country and provided bases for French columns that swept the country to search for guerrillas or collect taxes in money and supplies. But when Suchet left Aragon to campaign in a neighboring province, he had to halve the garrison, usually leaving at least 10,000 men.

These interludes provided an opportunity for the guerrillas to revive their activities. During these periods of reduced strength in 1810 a partisan chief engaged in an unsuccessful siege of a town, destroyed a detachment of 160 troops, and took 170 prisoners when he overwhelmed another small force. Later, guerrillas failed in attacks on a town and on a convoy escorted by only eighty men but captured a garrison of fifty-four soldiers and bested an escort of over 300 men to capture a convoy. Then partisans defeated a battalion of green troops marching to join their veteran regiments and captured more convoys. Another band defeated a tax-collection detachment, enriching themselves and impoverishing the French by the capture of 8,000 sheep. These samples of guerrilla activities all occurred during the three intervals in 1810 when Suchet had had to reduce his garrison to support campaigns elsewhere.

After they returned, the French troops took the offensive and harried the partisans, often eliminating whole bands, in one instance capturing the leader, or driving them entirely out of Aragon. When the partisans fought the French, as they sometimes did, they rarely had much success, one experienced leader losing a defensive battle when he outnumbered the French two to one. But the guerrillas usually proved elusive; on two occasions, when converging French columns seemed to doom the band of the important partisan leader Mina, the Spanish chieftain dispersed his men into small groups, which evaded the relatively concentrated French forces.

So the French controlled Aragon fairly well, alternating between the offensive and defensive strategies, depending on their troop strength in the province. This pattern had the disadvantage of providing only sporadic control in some areas. And after the French withdrew, the guerrillas would frequently return, reestablish their authority, and take vengeance on officials who had sworn loyalty to the French. On one occasion when the partisans captured a town mayor whom they deemed especially devoted to the French, they burned him alive. Yet these sweeps of the country did disrupt the guerrillas' base and facilitate the collection of the taxes and supplies needed to support the French army in Aragon and its campaigns in neighboring provinces.

In September 1811 Suchet had reduced his forces in Aragon to 7,400 men in order to have the largest possible force for a campaign to conquer Valencia. At this moment a force of 6,000 guerrillas entered Aragon from the south and besieged the town of Calatayud, held by 800 green men and convalescents. While 3,000 partisans prosecuted the siege, driving the garrison into a fortified convent, another 3,000 partisans occupied a pass and defeated the attack of a force of 900 trying to get through to relive the town. When a mine breached the wall of the convent, the garrison surrendered. The next day a second and larger relieving force arrived and found that the guerrillas and their prisoners had departed.

Meantime, the partisan chief Mina had invaded northern Aragon from Navarre on the west, overwhelmed a post held by 100 men, besieged another, assailed a relief force of 1,000 men on the march, and, having killed 200 and wounded 271, accepted its surrender. He then went on to occupy the second largest city in Aragon when the garrison evacuated on his approach, and levied a substantial contribution on the city before returning westward, evading two large pursuing columns in the process. These events, together with the loss of more posts and two indecisive battles between guerrillas and substantial French columns, demonstrated the high level of tactical skill the partisans had attained after three years of campaigning.

These events inspired Napoleon to create a special army, intended at 36,000 men but much smaller in fact, to extirpate the partisans in northeastern Spain in one quick campaign. This French operation in the winter and spring of 1812 collided with a renewed guerrilla offensive supported by the no longer passive people of Aragon; the partisan successes had given them hope. The French attained one major victory when they crushed one of the bands that had taken Calatayud in 1811, taking over 1,100 prisoners. Otherwise the French encountered a series of reverses. Mina concentrated against one of two columns pursuing him and defeated it decisively, capturing all of its artillery; a month later Mina attacked three battalions on the march, defeated them, and compelled them to retreat. An effort to capture another partisan chief with four converging columns ended with the defeat of French detachments ranging in size from 105 to an entire battalion; this chietain then departed because of the difficulty of continuing his operations with the burden of 1,000 prisoners. The French suffered another kind of loss when guerrillas captured a convoy with 3,000 pairs of shoes, 2,000 shirts, and 80,000 francs. That the officials of one city invited the garrison officers to a banquet so that the partisans could take the town easily and capture the officers and garrison shows the degree of weakness in the French political position. Further, Spanish forces had the effrontery to conduct a raid into France, defeat a French battalion, levy contributions on two towns, and return to Spain driving a herd of 2,000 cattle and sheep.

The setbacks of the spring of 1812 established the pattern for the decline in French control in Aragon. With the Russian campaign beginning, Napoleon had no troops available to increase the ratio of force to space in Spain and the guerrillas adroitly exploited the weakness of the French defensive position. Some of their raids helped them as well as hurt the French as when they captured convoys or in the case where partisans entered a town where the French had siege artillery stored in the bull ring, spiked nineteen guns, and made off with six howitzers and some horses. Ultimately the guerrillas outnumbered the French more than two to one and matched them in tactical mastery except in battles where the French could make use of their better understanding of the employment of cavalry and artillery. That the French lost 3,400 men in the first ten months of 1812 testifies to Spanish skill and the attrition of many small and a few large defeats.

The French strongholds that helped them hold the country when they had superior strength became a liability when they found themselves continuously on the defensive. The posts consumed many men in small garrisons that frequently had too little strength to venture outside their walls to attempt to control the surrounding country. Thus, many French forces lost their mobility while the partisan forces had ample freedom of movement to concentrate against inviting targets; the small posts had lost much of their defensive strength once the Spaniards had learned the siege technique of mining or had acquired artillery. Nevertheless, the fortified defense still showed its traditional power. For example, a force of 700 guerrillas failed to capture a walled fort held by twenty-two determined men. Daunted by the walls, the Spaniards spent three days digging a mine that breached the wall; yet when the attackers could not get through in spite of sustaining thirty casualties, they abandoned the siege. But not all French garrisons displayed such fortitude.

Often the French relieved a besieged fort only to use the occasion to withdraw the garrison from its exposed position and abandon the post. This accelerated the process of turning Aragon over to the Spaniards, who dominated the area around weak garrisons and had undisputed control in areas the French had evacuated. In regions where the French were strong, the partisans took the peasants' animals so that they could not transport the tax in grain to French depots. In areas where the French were weaker, the peasants fled with their valuables on the approach of a tax-collecting column. The guerrillas also taxed the peasants they controlled but at a lower rate than the French.

So gradually the French base area shrank and that of the guerrillas expanded, the partisan forces increasing in proportion to the extension of their base. The process had something in common with the French offensive at the end of the Hundred Years' War when the French slowly captured the cities and castles of northern France and drove out the numerically weak but defensively strong English. By the spring of 1813 the Spaniards controlled over half of the ad-ministrative districts in Aragon, and the French could do little more than try to keep open their communication routes. At this point Napoleon ordered another campaign against the guerrillas, using troops that he planned later to deploy against the British. The emperor entrusted the campaign to General Clausel, a talented officer inexperienced in dealing with guerrillas. The general directed a major effort against Mina who had begun Clausel's operation by wrecking two French battalions, netting 1,000 prisoners. Faced with Clausel's offensive, Mina, divided his forces and the French general directed his troops against one of these in two columns. One came up with Mina, fought a costly battle, and induced Mina to retreat by dispersing his force. Although Clausel believed this battle "decided nothing," he sent the optimistic report to his superior that he had defeated Mina, a type of reporting also characteristic of Suchet. Thus ended the last campaign against the guerrillas; the French soon evacuated Aragon after the British defeated their army and came close to the French frontier.

Though many partisan chiefs were Spanish regular officers, Mina, the most celebrated leader, was in many respects representative of the commanders who wrested control of so much of Spain from the French occupation forces and the feeble government of King Joseph. A young farmer when the French invaded, Mina became an exemplary organizer and strategist. In two years he asserted that he had engaged in 143 combats, taken fourteen fortified posts, and captured 14,000 prisoners, the latter indicating conduct toward his enemies more humane than most of his fellow guerrilla leaders. He excelled in his ability to concentrate quickly for a raid and retreat rapidly, even, as he had shown against overwhelming forces, by scattering his men whom he had well enough organized and disciplined that he could reassemble them when safe to do so. Like the other Spanish commanders, he made good use of the rugged terrain of Navarre and northern Aragon to evade his opponents.

The thorough Mina so organized the countryside he controlled that he had his own gunpowder manufactures. Ultimately he so completely interdicted com-munications through the territory he dominated in northern Spain that he sold passes to merchants and others who wished to use the roads. This revenue enabled him to pay his men, which, in turn, helped him confine his depredations solely to the French. This policy complemented the firm rule based on his army and conserved his political position with the people by diminishing the burdens which the war placed on the small farmer who provided his most reliable supporters. Eventually he could clothe his men in captured French uniforms and meet many of his other needs through a trade with the occupiers carried on through intermediaries. Eventually he so organized some of the routes from France into Spain that he confiscated only war materiel, allowing other goods to pass—after he was paid a tariff.

So the skill and tenacity of the Spanish guerrillas played a major part in defeating the French efforts to control Spain. The French had met such resistance elsewhere, but never on such a scale nor prosecuted so unremittingly. Antoine Henri Jomini, an officer who served with the French in Spain and who was a renowned interpreter of the warfare of Napoleon and Frederick the Great, commented on the difficulties the French encountered.

The invader has only an army: his adversaries have an army, and a people wholly or almost wholly in arms, and making means of resistance out of every thing, each individual of whom conspires against the common enemy; even the noncombatants have an interest in his ruin and accelerate it by every means in their power. He holds scarcely any ground but that upon which he encamps; outside the limits of his camp every thing is hostile and multiples a thousandfold the difficulties he meets at every step.

These obstacles become almost insurmountable when the country is difficult. Each armed inhabitant knows the smallest paths and their connections; he finds everywhere a relative or friend who aids him; the commanders also know the country, and learning immediately the slightest movement on the part of the invader, can adopt the best measures to defeat his projects; while the latter, without information of their movements, and not in a condition to send out detachments to gain it, having no resource but in his bayonets, and certain safety only in the concentration of his columns, is like a blind man: his combinations are failures; and when, after the most carefully-concerted movements and the most rapid and fatiguing marches, he thinks he is about to accomplish his aim and deal a terrible blow, he finds no signs of the enemy but his campfires: so that while, like Don Quixote, he is attacking windmills, his adversary is on his line of communications, destroys the detachments left to guard it, surprises his convoys, his depots, and carries on a war so disastrous for the invader that he must inevitably yield after a time.

Jomini then illustrated the ubiquity and dexterity of guerrillas. He had camped the companies of an artillery train "in the midst of four brigades distant from the camp from two to three leagues, and no Spanish forces had been seen within fifty miles. . . . nevertheless," he continued, "one fine night the companies of the train—men and horses—disappeared, and we were never able to discover what became of them: a solitary wounded corporal escaped to report that the peasants, led by their monks and priests, had thus made away with them." The war, he wrote, "presented a thousand incidents as striking as this. All the gold in Mexico could not have procured reliable information for the French; what was given was but a lure to make them fall more readily into snares."

He prescribed an adequate ratio of force to space and a persisting strategy as the means of victory in such a war. "No army, however disciplined, can contend successfully against such a system applied to a great nation, unless it be strong enough to hold all the essential points of the country, cover its communications, and at the same time furnish an active force sufficient to beat the enemy wherever he may present himself."

Having thus described military means similar to those employed by Alexander the Great in Bactria and Sogdiana, Jomini turned to the political component in such a struggle, which Alexander had exploited with success by his marriage to Roxana, a local princess. Since Napoleon, having replaced the Spanish king with his brother, had no such resources, Jomini looked to the local level. "If success be possible in such a war, the following general course will be most likely to insure it—viz.: make a display of a mass of troops proportioned to the obstacles and resistance likely to be encountered, calm the popular passions in every possible way, exhaust them by time and patience, display courtesy, gentleness, and severity united, and, particularly, deal justly."

Most French commanders relied on ruthless severity and even terror, which sometimes intimidated the Spaniards but did not quench their hostility. From Suchet's regime in Aragon, Jomini drew his political prescription for dealing with guerrillas. Suchet, not exemplary in his use of military means against guerrillas, showed his ability in his political measures. Fortunate in beginning his rule with 20,000 men available for seven months to crush only an incipient resistance by inept partisans, he could then proceed to conciliate the Spaniards. He then shrewdly placated much opposition by attracting prominent men to his administration, ruling through the existing lower officials, doing much to mollify the church, and curbing erratic and brutal behavior by his soldiers. He left the peasants alone if they paid their taxes and did not actively resist. The general realistically sought only acquiescence and applied force vigorously against those who opposed the French, for example, routinely executing priests found armed. His policy succeeded as long as he had adequate force and did not have to cope with invasions of guerrillas from neighboring provinces not as effectively subdued as his. His inability to recruit more than 400 men into a Spanish military force he established to aid the French indicates his failure to make foreign rule popular. Suchet might well have had somewhat more political success had he not had to support his army and its operations in other provinces on the heavy taxes he had to collect in Aragon.

With British intervention the French faced another difficulty because the British supplied the Spaniards and fielded their own capably commanded armies there. Jomini saw the key role played by British in providing "a regular army of respectable size to be a nucleus around which to rally the people." He particularly saw the role of these forces in diminishing the French ratio of force to space when he asked: "What force will be sufficient to be superior everywhere, and to assure the safety of long lines of communication against numerous bodies?" Alexander did not have to contend against this kind of problem nor did the English in the long, methodical conquest of Wales.[20]

So the British army and the Spanish and Portuguese regular forces they supported kept many French soldiers concentrated and so aggravated the French problem of having a force adequate for military conquest but not equal to the task of political pacification. And the skill of the British commander also played an important part, for the duke of Wellington showed that he, too, understood the merits of retreat and the value of a fleet at one's rear.

The French had a problem familiar to conquerors of the Middle Ages. The English in Wales had faced the same obstacles and had overcome them by a gradual process of subjugating small patches of territory and consolidating their mastery by castle building. But since this procedure took literally almost two centuries, it was not the method for a quick consolidation of King Joseph's rule. The Turks and Mongolians had attained immediate results by massacring a large proportion of the population, which combined the logistic strategy of depriving the enemy of fighting men with the political program of terror. But the French would have had difficulty accepting such a strategy, if only because they were still nominally Christian. Though Christians had shown no compunction about massacring infidels or heretics, the Spaniards qualified on neither count, and the French culture would have precluded the wholesale adoption of a Turko-Mongolian strategy.

Thus, the French used a combat persisting strategy to fight and failed to win a war that exhibited the ascendency of a raiding strategy over a defensive persisting strategy. By initially attempting to occupy the whole country and then steadily extend their sway, the French had really placed themselves on the defensive against the raiding guerrillas. In the English conquest of Wales, on the other hand, the invader had used an offensive persisting strategy by concentrating on a small area and pacifying it before advancing farther. Through domination of each successive region, the English had made this also a logistic strategy of depriving the Welsh of a portion of their base area and also of harnessing its resources to their needs. The French only apparently deprived the Spanish guerrillas of their base area; the superficial French control actually left much of the country to their adversaries.

With a much higher ratio of force to space or with a more substantial political base, the French might have triumphed. Over time patience and carefully considerate behavior by French soldiers and locally recruited troops might have gradually legitimized King Joseph's rule. But with a skillfully commanded British army in the field as well as Portuguese and Spanish forces and the feeling of urgency to complete the task promptly, the French persisted with their too thinly applied persisting strategy. The size of the Iberian Peninsula and the implacable hostility of so many Spaniards doomed the French efforts.

The Foundations of the French Conquests

The war concluded in 1814 with a number of large armies marching into France in a coordinated campaign. Against these Napoleon maneuvered a substantial number of men trying, without success, to exploit his central position to halt the allies. The numbers of soldiers, though large, did not really differentiate these operations from those of earlier times, especially when Louis XIV's France made its best effort against the armies of Britain, Holland, and the emperor. But the coordination of the French armies and of the allied contingents and the conception that all armies of each side functioned in the same theater as part of a single force distinguished these maneuvers from those times when separate armies received separate missions and performed largely independently.

The ability of these armies to disperse and impose battle upon one another contrasted with the campaigns of old. The tactical flexibility of all of the armies, in which they often fought with discontinuous fronts and easily moved infantry units on the battlefield, presented another marked departure from the past. But with all armies organized alike and equally well articulated, the offensive lost the strength it had acquired when the French had a monopoly on these methods. For example, on the second day of the Battle of Bautzen in May 1813, Napoleon concentrated two corps on the field of battle, sending them into the flank and rear of the Russo-Prussian army. One corps engaged the men guarding the allied flank while the other reached the allied rear. But the outflanked troops counterattacked and protected themselves well enough to escape without serious loss. Yet this attack, though poorly executed, would in the past have inflicted a defeat such as Frederick's on the Austrians at Leuthen had not the Prussians had the articulation and tactical mobility that had long characterized the French.

With both armies possessing the same tactical and strategic capabilities, the traditional ascendancy of the defense between similarly constituted armies using a persisting strategy reasserted itself. The new strategy exploited the ability to compel battle by trying to concentrate against weakness to make an opponent fall back. Individual battles thus became important and occurred at a frequency unknown in previous wars. But battles lacked the tactical importance of serious attrition, the proportion of casualties rising only about 1 percent from the 12.5 percent for victors and 21.9 percent for vanquished that had characterized combat in the first six decades of the bayonet era. Even when the French had a better commander and a distinctively better tactical system, victory failed to inflict significantly greater casualties on disciplined, moderately well-articulated forces of regular troops. The spread of the improved French articulation only buttressed the resilience of the defeated armies. So commanders no longer had the opportunity for victories like Hannibal's at Cannae or Alexander's at Issus and Arbela—armies had better training and articulation and both sides lacked the dominant weapon system that heavy cavalry had provided in Alexandrian combat.

Without the possibility of the major attrition of some ancient contests, battles increased in frequency, but not because their tactical consequences made them ends in themselves, the role that Alexander and Hannibal had properly and successfully given them. Nor were the political consequences of an individual battle generally significant. The incidence of battles grew because they had become the major tool in carrying out the traditional late seventeenth- and eighteenth-century strategy of acquiring and consolidating control of an enemy's territory. With the effects of defeat mitigated by improved articulation, generals risked conflicts more readily and their very frequency helped to meliorate the éclat of victory—and the opprobrium attached to the vanquished.

The new strategy did depend on an adequate ratio of force to space. In a large area, such as European Russia, even the enormous aggregation of armies that Napoleon used in 1812 could not compel the enemy to give battle. In so much space, even large, well-dispersed bodies of troops occupied relatively little more room than those of Turenne and Montecuccoli when they had maneuvered along the Main in 1673. Even Napoleon's army in Italy in 1800 had great difficulty in gathering the fruit of its turning movement by blocking Melas's retreat. The far greater ratio of force to space in the Ulm campaign made it much easier for Napoleon to block the Austrian retreat. As Napoleon's campaign in Austria in 1805 could have shown, had the Austrians been less willing to make peace or had Napoleon asked a great deal more, as his operation in Russia dramatically demonstrated, occupation of territory without political support required a greater ratio of force to space.

In the early days of their revolution the French had a political basis in the urban areas of Holland, the Rhine region of Germany, and north Italy that had provided meaningful help for their conquests. Their success in the Netherlands, including overrunning Holland, had a parallel in the Anglo-imperial conquest of a great deal of the Spanish Netherlands after the defeat of Marshal Villeroi at Ramillies in 1706. Much of the heavily fortified country yielded to the victors who represented the traditional Habsburg rulers. So also in the 1790s did the French program of political liberty and equality exercise an appeal among the middle class that helped them overcome the historically impregnable defenses of the Netherlands and Holland. This same political factor aided them in Italy and assisted them in coping with the much larger territory of Germany.

Yet the French dissipated this asset by allowing their troops to forage and loot in the manner of soldiers of the Thirty Years' War. As earlier, the Spanish Netherlanders, disillusioned with their new rulers, later welcomed back the French as representatives of the new Bourbon king of Spain, so territories occupied by the French developed an antipathy toward their ill-behaved conquerors.

The disorganization of the improvised revolutionary armies and the lack of money to buy supplies for the troops caused the men to fall back on marauding. After a century of scrupulous regard for civilian property, the French soldiers' looting produced a particularly hostile reaction among the public, especially when the allied armies adhered to what had become traditional policy. At the outset of the war in the Netherlands, for example, General Dumouriez commented: "I fear the dreadful consequences of a retreat in a country where we have raised the inhabitants against us by pillage and indiscipline."[21]

Even in France at that time, the troops alienated civilians from the new government of liberty and equality. Pointing out this result, one soldier reported that many French peasants had told him, "with tears in their eyes, that they preferred the ancient régime a thousand times more than our constitution, since at least then no one carried off their property." The government sought to control the troops but faced the same difficulties encountered in the Thirty Years' War. The great Lazare Carnot, who had charge of the republic's war effort, noted that he and "the generals found it impossible to stop the disorders; the drunken soldiers heard nothing, and the number guilty was too great to think of a violent punishment, which moveover, would have been impossible to execute in such a circumstance." When trying to move these men toward the enemy, Carnot found that "they were almost all drunk, more or less. . . . The soldiers' packs were so full of things they had stolen that they could no longer carry them."[22]

Seeing such military evils result from a return to the old methods, Carnot concluded: "If every soldier who steals a pin is not shot on the spot, you will never accomplish anything." But the French soldiers continued to squander much of the republic's political capital and undermined this vital basis of their conquests. Just as Antiochus VII of Syria converted his welcome in Mesopotamia into aversion, so the French alienated their supporters.[23]

When the behavior of Napoleon's troops provoked an uprising in Milan in 1796, this typified the conduct of French troops. In the same year one French general reported from Germany: "I am doing my best to control the plundering, but the troops have not been paid for two months, and the ration columns cannot keep up with our rapid marches; the peasants flee, and the soldiers lay waste empty houses." Another general also reported from Germany that "the soldiers mistreat the country to the most extreme degree; I blush to lead an army that behaves in such an unworthy manner."[24] When Prussian troops invaded France in 1814, they took revenge for these earlier depredations. The result: the Prussians antagonized the otherwise apathetic French populace, converting them into active opponents. But the war ended too quickly for this hostility to affect military operations. The lack of money, discipline, and good management that had permitted this behavior on the part of the French soldiers had contributed to the erosion of the good will felt toward the French in the Low Countries, Italy, and Germany and the squandering of valuable political capital.

Initially, popular political support had provided one of the keys to the early French success in overcoming opposition in areas that had long defied French control. But in the largely rural Austrian empire the French could have found few allies and would have faced a serious problem in garrisoning and dominating such a large area. In Russia their campaign amounted to nothing more than a spectacular raid, and in Spain the French showed that against essentially national hostility they would need time as well as more ample forces if they were to subdue the country quickly without massacring a substantial part of the population.

An adequate ratio of force to space permitted the new battle-oriented strategy to conquer territory rapidly. But areas small enough to fall to this strategy might still be too large if the invader faced substantial political opposition. Then the invader would need either a political program to win support or an even greater ratio of force to space, one responsive to political rather than military needs. In Spain the French encountered too much political antagonism for their force, a situation not unlike that which faced Hannibal in Italy and Alexander in Bactria and Sogdiana.

The transformations of warfare during the era of the French Revolution, together with the ratio of force to the geographical area involved, go far toward providing the reasons for French victories. When one adds the political factors influencing the receptivity of the defeated to the rule or hegemony of the conquerors, these three offer a convenient, if overly simple, means of understanding the resulting unprecedented, if transitory, expansion of French territory and influence. The French success in conquering the Netherlands and adjacent areas of Germany and Italy illustrates the operation of all three of these factors. In Spain, where they had the military means to conquer and the forces to occupy such a large country, they failed because they lacked a political base. In Russia, where they had only military supremacy, Napoleon's invasion became a mere raid, a persisting strategy being beyond military means alone.

In their search for the explanations for the success of Napoleon and his revolutionary predecessors people have found a few reasons that seem to lack validity. Some believed that Napoleonic armies marched more rapidly than those of the old regime. His men did march very swiftly on occasion but not faster than, for example, those of Tilly and Gustavus. Napoleon's usual rate of march did not differ from the twelve miles per day that had characterized armies since ancient times. He did march more quickly than this more often than did generals of the earlier centuries because the new strategy of dispersal and concentration created more occasions for rapid marches. His greater mobility, displayed in the long advance that, for example, played such a role in the Ulm and Austerlitz campaigns, made observers think that in finding food and fodder along the march route, he differed from his predecessors. He lived on the country, whereas they depended on supplies brought from the rear. But earlier armies, too, unless engaged in a siege, lived on the country in essentially the same way. And the spread of the cultivation of the potato had helped men find food in the area where they campaigned. Essentially as nutritious as bread, the potato required no milling into flour or baking in ovens as preparation for eating.

It is true that the armies of the revolution, and often Napoleon's also, took food and loot in a manner reminiscent of the soldiers of the Thirty Years' War. But the French paid a significant political price for this reversion to the older method of supply, facing guerrilla warfare in Italy as well as Spain and sacrificing real indigenous political support elsewhere.

But the method of supplying armies differed not at all; the only variation lay in the means of collecting the supplies. All armies in this period usually lived on the country just as armies had throughout the history of warfare. Because he engaged in fewer sieges, Napoleon relied less on magazines and supply convoys to support a stationary army. He continued to depend on contributions, and for the first twelve years of his rule foreign nations bore the costs of his wars, just as Saxony had paid so much of Frederick's costs in waging the Seven Years' War.

Observers also thought that Napoleon attained more because he had no limitations on his means or his objectives. He did accomplish more because of his unsurpassed military genius and because of the kind of army evolved by the work of eighteenth-century French military reformers and from the ideas of Bourcet and Guibert. The new armies and the combat strategy that he pioneered gave him military means not at the disposal of those who came before him. He had ambitious political objectives, and, to a degree, these expanded to meet the higher effectiveness of his military machine. For a time he dominated the non-Austrian part of the old Holy Roman Empire and made Austria an unwilling ally. This goal was beyond the capacity of Louis XIV, whose armed forces lacked the capabilities of Napoleon's; further, the king had no political base that could have helped to reconcile the states of the empire to his hegemony. But Napoleon exploited the political achievements of the French Revolution, and the ideal of political liberty and equality exercised enough influence to enable him to have a tenuous political base upon which to found what proved to be a very ephemeral European empire. Without the feeble political opposition that faced Alexander the Great, Napoleon could not reproduce the Macedonian's imperial triumph.

Napoleon's aims in dealing with Austria remained moderate and conventional. But when he raised his political objective in Spain to the overthrow of the ruling house and the introduction of French revolutionary ideas, he found that he had adopted, as he did in Russia, political objectives beyond his military capacity. Perhaps he had more ambitious and less realistic goals than any French monarch since Charles VIII and his successors had aimed to conquer Italy, but he had more military means than they since the art of war had advanced faster in France than elsewhere. Still, Napoleon did not employ all of the means at his disposal. Despite the great wealth of France and the conscription of soldiers, the proportion of men under arms remained fairly small, less than in Britain, for example, and French allies and subject and satellite states bore a large part of the cost of his wars.

The Military Legacy of the Napoleonic Era

The changes in warfare from 1792 to 1815 did not affect the essentials of tactics. Missile-weapon infantry still deployed in lines in the traditional manner for heavy infantry, and the predominance in fire continued to decide the contest. The bayonet still was a threat in fending off cavalry attacks and was used occasionally in infantry combat. The eighteenth-century idea of returning to shock action between infantry formations through the impetus of a column had few trials and fewer successes. In repelling an effort to employ the bayonet for shock action against infantry, the defender enjoyed the benefit of firing volleys while stationary as well as receiving a charge in a chosen position with ranks undisordered by any march to deliver an attack. Depth of formation proved no antidote to these advantages of the defense, and additional men in the rear added no impetus to those in front, who had to face the salvos of hostile fire before reaching the opposing line of muskets and bayonets.

Thus the defensive remained stronger in combat between the same weapon systems. And cavalry, its pistols dominated by muskets and its charge with sabers overmatched by a line of musketeers with bayonets, remained the inferior weapon system. Although the greater mobility of artillery enabled it to accompany the attack more often, it continued to contribute more to defense than to offense. With full-size balls at a distance and cannisters of smaller projectiles at 400 yards or less, it powerfully augmented the volleys of the musketeers. Thus, the relative power of the weapon systems had not changed, as shown in schematic 6.1., in which D is the ability to defend successfully.

infantry —————————— D ————————▶ cavalry

Schematic 6.1. Combat Relationship between Infantry and Cavalry

But cavalry could refuse battle and its greater mobility assured it a continued, if shrunken, tactical place in armies while infantry in linear formation remained vulnerable to a cavalry assault in its flank and rear. Battles in Spain and Portugal illustrate these tactical variables, as thoroughly drilled British units with good training in firing met those of the French trying to hold Spain for Napoleon's brother. At the Battle of Albuera, for example, about 22,000 French, under the capable command of the veteran campaigner, Marshal Soult, met a British, Spanish, and Portuguese force of 35,000 commanded by the one-eyed British general, Beresford, who, as a Portuguese marshal, had effectively reorganized the Portuguese army. Marshal Soult sent a small force to attract the attention of the allies by attacking their front while he directed his main army to his left to turn the allied position. But before the French could attack the allied flank and rear, the alert Beresford had redeployed the bulk of his men and formed a new line to resist the French assault.

The French corps that conducted the attack had four battalions, one behind the other, each formed with fifty files and nine ranks. On either side of these battalions, the French division commander deployed a battalion in line, 150 men in three ranks. In part to protect the flanks of his division from a cavalry charge, he posted on each side of the deployed battalions an additional battalion with a front of twenty-five men and eighteen ranks deep. On each side of the division a dozen cannon supported the attack, firing at Spanish troops 500 yards distant; the Spaniards had ten guns. The French division, keeping its mixed formation, came within sixty yards of the Spanish line where they halted and returned the volleys of the steady Spanish infantrymen. A British force of four battalions aided the Spaniards by forming on their right, angling forward, and firing into the French flank.

At this moment, when a sudden thunderstorm completely obscured the battlefield, a French cavalry force charged the flank of the British battalions, formed in a single line two ranks deep, and completely defeated three of the battalions, only one succeeding in forming a square and protecting itself. Both sides then reinforced the battle, six British battalions relieving the Spaniards and the French pushing forward a second division that, when intermingled with the first, created a mass with a front of 400 and depth of twenty, not at all a typical French formation. Of the 3,000 British troops in a double line, about 2,100 could fire on the French from as close as sixty yards away, directly in front of the French formation, to as much as 200 yards away when firing at an angle from the flanks. The French front of 400 could bring into action the first two ranks, 800 musketeers, but probably not more because of the traditional difficulty in securing fire from the third line, which Napoleon would soon eliminate because it usually functioned as a reserve for the first two lines rather than contributing its fire. French artillery could fire some rounds but, stationed behind the infantry and at longer range, could offer little more. The British had seven guns that could fire on the French, and they had great effect on the vulnerable target of the closely packed infantry.

In the battle, which lasted forty-five minutes until the French retreated, the British suffered 1,500 casualties, half their strength, and the French 3,000 of their 8,000. British artillery accounted for about one-third of the French casualties, and the French artillery inflicted 300 or 400 casualties on the British. Musket fire caused the remainder of the casualties. If the British had compressed their line as the center suffered losses, they would have had an average of about 1,850 muskets firing throughout the engagement; if they let the French shoot away their center without drawing in their flanks to fill the gaps, only 1,350. If the French third line did not fire, they would have kept 800 muskets in action continuously, the rear ranks filling the places of the fallen in the front two ranks. As a result of the firing, each veteran soldier on both sides fired as many as fifty rounds and accounted for about one or one and a half enemy soldiers.[25]

The casualties in this battle roughly fit Lanchester's hypothesis. Assuming that the British kept closing their line so as not to present a gap opposite the French mass, they had an average of 1,850 men firing against 800 French. The approximately 1,150 British casualties to musket fire amounted to a little over half of the 2,000 French losses attributable to small-arms fire. The casualties, which reasonably conform to the numbers firing, do not reflect the likely superiority of the British troops in musketry, but fresh French soldiers with unfouled muskets, as well as the protection offered by the bodies of the fallen, may well account for the failure of a qualitative difference to make itself felt. If, however, the French had continued the battle, even in their inefficient formation, they would ultimately have so shrunk the British line as to have more men firing and then they would have quickly extinguished their opponent. But their defective array for using their muskets would have caused the French to suffer far more casualties than Lanchester's law would indicate. That the French masked the fire of so many of their men would explain this divergence.

This battle is representative in many respects, beginning with Soult's turning movement, which at least succeeded in directing his subsequent frontal attacks against a position where Marshal Beresford had not planned to receive them. The failure of the deep French formation to close with the bayonet vindicated the opponents of shock action and the skeptics of the argument that depth could provide impetus to the attack. When faced with enemy volleys, the front ranks halted and returned fire, the rear ranks standing still, protected from fire by their comrades in front. On occasion in the war in Spain and Portugal, when British troops charged after their fire halted a French column, the dense French formation became badly disordered and demoralized, its additional depth contributing nothing.

In many of the combats in Spain, the French attacked in column without deploying in line. In some instances the commanders chose to do this, but often they were forced into it, having misjudged the location of the enemy, frequently because the defending British placed their line on the slope of a hill away from the French. In this case, when the French columns of maneuver came over the crest of the hill, they came immediately under the fire of British volleys. Thus the French commander would find that he had waited too late to deploy into line and preferred then to fight in column rather than to carry out the maneuver into line under fire.

The successful attack of the French cavalry clearly exhibited why cavalry, though an inferior weapon system, could still use its better mobility and ability to fight as it marched to attack infantry's vulnerable flank.

Battles witnessed many repetitions of the Battle of Albuera's instance of combat of formations standing as close as forty yards apart and firing at each other until one gave way. In almost every occasion the column formation failed to close with the enemy, though it usually had greater numbers and more strength concentrated at the potential point of contact. The combats, however, did demonstrate the value of effective numerical preponderance when missile weapons and a linear formation enabled one side to bring more men into action.

With the abandonment of continuous lines and, often in the French army, a deficiency in the drill and firing practice originally used with linear formations of missile-weapon infantry, the distinction tended to blur between line and light infantry. Light infantry learned to fight in line, and line infantry learned to use the skirmishing tactics traditional for the missile-armed soldier. By the end of the Napoleonic wars light and heavy infantry could readily substitute for one another and had really formed a general-purpose infantry that could use two different tactics.

Increasingly Napoleon, originally an artillery officer, gave a more effective offensive role to the artillery. The artillerymen learned better how to bring their guns forward on the battlefield and unlimber them as close as 300 yards from enemy infantry. At this range the gunners would still have relative immunity from musket fire while able to shoot cannister or the larger grape shot effectively at the enemy infantry. Used in this way, the fire of the artillery had such a destructive effect that the infantry had little to do but exploit the artillery's success. Concentration of large numbers of guns in one place facilitated this use of artillery fire in the offensive, and when generals applied the artillery doctrine conceived before the French Revolution, they made the same use of artillery's ability to concentrate as infantry commanders did with their battalion columns.

Intrepid artillerymen, by bringing more of their guns forward on the battlefield, had given increased value to mobile missile weapons. The weapons drawn forward by the horses fired a much larger load of missiles than the small infantry guns introduced by Gustavus Adolphus, accentuating the predominance of the heavy, powerful mobile missile weapons as compared with the portable musket. At the Battle of Friedland in 1807, for example, thirty French artillery pieces advanced with a division in an attack against the Russians. Beginning effective fire at extreme cannister range, the French artillery moved forward in stages until it had reached first 120 yards and finally sixty yards where the guns tore bloody gaps in the line of Russian infantry. This climaxed a twenty-five-minute struggle in which the artillery inflicted 4,000 casualties and compelled the sturdy Russian soldiers to retire. When Russian cavalry then charged the artillery in the flank, the French commander redeployed his guns in time to fire two salvos that routed the horsemen. The artillery then followed the infantry across a river into a village where it did terrible harm to Russian infantry crowded in the narrow streets.

In spite of such an exemplary use of guns, which showed the part they could play on the offensive, artillery still remained stronger on the defensive, where it had much greater certainty of finding suitable targets. The menace of the improved artillery led commanders, particularly the shrewd British commander, Wellington, to place their infantry beyond the crests of hills, where they had cover against artillery fire from a distance but had the crest of the hill within good musket range to bring assaulting infantry under fire when it appeared. Except in sieges, artillery remained a more effective but less mobile form of the basic missile weapon system.

The greater articulation of demi-brigades, brigades, and divisions and the battalion's facility in maneuver and deployment remained an enduring tactical legacy of this period. Upon these innovations and the resulting tactical mobility rested the novel ability of infantry to concentrate upon the battlefield and to spread out to envelop and turn an enemy position. These alterations also explain the ability of defenders to change front and extend to resist attacks in flank and rear as well as infantry's increased capacity to cope with cavalry and the foot soldier's great resilience in defeat.

The period of the French Revolution and Napoleon affected the supply of armies hardly at all; yet the provision of men for the armies had changed considerably. Except in Britain, compulsory service played a greater role and armies became increasingly national. The military entrepreneur, like the foreign recruit, dwindled into virtual insignificance except in the form of the heterogeneous armies of the extensive French empire, where its diverse territories and satellite kingdoms provided national contingents. Particularly in Prussia and France did militias have an important role as forces in the field and a source for manpower for the armies. In varying degrees in all armies national feeling and dynastic loyalty played a role in animating soldiers, many of whom also fought well because of the cohesion provided by their regiments and the leadershp of their officers. Essentially the French revolutionary model had spread, as many soldiers were coerced into the army and many were inspired by the cause of their country.

The revolution in strategy, depending much on that in tactics, altered war profoundly by resting strategy on combat or its threat to a degree heretofore unknown between armies composed of similar weapon systems. Dispersion and concentration against an opponent's weakness animated a strategic environment in which battle must occur if one, rather than both, contestants wished it, unless the reluctant army retreated. This gave new resources and the ability to force a decision to the strategic offensive and, though battles figured prominently, enabled successful campaigns to engulf and hold large sections of the enemy's territory. Larger armies in relation to the space of the traditional territorial prizes and campaigning areas had much to do with these greater conquests, but the new combat strategy made a fundamental contribution to the speed and scale of the strategic successes and, consequently, to reducing the effort required for victory in war.

The Tactics of Warfare at Sea

The naval contest between France and Britain continued the pattern established in the previous century. Britain blockaded French merchant and naval vessels, and the French navy continued to stay inferior to the British, mostly because, with their squadrons always bottled up in their ports, officers and men lacked experience at sea. The French sought to avoid battles or to make them indecisive while accomplishing a strategic objective.

The first major combat of the war occurred in late May 1794, when the courageous and competent Admiral Villaret de Joyeuse with the twenty-six men-of-war of the Brest fleet sallied to cover the arrival of a French convoy of 130 ships bearing wheat, sugar, and coffee. When the opponents met, the French had the advantage of the windward position and for two days kept Admiral Howe, a sailor with more than fifty years service, and his twenty-six British war vessels at bay. Even when Howe secured the windward position, stormy weather prevented battle for two more days.

On June 1, with weather improving, the British engaged in the usual manner by turning each of the ships in their line obliquely toward the parallel French line. The enterprising Howe apparently intended that his vessels pass through the intervals between the French warships and engage them on the leeward side, hampering their escape. But only eight ships carried out this maneuver. The bulk of the combat involved these vessels on which the French also concentrated by bringing some of their ships upon the British leeward side, catching their adversary between two fires. Yet the British won, due to the proficiency of their crews and the French weakness in officers, many of their best men lost on account of the revolution.

The French escaped, with one ship sunk and six captured. The British celebrated this combat as the Glorious First of June, a great tactical victory because of the losses inflicted on the enemy. The French also celebrated their strategic victory, for their convoy arrived unscathed.

Off Cape St. Vincent on the Spanish coast in 1797 another battle took place. The Spanish Mediterranean squadron of twenty-four vessels entered the Atlantic, escorting a convoy as it moved to join the French Brest fleet covering a French attempt to send an army against Great Britain. The Spanish admiral, who had good ships but not enough sailors and few with adequate sea experience, had no illusions that he commanded a fleet fit to fight. In spite of having only fifteen ships of the line, the British admiral, Jervis, a strict disciplinarian who knew the weakness of the Spaniards, attacked the enemy squadron, which he found divided into two parts, the smaller, eight men-of-war, forming a separate group in the rear. Sailing his line through this gap in the Spanish formation and delivering a succession of broadsides against the rearmost ships of the lead Spanish division, the British then turned not toward the smaller group but against the rear of the larger section heading the Spanish fleet. In spite of efforts of the Spanish rear contingent to come up and of the ships of the lead group to turn back, the British overwhelmed four Spanish vessels and secured their surrender. The victorious admiral then broke off the battle to protect his captured warships as the far more numerous Spanish men-of-war at last concentrated against the British between the two parts of their fleet.

By breaking through the substantial gap between the two sections of the Spanish fleet, Admiral Jervis had concentrated a two to one numerical advantage against the Spanish ships he attacked. Thus he had used a method like Rodney's to win a victory comparable to that at the Saints against a fleet almost double his strength. The first-class seamanship of the British helped them against the Spaniards, whose vessels had little recent sailing experience. Better drilled British gunners aided also, as evidenced by a British seventy-four-gun ship meeting, surviving, and damaging the gigantic *Santissima Trinidad*, a four-decked ship of 130 guns, the largest warship of the time.

Successful penetration of the enemy line contributed to the victory at Camperdown in 1797, when the aggressive Admiral Duncan's sixteen British ships met the same number of slightly smaller Dutch vessels. Fearing the Dutch might escape, the British, in two divisions, did not wait to form but rushed headlong at the Dutch line, some British men-of-war secured a leeward position, hampering Dutch withdrawal, taking some ships from two sides, and creating two separate close battles in which the British took nine Dutch vessels in a hard-fought contest. This victory caused the French to abandon plans for a landing in Great Britain.

In 1798 at Aboukir Bay in Egypt Admiral Horatio Nelson with fourteen British ships attacked an unready French fleet of thirteen vessels, all at anchor. Concentrating two men-of-war to one on the head of the French line, the British had an especial advantage because the French ships, with sailors ashore fetching water, were so short-handed that they could fire only one of their broadsides.

Since Admiral Nelson's two to one concentration against the head of the French line failed to include one French ship, the seventy-four-gun British *Bellerophon* had to face the 120-gun French flagship, *Orient*. Although the powerful broadsides of the *Orient* knocked off all the masts of the *Bellerophon* and inflicted enormous casualties, victory went to the British. The *Orient* caught fire and blew up when the fire reached her powder magazines. The *Bellerophon* used a single sail to pull away from the danger. Other French vessels, though badly battered, fared somewhat better in that one by one they surrendered and the British concentration moved gradually down the anchored French line until only two French ships escaped. This victory captured no convoy nor frustrated any invasion attempt but shifted the naval balance of power by destroying a major part of the French Mediterranean fleet.

The battle showed Nelson's preeminent traits as a tactician and inspirer of his captains and seamen alike. A captain at age twenty, rising by charm and ability rather than influence, he had already lost an eye and an arm in service to his country and, playing a brilliant role in the Battle of Saint Vincent, earned the command in the Mediterranean, which gave him the opportunity to lead his fleet at Aboukir Bay. He would later display his mastery of naval tactics against Admiral Villeneuve, who had reached the rank of rear admiral at age thirty-three in part because the navy had lost so many officers to death or emigration. Villeneuve had fought at Aboukir and had led the two ships that escaped.

The tactical trends begun at the Battle of the Saints and exhibited in these later conflicts reached their culmination at the Battle of Trafalgar in 1805. Here Admiral Nelson, his fleet reduced to twenty-seven men-of-war as six were replenishing their water, met Admiral Villeneuve's Franco-Spanish fleet of thirty-three vessels. Nelson attacked in two groups, one, which he commanded, directed at the center, and the other, the larger division, at the rear of the enemy line. Exploiting his windward position and not waiting to form either of his two divisions into a line, Nelson aimed to have his vessels break into Villeneuve's line and have his concentration of greater force overwhelm the center and rear before the head of the enemy line could turn back and enter the fight. Thus Nelson pitted all twenty-seven of his ships against twenty-three of the enemy. Since all ships could fire at all others, the British advantge, by Lanchester's theory, compared as 27^2 to 23^2, or 729 to 529. The dominance given the seasoned British by their better seamanship and gunnery made the odds in their favor greater than those indicated by Lanchester's augmentation.[26]

Thus the perceptive Nelson perfected the concept of breaking the enemy's line begun by Rodney at the Battle of the Saints by initially employing a perpendicular approach rather than attempting to make the penetration from the traditional parallel line of battle. He did by design what Admiral Duncan had improvised at the Battle of Camperdown. But, unlike Duncan, he directed his squadrons to secure concentration of greater force against the enemy's rear. By abandoning the line arrangement for his two divisions and approaching the enemy in the same formation in which he sailed, Nelson emancipated himself from the concept that fleets must maneuver in the same way that they fought, with their broadsides to the enemy. He also decentralized control, assigning full authority to his subordinate to execute the plan and giving complete discretion to the captains of his vessels to carry out his aggressive scheme to reach the windward side of the enemy line and sink or capture as many as possible. In reaching the far and leeward side of Villeneuve's line and blocking the traditional French tactic of retreat, Nelson successfully and fully systematized an evolving tactic that had something in common with the envelopment and the turning movement on land. Since ships had no primacy on the defense, a mere concentration of greater force could attain victory more readily than concentrations in frontal battles on land. Thus admirals needed no flank attack and—since except for briefly exposed heads or tails of lines fleets really lacked any such vulnerable side—could deliver none.

In Nelson's abandonment of the combat formation of the line for attacking the enemy in the arrangement in which the fleet sailed, an obvious parallel exists with the changes in land warfare that occurred at the same time. By his decentralization of command to the commander of a division of the fleet and to the captains, he secured an articulation like that which characterized French armies. And just as French armies maneuvered their battalions in column but usually deployed them into line to fight, so British men-of-war advanced toward the opposing fleet separately and directly, but, on engaging, they turned their broadsides to their enemies. On their way through the hostile line, the ships took advantage of the sailing ship's analogy of the flank attack, a broadside against the bows and, particularly, the vulnerable sterns of the vessels they passed.

So Nelson's plan for the conflict marked a transition from a rigid linear arrangement, which made decisive engagement difficult, to a decentralized attack in sailing formation, which facilitated forcing close battle on the enemy. This change has close parallels with the transformation of land warfare from unitary armies in linear array, which could not compel battle, to the dispersed divisions of the French army, whose battalions could maneuver in column but fight in line.

The discerning Admiral Villeneuve, conscious of British superiority, anticipated Nelson's tactics and sought to provide for it by allocating twelve of his thirty-three ships to a reserve, which he stationed in a second line to the leeward of his main line. When the fleets met in a light wind off Cape Trafalgar, the pessimistic Villeneuve reversed the course of his fleet to keep close to the Spanish port of Cadiz as a refuge in defeat. In the process of carrying out this maneuver, his reserve ended up as the rear of his line, out of position to carry out its purpose.

Nelson's battle went as he intended it. His ships reached and pierced the Franco-Spanish line exactly as planned and had overwhelmed the enemy rear and center before the head of Villeneuve's line could turn and sail back to help their outnumbered compatriots. The allies lost seventeen ships captured, one blown up, and about 14,000 men killed, wounded, and captured, including two

Spanish admirals killed and Admiral Villeneuve a prisoner. Although a storm sank all but four of the captured vessels, the loss of so many ships and men completed the ruin of Franco-Spanish sea power and removed the possibility of any future threat of an invasion of Britain. Released soon after his capture, Villeneuve committed suicide upon his return to France.

The Strategy of Warfare at Sea

The change in tactics, which culminated at Trafalgar and substituted battles with significant attrition for the relatively innocuous combats in which the French had long defended so well, had no parallel in strategy. But before the Battle of Trafalgar, the long war of blockade and raiding had included an intermittent menace of an invasion of Great Britain by the French army. The first of these threats materialized in December 1796, when a French convoy carrying a force of 14,000 men slipped out of Brest and would have landed the men in Ireland had a severe three-week storm not scattered the French ships. To renew this effort, the Mediterranean fleet of France's ally, Spain, left Cartagena for Cadiz, where the British squadron from Lisbon intercepted it off Cape St. Vincent and defeated it in battle. The British then blockaded the remaining ships in Cadiz.

The British faced three squadrons that could support an invasion, the Spanish at Cadiz, the French at Brest, and the fleet of France's Dutch ally. The British had ships watching each of these but understood that if any one of these squadrons should elude its blockading flotilla and sail to another of the blockaded ports, the French and their allies would have two fleets to the British one and the potential to control the sea. Since only enemy control of the channel between France and England created the crucial menace of invasion, British strategic doctrine prescribed that when any enemy ships eluded its blockading squadron, that force should sail immediately to the English channel and join the ships blockading Brest and guarding the channel.

When Spain entered into the war on the French side and changed the balance of naval power, the British had to give up their base in Corsica and withdraw from the Mediterranean, but in 1798 they reentered that sea in force when General Bonaparte led an expedition from the French port of Toulon to Egypt. Although the French army gained control of Egypt, in August 1798, when Admiral Nelson destroyed much of the French Toulon squadron at Aboukir Bay, the British regained control of the Mediterranean and secured for themselves a new base on the western Mediterranean island of Minorca. Yet the immediate French effort to retrieve the situation displayed the difficulties always inherent in the British strategy of blockading hostile fleets in widely separated ports.

The French ordered their ships at Brest to the Mediterranean. In April 1799, when a strong offshore wind drove the blockading fleet far to sea, Admiral Bruix sailed twenty-five men-of-war with the wind out of Brest and past the British blockading squadron. Following the doctrine of covering Great Britain against invasion and, misled by a French ruse, the British admiral promptly positioned his force to protect Ireland. The French admiral, commanding the best-manned fleet the French had sent to sea since the revolution, then, as ordered, took his ships toward the Mediterranean and, evading the British squadron blockading Cadiz and the small force at Gibraltar, led it to Toulon.

To deal with the menace presented by the new Toulon fleet, the British Cadiz blockading squadron entered the Mediterranean, raising British forces there to thirty-seven ships of the line. But when the Spanish Cadiz fleet of seventeen men-of-war followed its blockading squadron into the Mediterranean and went to Cartagena, Britain's enemies possessed forty-two vessels. Apprehensive about his unfortified base on Minorca, the British admiral positioned his fleet to cover his base as well as to place it in a central position between Toulon and Cartagena to prevent a concentration of the two hostile fleets and to attack the first that came out. Still, since such a central position did not serve to close Toulon, a second squadron of sixteen vessels guarded the routes to the eastern Mediterranean to protect British and Turkish efforts to defeat General Bonaparte's forces in Egypt and Syria.

For the first task for their new Toulon fleet, the French sent it with a convoy of troops and supplies to relieve a French army besieged in Genoa. When the British admiral between Cartagena and Toulon left this station to follow Admiral Bruix to Genoa, Bruix sailed from Genoa, slipped past the British squadron, and went to Cartagena, where the Spanish fleet came out to join him. With forty ships of the line the French admiral then headed into the Atlantic with Admiral Keith and the British Mediterranean squadron on his heels. When Admiral Keith joined the British before Brest the day after Admiral Bruix arrived, he restored the balance of naval power in the channel. Had he mistaken the French destination and, for example, sailed toward Egypt, the French and Spanish would have had supremacy in the channel.

Thus, with so many French and Spanish ships blockaded in Brest, the British had a much simpler strategic problem. Yet the whole campaign showed the complexity of the situation created when one of these blockaded enemy squadrons escaped. Superficially the British had interior lines when the French had to divide their ships between their Atlantic and Mediterranean coasts and the British had bases between them at Gibraltar and Lisbon. Yet as long as the French fleets remained in their ports, the British could not use their interior lines to concentrate and take the offensive against the separated French naval forces; the French ships did not even have to defend themselves because their elaborately fortified bases protected them from the hostile navy. Thus interior lines availed the British nothing on the defense and little on the offense because, when a blockaded squadron eluded its blockaders, the British admiral would usually not know where the French were and hence could have no idea where to concentrate. Further, the large distances between the fleets meant slow communication, even though a line of frigates along the coast might speed up the transmission of the news of the French escape.

So not only could the British not take the offensive against squadrons in protected harbors, but once a French fleet evaded its blockading squadron, the

French held the initiative. Under these circumstances the British found themselves in a fundamentally defensive combat strategic situation. And this condition really was inseparable from their powerful logistic strategy of blockade. The French squadrons, with the strong land defenses of their fortified bases assuming the full burden of protecting their ships, had the advantage of the offensive, the ability to make a sortie whenever the wind or weather favored them. The French men-of-war that broke the blockade had a choice of sailing to at least two other ports where their arrival would give them an opportunity to unite their forces and effect a concentration in menacing strength. Thus the French had strategic opportunities not unlike those of a commander on land who had the ability to exploit interior lines to concentrate against successive enemy armies.

When General Bonaparte took command of all French forces, he also undertook to exploit this strategic opportunity to make possible an invasion of England. In the spring of 1805, with his troops poised opposite England, Napoleon began a naval campaign to gain enough predominance in the channel to enable his army to cross to England. Napoleon's strategy had the distinctive feature of planning a concentration in the West Indies. In this way he could both concentrate his ships with less danger of meeting a British fleet and distract the enemy. Because the wealth of the West Indies had made them traditional objectives of French and British expeditions, the British could not disregard the possibility of a French concentration there. Thus Napoleon's strategy might draw the British navy to the West Indies just as he implemented a concentration in the channel to cover an invasion. As in land warfare, where distraction often could create the weak point against which to concentrate, Napoleon sought to apply the same principle at sea.

His shrewdly conceived plan faced the difficulty that for decisive results he had only one possible objective: the channel. Aiming at an obvious goal severely handicapped concentration against weakness. And British doctrine had long stressed that blockading fleets should repair to the channel if they lost their blockaded enemy squadron. Further, the vagaries of wind and weather made naval operations even more uncertain than those on land. In addition, at sea Napoleon relied not on veteran soldiers under seasoned commanders but on sailors who had served more in port than at sea and admirals who lacked the successful operational experience of his generals.

Napoleon planned for the Toulon fleet to escape, pick up the Spanish ships at Cartagena, then those at Cadiz, and all sail to the West Indies. The Brest ships would also escape, release those at Ferrol in northwestern Spain, and rendezvous in the West Indies. The whole armada would then sail for the channel and cover the invasion. If the Brest squadron failed to escape to the West Indies, the combined Toulon, Cartagena, and Cadiz fleets would sail to the channel, release the ships at Brest, and seek to gain naval supremacy for the invasion.

On March 30 Admiral Villeneuve eluded Admiral Nelson's blockading squadron and escaped from Toulon, but when he reached Cartagena, he found the Spanish vessels unready for sea. Fearful of Nelson and realistic about the readiness of his ships for combat, he did not wait but sailed into the Atlantic and, too strong for the British force watching Cadiz, added the eight ships at Cadiz to his fleet before sailing for the West Indies. Nelson did not immediately pursue, stationing himself to block Villeneuve's passage to the eastern Mediterranean. The small British force at Cadiz, following the doctrine, sailed north to the channel, and Nelson soon set sail for the Straits of Gibraltar.

Headwinds kept him from reaching Gibraltar until May 6, almost a month after Villeneuve had passed. Hearing no report of Villeneuve's heading for the channel and concluding he must have gone to the West Indies, Nelson set off in pursuit. This part of Napoleon's plan had worked well, but since the Brest squadron had not made its escape, Napoleon changed his strategy and ordered Villeneuve to wait only a little longer for it and then, if it had not appeared, return first to Ferrol to pick up warships and then sail to the channel to unite with the Brest fleet.

Three days after receiving Napoleon's orders, Villeneuve heard of Nelson's arrival in the West Indies. Apprehensive at Nelson's presence and aware that the emperor's strategy had indeed distracted the enemy, Villeneuve immediately set sail to release the sixteen ships of the Ferrol fleet and proceed to Brest. Three days later Nelson learned that Villeneuve had started for Europe; assuming that the French aimed for Cadiz, he, too, sailed in that direction. But from the captain of a frigate that chanced to observe the French fleet en route, the British admiralty found out Villeneuve's true course and sent eight vessels to strengthen Admiral Calder at Ferrol, with orders to patrol 100 miles to the westward to intercept Villeneuve.

In ordering Calder to take a westward position to meet the Franco-Spanish fleet far from Ferrol, the British admiralty took an effective step to prevent a conjunction of Villeneuve's force with the Ferrol squadron. The Spanish admiral at Ferrol would inevitably learn of Villeneuve's proximity too late. In fact, his position gave Calder interior lines between the two forces, though the variability of the wind could mitigate the advantage. An offshore wind, for example, could bring out the Ferrol squadron but give it a windward position and prevent Calder from attacking. But the same wind would hold back Villeneuve and favor Calder's concentration against him. An on-shore wind would bottle up the Ferrol ships but handicap an attack against Villeneuve. Nevertheless, the distance between the two enemies would do much to prevent their concentration unless Villeneuve could slip past Calder into Ferrol.

On July 22, a week after a reinforcement of eight ships had brought his squadron to fifteen, Calder sighted Villeneuve's twenty ships off Cape Finisterre. Although the wind came from the west, Calder, an adequate commander who clearly grapsed the situation, took the leeward position, which blocked Villeneuve's approach to Ferrol, a naval analog of situating an army on an enemy's line of retreat. Nevertheless, Calder took the offensive, and, with both fleets maneuvering in the traditional lines, he sought to attack the rear of the French squadron. But when Villeneuve had the head ship lead his line around on the opposite course, the foremost parts of the two lines fought an indecisive engagement in a dense fog. Though he had captured two ships of his opponent, Calder, conservative in his approach and concerned about his prizes and the Ferrol fleet, avoided further action in the next two days, and Villeneuve, equally relieved to avoid battle, finally passed him and sailed for Ferrol.

Nelson had reached Gibraltar three days before Calder met Villeneuve and, on August 3, three days after Villeneuve entered Ferrol, Nelson set sail to the channel where Calder had already gone. Napoleon's plan had distracted Nelson, but Villeneuve had inadequate time to exploit it. With his squadron enlarged to twenty-nine ships, Villeneuve sailed from Ferrol on August 13 in response to the emperor's orders to go to Brest and then around Ireland and Scotland to unite with the Dutch fleet. With twenty-nine ships, he would have to face in the channel the twenty-seven British men-of-war, which had a central position between his and the twenty-one in Brest. Nelson sailed toward the channel with twelve. After five days at sea, the discouraged and anxious Villeneuve, who knew that the Spanish ships in his squadron were even less fit than the French, abandoned the plan and sailed for Cadiz, intending to return to the Mediterranean.

If the Brest fleet had escaped to the West Indies or Villeneuve had displayed the energy and confidence characteristic of so many French marshals, Napoleon's plan might have worked. But the superlative combat skill of the veteran British sailors and captains would very likely have nullified even such hypothetically vigorous French leadership and a strategy good enough to distract Nelson. Napoleon did not renew the naval campaign because, before the end of August, he prepared to launch one on land that would lead him to Ulm and Austerlitz.

With the end of the invasion threat, the British resumed their blockades. After the menace of having the Toulon and Cadiz fleets unite in the West Indies, the task seemed routine. But Villeneuve's effort to return to the Mediterranean and reestablish a powerful French naval presence enabled the British to assume the offensive with a combat strategy. After Villeneuve left Cadiz, Nelson engaged him in battle off Cape Trafalgar, where he destroyed half of Villeneuve's fleet. After the memorable year of 1805, the French navy no longer seriously threatened the British blockade nor an invasion of the United Kingdom.

Napoleon then used his command of most of Europe's major seaports to blockade the British, closing those he controlled to British ships and goods. The British then forbade neutral ships to trade in those ports unless the neutral ships first came to British harbors, paid for a license to trade with Napoleonic ports, and paid a duty on their cargoes. Napoleon retaliated by treating as British any neutral ships that complied with this British rule.

Napoleon's measures seriously hurt British trade, even with a great expansion in smuggling. But when the British gained the American and Asian markets of the blockaded French and Dutch, their trade and exports increased and their flourishing commerce helped finance their long war against Napoleon, including the provision of crucial subsidies to their continental allies. The crippling of French commerce correspondingly weakened Britain's opponent. Napoleon's logistic strategy thus failed while that of the British worked as well as it could, given the existing state of international trade.

The British navy found its other principal use in the support of combat operations in Spain and Portugal, where it transported and reinforced the British armies and supplied them and their Portuguese and Spanish allies. Better sea supply routes and the opportunity to retreat by water gave Napoleon's enemies an important advantage in Spain.

7

TECHNOLOGICAL CHANGE AND DOCTRINAL STABILITY, 1815–1914

The Continuation of the Napoleonic Tradition in Radetzky's Victories

In spite of significant technological progress that changed missile weapons and logistics, nineteenth-century warfare retained the essential character of the French Revolution and Napoleon. The infantryman with his bayonet-tipped musket remained the predominant weapon system. Cavalry continued to have a role in combat, relying largely on shock action with the saber, and kept its strategic missions of reconnaisance and raiding communications. In strategy, the new capabilities evident in Napoleon's campaigns manifested themselves as the tactical system of deployment, and the articulation, dispersion, and numerical strength of armies continued to reflect the methods of the wars that began the century.

The campaigns of 1848 and 1849 in Italy clearly exhibit this consistency. A mixture of largely Sardinian regular troops and hastily assembled Italian volunteers attempted to take advantage of turmoil in Austria to drive the Austrian army from Milan and the old territory of Venice. Faced with popular rebellions in Milan and elsewhere, the Austrians fell back to the Mincio and awaited additional forces from Austria. Charles Albert, the king of the Italian state of Sardinia, a vascillating man of mediocre abilities, commanded the Italian forces. Except for showing exceptional bravery during a siege in his youth, the king lacked any military experience. Yet his army had good training, and all of the forces he led eastward against the Austrians had great zeal for the popular cause of expelling the Austrians from Italy. With some largely raw volunteers and forces supplied by Naples and the pope, he outnumbered the Austrians.

The Italians faced Austrian regulars who had excellent training under a commander the men revered as Father Radetzky. Fighting in all of the wars since 1792, Radetzky had served with distinction as Schwarzenberg's chief of staff in 1813 and 1814. In 1834 he had assumed the Italian command and two years later, at age seventy, received promotion to field marshal. He had expertly trained his command and fostered its morale; now, at age eighty-two, he faced the great opportunity of his career, displaying undiminished mental capacities and so much physical vigor that his staff had trouble keeping their horses up with his. The field marshal, served by an excellent staff, would show that he had not forgotten the Napoleonic tradition in warfare.

When King Charles Albert led his army over the Mincio at Goito and advanced to Verona, Radetzky, whose reinforcements had come, halted him. The field marshal then marched northeast to Vicenza where, using his interior lines between the two enemy forces and concentrating 30,000 men he drove back 20,000 papal and Neapolitan troops. Able now to concentrate his augmented army against Charles Albert, Radetzky took advantage of the Sardinian dispersal over a forty-five-mile front to concentrate in their center, defeat them at Custozza, and drive them back to the frontier, retaking Milan and ending the campaign for the year. Strauss celebrated the victory of Custozza by composing the Radetzky March.

In March 1849 Charles Albert concentrated his army near Novara, preparatory to a crossing of the Ticino in an effort to recapture Milan. The field marshal assembled his troops east of Pavia, giving the impression he again intended to retreat. Radetzky had 70,000 men, his opponent 65,000, large forces to operate on a thirty-mile front along the Ticino.

With the Sardinians concentrated on the north side of the theater of war and the Austrians on the south, each army had the opportunity to turn the other by marching past its flank and taking up a position in its opponent's rear. Each had a force large enough to block his enemy's retreat and compel him to assume the tactical offensive to recover his communications and base area. Though whichever moved first and fastest could expect to turn the other, Radetzky had the more favorable position because, even exclusive of his route of withdrawal south of the Po, he had more distance between the Sardinians and his line of communications and retreat than Charles Albert had separating his rear from the Austrians. The field marshal, planning to make the most of this opportunity, had kept the forces of his strong left well to the east of Pavia so as not to arouse the king's apprehensions.

The first Sardinian division crossed the Ticino and advanced toward Milan without opposition. Radetzky marched his troops rapidly to Pavia, supplemented its bridge with two on pontoons, and crossed the river quickly. General Ramorino, the commander of the Sardinian division left to delay the Austrians should they cross at Pavia, promptly violated his orders and retreated south of the Po. (After the war the Sardinian army court-martialed and shot him.) Since the Austrian advance to the south presented a more serious threat to the Sardinians than Charles Albert's in the north to Radetzky, the Sardinians promptly moved south to form a front against the Austrians. The armies came into intermittent contact along the eight miles between Vigevano and Mortara; Charles Albert's army held its own until an Austrian corps captured Mortara. Its position turned, the Sardinians fell back on Novara, offering battle south of the city.

Though pushing north toward Novara, Radetzky directed one corps toward Vercelli to block the Sardinian retreat. At Novara three of the four Austrian corps met the Sardinians in an essentially frontal battle that had ended before the Austrian corps directed toward Vercelli arrived to turn the Sardinian flank. Victory belonged to the Austrian rank and file who were by then battle-seasoned as well as thoroughly trained. Success elevated their morale—as did their well-placed confidence in their field marshal. His army vanquished, driven off its line of withdrawal and with its back toward the foothills of the Alps, Charles Albert abdicated in favor of his son, who concluded an armistice preparatory to a peace. The former king, who had shown such inflexible devotion to Italian liberty, died three months later in a Portuguese monastery. The victorious Radetzky died nine years later, quite infirm but still on active duty.

Radetzky's campaigns do not differ from those of the Napoleonic era. In 1848 he had used his interior lines to defeat one of the two forces opposed to him. Then, turning against the other, he had exploited their excessive dispersion to beat them in battle and drive them back westward across northern Italy. In 1849 he had carried out a turning movement that, after he had fought a successful engagement to drive the enemy army from its communications, had placed him athwart the Sardinian line of retreat. Such a conclusive victory and strategic position within the borders of a small country insured peace on the liberal terms the Austrians offered.

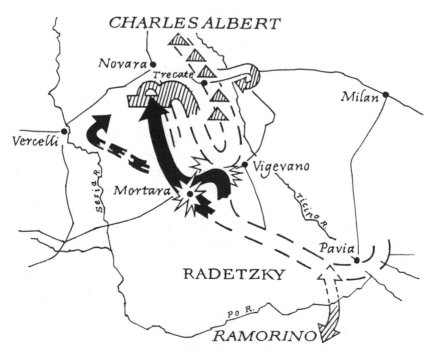

Diagram 7.1. Radetzky's Turning Movement

The Mid-Century's New Infantry Weapons

Radetzky's battles resulted in few casualties, barely 4 percent for the victor and 6.5 percent for the defeated. The principal weapon remained the muzzleloader, improved in reliability by the substitution of the percussion cap for the flintlock. But armies already had a rifle suitable for military use. Using an oblong bullet smaller than the barrel, the rifle loaded easily because the projectile had a smaller diameter than the barrel. This simple Minié bullet had a hollowed out rear so that when the force of the explosion of the powder entered the hollow, the rear of the bullet expanded to grip the rifling as the bullet traveled out of the barrel. This made a gas-tight fit and allowed the rifling to impart a stabilizing spin to the bullet. Together the tight fit and the spin doubled both the range and the accuracy of the muzzleloading rifle as compared with the traditional smoothbore. Yet because the bullet easily slid down the barrel, the rifle had a rate of fire equal to the unrifled weapon.

In 1859, when France and Austria fought, the French took the offensive against the Austrian rifles. Yet the French won the largely frontal battles in which commanders on both sides displayed neither the competence nor subtlety of Radetzky. The French regulars, with good training and full of confidence, followed their doctrine for compensating for the inferiority of their weapons by closing with the enemy as rapidly as possible and bested the Austrians.

The French doctrine of 1859 did not really vary much the tactics that armies had institutionalized after the Napoleonic wars. Recognizing that line and light infantry were interchangeable, the altered tactical doctrine gave a greater importance to skirmishing. Formerly skirmishers had simply preceded the line; by mid-century they assumed the main burden of the attack, with the formed troops held back to support them. The initiative of the individual and small-unit leaders played a greater role, which the skillfully trained and confident French regulars could carry out easily.

In spite of the hard-fought battles and the lethal Austrian weapon, the victorious French lost only 10 percent of their force, the defeated Austrians less than 17 percent. Reflecting that the French assumed the tactical offensive, their killed and wounded approximately equaled those of the Austrians, prisoners accounting for the difference in losses. In combat between these professional armies, casualties had declined below the level experienced during the eighteenth century and the Napoleonic wars. Excellent drill and discipline, together with improved articulation and tactics, doubtless explain this further decrease in the percentage of men killed, injured, or captured. The introduction of the breech-loading rifle doubled the rate of fire of the infantry, and soldiers had always set a higher value on the rate of a soldier's fire than on its accuracy. Following a long delay, due to the lack of workmanship adequate to make a breech capable of containing the gases of the explosion, the Prussians developed a barely satisfactory breechloader with which they gradually equipped their army in the 1840s and 1850s. In addition to its greater rate of fire, the breechloader enabled the soldier to fire from a prone position since he no longer had to work a ramrod and did not require the aid of gravity to load his powder. Instead he placed the entire cartridge in the breech, and the hammer and firing pin exploded the percussion cap and ignited the integral powder charge. The ability to fire while prone automatically gave the defender a substantially augmented advantage over the attacker, for the defender no longer needed field fortifications to gain considerable protection from the attacker's fire.

Troops in a prone position could not use their bayonets to defend themselves against cavalry. But since a breechloading rifle had at least double the rate and twice the accuracy of fire as well as double the range of the smoothbore muzzleloader, riflemen could defend themselves with their firepower alone. Cavalry's shock action had very little opportunity against this revolution in infantry firepower. Long the weaker weapon system against the bayonet-armed musketeer, cavalry lost most of its tactical value when soldiers were equipped with breechloading rifles.

The new rifle also devalued artillery. No longer could artillery unlimber within 300 yards and shoot at the infantry with relative impunity. Not only could rifles sighted to 1,000 yards shoot the gunners, but also soldiers in a prone position provided poor targets for cannister shot. But shrapnel shells gave artillery a means to retrieve the role that cannister shot had given it in the Napoleonic wars. These shells, filled with small projectiles, contained a powder charge exploded by a time fuse. This explosion burst the shell, scattering small projectiles; the forward motion of the shell carried the small projectiles forward, strewing them from above over a substantial area of the ground below. But the fuses of mid-nineteenth-century shrapnel lacked enough accuracy to insure that the shrapnel would explode in the air above the troops at which the gunners aimed, even if the gunners had correctly gauged the range.

The French created a new weapon, the *mitrailleuse*, to furnish the offensive firepower that artillery and its cannister could no longer provide and shrapnel's inaccuracy made too uncertain. Built at the direction of Napoleon III, an author of a work on artillery, the *mitrailleuse*, consisted of a bundle of twenty-five rifle barrels mounted on an artillery gun carriage. Fired mechanically in rapid succession and quickly reloaded simultaneously by a crew, its barrels could fire 125 shots per minute, delivering aimed fire for almost two miles. Used in 1870 to prepare the way for an infantry assault, it failed to have much effect against prone troops and since Napoleon III had kept it a secret and not issued it to the army, the artillerymen were unfamiliar with its use and the enemy artillery made it a special target. A similar weapon, the Gatling gun, was used, too, but it only functioned to augment infantry's already awesome firepower.

By the 1860s technological alterations had reinforced changes that had taken place with the introduction of the flintlock and bayonet. The new weapons consolidated the supremacy of the missile infantryman and further devalued shock cavalry as a weapon system. Artillery acquired rifled and breechloaded barrels, but these improvements only counterbalanced the new defensive strength of prone infantry with breechloaders, leaving artillery still a powerful but relatively immobile missile weapon system, indispensable for sieges but otherwise far more formidable in defense than offense.

The Prussian Staff and Manpower System

Just as the French regulations of 1791 contributed to creating profound alterations in tactics and strategy, two fundamental changes in the use of manpower had a major effect on the scale of operations and the management of armies in the nineteenth century. One, the perfection of the commander's staff, vastly improved the conduct of military operations. Evolving over several centuries, the quality and significance of the staff had received a strong impetus in the armies of Napoleon; the next stride in its improvement came in the Prussian army. By the eighteenth century the quartermaster was an important staff officer, with charge of the supply and movement of armies. In the Prussian army this responsibility led to the quartermaster's taking on virtually the entire burden for the conduct of operations, and, as the Prussian army evolved, he carried out his duties so well that his staff assumed, very properly, a significance hitherto unknown.

With huge forces dispersed over considerable areas, armies needed better management than the old organization could supply. The staff needs of a commander of a concentrated army of 40,000 men differed markedly from those of 200,000 spread over a wide area. The Prussian army developed a larger staff composed of men who had received uniform training, so that all had the same doctrine and vocabulary. Serving on the staffs of army and corps commanders, these officers understood one another readily and gave their commanders consistent recommendations. Coordinated by a chief who could represent their views to the commander, the staff could provide counsel and carry out the commander's orders. As advisors and executants, the staff came to represent the commander and gave orders in his name. Coordination and management improved because of harmony and communication between the staffs at different command levels.

By the middle of the nineteenth century the Prussian staff fully applied these principles and, as a corps of specially trained men who alternated staff and troop duty, executed its tasks very well. The staff made plans, issued orders and supervised their execution, and managed all aspects of the army and subordinate units, including operations, intelligence, personnel, supply, and movements. The excellence of the Prussian staff, though not always their quartermaster-based organization, became a model that armies worldwide began to emulate. By the twentieth century all European armies had a trained, adequately staffed management team to assist the line commander in his traditional duties of planning, fighting, marching, and caring for the men and horses.

Just as the Prussian staff represented a major step forward, so also did the Prussian innovation in providing manpower. The Prussian system had such distinctiveness that it differed in kind rather than degree from most militias and other similar systems that many armies employed.

The Prussian army of Frederick the Great, containing many foreigners to avoid taking Prussians from productive employment, had also drawn in rural citizens who, after receiving training, had returned to their villages on furlough. Recalled periodically for additional training and to bring their companies up to full strength for maneuvers, these soldiers, though lacking the training and esprit of long-service regulars, had economized the state's resources in a tangible way: they did not require pay when on furlough and their villages did not lose all of their labor.

When Napoleon defeated and imposed peace on the king of Prussia, he limited Prussia's army to 42,000 men and forbade any reserve. But the Prussians unobtrusively furloughed from each company a few men each month and filled their places with untrained men. Between 1808 and 1813, 36,000 Prussians not on active duty had received training. When war came again, these trained reservists rejoined their companies, bringing them to war strength. These men differed markedly from militia or the large number of green recruits from whom the Prussians created the bulk of the armies for their war with Napoleon. The 36,000 trained men recalled to duty served in the regular unit in which they had trained and under professional commissioned and noncommissioned officers alongside of soldiers already a part of the unit. In addition, these reservists participated significantly in the culture of the unit because they had trained there and knew most of their officers, sergeants, and many of the privates with whom they served. Thus, these civilian soldiers nearly doubled the size of the Prussian regular army without appreciably diluting its quality.

At the end of the Napoleonic wars, Prussia fundamentally altered its old system of a long-service professional force, only the officers and noncommissioned officers remaining career professionals. Instead, the army conscripted 40,000 men each year, keeping the infantrymen for three years, the cavalrymen and artillerymen for longer periods. Each year the army brought in all drafted men at the same time, simultaneously discharging those who had completed their service.

After discharge, the conscripts entered the reserve for a period of two years. Called up each summer for maneuvers, they brought their units to war strength and had the same advantages of familiarity with their leaders and fellow soldiers that had characterized the reservists trained between 1808 and 1813. The Prussians further reinforced this unit spirit by giving each regiment a geographical region from which to draw their recruits, so the men enjoyed another common bond that supported their morale and motivation. The Prussians' systematic, universal application of the plan used to prepare to fight Napoleon had its origins in the old system of furloughing native Prussian soldiers.

The Prussians also had a militia, the Landwehr, and they required a reservist who had completed his two years of reserve service to spend seven in the Landwehr. The Landwehr and the active army and its reserves constituted the Prussian field army. Exclusive of professional officers and noncommissioned officers, who provided the cadre of the active army, and the reserve officers, who led the Landwehr, the Prussian army would have had the strength shown in table 7.1. if all had served three years and no soldier died, emigrated, or suffered disability.

The Prussians also had another formation in which men discharged from the Landwehr served for eight years. They did not intend that these older men take the field but expected them to garrison fortresses, help resist invasion, and provide a pool of trained manpower for replacements in a long war.

TABLE 7.1.   The Initial Prussian Cadre, Reserve, and Militia Force

	Years of Service	×	Number Available	=	Total
Active army	3		40,000		120,000
Reserves	2		40,000		80,000
Total active army and its reserves					200,000
Landwehr	7		40,000		280,000
Total field army					480,000

This system of reserves increased the number of active army privates by 40 percent without significantly diminishing unit quality because the reserves returned to the unit in which they had served for their period of active duty. Thus, the army remained essentially a long-service force, for professionals supplied all of the leaders. On the other hand, the army also had much of the character of a militia or citizen force, but one composed of thoroughly trained men and led by a cadre of regulars.

Besides the advantage of professional leadership for the active army and its reserves, the Prussians had many of the benefits that long, continuous service gave to regular forces. Although not all men had served together, many had, and with a local basis for recruiting many more knew each other in civilian life. For these reasons Prussian units enjoyed most of the morale, sei.se of community, and cohesion characteristic of long-service professonal soldiers. Although it lost some unit esprit and competence by using reserves, the Prussian army gained far more in the large augmentation of its numbers at a trivial cost. This method also economized on the budget, because the government did not have to pay the conscripts the wage necessary to bid them away from civilian employment. Of course, the economy had to do without the labor of the active soldiers, but neither the economy nor the army's budget suffered any consequential loss because of the reserves, who followed their civilians pursuits for most of the year.

The Landwehr, which provided the other half of the field army, also had the advantage of a negligible peacetime cost. As a militia, the Landwehr had great effectiveness because all its members had undergone a substantial period of extended active-duty training. The Landwehr officers, drawn from the educated classes, had received one year of training before assuming their duties as militia officers. Although actual practice varied somewhat from the model, Prussia had provided itself with a trained military force of nearly half a million soldiers at a modest cost. Smaller and less populous than the other continential military powers, the Prussians in their system had a military force comparable to those of her powerful neighbors.

But at mid-century, when Prussia mobilized to face internal and external crises, the Landwehr proved a serious disappointment. Lacking a peacetime existence, the Landwehr was a confused mass, the officers ignorant of their duties and the men not knowing their places. The Prussians then concluded that only a force existing in peace and based on a cadre of professionals could effectively take the field in war. In 1861 they reformed their army, taking account of population growth by expanding the annual conscript contingent to 63,000, and, more significantly, increasing the reserve service to five years. They gave the service in the Landwehr an auxiliary role only. The new model of the Prussian army relied almost entirely on a cadre-based field force (table 7.2).

TABLE 7.2.   The Prussian Cadre and Reserve Force

	Years of Service	×	Number Available	=	Total
Active army	3		63,000		189,000
Reserves	5		63,000		315,000
Total active army and its reserves					504,000
Landwehr	4		63,000		252,000

As a result of this reform the active army and its reserves equaled in numbers and far exceeded in quality the old active army and Landwehr together. In addition, Prussia improved the Landwehr by assigning to it regular officers and replacing them with some reserve offices in junior positions in the mobilized active army. In its active army and its reserves the Prussians had successfully combined the characteristics of professionals with the low cost and large numbers of a militia and retained most of the benefits of each system. By the development of an effective reserve for its active army, Prussia had profoundly affected the logistics of its own manpower, having a monopoly of the application of this system on such a large scale and with such effectiveness.

But all nations immediately felt the effect of the electric telegraph and the steam railway. Cheaper and more rapid and reliable than the Chappe visual telegraph, by the 1860s the electric telegraph had linked all major points in

Illustration 7.1. Steam Railroad and Telegraph

European countries. The result meant almost instant communication between armies and between commanders and their headquarters. The telegraph also expedited mobilization once communities with reservists or militia had that type of communication. By the 1860s the steam railroad provided rapid, inexpensive communication between all major cities in Western Europe. It not only facilitated the mobilization and concentration of armies but also could supply armies from a base, long a monopoly of water transport.

In 1850 the Austrians used the railway to transport to Bohemia 75,000 men who, perhaps together with the impending arrival of Field Marshal Radetzky to take command, had helped the Prussians decide not to pit their army and imperfectly functioning Landwehr against Austria's seasoned regulars and formidable field marshal. A few years later, in their brief war with Austria, the French moved, in three months, over 600,000 men and 129,000 horses by train. Yet the railroad, like the telegraph, was fragile and could not immediately serve an army invading a hostile country that had disabled its railroads and telegraphs as its armies retreated.

The New Prussian Army in Action against Austria

The new Prussian manpower system received a thorough test in 1866 when Prussia fought the Austrians in Bohemia. The competently planned mobilization of Prussian reservists went smoothly, and the armies concentrated quickly and effectively using the railroad. The excellent Prussian staff had planned skillfully and supervised the strategy's execution equally well. For chief of the general staff King William I of Prussia had wisely chosen his son's former aide-de-camp, Helmuth von Moltke. This extrordinary soldier had made his way up through the peacetime Prussian army. That he remained a second lieutenant for twelve years reflected no lack of confidence in him, for his superiors had sent him through the three-year war school and appointed him to the general staff. The scholarly Moltke had published several historical works and one novel and had broadened his background by service in the Turkish army. His taciturn manner and complete mastery of social graces masked a profound understanding of military operations gained through his excellent education and tireless independent study. King William, a combat veteran of the last years of the Napoleonic wars, largely left military operations to his chief of staff just as he depended in politics and diplomacy on his superb chancellor, Bismarck.

In the Austrian army Moltke faced a basically long-service professional force with a higher peacetime strength than Prussia's and requiring far less augumentation by mobilization. Emphasizing speed of mobilization, the Prussian staff concentrated its forces in three armies covering the 200 miles from Silesia to the borders of Austria's ally, Saxony. The Prussians thus had to advance into Bohemia on exterior lines, a situation which the Austrians, plagued with supply diffculties and poor staff work, made no effort to exploit. The Austrian commander, Benedek, though he had played an honorable part in the Austrian defeat at the hands of the French in 1859, displayed a lack of energy and was almost despondent about the campaign.

The two westernmost Prussian armies soon united, and in a week the two forces had drawn within supporting distance. They then moved separately against the Austrians, joining together on the battlefield of Königgrätz, where one force held the Austrians in front while the other attacked the flank. But the Austrians, with a well-articulated army of veteran regulars, succeeded in withdrawing in good order, ultimately directing their troops to Vienna where they met reinforcements from Italy. The war would have continued had not internal political difficulties as well as the initial defeat prompted the Austrian emperor to accept the very limited political concessions sought by the Prussians and their Italian allies. Hostilites lasted only seven weeks.

The war demonstrated the effectiveness of the Prussian army of conscripts led by a cadre of regulars. Inexperienced in battle and facing Austrian combat veterans who had a minimum enlistment of seven years, the Prussians had fought well. Their staff had managed the mobilization capably and competently directed the movements of the armies and their constituent corps and divisions. Though outranged by the Austrian muzzleloading rifle, the Prussian breechloader proved its worth. In spite of having half the range of the Austrian rifle and such a poor seal at the breech that it could emit a flash that might deprive the soldier of sight in one eye, its higher rate of fire complemented the cover provided by firing in the prone position to demonstrate its decisive predominance over the muzzleloader and the Austrian soldiers who had to stand to reload.

As in the earlier battles between the French and Austrians, the skirmish line dominated the offensive deployment and gradually absorbed the formed troops. The Prussians, having substituted the company for the battalion column for maneuver, found that they had made a wise choice. But even with these small, relatively open formations, they discovered that on many occasions soldiers displayed an anxiety to go forward and join the skirmish line where they could seek cover and return fire. The breechloader simplified this development because it enabled the Prussian skirmishers to lie prone when they could find no better cover.

Artillery demonstrated its value on the defense when the proficiently served Austrian guns provided excellent protection for their army as it extricated itself from its difficult position at the end of the Battle of Königgrätz.

Decisive Turning Movements in the Franco-Prussian War

The Prussian army contrasted sharply with the French army in the war of 1870. Though both armies had adequate combat experience, the Prussian army had breechloading artillery, which had the advantage over the French army's muzzleloading guns. On the other hand, the French, who had attributed Prussia's victory over Austria to the breechloader, had armed its men with a much superior breechloading rifle. With a rifle with a longer range and an excellent seal at the breech, French soldiers had no temptation to emulate the Prussians and fire from the hip to save their eyesight. The French army, though it had some reserves, remained a long-service professional force similar to Austrian's.

It was intangibles more than weapons and manpower systems that separated the two armies. Not only did the Prussians have an incomparably better staff, but its members had received an education that gave adequate attention to the conduct of large-scale operations. The French army, unlike the intellectually active force of the previous century, stressed courage and small-unit leadership. Military education had decreased in quality, and fewer officers had attended the schools. The army promoted many officers from the ranks, some of whom were and remained illiterate. Long successful in colonial wars, the French emphasized the virtues required in those operations, neglecting the mastery of logistics and strategy needed for the conduct of major campaigns. Success in the Crimea against Russia and in Italy against Austria, achieved in spite of poor staff work and unimaginative campaigning, confirmed the view of most of its leaders that the army worked well enough. With a better rifle and excellent morale, the army and nation believed that the trained French professional soldier would triumph.

But when war came the French army lacked the organization and planning to begin a campaign promptly. It had dispersed its regiments around the country, separated from sparse reserves, and kept its supplies in a few large depots. For active operations the mediocre staff had simultaneously to assemble active and reserve forces, combine them into divisions, corps, and armies, distribute supplies, and concentrate the men for the campaign. Even with excellent plans this would have proven virtually insuperable, but the staff lacked adequate plans.

In Prussia each corps headquarters controlled a region and mobilized the troops within it, the corps' drawing their reserves from the immediate vicinity. With men, materiel, and supplies in the region and under corps control, mobilization took place quickly, and each corps moved to its place in the concentration according to a plan prepared and administered by the general staff of the army. The railroad and the telegraph assured that this process occurred simultaneously and relatively smoothly throughout Prussia and its German confederates.

The Prussian army had many more men than four years earlier when it fought Austria. In the interim it had discharged four additional annual contingents of 63,000 men into the reserve, making the new system adopted in 1861 fully effective. So, on the frontier between the Rhine and Luxembourg, King William of Prussia and General Moltke concentrated over 450,000 men; the French, under Emperor Napoleon III, had only half that number to resist the Prussian advance against the part of the French frontier that was unobstructed by the Rhine or the Vosges Mountains. Though interested in military affairs, the ailing French emperor had little taste or talent for army command and lacked both an effective general staff and a brilliant chief to direct his campaign. The emperor, an astute politican and possessed of many good qualities, did not possess either the temperament or the health to lead an army. But since a Napoleon's place must be with the armies, he took the field in person, ill-served by inadequate subordinates.

Having concentrated the bulk of his forces along the frontier east of Metz, Napoleon III, finding his supplies in a tangle and his army unready to take the offensive, waited for the Prussians to act. Moltke, with his armies closer together but otherwise arranged much as in the Bohemian campaign four years earlier, expected to withstand a French attack with his central army while seeking to envelop the French with the other two.

The failure of the French advance to materialize and the necessity of making the first move did not alter the basic concept that he intended the broad distribution of his larger forces to facilitate. But on August 6 General Steinmetz, the overly aggressive and insubordinate commander of the small First Army on the Prussian right, attacked the French at Spicheren, where they not only had a strong position but also greater numbers within reach of the battlefield. For much of a day, Prussian assaults failed so conclusively that General Frossard, the French commander, did not call very urgently for reinforcements. But Frossard had exhausted his reserves at hand when at last a Prussian turning column appeared and forced the French to withdraw.

The Germans, in spite of their heavy casualties, celebrated victory, even though it bore no relation to von Moltke's strategic objectives. French morale suffered correspondingly because, though they had successfully resisted frontal attacks, they had retreated. A small action at the frontier town of Wissembourg, where three Prussian army corps, totaling 50,000 men, surprised and defeated 6,000 French troops, had a similar effect on the morale of both sides. Both engagements exhibited the tactical power of the breechloader in the defense and the value in the attack of the Prussian rifled artillery with shells that exploded on impact.

But, simultaneously with the August 6 Battle of Spicheren, the Prussian Crown Prince's Third Army on the Prussian left forced its way through the Vosges Mountains in a battle at Froeschwiller brought on by corps commanders against the Crown Prince's desires. In the rugged terrain of these frontier mountains Marshal MacMahon's French army occupied a position so strong that, confident the Prussians would not attack, he had not directed his troops to entrench. In MacMahon, a veteran of warfare in Algeria, the Crimea, and Italy, the French had a solid but not brilliant marshal. But, contrary to the will of either commander, a battle began when, one Prussian corps after another having involved itself in attacks on the French, the Crown Prince had to intervene to give form to a battle that had evolved from the independent decisions of subordinates.

Eventually superior numbers enabled two Bavarian corps to engage and outflank the French division on the Prussian right while persistent, unsuccessful frontal assaults continued to engage the French center. On their left the Prussians had concentrated an entire corps to cross the river and attack the French occupying terrain ill-adapted to the defense. Soon the French saw "a black swarm of Prussians emerging at the run from the Gunstett bridge with every appearance of disorder. From this ant-heap, as if by magic, company columns shook themselves out and rapidly and without hesitation took up a perfectly regular formation." Soon the French right flank had to withdraw to avoid envelopment.[1]

Marshal MacMahon extricated his threatened army with difficulty and retreated southeast. Of his 42,000 infantry he lost 11,000 killed and wounded and 9,000 prisoners. Of their 89,000 infantry the Prussians lost only 10,500, all killed and wounded. As Lanchester's theory would suggest, greater Prussian numbers inflicted a very high level of casualties on their weaker opponent, in spite of the benefits that the defensive offered the French.

This major battle shows the excellence of the French professional army. One regiment, for example, did not retreat until it had lost 1,775 killed and wounded of its original strength of 2,200. Prussian infantry, at a disadvantage with their inferior rifle, displayed superb training in maneuvering and attacking in company column. Yet soon the Prussian attacking formations dissolved into a skirmish line in which the men lay prone or sought cover to return fire. With breechloading rifles men no longer stood within 100 yards and fired at each other until one side withdrew. But unable to keep men together in formation, officers could no longer exercise the same control of the attack. In developing tactics to combat the Austrian rifle, the French had altered their tactics to rely more on individual initiative and less on formations responding to higher command, thus requiring junior officers and noncommissioned officers to play a more prominent role in tactics. The Prussians had the same experience as their formations became skirmish lines and the initiative and leadership passed to subordinates.

The increased strength of the defense gave the artillery a more important role in the offense. The Prussians had improved their gunnery after its poor performance against Austria four years earlier and completed the re-equipment of their artillery with steel, breechloading, rifled guns. Firing shells that exploded on impact, Prussian guns had proved better than the bronze, muzzle-loading French rifled cannon in range and rate of fire. The principal French disadvantage, however, stemmed from their poor choice of ammunition. They initially relied exclusively on shrapnel shell, which had a time fuse that, in addition to its erratic performance, permitted no burst between 1,700 and 3,300 yards. Though the French later switched to percussion-fused ammunition, these deficiencies had enabled Prussian artillery to silence the French guns and inflict serious casualties upon the unentrenched defending French infantry.

The cavalry on each side played little role, the Prussian horsemen for the most part staying off the rifle-dominated battlefield. French cavalry attacked on two occasions, committed on unfavorable terrain as a last resort to help cover a retreat. The first charge initially looked irresistible, but the Prussian infantry, already behind hedges, walls, and trees, brought the horsemen under rapid, accurate fire. The attempt ended in an unsuccessful effort to get through the streets of a village. The second try, over even worse ground, fared no better, the infantry shooting the cavalry from cover. Probably no saber cut any infantryman and no infantryman had occasion to defend himself with his bayonet. The era of shock action in the traditional sense seemed to have ended, and cavalry, a large target in any case and usually unable to take cover, had lost its tactical role.

With the introduction of the breechloading rifle, only one weapon system existed on the battlefield, the light or missile infantryman, who no longer even needed a bayonet or had to stand and form squares to resist cavalry. The rifleman's tactics increasingly resembled those long customary for light infantry. Soldiers left their formations to fight as skirmishers, increasing their security without diminishing their firepower.

Before the war Moltke had written: "It is absolutely beyond doubt that the man who shoots without stirring has the advantage of him who fires while advancing, that the one finds protection in the ground, whereas in it the other finds obstacles, and that, if to the most spirited dash one opposes a quiet steadiness, it is fire effect, nowadays so powerful, which will determine the issue." The initial battles demonstrated the truth of his judgment, for the tactical results displayed the traditional preponderance of the defense in combat between similar weapon systems. Similar to but less mobile than the infantry in its battlefield role, the improved artillery still proved stronger in the defense than on the offense. In lieu of a diagram showing the supremacy of infantry over cavalry, schematic 7.1 best exhibits the tactical realities of 1870.[2]

missile infantry ─────── D ───────► missile infantry

Schematic 7.1. The Dominance of Light Infantry and the Defense

But tactical realities did not determine the campaign. High ability opposed to gross incompetence readily gave the decision to strategy. When Napoleon III learned of the defeats of his armies on August 6, he completely lost his nerve. Already ill with kidney stones and now faced with events that might cause the overthrow of his shaky regime, he showed the effects of his burdens, officers who came in contact with him during this period describing him as "much aged, much weakened, and possessing none of the bearing of the leader of an army."[3] At first directing his army to move west as far as Châlons, he countermanded his order when he realized the political impact of such a withdrawal. Because he felt uneasy about uncovering Paris, the emperor rejected a march south to join MacMahon's retreating army and the forces at Belfort, a flank position from which the concentrated French could have menaced any march on the fortified city of Paris. So the armies along the frontier fell back to the fortress of Metz.

Napoleon did decide to turn over the control of operations to one of his marshals and selected Marshal Canrobert who had commanded in the Crimea. But, when Canrobert, understanding his limitations, declined, the emperor selected Marshal Bazaine. Rising from the ranks in the foreign legion, Bazaine had displayed ability and great courage as a junior officer. He had fought in the Crimea and Italy and had his first independent assignment in an essentially colonial war in Mexico. Unfit for leadership of a large army, Bazaine exemplified the Peter Principle in action: he had risen well above the level at which he could perform competently. He aggravated the situation because, miffed with the emperor's choice of a chief of staff for him, he ignored his staff and tried to run the army with his aides. Further, he had trouble acting as if he had control because the emperor remained nearby and made suggestions.

The French army moved slowly to Metz because, following security measures learned combating insurgents in Africa, it closed up its columns every night, instead of bivouacing along the road and resuming the march the next day. Even the cavalry followed the Algerian practice, keeping concentrated close to the infantry, and so did little reconnaissance to ascertain the position of the Prussians. Meanwhile, Marshal MacMahon, intent on keeping away from the Prussians after his defeat at Froeschwiller, moved his army eastward, ignoring directions to draw close to the forces concentrating at Metz. By August 10 he had reached a railroad and used it to send his army to Châlons.

By August 9 the Prussians had learned the directions of the French retreats, and Moltke ordered an advance of all three armies on a fifty-mile front. Moltke had no specific plan, but his broad distribution would enable him to turn the French when he met them, his excellent staff could rapidly concentrate his forces against a point of French weakness. His directive sent one toward Metz and two, the Second and Third armies, on routes that led them south of the fortress and small city. Virtually all of the huge Prussian force followed on a broad front. With reinforcements sent to Metz by rail, the French had 180,000 men, the Prussians 2.5 times as many.

By August 13 Prussian infantry from the Second Army had crossed the Moselle south of Metz, and three days later the Third Army infantry had done the same. Moltke's wide dispersion then presented an opportunity for a turning movement. Napoleon III had long realized this possibility and had already had pontoon bridges constructed over the Moselle at Metz when he urged an immediate withdrawal from the fortress on August 13. In spite of the three permanent bridges, Marshal Bazaine delayed his retreat until August 14 because high water had damaged the pontoon bridges; then Bazaine, managing matters himself, forgot to use one of the bridges. Moving such a huge army through the streets of a small town and over six bridges took more than a day, and the Prussians interrupted the withdrawal with an assault. Again Prussian subordinate commanders attacked without orders and, though the French rear guard easily repulsed them, Bazaine suspended his retreat for twelve hours.

When the French army finally passed through Metz, its progress continued slowly. Still ignoring his staff, Bazaine directed it westward using only one road, even forbidding the use of a second road. But despite the slow advance and the presence of a few Prussian cavalry patrols, the road west still remained open on August 16. Yet the almost lackadaisical Bazaine failed to order a resumption of the retreat until the afternoon of the 16th. Comfortable with his army all concentrated and feeling secure when near the powerful fortress of Metz, Marshal Bazaine failed to exhibit any feelings of urgency or to take the most elementary steps to extricate his army from what had become a most dangerous situation.

Beginning to grasp the enemy's vulnerability on August 15, Moltke ordered the Second Army to advance rapidly north and west to attack the retreating French army. But assuming that the French must already have reached Verdun, the Second Army commander sent most of his troops west. Nevertheless, with the French virtually inert outside of Metz, this proved exactly the direction needed to complete a turning movement such as Napoleon I had accomplished at Ulm. Yet, as with Radetzky's turning movement at Novara, the Prussians would require a battle to consolidate their decisive strategic position.

Bazaine's army never began its afternoon march west because two Prussian divisions attacked them as they waited along the Verdun road. The aggressive and able Prussian commander, unable to believe that the French would move so slowly, sought to cut off what he supposed was the French rearguard. Reinforced by two more divisions in the afternoon, he maintained his assault all day along the road from Rezonville to Mars-la-Tour. Marshal Bazaine, who had greater numbers, with two corps engaged and two in reserve, could readily have extended his right to the west and defeated the Prussians while opening the road to Verdun. But the marshal kept the bulk of his men concentrated on his unthreatened left to protect his connection with Metz. He did not want to lose the safety of withdrawal into the fortress. After a bloody, all-day battle, in which the French lost almost 14,000 and the Prussians nearly 16,000 men, the French remained in their positions, but the Prussians had blocked the road west in two places.

Yet two to three miles north lay another road for the retreat to the west. Still Bazaine, unwilling to leave the security of Metz, decided to spend August 17 falling back to a line of battle facing west. From here, after he had replenished his ammunition and supplies from the stocks in Metz, he planned to resume his withdrawal later. While the French used the 17th to make their slow retreat toward Metz, Moltke issued orders to exploit the situation. Not realizing that the French were falling back eastward as if to expedite their entrapment, and so only hoping to push the French north toward the Luxembourg border, Moltke brought the First Army across the Moselle south of Metz and the entire Second Army north toward the site of the previous day's battle.

The commander of the Second Army, ignorant of the whereabouts of Bazaine, ordered his army north on the 17th, realizing that "whether it will be eventually necessary to make a wheeling movement to the right or the left cannot be decided at present." Certain the French had already escaped westward, the commander, expecting to meet a rearguard, had ordered his men to "set out tomorrow morning toward the north to find the enemy and fight him." But once again Bazaine's timid inertia had confused the Prussians. Insofar as the Prussians needed a battle to keep Bazaine from leaving Metz, they had fought it on August 16 between Rezonville and Mars-la-tour. Yet they began another engagement anyway, almost as if they expected to have to fight to achieve what Bazaine had given them gratis by backing his army toward Metz.[4]

Across the French line of retreat and ready to have the advantage of the tactical defensive if the enemy tried to escape, 188,000 Germans attacked 112,000 entrenched Frenchmen in a contest that opened when the French returned fire. A German officer reported: "Everywhere, along the whole range, guns sent out flashes and belched forth dense volumes of smoke. A hail of shell and shrapnel, the latter traceable by the little white clouds, looking like balloons, which remained suspended in the air for some time after bursting, answered the war-like greeting from our side. The grating noise of the mitrailleuses was heard above the tumult, drowning the whole roar of the battle." During the day the Prussians and their German allies made a number of assaults. One of them, seen from the Prussian side, revealed "masses of infantry, cavalry and artillery crowding into the ravine, some of them pressing on to the front, others falling back under pressure of the enemy's fire as the range got shorter, wounded and unwounded men, infantry in order and in disorder streaming in opposite directions and jumbled together, the echo of the shells as they burst in the wood or above the trees, the whistling of the bullets from either side as they rushed overhead, and over the whole a column of dust which darkened the sun."[5]

The numerically superior Prussians, by extending their line and turning the French right flank, drove Bazaine into the security of Metz, where he had yearned to go all along. The Battle of Gravelotte-St. Privat again demonstrated the tactical power of the defense. When the Prussian Guard, an elite unit of almost 30,000 infantry, attacked in formation, it lost 8,000 killed and wounded in the little over twenty minutes before the aristocratic guardsmen fell into the prone position, returned fire, and refused to advance farther toward the French line. The French suffered negligible casualties in repelling this assault, and their infantry, firing their excellent breechloaders, accounted for the bulk of the losses of the Prussian Guard.

Strategically redundant, the battle cost the Prussians 20,000 men and the French 12,000, each losing a little over 10 percent of the forces engaged. Bazaine promptly fell back within the safety of the fortress of Metz. With most of the Prussian troops east of the Moselle, Bazaine could fairly easily have marched out of Metz to the southeast; but, insofar as he had any plan to leave, he wired the emperor that after giving his troops rest for a couple of days, he intended to move northwest in the direction where the Prussians had substantial strength. But Bazaine made no effort to escape from Metz in any direction.

Thus Bazaine lost half of the French armies. In addition to illustrating the Peter Principle and displaying the profound influence that an incompetent performance could have on history, Bazaine showed a general wilting under the responsibility of command. He had become what the French call *fatigué*. Overcome with responsibility and adversity, he lost the power of decision and readily clung to the familiar fortifications of Metz and the temporary refuge that they offered.

Promptly organizing the blockade of Metz, Moltke sent a force west. It moved abreast of the Third Army in the south that, after defeating MacMahon at Froeschwiller, had remained south of Metz not participating in the bottling up of Bazaine. Moltke directed these two armies on Châlons.

After vacillating, the French at Châlons decided that the army under Marshal

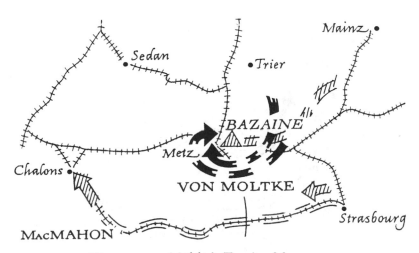

Diagram 7.2. Moltke's Turning Movement

MacMahon should march northeast toward Metz to relieve the unwilling Bazaine. MacMahon's route, chosen to enable him to draw supplies from the
railroad, led him toward the Belgian border, which he would have to skirt on
his route to Metz to meet Bazaine's hypothetical but unattempted sortie to the
northwest. Realizing his peril, MacMahon wished to turn back but continued
to move forward in response to an emphatic telegram from Paris that warned
of revolution if the army abandoned Bazaine. MacMahon then pushed on, taking
with him Napoleon III, sick, *fatigué*, and expressing his reservations about such
a move.

When Moltke realized the direction of the march of MacMahon's force,
he exploited his interior lines between the inert Bazaine and the advancing
MacMahon and turned his two armies to the right and headed them north to
turn the enemy and press MacMahon against the Belgian frontier. This he successfully did, compelling the surrender of the French emperor and over 100,000
men at Sedan, their retreat cut off on three sides by the enemy armies and on
the fourth by the Belgian frontier. A two to one numerical predominance and
a high ratio of force to space simplified a task that Napoleon I had found arduous
with relatively few men in the Marengo campaign.

MacMahon had known what he risked by his march to Sedan, but leaders
in Paris, aware of the political dangers yet failing to appreciate miltiary realities,
had ordered the army to its doom. Again the Prussians had achieved a strategic
victory comparable to Ulm. The surrender of the emperor and the army brought
the overthrow of the empire and the proclamation of a French republic. The
republic pursued the war with vigor, conscripting hundreds of thousands of men,
equipping them with newly manufactured weapons and with imports through
ports kept open by the powerful French navy.

The subsequent operations centered on the Prussian seige of Paris and the
efforts of the French to raise the siege. The Prussians faced a difficult assignment
in blockading the populous, heavily fortified city with its huge garrison. At the

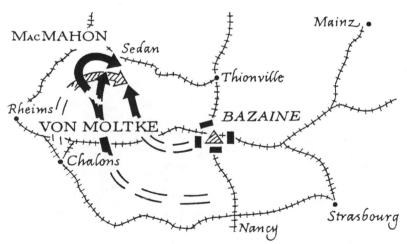

Diagram 7.3. Interior Lines and Turning Movement

same time they had to fend off the relief attempts by the large, though improvised, French armies. Bazaine's surrender of 173,000 men at Metz at the end of October augmented the forces for covering the siege of Paris and for coping with the attacks by irregular units on Prussian communications. The fall of Paris, at the end of January 1871, its food supplies exhausted, brought a peace in which the French ceded two provinces to the new German empire and paid an enormous sum of money.

French efforts to raise the siege of Paris had no chance of success. The Prussians not only had the advantage of the tactical defensive against both the Paris garrison and the relieving armies but also the superiority given them by their training and the improvement in their military skills through campaigning and combat. Against trained soldiers and commanders with battle experience and staffs that had perfected their methods in the opening campaigns, the French pitted improvised armies. With almost all of the regular troops surrounded in Metz or surrendered at Sedan, the French lacked any significant cadre of regulars upon which to build new armies. In spite of using sailors and retired officers, they could not create overnight forces capable of taking the offensive against thoroughly trained and expertly led Prussian combat veterans.

Thus the victories at Metz and Sedan decided the war. Over 2,000 years before, an incompetent Roman commander had given Hannibal the opportunity to destroy the Roman force at Cannae. Yet this battle had not decided the war because the Romans raised new armies and the bulk of the Italian population continued to resist the Carthaginians. And the French responded in the same way. But a major difference lay in the ratio of force to space. In trying to dominate about one-third of France, the Prussians dealt with an area about half again the size of the part of Italy Hannibal sought to control. The Prussians had enough force to pursue a combat persisting strategy, for they had nearly a million men. The Prussians had a force adequate to dominate enough of France to achieve for their political objectives. As did the Carthaginians, the Prussians had limited goals; if, as Napoleon had in Spain, the Prussians had sought to control all of the huge country and impose on its people a Prussian king, they doubtless would have encountered problems similar to those Napoleon had, including the intervention of foreign powers that would have objected to such a radical shift in the balance of power.

A Summary of the Tactics, Logistics, and Strategy of the Franco-Prussian War

In the battles between the trained Prussian and French troops the victors lost 9.4 percent of their forces, the defeated just over 16 percent. Both of these percentages represent a substantial reduction from the numbers characteristic of the eighteenth century and the wars of Napoleon. This decline in casualties occurred in spite of the heightened lethality of the weapons used, numerous Prussian frontal attacks, and the demonstrated increase that the breechloading rifle gave to the power of the tactical defense. The good doctrine and training provided the troops, together with the tactics employed, most likely offer the principal explanation for this significant change.

The Prussians, who almost always assumed the offensive, used their small company columns to take advantage of the ground and usually deployed at a considerable distance. The attackers soon all became skirmishers, and advances took place as a series of rushes by parts of the line. These offensive tactics, also used by the French, diminished the exposure of troops to the more deadly new weapons. The attackers, like the defenders, also secured protection from the prone position that the breechloader made possible. Adaptation to the new weapons, as well as the greater opportunity for cover that they offered the troops, resulted in reduced casualties for both attackers and defenders. Ample training, improved articulation, and unit cohesion help account for the low casualties among the defeated.

Logistics changed very little during the Franco-Prussian War, the Prussian and, to a large extent, the French armies living on the country in the traditional manner. The railways, having expedited Prussian mobilization and concentration, contributed very little to supply. French fortresses blocked the railway lines, and not until January 1871, when the war had nearly ended, did the Prussians get a second rail line working between the German frontier and the Paris siege. The one line that began operation in late September did help feed the besiegers of Paris, transport the siege artillery, and enable the accumulation of ammunition for a bombardment of the French capital.

Yet supply for the huge armies of Prussia and its German allies rested primarily on the dense population and great agricultural productivity of France. Beginning the campaign at the harvest season helped Moltke's armies, but when they faced the traditional dilemma of feeding a besieging army, the Prussian soldiers utilized their agricultural background by digging potatoes and harvesting and milling wheat. Requisition, purchase, and some contributions placed the produce of France at the disposal of the Prussians. Even when armies had access to a railroad, the supply organization had not solved either the problem of storing at the railhead the large quantity of supplies that the railroad could deliver or of transporting them to the troops.

In spite of the increased rate of fire of rifles and field guns, ammunition supply did not tax the logistical organization. Prussian small-arms ammunition expenditure for the war averaged only fifty-six rounds per man, less than each soldier carried, and artillery used only 199 rounds per gun, a consumption that only slightly exceeded that borne by the gunners and the additional rounds conveyed by the corps. Ammunition use remained essentially at its customary level and, as always, presented no hardship for supply.

The strategy of the war exhibited Napoleonic elements to a degree that surpassed in extent and compression in time any that Napoleon had ever achieved. His triumph over the Prussians at Jena and over the Austrians at Ulm had much in common with the two Prussian successes, but Moltke accomplished two such victories in only a month's time. The excellence of the Prussian staff in managing armies of unprecedented size contributed to capturing two formidable armies, as did Moltke's Napoleonic method of spreading his forces so that they had an opportunity to turn an opponent. Numerical predominance of at least two to one might easily have provided a decisive factor in making possible such strategic turning movements.

But all of these together could not have produced momentous defeats of this kind had Marshal Bazaine not displayed such exemplary incompetence, complete failure of nerve, and the inability to bear the responsibility of command. Success in colonial wars and subordinate command had failed to equip the marshal for high command, even though these had amply exhibited his bravery and his capacity to lead much smaller units. The lack of adequate training in strategy and large-unit command furnished no remedy for Bazaine's limited and inappropriate background. Although Marshal MacMahon's disaster at Sedan owes much to political motives determining the strategy for an army, the marshal should have resigned his command rather than lead his men on such a dangerous, doomed march.

The French army that failed in 1870 differed markedly from that of the eighteenth century, which had developed the regulations of 1791. Curiously enough, the royal army that reserved high command for the more exhalted aristocrats far outperformed the imperial one that opened its high ranks to talent. Too much success had doubtless made the French military and civilian leaders complacent and overconfident, but the absence both of the intellectual ferment of the eighteenth-century army and of the Prussian study of history and strategy distinguish the force that failed to have adequate commanders in 1870. Napoleon III must also assume blame for so dramatic a failure. But French failures should not dim the luster of Prussian success; even Napoleon and Hannibal had required inept opponents to win great victories.

The Strategy of the American Civil War

The American Civil War of 1861–65 exhibited the degree to which Europeans in the Western Hemisphere could employ continental military methods in a war on a European scale. In seeking to establish their independence, the Southerners or Confederates created an army that reached almost 300,000 men. This proved a match for the U.S. or Union forces that in the absence of a large regular army also created a modern force from civilian material and ultimately fielded over 600,000 men. Guided by a tiny cadre of well-educated professional officers, both became comparable to the best of Europe, and generals on both sides had competence equal to or greater than that of Radetzky or Moltke.

The operations of the war not only exhibited the generals' mastery of Napoleonic warfare but also made exemplary use of the telegraph and the railway to control and carry out strategic movements. Whereas the French had used the railway for supply and movements to the front in 1859 and the Prussians and

French had used it for mobilization and concentration, the Americans, particularly the Confederates, utilized trains for major strategic concentrations. On three occasions they moved large forces hundreds of miles by rail to reinforce an army and to carry out a major offensive. The railways and the rivers navigated by steamships provided new and significant lines of operations.

The first of these Confederate movements, the Shiloh campaign, illustrates clearly the use of the railway and the telegraph in the dispersal and concentration of troops over an unprecedented area. The Confederates fought on the strategic defensive, and this campaign has its clearest parallel with Napoleon's defense of his Mantua siege against Field Marshal Würmser's first advance. In March 1862 the U.S. commander in the West, H. W. Halleck, a thorough student of Napoleonic warfare, had sent an army under the energetic U.S. Grant up the Tennessee River. Halleck, fearing a Confederate concentration against Grant, urged the deliberate General Buell to expedite his march from Nashville to join Grant and telegraphed Grant about the possibility of an attack. Meanwhile, the Confederates in the West had begun concentrating their scattered forces in northern Mississippi.

They used the telegraph to order troops from the Mississippi River, eastern Tennessee, and Arkansas to this point. Meanwhile, Confederate President Jefferson Davis, who saw the opportunity to strike Grant before Buell had joined him, ordered troops from Charleston, Mobile, and New Orleans. All of these forces used railroads, or a combination of railroad and river steamers, for their movements, except those from Arkansas, which arrived too late. The smallest and most distant force, that from Charleston, also failed to arrive in time in spite of the use of trunk-line railways. The Confederates then carried out a Napoleonic campaign.

These armies concentrated near Grant's without his knowledge and in early April carried out a surprise attack, the Battle of Shiloh. The Confederates had little choice but to make an amateurish frontal assault, since Grant had his back to the river, thus securing his flanks. On the first day of the battle Grant staved off the Southerners and on the second day made a strong counterattack, aided by reinforcements from Buell who had reached the Tennessee River only a few miles down stream from Grant.

The interest of this campaign lies in its all-embracing strategic concept in an area so vast that only the telegraph, railway, and steamer made its implementation possible. Clearly both participants had so firm a grasp of the Napoleonic method that they could expand it in accord with the possibilities of the new modes of communication.

These up-to-date means of communication and transportation proved particularly important for supply. Compared to Europe, the American South had a sparse population that engaged in agriculture of low intensity and initially had much of its production devoted to cotton and tobacco. Thus the large stalemated armies became absolutely dependent on water or rail transporation.

Besides adapting the railroad and the telegraph to the exploitation of concentration on a single line of operations, the contestants also displayed a particular affinity for the strategic turning movement, as exemplified by Napoleon's Marengo and Ulm campaigns. Although they often attempted to reach their opponent's rear, they almost always failed. Yet lack of force did not cause these failures because, in spite of the vast size of the theater of war, each army had enough men to block the enemy's retreat. Rather, the intrinsic difficulty of executing such a maneuver against an alert opponent accounted for the general lack of success.

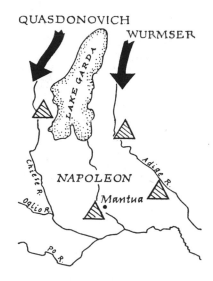

Diagram 7.4. Napoleon's Situation before Würmser's First Relief of Mantua

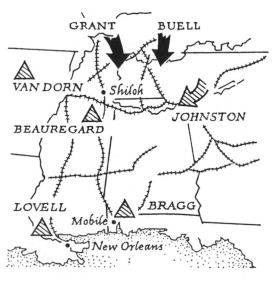

Diagram 7.5. Analogous Strategic Situation in March 1862

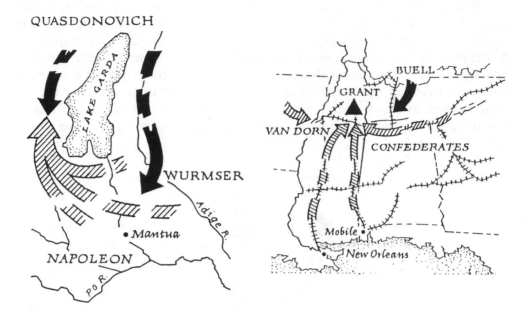

Diagram 7.6. Napoleon's Concentration against Quasdonovich

Diagram 7.7. Confederate Concentration against Grant

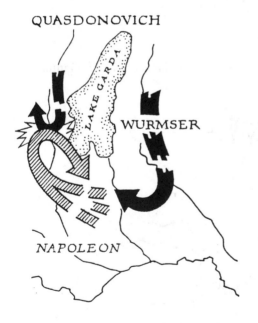

Diagram 7.8. Napoleon Drives Back Quasdonovich and Turns against Würmser

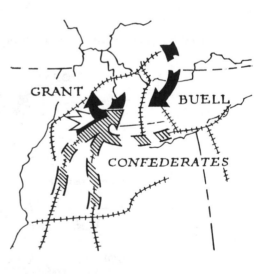

Diagram 7.9. Hypothetical Outcome if Confederates Had Defeated Grant before Buell Joined Him

U.S. Grant, general in chief in the last year of the war, succeeded twice in executing such a maneuver. Grant had proven an apt pupil in the school of experience and knew how to use capable subordinates. In the first instance he faced an opponent holding Vicksburg, a fortified city on the Mississippi River. Having failed in an earlier effort to turn this position when Confederate cavalry had broken his rail communications, Grant stuck to this secure river line. He finally carried out his turning movement by marching down the river bank opposite Vicksburg, using the navy to cross below the city, and heading north to its rear. At this point the Confederate commander, Pemberton, after a battle with Grant's army, withdrew to Vicksburg and shut himself up within its fortifications. Like Bazaine in Metz, Pemberton ultimately surrendered, losing his army as well as the place. In calling Pemberton his best friend, Grant gave the Confederate his due credit, but the Union general's fine conception and execution place this campaign among the best examples of the strategic turning movement.

Grant carried out another at the end of the war when he pursued General Robert E. Lee's army as it retreated from the Confederate capital, Richmond. Unable to reach his base by retreating directly away from Grant's much larger force, Lee had to move diagonally, which enabled Grant to keep up with him on a parallel route always staying between Lee and his base. Then Grant displayed the Americans' grasp of the role of cavalry by sending his mounted force ahead to delay Lee by fighting dismounted. Grant then moved in front of Lee and, at the little town of Appomattox, concluded the campaign with capitulation. Because Lee was the Confederacy's premier general and his army its largest, peace followed.

Lee himself had an exemplary mastery of the art of war and astutely used the strategic turning movement on the defensive. In the Second Bull Run, Antietam, and Gettysburg campaigns, he had forced his opponent back by threatening his rear. On all three occasions a battle resulted, but, in at least the first two, Lee had intended to avoid a contest, wishing rather to use the maneuver not to block the enemy's retreat but to force him back without the losses an engagement would entrail.

In his Antietam and Gettysburg campaigns, Lee lacked the line of communications necessary to hold the area into which he had advanced and made a brilliant use of the turning movement on the defensive. In each case his threat of reaching the rear of the much stronger opposing army forced the enemy back. Thus Lee's maneuver to menace the hostile rear, really a raid, functioned as a distraction; it differed little from one of Gustavus's or Wallenstein's raids or the king's attempted use of a threat to Frankfort to draw Tilly away from Magdeburg. Lee's mastery of the turning movement for defensive as well as offensive purposes, like his use of interior lines, placed him in the forefront of Civil War soldiers in his ability to apply the best elements found in the Napoleonic revolution in strategy.

In tactics, too, the armies of the North and South exhibited their debt to France, but here the Americans modified the lessons. Although the combatants

Diagram 7.10. Grant Turns Vicksburg

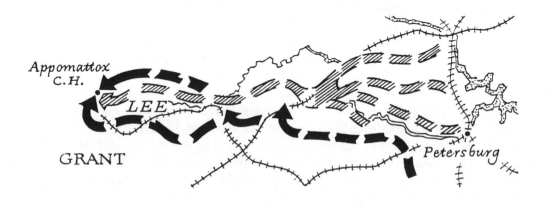

Diagram 7.11. Continuous Turning Movement

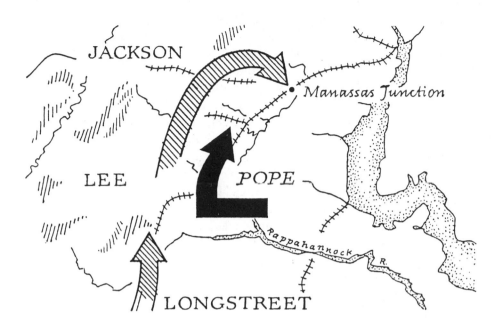

Diagram 7.12. Second Bull Run Turning Movement Forces Pope Back

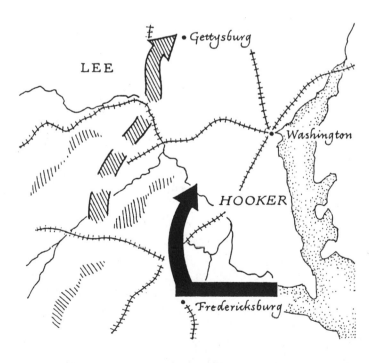

Diagram 7.13. Gettysburg Turning Movement Forces Hooker Back

had few breechloading or magazine rifles, they did ultimately equip themselves almost exclusively with muzzleloading rifles.

Armies on offensive and defensive entrenched more and more as the war progressed. The range of the rifle impelled soldiers to seek cover when they approached the enemy, the increased vulnerability of attackers and the enhanced security of the defenders markedly augmenting the power of the tactical defensive. By the end of the war both entrenched, and the often-stalemated armies frequently faced each other for several weeks in situations reminiscent of the long confrontation of Vendôme and Eugene at Luzzara. The railway helped permit these large armies to remain immobile so long.

The engineering orientation of the U. S. Military Academy, which leaders on both sides had attended, and the doctrine taught there reinforced this stress on field fortifications, which, in turn, was a response to the expanded danger of men equipped with rifles. So, as experience augmented training, the armies became almost Roman in their outlook, if not in their specific use of the entrenched camp.

The Americans completely avoided the European misconception that heavy cavalry still had a role on the battlefield, owing this insight to the weak cavalry tradition of their forested country and their realization that cavalry could not charge rifle-armed infantry. Nevertheless, both sides had much cavalry, the Confederates exceeding their opponents. When confronting infantry, cavalry customarily dismounted to fight. By equipping these men with rifles, in addition to pistols and sabers, the Americans had restored to their nineteenth-century cavalry the dismounted defensive power lost when the cavalry gave up the lance. Unlike the lance, soldiers could attach a rifle to their saddle, leaving their hands free for reins and saber or pistol.

Strategically, these versatile mounted infantrymen readily filled the role of light cavalry. In addition to reconnaissance, this mounted force proved particularly valuable as raiders. The excellent Southern cavalry so effectively exploited the vulnerability of railroads and the dependence of the armies on them that they halted two advances by major Union armies simply by raids against their rail communications. These armies thus suffered the same fate as two of Frederick's Prussian armies, victims of the skillful logistic strategy of the Austrian field marshals, Traun and Daun.

In spite of successful campaigns, especially in the West, where their armored steamers controlled the important navigable rivers, the Union had little success in dominating a country greater in size than France, Germany, and the Austrian Empire together. Faced with, in addition to cavalry raids, a hostile population, which engaged in guerrilla warfare against the invader's communications, the United States had to use a third of its forces to garrison the 200,000 square miles it had occupied by 1863.

Thus, the Union's persisting strategy became fundamentally a logistic strategy of occupying the country to weaken the Confederates by depriving them of recruits and agricultural and industrial resources. But combating guerrilla warfare and the raids of the Confederate cavalry absorbed so many Union troops as to defeat this logistic strategy. The Union needed too many men to control the country in view of the political opposition in the occupied areas. So the United States had a militarily adequate ratio of force to space but not enough force to meet the requirements imposed by the political situation. And though the Union forces had seized far more land in the Confederacy than the Prussians would later conquer in France, they still had not taken enough to exchange the land for their war aims: the extinction of the Confederacy and the abolition of slavery.

In 1864 the Union sought to overcome the apparently insuperable obstacles of their inadequate ratio of force to space by resorting to a strategy of raids, implementing a raiding rather than a persisting logistic strategy. These raids, aimed at breaking the South's railways, which supplied the Confederate armies with food, clothing, and munitions.

The first raid by an army of 60,000 men, led by the brilliant, innovative, and politically astute General W. T. Sherman, marched more than 250 miles from the inland city of Atlanta to meet the Union fleet on the Atlantic coast at Savannah. Initially uncertain as to Sherman's purpose, the Confederate commander, General G. T. Beauregard, showed his grasp of military history as well as his understanding of the inadequacy of Sherman's force to control the region between Atlanta and the sea by exhorting his subordinates by telegraph to "adopt Fabian system" and reminded them that "Hannibal held heart of Italy for sixteen years and then was defeated." But Sherman and Grant understood the situation as well as Beauregard and intended a raid only. This and following raids succeeded at the same time that the U. S. army and navy finally closed the ports through which merchant ships had long managed to evade the Union blockading squadrons.[6]

But the Union's logistic strategy never had a chance to demonstrate its effectiveness, nor did the Union army ever have to test its ability to overcome guerrilla resistance. In spite of the North's unlimited political objective—the subjugation of the South—the Confederacy collapsed rather suddenly when wholesale desertion struck its forces and the attenuated armies themselves capitulated. The Union president, Abraham Lincoln, contributed to this by mitigating the harshness of his unconditional surrender by inviting the rebelling states back into the Union without any political penalties other than that they abolish slavery.

Although the South had left the Union primarily to conserve slavery, it realized that a continued struggle would further undermine race relations. Most black slaves welcomed the Union armies, and many willingly enlisted in the invading armies. A continued war, especially one relying primarily on the activities of guerrillas, could only pit Union troops aided by slaves against the Southerners and destroy any semblance of the social organization of the races that slavery had exemplified. The raiding forces, especially Sherman's army, also showed the Confederates, as general Sherman had anticipated, that they had lost their territorial integrity and the depredations of the raiders had much of the effect of the traditional raid to extract political concessions. Such a strategy had failed to defeat France in the Hundred Years' War, but it had helped wring concessions from the king of France. It proved effective also in the American Civil War, depressing the morale of the southern populace.

So the Confederates surrendered. Slavery, which almost alone had separated the two sections, proved an inadequate basis for continuing a costly struggle against an enemy not so distinct except in its attitude toward slavery.

Thus the North had faced an almost impossible military assignment in subduing such a huge and hostile country, a task not much easier than that encountered earlier by the British in the American Revolution. By directing raids against factories and foundries as well as railroads, the Union had adopted a most effective logistic strategy, which relieved its forces of the need to occupy the country, an insuperable obstacle to their original persisting, logistic strategy. Such a raiding strategy would have compelled the disbandment of the South's principal armies but would have left them in existence as smaller forces dispersed throughout the Confederacy. The Union would not have controlled more territory than it occupied and could still have faced a situation comparable to that of the French in Spain, mitigated, however, by the lack of need to keep large forces concentrated to oppose hostile armies.

But the South's abandonment of the war prevented the working out of these military consequences. The Union's successful campaigns and its raids in the end had an effect more comparable to Alexander's victories over Darius, which gave him the Persian Empire, than to Hannibal's military triumphs over the Romans, which failed of decisive result due to Roman political strength.

Two Instances of Combating the Raiding Strategy of Guerrilla Warfare

In the nineteenth century, in building and retaining their worldwide empires, Western nations fought many wars against opponents who utilized a raiding strategy or guerrilla resistance. At the end of the century they conducted two of these against people European in culture. In an effort to retain control of its old colony of Cuba, Spain waged such a war against insurgents who were Spanish in language and culture, and the United Kingdom faced guerrilla resistance in southern Africa after it had defeated with a persisting strategy the two republics there established by Boers, descendants of Dutch settlers. Both countries conducted their operations against opponents who employed a guerrilla warfare of raids against weak detachments of the occupying forces and also directed their raids at railroads and other logistic objectives.

Spain and the United Kingdom both followed the strategy of impeding the movement of guerrillas. The Spaniards divided Cuba into three segments by building two lines of forts and blockhouses. They then planned successive concentrations in each geographical compartment to attain the ratio of force to space necessary to overwhelm the guerrillas. Many difficulties, including complications with the United States that ultimately led to war, prevented the completion of this strategy.

The British, in a far larger country but one characterized by open grazing land, followed the same approach on a more ambitious scale, likewise an extension of Alexander's method in Bactria and Sogdiana and comparable to William the Conqueror's in England. The Boers, skilled, active adversaries, almost invariably mounted, broke British railway lines 250 times in twelve months. They conducted many other raids, including one, during the early, persisting phase of the conflict, in which they captured and held for twenty-seven days the waterworks of the major city of Bloemfontein. This powerful application of logistic strategy forced the British troops in the city to resort to polluted wells, which constituted a major factor in the subsequent doubling of the death rate from typhoid fever.

The British responded by building across the country many lines of barbed wire, guarded by blockhouses placed close enough together to keep the wire lines under rifle fire. They facilitated this extensive program by producing movable iron blockhouses, which a crew of two or three dozen soldiers and laborers could erect in a day. Ultimately the British used 9,000 blockhouses to cover a network of 5,000 miles of barbed wire lines, which subdivided the extensive country into many compartments. These lines effectively inhibited the movements of the raiders and made easier the work of mobile columns that swept the compartments, capturing many guerrillas. The ample British resources combined with the conciliatory political offer made to the Boers enabled them to overcome adroit and determined resistance in two years.

In addition, the British and Spanish used a logistic strategy against their opponents, whose base area lay in the country these powers sought to subdue. They burned farms and crops and drove off cattle, acting much as William the Conqueror in his devastation of the north of England. But, unlike William, each nation coupled this with a policy of bringing friendly civilians and women and children into camps and providing them with food and housing. Although the camps lacked an adequate supply of either and received much humanitarian criticism, this practice did protect many civilians from the full rigor of the logistic strategy and had the political advantage of partially shielding the supporters of the Spaniards and British from the effects of the program of terror implicit in such a logistic strategy.

European Weapons, Armies, and Doctrine on the Eve of World War I

From the end of the Franco-Prussian War until 1914 weapons improved further. The breechloader became a magazine rifle with which, by working a handle, the rifleman could feed bullets into the chamber from a magazine holding from five to ten rounds. A trained soldier could fire sixteen aimed shots per minute from a rifle equipped with some versions of an eight-shot magazine.

In 1883 British investors backed Hiram Maxim, an American electrical engineer who invented an automatic gun. The Maxim, or machine gun, used the recoil caused by the first shot to reload and recock the gun, allowing continuous firing at the rate of 600 shots per minute. A cloth belt carried the ammunition, and the gun had such a capability for sustained fire that Maxim's model had a water jacket to keep the barrel cool. Intrinsically a light and handy weapon, the machine gun with its water jacket and extensive ammunition supply was a mobile rather than a portable weapon, and armies assigned only a few of these formidable guns to each battalion, as they had the old battalion guns.

By the end of the century artillery had undergone a transformation. The steel breechloading cannon of the Franco-Prussian War had lacked a recoil mechanism, which meant that the gun bounced when fired and required re-aiming after each shot. In addition, the cannon carried no useful shield because the gunners had to stand clear when the gun fired. By the end of the century cannon had a recoil mechanism based on compressing a spring or a gas and cushioning with a hydraulic shock absorber. This kept the gun carriage steady by allowing the barrel to move, thus dissipating the energy of firing and permitting repeated shots without re-aiming; gunners could now remain behind a motionless shield. The typical field gun had a bore of three inches and in a minute could fire six, and in an emergency as many as twenty, shells weighing fifteen to eighteen pounds to a range as far as 7,500 yards. In addition to shells that exploded on contact, guns fired shrapnel shells with precise and reliable fuses that permitted the shells to explode over distant bodies of troops, showering them with small bullets. Like the rifle and machine gun, artillery had a smokeless explosive that improved battlefield visibility and helped to hide the location of the weapon firing.

Although this increase in firepower should have further augmented the power of the tactical defense, soldiers tended to think otherwise. Some believed that the firepower of a larger number of attackers could overwhelm the de-

Illustration 7.2. Maxim's Gun

fenders, overlooking Moltke's reaffirmation of the defender's advantage in a fire fight. Others saw that since the defense would require fewer men, armies could concentrate more troops for the decisive turning movement that had played such a prominent role in 1870. The greater range and rate of fire of the new weapons would, they believed, make envelopment more effective as converging fires overwhelmed the defenders. Few, if any, reasoned that, if the strength of the defense enabled the concentration of more for the turning movement, armies needed fewer men to delay or halt the turning force.

This defective reasoning contributed significantly to the emergence in European armies of a belief in the offensive. A realization of the importance of morale also had a major role in this cult. Historical examples abounded of numerically superior, well-armed troops defeated by soldiers with confidence in their ability to win and press home their attack. Almost without casualties, Roman veterans had defeated larger armies that lacked the skill and confidence of the legionnaires. But many carried this valuable insight to an extreme wholly unwarranted in view of the increase in firepower.

Naturally each nation believed its soldiers possessed the better morale and determination needed to overmatch its opponents, an outlook fostered by the prevailing nationalistic, racist, Darwinian, and somewhat romantic climate of opinion. Some thoughtful officers and civilians dissented and pointed to the power the defense exhibited in the Boer and Russo-Japanese wars. But the offensive doctrine represented the dominant culture, and one extreme devotee of this school even disparaged using interior lines to concentrate larger numbers, believing that "the days of eighteenth century tricks and strategems are past and done with. . . . The essence of successful leadership in the future will be . . . a rapid and sustained advance which will overrun all opposition by its very momentum."[7]

This statement has a medieval flavor and certainly disparages the concept of winning with the least effort. Just as the archetypical medieval commander, conditioned by jousts, tournaments, and the culture of chivalry, tended to see battle in terms of the frontal charge by cavalry, so many early twentieth-century soldiers, led astray by the valid and important emphasis on morale, by a misinterpretation of the effects of augmented firepower, and by the climate of opinion, came to the implicit assumption that the tactical offensive had greater strength than the defensive when both contestants employed the same weapon systems. Though not ignoring the eighteenth-century strategems of turning movements and concentration on interior lines, by 1914 armies planned to assume the offensive in war.

Although armies derived their tactics from the experience of the Franco-Prussian War, a lack of realism soon emerged. Since commanders could not control an attack carried out by skirmishers, they had a motive to continue a role for battalion and company columns. A nostalgia for the more dramatic attacks of the past also affected tactical thinking, as did a belief in the near-invincibility of a force convinced of its dominance and endowed with a better will to win. Writers even mentioned shock action and infantrymen using bayonets against each other. So offensive tactics combined, in an unsatisfactory blend, the realism of the Franco-Prussian War with older ideas. Nothing better illustrates the delusive element in tactical thinking than the continuation of large forces of cavalry dedicated to shock action on the battlefield. As late as 1914 the Germans even armed their cavalry with lances. Armies, recognizing the importance of artillery and the effectiveness of the perfected shrapnel, did, however, plan an artillery bombardment to prepare for the attack.

The improvement in the railway system and the extension of its lines affected logistics somewhat by increasing the railway's impact on mobilization and making the supply of enormous armies possible. Although the development of the motor truck very much raised the efficiency of road transport, armies made little use of this expensive, still relatively scarce, and unreliable vehicle and continued to depend on the horse. The bicycle found some use in inexpensively augmenting the strategic mobility of infantry. The wireless telegraph made possible significantly better communications between the units of dispersed armies, and the telephone improved the utility of wire communications. All armies had some dirigible airships and a few of the primitive airplanes then available, though not enough to carry out reconnaissance on the broad fronts envisioned.

The achievements of the Prussian staff led all armies to adopt a similar system. Though varying in their effectiveness, all staffs could manage the movements of large numbers of men and coordinate their involvement in combat. Other nations soon appropriated the Prussian manpower system of a cadre of professionals who trained conscripts that, together with their reserves, constituted the active army. All created militia formations of trained men modeled somewhat on the Prussian Landwehr. The details varied greatly, but all countries except Britain emulated this successful and inexpensive system of having large, thoroughly trained, and professionally led armies ready for war.

By 1914 the three principal continental armies had enormous infantry forces, divided into divisions of twelve battalions each (table 7.3).

The German and French armies could mobilize fully and concentrate in three weeks; the Russians, with a far larger country, required more time. The

TABLE 7.3.   The Strength of the German, French, and Russian Armies in 1914

	Germany		France		Russia	
	Numbers	Divisions	Numbers	Divisions	Numbers	Divisions
Active						
Peace	750,000	51	800,000	48	1,250,000	79
War	1,700,000		1,600,000		2,200,000	
Units from excess reserves		31		25		35
Landwehr		36		12		
Total	5,300,000	118	4,400,000	85	5,000,000	114

French forces, for example, had, in addition to infantry weapons and horses for traction, approximately 4,500 artillery pieces, 2,100 machine guns, 19,000 motor vehicles, and 200 airplanes. The budgetary cost of the completely mobilized forces amounted, in 1984 dollars, to a little over $200 per man per year and about $30 per capita per year for the 40 million people in France. The new manpower system created a huge army with unprecedented firepower for a very modest cost. This low cost is all the more impressive in view of the ten cavalry divisions that, like the other powers, France kept at almost full strength.

Revolutions in industry, agriculture, and commerce made these large forces realistic. The growth of the market, made possible by railroads, steamships, and improved highways, permitted the efficiency of an expanded divison of labor, a productivity importantly aided by such developments as steam power, electricity, and improved metal working. Scientific and mechanized agriculture increased output and the efficiency of labor in food production. Whereas maintaining 3 percent of the population under arms had taxed the resources of Western European nations at the end of the eighteenth century, increased productivity and better financial institutions made 10 percent under arms a readily attainable goal in 1914.

The broad deployment of armies, developed in the Napoleonic wars and practiced with such dramatic success by Moltke, continued as the standard approach. Strategic viewpoints changed little, but by 1914 generals believed that any war would end quickly in a few decisive campaigns. The faith in the power of the offensive reinforced the precedents set by the short wars of the middle of the nineteenth century. Had they adequately examined the protracted American Civil War, European miltary leaders might have drawn a different conclusion, but most tended to dismiss that war as a struggle between amateurs in which a quick decision was beyond the capacity of the inept combatants.

The results of European military thinking between 1871 and 1914 contrast markedly with those of the rationalist environment of the eighteenth century, which had produced the ideas of Guibert and Bourcet and the French regulations of 1791. Many soldiers seemed to have overlooked the principle of winning with the least effort and to have forgotten the traditional ascendency of the tactical defensive in combat between similar weapon systems. But the war which began in 1914 would exhibit that neither the new weapons nor the emphasis on morale had abrogated the lessons of the past.

The Revolution in Naval Materiel and Its Use in the Russo-Japanese War

The revolution of steam, electricity, and improved metallurgy and manufacturing affected transportation and warfare at sea as much as it did logistics and weapons on land. In fact, the wireless telegraph had a greater impact at sea because it gave ships a long-distance means of communication with the land and each other that they had hitherto lacked.

By the 1830s sailing ships began to carry steam engines, first using side wheels for auxiliary propulsion and gradually adopting the more efficient screw propellor. As steam pressures increased and engines became more efficient, ships could conveniently carry enough fuel to rely entirely on steam propulsion. By the twentieth century steamers had superseded sailing vessels for moving most cargo and, where speed had more importance, entirely in carrying passengers. Steamers attained greater speed not only because of the consistency with which they could maintain a given speed but also because of their routes. Rather than taking detours to avail themselves of favorable prevailing winds or currents in the sea, steam vessels used the most direct route.

The increased speed of the steamer as well as its more direct route and certainty of operation so augmented the celerity of the movement of ships and fleets that the revolution in propulsion markedly augmented the ratio of naval force to space. When coupled with the wireless, which transformed communication among ships at sea and facilitated scouting and the movement and concentration of forces, the alteration in the ratio of force to space gave the dominant sea power far greater advantages than it had before. This change had an effect fully comparable to that wrought by the transition from galleys to sail. It meant that wireless-equipped scouts needed only to observe a blockaded harbor, confident that they could continue to observe a fleet attempting to elude the blockaders and use their wireless to call in their big ships to engage the squadron attempting escape.

On the other hand, steam complicated the problems of supply, which, in turn, affected the ratio of force to space in a way contrary to that of steam propulsion itself. Dependence on a base for frequent replenishment of coal meant that a higher proportion of a fleet would have to devote itself to going to and from a supply port for fuel. Even though it could do this far more rapidly than a sailing ship, the steamer obviously differed markedly in its dependence on a base from a sailing ship, which carried no fuel at all. This, in turn, reduced the ratio of force to space by diminishing the number of ships on a particular station. Bases thus became far more critical because operations very distant from a friendly port would far more drastically diminish the force of the dominant power than would have been the case in the age of sail.

The same factors also inhibited commerce raiders, making their escape to the ocean more difficult and, as merchant ships gradually equipped themselves with wireless, ensuring that the cruisers of the power with command of the sea would learn from the last communication of the victims where to search for the commerce raider. Further, the commerce raider itself would find that steam had deprived it of that independence of bases and supplies that sailing ships had enjoyed. This not only made it far more dependent on friendly ports but provided another opportunity for the dominant power to learn of its whereabouts.

Iron and then steel provided another source of enhanced efficiency in water transport. Iron ships weighed less for a given degree of strength and proved more durable and often less expensive to repair. Naval architects even made sailing vessels of iron, capitalizing on one form of efficiency while designing a ship to carry a cargo for which a slow passage with wind for fuel constituted the least cost combination. Better mechanical appliances for setting the sails reduced crew sizes and helped to keep sailing ships competitive for some services. Railroads enabled land transportation to close the gap in costs between land and water transportation, but water retained a substantial advantage.

All of these changes affected warships. But hardly had navies added auxiliary steam engines to their ships of the line and frigates when advances in guns revolutionized naval architecture. The rifled cannon and the development of an explosive shell meant that the projectile could pierce a wooden ship and blow up inside. This, together with the longer range and more accurate fire of artillery, made the warships of the past too vulnerable. Wooden sides, thicker at the waterline, no longer sufficed to protect vessels adequately. In 1859 the French launched a ship with its waterline and part of the sides protected by wrought-iron armor plate almost five inches thick. Except for this metal armor and steam engines that gave her a speed of thirteen knots, she differed little from previous vessels. The British replied the next year with a similar ship, but built entirely of iron. Both had armor adequate to resist any gun then available, but the ordnance designers soon produced more powerful guns and naval architects then fitted thicker armor.

There followed three decades of experimentation, with armored warships mounting increasingly powerful guns and thicker armor. Designers improved the quality of armor first by backing a hard, brittle plate with one of softer, tougher wrought iron and then by bonding a hard plate to a resilient steel plate. Finally, by the end of the century, steelmakers had produced single plates, hardened on the face but gradually containing less carbon until its back consisted of resilient steel that resisted cracking. Armor plate for ships changed little thereafter.

The breech-loading cannon came to dominate naval ordnance, new breech designs permitting rapid opening and closing and a gas-tight seal. Slower-burning explosives made longer barrels more useful, these explosives giving to the projectile a continuous impetus at a relatively constant pressure. Since raising velocity contributed more to piercing armor than raising projectile weight, guns became smaller in bore but with a longer tube, thus boosting the shell's velocity and capacity for penetration. The well-tempered steel projectiles, designed to break through armor, carried a relatively small, but still quite formidable, bursting charge, fused to explode after piercing armor.

Designers mounted big guns in turrets, or their equivalent, the stationary barbettes within which, covered by an armored hood, the gun moved. These could rotate to fire over an arc of as much as a full circle. Battleships tended to carry their smaller guns in casemates on either side. By the end of the century, 6-inch guns, firing 100-pound shells, and those of smaller bore could fire six or more shots a minute, larger guns with heavy ammunition and cumbersome explosive charges firing as slowly as one round a minute.

By this time the new ships of the line, called battleships, displaced from 10,000 to 15,000 tons, about five times the displacement of the wooden ships of a century earlier. British vessels carried four 12-inch guns, firing 870 pound shells. The battleships mounted these in pairs in a barbette at the bow and the stern, enabling two guns to fire ahead or astern, and four on either broadside. These ships mounted twelve 6-inch guns in casemates, six on each side. Armor as thick as twelve inches protected the big guns, six inches the smaller, and the waterline had as much as twelve inches with a second sloping plate behind, an inch or more thick. This thick side armor did not extend to the ends, but was over the area between the barbettes where it protected the magazines and engines.

The battleships had a speed of eighteen knots and filled the role of the ships of the line. Their design still required fighting broadside to broadside, and the increased range of the guns obviated the perpendicular approach used by Nelson so effectively at the Battle of Trafalgar. If an attacking fleet approached a defending line perpendicularly in line abreast, it could only use half of its guns. If the defenders began firing at 6,000 yards, the attackers must receive ten broadsides, replying with only half as many guns. Admirals realized that in spite of the rams that still equipped all ships, they must return to the combat in parallel lines. The ability of barbette or turret-mounted guns to fire very obliquely would enable most, if not all, guns on ships in a line to bear on hostile ships making a perpendicular approach and following one another. Not only would this ability to concentrate fire at long range rule out such an attack, but it made admirals hope for an opportunity to lead their vessels across the head of an enemy line where they could concentrate the fire of many ships on the enemy's lead battleships.

Whereas in the days of wooden sailing ships the frigates and smaller ships had been little more than smaller replicas of the ships of the line, the smaller vessels in the age of steam and steel, called cruisers, carried no armor beyond a deck that curved down at the sides below the waterline to give some protection to engines and magazines. Instead of having armored barbettes, cruisers placed their guns on pedestal mounts, often with shields, on the deck. With speeds of twenty-one to twenty-three knots, cruisers ranged in size from 2,000 tons to almost that of battleships. Guns of four to six inches predominated.

At the turn of the century an intermediate type of warship became important. The armored cruiser ranged in size from 8,000 tons up to that of the larger battleships and, with armor about half as thick as that of battleships, could rely on resisting the shells of cruisers. With guns as large as ten inches, mounted like those on battleships in barbettes and casemates, it could count on smashing other cruisers. By making these large ships relatively narrow and giving them great power, the designers had also given them the speed of smaller cruisers.

Smaller than cruisers, torpedo boats depended on high speed and the torpedo. Developed in the latter part of the nineteenth century, the torpedo really amounted to a tiny boat about twenty feet long that, using compressed air or steam, ran under water at a predetermined depth. Aimed at ships as much as a mile away and traveling at a speed of twenty-five or more knots, it struck the ship below the waterline, detonating a substantial explosive charge. Because it struck the vulnerable underwater part of a vessel, it was so dangerous that in the 1880s the French navy actually considered depending primarily on torpedo boats. For the first time in history a small ship could attack the largest with some prospect of success.

But these boats gave rise to torpedo boat destroyers, equally fast but larger and mounting guns to destroy torpedo boats. By the end of the century torpedo boat destroyers, by then called simply destroyers, had merged with torpedo boats, grown in size, and, smaller and faster but less seaworthy than cruisers, had in part joined cruisers as scouts for the fleet and protectors of trade routes. But all ships, including battleships, carried torpedoes.

This entire revolution in naval architecture and the transition from sail to steam and wood to steel had occurred without any of the major forces of new ships engaging each other in battle. The Russo-Japanese War of 1904 and 1905 saw these modern fleets in battle and exhibited a decisive influence for interior lines of operations at sea when Japan's strategic position enabled it to defeat the stronger Russian battleship force.

At the beginning of the conflict the Russians had, in addition to several battleships confined to the Black Sea, fourteen modern capital ships, mounting 10- or 12-inch guns. Their greater number of well-designed and adequately armored vessels gave the Russians a decisive superiority over the Japanese, who had only six ships, although all were newer, faster, and larger than the Russian ones and all were armed with 12-inch guns.

The Japanese began the war when the Russians had seven of their battleships in the Baltic and seven at Port Arthur, their base in Manchuria. This disposition placed the Japanese fleet squarely between the two halves of the Russian capital ship force. The Japanese immediately attained naval supremacy in the Far East with a surprise torpedo boat assault against the Port Arthur fleet prior to the declaration of war in February 1904. The damage resulting from this attack temporarily disabled three Russian battleships and enabled the Japanese to blockade the Russian squadron from their adjacent bases in Japan and Korea.

Able to use their central position to concentrate against the Russian Asiatic fleet, the Japanese attempted to destroy it before the Russian ships from the Baltic could arrive. The Japanese army provided the primary means to accomplish this through the application of a logistic strategy analogous to that employed by Alexander against the Persian navy, but the Japanese command of the sea greatly facilitated the army's task. In addition to ensuring efficient supply by water, the Japanese navy, like the Persian fleet in the Marathon campaign, could give the army the initiative to choose among different landing places without any apprehension that the Russians could cross the sea to attack the Japanese in Korea or their home islands.

The Japanese landed an army in Manchuria, on Port Arthur's peninsula, between that base and the mainland, thus cutting it off from the main Russian armies. The Japanese army then moved to besiege Port Arthur and, by capturing it, thus destroy the Russian fleet there. While the army moved slowly against

Map 7.1. Theater of Operations in the Russo-Japanese War

powerful opposition to besiege and capture the Russian fleet's base, the Japanese battleships bombarded the harbor to disable more ships, sought to sink ships of their own in the harbor's channel to bottle up the Russian flotilla, and laid mines outside the port. Meanwhile, the brilliant and energetic Russian commander, Admiral Makarov, diligently exercised his squadron to bring its proficiency up to a level comparable to that of the Japanese; in this way the admiral prepared to engage it when he had completed the repair of his damaged ships.

Soon the Russian coast defense guns forced the Japanese to give up their bombardments and none of the sunken Japanese ships were able to block the harbor entrance. The Russian defenders had again demonstrated the traditional primacy of coastal fortifications over naval attack. Only the minefields succeeded when in April the mines sank a Russian battleship; 600 men, including the irreplaceable Admiral Makarov, were lost. His successor, the competent but pessimistic Admiral Vitgeft, remained on the defensive and concentrated on employing the fleet to aid the army in its defense against the besieging Japanese forces.

Doubtless Admiral Makarov would have made the most of the impressive success of the Russian mine warfare program that on May 15 sank two Japanese battleships within a few minutes of each other. With a third of the Japanese capital ships sunk and the three damaged Russian ships repaired, the Russians had an advantage of six to four in these ships of the line. But Admiral Vitgeft did not act until August when, with the Japanese army closing in on Port Arthur, he felt he had to leave to save the fleet. Thus the Japanese army's siege compelled the navy to fight—just as sieges had traditionally placed intense pressure on a relieving army to assume the tactical offensive to raise a siege. Since the Russian armies in Manchuria lacked the strength to relieve Port Arthur, the Russian admiral had to risk battle.

In spite of their inferiority in capital ships, the Japanese had to fight if they were to exploit their interior lines to prevent the enemy from concentrating its two fleets. To allow the Russians to steam north to their secure port of Vladivostok would concede overwhelming preponderance to the Russians, for Vitgeft's squadron could securely await the arrival of the Baltic fleet that the Russians were about to send to the Far East. To refuse to fight would constitute the first step in giving command of the sea to the Russians and the cutting off of the Japanese armies in Manchuria and Korea from their base in Japan. To try to fight the Baltic fleet later, while blockading Vladivostok, would have placed the Japanese in the same situation as Admiral Calder off Ferrol when Villeneuve approached from the West Indies—and without the advantage of a prevailing wind that might keep sailing fleets apart. In exploiting their interior lines, the Japanese army and navy had concentrated against the Port Arthur squadron. The army's costly siege and assaults had done their part; now the navy must drive the fleet back into Port Arthur to complete its destruction when the port finally fell. Admiral Togo, the excellent Japanese commander, as well as his government completely understood the strategic situation and what it required.

To compensate for its weakness in capital ships, the Japanese battle line did have four armored cruisers. These faster, smaller ships mounted less powerful guns and had thinner armor: three mounted four 8-inch guns and one carried two 8-inch guns and one 10-inch. The Japanese battleships each mounted four 12-inch guns, and four of the Russian capital ships carried four 12-inch guns and two had four 10-inch guns. Since the shell of the 10-inch gun weighed about twice that of the 8-inch and that of the 12-inch about three times as much, the guns of the armored cruisers had little prospect of piercing the armor of the big ships nor could the cruisers' armor, less than half as thick as that on the battleships, have much chance of resisting penetration by the big guns of the opposing fleet.

On August 10, 1904, the Russian squadron came out; at 12:30 P.M. the hostile fleets sighted each other. After some complicated maneuvers, in which the greater speed of the Japanese squadron enabled Admiral Togo to attempt to steam across the vulnerable head of the Russian line, the Japanese found themselves astern of the Russians with nothing accomplished. Admiral Togo then overhauled Admiral Vitgeft on a parallel course and at 5:30 P.M. opened fire at 8,000 yards, a long range for the guns and fire control equipment in use and a range that favored the Russians because of their greater number of big guns.

After an hour of firing the combat seemed indecisive. The Japanese had shot better than the Russians and, because of this and their greater number of guns, scored more hits. But the heavy armor of Admiral Vitgeft's ships protected them while the Russian armor-piercing shells disabled five of the seventeen heavy guns in the Japanese fleet. Since Japanese fire had eliminated only four of the twenty-three operational big guns in the Russian squadron, it seemed as if Russian heavy gun superiority was, as Lanchester later theorized, gradually becoming cumulative.

But then two Japanese 12-inch shells hit the control area of the Russian flagship, killing the admiral, jamming the rudder, and causing the ship to turn. Thrown into confusion by the erratic behavior of the flagship, the Russian squadron fled, all ships reaching Port Arthur except the damaged flagship, which steamed to a Chinese port. Admiral Togo, having driven the enemy fleet back into the arms of the army, had made no effort to destroy the fleeing Russian ships other than to launch his torpedo boats in an ineffectual attack. Rather than risk his irreplaceable battleships in prolonging the battle in fading light, he was content, as the Byzantine Belisarius had counseled, to reap the strategic fruits and conserve his fleet for its inevitable combat with the Russian ships from the Baltic. Admiral Togo doubtless founded his caution on his realization that the Japanese, dependent on water communications for their campaign on the continent of Asia, could lose the war at sea; the Russians could not.

The weakened Port Arthur squadron, not venturing to sea again, came under fire of the Japanese army's siege artillery in December and, in January, along with the army, the battered remains surrendered to the Japanese land forces.

The Baltic fleet did not arrive until May 1905, and it was completely inadequate to cope with the incomparable Admiral Togo's refitted ships and their war-seasoned officers and men. Further, in a misguided effort to strengthen the squadron, the Russian admiralty had burdened it with a collection of naval antiquities. When some of these joined up in the Far East, they reminded an eye-witness of "owls that had been shooed out of their trees into the blinding tropical sunshine." In addition, sending so many ships had stretched the available skilled naval manpower so thin that even the best ships had many untrained men and, consequently, very low proficiency in gunnery and other combat duties.[8]

Having learned the location and course of the Russian fleet by wireless from his scouts, Admiral Togo placed all eight of his armored cruisers in his line of battle and met the slow-moving Russians in Tsushima Strait. He then used his greater speed to force battle relentlessly over a two-day period and totally defeated the Russians, sinking six and capturing two battleships. The fighting took place at ranges of 4,000 to 8,000 yards. The Japanese navy exploited their interior lines to defeat first one enemy fleet and then the other, but the army had played a crucial role in destroying the Port Arthur fleet.

Although the Russo-Japanese War little affected the thinking of the offensive-minded armies of Europe, the navies learned a great deal. The British drew the most influential conclusion, seeing the battles of ships in parallel lines at long range as confirmation of their view that they must press their efforts, already underway, to improve gunnery. Long had navies depended on the gunnery method, customary with wooden ships of the line, which relied on each gunner's aiming his own gun. But at long range, when a gunner shot at a moving target from a platform that moved, rolled, and pitched, this no longer sufficed. Wishing to fire centrally controlled salvos and to observe and correct their fire as often as possible, the British introduced a ship, the *Dreadnought*, which fired eight 12-inch guns on a broadside. Firing half the guns in each salvo, the *Dreadnought* could correct its aim twice as often as a vessel with only four guns on a broadside or fire twice as many guns in each broadside. By 1914 all navies had adopted the *Dreadnought* type and used on their bigger ships centralized aiming and control of guns, aided by computers and relying on powerful range finders mounted on stout masts. They observed the fall of their salvos, correcting their aim after each group of shells landed.

The British also concluded that the armament of 6-inch, rapid-firing guns could contribute little to a long-range battle between armored ships. So on the *Dreadnought* they eliminated this armament, keeping only a number of 3-inch guns to cope with torpedo boats. Other navies, which, like the British, had been enlarging the smaller guns carried, generally followed the British lead in relegating the smaller guns to the role of dealing with the torpedo attacks of torpedo boats and destroyers.

At the same time, the British introduced a new type of ship, the battle cruiser. Like the *Dreadnought*, it concentrated its firepower in a larger battery of big guns, thus attaining the gunnery advantages of more big cannon. Whereas their armored cruisers had carried guns of 6, 7.5, and 9.2 inches, the new battle cruisers had 12-inch guns. But since the British did not provide their battle cruisers with armor any thicker than that on armored cruisers, they had ships not armored to resist the guns of comparable ships. This new ship made armored cruisers obsolescent and gave the British an advantage as long as they possessed the only battle cruisers. But a rivalry with the Germans began, and the Germans provided their battle cruisers with armor almost as thick as that on battleships.

The decade before the outbreak of war in 1914 witnessed a naval race between the British and Germans, in which battleships increased in size by 60 percent and the British eventually mounted on their battleships 15-inch guns firing shells weighing 1,920 pounds. But this race did not include the submersible torpedo boat or submarine. This vessel submerged by letting water into tanks and surfaced by expelling this water with compressed air. Although originally stressed by France because of the threat submarines presented to a British blockading squadron, all navies built them. In accord with their policy of having the largest navy, the British had the largest number, followed by the French.

Perfected by 1914, a submarine displaced several hundred tons and carried about a dozen torpedoes, four of which it could fire simultaneously by aiming the boat. It also carried a gun of three or four inches. A diesel engine propelled it on the surface at as much as twelve knots, and the batteries, recharged on the surface by a diesel engine, could propel it submerged as fast as nine knots for a brief period. A submarine could submerge to 200 feet, but to fight it must remain close to the surface to use the periscope to see its target and aim its torpedoes.

Although navies had no means of attacking a submerged submarine, they did not know how effective a submarine might be, even though the improved models available at the start of the war could cruise on the surface long enough

Illustration 7.3. The Large Battle Cruiser H.M.S. *Tiger*

to remain at sea for two weeks. The submarine's tactic was to spot its target while cruising on the surface and then submerge to make an attack. But its slower speed once submerged and the fact that its torpedo was visible from the attacked ship, which could then change its course, meant that most naval authorities believed that the submarine would prove relatively ineffective.

8

THE APOGEE OF THE DEFENSE:
WORLD WAR I,
1914–18

The German Concentration on Interior Lines
and Effort to Turn the French

In 1914 Britain, France, and Russia went to war with Germany and Austria. All European armies had excellent staffs and virtually the same weapons and doctrine. Only Britain retained a small professional force without significant reserves or a large trained militia. In the campaign in France and Belgium the British army displayed the high quality attainable with a long-service professional force. But the British army was so minute compared with the continental ones that when asked earlier what he would do if the British landed on his coast, German Chancellor Bismarck supposedly said that he would have them arrested.

The British had both a powerful field gun and a good howitzer for high-angle fire, especially useful in siege warfare. The French field gun, the 75-millimeter, had elements of superiority over the British gun, including barely two-thirds of its weight. The French army had yet to receive any of its powerful new 105-millimeter howitzers. The German field gun lacked the range and power of the British and French guns and its howitzers also compared unfavorably with those of the allies; still the Germans had their 105-millimeter howitzer in ample numbers. The armies, however, had such great firepower that differences in weapons mattered little.

Their awesome firepower notwithstanding, all combatants planned to take the offensive, but the Germans had the most sophisticated strategy. Named for the chief of staff who devised it, the Schlieffen Plan exploited Germany's interior lines between Russia and France to concentrate first against France while Austria held the Russians at bay. The plan also relied on Russia's vast size to slow its mobilization and prevent the Russians from using all of their forces until the Germans had defeated the French and could use their railroads to reconcentrate against the Russians.

To defeat the French, Schlieffen had relied on a gigantic turning movement reminiscent of Napoleon's Ulm campaign. Instead of the less than 200,000 men used by Napoleon, the Germans envisioned the use of five armies totaling 1 million men with four of them marching through neutral Belgium. One would circle west of Paris, another just to the east, and the remaining three were to advance to make a front that would move west, then south, and finally east. Expecting, as did Napoleon against Mack and the Archduke Ferdinand, to attain strategic surprise, the Germans intended for these five armies to reach the enemy's rear and compel the French forces along the French-German frontier to attack to recover their communications. Faced with German armies and fortifications to the east and, in their rear, the three-fourths of the total of the available German forces that had carried out the turning movement, the French, so the German staff anticipated, could not escape.

But the plan had two important difficulties. Paris, a large, fortified city, presented a serious obstacle to the turning forces. In additon, feeding the enormous number of men and horses in the turning force depended, in the long run, on the railroad service available from Germany through Belgium into France. Even fertile France could not support such a vast horde and its many horses necessary to carry out the campaign.

The French, however, had the advantage in commanders. Moltke, the sixty-six-year-old chief of the German staff, bore the name of his famous uncle but lacked his high ability. A careful staff officer, he had modified the Schlieffen Plan to reduce the size of the turning force to one more consonant with logistic realities. The French generalissimo, Joseph Joffre, a sixty-two-year-old engineer officer, had been engaged in building railroads in Senegal when the French occupied Timbuktu. Given command of a small force to march to Timbuktu, Major Joffre pressed on with typical determination, even when he learned of the defeat of the French detachment there and the death of its colonel. He led his men nearly 500 miles up the Niger River, restored the situation, and consolidated French control of Timbuktu. Thereafter he received line as well as engineer appointments. So, like Marshal Bazaine, he had seen much colonial service, but in every other respect the portly Joffre emerged as the antithesis of Bazaine. Throughout the campaign he displayed a decisiveness and imperturbability in the face of adversity that should always characterize a commander faced with important responsibilities. Like Moltke, Joffre had an excellent staff.

In less than three weeks the French and German armies had mobilized and concentrated, and the Germans moved through Belgium, overwhelming the tiny Belgian professional army and overcoming fortifications with 305- and 420-millimeter siege mortars. The French completed their concentration on their frontier and, as they had planned, attacked to gain the initiative and recover the territory ceded to Germany in 1871. Here the augmented power of the defense first demonstrated itself when the Germans repulsed the French assaults and the French stopped the German counterattacks. One French division, regulars of the Foreign Legion, lost 11,000 of its 17,000 men in its unsuccessful charges and when shrapnel fire on a bridge cut off its retreat.

Early in the third week of August, as his attacks on the frontier failed, Joffre began to realize the magnitude of the German turning movement through Belgium. The French had anticipated this possibility and had stationed the Fifth Army, eight infantry divisions of twelve battalions each, to protect their left flank. In addition, the four regular infantry divisions of the British Expeditionary Force took position on the left of the Fifth Army. But clearly this force could not cope with the German move, even after Joffre had added three divisions to the Fifth Army.

The Germans had numbered the five armies of their turning force one through five from the flank inward. The two innermost, the Fifth and Fourth, faced and had repulsed the attacks of the French Fourth and Third armies, adjacent to the Fifth guarding the French flank. The remaining three German armies, emerging from Belgium, readily drove back the French Fifth and the British Expeditionary Force. Joffre now ordered a retreat west and south, in which the British opposed the German First Army, the French Fifth opposed the German Second, and the French Fourth, divided into two armies, retreated before the German Third and Fourth.

Meanwhile, the French generalissimo brought more of his own units without cadres into the field and used the railroad to move troops from his right to

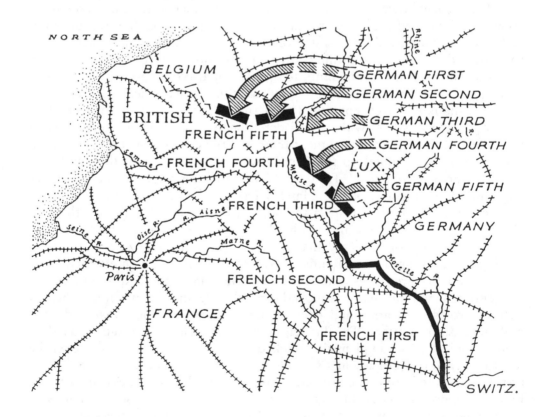

Diagram 8.1. Opening Turning Movement of World War I

left. Though lacking a subtracted force held back in reserve, Joffre could find reserves in troops not inextricably involved in combat with the Germans and, just as did Napoleon in his first defense of Mantua, promptly called them to the threatened points.

Joffre based his response on the important strategic mobility that possession of the excellent French railways gave him. Whereas the German turning forces found only destroyed railways as they advanced, Joffre used his railways to create a new army, the Sixth, which he placed at Paris. The intact railways thus provided the defending French general with strategically offensive troops, and he used this capability to prepare a counteroffensive. Tactically offensive troops, as exemplified by cavalry, required both better mobility and the ability to go into action without delay to attack the enemy's flank or rear. But in a movement exclusively for strategic purposes, offensive troops needed only better mobility because only tactical conditions required quick deployment. To create a strategic concentration of force or to reach the enemy's strategic flank, greater mobility, such as the railway provided, sufficed to give the advantages that under tactical conditions necessitated their immediate exploitation by a prompt attack, one not held up by any elaborate requirements for deployment.

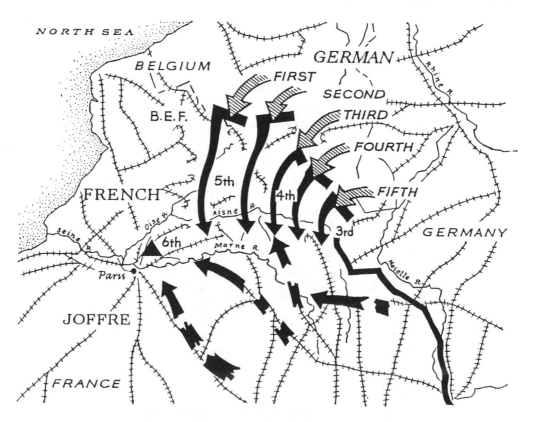

Diagram 8.2. Joffre Exploits His Strategic Mobility

As the huge German turning movement advanced rapidly in pursuit of the retreating French and British, the Germans turned south and passed all of their armies east of Paris, where they left on their flank the new French army, the Sixth. The strategic mobility provided by the railway had thus enabled the French to turn the turning movement. After nearly two weeks of falling back, Joffre counterattacked toward the Marne River on September 6. Although the German First Army faced some units to cover its right flank against the attack of the French Sixth Army, the vigor of the allied attack and a gap between the German First and Second armies brought about a German withdrawal on September 9.

Within a week the German First, Second, Third, and Fourth armies fell back twenty-five to thirty miles and began, like the combatants of the American Civil War, to entrench their defensive positions as did all Germans from their First Army eastward to the Swiss frontier. When allied assaults failed to drive back the German First and Second armies, Joffre attempted to outflank the German line; but Falkenhayn, the new German commander, sought to do the same and within a few weeks both French and German flanks had reached the North Sea. The Germans attacked near the coast and the allies counterattacked, both without much effect on the battle lines that both combatants had now entrenched from Switzerland to the sea.

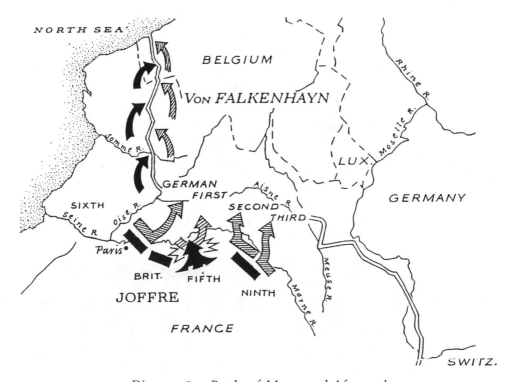

Diagram 8.3. Battle of Marne and Aftermath

The Tactical, Logistical, and Strategic Conditions of the War

The tactics of the campaign confirmed the experience of 1870–71, except that tactical defense had increased its supremacy. On one occasion British regulars, expertly trained in marksmanship with rifles holding ten shots, had defeated a German attack at a range of 900 yards. In another instance the British had turned back so many German charges that their rifles became so hot that many would not function. But at that point German courage or manpower failed, and the Germans did not make the attack that might have overrun the British. In the first month the allies had suffered 250,000 casualties, the Germans somewhat more.

With millions of men entrenched from Switzerland to the English Channel neither side had a flank that its opponent could turn. Frontal attacks, if they could break through, remained the only means that would create flanks that could then be turned. The machine gun demonstrated its worth, and all armies increased the numbers of the relatively immobile water-cooled, belt-fed models and added light, portable automatic rifles. Although the latter, relying on air cooling, could not maintain sustained fire, their brief bursts at a high rate augmented the infantry's firepower.

Shrapnel proved so effective that armies eventually adopted steel helmets in defense. But the deep trenches gave such increased protection from shrapnel that artillery came increasingly to rely on high-explosive shells, which could wreck the trenches. Barbed wire became an effective defense, taking the place of the ditch and wooden *chevaux-de-frise* obstacles of old. Thick barriers of barbed wire soon secured the entrenchments, the broad belts of resilient wire requiring many high-explosive shells to open gaps for attacking infantry.

In August 1914 the soldiers of the huge German turning force had found enough to eat in the fertile and densely populated area of France in which they campaigned. But the horses were less fortunate, as soldiers found relatively little hay. By early September the horses of some of the artillery could no longer keep up with the advance. The Battle of the Marne occurred just as the horses in the German army had reached the limit of their endurance.

Ammunition presented a serious supply problem. The armies used artillery shells at four times the rate in 1870 and consumed twelve times as much small-arms ammunition as in 1870. Railroads transported the ammunition to the point at which Belgium or France had disabled the railroads, and from there it moved to the Germans by road. The very speed of the advance, which constantly brought the troops into unforaged areas, meant that wagons could not have gone rapidly enough to meet the extraordinary demands for ammunition. A small group of German motor trucks, together with requisitioned motor vehicles, maintained ammunition supplies. But by the time of the Battle of the Marne, 60 percent of the motor trucks had broken down, casualties of hard usage.

In view of the state of the horses and motor transport in the German armies and the long distance from German railheads, it is doubtful that the Germans could have continued their advance much beyond the Marne. The exhaustion of the troops after so long a march also tended to make further advances difficult. Most of the soldiers, civilians barely a month before, had performanced extraordinarily, but the experience of one unit showed the effect of three weeks of uninterrupted marching. An officer wrote: "Before the war I should have regarded such powers of endurance as beyond the capacity of the most robust peasant lads . . . how the men's feet have suffered. From time to time we had to examine them; and it was no pleasure to look at the inflamed heels, soles and toes of my wretched young lads, whole patches of skin rubbed off to the raw flesh." But except for the fatigue of the marching, the French did not suffer from these logistical difficulties: they always fell back onto their own elaborate railway network, which tapped supplies of food, fodder, and ammunition.[1]

The ambitious effort to carry out a turning movement with a million men had failed. Even if the logistical problems created by so many soldiers had not doomed it, its success would have depended on the enemy command. The taciturn Joffre not only maintained his nerve but continued to sleep ten hours a night and take time to dine well. On one occasion, after enjoying a sumptuous repast, Joffre received a report that the Germans had captured an important town. Apparently quite unperturbed, the generalissimo, patting his ample stomach, only remarked that it contained one thing the Germans would not capture. His excellent staff and his own timely and decisive responses meant that he saw, and promptly moved to cope with, the danger presented by the German turning movement. In exercising his command, Joffre displayed a ruthlessness that belied his benign appearance. In two months he removed eighty commanders of divisions and higher units; some were promoted, but most were moved to make way for others he regarded as more able.

The very numbers of soldiers, which created logistical problems for the Germans and would have given them an adequate ratio of force to space to block the retreat of the French had the German turning armies reached their enemy's rear, may also have ensured a deadlock. With cavalry almost irrelevant, the tactical power of the defense at an apogee, and an unprecedented ratio of force to space, a decisive campaign may well have been beyond the reach of the contestants. Because of so many men with such a large amount of defensive firepower, a deadlock may have been inevitable, barring extraordinary incompetence. And thoroughly trained, effective staffs would have made it difficult even for a Bazaine to have mismanaged enough to insure disaster.

The ratio of force to space had long played a major role in determining the outcome of military operations. In campaigns from the French Revolution through the Franco-Prussian War the combatants had had a ratio of force to space great enough to attain a quick decision when at least one contestant had dispersed its armies, used its capacity to march rapidly when near the enemy, and made the most of its ability to deploy quickly from column to line. With a ratio of force in relation to space too low, the new armies and new strategy could not compel an enemy either to fight or to retreat directly to its rear. Thus, when Napoleon entered Russia, the theater of operations had so much space in relation to his forces that he could not make the Russians fight against their will.

The high ratio of force to space dominated operations in France during the four years of World War I and, along with the unparalleled primacy of the defense, strongly influenced events in other theaters. Just as too little force to space could render operations indecisive, so did too much, as operations in the fortified Netherlands had long demonstrated. Without flanks, the primacy of the tactical defensive over frontal attacks asserted itself and produced a stalemate. The numbers engaged, the constant contact on long fronts, and the frontal attack as the only tactical expedient greatly increased casualties. The French, for example, usually on the offensive against the Germans, lost more than one million men killed and wounded a year. For the four years of war the battle deaths numbered 1,385,000 for the French empire, 947,000 for the British, 1,700,000 for the Russians, and 1,808,000 for the Germans. Italy lost 460,000, the United States 115,000 dead. Of the 65 million mobilized by all belligerents, the killed and wounded in battle approached 29 million.

Many of these immense casualties resulted from vain attacks, often conducted by French and British generals against entrenched German defenders. In retrospect these seem, and frequently were, foolish, but the competent soldiers who conducted a number of them found it difficult to grasp the almost absolute supremacy of the entrenched defensive, so at variance with prewar conceptions. Nor could they easily give up the idea that greater numbers could not prevail, pierce the front, and emancipate the armies from the tyranny of the siege warfare which so favored the defensive.

The German Exploitation of Interior Lines and a Turning Movement to Defeat the Russians

In defending East Prussia against a Russian attack, the Germans conducted a campaign based on the brilliant success of those elements that had characterized Napoleon's operations. Holding East Prussia with small forces and facing a coordinated Russian advance by Rennenkampf's army from the west and Samsonov's from the south, the German commander, Prittwitz, planned to utilize his interior lines first to drive back Rennenkampf and then to turn against Samsonov who was advancing more slowly. The Russians, with larger numbers and expecting his move, planned for Samsonov to reach Prittwitz's rear and block his retreat.

When his attack against Rennenkampf failed on August 20, Prittwitz panicked and telephoned supreme headquarters his intention to withdraw to the Vistula River, thus abandoning most of East Prussia. General Moltke promptly relieved Prittwitz and sent General Paul von Hindenburg, a veteran of Königgrätz and the Franco-Prussian War, to replace him. Hindenburg had served on the general staff and on the faculty of the War College and had commanded a corps during peace. Hindenburg brought to command a calmness and resolution not unlike Joffre's. Moltke sent Erich Ludendorff, a forty-nine-year-old career staff officer, as Hindenburg's chief of staff. Ludendorff had just distinguished himself by leaving the Second Army staff to head the brigade that captured the powerfully fortified Belgian city of Liége. General Ludendorff, a keen, sensitive, brilliant staff officer, displayed a mastery of operations and dominated the team while Hindenburg supplied stability in adversity and a balance in a relationship that Hindenburg described as a happy marriage.

By the time Hindenburg and Ludendorff arrived, Prittwitz's staff had made a new plan. Its author, Lt. Colonel Hoffman, knowing that Rennenkampf and Samsonov were hostile to one another, believed that the Germans could safely ignore Rennenkampf and concentrate their forces against Samsonov's menacing march toward their rear. Interception of unencoded Russian wireless messages confirmed that Rennenkampf planned no rapid advance.

Hindenburg and Ludendorff approved the plan. It moved General François's corps by rail from its position opposite Rennenkampf all the way to Samsonov's left flank while the other two corps marched south toward Samsonov's center and right flank. The Germans left only a cavalry division and six battalions of infantry to hold back Rennenkampf. The two corps that marched south exploited the traditional strategic situation of interior lines. François's corps, which used the railroad to reach Samsonov's left, traveled a circuitous route and moved much farther. But rail transport more than compensated for the additional distance to reach a strategically important position. As with Joffre's reconcentration of his force and creation of the Sixth Army on the German flank, the railroad gave the defending commander strategically offensive troops, enabling him to concentrate more rapidly and turn the attackers.

On August 25 the Germans began their advance, the forces from the north striking Samsonov's right and François attacking his left. When the Russian corps opposing François withdrew to the south, the energetic and aggressive François pushed forward into the Russian rear, distributing his army to block their retreat. To make his turning movement effective, he covered a thirty-seven-mile front with only twenty-five battalions. But when the disorganized Russians sought to withdraw, the firepower of this thin screen proved adequate to contain the Russians. As a result of this campaign at Tannenberg General Samsonov surrendered 125,000 men and 500 guns. He himself did not surrender but walked into the woods and shot himself.

The Germans then turned against Rennenkampf who, when he realized the Germans threatened to turn his flank, retreated promptly and rapidly eastward. Excellent German commanders and staffs, with the aid of interior lines and the first-rate mobility that the railroad gave the defender, had defeated in the Napoleonic manner the medicore leadership of an essentially improvised Russian offensive.

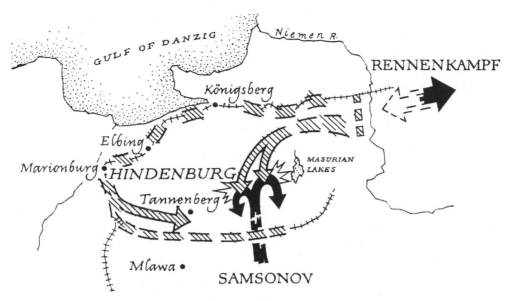

Diagram 8.4. German Use of Interior Lines and Railway for Turning Movement

The Opening Naval Campaigns

Although the entrenched deadlock on land represented stability only in terms of prewar expectations, the allied predominance on the surface of the sea conformed to the sailors' prewar anticipations. Against a 50 percent British superiority in *Dreadnought*-type battleships and a two-to-one dominance in older battleships, the German fleet stayed in its bases. With a strong force of cruisers, the British maintained a blockade of both the German fleet and commerce by keeping their main battle fleet in its base. Because of their nearness to Germany, the British Isles gave the navy ample nearby bases, thus conferring on it all of the advantages of the increase in the ratio of force to space brought about by steam and wireless but with none of the logistical disadvantages of the dependence on distant bases for fuel.

With the British Isles themselves by their geographical position, blockading Germany, the British easily maintained their persisting logistic strategy of blockade at a distance from German ports. The French fleet, more than a match for those of Austria-Hungary and Italy even without British aid, controlled the Mediterranean, a task much simplified when Italy at first remained neutral and then joined the French and British in the spring of 1915.

The Germans and the British each had naval forces stationed worldwide at colonial bases. The British navy immediately addressed the task of tracking down and destroying these German ships to prevent their attacking British commerce. This they essentially completed by the end of 1914. These operations saw the new classes of cruisers in action and again witnessed the changes steam and steel had wrought in naval warfare.

In the fall of 1914 the German Asiatic squadron of five cruisers crossed to the coast of Chile where, off Coronel in early November 1914, it met a British force of four cruisers. Two modern armored cruisers, each with the power of their broadsides concentrated in six 210-millimeter guns, constituted the backbone of the German squadron. The British also had two armored cruisers of an older, though faster, design that together had a broadside of only two 9.2-inch guns and many 6-inch. In spite of this inferiority and with a large number of reservists among his crews, the aggressive, one-eyed British admiral, Craddock, sought to engage, believing that he followed orders. Glad to oblige, the perceptive German Admiral Spee led his ships on a course parallel to Craddock's, but the British ships were silhouetted by a setting sun behind them and his were obscured by darkness, accentuated by a squall. In an hour he had sunk both British armored cruisers with all hands; the Germans suffered only six hits and virtually no damage to their ships.

Although Admiral Craddock had acted in the tradition of the British navy, he no longer enjoyed the benefit that the British had so often exploited in their combats with the French and Spaniards. Instead of bringing a sea-seasoned force against an enemy long in port, he led reservists in old ships against thoroughly ready and more modern German ships that had won a gunnery prize while serving on the China station. In addition, by 1914 the ships and their weapon systems had relatively more importance than the men when compared with conditions at the Battle of Trafalgar for example.

Suspecting, correctly, that Admiral Spee would head for the Atlantic, the British admiralty took drastic steps. Instead of assembling a more numerous fleet of armored cruisers, it took the chief of the war staff, the proficient but pedantic Vice Admiral Sturdee, and sent him to the south Atlantic with two battle cruisers. When he reached the Falkland Islands off the Argentine coast, Sturdee, who had early favored sending the battle cruisers, joined three British armored cruisers as well as two small, unarmored cruisers and an old, slow battleship that Craddock had dropped from his squadron. Over the protests of his engine room staff, who wished to perform maintenance work, Admiral Sturdee kept all of his ships, except the battleship, ready to raise full steam in only four hours.

When, on an early December morning, Spee came to reconnoiter the Falklands anchorage, he did not suspect the concentration of force, even when he could see clouds of smoke beginning to shroud the harbor. This smoke resulted from Admiral Sturdee's frantic efforts to raise steam for full speed while the old battleship sought to keep the Germans at bay with inaccurate shots fired at the Germans over an intervening spit of land. When Sturdee had steam enough for fifteen knots, he led his battle cruisers out of the harbor. As these big ships emerged from the harbor's smoke and Spee could see the characteristic tripod masts of battle cruisers, he knew that he was doomed. Signaling his three small cruisers to scatter, the courageous Spee prepared to cover their flight by using his two armored cruisers to engage the two battle cruisers. He faced the insuperable odds shown in table 8.1.

TABLE 8.1.   Comparison of Ships at the Battle of the
Falkland Islands

	German Armored Cruisers	British Battle Cruisers
Displacement	11,420 tons	17,250 tons
Speed	21.5 knots	25 knots
Big guns	16 x 210 mm (8.27 in.)	16 x 12 inch
Thickest armor	4 inch	7 inch

Sturdee signaled to two of his armored cruisers and his two smaller cruisers to pursue the smaller German ships while, with his battle cruisers and the *Carnarvon* with four 7.5-inch guns his strongest armored cruiser, he followed the German armored cruisers. For their task the British had clear weather, a calm sea, and the long day characteristic of the month of the summer solstice. Reaching twenty-five knots and easily overtaking the Germans, Sturdee slowed and, seeking a superfluity of superiority, waited for the unexpectedly slow-steaming *Carnarvon* to catch up. After availing himself of the opportunity to give his men an early lunch, Admiral Sturdee gave up on the *Carnarvon*, and, with well-fed men, the suitably named admiral, in his appropriately christened flagship *Invincible*, increased speed again and engaged the Germans at 12,000 yards, a range at which their 210-millimeter guns could hardly pierce his armor.

In a few minutes his heavy guns had smashed the barbettes and casemates of the German ships, slowed their speed, and rendered them literally inoffensive. But to sink such ships proved difficult because of the subdivision of the hulls into numerous water-tight compartments and the difficulty of hitting the water-line. In order to sink both the German ships, the British had to expend 60 percent of their 12-inch gun ammunition. Like the British at Coronel, the German ships left few survivors, Admiral Spee going down with his flagship. The British ships demonstrated their invulnerability at long range: the *Invincible* sustained twenty-two hits but suffered only one sailor wounded.

While Sturdee engaged Spee and his armored cruisers, the other British armored cruisers overtook two of the smaller German cruisers, though one of the British ships had to burn much of its woodwork to gain a hotter fire and a little more steam. The small German cruisers suffered a fate similar to the armored cruisers when 3,300-ton, unarmored ships with 105-millimeter guns faced armored ships of 9,800 tons with 6-inch guns. The third German cruiser escaped.

The actions at Coronel and Falkland Islands exhibited the primacy of materiel in the naval warfare of steam and steel. In their many conflicts with the French in the late seventeenth and eighteenth centuries the British had fought with inferior ships, but their far greater skills gained in constant service at sea far overbalanced the better quality of the French vessels. By 1914, however, all navies could gain in port and in peacetime exercises more of the skills needed to operate range finders, master mechanically aided gun-loading routines, and operate steam engines.

Battles in parallel lines had proven decisive at Coronel because of Craddock's determination to use his higher speed to engage a more powerful force and, as with the Japanese in their second battle with the Russians, because of Sturdee's use of his greater speed at the Falkland Islands to engage Spee's weaker and reluctant squadron. But when the German and British battleship fleets met in the traditional lines, the Germans showed that they could emulate the French of old and escape.

Allied Naval Predominance Confirmed: The Battle of Jutland

The Battle of Jutland took place on May 31, 1916. The German battleship fleet moved to cover an attack on British shipping to Norway at the same time that Admiral Sir John Jellicoe's British fleet made one of its periodic sweeps in the North Sea. The British had twenty-eight *Dreadnought*-type battleships, the Germans sixteen. The British vessels tended to be larger and faster than the German and had greater firepower. British ships had broadsides of eight 12-inch or ten 13.5-inch guns, though one had a broadside of fourteen 12-inch guns and six had broadsides of eight 15-inch guns. German vessels had broadsides of eight 11-inch or eight to ten 12-inch guns and had somewhat thicker armor than the British, better fire-control equipment, and more effective armor-piercing ammunition; but British armor plate offered more resistance than German plate of the same thickness.

The British had nine battle cruisers, the Germans five. The British ships had higher speed and bigger guns but much thinner armor than the German ships. The whole British force had much greater speed than the German because, in an effort to compensate for their marked inferiority in numbers of *Dreadnought*s, the Germans brought with them six slow pre-*Dreadnought*s carrying four guns on a broadside.

The fleets discovered each other when the German scouting squadron, including all five of its battle cruisers, met the British scouting force with six of its nine battle cruisers. The battle cruisers began firing at each other at a range of over 16,000 yards. The engagement demonstrated the flaw in exposing British ships with armor suitable for armored cruisers to the German 11- and 12-inch guns: one of the smaller British battle cruisers blew up, a shell having apparently pierced a barbette, igniting a magazine. Soon after, one of the largest British battle cruisers suffered a similar fate, breaking in half as the explosion of her magazines sent a cloud of smoke more than 1,000 feet in the air.

The afternoon engagement led the aggressive British battle cruiser squadron toward the German battleships, but when the British battle cruisers came in range of the German battleships, they turned and the Germans then became the pursuers. The British battle cruisers however, led the unsuspecting Germans toward the British battleships which the careful Admiral Jellicoe had deployed from six squadrons abreast into a single line that headed across the path of the German battleship fleet, also in line. When the German battle line came within range, the Germans found the far more numerous British fleet in a position to concentrate its fire on lead German ships, which were unable to reply with their full broadsides. The Germans, however, had practiced a maneuver to extricate themselves from such a predicament, and each vessel turned 180 degrees and began steaming away from the British.

Still, the course of the British fleet carried it between the German fleet and its base. As the Germans turned toward home to escape from the unexpected and unwanted battle, they again steamed their line directly toward the British and again its ships made their 180-degree turns. On its new course the German line converged toward the British, but when German vessels saw the British in the fading light of evening, they turned away.

Reluctant to fight at night when torpedoes and mines as well as chance might nullify his preponderance, the prudent Jellicoe did not press his advantage. Aware that he had nothing to gain strategically by defeating the Germans and much to lose—even, hypothetically, allied naval predominance and, consequently, the war itself—he displayed a commendable caution in following the same reasoning as had Admiral Togo after his victory on August 10, 1904. So the battered German fleet passed Jellicoe's rear during the night and reached its base.

Tactically the Germans secured a victory, sinking three British battle cruisers at a cost of only one battle cruiser and one old battleship. The British loss of three armored cruisers and the German loss of four small cruisers helped raise tonnage of ships forfeited to 111,980 for the British and 62,233 for the Germans. But as after so many battles with the French, the British preponderance remained undiminished, and the results of the battle did not tempt the Germans to fight again. The British gave prompt attention to improving their fire-control equipment, their ammunition, and the security of their magazines against explosions in a barbette.

The Submarine as a Commerce Raider

Throughout the war the Germans found themselves in an analogous situation to that experienced by the French in their numerous wars with the British. But with fast, wireless-equipped British steamers observing the sea lanes outside of the defenses and minefields of German harbors, the Germans faced a far more stringent blockade than any that the French had to contend with. Further, the industrial transformations that made possible the new ships also made the German economy dependent on overseas commerce to an extent not imagined in the eighteenth century. In addition, the Germans found that the changed circumstances prevented any emulation of the devastating logistic strategy of raids against British commerce at which the French had long excelled. The relative independence of wind and weather enjoyed by the blockading ships made it far more difficult for a commerce raider to slip out into the Atlantic, as French ships had so often done in the past. And the reliance of commerce raiders on coal, rather than wind, further crippled the German effort to pursue a traditional raiding strategy. Moreover, the greater effectiveness of the blockade made it virtually impossible to return to a German port with captured British ships, an inducement and a gain that had long helped French commerce raiding.

The submarine provided the means for the Germans to continue the weaker naval power's application of the logistic strategy by means of raids. The submarine began the war with a spectacular success. Sighting a squadron of three British armored cruisers of 12,000 tons each, a German submarine submerged and torpedoed one ship. As it slowly sank, the other two stood by to pick up survivors. This unwise act enabled the German submarine captain to make a second and then a third successful attack, sinking 36,000 tons of powerful surface vessels.

But warships promptly learned to counter submarines by keeping a sharp lookout for torpedoes, maintaining a high enough speed to prevent the submarine from closing in, and adopting an erratic course to make it unlikely that a submarine could count on a torpedo's course intersecting that of the target vessel. If warships spotted a torpedo approaching them, they often not only avoided it but also turned toward its source and sought to ram the submarine before it could dive to a safe depth.

On the other hand, in a largely unexpected development, merchant ships proved vulnerable to submarines. On the surface submarines used their deck guns to force the surrender of merchant vessels. The small submarine, however, could not carry enough sailors to man captured ships, and even if they could, the tight blockade virtually precluded taking their prizes back to Germany. So submarines sank their captures, allowing the crews to escape in lifeboats.

The British then resumed the old practice of arming their merchant ships. Although civilian seamen did not compare with German sailors as gunners and the merchant vessels carried an assortment of often-obsolete guns, the fragility of the submarine made it hazardous for one to engage in battle with an armed merchant ship. In addition, the British equipped some merchant ships with concealed modern guns and manned them with naval crews. These vessels, mistaken by German submarine captains for unarmed merchant vessels, easily sank the submarines.

Since German captains could not tell whether merchant ships carried powerful concealed guns manned by trained crews, they began torpedoing some merchant ships, without warning. This practice had the disadvantage not only of using up torpedoes, and submarines could carry only a few of these bulky projectiles, but also defied the long tradition and accepted international law of not attacking civilians. Since neutral vessels carried important cargoes and offered valuable targets, the Germans attacked them also. Because this warfare involved the Germans in disputes with the United States, the only great power still neutral, the German government vacillated in the rigor with which it applied this policy.

The Germans quickly realized that the submarine offered a very effective naval weapon against the predominant sea power of their opponents, and they set to work to apply vigorously the logistic strategy of submarine raids against commerce. Beginning the war with only twenty-eight submarines, compared with fifty-six for the British, by January 1915 the Germans had 160 under construction or on order. Sinking only 3,382 tons of merchant ships in 1914, the German and Austro-Hungarian submarines sank 1,193,004 tons of merchant ships in 1915, a loss that the allies essentially replaced by new construction. The Germans began 1916 with sixty-eight submarines (compared with twenty-four at the beginning of 1915), having more than replaced the twenty-three they had lost since 1914. In 1916 the Germans sank 2,209,709 tons of shipping, more than double the new tonnage added by the allies. So the Germans had created a force to attack allied commerce that equaled or surpassed the best successes of the French commerce raiders in the seventeenth and eighteenth centuries.

The Dominance of Artillery in Siege Warfare on Land

Faced with siege warfare, each combatant reacted quickly to augment his supply of the siege's premier weapon—artillery. All rushed old weapons to the front; though these old cannon had slow rates of fire and primitive recoil mechanisms, they filled the gap until factories could deliver new ones, and they amply demonstrated that obsolete weapons could kill enemy soldiers quite effectively. The belligerents also stripped unthreatened fortresses of their guns. Initially the Germans had a distinct advantage in howitzers, which had especial value for siege work because of their weightier projectiles and suitability for high-angle, indirect fire at distant targets that the gunners could not see. But the French rushed their 1913-model howitzer into production and manufactured a huge variety of the heavier weapons so valuable in attacking field fortifications.

The French had particular good fortune in the numbers and types of their coast-defense artillery. In establishing their coast defenses, they had provided a larger number of guns on a cheap mounting rather than choosing a few well-protected guns on expensive mounts. They positioned the gun's mount on a curved railway track, the motion of the carriage along the track providing both the major part of the aiming in azimuth and the absorption of some of the recoil. Since they had intended their coast artillery largely for defense against the British navy, they quickly removed the guns and brought them to the front, where the adoption of the simple railway-track type of mounting and the greater number of guns originally made possible by the inexpensive mount proved the perfect choice to provide super heavy siege artillery for the unanticipated kind of war that had developed.

The British, who relied for defense on their navy, had no fortresses or coast defenses from which to withdraw artillery. This, and their initially small army, meant that for much of the war the rapidly expanding British armies suffered from a lack of artillery as manufacturing continually lagged behind need. Shortages of ammunition plagued all of the belligerents, especially the French and British who attacked on the more artillery-intensive western front in France.

Not until 1916 did the armies have ample numbers of heavier guns and the necessary supplies of ammunition to go with them. Russia, with forces very large in relation to its industrial productive capacity, never adequately provided for its armies with respect to the new, enlarged requirements for artillery.

The expansion of the artillery in size was perhaps more impressive than its increase in numbers. A gun had the longest barrel, more than thirty times the bore; next, a howitzer, twenty to thirty times the bore in length; and last, mortars, with a length of less than twenty times its bore. The weight of a cannon was proportional to its length, the shorter, lighter versions weighing less, firing a shell of the same weight as the longer but at a lower muzzle velocity and, consequently, a shorter distance. The shorter guns, the mortar and the howitzer, had their principal use in delivering high-angle fire over intervening hills and against entrenchments. The longer range guns had great utility for shooting at targets in the enemy rear, such as railway lines and supply installations.

In 1918 the Germans introduced a gun that could shoot 75 miles, almost four times the range of the biggest guns. They accomplished this by modifying a 380-millimeter gun to fire a 210-millimeter shell and adding a long smooth-bore extension to the barrel. The long barrel, light shell, and powerful charge gave a muzzle velocity double that of a conventional gun, which enabled the shell to reach the limited wind resistance of high altitude to attain its extraordinary range. But it had only enough accuracy to hit a target the size of a city. They used this gun to bombard Paris, an attack with psychological rather than military significance. The Paris gun created a sensation and the French and Italians began work on such guns, which they did not complete in time for use in the war.

Table 8.2 omits the Paris gun but summarizes most of the other artillery used by the French and Germans during the war. The measurements of the bore are in millimeters. The 75- and 77-millimeter field pieces accounted for about half of all the cannon on each side. Their shells weighed from 13 to 17 pounds. The shell in the 520-millimeter howitzer weighed 2,800 pounds. The larger cannon required railway mounts.

The Development and Utility of Air Forces

Flying had developed in the decade before the outbreak of the war. Gas-filled airships had advanced the most rapidly, even engaging in carrying passengers, and armies and navies had recognized their value for reconnaissance. Their ability to remain aloft for several days made them especially valuable for this task, the Germans, in particular, developing this speciality. But their utility was limited during war: the dirigibles were vulnerable to ground fire and sometimes powerless to maintain their course in the face of adverse winds. The Germans eventually used them to carry two tons of bombs to drop on British cities. These air raids proved to be no more than a nuisance because the Zeppelin dirigible airships,

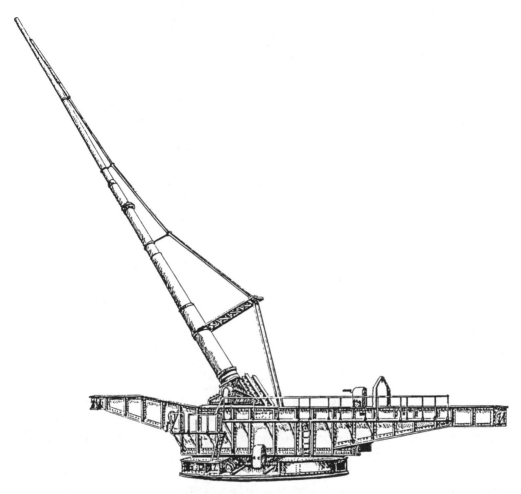

Illustration 8.1. Paris Gun

flying at night for greater safety, often missed the cities entirely, dropping their loads in open country. Ultimately the Germans substituted airplanes in these raids and then abandoned these attacks altogether. Aimed at British civilian morale, these raids delivered 300 tons of bombs and killed 1,400 people, few of them soldiers or sailors.

Winged aircraft proved of greater military significance during the war. By 1913 a plane had flown 126 miles an hour and another had ascended to 15,000 feet; the Russians had built a four-engine airplane with a cabin that could carry sixteen passengers. But the few hundred aircraft that the belligerents possessed at the outset of the war had more modest capabilities. Intended essentially for

TABLE 8.2.   Some World War I Artillery

Class	German	French
Light	77 howitzer 77 gun 105 mortar 105 howitzer	75 gun 105 howitzer
Medium	105 gun 130 howitzer 150 mortar 170 howitzer	105 gun 120 howitzer 155 howitzer
Heavy	150 gun 170 gun 210 mortar	140 gun 145 gun 155 gun 160 gun 202 gun 220 mortar 220 gun 240 howitzer
Super-heavy	280 howitzer 305 mortar 420 mortar 280 gun 380 gun	370 mortar 240 gun 274 gun 305 gun 340 gun 400 gun 520 howitzer

reconnaissance, their speeds rarely exceeded seventy miles an hour, and some could climb no higher than 3,000 feet. But since they proved easy and inexpensive to build and rather simple to learn to fly, armies quickly expanded the number of their aircraft.

The allies enjoyed superiority in the air because of French leadership in the development of the airplane and because the allies manufactured far more aircraft than Germany and its allies. Compared to German production of about 48,000 planes, the French built approximately 51,000, the British around 52,000, and Italy, who joined with the allies in 1915, about 20,000. The French manufactured 92,000 engines, many of which went to their allies. Russia and Austria-Hungary made very few. The United States produced 15,000, but practically none of these reached combat. In 1918 the combatants had as operational aircraft about 5 or 6 percent of their total production during the war. The allies had so great a preponderance in 1918 that in France the French had 260 squadrons and the British 100 compared with 200 for the Germans.

Captive balloons, used as far back as the French Revolution, provided the basic means of aerial observation for artillery; but aircraft supplemented these, eventually carrying wireless telegraphs to communicate with the artillery. More typically, the airplanes provided reconnaissance to observe enemy troop and artillery movements and concentrations. In a war with continuous fronts, planes performed the reconnaissance duties traditionally reserved for the light cavalry. Airborne cameras and subsequent expert study of the photographs made for effective observation by the new light cavalry of the air.

In September 1914 the French created the first unit of airplanes devoted to bombing. Even though the armies had studied air bombing and the Italians had used it as well as air reconnaissance in their 1911 war with the Turks, the French were not ready and had to improvise bombs from 90-millimeter artillery shells. Soon all combatants began bombing and developed specialized aircraft. Typically they bombed objectives, such as railway terminals, beyond the range of artillery and attacked troops and artillery with bombs and machine guns. Planes assisted ground offensives by attacking targets that the artillery had missed, but the inaccuracy of aerial bombing made these efforts relatively ineffective. Aircraft with machine guns did prove useful against troops in the open and thus fulfilled the tactical role of light cavalry as well.

The French also made a major effort at strategic bombing, aiming for the iron ore of Briey Basin. Captured by the Germans in 1914, this region supplied the raw material Germany needed to make steel. In a sustained two-year effort the French bombed the railway terminals through which the ore traveled. In the course of the campaign they dropped 1,800 tons of bombs, six times as much as the Germans dropped on England. But after the war the French found that their effort had had no effect. Of 1,300 bombs dropped on one railroad station, only 100 had hit the target, and these had not impeded ore transport. The French concluded that they would have had to drop 180,000 tons to block rail transit from the Briey basin unless, of course, they had bombed more accurately.

But during the war, unaware of the ineffectiveness of their bombing, the belligerents constantly enlarged and improved their bombers. By 1918 the Germans had a plane that could drop a one-ton bomb thirteen feet long on London. The huge British four-engine Handley-Page, which did not see action, could carry 6,900 pounds of bombs on a short flight.

Defense against bombers relied primarily on attacking them with other aircraft. Bombers then attacked at night, when the defending planes had small chance of seeing them and even less of attacking. But dropping bombs at night further reduced the already dismal accuracy of the bombardiers.

One of the first effective uses of antiaircraft fire occurred when a French infantry unit shot down a German airplane with a volley of rifle fire. Soon machine guns mounted for high single fire provided defense against low-flying aircraft and similarly mounted field guns engaged targets at high altitude. But antiaircraft weapons failed to have much success against targets moving in three dimensions. Even with searchlights, they were less effective at night. Defending aircraft and the inaccuracy of the bombers, not antiaircraft guns, provided the best defense against an air strike.

So, early in the war, planes fought each other. In spite of the novelty of combat between aircraft, the basic pattern developed rather quickly. Pilots and observers in reconnaissance aircraft armed themselves first with pistols and rifles and then with air-cooled machine guns. Planes with the engine behind pushing and an observer armed with a machine gun in front proved the best combat aircraft because of the wide, unobstructed field of fire open to the observer.

But the lighter single-seat planes with the engine and propeller in front had greater speed and maneuverability than the two-man pusher planes. A French pilot, after trying unsuccessfully to synchronize a machine gun to fire through the propeller, placed steel plates on his propeller; these deflected the bullets that hit them from the forward-firing machine gun. Since most bullets missed the propeller, he could use the faster, more maneuverable tractor plane for combat and aim his machine gun by aiming the plane.

The Germans then developed a workable synchronizing gear, which enabled the machine gun to fire through the propeller. This became the standard type of combat or fighter or pursuit aircraft by the middle of the war. By 1918 fighter planes had two rifle-caliber, air-cooled machine guns firing through the propeller and could attain speeds of 130 miles an hour. The reconnaissance airplane was similar, except that it carried an observer and, with its greater weight, had less speed and maneuverability. Most bombers had much in common with reconnaissance planes, though a few had two, three, or even four engines.

Thus air warfare came to resemble the naval warfare of ancient times when light, maneuverable galleys aimed the ship to sink their opponent by ramming. Instead of a ram, the aircraft directed a stream of machine gun bullets at its opponent. The method of fighting also put greater emphasis on individual combat, a characteristic altered only somewhat by the organization of planes into squadrons. When squadrons fought each other, a melee resulted.

In the air fighting of World War I bombing and reconnaissance aircraft played a major role. Their greater size and weight and slower speed gave these planes something in common with the merchant ships of old. Although the

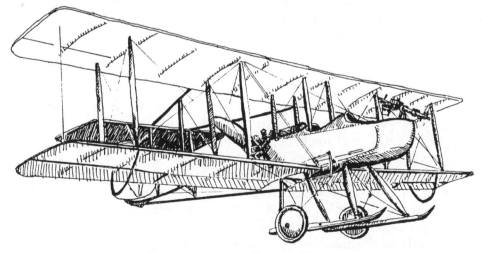

Illustration 8.2. Pusher Airplane

Illustration 8.3. Sopwith Camel, Tractor with Synchronized Machine Guns

observer had a machine gun and later bombers and observation planes had forward-firing machine guns, these weapons did not provide all-around protection. Fighter planes used their greater speed and maneuverability to attack the slower airplanes from an unprotected angle just as a galley would have rammed the side of a merchant ship. And bombers, with their cargo of explosives, were, in a sense, the armed merchant ships of the skies.

Since only bombers and observation planes could carry out the fundamental purpose of aircraft, fighter planes played a defensive role in attacking them and also had an offensive mission in escorting the more vulnerable airplanes, much as escorts had protected merchant convoys. In terms of tactical success, the attrition from combat, the defenders had an advantage because they could attack the vulnerable bombers and reconnaissance planes. Often defending fighters had another defensive advantage, fighting closer to their own airports. This enabled them to go into combat with more fuel and so fight longer before having to return to their base. Also the pilot and the airplane had a chance of seeing action again if downed over their own territory. But the damage done by bombing and the information gathered by reconnaissance also constituted a tactical benefit as well as the strategic result that this offensive action might yield.

In spite of their preponderance in numbers, the allied air forces did not gain command of the air in the way that their fleets controlled the sea. The Germans had too much strength, and their aircraft were too elusive for a blockade to succeed. Efforts to keep a constant patrol above an enemy airport, for example, required constant relays of aircraft, a difficulty sailing ships did not encounter in maintaining a close blockade of a port in earlier times. Such relays usually meant that the blockading air force had so few aircraft above an airport at a time that the inferior air force could easily achieve superiority over its own air fields. Air attacks against aircraft on the ground proved effective but difficult to execute without the enemy's knowing of the attack and having fighters in the air. Antiaircraft defenses of machine guns and field guns adapted for high-angle fire also helped thwart such attacks by a stronger air force.

Thus, strategically, the war in the air involved both raids and defense against raids; the stronger air forces conducted more raids. The allies complemented their offensive on the ground with an offensive in the air. This caused them to sustain heavier losses than the Germans, in spite of their greater numbers that in the unobstructed combat area of the air should have given them a decisive advantage as they would have more guns shooting at fewer targets.

Popular attention fixed itself on the fighter pilot and usually ignored the more prosaic bomber pilot and his crew. The heroism implied by single combat attracted popular imagination and provided the heroes that the butchery of the static trench warfare seemed to deny. Dubbed "aces," these pilots counted the number of enemy aircraft shot down. These required confirmation by another observer or by finding the wrecked plane on the ground. Inexperienced pilots, often inadequately trained, proved easy victims for those who had survived long enough to acquire skill in flying and combat maneuvers. Thus, the leading German ace, Manfred von Richtofen, shot down eighty enemy planes before he himself, exhausted by constant combat, succumbed. Edward Mannock, the most successful British ace, accounted for seventy-three enemy aircraft before he died. William A. Bishop, a Canadian, downed seventy-two enemy planes and survived the war, as did the leading French ace, René Fonck, who bagged seventy-five.

The Tactics of Trench Warfare

The Germans, standing on the defensive in France in 1915, fortified their front with care. It consisted of a line of trenches. The fire of the infantry and machine guns of the first trench commanded the terrain before it and then connected to a second trench line, 200 yards behind it. Seven hundred to 1,000 yards in the rear the Germans placed another line of machine gun posts protected by concrete. The German doctrine, laid down by the solid, methodical chief of staff, Falkenhayn, required a defense of this line at all costs, with counterattacks to recover any loss. Although this constituted the standard response in defending a siege of a city, it hardly had much relevance where the Germans had behind them thousands of square miles of captured territory.

In the spring of 1915 the British tried to break through with a surprise thrust following a thirty- to forty-minute bombardment. In one instance they got through, but reserves and the line of machine gun posts then held up the advance until more reserves arrived and created a new front. The British might have advanced farther, but they delayed while they awaited orders from the generals in the rear. By the time messengers carried back reports and returned with orders, the situation had changed. Usually lacking any vantage point, like a hill, from which they could observe, and commanding a battle over a front several miles long, generals had neither adequate knowledge of events nor the ability to communicate quickly enough to control the fight. Defenders faced the same difficulties. Gradually commanders learned that trench warfare required decentralization of command, with more authority given to small-unit commanders.

In another assault the British infantry had to advance only the 200 yards from the attackers' to the defenders' trenchlines. They moved forward in six successive lines or waves with the men three paces apart. The German infantry and a few machine guns shot down the first three waves, and German artillery, firing on the British trench, shot the fourth as it climbed over the top to begin its charge. The last two waves failed to attack at all. In this and a subsequent renewal the British lost 6,340 men, the Germans only 902.

The attack in waves reflected a linear system traditional since the seventeenth century. Prewar doctrine in all European armies had stressed the need for the attackers to establish fire supremacy over the defenders; maximum firepower required this linear array. The doctrine had envisioned advances in rushes after prone infantry had overwhelmed the defenders' fire, but since it had also assumed advances from greater distances, the actual assault from 200 yards represented the final rush. Instead of running, however, the attacking infantry walked advancing at a predictable rate to allow the artillery to keep the defending positions under fire until the last moment. Prewar doctrine had neither reckoned on such thorough entrenchments nor realized the volume and effectiveness of the defending fire. The British use of many troops and officers, only recently enlisted and without prewar training, made their tactics cumbersome and rigid.

In both attacks the artillery failed to impair the German position or even seriously damage the barbed wire, even though the British had one gun for each seven yards of the front on the narrow sector on which they made the assault. Most of the British artillery consisted of field guns firing eighteen-pound shells, which lacked the power to damage seriously the German field fortifications in so short a bombardment. The inaccuracy of the fire of the guns constituted a more important cause of failure. Most shells missed the trenches and the barbed wire because each gunner had not registered, that is, fired on the target before and observed and adjusted its fire to be sure to hit its mark. But the registration of 600 guns takes time. Without registration the bombardment lacked accuracy; with registration the attack would not have had the element of surprise.

Instead of relying on a surprise infantry assault, the French approached the problem of attacking the entrenched German positions as if it were a siege. Joffre, an engineer officer, prescribed the solution as one of artillery conquering and infantry occupying the ground. He abandoned surprise to attain the advantages of the prolonged bombardment characteristic of sieges. But since Joffre's long bombardment required immense stocks of ammunition, his offensives had to wait until he had accumulated these. After unsuccessful efforts in the winter and spring of 1915, in the fall he attempted two major efforts, one in cooperation with the British in the north.

In the second, in Champagne on an eighteen-mile front, Joffre concentrated twenty infantry divisions for the attack with eight infantry and six cavalry divisions in reserve to exploit a breakthrough. The German defenders had only five divisions. In addition to an enormous number of field guns, the French had 850 of heavier caliber for a three-day bombardment that obliterated the German trenches. The infantry attack broke through the German trench line on about half the front, and on eight miles of these the thrust carried them through the line of concrete machine gun positions. But the Germans, aided by the time provided by the three-day bombardment, had strengthened their defense by building another line in the rear, 2,500 to 3,000 yards behind the first line. To attack this the French had to delay to move up their artillery to conduct another bombardment.

This new German line proved less vulnerable to artillery fire because the Germans had located it on the far side of hills. When they had built their original line, they had placed it on the forward slopes of these hills, assuming that the infantry needed a good field of fire to repel an attack. But they had learned that their firepower could halt infantry with only a few hundred yards as a field of fire. Trench lines on the far slopes offered excellent protection from the fire of the hostile artillery because the position offered the Germans shelter from direct fire and hindered the French observers who were trying to correct the fall of the shells from howitzers and other weapons employing indirect fire.

The French also attacked in waves, but with their better trained troops and more professional officers and noncommissioned officers, they gave more initiative to subordinates to maneuver and to exploit weaknesses in the German position, procedures also quite in consonance with the traditions of siege warfare. Yet their whole concept tied the infantry to the artillery and thus inevitably introduced a ponderousness and rigidity into their offensive efforts.

This precaution of using the far slopes differed little from that used in the Napoleonic Wars by the duke of Wellington to protect his infantry from French artillery. In addition, the Germans immediately began digging two new defensive lines in the rear of their second line. They did not need these however, because their advantageously located second line supported by their artillery repelled the renewed French assaults.

The French attacks in the north fared no better, nor did those of the British who, without the French advantage of an ample supply of heavy artillery, tried the long-bombardment technique. Even though this killed many defenders and smashed the German entrenchments, the defense, having basically redundant firepower, could turn back an infantry charge with only a fraction of its force intact. One German machine gun, for example, fired 12,500 rounds in one afternoon. This occurred in an attack in which the British suffered over 8,000 casualties in spite of a bombardment that lasted four days and used over 250,000 shells.

In these fall offensives the British lost 50,000 men, the Germans 20,000. Against the French, the Germans lost 120,000 to 192,000 for the French. The German counterattacks and their insistence on not abandoning any territory cost them heavily against the more skillful and powerfully armed French.

The allies kept cavalry divisions in reserve to exploit the breakthrough that never came. At a later date British cavalry charged the entrenched positions in the mistaken belief the Germans were retreating. A German wrote: "We could scarcely believe our eyes when English squadrons rode towards us." He explained that German soldiers "stood up as on a rifle range and, laughing, greeted this rare target with a hail of bullets. The survivors turned and galloped back with many empty saddles." At another point the cavalry gave the Germans no sporting opportunities, for, as the German soldier added, "A few batteries fired into a mass of cavalry and our machine guns completed their destruction. Countless riderless horses galloped over the battlefield and we captured many."[2]

The War in 1915 and 1916

The logistics of this war differed from all previous wars in that rail transportation provided the food, fodder, and enormous quantities of ammunition the stationary armies required. Sieges had always presented supply problems, but without the railroads the armies could not have remained immobile, besieging each other. The belligerents harnessed their industrialized economies to furnish the needs of more than 10 percent of their populations under arms. These armies could not, for the most part, live at the enemy's expense and required ammunition and new and replacement weapons in unprecedented quantities.

Allied strategy responded to this new relationship between war and the economy when the British blockaded Germany. This logistic strategy could not decide the war because Germany had industry, a substantial agriculture, coal and iron, and land connections with Eastern Europe as well as water communications with Scandinavia. But the blockade did limit German food supplies and such overseas imports as cotton, rubber, and oil. Germany armed its soldiers and fed its armies and civilian populations but not without substitutions, inconvenience, some hardship, and damage to morale. The allies, on the other hand, used their command of the sea, overseas investments, and credit to import lavishly the requirements of their industries, armies, and civilian populations.

The Germans continued to make the most of their interior lines. In 1915 they went over to the defensive in France and concentrated against Russia. Here the opposing armies covered a front of about 700 miles, over double that from Switzerland to the sea, and each had forces fundamentally comparable in strength to those in the West. The 1914 Russian and Austrian offensives had collided head-on, and, after a Russian advance, the front of the Russians against the Germans and Austrians had stabilized in the late fall. The Germans and Austrians intended for their 1915 offensives to beat back and weaken the Russians, removing the threat to Austria.

First distracting the Russians by an offensive on the northern extremity of the front, in early May the Germans and Austrians attacked farther south where only six Russian divisions held a front of twenty-eight miles. With only a single trench line, the Russians faced fourteen Austrian and German divisions supported by 1,500 guns. Surprised and their entrenchments seriously damaged by a skillfully planned and accurately aimed bombardment lasting four hours, the Russians

Map 8.1. Central and Eastern Europe (shading shows Germany and its allies
as of early 1915)

gave way, and the Austro-German troops pushed forward eighty miles in twelve days. Since this advance threatened the flank and rear of neighboring forces, the Russians fell back on a 250-mile front, re-establishing themselves with a new line of entrenchments.

The lower ratio of force to space on the Russian front permitted the breakthroughs that had eluded allied commanders in France. With a succession of such offensives the Germans and Austrians drove the Russian armies from Poland, inflicting heavy casualties. The Germans and Austrians then turned against Serbia in the fall, occupying its territory, though its army escaped to the Adriatic where it boarded allied ships. Thinking they had destroyed Russia's offensive capacity, Germany then turned against France, fighting a long, costly, and indecisive struggle at Verdun in the winter and spring of 1916.

The allies sought to secure concentration in time when Joffre called a conference in December 1915 when Russia and Italy as well as France and Britain agreed to simultaneous offensives for June 1916.

But the allies failed to exploit their own interior lines. In the fall of 1914 the Ottoman Empire had entered the war on the side of Germany and Austria. Its territory included present-day Turkey, Syria, Lebanon, Iraq, Palestine, and Arabia. British and Russian forces soon engaged the Turks. Since in early 1915 belligerent Serbia as well as neutral Bulgaria separated the Ottoman Empire from Austria and Germany, the allies had the equivalent of interior lines because they could concentrate either against the Germans and Austrians or against the Turks. With their predominance at sea, the allies could readily have brought overwhelming forces against the Ottoman Empire and driven it from the war. Such a success would then have released the resources employed against the Turks throughout the war for use against Germany and Austria.

Instead, the allies attempted to open the straits into the Black Sea with their navies and, when that failed, landed troops where the Turks expected them in an attempt to capture the Gallipoli Pennisula and open the Dardanelles straits. When this too failed, ending in an entrenched siege like the western front, the Allies withdrew their troops, landing some of them at Salonika in Greece. Meanwhile, Bulgaria entered the war on the side of Germany and Austria and participated in the defeat of Serbia, thus opening railroad communication between Germany and Austria and the Ottoman Empire over which flowed German munitions and assistance. The allies thus lost their central position between the Turks and Germans and Austrians.

To have defeated the weak Ottoman Empire first and then concentrated all resources against the stronger Austro-German combination would have been an orthodox application of the concept of interior lines. First accomplishing the easier task of defeating the weaker antagonist would have increased the power brought against the more formidable opponent. Clausewitz, the justly renowned German authority on war, stated the argument against this approach when he pointed out that one should aim at the enemy's main power. Only an attack on

Germany met this requirement, for Austria as well as the Ottoman Empire must fall if the allies vanquished Germany. But the overthrow of the Ottoman Empire would neither defeat Germany nor end the war.

The argument based on interior lines does seem stronger, however, since initial concentration against the Ottoman Empire would ultimately enable the concentration of larger forces against Germany. To conquer the weaker opponent first would have required the least effort, a factor of especially great importance in view of the overwhelming tactical primacy of the defense. But such a debate did not determine allied strategy. Rather, the dominant position of France and its desire to expel German armies from its soil meant that the allies would focus their efforts there, even though they had temporarily diverted rather large land forces to open the Dardanelles and kept significant forces in the Balkans facing Bulgarian and German armies throughout the war.

The 1916 simultaneous offensives did put pressure on Germany when the Russian offensive in June seriously defeated the Austrians just as other Austrian armies were engaged in an offensive against Italy, and the Germans still found themselves involved in their protracted offensive against France at Verdun. At the end of June the French and British completed the simultaneous operations by joining the fray with a combined attack in France along the river Somme. This Somme offensive turned out to be another costly, inclusive struggle, which lasted five months.

The British bore the principal burden, attacking on a fourteen-mile front, the French on only nine miles. The British had created large armies from volunteers during the period since 1914. These men had the advantage of enthusiasm but the disadvantages of inexperience and of few regular commissioned or noncommissioned officers to lead them. The British began with a bombardment that lasted seven days and consumed over 1.6 million shells. The German defenses, with telephone wires buried six feet deep and dugouts for the men twenty to thirty feet in the ground, rightly merited so much attention from the British artillery. The barbed wire, strung on steel stakes and frames, consisted of two separate belts, each thirty yards broad. The shelling eventually demolished all of this, even caving in many of the deep shelters, often suffocating the men. But the colossal bombardment would have sacrificed surprise, even if the elaborate British preparations had not already warned the Germans. The defenders thus had ample notice to move reserves to the threatened point and begin the construction of additional lines of defense.

And when the assault came, the remaining Germans came out of their dugouts and set up a defense line in the shell holes. The attackers, coming in waves, thus met rifle and machine gun fire deadly enough to inflict on the British on the first day 57,000 casualties, about 40 percent of the men engaged. Such assaults had restored losses to the level of the eighteenth century when Frederick suffered 43 percent casualties in his unsuccessful offensive battle at Kolin and losses over 30 percent in three other battles.

Even in shell holes the defenders had cover that completely neutralized the numerical advantage of the attackers. If all men in both forces could have fired on each other, the N-square law should convert the three-to-one numerical superiority of the attackers into a predominance of nine to one, assuring the rapid elimination of the defenders. But the cover provided by holes in the ground more than counterbalanced greater numbers. The attacking troops lost more heavily.

The terrain also aided the Germans, one contemporary observing "almost in every part of this old front our men had to go up hill to attack.... The enemy had lookout posts, with fine views over France, and the sense of domination. Our men were down below, with no view of anything but stronghold after stronghold, just up above, being made stronger daily." So the German positions gave them a psychological as well as a physical advantage.[3]

The allies really had no hope of a breakthrough because the German second line, 2,000 yards in the rear, had as great strength, including complete belts of barbed wire, as the first and 3,000 yards behind this second line the Germans had a reserve line already constructed. In addition, General Falkenhayn had not relaxed his determination to yield no ground. He had packed the front line with men and, warned by the long bombardment, had reserves at hand to counterattack. He had reaffirmed his principle that "not one foot of ground must be given up, and if lost must be retaken by immediate counter attack at all costs."[4]

This defensive philosophy caused heavy German losses by keeping large numbers of men under the fire of the more powerful hostile artillery and losing many more in counterattacks. In the five-month battle, really a siege, the British lost about 420,000, the French about 200,000, and the Germans, whose losses are uncertain, probably somewhat less than 600,000. The territory of France that the Germans fought so hard to retain had cost them dearly, going far to nullify the great advantages that the tactical defensive gave them in any conflict in which only attrition could measure the outcome. Greater allied strength in infantry and artillery and German exposure to the bombardment and in counterattacks offset to some degree the power of the tactical defense to inflict greater casualties.

The Search for a Technological Solution to the Tactical Deadlock

Although generals lost literally millions of men in struggles in which they often measured the results in terms of a few square miles gained or lost, they faced a situation unprecedented in the history of war. For hundreds of years generals had lived with and understood stalemates based on the strength of castles or fortresses and on their inability to force battle on an enemy endowed with ample space in which to elude a combat-inclined adversary. Then for a century warfare seemed to conform to the Napoleonic model where the attacker could force on the defender either battle or retreat. But suddenly generals faced a deadlock brought on by a huge increase in the ratio of force to space and an augmentation of the power of the tactical defense.

Soldiers found it difficult to abandon the thinking of a lifetime, one reinforced by the prewar illusions that firepower had enhanced the power of the offensive and that morale and the determination to win could impose one's will on the enemy and attain victory. "Firepower kills," the aphorism of French General Pétain, seems in retrospect only to display his mastery of the obvious. But it made sense in World War I as an antidote to the prewar overemphasis on morale and the will to win. A German officer fighting the Russians displayed the reorientation of view needed when his unit repelled a Russian attack. His men, elderly reservists, overweight, balding, and not displaying many soldierly qualities, had shot down the Russians in spite of vision corrected by spectacles. What particularly shocked the German officer was that the Russians carried out their attack with guard units, elite forces with more aristocratic officers and more courageous and physically robust men. The climate of opinion that had given credence to the concept of survival of the fittest had difficulty adapting to the unfit with machine guns mowing down the fit.

In spite of the natural difficulties in coping with the unexpected and unprecedented tactical conditions they faced, staffs and individuals sought solutions to the tactical problem. Artillerymen, for example, suddenly elevated in importance, had not expected the situations they confronted. Most had planned to use their field guns to shoot at targets they could see; instead, they found themselves engaged in siege warfare, firing at targets they could not see and dependent on observers distant on the ground or aloft in an airplane or balloon.

From the siege artillery, the artillerymen readily learned the technique of indirect fire and then turned to the issue of dispensing with registration. If the artillery could eliminate registration, the gunners could supply the infantry with a surprise and precise bombardment, which they could keep brief because it would have great accuracy. To do this they faced the problem of each gun's having a different muzzle velocity, depending on how many rounds it had fired and small variations in manufacture. The temperature of the explosive also affected the muzzle velocity, cool explosives of a cool day having a different propulsion power than the warm explosives of a warm day. The wind aloft and the density of the air affected the flight of the shell once fired.

The French artillerymen learned from the coast artillery how to deal with these problems. They determined the muzzle velocity of all pieces, calculated the effect of subsequent wear, determined the result of the temperature of the explosives, and learned to send aloft small balloons to discover air density, wind velocity, and direction. With excellent maps and a surveyor's location of each gun, the artillery could calculate in advance the aiming of a gun with a known muzzle velocity under various conditions of temperature, wind, and air density. With this new skill, additional artillery could secretly move to the area of a projected offensive and calculate how they would hit their targets with the first shot. By 1918 artillerymen could dispense with registration and could give their commander a surprise bombardment of great power and accuracy, providing the enemy did not detect the arrival of the new artillery batteries.

New weapons proved useful but did not alter the tactical balance. The hand grenade, the flame thrower, and the small portable trench mortar proved valuable and probably aided the attack more than the defense. But the proliferation of the light, portable, air-cooled machine gun gave more firepower to the defense.

The Germans introduced poison gas on a large scale and, in part because of the preeminence of their chemical industry, kept a lead in developing more lethal varieties. Dispensed at first from cylinders in the attackers' trenches and later in artillery shells, poison gas turned out to be a deadly but tricky weapon. Its use depended on the wind. Soldiers soon had masks that protected them from the asphixiating gas, and gas did not prove decisive. If used as a surprise in great quantities in an adequately supported attack, it could doubtlessly have provided a big breakthrough, but the Germans overlooked this opportunity. In fact, gas seemed so unlikely to alter the balance of strength against a prepared opponent that no belligerents used it in World War II.

The French and British both began early to seek a way to apply the principle of the Holt agricultural tractor to trench warfare. The Holt tractor ran on a track, which enabled it to operate off roads, a capability that the armored car lacked. Initially, the British and French took different approaches and did not share their activities with each other.

Lt. Colonel Swinton of the British army suggested the idea of a tracked machine gun vehicle that could cross trenches, while in the British Admiralty the Landship Committee had designed one. Produced in early 1915, the landship weighed twenty-eight tons and had a length of twenty-six feet. A lozenge-shaped, armored box, its track ran all around it to give it maximum trench-crossing capacity. On each side, mounted in sponsons, it carried either a machine gun and a navy 57-millimeter gun or two machine guns. If armed with a 57-millimeter gun on each side, the British called it a male; if machine guns instead, a female; and if it had a six pounder on one side and machine guns on the other, it was called a hermaphrodite; all types carried two machine guns in addition to those in the sponsons. With first a 105- and then a 150-horsepower engine, it had a top speed of four to five miles per hour. Since the designers of the Holt tractor intended it to pull plows, the track design did not lend itself to high speed, regardless of the amount of power the landship had. When first shipped to France, for security reasons it was called a water reservoir, soon shortened to tank.

The French tank also had its origin in the fall of 1914, the idea of Colonel Estienne. An artilleryman, the colonel wished to enable the artillery to follow the infantry in the attack. Both of his models, developed by different manufacturers, consisted of a 75-millimeter field gun in an armored box on a Holt tractor. One model weighed fifteen tons, the other twenty-five. Both had machine guns and a speed of about five miles per hour. The French design showed less imagination because the box extended beyond the tracks, limiting its ability to cross trenches or negotiate uneven terrain. Rather than a trench-crossing machine, the French had really produced a self-propelled gun.

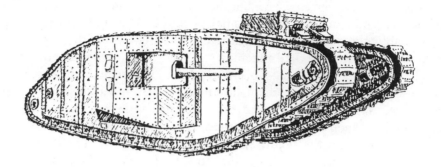

Illustration 8.4. Prototype Landship

The two allies kept secret from each other, as well as from the Germans, their tank developments. The French displayed more enthusiasm than the British for these tracked vehicles, ordering 800 before they had even seen an experimental machine, and planned to accumulate a large number to employ in a major surprise offensive. But the British warned the enemy of their existence when they used a few of theirs in the latter part of the Somme offensive. Fortunately, the Germans proved as skeptical of them as most British commanders and made no significant effort to provide themselves with tanks. Even if they had, Germany would have worked at a severe disadvantage because France had led in the development and manufacture of the motor car, only recently losing to the United States its position as the world's leading automobile manufacturer. Since the British also had a large automobile industry, the allies had an overwhelming predominance of manufacturers that could easily convert to fabricating tanks.

Meanwhile, Colonel Estienne worked with the Renault automobile company to produce an armored vehicle entirely different from the landship or the self-propelled gun. Weighing only six and one-half tons, the new tank had a track that extended beyond its body in front giving it good trench-crossing capabilities for its small size. Lower than either the British or earlier French machines, it had on top a turret, which could traverse 360 degrees. The turret carried either a 37-millimeter gun, for shooting at machine gun emplacements, or a machine gun. The tactical plan envisioned one tank with a cannon working with two armed with machine guns.

Most tanks have followed these design principles ever since, and the French, realizing they had the right concept, ordered 4,000 of these Renault tanks. Both the British and French had large numbers ready for use in 1918, had organized and trained men to operate them, and had a fairly clear idea of their role in an attack.

The German Quest for Victory through a Logistic Strategy Using Submarines

By January 1917 the German navy had 111 submarines compared with sixty-eight in early 1916. Their navy believed that if it disregarded any restrictions on torpedoing merchant ships, it could sink 600,000 tons of shipping per month. This would drive the British from the war because the submarines could sink so many more ships than the allies could build and thus interrupt the imports and exports necessary to keep Britain's industries going, its people employed, and its armies provided for. Consequently, at the end of January 1917, Germany resumed unrestricted submarine warfare against merchant ships, realizing that it would probably bring the United States into the war. But if Germany closed the sea lanes, U. S. participation would have little meaning, and the American navy, strong in battleships and armored cruisers but weak in the destroyers useful against submarines, could do little to combat the submarine.

The German submarine strategy, sound in its calculations, foundered on two related variables, one tactical, the other strategic. By 1917 the British navy could track a moving submarine with a hydrophone, which could hear the propellers and give an approximate location of the submarine. It could also attack the submarine with depth charges. The attacking destroyer dropped these cylinders filled with explosives in an area where they believed they had located a submarine, setting them to explode either at the likely depth of the submarine or at various depths. A depth charge did not need a direct hit to disable a submarine because water, an incompressible fluid, readily transmitted to the submarine's hull the pressure created by the explosion.

The convoy, long ago used by the British navy to protect merchant ships against the commerce raiders of France and other opponents, provided the strategic means to protect the merchant ships and to bring the warships with hydrophones and depth charges into contact with the submarines that must attack ships in convoy if they attacked at all. The data on ship sinkings reflect both the realism of German expectations—initial sinkings far exceeded British construction output—and the effectiveness of the British response—sinkings of merchant ships declined and submarine losses increased (table 8.3).

The New German Method of Defense

At the end of 1916 the French government had removed Joffre, the repeated failures and enormous casualties of his offensives dimming the luster of his achievements in 1914. To dispose of Joffre in a genteel manner, the republic revived for him the old royal and imperial rank of Marshal of France, the conjunction of its ancient glory and Joffre's real achievements making this a felicitous means of laying him on the shelf and of giving real dignity to the rank, its seven-star insignia, and the new marshal.

The government replaced him with Nivelle, a confident junior general who began a new offensive in April, supposedly with a new method. But it fell dismally

TABLE 8.3.   The Submarine War, 1917–18

Time Frame	Tonnage of Merchant Ships Sunk (in thousands)		Number of Submarines Sunk
1917			
January	293		2
February	468		4
March	511		4
April	840		2
		convoys inaugurated	
May	551		6
June	633		4
July	495		6
August	490		4
September	316		10
October	429		8
November	260	convoying complete	9
December	353		7
1918	1,103		88
January–November 11			

short of anticipations, in spite of having over 5,000 cannon for a twenty-five-mile front, almost one gun for every eight yards of the assault frontage. The contrast between the expectations that Nivelle had raised and the emphatic failure of his offensive demoralized French soldiers, who said they would defend but no longer attack. The government then gave the command to General Henri Philippe Pétain, who had begun the war in August as a colonel but by October 1914 had so excelled that Joffre had promoted him to command of a corps. In 1915 Pétain received an army command and in 1916 successfully conducted the defense of Verdun and had the reward of an army group. Just before his sixty-first birthday Pétain, a perceptive student of the combat realities of the war, took over the French army. A believer in the supremacy of firepower and the primacy of the defense and acting promptly and wisely, he gradually restored the morale of the army. Thus the French army had a small offensive role in 1917 and, because rigid security kept their crisis of morale from the Germans, no major defensive tasks.

But the Germans had to face attacks from the British, who had markedly strengthened their artillery and augmented the quality and quantity of their ammunition. Beginning their bombardment in early May, the British, having a six-to-one superiority in aircraft against which even Baron von Richtofen's squadron of red-painted airplanes could not prevail, made extensive use of artillery observation from aircraft. The steadily accelerating shelling by over 2,300 cannon obliterated the German positions. The German garrisons, with the realistic fear of being entombed in their dugouts, took refuge in shell holes, where they lived a precarious and uncomfortable existence while British artillery demolished the empty trenches. After a final seven-day bombardment in which over 3 million shells landed on a six-mile front, the British, who, like besiegers of old, had spent a year tunneling under the Messines Ridge, exploded nineteen deep mines under the German lines. The force of the 1 million pounds of explosive, felt twenty miles away, enabled the British to take Messines Ridge, the Germans losing more men than the assaulting British.

Before the British resumed their attack toward nearby Passchendaele, the Germans introduced a new system of defense, which they had perfected during the more than three months that this Passchendaele campaign lasted. The method had already received the endorsement of the new leaders of the German army, Field Marshal Hindenburg and his associate, General Ludendorff, the victors of Tannenberg and architects of victories against the Russian armies. Whereas General Falkenhayn, whom the government had removed in the summer of 1916, had insisted on holding every inch of territory, Hindenburg and Ludendorff encouraged an elastic defense. Instead of cramming the front trenches with men— to be casualties of a bombardment—the new German doctrine prescribed an outpost line of a few squads with light machine guns to hold the front. As soon as a bombardment began, the troops in both the outpost and the second line, 2,000 yards behind, were to leave their trenches and underground dugouts to take refuge in shell holes. In fact, the tremendous power of British artillery had made the trenches, dugouts, and concrete machine gun positions useful only to attract enemy artillery fire.

Behind the outpost and second line, the Germans had three additional lines with a sixth on which they had begun construction. But they planned to halt the attack in the zone between the second and third lines in which their reserves would conduct counterattacks. Well could the German army group commander confide to his diary: "My mind is quite at rest about the attack, as we have never disposed of such strong reserves, so well trained for their part, as on the front attacked."[5]

The British began their renewed drive on a fifteen-mile front with a ten-day bombardment by 2,300 guns that expended 6 million shells amounting to 65,000 tons of metal. As the British slowly ground through the German defenses, the defenders gradually perfected the technique of a lightly held front line to absorb the shelling and of troops dispersed in shell holes to avoid acting as the targets of the British gunners. The Germans also improved their use of artillery in the defense and conducted their counterattacks either promptly, before the advancing British had dug in, or after a day or two when German artillery could give proper support. In any case, the British would have had to move slowly because each advance of 2,000 or more yards usually required a halt of as many as three days while the artillery proceeded forward to positions from which it could bombard the next German position. Throughout this four-month struggle the thoroughly cratered and quite soggy ground impeded the movement of the guns and the provision of an adequate supply of ammunition.

Again the terrain favored the Germans, this time because the elaborately drained, low-lying ground quickly became a morass when artillery fire destroyed the drainage. Behind the lines the British soldiers had to lay plank walkways to protect themselves from sinking into the mud. On at least one occasion a soldier missed his step and went into the mud where he began to sink into the mud, his comrades helpless to save him. As the mud was about to swallow him he appealed to his fellows to shoot him, a death he thought preferable to suffocation. The higher commanders often remained quite ignorant of these terrain conditions, which so handicapped the offensive. A British officer from headquarters, for example, coming to the front toward the end of the long campaign, first became apprehensive that his automobile might become stranded and then, grasping the real nature of the terrain, burst into tears and exclaimed: "Good God, did we really send men to fight in that?"[6]

As a result of their successful experience with this form of defense, the Germans prescribed it for all units on the western front. Ironically, the French, who usually assumed the offensive and, on the defense, sought to protect their own soil, had first adopted this method of elastic defense. As originally constituted, it had used as a main line of defense a system of strongpoints placed 200 yards apart and organized for all-around defense. Ahead of these strongpoints the French maintained an outpost line and, behind, a third line with shelters for reserves who would counterattack. Constrained by Falkenhayn, the Germans had not used such a procedure until 1917, and when they did they elaborated it in depth, thoroughness, and sophistication.

The new German defensive arrangements fully proved themselves. The thinly held front line of troops, dispersed in shell holes once the bombardment began, significantly reduced German losses in spite of the awesome power and nerve-racking length of the British bombardment. But this front line still proved formidable and inflicted heavy casualties on the attackers. The main burden of the defense, however, fell on an area of one to three miles in depth between the second and third lines. Here, on terrain usually protected by hills from direct British observation, with defensive positions adequately camouflaged against air reconnaissance, and at the limit of British light artillery the Germans made their main defensive effort. In addition to machine guns, many in concrete emplacements, the Germans used their artillery, which enjoyed excellent fire control and communications in areas with which they had thorough familiarity. They counted on depth, each regiment deploying its three battalions one behind the other. Behind this battle zone they had a further defensive line, occupied by each regiment's rearmost battalion, to protect their artillery, and other lines farther to the rear laid out if not already built.

In addition to the strength supplied by depth, the power of well-directed artillery, and the surprise that faced attackers from camouflaged defensive positions, the German defense placed a fundamental reliance on counterattacks. Their thin front enabled them to maintain large reserves, far behind the principal area of the British barrage. The sufficient notice of attack provided by the long bombardment enabled the Germans to strengthen these reserves most amply. Since the counterattack had such a fundamental role in this new German concept of the defense, the reserves practiced their approach marches to their counter-attacking positions.

As an ideal response, the Germans envisioned an almost immediate counterattack that would take the attacking British by surprise and find them disorganized by their offensive efforts. To assure the timeliness of this assault as well as the responsiveness of the whole defense, the commander of the regiment's foremost battalion commanded the sector, including the battalions behind. The front-line division commander exercised similar control over divisions committed in his sector. Thus the Germans secured excellent decentralization of command, a change demanded by trench warfare. If the immediate counterattack failed in spite of the advanced preparations and excellent artillery control, the Germans prepared a more deliberate assault with more troops and artillery, which still would enjoy the advantages of better organization over the allied forces that had to occupy and fortify their newly won territory, even if they were not giving their principal attention to continuing their offensive.

But these counterattacks did not have as their primary objective the recovery of territory, though retaining their favorable terrain, fortified zone, and established artillery positions did indeed constitute an important advantage of holding territory. Successful counterattacks against unprepared foes not only defeated the assault but also inflicted adverse attrition on the defenders, often netting the Germans many prisoners.

By their decentralization of command, the Germans improved the effectiveness of their already well-articulated units. Combat in which small groups occupied separate defensive positions or shell holes required a decentralization and articulation within a battalion not anticipated before the war. Not only did the companies of the battalion and their captains and the company's platoons and their lieutenants acquire undreamed of antonomy and responsibility, but also the sergeants of the platoon's subdivisions had significant opportunity for maneuvering their units of a dozen men and displaying an initiative quite foreign to earlier ideas of a sergeant's responsibility.

Such perfected articulation strengthened the resilience of the battalion and, on the defense, enabled it to concentrate against the strength of the enemy's attack as well as, in the counterattack, to concentrate to exploit British weakness. The telephone and the elaboration and decentralization of the means of artillery control enabled the guns to play a role on the defensive essentially comparable to that in the past when they could fire cannister against attacking lines they could see. The guns could participate in the counterattack very effectively because the assaulting enemy troops had already come close to the guns, meaning that the counterattacking Germans would not likely advance beyond the support of their artillery. However different this kind of warfare seemed from that of the eighteenth and nineteenth centuries, it but constituted a logical extension of the trends begun in the French army in the latter part of the eighteenth century.

The New German Doctrine for Attack

In 1917 the Germans adopted a new method of attack, which also owed something to French inspiration. The initial French system, which the Germans employed and the British had adopted, involved using attacking infantry in successive lines or waves of men. These often advanced according to a predetermined timetable, the use of lines or waves facilitating control by higher headquarters as well as the coordinating of the movements of the infantry with the fire plan of the artillery. Ultimately, the artillery fired a barrage that placed a curtain of exploding shells before the attacking infantry; the curtain also moved forward according to a preestablished timetable, and behind it the infantry advanced, following the artillery's schedule. Such a subordination of infantry to artillery exemplified Joffre's siege warfare principle that artillery conquered and infantry occupied.

Captain Laffargue, a French officer who experienced this attack in its most primitive form in early 1915, promptly wrote a pamphlet. He alluded to the value of infantry in line: "To have experienced the influence of an alignment in those first critical minutes of an assault is to appreciate its capital importance." It worked "to drag on with it any hesitating individuals, to restrain the too impetuous and to give to all that warm and comforting feeling of mutual confidence." Nevertheless, he favored using small groups armed with machine guns and grenades that would go ahead of the line and push through weak spots and thus be able to attack enemy machine gun positions from the rear and penetrate deep into the hostile position.[7]

In a sense tactics using lines, dictated in part by the role of artillery and the difficulty controlling its fire, had reverted to the linear system of the late seventeenth and the eighteenth centuries when battalions in line kept contiguous to and aligned with their neighbors. Laffargue advocated a parallel to the adoption of the battalion column, which could maneuver on the battlefield and concentrate against the weak points in the enemy line. Of course, he envisioned a squad of skirmishers, but the same principles—better articulation and the ability to concentrate against weakness—animated his ideas.

French headquarters printed and distributed Laffargue's pamphlet but did not implement its principles as their basic offensive doctrine. Laffargue's method required decentralization of command down to squad leaders and further deprived generals of control over the battle, a command that they still partially exercised through the artillery's fire plan and infantry in waves. On the defense, the Germans had discovered the same need for initiative and control on the part of the low-level commanders. Laffargue's ideas also contradicted Joffre's siege warfare approach in which the infantry followed the artillery.

In 1916 the Germans obtained a copy of Laffargue's pamphlet and, because its ideas fit so nicely with those they already were evolving, translated and diffused it within the army. By 1917 the German army, which had never fully conceived of the offensive as siege warfare, began using infiltration tactics like Laffargue's as the doctrine for infantry in the offensive. Just as with their new system of defense where defenders fought in shell holes rather than field fortifications and reserves sought to make surprise counterattacks, the German offensive doctrine made use of principles applicable to open rather than siege warfare and refused to let artillery subordinate the infantry's action to its needs.

The defenses, which disposed troops in depth and, in spite of a reliance on trench lines, consisted of a series of strong points, lent themselves to penetration by infiltration tactics. The strong points, covering gaps with fire, depended on observation, which in turn could suffer impairment from fog, smoke, and gas as well as from artillery fire that could drive observers to cover.

Infiltration tactics abandoned waves in favor of groups that pushed through weak spots. Instead of delaying the advance of a wave until the assaulting force had overcome a defending strong point, the attackers infiltrated the defense, pushed forward, and left the conquest of the strong points to the troops that came behind. The old ideas of concentration against weakness and of turning and enveloping hostile forces animated these tactics. The Germans indoctrinated troops with the principle and drilled them in the application of the new form of attack, spending the winter of 1917–18 retraining a large part of their army. The basic element of attack became about a dozen men with light machine guns. They divided their units into those composed of the more and those of the less competent and well motivated. Concentrating their offensive training on the better men, the Germans created many divisions of trained assault troops, leaving the men with less enterprise, courage, and skill to hold defensive positions. Fifty-six of the 192 divisions then on the western front became attack divisions.

The soldiers of 1918 had steel helmets to protect them from shrapnel and the splinters of high-explosive shells. They carried magazine rifles and hand grenades. They could hurl these small bombs, which had a short time fuse before they exploded to throw antipersonnel fragments. The grenades reproduced, in miniature, the capabilities of the howitzer. Some soldiers had grenade launchers to give increased range. In the German army platoons had sections of about a dozen men. In each section one squad of five served and supported a light, air-cooled machine gun. The other squad consisted of infantrymen only, with the machine gun usually providing fire and the infantrymen often constituting the maneuver or offensive element of the section.

In the infiltration tactics the battalion still comprised the assault formation, and it helped the infantry section with water-cooled machine guns, flame throwers, a French innovation that projected burning petroleum under pressure, and portable mortars that were like grenades but more accurate and powerful. Often engineers equipped to build light bridges prepared the way for men, artillery, and vehicles following. The battalion also had its own artillery, the army's older, shorter, and lighter field pieces. These, the army's most easily moved artillery, accompanied the battalion in the advance.

In the attack the first group of infantry located the enemy positions, the second found and pushed through the weak spots, and the third supported the second and protected its flanks. The remainder of the division followed, reducing the bypassed strong points by using the gaps made to envelop them. The lead units kept up their advance without respite, constantly probing for and exploiting weak spots in the enemy defenses. The whole offensive doctrine had the goal of breaking completely through the allied defensive zone.

Aircraft played a major role in this offensive. Like the infantry and artillery, secretly concentrated in sufficient numbers to have numerical superiority, the planes aimed to protect their own troops, to keep away allied observation aircraft, and to supplement the artillery and attack targets of opportunity, especially allied reserves in motion on the roads.

In the latter part of 1917 the Germans had made several trials of the new tactics. Of one of these, a competently prepared counterattack against the British in November, the *British Official History* said that the Germans advanced "in small columns bearing many light machine guns, and, in some cases, flame throwers. From overhead low flying airplanes in greater numbers than had been seen, bombed and machinegunned the British defenders, causing further casualties and, especially, distraction at the critical moment." The *Official History* also pointed out that few strong points "appear to have been attacked from the front, the assault sweeping in between to envelop them from flanks and rear."[8]

The mating of the infiltration tactics with other measures to secure an effective offense became known as the Hutier system, for the methods had worked well in an attack by General Oskar von Hutier in an offensive against the Russians in September 1917. The attack relied on surprise. The ability of the artillery to fire accurately without giving away its presence or location permitted a surprise concentration of artillery. The accuracy of the fire, made possible by the improved artillery methods, rendered a long bombardment unnecessary in order to damage the defenses seriously. The short, intensive bombardment used in the von Hutier system also relied on a large proportion of gas and smoke shells. Not only did these reduce the effectiveness of the defenders, who had to wear masks, and obscure observation, but also the small charge in gas and smoke shells limited disturbance of the ground and destruction of roads, thus facilitating the move forward of German artillery, reinforcements, and supplies. After the initial barrage, the artillery supported the infantry and conformed its fire to the infantry's movements; the infantry conquered with the aid of the artillery rather than the artillery conquering and the infantry occupying. In this way the artillery integrated its doctrine with the new infiltration tactics that, with surprise, lay at the heart of von Hutier's success.

With the failure of the submarine-based logistic strategy, the Germans planned to win the war in 1918 with combat strategy. The Russians having left the war, the Austrians concentrated against the Italians, and the Germans, rather than joining in a concentration to drive Italy from the war, threw their whole force against the Anglo-French armies. Instead of avoiding attack and trusting to the proven power of the defense and the exploitation of the resources of

Russia and Eastern Europe, the Germans chose the offensive because the United States was creating a large army very rapidly. With a population nearly double that of Germany, huge financial, industrial, and agricultural resources, and weapons and expert guidance from the French and British, the United States seemed as if it could field virtually invincible armies in 1919.

Ludendorff did not base his belief in a successful combat strategy on his greater numbers: he had for operations in France only 207 divisions against the Allies' 169, all divisions then numbering nine rather than twelve battalions. He counted on his new tactical methods and on pitting fresh, retrained divisions composed of his best men against tired allied troops, depleted by four years of unsuccessful offensives.

The Campaigns of 1918 on the Western Front

The German offensive in March 1918 aimed at the joint between the French and British fronts. General Ludendorff directed the main effort against the British, because he believed that the French would offer a stronger resistance due to their more powerful artillery and excellent tactical skill. His drive sought to force the British back toward the coast. He distracted the enemy by preparing three additional attacks, two against British forces and one against the French. Ludendorff held back his reserves at so great a distance that he could commit them anywhere. But he had assembled 6,000 guns on a forty-three-mile front, moving them in at night with the noise of their wheels muffled by wrappings of burlap. Just before the offensive, the reserves came up, marching at night.

When the assault began early on the morning of March 21, the Germans had sixty-three divisions on this forty-three-mile front. The attack was almost a complete surprise, the British only learning of it with certainty the night before. A mist aided the smoke and gas shells of the five-hour, intense bombardment, and the Hutier system worked superbly, especially on the thinly held front of General Gough's Fifth Army.

The power and accuracy of the bombardment inflicted severe casualties, tore gaps in the barbed wire, and wrecked field fortifications. Following their moving barrage, the exceptionally trained German assault troops took advantage of the impaired visibility to infiltrate past the dazed British defenders. In a number of parts of the line they made very deep penetrations, turning the strong points that held out and in places going all the way through the defenses and reaching the open country behind.

The successful attack overwhelmed the Fifth Army, the German capture of 2 million bottles of whisky properly illustrating the extent of its victory. Actually, the sumptuousness of British supply diverted as well as nourished German troops. In 1916 a diarist noted that the men looked forward to an offensive because of "the prospect of loot. . . . A pot of English marmalade or a razor is more important than a British officer's notebook." By March British opulence had become quite demoralizing. The diarist noted that the troops had come to feel that "the English made everything out of either rubber or brass, since these were the two materials we had not seen for the longest time."[9]

To the south of the British Fifth Army the German offensive embraced a French army, against which the attack went surprisingly well. Yet Ludendorff's plan envisioned driving the British back toward the coast, and he needed success in the north, where the British Third Army of the capable General Byng held up the German advance.

Meanwhile, in the south against the remains of Gough's army and the retreating French, the Germans had advanced nearly forty miles in six days. After sending reserves against Byng without overcoming his stubborn defense, Ludendorff began to reinforce the flourishing effort in the south. Thus, belatedly Ludendorff began to apply to strategy the path-of-least-resistance principle, which had animated the infiltration tactics. This he had already enunciated by acknowledging that tactics and the power of the defense must determine strategy when he wrote that "tactics had to be considered before purely strategical objectives which it is futile to pursue unless tactical success is possible." But stiffening British resistance and the power of a French defense reinforced by seventeen infantry and four cavalry divisions from General Pétain halted the belated effort to reinforce and exploit the initial success in the south. By the end of March the Germans no longer had any chance of separating the allied armies.[10]

The Germans had won such a decisive victory that the defenders suffered greater casualties than the attackers. German troops had broken clear through the defenses and reached open country on a broad front. But the offensive had failed. To a large extent logistical limitations prevented German tactical success from yielding the strategic results that one would expect from the breakthrough by a huge concentration of tactically skillful fresh troops. Handicapped by broken ground, destroyed bridges, their vast numbers, and large requirements for ammunition, the German reserves, artillery, and supplies could not keep pace with the tactical success of the breakthrough.

Behind the allied front lay the French railways, which provided supplies and brought up the French reserves sent by Pétain. Just as in 1914, access to functioning railways gave to the defending allies greater strategic mobility. The defenders had rail-borne, strategically offensive troops while the attackers labored with largely horse-drawn transport on an inadequate network of damaged roads.

Yet Ludendorff persevered, assailing the British farther north in the second and third weeks of April. He attained some tactical triumphs but made no breakthrough. But his victories had given the allies their first unified command when General Ferdinand Foch, the French representative on an allied committee, received first a coordinating assignment and then command of the allied armies. A former member of the War College faculty, Foch had risen from corps command to army group commander in 1914. Shelved along with Joffre, at age sixty-seven he became the allied commander. Lacking the realism and operational skill of Ludendorff and still a devotee of the concept of the supremacy of morale and the offensive, Foch nevertheless suited the needs of the moment. His conviction that victory belonged to the commander who would not admit of the possibility of defeat, his optimism, his anxiousness to resume the offensive, his comprehensive view, and his ability to work with the allied commanders all made him the right man for the place and time.

Still pursuing the objective of driving the British to the English Channel, Ludendorff next attacked the French to draw allied reserves south, preparatory to his final drive against the British in the north. The Germans again practiced thorough and effective security measures, once more deploying troops at night and muffling the wheels of their artillery as they moved the guns into concealed positions under cover of darkness. They even took air photographs of their own positions to inspect the efficacy of their camouflage.

When French reconnaissance discovered no signs of an offensive, it confirmed their conviction that the Germans would never attack against the formidable terrain of the Chemins des Dames ridge. Due to their certainty that the Germans would again strike in the north and because of the strength of the terrain, the French held the zone very lightly, eleven divisions on a fifty-five-mile front, and had most of their men concentrated in the forward defenses to make the most of the advantages offered by the ridge and the swamp in front of it. Only on the evening before the German assault did the local commander learn from a prisoner of the impending attack. In ordering distant divisions toward the threatened sector, the French took the only countermeasure available.

On the morning of April 27, after the usual hurricane of shells, the Germans, with forty-one divisions on a forty-mile front, broke completely through the shallow French defenses, advancing thirteen miles in one day. The effect of the well-aimed bombardment on the strongly held forward trenches accentuated the effect of infiltration tactics against a line thinly held and with little depth. Surprised by his achievement, Ludendorff pushed forward, creating a deep salient before his supply difficulties and the arrival of French reserves by rail recreated an entrenched front.

The unexpected and impressive German success resulted in the relieving of the French army group commander and the government's decision, later reversed, to replace General Pétain. For Ludendorff his deep salient, with vulnerable communications, proved an embarrassment. He could not withdraw because the acquisition of so much territory constituted evidence of victory. So he tried to connect it with his large salient created in March. These efforts accomplished little. He then planned to extend his new conquest east through an attempt to take the city of Reims. This attack would draw more allied reserves away from the north and would be his last offensive before returning artillery north for the final assault against the British, which he planned for August.

But Ludendorff's successive attacks consumed his reserves of fresh troops trained for offensive action. He had enjoyed tactical victories in three of his four offensives, but strategic achievement eluded him and had to continue to escape him because of the greater mobility of allied reserves. The better communications enjoyed by the retreating forces ensured that the allies could reconstitute the front and restore the entrenched stalemate after any tactical defeat. The course of operations reinforced Foch's confidence, an attitude shared by the adequate British commander, Field Marshal Sir Douglas Haig, who with an improved staff gave an excellent performance in 1918. The arrival of significant U.S. forces in France sustained the morale of the allied rank and file while Ludendorff's offensives depleted the confidence of his best men employed in the front ranks of these successive drives.

German security measures for their attack on either side of Reims lacked the care of earlier offensives, as allied air observation noted increased troop movements and air photographs revealed badly camouflaged ammunition supplies. Foch moved fifteen divisions into the area and alerted another eight. These he kept in reserve under his own control. He also added nine squadrons of aircraft to those available. In addition to their role in allied reconnaissance and inhibiting German air observation, allied aircraft had attacked communications links with bombs and used their machines guns to shoot troops marching or deployed in the open.

The magnetic and combative General Gouraud, commanding the French Fourth Army, made the best use of the intelligence of a German concentration. The red-bearded general planned, reluctantly, to follow a version of the German defensive model and leave only a few men in his first line when the Germans attacked. He supplemented his air reconnaissance with aggressive patroling. On on July 14 a raid brought in twenty-seven prisoners, one of whom revealed that the attack would take place the following day, the bombardment to begin ten minutes after midnight. The prisoner's anxiety to keep his gas mask convinced his interrogators that he believed his story of a Hutier bombardment heavy in gas shells soon, and General Gouraud made plans accordingly.

At midnight, ten minutes before the prisoner said the German bombardment would begin, French artillery began firing on the areas where the gunners expected the attacking German troops to assemble. Then, as expected, the German bombardment began with one gun for every eight yards of front, firing rapidly. In Paris, 100 miles away, citizens could hear the roar of the guns and the noise of the exploding shells; in the streets of Châlons near the front the flashes so illuminated the sky that night seemed day.

After four hours of shelling, the German infantry moved forward and easily overran the first line. Vaguely uneasy over the few French casualties they found but not realizing that the French had essentially evacuated their first line, they pushed on to exploit their victory. Late in the morning, at the limit of the range of their field artillery, they reached the strongly held French second line where, behind their barbed wire, the French opened fire with rifles, machine guns, light mortars, and 1,500 cannon. The Germans suffered heavy losses before they could retreat to the shelter of the French first line.

The other German attackers did not encounter the same emphatic failure, but the offensive failed to make a real impression on the French defenses. At this point, July 18, Foch used his reserves to counterattack on the west side of the salient created at the end of May. Without elaborate preparations and with only a very brief bombardment, twenty-one divisions attacked newly built German defenses, manned by units from which the Germans had culled many of the more courageous and better motivated men to create the formidable units used on the offensive. The attack would doubtless have succeeded anyway, but the French use of 700 of the small Renault tanks and 120 of the large self-propelled field-gun models ensured that the French easily overran the German first line.

Tanks had enjoyed success earlier. In the fall of 1917 the British, dispensing with a preparatory bombardment, had won at Cambrai when infantry cooperating with 200 of their landships had broken through the defenses of the surprised Germans with comparative ease. Now, as at Cambrai, infantry and tanks worked together, the tanks flattening barbed wire and their cannon destroying machine gun positions while the cooperating infantry protected the tanks from infantry. One French writer described his small unit as coming over a rise in the ground and seeing a French tank surrounded by German soldiers who had halted the tank by wedging a piece of wood in the tracks. The tank could not fire on the infantry because they were too close and the German soldiers were seeking to pry open the tank with their bayonets and trying to insert a hand grenade in the tank's ventilator. The absorbed German soldiers did not notice the approaching French infantry who opened fire on the Germans around the tank, killed or wounded most of them, and rescued the tank. To provide protection against infantry, French tank doctrine prescribed platoons of three tanks, two with machine guns to protect each other and the third, to use its cannon against German machine gun positions.

Together the French tanks and infantry in Foch's big counterattack overran the German positions until they reached the line of the field-gun batteries. Here the tanks stopped, their thin armor vulnerable to the fire of high-explosive shells from the German 77-millimeter field gun. But the turning movement against the salient caused a rapid German retreat from most of the gains of their May success.

Foch immediately planned more offensives, not aiming at the knockout blow to which Ludendorff aspired, but to push back the Germans from the lateral railways. Compared to earlier offensives, those of 1918 more realistically sought limited objectives. The allies discontinued them when they had attracted the enemy's reserves and promised to settle into the mold of their earlier protracted and costly offensives. So Foch's new approach avoided the earlier, prolonged indecisive struggles that had pitted a well-organized defense against a powerful offense. On August 8 Foch's second, an allied but largely British, offensive began. Attaining complete surprise, relying on over 400 tanks rather than a long bombardment, and using 1,700 aircraft, the allied forces had brilliant success against the understrength and somewhat demoralized divisions that the Germans used on the defensive. Assisted by the tanks, allied tactics relied on ideas and practices from the German infiltration method. The unexpected and triumphant offensive completely demoralized Ludendorff, who declared that Germany must make peace. The French made the same estimate when, after his second victorious offensive, they elevated Foch to the rank of Marshal of France.

Less than two weeks after the conclusion of the British and French offensives in the north, the U. S. army successfully attacked the German salient south of Verdun. And almost immediately after the conclusion of this offensive, U. S. forces joined the French in another attack. In barely two months, Germany, its armies beset by Marshal Foch's offensives, driven from France, and deserted by collapsing allies, sought an armistice.

A Turning Movement through Superior Mobility: The Megiddo Campaign

The German retreat before Foch's sequence of offensives in France coincided with a series of allied victories on other fronts. An Italian offensive drove back the demoralized and disintegrating Austro-Hungarian troops, and a French, British, Italian, and Serbian combined army under a French general drove Bulgaria from the war, advanced to the Danube, and prepared to invade Austria-Hungary against only token opposition. Yet the success of small forces in Palestine, which led to the withdrawal of the Ottoman Empire from the war, had the greatest military significance. The British commander, Sir Edmund Allenby, who had begun the war in France as a division commander in 1914 and succeeded to corps and army command before his transfer to Palestine, executed a campaign of virtually unsurpassed brilliance that embodied almost all of the classic elements of decisive victory.

In September 1918 General Allenby with 57,000 infantry held a line sixty-miles long running from the Mediterranean eastward to the Jordan River and south along the Jordan to the Dead Sea. He faced 32,000 entrenched infantry, largely Turkish, led by a capable German, General Liman von Sanders. Allenby had overwhelming air supremacy and 12,000 cavalry against only 4,000 mounted Turks.

Because an attack on the east of the line over favorable terrain against the Turkish rail communications seemed the obvious move, Allenby encouraged this supposition while planning to attack the Turk's western flank.

To support his plan the British general had engaged in a most elaborate and successful game of distraction. All summer he kept his cavalry behind the eastern part of his front, and when he moved them westward, he replaced them with dummies that at a distance seemed to be grazing horses. Troops visibly marched east by day and back west at night, repeating the process again the following day. When hills concealed the road, mules drew sledges east by day to raise dust and simulate marching troops. Dummy camps housed these phony reinforcements for his eastern flank. To add verisimilitude to the impression created by these crude measures, Allenby had agents east of the Jordan buy forage, presumably for his cavalry in an offensive on the east flank; he established active wireless nets linking nonexistent headquarters that had no troops; and he reserved and apparently occupied a suite in a Jerusalem hotel to indicate that he had moved his headquarters eastward.

Attentive also to his security, he set up a telephone network to warn of German reconnaissance planes and had his air force on alert to shoot down any that might observe behind his lines. To complete the assurance of the interdiction of air observation, British aircraft maintained patrols over German airfields to keep all aircraft grounded, essentially a blockade of their airports.

By September 18 Allenby had a four-to-one numerical predominance on the westernmost fifteen miles of his line; the Turks outnumbered the British on the remaining forty-five miles of the front. With such a concentration and the relatively low ratio of force to space along the whole front, Allenby could expect a breakthrough, even though his 540 artillery pieces gave him only nine guns for each mile of the entire front.

Early in the morning of September 19, after a fifteen-minute bombardment, British troops attacked and in three hours broke through the Turkish front, driving the retreating Turks north and east. This opened a door through which Allenby sent his cavalry. Without infantry to stop them, the cavalry rode up the coast and turned eastward near Megiddo, riding into the Turkish rear. One division rode the seventy miles to Beisan on the Jordan in thirty-four hours.

When the cavalrymen reached the Turkish rear, they dismounted and, using rifles and machine guns carried on pack horses, blocked the retreat of the Turks. Allenby, a cavalryman, used his horsemen as mounted infantry, standard doctrine in the British army. The British owed much to their study of the American Civil War, where the cavalry of both armies marched on horseback but usually fought as infantry. Yet this tactic, and the strategy that depended on it, also relied on the portable rifle, which the cavalryman could carry attached to his saddle, and on the supremacy of the defensively dominant infantryman equipped with it. During the 300 years when the pistol and saber had provided the principal cavalry arms, dismounted cavalrymen, some of whom had muskets to fight as light infantry, could not have adequately coped with hostile infantry and, particularly, cavalry; to have resisted a cavalry charge, they would have needed their bayonets and the thorough drill and volley firing techniques of the heavy infantry. But the rifle had restored to cavalry its dismounted defensive strength, enabling the British troops, doubtless without realizing it, to emulate an aspect of the English tactics of the Hundred Years' War in which the knights had left their horses to offer a stronger defense as infantry.

Yet Allenby had done more than make his cavalry more effective in combat by dismounting them. In his offensive he had used the superlative strategic mobility of cavalry—really mounted infantry—to turn the enemy. He had used cavalry's latent capability as strategically offensive troops to carry out a turning movement and, just as Napoleon in his Marengo campaign, had reached the enemy's rear, blocking his line of withdrawal and compelling him to assume the tactical offensive. The large size of his cavalry force and its great firepower as

infantry enabled him to block partially the retreat of the Turks to the north and
secure the surrender of many of them.

But by attacking on the Turks' west flank where they least expected it—
because they were less vulnerable there—he had failed to block the Turkish
route of withdrawal fully. But as the Turks fled westward through the mountains,
Allenby's aircraft attacked. In the deep gorge from Nablus to the Jordan, the
aircraft used machine guns and small bombs against the retreating Turks. The
aircraft killed artillerymen and transport animals that then obstructed the road.
The immobile column made an excellent target. The demoralized Turks, unable
to reply to the attack of the aircraft, were anxious to surrender.

Having used an elaborate and effective distraction to create a weak point
against which to concentrate, Allenby had pierced the Turkish line. He then
used the higher strategic mobility of tactically innocuous cavalry to take advantage of his breakthrough to carry out a turning movement against the Turks.
This he could advantageously exploit by converting his tactically ineffective
cavalry into defensively formidable infantry. Using his cavalry on the strategic

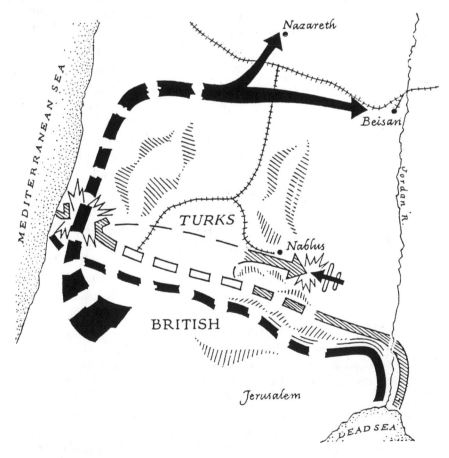

Diagram 8.5. Allenby's Distraction, Breakthrough, and Turning Movement

offensive to turn the Turks and as infantry on the resulting tactical defensive, Allenby had made the most of his old-fashioned cavalry. In completing the victory, his new-model light-cavalry biplanes had shown how effectively they could emulate the tactics of the Parthian, Turkish, and Mongolian light cavalry of old.

As a result of the campaign of Megiddo, the British advanced 360 miles in less than six weeks, taking 75,000 prisoners at a cost of 5,000 casualties. General Allenby justly became Field Marshal Viscount Allenby of Megiddo.

Summary of the Changes in Weapons, Tactics, and Logistics

Tactics had changed during the war as infantry in a skirmish line, which played such a role in the Franco-Prussian War, became articulated through the use of a squad of about a dozen riflemen, one of whom had a light-weight portable machine gun. The new format combined squads into a platoon under an officer, and platoons combined into the constituent companies of the battalion. This organization extended the articulation that armies had long possessed from the battalion upward to army headquarters as well as made the skirmishers into an articulated and better controlled force. This new structure, like infiltration tactics, became standard in all armies after the war.

This new organization incorporated in the battalion the principle that Guibert had enunciated for the army down to the battalion. Thus the component parts of the battalion could concentrate and act on the offensive to take advantage of the enemy's weakness in a way that Napoleonic armies had used battalions and larger units. This concept applied on the defense also, for, in the perfected German method of defense, German doctrine expected the small groups occupying shell holes, for example, to exercise initiative to move to another hole when brought under artillery fire and to move as well to take up the most expedient positions to repel the attack of the hostile infantry. The employment of mobility and concentration on the defense proved more difficult because of greater enemy numbers and artillery.

This new doctrine increased the responsibilities, initiative, and competence expected of noncommissioned as well as junior commissioned officers. Correspondingly, it deprived higher commanders of control of a battle that they usually could not, in any case, observe well enough to command as had higher officers in previous generations. Although this marked improvement in tactics and organization appeared in response to the increase in firepower, it conformed to principles nearly as old as warfare itself and used methods that armies had explicitly applied for more than a century.

The enhancement of firepower had made field fortifications standard practice, troops on the offensive as well as the defensive digging in promptly and then steadily elaborating their defenses. The continuous trench or breastwork of the traditional defense gradually gave way to a succession of strong points with the intervals covered by machine gun fire and, if the defenders had time to arrange it, by the fire of their own artillery. The light portable machine gun grew in numbers, and gradually the rifle became a supplement to the machine gun rather than the reverse. The expansion in numbers of these portable machine guns is primarily responsible for the growth in the number of machine guns of all kinds in the French army deployed against the Germans from 2,100 in 1914 to 65,000 in 1918.

With a high ratio of force to space, real siege warfare had resulted. To have enough strength to compel the enemy to resort to siege methods, commanders liked to have one division for every three miles of the front they must defend. This meant that they had about 4,000 men per mile holding the line with reserves at hand for reinforcement, counterattack, or, at worst, the reconstitution of the front should the attack attain a breakthrough. This number amounted only to about a fourth of the average strength arrayed for a Napoleonic battle, though this exaggerates the disparity by excluding aircraft as well as the reserves at hand to support the World War I divisions. Further, the comparison neglects the elaborate field fortifications that Napoleonic armies lacked. Of course the thinner defense in men had an ability to deliver a far greater volume of much more accurate fire.

To overcome such high ratio of firepower to space and the field fortifications associated with it, one formula called for the attackers to have three times as many men, six times as much artillery, and eighteen times as much ammunition as the defenders. But unless the attackers achieved surprise, the defenders would lay out a succession of defense lines in their rear and build them as rapidly as the attackers fought their way through the initial lines. The necessity of moving forward and properly emplacing their essentially siege artillery meant that in the absence of surprise and a breakthrough the attack must halt every 2,000 or 3,000 yards.

Although tactics represented an extension of the implications of the absolute supremacy of the light or missile-armed infantryman, the introduction of two new weapon systems, the airplane and the tank, constituted the war's real revolution in tactics, even though neither had affected the course of operations in a major way. At the beginning of the eighteenth century, when the musketeer acquired a bayonet, he became virtually immune to frontal attack by cavalry. With his bayonet he could resist the shock action of the cavalry's saber and with his musket he could defeat the cavalry's pistol. But by the end of World War I, his more formidable, magazine rifle-armed successor had become completely susceptible to injury by a new kind of cavalry: the tank. His rifle and bayonet made no impression on the tank, which could charge him like the heavy cavalry of old and destroy him with its machine gun and armored invulnerability. Likewise, he found his rifle virtually useless against the rapidly moving target of the aircraft, which bombed him or shot him with its machine guns, keeping, like the light cavalry of old, its distance and relying on its missiles. In the early 1700s the bayonet-armed musketeer had embodied, with respect to the cavalry, the capabilities of both light and heavy infantry. Two centuries later he had neither, having no more defense against the charge of the tank than light-infantry bowmen against the armored cavalry of old, and being no better able to cope with the aircraft than Roman swordsmen with Parthian horse archers.

In the siege warfare of the western front the field artillery had stopped the tanks, but only after the tanks had overwhelmed the infantry of the forward defensive zone. The war had not provided even the Germans, who alone had faced tanks, with much time to consider how to cope with them. The aircraft, on the other hand, early attracted a defensive measure consisting usually of machine guns or field artillery mounted to fire at aircraft. But the difficulties of firing at a rapidly moving target made such antiaircraft weapons relatively ineffective.

When the war ended, the tank and the aircraft had an apparent tactical supremacy over the infantry with which armies had not had to deal during the war itself. Although armies had not fully appreciated the possibilities of the new weapons nor grasped how best to use them, the growth of the French army's aircraft from about 200 in 1914 to 3,300 in 1918 reflects a faith in their utility as does its 4,600 tanks at the end of 1918.

But, as with the light and heavy cavalry of the past, not all terrain suited the use of aircraft and tanks. Just as the forests of Syria had thwarted the Parthian cavalry, thus also did forests handicap both the movement of tanks and observation from aircraft. Mountains had an almost equally inhibiting effect, the tanks having to keep to the valleys and the aircraft having difficulty finding suitable targets on the uneven and often wooded slopes of mountains.

This resulted in limiting the potential supremacy of the new weapon systems to level terrain. In the same way that mountains enabled the Armenians to maintain their independence against the armored cavalry and skilled horse archers of the Parthians, so also would terrain limit tanks and aircraft. Aided by their mountains, Swiss militia, without armor and only equipped with halberds, had protected themselves against the formidable professional cavalry of their lowland neighbors; in spite of primitive weapons and fighting on foot, the Welsh, Irish, and Scots had long confined their powerful mounted invaders to the lowlands; so also could the terrain again bifurcate warfare. The new weapons could dominate level terrain while the rifleman, the machine gunner, and artilleryman, the premier weapon system of the nineteenth century, would continue supreme in the mountains and forests.

The railway naturally dominated the logistics of the concentrated, stationary armies on the western front and controlled all of the large armies elsewhere. But the motor truck had shown its value in supplying the Germans with ammunition in 1914 and exhibited its potential later when the French used trucks in great numbers to supply Verdun in the absence of a railroad. In September 1918 the French used trucks at night to transport over a third of a million U.S. troops fifty miles in six days. Recognizing their value, the French increased their numbers of trucks from 19,000 in 1914 to 88,000 in 1918. Clearly they had

proved their logistical value during the war and had provided a valuable supplement to the railroad in meeting the enormous supply requirements of the
huge stationary armies as well as displaying the potential for strategic movement
of troops.

As the early operations in East Prussia showed, nothing about the increase
in firepower since the Franco-Prussian War precluded capitalizing on interior
lines or executing the kind of turning movement that had characterized operations since Napoleon's Marengo campaign. In fact, the increase in firepower,
by enhancing the power of the defense, had improved the potentiality of the
turning movement, relying as it did on forcing the enemy to assume the tactical
offensive to recover his communciations. When, in the Tannenberg campaign,
General François's corps had reached the Russian rear, his thinly spread forces,
an average of a battalion every mile and a half, had prevented the retreat of
many times as many Russians. Of course, so few could not have held back a
deliberate attack by so many, but the disorganized Russians, beset on the east
and north, could not mount such an attack.

Nevertheless, the disappearance of flanks on most fronts precluded the
exploitation of the benefits that the augmented power of the defense gave the
turning movement. General Allenby's brilliant Megiddo campaign exhibited this
advantage again, an opportunity that he created by his innovative use of cavalry
as strategically offensive troops and his exploitation of their power on the tactical
defensive when dismounted.

Still most battles had only tactical significance, their attrition measuring the
outcome as it had in much of pre-Napoleonic warfare. Often almost incredible
in extent and duration, few battles on the western front produced the strategic
result of a breakthrough and a threat to the defender's flanks that forced withdrawal. When western frontal battles attained a breakthrough, the penetration
failed to have much strategic importance.

In their strategy the Germans made the most of their interior lines, a situation
magnified by the benefit of fighting a poorly coordinated coalition that could
not take advantage of the concentration in time made possible by simultaneous
advances. After concentrating against first Russia and then Serbia in 1915, the
Germans launched a major campaign against France in early 1916. The allied
operation on the Somme, Austrian involvement in an attack in Italy, and the
successful Russian offensive in the summer did not prevent the Germans from
abandoning their Verdun operation, standing on the defensive and concentrating
against and defeating Romania when it entered the war in the summer of 1916.
In 1917 Germany and Austria again made use of their interior lines to concentrate
against and strike Italy a nearly crippling blow. Except against such a well-
conducted operation on exterior lines as the allies had waged against Napoleon
in 1813, interior lines of operations clearly conferred a meaningful strategic
advantage, especially when fighting a coalition.

The railroad strengthened the strategic defense not only because its destruction complicated the logistics of an advancing army but also because control

of undestroyed railways, by conferring superior mobility, gave strategically offensive troops to the defenders. The Germans demonstrated this in their Tannenberg campaign when they used their East Prussian railroad to move a corps not just from one army to another but to the far flank of Samsonov's army to carry out their turning movement. Just as the Germans made this strategic maneuver by rail, so Joffre made equally good use of his comparable advantages to create a new army at Paris in a position where it could turn the German turning movement. Operations in 1918 again exhibited the critical advantage the defense gained by its railroad mobility when the allies promptly concentrated the necessary troops to seal a breakthrough that the Germans sought to exploit on foot and with horsedrawn artillery and supply vehicles.

Aircraft affected strategy because it performed light cavalry's role of reconnaissance as well as improved on it through the aerial photograph. In fact, in the siege warfare of fronts but no flanks, armies would have had no reconnaissance at all without aircraft and balloons since cavalry could not reconnoiter under those conditions. Aircraft could also replace light cavalry in conducting long-distance raids. Reliance on inaccurate bombs and the airplane's limited carrying capacity for explosives meant that damage by aircraft failed to have the thoroughness of destruction brought about by men on the ground. Raiding aircraft also could not live at the enemy's expense, nor could they bring off booty; nevertheless, railways proved vulnerable to bombing, and aircraft machine guns as well as their bombs could attack troops and vehicles on roads and trains in motion. Clearly, aircraft proved an admirable replacement for carrying out the strategic roles of light cavalry.

With a maximum speed of five miles an hour and a range of only fifteen to twenty-five miles, tanks had no strategic role. Since they required rail transportation for their strategic movements, their mobility had tactical significance only. The fragility of their tracks and their liability to mechanical breakdowns further limited their movement under their own power. Gas, which had proved so lethal, continued to be a concern of all armies, but never again saw major use.

In the two decades between the world wars military thinkers balanced the lessons of the siege warfare of 1914–18 with the possibilities inherent in the presence of two new weapon systems.

Although the emergence of the submarine and the aircraft had each moved sea warfare into a third dimension, the sailors had fewer changes to digest. In fact, the war had developed the capabilities of the submarine rather fully, which, in turn, had stimulated the invention and use of hydrophones and depth charges. In spite of defects in armor placement, the design of warships and their method of gunnery control had proven fundamentally sound. Navies had even pioneered the use of aircraft at sea before the war, and the British, who had begun work on a seaplane carrier before 1914, converted other ships during the conflict, one into a ship on which planes could land as well as take off. Aircraft at sea, as on land, would see substantial development and controversy as to their potential during the ensuing two decades.

The expansion of the scale and intensity of land operations and the greatly augmented economic drain of this effort gave seapower added importance, given the role of seaborne commerce in providing products needed to support the more industrialized contest of 1914 to 1918. In former wars British blockades had hurt France's economy somewhat but had never had the effect that the blockade had on Germany, of reducing food consumption and handicapping industry because it had diminished or shut off the supply of such critical supplies as oil or copper. Never, too, had France's raiding strategy of attacking English ships come as near seriously menacing the British economy and ability to carry on the struggle as had the German submarine campaign against the allies. The navy's logistic strategy had acquired a new and perhaps decisive power in the industrial age.

9

PRELUDE TO RENEWED CONFLICT,
1919–39

The Full Development of Four New Weapon Systems

During the period between World Wars I and II no major European power engaged in large-scale warfare with an opponent comparable in power. Nevertheless, the era saw many changes, and all major armies and private manufacturers pursued the development of the weapon systems introduced in World War I. These taxing and difficult decades of economic depression, dictatorship, and apprehension of war saw, like the dissimilar period before the outbreak of the wars of the French Revolution, the emergence of new ideas, as soldiers coped with understanding the lessons of the world war and the implication of the new weapon systems. World War II would test the ideas and the improved materiel.

Aircraft advanced rapidly, in part because its commercial possibilities, often supported by government subsidies, encouraged development. The representative fighter airplane of 1918 had an engine of 200 horsepower and a speed of 130 miles an hour. By 1939 power had increased fivefold, and some aircraft could travel over 350 miles per hour. This increase in velocity resulted not only from more power but also from the reduced wind resistance of one, rather than two, wings and retractable landing wheels. Other measures, such as the use of a twelve-cylinder V-type engine with its narrow cross section, rather than the bulkier rotary or radial, also diminished wind resistance on fighters. Metal had largely replaced wood and fabric, and the aircraft had become bigger and heavier. Although they lacked the maneuverability of the old biplanes, the new fighters compensated by their far greater speed and firepower. Whereas 1918 fighters had two rifle-caliber machine guns, the 1939 models boasted as many as eight or their equivalent in larger-bore weapons. Most fighters could also carry a few small bombs.

Bombers followed similar development, evolving into light, medium, and heavy with one to four engines and bomb loads up to several tons. Fighters had a top speed 50 to 100 miles per hour greater than bombers. The dive bomber specialized in diving toward its target at a steep angle and dropping its bomb more accurately because of the proximity to the target. Although aircraft had much improved bombsights, even dive bombing remained inaccurate when compared with artillery fire, which customarily dealt with known ranges and gun capabilities and could usually correct the aim of successive shots. Observation planes continued as a specialized type, but often smaller bombers performed their duties.

Countering aircraft from the ground, which had begun even before World War I, continued during the conflict, and reached a measure of perfection in the interwar period. For high-flying planes, the air defenses tended to use a high-velocity gun of between 3 and 4 inch bore, usually firing shrapnel shell timed to explode at the height of the aircraft. But aiming at a target moving in three dimensions at an unknown speed and range presented a difficult problem.

Air defense counted on hearing the engines of the approaching plane by means of receivers that an operator could move until he found the exact direction of the sound. This permitted the aiming of an optical range finder, and at night also searchlights, in the proper direction. When the range finder tracked the target, a primitive mechanical computer, knowing the range, calculated speed and direction and the point at which the artillery should shoot, so that its shrapnel shells would intercept the aircraft and explode at the right moment. With this information transmitted to the guns, the gunners set their time fuses, aimed their weapons, and began firing.

With good visibility the system proved very effective against planes at high altitude, but it had no applicability for defending against a fast approaching low-level attack, such as that which British aircraft had used against the retreating Turkish troops during the Megiddo campaign. For defense against low-flying aircraft, the infantry had used machine guns during World War I. This defensive solution—volume, rather than accuracy, of fire—continued as the line of development after the war, with the addition of larger machine guns of 20 to 50 millimeters shooting bullets that exploded on impact. These lighter antiaircraft weapons and the smaller-bore machine guns, often mounted in groups, dispatched a high volume of bullets very lethal to aircraft. For aiming they depended either on a gunsight and the gunner's eye and judgment or on a rudimentary fire control system. They compensated for this inaccuracy by the number of rounds fired and by the aid of tracer bullets, which the gunners could see as they passed through the air toward the target. Armies towed such weapons or mounted them on motor trucks or tracked carriers.

If it chose to provide many antiaircraft guns, a navy or an army could protect itself with an antiaircraft defense so formidable as to justify the continued validity of the old principle that the man on foot had the advantage over the man mounted. Considering the great cost of the plane, its highly trained pilot, and the necessary support of its specialized ground crew, the antiaircraft guns did not have to shoot down many aircraft to have the best of the engagement on the basis of attrition. But aircraft did not wish to attack antiaircraft guns any more than in earlier times light cavalry wished to attack light infantry; like the light cavalry of old the airplanes aimed at vulnerable and defenseless weapon systems and logistical equipment and installations.

To cope with the Moslem horse archer, the Crusaders had used the crossbow. The antiaircraft guns fulfilled the role of the crossbow but with less effectiveness and with the very serious drawback of lack of mobility. Whereas the crossbowman had all of the mobility of an infantryman, no infantryman could carry a useful antiaircraft weapon. To give mobility to an antiaircraft gun capable of defending against low-flying aircraft required towing or mounting it on a truck or tracked vehicle. This ability to move could exceed that of the infantry on foot but at a substantial cost in resources and flexibility. A battery of powerful guns for defense against high-altitude attack and its associated complex fire-control apparatus could not go into action as promptly as could self-propelled antiaircraft machine guns accompanying troops on the march or deployed. The inaccuracy of high-altitude bombing did, however, substantially mitigate the difficulties of defending troops against this danger. Unlike the situation with the crossbowman, the weapons available limited antiaircraft protection for troops in motion to defense against low-flying aircraft and only succeeded in doing this by employing costly motorized mounts or traction. Not surprisingly, many armies acted as if they underestimated the tactical menace presented by the light cavalry of the air.

The quality and capabilities of tanks also made substantial progress during the interwar years. The French stayed with the successful design of their Renault, and British arms producers, who did a considerable export business, followed the French in producing small tanks with a turret having a 360-degree traverse. Soon manufacturers turned out durable tracks and suspension systems, which permitted speeds of 20 and then 30 miles an hour. Tanks usually weighed between six and twelve tons and had machine guns and a gun not unlike the 37 millimeter originally used on the Renault. Armor, usually between 10 and 20 millimeters thick, provided a comfortable margin of protection against small-arms fire.

Armies tended to divide tanks into two classes, intending to use slower ones with thicker armor to assist infantry in their assaults and faster ones with thinner armor to play a part vaguely analogous to cavalry. Yet, in relation to the light infantry rifleman and machine gunner, both played the role of heavy cavalry. As did naval architects, tank designers faced a substitution relationship between speed, armor, and firepower.

With greatly increased durability and mechanical reliability and road speeds of twenty miles an hour, the tank of the 1930s had a greatly augmented tactical value as well as real strategic mobility. To counter this enhanced potential, all armies sought a defense. Just as Roman armies, medieval militias, and Swiss infantry had adopted pikes to protect themselves against the charge of heavy cavalry, armies searched for the proper weapon to deal with the tank. They sought a gun with greater mobility, less cost in terms of crew size, more modest traction requirements, and greater ease of entrenchment and concealment than the field gun.

During World War I the Germans had introduced an enlarged rifle with a bore about two-thirds greater than their standard infantry rifle. Bearing about the same relation to the infantry rifle as the Spanish musket to the arquebus, this weapon could be fired by one man, though with difficulty, and the high velocity of its steel bullet enabled it to pierce tank armor. But the thicker armor of the postwar tanks soon rendered this solution obsolete.

The ability of a bullet to pierce armor depended on the bullet's energy, a product of its weight and the square of its velocity and, to a degree, the size of the hole it must make. Since a bigger projectile must make a larger hole in the armor plate and so encountered greater resistance, a smaller, lighter projectile at a high rate of speed performed this task better than a larger, heavier missile at a low rate of speed that had the same amount of energy. But a high velocity required a long, heavy barrel and a carriage strong enough to take the recoil of the explosive charge to create the velocity.

Only a small cannon could provide these characteristics. Most armies adopted a low, easily entrenched, shielded gun of 25 to 50 millimeters, lengthening its barrel and muzzle velocity or enlarging its bore and weight of shell as the armor on tanks improved. But even the earlier and smaller models of this cannon weighed from a quarter to a half ton and required a truck, tracked vehicle, or a horse to tow it. As with the antiaircraft gun, the antitank gun provided good protection but at a sacrifice of tactical mobility for the infantry even greater than that imposed by the undrilled medieval urban militia. But, with direct fire, the antitank gun could shoot accurately and rapidly at its conspicuous target and presented, even unentrenched, a difficult target for the tank gun to hit. Less costly, somewhat easier to implace, and slightly more mobile than field guns, the antitank gun still involved essentially the same high costs to move and time to place into action as the antiaircraft gun.

So in creating their defenses against aircraft and tanks, armies, had had to resort to the use of artillery, handicapping their tactical maneuverability with

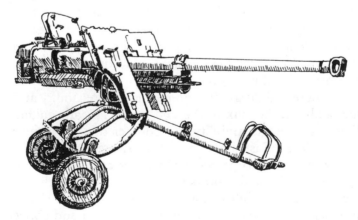

Illustration 9.1. Small-Bore, High-Velocity German Antitank Gun

mobile weapon systems rather than the portable crossbow and pike of earlier times. With missile weapons, mobility had varied inversely with weight that in turn, had varied directly with power. Crossbows used in sieges, for example, had vastly exceeded in force those carried in the field but required animal traction to move them. Thus power and mobility had an inverse ratio (schematic 9.1). The arquebus belongs on the upper part of the curve with the Spanish musket, Gustavus's light regimental gun, and various heavier pieces fitting in order below it on this curve of the substitution relationship between mobility and power. Various antitank guns would fall along this curve as would antiaircraft guns and artillery from the light-weight field gun to the heaviest railway pieces.

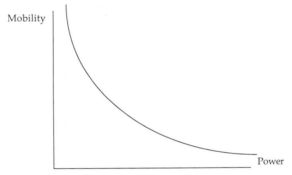

Schematic 9.1. Substitution Relationship between Mobility and Power

The available defenses against the tank and the airplane admirably suited the siege warfare of the western front of World War I. But for mobile warfare, these guns required traction or self-propulsion like artillery, suffered from the same disadvantages of delay in getting into action, and, because of their mission to combat weapon systems of much greater mobility, had their principal utility on the defense only.

The antiaircraft and antitank guns had so much in common in their ballistic characteristics that they could have readily exchanged targets by using each other's ammunition. But the gun mountings precluded the happy solution of a common weapon system that could concentrate its fire against the momentarily more menacing of its two mobile opponents. Whereas the antiaircraft gun necessitated a tall mounting to permit high-angle fire, the direct-fire antitank weapon required little elevation and needed, instead, to be as low as possible so as to present a small target to tank gunners and to facilitate easy entrenchment. Nevertheless, especially with an opportunity for more elaborate entrenchment, antiaircraft weapons could serve very effectively against tanks, and heavy antiaircraft guns also made good field artillery.

So the traditional matrix of four weapon systems (schematic 9.2) had returned in a different form.

The 1920s and 1930s had perfected that shown in schematic 9.3.

Initially tanks and aircraft could not fight each other at all. The tank guns could not fire at aircraft, and the tank presented an unpromising target for

	Foot	Mounted
Shock	Heavy Infantry	Heavy Cavalry
Missile	Light Infantry	Light Cavalry

Schematic 9.2. Traditional Weapon Systems Matrix

	Fixed or Mobile	Mounted
Close	antitank gun	tank
Distant	antiaircraft gun	aircraft

Schematic 9.3. 1930s Weapon Systems Matrix

aircraft. A small target, and therefore hard to hit with a bomb even when not in motion, the tank's armor protected it from the aircraft's machine gun. Even though tanks usually only carried thin armor on the roofs of their hull and turret, the acute angle at which bullets from aircraft struck the roofs enabled them to deflect the bullets from the aircraft.

But in the early 1930s the situation changed. The French mounted a 20-millimeter cannon on a fighter airplane. This weapon could pierce a tank's horizontal armor. By 1939 the French, Germans, and Russians, who most closely tied their air forces to the requirements of their armies, had armed their fighter planes with at least one 20-millimeter cannon. This change in aircraft enabled them to attack the tank, and the tank, except for a machine gun fired in the open from the top of the turret, could not defend itself against a diving aircraft shooting its cannon. Just as Moslem light cavalry could keep away from Byzantine or Crusader heavy cavalrymen and destroy them with their bows, so also could aircraft now deal with tanks.

During the later Middle Ages the four weapon systems had borne the relationships to one another shown in schematic 9.4, in which D stands for the ability to defend against an attack and A the ability to attack successfully, both in the direction of the arrow.

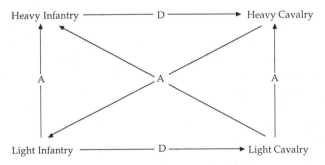

Schematic 9.4. Traditional Weapon Systems Capabilities

By the late 1930s four new and fully developed weapon systems had acquired almost exactly corresponding relationships (schematic 9.5).

This diagram does overstate the symmetry betwen the medieval and modern situations in that, for example, tanks would rarely have the need or opportunity to attack antiaircraft guns in the way medieval heavy cavalry would ride down crossbowmen. It also ignores the ability of antiaircraft guns, when properly alerted and positioned, to defend against tanks. Artillery has no formal place in this diagram but was very definitely present and had facilities superior to aircraft for attacking antitank guns. Insofar as heavy antiaircraft guns could function as field artillery, they could attack antitank guns.

The appearance of the airplane and tank also restored the original differentiation of mounted troops into heavy and light, a distinction eliminated in the sixteenth century by the adoption of the pistol and saber. This reversion to the old dichotomy gave the tank the opportunity to have the same advantage on the defensive against other tanks enjoyed by the dismounted medieval knight when he defended against cavalry. The equipment of some French tanks with 37- or 75-millimeter cannon and many British tanks with a 57-millimeter gun gave the early tanks a weapon capable of piercing the armor of another tank.

After the war the continuation of gun armament on most tanks confirmed for the new heavy cavalry a defensive power comparable to the dismounted heavy cavalry of old. The stationary tank defending against a moving opponent had the defense's traditional benefit of choice of ground and use of cover as well as a good field of fire and the opportunity to shoot deliberately, which gave overwhelming predominance to riflemen defending against the same weapon system. Of course, the less expensive antitank gun enjoyed the same advantages over the attacker, but, like the defensive superiority of King Edward's dismounted knights over Welsh spearmen with less body armor than knights, the more costly, fully armored tank could give a better performance than an antitank gun that had only a shield and a low silhouette. This ability of tanks to defend against other tanks gradually led designers to arm almost all tanks in addition to machine guns, with a higher velocity gun capable of piercing tank armor as well as firing explosive shells at infantry machine gun positions.

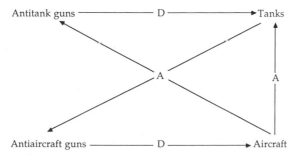

Schematic 9.5. 1930s Weapon Systems Capabilities

On the other hand, aircraft lacked the ability to dismount for the defensive, which had characterized the light cavalry of old. Whereas mounted bowmen could leave their horses and take defensive advantage of the terrain and the superiority of the man on foot over the mounted man or assume their place as bowmen on the walls of cities or fortifications, aircraft lacked the old versatility of fighting dismounted, which the tank had given back to the heavy cavalry, and all cavalry had possessed if armed with a rifle in addition to saber and pistol.

As in the Middle Ages, the schematic of weapon system capabilities is relevant only to terrain suitable for fighting mounted in aircraft and tanks. In wooded or mountainous territory, unsuitable for mounted warfare, the infantryman with his rifle, machine gun, and mobile field artillery still reigned supreme just as he had in the nineteenth century. But if, on level and unobstructed terrain, such a nineteenth-century army should meet a force largely composed of aircraft and tanks, it would suffer the fate of the Romans at Carrhae when Parthian light cavalry used its bows to decimate the Romans. Such an army of rifle-armed infantry would fare even worse than the Romans unless their artillery could protect them from tanks the way Roman heavy infantry kept at bay the Parthian heavy cavalry.

But in territory appropriate for mounted combat, commanders faced basically the same problem as medieval soldiers, that of uniting the various weapon systems to protect against their vulnerabilities and accentuate their strengths. Commanders had wrestled with this dilemma until, in the sixteenth century, they had reached the combined-arms synthesis of pikemen aided by arquebusiers with cavalry at hand to fill the role of offensive troops. Commanders and military thinkers had barely two decades to solve this combined-arms puzzle before they took their new weapons systems into another world war.

Even if soldiers had promptly discovered the right combined-arms synthesis for the new weapons, the existence of the new weapon systems enhanced the power of the offense because again, on suitable ground, generals commanded heterogeneous armies composed of weapon systems each of which had an intrinsic preponderance over one of the enemy's and an inferiority with respect to another in the enemy army. Even if both armies had devised the perfect array, the presence of different weapon systems provided occasions that had not existed for over two centuries, opportunities from which exceptional talent on one side or blundering on the other could create an advantage for the offense absent when homogeneous armies had struggled indecisively against each other during World War I.

The existence of a weapon system that had a superiority over another, as the antitank gun had over the tank, assured the continued tactical primacy of the defense, but the requirements of combination, the vulnerabilities created by the lack of combination, and circumstances produced by various concentrations of different weapon systems had clearly furnished the tactical offensive with a scope that it had lacked since the early sixteenth century.

The radio increased commanders' control and improved articulation. By the late 1930s aircraft, tanks, and troops in the field all carried radios. They not only had much more widespread use than the wireless telegraph in the First World War, but also the voice communication of the radio enhanced the utility of communication without wire.

In the 1930s most nations discovered how to reflect a radio beam back from an object to determine its location. Called radar, it had its primary use in searching for aircraft. Because of improvements during World War II it substituted in air defense first for the aural system of detecting the approach of aircraft and their approximate location and then for the optical system of ranging and aiming. Although radar had greater accuracy and could function at night without searchlights, aircraft could befuddle it by throwing out strips of metal foil that would reflect back the radio beam. But radar provided a better air defense than the sound, optical, and searchlight method.

Artillery and small arms remained much as they had since the turn of the century. Except for antiaircraft and antitank weapons and better communications, armies entered World War II armed very much as they had ended World War I.

The French in Morocco: New Weapons and Old Strategy

But the new weapon systems of World War I had trials during the interwar period from which some soldiers gleaned lessons about their potential. French operations in extending France's control over Morocco furnished both the most sustained and most limited use of the new weapons. The French campaigned in Morocco for twenty-six years, using an approach that they had perfected during their nineteenth-century colonial conquests. Their initial entry into Africa, however, in Algeria in 1830, had been very brutal. In their efforts to subdue Algeria in the 1830s and 1840s, the French had improved the mobility of their forces by dispensing with artillery, lightening the loads of the infantrymen, and using pack mules instead of wagons. But even by raising the mobility of their columns to that of their opponents and adopting the practice of trying to surround them, they still found the guerrillas too elusive. This simply confirmed the experience of their commander in Algeria, Thomas-Robert Bugeaud, who had served in Spain during the French occupation in the Napoleonic wars and had fought the Spaniards in the contest that had given guerrilla warfare its name.

So Marshal Bugeaud adopted an extraordinarily ruthless yet impressively effective strategy. Marching his more powerful forces through the country, he not only destroyed grain stocks, including those secreted underground, but also took livestock, burned the fields at harvest time, and cut down fruit trees. Although he thus used a raiding logistic strategy against his enemy's base area (where he burned tents and dwellings and destroyed furniture and utensils), he employed counterraids that, like the strategy of the ancient Greeks, sought to secure political objectives through destructive raids. In this case, Bugeaud sought the submission of the chiefs of the different tribes, through whom the French would rule the country. The chiefs who acquiesced and paid taxes received political support from the French as well as the courtesy and status appropriate to the dignity of partners in the rule of the country. But those who refused to comply or subsequently revolted, the marshal treated with merciless severity.

The logistical and political strategy of raids provided the requisite rigor because Bugeaud, not employing the later policies of the Spanish in Cuba and the British in South Africa, did nothing to shield civilians from the cruel effects of his logistic strategy. So these raids differed little from those employed by the Turks in Anatolia after their victory at Manzikert. The logistic strategy itself produced tragedies, a French general observing, in a return to a devastated village, "heaps of bodies huddled together, frozen to death during the night." But such an event accorded with the intentional, systematic employment of terrorism that had much in common with that of the Mongols in the Khwarizmian empire. One French officer characterized the policy as to "kill all the men over the age of fifteen" and deport women and children. "In a word, annihilate everyone who does not crawl at our feet like dogs."[1]

When several hundred natives took refuge in a cave, the French commander built a fire at the mouth and asphyxiated them. Later another commander walled up the mouth of a cave filled with people. One French soldier had written that the barbarous methods used in Algeria would "make the hair on the head of an honest bourgeois stand straight up." And this proved true when the French press reported the atrocities and the kind of warfare waged in Algeria. Marshal Bugeaud then resigned after six years of command, but his method had conquered much of the country. Within another twenty years the French had consolidated their rule.[2]

But in extending their colonial empire in the nineteenth and twentieth centuries, the French did not apply Bugeaud's repugnant model. Though they retained the marshal's emphasis on mobility for forces and his political approach of rule through local chiefs and princes, they used a strategy more humane and, when skillfully applied, apparently little less effective. They developed their strategy of conquest during the later nineteenth century in the course of subduing Indo-China and Madagascar. They applied these methods in the twentieth century in Morocco under the leadership of General Lyautey, a determined and resourceful soldier and astute administrator with a talent for self-advertisement. In his long command in Morocco he showed that he had profited from his service in Indo-China and his responsible posts in Madagascar and Algeria.

Beginning their operations in Morocco in 1908, the French began a methodical application of methods of conquest that harmonized with the ideals of their bourgeois republic and furnished a good means of reconciling the people to their rule. The French forces, representing the sultan whom they controlled, extended their domination by a system of slow penetration. In doing this they depended on ruling through the local authorities and exploiting the divisions or factions among the people of the region they sought to control. At the same time they followed a policy of respect for local laws, religion, and customs, and, to make their rule attractive, relied on the sale of goods at artificially low prices, the provision of free medical care, and constructing valuable public works such as roads and wells. These economic incentives helped to reconcile the populace to French rule but failed to counterbalance motives for resistance.

To permit these political and economic measures to work, the French usually employed military action first. They customarily concentrated large forces against a relatively small, unsubdued area that they often sought to surround and overwhelm by an unexpected advance from all sides. When the concentration of force had secured the submission of the native authorities, the French maintained a high ratio of force to space, augmented by the construction of strong points, and patroled the newly conquered territory while giving their political and economic measures an opportunity to reconcile the vanquished to the rule of the French and the sultan.

This method of conquest, in its military strategy so like that of the English in Wales centuries before, employed a persisting strategy that embodied, in its gradual diminution of the area under enemy control, a large logistic element. Also, as in Wales, the lowlands had greater productivity than the highlands, which permitted the application of a logistic strategy to subjugate specific areas. Often indigenous armed forces dwelt in mountainous areas but maintained themselves by grazing cattle in the lowlands and levying taxes or tribute on the agricultural and commercial population of the lowlands. French mastery of the lowlands often vanquished the forces in the nearby mountains, cutting off the pasturage and the supplies that the mountaineers had drawn from the sedentary population. This system of conquest also relied on recruiting and training troops in the regions already subdued and using them to garrison this territory as well as to play a major role in the subjection of new areas.

The French under Lyautey, elevated to marshal in 1921, had used this process of slow subjugation for over a decade and a half when in 1925 they confronted Abd-el-Krim, who controlled the Riff Mountains in the northern or Spanish part of Morocco. Having earlier defeated the Spaniards, wiping out many of their posts and virtually destroying a force of 20,000 men, Abd-el-Krim had developed a regular army with machine guns, artillery, and even a few aircraft. With this force he moved south and attacked the numerically inferior French along an extended front south of and parallel to the frontier between the French and Spanish zones of Morocco.

Abd-el-Krim drove back the outnumbered French, capturing two-thirds of their fortified posts in this mountainous region, but he failed to push their forces back very far. The French owed much to their superior artillery, their methodical approach, and their discipline, training, and combat experience. Their greater number of planes also aided their defense, but, even though a raid by three squadrons of bombers played a key role in the successful evacuation of one post, the few aircraft available did not make a major contribution to the triumphant defense. They did occasionally prove useful in supply, dropping water in the form of blocks of ice to the garrison of one beleaguered post and, on another occasion, bringing a quantity of medals to the front so that a general could raise morale by awarding them on the spot.

Abd-el-Krim's achievements brought prompt reinforcements from France and a combined Franco-Spanish campaign in which Marshal Pétain, the commander of the victorious French armies in 1918, took the field in person as did General Primo de Rivera, the Spanish prime minister. Marshal Pétain brought more men, aircraft, heavy artillery, and tanks. In the fall of 1925 and spring of 1926 these powerful forces overwhelmed Abd-el-Krim's army and took him prisoner. Warfare returned to the slow penetration model that the French had followed systematically since 1911.

For this war tanks proved of limited value because the French had already overrun most of the level areas where these vehicles could have made a significant contribution. The French had based their original conquest of the lowlands on their better training, discipline, and organization, importantly aided by their virtual monopoly of modern rifles. By the time the Moroccans acquired modern rifles and had mastered combat as skirmishers—a situation in which tanks would have helped immensely—the French had already won most of the suitable terrain, and the majority of the rest of the operations took place in mountains as high as 10,000 feet, where tanks could not work effectively. In one desert campaign at an oasis, however, tanks did prove their value in spite of the obstruction presented by numerous palm trees.

In 1934, at the conclusion of the campaigns to pacify Morocco, the French successfully used motor trucks. In the south where the firm, level, treeless land bordered the Spanish colony of Rio de Oro, 100 motor trucks, each carrying fourteen men, made up the main force of a column that included motorized machine guns and 37-millimeter and 75-millimeter guns. In a sudden, surprise advance this column moved over the smooth ground to carry out a turning movement against native troops mounted on horses. Moving forward at the almost leisurely pace of sixty miles a day, the French took position south of their opponents, cutting off their retreat across the Spanish border and compelling their surrender when the natives found themselves hemmed in between motorized forces in the south and foot-marching infantry advancing from the north. Substituting motor trucks for horses to secure their greater strategic mobility, the French had reproduced Allenby's Megiddo turning movement and again shown the importance of mounted infantry armed with rapid-fire, rifled weapons.

Since the mountains usually lacked any tree cover, aircraft made a significant contribution through one of the traditional strategic missions of light cavalry, reconnaissance. Aerial photographs made possible the careful planning before several of the characteristic quick, surprise advances in which comparatively large forces engulfed a small area. Air attacks against the enemy troops would have played a small role because the French were relying on minimum force, seeking to pacify rather than destroy the foe. But in one instance, when an enemy force entrenched on a high mountain had repelled an attack and easily held out against a month-long siege and bombardment, air reconnaissance did contribute in a meaningful way to combat. Aircraft aided the search for two secret springs upon which the besieged depended for their water supply and helped the artillery shell them. In an application of logistic strategy remarkably like and ultimately much more successful than that of the Persians at Plataea, the French compelled the besieged Moroccans to surrender after they lost their springs and their water.

Tactical and Strategic Use of Aircraft

In the Italian war against Ethiopia in 1935–36 aircraft played a premier role. For attack on supply routes and troops the Italians had modern tri-motor bombers, some with top speeds of 200 miles per hour and the capacity to carry more than 2,600 pounds of bombs. Italian planes scored their greatest combat success when they attacked 20,000 defeated Ethiopian troops retreating over flat, open ground. Italian aircraft sprayed the hungry and demoralized Ethiopians with blister gas and dropped seventy-three tons of bombs, the equivalent in weight to more than 10,000 75-millimeter shells. The uncounted corpses of the Ethiopians numbered in the thousands. Without antiaircraft guns, the Ethiopians proved as defenseless as Romans or Crusaders on foot when assailed by horse archers and, without armor, even more vulnerable.

Italian tanks proved useful in the war, but the Italians' greater numbers and immense preponderance in firepower provided the decisive element in their victory and conquest of the key centers of the huge country. For the final push to the Ethiopian capital over 12,000 Italian troops traveled the 200 miles in 1,785 automobiles and trucks. But damage to the road so delayed the motorized column that the trek took ten days.

In the Spanish Civil War government bombers and fighters provided major, if not crucial, assistance in turning back an advance by two largely motorized Italian divisions accompanied by fifty tanks. Confined to the roads by heavy rains, the columns of the advancing motorized forces presented a perfect target for the government airplanes near Guadalajara in 1937.

In spite of bad weather, bombers and fighters carrying bombs effectively assaulted the road-bound Italians. Damaged and demoralized by the air attacks and halted by stiffening resistance in front, the Italians had difficulty retreating because of their damaged vehicles. A blocked road junction, cratered by bombs and blocked by demolished trucks, was particularly effective in impeding the retreat. The soldiers abandoned their vehicles and walked across the muddy fields; most made good their escape, but others, moving in small groups, presented excellent targets for fighter planes whose four machine guns mowed them down, just as Turkish light cavalry shot Crusaders marching through Asia Minor.

A Russian Cannae

In 1939 on the level, treeless terrain on the border of Manchuria and Mongolia, Japanese and Russian troops clashed over a small piece of disputed territory. Both forces, in army corps strength, had a substantial number of aircraft and tanks as well as antiaircraft and antitank guns. Entrenched in the area for nearly two months, the contestants demonstrated the power of the antitank gun as both sides halted the assaults of the other's tanks. In one unsuccessful attack the Japanese lost half of their seventy-three tanks, and the Japanese 37-millimeter antitank gun proved quite capable of defeating the larger Russian tanks that, though they weighed as much as thirteen tons, had armor less than an inch thick.

The Russians, with more troops, eventually defeated the Japanese, who had not believed that the Russians would concentrate such powerful forces 500 miles from a railroad. But with over 4,000 motor trucks, the Russians supplied 57,000 men. Yet such a supremacy in infantry should hardly have proved decisive against 30,000 entrenched Japanese, well equipped with machine guns and artillery. The Russian success depended on the wise use of their 498 tanks and 346 armored cars against which, at this stage in the prolonged battle, the Japanese could only contend with their field artillery and inadequate numbers of antitank guns. The Russians won when they concentrated their tanks on either flank and, overwhelming the Japanese defenses, pushed through into the rear and enveloped the defending Japanese infantry. The tank forces thus surrounded a substantial part of the Japanese forces. This battle at Khalkin Gol had much in common with Hannibal's victory at Cannae in that the envelopment of the Romans by the Carthaginian heavy cavalry played the most significant part in Hannibal's victory. Japanese killed and wounded in the whole campaign numbered 17,000, nearly double those of the Russians.

The Navies' Response to the New Weapons

After World War I naval architects realized that their ships had totally inadequate armor against long-range gunfire. The steep angle of descent of shells fired from 15,000 to 20,000 yards enabled shells to pierce decks protected only against projectiles striking at a shallow angle. The remedy involved not only thickening the decks but also using face-hardened armor instead of the ordinary steel, which had initially seemed appropriate for deflecting glancing blows. Naval architects also improved the extent and the sophistication of the defense of all warships against underwater explosions. Otherwise, the all-big-gun ships had stood the test of the war.

Reconstruction of existing battleships as well as new construction embodied these lessons. New battleships, which rose in displacement to over 40,000 tons, carried a higher percentage of their weight in armor and increased in speed from twenty to twenty-one knots to twenty-seven to thirty-one knots. Since many cruisers had no greater speed than thirty-one knots, the new capital ships blurred if they did not abolish the distinction between battleships and battle cruisers. Designers altered the secondary armament on battleships, originally intended to protect against torpedo boats, to add antiaircraft guns and, in some instances, to make the secondary guns dual-purpose, suitable as heavy antiaircraft guns as well as for defense against destroyers.

The changes that safeguarded ships against torpedoes and long-distance gunfire also provided admirable protection against aircraft attack. Decks strong enough to withstand the plunging fire of armor-piercing projectiles offered ample defense against contemporary bombs, and improved underwater defense against torpedoes and mines did much to shield ships against the mining effect of bombs that missed the ship but landed alongside. Converting the secondary armament into antiaircraft guns or adding heavy antiaircraft guns gave an ample measure of security against the inaccurate bombing of high-flying aircraft, and the automatic 20- to 40-millimeter guns that the armies used against low-flying planes supplied the same kind of safety for ships. But admirals failed to grasp the really enormous number of small guns that World War II would reveal that ships needed to offer the amount of fire to defend adequately against the far more menacing attack of low-flying aircraft.

During the interwar period cruisers and destroyers all adopted the turret mounting, usually two or three guns together. Cruisers, typically with a speed of about thirty-two knots and ranging in size from 5,000 to 10,000 tons, varied little from battleships in their essential concept of six or more guns, usually six or eight inch, and a secondary armament of dual-purpose guns to deal principally with aircraft and also with torpedo boats. They carried thin armor but disposed it much like battleships. Destroyers had increased in size and ranged from 1,000 to 2,500 tons, with about 1,800 tons typical. They looked like small cruisers and, except for their lack of armor and their higher speed of thirty-five or more knots, differed very little from cruisers. Their turret guns, usually four to five inch, could engage aircraft as well as surface targets. They, too, carried smaller antiaircraft guns for dealing with low-flying aircraft.

In spite of some spectacular tests conducted in the United States, the bombing of ships, especially in motion, by aircraft at high altitudes would prove ineffectual. Most navies thus relied on the dive bomber and the torpedo airplane. During World War I the British had successfully launched a torpedo from an aircraft to sink a Turkish merchant ship. Clearly this means of attacking the buoyancy of the ship offered several advantages over hitting armor plate with bombs. While dive bombers engaged the attention of a ship's air defenses and their bombs damaged the ship's antiaircraft armament, the slow-flying, vulnerable torpedo airplanes flew in low and launched their lethal underwater missiles. Bombs, however, would prove effective against unarmored ships.

But the aircraft carrier wrought the real revolution in naval warfare. As developed when the British converted to carriers three 30-knot ships of 18,000 tons, the aircraft carrier had a flat deck over all or virtually all of its whole surface on which planes could land and from which they could take off. When a 30-knot ship steamed into the wind, an airplane flying into the wind could have very little motion in relation to the deck when landing or taking off. As planes increased their speed, cables stretched across the deck engaged a hook on the aircraft and arrested its progress during landing.

The aircraft outranged the ships' guns. At a distance of 100 miles, a fast, unarmored aircraft carrier could launch its planes against any surface ships without having to fear engagement by the enemy's guns. The reliance on missile weapons for sea warfare had not changed, and the greater range of aircraft from a carrier gave it a potential superiority over the gun. The British provided themselves with seven aircraft carriers, half as many as they had battleships; the United States and Japan, the other major naval powers, also had seven and France, one. In the mid–1930s, when the British began to modernize their fleet, they planned an equal number of new carriers and battleships, five of each.

That planes from land could fly far out over the sea also altered the naval situation, and the larger, land-based aircraft had longer range than those on carriers, often performed better, and, without the need for an expensive ship as a base, lower cost. Astride the Mediterranean, Italy felt no need for carriers. Just as they underestimated the need for air defense against low-flying aircraft, so also did admirals fail fully to grasp the extent to which the aircraft carrier could alter war at sea.

Insofar as the range of the carriers' aircraft and their reconnaisance capabilities made them essentially different from battleships or cruisers, for the first time since the galley and the temporary co-existence of heavy gun tactics with boarding tactics, navies had heterogeneity in the weapon systems. Just as armies were returning to heterogeneity from the era of the single weapon system (the rifle-armed infantryman), so navies, too, faced the problem of understanding the interrelation of two rather distinct weapon systems. It is not surprising that the sailors, like the soldiers, had difficulty in immediately finding the best doctrine.

In antisubmarine warfare navies made a significant advance, introducing a device that sent out an underwater sonic wave that, when reflected from the submarine's hull, gave its range and direction. Called asdic by Britain and sonar by the United States, this device could find stationary as well as moving submarines and correspondingly increased the power of surface ships to cope with their undersea enemy.

Radar could also have value against submarines, which still had to remain on the surface most of the time. Observation at night by radar gave surface ships another advantage in detecting the submarine. When carried in airplanes during World War II, radar extended its reconnaissance ability. But radar not only had benefits for reconnaissance; it soon acquired sufficient sophistication and accuracy for use in fire control for the main armament as well as the antiaircraft guns. Navies embraced radar with enthusiasm.

Doctrinal Diversity

Although armies had much the same composition as in 1918, ideas about warfare had changed. The enthusiasts for the tank insisted that it could and should play a far different role than it did in 1918, when it primarily helped the infantry overcome the machine gun. While orthodox thinking continued to view the tank as a slow-moving heavy cavalryman helping the light infantry, tank theorists envisioned a completely motorized force of infantry and artillery in which a large number of tanks would provide the striking power.

Although British writers including J. F. C. Fuller and B. H. Liddell Hart and the small British army pioneered these ideas and though the French also created a motorized division with tanks in 1933, the German army implemented the new theories on a large scale and incorporated them into their army's doctrine. In 1935 the Germans created their first Panzer, or armored, division, whose organization initially called for over 500 tanks, two battalions of infantry carried in motor trucks, and motorized artillery and antitank guns. The large number of tanks, aided by the infantry and artillery, provided a powerful tactical offensive capability for breaking through a defense. The motorization of the entire unit gave it a strategic mobility to exploit the penetration of the enemy's defenses. If planning a relentless push into the enemy's rear, bypassing obstacles, or overwhelming them with the offensive power of so many tanks, the Panzer division could strike the enemy's communications and disrupt the movement of supplies and reserves. The doctrine of the tank enthusiasts envisioned the strategic co-operation of the air force in attacking the defender's communications, troop movements, and headquarters and its tactical assistance in battle, with dive bombers augmenting or replacing artillery fire. The radio would permit command and coordination of the air as well as the ground forces. Thus the Germans envisioned a Parthian army, aided by heavy and light infantry, mounted for strategic mobility.

The Germans created additional Panzer divisions in succeeding years, even though the higher commanders of the army had misgivings and lacked any clear idea of what would be the consequences of their employment. Well might soldiers hesitate, for no comparable combat formation had existed since the Middle Ages. When knights pursued Viking raiders mounted on stolen horses, the equivalent of the tank and the motorized infantry elements of the Panzer division had existed but in the opposing forces. English armies raiding in France had, in addition to their heavy cavalry, longbowmen and even a few spearmen mounted for strategic mobility. But these concentrated forces, minute in relation to the space in which they operated, controlled no territory beyond their camp and supplied themselves by moving from place to place. Nothing in their use had any relation to the purposes that Panzer division proponents proposed for comparable, but much larger, twentieth-century forces.

The Russians, who had adopted and then temporarily discarded a similar theory of tank warfare, had successfully employed tanks during their undeclared war with Japan. The battle at Khalkin Gol had exhibited the power of tanks as an offensive weapon under other circumstances than the siege warfare of the western front in 1917 and 1918. The tanks' offensive characteristic of greater mobility and the capacity to fight without time-consuming deployment had enabled them to envelop the Japanese forces and attack their flank and rear. Clearly, after any breakthrough of a front, tanks could use the same formidable offensive attributes they had displayed at Khalkin Gol and return to the offensive the power that Alexander the Great's heavy cavalry and his brilliant doctrine for its employment had endowed it. But the battle at Khalkin Gol only exhibited the tactical virtuosity of tanks; it said nothing about strategy and the impact of the deep penetration some envisioned for Panzer divisions.

The French, who had, for most of the period between the wars, the strongest and most modern army, displayed even more skepticism about any role for the tank other than as an aid to the artillery and infantry in the siege warfare, which they expected again to characterize the operations of large forces along their frontiers. They, too, formed armored divisions, but in fewer numbers than the Germans and with fewer tanks in each division. Nevertheless, they had similar ideas for their use, but at least an equal lack of clarity about the result. Unlike the Germans, who allocated all of their tanks to Panzer divisions, the French kept over half of their ample supply of tanks for assignment to infantry divisions to aid in their attacks or counterattacks. Like the Germans, the French motorized a few of their divisions, carrying infantry in trucks and towing artillery with motor vehicles. Like the Germans, the bulk of the French army remained unchanged from 1918, consisting of marching infantry with horse-drawn artillery and much horsedrawn transport.

The more drastic enthusiasts for the airplane did not see it as a weapon system that restored light cavalry to the army and, at sea, because of its long range, replaced the navy's big gun. Rather they perceived the aircraft as a unique and all-powerful weapon system that could win wars virtually unaided. The theorists of the supremacy of the airplane, led by the Italian Giulio Douhet, soon evolved a clear doctrine for its use.

These radical advocates of the primacy of aviation believed in the bomber and usually in the futility of any defense against it. Since some bombers would always reach their target, only a passive defense of shelters made sense, the principal countermeasure lying in taking the offensive with one's own bombers. But the bombers, rather than aiming at the hostile army or navy, would strike at the enemy's industries and population centers. Such attacks would, Douhet believed, win the war unaided, rendering the combat of armies and navies redundant and any diversion of airpower to attack them a foolish dispersal of effort.

This doctrine was essentially a logistic strategy of using aircraft to destroy the economy that maintained the enemy's armed forces. It also embodied a political program in that the extreme advocates of air power believed that the bombing of large cities would terrorize the citizens and bring a demand for peace. Thus the strategy for victory through air power alone unconsciously emulated that used by the light cavalry powers of old, the Turks and Jenghiz Khan. Their raiding, logistic strategy had aimed at killing much of the hostile population, thus depriving the defenders of manpower for their armies and basing their political program on the terror inspired by their raids. The Turks had thus conquered Asia Minor from the Byzantines, using raids by their horse archers in much the same way that the many air power advocates proposed to use their bombers.

These radical ideas dominated no air force or strategy, but they had great strength in Italy, Britain, and the United States. In France, Germany, and Russia, where the army had the dominant role in national defense, the air force remained strongly tied to the mission of serving as the army's light cavalry.

Thus two decades of peace had improved the weapons available in 1918 and had given soldiers and military experts an opportunity to assess and devise doctrines for the tank and airplane. But the soldiers had found no consensus, and World War II would act as a proving ground for different ideas rather than, as in World War I, a graveyard for the consensus.

10

THE CLIMAX OF MODERN WARFARE: WORLD WAR II, 1939–45

The German Victory over Poland

World War II began on September 1, 1939. Germany initially fought France, Britain, and Poland. The Germans reproduced their strategy of 1914 but exploited their interior lines to concentrate first against the weaker Polish army to achieve a quick victory while France was mobilizing. The Germans had forty-eight active divisions against the Polish army's thirty active divisions and ten formed in the manner of Landwehr. The Germans had a far greater number of tanks, and the Poles had few antitank guns. Since the German-Polish frontier stretched for 1,750 miles, the Poles did not have a ratio of force to space adequate to create even a tenuously stable front, comparable to that on the eastern front in World War I, much less an entrenched stalemate, like that on the western front in the same war.

Better trained and armed and with more competent staffs, the Germans secured concentration in time on September 1, 1939, by advancing simultaneously from the west and the north. With much of the Polish army held back to counterattack, the fully deployed Germans initially made rapid progress. In the south, where the Germans had concentrated and the Poles had their weakest forces, the Germans reached the Vistula River, south of Warsaw, an advance of 140 miles, in nine days. This enabled them to turn north along the west bank of the Vistula and, meeting their armies driving south, reach the rear of the bulk of the Polish troops. Turning the enemy from both sides, the Germans carried out a strategic envelopment. The Germans in the Polish rear readily resisted the disorganized attacks of their adversaries, who sought to recover their communications and reach Warsaw. The campaign ended on September 17 when, by prearrangement, the Russians advanced from the east to claim their share of Poland.

Diagram 10.1. German Strategic Envelopment with Simultaneous Advances

On September 17 the French army completed its mobilization and concentration, ready to face a force of largely Landwehr-type German divisions aided by good permanent fortifications strengthed by antitank barriers. The defeat of Poland and the intervention of Russia caused France to discard any intention for an offensive to aid Poland and to take up a defensive posture instead. Although the armies faced each other, they did not entrench within a few hundred yards and engage in skirmishing and exchange of artillery fire. Instead, as armies not actively campaigning had done for thousands of years, they kept away from each other. The French made the most of this opportunity to train their men. Conditioned by the experience of World War I, the newspapers christened this period of inactivity and absence of contact a "phony war."

In the campaign in Poland, German tanks had proved invaluable, exhibiting a far greater utility than allied tanks had displayed in 1918 against the deep and elaborately fortified German defenses and their dense concentrations of field guns. The vastly larger and much better German air force carried out well the traditional strategic duties of light cavalry, not only in reconnaissance but also in disabling Polish railways and in effective attacks on highway traffic. The German use of motor vehicles for supply and for the movement of troops contributed to their rapid victory, and their fourteen armored or fully motorized divisions played a major role, the significance of which many observers at the time failed to appreciate.

The French and German Armies

Having won in the East, the Germans now faced the French in a campaign that did not begin until May 1940. The peace treaty of 1919 had limited the German army to 100,000 men, and so the Germans lacked the French reserves of weapons and trained manpower. But the Germans had used this interlude for training and forming new divisions, and when the campaign opened, they had 136 divisions, including ten Panzer divisions, deployed against the French. Constrained by Italy's hostile neutrality, the French deployed only ninety-four of their 110 divisions against Germany. But in many essential respects the Germans faced much stronger forces.

Believing in the tactical power of the defense, the Anglo-French allies based their strategy on the assumption of a long war, the effect of a logistic strategy founded on the blockade, and when the British had sufficiently expanded their air force, the bombing of German industrial centers. In no case did the French plan an offensive until the British had gone through the same process of creating a large army, which had taken them the first year and a half of World War I. And the French themselves had much to do to bring their army up to an acceptable standard.

The German occupation of a small part of northern France in 1914 had deprived France of much of its steel industry. To avoid the workings of such an unintended logistic strategy, the French stressed protection of their territory. Since conservation of manpower harmonized with this strategy, the French fortified their new frontier with Germany, one they had not occupied since the Franco-Prussian War. In this case they not only planned to substitute the capital represented by the fortifications for the labor of additional troops to defend the border but also to save the lives of Frenchmen who would have died defending the border had they lacked permanent fortifications.

Strengthening the defenses against Germany proved easy in the east where the Vosges Mountains lay west of the barrier of the Rhine River, but the boundary from the Rhine to Luxembourg offered no such easily defensible obstacles. So French military engineers lined much of this stretch of the border with formidable fortresses that embodied all of the lessons of World War I. Thus France had fortified all of its German frontier, the more vulnerable parts in greater strength. Since in 1914 the plunging fire of heavy howitzers had pierced the gun turrets on Belgian fortifications, the new ones had turrets with armor as much as fifteen inches thick. To protect the turrets from the mining effects of the near miss of a heavy projectile, the engineers surrounded them with rock and concrete and paved this with blocks of cast iron one meter square. Because of mechanical aids for ammunition movement and loading, the fortress guns had a sustained rate of fire much higher than that of field artillery.

With elaborate underground habitation for the garrison, the gas-proof defenses covered barbed wire and antitank barriers with interlocking fire of weapons from machine guns through 135-millimeter guns. These defenses merely provided the first and second line for troops that would dig in among and to the rear of the forts. Since no existing artillery could seriously damage these steel and concrete defenses, the French could, in effect, man their first line strongly, secure against most of the effects of the intense surprise bombardment characteristic of the Hutier system of offense. Any effort to pierce this line, named after the minister of war, André Maginot, must become a protracted struggle in which the defender had the advantage and primacy in artillery would determine the outcome.

The French depended on their artillery, having about 11,000 field guns, approximately 50 percent more guns per division than the Germans. Both armies still used mainly World War I artillery with some improved pieces, retaining the field gun as well as the howitzer. Added to their 5,600 75-millimeter field guns, the French had 6,000 25-millimeter antitank guns. With a muzzle velocity of about 3,000 feet per second, this gun could fire a shot that would pierce any German tank. They supplemented this antitank gun with more than 1,000 new 47-millimeter antitank guns, powerful enough not just to penetrate the armor of any German tank but, hypothetically, for the projectile to continue its trajectory and pierce the armor again on its way through the enemy tank.

Tanks provided another element in French supremacy. Against about 2,600 German tanks the French deployed approximately 3,000. In addition, they had 500 renovated World War I Renault tanks and some tankettes with machine guns. Both sides had armored cars, the Germans somewhat more than the French. French tanks tended to be larger than the German counterparts, the increased size providing much thicker armor and a more powerful gun at some sacrifice in speed. Consider this comparison of the German light tank with the French R–35 light tank, shown in table 10.1. The small German gun had a much higher muzzle velocity than the larger French one but had less chance of piercing the thicker armor of the French tank than the slow-moving projectile from the French gun had of penetrating the German's thinner protection. Both tanks underwent improvements and weight increases before production ceased. The French had another light tank with higher speed and somewhat thinner armor, some of which had a high velocity gun and armor comparable to the R–35.

TABLE 10.1.   Comparison of French
and German Light Tanks

	German	French
Weight (tons)	7.2	9.8
Speed (mph)	25	13
Thickest armor (mm)	30	45
Gun (mm)	20	37

The comparison of medium tanks does not differ, when one matches the German model III with the French S–35 (table 10.2). In 1939 the Germans began equipping their new models of this tank with a short 50-millimeter gun similar

TABLE 10.2. Comparison of French
and German Medium Tanks

	German	French
Weight (tons)	18	20
Speed (mph)	20	25
Thickest armor (mm)	14.5	55
Gun (mm)	37	47

in power to the French 47-millimeter gun, thickened the armor to 30-millimeters, and increased the speed to 25 miles per hour.

The French also had the Char-B, a heavy tank weighing 32 tons, with a speed of 17 miles per hour, armor 60 millimeters thick, and an armament of a 47-millimeter gun in a turret and a 75-millimeter howitzer in the hull. The Germans had nothing comparable in weight, though they did have an 18-ton medium tank with a 75-millimeter howitzer in the turret.

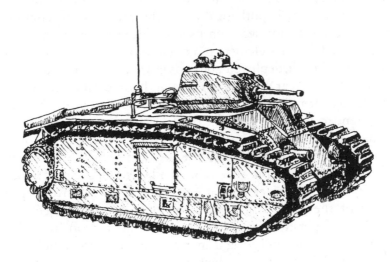

Illustration 10.1. Char-B Tank

These comparisons omit a great deal. For example, the armor on French tanks had more slope and therefore more resistance than the armor on the German tanks. But the French decision to economize on manpower and have smaller crews in their tanks had a major effect on their fighting capacity. The turrets on the German tanks, larger and therefore more vulnerable, provided working space for a crew to man the gun; in French turrets only the commander could work the gun, a difficult task, especially while trying to command and direct the tank.

Although German and French doctrine, like their weapons, had far more similarities than differences, they did vary significantly. Whereas the Germans clung faithfully to, and sought to improve, their decentralized infiltration tactics of 1918, the French retained a preference for centralization of command and control, including the selection of artillery targets. For example, the French version of the infiltration tactics kept subordinate units more responsive to higher headquarters by having the attacking units envelop and attack strong points rather than bypass them in a drive into the hostile rear. The French preference for a tightly controlled, methodical battle reflected their conviction, based on their experiences in 1918, that an attacker could not make a strategic penetration of an enemy front because the defender could always use the better mobility of his reserves to re-establish the entrenched line of defense; the Germans, on the other hand, continued to strive for a breakthrough like those they had achieved in 1918, after which they proposed to aim at "subsequent operations of encirclement."[1]

So French offensive doctrine, which showed links with Marshal Joffre's siege warfare approach, lacked the progressiveness evident in their materiel. Though the French had not renounced the offensive, they clearly recognized the primacy of the defensive and tied their offensive doctrine to the dominance of firepower, which World War I had taught. The Germans did not, of course, discount either the superior power of the defensive or the awesome firepower on which the French army relied and with which they had so amply supplied themselves.

And, in addition to the French, the Germans would have to fight the nine divisions of the British professional army, which had over 600 tanks. Because of its excellent training and weapons, this force, like its much smaller counterpart in 1914, could make a disproportionate contribution. When the French and German armies fought in May 1940, both resembled their 1918 predecessors in that most of their divisions marched on foot and horses drew their artillery. Each army had seven fully motorized infantry divisions in which all soldiers could ride. The Germans also had ten Panzer divisions with 200 to 300 tanks each. The French had three light mechanized divisions developed by the cavalry, three armored divisions created under the auspices of the infantry, and one more of each of these in the process of formation. Both kinds had about 200 tanks. But the French also had five cavalry divisions, which had some tanks, tankettes, armored cars, and motorized infantry as well as horse cavalry. Altogether the Germans had seventeen and the French eighteen fully motorized divisions, the French having a higher proportion because of their smaller army. In addition, each French army had some tanks that it could employ to attach to infantry divisions or use as a unit; the Germans, on the other hand, had reserved all of their limited number of tanks for their Panzer divisions.

The different German concept of the use of the tank had more importance than variations in the quality and quantity of the material. Many of the French leaders continued to view the tank as they had in World War I, as a helper for the infantry and artillery in making a breakthrough. The French, who planned on using their armored divisions in this way on the offensive against an entrenched defense, did envision a more versatile role for the cavalry's light mechanized divisions, including rapid exploitation of a breakthrough. But the withholding of over 1,000 tanks from these two types of armored divisions reflected the dominance in their thinking of the concept of the tank as the partner of the infantry and artillery in a methodical attack. The Germans, however, had concentrated all of their tanks in ten powerful Panzer divisions. Though the German higher commanders, who had thus concentrated their tanks, had no very clear idea of the potentiality of these divisions, their subordinates did, and the existence of these divisions and their concentration in corps provided the German tank forces with an entirely different potential than that of the French.

In the air the Germans did enjoy superiority in materiel. The French had not stressed their air force as long as had the Germans and had aggravated their delay in rebuilding it by a reluctance to place a model in production, knowing that they could have a better airplane if they waited. This meant that the French fought with inferior numbers of largely out-of-date aircraft. The French had about 200 bombers compared to 1,700 German bombers, for example. In reconnaissance and fighter aircraft the French had about seven for every German ten. Most French fighter squadrons had old airplanes barely capable of 300 miles an hour compared with 350 miles an hour for the German fighters. Aircraft from the large wartime production of modern fighters only began reaching the operational squadrons just as the 1940 spring campaign commenced.

British aircraft in France more than doubled the number of allied bombers and added about 20 percent to their fighter strength and somewhat more to their quality. By the spring of 1940 British aircraft production exceeded that of Germany, but the allies would need a year before this preponderance in production could create a parity in the air. The claims of the air enthusiasts and the scoffing of the skeptics had created uncertainty about the effect of aircraft on war. Inferiority in the air caused great unease for many allied commanders, even though they had no definite ideas about the consequences of this disparity.

The French did not expect the Germans to attack along their frontier, anticipating that, as in 1914, they would attempt a turning movement through Belgium. But at the same time the French did not elaborately fortify their Belgian frontier, even though a major French industrial region bordered Belgium. Rather than make this important area a battleground, the French planned to move their forces forward rapidly into Belgium and engage the Germans as far as possible from the French border. Not only did this strategy protect the French industrial region, but also it assured the maximum support of Belgian industry and the powerful army of more than twenty divisions that Belgium had created in the period between the wars. If, as the French suspected, the Germans also moved through Holland, Germany would face ten Dutch divisions. Exclusive of the Dutch, allied dispositions provided about one division for every two miles of the gap between Antwerp and the rugged country of the Ardennes. The experience of World War I had shown that such a high density of force could, if not surprised, resist a breakthrough, even if the enemy had a three-to-one predominance in artillery—and the allies had stronger artillery, nearly twice the German strength without counting the artillery in Belgian forts.

The German generals planned to do exactly what the French expected—repeat their 1914 plan of a giant turning movement through Belgium. Having a healthy respect for allied firepower and the tactical strength of the defense, they made their plan without much enthusiasm, choosing it because a struggle against the Maginot line seemed even less desirable. By bringing in the Dutch and Belgians, this plan would increase the strength of their opponents to at least 136 divisions, a force equal to their 136 divisions but greater in artillery and tanks and having the advantage of the defensive and of Belgian and Dutch fortifications.

But the Germans had one benefit, which they had underestimated: their army possessed better morale and far greater tactical skill than that of their opponents. Part of this primacy rested on a change in the French army. In the 1920s, in part for political and ideological reasons, the French had ceased to rely on an active army cadre filled with reserves on mobilization and instead had created a regular force to train conscripts and another to form a skeleton of regulars upon which most of the reserves would form when activated. This system provided a far less satisfactory organization than an army in which the units trained their own reserves and to which, when recalled, the men returned and found familiar leaders and comrades.

On mobilization the active French divisions, composing a little over half of the divisions not specialized to holding fortifications, gave up two-thirds of their officers, replacing them with reservists. But they retained two-thirds of their noncommissioned officers and 55 percent of their privates, filling these vacancies with reservists. If these divisions could have an opportunity to train together after mobilization, their effectiveness would soon come close to that of the active divisions of 1914, in spite of the very high proportion of reserve officers. In addition to these divisions, the French army formed about a quarter of its field divisions from 23 percent regular officers, drawn from the active divisions, and 17 percent career noncommissioned officers from the same source; reservists constituted the remainder. Reservists supplied virtually all of the privates. A second-class reserve division, much like the old German Landwehr, composed about a fifth of the army's mobile divisions. These, except for about 5 percent regular officers, had only reservists, the oldest of the reservists who had received the briefest active duty training long before. These formations also lacked the experience of serving together and well-trained leadership.

In addition, because of the low birth rate during World War I, between 1935 and 1938 the French army had trained and discharged to the reserve only half as many men as it had in the comparable years before World War I. The larger numbers discharged in earlier years had received only one year of training rather than the two adopted in 1934 and customary from 1905 to 1913. Some reservists serving in the army had originally received their training as sailors or airmen. Thus the organization and training of the French forces in 1939 fell significantly below their standards in 1914. The Germans, on the other hand, though they had barely fifty active divisions, had recruited, trained, and formed these in the traditional manner on a regular cadre and drawn the men from the same geographical region. Most of these had also served in the Polish campaign.

Thus, none of these French divisions, not even the active ones, had the qualities of the conventional German division. French soldiers had all received at least one year of training, but usually they had not drilled nor served much with one another before their 1939 mobilization and did not know their leaders. And the reservists who supplied two-thirds of the officers of the active divisions did not have the skill of regulars nor the familiarity with their fellow officers or noncommissioned officers.

The French active divisions, though composed of seasoned men, had defects not often experienced since the seventeenth century, when military contractors still assembled forces of veterans who often did not know each other or their commanders. And the French army largely lacked the cohesion provided by regional recruiting whose virtues a French Revolutionary soldier had extolled thus: "We would like to serve altogether, for when a soldier is known and loved, defeats are less disastrous and successes more flattering."[2]

In addition to all of the defects of the active divisions, the first level of reserve divisions, with almost all reserve privates and less than a quarter active officers and noncommissioned officers, had fewer experienced leaders and, perhaps more important, fewer professional soldiers as well as reservists who had not served in the same unit together. Lack of prior service together would handicap the officers working with each other as well with the other ranks. In addition to all of the foregoing flaws, the second level of reserve units had an almost total absence of thoroughly trained and experienced leadership.

So this system of separating training from the combat formation deprived a unit, when mobilized, of a sense of community derived either from previous service or from their recruitment from the same village or region. Upon activation, the units of the French army had no unit esprit or cohesion; were unfamiliar with their fellows; and had amateurs filling the majority of command and leadership positions.

The French high command realized these weaknesses of an army characterized by their chief of staff as initially "composed of very excitable reservists" and had resolved that the army must limit its operations to the defensive until the men had seen enough service to give the commanders and soldiers adequate competence and the units a sense of community. The French army's doctrine for the offensive minimized the effects of these deficiencies in their army's personnel because they saw these operations as methodically and deliberately executed, controlled by division and higher headquarters, and dependent on the artillery that, firing from the rear against targets not seen, relied more than the infantry on proficiency acquired through training and less on tactical experience and unit morale. Of course, the lessons of World War I had taught the primacy of the defense and the need for the carefully planned, artillery-dependent attacks, but the manpower system of the French army reinforced these doctrinal decisions by giving the high command little alternative at the outset of operations and almost imposing an initial defensive stance.[3]

The "phony war" provided the French with an invaluable interlude to prepare their army. Serving and training together, the soldiers and their leaders made marked progress in developing their skill, their ability to work together, and their unit cohesiveness. Still, the units had only a brief time compared to those, in the German army, which had existed for a long time and had given their reservists their initial two years of instruction.

The Germans also used this time well. Almost half of the divisons the Germans employed in the spring campaign had received the bulk of their training in a program extending from October 1939 into April 1940. The new units did have a number of battle-seasoned officers and noncommissioned officers transferred from the forces that had fought in Poland. Not only did the Germans rely on the lessons learned in Poland to animate the training of the new units, but also the veteran formations went through a rigorous program of instruction and practice to remedy the deficiencies noted in combat with the Polish army.

But the additional instruction merely increased the value of an incomparable asset: combat in Poland. That campaign accomplished training that even the most elaborate maneuver could not approximate. In addition to the combat knowledge gained by the front-line soldiers, commanders and staffs gained experience moving and fighting large numbers of men in actual conditions. Maneuvers can test communications well and supply arrangements somewhat, but a campaign on a large front against a determined foe nearly equal in numbers and involving opposed advances of 250 miles tested and educated every element in the German forces.

The combat with the Polish army, which cost the Germans 30,000 killed and wounded, provided an opportunity that training had had increasing difficulty in simulating. Artillerymen found peacetime practice of high value because they shot at targets they could not see, exactly as they would in combat. But the infantry, which maneuvered by squad, platoon, and company, could not so nearly simulate combat in training. In the heyday of the linear system, Frederick the Great's infantry, carefully and thoroughly prepared but without previous combat, demonstrated its superiority over Austrian veterans. But practice of firing, of forming, and of marching in alignment presented few differences from combat when compared with the unstereotyped response needed for attack with infiltration tactics and in a defensive relying on some movement.

Combat with the Poles thus provided an occasion for acquiring skill unavailable in any other way. The two army group commanders who had the principal responsibility in the campaign against France had led the German army groups in Poland and four of the five commanders of the key armies had the same assignments in Poland. No French commander had a comparable background, and this fundamental difference affected all of the corps and divisions that served in Poland. When the Germans attacked, they displayed a much greater level of operational skill, much of it due to their campaign in Poland.

Yet the training the Germans received in actual combat would be a perishable asset because when they fought in Belgium, the allies would quickly acquire the same advantages, an opportunity that their strength and firepower seemed destined to assure them because these appeared certain to halt the German advance.

French and German Plans

After Germany defeated Poland, Adolf Hitler, to the dismay of his generals, ordered an immediate attack on France through Belgium and Holland. With many troops still inadequately trained and motorized equipment undergoing repair after the Polish campaign, the leaders of the German army felt unready to take on the French. By postponements, obstruction, and procrastination, and with the help of some bad weather, they managed to defer the offensive until May 1940. The plan of campaign drawn up in the fall had envisioned a limited objective, which they would attain by a drive into Belgium with the main forces pushing west toward Ghent and the coast. It did not occur to the German general staff to attempt a decisive campaign, such as their 1914 plan had envisioned. The four years' duration of World War I, after opening operations with Schlieffen's abortive decisive campaign, an understanding of the supremacy of the defensive, and an appreciation of the strength of the French army kept the German staff from considering any initial objective more ambitious than a push to the coast and the occupation of most of Belgium.

French plans, as finally perfected by General Maurice Gamelin, the French chief of staff, placed the ten high-quality divisions of the French First Army on the twenty miles of the front north of Namur with the nine divisions of the

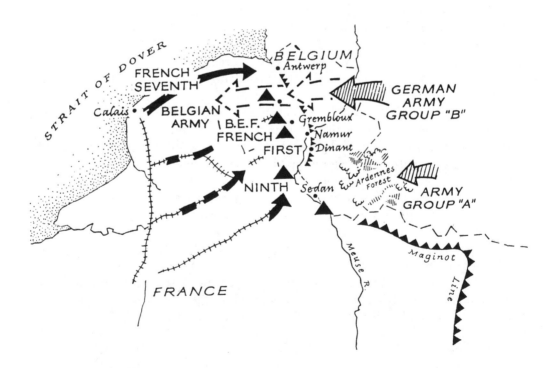

Diagram 10.2. First French and German Plans

British Expeditionary Force and fourteen divisions from the Belgian army covering the remaining distance, over forty miles, to Antwerp. Other Belgian divisions, retreating from forward positions, could expect to strengthen this force. In addition, the French Seventh Army, with seven divisions, would advance along the coast beyond Antwerp, where it would link up with the Dutch and have a position on the flank of the German advance. Since General Gamelin had served on Marshal Joffre's staff in 1914, the role of the Seventh Army may have owed some of its inspiration to Joffre's creation of the Sixth Army and his placing it on the flank of the German advance in 1914. Expecting the French forces to move rapidly to meet the Germans as far east as possible, the plan called for the French, British, and Belgian armies to hold on the line of the Dyle River between Antwerp and Namur.

South of Namur, Gamelin planned for his Ninth Army to move forward to hold the formidable barrier of the Meuse River from the French frontier north to Namur. He expected the Germans, advancing through the hilly and forested Ardennes region, to take more than a week to reach the Meuse and to arrive in very modest force because of few roads and the mountainous and forested terrain of the Ardennes. Since the Ninth Army would face comparatively weak opposition and have ample time to entrench the line of the Meuse, it had less than half the number of divisions per mile allocated to the other allied armies advancing to meet the Germans. The Germans as well as the French had long acknowledged that the terrain of the Ardennes did seriously handicap, if not preclude, the movement of large forces. The French Second Army, already in position, held the French-Belgian frontier, forming a link between the Ninth Army and the soldiers posted along the Maginot line on the Luxembourg border. All of the armies formed the French first army group under General Billotte.

Most of the remainder of the French army deployed against Germany lined the French-German frontier and watched for a possible German move through Switzerland. The distribution of men did not suit Gamelin's subordinate, General Alphonse Georges, who commanded the forces facing Germany.

The two French generals, Gamelin, sixty-eight years of age, and Georges, sixty-five, disagreed about Gamelin's plan and disliked each other. They differed in other respects, too. Gamelin, after he had left Marshal Joffre's staff, had successfully commanded a division and briefly a corps. Georges, on the other hand, had been wounded leading a battalion in France in 1914 and spent most of the war in staff assignments. While Gamelin's scholarly manner and aloof air kept many at a distance, Georges had a wide circle of acquaintances and admirers. The men who knew him regarded the energetic and outspoken Georges as well fitted for command, in spite of a near-fatal incident at Marseille in 1934, when Georges and the French foreign minister greeted the king of Yugoslavia. Having met the king at the dock, the three drove slowly through the streets in an open car, receiving the cheers of the welcoming crowd; an assassin stepped up to the car and shot both the king and foreign minister. With the car stopped, Georges courageously stepped out and, when he grappled with the gunman, the man shot him several times in the body. The doctors saved only Georges, and the general never seemed fully to recover.

Georges believed that the army group covering the Maginot line and the Rhine had too many divisions, but when he could not persuade their army group commander to part with some, he did not order him to give up any of his divisions. But Georges's unease extended to the whole scheme that committed so many troops and left so few for a subtracted reserve.

As a result of these commitments, Gamelin had three divisions that he might employ anywhere and Georges had twenty-one divisions as a subtracted reserve. Five of these, including an additional armored division in the process of formation, had not reached a state of full combat readiness. Of the twenty-one, the plan posted six as a reserve for the Belgian front and five near Switzerland in case the Germans should attempt to turn the frontier fortifications by entering that country. This left only ten divisions, including one motorized and two armored, placed along the center of the long line between Switzerland and the sea.

Gamelin felt no apprehension because the whole distribution of forces, including earmarking so many reserves, recalled the occasion in World War I in which Gamelin had played a significant role at Joffre's headquarters in 1914. His experience then had shown him that every soldier not irrevocably committed in combat constituted a reserve, a concept Joffre had used when he moved troops from the Lorraine and Alsace fronts to oppose the German turning movement and create the Sixth Army. Knowing that the railways could transport a division anywhere in France in four days and having helped to employ these strategically offensive troops in 1914, Gamelin apparently dismissed the concerns of a 1914 battalion commander.

And Gamelin's plan fit the circumstances. In a long war, conservation of Belgian territory, manpower, and resources would prove important, and only prompt action and strong armies could do this. The other terrain suitable for large forces, that between the Rhine and Luxembourg, had the powerful fortifications of the Maginot line, well supported by the mobile armies posted there. Adequate troops guarded the less heavily fortified areas unsuitable for large forces, the Rhine frontier and the Vosges in the south and the Ardennes region between the Maginot line and the level, prospective battleground in Belgium.

That the Germans initially planned to do exactly what Gamelin expected and shared his confidence in the ability of the French to defend successfully endorsed Gamelin's plan and would have completely belied Georges's misgivings had the Germans not radically changed their whole approach to the campaign.

The New German Offensive Plan

Two of the ablest soldiers of World War II played a major role in changing the German plan. When General Gerd von Rundstedt, commander of the southern army group in the Polish campaign, took over Army Group A facing the Ardennes, he had as his chief of staff General Erich von Manstein. In their service in World War II, both men established well-deserved reputations for great skill in operations. The aristocratic Runstedt, recalled from retirement at age sixty-three to command an army group in Poland, had already displayed his skill, for which his peacetime career and World War I service as chief of an army corps staff fighting the Russians had prepared him. Also a staff officer in World War I, Manstein, ten years Runstedt's junior, had served on the general staff of the army and as Runstedt's chief of staff in the Polish campaign during which their army group had distinguished itself.

When Runstedt and Manstein learned of the plan for the offensive into Belgium, Manstein prepared and Runstedt signed a series of memoranda of protest, proposing to shift strength to Army Group A and envisioning the possibility of breaking through to the south and west and cutting off the allied forces in Belgium.

In November Manstein conferred with General Heinz Guderian, who, as a lieutenant on staff and school assignments in the 1920s, had studied the role of tanks and developed profound ideas about their employment. He had risen rapidly in the 1930s, had published a book on tank warfare in 1937, and had become the German army's leading exponent of the role of the Panzer division. Having begun World War I in charge of a wireless detachment, Guderian had capitalized on this background to ensure that German tanks had an excellent system of radio communication. The superb articulation, which this assured, helped the Panzer divisions realize Guderian's aspirations for them.

Initiating the conference to learn whether Panzer divisions could move through the Ardennes, infantryman Manstein learned a great deal from Guderian's vision of the deep penetration possible if Panzer divisions broke through. Manstein's new memoranda reflected what he learned from Guderian but also led to the importunate chief of staff's reassignment to command a distant corps.

A piece of apparent bad luck helped Manstein and the Germans. A German officer carrying parts of the plan for the campaign into Belgium visited the officers' club at an air base and, in the convivial atmosphere of the bar, accepted an invitation for air rather than rail transportation to his conference. Lost in bad weather the next morning, the officer's light plane landed in Belgium; when his cigarette lighter did not light, he failed to destroy all of his plans before the Belgian army seized them and notified the French.

This incident and its compromise of the German plans helped Hitler decide to postpone his offensive and gave the German staff both the time and additional motivation to study their concept for the offensive. In their reexamination, Manstein's ideas looked better. At the same time, Hitler learned of Manstein's proposals and promptly sent for the author, as Hitler recognized a concept similar to one he had had for some time but which the former First World War corporal could not clearly formulate. Embracing Manstein's ideas, Hitler immediately ordered the staff to draw up an appropriate operational plan.

The now receptive staff executed a design that concentrated forty-five divisions, including seven of the army's ten Panzer divisions, with Army Group A opposite the Ardennes. Army Group B, carrying out the original scheme with only twenty-nine divisions, provided a distraction to convince the French that the Germans were launching their main attack on the terrain north of Namur. The new plan devoted much attention to the question of breaking through along the Meuse, where the Panzer divisions would meet French troops already dug in. Many German generals did not believe that they could cross the Meuse unaided and thought they would have to wait until the infantry completed their nine-day march and, with artillery support, could conduct an orthodox breakthrough of the kind perfected during World War I. But while many German generals thus made the same assumptions as General Gamelin, others, like General Guderian, believed that the Panzer divisions could cross the Meuse in the face of entrenched resistance.

In fact, the staff had given so much attention to the surprise concentration and to solving the problem of the breakthrough that they included nothing about the action that would follow success. In a way, World War I had made the penetration of the continuous front so difficult, so elusive an achievement, that it had almost become an end in itself. The forces carrying out the breakthrough could turn south against the French armies along the Maginot line, or

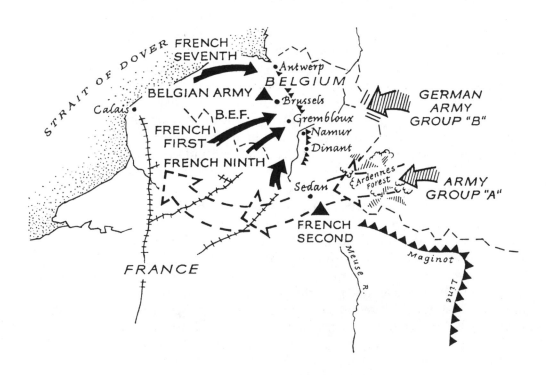

Diagram 10.3. Final French and German Plans

west toward the English channel, or even drive toward Paris. But in the absence of explicit directions, the Panzer leaders expected to follow von Manstein's original objective and aim for the coast.

The German Breakthrough in May 1940

Early on May 10, 1940, the Germans began their offensive, attacking Holland and Belgium according to the strategy painstakingly evolved during the period since the Polish campaign. Dismissing intelligence that the Germans had concentrated most of their Panzer and infantry divisions opposite the Ardennes, General Gamelin ordered his armies forward into Belgium. Unlike the gloomy General Georges, the smilingly confident Gamelin hummed military music as he gave the order to counter the German offensive. The motorized units of the French Seventh and First armies reached their objectives the first day, the foot troops marching slowly behind, with some tanks moving on railway flat cars.

The German air force opened the campaign by striking fifty French airfields, destroying four and damaging sixty French aircraft in addition to inflicting losses on British, Belgian, and Dutch planes. The second day such assaults destroyed three French planes and damaged a few others. These attacks cost the Germans heavily: one flight lost seven of twenty-one medium bombers to French fighters and one to antiaircraft fire. The main German air effort seemed concentrated against the Dutch, as the allied troops advanced into Belgium unmolested.

The German plan to avoid attack on the fortified French border confined the initial fighting to combat with the Dutch army and to overcoming Belgian frontier fortifications. The main armies would not meet in Belgium until both had reached the Dyle line. Even less fighting occurred in the Ardennes as most Belgian forces withdrew northward, leaving the Germans a march of as much as sixty-five miles from the Belgian border to the Meuse River. Thus the Germans faced no determined opposition in the uneven and forested Ardennes, terrain quite unsuitable for the large numbers of tanks that led their drive.

Since seven Panzer, three motorized, and thirty-five infantry divisions had to pass through an area of inadequate roads, the German staffs had planned with exceptional thoroughness, and the excellently prepared units executed the movement so expertly that the thousands of vehicles proceeded on their ambitious schedule with few difficulties.

The German columns entering Belgium presented a tempting target for the few allied bombers, and the British promptly attacked at low altitude with their obsolete single-engine Fairey Battle attack bomber. On May 10 the British lost to antiaircraft or German fighter planes thirteen bombers. The next day the British squandered all eight of their aircraft against the same target, and they and the Belgians suffered heavy losses in strikes on German columns farther north.

On May 12 the experience of six French Breguet light bombers illustrated the difficulties of the attackers. Coming in at tree-top level, these fast, modern

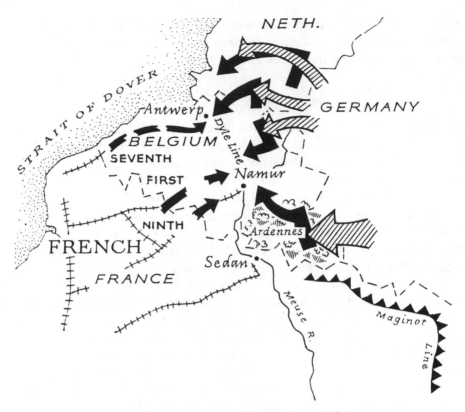

Diagram 10.4. German Advance into Belgium

aircraft assaulted a German column on the march. But with a torrent of shells German 20- and 37-millimeter automatic antiaircraft guns shot down five of the six and disabled the one that succeeded in returning to its base. One plane dropped bombs on truckloads of German soldiers, and another French bomber crashed into the German column. The German stress on air defense made their columns virtually invulnerable to allied air attack, even without the aid of the fighter planes that so successfully protected the huge concentration marching into the Ardennes. Later French raids from higher attitude proved safer for the French but inflicted little damage on the Germans.

The fighter airplane compounded the problems of the bomber, as the fate of twelve outdated German J–87 dive bombers graphically showed. Effective as bombers in spite of their fixed landing gear and low speed, these planes, when returning from a raid, met five slow French fighters. The French fighters, with a 100-mile-an-hour superiority in speed and an armament of a 20-millimeter cannon and two machine guns, shot down all of the even more outmoded German bombers and immediately engaged and drove back a group of outward-bound dive bombers, all without the loss of a single fighter.

Although these incidents exaggerate the plight of air attackers, they do illustrate the effectiveness of an adequate antiaircraft defense manned by well-trained gunners and confirm the analogy of light infantry opposing light cavalry.

These air operations also reaffirmed the experience of World War I, which had amply demonstrated the vulnerability of bombing and reconnaissance planes to attack by fighters, planes specifically designed to fight other aircraft.

Meanwhile, the movements of the armies of both adversaries developed according to their plans, except that German success against Belgian and Dutch defenses committed French troops earlier than the French had expected. To hold the Germans until the French First Army completely closed up to the Dyle, its two armored divisions proceeded east of the Dyle where they engaged the first of the two stronger German Panzer divisions pushing toward the Dyle. The inconclusive result of this first major battle between tanks halted the German movement. Again, defense exhibited its predominance in combat between the same weapon systems. Farther north, when the French Seventh Army reached Dutch territory and found the Dutch army driven back, it withdrew toward Antwerp, ending Gamelin's hope of having an army in a flank position to threaten the German advance.

But on May 13 and 14 Belgian operations followed Gamelin's plans with the French armored divisions falling back before their stronger German counterparts but holding the Dyle line until all of the French First Army had arrived on the 14th. With powerful allied forces digging in from Antwerp to Namur, the Germans halted, with their initial, tentative attacks repulsed. The situation had apparently stabilized.

In the Ardennes, however, events conformed to the German plan. Protected against allied aircraft, the German march through the Ardennes encountered only limited resistance from the five French cavalry divisions sent to delay the progress of a force the French expected but that they had believed would consist largely of infantry in fairly limited numbers. Basically reconnaissance units, the cavalry divisions included artillery, troops carried in trucks, tankettes with machine guns, and a few light tanks as well as horse cavalry. These weak formations delayed the Germans only briefly, largely because the huge mass of Panzer divisions almost automatically turned or enveloped any positions the French took up. For example, tanks exhibited their tactically offensive qualities when, halted by French 105-millimeter howitzers, they passed around the flank and attacked the rear of these guns, so dangerous to the small, thinly armored German tanks. Even in unsuitable country, tanks proved well adapted to executing the infiltration tactics German infantry had learned so well.

By the evening of May 12, after three days of marching, the Germans had reached the Meuse. During the night of May 12-13 the Panzer division vehicles turned on their headlights and closed rapidly to the river, planning to attack the next day. Two Panzer divisions would reach the Meuse in the north at Dinant, two in the middle at Monthermé, and three in the south at Sedan. Although Georges and Gamelin realized that they faced a stronger than expected force in the Ardennes, neither yet comprehended the German plan. On May 11 Georges ordered his reserves forward as originally planned but did send five infantry and two armored divisions to the Second Army, basing this action on his earlier

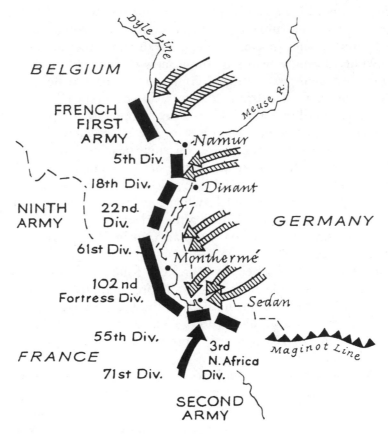

Diagram 10.5. Panzer Divisions Reach the Meuse

misgivings about the weakness of the center of his array of armies. He had
strengthened the Second Army because he doubtless assumed that the Germans
would direct any turning effort toward the flank of the Second Army, with the
objective of reaching the rear of the forces facing the German frontier, thus
attempting the same maneuver they had tried in 1914.

By his commitment of his reserves, Georges began to strengthen the southern
part of the Meuse, a part of the front where, though Georges did not realize it,
he had even less force than planned. The French held the area around Sedan,
toward which three Panzer divisions moved, with two of their second-class
reserve divisions. Not only did the units have a mere twenty regular officers, but
their morale and training had serious deficiencies. The effectiveness of both of
these divisions, composed of men who had received only a year and a half of
training more than a decade earlier, depended on the success of the training
program they had undergone since their mobilization in September. The quality
of these programs varied among the different units, and those of the two divisions
at Sedan had failed to realize most of the potential benefit of the seven months
available for training before May 10. In addition, these units did not have their

full complement of antitank and antiaircraft guns. Even had they received good training, these formations had as their only mission the guarding of quiet sectors of the front.

Farther north, near Dinant, an active motorized division connected the Ninth Army with the right of the First Army north of Namur and had two reserve divisions of the first class marching to take up positions on its right. These better quality reserve divisions had 23 percent regular officers and 17 percent regular noncommissioned officers. Although both of these divisions had a long way to go to reach their destination, they had counted on ample time, since the French did not expect the Germans on the Meuse before May 16 nor anticipate that they could launch an attack until even later. But the Germans had arrived earlier, and, in spite of one division's rushing two of its battalions forward by truck, all French troops had not arrived by the time the Germans reached the Meuse. On the morning of May 13, three of the Ninth Army's divisions had only nineteen of their twenty-seven battalions on the Meuse, which the French held with less than one division for every six miles of front, even counting a weak cavalry division, a minimum ratio of force to space by the standards of World War I's western front. Exclusive of the cavalry divisions, one division had fifteen miles to hold, another twenty-one. French doctrine allowed no less than one division for every five or six miles of front.

Against these inadequate forces at Dinant on a hastily and incompletely occupied line, the two German Panzer divisions gained an immediate and important victory. Even on the night before their assault on May 13, German soldiers, under the command of the able and aggressive General Erwin Rommel, had already crossed the river. All of May 13 the expertly led, combat-seasoned Germans pushed men across the Meuse, supporting their attacks with artillery and with the fire of tank guns from the river bank. Courage, competence, and persistence enabled the Germans to establish themselves on the far bank; the engineers built pontoons and began ferrying antitank guns and tanks to the other side.

By the end of May 13 the Germans had pushed two miles inland from the Meuse and held three miles of the bank, though they still had to cope with pockets of French resistance within this perimeter. Two poorly organized French counterattacks, one with tanks from a cavalry division, failed to drive back the Germans. The next day the Germans withstood another feeble counterattack while expanding their bridgehead and using their newly completed pontoon bridge to bring tanks across. Three infantry divisions then joined the two Panzer divisions in enlarging the bridgehead to a depth of ten to twelve miles. Even though the French had brought up another division, the swelling of the bridgehead so extended their lines that they had barely one division for each ten miles of front.

Having abandoned the river line at Dinant, the thinly stretched French forces now faced the menace of a breakthrough by an enemy whose two Panzer divisions included more than 500 tanks. The only reserve at hand, the French

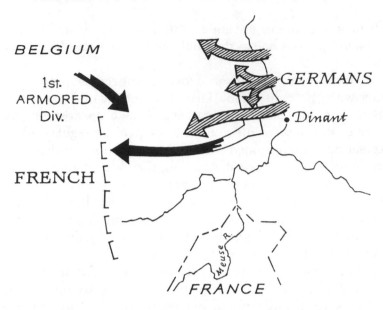

Diagram 10.6. French Fall Back from Dinant

First Armored Division, had moved up slowly, initially because of delays imposed by German air attacks on the railways, then by a wait pending a decision to commit it at Dinant or keep it in support of the Dyle defenders, and finally by slow staff work and clumsy arrangements for fuel supplies. By the evening of May 14 the division had reached a position to counterattack the next day, but by then it faced a stronger enemy, which had added to a victorious Polish combat background the daring and well-conducted crossing of the Meuse.

In contrast, to the south around Monthermé, events conformed to the French plan. Here, on May 13 one of the two German Panzer divisions tried without success to cross the river; it was joined on the 14th by two infantry divisions just to the south whose efforts to cross also failed. The French fortress division, an active unit which held the middle sector of the Meuse, had occupied its position since the beginning of the war. These well-trained soldiers had the advantage of thorough familiarity with their positions, the aid of good fortifications along the river bank, and excellent points of observation for artillery. When the German infantry tried to cross in rubber boats, French machine guns and well-directed artillery fire turned them back, puncturing their boats when it did not kill or wound the occupants. In two days a few Germans reached the far bank but maintained themselves only precariously against French artillery fire and counterattacks.

Lacking surprise or supremacy in artillery, the Germans experienced no better success than soldiers in World War I in attacking adequately defended lines under similar circumstances. Dug in well, these few Frenchmen, representative of the active divisions in the French army, showed that on familiar ground in a fortified defense, soldiers sufficiently trained but lacking in combat experience could perform well. And this these defenders of the Meuse did when their artillery followed their observers' directions and the machine gunners swept the river from concrete emplacements and well-concealed, entrenched strong points. The German primacy in tactical skill, largely derived from the Polish campaign, availed them little. Neither could the numerous tanks of the Germans help them against the barrier of the Meuse.

But in the south, near Sedan, even greater success rewarded German efforts than they had enjoyed in the north near Dinant. Here three Panzer divisions planned to cross the river against the resistance of the two poorly trained second-class reserve divisions. Each of the three Panzer divisions planned assaults, but the central division, the First, had an engineer and four infantry battalions added to its three infantry battalions as well as the support of artillery from the other two divisions. Only one of the French divisions, the Fifty-fifth, would receive the blow of all three Panzer divisions, which the corps commander, the armor specialist, General Guderian, planned for 3:00 P.M. on May 13.

The French corps commander did not believe that the Germans would attack on May 13 because he thought that they would await the arrival of their heavy artillery. But General Guderian, an exponent of tactical aviation as well as of the Panzer division, had the support of 300 high-level bombers, 200 dive bombers, and 200 fighters. Because he could substitute these for heavy artillery, he planned to execute immediately a classic World War I assault. Against the ensuing, powerful German air effort, the French had only enough fighter aircraft to fly 250 sorties over the entire front of the Ninth and Second armies, losing twelve aircraft and believing that they shot down twenty-one German airplanes.

Before the German infantry attempted to launch its rubber boats across the sixty yards of the Meuse, the German medium bombers had begun their raids from a high altitude at 7:00 A.M. At noon 120 dive bombers each dropped two 500-pound bombs. Since a 500-pound bomb weighed as much as a 10-inch shell and contained far more explosive than the thick-walled shell, the aircraft subjected the French troops to a bombardment equivalent to that from many batteries of super-heavy artillery. Though the bombers lacked the accuracy of the artillery, their huge bombs did considerable damage, raised clouds of dust, panicked many of the older French reservists who composed the division, and drove a large number of artillerymen to seek cover rather than continue their fire against the Germans concentrated on the east bank of the Meuse. This intensified air bombardment continued for three hours and then shifted toward the rear of the French positions.

The 3:00 P.M. attack of the First Panzer division met with immediate success. Opposed only by a few desultory artillery rounds and weak machine gun fire, the proficient and skillfully led German infantry crossed easily and quickly overwhelmed the outnumbered and thoroughly demoralized defenders. By 4:00 P.M. German engineers had a ferry in operation and had begun their bridge a half hour later. The assaults of the other two Panzer divisions, unsupported by the air force, failed to get more than a few men across, facing entrenched defenders and strong artillery fire. But the First Panzer division made such progress during the night that the Germans had bridgeheads three miles wide and four to six miles deep.

The Germans owed part of their achievement to the disintegration of much of the French Fifty-fifth Division. Entering their first combat with deficient morale and cohesion and ineffective training, many of the French soldiers fled in panic during the night after facing the powerful air bombardment and the quick triumph of the First Panzer Division's attack. Mistaking their own tanks for German, the fleeing soldiers of the Fifty-fifth spread demoralization in the rear and to the Seventy-first Division on their right, which had faced neither bombardment, attack, nor defeat in its defense of the river and had even used its reinforced artillery to help the Fifty-fifth.

While the disheartened French troops fell back during the night and early morning of May 13–14, General Georges learned of the extent of the disaster. At 3:00 A.M. on the 14th visitors to his headquarters found him in tears at the realization of the collapse of the front, a reverse coming on top of the unexpectedly rapid German advances in the Ardennes and in Belgium and Holland. Even though he had just ordered two divisions to the right of the Ninth Army and had accelerated the move of the armored division already ordered, he knew that these and most of the reserves previously directed to the Second Army could not intervene on May 14. Although Georges looked physically sick on the 14th and his conduct betrayed the strain he felt, he and his staff continued to function; General Gamelin, who emulated Marshal Joffre's fabled calm demeanor, did not feel it necessary to interfere. On May 14 Georges, having exhausted the bulk of his reserves, ordered the withdrawal of a corps and a division from the forces guarding the fortified Franco-German frontier.

Events at the Sedan bridgehead on May 14 fully justified General Georges's early morning apprehensions, even though the French corps commander soon

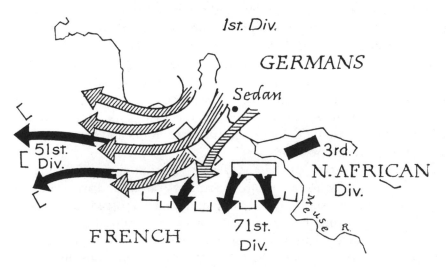

Diagram 10.7. Panzer Breakthrough at Sedan

counterattacked with an infantry regiment supported by a tank battalion. The French initially succeeded against German infantry and tanks, but German tanks counterattacked and drove back the French infantry and armor with heavy losses. And this counterattack turned out to be but a prelude to the break-up of the Seventy-first Division, which, deserted by its sick commander, melted away.

Grasping the French weakness, the forceful and perspicacious General Guderian ordered two of his three Panzer divisions to launch an offensive westward, leaving his infantry regiment and one Panzer division to protect his bridgehead from a weak counterattack by local reserves and the assault expected from strong French forces that the German air force had observed heading toward Sedan by road and rail and whose movement their air strikes had failed to halt. Although the Panzer divisions attacking westward faced a second-class reserve division, a colonial brigade of professional troops, and a cavalry division that the French had pushed into this breach, the Germans succeeded in pushing west more than six miles, and during the night both Panzer divisions completed moving up, ready to resume their assault on the morning of the 15th. Guderian's commanding officer, anxious about a French counterattack from the south, demurred at such a daring advance, but Guderian prevailed.

Well might the German commander have displayed fear, for the allied air forces had shown during the day how seriously they regarded the crossing of the Meuse at Sedan. During May 14 the allies carried out five separate raids against the bridges at Sedan, one with sixty-seven obsolete, single-engine, British bombers having an escort of more than that number of allied fighters. But German antiaircraft guns and fighter airplanes inflicted terrible losses, destroying thirty-two British and seven French bombers and probably forty of the fighters involved. The bridges were difficult to hit and survived with only minor damage. The losses of the day virtually crippled the allied bomber forces. Since, with an ample output of fighter aircraft, they could replace their fighter losses, allied air capabilities became essentially one of defense against German aircraft, though the fighters, particularly the cannon-armed French, carrying small bombs, could still attack vehicles and troops on the roads.

On May 15, the sixth day of the German offensive, the French faced an entirely new situation, with substantial German footholds around both Sedan and Dinant. The expansion of the bridgeheads had thinned the French defensive front and reduced their ratio of force to space, and the Germans had all of the tanks of their Panzer divisions over the river, 800 at Sedan and over 500 at Dinant. Such a concentration of tanks could not fail to overwhelm a thinly held front protected by only the hastiest of entrenchments, few antitank guns or mines, and no special physical barriers. Further, with initiative and superior forces, the Germans within each bridgehead possessed interior lines and the ability to concentrate against one face of their salients while standing on the defensive on the other two.

At Sedan General Guderian exploited this position to continue his attack westward on May 15, overcoming determined resistance. Directly in his path, the colonial brigade resisted until it lost 30 percent of its men, the Germans killing two of its colonels and capturing the third. Farther south an ably commanded, thoroughly trained French active regiment, part of the reserves dispatched two days earlier, defended all day, retreating only after losing a third of its force and, in disabling twenty German tanks, all of its antitank guns. In its defense it had the aid of three immobilized French 32-ton Char-B tanks, almost twice the size of the biggest German tank, which, many times in the campaign, demonstrated both the wisdom of the French policy of armoring their tanks well and the inadequacy of the Germans' 37-millimeter antitank gun. The defeat of these units let the Germans through, enabling them to turn the line held to the north by a second-class reserve division. Against such competently led combat veterans with 500 tanks, the thin line of French defenders failed; General Guderian's Panzer divisions broke completely through to the west on May 15.

At the same time that Guderian's concentration pierced the improvised French defense, his remaining forces held the southern flank of his bridgehead against a counterattack on which General Georges had insisted the day before. This tardy offensive, conducted by a motorized and an armored division that Georges had ordered from his reserve on May 11, would have had little chance of success against a division and a half of German combat veterans even if the French had not so mismanaged it that the corps commander relieved the general leading the armored division. Schooled for prepared, methodical attacks, the French had difficulty improvising. On May 16 a German motorized division arrived to take over these defensive duties, releasing the Panzer division to join Guderian's other two and reinforce the drive westward.

On the 15th, in the vicinity of Dinant, the Germans enjoyed a victory similar to theirs at Sedan as their two Panzer divisions drove due west while their three infantry divisions held the bridgehead. These Panzer divisions, with the dynamic General Rommel leading his from the front, conducted their offensive against French forces that were in the process of withdrawing from the Meuse to establish a new line about fifteen miles in the rear. But the Panzer divisions advanced so rapidly that the lead German division caught their most serious opposition, the French First Armored Division, refueling. Inflicting heavy losses on the French tanks of this active division, the lead Panzer division pushed on, leaving it to the following Panzer division to complete the virtual destruction of the French unit. The 150 French tanks proved formidable, but the more experienced Germans, with 500 tanks in their two divisions, won fairly easily, suffering losses of less than 20 percent of their tanks engaged compared with nearly 80 percent for the French. In spite of facing French heavy tanks with basically invulnerable frontal armor, the Germans evened the odds with their exceptional skill, and the loss rates approximated those expected according to Lanchester's N-square law.

Meanwhile, the French withdrawal from the Meuse opened the way for the two Panzer divisions, which had been stymied for two days trying to cross the central Meuse near Monthermé. The French fell back to protect their flanks, and their retreating infantry proved very vulnerable to the advancing German tanks. Just as heavy cavalry of old could overtake and ride down light infantry, so did the German tanks overwhelm marching French infantry and wreck their guns and transport along the roads. The speed of the advance of the tanks and their accompanying motorized infantry and artillery constantly took the French by surprise, in the same way as the tanks from the force pushing on from Dinant had caught the French tanks refueling. In one day the German force from the central Meuse moved forward thirty-seven miles.

Just as German aircraft had struck at French forces marching to reinforce the front, so did the German light cavalry of the air also attack retreating French men and vehicles with much of the same effectiveness as the primitive British aircraft against the retreating Turks in 1918. Having displayed their tactical value in attacking retreating troops after battle and in their bombing at Sedan of French forces deficient in antiaircraft defenses, from the beginning of the campaign the German air force carried out the traditional strategic role of light cavalry when they penetrated deep in the French rear to raid the railways and soldiers and vehicles using the roads.

Diagram 10.8. German Breakthrough

The Causes of the German Breakthrough

The Germans accomplished the crossing of the Meuse by concentrating against the point of allied weakness opposite the Ardennes, a strategic surprise facilitated, if not made possible, by the distraction provided by the strong attack through Holland and Belgium. Of course, the conviction, initially shared by both high commands, that the Ardennes did not provide a suitable route of invasion also contributed to the unexpected character of the move.

But the German plan depended on carrying out an assault against the Meuse with infantry under traditional World War I conditions of the primacy of the defensive. Without overwhelming predominance in artillery or tactical surprise, they succeeded because of the comparatively low density of French force to the length of the front and the skill with which the Germans applied the principles of infiltration tactics against the strong points with which the French defended their shallow line. Here the splendid training of the German troops and the combat experience of many of them made a perhaps decisive contribution. Although aircraft playing the role of artillery made possible the quick victory at Sedan, the forces at Dinant won without any significant help from their bombers. The only German failure occurred on the middle on the Meuse line. Here the Germans met, in well-prepared defensive positions, a French active division that had a third of its officers and a majority of the enlisted strength serving together on active duty during peace, six months of training together, and thorough familiarity with its strong position.

When the successful German attacks had driven the French back several miles, an impressive advance by the standards of World War I, the attackers did not, as had their fathers in 1918, face the obstacle of inferior mobility compared with the defenders, who had undamaged roads and ready access to rail transportation. Neither elaborate trenches nor intense bombardment had seriously impeded the attackers' road mobility, and the Germans had enough tracked and wheeled transport both to move and supply their Panzer divisions. Thus they had mobility equal to or better than the defenders' and would not repeat their World War I experience of breaking through only to find that the enemy had moved more quickly and reconstituted the front.

But the contrast with World War I did not end here. Once the German infantry had captured the far bank of the Meuse and the engineers had built a bridge over that perfect antitank barrier, the formidable German concentration of tanks on this front altered the tactical situation dramatically. With so many tanks on such narrow frontages the Germans could readily overwhelm French antitank guns and field artillery, unaided as they were by antitank barriers or mines. In addition, tanks had ideal attributes to apply the principles of infiltration tactics by concentrating against weak points, making deep tactical penetrations, breaking the way for the infantry, and taking strong points in the flank and rear. With their superb mobility, machine gun and cannon, 360-degree traverse of the turret, and their ability to move and fight in the same formation, tanks constituted the perfect tactically offensive troops. Radio communication among the tanks gave them an articulation hitherto unknown in war.

The crossing of the Meuse by the tanks of the German Panzer divisions gave the Germans such an overwhelming tactical advantage that they broke through the French front in three places. The next day the Germans began to exploit a breakthrough of the front. They had attained this in March 1918 but had achieved no strategic result because the allies had used their greater strategic mobility to halt the German advance even though it penetrated forty miles. There the French and British had confronted the Germans with a new line created by reserves brought by rail.

In May 1940 the situation differed completely. By the time the Germans had established the two bridgeheads from which they could readily advance, the French had not ordered any reserves by rail in numbers adequate to deal with the strategic menace the Germans presented. And the French had not directed even those reserves en route so that they could resist the westward-facing German armored corps.

In addition to wheel or track mobility for all of their forces, including the infantry's antitank and antiaircraft guns, the Germans had the advantage of their strategic situation with most of the uncommitted French troops stationed to the east along the German border. Because French reserves lay to the east of the westward-advancing Germans, the reserves would have to come from a direction that compelled them to overtake the Germans to oppose them in front. This proved an impossible task for the rail-borne soldiers when the enemy rode on paved French roads. So French divisions would arrive not in front of the Germans but on their flank. Although this placed them in a threatening position from the German point of view, the French would have to take the offensive to exploit it. In 1918 they had needed only to defend to thwart the breakthrough. And the French commanders did not believe that their troops were yet prepared for a methodical, much less an improvised, offensive.

Thus the attackers' better mobility and the disposition of the defenders' reserves doomed the French to employing the tactical offensive rather than having it as their advantage as in 1918. This situation, of course, typified that imposed on the defenders by a strategic turning movement.

The German Turning Movement

With the deep German advances of May 15 the French high commanders realized that they faced a breakthrough. To reconstitute the front, the French needed to know in what direction the Germans planned to move. Generals Georges and Gamelin, remembering World War I, assumed that the Germans would proceed to take in the rear the armies facing the German frontier. For this reason, when he had deployed his reserves, Georges had sent eight divisions to the Second Army south of Sedan but dispatched none to the Ninth Army, which faced eastward on the Meuse. It is doubtful, however, that the reserves could have reached the scene in time. So on May 16, when the Panzer divisions resumed their advance westward, the Germans encountered little but the remnants of the retreating Ninth Army. Georges ordered an additional three divisions from the forces facing Germany, but these would take several days to arrive in the combat zone.

On May 16, the first day of their strategic exploitation, one German Panzer corps moved forward forty miles and another almost fifty. Again, in their advance the victorious Panzer divisions captured or destroyed enemy artillery and transport. When one Panzer division captured 10,000 prisoners and disabled or captured 200 tanks, the situation resembled battles of the seventeenth century and earlier when the victorious cavalry had slaughtered the defeated infantry. The long advance of May 16 took the Panzer divisions and motorized and foot-marching infantry that followed a good way toward turning the allied armies on the Dyle in Belgium. Having only just halted the Germans on the Dyle, the allied forces, because of this threat, had to begin a retreat westward, one done slowly to respond to the pressure of the closely following Germans. In withdrawing, the allies did not desert the Dutch, who had already capitulated on May 14.

On the 17th, the Germans halted for rest, resupply, and repair of equipment. This delay also reflected their anxiety about the exposed southern flank their move had created and the need for their foot-marching infantry to keep up and protect the rear of the advancing Panzer and motorized divisions.

Germans faced continuing French local counterattacks. Again they encountered problems with the French heavy tanks, one withstanding twenty-five hits from German antitank guns, a twenty-sixth shot immobilizing it by breaking its track. The Germans finally defeated one counterattack by using high-velocity 88-millimeter antiaircraft guns as antitank guns. But the armor on other French tanks proved equally troublesome, a tank of less than half the size of the heavy tank weathering forty-two hits by German antitank guns. But French counterattacks failed to drive back the Germans because the dispersal of French reserves around the perimeter of the German breakthrough meant that no more than one armored division ever struck at the same point. If the French had waited to concentrate their armored divisions and support them with infantry divisions, the Germans would have advanced almost unimpeded. But the alternative—counterassaults by reserves as they arrived—proved hardly more effectual, for the Germans had little difficulty repelling these weak, localized attacks.

In the next three days, May 18–20, the Germans reached the coast through a gap forty miles wide in which the French could place only a few troops to oppose the Germans, reinforced by Panzer and motorized divisions from the army group that had entered Belgium and Holland. Moving slowly on the 18th and 19th, the Germans completed the defeat of two French armored divisions and captured 110,000 prisoners, including an army commander and his staff. Accelerating their advance to sixty miles on May 20, the Panzer divisions reached the coast, concluded their turning movement, and enclosed the French, British, and Belgian troops against the Channel.

On May 19 the French government replaced General Gamelin with General Maxime Weygand. Though seventy-three years of age, Weygand looked and acted like a man in his fifties. His preference for 100-yard sprints rather than jogging exemplified the energy with which he approached his task of taking command against the Germans, and his vigor and aggressiveness showed his debt to his mentor, Marshal Foch, whom he had served during World War I as chief of staff.

General Weygand faced circumstances typical of the commander of a turned army, one like the Austrians before Marengo or in the Ulm campaign and like that of Bazaine in Metz. But Weygand's situation differed in that he had sustantial forces that the Germans had not enclosed on the coast and so could threaten the turning German divisions from the south as well as the north. So he attempted to organize counterattacks against the German Panzer turning force, with elements driving against both sides of the tenuous corridor that ran from the coast back to the Meuse. Vulnerable as this line of communications seemed until infantry marching on foot should arrive to protect it, the allies lacked the strength to exploit its weakness. With most of their armies facing east against the Germans advancing into Belgium, the first attack from the north could muster only one French and two British divisions, and when it took place on May 21, only two British infantry battalions and less than 100 tanks carried it out. A later French assault from the north had no more power. These amounted to no more than pinpricks to the Germans. The French attacks from the south came even later, dependent on the arrival from the east of divisions by rail that had to detrain, organize, and deploy. These weak assaults from the south enjoyed no more success than those from the north.

So, unlike the usual situation in a turning movement, the Germans did not have to defend against a determined effort by the allied armies to escape south.

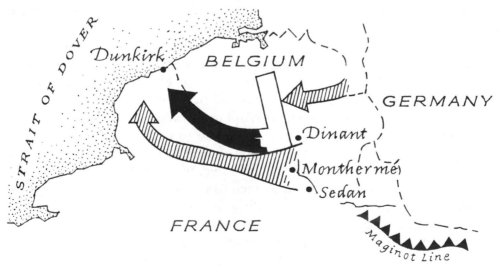

Diagram 10.9. Strategic Turning Movement

The capitulation of the large Belgian army soon further crippled the ability of these armies to counterattack toward their rear. Engaged with the German invaders of Belgium, the allies could barely disengage enough forces to guard their rear from the turning Panzer divisions that, in turn, had to protect their own rear against the French armies assembling south of them along the Somme River. Although the French troops in the south arrived and took up their positions so slowly that the Panzer divisions could have used some of their strength to attack successfully the rear of the allied troops retreating from Belgium, the Germans withdrew many of their Panzer divisions from combat to rest them and repair their equipment to prepare for the ensuing campaign against the main part of the French army, which first Georges, and then Weygand, was moving northward to positions between the Meuse and the English Channel.

This turning movement differed from that at Ulm in that the allies could attempt an evacuation by sea. Bad weather, much smoke, and British fighter aircraft from across the Channel thwarted the efforts of the German air force to keep ships from picking up the troops at Dunkirk, enabling the allies to evacuate 227,000 British and 110,000 French troops at a cost of the sinking of six British and two French destroyers and the loss of several noncombatant ships, leaving behind many of the French soldiers whose fighting had kept the Germans at bay. But these evacuated forces, having abandoned their artillery and transport, could not immediately reenter combat.

As soon as the last allied soldiers left by sea or surrendered, the Germans began an offensive against the French armies, most of whose soldiers deployed from the Meuse to the Channel. Outnumbered two to one and with only about fifty divisions on a hastily entrenched 225-mile front, the French could not prevent concentrations of Panzer divisions from breaking through and turning the defending armies. In spite of basically unspecified German political goals, the French, with Italy also entering the war on the German side and attacking with thirty-two divisions, asked for an armistice.

A defeat that drove the French south of Paris had a different result in 1870 because in the Franco-Prussian War only a small part of the potential military force of France had suffered defeat when turned at Metz and Sedan. In 1940, with complete mobilization, the Germans had overcome all of the potential as well as actual military forces of France. And with several times as many soldiers as in 1870, the Germans had an army adequate to occupy all of France. The French, made complacent by the strength of their army and fortifications and by the acknowledged primacy of the defensive, were so demoralized by their rapid defeat that they felt no immediate inclination to emulate the Spanish against Napoleon and offer guerrilla resistance. Instead, like the Prussians who had also believed in the invincibility of their army only to be defeated by Napoleon in 1806–7, the French yielded to their conqueror even more quickly than the Prussians did to the French in 1807.

The German Victory: Napoleonic Warfare
with Four Weapon Systems

Could the French have prevented their defeat? If General Billotte, the First Army group commander, had promptly and energetically used the Seventh Army as a reserve as soon as it fell back from Holland, joined it to his own armored divisions, and even had some access to British and Belgian reserves, he could have had a formidable force with which to counterattack or to block the path of the German Panzer turning movement. But even if the vigor of the German attack from the east had not prevented this or, as it did, had made General Billotte believe that it was unwise, this powerful intervention probably could not have changed the outcome. Billotte would have inevitably underestimated the speed of the German advance and, failing to get ahead of the Panzer divisions, would have faced the difficult problem of organizing a counterattack rather than the far easier task of the defense. The Germans had such a concentration of force and so much tactical skill that it is difficult to conceive that they could not have fended off such an attack while at least two Panzer divisions completed their race to the sea.

A conversation between Generals Gamelin and Weygand implies another possibility. In his brief exchange with General Weygand when he replaced him in supreme command, Gamelin reported that Weygand said that he possessed the secrets of Marshal Foch's success. Gamelin thought of replying that he had had those of Marshal Joffre, but they had not proved equal to the occasion. If Gamelin, who had served capably on Joffre's staff in 1914, had reacted with the promptness, perceptiveness, and energy of the marshal, would the campaign have turned out differently? Gamelin could hardly have grasped the German plan before the Germans had begun consolidating their Sedan and Dinant bridgeheads on May 14. In 1914 Joffre had allowed a week to create the Sixth Army and complete his redispositions and did not, in fact, begin his counteroffensive for eleven days. Such a timetable for a response, adequate for 1914, would have been too slow for 1940: the Germans reached the coast in six days.

Since Gamelin left the conduct of the campaign to Georges, his realization of the breaking of the Meuse front early on May 14 constitutes the likely time of a drastic French reconcentration of their forces. But the strategic ambiguity inherent in a situation in which the Germans could use their breakthrough to turn either flank of the French army necessarily confused the enemy. Georges still believed that the Germans intended to turn the French armies facing the German frontier rather than the allied in Belgium and had thus directed most of his later reinforcements to the Second Army facing north at Sedan. If he had correctly grasped the German objective on May 14 and ordered fifteen, or even twenty, divisions from those behind the frontier fortifications as well as redirecting, as he did, reserves already dispatched to the Sedan area, could they have arrived in time?

Since the French allowed four days for a rail movement, these fifteen or twenty divisions could, hypothetically at least, have headed off the dash of the Panzer divisions to the sea because the German air force had enjoyed little real success in significantly retarding the rail transport of French troops. The actual record of the movement of divisions laterally along the front supports this rate of transport by rail, one division getting one regiment into action as quickly as two days after starting. But in conveying troops west by rail, the French high command detrained these divisions some distance from the enemy in order to organize them after their journey and deploy them for action. This process took time, and clearly these French troops could not have interposed themselves between the Panzer divisions and the Channel quickly enough to cope with the onrushing, fully deployed, and completely motorized Panzer divisions.

But had German air reconnaissance seen such a massive troop movement, the apprehensive German high command would likely have halted the advance to the Channel to avoid exposing so extensive a flank to attack by so formidable a concentration of French troops. Still, if the German high command could have displayed the courage of the convictions of General Guderian and the other Panzer leaders, they could have completed their turning movement and held their long southern flank with the original breakthrough force of seven Panzer divisions and two motorized divisions. The newly arrived two Panzer and one motorized divisions from the northern army group should have sufficed to protect their corridor from the forces in Belgium. Hence, the original nine divisions could have thus given their almost undivided attention to this flank because the allied forces in Belgium could not have disengaged enough men from the German armies attacking them from the east to overcome the three divisions left to protect the northern flank of the Panzer corridor. On the defensive, the German mobile divisions facing south could readily have defended their 100-mile-long flank against the attack of twenty infantry divisions, which had to face the barrier of the Somme over much of this front.

So even if a hypothetically prescient General Georges had reacted in a dramatically emphatic way on May 14, the French could hardly have blocked the advance to the sea and the completion of the German turning movement. In 1914 Marshal Joffre used the railways to respond to a strategic surprise that itself had an inadequate logistic base, but in 1940 the railways could not prevail against the motor vehicle for moving and supplying men and guns and the tank for providing a weapon system ascendant over the light infantry whose defensive power had dominated the battlefields of 1914.

Thus the Germans founded their success on the exceptional strategic mobility of their Panzer divisions. But this mobility extended far beyond the traditional role of cavalry as strategically offensive troops, which had for several centuries helped to convince commanders of the need to adopt the slow and cumbersome method of marching in the battle formation that in the late sixteenth century the duke of Parma had used to foil King Henry IV's cavalry.

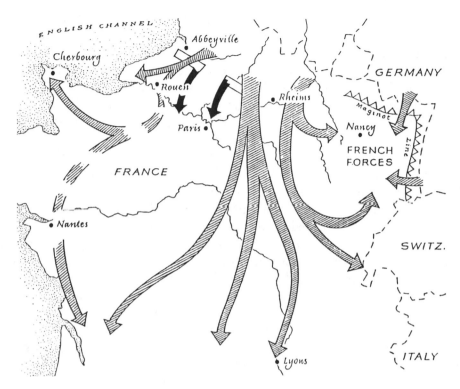

Diagram 10.10. Final German Offensive in France

The large forces represented by the Panzer divisions and their ability to fight dispersed gave them the capability to carry out a strategic turning movement. Their campaign had a recent and dramatic precedent when Allenby had used the greater mobility of a large number of cavalry to turn the Turks in his Megiddo campaign. Just as Allenby had used the horse to make a strategic movement of troops that arrayed themselves tactically as infantry, so the motor truck and the tracked vehicle moved German infantry and their artillery, antitank guns, and antiaircraft guns, an operation anticipated, ironically, by the French motorized turning movement in Morocco six years before. The Panzer division came well equipped to take advantage of the tactical primacy of fighting on the tactical defensive that the turning movement traditionally conferred. The Panzer division's infantry, artillery, and antitank guns had made good use of these defensive capabilities when they turned back the many small-scale French counterattacks launched from the time they crossed the Meuse until after they reached the coast.

Invaluable tactically, especially in the initial breakthrough, the tank in one sense contributed less to the decisive strategic results that the campaign produced than did the motor truck and the tracked vehicle. These vehicles not only conveyed the infantry and their antitank and antiaircraft weapons but also supplied the Panzer divisions' requirements for ammunition and fuel. Without the logistical revolution of the truck, the tanks alone could not have reaped the strategic harvest of their tactical capabilities.

True, the 1940 tanks had the strategic mobility that the short-range, unreliable machines of 1918 lacked. But without the trucks to supply them, tanks could still have made no deep strategic penetration; and even if they had the trucks for their logistic support, such a drive could have amounted to nothing more than a destructive raid, such as Henry IV wished to execute against Parma. Only with the truck and its defensively predominant infantry, artillery, and antitank and antiaircraft guns could tanks have had the necessary defensive capability and the ratio of force to space to carry out a strategic turning movement. And only with the truck could the infantry and their mobile weapon systems have had the mobility needed to keep ahead of French reserves moved by rail.

The German victory also depended on many familiar elements in warfare. The strategic surprise made possible by the diversion of the strong even ostentatious push into Holland and Belgium and abetted by the French confidence in the difficulties of the Ardennes contributed much to German success. The Germans' tactical skill complemented their organization for strategic mobility and their masterful combination of distraction and concentration against weakness. Panzer infantry, largely veterans of combat, carried out the daunting crossings of the Meuse against troops lacking similar experience and comparable training and leadership. At Sedan, however, the Germans made use of an intrinsically superior weapon system when they employed their bombers against French infantry that lacked enough antiaircraft guns. The defending French reservists displayed the same demoralization expected of heavy infantry of old that, when attacked by horse archers or pistoliers, could make no reply.

When the Panzer divisions had crossed the barrier of the Meuse, they repeated again and again the theme of the use of a predominant weapon system. French divisions had enough antitank guns to withstand a tank-supported infantry attack on a broad front, such as had characterized the victorious allied assaults in World War I. Yet they lacked the number of antitank weapons needed to resist the enormous concentrations of German tanks at their three bridgeheads over the Meuse or often at the disposal of the Germans throughout their drive to the coast.

The parallel that clarifies this aspect of German tactical success is the use of large bodies of heavy cavalry against a mass of light infantry supported by a few pikemen and by the occasional rush of a few heavy cavalry. Predictably, the heavy cavalry slaughtered the light infantry in combat and during their retreat. Alexander's stirrupless heavy cavalry enjoyed such success against the flank and rear of heavy infantry, and it is hardly surprising that the tank unit with radio communication, superbly articulated and the ideal offensive troops, overwhelmed the light infantry. When they faced more formidable opposition, the concept of infiltration tactics enabled them to exploit their mobility to take artillery and antitank guns in the flank and rear. When they could not turn a point strong in antitank guns, they concentrated their infantry and artillery to take the position, thus carrying out an operation with a parallel to light infantry defeating heavy infantry. And German attention to making the most of the capabilities of the new weapon systems extended to equipping themselves with even more antitank guns than the French. In this way they had an ample number of a dominant weapon system essential to a successful defense against the powerful French armored forces.

The German aircraft, the light cavalry of the air, played an important but not decisive role. They scored high in their strategic role against marching troops but could not appreciably slow, much less prevent, the strategic movement of French troops by road or rail. The crossing of the Meuse at Dinant without air support against first-class reserve divisions indicates that German infantry may not have required the tactical support of aircraft to have crossed against the second-class reserve divisions at Sedan.

Clearly, many other familiar elements contributed to the German victory. The use of aircraft in the crossing at Sedan, whether essential or not, exhibited the degree of concentration practiced, not just in bringing seven Panzer divisions against the Meuse but in the concentration represented by the Panzer division itself. The Germans skillfully employed the tank as a tactically offensive weapon system and articulated their tank units well with radios. By combining tanks with other motorized weapon systems in the Panzer division, aided by aircraft, they had created a strategically offensive army with enough force to space in the theater of operations to carry out the strategic turning movement. Thus, they intelligently united the new logistic capabilities with the traditional mounted weapon systems, revived in the form of aircraft and tanks, and their new, unmounted counterparts, the antitank and antiaircraft guns. When joined with the concepts of Napoleonic warfare, made almost obsolete by the siege warfare of World War I, this resulting blend of new and old elements had produced a transformation of warfare comparable to that of Napoleon. Thus, the German army overthrew the tyranny of an excess of force to space that had ruled in this region from 1914 to 1918.

So, rather than a French failure, the German army's comprehensive mixture of old and new elements accounted for the dramatic outcome of the campaign. That in a campaign of a little over a month the French lost approximately 290,000 killed and wounded and the Germans about 138,000 indicates the level of effort required for the Germans to attain their extraordinary victory.

Although General Georges displayed the symptoms of collapse under pressure, his performance differed markedly from Bazaine's seventy years earlier. He continued to function as did his staff. The French did not owe their defeat to him or to Gamelin's plan or his failure to intervene, because a more vigorous response earlier would hardly have altered the outcome. Once a brilliant union of the classical elements of distraction and concentration against weakness had brought the Germans across the Meuse, the French faced the tactical innovation of a large number of tanks on a narrow front; the strategic departure of the mobility of the Panzer division combined with its great power on the tactical offensive and defensive; the logistic revolution made possible by the motor truck; the valuable tactical and strategic aid of larger numbers of powerful aircraft; and the strategic innovation of the concentration of Panzer and motorized divisions to create a force of strategically offensive troops so powerful that it could carry out a major strategic turning movement.

With traditionally important factors added to such major tactical and strategic departures, surely no French command could have foreseen and coped with the campaign of May 1940, the full concept and implications of which many of its German originators and executants had difficulty grasping fully.

Air Power in a Decisive Role: The Battle of Britain

With much of the equipment of its small army left in France, Britain had deficient means to resist the victorious German army on the ground. Britain's defense depended on the ability of the Britain's navy to interdict a passage of the English Channel by the German ground forces. In terms of naval power alone, this task presented no difficulties because the navy had convenient bases and a large number of cruisers armed with 8- or 6-inch guns as well as 4-inch antiaircraft guns. All of these weapons could sink troop transports as could the 4.7-inch guns carried by most destroyers. Against small craft the ships' automatic antiaircraft guns firing 2-pound explosive bullets would prove very effective as well. Faced with intensive patrols by such ships, the Germans had no chance of launching an invasion of the British Isles.

Napoleon, like the French on several occasions before him, had faced a similar problem but one in which he had the potential of naval supremacy if he could concentrate more ships in the Channel than could the British. But compared to the British, the Germans had a negligible navy, and even if the Italian fleet had proven willing and able to emulate the French Mediterranean fleets of old and come to the Channel, the Germans and Italians had no hope that their combined fleets' eight battleships could match the fourteen British battleships and battle cruisers.

The Germans, however, had a more powerful air force and could use this to drive away the British fleet and open the way for the movement of their army. Operating over the sea, as over the land, as light cavalry, the German bombers could expect to defeat the warships. Although the ships, like armies, had antiaircraft defenses, the far more numerous aircraft could expect to prevail. In the summer of 1940 the Germans had about 1,300 bombers available to operate over the English Channel, and about 300 of these were dive bombers that had the accuracy to hit the lightly armored cruisers and unarmored destroyers with heavy bombs. Such numerical advantage of aircraft against ships would ensure German mastery in an extended contest between the sea and air forces because the Germans could replace their aircraft losses from the steady production of new planes and the stream of newly trained pilots. The British had no comparable flow of new ships.

Doubtless such a contest would have been a long, grueling struggle with adverse weather constantly handicapping the aircraft. The British also would likely have kept many ships in port, ready to sortie if the Germans had begun to dispatch their invasion forces. Here they would have presented easier-to-hit stationary targets but would have had the support of ground-based antiaircraft guns and greater access to protection by fighter aircraft. Even with a victory against the royal navy, the German invasion vessels could not have crossed completely unmolested. After they came ashore, the Germans would have faced the problem of continuing to land and supply enough men so as not to have the British ground forces halt them on the narrow landing fronts and bottle them up near the beaches without a port for supply.

But before the British and Germans could wage these campaigns, the Germans first had to deal with the British aircraft. The German air force could not easily attack the British navy as long as the British had a powerful fighter-plane force available with bases that enabled them to fly over the Channel. The Germans had found this out when they had tried to use their air force to prevent the evacuation of British and French troops from the French coast near Dunkirk. The British fighters intervened from their bases in England and contributed a great deal to the success of the evacuation.

So the German air force had first to defeat Britain's air force before it could begin its contest with the navy. For this struggle fighters would play a crucial role, and the Germans had about 800 of their excellent Messerschmitt 109 single-engine, monoplane fighters. To counter these the British had about 600 modern single-engine, monoplane fighters. The Spitfire, a match for the Messerschmitt, constituted less than half of these British aircraft. The Hurricane, which provided the remainder, had firepower comparable to the Messerschmitt or Spitfire but had about 10 percent less speed than these other two fighters; this placed it at a significant disadvantage in comparison with the German plane. Both air forces had combat experience.

The Germans planned to compel Britain's air force to fight by bombing their airfields with bombers heavily escorted by fighters. Although the British kept many fighters on fields out of reach of the Germans, this strategy would require the British to fight rather than have their aircraft attacked on the ground and their ground installations bombed. To combat these raids and avoid loss of planes on the ground, the British had radar as well as ground observers to detect approaching hostile aircraft and used control from land to direct the fighters to intercept the German bombers. In addition, the British obtained intelligence of German intentions through decoding messages. Thus, the British aircraft could remain on the ground except when actual combat threatened.

In this contest Britain's air force had a number of advantages. Though inferior in the number and quality of its fighters, it had almost 300 in reserve and a production of 475 per month compared with German output of only 200 per month. Replacing pilots at the rate of the loss of aircraft presented a serious problem, but one the British solved, in part because in fighting over their own territory many of their pilots could parachute to safety and fly again. In addition, they could draw on the navy, use pilots manning their few remaining obsolete fighters, and begin retraining bomber pilots into fighter pilots. Fighting on the strategic defensive provided another benefit besides saving pilots: like steam warships operating far from their bases, German fighters, in coming to engage the British near their own airfields, used up much of their fuel and in some instances had only about twenty minutes of combat time over British territory. For the Germans, a shorter time in the combat area equated to having fewer planes.

Tactically the British had to act on the offensive. But since they had as their objective the slow, vulnerable bomber, an aircraft in many ways comparable to a merchant ship on the sea, they pitted their superior fighter weapon system—the galley of the air—against the inferior bomber. The German bombers could rarely bring more than one or two of their defensive machine guns to bear against the eight forward-firing machine guns of the small, fast-flying Spitfire and Hurricane.

To control operations the British had a good system of ground observers and radar stations to warn of the approach and course of the German aircraft. This intelligence enabled them to concentrate fighter aircraft, dispersed at many different airfields, against the hostile formations reported and located by the warning system. The tactical offensive also gave British fighters some advantage of the initiative against the German fighters, which had to stay close to their bombers to protect them. The British tried to use their slower Hurricane fighters against bombers and reserve the Spitfires to engage the German Messerschmitts. The Hurricanes had ample speed and firepower to deal with bombers.

After a period of attacks in less than full strength, the Germans opened their major air campaign on August 12, 1940, with raids on British radar stations; some were damaged, but only one was disabled. The Germans began their main offensive the next day with flights by nearly 1,500 aircraft. The British fighters met them and shot down forty-five, losing only thirteen. Both sides overestimated the other's losses, the Germans, for example, believing that in a week they had shot down 300 British planes instead of the 99 actually destroyed. After a small effort on August 14, the Germans attacked the next day, making 520 bomber flights and 1,270 by fighters. The British lost 34 aircraft to German losses of 75. The next day the Germans again made a great effort, 1,700 flights, and lost 45 planes to 21 for the British. But the Germans, again overestimating enemy losses, thought they had reduced the total of British fighters to 300; in fact, the British still operated over 600 as they showed on August 18 when they shot down 71 German planes to their loss of 27. From August 8 through 18 the Germans lost 363 aircraft and the British 181 in the air and 30 on the ground.

Disappointed in their expectation of a quick victory, the Germans continued their strikes on airfields, including the ground control centers that directed the

British fighter effort. From August 24 through September 6 the Germans made thirty-three large attacks and, using a higher proportion of fighters and few of their vulnerable dive bombers, had lost 380 aircraft compared to 286 for the British. Both air forces had lost heavily, and the men had difficulty maintaining the grueling pace of the campaign.

On September 5 the Germans began bombing London in retaliation for a British raid on Berlin. But bad weather limited the German effort until September 15, when they made almost 1,000 flights over Britain, losing 60 planes to 26 for Britain's air force, which had half its downed pilots survive. At this point the Germans realized that they could not defeat the British fighters, abandoned their plans for an immediate invasion, but continued the air offensive. During the period August 11 through September 30, both combatants lost heavily, but each thought they had inflicted greater aircraft losses on the enemy. During the period from August 5 to September 20 the Germans lost 1,155 planes, the British, 666. But the British lost 422 pilots killed, wounded, and missing and maintained their operational strength at a fairly constant level throughout this campaign, called the Battle of Britain. On August 5 they had 373 Hurricanes operational and 257 Spitfires; on September 20 they had 391 Hurricanes and 237 Spitfires. Aircraft production and the provision of new pilots had matched the losses. In view of the British skill in combat and operations and their resources in men and materiel, the Germans clearly had little chance of winning the Battle of Britain.

The attacker had lost more heavily, even with greater numbers, because he had to expose his bombers to the fighter, a better weapon system. If the Germans could have pitted fighter against fighter, each the same distance from its base, the Germans would have had the best of the contest because they had a slight advantage in numbers and a significant one in the preponderance of the Messerschmitts over the Hurricanes; the combat of fighters, without any advantage for the defense, would have occurred under the conditions for which Lanchester formulated his N-square law. But the British had no reason to accept a challenge to fight on such terms. Just as the ancient Greeks used to devastate an enemy's territory to compel him to fight or lose his crops, so the Germans had to attack airfields, ports, or London to make Britain's air force fight; and such attacks required them to expose their vulnerable bombers and employ fighters far from their airfields and over the enemy's territory.

Had the British lacked the Spitfire, the Germans might have prevailed. Slightly older in design than the Spitfire and a bulkier aircraft but with the same engine, the Hurricane fell enough short in performance of the best German fighter to place the pilot at a serious disadvantage. The British withdrew it as a fighter during the war whereas the Spitfire, like the Messerschmitt, continued in service until the end of the conflict, receiving successive improvements that increased its speed by 100 miles per hour. The French air force had suffered severely from having older designs predominate among its aircraft, and the Russians and the Italians would have the same problem at the outset of hostilities. The Russians recovered by introducing new designs, but the Italians did not.

Just as Admiral Sturdee and his battle cruisers had easily sunk the German armored cruisers off the Falkland Islands in 1914, so a pilot in a superior aircraft, because of a combination of some or all of the attributes of speed, rate of climb, armament, or maneuverability, would have a similar advantage. But the pilot would owe his dominance not to having a different type, as in battle cruiser against armored cruiser, but to a more modern design. As weapon systems grow older, they have tended to last longer as the rate of development decreases. In World War I aircraft became obsolete in two years or less, but in World War II some aircraft continued in service throughout the war. Ships exhibited the same phenomenon, modernized World War I battleships doing good service in World War II.

If the Germans had defeated the fighters of Britain's air force, they would then have had to turn their exhausted and depleted forces to exploiting their victory by attacking their adversary's navy. The Germans apparently believed that they could begin their invasion immediately after defeating the enemy fighters. But it is doubtful that even unmolested German bombers could have prevented British warships from intercepting German invasion flotillas. The enormous firepower of cruisers and destroyers would have found a multitude of vulnerable targets in a convoy of troop transports and barges.

The Germans would perhaps have displayed greater wisdom to use their hypothetical air preponderance, if they had been able to maintain it in the face of greater British fighter-plane production, to mount a sustained campaign against enemy warships while expanding their number of invasion craft and, consequently, the size of their invasion force and the breadth of its front. This doubtless would have involved a delay until the spring when invasion craft and airplanes would have had good weather. But the increase in the width of the German invasion frontage, in men involved, and in loss of British warships in the interim would probably have more than counterbalanced the larger number of defending troops the British would have had by the spring.

The Germans, however, might have found that they could have made the best use of their air superiority by employing it to implement a logistic strategy of blockade by attacking British shipping and ports while, by maintaining the threat of invasion, continuing to divert enemy warships from the protection of convoys against the attacks of German submarines.

The Strategic and Tactical Conditions of the Russo-German War

The German use of their Panzer and motorized divisions to turn the allied forces in Belgium provided the strategic model for the use of the motor truck and the new weapon systems during the remainder of the war. The Germans applied this model in 1941 in their war with Russia. To carry out this strategy the Germans increased their number of motorized divisions to fourteen and, by reducing the number of tanks, their Panzer divisions to nineteen. This significantly decreased the ratio of the heavy cavalry tanks to the infantry, artillery, and antitank and antiaircraft guns and gave more emphasis to the element of strategic mobility in the Panzer division and less to its tactically offensive, heavy cavalry element, the tank. Just as Alexander's Companion cavalry had constituted only a small part of his army, so tanks provided only a tiny fraction of the whole German army and, now, a lesser proportion of the motorized and armored forces. The Germans had an army far different from the heavy–cavalry–centered medieval model.

To accomplish their now thoroughly understood turning movement strategy, they planned to break through in two places, rather than the one in France, where the sea acted as a barrier. The two groups of Panzer and motorized divisions would drive deep into the enemy rear and unite behind, while infantry divisions on foot marched in the track of the mechanized and motorized forces to furnish adequate strength to block the retreat of the divisions encircled by the double turning movement, often called a strategic envelopment.

The Germans faced less favorable conditions than they had encountered in France. They would have a lower ratio of force to space, which would facilitate breakthroughs just as it had in World War I but would impose serious logistical problems and make it more difficult to envelop as great a proportion of the hostile forces as they had turned in May 1940. Further, a lower ratio of force to space would augment the difficulty in blocking or containing the enveloped forces. The climate was difficult: much of Russia lay north of France and all of it far from the warmth of the Atlantic Ocean. In addition, Russia possessed large rivers with many tributaries. The poverty of the country, like its low population density, meant the Germans would find less food and forage, fewer bridges and roads, and more unpaved roads, undrained marshes, and uncut forests. These terrain conditions would inhibit but not preclude the success of the German mounted warfare upon which they depended for strategically decisive victories.

On the other hand, the comparsion with the German campaign against the French extended to the tactical level where the Germans, after their operations in France, had markedly enhanced their already high level of tactical skill and the experience and competence of their commanders and staffs. The deficiencies of the Russians when compared with the French intensified this contrast. Inferior to the French in World War I, the Russian army suffered almost total dissolution as a result of the conflict and the ensuing Bolshevik Revolution. When by the late 1930s the Russians had rebuilt and rearmed their army, the Russian high command, purged of high officers suspected of political unreliability, lost a high proportion of its more experienced and better trained commanders.

The Germans had to rely on their skills to offset Russian predominance in artillery and tanks, as the Russians had added to their traditional passion for large quantities of powerful artillery an enthusiasm for armored forces. Although many of these tracked vehicles represented obsolete designs and a considerable number were not ready for action and required repair, the Russians certainly had a three to one numerical advantage against the 3,500 tanks in the German armies attacking Russia. One of the many Russian light tanks, the BT7, compared with the German Model II light tank as follows (table 10.3).

TABLE 10.3.   Comparison of Russian
and German Light Tanks

	German	Russian
Weight (tons)	7.2	13.8
Speed (mph)	25	33
Thickest armor (mm)	30	22
Gun (mm)	20	45

But the Germans had few of these light tanks, two-thirds of theirs being two similar models of medium tanks weighing about twenty tons. The Russians had an excellent new medium tank, the T–34, in production, but had significantly fewer of these medium tanks than the Germans. The best example of each tank available in 1940 compares as follows (table 10.4). The armor on the Russian tank sloped much more sharply than the armor on the German tanks, and its gun had over double the armor-piercing power of the much shorter 75-millimeter and somewhat more than the longer-barreled 50-millimeter guns on the German tanks. The diesel engine on the Russian tank gave it twice the range of the gasoline-fueled German tank and reduced the hazard from the fuel's catching fire. For its size the Russian T–34 was probably the best tank of World War II.

TABLE 10.4.   Comparison of Russian
and German Medium Tanks

	German	Russian
Weight (tons)	21	28
Speed (mph)	27	33
Thickest armor (mm)	60	60
Gun (mm)	50 or 75	76

In addition, the Russians had a heavy tank in production, the 47-ton KV with armor 110-millimeters thick on the models produced in 1941. It, too, had a powerful 76-millimeter gun but a speed of only twenty-one miles per hour. Nevertheless, it had more speed, range, firepower, and armor protection than the French heavy tank, which the Germans had found so formidable and which had convinced them to increase the armor on their tanks and to mount more powerful tank guns. But the Russians had altogether only about 1,500 of their T–34 medium and strong KV heavy tanks.

The two armies had about the same strength, the Germans having expanded theirs by equipping eighty-eight divisions with French weapons. Leaving almost fifty divisions in subjugated countries, campaigning in Africa, and guarding against Britain, the Germans deployed about 145 divisions in the East. The Russians, fully mobilized, had about the same number available in their western provinces. The Russians had more aircraft, and their production was greater, but they had older fighter planes. Both their air and ground forces lacked the extensive German operational and combat experience.

In doctrine the armies differed little, the Russians, like the Germans, knowing that tanks were not primarily helpers of the infantry in overcoming the machine gun. But the purge of so many higher commanders had caused a reorganization of Russian armored forces, and when the war began, the Russian army had yet another restructuring underway, one basically intended to restore a disposition of armored forces similar to that of the Germans. They had not completed these changes, and the outbreak of the war found their armored force unready.

In attacking Russia with over 3 million soldiers the Germans did not repeat Napoleon's raid of 1812, but they did lack the forces necessary to conquer the entire country. Their situation had much in common with the Prussian campaign against France in 1870–71 in that they had the troops to dominate much but not all of the country. European Russia had about eight times the land area of France, and the Germans and their Balkan allies had five or six times as many men as those available to the Prussians and their German allies seventy years earlier. If they could defeat the Russian armies, they could expect to conquer European Russia, beat back the counterattacks of improvised armies, and impose a peace.

But their situation had many ominous variations from that of 1870. Germany had Italy as an ally, but Russia had Britain, aided by the United States. Russia had more than double the population of Germany, whereas in 1870 Prussia and its German allies together had about the same population as France. In addition, the Russians had still more men of military age and considerable reserves of trained manpower not represented in the armies deployed against Germany as well as the forces in the Far East, which had defeated the Japanese in such an exemplary fashion at Khalkin Gol. Further, Asiatic Russia contained significant population centers and a powerful heavy industry. If a comparison of force to space included Asiatic Russia, the country had forty times the land area of France, presenting an insuperable obstacle to any conquest not founded on a strong political base or an exercise of the Turko-Mongolian strategy of massacre and terror over a hitherto unprecedented land area.

And the Germans lacked a political program to appeal to the Russians, even though many Russians harbored considerable ill will toward the regime of Joseph Stalin. But Adolf Hitler aimed at the complete overthrow of Stalin's government and the annexation of a large part of European Russia, including the most productive agricultural, industrial, and mining regions.

The Germans had objectives too ambitious to be attained by the limited military action of 1870–71. And not only did they have no attractive political program but also they treated the conquered Russian population in a way which helped to arouse their animosity. Also, curiously, Hitler could not rely on the political strategy of terror or the logistic strategy of extermination of military manpower. Although Hitler had no aversion to slaughtering the Russians, whom he regarded as racially subhuman, he wished to conserve the agricultural output of the country as a resource for Germany, something not possible if he depopulated Russia. It is doubtful that German means and methods equaled the requirements of their political and economic objectives in attacking Russia.

In fact, the almost unlimited German political goals, their ethnic and ideological hostility to the Russians and their regime, the brutality the Germans earlier displayed, and the example of France, supine at the feet of Germany, motivated the Russian leaders, people, and soldiers to offer a desperate resistance. German soldiers, aware of both the depth of their antagonist's hatred and their great strength, knew that they, too, fought for their very existence in an unlimited war. The subsequent Anglo-American demand for the unconditional surrender of their opponents made formal what the Germans had already comprehended. So combatants on both sides in World War II fought not only with ideological and patriotic zeal but also with the knowledge that they struggled for their existence.

The Strategic Envelopments of the 1941 Campaign in Russia

The Germans and Russians each disposed their forces in three army groups. The Germans clearly had the better leaders. In the north the aristocratic Field Marshal Leeb faced Marshal Voroshilov; both were veterans of World War I but Voroshilov's background was with the war ministry and in political participation, Leeb's, the successful command of an army group in France. In the center the thin, hard-bitten Field Marshal Bock, who had headed an army group in both Poland and France, met the ablest of the Russians, Marshal Timoshenko. In the south Germany's best leader, Field Marshal Runstedt, confronted Russia's weakest, the colorful World War I cavalryman Marshal Budenny, noted more for his imposing mustache than his ability to head an army group.

The German advantage in trained, tested, and competent commanders extended down to the platoon and squad level. At the apex both Hitler and Stalin exercised supreme command, aided by good, though on the Russian side inadequately prepared, staffs. As chief of staff, Stalin had the decisive, perceptive, and innovative Georgi Zhukov. A World War I cavalryman turned armor expert, Zhukov had made his reputation by his classic victory over the Japanese at Khalkin Gol in 1939. He lived up to his early promise and became Stalin's indispensable advisor and his commander in critical situations. But considering the strategic capabilities the Germans had exhibited in France, Stalin, in view of the immense space at his disposal, would have displayed more wisdom had he not concentrated his forces so near the German frontier.

The Germans began their offensive campaign on June 22, 1941, the weakest of the three army groups driving northeast toward Leningrad, the strongest east in the direction of Moscow, and the third southeast into the level, fertile, agricultural area of the Ukraine and eastward toward the industrial region north of the Crimea. They had divided their thirty-three Panzer and motorized divisions into four groups, assigning one each to the northern and southern army groups and two to the central army group, which posted one on each flank.

Facing an undeployed enemy, tactically surprised, the two mechanized groups in the center advanced nearly 200 miles in five days, meeting at Minsk; together with the infantry marching in their wake, they encircled huge Russian forces. Although half of the Russians escaped through the necessarily thin lines of the encircling forces, the Germans took 300,000 prisoners and captured 2,500 tanks and 1,400 artillery pieces. The Germans had won a victory over the Russians comparable to that over the Anglo-French allies a year earlier. They had achieved this without analogous strategic surprise or a position similar to that which they had the year before on the flank of the allied army in Belgium. They had accomplished victory by an exploitation of the tactically offensive qualities of the tank and the strategically offensive capabilities of the Panzer and motorized divisions.

Having completed this operation, the Germans promptly repeated it, driving over 100 miles farther east, capturing Smolensk, and surrounding another large Russian force by July 26. But at this point the advance had to halt for logistic reasons. Although the Germans drew a large part of their subsistence from the Russian countryside, they depended on motor trucks to provide the huge quantities of ammunition and the fuel that their motorized armies required. The Germans had only enough trucks to supply the troops as far as Smolensk, a situation aggravated by the consumption of fuel and ammunition in resisting Russian counterattacks.

Before the army could resume its advance, the Germans had to restore railway service, a task complicated not just by having to rebuild bridges but also by the necessity of altering Russian railways to the narrower German gauge. This chore, and the operation of captured segments of Russian railroads, proved harder than anticipated. Their railway troops, inadequate in any case, encountered unexpected obstacles in such mundane matters as water tank locations and the need to change the gauges of sidings as well as the main lines. Bypassed groups of Russian soldiers and armed, hostile civilians also caused problems. Throughout the summer and fall the failure of rail traffic to approach needs halted and delayed the German advance.

While the central army group gained such significant strategic victories, the army group in the north initially made rapid progress, advancing 400 miles by the middle of July. But the move toward Leningrad then halted, not only for logistic reasons but also because of the particular difficulties in the heavily forested area of northern Russia. Here the tanks proved so ineffective that the German command withdrew the mechanized group in September. Without tanks the war in the north came to resemble World War I, and even exceptional German tactical skill could not capture Leningrad against the power of the defense, Russian determination, and the lack of any ambiguity as to their strategic objective.

In the south, against the greater numbers of the Russian armies there, the Germans, with the aid of their Romanian and Hungarian allies, proceeded slowly in spite of the better terrain for tanks. But by early August they had encircled a large body of Russian troops and had reached the Dnieper River. This advance and that on the north to Smolensk had created a Russian salient extending as far east as Kiev. Using one of the mechanized groups from the central army group to drive south and that from the southern army group to drive north, the Germans broke through in late August and enclosed a huge Russian force. In spite of counterattacks and their own efforts to escape, the Russians lost part of five armies to the Germans who had taken over 600,000 prisoners by the end of September.

While this brilliantly successful operation took place, the Germans so improved the supply situation of the central army group that, strengthened to seventy divisions and with three of the four mechanized groups, it began a drive toward Moscow at the end of September. Again breaking through and sending forward two mechanized groups, the Germans once more surrounded a large number of Russian troops when they reached Vyazma on October 8. Yet the liquidation of these stubbornly resisting forces and the capture of an additional 600,000 prisoners took until the end of October.

The advance to Moscow, however, meant long lines of road transportation, a situation aggravated by the mud of the predominantly unsurfaced Russian roads. Unlike wealthy and densely populated France, Russia had few surfaced roads, and the invading armies soon wore these out. Until freezing temperatures solidified the mud, motor transport encountered almost insuperable difficulties. And the frost, which came early in November and arrived in one area with a sudden drop to four degrees below zero Fahrenheit, compounded the problems of the still poorly functioning railways, freezing water pipes on at least two-thirds of the German locomotives. So a dramatic decrease in rail transportation offset improved road conditions.

Nevertheless, the Germans pushed on toward Moscow and drove beyond the Dnieper in the south. But in early December they met strong Russian counterattacks, coordinated by Zhukov, which threatened the flanks of the forces near Moscow. These, and counterattacks along the whole front, compelled the Germans to assume the defensive during the winter and caused them to lose some ground to the Russians who, driven back on their intact railways, had sufficient supplies and better strategic mobility. The German troops lacked adequate provision for winter campaigning, a condition intensified by the inability of their deficient transport to supply special clothing and equipment.

In 1941 the Germans, applying a combat strategy, had attained brilliant tactical and strategic successes when they had encircled several major Russian armies. In fact, piercing a front, a relatively easy task with an average of only about one division for each six miles of front, almost inevitably led to a strategic disaster for the Russians whose troops could not retreat on foot as rapidly as motorized forces led by tanks could advance into the Russian rear. Only a large reserve of Russian motorized forces could have blocked the advance of the German mechanized forces or counterattacked on their vulnerable flanks. The Russian command had neither the understanding nor the capacity to create and use these appropriately.

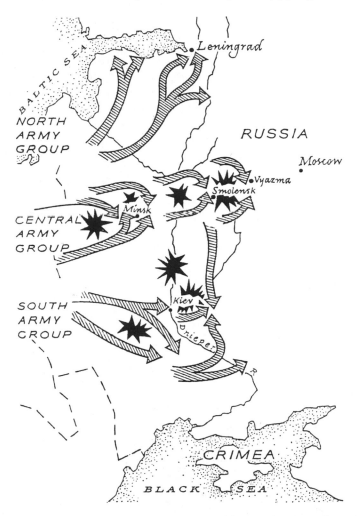

Diagram 10.11. German Successes at Minsk, Smolensk, and Vyazma

The Germans had displayed superb tactical and operational skills, which had completely overmatched the inexperienced, often bumbling, leadership of the Russian armies. But, as in France, the Germans met unpleasant surprises from enemy materiel. In one case, early in the campaign of Army Group North, a motionless Russian 47-ton KV tank commanded the road used by German supply vehicles. To eliminate this roadblock the Germans brought up successively a dozen of their new 50-millimeter antitank guns, a weapon with triple the power of the 37-millimeter gun that had proven so ineffectual against French tanks. Not only did these prove unable to pierce the thick armor of the KV, but the Russian tank used its turret-mounted 76-millimeter cannon to smash all twelve of the antitank guns firing on it and, before it could fire a single shot, a very powerful but vulnerable 88-millimeter antiaircraft gun. The Germans ultimately fired on the tank from behind with armor-piercing ammunition from another antiaircraft gun.

Yet the already combat-honed skills of the Germans usually compensated for Russian preponderance in numbers or quality of materiel. This proved equally true of the air force, where tactical surprise enabled the Germans to wreck enormous numbers of Russian aircraft on the ground. Nevertheless, these losses of aircraft cost the Russians few of their trained pilots, an important factor because the Russians were producing new high-performance fighters and bombers at a greater rate than the Germans. By the end of 1941 both sides had lost heavily, and each had only about 1,500 aircraft operational. But the Russian air force recovered its strength more rapidly and came to have a steadily increasing primacy as it augmented its greater numbers with improved aircraft and skill developed in combat.

The Russians suffered about 3,000,000 casualties in the 1941 campaign compared to about 800,000 for the Germans. The loss of 800,000 men had doubtless offset the German gain in effectiveness through additional combat experience whereas the Russians who had survived had learned valuable lessons and gained practical experience and a grasp of the German tactical and strategic method. When the Germans began the campaign, they already had such a high level of skill, and the Russians so comparatively little proficiency that the Russians inevitably benefited far more from the fighting than the Germans.

Thoroughly organized Russian production replaced the guns and tanks in spite of factories forfeited to the Germans, and the huge population still under Russian rule meant Stalin could raise new armies to replace those destroyed. Most of the officers and men of the new forces lacked experience and adequate training, but the higher commanders, who replaced those relieved for failure, had a good understanding of the kind of warfare the Germans had perfected in France and practiced so well against the Russians.

As the Russian commanders improved in ability, the Germans began to lose the advantage they had had with their commanders. In fact, the same situation existed with the troops: surviving combat gave troops experience and skills. When they had their greatest predominance in the summer and fall of 1941, the vast size of the theater of operations, which had enabled the Russians to retreat and to use newly created units to strengthen new fronts, defeated the Germans because of the logistical limitations of their armies. A century earlier even such gigantic armies, if in motion in a country as large and well populated as Russia in 1941, could probably have found enough food and forage to have lived off the country. But the fuel and ammunition requirements of the German motorized forces meant that they had ultimately to depend on the railroads for supply. The continuation of operations in the winter, which precluded dispersal to winter quarters, also aggravated German supply problems. During the summer and fall the need to reconstruct the railroads to supply the trucks, which could support the mechanized groups about 300 miles beyond the railhead, meant that the Germans would have had to advance in a series of bounds, even if the mud of the primitive Russian roads had not inhibited their movement just as it had the horsedrawn transport of the armies of earlier times. Thus, logistics circumscribed the depth of German penetration in 1941 and hence limited the number of strategic encirclements that the Germans could execute.

The Debacle of the German Logistic Strategy of 1942 and the Conclusion of the Russo-German War

Combat strategy failed to bring a decision in the vast spaces of European Russia, and in 1942 the Germans turned to a logistic strategy. Planning to use their operational primacy to carry out a deep advance, they aimed to occupy the Russian oil-producing areas in the region between the Black and Caspian seas. Without fuel and lubricants, the Russian armies would have to revert to the supply and combat capabilities of a World War I army, leaving the Germans to enjoy the advantages of a monopoly of air, armored, and motorized forces by 1943. In the process the Germans would augment their own inadequate stock of petroleum, an objective that actually had greater priority with the German command than the impact of the seizure of the oil fields on the Russians.

The Germans did not begin their operation until June 1942, because they had to reinforce their armies with men and materiel to replace the losses of the previous year and those sustained combating the Russian winter and spring attacks. Since they had held most of their territorial gains in Russia, they did begin their offensive in a good position. They had accomplished this by abandoning the concept of the continuous front, which was difficult to sustain with such a low ratio of force to space. Instead they blocked communications routes with large, heavily fortified, and virtually impregnable strong points from which they could counterattack the flanks of Russian forces that pushed between them. Those strong points that the Russians surrounded, the Germans supplied by air. This system of defense had something in common with that of fortified cities in the Netherlands in the sixteenth and seventeenth centuries, which usually succeeded in thwarting the offensive efforts of such commanders as Alba, Parma, Luxembourg, and Marlborough.

In June a German mechanized army drove forward to the Don River at Voronezh and turned south while another army, farther south, pushed eastward and then also turned south. These advances enveloped some Russians but not as many as in 1941. The mechanized forces then pushed south toward the oil fields while foot-marching troops moved southeast along the Don to guard the flank of the principal drive. By early August the mechanized forces had crossed 400 miles over level, treeless terrain and had reached the limit of their push until the Germans could reopen the railways for their own use.

The mechanized forces heading to the oil fields made some additional progress in the ensuing months, but strong Russian resistance, aided by the tactical and strategic attacks of powerful bomber forces, limited this German drive. The terrain also assisted the Russians, the mountainous topography of the Caucasus region inhibiting the ability of the tanks to turn strong points and an area of forested mountains providing an effective shield for the Grozny oil fields.

Meanwhile, the German forces guarding the flank had passed the Don and reached the Volga near Stalingrad. Hilter, who increasingly exercised more control over German operations, made a point of the capture of Stalingrad, which lay on the west bank of the broad Volga. The Russian command made an equal point of holding it, and Hilter's decision led to the commitment of large German reserves to attack the city, a natural fortress since its many masonry buildings lost none of their value as fortifications or obstacles when artillery fire or bombs had demolished them. The city itself lay on the west bank of the Volga River near the end of its 2,500-mile descent to the Caspian Sea. The inability of the Germans to force a crossing of this formidable obstacle protected Stalingrad's flanks.

This absorption of German reserves in an unavailing effort to overcome Stalingrad only accentuated the weakness of the whole German plan, an expansion of the front and the creation of a 300-mile-long flank from Voronezh to Stalingrad. The lengthening of the front compelled the Germans to hold this long flank of their extended advance with allied Hungarian, Italian, and Romanian troops. These forces lacked the proficiency of their German counterparts and did not have the numbers necessary for the task; one division had to hold a front of forty miles.

The Russian command, noting this weakness and finding the points of German concentration quite obvious, moved up its reserves to positions along the Don and south of Stalingrad. With Hilter oblivious to this transparent maneuver, the Russian reserves, with the brilliant and experienced Zhukov in command, attacked on November 19 and 20, overwhelming the Romanians on the north of Stalingrad and breaking through the thin German line on the south. On November 23 the enveloping mechanized forces met behind the Germans still besieging Stalingrad. While these Russian forces stood on the defensive to keep the Germans from retreating, a second group drove in to create a new line to the westward to fend off relief efforts. The Russians had created strategic defensive lines of circumvallation and countervallation, much as the Germans had done on their drive to the sea in France and had employed against surrounded Russian forces the previous year.

Just as an unsuccessful German relief offensive began in mid-December, the Russians unleashed another offensive on the Don east of Voronezh, which overwhelmed the thin line of Italian defenders, but failed to reach the Black Sea and thus turn both the German armies still near the oil fields and those seeking to open a route to the Stalingrad forces. Despite further Russian offensive efforts, which miscarried in part because of their distance from their own railheads, the Germans near the oil fields managed to extricate themselves. But the German army at Stalingrad could not escape and surrendered at the end of January 1943. The Germans had tried to supply the trapped army by air but only lost many of their transport aircraft to Russian fighters.

The Germans had lost about 300,000 men to the initial Russian counter-offensive, one which exploited the weakness of the German position at Stalingrad, and many more prisoners as a result of the subsequent Russian offensives that took advantage of the unwise German advance so far into southern Russia. Even if the long flank along the Don had not made the German position hopelessly exposed to strategic disaster, the great extension of the German front had so attenuated their forces in relation to the length of the line as to deprive them of the ability to use the power of the defense in anything approximating a continuous front. Their thinly held line would have little power of resistance, and any Russian attack would have exhibited its vulnerability to penetration and exploitation by mechanized forces.

After withdrawing during the winter of 1942–43, in the face of Russian offensives, to the starting line of their 1942 offensive, the Germans attempted to pinch out a Russian salient at Kursk in July 1943. But since the Russians had prepared elaborate entrenchments and minefields to defend against this obvious move and held immense reserves at hand, the offensive failed with heavy German losses. A battle in which counterattacking Russian armor met attacking German armor resulted in combat involving thousands of tanks.

Thereafter, German-Russian operations took the form of a series of Russian offensives in which mechanized forces made deep penetrations until compelled to stop by an advance too far from their railheads. Long halts to rebuild communications followed each forward movement. In spite of growing German weakness, increasing Russian skill, and the provision of many trucks by the United States, the Russians never succeeded in making any strategic envelopments of German forces quite comparable to those that the Germans had carried out against the Russians in 1941. Still, the armored and the motorized division had profoundly altered warfare, which still superficially seemed to resemble World War I. Large concentrations of artillery and infantry attacks played a major role in the Russian breakthroughs conducted in the same fashion as in World War I. But at that point the mechanized forces exploited the tactical success to move forward as far as 400 miles. Without the mobility of wheels and tracks, many of the advances might well have gone no farther than those of the earlier world war. The greater strength and mobility of the attacking mechanized forces compelled the Germans to fall back until a combination of their reserves on the defensive, counterattacks, and full extension of the Russian line of motorized communication forced a halt.

Distraction, Concentration, and Turning Movement Again: The Landing and Campaign in Normandy

When the British returned to France in 1944, in company with forces from the United States and under an American general, the organization of the Anglo-American armies and their strategy conformed to the model pioneered by the Germans in 1940 and applied by the Germans and Russians. The Anglo-American allies had to leave Britain by ship and go ashore on the defended coast of France, a monumental logistical task involving 5,000 ships and requiring a large number of specialized landing vessels and the subsequent construction of artificial harbors on the French coast. With forty-five divisions available, the allies faced fifty-eight, mostly weaker, German divisions, of which half consisted of immobile fortress divisions and ten were understrength Panzer divisions.

Although command of the sea gave the Anglo-American invaders the same strategic advantage of the initiative the Persians had enjoyed in the Marathon campaign and the Japanese had in their landing to besiege Port Arthur, they could not make an untrammelled choice because the soldiers did not wish to forego the protection offered by their fighter aircraft based in England. Nevertheless, because of their landing craft and prefabricated harbors, they could emulate the Persians and land on the beaches.

By effective security measures, the allies kept their plans and dispositions secret. They created a valuable distraction by using a radio net to fabricate the impression of large forces in southeastern England opposite the French coast around Calais. This diversion successfully confused the German high command and aided the Anglo-American landing farther west.

The German command could not agree on whether to guard the coast heavily or hold back large reserves to concentrate against the landing area in a counterattack. Field Marshal Rommel, who had distinguished himself in North African campaigns, had immediate charge of the defense; he believed that the vastly better enemy air forces could virtually immobilize his reserves and chose to concentrate on protecting the coast. But when the attack came on June 6, 1944, German troops proved inadequate to prevent the disembarkations along a forty-mile section of shoreline between the ports of Le Havre and Cherbourg. And when German reserves arrived, they lacked the necessary strength to drive the allies back into the water. But they did contain the invading forces after they had established a line stretching 100 miles westward from the coast near Caen to the sea and embracing Cherbourg's peninsula and the port itself, which fell to the allies at the end of June. The British and Canadians held the eastern end of this line, the Americans the western.

In early July the Anglo-American-Canadian armies had thirty-four divisions; the Germans had probably a third as much strength distributed in smaller divisions. Thus the Germans had a low ratio of force to the length of the front they held. Although the huge British and American air forces had broken the bridges over the Seine and other rivers and had thus seriously hindered the movement of German reserves, the Germans could still travel by road and had substantial numbers of uncommitted troops that they held back on the Channel coast near Calais to resist a feared second landing. So the Germans tended to think that the landing in Normandy corresponded to the distraction of the Persian landing at Marathon, whereas the radio net in England opposite Calais, together with other deceptive measures and German preconceptions, constituted the real allied distraction.

The Germans concentrated a larger number of men on the eastern end of their line, where an allied breakthrough could turn their entire position by interposing the forces breaking through between the German army and their homeland. The experienced General Sir Bernard Montgomery, the allied ground force commander, encouraged this concentration by constant threats to Caen. In this operation the arrogant, controversial, and quite capable Montgomery showed a performance equal to his methodically gained victories against the Germans and Italians in North Africa. On July 18, after the British and Americans had each pushed forward slowly against strong opposition, Montgomery attacked on both sides of Caen, using in one attack three British armored divisions. As had the Germans in crossing the Meuse at Sedan in 1940, he substituted air bombing for the heavy artillery barrage, 2,000 heavy and medium bombers deluging a small area with bombs. The noise so deafened the Germans who survived that the British could not interrogate some of their prisoners for twenty-four hours.

But the Germans had too much depth in their defensive position. They contained the assault that, had it succeeded, would have sent three armored divisions and the bulk of the Anglo-Canadian forces into the German rear into a position to block a retreat east. Still it accomplished its other purpose—to draw eastward both German reserves near the front and distract the attention of their high command. Just as Allenby in his Megiddo offensive of 1918 had found it easy to convince the Turko-German command that he planned to attack on their most vulnerable flank, so did Montgomery have the same success in mid-July 1944.

On July 25 U.S. forces struck the thinly held German positions before them, also relying on an air bombardment, which dropped 4,200 tons of bombs on an area of less than five square miles. The bombs dropped equaled in weight 17,000 10-inch shells or 500,000 shells from 75-millimeter guns and exceeded

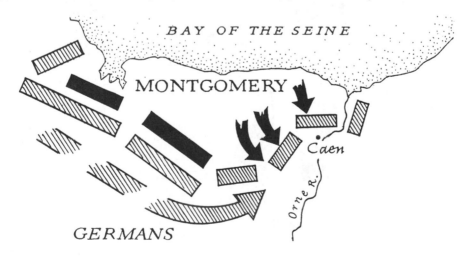

Diagram 10.12. Montgomery's Distraction

either in power because the thin-walled bombs held far more explosives. Three infantry divisions accomplished the breakthrough of the German position, and one motorized and two armored divisions promptly pushed through the gap.

U.S. reserves then poured through the opening, three divisions, including two armored, driving west toward Brest and others going south and east. This dispersal of force, largely to acquire relatively undefended territory and to besiege well-garrisoned but potentially significant ports, varied from the German practice, which usually concentrated on turning the enemy. Yet the Germans, although threatened by troops moving toward their rear, mounted counterattacks to reach the sea and cut off the allies who had broken through. And they succeeded in bringing reinforcements from the Calais area in spite of the activity of the large and skillful Anglo-American air forces and accomplished this by often limiting their moves to the night, a practice the French had used in 1940 to protect their movements from the German airplanes.

But the Americans holding the flank of the breakthrough proved too strong on the defense, and while they repulsed the German counterattack, the British and Canadians maintained unrelenting pressure on the German troops facing northward, just as the American divisions lapped around the open flank of the counterattacking Germans, reaching Argenten by August 13. The Germans extricated themselves from this pocket, created by the American turning movement, with 50,000 captured. In spite of a vigorous pursuit and the difficulties of crossing the Seine with allied troops right behind them and air forces above them, many escaped to the French frontier. Nevertheless, the Germans sustained enormous losses, the extent of which a Panzer army revealed when it reported its strength

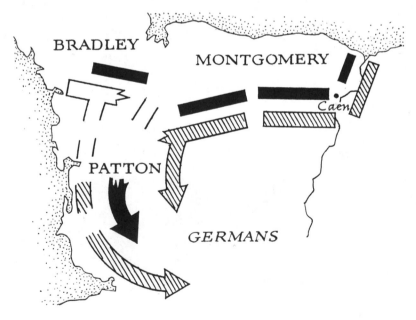

Diagram 10.13. Breakout and Turning Movement

at only twenty-four tanks and 1,300 men. German casualties in men from the landing until the end of the campaign exceeded 500,000. In fact, allied successes virtually denuded the German frontier of troops, but an advance of 300 miles so stretched supply lines, even for the heavily motorized American, British, and Canadian armies, that the Germans had time to bring up men to reconstitute their front.

Thus, as in the past, logistics exercised a constant sway over military operations. Rather than finding themselves trammeled by the need to keep moving to find supplies or to avoid regions already well-foraged or of low productivity, those that achieved the major victory in Normandy found themselves tethered by supply lines to a base. In fact, the need to open ports to increase unloading capacity or to shorten land communication lines exercised an important influence over strategic decisions made about subsequent operations as well as plans for this campaign itself.

The British Inauguration of Mounted Warfare in North Africa and the Defeat of the Italians

North Africa provided the theater for a somewhat different kind of warfare. Medieval in its mounted character and use of foot soldiers in fortified strong points, it differed in that both sides made extensive use of the light cavalry of the air. A low ratio of force to the available space also distinguished it from the warfare in Europe.

The Italians from their colony in Libya fought the British who controlled Egypt. Marshal Graziani, who had displayed ruthlessness in his victorious campaigns against Libyan insurgents and in the Ethiopian war, commanded the much stronger Italians. In General Wavell the British had as their commander a mature, scholarly soldier who understood how to reconcile his immense responsibilities with his meager resources.

Operations began in September 1940 when 80,000 Italians advanced about eighty miles into Egypt to Sidi Barrani, meeting only outposts of the British army concentrated well to the eastward. On reaching Sidi Barrani, the Italians halted and dug in their predominantly infantry force into a group of six heavily garrisoned strong points. Without control of the sea, the Italians faced supply difficulties because of the barrenness of the country, which included inadequate water supplies, and their shortage of motor transport. Neither contestant had first-class weapons because both countries had relegated their obsolete equipment to the secondary theater of Africa. The British had armored cars with machine guns only, and both adversaries had simlarly armed tankettes. Each also relied on essentially comparable and quite out-of-date biplane fighter aircraft of low speed and limited firepower.

The Italian force at Sidi Barrani constituted the easternmost end of a series of strongly garrisoned Italian posts that extended back to Benghazi, more than 300 miles inside the Libyan border. When the British received reinforcements, they determined to attack Sidi Barrani in spite of having only 30,000 men against 80,000 Italians. But the British had received new monoplane fighters, which gave them air supremacy, and fifty Matilda infantry support tanks. At twenty-six tons, twice as heavy as the best Italian tank, the fifteen-mile-an-hour Matilda had essentially invulerable 3-inch armor and mounted a 40-millimeter antitank gun of exceptional power. More important, the British had no foot-marching infantry, their forces consisting of only an armored division and a motorized division. General Wavell gave full latitude in carrying out this operation to his subordinate, the aggressive yet prudent General O'Connor.

Making a moonlit march across the desert in early December 1940, O'Connor's two divisions moved around the Italian fortified positions, passing just north of the outermost of these. The armored division reached the coast easily in the morning where it overcame a heavily defended post twenty miles behind the Italian position at Sidi Barrani. Meanwhile, the infantry division, supported by the Matilda tanks and field artillery, struck the Italian Sidi Barrani strong points from the rear. Turned, caught unaware, demoralized by attacks from their rear, and deficient in antitank guns, the Italians surrendered 40,000 men and 400 guns.

Surprised by and unready for their easy victory, the British did not resume their advance until early January. Then O'Connor repeated his turning movement around the southern flank against the Italians dug in to defend a pass along the coast, capturing 129 tanks, 45,000 prisoners, and 462 guns. A similar maneuver later in the month against the next fort yielded 30,000 prisoners and 87 tanks. At this point the British, their forces much depleted by mechanical breakdowns and combat losses, sent most of the remaining armored force west to head off the retreat of the last Italians in eastern Libya.

Sending in advance a faster force of untracked vehicles, composed of some armored cars, a few infantry in trucks, and a small number of towed field and antitank guns, O'Connor's small advance force reached the coastal road ahead of the Italians. Since the Italians had naturally concentrated their strength at the

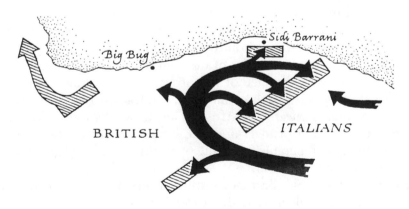

Diagram 10.14. British Turn Sidi Barrani

rear of their retreating column, the small British contingent held up the Italians until their tanks arrived. Although they had used up their Matilda tanks, they had a few fast, thinly armored tanks also equipped with the powerful 40-millimeter gun. These took positions behind the crests of hills, where they could fire at the Italian tanks on the coastal highway without exposing any part but the turret. The 3,000 men in the British mechanized force captured 20,000 prisoners and 120 tanks.

In this operation the infantry in trucks and the towed artillery and antitank guns played the medieval role of spearmen who mounted themselves on nags for strategic mobility but fought on foot. The tanks, when they took up positions that exposed only their turrets, behaved in a manner analogous to medieval cavalry dismounted to fight as heavy infantry. In this instance, the tanks functioned as emplaced antitank guns. In catching the Italians as they attempted to make their way along the coast road, the British had pressed them against the sea as well as blocked their retreat, thus even giving something of a medieval character to the turning movement. This operation has parallels not just with Allenby's campaign and the French motorized movement in Morocco but also with the role of cavalry in Grant's successful pursuit of Lee to Appomattox.

The sum of their series of defeats inflicted on the Italians represented a stupendous victory for 30,000 men over an army many times its size with comparable weapons. Although the British suffered less than 2,000 casualties, the Italians lost 130,000 as prisoners, nearly 400 tanks, and over 800 guns. Yet the bulk of the Italian losses consisted of infantry fitted out with rifles, machine guns, and artillery, a force well adapted to the siege warfare conditions of World War I but of limited value in the mounted conflict that the British had inaugurated. Although the Italians had more tanks than the British, they never concentrated them nor separated them from their foot soldiers to exploit their mobility as did the British. The Italians did not concentrate their antitank guns, effective against the thin armor of most British tanks. The infantry armed after the manner of World War I had played a major role in Europe where it denied territory to similarly outfitted enemy infantry. In North Africa, where the sea protected one flank, and the other, in such a huge country, must necessarily remain open, such infantry seemed only to complicate logistics and provide casualties in defeat.

The Warfare of the Mounted British and German Armies

No sooner had the British driven back the Italians and transferred some troops to another theater than German Panzer and motorized forces arrived to aid the Italians, who had reinforced their African army with an armored and a motorized division. Led by General Rommel, who had distinguished himself commanding a Panzer division in France, the Germans drove the surprised and unready British back nearly to the Egyptian border so quickly that they surprised and captured

General O'Connor. A stalemate ensued as both strengthened their armies. General Rommel, who displayed dash, daring, and tactical skill, controlled the operation of the Italian and German forces. He faced capable opponents when the government replaced Wavell with India's leading soldier, the likeable but prickly General Auchinleck, in 1941 and supplanted him in 1942 with the charming and confident General Alexander.

The British were not so fortunate in their operational commanders, none nearly matching O'Connor until General Montgomery received the command in the summer of 1942.

After Rommel's appointment and initial victory there followed an eighteen-month seesaw struggle in which German and Italian forces, largely armored and motorized, successfully fought the usually stronger British. The British not only had more tanks but, on the whole, better equipment. Their new, higher-speed tanks had 40-millimeter armor compared with the 30-millimeter armor on German tanks, and their excellent 40-millimeter tank and antitank guns had armor-penetrating power comparable to the German 50-millimeter gun. The British, who continued to discriminate between their fast tanks and those designed to accompany infantry, also had their Matildas with 75-millimeter armor and a smaller infantry tank with armor 65-millimeters thick. Both had the excellent 40-millimeter gun. The Italian tanks, smaller than the British and German, had no more speed than British infantry tanks and lacked their thick armor. When the Germans improvised thicker armor on their tanks and introduced a few with 50-millimeter armor, the British acquired an American 28-ton tank with sloped armor 57-millimeters thick. This tank's 75-millimeter gun also countered the improved 50-millimeter gun on a few of the new German tanks. In addition, the Germans had more light tanks without any effective guns.

The Germans suffered inferiority in antitank guns, too. Initially two-thirds of their antitank guns consisted of the 37-millimeter, which had proven so inadequate against the French, could only pierce the thinly armored fast British tanks at close range, and had little value against the slow British infantry tanks. When the Germans obtained some of a superior 50-millimeter, the British had reequipped many units with their new, more powerful 57-millimeter antitank gun.

The Germans coped by using their 88-millimeter antiaircraft gun as an antitank gun. In spite of its bulk, occasioned by its mounting for high-angle fire, they used it effectively by careful siting and emplacement. This powerful, high-velocity gun, which had the same bore as one used on the imperial German navy's early destroyers, fired a twenty-pound shell, compared with the 4½-pound shell of the 50-millimeter antitank gun, and had very nearly the same rate of fire. The Germans had no monopoly on such an antiaircraft gun, the Russians having an 85-millimeter, the French, Americans, and Italians a 90-millimeter, and the British a 94-millimeter antiaircraft gun, all with characteristics essentially similar to the German gun. But the Germans in Africa had a need to make this expedient improvisation and did so very skillfully.

In spite of great inferiority in numbers and some in materiel, the Germans and Italians held their own. They owed much of their achievement to the Germans' first-rate tactical skill, particularly their better grasp of the importance of concentration of their tanks and to their appreciation of the supremacy of the defense. While the cliché of attacking and destroying the enemy influenced British doctrine and contributed to an almost exclusively offensive attitude in the British armored forces, the Germans knew how to combine their antitank guns with their tanks and invite British tank attacks against defensively deployed tanks and antitank guns.

For example, in June 1942 Rommel's army carried out a turning movement around the desert flank of the British position, a maneuver that typified almost every offensive operation on either side. When the resistance of British tanks proved too strong to enable him to reach the coast, Rommel went on the defensive in a place that still threatened British communications. The British responded by trying to drive him out with tank attacks. The Germans repulsed these with a combination of the fire of tank and antitank guns. After a period on the defensive, during which the Germans had inflicted appalling losses on the British, they could resume the offensive, complete their turning movement, and drive the British well back into Egypt. The Germans had thus exploited with their tanks, aided by antitank guns, the traditional advantage of the turning movement of imposing on the turned force the disadvantage of assuming the tactical offensive. In this case the threat of completing the turning movement proved adequate to compel the British to take the offensive.

And tanks on the defensive enjoyed substantial benefits over those attacking: the defender knew his field of fire, and the crew could give their undivided attention to the gunnery. In addition, the defending tank almost invariably settled in beyond the crest of a hill or ridge so that it exposed only its comparatively small and well-armored turret to the fire of its completely visible assailants. Thus tanks on the defensive had the benefit that dismounted heavy cavalry had traditionally enjoyed in defense against a charge of mounted heavy cavalry. The Germans, rather than the British (who had employed this tactic so masterfully against the French at the Battle of Crécy and in their last turning movement against the Italians), made the most extensive use of this tactic of employing tanks on the defensive, supplemented by the emplacement of towed antitank guns and their formidable 88-millimeter antiaircraft guns. The British soon became wary of attacking or even pursuing the Germans and learned to use the Crécy tactic effectively themselves. On one occasion, for example, the Germans overwhelmed British defenders, inflicting 3,000 casualties, but lost nearly half of their tank force in the process. Like Pyrrhus, they could not afford more such victories.

Infantry played a role on the entrenched defense, sometimes in lines, often in an array of strong points prepared for all-around defense. Antitank guns and field artillery provided protection against tanks as did a liberal use of land mines. To guard one line, for example, the British planted 500,000 mines to halt tanks, and these defenses proved deadly to German and Italian armor. In particular, adequate antitank guns showed their mastery over both British and German tanks, four 88-millimeter guns destroying twelve of thirteen attacking British Matilda tanks in spite of their thick armor.

As in the stereotype of completely mounted medieval warfare, the struggles of tanks against tanks whirled around castle-like fortified positions that defended mine fields and interdicted the best routes for wheeled vehicles over the rugged desert terrain. The operations also had some comparability with the traditional association of heavy cavalry with pike squares on the battlefield. But in daylight the aircraft played the role of light cavalry by attacking with bombs and gunfire the ground forces, supply vehicles proving the most vulnerable.

The open flank, which extended hundreds of miles into the desert, provided so much space for combat that the forces, rarely much more than 50,000 men and 500 tanks, could not control the available area. Operations would have had much in common with those of the distant past, when armies had the ability to avoid action by moving to and fro in a theater of war large in relation to their size, had logistics not tethered the forces in a way unknown to armies whose horses could graze as they went from place to place. The need for fuel as well as ammunition, food, and water made these armies quite sensitive to communications and hence unable to move as freely as the mounted forces of old. The speed at which the mechanized forces progressed had, however, shrunk the area of operations when mobile forces maneuvered against one another and this, together with the greater distance at which combat took place, made possible unexpected engagements and the forcing of battle upon a halted enemy that wished to avoid fighting.

Thus control of the good coastal road, and the ports it linked together, dominated the strategy of mechanized forces, which depended on it to replenish fuel. The warfare then had the older characteristic of a low ratio of force to space but, having the constraint of communications to defend, still made the turning movement and defense against it the dominant strategic variable.

Turning movements traditionally depended on communications—or the equivalent—because communciations gave the turned force a rear and provided at least a strong incentive to take the offensive against the turning force to recover those communications. Yet turning movements also relied on the supremacy of the tactical defensive so that the turning force would gain tactical superiority, a condition met in North Africa because tanks on the defensive as well as antitank guns had prevailed against tanks on the offensive. But turning movements also banked on an adequate ratio of force to space, so as to have the ability to block the retreat of the turned, as Napoleon's experience in the Battle of Marengo, where he had brought to the battle barely enough force to win and interdict the Austrian withdrawal, demonstrated.

So in the North African campaign turning movements failed to trap the mounted forces. Exceptionally well articulated because of radio communciation, tanks and tank units constituted the ideal offensive troops, for in the relatively large spaces of the North African theatre, tank forces proved particularly elusive and hard to contain. With both contestants avoiding the mistake of attacking tanks arrayed for the defense, mechanized forces seeking to fall back used their mobility to pass around the flank of opponents trying to block them, or they employed their capacity for rapid concentration to overwhelm weak forces in their path.

Although the Germans and Italians as well as the British tried to rely on the predominance of the tactical defense, encounter battles between tank forces often characterized the intermittent but intense combat. Both sides lost heavily in tanks, each of two major struggles, for example, reduced tank forces of the combatants by over 80 percent. In one prolonged losing struggle, the Germans lost 230 of their original 260 tanks, and in their victory that carried them into Egypt, the Germans and Italians began the protracted battle with 560 tanks but had only fifty-eight when they crossed the Egyptian border. The British suffered comparable losses in both conflicts.

The tactical results of these engagements, that is, the attrition inflicted and suffered, had a predominant role in determining the strategic outcome. Armies could sustain their morale and continue fighting in spite of such catastrophic tolls because the losses in tanks did not reflect casualties in manpower. Crews often escaped unharmed from disabled tanks, and hard usage and rugged terrain meant that mechanical failures also provided a major source of tank casualties. The loss of tanks to damage and breakdowns meant that possession of the battlefield, the traditional indicator of victory, assumed a tactical importance as meaningful as the ransoming of prisoners after a medieval battle between knights. Since possession of the battlefield gave the victor control of the disabled tanks, they could repair many of them and thus significantly reduce their casualties while appropriating some of the enemy's derelict vehicles.

New and Improved Weapons

The war changed aircraft relatively little. Many airplanes in service at the beginning of the conflict continued, with improvements, until the end. Increases in engine power, speed, and carrying capacity represented the principal alterations. The British and the Americans used ever greater numbers of large, four-engine bombers of models that had existed earlier. They employed these mainly for strategic bombing programs.

Low-level ground attack aircraft underwent considerable development as the belligerents perfected methods of attack other than dive bombing. Flying low, planes with one and two engines dropped bombs on vehicles, railroad trains, and bridges and used rockets as well as machine guns and cannon against personnel and vehicles. Fighters, bigger and more powerful, armed with cannon and able to carry bombs or rockets, easily became fighter-bombers, able to perform both tasks with excellent facility. The Russians used these and more specialized ground attack aircraft in which they mounted a 37-millimeter cannon, which could pierce the thin horizontal armor of even large tanks. With such cannon, bombs, and rockets, airplanes proved deadly to tanks in the open, thus resurrecting a light cavalry superiority, which the Turkish horse archers had so decisively demonstrated against Byzantine heavy cavalry at Manzikert.

The war altered tanks to an important degree. At the beginning of the conflict tanks of 10 to 15 tons with 37-millimeter cannon of modest muzzle velocity represented the majority of modern tanks in European armies. By 1945 such tanks found little use. Instead, tanks of 25 to 35 tons with 3-inch, high-velocity guns played the major role in all armies, and the Germans and Russians had tanks of more than 40 tons, some mounting high-velocity guns larger than 3 inches. Armor plate became thicker as well, 4 inches becoming as common as 1½ inches was at the outbreak of the war. Speed changed little, 20 to 30 miles an hour remaining typical.

These modifications in tanks, especially the mounting of the larger, high-velocity gun, did not respond to the tank's original purpose: attacking infantry and its machine guns. Rather, the ability to defeat infantry became a by-product of a tank designed to fight other tanks. The use of tanks for counterattacks and even in defense made it essential to equip armies with tanks that could defeat the enemy's tanks. The Germans and the Russians also adopted the self-propelled gun, essentially a turretless tank with a powerful gun mounted in the hull. This gun thus lacked much traverse, but it enabled the chassis of smaller, well-proven tanks already in production to carry guns and armor capable of dealing with the larger antitank tanks.

Armored cars continued in use, and armored personnel carriers grew in numbers. These, often having wheels in front with tracks in the rear to provide cross-country mobility, carried some of the infantry accompanying the tanks in armored divisions. Since many of these had some armor on their sides and carried a machine gun, they could perform some of the tank's mission of attacking an infantry armed only with rifles and machine guns.

Tanks had evolved much as had the armored medieval heavy cavalryman. Because heavy cavalry fought each other, the horsemen had exceptionally powerful war-horses and plate armor, expensive improvements not critical for riding down light infantry with bows or successfully attacking the flank or rear of heavy infantry formations. So also tanks acquired guns of far greater power than needed to attack machine gun positions; they became larger not only to carry these bigger guns but also because of the thicker armor required to resist the more powerful guns of the opposing tanks and the infantry's antitank weapons.

The development of the thickly armored antitank tank quickly made existing antitank guns obsolete. Three-inch field guns proved useful as antitank guns as did heavy antiaircraft guns. The progression in British antitank guns well exemplifies the growth in power of guns designed for the antitank role. Beginning the war with an effective, high-velocity gun firing a 2½-pound shot, the British progressed through one with a 7-pound projectile to end the war with a gun firing a 17-pound shot. Since they accompanied this rise in projectile weight with a small increase in muzzle velocity, they had enhanced muzzle energy more than 7 times. Yet economies of scale meant that the weight of the gun grew only a little over 2½ times. Nevertheless, the resulting antitank gun weighed more than the field guns of the same bore and weighed as much as the standard howitzers firing a shell nearly twice as heavy. To cope with the thick armor of the large antitank tank, the antitank gun had become as heavy and immobile as the traditional artillery piece.

But another change, and an important one, carried the antitank weapon back to the mobility of the shoulder-fired antitank rifle of World War I, which, in turn, had differed little in portability from the pike used long before to resist the charge of the heavy cavalry. One man could carry, and one or two men could fire the antitank rocket, nicknamed the bazooka in the U. S. army. This became available during the middle of the war and proved effective in piercing tank armor. Since, with its low velocity, the rocket-powered projectile could not penetrate tank armor, the bazooka relied on a special type of shaped charge in its projectile. The charge had a deeply concave figuration so that, upon combustion, the force of the explosion focused at the base of the vacant conical space, which was at the point of the projectile. Here the heat of the explosion melted the armor, piercing a small hole through which passed much of the blast of the explosion together with some particles of the melted armor. In the confined area of the inside of a tank this explosion often had a disastrous effect on the crew and on interior components of the tank.

The portability of the bazooka rocket launcher with its special projectile enabled skillful and courageous soldiers to ambush tanks, effectively firing at them from the sides with bazookas too small to penetrate the tanks' thick frontal armor. So infantry had regained an antitank capability by the end of the war, which, however, lacked sufficient potency to render redundant for antitank defense either the powerful, high-velocity antitank artillery piece or the mobile tank fighting from covered positions on the defensive in a role comparable to dismounted medieval cavalry.

In the recoilless cannon infantry gained a portable, flat-trajectory weapon to complement the light mortar that it had acquired in World War I. By allowing some of the force of the explosion of the shell's propelling charge to escape from the rear of the small cannon, the designers provided a gun in which the rearward escaping gases so exactly nullified the recoil caused by the ejection of the projectile from the barrel that such a cannon had no recoil. Because the barrel did not have to contain the full force of the explosion, the weapon had so little weight that a gunner could fire a 57-millimeter version from his shoulder, the back blast eliminating any recoil.

Infantry thus acquired a portable or mobile cannon whose capacity for direct fire complemented the indirect fire of the infantry's similarly light-weight mortars. But recoilless cannon had a number of defects. The escape of gases to the rear not only made them dangerous to fire but also immediately revealed

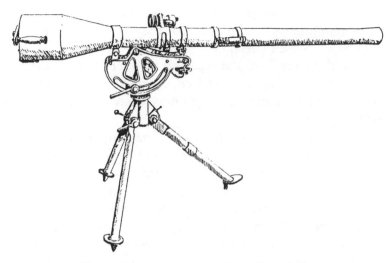

Illustration 10.2. 75-mm Recoilless Rifle

their location to the enemy. Their low-muzzle velocity and limited range inhibited their use as infantry weapons, primarily by depriving them of much armor-piercing ability in spite of some having bores greater than four inches. So, for use against tanks, recoilless cannon had to rely on shaped charges whose effect the rotation of the shell diminished. The bazooka's rocket, stabilized in flight by fins rather than the spin characteristic of the shell, proved a better antitank weapon. Nevertheless, the infantry gained a versatile weapon that augmented its antitank capability.

Rockets had many other uses, for example supplementing artillery when an area was the target. They also had utility on aircraft, as fighters employed them against formations of bombers, and low-level bombers and fighter-bombers fired them against targets on the ground. The Germans also used a ballistic rocket, called the V2, against English targets. This 8-ton rocket, which carried 1,000 pounds of explosives and had a range of 200 miles, rose to a height of eight miles before descending at a speed that defied interceptor aircraft or antiaircraft guns. It lacked accuracy, a sizable city being the smallest target at which it could aim with much prospect of obtaining a hit.

The development of small radar sets permitted their installation in a shell, the radar detonating the shell when it approached an object. This expensive fuse improved the performance of the shell but had greater value against high-flying planes because it eliminated the need for precise altitude calculations. If the shell with a radar-operated proximity fuse could pass close to the enemy aircraft, the fuse would explode the shell at the right time and altitude.

Most of these changes improved on existing methods. Radar for controlling antiaircraft guns, for example, substituted for aural detection, optical observation and ranging, and for searchlights. But the provision of infantry with portable antitank weapons, particularly the rocket, made a significant change in that it

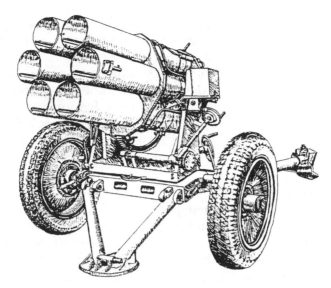

Illustration 10.3. Rocket Launcher

could emancipate the infantry from dependence on the powerful towed artillery piece that the antitank gun had become. An improved bazooka could thus give back to the infantry the heavy infantry role that pikemen had filled in resisting cavalry from the late Middle Ages until the advent of the bayonet.

The German V2 ballistic missile also represented an innovation in that, with its range of 200 miles, it reached far beyond what artillery could attain, yet did so with the invulnerability of the artillery shell. But because of its inaccuracy and its relatively small, 1,000-pound warhead, it lacked much importance during the war. Yet as a weapon in its infancy it, like other rockets used in the war, had the potential to evolve.

World War II completed a transformation of artillery. Originating in ancient times as essentially static weapons for aid in the attack and defense of fortified places, artillery played a negligible role elsewhere, if only because even artillery pieces such as catapults and cannon, which had a reasonable degree of mobility, could not maneuver with the mobile light infantry, armed with a less effective but portable version of the same weapon system. Even with the introduction of much lighter and more mobile pieces during the Thirty Years' War, artillery still played only a circumscribed role on the offensive and could hardly employ the skirmishing tactics of the light infantry.

Eighteenth-century improvements in power, accuracy, and mobility enabled artillery to contribute more to the offense. Well-placed guns could prepare an attack by bouncing cannon balls diagonally through lines of defending infantry. Their enhanced mobility enabled aggressive gunners to push their lighter pieces forward in support of the infantry or even have the teams pull them to positions in front of the infantry and bring the opposing foot soldiers under fire with cannister shot. The defending infantry, remaining standing to resist a cavalry attack and to be ready to reload its muzzleloaders rapidly, suffered severely from the cannister shot of artillery whose fire proved effective even when delivered from beyond the range of the smoothbore muskets.

But nineteenth-century technological developments again devalued artillery's offensive capabilities. The rifle so outranged the smoothbore artillery's cannister shot that the old smoothbore artillery lost its offensive potency once the infantry could shoot the artillerymen. The breechloader, which enabled infantry to fire faster while lying prone, completed the depreciation of artillery, for its gunners were left standing and even more vulnerable to an increased volume of infantry fire.

The new long-range rifled artillery did not restore the balance because it had to rely on shrapnel shells. These projectiles, filled with small missiles and a powder charge to burst the case and propel the shrapnel down on the opposing troops, would have proved effective had they possessed fuses accurate enough to assure the shell's exploding above the enemy troops. This problem led the French in the 1860s to develop their multibarrelled, 125-shots-per-minute *mitrailleuse* to replace the cannister. For this reason the French deployed the *mitrailleuse* with their rifled artillery, which could not shoot very tellingly at rifle-armed infantry. But the *mitrailleuse* failed to provide the expected offensive firepower.

Refinement in fuses by the end of the century enabled the rifled artillery to realize the full possibilities of shrapnel, and, with excellent recoil systems permitting a shield on the gun, the new rapid-fire artillery recovered the power to attack infantry that it had enjoyed in Napoleon's day.

Still, in World War I the new artillery failed to utilize fully its recovered offensive potential. Not only did the rifle bullet drive the infantry underground and so give the soldiers protection from artillery, but also, in the absence of mobile warfare, the new field guns could not use their mobility. Artillery played a major offensive role in the war, of course, but only in its oldest and most traditional character, as the essential weapon in the siege warfare that typified most major operations. Nevertheless, the percentage of casualties attributed to artillery fire far surpassed the levels of previous eras.

The siege multiplied heavy guns and provided the infantry with its own small, mobile cannon, grenade launchers, and mortars, completing the infantry's array of gunpowder missile weapons by giving it explosive bullets and indirect as well as direct fire. Most of these weapons functioned as portable weapons with which the infantry could maneuver.

The aircraft of World War I acted as a rival or supplement to artillery, and aircraft certainly expanded this role as its speed and weight-bearing capacity improved. Bombs carried a much higher proportion of explosives in relation to their weight than artillery shells, because they did not have to withstand the force of discharge from a cannon. On the other hand, bombs lacked the accuracy of artillery fire.

The division of labor that evolved between artillery and aircraft during World War II meant that armies relied on bombs when ground units lacked artillery, and bombs also substituted for World War I's heavy artillery and long-range guns. So though bombs often played a major role in tactical situations, aircraft normally reserved their tactical use of bombs for attacking tanks or infantry in the rear and for carrying out the strategic light cavalry role of raiding communications and supply depots.

In the interwar years the spread of motorized traction for artillery increased its strategic mobility but not its tactical role. The dramatic change came when the tank chassis furnished self-propelled mounts for howitzers, which provided indirect fire while keeping up with the infantry's tactical movements. These self-propelled howitzers had enough armor to continue the shield tradition and give crews protection from small-arms fire. Usually they carried a machine gun in addition to their cannon. But the type was not well defined: for example, the Russians mounted a rather high-velocity 76.2-millimeter gun on a tank chassis and armored it with plate thicker than necessary to resist small arms. Self-propelled antitank guns and field guns for antitank use, some as thickly armored as tanks, further blurred the distinction between self-propelled artillery and tanks. By the end of the war some tanks mounted more powerful guns than most self-propelled artillery; one Russian tank had a high-velocity 122-millimeter gun for instance. The French, British, and Americans produced authentic hybrids, tanks with a light howitzer or gun in the hull and an antitank gun in the turret. These tanks could function as self-propelled artillery, particularly in providing direct fire at close range.

All of these provided a great variety of self-propelled artillery, some well adapted for indirect fire and some useful only for direct fire. As such they often had more tactical mobility than infantry and always more unaided strategic mobility. Therefore, they do not fit neatly into the categories that had existed for centuries.

If one defines the primary duty of heavy cavalry as attack against light infantry, all of these self-propelled guns can be seen as heavy cavalry. But if heavy cavalry must also fight other heavy cavalry, then only those with high-velocity guns constitute heavy cavalry; the self-propelled howitzers remain infantry. But if, as is inevitable, heavy cavalry must sometimes charge heavy infantry, the fire of the self-propelled howitzers could prove valuable against hostile antitank guns. And on the kind of battlefield where infantry, armed neither with antitank nor antiaircraft weapons, had no place, the self-propelled howitzer had great effect against the heavy infantry with antitank weapons and menaced even more the light infantry with antiaircraft guns.

Clearly, the usual categories no longer applied to self-propelled artillery that under many circumstances could function in different groups. When howitzers used indirect fire against antitank guns, they operated as did light infantry with bows or arquebuses against pikemen. When they fired at antiaircraft gunners, they performed somewhat as heavy cavalry riding down the light infantry. These two roles account for much of the difficulty of fitting them into a traditional matrix. So the versatility of self-propelled artillery deprives their classification of elegance and mars the symmetry of the relationship among modern weapon systems but easily explains their World War II and present popularity, even though they are far more costly than the traditional towed gun.

The Interaction of Technology with Strategy

It is important to resist explaining the outcome of campaigns with an interpretation that bases itself solely on the quality and quantity of these new weapons. Consider the German campaign of May and June 1940. Faced with an enemy equal in numbers with artillery of comparable quality but far greater in quantity, the Germans won. Of the new weapons, the French, Belgians, and British had an adequate stock of antitank guns, which had a full mastery over German tanks, and a larger supply of tanks that with their greater average weight generally had more powerful combat qualities.

Only in aircraft and antiaircraft guns did the Germans have greater numbers and enjoy superior performance. Yet airplanes had no decisive effect and, though useful tactically, failed greatly to reduce French strategic mobility. They made a spectacular contribution to the crossing of the Meuse at Sedan, but even had the Germans failed without them, the troops crossing in the north at Dinant could have turned the other two French positions on the Meuse, Sedan as well as Monthermé. So German technological primacy in the air did not determine the results of the campaign any more than did their greater number of antiaircraft and antitank guns.

Technology's principal impact came through restoring the four basic weapon systems that had so long conditioned tactics, a process completed when the tanks of World War II acquired the strategic mobility characteristic of heavy cavalry and when aircraft had the necessary cannon and rockets to emulate the light cavalry of old to assail heavy cavalry tanks. The motor truck added a new dimension to war, giving mounted strategic mobility to the infantry and its artillery and the new dismounted weapon systems, the antitank and antiaircraft guns. In addition, the truck solved the problem of supplying ammunition, fuel, and food in mobile warfare with a high ratio of force to space.

The return of the four weapon systems did not restore the warfare of the remote past. Earlier generals had prepared for battles, usually through joint consent, by deploying their weapon systems on a battlefield a mile or more in width so as to place themselves in a mutually supporting array. But the strategic situation in World War II—a high ratio of force to space and a Napoleonic dispersion—precluded a return to the tactical as well as the strategic environment of ancient or medieval times or the Thirty Years' War.

These Napoleonic conditions multiplied the tactical problem of maintaining the proper mixture of weapon systems. Dispersion of forces, introduced during the wars of the French Revolution and Napoleon, had occurred when armies had infantry and heavy cavalry only, and the infantry had defensive predominance over the cavalry. The situation differed markedly in 1940, when the dispersal of armies meant that the new mounted forces could concentrate on a narrow front and overwhelm the defenders just as a large number of heavy cavalry could have swamped a few pikemen or a multitude of Turkish horse archers could have had the best of a much smaller force of crossbowmen. Lanchester's insight about the advantage conferred by numerical superiority when troops have missile weapons helps explain why greater numbers of tanks, for example, could prevail over fewer antitank guns in spite of the benefits conferred by the immobile defense.

Since generals could no longer count on fighting a battle against an enemy with a comparable mixture of weapon systems, the strategic distribution of the varieties of mounted and dismounted forces assumed an importance that it had never had in the past, when armies possessed a similar composition of the different varieties of troops. When the Germans concentrated all of their tanks to make a strategic team with fully motorized infantry weapons to create the Panzer divisions and then provided for coordination with their air force, they created a strategically powerful union of mounted forces with the dismounted antitank and antiaircraft guns, for which they had provided strategic mobility. The French had done this, too, but the Germans used this combination to implement Napoleon's most important maneuver.

Generals always found difficulty in executing a turning movement when their strategic mobility was the same as their adversaries'. This meant that a perceptive and reasonably alert enemy could always avoid a turning movement. But Panzer and motorized divisions concentrated together gave German generals the superior strategic mobility needed to turn a wary enemy. They pioneered it in France and practiced it again and again in Russia, using its strategic double envelopment form. The Panzer division complemented its high strategic mobility with the presence of so many tanks, the tactically offensive heavy cavalry whose decisive impact Alexander the Great had demonstrated. And, like Alexander's army, a Panzer division possessed a good proportion of all four weapon systems. The Germans knew how to integrate these tactically as well as had Alexander, and, in addition, they employed the dispersion of Napoleonic battles and possessed the high level of articulation perfected in World War I, augumented by the radio.

These Napoleonic successes depended on their adversary's having large numbers of soldiers lacking the strategic mobility of Panzer and motorized divisions. In the initial conflicts in the North African desert, the British reproduced these turning movements against Italian infantry. But when the Germans arrived and the Italians sent their armored and motorized divisions, the warfare of the reincarnated four weapon systems appeared in its purest form. Infantry had little relevance apart from its antiaircraft guns and the ability of its field, antiaircraft, or antitank artillery to defend against tanks and planes. Further, all divisions, except the garrisons of forts and cities, had mounted strategic mobility.

Yet, although neither side had better strategic mobility, turning movements did occur, just as in the past generals had reached their opponent's rear without the benefit of better mobility. But the low ratio of force to space prevented these from having the decisive effect of blocking a retreat, in spite of the armies' extraordinary dependence on communications engendered by the desert and the high consumption of fuel as well as ammunition. The vast size of the theater of war caused this low ratio of force to space as did the small forces resulting from the secondary importance both combatants assigned to combat in Africa. But the high relative cost of the mounted weapon systems, and the trucks and tracked carriers used to provide strategic mobility to the dismounted antitank and antiaircraft guns and their gunners, so raised the expense of the forces that this implied smaller numbers. The mounted armies in North Africa had much in common with those of the Byzantines, which had contrasted markedly in size with the larger, essentially infantry forces of the earlier Roman Empire.

Of course, the new warfare in either its desert form or that introduced in France in 1940 did not always prevail. In the forested regions of northern Russia, for example, the terrain reduced the tank and the airplane to the role of auxiliaries. Here warfare did not differ much from that of World War I.

Strategic Bombing

The British and the Americans both invested immense resources in creating huge heavy bomber forces with which to try to win the war with the logistic strategy of crippling the enemy's economy. But neither had enough aircraft ready when they entered the war; the British had only a small number of two-engine heavy bombers of limited carrying capacity.

Bombing by the small British long-range bombers in 1939 and 1940 revealed unanticipated problems in executing the air raids to implement the strategy. Accuracy in dropping bombs proved very difficult to achieve, and even finding the target city occasionally became too challenging. In addition, unescorted bombers, in spite of their defensive machine guns, displayed an unexpected and disastrous vulnerability to fighter aircraft. In one early raid, for example, in which twenty-two British bombers took part, fifteen failed to return. Thus British bombers had the same experience against fighters as had the Germans in their attack on Britain in the summer of 1940. Since fighter planes lacked the range to accompany the bombers, the British soon adopted the plan of bombing at night when interceptor aircraft lost most of their effectiveness and antiaircraft fire depended on the uncertain and frequently ineffective assistance of searchlights.

But bombing at night aggravated the problems of finding the target and bombing accurately once aircraft reached their destination. Aerial reconnaissance of early night bombing efforts revealed that only one bomb in ten fell within a mile of the goal. British bombing showed little improvement over French night bombing of the Briey Basin in World War I. These problems led the British to modify their purpose in bombing enemy industry. Instead of striving to hit specific factories or railway yards, they directed their missions at whole areas, aiming their attacks at the work force instead of the capital—the buildings, machinery, and tools. The cities, morale, and lives of the workers thus became the logistic target of night air raids.

But this change in logistic objective also altered the character of the bombing. Night area bombing necessarily tested the political part of the strategic bombing theory—compelling the enemy to abandon the war through the terror of the raids. By destroying property and killing civilians, many exponents of air power believed that the raids would, as had the actions of the Turks in Asia Minor and the Mongols in Khwarizm, terrorize the enemy into surrender. But the German air raids against British cities in 1940 had failed to have this result. Instead, British civilian morale and determination had, if anything, stiffened. Thus, the British had no reason to expect the Germans to react differently, and, in fact, they did not.

By 1943 the British had the resources to pursue the strategy of demolishing cities. Their production of four-engine bombers had expanded until they had 700 to 800 bombers available. By the use of radar and radio beams they had so improved their accuracy that instead of 20 percent of the bombs falling within five miles of the aiming point as in 1941, 60 percent fell within three miles of the target in 1943. This level of accuracy sufficed in bombing a large city. The British had also adopted the practice of using a large proportion of 4-pound incendiary bombs, combined with some high-explosive bombs to wreck buildings and make the city unsafe for fire fighters.

The British also refined their methods when they concentrated a night's raid on one city and learned to bring the entire force of 400 or 500 aircraft over the city in two to three hours, thus securing concentration in time as well as space. In addition, they had strips of metallized paper that, when dropped from the aircraft, would foil the German radar by cluttering the screen with reflections. This technique seriously handicapped both German antiaircraft fire control and the direction of night fighters from the ground.

In the summer of 1943 the British brought all of their latest techniques to bear upon the port and industrial city of Hamburg, Germany's second largest metropolis. On the night of July 24–25, 791 bombers, almost all four-engined, attacked the city. The British lost only twelve planes. Three nights later 787 aircraft dropped 1,200 tons of incendiary bombs as well as high explosives. A gigantic fire resulted in which air rushing in to feed the flames created winds sufficient to uproot trees and sweep much into the fire, including human beings.

The fire suffocated or killed with its heat, which exceeded 1,400 degrees Fahrenheit, many civilians who would otherwise have been secure in underground shelters. The raids and the ensuing fire overwhelmed the city's fire department and civil defense capabilities. The bombings resulted in the obliteration of over nine square miles of the city and destruction of or damage to 300,000 houses. A third raid, handicapped by bad weather, did little additional damage. At Hamburg the attack on cities, civilians, and morale had reached a level close to perfection. Fatalities due to the raid exceeded 40,000, almost all civilians.

Yet this exemplary application of the political strategy of terror, and others like it on a much smaller scale, failed to bring peace. Doubtless the better German preparation and the more modern construction of other cities help explain the lack of success of future raids in inflicting the high rate of casualties of the Hamburg experience. The failure of the morale of the German public to succumb to the terror of the raids owed much to the power of the German government, its control of radio and newspapers, and its competent efforts to influence public opinion. The unlimited war aims of their adversaries undoubtedly contributed also. Yet the outcome does present a puzzling contrast to those attained by the Turks and Mongolians, and the answer to the question lies outside the limits of this work.

The pure logistic strategy received a second chance in 1942 when U.S. bombers arrived. With a more accurate bombsight and bombers with more defensive machine guns, the Americans expected to adhere to their original doctrine of accurate daylight bombing to destroy critical logistic targets and to cripple the enemy's economy. So in early 1943 the American bombers began small unescorted daylight raids into Germany. These planes suffered heavily, one strike by fourteen aircraft losing four. But in spite of continued heavy losses, the U.S. bombers persisted, believing that when they had a large force, the machine guns of the many bombers would provide adequate protection.

On August 1, 1943, 147 aircraft assailed the Romanian oil fields but lost 54. On August 17, 315 planes attacked two more logistically vital targets, a Messerschmitt aircraft works and a ball-bearing factory. Meeting antiaircraft fire and 300 defending fighters, they lost 60 aircraft, shooting down 27 German planes. The American belief that they had downed 288 German fighters provided them with their only encouragement. The raids proved to have inflicted little damage on the targets, in spite of the 724 tons of bombs dropped, and such losses would soon have eliminated the American bomber force.

In October 291 U.S. bombers made another deep raid against the ball-bearing factory, losing 60 aircraft and not significantly impeding German production. This culminated a week's activity that had already cost 88 aircraft. The doctrine of unescorted day air raids had apparently failed again. And although the U.S. bomber fleet grew, so did the German fighter force, increasing from 1,100 fighters in early 1943 to 1,600 at the beginning of 1944.

And the British did not prove able to repeat their Hamburg success. The Germans learned to cope with the confusion caused by the metallized paper and their antiaircraft guns recovered some of their effectiveness as did the ground control of night fighters. These fighters, directed toward approaching bombers spotted by ground radar, used their own radar sets to close in on and shoot down British bombers. British losses in the fall of 1943 averaged more than 5 percent per raid, thus coming perilously close to the 7 percent that Britain's air force believed would preclude continuing their raids. Further, the British could not burn more cities as they had Hamburg. An effort against Berlin failed because the less compact city's more modern buildings resisted a fire storm like Hamburg's.

In 1944 the Anglo-American air forces diverted much of their energy to supporting the impending landing of their armies on the continent. Their reduced activity deep over Germany diminished their losses, especially among the Americans, but the British continued to have difficulties. In March 1944, for example, a British raid of 791 planes lost 94, and many more aircraft received enough damage to require extensive repairs. The 55,000 fatalities suffered during the war by the British bomber command well attests to the heavy cost of night bombing.

But in the spring of 1944 the Americans decisively overcame the German daylight air defenses by escorting the U. S. bombers. They fit additional gasoline tanks to fighters, the auxiliary tanks supplying the fighters with fuel until they drew near the target. The fighters then dropped the tanks, engaged the German fighters, and protected the bombers and inflicted heavy losses on the German planes. The normal fuel load of the fighters sufficed for the period of combat and the return flight.

By the summer of 1944 the allies had increasingly large numbers of four-engine bombers to carry out regular raids. By then the Anglo-American bombers had dropped about three-quarters of a million tons of bombs on Germany. Yet German arms production had doubled between 1942 and 1944. The more complete mobilization of the German economy and the labor of prisoners and foreigners had more than compensated for the limited results of the bombing.

In September 1944 the success of the armies in their campaign in France enabled the Anglo-American air forces to give full attention to an undiminished and unremitting attack on Germany. Although the Americans had, to a degree, adopted the British outlook when they compensated for poor visibility by bombing cities by radar, they still sought logistically important targets. Transportation facilities and synthetic oil plants received consistent attention on the assumption that the German economy and army could not do without these vital logistical sinews.

The air forces had unprecedented resources for this campaign. The British had 1,000 heavy bombers and the United States had 2,000 in the United Kingdom and another 1,200 based in Italy. They possessed an ample supply of fighters to escort the American bombers, and the British had airborne electronic equipment to paralyze the night air defense by jamming German radars and radios.

The campaign had a powerful effect. In the last months of 1944, for instance, the British dropped four times as much bomb tonnage as in the same period in the previous year. From the middle of 1944 until the end of the war the following spring, the British and Americans dropped nearly 2 million additional tons of bombs. The effort of the United States to apply in daylight the original concept of the logistic strategy had proved no more significant than the smashing of dwellings and the killing of civilians. They had tried bombing German aircraft factories but without much success due to the dispersed nature of the industry. German aircraft output reached its peak in September 1944, when the industry produced 3,538 aircraft, and the fall of 1944 the factories reached their highest production for a comparable period.

But attacks on the new targets, the railways and synthetic petroleum plants, did yield important results. Coal shipments from the Ruhr mines fell by 75 percent, which reduced industrial production, including steel. The bombing, together with the loss of the Romanian oil fields, caused the output of gasoline to fall so disastrously that the Germans had to curtail flying times in pilot training and ultimately found all military operations seriously hampered.

The pure logistic strategy, pursued by reasonably accurate bombing in daylight from aircraft protected by fighters with extended range, did prove effective. But it came at a time when the allies had already defeated Germany at sea and were completing its defeat on land. Yet it is difficult to see how the bombing forces could have implemented such an ambitious logistic strategy sooner. Only the accuracy of day bombing could have secured the hits necessary to disable oil and transportation targets. And factories and railways proved so resistant to destruction and so readily repaired that only large-scale and continuing day bombing could have effectively smashed them. But these raids carried out earlier would have had to face the undiminished vigor of the German air defense, and concentrating on these targets would have helped the Germans to make a comparable concentration of their air defenses.

The Anglo-American strategic bombing forces, as originally constituted, probably lacked the resources to carry out this campaign in 1943. Only a differently structured force, one with fewer bombers but emphasizing large numbers of fighters with extended range, could have executed such a logistic bombing campaign in 1943. It then might have appreciably shortened the war. To a degree this bombing campaign paralleled the blockade at sea: without naval supremacy there can be no blockade, only raids that harm but rarely close sea lanes.

In a final analysis, the strategic bombing program did not contribute much to winning the war. The British could probably have made better use of some of the nearly one-third of their war effort that they devoted to strategic bombing. The United States could have made a similar reduction in its large commitment to its air force. These savings would doubtless have exceeded those that the Germans could have made from the resources devoted to air defense and to rebuilding damaged factories and railways, even though these tasks absorbed perhaps 2 million people and half of Germany's air force.

With the British building 40,000 aircraft in 1944, including many with two and four engines, and the Germans and Russians each building the same number, though with a far higher proportion of smaller, single-engine aircraft, Britain and Russia had an adequate number of aircraft for tactical superiority without drawing on the European theater's share of the U.S. production of 100,000 aircraft that year.

A comparison of the aircraft involved illustrates the immense effort required for strategic bombing. In 1944 the British and Americans had 4,200 four-engine bombers for their campaign against 1,600 German fighters. Since the bomber weighed six times as much as the fighter, one may compare the two forces as having a resource cost ratio similar to their weight, 252 to 16 or almost 16 to 1. True, the bomber had only four engines and a crew of seven or more, but of less average skill than the fighter pilot. Since, however, 3,200 of the bombers had two crews, the 16 to 1 resource ratio may not vary too much from the actual. Of course, if only because the Germans had an elaborate antiaircraft defense and the British and Americans had fighter aircraft committed to escorting the bombers, this ratio does not pretend to compare the total resources employed. But it does illustrate the immense cost of the strategic bombing program.

In a sense, the two atomic bombs dropped on Japan at the end of the war only did what ordinary explosives had already done in Japan and Germany. With an explosive force of not more than the equivalent 20,000 tons of that used in bombs, one air raid with one aircraft accomplished what earlier required several raids of 1,000 airplanes. But the atomic bomb stood for more than an increase in efficiency; it brought about so great a change in degree that it represented a difference in kind. The rapid postwar growth in the power of nuclear bombs and the reduction in their bulk accentuated the difference in kind between the new bombs and the old.

Combat at Sea with Two Types of Capital Ships

In its main outlines, World War II at sea differed little from that twenty-five years earlier. Faced with Britain's even greater supremacy in battleships, the Germans made no effort to maintain a battle fleet. Instead, the German navy used its battleships as raiders. Such raids presented a serious menace because the great firepower of a battleship could quickly destroy a substantial number of merchant ships in convoy. The search for these raiders shows not only how steam propulsion and the wireless had augmented the ratio of force to space but the degree to which the airplane, based on land as well as at sea, had accelerated a trend begun when the sailing ship superseded the galley.

The most spectacular of these raids occurred in 1941, when the large, new German battleship *Bismarck* steamed into the Atlantic. Since the British had thirteen battleships and three battle cruisers, a single German battleship should not have presented a serious threat to British shipping. But eleven of the British battleships dated from the era of World War I and had speeds of twenty-four knots or less. The two new ships had speeds comparable to the *Bismarck* (thirty knots), but the shipyards had completed them so recently that the crews had not used their guns enough for the men or loading equipment to maintain a full rate of fire. In fact, the British had planned to depend on two fast, modern French battleships to help cope with the *Bismarck*, but the defeat of France eliminated this resource. So the British had to rely on their new ships and their battle cruisers, the only ships with enough speed to engage the *Bismarck*.

When, in May 1941, the British knew that the *Bismarck* had gone to Norway and was ready to make a raid, the British created two squadrons to intercept it and protect the eleven convoys at sea in the north Atlantic. They paired the new *King George V*, with ten 14-inch guns and 14-inch armor, with the battle cruiser *Repulse* with six 15-inch guns and 9-inch armor, and then teamed the *Prince of Wales*, so new it put to sea with workmen on board, with the battle cruiser *Hood* with eight 15-inch guns and 12-inch armor. The *Hood*, as large and fast as the *Bismarck* and with side armor as thick, represented a design originated during World War I and lacked adequate deck protection, especially against guns like *Bismarck*'s eight 15-inchers. The *Repulse* with its thin armor could not face the *Bismarck*, but, on the assumption that the Germans would concentrate their fire on the *George V*, the *Repulse*'s six 15-inch guns could give the two smaller British ships fire predominance. Although British admirals knew of the *Hood*'s deficiencies, they did not believe that they disqualified the *Hood* for fighting the *Bismarck*.

When the *Bismarck* and a cruiser went to the coast of Norway, British aircraft observed them en route and later ascertained when they departed. In Admiral Tovey the British had a talented commander who had earned combat distinction at the Battle of Jutland. The admiral himself, in the *King George V* accompanied by the *Repulse* and the aircraft carrier *Victorious*, then covered the waters east of Iceland and sent two cruisers to observe the passage between Iceland and Greenland, backing them with the *Hood* and the *Prince of Wales*. These cruisers spotted the *Bismarck* and followed it, using radar to observe, while radioing its location. In the late afternoon of May 24, 1941, the *Hood* and the *Prince of Wales* intercepted the *Bismarck* and closed the range rapidly by taking an almost perpendicular approach toward the German ships. The *Bismarck* fired at the *Hood*, the leading British ship, and hardly had the action begun when the *Hood* blew up just as had three British battle cruisers at the Battle of Jutland. Because of the end-on approach, it is likely that one of the *Bismarck*'s 15-inch shells struck a magazine without having to pierce the thick side armor of the *Hood* before striking the thin plates behind.

Firing her ten 14-inch guns slowly because of her barely completed condition, the *Prince of Wales* promptly withdrew, leaving the *Bismarck* with a hit that punctured an oil tank. Leaking oil, the German admiral abandoned his cruise, deciding to steam south before turning toward the German-held French coast. With the cruisers still following, aircraft from the *Victorious* knew the *Bismarck*'s location and attacked with torpedo bombers. They secured at least one hit, but the small torpedo carried by the obsolete British carrier aircraft affected the *Bismarck* very little.

The *Bismarck* then eluded the shadowing cruisers and steamed toward the French coast. The British continued their search but did not locate the ship until a land-based reconnaisance plane found her on the morning of May 26. But the *Bismarck* was to the east of Admiral Tovey, who had with him the *George V* and the slow but powerful and well-armored old battleship *Rodney*. The British, however, had sent northwest from Gibraltar the modern aircraft carrier *Ark Royal* and the old battle crusier *Renown*, like the *Repulse* quite thinly armored. In spite of a heavy sea, which caused the carrier's deck to rise and fall as much as fifty feet, the aircraft carried out two attacks, hitting the *Bismarck* with two torpedos. These damaged the *Bismarck*'s rudder and prevented her from continuing her course toward the French coast or steaming at more than ten knots.

When Admiral Tovey overtook the *Bismarck*, the *Rodney* proved the most formidable antagonist as she maintained a high rate of fire with her nine 16-inch guns. The British ships soon wrecked the *Bismarck*'s barbettes, and when the *Rodney* closed the range to 5,000 yards, some of its 16-inch shells went through the unarmored portions of the *Bismarck* and landed in the water far beyond. Others hit the armored portions of the ship and completed the destruction of the *Bismarck*'s offensive power. The *Rodney*, so old-fashioned she still carried torpedoes, actually struck the *Bismarck* with one of the exceptionally large ones fitted in this battleship. Nevertheless, like the German armored cruisers at the Battle of the Falkland Islands, the *Bismarck*, though defeated, proved difficult to sink with gunfire. A torpedo from a British cruiser finally completed the task.

The *Bismarck* campaign exhibits both the importance and the limitations of aircraft and aircraft carriers. North Atlantic weather in the form of large waves and bad visibility limited the utility of planes and their carriers. With smooth sea and cloudless skies, the carriers *Victorious* and *Ark Royal*, each transporting as many as sixty aircraft, could, hypothetically, have found and sunk the *Bismarck* while keeping well out of range of her guns. But the climatic conditions kept the carriers from superseding the battleship. Nevertheless, the land-based reconnaissance planes and the successful attack by the *Ark Royal*'s torpedo bombers played an essential role in the destruction of the *Bismarck*. That the *Ark Royal* had the battle cruiser *Renown* as an escort also showed the interdependent nature of the aircraft and gun ships. If the powerful German cruiser that accompanied the *Bismarck* had found the *Ark Royal*, the carrier would have needed the battle cruiser for protection.

In the Mediterranean, the sea and the climate favored aircraft carriers, but with so many operations occurring close to Italian territory, land-based planes also presented a serious threat. Unlike the armored battleship, the unarmored aircraft carrier had no passive defense other than water-tight compartmentation of its hull to protect it from torpedoes and mines. The new British aircraft carriers did have armored flight decks, but few of these ships were available during the critical 1940–42 period. In addition, the British rarely had more than one carrier available with their Mediterranean fleet. However, they did make good use of their old, slow battleships, which with eight 15-inch guns made them better than the old, smaller, but much faster Italian battleships that mounted ten 320-millimeter guns and not much inferior to the two new, fast Italian battleships that carried nine 15-inch guns. Thus, the Italians had ascendancy in squadron speed, the British in battleships and carriers, of which the Italians had none.

The Italians enjoyed a central position between the British squadron based at Gibraltar and the larger British force in Egypt. Since the weaker British force did not remain in their ports, the Italians had an opportunity to use their interior lines, greater strength, and the higher speed of their ships to concentrate against the British and inflict a crushing defeat. But the improvement in observation made possible by aircraft and radar meant that even the slower British fleet would have adequate warning of the Italians' approach and could, as with armies, refuse action by retreating, a task made easier by the British carrier-borne aircraft. Yet the naval war did not develop in this way, each fleet instead giving primary consideration to protecting the lines of supply of its armies fighting in Africa and attacking those of the other.

So neither combatant controlled the sea, each menacing the other's key supply routes. These intersected, the British route through the Mediterranean to supply forces in Egypt crossing the Italian route across the sea to support its forces in Libya. The fleets met to attack and defend convoys. Initially, the British had the old carrier *Eagle* with a fleet based in Egypt. This ship opened operations by sinking an Italian destroyer and freighter in a North African port and then supported the British fleet when it met the Italian, each fleet at sea to escort a convoy. Aircraft from the *Eagle* attacked but failed to harm any Italian ships. Italian land-based bombers struck the British ships at high altitude but only one bomb scored a hit on a cruiser and others slightly damaged with near misses the carrier *Eagle*. Fortunately for the Italians, the high-altitude assaults proved ineffective; their airmen had mistakenly attacked their own fleet as well as the British.

Later, the single British carrier sank four more Italian destoyers before it made perhaps the greatest coup of the war. The calculating but audacious British Admiral Cunningham, Britain's premier admiral of the war, determined to take the offensive against his more powerful opponent. To nullify the stronger Italian air force, he planned to use his carrier aircraft at night. So, launching its aircraft far from land, on the night of November 11, a single carrier assailed the Italian fleet in its fortified anchorage at Taranto. In two waves, with flares to illuminate the harbor, torpedo bombers scored three hits on a big, new Italian battleship and one each on two of the older but thoroughly modernized Italian battleships. The torpedoes sank two and disabled a third, crippling half of Italy's battleship strength with a loss of only two aircraft.

Illustration 10.4. Torpedo Plane

The successful air strike against the Italian fleet in Taranto Harbor accomplished the purpose of a naval bombardment without exposing battleships to powerful coast defense guns. During World War II coast defense guns had maintained their long-established dominance over sea attack because their guns still had the advantage of firing from a fixed platform and, before radar, the benefit of better range determination as well as strong protection against hostile fire—easier to provide on land where weight did not exercise the same constraint as at sea.

Although over the centuries navies had successfully carried out surprise night attacks against defended harbors, the victory by the British torpedo bombers differed from ones achieved by surface vessels slipping past defenders' guns in the dark. Rather, the aircraft challenged an entirely different order of defenses, the antiaircraft guns and fighter aircraft of the defenders of the port. Even had surprise and darkness not rendered these ineffective, the British attack would have altered the circumstances that had so long prevailed; instead of exposing capital ships to shore gunfire to strike at the ships in the anchorage, as the Japanese had done at Port Arthur, the British risked only the readily replaced aircraft in an attack that disabled half of the capital ships in the Italian fleet.

Of course, the Italians could have counterattacked against the carrier and its escorts but this would have required not only a sufficient force of the dive and torpedo bombers adapted to this task but also sufficient reconnaissance aircraft to find the distant British squadron, no longer visible to observers in the gun positions on shore.

So the aircraft carrier, a companion to the battleship as a capital ship, had pierced the virtual invulnerability of a fortified port without, however, completely overthrowing the primacy of a properly prepared defense nor eliminating the attackers's risk of losing capital ships to an attack by aircraft stationed to defend the port. Still, the emergence of the carrier had markedly increased the cost of defending a naval base while reducing the resulting security. On the other hand, warning of an impending attack could enable the defenders to avail themselves of the ability of shore-based aircraft to concentrate rapidly to strengthen the port's air defenses and strike at the hostile aircraft carriers.

But the British made the main use of their carriers in their operations against the powerful Italian fleet when they found it at sea. Less than a week after the victory at Taranto, as the British Gibraltar squadron escorted a convoy, its planes observed an Italian squadron, and when the aircraft from the single carrier attacked, the Italians withdrew without loss. In March 1941, when the British were convoying troops and supplies to Greece, the Italian fleet sortied to strike these convoys, bringing out fourteen destroyers, eight cruisers, and its only operational battleship, the modern, 30-knot *Vittorio Veneto*, armed with nine 15-inch guns. This force seemed adequate in view of the British weakness in cruisers and given the Italian belief that the enemy had only one battleship able to put to sea.

Aware that the Italians would attack so valuable a target as troop convoys, Admiral Cunningham ordered four cruisers and four destroyers from Greece to meet his fleet from Egypt south of Crete. With him Admiral Cunningham had nine destroyers, a carrier, and three, not one, old 24-knot battleships, each armed with eight 15-inch guns. The British captains and men, inspired by their bold and victorious admiral, approached battle with zeal and confidence. A British carrier aircraft spotted a squadron of the Italian cruisers just as a sea plane launched by the Italian battleship observed the British cruisers. Each saw only part of the other's fleet.

When the British cruisers sighted the Italian cruisers, which had the advantage in numbers and in size of guns, the British cruisers retreated toward their advancing battleships. The Italians pursued, until, apprehensive about British aircraft based on Crete, they turned back; the British cruisers followed until they met the *Vittorio Veneto*. As the British cruisers retired, covered by a smoke screen, the first of the attacks by the British carrier aircraft took place. Although it failed to harm the *Vittorio Veneto*, it convinced the Italian admiral of the wisdom of setting a course back to Italy, which he promptly did at high speed, followed by the British cruisers and, at a considerable distance and a slower speed, the three British battleships.

The Italians would have escaped the stronger British squadron had not a second strike by carrier torpedo planes hit the *Vittorio Veneto* and slowed its speed to nineteen knots; and a third attack, in early evening, virtually stopped the 10,000-ton cruiser *Pola*. The Italian admiral continued his retreat but sent back in the dark two other cruisers like the *Pola* to aid that stricken ship. Without radar, the three Italian cruisers, each with eight 8-inch guns, did not detect the night approach of the three British battleships, each with eight 15-inch guns and armor virtually impervious to 8-inch guns. The Italian ships first learned of the presence of the British when searchlights illuminated one of the Italian cruisers and she was hit with two simultaneous broadsides of 15-inch guns fired from only 4,000 yards away. When two battleships had thus quickly demolished one cruiser and the third battleship another, the three ships opened fire on the third Italian cruiser, hitting it with at least fifteen big-gun shells. In addition to destroying three cruisers in this night action, the British ships also sank two destroyers.

After this disastrous battle off Cape Matapan, the Italian fleet gave up all efforts to attack British convoys, leaving this task to the Italian and German air forces. In the subsequent operations German land-based dive bombers proved their effectiveness, seriously damaging four carriers in air strikes and sinking three cruisers and a number of destroyers and damaging others.

So the presence of German and Italian land-based aircraft, the telling British use of their old battleships, and the paucity of British carriers meant that the naval operations in the Mediterranean followed the model exemplified in the cruise of *Bismarck*. Since neither battleships nor carriers had primacy, there ceased to be a single ship of the line. If ships of the line, or capital ships, are simply the strongest ships, then both carriers and battleships constituted capital ships. The fragile carrier, which provided reconnaissance and the ability to strike at a range far greater than the biggest gun, complemented the stout, well-protected battleship and its ability to overwhelm any other class of ship that came within range of its powerful guns.

The British succeeded in consistently defeating the Italian fleet because of their preponderance in both types of capital ships. Although they never had more than three or four of their old battleships, the British maintained their primacy over the four faster but weaker old Italian battleships and near parity, except in speed, with the two new Italian ships. Their willingness to risk their old ships also contributed to their success. And a single carrier, when their opponent had none and only very ineffective aid from its land-based aircraft, gave the British a comparable predominance in carriers also.

In the Pacific, however, the carrier rarely had to share with the battleship the distinction of being the capital ship. In the large spaces of that great ocean, with much of its climate congenial to air operations, the greater range of the carrier's aircraft, as compared with a ship's guns, made it the capital ship. Since battleships met only twice, the combat of the carriers, in which the aircraft aimed at the opposing carriers, decided the command of the Pacific and the outcome of the naval war.

As in the Atlantic and the Mediterranean, the torpedo-carrying aircraft proved the key weapon for attacking armored ships in the Pacific. Originally designed for launching from a torpedo boat on the surface, the torpedo, though still formidable in its original role, had far greater influence on naval warfare when launched by a submersible torpedo boat, the submarine, or by an aircraft, an airborne torpedo boat.

The aircraft carrier also changed the nature of the protection of capital ships. Even with their armored flight decks, British aircraft carriers, like their unarmored U.S. counterparts, depended primarily on the active defense of their antiaircraft guns rather than the armor plate of the battleship or, earlier, the thick sides of the ship of the line. Much more vulnerable because of the absence of the passive defense of armor, the carriers gained in defensive power because other ships could aid them. The antiaircraft armament of destroyers, originally intended to combat surface torpedo boats, helped protect carriers from air attack as did the antiaircraft armament of cruisers. The British and U.S. navies even had antiaircraft cruisers. In addition, the carriers also had fighter planes that helped to protect them and other fleet units from the attacks of carrier planes.

The German Submarine Campaign

And aircraft also played a major role in the war against the submarine, which, as in World War I, constituted the naval struggle in which the issue was really in doubt. The World War II submarine campaign began where that of the first left off, except for the asdic or sonar submarine detecting device, which proved far better at finding submarines than the hydrophone of 1918. The Germans, after initial difficulties with faulty torpedoes, benefited from an electric torpedo, which left no wake, and from homing torpedoes, which used magnetic and acoustic devices. The typical German submarine displaced about 500 tons, could dive almost to 500 feet, and had a 16-knot surface speed and a cruising range of over 8,000 miles.

But as at the beginning of World War I, the Germans, with only fifty-six submarines, not all of which were well suited to Atlantic operations, lacked the force to strangle British commerce, and the British needed many more escort vessels to baffle the German attacks. Nevertheless, in the first six months of the war, the Germans sank an average of over 140,000 tons of shipping per month. This amounted to about half of the average monthly loss from all causes in 1918. Most submarine successes came against single ships, those the British excluded from convoys because they had too much speed to need protection or so little, that, in the interest of transport efficiency, the British admiralty barred them from convoys.

In March, April, and May of 1940 losses dropped about 60 percent because Germany committed many of its submarines to support of their invasion of Norway. But in June of that year, with a force of fifty-seven submarines available and most of them replenished and sent to sea simultaneously, ship losses amounted to over 350,000 tons. Other weapon systems, such as surface raiders, aircraft, and mines, pushed this total to nearly 600,000 tons. This campaign owed part of its success to a new strategy introduced by Admiral Dönitz, the commander

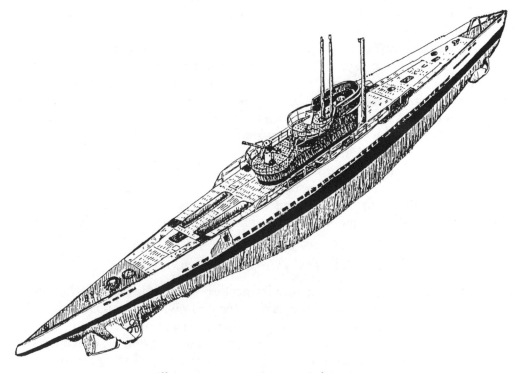

Illustration 10.5. German Submarine

of the German submarine forces. A World War I submarine commander, Dönitz had assumed command of German submarines in 1935. A fine leader and prescient planner and strategist, he had early decided to respond to the concentration of the defense in the convoy with a concentration by the submarines. So, when a submarine sighted a convoy, it did not attack but radioed its position. Other submarines, often ordered from the shore by Admiral Dönitz himself, then assembled, and all attacked together. In one particularly successful application of this strategy, seven submarines sank seventeen ships from a convoy of thirty-four that had an inadequate escort of only four warships.

The Germans also employed the new and very effective tactic of striking at night on the surface. This gave the submarines a far better opportunity to observe and the advantage of high surface speed, about double the rate of progress of the average convoy. Not only did the submarine's small conning tower make the submarine difficult to see, but surface operation nullified the asdic. Better tactics complemented better strategy to cause the allies to lose 1.5 million tons of shipping in the period June through October 1940. During this time the Germans also began to reap the important, long-term benefit of having bases on the Norwegian and French coasts, which enabled submarines to make shorter voyages to and from the shipping routes, thus increasing the number of German submarines attacking merchant ships.

But sinkings declined as the British strengthened convoy escorts after the threat of a German invasion waned and the German submarines sent out in June had to return for replenishment. The British also increased aircraft patrols. Even slow, lumbering flying boats presented a serious menace to submarines because the aircraft carried depth charges or bombs and the submarines had weak antiaircraft armament. In addition, often an even slightly damaged submarine could not safely submerge. Thus air patrols forced submarines to submerge and made it hard for them to track convoys.

In 1941 the submarine war against commerce followed the pattern established late in 1940. The monthly toll in 1941 amounted to a little less than 200,000 tons. The Germans had lost only thirty-one submarines since the war began, but they had so neglected to accelerate building that they had barely replaced their casualties. The British offset the addition of Italy's fleet and the increase in the number of German submarines during 1941 by building still more escort vessels, acquiring fifty old destroyers from the United States, and securing some direct escort aid from the U.S. navy. This enabled them to strengthen escorts and extend convoying all the way across the Atlantic rather than limit it to either end of the voyage.

In 1942 allied ship losses to submarines surged to two and one half that of the 1941 monthly averages, though they still fell about 200,000 tons short of the 700,000 tons per month that the Germans had calculated would give them victory. The German navy owed its success in part to a growth in the number of submarines. At the beginning of 1942 the Germans had 249 submarines with 91 operational; at the end of the year they had 212 operational out of 393 available. The building program and crew training together had dramatically augmented German naval strength.

Admiral Dönitz's winning strategy of concentration against weakness provided the other factor in the increase in sinkings. As soon as the United States entered the war, Dönitz dispatched submarines to the North American coast where they found a happy hunting ground of unconvoyed ships. When the U.S. navy organized convoys, the admiral shifted his vessels to the Caribbean and then again concentrated on the North Atlantic sea lanes, weakened to provide escorts for the new convoy routes. Late in the year, he sent significant forces to the south Atlantic, using some new long-range submarines and large supply submarines that rendezvoused at sea to provide the smaller combat submarines with fuel and supplies.

Against this powerful offensive the British replied with an improved radar that could detect an object as small as a submarine conning tower. The British also built a radar set compact enough to fit into an airplane. Submarines thus became vulnerable to discovery on the surface at night; aircraft could attack at night by using an 80-million-candlepower searchlight to illuminate a submarine originally found with radar. The Germans responded by mounting on their submarines a receiver which could detect the presence of radar. This enabled the submarine to dive in the presence of radar-equipped aircraft or ships. The British responded in the fall with a radar of a different wavelength, which defeated the detector. Surface travel remained hazardous for the submarines, especially as the British continually added to the number of their air patrols and the scope of their coverage.

The year 1943 promised to be a continuation of 1942 for the Germans. Though they had lost eighty-seven submarines in 1942, they had increased their total numbers from 249 to 393. This growth meant that enough German crews and commanders survived to augment their proficiency in spite of the multitude of newly trained men required to man a force that had expanded so rapidly. But in the steadily growing numbers of allied escort vessels, skill advanced more quickly because, compared to submarines and convoyed ships, escort vessels suffered negligible losses. So, comparatively, the skill of the defending ships increased more than that of the attackers.

As 1943 began, the Germans had a reasonable expectation of greater success as they now produced thirty submarines per month. In mid-March two allied convoys approached several German submarine groups, called wolfpacks, together totaling more than forty submarines. In a five-day struggle the submarines sank twenty-one ships aggregating 141,000 tons. In March the German submarines sank 490,000 tons of shipping in the north Atlantic alone. But this marked the high point; improved Anglo-American skill and methods, together with more escorts, henceforth overmatched the Germans.

The British had carried a few aircraft with convoys by using the long, unobstructed surfaces of grain or oil ships to launch and recover a complement of three or four old, slow Swordfish single-engine carrier aircraft. But as early as December 1941 they had put into action a freighter converted into an aircraft carrier. It carried only about a dozen aircraft, which it had to launch with a catapult, but it provided planes to aid a convoy. The first of these carriers, the *Audacity*, joined twelve other escorts to bring a thirty-two-ship convoy from Gibraltar to the United Kingdom. Nine submarines attacked and sank the *Audacity* and a destroyer, but the convoy lost only two ships and the escort sank five of the submarines.

By April 1943 the British and Americans had several escort carriers, which enabled many convoys to have air protection even in the mid-Atlantic area too far for land aircraft to patrol. In addition, they had formed support groups of six to eight escorts that, rather than protecting a particular convoy, could come to the assistance of any convoy meeting the attack of a wolfpack. These support groups enabled the British and United States navies to employ the defender's principle of concentration against strength to counter Dönitz's offensive wolfpack concentration against a single convoy.

In early May 1943 over twenty submarines attacked a convoy whose defenders had the augmentation of a support group. The submarines succeeded in sinking twelve ships but at a cost of seven submarines. When the submarines then concentrated against another convoy, they sank three ships but lost one submarine to the planes of the escort carrier *Biter*, another to a land-based aircraft, and a third to the combined action of an escort and a land-based aircraft. A submarine concentration against a third convoy met the *Biter*, sent to aid that convoy, and the Germans sank only two ships, at a loss of two submarines sunk and others damaged. Another convoy, attacked by four different wolfpacks, suffered no casualties but the attackers lost five boats. In a period in May twelve convoys crossed the north Atlantic, losing only five ships; but the Germans lost thirteen submarines.

This represented the pattern of the future, as enhanced Anglo-American skill, aircraft from land bases and escort carriers, and adequate numbers of escorts defeated the German offensive. When the British, by enlarging the size of convoys, had proportionately expanded the size of the escort, they proved again to have strengthened the defense because the increased number of ships vulnerable to sinking had not, as it turned out, correspondingly augmented the defender's tasks or the attacker's opportunities.

In May the Germans sank less than a quarter of a million tons of shipping but lost forty-one submarines. Thereafter, the rate of loss of merchant ships fell as the defense had clearly triumphed. In all of 1943 the Germans sank barely 2.5 million tons of shipping in a year in which their enemies reached a building rate of over 14 million tons a year. The Germans had suffered defeat in the raiding war against commerce, just as the French had two centuries before. Technological advances played a role unknown to that struggle as did, here and elsewhere, the British ability to decipher messages encoded by the German cipher machine.

In fact, the German submarines were really on the defensive against the air patrols of radar-equipped land- or carrier-based aircraft. Land-based aircraft relentlessly harassed German submarines in the Bay of Biscay off the French coast, finding them with radar and attacking with bombs and depth charges. The Germans tried running submerged except to recharge their batteries and, when detected on the surface, either diving or fighting back with an augmented antiaircraft armament. Neither method of defense proved effective enough to prevent the loss of fifteen submarines in a five-week period in July and August 1943.

The aircraft, the light cavalry of the air, proved potent at sea against a ship that lacked the surface ship's array of antiaircraft weapons and the armored ship's protection. But the planes did not owe their success solely to the speed of their approach; aircraft with radar had a special advantage over a ship equipped only with a detector ineffective against the radar's frequency.

The Germans responded by developing the snorkel, an air intake above the surface but small enough to elude radar observation. This enabled the submarine to operate its diesel engines while submerged. Still, this only constituted a defensive measure and consistent submerged operation reduced crew morale and limited the submarine's observation. Toward the end of the war the Germans introduced a larger combat submarine capable of sixteen knots under water. Yet this did not alter the balance of power between the submarine and the escort nor, doubtless, would the submarine the Germans had developed, which had a hydrogen peroxide engine and needed no snorkel.

The submarine suffered defeat in World War II for the same reason it had in the first: the convoy. Germany's enemies lost 2,775 ships, but only 27 percent of these were steaming in convoy when sunk. Submarines destroyed 14,573,000 tons of shipping at a cost of 781 German and 85 Italian submarines. In World War I the Germans lost 178 submarines and the allies almost as many tons of merchant ships. The Germans had made a bigger effort but secured proportionately smaller results. Their enemies, too, had committed more resources to the defense. Defensive weapons had improved more than those of the offensive, asdic proving more telling than the hydrophone and aircraft and radar so adding to the power of the defenders that they could go to the offensive against the submarines. Better torpedoes and submarines could not counterbalance these.

The Germans had used an effective strategy when they concentrated successively against enemy weakness—unconvoyed areas in the central Atlantic, the North American coast, the Caribbean, the South American and African coasts, and even the Indian Ocean. Using the wolfpack to counteract the convoys proved a good strategy, but it failed to prevail against stronger escorts aided by aircraft and radar and, later, by the defensive concentration of support groups.

Skill also had a part in the defeat of the submarines. The Germans lost so many submarines, 237 in 1943 alone, that they had constantly to send into battle commanders and crews who lacked much actual experience. But because they aimed to sink the merchant ships rather than their escorts, their escort ship and aircraft opponents suffered negligible losses. Increasingly the German submarines faced veterans—commanders, sailors, and aircraft pilots with successful experience sinking submarines.

The balance of forces changed during the submarine war and new weapons, tactics, and strategy played a role. Unlike the surface naval war in which initial fleet strength and building programs decided the result, the belligerents had to fight this crucial war to determine its outcome.

So the Germans failed in their effort to apply a logistic strategy that could not only have proved decisive against the United Kingdom but also could have established a blockade sufficient to prevent the United States from supporting armies in Europe. The British, on the other hand, masterfully applied their logistic strategy of blockade, but, as in World War I, it did not prove decisive. The German access to the resources of Europe, including the oil fields of Romania, and their reliance on substitutes enabled them to maintain their war effort in spite of the blockade.

In Asia, however, logistic strategy had multiple triumphs. Not only did U.S. submarines have impressive success against Japanese commerce, but also, at the end of the war when the Japanese had already lost the bulk of their merchant marine, the U.S. navy established a fairly effective blockade of the Japanese islands. Such a blockade, if total, would have reduced Japanese steel production to a trickle and, in the absence of increased food production, Japanese daily food consumption to 1,200 calories per capita. But such a powerful application of a logistic strategy against an island nation did not suffice; the U.S. air force added the logistic strategy of strategic bombing. Yet in spite of the success of the navy's logistic strategy and the destruction wrought by that of the air force, the United States also planned to attain victory by the combat strategy of invasion as well. But Japan made peace before that campaign began.

11

AFTER THE WORLD WARS: CONSOLIDATION AND TECHNOLOGICAL CHANGE, 1945–85

Changes in Weapons

The period since World War II has witnessed a rapid growth in new and improved weapons as governments sponsored and liberally supported their systematic development. Most of the weapons evolved from those originated before or during World War II. The mature ones underwent the least modifications, artillery, ships, and tanks seeking further improvement rather than drastic alteration. Nuclear power for submarines constituted the exception here, because it made submarines relatively independent of need for contact with the surface to operate air-breathing engines. This ability gave submarines the means to attain greater speeds because they could use full power under the surface. Routine underwater operation enabled naval architects to design their ships for maximum subsurface speeds. Of course, nuclear submarines also had great range because their nuclear fuel lasted for years, and the ships could carry enough oxygen for the crews to remain submerged for long periods of time. An early nuclear submarine demonstrated its capabilities by cruising to the North Pole under the ice.

Artillery changed little, but, with the abandonment of horse traction and the stepped-up usage of self-propelled tracked mounting, armies employed larger-bore howitzers than those used in the world wars and abandoned the World War I field gun entirely.

The jet engine, introduced by the Germans and the British at the end of the war, dramatically increased the speed of aircraft. From 450 miles an hour for fighters with reciprocating engines at the end of the war, jet fighter and bomber aircraft soon routinely flew at 650 miles an hour, and many fighters could attain speeds more than double this. Planes grew larger until fighters rivaled many World War II bombers in size; bombers themselves grew proportionately bigger.

Except for the revolution in submarine capabilities, these changes were of degree only. As with most other weapon systems, the progress in infantry extrapolated earlier trends. The quest for a greater rate of fire, a characteristic

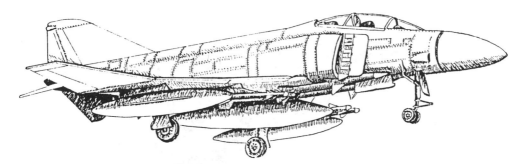

Illustration 11.1. Jet Aircraft

since the muzzleloader, reached its apex when armies equipped every soldier with a small, light machine gun.

But the postwar period became the age of the rocket; it actually began during World War II, with the use of rockets in aircraft, to supplement artillery, and with the German development of the V2 long-range ballistic rocket. By the 1960s ballistic rockets had achieved greater accuracy and extended their range to over 5,000 miles. Such missiles still defied antiaircraft defense and could carry a nuclear warhead far more powerful than the two bombs dropped in World War II. This provided Britain, France, Russia, the United States and probably other states with an irresistible offensive weapon for strategic attack against population centers. It made fully effective the original concept of a strategic air attack that would cripple a country's war-making potential and terrorize its people into submission. Subsequent improvements enhanced accuracy and enabled a single rocket to carry several independently targetable warheads. Accuracy reached the level where planners envisioned the possibility of attacking enemy rockets before they could fire.

The guiding of smaller rockets had a major impact on traditional modes of combat. The antiaircraft defense against high-altitude attack, for example, substituted a missile for cannon to fire at high-flying targets. The radar found and tracked the enemy plane in the same way it had controlled cannon, but, instead, the defenders shot a missile containing an explosive charge of several hundred pounds. An additional radar set tracked this missile and, from a computer, sent commands that moved the missile's directing fins, guided it to intercept the attacking aircraft, and then ordered it to explode when near the aircraft. No jet plane could fly higher or faster than this rocket-powered missile.

Other systems of guidance aimed a radio beam at the target, a rocket traveling along the beam until it intercepted the moving aircraft. Other missiles directed themselves by seeking a heat source, such as a jet aircraft's exhaust. Still others made use of television images. A rocket could use more than one system of guidance in sequence, receiving direction, for example, until near enough to home in on a source of heat.

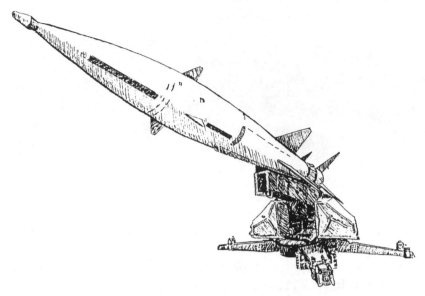

Illustration 11.2. Antiaircraft Rocket

Soldiers could use such missiles to fire at one another, and aircraft could fire them at ground targets. But these missiles had particularly great utility for air defense and for combat between planes, which could now engage one another at distances too great for the machine guns or cannon of World War II. Ships could combat each other with flying missiles that could remain almost invisible to radar and difficult to shoot down as they traveled a few feet above the surface of the water. Aircraft could launch such missiles against ships.

Missiles changed aircraft little, but missiles and the aircraft carrier wrought a profound modification in warships. The expectation of combat at great ranges, with aircraft or with missiles, led to the gradual demise of the gun as the primary armament of ships and of the armor needed to give protection against gunfire. Warships became unarmored vessels loaded with antiaircraft and, often, anti-submarine weapons, together with the large amount of electronic equipment needed to guide their missiles and detect the enemy. By the standards prevailing for nearly a century, warships had become incredibly fragile as they depended on the active defense of their missiles and their associated detection and guidance equipment rather than the traditional passive defense of armor plate, protective decks, and sturdy construction. The limited naval combat occurring since World War II confirmed this fragility. The aircraft carrier, so dominant in the Pacific in World War II, remained the capital ship of the U. S. navy, but no other country contested its supremacy in this kind of warfare. Other nations relied almost exclusively on attack with missiles and defense against missiles and aircraft.

Air forces continued to depend on bombs and supplied guidance to some of these. But, unlike the warships, the large, stoutly built jets had more resistance than their World War II counterparts.

In spite of a great proliferation of sophisticated electronic surveillance equipment and rockets with complex guidance systems, warfare on land changed little. In fact, the rocket reinforced some of the changes that had originated during World War II by increasing the infantry's capacity to resist the mounted weapon systems. The improvement of the bazooka antitank rocket and the recoilless cannon enhanced the infantry's ability to deal with tanks. In the 1950s the French used a missile guided by commands sent along a wire payed out by the missile as it moved toward the target. This apparently primitive approach assured continuous contact with the missile and allowed the operator to direct it against a moving target. With a shaped charge, this wire-guided missile proved effective against tanks at a range greater than a mile. The smaller models of these weapons were portable.

The infantry acquired a portable antiaircraft missile that a soldier could fire from the shoulder. Heat-seeking guidance aimed a small, rocket-powered missile toward the exhaust of the attacking aircraft. Thus infantry acquired its own significant protection against low-level air attackers and could play the role of Crusader crossbowmen in fending off the light cavalry of the air.

This provision of infantry with economical, portable weapons gave them the capacity to fulfill the roles of the light and heavy infantry of old, but it did not bring about a reemphasis on the function of the infantry. In spite of the value of the portable, heat-seeking antiaircraft missile, the mobile, radar-directed weapons, including the small automatic cannon so effective in World War II, still seemed needed for air defense. And the greater effectiveness of the tank in an antitank role, coupled with its versatility, made soldiers prefer this powerful weapon system. Just as dismounted English knights had withstood French heavy cavalry at the Battle of Crécy, so stationary defending tanks proved superior to moving tanks in the attack. In the fourteenth century the English could have obtained the same results with Welsh spearmen whom they could have given strategic mobility by mounting on inexpensive horses. But a comparable resistance to French cavalry would have required more spearmen than dismounted men at arms and the spearmen lacked any capability to act as cavalry. So just as had the English centuries before, armies placed more reliance upon tanks and strove to reach the ideal of all-mounted forces.

In fact, the warfare of the North African desert seems to have forecast the future, as European armies came more and more to resemble the largely mounted Byzantine army with its costly armored cavalry equipped also with bows. So armies mounted a high proportion of their soldiers in aircraft, tanks, or self-propelled artillery. They also made extensive use of tracked, armored carriers for moving infantry, vehicles that could fight and fill the role of the horses used to carry Welsh spearmen. Like the Byzantine heavy cavalry, the tanks of the European armies could charge with great power or capably conduct the tank's equivalent of the horseman's dismounted defense against a heavy cavalry charge of enemy tanks. Rather than having antiaircraft weapons placed on tanks in imitation of the bows carried by Byzantine heavy cavalry, self-propelled antiaircraft guns accompanied the tanks. The armies retained infantry but often as mounted infantry, carried in lightly armed and armored tracked carriers, derived from the half-tracked vehicles that carried the armored-division infantry of World War II. Dismounted, these infantrymen could use their antitank rockets, machine guns, mortars, and recoilless cannon to attack or defend against other infantry and so protect their own or operate against enemy tanks and other vehicles, thus blending nineteenth-century combat with post–1945 mounted warfare.

Yet the emphasis on guided rockets for infantry's combat against aircraft and tanks and the use of rockets in combat between aircraft reversed a long-standing tradition in Western warfare. For centuries soldiers had valued volume of fire over accuracy, but, in spite of the extension of this trend to the equipment of all soldiers with automatic rifles, the guidance of rockets emphasized accuracy at the expense of rate of fire, and the cost of the ammunition precluded a resort to a high volume of fire.

Armies placed such great stress on new or improved weapons, greater accuracy, and more effective electronic surveillance that it often seemed as if the quality and sophistication of weapons would determine the outcome of battles. But in the many small conflicts throughout the world in the post-World War II era, leadership and training, together with skill gained in combat, still made the same contribution to victory that they had always made. This occurred in spite of the growth in the automatic attributes of weapons that reduced the manual skill demanded for their most proficient use. No longer, for example, did soldiers require strength and expertness to shoot longbows, well-honed and slowly acquired facility for reloading muzzleloaders, or even dexterity in working the bolt of a rifle and bringing the weapon promptly back on the target; riflemen needed only to aim, pull the trigger, and exchange full for empty magazines.

But new weapons demanded a higher level of logistic competence. The complex weapons, particularly electronic guidance and surveillance equipment, necessitated knowledgable repairmen to keep them working. And, in spite of this attention, the new and relatively untried apparatus proved unreliable. In one aspect, armies had returned to the day of the matchlock when only half of the weapons fired when the arquebusiers pulled the triggers. But, unlike the matchlock, modern weapons that failed to function properly performed below their designed capacity and so compelled the armies to provide competent repairmen.

In the helicopter armies acquired their own light cavalry. Able to rise and descend vertically and hover in the air, the helicopter almost exactly reproduced the capabilities of traditional light cavalry. Armed with machine guns and rockets, it proved extremely effective against infantry and, particularly when armed with wire-guided antitank missiles, deadly to tanks. It could also carry a dozen or more soldiers. But the slow bulky helicopter was at least as vulnerable to antiaircraft fire as light cavalry to the light infantry of old, so much so in fact that it had little combat use against forces provided with antiaircraft defenses. But its logistic value in furnishing rapid movement, overcoming difficult terrain or passing over water, and flying over enemy territory not defended by antiaircraft weapons made it quite valuable nonetheless.

Illustration 11.3. Helicopter

The All-Mounted Army

Armies also had tactical nuclear weapons with warheads small enough to fit into field artillery projectiles. Such great power in a small bulk would have consequences hard to calculate, especially in view of the radiation inseparable from such explosions. A single nuclear shell or bomb could reproduce the effects of a virtually unprecedented concentration of artillery. Since for nearly two centuries such concentrations had played a major role in the offensive, tactical nuclear weapons obviously gave the offensive an opportunity for surprise because it could dispense with a concentration of artillery, always troublesome to conceal.

But since offensive action had traditionally required concentration of forces, the defensive reaped a major advantage from the new weapon in that it could promptly deliver a nuclear weapon against the enemy concentration. Thus the defense, even if caught unaware, had no need to carry out a counterconcentration to deal with an enemy offensive. Since the increases in firepower in the nineteenth and twentieth centuries had usually strengthened the relative power of the defense, it seems logical to assume that the addition of nuclear weapons would have the same outcome.

But European armies did not plan routinely to have recourse to tactical nuclear weapons on the defensive. The apprehension that such tactical employment could lead to strategic use, and the resulting destruction of cities and killing of millions of civilians, made armies plan to fight without them as well.

The possibility, however, of the employment of tactical nuclear weapons gave added impetus to the trend to the all-mounted force. Increased mobility would make it easier to seek safety through the dispersal of forces because mounted forces could reconcentrate more rapidly than those on foot. The protection from a nuclear explosion offered by a tank or an armored carrier also made these weapon systems more attractive.

The new mounted armies stressed tanks to a degree unprecedented in World War II and not seen since medieval armies placed comparable emphasis upon heavy cavalry. They followed more closely the Crusader or Byzantine model rather than the Turkish light-cavalry army of the Middle Ages, in part because cost ratios had changed dramatically. Equipping the armored heavy cavalryman and his robust warhorse amounted to a great deal more than outfitting the light cavalryman with his simpler equipment and less expensive horse. But by the 1960s, however, a jet fighter bomber cost about ten times as much as a tank and had greater requirements in skill for the pilot and for logistical and maintenance facilities. The heavy cavalry tank had become so much less expensive than the light cavalry of the air that tanks proliferated in spite of the greater security aircraft offered against tactical nuclear weapons.

The mobile armies with many expensive fighter bombers, vast numbers of large, sophisticated tanks, self-propelled artillery, and armored carriers for infantry had far fewer men than the armies of the European powers on the eve of the World War II. Quantities of electronic surveillance and guidance systems and costly ammunition added to the capital intensive nature of these armies in which millions of trained reserves no longer played the vital role they had in 1914 and 1939. This, too, constituted a rational response to economic realities in one of the wealthiest parts of the world. The high cost of labor, because of its productive civilian alternative uses, made capital-intensive armies sensible. In one area, however, European powers neglected capital investment in defense. The tradition of permanent fortifications, which had such great importance in Western Europe since the castle and the walled town, suffered neglect in the defensive planning of the Germans and French. Even the formidable underground fortifications of the Maginot line languished unheeded, in spite of the defense they offered against even nuclear blasts and radiation.

The Israeli-Egyptian War of 1973

The European and American mounted way of war and the up-to-date missile-oriented weapon systems had a number of trials in the Middle East in the wars between the Arabs and the Israelis. These had not only shown the new weapons in action but also proved that modern technology had not devalued skill and combat experience. The tendency to apply a technological determinism to predict victory received its rebuttal from the easy successes of the Israeli army.

But one campaign, in which the antagonists were fairly evenly matched, gave the capabilities of the weapons and the characteristics of the doctrines an opportunity to display themselves without the bias of distinctly superior tactical skill on one side. By 1973 most of the contending armies in these Middle East wars had ample supplies of modern weapons and the doctrine, training, and combat experience to use them well. As the Russians supplied the bulk of the Arab weapons, the United States provided the majority of Israel's armaments, and most had some British and French equipment also. Each army's weapons differed in detail but not in fundamental characteristics. But U. S. tanks did tend to have greater size, thicker armor, and a smaller gun than the Russian tanks.

Since Israel lay between Egypt on its west and Syria and Jordan on the east, the Egyptians and Syrians carefully coordinated their unexpected inauguration of hostilities to offset Israel's interior lines by a concentration in time through a simultaneous attack. They succeeded, securing tactical surprise but, in view of their strategic situation and obvious objectives, attained no strategic surprise.

The contest of the Egyptian and Israeli armies well exhibited both the changes in warfare made possible by new weapon systems and the continuity in tactics and strategy that seems inevitably to characterize at least some aspects of operations in any era. Both armies had such large numbers of tanks that although each retained the armored division, both distributed tanks among all of their divisions, much as the French had done in 1940. But all divisions had motor transport, and many infantrymen rode in thinly armored tracked carriers.

The Suez Canal, at all points at least 200 yards wide, divided the Egyptian and Israeli forces. Both armies had fortified this waterway, each side having erected an earthen embankment at least fifty feet high along the bank of its side. These seemingly archaic fortifications provided a physical barrier to soldiers and vehicles, protection for the road behind, and a commanding location for guns or strong points. They were difficult to damage with artillery fire. But, for defense of the canal line, the Israelis relied primarily on tank and motorized infantry forces posted behind their embankment. Though the Israelis had a road network to facilitate their lateral movement and concentration, tracked and even wheeled vehicles could pass over most of the treeless terrain near the canal.

On the afternoon of October 6, 1973, the Egyptians and Syrians began hostilities against Israeli armies that were without their reserves. In a well-planned operation, guided by an excellent staff, 8,000 Egyptian infantry used small boats to cross the canal on a fifty-mile front, avoiding only the swamp region in the north and the lakes in the south. The Egyptain soldiers had the support of almost 4,000 guns, including those in tanks, which fired over 10,000 shells in the first minute of the attack. With ladders the soldiers climbed the sloping sides of the Israeli bank and pushed beyond it a little over a half mile. Each soldier pulled a little cart to help him carry his rifle and principal weapon system.

Some soldiers carried wire-guided antitank missiles with a range as great as 1,100 yards, and others carried antitank rocket launchers, like bazookas, with a maximum range of about 200 yards. If enemy tanks should approach too close for the guided missiles, they would have reached the effective range of the rocket launchers. The system of defense had much in common with that of the Swiss when they armed their outer ranks with long pikes and the inner ranks of their square with halberds to combat knights who got past the pikes.

In addition, many of the Egyptian infantry carried a heat-seeking antiaircraft missile effective against low-flying aircraft. For defense against a high-level attack the Egyptians had radar-controlled, long-range antiaircraft missiles close to their bank of the canal, which could readily protect their infantry as long as they remained near the canal's far bank.

With the development of portable antitank and antiaircraft weapons, infantry had recovered the capabilities that they had possessed centuries before. Just as pikemen could defend against heavy cavalry and crossbowmen could inflict serious casualties on horse archers, so the Egyptian infantry, with the aid of the stationary antiaircraft missiles east of the canal, could resist the Israelis who, much like the Parthians or Mongols of old, favored mounted warfare. Because combat had expanded to three dimensions, the Egyptians could adopt an uncomplicated array, the soldiers with antiaircraft missiles taking their position behind those with the antitank weapons.

As the Egyptians steadily reinforced their army on the far bank of the canal, the superlative Israeli air force attacked, losing half of its planes to the air defenses. The antiaircraft missiles carried by the soldiers proved accurate but often failed to disable the aircraft because its small warhead exploded where the hot gasses of the jet left the engine. But the explosion inflicted substantial damage and the comparative cost of the two weapon systems, infantryman with a small missile and a pilot with an expensive airplane, meant that damage to the aircraft constituted a major tactical victory. In one attack 80 percent of the Israeli planes suffered damage. When the Egyptians brought over self-propelled, four-barreled, 23-millimeter radar-directed automatic antiaircraft guns, they had a complete air defense, which reinforced the decision of the Israeli air force to avoid attacks on the Egyptians east of the canal.

The assaults of the Israeli armored forces suffered a similar fate when they charged the infantry. The well-trained and confident Egyptian soldiers withstood a number of small tank attacks during the afternoon in which the counterattacking Israelis lost almost all of their tanks. Meanwhile, the Egyptians reinforced their infantry with recoilless rifles and 85- and 100-millimeter antitank guns. They also had small, lightly armored vehicles that carried antitank missiles, one having a small antitank gun. Stronger Israeli tank assaults in the evening and the following day suffered the same fate as those launched immediately, one losing 90 percent of the assaulting tanks in ten minutes. The armored division making these attacks lost two-thirds of its strength.

The next day, October 8, the Israelis, reinforced to three divisions, made a renewed counterattack. Overconfident and misled by the lack of intelligence caused by the Egyptian's antiaircraft defenses limiting air reconnaissance, the Israelis, supported by only four artillery pieces, launched counterattacks of inadequate strength and with confused objectives. Only one division actually participated, and it lost half its tanks. In these local counterattacks the Israelis lost as many as 250 tanks. After this they kept their distance and remained on the defensive.

But the Egyptians made no effort to exploit their successes, instead staying close to the canal, building bridges, bringing over 800 tanks and nine divisions, and deepening their bridgehead only very circumspectly. In spite of their great superiority, they adopted this essentially defensive posture because the success attained and the ground gained met their political objectives for the campaign.

Having proved their defensive might, they were reluctant to advance and engage in the kind of mounted warfare in which the seasoned Israelis excelled.

While the Egyptians built up their strength on the east bank of the canal, they had tried to retard the arrival of additional Israeli troops by sending a force of small amphibious tanks over the canal and eastward to block passes. But Israeli tanks reached the positions first and easily defeated these fragile Egyptian tanks. Thirty Egyptian helicopters, each carrying about twenty-five soldiers, landed men well east of the canal. Armed with antitank rockets, these units blocked the main roads to delay Israeli reinforcements. But the small Egyptian detachments imposed only brief delays on the powerful Israeli forces when they appeared.

The helicopters performed their function well, even though the Israelis shot down a number when they made later flights to reinforce the blocking units. The loss of these helicopters confirmed their vulnerability when opposing armies had elaborate antiaircraft defenses. Anticipating this, both combatants generally limited their use of helicopters to logistic tasks.

If this Egyptian judgment in favor of the defensive needed any support, it received it from the experience of one force that had pushed a deep thrust into Israeli territory. Three battalions with about 200 vehicles, including tanks, trucks, and armored carriers for infantry, having advanced ten miles from the canal, received Israeli air strikes that, together with the resistance of an infantry battalion and twenty tanks, destroyed half the Egyptian vehicles before they returned to the canal.

But the distress of the Syrians who faced a successful Israeli offensive concentration induced the Egyptians to abandon the defensive and to carry out on October 14 an offensive against the Israelis who, though inferior in numbers, had 800 tanks. Bringing across the canal some of the radar-guided antiaircraft missiles and reinforcements of infantry and tanks, the Egyptians attacked all along the front in what proved to be little more than a demonstration. Without any concentration of troops, they met the Israelis in essentially equal force everywhere, their attacks showing the effectiveness of tanks on the defense.

Israeli tanks occupied previously selected defensive positions, including some excavated for the purpose, and, exposing only their turrets and guns, had a great advantage over the fully visible and vulnerable Egyptian tanks making the attack. The Israeli tanks gained added security from the Egyptian howitzers and artillery by moving from one previously chosen protected position to another. The Israeli tanks also counterattacked against the flanks of the advancing Egyptian tanks and displayed their dominant tactical skill in maneuvering and shooting with their tank guns. For the day's unsuccessful attacks the Egyptians lost 260 of their 1,000 tanks, the Israelis less than one-fourth as many, the majority of which they soon repaired.

Machine guns proved invaluable in coping with the Egyptian infantry armed with wire-guided missiles. Machine gun fire made it difficult for the Egyptian infantry with missiles to move and even harder for the soldier to keep his head exposed to guide the missile to its target. Israeli field artillery, too, served this purpose and also displayed its value against the thinly armored vehicles that carried missiles.

In spite of progress by some of their columns, all of the Egyptians fell back to their starting points by the following day. The Israeli air force, which had already attacked some of the most advanced formations, provided one motive for this withdrawal, the Egyptian command thus adhering to the old Byzantine rule of not separating the heavy cavalry from the light infantry. Limited expectations for such an offensive without any concentration of force must have constituted another reason. Only part of the Egyptian army had engaged, those held back equaling the number that had originally resisted the Israeli counterattacks. A soldier as astute and orthodox as General Ismail, the Egyptian commander in chief, could hardly have entertained other expectations from the kind of offensive undertaken, with the limited troops engaged, than the few modest gains made and the casualties incurred. The Israelis attempted no pursuit, carefully avoiding the formidable Egyptian antitank and antiaircraft defenses along the canal.

But the Israelis did plan a counterattack against a spot where they found a small gap in the Egyptian line east of the canal. This weak point, north of the larger lake, coincided with one of their own preplanned crossing points where they had made a less formidable embankment on the canal and near which they had stored bridging equipment with a designated route for it to the crossing site. Concentrating their forces, the Israelis reached the canal bank before the surprised Egyptians could prevent them. There ensued a struggle of several days in which the Egyptians used their powerful infantry and tank forces north of the lake to counterattack and the Israelis, in turn, struck to the north in an effort to protect their flank to and to clear their route to the canal bank. Much fighting occurred in an area known as the Chinese farm. But their blow to the north also had created the impression that they wished to drive north, east of the canal, to assault the flank of the Egyptian Second Army defending the east bank of the canal between the lake and the swampy area on the north end of the canal.

This distraction worked well, the Egyptian command discounting the possibility of a crossing even when they detected Israeli troops on the west side of the waterway. The Israelis prevented discovery of the extent of the forces that had crossed by concealing their infantry in the vegetation on the west side of the canal and placing most of their tanks in captured aircraft hangars. Their failure to install their mobile bridges as quickly as they expected also contributed to obscuring their objective because the Egyptians knew that the Israelis could not support a major force west of the river only with ferries on the canal.

Yet this Israeli offensive presented a major threat to the Egyptians who, in order to conduct their abortive one-day offensive, had substantially diminished the powerful armored reserves that they had originally kept west of the canal. While the Israelis struggled to drive north against the Egyptians east of the waterway to continue the distraction, expand the corridor to their bridgehead, and clear a way for a prefabricated bridge, the small Israeli force west of the canal sent out some of its tanks to attack the stationary but unprotected anti-aircraft missiles established there, destroying three and forcing another to move in haste. Thus, they began to prepare the way for the later employment of the Israeli air force by attacking the weapon system deadly to aircraft but defenseless against tanks and other ground forces. A battery of long-range 175-millimeter guns, brought across the canal for this purpose, fired at the nearby antiaircraft missile sites, causing some damage and compelling the Egyptians to move the missiles.

Concentrating three divisions at this point, the Israelis planned to use one to stand on the defensive to defend their communications and the other two to carry out a turning movement against the Egyptian Third Army, which had most of its men deployed on the east side of the canal south of the lakes. With the canal bridged and the turning forces crossing on the night of October 17, the Israelis were ready to begin their strategically decisive movement the following day. The situation had much in common with the German crossing of the Meuse in May 1940. The Egyptian high command, like the French, focused their attention on a false menace—the Israeli threat to push north on the east bank of the canal—just as in 1940 the German push into Belgium had distracted Generals Georges and Gamelin. But in 1973 the Egyptian army, having ample motorized troops, did not face an enemy with superior strategic mobility as did Gamelin and Georges.

On October 18 the initial Israeli division drove due west and, despite strong resistance from Egyptian tanks in defensive excavations supported by antitank missiles, managed to push far enough to have a sufficiently secure position to turn south the next day. The Israelis also destroyed three more missile sites and fended off air strikes on their bridges, including one in which they shot down the five attacking helicopters. Meanwhile, General Ismail, aware of the Israeli bridges, sent his chief of staff to the front to investigate. On October 18 the chief of staff visited the front and formed a gloomy estimate of the Israeli menace.

On October 19, as the lead Israeli division drove south until powerful Egyptian opposition halted it after an advance of about six miles, the Egyptian chief of staff reported such a serious Israeli threat that he recommended the withdrawal of all forces west of the canal. General Ismail rejected this advice and ordered his two armies to drive back or at least halt the Israeli advance. He did not, however, establish a separate headquarters to coordinate forces fighting on the west bank of the canal nor order any specific concentration of troops.

The following day the lead Israeli division bypassed the strong point that had stopped it the previous day and pushed south fifteen miles. Since the Egyptians had withdrawn most of their stationary antiaircraft missiles to prevent their loss to the advancing Israelis and still had most of the infantry-carried missiles for low-altitude defense west of the river, the Israeli air force could render excellent assistance to the advance that day.

But the drive south on October 21, meeting the resistance of two-thirds of an armored division, covered only a few miles. The second Israeli division, following in the rear, overcame the resistance of the Egyptian strong points that the lead division, in applying the principle of the infiltration tactics, had bypassed on its push southward. On the following day, despite heavy opposition and only through passing around much of it, the lead division turned east and arrived at the west bank of the smaller lake, having thus reached a spot as far south as ten miles from the southern mouth of the canal.

On October 23 the lead Israeli division, reinforced by infantry from the Syrian front, drove south to the shores of the Gulf of Suez as did elements of the following division pushing south farther to the west. Thus, the Israelis had both an outer and inner ring around the rear of the Egyptian Third Army, which was holding the town of Suez on the west bank of the canal as well as their bridgehead on the east. The Israelis had trapped two infantry divisions and parts of two others, a total of about 40,000 men. This final, decisive day of the campaign occurred when the combatants had agreed to a cease-fire, proved difficult to enforce because of the intermingling of units resulting from the Israeli tactic of bypassing Egyptian strong points.

In six days the Israelis had driven over fifty miles to complete the turning of the Egyptian army. Two divisions had overcome the persistent and continuing opposition of at least equal forces, including portions of two divisions strong in tanks. They had succeeded not only because of their combat-honed tactical skills but also because of the dominance and support of their air force, the disorganization of their unconcentrated enemy who had to improvise a defense, and the dispatch by the Egyptain forces west of the canal of their antitank missiles to units on the east bank.

The Israelis had prevailed, just as had the Germans in 1940, but a more formidable task lay ahead of them than faced the Germans in 1940. The city of Suez and the canal shielded the rear of the Egyptian Third Army and its well-developed defensive positions protected its eastern front. And the Third Army, with adequate supplies of food and ammunition, differed greatly from the allied forces in Belgium in 1940. Instead of an army compelled to retreat because of the threat to its rear and deserted by its Belgian allies, the Egyptian Third Army, with the soldiers' morale elevated by their brilliantly executed crossing of the canal and their victory over Israeli counterattacks, had the morale as well as the material means to resist.

Since both the Israeli turning force and the Third Army had sufficient supplies, the situation resembled a seige more than a turning movement. And the two Israeli divisions that held the lines behind the Third Army on the west bank faced a relieving force of five Egyptian divisions. But the cease-fire precluded a reenactment of any famous sieges or of the great frontal battles that pitted the covering force against the relieving army.

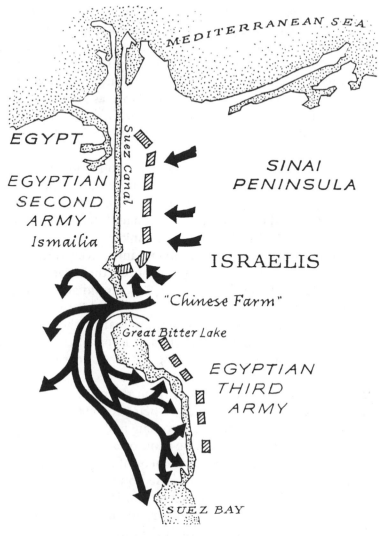

Diagram 11.1. Israeli Counterattack and Turning Movement

The Tactical Mixture of Old and New

Aided by the distraction of its apparent effort to attack the southern flank of the Egyptian Second Army, the Israeli offensive had attained strategic surprise. By skillfully applying Guibert's offensive formula of distraction to induce the enemy to create a weak point and by using a concentration to exploit it, the Israelis had gained a victory over a capable, well-led enemy, larger in numbers. But Egyptian preparations, tenacity, and imperturbable leadership made Israeli success difficult and mitigated the effects of the winning turning movement. As in Caesar's victory at Ilerda, political factors mingled with military in the outcome that, like Marengo, showed that the defeated had not lost their powers of resistance.

Egyptian tactics displayed a mastery of the employment of the fully revived infantry weapon systems of the past. Like the generals of the seventeenth century who displayed their confidence in the defensive power of pike and musket when they had secure flanks, the Egyptians also took a position with a water obstacle at their rear. Their infantrymen, with antitank and antiaircraft weapons, justified their faith in the traditional primacy of the defense as it pitted the dismounted man against the mounted when the infantryman had the appropriate weapon system to defend against his mounted opponent. In addition, the Egyptians strengthened their infantry defense with tanks. These not only played the role of dismounted cavalry by taking positions with good fields of fire that exposed only their turrets but also mounted local counterattacks. The excellent articulation of the Egyptian infantry, improved by radios and complemented by a defense in depth, shielded it from the disruption and defeat that pikemen would have suffered if cavalry had penetrated their ranks.

The Suez Canal protected the Egyptian flanks, even though this was not literally true, because the Egyptians had anchored their flanks on a swamp in the north and the Gulf of Suez in the south. But should an Israeli assault pierce the Egyptian front, the attackers would face the canal rather than have an opportunity to break through and then attack the rear of the Egyptian defenders on either side. This barrier failed the Egyptians, in part because the Israelis had prepared crossing sites in advance, including the placement of bridging material nearby.

Israeli defensive tactics, based primarily on the old concept of dismounting cavalry, used the depth available to them. Their protected tanks could use their guns effectively against the attacking Egyptian tanks as well as employ their mobility to counterattack any vulnerable flank of a force of Egyptian assaulting tanks. But the Egyptians could have employed infantry to attack the tanks and could have attained a tactical supremacy based on the accuracy of a missile that the operator could guide to hit the turret of the Israeli tank.

Israeli machine guns, however, inhibited such use of Egyptian antitank missiles because of the vulnerability of the operator. This employment of small arms fire, plus the use of field artillery, exhibits the coexistence of the single, light infantry weapon system warfare of the late nineteenth and early twentieth centuries with the warfare based on the customary four weapon systems that had again become dominant since the last years of World War I.

As the successful use of Israeli artillery against Egyptian antiaircraft missile sites exhibited, late nineteenth-century warfare presented the same menace to antiaircraft weapons as it did to antitank weapons. Against the stationary antiaircraft missiles, as against the portable missile carried by a soldier, rifle and machine gun fire would have had a disastrous impact on the personnel using the weapons. The new antiaircraft light infantryman, like the heavy infantry with antitank gun and missile, required protection against the apparently obsolete rifle-armed light infantry. And the most effective safeguard could only come by reinforcing the antiaircraft and antitank infantry with nineteenth-century riflemen and their machine guns and artillery. By thus mixing the old and the new, the antiaircraft and antitank weapons could have a defense based on exploiting the superiority on the defense of the rifleman and machine gunner against similarly armed soldiers.

In the traditional relations, largely restored by the introduction of tank, aircraft, and antitank and antiaircraft weapons (schematic 11.1), A stands for the ability to attack in the direction of the arrow and D for the ability to defend in the direction of the arrow.

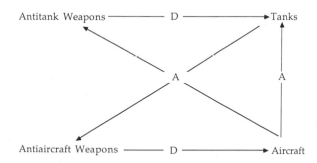

Schematic 11.1. 1930s Weapon Systems Capabilities

But the infantry and artillery which dominated warfare in the sixty years before 1918 also belong on this schematic. Typically the artillery would now have only howitzers, and the infantry would have recoilless rifles as well as machine guns and light mortars. Yet, for simplicity, the new schematic will attribute to them no antitank capability. Schematic 11.2 is transitional, introduced only to clarify the process of adding infantry and artillery. In order to make a place on the new schematic, 11.2 does not show the tanks' attack relationship to the antiaircraft weapons nor the aircraft's ability to assail antitank weapons.

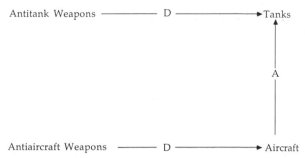

Schematic 11.2. 1930s Weapon Systems Capabilities

The new schematic 11.3, has added to 11.2 the infantry and artillery, abbreviated "inf. & arty.," and their relationships with the more modern weapon systems. Thus, the World War I infantry remains vulnerable to the tank and aircraft but can attack the antitank and antiaircraft weapons. If the antiaircraft

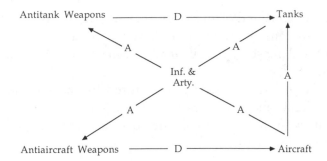

Schematic 11.3. Relation of World War I Infantry and Artillery
to 1930s Weapon Systems

weapons are self-propelled, the old infantry can only defend against them because it cannot overtake and attack them unless they halt and deploy to engage aircraft. From the standpoint of World War I infantry, antiaircraft guns on an armored carrier, like antitank guns similarly mounted, do not differ in kind from a tank.

So the intermingling of the old and the new, possible only where terrain permits the employment of the new, has presented commanders with more and, therefore, more complex, interrelationships among the weapon systems, creating essentially unprecedented problems of combination for mutual support and further complicating the offensive task of exploiting the vulnerabilities of the opponent's synthesis of his weapon systems.

Other conflicts in the period since 1945 took place outside the Western world, though Western powers participated. The United States carried the burden in Korea of struggle much like World War II. The British in Malaya and France and then the United States in Indo-China, among other instances, fought against the raiding strategy of guerrillas rather than engaging in the persisting kind of conflict characteristic of the formal Arab-Israeli wars and that of most European wars for the preceding three centuries. In these and other conflicts terrain limited the use of the new mounted weapon systems and often made the operations resemble those of the more remote past.

12

CONTINUITY AND CHANGE

The themes in warfare in the Western world recapitulated in this chapter focus on the nature of military operations and help explain why wars have been typically protracted and so often indecisive. So many different operational elements affect the outcome of a battle, campaign, or series of campaigns that rarely can all favor a quick result. And when even wise commanders blunder and the inept often do not understand their situation at all, the human element of command, as well as many other behaviorial aspects of warfare omitted in this treatment, will, like Clausewitz's friction, inhibit the attainment of an early military decision. These intrinsic attributes of warfare often so severely tried the political patience and so depleted the economic and moral resources of the combatants that wars fell short of producing significant political consequences. Often failing to grasp the inherent military obstacles to victory, combatants frequently overestimated the contributions of nonmilitary variables. The following summary should assist in describing many of the military factors that helped to extend many conflicts.

This summary chapter begins by showing the consistencies among land, sea, and air warfare in terms of the strategic distinctions used throughout. Since this book has primarily to do with armed strife on land, this chapter concentrates on this most prevalent form of warfare by devoting sections to tactics, logistics, and strategy—essentially the same organization as Chapter 1. Each section begins with a chronological overview and summarizes the main themes. The section on strategy concludes with a recapitulation of alternatives confronting commanders.

SEA AND AIR WARFARE

Chronological Survey

Naval warfare has exhibited far fewer changes than that on land, though this is the branch of war that gunpowder influenced first and most profoundly. On land cannon forced only a redesign of fortifications and handguns began to substitute for bows; at sea gunpowder wrought a revolution. In the sixteenth century missile action began to supplant the shock action of combat by soldiers on adjacent decks and ramming galleys. By the end of that century naval warfare had become one of combat with missiles; large, lumbering ships with the greatest number of the heaviest guns became the dominant combat ship.

Ships had to fight in line ahead to use their broadside-mounted guns rather than in line abreast to facilitate ramming. As the tactics of battles developed, admirals learned to concentrate against a smaller portion of the enemy line. Fighting took place at close range and numerical superiority played a major role because, among the ships engaged, all could fire at an enemy. At the Battle of the Nile, for example, Nelson's concentration of two ships against one at the head of the French line assured the British a quick and overwhelming victory.

But gunpowder affected only tactics. The reliance on sailing ships with better capabilities for sailing and navigating revolutionized naval logistics. Yet though this alteration facilitated the blockade, naval strategy did not change. The stronger power still sought by the persisting strategy of the blockade to interdict enemy commerce and ensure safe troop movements by ship; the weaker power had to rely on the raiding strategy of sending small fast ships against the dominant power's commerce. Navies continued to guard and attack sea communications and carry on overseas expeditions, both exemplified in the early Persian campaigns against Greece. The Marathon campaign showed the strategic advantage conferred on an army by command of the sea, enabling the army commander to concentrate fully against weakness without any concern that his enemy, weaker at sea, could attack him.

The introduction of the iron steamship and more powerful and longer range guns in the nineteenth century did not modify tactics or strategy in any fundamental way. But the increase in the speed and reliability of ship movements brought about by steam, together with the enhanced power of rapid concentration conferred by the wireless, raised the ratio of force to space, thus benefiting the stronger power. On the other hand, the dependence of steamers on coal and later oil fuel decreased the ratio of force to space for navies operating far from a base because of the frequent need of steamers to return for fuel.

The naval age of steam, steel, and the wireless also profoundly affected the weaker power's raiding strategy against commerce. The wireless inhibited commerce raiding because it permitted instant reporting of the whereabouts of a raider. And the logistic tether of fuel for steamers trammeled the raider's movements, further diminishing its power. In addition, the distant blockade maintained from adjacent bases by the British in World War I also hurt the commerce raider because the wireless and the independence of steamers from winds enabled the blockading power to move promptly to intercept any raider putting to sea. The growth in the size of ships removed many shallow estuaries as bases for small raiders and the increase in the expense of the steamers meant that the cost of raiding squeezed out many small entrepreneurs. Only the government remained in the business, which further simplified the task of protecting commerce from raiders.

But in World War I, the submarine employed another dimension of the sea for temporary concealment and fighting and revived the raiding strategy at a time when the navy's fundamental logistic strategy assumed greater significance, for war had come to depend so much on industrial production and critical supplies brought from overseas. Directed against the United Kingdom, the raiding strategy with submarines promised victory to the Germans until the strategic concentration of force of the convoy and the tactical strength conferred by the development of the hydrophone and the depth charge defeated the raiders. The same strategy failed again in World War II for essentially the same reasons.

In World War II the airplane affected naval tactics by outranging guns and causing the vulnerable aircraft carrier to share with the battleship the role of capital ship in the Mediterranean and Atlantic and supersede the battleship in the Pacific. The range of land-based aircraft so exceeded that of coast defense guns that, without air superiority from carriers or adjacent land bases, fleets could no longer hover menacingly off a hostile shore. But the aircraft, based on land as well as at sea, further augmented the ratio of force to space that the wireless-equipped steamer had already increased, in spite of the fewer number of ships available, at least as compared with the days of sailing navies. The Battle of Britain presented an opportunity for land-based aircraft to demonstrate that they could command the English Channel, but the size and efficiency of Britain's air force prevented that trial between aircraft from the land and the navy.

Aircraft also proved their worth as raiders against commerce, particularly when the Germans used planes in an attempt to interdict sea communication between the United Kingdom and Russia. Yet their greater speed gave them a more significant function in acting against submarine commerce raiders.

The power of small inexpensive aircraft against the surfaced submarine presented an apparent anomaly unless one remembers the danger a horse archer posed for the powerfully armored and mounted Byzantine and Crusader heavy cavalry. Difficult to hit because of its speed, the aircraft proved dangerous to the submarine that on the surface combined the disadvantages of low speed, small defensive firepower, and considerable fragility. As long as the submarine had to use the surface, it suffered the same disadvantage of any raider when confronted with a better weapon system with greater speed.

None of this changed naval strategy, the dominant power continuing to rely on the persisting logistic strategy of blockade, and because of the submarine and the aircraft, the weaker could continue its raiding logistic strategy. Likewise, command of the sea as before permitted the supply and movement of armies over the sea and still, as the Anglo-American Normandy landing demonstrated, gave the advantage of the initiative as demonstrated in the Marathon campaign. The British also employed raids against the German-held coast, such as the one at Dieppe on the French coast in 1942, to distract the Germans by arousing apprehensions about the security of the coast. Unlike the French when they lacked command of the sea in the Hundred Years' War, the Germans attempted no seaborne raids on the British coast, leaving retaliation to their aircraft and their flying and rocket bombs.

Aircraft made their military debut in World War I, making their principal contribution as often the only available means of reconnaissance in combat along a continuous, fortified front. They also carried out raids against communications, though limited bomb loads and poor accuracy restricted their effectiveness in this strategic role. Appropriately, one of the aircraft's greatest tactical successes occurred in Palestine, where Crusaders had faced Moslem light cavalry. In 1918 British planes had caught Turkish infantry on the march, just as Turkish horse archers had assailed early Crusaders on the march in Anatolia. The British light cavalry of the air had kept their distance and shot and bombed the helpless men and animals of the marching Turks who, like the Crusaders, lacked any weapon system to reply to their rapidly moving, deadly, and inaccessible assailants.

During World War II the combatants integrated their improved airplanes into land operations by confirming them in the traditional tactical and strategic functions of light cavalry. An effort to extend airpower beyond this role, the expensive Anglo-American experiment of trying to win the war in Europe with a logistic and political strategy of bombing industries and cities, failed to have a decisive effect on the outcome of the war.

The nuclear bomb, combined with the long-range aircraft and cruise and ballistic missiles, has given a paramount place to air power's strategic bombing and its logistic and political objectives. Otherwise, the mission and the capabilities of aircraft have remained the same. Guided missiles affected air war as they did that on land and sea, and aircraft would participate in the use of tactical nuclear weapons on land. At sea the missile gained ground at the expense of the carrier-borne aircraft, if only because it provided a less expensive means of outranging the gun, but this merely continued the trend toward greater range and accuracy that, along with expansion in power, had continued since the sixteenth century.

Recapitulation of the Characteristics of Naval Warfare

Writers on strategy often distinguish sharply between warfare at sea and warfare on land and sometimes have claimed primacy for the domination of one element or the other. But the similarities seem to have outweighed the differences. Both employed raiding as well as persisting strategy in an effort to dominate a given area. Warfare at sea had as its strategic objective the essentially logistic goal of depriving the enemy of the benefits of sea communications and of assuring them to friendly forces. Control of the sea bestowed the advantage of the ability to move and supply land forces. This conferred a special benefit because even after the revolution in logistics in the nineteenth and twentieth centuries, water communications remained the least expensive mode of supply. In addition, the navy could effectively collaborate with the army by landing troops at both unexpected and strategically important points. Yet the more elaborate equipment of armies complicated the task of carrying out such an overseas invasion in that conveying a motorized army magnified the number of ships needed for the landing.

World War II again demonstrated the traditional effect of the mobility provided by sea power on the strategy of warfare on land. When Field Marshal Montgomery's British, Canadian, and U. S. armies landed in France in 1944, they again showed the sea as a highway for the dominant seapower but, as in 1940, an impassable moat for the weaker. If, in 1944, the Germans could have gained mastery of the sea, as had the Greeks after defeating the Persian fleet, Montgomery's forces would have had to make a hastier and more complete retreat than did the Persians after they lost command of the sea. In building a navy to resist Viking raiders, the English had shown the value to operations on land of contesting mastery of the seas. History teems with examples of the use of the strategic mobility provided by low-cost sea transportation; the British, for example, used the sea to send troops to the Iberian Peninsula to fight Napoleon and to withdraw them when defeated. In World War II in Italy, for instance, the allied forces pushing north against the Germans integrated seaborne movements closely with those on land when they attempted a turning movement. But the Germans concentrated against the men landing at Anzio, thus protecting their communications and bottling up the landing force, just as the Turks in 1915 had contained allied landing forces that had exploited the interior lines made possible by sea power.

In modern times, sea power has become increasingly important in its ability to pursue the logistic objective of taking away the enemy's economic advantages of overseas trade and important imports. To illustrate, in the Napoleonic Wars British domination of the sea not only protected the United Kingdom from invasion by the superior French armies but also enabled it to blockade France and, to a degree, the entire continent of Europe to deprive France of the products as well as the economic benefits of overseas business. Further, the command of the sea allowed Britain to appropriate the trade of French and Dutch colonies as well as use its strategic mobility on water to concentrate against and conquer many of these valuable possessions.

The British could carry out this persisting strategy of blockade, which included bottling up squadrons of French warships as well as interdicting commerce, because they had an adequate ratio of force to space. The proximity of their bases to the blockaded ports and their huge fleet helped them to reduce to a trickle overseas trade from French ports. A smaller fleet, or one more distant from its bases of supply and repair, would have markedly diminished the effect of the blockade. And if both the British and French had had far smaller fleets, the British could have done little more than raid French commerce even though they could have blockaded the few ports harboring the principal squadrons of French warships. Thus, the ratio of force to space conditions warfare at sea just as it does on land and so provides one requisite for the pursuit of a persisting strategy.

In combating the British blockade, the French also used a persisting logistic strategy when they closed the ports of Europe to British imports as well as continued their traditional logistic strategy of sending raiders against British merchant ships. The French left a great deal of their raiding to private enterprise, with the capture of British ships and cargoes as an incentive to induce entrepreneurs to wage war on behalf of France. Except for official sanction, this sea warfare differed little from piracy and, in the economic motivation of its executants, paralleled the raids of Vikings into Western Europe and of barbarians into the Roman and Arabs into the Byzantine empire.

Against the French raiders the British armed their merchant ships and escorted groups of them with warships. The delay imposed on some ships by waiting for the departure of the convoy raised costs, but the expense doubtless proved less than the losses that were prevented. The efficiency of sea commerce made sailing in protected flotillas possible because a few ships covered only a small sea area and, compared to a convoy on land, carried much merchandise in a little space. So a procedure that concentrated too much force for raiders to cope with, difficult to employ on land, proved effective at sea against raiders that rarely operated in squadrons of formidable size.

But neither British nor French logistic strategies had a serious effect on the ability of either combatant to maintain its army and navy. And the strategies differed only slightly from those employed on land because the stronger naval power used a persisting combat strategy to control the seas so as to follow a logistic strategy of blockade. The weaker French had most often resorted primarily to raids against merchant ships to implement a logistic strategy.

After the Industrial Revolution made economies more dependent on imports, sea power's logistic strategy became more important. Petroleum and copper, for example, minerals that Europe could not supply in the quantities needed for large-scale warfare, played a major role in twentieth-century conflicts. Against island nations such as the United Kingdom and Japan, a logistic strategy, implemented by a total blockade, could virtually win a war by crippling industrial production and diverting resources to agriculture as blockaded nations sought self-sufficiency in their food supply.

The airplane and the submarine gave the weaker power new tools for its raiding strategy against the dominant power's commerce, a task made difficult for surface raiders dependent on fuel for their boilers and liable to have their location reported by wireless. But the new air and submarine means of raiding, like the new modes of attack and defense at sea, did not basically change the fundamental objectives of naval strategy nor the manner in which the belligerents followed them.

Thus naval strategy has remained essentially unchanged, as have tactics since the sixteenth-century transition from shock to missile action. The same strategy matrix used for land warfare applies to much of naval strategy, with persisting and raiding combat strategies and the same divisions for logistic strategy. These categories better suit the navy's action against the hostile power and its army than against the opposing fleet. For example, the uses of a logistic strategy against the hostile fleet that had impressive success—Alexander's campaign to capture the bases of the Persian fleet and the siege and capture of the Port Arthur fleet—both depended on the army.

In assailing the hostile country and army, however, the Normandy landing, like that of William the Conqueror, exemplified combat persisting strategy just as many British blockades show a logistic persisting strategy and French commerce raiders and German submarines demonstrate the use of a logistic raiding strategy. Combat raiding strategies against the enemy country and army are more rare, the Dieppe raid constituting a recent example. But the Persian landing at Marathon could readily fit into the class of combat raids because, as a distraction, the Persian commander had no aim to persist at that point any more than did the British who landed at Dieppe or French raiders on the English coast in the Hundred Years' War.

Summary of the Attributes of Aircraft in Warfare

Writers on strategy often distinguish between warfare in the air and warfare on the land and sea. After the military airplane had just come into use, many writers and theorists thought that this weapon system alone could drive ships from the surface of the sea and win land wars unaided. In its tactical role of restoring light cavalry to the armies, it proved quite effective, but it did not render other weapon systems obsolete any more than had Turkish light cavalry when pitted against Byzantine and Crusader combined-arms armies.

For the strategic role of light cavalry for reconnaissance and for interdicting communications, the airplane is invaluable. It can fly over terrain obstacles and opposing forces. Without the light cavalry of the air, the continuous fronts of World War I would have precluded any reconnaissance or raiding of communications. This ability to fly over the deadlocked front helped convince General Douhet, an early exponent of victory through airpower, that a raiding strategy executed by aircraft provided the means to carry out an effective offensive in the presence of too high a ratio of force to space to permit a decisive application of a persisting strategy on the ground. Accordingly, just as commanders had to resort to raids when they had too low a ratio of force to space to aspire to a persisting strategy of dominating the ground, so they could use air raids as an antidote to too much force to space.

Using airplanes to perform the light cavalry's traditional role of executing a raiding logistic strategy against armies' communications proved important. But air raiders against communications lacked the precision and, consequently, the effectiveness of surface raiders. Bridges, for example, which traditional raiders could have destroyed with a small amount of well-placed explosives, proved extremely hard targets for aircraft to hit and often were resistant to bombs. For instance, the destruction of each of the major bridges bombed by the Anglo-American air forces in 1944 prior to the landing in Normandy required an average of 220 tons of bombs.

In carrying out its raids, most bombing aircraft lacked the preponderance in speed usually possessed by mounted raiders on land. Aircraft carrying bombs traditionally had more bulk and lower speed than observation or fighter aircraft, and, in the latter, the larger bomber faced an aircraft greater in speed, one designed as a weapon system to be dominant over the bomber. Though not without defenses and often moving in convoys accompanied by fighter aircraft, bombers lacked the elusiveness customary for raiders. The situation of the bombers is analogous to, but not exactly parallel to, that of heavy cavalry assailed by light cavalry. This disadvantage made air forces particularly anxious to defeat the opposing air force so its bombers could raid without danger. So although in its strategic role the air arm relied exclusively on the raid, in its combat with other aircraft it, like navies, adhered to a persisting strategy to attain such a mastery of the air that its aircraft might fly unmolested by the enemy.

In addition to facilitating air raids and reducing their cost, substantial control of the air made easy its use for logistic purposes by unarmed aircraft. This capability had limited logistic value because the expense of air transportation far exceeded that of other means. To illustrate, in the United States in the 1960s rail travel per ton-mile cost four times as much as water, truck travel five times as much as rail, and conveyance by air over three times as much as truck.

But movement of men and goods by air had the advantage of speed as well as the ability to fly over enemy-held terrain. Aircraft could function in the absence of rail, road, or water routes of communication. Thus the Germans sought to supply their army at Stalingrad by air, an attempt defeated, with heavy loss of aircraft, by the Russian command of the skies. But under more favorable circumstances, other, less ambitious efforts by air succeeded. On occasion, bombing planes temporarily diverted to transport service could have helped to alleviate critical shortages for all of the belligerents.

Command of the air not only permitted the dropping of groups of parachute raiders but also made possible the carrying out of a substantial campaign. In 1941, after the Germans had conquered mainland Greece, they used their air force to carry paratroopers to the island of Crete. In spite of their disadvantage of being essentially World War I infantrymen facing soldiers supported by tanks and artillery, these troops, reinforced by sea-borne forces, captured the island. A later Anglo-American effort in the fall of 1944 to use parachute troops to create a corridor for an armored advance, however, did fail in spite of complete air supremacy and the substantial number of parachute troops used. In combating the German armored forces the lightly armed paratroopers had many of the disadvantages of light infantry defending against heavy cavalry.

In its larger strategic role, the aircraft in World War II adhered to a logistic raiding strategy against Germany's economy and, in attacking population centers, also a political strategy of terror. This use of bombers had something in common with that used earlier by the Turks in Asia Minor and the Mongols in Khwarizm. In view of its cost in terms of resources and its failure for most of the war to do decisive damage either to the enemy economy or morale, this logistic strategy should have caused much controversy after the war as to the value of its future use. But the atomic bomb obviated this dispute, and it, and the ballistic missile to carry it, changed strategy dramatically.

Since only a few planes with nuclear bombs need to get through the defenses to do tremendous damage, a Turko-Mongolian strategy promises to be as effective as of old. The ballistic missile, against which no defense seems presently feasible, has increased the ability of the raiders to have the assurance of inflicting ruinous damage, and its range has guaranteed that every country is vulnerable to this devastating attack. In fact, the political result of the dread inspired by this kind of war has perhaps prevented a war between the powers so armed. Thus, the threat of such a logistic raiding strategy, one aimed at people as well as things and embodying the element of terror, has proven as potent in preventing war as its application had been in giving victory to the Turks and Mongols.

The difference between this strategy, based on nuclear bombs delivered through the air, and the destruction wreaked by Turkish and Mongolian cavalry lies in the capability of both sides to follow the same strategy simultaneously. It diverges from the navy's application of a logistic strategy in that its effect will be more rapid and far more horrible than a blockade against even the most vulnerable island power.

Thus, in the age of the air-delivered nuclear bombs, not just the counterraid but also the mere threat of such raids has proven for more than three decades the most telling defense against raids yet devised.

As light cavalry, the air forces fought as part of the army, as had navies when they served the land forces by controlling the sea and moving and supplying armies. In addition, air forces and navies had larger, independent strategic roles, as did armies. Such actions in the air and on the sea carried out a logistic strategy of disabling the enemy's economy exactly as armies did through territorial acquisitions or, usually less effectively, by raids. Navies pursued their independent mission first using a combat strategy against the opposing fleets to gain dominance and then resorting to the persisting strategy of blockade; with less results, they had to rely on raids against hostile commerce alone; air forces adhered to a persisting combat strategy to gain air mastery to allow their raiders to operate unmolested; also less effectively, they depended solely on contested raids. Following a comparable sequence, armies also oriented on the enemy armies, using combat or logistic persisting strategy, or a combination of the two; if they succeeded, they won the war directly by occupying the enemy country. If they lacked the means to implement a persisting strategy, they too employed raids, even to weaken the enemy's economy.

All three branches of the service have also used raids, and armies and navies have access to a persisting strategy as well, to pursue political objectives directly. The sea has experienced economic raiders in the form of pirates and privateers. In capturing enemy merchant ships navies have, like armies, tried to live at the enemy's expense and make war support war.

So air forces had to count on the strategy of raids in carrying out their objectives, whereas navies and armies had a choice of methods, the raid on commerce or the persisting strategy of blockade. Thus, it may prove helpful in strategy to abandon any exclusive reliance on treating land, sea, and air warfare as different. Instead, strategic means and strategic ends may be as useful and as enlightening as those distinctions based upon the element in which warfare takes place.

But there has been a relationship between the larger strategic goals of warfare on the land, sea, and air. The navies' blockades, like the air forces' raids against economic targets, usually had as their military effect the weakening of the enemy armies and facilitating the task of the friendly armies. All military strategy must aim at the domination of people and the land where they dwell. If military means must be applied to military ends to achieve political goals, then the armed forces must have the land, sea, and air forces of the enemy as their objective and may attack them by a persisting or raiding strategy with forces deployed in all three elements, using either a combat or logistic strategy or a combination, whichever requires the least effort and presents the greatest promise of victory.

TACTICS

Chronological Summary

In 2,500 years the tactics of combat in Europe have undergone numerous transformations, many of which were more cyclical than linear in character. A chronological summary of some themes in tactics begins with the Greeks, who used primarily homogeneous armies of heavy infantry that lacking much articulation fought frontal battles. When they occupied an uphill position, the defenders enjoyed tactical primacy on the defense, and since neither side had better mobility and armies were small in relation to the space in which they operated, battles occurred only by mutual consent. Thus, between homogeneous armies, the tactical defense benefited from a predominance based on its ability to resist frontal attacks.

The preponderance of the defense in Greek warfare received reinforcement from the supremacy of fortifications; these accentuated the strength of the defense against frontal attack and brought more capital to the aid of the soldier's labor in combat. Yet by the time of Alexander the Great, the Greeks had developed a sophisticated way of war based on a mutually supporting use of the four basic weapon systems. The heavy cavalry, a weapon system essentially unknown to the Persians, provided the tactically offensive troops: by using their greater mobility and ability to fight without any significant delay to assume their combat formation, they attacked the flanks and rear of the redoubtable Greek heavy infantry in Persian service. In doing this, they also exploited their capability to attack light infantry and to overcome Persian light cavalry in shock combat.

The Alexandrian tactical scheme of employing all four weapon systems, using heavy cavalry to attack the flank and rear of the heavy infantry, dominated warfare in the Mediterranean basin until the time of the Romans, who modified it by depending more on their well-articulated, sword-armed infantry. Arrayed in several lines and incorporating the concept of a reserve, Roman infantry could maneuver and even cover its flanks against cavalry. Relying on allied cavalry, the Romans defeated their opponents and, with their orderly system of war and excellent engineering and field fortifications, controlled the lands bordering on the Mediterranean.

For several centuries the tactical skill of the Romans' professional infantry formations provided a fundamental basis for their victories over variously armed barbarians. But the impetuosity of the barbarian cavalry charge made the Romans adopt the long spear or pike and, in part to cope with raiders, steadily increase their proportion of cavalry. The modified Roman methods mixed with the national formulas of various barbarian groups, which all involved some form of foot and mounted combat, to create great tactical diversity as the age of the Roman Empire gradually passed into the Middle Ages.

The sophisticated warfare of the Eastern Roman or Byzantine Empire had as its foundation employing the tactical diversity of its army to bring the superior weapon system into action against the inferior. Thus against mounted opponents, Byzantine armies used infantry strengthed by dismounted cavalry, and against heavy infantry, they depended on their bowmen, both on foot and mounted, to weaken the barbarian host and prepare the way for their heavy cavalry's charge in the flank. An early disaster at the hands of the mounted Parthians and a long tradition of war against mounted Asiatic opponents had taught these Romans the lessons of exploiting and defending against the preponderance of one weapon system over another.

In Western Europe the introduction of the stirrup helped give heavy cavalry a prominence that the weakness of its natural enemies accentuated. In fact, the power of the stirrup-stabilized heavy cavalryman came near to nullifying the traditional advantage of the footman over the horseman, one almost always magnified by the foot soldier's usual posture of defense against the mounted warrior. Only good infantry equipped with long spears could resist the new cavalry. The absence of light cavalry in the often thickly wooded areas of the West protected Western European heavy cavalry from a menace to which Byzantine cavalry succumbed at Manzikert, and the lack of a regular infantry that trained together to fight in the field meant that the stirrup-stabilized heavy cavalry had a disproportionately predominant role in the field army. Since the defense relied much on fortifications, infantry had its appropriate place in the attack and defense of castles and cities.

But heavy cavalry notwithstanding, the defense dominated because of the strength and increasing sophistication of fortifications, the low ratio of force to space, and the lack of a government that could field professional armies or practice a persistent and systematic way of war. And in spite of an emerging feudal political synthesis, Western Europe did not have the tactical uniformity that had characterized the Mediterranean area when Alexandrian or Roman warfare prevailed.

Regional diversity characterized European warfare. Spaniards used light cavalry with javelins in raids against the Moslems in Spain; the English employed light infantry with longbows against the heavy infantry of the Scots; Crusaders utilized light infantry with crossbows to defeat Turkish light cavalry in Syria and Palestine; and towns, often having an immobile, usually undrilled, heavy infantry, armed themselves with pikes to resist heavy cavalry. The heavy cavalry provided the only constant, fighting either mounted or on foot as an elite but not well-articulated heavy infantry.

When the Swiss evolved a thoroughly drilled, pike-armed heavy infantry that could maneuver in large squares and also withstand the charge of heavy cavalry, Western Europe acquired a necessary ingredient to bring forth a new combined-arms synthesis. Joining this variety of weapon systems with the development of more professional military forces in France and Italy and the emergence in fifteenth-century Italian wars of a school of leaders who consistently pursued victory with the least effort without depending solely on the defensive, Western Europe had all of the requisites for field forces that, like the Byzantine, would have supremacy over any regional system of warfare.

The heavy infantry lacked Roman articulation but safeguarded its flanks by avoiding a linear array, each large square having a capacity for all-around defense. The light infantry, initially valuable for skirmishing, harassing the cavalry, and shooting horses, became an indispensable part of the infantry team by the late sixteenth century, when the invention of the pistol introduced light-cavalry tactics to Western Europe and gave the light-infantry arquebusiers the mission of protecting the heavy infantry from the pistoliers. The immobility of the infantry and its consequent deficiencies in carrying out attacks accentuated heavy cavalry's traditional role as the offensive troops.

The combined-arms tactical synthesis of 1600 had the same rationale as its predecessors, the Alexandrian and Roman, resting on the mutual support of each arm to protect another against a stronger weapon system. And, just as in Alexander's method, commanders relied on the higher mobility of the heavy cavalry to defeat the intrinsically stronger heavy infantry, either by charging a dispersed and so vulnerable infantry, or by using the mobility of the horsemen to attack a flank or rear unready to receive a charge. The technique differed from the ancients only in that cavalrymen with pistol and saber provided the most effective dual-purpose weapon system history had thus far seen. Yet the versatility of cavalry did not alter combat conditions, only forcing on the infantry closer and more sophisticated methods of mutual support.

The seventeenth century witnessed the complete restoration of the full capabilities of ancient warfare, operations Alexandrian in their reliance on cavalry and Roman in their persistence and dependence on fortifications and seigecraft. Linear tactics and even Roman words of command exemplified changes that created long-service professional armies that received fairly regular pay and obtained their supplies through a well-organized commissariat. Nevertheless, in spite of the predominance of linear infantry formations, the tactics varied from

Rome's in one important respect: the light infantry musketeers, rather than dispersing ahead of the heavy infantry as skirmishers, had an important place in the line. Instead of individual fire, volleys on command characterized the actions of musketeers, and the light infantry had a place in the battle that had more in common with Persian practice and the English use of their longbowmen.

The strength of fortifications and the even match of the contestants in numbers, skills, tactics, and resources kept such warfare indecisive. Yet when employed against non-European opponents with weaker political organizations, these methods met the same success enjoyed by the Romans in their wars against barbarians or the Macedonians and Syrians. In India, for example, the Europeans in the eighteenth century found their tactical system well adapted both to the terrain and to coping with the Indians who gave considerable emphasis to cavalry.

Still, no sooner had ancient warfare returned in all of its essentials than a simple innovation—the bayonet attached to the musket—merged light and heavy infantry and consequently devalued cavalry as a weapon system. The effectiveness of the flintlock musket meant that in combat between infantry missile action superseded shock action, and battles increasingly consisted of infantry arrayed in thinner, linear formations to develop the maximum firepower. Nevertheless, cavalry remained important: its tactically offensive characteristics of greater mobility and ease of taking up combat formation still enabled it to attack the flanks and rear of the infantry formations, now even more vulnerable because of the adoption of a linear system. With cavalry deployed on the flanks, combat resembled that of the ancient Persians.

But the supremacy of infantry and its continuance of the traditional dominance of the defensive when similar weapon systems fought augmented the tactical strengths of the defensive. Armed only with saber and pistol, dismounted cavalry, however, could no longer withstand the charge of mounted horsemen nor have parity with infantry. Only dragoons, also armed with muskets, could function effectively as infantry. And the power of even more sophisticated fortifications further increased the tactical resistance of the defensive.

But constant indecisive wars and the scientific spirit of the age helped animate and guide a successful search for a new way of war, one which flowered during the French Revolution. In tactics, the column, which furnished both battlefield mobility and the ability to deploy rapidly into the linear combat formation, gave infantry a hitherto unknown offensive power. Compared with opponents in a linear array, an army with infantry in columns possessed tactically offensive capabilities because its columns, marching more quickly than troops in line, could move fast enough to reach the enemy flank or rear and could deploy hastily enough to attack before the enemy could re-form to resist the threat. Equally, columns could maneuver on the battlefield to enable commanders to concentrate infantry to exploit weak points in the enemy array.

This enhanced infantry articulation, based on improved drill and well-conceived, simple evolutions, also contributed to the defensive supremacy of the bayonet-armed musketeer and made infantry on the march much less vulnerable to cavalry. This additional security helped to make unnecessary the cumbersome system of marching in readiness for battle when near the enemy in order to have defenses against a sudden attack by cavalry. An army whose infantry could form quickly, either to resist cavalry or to draw up for battle if surprised by enemy infantry, could move more swiftly because it could retain the speedy pace of the march formation even in proximity to the enemy. Such mobility and capacity for rapid concentration made it safe to disperse and, by using the fire of the musket to cover small gaps, unnecessary to deploy in a rigid line, which was difficult to form properly and impossible to move quickly. The shift from the shock action of the linear deployment of the ancients to reliance on missiles gave eighteenth-century linear infantry a flexibility denied to the Greek or Roman who had to avoid gaps so as not to expose any flanks to hostile swords- or spearmen.

Such newly constituted armies had greater strategic mobility when they were pitted against armies that continued to march in the old battle array. In both tactics and strategy the infantry of an army formed on this new model had the offensive capabilities long a monopoly of cavalry, a weapon system now inferior to bayonet-armed musketeers. When, however, this type of infantry organization became the archetype for nineteenth-century Europe, its ubiquity deprived either combatant of tactically offensive infantry and further devalued cavalry. But armies changed even more as the rifle and the breechloader eliminated cavalry as a tactically significant weapon system. Tactically, armies became truly completely homogeneous, composed of bayonet-armed riflemen and their slower-moving missle weapon companion, the artillery. The bayonet had become redundant because the range and rate of fire of the rifle virtually precluded shock action between infantries as well as cavalry against infantry. Nevertheless, armies retained cavalry for its strategic value and cherished the illusion that it still had tactical importance. Cavalry had too long and glorious a history to enable officers from rural backgrounds, where the horse still had a dominant role in the culture as well as the economy, to give it up easily.

Not since the early Greeks had all European armies so exclusively utilized essentially a single weapon system. They did not base this usage on ignorance of alternatives, a conservative adherence to old methods, or the unsuitability to terrain of any other. Rather, late nineteenth-century warfare no longer had any other weapon system that had serious value in combat. Since cavalry had no tactical use even for attacking the flanks of infantry, armies with only light infantry lacked a weapon system with better mobility. And with all forces employing the quick-moving, rapid-deploying French revolutionary column, no army had any body of infantry that had better mobility than any other. So, without any differential mobility among its troops, no army possessed any tactically offensive component. The tactical defensive had attained unprecedented predominance.

World War I exhibited this conclusive primacy of the defensive when it produced casualties in unheard-of total numbers, as generals struggled with a situation both unique and much at variance with their preconceptions. The losses came not so much from the deadliness of the new weapons or a high proportion of losses in a few days; rather, like the seige warfare of the past, the entrenched armies suffered moderate casualties that persisted day after day and month after month. Because 10 percent of populations were under arms, rather than the 2 or 3 percent of wars in the previous two centuries, casualties as a percentage of population rose to an extraordinary level, even when casualties as a percentage of those engaged in a particular battle usually remained, for periods of time comparable to the battles of old, quite low. The paradox of a declining ratio of losses accompanying growing lethality of weapons—explained largely by improved articulation, increasing homogeneity in respect to weapon systems, and the lower density of the troops in combat—received reinforcement from the entrenching that caused armies quite literally to disappear from view.

But from a situation in which similarly constituted, homogeneous armies struggled ineffectively against one another in prolonged, costly battles came a new sophistication in tactics. The concepts of mobility and concentration that in Napoleonic times commanders had employed for battalion columns marching erect on a smoky battlefield proved applicable in trench warfare to units as small as a dozen men moving from one covered position to another as they probed for and exploited a weakness in the enemy's defense. These infiltration tactics used on a minute scale the principle of concentration against weakness, and the small infantry groups, by their successful penetration, created openings that provided them with enemy flanks and rear to attack.

The doctrine of avoiding frontal assault and bypassing opposition proved fundamental to these tactics, as the attacking forces concentrated against weakness and reinforced success to pierce a deep defense, leaving to the reserves following the lead formations the task of completing the defeat of strong points avoided by the first groups of attackers. Infiltration tactics required this perseverance in pushing to the rear because the defense had organized in depth, just as castles had a series of walls, with an array of positions that like the towers on the castles of old interdicted the intervals between them and protected each other by their fire. Although barbed wire provided the physical barrier offered by walls and ditches in former times, defenders relied primarily on fire and more and more placed dependence on a succession of defenses and counterattacks to drive back the infiltrating enemy. Just as the attackers concentrated against weakness, the defenders sought to concentrate against strength.

Artillery played an augmented role in the offensive, and not only because initial tactical concepts had used the techniques of siege warfare as a model for the offensive against entrenchments. The accuracy possible with sophisticated control of indirect fire from calibrated weapons shooting under known conditions enabled artillery's high-explosive shells to support an offensive in a way impossible earlier. Yet the very immobility of the artillery, aggravated not only by the destruction of roads and bridges but also the obstruction of open fields by trenches and the craters created by its own fire, limited the range of an offensive. The attack had to await the difficult forward movement of the artillery.

But no sooner had a new era in warfare begun than the airplane and the tank reversed the trend toward homogeneity and took warfare back to the condition of four weapon systems, a situation that had not prevailed since the early days of the pistol in the sixteenth century. Armies soon had the same heterogeneity as in Alexander's times. Just as at the beginning of the sixteenth century, during and after the war commanders and military thinkers sought to assess their relative importance and devise the best combinations for the use of these new weapons.

In spite of their relatively small numbers, tanks had a major impact. With the same offensive characteristics as the armored heavy cavalry of the stirrup era, they enjoyed the advantage of the progress in discipline and articulation that had occurred since the Middle Ages. The use of the radio augmented this trend toward enhanced articulation and helped the tanks apply the concept of the infiltration tactics, for the execution of which they had, intrinsically, admirable attributes.

The strategic dispersal that had typified armies since Napoleon's day, also strengthened the effectiveness of tanks because, unlike the situation in the contests of old, most of the forces of each combatant did not necessarily participate in any given battle. Tanks could concentrate at one point and have a tactical predominance over the proportionately fewer antitank guns assembled there. In addition, when compared with the tank, the first antitank guns, as mobile rather than portable weapons, had less tactical mobility than the pike formations of earlier times. They could not take the offensive as had the heavy infantry at Pharsalus and Bannockburn.

Aircraft not only reproduced the properties of light cavalry but had the tank's advantage of radio communication. Also the aircraft enjoyed, even more than the tanks, those qualities of the capacity for rapid concentration and a comparative superiority in mobility over the antiaircraft gun greater than light cavalry had had over light infantry. Although airplanes had more prominence in their strategic light cavalry role, they could make serious tactical contributions.

But most forces fighting in World War II consisted of World War I infantry and artillery supported by antitank and antiaircraft guns. The tank and motorized forces constituted a small minority of the total, the air forces sometimes a somewhat larger proportion. After World War II armies gradually added to their motorized forces until marching infantry virtually disappeared. At the same time armies so increased the number of tanks that nearly every division had a significant number. Concurrently, artillery became self-propelled as did all antiaircraft guns, and the infantry became mounted infantry, or dragoons, when it received tracked carriers with bullet-proof armor and weapons of its own. Helicopters with machine guns and rockets, also able to transport infantry, completed the all-mounted division. Infantry equipped with portable antitank and antiaircraft missiles gave these weapon systems a mobility comparable to the pikemen and crossbowmen of old and, through their armored carrier and helicopter transport, mounted tactical as well as strategic celerity.

With light cavalry in the form of helicopters as well as aircraft from the air forces, postwar European armies had a certain Parthian character, but the presence of antiaircraft and antitank weapons actually made them more Byzantine. Armies shrunk in size as they adopted the more expensive mounted way of war. In this respect they also resembled the almost exclusively mounted armies of the Byzantine Empire and medieval Western Europe. And tanks also followed the Western medieval model as armies apparently planned to rely on the charge of their tanks. Consistently, the tank more and more followed the World War II trend of the antitank tank with all its features directed toward combat with a similar weapon system. With so many tanks in the armies and all depending on them to contribute significantly to antitank defense, tanks would have little choice but to fight other tanks.

Technology and the Four Basic Weapon Systems

The foregoing summary stresses the theme of the four basic weapon systems and how soldiers utilized those at their disposal. Terrain had much to do with their applicability as did their cost and the society providing the armed force. Overwhelming tactical success rewarded the employment of a more powerful weapon system against an inferior, as Byzantine practice exemplified. In heterogeneous armies commanders sought to make their own different weapon systems mutually supporting while seeking to assail with a better one an opponent's isolated weaker weapon system. Such heterogeneity, compared with a homogeneous army, complicated the tasks of a commander, providing more opportunities for blunders and a greater scope for ability.

But not all periods had every weapon system available to them, even when terrain suitable for their use existed. The development of the pistol eliminated the distinction between light and heavy cavalry, and the introduction of the bayonet at the end of the seventeenth century merged light and heavy infantry. This inaugurated an era of a century and a half in which European soldiers warred with only dual-purpose infantry and cavalry. Then rifles and breech-loaders gave infantry the power to eliminate cavalry's role in combat. The age of dual-purpose infantry as the only weapon system lasted until World War I, when the tank restored heavy cavalry and the aircraft the light cavalry. These gave rise to the modern analogs of the heavy and light infantry, the antitank and antiaircraft gun.

So technological change made possible these innovations, which created a unique period in warfare from 1700 to 1916 when soldiers had two, and then only one, weapon systems. Earlier, combat had undergone alterations through the impact of the stirrup and, in the more remote past, through such fundamental innovations as domesticating the horse for war, using iron rather than bronze weapons, and improving the bow. Clearly technology supplies a major theme for understanding tactics because of the huge modifications in combat that often rather simple concepts have made. In modern times technology first eliminated and later restored the four weapon systems of ancient and medieval warfare.

Thus the most dramatic effects of technology have occurred in the form of a few simple innovations, such as the bayonet, which affected the conduct of combat and the role or continued existence of a weapon system. Such important inventions as the flintlock changed tactics less because, like the handgun in its early stages, it only improved on an existing weapon or method of combat, a difference in degree rather than in kind. The stirrup worked a change of such great magnitude in the capability of the heavy cavalryman that this change might well have equaled a difference in kind; one might say the same about the crossbow in enabling men deficient in strength and skill to employ a strong bow nevertheless to use one of great power with considerable accuracy.

Gunpowder, curiously enough, worked its revolution in warfare on land only gradually. Fortifications quickly accommodated to the siege cannon, and handguns long performed no better than bows. But the facility with which the cavalry could use the pistol, a one-handed weapon, made it relatively easy, since the horseman also had a saber, to create a dual-purpose cavalry. This made gunpowder's first major impact on combat on land. The musket's easy conversion to a short pike by the addition of a bayonet probably gave this weapon its first serious combat advantage over the bow. Artillery more and more affected the battlefield but not enough to see it as different in kind, rather than degree, from the musket. A study of the era of artillery in microcosm might well show the need for an entirely new classification of weapon systems, one using more sophisticated distinctions. But the rifle, depending on the simple concept embodied in the Minié bullet, and the breechloader completed the destruction of cavalry's tactical value, a difference in kind that constituted another of gunpowder's major effects on warfare.

The existence of various weapon systems provided opportunities to employ the concept of economy of force—using no more resources than are necessary to carry out a task. Such frugality leaves uncommitted or unexpended assets available for other purposes. This idea, usually applied in the context of having the largest possible concentration for the main offensive or defensive effort, also had relevance in choosing among weapon systems so as to have the greatest combat power through least cost combinations.

The Economics of Force Composition

Only recently have elaborate cost calculations come to play an explicit role in the composition of forces. But such considerations have long been important. The replacement of the crossbow by the initially less effective but cheaper handgun exemplifies the influence of expense, as does the continued use of the matchlock musket rather than the more effective but more expensive wheel lock. Still, comparing prices has often involved more sophisticated tactical thinking than a mere examination of the charge for handgunners and crossbowmen and the number of handgunners needed to take the place of a given number of crossbowmen.

For example, if in the fourteenth century, an English army had as its only combat mission the resistance of a mounted charge by French cavalry, the English king could have used inexpensive Welsh pikemen. Suppose three of these pikemen could substitute, as infantry, for two dismounted knights, and a spearman with a nag to ride for strategic mobility involved only one-fourth the expense as a knight. If these assumptions were true, the English king could have met his combat needs with spearmen at 37.5 percent of the price for knights—two knights cost eight units of money and the equivalent combat capability through three spearmen incurred the expenditure of only three units.

But if the English king also had to face French crossbowmen as well as French knights, the spearmen alone would not suffice: the French could employ William's method at Hastings of shooting the immobile spearmen with crossbows until gaps appeared in the forces into which the French knights could charge. To cope with this menace the king would need some English knights who could remain mounted to ride out and disperse the French crossbowmen just as, at Bannockburn, Scottish knights had ridden over the English longbowmen.

When the king made the decision as to the proportions of high-priced knights and low-priced spearmen, expenditure and combat considerations would cooperate. Knights and spearmen could replace one another to resist a charge, but spearmen could not do the knights' work of driving off the crossbowmen. In addition, the English king would value knights because some on foot among the spearmen would strengthen their defense, and he could also use the mounted knights for reconnaissance and for dealing with any rural militia that might impede progress. So he might replace two knights with three spearman if he planned to use only a few spearmen. But when he thought of supplanting more knights with spearmen, other considerations than merely resisting a frontal charge would cause him to value knights more highly, and as the substitution process continued, the king would approach, and even exceed, having four and then more spearmen take the place of one knight. Finally, he would have an irreducible minimum of, say, 10 percent of the force that must be knights to deal with the crossbowmen. Because of this changing estimate of the worth of spearmen as their number increased—an example of the law of diminishing returns—the graph in schematic 12.1 of the king's hypothetical rate of substitution between spearmen and knights is a curved rather than a straight line.

This graph shows that the English king believed that he needed to keep some knights mounted to deal with the bowmen and leave the remaining dismounted knights, or their equivalent in spearmen, to resist the charge of the French knights. But between the extremes of 90 percent spearmen and 10 percent knights and all knights, the English king had a choice, because the curve graphs equal combat value, each combination of knights and spearmen having, in the king's estimation, the same effectiveness for meeting the French in battle.

In making the choice, the king could compare the price of knights and spearmen, trying various mixtures until he found one that involved the least

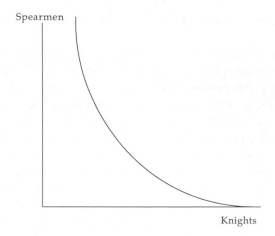

Schematic 12.1. Marginal Rate of Substitution between Spearmen and Dismounted Knights, Exhibiting a Curve of Equal Combat Effectiveness under Certain Conditions

expenditure. In the graph in schematic 12.2, the tangential line exhibits the one-to-four ratio of the charge for a spearman to that for a knight, showing that the least cost combination consists of about 16 percent knights and 84 percent spearmen.

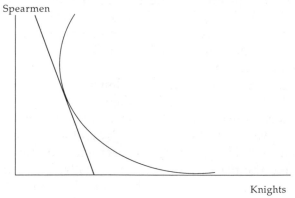

Schematic 12.2. The Role of Cost in Choosing the Optimum Combination of Spearmen and Dismounted Knights

The king also had another alternative. He could replace knights with long-bowmen mounted on nags for strategic mobility. In a good defensive position with some natural or artificial cover, the longbowmen could defeat French cross-bowmen. In addition, English experience in Scotland had shown that longbow-men could help significantly to defeat a cavalry charge. Further, since many longbowmen had swords or axes and some protection for their bodies, they could make some contribution as heavy infantrymen. On the other hand, if the king depended on the longbowmen for defense against crossbowmen, and the spearmen and dismounted cavalry thus had to withstand missiles from the French crossbow until the longbowmen had driven them off, the better armor of the dismounted knights would add to their value compared with the more vulnerable spearmen.

A similar graph could exhibit the combat substitution relationship between knights and longbowmen and a choice based on the least cost combination, again shown by a line charting the expense ratio between the two weapon systems. To graph the relationship among knights, spearmen, and longbowmen would require a three-dimensional figure with the price relationships reflected by a plane rather than a line. Of course, other considerations besides costs, and the needs of the entire campaign rather than just the battle, would also have weight; an absolute shortage of one weapon system would constrain choices as would political, cultural, and other factors.

In fact, at the Battle of Crécy the English had almost two-thirds of their force in longbowmen, most of the remainder in knights, and only a few spearmen. To defeat the French crossbowmen the king depended exclusively on his long-bowmen who, from their uphill position, defeated the brief attack of the cross-bowmen. The longbowmen then made a powerful contribution to the defeat of the French mounted charge, their arrows bringing down many horses.

In an actual example of constructing a force to meet a specific opponent, Gonzalo of Cordoba landed in Italy with an army suited to the kind of raiding warfare that the Spaniards and the Moslems had long waged against each other in Spain. But when this force of light cavalry genetours and heavy infantry with sword and shield met the French heavy cavalry and Swiss pikemen, they promptly suffered defeat. Gonzalo then reconstituted his army to meet the French. Retaining many of his javelin-armed genetours to execute the strategic missions of light cavalry, he trained some of his men to use the pike to provide essential help to his swordsmen in resisting the French cavalry, and he added arquebusiers to his heavy infantry to defend the entrenchments he used so prudently to stymie the powerful French cavalry. Thus, he rebuilt his forces to deal with a new adversary, combining various weapon systems with different characteristics to meet tactical and strategic needs. Unable to pay his Spaniards much less hire mercenaries because of lack of funds, he certainly must have taken scarcity and cost constraints into consideration as he refashioned his army to oppose French heavy cavalry and their formidable Swiss pikemen.

A recent example of a choice similar to that hypothesized for the Crécy campaign involves the comparable problem of antitank defense. The tank is clearly the best antitank weapon. Not only do its armor and powerful gun make it exceptional for this purpose when defending in a covered position, but its armor protects it from some of the effects of field artillery fire. Its mobility, in spite of the battlefield's small arms and artillery fire, also makes it the predom-inant weapon system to oppose the tank.

But modern armies have elected to have a good proportion of infantry armed with guided and unguided antitank rockets, a choice equivalent to the hypothesis that King Edward could have brought Welsh spearmen to the Crécy battlefield. In preparing for World War II the French and Germans both had more antitank guns than they did tanks, the Germans having proportionately and absolutely many more than the French. More recently, in crossing of the Suez Canal, the Egyptians employed so many infantry with rocket launchers that with little aid from tanks they repelled the initial attack of the Israeli tank forces. The effectiveness of the infantry in antitank defense came as no surprise to the Egyptians, and the preference for infantry, rather than the more costly tanks, resulted from the comparative costs of the two weapon systems. To buy, maintain, and man a tank involved vastly greater expense than using enough infantrymen with rockets to provide the same level of antitank defense. So a mixture of the less effective but more efficient infantry and the more formidable and more versatile tank provided an equally telling defense at a lower price than relying entirely on the tank.

These considerations have implicitly controlled force composition throughout 2,500 years of warfare. The elite Companion cavalry, for example, formed a very small proportion of Alexander's army, just enough, but not more, of these well-trained, expensive heavy cavalry to perform their essential tactical mission. Other less costly cavalry completed the necessary complement of mounted men for duties other than shock action. In the 1930s a French general made a similar point when he said that France would make a mistake if it gave up cavalry because this would involve the sacrifice of a natural advantage in higher quality horses. If he expressed anything more than a sentimental regard for the horse and a nostalgia for cavalry, he indicated that a plentiful supply of good horses made it inefficient for France to depend entirely on tanks and mechanization. And in World War II the French army, like the German and Russian, did employ a few horse cavalry as well as tanks and did use horse-drawn transport as well as trucks.

The Role of Articulation and Offensive Troops in Concentrating against Weakness

Although soldiers long devoted much implicit thought to the least cost combination of weapon systems, they often gave very explicit attention to the best tactical array. The Spartan and Theban flank attacks exhibit the results of this with homogeneous armies as Alexander's system does with a completely heterogeneous army. With the understanding by generals early in our era of the concept of the reserve and of the role of the general as commander instead of combat leader of his men, these points have required no elaboration or special emphasis in this book other than to point out that commanders have had as reserves troops other than those explicitly held out of combat for this purpose. In addition to the subtracted forces, all men not inextricably involved with the enemy constituted reserves. Alexander demonstrated this kind of reserve at Arbela when he led men orginally posted on the right to the aid of his hard-pressed left. Because active combat often made it difficult to extricate men already committed, this concept had more applicability to strategy, and Napoleon's use of such reserves against Würmser and Joffre's employment of them in 1914 illustrate the concept. On the other hand, the tactical problems that commanders faced have involved several of the themes of this book.

The defense had primacy not only when facing a weaker weapon system but against a similar one, as long as each faced the other's front in combat. Thus, one is tempted to define the problem of tactics as how best to overcome the dominance of the defensive when lacking a superior weapon system. To attack weakness provides the obvious answer.

The flank and rear of the formation of hostile soldiers furnished the most obvious points of weakness and, realizing this, the Spartans and the Thebans directed their assault at their opponent's flank. To carry it out, they improved the articulation of their armies and, by subdividing their phalanx, they articulated it, exemplifying another theme, and so created a power to maneuver and strike the enemy flank. The Romans had better articulation, which facilitated the provision of a reserve that they could also use to defend by concentrating against strength, as Scipio did to defeat Hannibal's outflanking moves at Zama.

Articulation, particularly important for shock infantry that had to prevent gaps in its line, dwindled in the Middle Ages, when militia often lacked the drill of the Greeks and Romans and when professionals did not serve in permanently embodied units. Yet, though medieval infantry usually lacked enough articulation to conduct a flank attack, cavalry, with its more modest reliance on a careful array, suffered less than infantry from this decline.

The Swiss had good articulation but needed it less because they did not use the awkward linear deployment. Still, they sometimes used the mobility of their squares to attack an enemy's flank. Their imitators did not adequately emulate their articulation, only adopting their solid formation. Better articulated linear arrays returned when the Dutch and Swedes adopted the Roman model. This placed a premium on articulation, if only because of the far greater difficulty of arranging and maneuvering a line of infantry compared with a solid, rectangular mass. But articulation into battalions of 500 did not reach the Roman level with its centuries because tacticians did not use the companies within the battalion to maneuver separately.

The armies of the French Revolution and Napoleon, divided into divisions and corps able to act independently, also provided improved tactical articulation through organization in brigades, demi-brigades, and battalions. Thus able to maneuver independently on the battlefield, rather than to keep its place in a rigid linear array on a field of battle, the battalion as part of the articulated division became a fundamental unit for maneuver, which readily deployed into line and so markedly facilitated concentration and assailing the enemy in flank and rear. But useful articulation still did not extend below the battalion level.

In the nineteenth century, with the merging of the roles of skirmisher and the line, the company assumed tactical importance, and a trend began to push workable tactical articulation down below the battalion level. This line of development nearly reached its apogee in the last year of World War I, when a company's platoons and a platoon's sections and their squads all became separate units in executing the concentration against weakness that animated the infiltration tactics. The new organization dispersed soldiers and decentralized combat command under conditions in which all men sought cover—or at least crouched—to avoid the ubiquitous rifle and machine gun bullets. This scattering did, however, deprive higher commanders of much of their control over their units, the initiative of subordinates taking its place. In World War II a portable battery-powered radio, sometimes available even in squads, restored a considerable measure of central command and provided armies with an undreamed-of level of articulation. In armored units usually every tank had a radio.

Improved articulation and its extension to ever smaller units also often enhanced individual performance because of the impact of the permanently constituted tactical group. Such subdivision facilitated the creation of social bonds among the soldiers, provided reinforcement of morale, and enforced standards of effective soldierly behavior.

The advance of articulation increased the ability of infantry to attack the weakness of an opponent, exemplified in the infiltration tactics of completely articulated battalions in having the capacity to move men past the flanks of hostile strong points, and, in turn, to maneuver with agility to protect its own flanks and rear against a hostile assault. Cavalry, relying on the charge and needing a less careful array than infantry, had had, even after the caracole method of firing introduced more drill, fewer requirements for articulation. But the radio gave tanks and aircraft a degree of articulation that cavalry had never had.

Concentration of a stronger force at one point on a battle front provided another method of assailing weakness, but it did not avail much in shock action because greater depth in a formation added little to the strength of its attack. Yet Marlborough's battles exhibit success in concentrating against a weak spot in a front. He achieved this because he combined with concentration an often-essential concomitant theme, distraction to cause the enemy to create a point of weakness. At the Battle of Blenheim, for example, his strikes at the enemy flanks lured the French into weakening their center, already lacking some defensive strength because among the troops posted there, the French had a relatively high proportion of pistol- and saber-armed cavalry, a weapon system that was unable to fight effectively dismounted and so had no advantage on the defensive. He then assembled troops strong in cavalry and conducted a devastating breakthrough of the French center. Such a success, which did not require maneuvering against the adversary's flank, depended little on sophisticated articulation but much on the cavalry's mobility and ability to attack rapidly.

The French revolutionary system of using columns for battlefield maneuver before quickly deploying into line for combat facilitated such frontal concentration against weakness, again showing the interdependence of articulation and tactical concentration. At the Battle of Austerlitz, for instance, Napoleon, having distracted the allies and induced them to concentrate on his right, broke their center with an assault strong in his readily concentrated and more rapidly marching infantry displaying its enhanced mobility and articulation. Late in World

War I infantry reached an unprecedented peak of articulation and, in its ability to exploit frontal weakness through infiltration tactics, created vulnerable flanks and opportunities to reach the rear. On the defense the Germans had learned to employ essentially comparable mobility as well as to use counterattacks to resist the attacker's larger force. In the absence of flanks, infiltration tactics provided the only means of assailing weakness.

But next to implicitly emulating the Parthian triumph with a superior weapon system, the best commanders had traditionally favored an attack against a weak flank or rear. Here the concept of offensive troops helps to understand this theme and is really a part of it. Alexander's shock cavalry exemplified offensive troops when they charged the flank of the Persian hoplites at the Battle of Granicus.

To carry out this successful assault Alexander's Companion cavalry had two requisites, greater mobility than the hoplites to enable them to reach their flank and the ability to conduct their assault without a time-consuming rearrangement into a combat formation. The heavy cavalry, however, did not have primacy as a weapon system over heavy infantry; it only acquired predominance when it assailed the hoplites' vulnerable flank and rear.

Heavy cavalry's attributes of mounted mobility and modest requirements for a battle array, which enabled it to fight as it marched, made it the premier offensive weapon system for the succeeding 2,000 years. Even in the centuries when heavy cavalry faced infantry using the Swiss square with its all-around defensive capability, the horsemen still remained the decisive arm because only they had the mobility and ability to go into action quickly, traits commanders needed to exploit any weakness in the hostile army's dispositions or any disorder among the heavy infantry.

Nevertheless, infantry could play the role of offensive troops. The Spartans pioneered this with their stylized march of part of their line, which brought it to right angles against the opponent's flank. They used drill and articulation to execute a maneuver that placed them against the hostile flank already arrayed for battle. They thus substituted a planned, practiced movement for better mobility. It succeeded when it attained surprise. The Thebans' Sacred Band used the same ingredients also to convert some of their infantry into offensive troops. Hannibal at Cannae and Zama used drilled and articulated infantry in place of greater mobility to attack the Roman flank, and he conducted the maneuver so as to bring the infantry against the hostile flank in battle array. It succeeded when the enemy did not expect it.

The medieval decline of trained articulated infantry used to working together again placed on cavalry virtually the entire offensive burden. In the eighteenth century the perfected Prussian drill permitted the oblique attack, which enabled an army in a rigid linear array to assail a hostile flank. Drill, more than articulation, substituted for better mobility, and the device of turning each platoon allowed the Prussian infantry to fight virtually as it marched. Frederick's method had much in common with those of the Spartans, Thebans, and Carthaginians in spirit and results.

The French revolutionary infantry column, which could rapidly deploy into line, supplied an infantry formation with the attributes of offensive troops. When formed in demi-brigades and these into the brigades that composed the divisions, the articulated division could concentrate against weakness and spread to reach exposed flanks. Untrammeled by the constraints of a linear formation, the columns could show greater celerity on the battlefield and yet almost instantly form into the line essential for combat with muskets. And even without deploying into line, they had some firepower and ability to resist the charge of cavalry. Troops thus marching and so arranged had an admirable capacity for passing around enemy lines and assaulting their flanks.

Accordingly articulation, completely attained through entire subdivision and controlled by a full chain of command, together with drill and training, endowed armies and their parts with an enhanced capacity to maneuver. Good leaders used this capability to concentrate against frontal weakness and, particularly, to assail vulnerable flanks and rear. At the Battle of Breitenfeld, for instance, Tilly sought to use his infantry to exploit the opportunity presented by the flight of the Saxons to fall upon Gustavus's vulnerable flank. But the imperial general's unwieldy and inadequately drilled formations proved unable to move fast enough to prevent the better trained and articulated Swedes from facing toward their flank and winning the battle.

Thus articulation facilitated concentration against weakness; and if an army had a distinct advantage in this attribute, as did the Prussians through their intensively perfected drill or, later, the French with their articulated divisions and separately maneuvering, quick marching battalions, its infantry could have enough of the offensive attributes intrinsic to cavalry to enable the foot formations to function as offensive troops in reaching an adversary's flank or rear.

In the nineteenth century the universal adoption of the French tactics and organization meant that all armies again reached the same level of facility of employment, which meant that defenders could move their men with equal dispatch to protect their flanks. Thus infantry again lost its offensive quality, just as earlier the Sacred Band and Scipio's articulated reserves had countered the Spartans' and Hannibal's attempted envelopments.

With the reappearance of the heavy cavalry in the form of the tank, offensive troops returned to warfare because a tank could use its high mobility and ability to fight virtually in march formation to reach the flank and rear of opposing forces capable of withstanding the tank's frontal attack. Aircraft also functioned as offensive troops, though like the light cavalry of old planes had difficulty providing the decisive element, except against an opponent in open terrain without antiaircraft weapons.

Battles and Casualties

Battles have figured conspicuously in all military history, if only because of the drama they provided. Yet they usually contributed less to the outcome of a given war than the prominence accorded them would suggest. They derived their intrinsic or purely tactical significance from their attrition (the casualties suffered). Victors traditionally experienced less attrition and the seriously disorganized vanquished more. Yet the strategic effect of battles often depended on their psychological impact and the political situation. Caesar's victory over Pompey at Pharsalus, far less devastating than that of Hannibal over the Romans at Cannae, exhibits this dependence of battles on their nontactical consequences as does a comparison of the results of Cannae with those of Alexander's two victories over Darius III. British battles won in the Hundred Years' War, like three of Marlborough's against the French and most of those of the Austrians and Prussians against one another in the Seven Years' War, show the limited effect of famous victories on the course of a war. In modern times, in the new strategic environment of the turning movement, more battles, such as Marengo and the German crossing of the Meuse in 1940, have had major strategic importance.

Even though battles underwent no fundamental change in their nature and they continued to rely for their significance on the strategic, political, psychological, and other elements of their context, they have grown in frequency in the last 200 years, in part from the greater ease of bringing them about and their often enhanced strategic importance. The smaller proportion of casualties suffered by the defeated has doubtless made generals more willing to risk conflicts.

That battles increase in number as their tactical meaning has declined does not present an anomaly in view of altered strategic conditions but does contradict the obvious influence of two factors that should have caused an elevation in casualty rates. A change in the last two centuries to almost total reliance on powerful missile weapons used by essentially unarmored combatants should have raised the defeated's losses just as should the steady increase in the deadliness of the weapons used.

Yet since the early seventeenth century, the number of casualties of the vanquished has fallen more rapidly than those of the victor, and on occasion victory in terms of ground gained or who retreated has meant defeat when measured by attrition. But with steadily more lethal missile weapons, casualties should have multiplied, and the numerically stronger adversary should have won more readily with greater losses for the defeated because more and more combat came to conform to the assumptions of F. W. Lanchester's N-square law. Longer range weapons and dispersed armies, which often allowed a larger force to utilize more of its men, should have brought combat closer to a situation in which each soldier could shoot at every other opponent.

When every soldier could fire at every other, the combat power of armies would vary, not directly, but as the square of their numerical strength. A notably larger force would under these conditions promptly exterminate a smaller. Though, of course, all men or weapon systems in each army could not shoot at every other, they could do so to an increasing degree; for example, indirect fire by artillery exposed more of the opposing army to danger. Yet many factors militated against the influence of conditions suitable to Lanchester's hypothesis.

The augmented value of a preponderance of numbers and the growth in firepower did not alter the strength of the tactical defense. The defender continued to enjoy the advantage of selected defensive ground, the use of natural and created defensive cover, and the capability to concentrate on using his weapons without the distraction and difficulty of also moving. The predominance of missile weapons in one way probably enlarged the benefit of the defense because, compared with shock action, the defender using missiles had even greater dominance, deriving more of an advantage from taking cover and availing himself of the opportunity to shoot more rapidly or accurately than the attacker. The artillery concentrations of World War I however did exhibit Lanchester's law at work, especially when the Germans, obstinately refusing to risk yielding any ground, remained under fire of much stronger enemy concentrations of artillery. But when the Germans exploited their fine articulation to adopt the system of elastic defense, which incorporated on the tactical level the defender's traditional strategic alternative of retreat, they restored the defense's preponderance and inflicted much higher casualties on the attackers.

In battles in ancient and medieval times the defeated usually suffered far greater casualties than the victor because the winner could often massacre the inadequately disciplined and poorly articulated troops of the vanquished army, use heavy cavalry to overrun light infantry, or employ light cavalry to attack vulnerable shock-action forces in retreat.

The return of the four basic weapon systems in the twentieth century has restored some of the old opportunities for the winner to inflict heavy casualties, amply illustrated by the success of Italian bombers against fleeing Ethiopians. Nevertheless, the influence of progressively improved articulation seems to have played a major role in countervailing the factors making for far greater casualties among the defeated. Inspired primarily by a desire to increase tactical mobility, enhanced articulation had two significant by-products. First, the smaller groups helped the army's cohesiveness and unit esprit. Second, the improved articulation permitted an army to cope better with the disorganization inseparable from defeat and retreat.

A comparison of seventeenth-century battles offers evidence for the significant effect of these two additional results. In the second half of the seventeenth century governments adopted permanently established armies, which in peacetime kept under arms most of their units at a high proportion of their wartime manpower strength. This change provided both better drill, training, and, consequently, articulation as well as enhancing unit identity, morale, and cohesion. This change goes far to explain the decline in the casualties of the losers in the battles in the latter part of the century as compared with the earlier era. In the Thirty Years' War defeated armies suffered a loss, on the average, of 37.4 percent of their strength. In the later battles between standing armies with greater articulation and sense of community the casualties of the defeated dropped to

27.6 percent. These figures argue strongly for these factors as causes for the decline in loss of men. In the next sixty-three years, a period signalized by the adoption of the bayonet, which rendered foot soldiers less vulnerable, casualties for the defeated decreased to 21.9 percent, a reduction for which the flintlock, uniformity of drill, and the perfection of the standing army must share with the bayonet the responsibility.

Yet articulation had barely grown out of its infancy in 1700. Its steady progress during the next two and a half centuries, coupled with more thorough and uniform training and discipline, paralleled the growth in dependence on firearms and the expansion of their range, power, and rate of fire. Instead of confusion and disorganization in defeat, increasingly better articulated armies could continue fighting effectively and carry out retreats more readily and with fewer casualties.

Groups of soldiers, fostered by the more minute subdivision occasioned by better articulation and permanently embodied units, often provided for better cooperation among individuals and sustained each soldier's motivation and performance because of his knowledge of the support of his fellows and his loyalty to them and to the group and its standards. Such an army bore defeat in battle better than many earlier ones, which readily disintegrated into an aggregation of individuals because they lacked both the maneuverability of the better articulated force and the cohesion supplied by such groups. They could do this even when deluged by the vastly greater firepower of the attackers in World War I and these conditions in the Second, aggravated by having to cope with an assailant's preponderance in tanks and aircraft.

This trend to lower casualties for the defeated also received reinforcement from the adoption of the breechloader that, while augmenting the rate of fire, enabled the rifleman to fire from a prone position. This, like the seeking-cover response to more bullets on the battlefield, helps explain the apparent anomaly of declining casualties seeming to correlate with enhanced weapon effectiveness. The increase in firepower together with the earlier adoption of the linear system permitted, particularly in the twentieth century, more extended fronts without men thickly packed at every point. This reduced density meant that a tactical defeat at one point in the front had a more localized effect and involved a smaller percentage of the defeated army.

One variation in the trend toward reduced casualties seems to have occurred in the armored combats in North Africa in World War II and in the recent wars between the Israel and the Arab states. The combatants, especially the defeated, sustained heavy casualties in terms of weapon systems, principally tanks. In the 1973 war of Syria and Egypt against Israel, the combatants lost over a quarter of their 1,300 aircraft and nearly half of their almost 6,000 tanks in a war lasting only a little over two weeks. Although these casualties seem high for such a short war, they did not appear exhorbitant when one realizes that a battle was in progress on almost every day of the war and sometimes more than one battle was fought each day. This amounts to any average daily loss of less than 5 percent of the total available tank forces and a casualty rate of 10 percent if commanders succeeded in committing half to battle and 20 percent if only a quarter engaged the enemy. This brief war did, however, involve relatively minor losses in terms of personnel, less than 20,000 fatalities, or about seven for every tank lost.

Thus the losses do not seem particularly heavy in view of the number of battles fought, a situation having something in common with the prolonged offensives of World War I and their large daily casualties. The frequency of the battles had much to do with the high ratio of force to space, one magnified by the great mobility of the all-mounted forces engaged. With the borders of the small state of Israel and key points, such as the Suez Canal and the Syrian capital, near the theater of operations, the belligerents acutely felt the danger of retreat in a war with armies having such rapidity of movement. This helps explain the tenacity with which dedicated soldiers on each side fought, the commanders, like so many of their men, displaying a reluctance to admit defeat and retreat. That the commander could show such persistence in the face of adversity testified also to the excellence of the discipline and the articulation of these thoroughly modern armies. The disinclination of combatants to withdraw also reflected the political context of the battles in which the opponents saw so much at stake. Still it is not clear whether these high casualties, also experienced in the mounted warfare in North Africa in World War II, are a necessary result of mounted war with formidable firepower and bulky weapon systems that, like the line infantry musketeer of the eighteenth century, may have a particular vulnerability because they cannot take cover as readily as men armed with breechloading rifles. The political and geographical circumstances, also found in Europe, may claim much of the responsibility for casualties, which, though they do not approach as a percentage the one-day battles of the eighteenth century and earlier, are very high because of sustained combat.

Independent of the level of casualties prevailing in a particular era or between individual armies or combinations of weapon systems, the significance of attrition varies. After catastrophic losses at the Battle of Cannae, the Romans avoided more battles but also recovered from their losses by drawing on the large reserves of militia available from the many towns under their sway. Similarly, after the heavy losses during some battles of the Thirty Years' War, commanders, like Tilly after Breitenfeld, hired more mercenaries. On the other hand, after the appalling disaster at Manzikert, the Byzantines could not readily replenish their army, having lost virtually all of their professional and highly skilled heavy cavalrymen, their expensive armor and fine horses, and, partly as a consequence, much of their main recruiting area of Anatolia. In World Wars I and II, on the other hand, when armies could convert civilians into soldiers fairly readily, some countries suffered such heavy casualties in the steady combat of the huge armies along continuous fronts that they began, quite literally, to run out of men suitable for military service. Thus, the availability of suitable replacements has, like the estimate of potential losses in defeat, conditioned the willingness of commanders and governments to risk battle.

Still, battles of tactical annihilation involving significant forces still seem to have become increasingly rare in modern times. This decline in the likelihood of valuable tactical results means that it is more than ever necessary to look to logistics, strategy, politics, and other contexts of the oft-recurring battles.

LOGISTICS

Chronological Overview

The supply and movement of armies changed little during most of the period of this study. Armies and their animals usually lived on the country in which they campaigned. Hence the population, concomitant productivity of the country, and the season of the year powerfully influenced the timing and direction of operations.

In his conquest of the Persian Empire had Alexander, for example, displayed less care and sophistication in his supply arrangements, he could have lost even without the Persians explicitly resorting to a logistic strategy. By minimizing the baggage and noncombat personnel, using supply lines for sieges, carefully preparing in advance, and subordinating his routes and objectives to the need of his army to live on the country, Alexander exemplified the best logistic system of the day, one that would endure into the twentieth century. He also showed his knowledge of the importance of logistics by his use of a logistic strategy to defeat the Persian fleet by utilizing his army to capture its bases.

During the past 2,500 years the method of obtaining food and fodder has ranged from plunder to purchase. The waste of supplies, the loss of men to desertion, and, often, the hostile reaction of the natives reinforced political considerations that frequently argued in favor of an orderly way of meeting an army's needs from enemy as well as friendly territory. Often armies levied political authorities for food and fodder or for the money to buy them from producers or merchants. In modern times armies have called this arrangement contributions and requisitions. In friendly areas and frequently in neutral lands armies paid for their supplies from their own resources and even did so in an adversary's territory where they wished to make a particular point of conciliating the public. Regardless of the method, the army could usually find most of what it needed for a campaign. Infrequent battles rarely exhausted the stock of missiles an army could carry.

Drawing supplies from a distance occurred largely during sieges and sometimes early in a campaign when winter consumption had depleted the resources at the scene of the prospective campaign. The efficiency of water transport by sea, lake, and river made supply from a base possible, even to meeting the needs of the animals. Carrying provisions over land could, with difficulty, feed only the men. The quality of the roads as well as the produce of the surrounding country had much to do with the practicality of conducting a siege. That cavalry played little part in a siege facilitated supply.

Improvements in roads and in agricultural productivity helped the movement and maintenance of armies, as did the shoeing and more effective harnessing of the horse and better ships and navigation. In the nineteenth century the steamer increased the rapidity and economy of river and ocean conveyance, and the railroad made a major change in land travel. Though more expensive than water transport, railroads were swifter. The proliferation of railways in the late nineteenth century probably had more impact on logistics than better water transport, because so many railroad lines meant that almost any army could draw supplies from a base, one fed in turn by an extensive road, rail, and water transportation system that tapped a wide agricultural region.

The high capacity and rapid pace of railways conferred a new strategic mobility on armies. First fully demonstrated in the American Civil War, railway conveyance of large forces for concentration of troops over great distances broadened the scope of strategic movement by the difference between the rate of foot-marching locomotion and that by rail. Because retreating armies routinely disabled the railroads, the defender often had better strategic mobility than the invader. The 1914 campaigns in France and East Prussia demonstrated the value to the defender of strategically offensive troops as did the rapid rail concentration of allied reserves against the German offensives of 1918.

Technological change, which had already often responded to the civil demand for better transportation, again, with the motor truck, affected logistics profoundly. More costly than the railroad, the truck could carry supplies and men where the railroad did not run, even right to the firing line. Trucks and railways made possible World War I combat between huge stationary armies that consumed enormous quantities of ammunition. In 1940 trucks furnished an essential ingredient in the German recipe for their stupendous strategic victory. Providing strategically offensive troops for the attacker, trucks had a versatility that overmatched the railways.

Aircraft transportation, more costly than the truck, has more and more proven a valuable supplement to the slower but less expensive water and ground transport. When rapidity in carrying men or supplies has had crucial importance or when forces are isolated, aircraft provided an essential mode of conveyance.

Thus technological change has had a profound effect on logistics and its impact has accelerated over the period of a hundred years. Unlike most weapon changes but similar to the application to warfare of the telegraph, telephone, wireless, radio, and data processing, most inventions that altered logistics came from civilian life. Here civil and military requirements differed little, and economic demand long successfully called forth improvements in transportation and communication of information. And, unlike the somewhat cyclical effect of technological change on tactics, new ways have modified the supply, movement, and management of armies in an almost exclusively linear way with constantly increasing facility and falling costs.

Alternative Manpower Systems

The significance of logistics, its demands always urgent whether the enemy was near or far, and the complexity inherent in the movement as well as the supply of armies meant that it played a premier role in the evolution of the modern army staff. Gradually developed over the years, the staff underwent a dramatic improvement in the nineteenth century, emerging as a fundamental planning and management instrument. Through the staff, commanders not only arranged to meet the logistic requirements of the huge armies but also coordinated intelligence and operational activities. The more complex manpower system introduced in the nineteenth century required the better management that the staff could supply.

The provision and training of manpower affects the outcome of battles, campaigns, and wars. Manpower systems have displayed great consistency throughout these 2,500 years of Europe's warfare. The Greeks used a militia, which, engaging in some practice together, had a measure of tactical proficiency and, because of its base in small cities, also had some cohesion and unit spirit. The Persians, on the other hand, employed a professional army of soldiers who had the greater proficiency resulting from continuous, essentially full-time service year after year. Constant warfare ultimately forced the Greeks to adopt a system of professional soldiers, too.

The Romans, starting like the Greeks with a militia, likewise began utilizing a long-service career army, one exemplary in its organization and discipline. These two models, militia and regulars, consistently reappear in succeeding centuries. The militia, inexpensive compared to a standing army, had the benefits of large numbers and potential reserves that stood the Romans in such good stead in resisting Hannibal's invasion of Italy. The career soldiers had greater individual skill, and additional tactical preponderance, provided by their ample experience in working together in units, which also gave the men greater mutual confidence and enhanced each unit's sense of community.

Militia could not fight long wars, especially those far from home, which explains why the Greeks and Romans ultimately adopted professionals. But militia excelled in transitory operations. A large number of raiders, such as Arabs and Magyars, many of whom came from civil life, did not really constitute a professional force. Militia had even greater advantages in defense against raids, because acting on the defensive, often with the aid of fortifications, placed fewer demands on the militia's limited tactical skill.

The military forces of the Middle Ages only superficially conformed to the militia or professional models. Although an urban militia had a basic similarity to the Greek pattern and, like it, depended tactically on dense masses of pikemen, the rural militia hardly deserved the name. Without drill and often with agricultural implements instead of weapons, it lacked even the cohesion of an urban force because of its dispersal in many tiny villages. Some rural militia, however, had better characteristics. The Swiss, for example, with their more compact valley communities possessed an armed and trained force, one hardly distinguishable from regular soldiers.

Medieval professionals differed markedly from the Greek and Roman model. Rather than having a permanently embodied and partially concentrated force, medieval armies decentralized their regulars into small garrisons and even individuals scattered over the countryside. This system produced soldiers with adequate, and often greater, skill but rarely furnished units accustomed to discipline and subordination, experienced in working together or possessed of much sense of community. The more frequent employment of individual professionals for a year's campaign, either directly or through military contractors, did little to mitigate the deficiencies of the medieval system of mercenaries, even though groups of men would remain together over the winter in anticipation of a contract for the coming year. Not until the latter part of the seventeenth century did European professional armies take the far more effective Roman form of regulars who lived and trained together year after year with the support of an organized and adequately funded commissariat.

So, just as in the later history of Greece and Rome, militias had lost most of their significance by the seventeenth century and only again assumed importance during the wars of the French Revolution and Napoleon. Though nations strengthened or recruited militias, the hurried conscription of men into the armies played a more consequential role, filling French ranks at the beginning of these conflicts and Prussian at the end. The improvement in deployment from column to line, which permitted battlefield maneuver in columns, overcame many of the disadvantages of the linear system because the columns had a mobility typical of the earlier dense formation of the Swiss. This change from an exclusively linear system simplified the task of rapidly converting civilians into soldiers. Less dependence on the rigid fire discipline needed for frontal combat between infantry lines also facilitated the task of using hastily trained civilians in combat roles.

In the nineteenth century the Prussians consistently applied to their armed forces a plan that merged the militia with professionals and secured virtually all of the advantages of both. By using civilian reserves to bring their full-time units up to strength, they combined militia and regulars in a meaningful way. The active units trained their reservists, who would otherwise have served in a militia, for three years, thus providing a uniquely well-trained group of civilians, and the actives could then call them back for brief periods of further duty as well as for wartime mobilization.

Because each regular unit had a base in a particular territory, recruits with a common background and, often, previous acquaintance or ties joined the local unit. By training them with the officers and noncommissioned officers under whom they would serve in war, the army created communities of soldiers and leaders based upon the foundation provided by the local system of recruitment. The annual mobilization brought everyone together for exercises simulating war conditions as well as nineteenth-century training and warfare permitted. Thus, the Prussians developed among the civilians in their units a strong sense of kinship and gave them training conditions that approximated those representative of a long-service regular force.

Still, by using a virtually complete cadre of career soldiers for their active army and its reserves, the Prussians had an army professional in competence but with the great size and low cost that had long commended a large militia. When the reserves joined their units, they more than doubled their size but hardly diluted their quality at all. Professionally led, thoroughly trained, and accustomed to working together, the mobilized Prussian active army had almost all of the attributes of a long-service force. Even the real militia, the Landwehr, composed of men all with substantial active-duty training and led in part by regulars, exceeded in proficiency most of the militias that Europe had seen.

This method proved its combat effectiveness in Prussia's mid-century wars when its cadre of professionals and its civilian reserves defeated Austrian regulars. Against France in 1870 the fully expanded Prussian system showed its full potential when it enabled Prussia to field an army twice the size of France's and in quality little below that of the French professionals. Without this huge French numerical inferiority, even Bazaine's egregious incompetence might have failed to defeat the French.

Most European nations used the Prussian system in the two world wars, and the lack of it in the United Kingdom and the United States delayed their full participation in these wars and caused their armies to suffer from a deficiency of thoroughly trained manpower. One of France's disadvantages in World War II stemmed from training men in one formation solely to serve in another that existed only upon mobilization for war. By overlooking the benefits of having the war units exist in peacetime, the French reproduced some of the difficulties inherent in the medieval type of decentralized professionals and that of the military contractors; again, trained men did not assure effective units until they had substantial experience working together in the groups with which they would serve in combat.

Since World War II, the reliance on large armies through a regular cadre and trained reserves has declined, only Russia providing, on the usual basis of a cadre of professionals and a large number of trained reserves, an army similar in numbers to those typical of the first half of the century. To furnish an army comparable in size, in relation to their populations, Israel and Switzerland use an essentially militia system that depends on trained manpower that undergoes repeated subsequent periods of service to conserve and improve their proficiency. The transition to a largely mounted force and the consequent reduction in the size of armies has had much to do with this change among Western powers. The active forces now constitute a far higher proportion of the much smaller mobilized strength envisioned at the outbreak of war, though most European states still conscript men of military age and so create large reserves of trained manpower. But the regulars again are coming to the forefront, as has often happened in the past.

Training has remained difficult, influenced by one factor that has simplified the task and another that has complicated it. Whereas mastery of the bow could require years to acquire the strength to pull and skill to aim accurately, the muzzleloading musket demanded only practice in the drill needed to load quickly and reliably. The modern automatic rifle, with excellent sights and a flat trajectory, demands little time or talent to learn its use. The utilization of the automatic features of artillery weapons also needs less training than the hand-operated and aimed guns of old, and mastering the operation of a tank, the task of a crew, is less daunting than learning to ride a horse while manipulating a lance and sword. Even flying an airplane may not call for more practice than gaining the skills to ride without stirrups while using two hands to shoot a strong bow with speed and accuracy. All of these changes have facilitated the task of turning civilians into accomplished soldiers.

On the other hand, it is much harder for many weapon systems to simulate battle. Whereas the heavy infantry of old could fence and the heavy cavalry could joust, modern soldiers, though they can practice and use simulators, miss much that the old training offered when it had some of the attributes of the scrimmage of an athletic team. Even eighteenth-century soldiers could repeatedly replicate their drill and know that they would use their laborously attained proficiency on the battlefield. The ambiguity of infiltration tactics removes the possibility of giving all of the necessary skills to infantry, and combat with tanks in motion offers little better opportunity to have drivers or commanders learn motions that they will repeat in combat. Even the artillery personnel, who can do in peace what they will do in war, encounter difficulties if their elaborate communications fail to function in battle as they do in peace.

Thus, the imparting of individual proficiency has become simpler, but relating that and the action of the group to actual fighting has become harder as weapons and tactics have changed. And as armies have become dependent on elaborate equipment, another complexity occurs: the provision of repair for weapons that lack the reliability of many of the unsophisticated weapons of old. Here, levels of competence equal and exceed those required of soldiers of old, but peacetime training for and experience in mending weapons do, as with many of the old combat skills, prepare the repairman for his wartime tasks reasonably well. Only the morale and motivation of the soldiers and the importance of the group, a subordinate theme in this book, have changed little over the centuries.

STRATEGY

Chronological Summary

The defense's tactical superiority lay in its primacy in frontal combat between analogous weapon systems. In strategy the defense relied on this tactical ascendency and found its predominance in persisting strategy in the supremacy of retreat over pursuit when similarly constituted armies faced one another. When an adversary used a raiding against a persisting strategy, the advantage of retreat over pursuit made the offensive stronger because the attacking raiders, as a part of their transitory presence, used retreat. Raiding is the strategic analog of the tactic of employing light troops against heavy, illustrated by Turkish horse archers defeating Byzantine heavy cavalry. The hit-and-run approach inheres in both the tactics and the strategy, except that in strategy the raiders, because of the primacy of retreat, need not have a more mobile weapon system.

So in both persisting and raiding strategy between armies of like composition the customary inability of the stronger to force battle on the weaker conditioned strategy during most of the period under study. That agile, spear-throwing peltasts could compel an army of hoplites to accept combat on their terms was an exception to the usual situation of battles by mutual consent, as was the extraordinary fate at Carrhae of the largely foot-marching Roman army at the hands of the mounted Parthians. Since, for the most part, armies had a sufficiently comparable make-up to give each side the same strategic mobility, the side withdrawing usually exercised its dominance.

The normally low ratio of force to space confronting most armies gave the inability to bring on battle special importance, because the more powerful army often lacked enough men to follow a persisting strategy of dominating a significant area and thus compelling its militarily weaker but politically strong opponent to fight or give up its country. Even if powerful enough to carry out a systematic conquest and the garrisoning of a country and its strong points, the aggressor might lack the financial resources or political patience or constancy that such a protracted campaign required.

The lack of capacity to coerce an enemy into fighting and the unwillingness or inability to attempt slowly to engross the enemy's territory led the more formidable army in warfare in ancient Greece to resort to the political strategy of using destructive raids to force political concessions from the weaker. This raiding strategy also had the military component of giving the defending army the alternative of suffering the desolation of its agricultural resources or fighting the invader on at least equal terms with respect to tactical conditions.

So only when each contestant believed it had the better chance of victory would a combat likely occur, unless political factors dictated a battle as, for example, it did when Pompey and Caesar fought at Pharsalus and Harold faced William at Hastings. Yet the evasiveness that the dominance of pursuit over retreat imparted to each army helped to give the offensive of a raiding strategy superiority over the defense. Ironically, the weaker contestant usually had recourse to a raiding strategy, which relied on retreat after assailing a weak portion of the stronger opponent's forces. The resistance against Alexander the Great in Bactria and Sogdiana used this raiding strategy, attacking a small detachment and then, too weak to face a major force of Macedonians, retreating to avoid further combat.

Ability to avoid battle with hostile forces provided one of the elements that made this offensive strategy by the weaker more powerful than the defensive by the stronger adversary. In addition to turning the primacy of retreat over pursuit to the advantage of the attacker, this raiding strategy could countervail much of the dominance of the tactical defensive, the other source of the predominance of the strategic defensive. Since marauders sought only an accumulation of small tactical successes, they could select their objective solely on the criterion of its weakness in comparison with their own forces. Such wide choice and almost complete ambiguity of goal confronted their opponents with the insuperable task of making themselves strong everywhere. Inevitably they failed, and the raiders, usually with a great preponderance of force in their assaults, frequently enjoyed a good measure of success in overmatching the primacy of the tactical defensive.

Alexander sought to impede the guerrillas' mobility through garrisoning communications focal points. Thus he hampered the retreat as well as the advance phase of the raids. This persisting defense later reappeared often as did guerrillas who used this kind of raiding strategy against opponents who so overmatched them that they could not use the persisting strategy's tactical defensive. The Romans, in their conquests against the determined resistance of barbarian tribes, applied a persisting strategy but coupled it with extensive use of fortifications and almost endless perseverance. Caesar exemplified Roman reliance on least effort, fortification, and patience when he defied the Belgae from his entrenched camp and so used a logistic strategy to disperse them, merely waiting until their supplies gave out.

Faced by Vercingetorix's shrewd scorched-earth logistic strategy and the Fabian dependence on raids to strike at foragers, Caesar retreated, accepting temporary defeat and adhering to his principle: "It was better to sacrifice an opportunity to injure the enemy if the injury would involve a loss on our part." But Vercingetorix, realizing the perseverance of the Romans and that they "would never put an end to the war," risked battle, lost, and took refuge in the town of Alesia. Here, with elaborately fortified lines of contravallation and circumvallation, the Romans successfully resisted the sorties of the besieged and the assaults of the relieving forces. Of course, this victory marked only one step in the Roman conquest, which involved garrisoning the country, establishing fortified posts, and suppressing subsequent insurrections and guerrilla warfare. The final Roman conquests owed as much to the excellence of their political institutions and the imperialism of their culture as to their powerful and patient persisting strategy.

Military operations themselves mixed raiding and persisting as well as combat and logistic strategies. The Middle Ages showed the role of fortifications, as castles supplemented cities, defending forces taking refuge in well-stocked cities or castles and defying more formidable opponents whose often primitive logistic arrangements precluded a prolonged siege.

The Hundred Years' War exemplified many aspects of medieval warfare when in the fourteenth century the English depended on a political raiding strategy, ultimately exacting concessions from the French. Both also applied a persisting strategy in southwestern France, which revolved around taking castles and cities that dominated the country. The French successfully employed the same methods Rome's Fabius had used against Hannibal; relying on the political sympathies of the local population, they avoided combat with the English army, an easy task because the English tactical doctrine depended on fighting on the defensive, and besieged the English-held castles and towns.

In the fifteenth century the English, finding political support in France, changed to a persisting strategy of systematic conquest of towns and castles. But they found France too large and too many of its townsmen and gentry opposed to their rule to conquer all of the country. Gradually the English forces became so attenuated that they could not resist a revived French effort, which also made use of a similar persisting strategy to drive them out.

Except in the obvious case of starving out the defenders of a castle or town, logistic strategy usually did not play a major role in wars. The defensive logistic strategy of scorching the earth provided the major technique and was used by the French and the Scots against the English. This destruction of crops, food, and fodder supplies cost little, if the defenders knew the raiders' route, for raiders and even invaders usually destroyed what they did not consume since all armies customarily used the approach of the raiding strategy, as had the Greeks, to attain both their political and military objectives.

The changes in warfare during the Middle Ages little affected the conduct of an offensive raiding strategy against a stronger adversary. Like the Romans, medieval monarchies faced marauders, such as the Vikings, who came seeking booty, and defended themselves with a persisting strategy of fortification and control of communication routes. The English used the same method on the offensive in their prolonged struggle to control Wales. Lacking the strength initially to garrison the whole country simultaneously, the English conquered Wales in small increments, each of which they then fortified. By having, through a combination of men and castles, a high ratio of force to space, they could have adequate defensive strength in the small, newly subdued regions. Thus their offensive persisting strategy defeated the guerrillas by depriving them of one of the elements that gave the raid offensive predominance. The consistency with the past, which the medieval experience with this kind of warfare exhibited, forecast the future when changes in weapons, tactics, logistics, and even strategy failed to alter the pattern of this raiding warfare.

The English reliance on castles, a practice the Welsh eventually emulated, naturally involved some sieges. But these lacked the importance that these operations came to have in campaigning with a combat persisting strategy. For pursuing such a combat strategy a siege had a special significance because it could compel the relieving army to fight. This accounts for the large number of conflicts that accompanied the French efforts to conquer northern Italy in the early sixteenth century. The importance of the fall of a town to besiegers, who increasingly had the monetary and organizational resources to continue long enough to take the town, often compelled generals, in order to save the town, to fight battles that they knew would have a very doubtful outcome.

The Thirty Years' War clearly exhibited the conditions of warfare when capable, dedicated opponents fought with a ratio of force to space inadequate for an army readily to control a major part of the large area of Germany under conditions in which neither could compel the other to fight. Gustavus Adolphus began in Protestant northern Germany, moving forward systematically with a persisting strategy. Yet the raid to live at the enemy's expense and devastate his country remained an important part of his strategy. Such a raid would have a powerful political impact, discrediting the opposing ruler and his cause and possibly securing the submission or at least neutrality of the area. Further, it could implement the logistic strategy of depriving the hostile army of the resources of a region in which he could otherwise have subsisted his army. Thus, Gustavus combined the persisting combat strategy of sieges with a logistic strategy of raids as well as with his slow acquisition of hostile territory in the north and the conversion of its resources to his own use.

In spite of the commitment of both Gustavus and his seasoned adversary, Count Tilly, to a combat strategy, for a long time no battle occurred. Each, instead, largely used the raid into his adversary's base area to protect himself by distracting his opponent. Thus, in 1631 Gustavus twice menaced Frankfort on the Oder and followed this with the threat of a raid into Silesia, in each case distracting Tilly from a dangerous advance against Magdeburg. The next year, when Gustavus threatened a raid into Bavaria, the new imperial commander, Wallenstein, distracted the Swedish king by moving north to menace the king's vacillating Saxon ally and the Swedish base area in the north. Thus, raid and counterraid had an important function in strategy when both contestants had vulnerable base areas and small, similarly constituted armies confronted one another in a relatively large area.

Battles occurred rarely because neither side would fight on the antagonist's terms. This happened when Gustavus defied Tilly from a powerful position at Werben and likewise challenged Wallenstein at Nuremberg. Wallenstein, baffled by the formidable Swedish position, resorted to the logistic strategy of interrupting Gustavus's supplies, to which the reinforced king replied in kind, each army suffering serious attrition before they parted.

The Thirty Years' War also exhibited the degree to which strategy depended on logistics. Though formed of career soldiers, the annually recruited armies largely consisted of aggregations of professionals rather than units that had the cohesion, articulation, and morale of personnel with long service together. This grew out of the residue of feudal methods of raising armies and of rulers' counting on independent contractors to supply their forces. Nor did they have an Alexandrian or Roman system of logistics since the contractors and their usually impecunious employers relied on war supporting war. Whereas Alexander's attention to logistics supplied and conserved his army while he persistently pursued his strategic objectives, the nourishment of men and horses exercised a tyranny over the armies of the early seventeenth century because their commanders often had to follow the immediate logistical needs of feeding and paying their soldiers rather than pursuing the aims dictated by the political and military objectives of the campaign. Often logistical requirements subverted political goals and handicapped military operations by alienating the civilian victims of logistical depredations.

The growth of the European population and the increase of production and the revenues of the governments permitted the larger armies more often to have a ratio of force to space sufficient to pursue persisting strategies. Though these conditions applied in the Netherlands, the immense number of fortified cities there meant that the combatants found the ratio of force to space so high that, without the support of the inhabitants of the enemy territory, the contending armies found progress slow, often consisting of a sequence of sieges.

In northern Italy the ratio of force to space favored more decisive warfare but the continued ability of the armies to refuse battle hampered combat strategy. In crossing the rivers, which constituted defensive barriers, armies used surprise, facilitated by distraction, to concentrate against weakness and accomplish their objective. An army on the offensive, when crossing a river, could often force back the enemy by taking up a strong position that controlled a foraging area, which had supplied the defender and now provided for the invaders. Thus, rather than raiding a foe's base area, such commanders as Eugene and Vendôme conquered it, converted it to their own use, and drove back the enemy. Their strategy, with its large logistic component, paralleled Gustavus's earlier in north Germany as it did the English conquest of Wales.

Campaigns in the mid-eighteenth century between the Prussians and Austrians in Bohemia, Saxony, and Silesia also benefited from a ratio of force to space that allowed the invading armies to pursue a persisting strategy of dominating the productive country. In these areas, crucial to Frederick's survival, the logistic element of a persisting strategy received ample illustration. To protect or recover these sources of revenues and recruits, Frederick fought offensive battles for motives having some parallel to that of an army attempting to raise a siege.

The Austrians, on the other hand, with strong cavalry and predominant light infantry twice used a logistic strategy to defeat Prussian invasions, once when Field Marshal Traun drove out a Prussian army by raiding its convoys and circumscribing its foragers and on another occasion when Field Marshal Daun raised the siege of Olmütz by destroying a huge convoy bringing the besiegers their supplies.

The wars of the French Revolution and Napoleon transformed warfare. The French tactical system of maneuvering in column but forming in line to fight changed the situation in which an army could march away while its opponent slowly deployed, thus frustrating an aggressive commander's desire for battle. This improved articulation and ability to go quickly from march to combat order meant that armies no longer had to march slowly in cumbersome battle formation to protect themselves from surprise attacks by infantry or cavalry. This accelerated the movements of French armies when near the hostile force.

The French armies, scattered in divisions and often united into corps comparable to an army, used their favorable ratio of force to space to spread out, not just to dominate the country but to impede an enemy on many routes of advance or to threaten a defender at many points. By keeping these widely dispersed forces conceptually a unit, they could quickly concentrate to avail themselves of a weak spot in the hostile dispositions or to resist an adversary's concentration. The new broad distribution of the armies distracted the enemy by creating ambiguity as to the direction from which the main advance would come, thus fully complementing the attacking army's ability and intent to concentrate against weakness.

A dispersed army, strategically offensive because of its better mobility on the march and composed of tactically offensive infantry as well as cavalry, had the capacity to force battle on its unwilling opponent. Never before could armies with the same weapon systems do this because of the higher mobility of retreat compared with that of pursuit and the inability of one concentrated army to engage another. But with an adequate ratio of force to space the dispersed troops of the new armies could compel the enemy to fight partial engagements, thus halting his movement until the whole of the army wanting battle could arrive.

So armies could coerce an adversary either into fighting or adopting the only alternative—retreating directly to the rear. No longer could a defending army, concentrated and quite small in relation to the theater of operations, avoid battle by moving just out of reach of an opponent. Defenders even lost the resource of defying an enemy from an impregnable position, for the widely spread French armies could envelop or turn such a position. But a dispersed army risked a hostile concentration against one of its parts.

In explaining the tactical and strategic possibilities of the newly organized army of the late eighteenth century, Guibert made explicit theories long implicit in the conduct of campaigns and battles. By extolling the virtues of dispersion as a means to distract the defender so that he created a weak point that the attacker could take advantage of by rapid concentration, Guibert generalized the idea of winning with the least effort through concentrating against weakness. This concept, which had long pervaded tactics, underlay both the use of a superior weapon system and attacks against flanks and rear; it also found exemplification in Marlborough's victories in which he relied on cavalry to deliver the attack against the weak point created by an earlier distracting assault. The ability to engage, made possible by dispersed armies of strategically offensive infantry, gave these theories more relevance than they had possessed in eras of battle by mutual consent. Equally, tactically offensive infantry, which could concentrate against a weak center or reach the enemy's flank or rear and so bring infantry into combat with other infantry on advantageous terms, promised more tactical success than had the frontal battles of the past between armies with secure flanks.

These dispersed forces, when combined with an adequate ratio of force to space, not only brought about much more decisive warfare but also made possible the use of interior lines of operations to concentrate against first one enemy army and then another. Formerly, when a hostile army could refuse battle, such concentrations would have little point and occurred rarely. When Consul Nero employed this strategy to bring a more formidable force against Hasdrubal, its success had rested on Hasdrubal's blunder, which compelled him to give battle. Prince Edward had concentrated first against the younger and then the elder de Montfort, but his victories depended on surprising one early in the morning and trapping the other against a river. Frederick the Great had also used interior lines but had to accept battle on the enemy's terms to use his concentration of force. Consequently, under normal circumstances, the ability of the enemy to refuse battle had usually deprived such concentrations of a large force of any consistent significance. Since the dispersed, easily deployed armies of the French Revolution could readily compel the enemy to fight or engage in a disastrous retreat, using interior lines to concentrate in space became a major strategic resource, equally applicable on the defensive and offensive. So generals could convert the possession of greater numbers into either battles with a high likelihood of victory or a damaging retreat by their enemy. That Napoleon began his career as a general by deliberately marching between two opposing armies so that he could fight them alternately demonstrated the high value that interior lines had suddenly acquired.

Disseminated armies, which concentrated rapidly against a threat, enabled Napoleon to block an enemy's retreat when he reached his rear. When, at the beginning of his Marengo campaign, Napoleon had reached the Austrian rear and occupied Milan and the surrounding country, he had acquired a base area in Italy that permitted him to maintain his position. Yet Napoleon had achieved no more than had Marshal Vendôme a century earlier when he had passed a river and established himself in an Austrian base area. But the situation differed in that, unlike Vendôme's, Napoleon's dispersed army had the ability to block the Austrian retreat, which he did in his victory at Marengo.

So the new strategic as well tactical capabilities of armies transformed the significance of reaching the hostile rear. No longer could one compact army march past another. And although armies still lived on the country and rarely needed supply lines except when concentrated for a siege, the position of Napoleon's army after his victory at Marengo proved so disconcerting for the Austrians, in spite of their ample base area and sea communications, that they agreed to evacuate northern Italy. In another turning movement in the Ulm campaign, the inferior Austrian forces had to fight or retreat directly toward the Rhine and France.

Strategy opened a road to a victory far more decisive than battles alone could provide. The Battle of Blenheim, in which the French forfeited two-thirds of their army to Marlborough's skillful combination of distraction and concentration, stands out as the only battle of its era in which the casualties, the tactical results, approximated those at Cannae. But strategy redeemed battles, which had steadily lost tactical significance. Turning movements could produce decisive strategic consequences in which the maneuver insured an impressive victory if the attackers could block the enemy's retreat in a defensive battle devoid of tactical importance.

The new capabilities of the armies joined to the adequate ratio of force to space made for decisive campaigns. When France united these with an appealing political program, unprecedented conquests followed.

Political factors had long exercised an influence over military operations, often dictating the amount of military effort required and giving significance to triumphs in battles and successful campaigns. The political weakness of Darius III had forced him to meet Alexander in battle and had made the invader's victories decisive in giving him control of most of the Persian Empire. On the other hand, Alexander's marriage to Roxana so conciliated opposition in Bactria and Sogdiana as to make his hitherto inadequate military measures equal to the task of controlling the country. Hannibal's annihilation of the Romans at Cannae led to no strategic result because of the political as well as the military strength of the Roman opposition to him. Such factors also influenced military decisions, as when the Satraps of Darius III declined to impose on their subjects the burden of a scorched-earth logistic strategy, which might well have defeated Alexander.

The Thirty Years' War showed how much opposition soldiers could engender by securing their food, fodder, and, sometimes, pay directly from the public, an evil aggravated by the waste as well as the destruction and pillage incident to this logistic method. The problem of political opposition fostered by the behavior of occupying troops did not originate in the Thirty Years' War, however; the fate of the invasion of Mesopotamia by Antiochus VII of Syria had amply illustrated this when in a winter of occupation his men had turned a welcoming population of Greeks, kindred in culture, into opponents who then sided with the Parthians to kill Antiochus and his men. The victimized peasants of the Thirty Years' War exercised no such decisive effect but often ambushed and killed soldiers when they had the opportunity and usually made every effort to avoid willingly providing supplies to marauding armies.

During their revolution the French overran the usually unconquerable Netherlands because their principles of liberty and equality appealed to the region's middle class. Having a comparable political welcome in northern Italy and Germany, the French readily converted military success into conquest because of a political appeal to the influential urban bourgeoisie. But by allowing their soldiers to supply themselves by preying on civilians after the manner of the Thirty Years' War, they soon squandered much of their political capital, though without the immediate and disastrous consequences that had followed Antiochus's similar blunder.

In their invasion of Spain the French possessed the military means and the requisite ratio of force to space to wage decisive campaigns and dominate the country. But they failed to conquer because they lacked a political base. The Spaniards rejected Napoleon's brother as king and opposed the French political program, which they perceived as hostile to religion. The behavior of French soldiers intensified difficulties with the public. With only two of the three principal components of French Revolutionary success, they could defeat the hostile armies but not control the country. The French confronted the weaker effectively using the raiding strategy of guerrilla warfare, a situation not unlike Alexander's in his initial occupation of Bactria and Sogdiana, but found no political means to reconcile the country.

In Russia the French had only their dominant military system. They faced an adamant tsar and a population for which they had no political attraction and had a ratio of force to space totally inadequate to compel the enemy to fight and insufficient to control much of the country. This absence of two of the three main requisites for success reduced the French to raiders trying to extract political concessions. Their primitive method of subsisting their armies aggravated the miseries of their retreat when they marched back over their route of advance and sought supplies from peasants who had learned to fear and hate them on their way into the country.

The transformation of warfare that occurred during the era of the French Revolution and Napoleon became the norm for nineteenth-century Europe. Radetzsky's Austrians and Moltke's Prussians achieved Napoleonic victories based on successful execution of strategic turning movements. Their armies, organized on the French model with force adequate to the space, could wage quick wars because of the limited political objectives which the victors sought.

This ability to compel battle but have the tactical defensive paramount helped to create the conditions in which the defensive reached its apogee in World War I. Then armies, on the average adequately commanded, liberally sustained by the new railway, which made possible the maintenance of huge stationary forces, and swelled by the effective manpower system which augmented regular troops with trained reservists, provided so much force to space that the armies covered the theater of operations and eliminated their flanks. From indecisive operations attributable in part to a low ratio of force to space before Napoleon, a high ratio contributed to the same result on the western front in 1914–18. With each army entrenched and its flanks secure, armies faced a situation in which a high ratio of force to space had allowed the tactical supremacy of the defense to nullify all of the strategic possibilities the offensive had gained in Napoleon's time. On the eastern front, however, where the Russians had too little strength to prevent breakthroughs of their front, the Germans and the Austrians had too little force in relation to the vast space of Russia. Only Russian political collapse brought victory in the east, an outcome in the west to which German political weakness and loss of morale also contributed significantly.

The siege warfare that resulted, even on the eastern front, gave artillery an unusual prominence, based on its traditional role in sieges. But this dependence on artillery, necessary to help cope with the firepower of magazine rifles and a variety of machine guns, constituted only one of the new weaknesses of the strategic offensive when confronted by the distinctly higher level of mobility conferred on the defense by the railroad. Whether in the war of movement in 1914 or the trench warfare and occasional breakthroughs of 1918, the defender's railroad-based mobility enabled him not only to supply his troops more readily but also to concentrate them more rapidly. For counterattack or for defensive concentration against enemy strength, the railroad gave the defenders strategically offensive troops, men who could make a strategic movement more quickly than their opponents who moved on foot. Although improved tactics made a breakthrough possible, if not easy or likely, inferior strategic mobility took away from the offensive the opportunity that tactical creativity had given it.

The fundamental alteration in logistics, brought about in part by the motor truck, and the revolution in tactics, caused by the return to the four basic weapon systems, provided the foundation for a transformation of warfare in many ways as profound as that of the French Revolution and Napoleon. Decisive campaigns became possible again in spite of a high ratio of force to space. This great change took place suddenly in the German campaign against France and its allies in May and June of 1940.

The strategic use of the tank in World War II provided a significant change from World War I, and this innovation depended as much or more on the motor truck than it did on the tank. By emancipating the large, relatively well-concentrated armies and their huge requirements for ammunition from the railroads, the motor truck, though its fuel created a new logistic demand, worked a revolution in supply. But motor trucks, and analogous vehicles with tracks, could move soldiers and their artillery in numbers and at a rate of speed comparable to the railroad. Further, the use of roads and the movement of men in tactical units with their weapons enabled soldiers to go into action more quickly than troops transported by rail.

With the tanks aided by aircraft contributing the principal offensive element and the truck-borne infantry with machine guns, artillery, and antitank and antiaircraft guns furnishing the primary defensive power, such a force, supplied by motor truck, had all of the elements to carry out a strategic turning movement on the Napoleonic model. When he had treated his cavalry as mounted infantry and used the better mobility conferred by horses to carry men and machine guns to the Turkish rear in 1918, General Allenby had relied on the vulnerable horse to carry a force with only the minimum defensive power. When, in Morocco in 1934, the French employed trucks for moving artillery, men, and machine guns, they increased their mobility and the defensive strength of the turning force as well. But neither had any tactically offensive ability because infantry could easily have halted the horses and trucks, placing the would-be turning force in the position of attempting to overcome the tactical primacy of the defense. With tanks, however, the turning force had tactically offensive capabilities that would enable it to overcome the opposition of infantry and all but large forces of antitank guns until it reached the enemy's rear where it could then go over to the defensive.

Meanwhile, aircraft attacked the enemy's supplies, hampered mobility, and provided intermittent tactical support. This strategic revolution, based on combining the mechanized tactical and logistical innovations of World War I, the Germans brought into existence in May 1940. Simple, even elegant, in conception and as obvious as the stirrup or bayonet once accomplished and its creation and implementation only the result of a happy mixture in which luck, enthusiasm, competence, and vision overcame conservatism, the execution of this campaign depended upon virtually every significant theme found in the western art of war in the previous 2,500 years.

This campaign marked one of the major transformations of warfare. World War I had introduced two new weapon systems, the light cavalry of the air and the armored heavy cavalry, but in World War II these weapon systems, no longer in primitive form, reached their operational maturity. The Germans made significant use of the tactical facility of planes when their aircraft, little impeded by weak French antiaircraft defenses, bombed the defenders of the Meuse and played a key role in the making of one of the important crossings of this river. The Germans also used their planes effectively in raiding the enemies' communciations and, like the British against the Turks in 1918, in attacking French and British troops in retreat along the roads. Germans tanks, though deficient in armor and firepower, performed admirably in articulated units connected by radio, which enabled them to envelop strong points or readily concentrate against a weakness in a continuous front. The tanks played expertly their heavy cavalry role of overwhelming light infantry and attacking heavy infantry in the flank and rear.

When the Germans had provided themselves with even more antitank guns than the French, they exhibited their grasp of the character of all of the weapon systems. French tank-led counterattacks almost inevitably met a strong resistance from the numerous though inadequate German antitank guns. Like the pikemen of old, the courageously and skillfully manned German antitank guns made a crucial contribution to stopping these attacks. Similarly, the Germans did not neglect defense against the weaker but still dangerous Anglo-French air forces. When the German columns on the road encountered strikes by enemy aircraft, they received them as the Crusaders had the Turkish light cavalry. Instead of crossbows, the Germans had antiaircraft machine guns and automatic cannon, some self-propelled so they could go into action immediately.

But the intelligent employment of the capabilities of the four weapon systems only represented the fruition of the changes begun during the First World War. In strategy the Germans harnessed the new logistics made possible by the truck to the strategic achievements of Napoleon, Radetzsky, and Moltke. In 1939 in Mongolia the Russians had demonstrated the power of the new logistics, using 4,000 trucks to supply an army of 57,000 men and over 800 tanks and armored cars 500 miles from a railroad. The Germans, by motorizing antitank and antiaircraft guns as well as some infantry and artillery and supplying all using trucks, reproduced Napoleon's Ulm campaign. When the Germans had attempted an Ulm maneuver on a vast scale in 1914, the better mobility of the French, who possessed functioning railroads, which gave them strategically offensive troops, would have defeated the Germans even had their plan lacked any other defects. But in 1940 the Panzer divisions and the accompanying motorized infantry divisions could keep ahead of the reserves the French delivered by rail. The French also possessed these more effective strategically offensive armored and motorized troops, but the Germans had concentrated theirs for a strategic turning movement.

The increase in the power of the offense, caused by the reappearance of light and heavy cavalry, contributed to German victories; a few men with rifles and machine guns could no longer delay many times their number because tanks could overrun them if they lacked adequate antitank guns. The wide dispersal of armies, characteristic of Napoleonic warfare, permitted the concentration of tanks in overwhelming numbers. German aircraft helped on occasion by attacking French forces that impeded the ground advance.

It proved impossible for the French to use the railways to reconstitute the front as they had in 1918. No longer did inadequate logistics prevent the Germans from exerting their full force against defending troops that in 1940 did not have the relative defensive power of those in 1914–18. The Germans also owed much of their success to the ruthlessness with which they concentrated. In forming armored and motorized divisions they had an organization that embodied concentration; by committing those powerful formations in only two operations, and the bulk of them in only one, they again concentrated. Their aircraft had such great mobility and range in relation to the size of the theater of war that they, too, provided another force that the Germans could and did readily concentrate. Finally, in their strategy the Germans concentrated against the weakness of the Ardennes front and insured its vulnerability by their convincing distraction in Belgium. Here they combined dispersion along an extended front with a surprise concentration.

The Germans combined these tactical, logistic, and strategic elements to execute a vast strategic turning movement, used in ancient times by Caesar and introduced in modern times by Napoleon. They daringly, and not without misgivings, utilized the splendid strategic mobility they owed to the motor truck to plunge deep into their adversaries' rear. Once behind the enemy, the Germans could exploit the tactical power of the defense to hold their position and ensure a disastrous evacuation by the enemy, immense booty in materiel, and many prisoners. With the completion of this campaign, the French and British had too little strength remaining to prevent the Germans from overrunning France, a task for which they had an adequate ratio of force to space and little popular opposition from the stunned French.

The Germans conquered France in spite of a competent adversary, equal in numbers and, on the whole, in materiel. Their achievement rested on the harmonizing of the new weapon systems much as the old masters of the art of war had united the earlier counterparts of the tank, plane, and antitank and antiaircraft guns. Combining this with the revolution in logistics and a thoroughly Napoleonic strategy, they defeated their opponent's powerful defense. And only in this way could they have overmatched the preponderance of the defense in a theater of war with a high ratio of force to space.

Thus, this campaign transformed warfare, and military operations entered a new era that endures to this day. During the remainder of World War II all the belligerents applied these tactical, logistical, and strategic principles. But none equaled the Germans who, having made such a just mixture of the weapon systems and pioneered the doctrines and the strategy, had also the advantage of the experience gained in their Polish and French campaigns before they further honed their skills against the Russians, another unseasoned opponent.

In subsequent European campaigns the combatants used the revived Napoleonic strategy, usually having a ratio of force to space large enough to wage a decisive campaign.

If an attacker attained surprise, a breakthrough of the front proved difficult to prevent because of the concentrated tank and motorized forces available for exploitation. The counterattack on the flank provided the only antidote to this strategic prescription, but even this defense inevitably involved the loss of significant amounts of territory and supplies. The Russian counterattack at Stalingrad exemplified this countermeasure, one applied also by the Anglo-American forces against a German offensive in December 1944. To use the counterattack to defeat a strategic penetration required motorized forces in reserve in some combination of a subtracted reserve of uncommitted units and of those near or in touch with the enemy which the commander could still withdraw and use to carry out this counterattack. To have the maximum effect, the counterattacking forces must use the same method of breakthrough and rapid advance that the enemy had initially employed. In this respect the Russian response to the German drive to Stalingrad and toward the oil fields showed the major achievement possible for counteraction of this type. Conceptually it had something in common with Marshal Joffre's effort to turn the German turning movement of 1914, for, in capturing the Germans in Stalingrad, the Russians executed a turning movement, even though two armies participated to make it a strategic envelopment.

The basic strategy of the 1973 campaign of the Egyptians and Israelis conforms to that which has characterized warfare since the 1790s, except for the siege warfare deadlock of 1914–18. Still, in spite of the Israeli success in turning the Egyptian Third Army in 1973, this event seems less likely to occur than in World War III if the armies in Europe should engage. These all-mounted armies, heterogeneous in their weapon systems, are homogeneous in the sense that almost every division, corps, and army has a similar composition. In this way they differ markedly from the armies of World War II. Thus, commanders can no longer as readily make a strategic concentration of tanks, which could overcome antitank defenses, as often happened in the 1940s. Further, with all troops having equal mobility, commanders cannot rely on differential mobility, which enabled motor-marching forces to turn the foot marching in World War II.

So the wars of the French Revolution and Napoleon inaugurated an era in which combat persisting strategy dominated warfare. With so much force in relation to space, raiders could find few vulnerable enemies to attack and even had difficulty reaching hostile communications to practice a raiding logistic strategy. Armies in retreat did practice some scorched-earth logistic strategy by destroying bridges, railways, and supplies they could not carry away. The advent of the airplane, however, had returned both raiding and logistic strategies to prominence by the Second World War through air raids on communications and against hostile cities, a trend that has continued since then.

The Classifications of Military Strategy

The concepts underlying military strategy have remained fairly constant for 2,500 years, though tactical and logistical conditions, among others, have conditioned what commanders could accomplish. Still, through this long span of warfare most contestants had the alternative of aiming at each other directly through employing a combat strategy or indirectly by attacking the other's supplies. Equally, and without excluding a choice between these alternatives, they had the possibility of defending or pursuing the offensive by raids or by risking battle and following a persisting strategy to protect their own or engross their adversary's territory. The matrix in schematic 12.3. clearly represents the classifications of strategy used in this work. Although this shows only military strategy, which aims at the hostile armed forces, it can, as schematic 12.4 exhibits, thus embrace military action not directed at strictly military ends.

	Persisting	Raiding
Combat		
Logistic		

Schematic 12.3. Strategy Matrix

This organization probably would not provide the best approach to a more general consideration of strategy. Nevertheless, it does embrace the other instances of the use of military force noted in this book. Raiding to extract political concessions directly, rather than by engaging the hostile armed forces, has appeared prominently when purely military measures promised less success. The frequently used strategy of the Greek city states and that employed by the English in the Hundred Years' War provided the most conspicuous illustrations of a political raiding strategy.

Such a strategy also appeared in the Turkish raids in Anatolia after the Battle of Manzikert and those of Marshal Bugeaud in Algeria in the nineteenth century.

	Persisting	Raiding
Military aims		
Political aims		
Economic aims		
Other aims		

Schematic 12.4. More General Strategy Matrix

In both of these examples many civilians died, the direct, rather than the incidental, result of forays that appropriated and destroyed property, and the terror inspired by this loss of life helped significantly in subduing these territories. Although raids directed primarily against property, like those of the Greeks and English, doubtless killed or injured people, these incursions aimed at property rather than at inhabitants. So although the political objective and military means did not differ, raids that include killing civilians among their objectives, like the Mongols killing urban populations in the Khwarizmian Empire, have often received a distinct categorization because they rely on terror. Actually, contemporary political terrorism, in execution often analogous to a military raid, does not differ in its essence from a political raiding strategy, which depends primarily on intimidating civilians by killing rather than destroying property. A persisting strategy that acquired territory could not qualify as an instance of using military action to secure political objectives directly because a persisting strategy almost always necessarily includes facing the major enemy's armed forces and must involve military strategy.

In fact, military and political objectives often combined in a way that made the distinction irrelevant. In the Thirty Years' War, for example, raids met supply needs by feeding the raiding army, implemented a logistic strategy by depleting the adversary's resources, overwhelmed the garrisons of small cities to carry out a combat strategy, and, through all of this damage, directly exerted intense political pressure. The Union raids in the last year of the American Civil War, carried out in pursuit of a logistic strategy, had as an important by-product and, perhaps, their most important result, a political effect—the Southerners' perception of the cost of continuing the war—and a psychological effect—altering the Southerners' estimate of the chances for victory. The strategic bombing in World War II deliberately mixed similar political objectives, along with the use of terror, with the execution of a logistic raiding military strategy.

A persisting strategy, in the absence of the tactical or strategic means of destroying the enemy army, had to aim at the acquisition of hostile territory which, if it did not constitute the political objective of the war, might provide something of value to the defender that the attacker could exchange for a goal of the war. If the attacker had ambitious political aims, he could have to occupy all of the enemy's territory, as was the case in World War II to secure unconditional surrender of Germany. In this instance Germany's numerous and powerfully armed enemies had both the preponderance of military power and the ratio of force to space to attain their unlimited objective as well as the motivation to use the needed military means for the time requisite to win such a total victory. The experience of such a triumph, largely attained through military means, a rare occurrence in war, has colored military and political thinking since that war by making unlimited political and military victory seem more attainable than a longer view of history would suggest. More restricted goals and, therefore, victories have usually characterized conflicts in the past, though Alexander's war against Darius III of Persia and Rome's in her conquest of Gaul offer two important exceptions.

In general, the strength of the motive behind political goals has affected the proportion of a country's resources devoted to the conflict and the extent of the defeat required to accede to the enemy's demands. An analogy with the economic concept of supply and demand would equate the political motive with a consumer's desire for a product and the military and other costs of a war with the cost of the economic good. Yet each of the two contestants functions as seller as well as buyer. Thus a triumphant attacker might attain impressive successes but find that the enemy still would not adopt his definition of defeat and that he had already expended all of the effort he believed his objectives were worth. In this case, military events would not have altered the political aspirations of either. But if this led to compromise, the degree of determination of each side would influence the outcome, which would fit the market parallel only very roughly as an instance of buying a smaller quantity but at a higher unit cost. Surely, only a coincidence would have made the degree of military achievement the victor was willing to purchase in exchange for his political goal equal the level of effort and military failure the loser would endure to concede defeat and accede to the stronger's requirements. But understanding the interaction among motives and objectives and military costs, outcomes, and prospects is not part of this book.

Sometimes political determination has not seemed proportionate to the stakes in a war. Whereas how much moral and combat support each combatant would contribute to the war would usually depend on political objectives, the intensity and length of the war effort tended to have a direct relation to the political costs of defeat. In the Thirty Years' War, for example, when the Holy Roman Emperor and the Catholic forces had defeated Denmark, they seemed to have intimidated their enemies and reconciled them to defeat. But the emperor's Edict of Restitution, seizing estates long Protestant, raised the stakes in the war and insured a continued struggle. In other ways, too, the length and intensity of the struggle may also affect political aims, a case of the means contributing to the determination of the end. This only roughly fits the economic analogy as an instance of a buyer, having already paid more than expected, demands more of the product as recompense for the enlarged outlay. The cost of World War I, in which the belligerents escalated their war aims, provides an excellent example.

Sometimes there has seemed little correlation between the objective and the intensity or duration of the struggle, as the War of the Triple Alliance graphically illustrates. In 1865, a war, ostensibly a dispute over territory, pitted Paraguay against Brazil, Argentina, and Uruguay. Paraguay displayed amazing political as well as military fortitude. In a struggle lasting over five years the triple allies totally defeated Paraguay, so overmatched that the numbers enrolled in the imperial Brazilian militia exceeded the entire population of Paraguay. If the time required for an allied victory appears exorbitant, the endeavors of Paraguay seem extraordinary: its government reduced the draft age to twelve, conscripted women, at first to substitute for scarce horses in pulling artillery and wagons, and followed a ruthless logistic strategy of destroying every village in the invaders' path and killing every animal. By the end of the war the population of Paraguay had declined by 55 percent, leaving less than 29,000 men, 107,000 women, and 87,000 children. The Paraguayan commitment to war bore little relation to the original political goals or the outcome.

History abounds with other examples of political goals limited by the inadequacy of the military means to reach them, just as it does of instances of the potentiality of military successes that lay beyond the scope of the available economic resources to sustain the military endeavor or exceeded the political willingness to expend the effort to achieve goals for the attainment of which the economic resources and military means existed. So, on the boundary between warfare and politics one may readily find, the Paraguayan example notwithstanding, analogs with consumer choice comparable to those alternatives in the selection of the combination of weapon systems to accomplish a given military task.

In seeking economic rather than political benefits, raiding characterized the strategy of barbarians, Arabs, Magyars, and Vikings. Of course, the same motive and concept underlies the robbery of a store or a bank. Although those seeking economic goals by military means usually placed almost exclusive reliance on raids, as did those using them to pursue political ends directly, the nineteenth century contains examples of major powers using a persisting strategy to forward economic ends when their armed forces seized a foreign nation's port and appropriated the proceeds of the customshouse to pay on a defaulted debt.

Since the problems of conducting and defending against such operations with political, economic, or other objectives differed little, if any, from those with military objectives, the treatment of military strategy alone usually adequately deals with these in their military aspects, even though they fall outside the province of this book.

The Influence of the Ratio of Force to Space

Some themes, such as the ratio of force to space, have an influence that pervades all four types of strategy. Unless attackers have an adequate ratio of force to the space of the theater of war so as to have the ability to make the defender fight or retreat directly to the rear, the army on the offensive is unlikely to have effective strategic means of compelling the enemy to fight, except under the circumstance of the defender's own choosing. A high ratio of force to space can, on the other hand, confront the attacker with the continuous fortified front, which has characterized much of the world wars.

A simple schematic may help clarify the relationship between these two variables. If the vertical axis in schematic 12.5 measures the amount of space and the horizontal the quantity of force, the zone near the line at forty-five degrees represents the strategically decisive ratio with which armies organized in the manner of those of the French Revolution and Napoleon could pursue a persisting strategy and compel battle or the enemy's retreat to the rear.

If the contending forces operated in more space, represented by the area well above the forty-five-degree line, they could not compel a decision. Napoleon faced this situation in Russia, and it resembled campaigning with the concentrated, unitary armies of earlier times. Just as Montecuccoli could avoid Turenne and neither Tilly nor Gustavus could coerce the other to fight, so Napoleon could not close with the Russian army except with its acquiescence. This low ratio not only favored raiding, if often left no alternative.

The ratio of force to space in the campaign of 1914 in France and Belgium belongs well below the forty-five-degree line. Here the contending armies had such a high ratio of force to space that an entrenched deadlock resulted. Without any flanks and no alternative to frontal attacks against an entrenched enemy, siege warfare ensued. But rather than the grid of fortified towns, which had typified the two centuries of siege warfare in the Netherlands, the combatants had so much strength that continuous siege lines covered the whole front. Earlier,

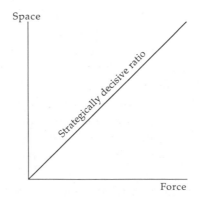

Schematic 12.5. The Influence of the Ratio of Force to Space

the need to relieve besieged cities had given the attacker an opportunity to make the defender assume the offensive against the covering army, but with continuous lines the attacker had no alternative but to take the tactical offensive. Of course, sieges themselves exemplify operations with this high ratio.

This potent influence of the ratio of force to space only holds true when armies have like composition with respect to their weapon systems. When, for example, the Romans campaigned against the Parthians in the relatively unobstructed terrain of Mesopotamia, the ratio of force to space mattered little. The mounted Parthians could use their greater mobility to refuse to fight or to compel the Roman infantry to accept battle regardless of the numbers on each side. But when armies have similar mobility, the ratio of force to space has a major influence.

When armies have comparable constitutions and mobility, the defense has two capabilities: it can resist frontal attacks, and it can take strategic advantage of the primacy of retreat over pursuit. When the armies pursuing persisting strategies represent a high ratio of force to space, as in 1914, the capacity to withstand a frontal assault becomes the defense's principal means of forcing a deadlock. When the ratio is low, as in most of the campaigns in the past, the defense uses its ability to avoid battle to frustrate the attackers. Commanders did not need to make this choice between tactical and strategic means, as the Romans showed when they defeated Hannibal by avoiding battle and by relying on their fortified cities.

As Hannibal's experience exhibits, the ratio of force to space affects what a victorious army may achieve. If small in relation to a politically antipathetic country, it cannot control it, even if it can always defeat the hostile forces. The experience of the English in the Hundred Years' War shows how the vast size of France swallowed up the English invaders. The length of time the systematic Romans required to consolidate their conquests offers another illustration of the effect of the ratio of force to space on a victorious army gaining a political result from its military supremacy.

The foregoing applies only to a persisting strategy; the situation with respect to a raiding strategy has no such complexity. Raiders can only function in the area well above the forty-five-degree line. Without a low ratio of hostile force in the theater of operations, the raiders would find their movements impeded and their persisting enemy strong everywhere. Thus raiding has greater strength on the offensive than persisting on the defensive but only with a low ratio of force to space.

The Supremacy of Retreat Over Pursuit

The primacy of retreat over pursuit has usually dictated strategy with more or less authority since the time of the ancient Greeks. This generalization, a major theme, applies only to the same weapon systems or, of course, when the pursuers have less mobility. Light infantry could, for example, outmarch heavy infantry, just as light cavalry could outdistance heavy cavalry. Mounted men had an even greater margin over dismounted. In withdrawal, men with the same weapon system could outrun their pursuers, if only because they could place obstacles, such as broken bridges and fallen trees, in the path of those following. In addition, the retreating force could leave a rear guard to delay the pursuers. The rear guard often might not need to fight much, for, by making the enemy change from march to combat formation and then resuming its retreat, the fleeing army would have gained ground in its march.

When armies had comparable composition, the weaker could retire, if it lacked the strength, inclination, or opportunity to use the tactical resource of resisting a frontal attack. Often, when favored by a low or moderate ratio of force to space, the withdrawing army could move in any direction, confident, until the end of the eighteenth century, that its opponent had no means of bringing it to battle because the weaker could march away while the stronger arrayed for combat.

This elusiveness, which often made the stronger powerless to force a contest on the weaker, fostered a resort to a raiding strategy and provided one of the fundamental conditions that made raids possible and assured their eminence on the offensive against a persisting opponent. Without the strategic primacy of retreat, raiders could often meet with disaster when trying to escape and on occasion even fail to reach their objective. Of course, the same conditions applied to raiders as governed the supremacy of withdrawal over pursuit, a low ratio of force to space and the possession of a weapon system equal or superior in mobility to that of the defenders against the raid.

Concentration against Weakness, Distraction, and the Principles of War

Napoleon once stated a salient theme in warfare: "The nature of strategy consists of always having, even with a weaker army, more forces at the point of attack or at the point one is being attacked than the enemy has." This principle, also applicable to tactics, has governed combat, logistic, persisting, and raiding strategies. Just as in battles where the combatants sought to attack or defend their weak flanks and rear and watch for a vulnerable point in their own or their adversary's front, so also in strategy did commanders look for weakness to exploit on the offensive and for hostile strength as a source of danger against which to concentrate their forces on the defensive. The enemy's logistic resources, usually more vulnerable than his combat forces, made the best target, and because a logistic strategy necessarily implied some combat (except for a scorched-earth policy on the defense), the relevance of the concept of attacking weakness differed little for a logistic strategy.[1]

In executing their mission, whether directed at the enemy's forces or his logistic resources, raiders sought to assail weakness. Defenders tried to confront or trap raiders with the strongest force possible. But forces employing a raiding strategy to win through the accumulation of many small combat or logistic victories had a facility for concentration against weakness superior to that of those using a persisting strategy. Such raiders, often weaker and using the primacy of retreat to avoid strong defending forces, could concentrate against any combat or logistic objective because they had to have no strategic aim other than the immediate results of the raid. With such ambiguity as to objective, a raiding strategy so distracted a defender and gave so many opportunities to the attacker that he could so readily concentrate against weakness as to make a raiding strategy stronger on the offensive than a defending persisting strategy. Since all forms of strategy usually involved at least the possibility of combat, the concept of having the greatest preponderance of force possible or having the most favorable strategic position had a universal applicability.

The idea of distracting the enemy almost constitutes a corollary to the offensive concept of assailing weakness and could aid the defender as well if he deceived the attacker into mistaking strength for weakness. Distraction served Gustavus well in his initial campaign against Tilly and later made possible the king's crossing of the difficult barrier of the Lech River; and Eugene used it to confuse Marshal Catinat and cross the Adige and then two more rivers. Recently strategic distraction has contributed to a more decisive operation. In May 1940 the German offensive over the most favorable terrain into Holland and Belgium drew French reserves into Belgium while the Germans themselves moved to attack through the Ardennes. Allenby's distraction of the Turks toward the east before his 1918 Megiddo offensive on the west and Montgomery's strong drive on the east of the Normandy beachhead before the breakout on the west in 1944 also threatened the obvious, thus reinforcing the preconceptions of the hostile commanders. Although not a requirement for a successful distraction, it did facilitate it and argued for an avoidance of the obvious in the search for a weak objective.

Because of the predominance of the tactical defensive, the offensive version of this rule—concentrate against weakness—has received more frequent statement than the defensive formulation—concentrate against strength. But often the concept has appeared in a general statement in the simple injuction to concentrate. This affirmation has the virtue of general applicability but fails to specify against what, and sometimes commanders have taken it to mean the enemy's main force when such a concentration would violate the doctrine to attack weakness when on the offensive. The principles of war used today in many armies provide an example of this more general rule to concentrate. Nevertheless, equally appropriate for tactics and strategy, they do lend themselves to exhibiting the properties a military operation must have to achieve an offensive concentration against weakness or to bring the maximum defensive force against the main hostile offensive effort. The U. S. army currently adheres to the following nine principles for success in warfare.

The principle of the *objective* states that the commander must have a clear idea of what he wishes to accomplish. That of the *offensive* holds that the defensive, no matter how strong, cannot achieve victory by itself. Only the offensive can dominate the enemy and attain victory. *Simplicity* points out that complex plans and operations present too many difficulties in execution, and that simpler plans will more likely achieve victory. *Maneuver* stresses mobility in combat and strategy. *Unity of command* emphasizes that divided commands risk failure because of a lack of coordination of effort and agreement as to the objective. *Surprise* has its value because a surprised enemy is psychologically as well as physically unready to make his best effort. *Security* states that a commander must avoid being caught unaware himself as well as keep his plans and his movements secret from the enemy. To do this involves good intelligence of the enemy's capabilities. *Economy of force* enjoins using no more force than needed to accomplish the mission. *Mass* or *concentration* complements economy of force: a commander must use the forces economized elsewhere to concentrate for the main offensive or defensive effort.

One may view all of these principles as the means to secure an appropriate concentration. A clear idea of the objective requires unity of command to execute a simple plan to concentrate economized forces against a defender's weakness or an attacker's strength. Such a concentration requires maneuver and cannot achieve surprise without security. Without surprise, the offensive effort will not find the enemy weak, nor will an enemy not caught unaware carry out an offensive against a defender who had concentrated to receive the attack. Either the attack itself or the subsequent adoption of the offensive to exploit the dominance produced by a successful defensive shows the relevance of the principle of the offensive.

The foregoing also includes by implication the concept of the initiative, an important idea, though not one of these principles of war. Concentration demands the ability to initiate action, to act as well as react. This quality, which usually belongs to the offensive and to the stronger force, normally depends on a good knowledge of the enemy, and without initiative commanders usually find surprise more difficult to attain. Thus, like the nine principles, initiative is implied in the concept of concentration, and all of these not only lend themselves to the accomplishment of the objective of concentration against weakness on the offensive and opposition against strength on the defensive, but also describe the means needed to attain success in almost any military operation.

Compelling the Enemy to Fight, Turning Movements, and Concentration in Space and Time

Several themes have their principal applications in a persisting combat strategy. This kind of warfare, characteristic in Europe for the past 200 years, has received the most study from military theorists and historians, but has also encountered great difficulties in execution. The army on the offensive with a persisting strategy, superior in combat strength but lacking a dominant weapon system, throughout history has most often lacked enough force in relation to the size of the theater of operations to compel battle, except on the opponent's terms when the attacker has usually had to meet the defender in a strong, often entrenched, position with secure flanks. Thus Tilly, eager for battle, found Gustavus Adolphus well prepared at Werben and consequently abandoned the assault. Very often the defender has shut himself up in a castle or fortified city.

That for centuries the attacker had few resources for forcing a battle has constituted a major theme of this book. He could, like the ancient Greeks or Hannibal in Italy, devastate the countryside in an effort to coerce his opponent to fight. But since invading armies consumed and destroyed much in the ordinary course of operations, this method rarely proved effective, especially as defending armies could often hover nearby and interfere with these foraging and destructive activities. Or the intruder could, as the French did several times in their early sixteenth-century Italian campaigns, use a siege to make the enemy fight. This had the advantage of making the relieving army assume the tactical offensive.

Commanders also sought to accomplish the harder task of entrapping an opposing force against an obstacle, thus compelling capitulation or an attack against the enemy army blocking the way. Prince Edward attained this when he caught de Montfort in Evesham, and King Henry IV of France thought he had achieved it against the wily duke of Parma until the resourceful duke escaped by building a bridge over the river. The higher potential in this strategy of making an opponent take the offensive with his back against an impassable barrier matched the greater difficulty of catching even a moderately alert adversary.

The low ratio of force to space, which so often prevailed, would have caused many of these frustrations for the attacker even had armies better means for ensnaring their opponent and forcing battle. For this reason strategy often relied on destructive raids to extract political concessions rather than to attain a military objective. Strategists found an alternative for a successful offensive in a persisting strategy that depended on the acquisition of territory by systematic conquest of the cities and fortified points in the country. The Romans used this approach to circumscribe Hannibal's area of control. But the method worked slowly and, in the absence of political support in the country, could require impossibly large armies to garrison the occupied territory. Gustavus used this form of the persisting strategy when he began his campaign in a Protestant area of Germany but then sought to dominate more territory than he could control and, in consequence, fell back on a raiding strategy embodying logistic and political objectives as well as the goal of compelling the enemy to fight.

The standard procedure of slowly gaining territory by taking cities and fortifying the country, which also embraced a logistic strategy, drove the enemy army from the region by inhibiting its mobility and, for the same reason, protected the newly acquired areas from incursions if the enemy adopted a raiding strategy. This approach also characterized operations in the Netherlands, where commanders faced the different problem of so much force, in the form of fortifications as well as soldiers, as to create a stalemate. When, as in northern Italy, Bohemia, Saxony, and Silesia in the eighteenth century, generals had enough force to control the theater but not enough to produce a stalemate, they could make quick progress with a persisting strategy in spite of their inability to coerce their weaker opponent to fight. To do this such commanders as Eugene and Vendôme avoided the defender's strong position and invaded and dominated the area from which he drew his supplies, making the defender withdraw to find food and fodder, or, as Frederick the Great felt compelled to do to save Saxony when he attacked the well-prepared Daun at Torgau, fight a battle on unfavorable terms. This strategy exhibited the logistic element almost always implicit in persisting strategy.

Battles thus normally occurred by mutual consent because of the elusiveness of the defender and usually depended either on a difference of opinion as to the likely outcome or on pressing political necessity. And so, in spite of the usual primacy of the defensive, commanders never abandoned hope of a tactically decisive battle that could give them, through attrition and psychological ascendancy, peace on their terms or at least the opportunity to dominate a large area abandoned by a weakened and discouraged opponent. Thus, generals always kept in mind the possibility of a tactical solution and labored to constrain their adversary to fight under disadvantageous circumstances while they sought to engross critical portions of his territory.

The development, during the wars of the French Revolution and Napoleon, of the strategy of dispersing armies and the means of rapid deployment from column to line diminished the paramount position of the strategic defensive by markedly increasing the difficulties of avoiding battle by other means than a retreat directly to the rear. This fundamental change also placed in the hands of the attacker the turning movement, which, like entrapment against an obstacle and the relief of a siege, gave him the advantages of the tactical defensive. Yet, the strategic turning movement offered much more than the attrition of a winning defensive battle fought to cover a siege. It had the potential to annihilate the enemy army by compelling its capitulation after it failed in its effort to drive the turning force from its path.

The strategic turning movement, a theme since the Napoleonic period, emulates tactics, for, just as in tactics where a movement past an army's flank to assault its rear promised great tactical rewards, so also did a strategic movement to the enemy's rear. Napoleon in his Marengo and Ulm campaigns achieved success with this turning movement and blocked the defender's retreat. The Austrian losses at Ulm in prisoners and stragglers enabled this victory to rank with the most decisive of battles. And in the same way the greater mobility of tactically offensive troops aided an attack on flank and rear, the greater mobility of strategically offensive troops enhanced the chances of a successful turning movement. The Germans in their 1914 Tannenberg campaign against the Russians used the railroad to carry out a strategic shift of troops to turn Samsonov's army, and General Allenby used the differential mobility provided by horses to accomplish the movement in 1918 and, by dismounting his cavalry, gave them the tactical defensive strength of infantry. But in 1940 the dominant strategic mobility of German Panzer and motorized divisions inaugurated an era of turning movements based on the better strategic mobility of motorized over foot-marching armies.

Without strategically offensive troops, commanders had to base their successful turning movements on strategic surprise. This Napoleon achieved in his Marengo campaign by his unexpected direction of approach and in the Ulm campaign by the breadth of his advance and the strategic possibilities this opened to him. The same advance on a broad front gave Moltke his opportunity to turn Bazaine in 1870. Clearly, strategic surprise had more importance than tactical surprise and, if only because it dealt with greater forces, was likely to yield far larger rewards.

Strategic turning movements also had great utility for defense against a persisting strategy. They could attain their effect not by the difficult task of actually reaching the enemy's rear but merely by threatening such a movement. Faced with this menace, the advancing enemy would fall back to protect himself, thus bringing on a retreat as significant in distance, if not in other results, as if imposed by a serious defeat in battle. The outstanding practitioner of this use of the turning movement was the Confederate general, R. E. Lee.

For concentration against weakness, interior lines of operations, another theme of this book, offered opportunities both to armies on the offensive and to defenders for counterattacks. The utility of interior lines depended on the ability of one side to compel battle or retreat to the rear, though the successes of Consul Nero against Hasdrubal, of Prince Edward against the de Montforts, and Frederick against Soubise and Charles indicated that luck could substitute.

To counteract the enemy's possession of interior lines, which gave him the capacity to concentrate in space, commanders sought to employ simultaneous actions on exterior lines—concentration in time. These presented difficulties, especially when the lack of a Chappe or electric telegraph precluded rapid communication. Simultaneous actions by distant armies proved easier on the offensive when the forces could arrange them by prior agreement rather than improvising the advances in response to an enemy's exploitation of interior lines. Even so, distant armies rarely found it convenient to act at the same time, and two forces doubled the chances of delay. Despite this, King John of England and the Emperor Otto accomplished a modest result on exterior lines in their campaign against King Philip of France, in spite of the dilatoriness of the emperor. Frederick's enemies seriously menaced him in 1757 and 1758, and Napoleon's opponents gained an impressive and important victory when they planned effectively and used concentration in time against him as they ultimately united their forces at Leipzig after a concentric campaign.

In the strategy to coordinate many campaigns interior lines may offer an important advantage. In World War I, for example, the Germans used the comparative isolation of their eastern and western adversaries to concentrate against

France in 1914, Russia and Serbia in 1915, and France in early 1916, improvise a concentration against Romania later in 1916, and strike against Italy in 1917. The allies could have used their sea power and the separation of Germany and Austria-Hungary from the Ottoman Empire to make a more powerful and efficacious attack to drive the latter from the war. In World War II the allies took advantage of the isolation of their European and Asiatic enemies to concentrate consistently against Germany.

Nevertheless, concentration in time has an intrinsic advantage over concentration in space if terrain and other conditions were comparable on the two fronts involved. If, for example, an army of 100,000 men on interior lines opposed two forces of 50,000 on exterior lines, the interior army could concentrate 75,000 against one of the units of 50,000, leaving 25,000 to hold in check the other 50,000. This would give the attacker an advantage of 1.5 to 1. But if the armies on exterior lines responded with a concentration in time, one exterior army of 50,000 could take the offensive against the holding force of 25,000, enjoying a predominance of 2 to 1 while its companion had to contend with a numerical disadvantage of only 1 to 1.5. Still, if the troops seeking to hold had good fortifications or terrain especially adapted to the defense, these could nullify the greater ratio of superiority. And the more effective unity of command, an important principle of war and one an interior army would be more likely to have, usually confers an advantage on the interior force. On the other hand, Frederick the Great, a successful practitioner of concentration on interior lines, noted another disadvantage of concentration in space, applicable to the logistics of his day, when he wrote: "These kinds of wars ruin the armies by fatigue and the marches that one must have his men make."[2]

Not only did the ability to compel battle or to force retreat directly to the rear give meaning to strategic concentration, but the almost exclusive dependence on missile weapons of increasing range added greatly to the consequence of numerical preponderance. The assumption underlying Lanchester's N-square law, that every soldier could combat every other, lacked reality when the Greeks fought each other hand to hand in deep formations. Even eighteenth-century lines of musketeers firing volleys often failed to conform to his necessary supposition. But dispersed armies with long-range, rapid-firing weapons and artillery using indirect fire gave authenticity to Lanchester's assumption and great point to his conclusion that when every opposing soldier could fight every other, the combat power of armies would vary, not directly, but as the square of their numerical strength.

Accordingly, in recent times numerical superiority has taken on greater significance and has given, especially in the case of dispersed armies, more import to strategic concentration, either in space through exploitation of interior lines or in time through coordinated or simultaneous advances or attacks. These forms of concentration of dispersed armies have offered defenders as well as attackers new opportunities. With a strategically decisive ratio of force to space and armies with the tactical capabilities and the dispersion to ensnare an opponent who did not retreat directly to the rear, strategic concentration in space or time and the turning movement have virtually superseded the older methods of combat persisting strategy: compelling the enemy to fight by devastating his territory, forcing him to raise a siege, or entrapping him against an obstacle.

The Nature and Objectives of a Raiding Strategy

Except through aircraft, combat or logistic raiding strategies had little place in European warfare after its transformation by Napoleon. But throughout its long span before Napoleon, combat and logistic raids played a prominent role and provided a major theme in war. Usually aiming at enemy economic or logistic resources or at weak, vulnerable bodies of troops, most raiders planned to avoid contact with the main army of their adversary and to withdraw once they had done their damage. They generally retreated when menaced by the main hostile force and, with alternative objectives, directed their marches into areas where they could avoid the major opposing army. The uncertainty of their goal and route of advance usually prevented interception, and by having other lines of withdrawal, the marauders proved equally elusive after reaching their target. On the offensive, this strategy differed much from a persisting strategy and its conquest of territory as a normal result. On the defensive, the raid's offensive character contrasted with the defender's customary defensive reliance on fortifications and willingness to give battle only in a strong position as well as the weaker defender's concern to cover his own territory rather than enter that controlled by the adversary.

Many raids had logistic objectives, but frequently in the process of devastation or carrying off booty the raiders had to engage in combat with civilians or small belligerent forces, and, in any case, nothing about raids confined them solely to logistical targets. Raiders might aim at enemy forces rather than their supplies. Such raids exemplified the application of the concept of concentration against weakness, and civilians and, often, an army's supply installations were weak. The Persian cavalry strike against the Greek supply convoy during the Plataea campaign exhibited concentration against weakness as well as the deliberate pursuit of a logistic strategy.

Raiders thus employed an offensive strategy of concentration against weakness. Sometimes they marched away from their adversary to raid his territory to distract him, as in the Thirty Years' War, and stronger armies used incursions as a means to compel battle, attacking crops, property, or weak opponents because the enemy's main force would not fight. The destructive marches of the Greeks and of Hannibal to coerce the Romans to battle also illustrated this objective.

But in the representative cases, when raiders had less strength than the enemy, they used the defensive's attribute of retreat to avoid the enemy's stronger forces while at the same time they sought to concentrate against the enemy's weakness. The Poitiers campaign exhibited the success of a weaker English army in eluding the French while carrying out a ruinous foray. The French only overtook the English at Poitiers because the English prince, encumbered by booty, sacrificed the ability of the retreating force to keep ahead of the pursuers. At Poitiers the English changed from retreat to the defensive's other resource, the tactical defensive, won the battle, and continued the withdrawal, triumphantly bringing away their spoils. Had he aimed at only destruction or at overwhelming isolated French combat forces, the English prince could have carried out his raid without battle. Intrinsically better mobility, such as the Magyar light cavalry enjoyed, facilitated a raiding strategy but, as the Poitiers campaign showed, incursions with a favorable outcome did not depend on this. Nevertheless, since such marauders usually lacked the strength or inclination to fight even a defensive battle with the principal hostile force, they more typically defended themselves with strategic retreat rather than the tactical defensive.

So raids provided a tactically and strategically offensive means for a weaker adversary to use against a stronger. The weaker did not need to have an offensive goal, as did the English raids in the Hundred Years' War. The Austrians employed this method defensively, largely by light infantry, to attack detachments of the army of Frederick the Great and to overwhelm supply convoy guards and destroy their wagons. In this way the weaker Austrians utilized raids to defeat two Prussian invasions. And the Austrians adopted raids to accomplish this winning logistic strategy, even though they defended in their own territory and so had to limit their objectives to the Prussian army rather than take the opportunity to assail far more vulnerable civilians. The Austrian light infantry's somewhat better mobility, as compared with the Prussian heavy infantry, did promote their victory, even though the two types of infantry differed little in equipment and none in intrinsic mobility.

These kinds of raiders, therefore, used offensive tactical means but combined them with the defensive's strategic ability to retreat to engage only less powerful hostile forces. Because the raiders might have the choice of coming by a number of routes and had a virtually untrammeled selection of objectives, as long as the objective had comparatively little combat strength, the raiders usually had better capabilities for concentrating against weakness than did a force pursuing a persisting strategy. So its intrinsic strength meant that both attackers or defenders employed raiding in either a logistic or combat strategy. Because of the comparative combat weakness of the means of supply, raids lent themselves to the pursuit of a logistic strategy. But, as the French learned in Spain, raiders could concentrate against weak combat forces and overwhelm them before reinforcements arrived.

A raiding strategy thus shared some goals with a persisting strategy. As a combat strategy, raiding strove for attrition through the accumulation of many small tactical successes. On the other hand, a combat persisting strategy planned to accomplish its attrition through winning one or more important battles. Each strategy also aimed to discourage the enemy and convince him he had slender prospects for winning the war. So whereas the victor in battle often tried to follow up his success with a pursuit to complete the ruin of the defeated, the raider immediately resorted to retreat. Thus, instead of extensive damage to enemy forces and the usual concomitant control of much territory, the raider counted only on the destruction of hostile combat and logistic resources that occurred immediately and depended on many such achievements for the material and psychological gains necessary to strategic success.

A persisting strategy that aimed at the adversary's main force also had, as a by-product, a logistic objective, since the occupation of hostile territory thus deprived the enemy of its produce and diverted these resources to the support of the attacker. Raids could also follow such an offensive logistic strategy but have much less effect because they could not deny all of the assets of the region to the enemy and could, as the English difficulties with their booty illustrated in the Poitiers campaign, turn little of the produce of the hostile territory to the use of the raiding power.

On the defensive raids could substitute for a defensive persisting logistic strategy of scorching the earth, as the Confederates had shown Union invaders. This resort to logistic raids had political as well as economic advantages, as the refusal of the Persian satraps to devastate their country illustrated. Of course, the two methods did not exclude one another, and an enemy attempting to subsist in a scorched country would find himself even more vulnerable to forays aimed at the remaining supplies; but raiders who reckoned on living on the country would have found themselves seriously handicapped by a previous application of a scorched-earth defensive, logistic, persisting strategy.

Consequently, raids had much in common with the combat and logistic persisting strategies of having the enemy's main army and territory as objectives. Still, exclusive reliance on raids, rather than as a means to implement some or all of a logistic element in a persisting strategy, differed markedly from a persisting approach. It meant victory accumulated through many small combat and logistic successes, which must consume more time than one which wins through decisive maneuvers or a few major battles. The added time and the resulting increase in cost meant that rarely did a stronger power depend primarily on raids unless it had such a low ratio of force to space as to render impractical aiming at the enemy's main force and territorial conquest. But raids did provide an offensive combat strategy for the weaker, which he could employ on the strategic offensive or defensive.

So raids provided a less effective method than a persisting logistic strategy of depriving the enemy of the benefits of his territory and proved virtually ineffectual in turning the opponent's land and resources to the advantage of the raiding power. Yet they did provide a way to accomplish this objective for a weaker party, and raids in pursuit of a logistic strategy had the same relevance for a stronger power as well; they could complement and markedly facilitate a persisting strategy by adding a logistic element to a primarily combat strategy.

Accordingly, raids functioned for the weaker adversary as a substitute for the more effective and less costly persisting strategies that were beyond their strength, and the stronger employed them not only to implement a logistic strategy but also to provide attrition in supplementing their main strategy and to furnish a form of distraction as well. As a major instrument for carrying out a logistic strategy, raids had equal applicability for the stronger and the weaker and on the offensive and the defensive.

Whereas a persisting defense had greater strength when resisting an offensive persisting strategy, it had less in opposing raiders, even when raiders were weaker than the defenders. The raiders derived some of their dominance from depriving the defenders of the utility of retreat, one of the two principal resources of the defense. Instead, to engage raiders with a combat persisting strategy, the defenders had to resort to the weaker pursuit, the raiders having appropriated the stronger retreat. Further, because of the raiders' broader choice of objective, they had better opportunities than a persisting force to concentrate against weakness and so overcome the power of the tactical defense, the defender's other main resource and one that he continued to retain.

So in employing their predominance on the offensive, raiders used the tactical offensive and depended on concentration against weakness, a concept they could readily apply because they had no settled objective. They obtained more of their strength from their capacity to use the defense's strategic ability to retreat and, typically, avoided involving themselves in combat so deeply that they frequently also enjoyed the tactical ability to retreat.

Yet raiders could only act on the strategic offensive: on the defensive, they would cease to be raiders if they pursued other raiders or attempted directly to halt a persisting invasion. So the raiders' methods did not vary between the offensive and the defensive. In either case they acted on the offensive, raiding their adversary's base area, the source of his strength and his place of greatest vulnerability. Even when they could not reach an opponent's source of support or found their own so threatened that they felt they must act to defend it, raiders continued on the offensive, directing their raids against a persisting invaders' army. In fact, if they did otherwise, they would deny their essence and cease to be raiders because without attack they could not execute a raid.

If two adversaries each employed a raiding strategy against the origin of the other's sustenance, the outcome would depend on their relative strengths and the comparative vulnerabilities of their base areas as well as political and other factors. If one of the opponents had an exposed source of maintenance and the other did not, then the vulnerable contestant could not pursue a raiding strategy against his protected opponent. The persisting defensive would offer the only alternative form of warfare against such raids. The Viking incursions over the seas into Western Europe illustrated this as did those of the Magyars, issuing from remote Hungary.

Raids traditionally had political and economic as well as military objectives. The Greeks adopted raids as a way to destroy crops to extract political concessions, the Vikings used them for economic ends, and the English in the Hundred Years' War for both reasons. Armies have utilized them with little else in mind than to live at the enemy's expense. Raids had a particular value in providing a means of defense to a contestant who was too weak in numbers or weapon systems even to employ the tactical advantage of the defense against frontal attacks in resisting his opponent's main force. So, ironically, too weak to use the tactical defensive, this defender adopted the tactical offensive in raids against a vastly stronger enemy, whom he lacked the power to resist in battle, to attain his strategically defensive aim. Of course, the weaker could do this because the offensively stronger raid had, as a part of its essence as a transitory operation, the ability to reckon on strategic retreat.

But a weaker contestant would never have reasonably availed himself of raids for defense were he strong enough to meet the enemy in battle and trust to the primacy of the defense in withstanding frontal attacks. Only if too weak to face the enemy in defensive battle would he have used raids, because, by not resisting the enemy directly, he exposed his country to hostile incursions, encroachment, and even partial or complete occupation. This choice very likely involved a longer and more costly war.

In summary, the stronger contestant resorted to raids for the following purposes:

> to gain economically;
> to extract political concessions;
> to deplete or destroy enemy supplies;
> to live at the enemy's expense; and
> to compel battle.

The weaker turned to raids for the following purposes:

> to gain economically;
> to extract political concessions;
> to deplete or destroy enemy supplies;
> to live at the enemy's expense; and
> to substitute for battle.

Guerrilla Warfare as an Application of Raiding Strategy

When the weaker employed raids as a means of combat strategy, he often utilized them to exert political pressure, attack enemy supplies, and live at his adversary's expense. The weaker could also combine the essentially logistic types of raids with a combat persisting strategy in which he counted on using the tactical power of the defense. When the inferior belligerent did not rely primarily on the tactical power of the defense and adopted some or all of the classes of raids, he engaged in guerrilla warfare, which constitutes another theme of this book. Such warfare could include either or both combat and logistic strategies, but, to meet the definition, it could not embrace a principal dependence on the tactical power of the defense in resisting the stronger's attacks. Instead, the weaker reckoned on the defense's power to retreat. And the raiders did not need to retreat by withdrawal or dispersal; they could discard their uniforms, blend in with the people around them, and become indistinguishable from civilians.

In action, the guerrilla warfare raiding strategy utilized the offensive principle of concentration against weakness. Exemplified in modern times in the Spanish resistance to Napoleon, guerrillas, markedly inferior in force to their opponents, avoided the hostile main armies and their strong detachments and directed their efforts toward small, isolated garrisons and weakly guarded supply depots and convoys. These they attacked and sought to overwhelm, and then they retreated promptly to avoid contact with enemy reinforcements. They also destroyed unprotected logistic installations, such as bridges. In an assault on a small garrison, they pursued an exclusively combat strategy. When they chose a wagon train and its guards, they had both a logistic and a combat objective. In wrecking an undefended bridge they had only a logistic purpose. Guerrillas had great opportunities for surprise, both strategically and tactically. A raiding strategy obviously facilitated surprise, as raiders had no settled line of operations nor obvious objective. Enemy troops on the march presented a vulnerable target for unexpected attacks.

But guerrilla warfare depended on the enemy's having a small ratio of force to space. If the hostile army had enough strength to deploy its troops in a continuous line, it virtually sealed its front against any but a major attack and protected its exposed rear against raiders. With adequate security to defend its line against attacks by the enemy's principal force, the continuous front offered no more vulnerability to the forays of marauders than to any attacks by a small force. An army strong enough to fortify and garrison most routes of communication in a zone of occupation also seriously handicapped a raiding strategy by limiting the guerrillas' routes of advance and evasion and exposed the guerrillas to the danger of being overtaken on one of their incursions.

Terrain played a vital role in the conduct of guerrilla warfare. Unmounted guerrillas facing mounted weapon systems still operated effectively in mountainous or wooded country because of its inhospitality to men on horseback. Because of the cover and concealment and the usually less well-developed roads in these areas, guerrillas often found such terrain a more advantageous place to operate against more powerful opponents whose greater numbers might inhibit the rapidity of their movements. The success of the Welsh against the English, like that of the Spanish against the French, exhibited the value of terrain to guerrillas.

Guerrillas required a base. Although they traditionally lived partially at their enemy's expense—because of their raids against supply depots and convoys— guerrillas still needed a place that provided them an assured source of supplies, such as Mina's secluded area and powder factory. Without such a base, the need for food, fuel, equipment, and ammunition would dominate their operations, place a severe constraint both on their movements and their choice of objectives for their raids, and could drive them from one raid to another in search of supplies until they had exhausted their physical and psychological resources. In addition, a base provided a place for rest and recuperation and a point to which they could retreat. Thus, the base had to be reasonably secure from enemy attack. The higher and more rugged part of Wales supplied such a location to the defenders against English invasions.

Guerrillas needed to conduct their operations among a people who were not overtly hostile to them. A populace antipathetic to the raiders increased the ratio of the stronger's force to space. Even Hannibal failed under such conditions. So, like many other military situations, guerrilla warfare had an important political requisite.

Guerrilla warfare had as its objective the defeat of the enemy, either physically or psychologically, through the accumulation of many small combat victories of attrition and logistical successes against his supplies. Victory could take the form of the enemy's abandoning his efforts entirely or his decreasing the amount of land he sought to dominate. This reduction would give the guerrillas complete control of a new area, enabling them, as it did the Spanish guerrillas, to expand their base and the region from which they could draw recruits for their forces. With these additional men they might have gained the necessary strength to overcome that which the enemy could have added by increasing his ratio of available numbers to the space of the contracted area.

Guerrillas thus pursued a distinctive kind of logistic strategy in that the domination of additional, politically sympathetic territory augmented their supplies and forces. But such success need not have diminished the enemy's combat capabilities proportionately, because, like the French in Morocco, he often drew, or could draw, the bulk of his revenues, supplies, and recruits from a base area beyond the contested region.

Hypothetically, this process of strengthening the guerrillas could have continued until the guerrillas had the more powerful force and could abandon raids in favor of an offensive persisting strategy, which would yield a quicker decision. Such an outcome would have depended on political support for the guerrillas in the areas abandoned by the enemy. For the same reason, the enemy could not have defended with guerrilla warfare against a persisting strategy because he would lack the political base necessary for the implementation of this strategy.

Defense and Offense against Guerrilla Warfare

Defenders have often relied on the combat strategy of aiming at the raiders by pitting pursuit against unimpeded retreat. Nevertheless, a combat strategy offered more promise than a logistic strategy because raiders lacked communications to attack and a scorched-earth defensive logistic strategy often was difficult to apply against raiders because of the ambiguity of their objective.

For thwarting raids with economic objectives, the Romans and Byzantines sought to capture the raiders by inhibiting their movement through the control of the focal points of communications and by trying to intercept their withdrawal. The frontier walls that the Romans built helped bar a retreat after the barbarians had crossed them on the inward part of their foray, and the mountain passes of Byzantine Anatolia facilitated this strategy. The fortification of the frontier and the communication hubs as well as such measures for a defense in depth as the Romans' walling their interior cities added the capital of strongholds and walls to the labor of soldiers and militia and increased the ratio of force to space, which further hampered raiders. The large resources employed to defend against raiders often small in numbers illustrated the dominance of raiding over a persisting defensive strategy.

Fortifying communication focal points and walling cities in a sense barricaded the whole country and constrained the raiders in a manner comparable to the way defensive works of the sixteenth, seventeenth, and eighteenth centuries in Holland and Belgium blocked the movement of armies. Of course, they did not restrict raiders to the degree to which these fortifications in this thickly settled area usually stopped invading armies and reduced their operations to a series of sieges, but the concept and the effect has obvious parallels.

Victims of Viking and Magyar incursions used similar strategies, except in France after the Vikings settled in Normandy. By doing this the Vikings moved their base area from overseas to a location immediately accessible to the heavy cavalry of the Franks. The Franks then attacked the Vikings' base area with counterraids and, because the Vikings had primarily an economic motivation, these raised the cost of further Viking raids above the benefits they produced. This halted any further aggressive activity by the Vikings and produced a political accommodation between the adversaries.

Because guerrilla warfare usually had a political motivation, it often presented to the defender a more serious problem, as political goals frequently provided a stronger inducement than economic ones. In addition, guerrillas usually functioned in areas politically sympathetic to them, whereas most economically inspired raids occurred in hostile regions. Instead of trying to combat the elusiveness of raiders by pursuing them as they retreated, the defenders followed the same model as those who resisted economically motivated raiders by attacking the guerrillas' requisites, a plan that offered the best means of dealing with the incursions of raiders. In Bactria and Sogdiana Alexander the Great relied primarily on inhibiting the mobility of guerrillas by controlling the focal points of communications and undermining their political support by his marriage to Roxana. These two measures sufficed to defeat the main guerrilla resistance in two years. Without this political component, the French failed in Spain.

Alexander's situation differed from that of the defenders against economic raiders in that he had taken the offensive in his initial invasion of Bactria and Sogdiana. Yet in occupying but not subduing the country nor in depriving the guerrillas of their base area, he then found himself on the defensive and suffering from the weakness of a persisting defense against a raiding strategy. Yet the defensive did give him control of communication hubs along valleys or river verges and the consequent ability to inhibit the movements of the guerrillas. His method differed little in concept from the British in South Africa, who found themselves operating on a largely level and treeless terrain. The British used their ample resources to erect 5,000 miles of barbed wire studded with 9,000 block-houses, which effectively inhibited the movement of the Boer raiders and rendered them vulnerable to pursuit.

Other examples of an invasion resisted by guerrilla warfare followed a different model, and, though initially lacking the defense's opportunity to facilitate pursuit by impeding the guerrillas' mobility, had the advantage of having far more affinity with a logistic strategy. And, against a defender using raids and its powerful element, retreat, an attacker could not expect a combat strategy, necessarily relying on pursuit, to have as much promise of success as a logistic strategy.

To apply a logistic strategy against raiders involved either the use of raids against their base area or the persistent occupation of territory. But to take the offensive against raiders required access to their base area, which medieval defenders against Viking and Magyar raiders lacked until the Vikings settled in Normandy. Here, because of the strength of the Vikings in combat and the power of the medieval defense, the French wisely used a raiding strategy to extract political concessions rather than attempting a persisting strategy.

The English conquest of Wales exemplified the strength of a persisting, inherently logistic strategy directed into the defender's base area, as well as the difficulties the stronger power could encounter in coping with this kind of opposition. Rather than fighting a few major battles, losing to the English, and then submitting, as much of the Persian Empire had done when Alexander invaded, the Welsh fought their invader in the same way as had the Bactrians and Sogdianians. But the English situation differed from Alexander's in that they used their persisting strategy on the offensive rather than the defensive.

Without the force needed to attempt the occupation of the country at one stroke, as had Alexander, the English went ahead slowly, following a persisting strategy and using a method that had many analogies with that of the guerrillas on the offensive. Whereas guerrillas on the offensive strove to win by accumulating many small combat and logistical accomplishments, the English, displaying of necessity the same patience, won by the gradual accretion of small bits of territory. In their deliberate and thorough procedures the English had much in common with the Romans' way of conquest.

But no other technique would likely have worked as well in view of the virulence of the opposition and the inhospitableness of the mountainous terrain to the heavy cavalry weapon system, one which played so prominent a part in the English forces. Nor did the English have any such ready political resource, like Alexander's marriage, for mitigating the zeal of their enemies.

A raiding, or counterraiding, strategy offered little promise to the English, not only because raids would have failed to overcome the political hostility of the Welsh but also because of their difficult execution. All of the unsubdued, mountainous country constituted the Welsh base area, and its rugged, often obstructed, terrain made raids difficult. Further, the English raiders would have trouble striking at the Welsh because their elusive opponent would drive off their flocks and leave few settled villages for the English to burn. Long before, the Persian King Darius I had faced a similar problem when he sought to make nomadic adversaries fight him. Finally, the exasperated king sent a messenger to them asking why they would not fight. The nomadic leader replied, my people have "neither towns nor cultivated lands, which might induce us through fear of their being taken or ravaged, to be in any hurry to fight you."[3]

So the English had to rely on the persisting strategy of impeding the mobility of their adversaries and increasing the ratio of force to space. They accomplished the latter by concentrating in a single, small area that they could command. They augmented their strength by building castles, and by placing them where they controlled the easiest route of communication, they used them to hinder the movements of the Welsh.

Usually they had limited their efforts to the level terrain where their cavalry could function, but in dominating the most fertile agricultural regions, they employed a logistic strategy against the Welsh by confining them to the less productive mountains. Sustained and apparently irreversible control of a valley gradually reconciled its inhabitants to English rule, as the castle and the strong forces the English placed there restrained Welsh raiders. This development, in many respects political and to a degree economic and cultural, enabled the English to extend their military control to another small part of Wales and then repeat the process. Further, the success of the English in one valley augmented their strength for their campaign in the next because they had added the revenues and resources of the conquered territory to those they already possessed. Also they reinforced their army by the addition of the indigenous Welsh spearmen and longbowmen, useful in battle as well as in the defense of castles.

This approach also exemplified the logistic element in a persisting strategy. With the implicit total political objective of a complete conquest of Wales pitted against the Welsh's strong commitment against such subjugation, acquisition of some territory could not compel a concession of political demands nor apparently demoralize the enemy and dim his hopes for victory enough to secure his quick subjection. But territory taken from the Welsh diminished their resources of military manpower and ultimately gave the English manpower as well as material resources. Thus, except in the initial conquest and in their defense against raids, the English followed an inherently logistic strategy in pitting their incremental persisting strategy against the Welsh, who could only combat the English with raids.

So the English attained their goal in spite of their apparent vulnerability to the guerrilla warfare of the Welsh, which did not differ in essence from the raids of the Vikings. Yet, unlike the Vikings, the Welsh suffered defeat because of the vulnerability of their base area to the English offensive persisting strategy. Thus the adversaries each assumed the offensive but with different strategies.

The Welsh suffered a severe handicap, despite their avoidance of the English combined-arms armies and their application of raids, because the raiders' ability to concentrate against weakness depended on their almost completely untrammeled choice of objective. Yet to resist the intrusion of the English into a small part of Wales immediately circumscribed the Welsh choice of object; unless they resorted to raids into already carefully defended England or the parts of Wales where the conquerors had already consolidated their rule, the Welsh had to direct their raids against the small area the enemy had recently occupied and fortified with one or more castles. In a country where researchers have identified 300 castle sites, one for every twenty-five square miles, the newly overrun region offered the most promise for raids unless the English, in moving too fast and attempting to engross more territory than they could readily dominate, had left vulnerable areas behind their advance. But in the newly lost territory, with their target obvious, the ratio of force to space very high, the tactical defense powerful in its castles, and the easy communication routes dominated by the English, the Welsh had lost many of the attributes that made raiding stronger than a persisting defense.

By using an offensive persisting strategy and concentrating in successive small areas, the English could defend because they had a high ratio of force to space in the newly conquered locality. Further, the whole strategy attacked two other guerrilla requisites, a base area and political support, because the English not only gradually encroached upon the Welsh base but also in the process won the acquiescence, if not the allegiance, of the inhabitants brought under their sway. Thus the offensive, by its concentration, overcame the disadvantages of defending over a broader, more thinly held front where the raiders had a wide choice of aims. Further, concentration decisively deprived the Welsh of the conquered region as a base, and the strong English presence furthered their political, economic, and cultural imperialism in a way that less control over more territory could not.

The defenders against Vikings, on the other hand, never had the certainty of the raiders' goals nor the ratio of force to space that the English enjoyed. Further, the invaders of Wales had the advantage of the strategic offensive into the hostile base area with each advance of their persisting logistic strategy weakening the Welsh and strengthening the English. By conducting their offensive so as to nullify the advantages of raiding, Hugh the Fat of Chester and the other border earls had success while the kings who advanced into Wales with big armies, attempting a combat strategy, simply demonstrated the primacy of retreat over pursuit. When the astute King Edward I used the great power of his monarchy to implement the logistic strategy long employed by the local earls, he quickly overwhelmed the remaining Welsh resistance.

To summarize the capabilities and vulnerabilities of raiders, raiders are stronger on the offense, when the ratio of force to space is low, against an adversary pursuing a persisting strategy and, when raiders oppose one another, neither has an advantage unless one can reach the adversary's base area and the other cannot. Thus, the characteristics of a raiding strategy deprive the defense of the predominance it enjoys between opponents using persisting strategies.

The dominance of raiders hinged, however, on certain conditions. When they had a base area secure from either raids or a persisting strategy, they used the defense's resource of retreat to avoid the enemy and took advantage of his low ratio of force to space and the ambiguity of the raiders' objective to concentrate against weakness. This compelled the defenders to bank on a combat strategy of pitting pursuit against retreat and attempting to protect themselves everywhere, both particularly difficult with a low ratio of force to space. With a high ratio of force to space, however, the raiders found their movements inhibited and the defenders in great numbers at many strong points.

When the raiders had a vulnerable base area, however, the defenders could assume the offensive either by counterraids, which would offset those of the raiders, or by a persisting invasion. With a sufficiently high ratio of force to space, the combat persisting strategy could count on defeating the raiders because they would find few vulnerable objectives and face a serious hazard from pursuit coupled with impediments to retreat. Further, with their base engulfed, the raiders would soon perish from lack of supplies and respite from movement.

If the invader of the raiders' base area lacked sufficient force to occupy it with an adequate ratio of force to space to execute such a campaign, he could accomplish the same goal by taking more time. In this, he relied on an incremental approach of creating a high ratio of force to space in the successive areas selected for conquest. In defending each such area, the high ratio of force to space would confront the raiders everywhere with strength and impede their retreat. Further, it usually removed ambiguity about the raiders' objective because the prospective loss of a portion of their base area normally induced the raiders to attack the area of recent conquest rather than continue raids into the invaders' own base area. Thus, after the English began their penetration of Wales, the Welsh concentrated on defending their base area and rarely raided the strongly defended English border areas.

Thus the strength of a raiding strategy depended in part on the vulnerability of the region used as a base. This requires dividing raiders into two classes, as shown in schematic 12.6, which exhibits the comparative strengths of raiding and persisting strategies, using A to mean dominance on the attack and D to stand for greater strength on the defense. The relations in schematic 12.6 assume

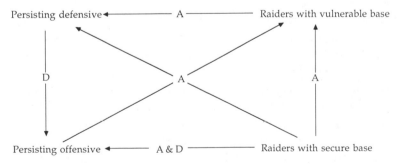

Schematic 12.6. Comparison of the Strengths of Raiding and Persisting Strategies

a ratio of force to space low enough for raiders to function, just as these relations also derive from the assumptions of the tactical primacy of the defensive and the ascendancy of strategic retreat over pursuit.

This comparison between persisting and raiding strategies has analogies in operations not explicitly related to guerrilla warfare, but that involve raiding or merely evasive opponents. The persisting strategy used in Wales had much in common with that introduced by Henry V in the latter stages of the Hundred Years' War when the English slowly and systematically conquered, garrisoned, and subdued territory in northern France. The English method also found parallels with Gustavus Adolphus's persisting strategy in north Germany. Confronted with an adversary who could move at will over much of Germany and who raided to deplete the resources of hostile princes and to subsist at the expense of his opponents, Gustavus used a method of conquering and fortifying the cities and transportation hubs that had much in common with that of the English in Wales. Faced with a problem that had analogies with that of the English, he used a comparable approach. Though it dealt with a different issue, a similar incremental persisting strategy characterized much warfare in the region of Belgium and Holland. The offensive persisting strategy of gradually occupying and fortifying the country provided a certain antidote to an elusive enemy that the compact, slow-deploying armies of an earlier day could not bring to battle.

Although possessing the greater financial and military resources of their wealthy and powerfully armed republic as well as the political strength of representing the sultan, the French deliberately employed in their conquest of Morocco in the twentieth century a persisting strategy identical to that the English had used in Wales. Slowly occupying successive lowland areas first, they pursued the same patient strategy and often exerted the same logistic pressures against their opponents in the mountains. They also followed a calculated program of reconciling the Moroccans to their rule by supplying free medical service and selling goods at subsidized prices. They recruited Moroccans into their army, and Moroccan troops under French command soon comprised the bulk of the forces used to extend French domination over other areas. With a unified, sustained campaign the French, at considerable financial cost, thus spread their control over the vast extent of Morocco in twenty-six years, compared with the two centuries the sporadic, partial, and occasionally misdirected English effort required to conquer the far smaller area of Wales.

The French did not use the English strategy as a conscious model, but they had discovered earlier in Algeria the difficulty of seeking a quick decision through a combat persisting strategy against their opponents. Algerian guerrillas had almost always eluded French forces sent to defeat them in battle. But the Algerians eventually succumbed to a logistic raiding strategy and its concomitant terror, though the French public found such a method repugnant. The slow procedure of using successive high ratios of force to space, coupled with political inducements, proved far more effective and had become the standard French approach by the time they undertook the conquest of Morocco.

The strategy of the French included the same logistic element found in that of the English when they diminished the enemy's strength by occupying his territory and then harnessed his human and material resources to the French military effort. It displayed the same patience and had much in common with the results of a successful guerrilla advance. As guerrillas added to their territory when they had compelled their opponent to contract his area of operation, so the French in Morocco and the English in Wales gradually augmented their strength and attenuated that of their opponents.

Guerrilla warfare necessarily constituted a protracted way of war and those opposing it also proceeded slowly. Just as guerrilla warfare was costly, because it took a long time and might expose some or all of the defending country to hostile occupation, so too was the technique of combatting it expensive, in terms of time and therefore of manpower as calculated by the number of men multiplied by the number of years they must campaign. Guerrillas would not use that method were they strong enough to face the invaders in battle, and those conquering them would not depend on such a necessarily patient strategy if they had the ratio of force to space to move more rapidly and therefore more economically.

Defense against guerrilla warfare involved using a persisting combat strategy based on directing military efforts at the requisites of guerrilla success. By blocking routes of communications and of retreat, the defenders inhibited the raiders, and, in the defense in depth, by adding the capital of fortifications to their mobile forces defenders restrained raiders by increasing the ratio of force to space. Thus they also contracted the hostile base area and usually, as had the Romans, facilitated the accomplishment of the political reconciliation of each group of the vanquished.

On the offensive, rather than relying primarily on the combat strategy of pitting pursuit against retreat, the opponents of guerrillas successfully employed an explicitly combat but implicitly logistic persisting strategy of conquering the territory from which the guerrillas drew their supplies. In the examples of the English in Wales and the French in Morocco, this conquest of the supply region did not differ from the political objective of the war. The vulnerability of the guerrillas' base area did, of course, make this strategy possible and would often make this the best defense against any sort of raiders. A raiding strategy against the raiders' vulnerable base area did also have promise, however, depending, of course, on, among other factors, the strength of the guerrillas' motivation.

Both attack and defense against guerrillas typically have had a political component. Each contestant sought to retain his political strength while at the same time subverting his opponent's. Guerrillas are particularly dependent on popular support, against which the French in Morocco, for example, explicitly directed a campaign to win the allegiance of the public to France and the sultan whom the French controlled.

Schematic 12.7 summarizes the alternatives for combatting a raiding strategy or guerrilla warfare.

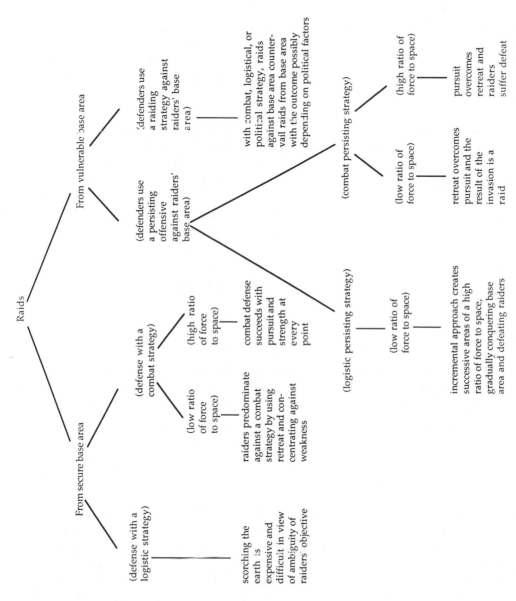

Schematic 12.7. Summary of Alternatives for Combatting a Raiding Strategy or Guerrilla Warfare

The offensive routine of gradual conquest of the base area through consecutive concentrations, fortification, and pacification did have an essentially political alternative, not shown in the diagram, which could produce quicker results. The Turks subdued the Anatolian provinces of the Byzantine Empire by raids that created such dread that they cowed the population in much of this large area in a matter of only five years. Terror supplied the political ingredient in the plan, but the Turks killed so many people and destroyed so much property that one may fairly say that they coupled with their political program a military logistic strategy aimed at human as well as physical resources. This strategy did, however, deprive their conquest of much of its immediate economic value. Later, when he had overrun the Khwarizmian Empire, Jenghiz Khan used much the same logistic strategy, except that, in killing the population of large cities, he aimed his logistic strategy at the human resources, accomplishing at the same time his political purpose of frightening into submission the inhabitants of the empire. Marshal Bugeaud had used this approach in Algeria and found that it worked, though not very quickly on the scale he applied it. On the other hand, the terror component of the strategic bombing of Germany in the Second World War failed to have a sufficient political effect to hasten the end of the war.

On at least two occasions the Romans demonstrated an even more extreme method of dealing with opponents. When they defeated Carthage, they removed the inhabitants, demolished the city, and plowed the ground with salt. In dealing with the rebellious Nasamones, the Emperor Domitian killed them all, having "forbidden the Nasamones to exist."

Summary of Alternatives Confronting Commanders

Land warfare in the Western world contrasted an almost cyclical pattern in its tactical development, one affected importantly but not exclusively by technological factors, with a stability in logistical methods until the Industrial Revolution and its associated changes in the nineteenth and twentieth centuries altered logistics profoundly. Strategy displayed significant constants while undergoing variations quite harmonious with the elements important in ancient times.

Several methods of organizing and interpreting 2,500 years war offer themselves. For example, the principles of war introduced into the British and U. S. armies in the 1920s could provide a means of supplying continuity and uniformity for explaining these eras of warfare and could lend themselves to teaching soldiers of the future what to avoid and what to do. Among many other different approaches, geography can account for much that has happened. For instance, instead of saying that the terrain of Mesopotamia permitted the Parthians to fight mounted, one could say that an army that did not fight mounted in such terrain would almost necessarily lose, if not to a combat strategy, certainly to a logistic strategy. Human factors, including the characteristics of successful commanders, could provide an entirely different and at least as powerful approach as any other.

The themes used in this book to explain land warfare since about 500 B.C. do not, like the principles of war, lend themselves readily to providing enduring generalizations applicable to the conduct of military operations and rules for generals. Nevertheless, to extract from this history some consistency is worthwhile, even though only modest success can possibly reward the effort and the most that one could induce would be methods by which good commanders exploited tendencies and probabilities whose prominence and reliability this book has already much overstated by proposing them as virtual laws of warfare. Four of these assumed a prominent place as constants over the whole period treated. Two of these familiar ideas are the primacy of the tactical defensive, qualified by the superiority of some weapon systems over others. Another is the supremacy of retreat over pursuit, which contributed to giving preponderance to the strategic defensive when adversaries used persisting strategies and to raiders on the offensive against a persisting defense. Finally, the ratio of force to space conditioned all strategic situations. In facing these contraints, soldiers learned how to overcome the impediments they presented and how to turn them to their advantage. Since this approach has underlain the presentation of the subject, it is appropriate to conclude with a summary of the alternatives facing commanders and how they could match their strategy to the obstacles and opportunities presented by the nature of warfare as revealed by these factors.

Choice of Strategic Objective

Military strategy, even as narrowly defined in this book, must begin with the objectives of military operations. These did not have to aim at the enemy army to accomplish the mission. The strategy of raids to extort political concessions, used by the English in the Hundred Years' War, demonstrated this as did the economically motivated raids used by the Magyars, Vikings, and others. Many other, less easily classified motives doubtless also caused military actions in pursuit of not-strictly military objectives. Those seeking nonmilitary goals have tended to employ a raiding strategy, not only because of its offensive primacy but because raiders usually avoided enemy armed forces, whereas a persisting strategy normally involved military strategy because of the need to meet the enemy armed forces.

Thus strategy that used military means began with a dichotomy illustrated in schematic 12.8.

Military strategy strove to gain political or other nonmilitary objectives by warlike means directed at the enemy armed forces. But one could apply armed force directly to attain nonmilitary goals, as the schematic displays. The principle of winning with the least effort usually governed this selection, just as it did in the subsequent choices in military strategy where political and other nonmilitary factors rarely lacked relevance.

But a strategy in pursuit of nonmilitary results, like that of raids for booty, was not primarily military, for military strategy, as defined here, had to aim at

Schematic 12.8. Choice between Military Strategy and Military Means
to Attain Nonmilitary Results

the enemy army. Nevertheless, in dealing with military strategy only, the following summary also treats many of the problems of executing and defending against warlike actions for nonmilitary purposes.

The Choice between Combat and Logistic Strategy

To attack the enemy army, the commander had two alternatives, combat or logistic strategy, and the ablest commanders usually decided by following what they believed would be the path of least resistance, thus trying to win with minimum effort. Saladin, for example, used a logistic strategy of scorching the earth to thwart the advance against Jerusalem of King Richard's Crusaders, adopting the strategy of hunger rather than steel as the least costly and most efficacious alternative against Richard, a shrewd warrior commanding a formidable host. The Germans tried to defeat the Russians with a logistic strategy in 1942 but did not have the combat capability to take and hold the Russian oil regions. But this failure tends to support their choice, for if the Germans lacked the power to take and hold significant territory, they also did not have the ability to destroy the Russian armies in the pursuit of a combat strategy.

In adhering to the principle of least effort in making military decisions, a commander customarily chose that of maximizing his chances for winning because using the least effort created the greatest difference between the power needed for success and that available. This idea had close kinship to a traditional principle of war, economy of force. The concept of utilizing the minimum of resources included not just avoiding waste but employing the maximum in what the commander believed to be the most important action. Economy of force implied no hostility to an ample margin, for, as Xenophon wrote, "a surplus of victory never caused any conqueror one pang of remorse."

The past abounds with examples of logistic strategy, and though Caesar said he favored hunger over steel, commanders did not necessarily find it easier to win with a logistic strategy, even if there existed a way of effectively attacking the enemy's means of supporting his army.

Thus a second dichotomy presents itself (schematic 12.9). The principle of least effort generally governed a military choice between these two alternative means of operating against the enemy armed forces.

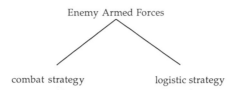

Schematic 12.9. Choice between the Two Most Basic Means
of Attacking the Enemy Armed Forces

Implementing a Logistic Strategy by a Persisting or Raiding Strategy

In carrying out a logistic strategy the attacker could employ either a persisting or a raiding strategy. A persisting strategy normally involved the occupation of logistically valuable territory. Although often this came as the significant by-product of a combat strategy, a combatant could, as the Germans did in 1942 when they tried to capture the Russian oil fields, incline his operations toward a territory of logistical importance rather than, say, that of political or diplomatic consequence. Such a persisting strategy habitually entailed a major application of combat strategy to attain it but presumably required less effort than aiming at the enemy armed forces directly through an exclusive reliance on combat strategy. For the defender, resistance against such a persisting logistic strategy rarely differed from a defense against a purely combat strategy.

On the level of addressing a logistic strategy to an individual army, Wallenstein and Gustavus, in their protracted stay at Nuremberg, showed the power of controlling the foraging areas adjacent to the hostile force. Since neither would retreat, both lost a large number of horses to hunger and many men to desertion. The result, in fact, was the equivalent of a battle, with hunger rather than steel the weapon of choice.

For attacking with a logistic strategy, raiding offered a valuable alternative to the occupation of territory. The success of a Persian cavalry raid against a supply convoy in compelling the Greeks to retire during the Plataea campaign, like the similar achievements of the Austrians on two occasions against the Prussians, exhibits the power of such a logistic raiding strategy as do many instances of the use of aircraft. The Union raids against Confederate railroads and industrial plants in the last year of the Civil War demonstrated a strategy leveled against the resources to support all of the hostile armies, as did the French strategic bombing of the Briey Basin in World War I and most of the strategic bombing in World War II.

Schematic 12.10 summarizes this section.

Combat Defense against a Raiding Strategy

Defenders could use either a combat or a logistic strategy against a raiding strategy. In coupling combat and persisting strategies to resist raiders, the defender combined pursuit with the blocking of routes of communications and

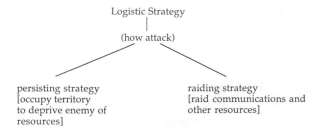

Schematic 12.10. Alternatives in the Employment of a Logistic Strategy
against Enemy Armed Forces

retreat. The Romans fortified the country in depth to inhibit the movement of raiders and counted on their frontier defenses and walls to hinder the raiders' retreat. These impediments often gave pursuit an advantage over withdrawal and permitted the defenders to overtake and defeat the raiders. The Byzantines used the same method, and Gustavus Adolphus, by his offensive persisting strategy in northern Germany, in which he conquered and fortified the towns, helped to close this territory to marauding hostile forces that would have had among their objectives the supplying of their armies while denying to the Swedish king the resources consumed or destroyed.

Not only fortified cities but castles and embattled villages and estates have played a major role in applying a persisting strategy against raids. In this aspect of the resistance a militia gave the defender a powerful means of economizing force. Used in lieu of professionals to man garrisons, militia soldiers could continue their civilian occupations except when faced with an actual threat, thus economizing on more expensive professionals. Both fortifications and militia raised the ratio of force to space, thus eliminating one of the essential conditions for the successful execution of a raiding strategy.

To protect their empire against barbarian raiders, the Romans even paid their professionals by giving them land in threatened areas and allocating to them no other duties than the safekeeping of the region where they lived. Thus the Romans, in a sense, converted their professionals into a species of militia, reversing the usual direction of the evolution of soldiery in ancient times. Militia could perform particularly effectively because they only needed to undertake the simpler task of the defense and often did so with the aid of fortifications. So these inexpensive fighters expanded the number of defenders while reducing their cost. And, for the Romans, richer than the barbarian raiders, the building of walls and forts, which also constituted a saving by substituting capital for labor, and the using of militia to man the battlements provided both an economy and a useful military complement because of the effectiveness of militia serving with the aid of these permanent defenses.

To defend with a raiding strategy involved counterraids, which were potentially powerful if the raiders had an accessible base area. In World War II air raids in retaliation for similar raids characterized both the mutual attacks of the Germans and the British and the German use of unmanned jet planes and rockets against the United Kingdom toward the end of the war. The failure of all these efforts as deterrents suggests these ideas on the utility of counterraids: they may motivate more raids by each side for revenge; the threat, as, for example, in World War II in which all antagonists were ready to use poison gas but none employed it, may have more effect than the execution; and much of this question lies in the affective, or behavioral, domain of warfare and also belongs to the political sphere.

Schematic 12.11 illustrates this section.

Schematic 12.11. Alternatives for a Combat Defense against a Logistic Raiding Strategy

Logistic Defense against a Raiding Strategy

Counterraids directed at the attacker's logistic resources for carrying out his raids constituted a means of executing a logistic raiding strategy to defend against the same strategy. Some of the British and American bombing of German aircraft factories in World War II included this as an objective, and their attacks against German facilities for preparing the rockets used against the United Kingdom had as their only purpose the crippling of these weapons by means of logistic raids by airplanes.

Defenders may employ a persisting logistic strategy by scorching the earth to destroy the resources upon which the raider must depend. For example, the French used this against English raiders in the Hundred Years' War. But such a strategy had a special difficulty when used against raiders. Since raiders frequently had unknown objectives and often many choices as to their route, scorching the proper piece of earth often presented an insuperable obstacle even if the defenders knew their objective. The alternative, destroying resources on all possible routes, would likely make the defense cost more than the damage the raiders would inflict. Against aircraft raiders, defenders had no such defense, nor would such a persisting logistic strategy avail against modern raiders with motor vehicles who would not rely on the country for supplies, though the destruction of bridges, for example, would have an effect.

Schematic 12.12 shows the foregoing alternatives.

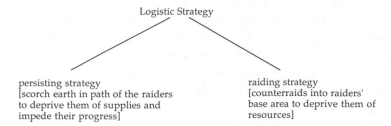

persisting strategy
[scorch earth in path of the raiders
to deprive them of supplies and
impede their progress]

raiding strategy
[counterraids into raiders'
base area to deprive them of
resources]

Schematic 12.12. Alternative Means of Using a Logistic Strategy to Defend
against a Logistic Raiding Strategy

Alternatives in Pursuit of a Combat Strategy

If commanders adopted a combat instead of a logistic strategy for the offensive, they have sought first to use the tactical means of opposing a superior weapon system to an inferior. The Turks used their horse archers against the Byzantine and Crusader heavy cavalry, and, employing tactics that appeared to derive from timidity, they avoided the charges of the heavy cavalry and won with the least effort. The Byzantines, consistent in pursuing their aims with a minimum of cost and risk of failure, accepted battle gladly when they could pit bowmen against heavy infantry, or heavy infantry and dismounted cavalry against the charge of barbarian heavy cavalry. Against the more powerful Western European cavalry from France they found that the strategic means of a logistic strategy required less effort and incurred less risk than the tactical means of combat.

When a commander had a weapon system with higher mobility, he had a simple task, as when Greek peltasts with javelins defeated Greek heavy infantry; the mounted Parthians easily forced battle on Roman heavy infantry in level, unobstructed terrain; or Italian bombers caught Ethiopian riflemen in 1935. Yet, with weapon systems whose predominance could only display itself on the defensive, this method proved more difficult to apply. At the Battle of Crécy, for example, the dismounted English cavalry had to count on the medieval knight's propensity for the impetuous charge. In World War II battles in Africa, the Germans won such victories by pitting antitank weapons and tanks situated defensively against assaults by British tanks.

But only occasionally did commanders have the opportunity for pitting a stronger weapon system against an inferior. Often the contestants had similar homogeneous armies. The more usual situation found heterogeneous armies composed of more than one weapon system in which tactics involved an effort to exploit a flaw in the mutual support between the weapon systems in the opposing army. Sixteenth- and seventeenth-century warfare abounded with battles in which the cavalry sought to ride down the arquebusiers or use their pistols against unaided pikemen, while the arquebusiers tried to fire on the cavalry or pikemen from positions protected by the terrain or their own pikemen. World

War II teemed with cases of tanks caught in the open by cannon or rocket-armed aircraft and tanks overwhelming infantry inadequately provided with antitank weapons.

But, important though some cases have been, only infrequently have any of these instances of the use of the superior weapon system against the inferior had a major effect on a battle, much less a campaign. In modern times, with the declining possibilities of significant tactical success, this key tactical variable rarely made an important difference. In 1973, for example, when the Egyptian infantry used surprise to take the east bank of the Suez Canal, of high political import for Israel as well as Egypt, the Egyptians could count on Israeli tanks and aircraft promptly attacking the infantry, even though the Egyptian army had elaborately equipped their men with antitank and antiaircraft guns and missiles. As a result of these weak, improvised assaults, the Israelis lost about 250 tanks but suffered no loss of strategic position. When, a few days later, Egyptian tanks assailed Israeli tank forces deployed defensively and supported by aircraft, the defenders easily repulsed the assault of the Egyptians, which placed their tanks at a serious disadvantage without giving them the aid of concentration of force. But once more the action had only a tactical result, the loss of 250 tanks, which again did not seriously alter the balance of forces nor cause any change in the strategic situation.

Nevertheless, combats between heterogeneous armies had greater complexity and opportunities for tactical success and defeat than warfare with essentially homogeneous armies of rifle-armed infantry, which characterized the period from the middle of the nineteenth century until almost the end of World War I. The tactical conditions of those years have had few parallels, one comparable time being the early warfare of the Greeks when heavy infantry dominated the battlefield. With these homogeneous armies, except in those medieval battles in which cavalry predominated and did not dismount, the tactical defensive usually had primacy because in combat between the same weapon systems the defensive had the advantage of being able to resist frontal attacks. Only after the French had developed the column, and the method of quickly deploying it, did the offensive have a preponderance between similar homogeneous armies, and then only until their opponents adopted the same tactical methods. Even then the tactical defensive retained its dominance in resisting frontal attacks, and in strategy retreat continued its primacy over pursuit. The new system of tactical deployment, introduced by the French and universally adopted in the nineteenth century, may have added slightly to the tactical strength of the offensive by conferring on infantry the ability to turn or envelop strong positions and to improve the chances of a frontal attack by rapid concentration of infantry on the battlefield.

The illustration in schematic 12.13 summarizes the points of this section. The choice between these possibilities hinged on the availability of the better alternative, a superior weapon system, which, in turn, depended on the composition of the armies and, more remotely, on such factors as the state of military technology and the terrain upon which the armies customarily fought.

Schematic 12.13. The Two Fundamental Offensive Possibilities in Combat Strategy

The Persisting and Raiding Alternatives for an Offensive Combat Strategy

In seeking to use a combat strategy to overcome the tactical strength of the defense, attackers used either a persisting or raiding strategy. In choosing between a persisting and raiding strategy a commander would not necessarily find the offensively predominant raids preferable to a persisting offensive. Though stronger on the offensive, raids often could not produce a decisive outcome quickly and, if this protracted the war, it could result in a higher cost. Yet, although winning with the least effort ordinarily governed the choice between the two strategies, the attacker had to resort to a raiding strategy when he lacked an adequate ratio of force to space to control the country because of its size and/or political opposition. In employing raids, the attacker necessarily followed the principle of aiming at weakness, for a raid has as part of its essence avoiding hostile strength and striking weak forces and vulnerable objectives.

For example, supply convoys often presented both a weak and a worthwhile objective. So a strategy of raids against them normally embraced a logistic as well as a combat element. This strategy would earn its victory though the attrition of the many small successes amassed in many raids. Yet, because the killing of civilians and the destruction of their property in a hostile country could frequently hurt the enemy as much as comparable damage to military resources, this strategy of winning through the accumulation of the results of many raids could include the political strategy of extracting concessions.

Schematic 12.14 shows the choices open to a commander pursuing a combat strategy. The executant of the persisting strategy has usually sought to destroy the enemy army, a more direct approach, if only by its psychological impact, to

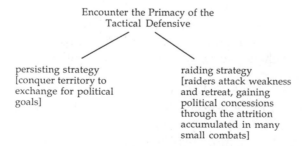

Schematic 12.14. Alternatives in Pursuing an Offensive Combat Strategy

winning the war or occupying much territory in a brief time. But in the representative case wise commanders using a persisting strategy counted only on acquiring territory. Such crippling victories of annihilation as the Prussians gained at the outset of their 1870–71 war with the French have rarely occurred in the absence of supremacy in weapon systems or doctrine such as those enjoyed, for instance, by Alexander over Darius, Hannibal over the Romans, the Parthians over the Romans, Napoleon over his adversaries early in his career, and the Germans over their opponents in 1940.

Even with the realistic objective of only taking enemy territory, the attacker using a combat persisting strategy has traditionally faced a daunting task. Because of the tactical power of the defense to resist frontal attacks, the often greater difficulty the invader had in supplying his army, and the defender's strategic ability to avoid battle by retreat, most military history and thought have dwelt on the tactical and strategic means of conducting a combat, persisting offensive. The defender had the choice of using a combat or logistic strategy, one either of a persisting invasion or of raiding, and often he blended some or all of these.

Varieties of Defense against a Combat Persisting Strategy

Scorching the earth could offer a powerful resistance to implementing a persisting logistic strategy, as when Vercingetorix burned barns to keep their contents from Caesar's army or when the French destroyed supplies in the path of the army of Emperor Charles V to resist an invasion of southern France. A raiding defensive logistic strategy could take the same form applied on the offensive by raiding an enemy's supplies, as the Austrians did against the Prussians.

Guerrilla warfare, another type of raiding strategy, had its value when the defender had no capability for opposing the invader, even against frontal attacks, and when he found the resources of retreat inadequate unless he dispersed his army. A guerrilla resistance, which implies that the enemy controls much of the defender's country, was expensive and—because of its tedious, incremental approach of attrition through raids—long and exhausting. So in spite of the strategic dominance of raids, guerrilla warfare required much political strength.

As a means of defense—relying on strategic retreat instead of the tactical defensive—guerrilla warfare used the tactical offensive to implement the strategic defensive. Employing raids to concentrate against weak combat or logistic objectives and availing themselves of the strategic and tactical surprise made possible by the ambiguity of a raid's objectives, guerrillas systematically concentrated against weakness. The guerrillas required a low ratio of force to space, but, as their achievements against the French in Spain demonstrated, they could succeed in spite of a ratio high enough to permit strategically decisive operations on the Napoleonic model.

Guerrilla warfare required either weapon systems with the same mobility as those of the invader or terrain that reduced the better mobility of the adversaries, as the obstructed countryside shielded the Irish from the mounted English men at arms and the mountains protected the Moroccans from the

French in their tanks and motor trucks. Finally, guerrillas must control some country to have a base for supply and for recuperation. With all of these requisites and a political determination greater than that of their opponent, guerrillas could win a costly victory through the attrition inflicted by the aggregation of many small logistic and combat successes.

Schematic 12.15 summarizes the foregoing alternatives. The raiding strategy of guerrilla warfare had an applicability for defense against a logistic strategy just as it did against a combat strategy. But defenders usually found that a persisting combat strategy gave victory with the least effort, avoiding the protracted, costly resistance of guerrilla warfare or the lesser sacrifices of a persisting logistic strategy. The Scots, for example, avoided combat and scorched their earth only after becoming discouraged at their chances of prevailing over the English in battle.

Schematic 12.15. Defender's Alternatives for Resisting a Combat Persisting Strategy

The Combat Persisting Defense

To implement a persisting combat strategy, a defender had to have only enough strength to face the invader in frontal combat in a position he chose. Thus, he could present his front to the enemy or retreat, either when he feared the consequences of a battle or when he could not fight in a sufficiently favorable situation. His adoption of the combat persisting strategy utilized the defender's strong tactical and strategic alternatives, as schematic 12.16 summarizes. Without ample political strength, a defender must emulate Darius III and risk all on battle rather than withdraw. With sufficient political power, the defender could imitate

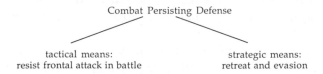

Schematic 12.16. Defender's Combat Persisting Alternatives against the Same Kind of Attack

either the Romans under Fabius combatting Hannibal or the Russian tsar resisting Napoleon in 1812.

But generally the defender had adequate forces to avoid the disadvantages of withdrawing too far. He often banked on a combination of the power of the tactical defense in frontal combat and the ability to avoid battle through exercising the supremacy of retreat over pursuit. Against such a defense, even if he had enough power to utilize a combat persisting strategy, the attacker habitually faced obstacles as intimidating as those encountered in combating the raiding strategy of guerrilla warfare.

The Offensive against a Guerrilla Defense

In using a persisting strategy against a guerrilla defense, the attacker routinely intermingled combat and logistic strategies just as did his adversary. A persisting strategy of controlling the country, especially its communication routes, inhibited the raiders' mobility, thus giving pursuit a chance of overmatching retreat. Similarly, in matching the guerrillas' strategy of attrition with a comparable incremental persisting strategy of gradually dominating the country by taking one piece at a time, the attacker deprived the guerrillas of a low ratio of force to space. As the attacker, using a persisting advance, invaded, fortified, and controlled the guerrillas' essential base area, the fundamental logistic element in the persisting strategy took away another of the guerrillas' requirements for success. The Romans followed this method in Britain as did the English in Wales. This approach also undermined the guerrillas' political as well as logistic support.

As Alexander demonstrated, if the offensive embodied a political component, it could deprive the guerrillas of their essential political support. Alexander, after trying terror without success, effectively employed this approach of placating the enemy. If the attacker had tried counterraids, either as a substitute for or a supplement to a persisting strategy, he could have, implicitly at least, decided against Alexander's political conciliation model because of the hostility such raids could arouse. Marshal Bugeaud applied a raiding strategy in Algeria so ruthlessly that it incorporated a political program of terror that intimidated the opposition. Clearly, since the two political approaches tended to exclude one another, the mixing of a persisting and a raiding strategy must have required much political discernment to succeed.

Schematic 12.17 illustrates the foregoing. This schematic, which exhibits the strategic ingredients of an offensive against guerrillas, overrefines the distinctions as actually practiced. The combat and logistic elements are ordinarily combined, and the difference between persisting and raiding provide the basic military distinction. The political component of the campaign often dictates the military strategy employed and, of course, the guerrillas must have an accessible base area.

Combat and Persisting Attack and Defense

In spite of defenders customarily offering battle only when they had an almost impregnable position, many wise, invading commanders accepted battle

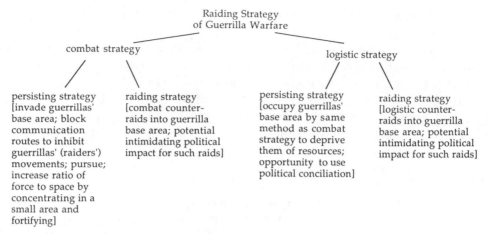

Schematic 12.17. Alternatives for Attacking against a Guerrilla Resistance

under such conditions, even without any advantage in doctrine or weapon system over their opponent or using offensive troops not available to their enemy. Frederick the Great often accepted battle on his adversary's terms, but not always victoriously, though he did rightly count on his oblique approach and well-drilled infantry to give him an approximation of offensive troops and a means to concentrate against weakness. The duke of Marlborough, on the other hand, in his four winning battles over the French, lacked any dominance in numbers, weapon systems, or organization. The duke won offensive battles, fought under circumstances preferred by the hostile commander, because of his skill and mastery of the application of the concept of concentration against weakness and his grasp of the importance of distraction in creating a weak point. His battles exemplify the role of these enduring themes as practiced in tactics.

Yet only one of Marlborough's victories yielded major strategic gains. In recent times strategy, rather than tactics, has offered the shorter road to a winning combat persisting strategy against an opponent employing the same strategy and constitutes the representative case of European warfare in the last two centuries. But in earlier times following a persisting combat strategy presented almost insuperable obstacles because the weaker army could easily elude the stronger, and the invader rarely had enough force to control a country hostile to his cause. Strongholds and fortified cities generally further complicated the attacker's task.

While hoping for a battle on favorable terms, which would result in a famous victory that might lead to a quick attainment of the aims of the war, commanders knew that they could not count on it. They sought to coerce the enemy into fighting an offensive battle under unfavorable conditions through sieges, which might compel the relieving army to assume the tactical offensive, by trapping an adversary against an obstacle, or by inducing him to fight by devastating his country.

If the invader had the money and patience, he could still follow a persisting strategy, even with a ratio of force to space too low to occupy a large part of the country immediately. He could take cities one by one and so garrison and fortify the conquered country as to deny the area to the defender's army as a zone in which it could maneuver. If pursued over a wide area, this gradual and necessarily slow persisting strategy nevertheless required much force, in the form of strongholds as well as garrisons, to hold the country, unless the invader could secure substantial political support. England's successful use of this strategy in the latter years of the Hundred Years' War ultimately foundered on the large forces required to hold even a small part of France when the English could not consistently muster many adherents to their cause.

With a ratio of force to space adequate to control the country without elaborate garrisoning, which existed in many parts of Europe in the eighteenth century, armies could more readily adhere to a persisting strategy by advancing into and dominating the area upon which the defending army depended for its supplies and so forcing its retreat.

And, of course, such success for a persisting strategy could also threaten the defending power's logistic resources or political position and compel it to assume the offensive and attack the invading army in a strong defensive position. Frederick the Great, faced with the loss of Saxony and consequently nearly a third of the revenues with which he supported the war, reacted thus when he attacked Daun at Torgau. Frederick's response and the significance of defeat he would have suffered had Daun won the battle also clearly illustrates the logistic element implicit in a combat persisting strategy.

The change in warfare in the era of the French Revolution and Napoleon made a combat persisting strategy relatively easy. Dispersed armies able to maneuver tactically in columns and deploy quickly into lines for combat readily threatened many points in a theater of war and forced their opponent either to fight or make a precipitate retreat out of the zone of operations.

This transformation made a combat persisting strategy the shortest route to victory and the characteristic strategy in virtually all European warfare to this day. The ability to compel the enemy to fight or conduct a disastrous retreat made possible the concentration in time of simultaneous advances on exterior lines and the use of interior lines of operations to concentrate in space strong forces for the defense or offense. The dispersal, which, when combined with quick concentration, enabled an army to prevent another from passing it without a battle, made the strategic turning movement possible. Though in the absence of strategically offensive troops, the turning movement was difficult to execute against an even moderately attentive enemy, it nevertheless offered another means to force on the enemy the disadvantage of assuming the tactical offensive as he fought to recover contact with his base area.

Yet besides giving strategy another method of compelling an adversary to fight in unfavorable circumstances (in addition to entrapment against a barrier, the siege, and devastation of territory), the turning movement promised more than the mere tactical result of the attrition of a losing battle, for it could snare and annihilate an entire army. It achieved this twice in the Franco-Prussian War, made possible by incredible and uncharacteristic French incompetence, and again at the outset of World War II when the German Panzer and motorized corps exploited their strategically offensive mobility to trap their opponents against the coast. Of course, one may see in the turning movement merely an enlarged instance of the old method of holding an adversary against an obstacle.

Schematic 12.18 recapitulates these possibilities and completes the array of choices facing commanders when they analyze military operations.

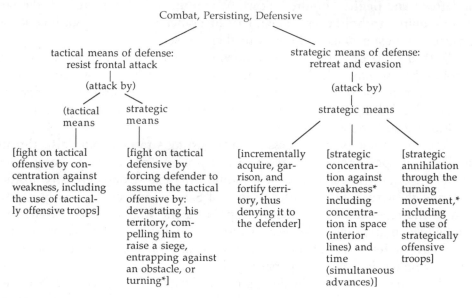

*Requires a strategically decisive ratio of force to space

Schematic 12.18. Alternatives Available When Attacker and Defender Both Employ a Combat Persisting Strategy

The idea of winning with the least effort guided the best commanders in choosing among alternatives and in combining more than one method. Schematic 12.19, essentially a consolidation of the preceding ones, summarizes many of the fundamental military ideas exhibited over more than 2,000 years of warfare in the Western world.

Continuity and Change

Schematic 12.19 summarizes the means of coping with the factors that have conditioned strategy for 2,500 years in the West. So, to simplify, one may say that it is possible to deduce the problems and opportunities of strategy from only three of the major constants revealed in this span of warfare. Thus the dominance of retreat and the usual superiority of the tactical defensive have given the defense primacy when both combatants use a persisting strategy, a low ratio of force to space favoring the use of retreat and a high ratio fostering reliance on the tactical defensive. Two of these same factors have favored the use of a raiding strategy that could exploit retreat when hostile forces had a low ratio of force to space and used the ambiguity of the raiders' objective to have more abundant opportunities for concentrating against weakness.

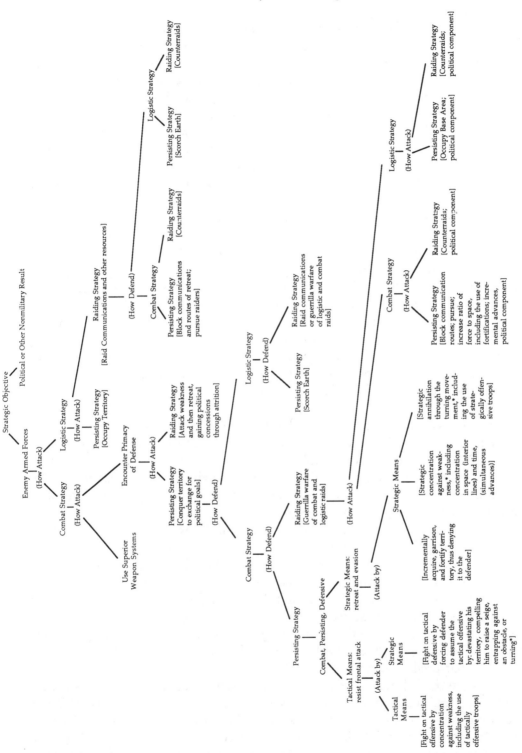

Schematic 12.19. Strategic Alternatives: A Summary

*Requires a strategically decisive ratio of force to space

The relative inferiority of the persisting and the power of the raiding of-fensive against a persisting defense goes far to account for the popularity of raids over such a long span of warfare. Yet the importance of raids to harm the enemy in any but small increments or to conquer any of its territory accounted for a continuing extensive reliance on a persisting strategy. In choosing between these two strategies commanders usually aimed at striking at their adversary's weak-ness. In fact, if schematic 12.19 has a theme, the word weakness concisely summarizes it. The army on the offensive, following the path of least resistance, tactically sought the enemy's weakness by employing the superior weapon sys-tem, aiming at the enemy's flank or rear, or bringing greater numbers against lesser. Even in compelling an adversary to fight to protect his crops, raise a siege, or recover his communications, the attacking army would have succeeded in forcing the defender to use the tactically weaker form, the offensive.

Often an attacker used the strategic resources of distraction or the turning movement, among other methods, to push an opponent back when a territorial gain would satisfy the goal of a campaign—though some have seen this as an unmanly sort of war. But using the path of least resistance avoided the enemy altogether and marred the theme of weakness, unless one defines keeping away from the enemy army as striking at weakness. Of course, the means—threatening the hostile army's rear or menacing a vulnerable province, for example—did aim at weakness. And in choosing a strategic rather than a tactical means to victory, the wise commander had perceived that his adversary had greater tactical than strategic strength.

Weakness also provided the theme for the defender who wished to shun it when he attempted to receive attacks in front, had the aid of fortifications, or retreated to protect his vulnerable flank or rear. In concentrating at an actual or expected point of assault, the defender also sought to avoid weakness, as he did when he tried to employ a better or, exploiting the primacy of the defensive, an equal weapon system against that of his opponent.

The enemy's weakness dictated the selection between a combat and a lo-gistic strategy. When Caesar pitted his stronger commissariat against that of the Belgae by waiting in his entrenched camp until they dispersed to find supplies, he capitalized on their weakness, as did the Spanish general Alba when he avoided his Dutch enemies until they abandoned the campaign for lack of money to pay their troops. So Caesar evaded his tactically dangerous opponents when they were concentrated, and Alba avoided fighting at all, each acting against his adversary's logistic weakness. Both followed this logistic strategy in spite of their own combat predominance.

Cost, in that a lower price reflects a comparatively greater supply, has always dominated logistics, but it also circumscribed tactics and strategy, just as it did the composition of armies. Victories such as those of Pyrrhus over the Romans and Marlborough's over Villars at Malplaquet cost in casualties more than they yielded in military or political results. And, of course, not just the price of victory or defeat but the availability of replacements enter into tactical and strategic cost calculations. The use of a raiding or guerrilla strategy offers an excellent example of consideration of costs constraining the theme of making use of the adversary's weakness and avoiding exposing one's own. Strategically better on the offensive against a persisting strategy, raiding or guerrilla warfare pits the stronger strategy against the weaker. But because guerrilla warfare depends on the accumulation of many small successes and does not directly seek to conquer territory, it usually takes longer to attain victory than a persisting strategy. This greater time and the losses incurred by the hostile occupation of one's territory raise the economic and political price of victory above that of a persisting strategy. This means that rather than face these costs, governments have often gambled on success with a persisting strategy and have relied on guerrilla warfare only as a last recourse. In fact, they sometimes accepted defeat rather than resort to it.

The concept of winning with the least effort readily unites the themes of weakness and alternative routes to victory with the consideration of costs. Although complicated by tension between long- and short-term considerations, insufficient information, and the effect of political and other nonoperational variables, the concept of least effort does adequately unite the aspects of military operations dwelt upon herein.

Strategists have argued about whether a general should aim at the enemy's territory or army. They have not often defined this as the alternative of a combat or a logistic persisting strategy nor have they always seen it as a choice between a political and a military strategy. This book has not directly addressed this question, embracing both approaches within the concept of combat persisting strategy. One reason for this procedure was the frequent lack of choice, as, for example, when an attacking army faced an elusive opponent with ample space in which to avoid battle. In this instance the army on the offensive, if it had enough men and resources, could only aim at occupying the defender's dominions. Of course, the sieges, so frequently inseparable from a strategy directed at territorial acquisition, could serve the double purpose of conquering the country and possibly bringing the enemy commander to battle in his effort to raise the invader's siege.

On occasion, the opportunity to choose did not present itself for different reasons, as in Frederick the Great's initial invasion of Silesia, when the inadequate garrison of the province could offer no resistance to the king's occupation of his political objective in the war. Having attained his goal, Frederick adopted the defensive. Sometimes an offensive aimed at the hostile army could result in obtaining some of the enemy's country. The strategic turning movement of modern warfare provides an obvious instance, because, when an adversary has thwarted it by retreat, it can yield the attacker a substantial territorial gain. The abortive German turning movement of 1914 illustrates this: it gave Germany much of France, including industrial areas and the iron ore of the Briey Basin, an advantage of potential political as well as actual economic value and one that forwarded a logistic strategy.

After his defeat of Darius III in the Battle of Issus, Alexander could have pursued the Persian king's army eastward into Mesopotamia. Instead he decided to continue his campaign along the coast, ending with the conquest of Egypt. Even had he not wished still to follow his logistic strategy against the Persian navy, Alexander might well have decided to exploit his victory by expanding his domains along the Mediterranean coast. Such a course would have immediately increased the political fruits of the war, removed a potential enemy in his rear when he eventually campaigned in Mesopotamia, and might well have augmented his resources for that subsequent campaign. Further, Alexander believed that he could expect difficulty in bringing Darius to battle in the distant reaches of his vast empire. Surely Alexander would have decided the question not on the basis of whether he should direct his campaign against the hostile army or its land area but by considering all of the variables relevant to conquering the Persian empire with the least effort.

Certainly commanders who faced this choice in the past have had to gauge the importance not just of logistical constraints but of economic, political, and other nonmilitary considerations. For this reason this book has made no effort to deal explicitly with this question, leaving it instead for an appeal to the theme of least effort to govern this decision as well as so many others.

Although this idea would likely dominate any organization of the topic of military operations, many different approaches other than the classifications used in the themes in this work suggest themselves. One may, for instance, stress tactics and divide combat strategy into technical and operational approaches. The technical would embrace a warfare oriented around capitalization on the qualities of weapon systems such as the Parthians used against the Romans. This avenue has more and more characterized warfare in the twentieth century as armed forces have developed new or improved versions of weapons. The operational would include the other aspects of combat strategy and stress other means of attacking or avoiding weakness. Almost exclusive emphasis on this latter category typified the period from the introduction of the bayonet until the early stages of World War I, an era of increasingly homogeneous armies.

Many other classifications and themes will occur to readers who can then create their own organizations. Also one may yet find a simple arrangement that will unite all elements into the elegant scheme sought by the theorists of two centuries ago.

Possibly such a complete, simple synthesis would permit a confident leap into the future, for even if the many elements of continuity found over 2,500 years do define the limits of change, they do not suffice to discern what lies ahead. Yet perhaps the most distinctive feature of the array of alternatives facing commanders is how little they have varied since ancient times. Only the strategic opportunities presented by the Napoleonic revolution really differentiate the present from the operational conditions of the past, though tactical nuclear weapons threaten the use of concentration, deprive major permanent fortifications of the importance they have long had, and, if used, would certainly have many unanticipated consequences.

Since the threat of precipitating a devastating nuclear war inhibits the employment not only of tactical nuclear weapons but also of military operations in which they might have significant value, there are unusual constraints on military action in Europe. This absence of warfare in Europe has accentuated the worldwide shift in the last decades away from the conflict of combatants employing persisting strategies, which dominated in Europe for the last two centuries and which the overseas campaigns of Europeans during this same period often featured. So long have Europeans fought each other in the combat persisting quadrant of the strategy matrix that they have come to call this conventional war and seen a resort to the raiding strategies so typical of the more remote past as unconventional. Perhaps this experience has helped them view the logistic and often raiding strategies of sea and air power as particularly distinct from those on land.

Yet the history of war in just the last 500 years presents a vast variety of tactical, logistic, and strategic situations to offer guidance for the present and the future. For example, in the future the variations in the number of weapon systems available, as a result of topographical, cultural, or resource constraints, could also reproduce tactical conditions best exemplified by the era between about 1500 and 1870. During this period the number of weapon systems useful in combat declined from four to three, when the adoption of both the pistol and saber united light and heavy cavalry in the same horseman, to two, when the bayonet joined to the musket combined heavy and light infantry into one soldier, to one, when the rifle virtually drove the horseman from the battlefield.

In Europe the concomitant steady increase in the ratio of force to space and the Napoleonic revolution in strategy and tactics somewhat obscured the effect of this change from four to one weapon systems. At first the versatility of the dual-purpose cavalryman probably augmented the power of the offense and weakened the defense because dismounted cavalry, with pistols and sabers rather than arquebuses and lances, could no longer function effectively as light or heavy infantry. But the advent of the bayonet and the appearance of a homogeneous body of infantry superior to cavalry turned the tables in favor of the defense. The adoption of the rifles and the resulting eclipse of mounted troops made armies completely homogeneous, deprived commanders of tactically offensive troops, and brought the tactical defensive to an apogee so evident in World War I.

Warfare around the world, with the variety of terrain and diverse combinations of weapon systems likely to appear, will certainly reproduce many of the tactical conditions that prevailed in the period from 1500 until 1914 as well as those characteristic of earlier periods when rarely did combatants use all four weapon systems. Thus, if one contestant had on suitable terrain weapon systems not available to the other, the tactical offensive may have a superiority of the kind exemplified in the Parthian triumph at Carrhae or the Byzantine victories over barbarians at Taginae and Casilinum. But if geography should constrain both combatants to a use of fewer than the four weapon systems available today, the tactical defense may well benefit. And should topography so inhibit mounted warfare as to eliminate the use of aircraft and tanks, the defense would recover that primacy it had in the period from 1870 to 1914.

Strategic conditions will likely reproduce the conditions of the remote past, with the amount of force in relation to the space in which operations occur varying markedly from the strategically decisive ratio. In early times sieges represented virtually the only instance of so high a ratio of force to space as to give the defense a decided advantage. Yet combat in the extensive urban areas characteristic of this century has added to the siege another situation in which the combatants would have so high a ratio of force to space as to make a decisive campaign quite difficult.

On the other hand, the opposite situation—a very low ratio of force to space, so typical of warfare in the Western world from the earliest times until the last 200 or 300 years—could frequently recur. With armies again unable to dominate much territory beyond their immediate area and opponents able to retreat in any of several directions, operational conditions would not deviate much from those that in recent years soldiers have come to associate exclusively with guerrilla warfare. But such strategic circumstances actually differ little from those that faced commanders for thousands of years when the ratio of force to space was so low as to leave no alternative but a raiding strategy.

These conditions may, as in the past, significantly reduce the decisiveness of military operations from the extraordinary level that they reached in the Napoleonic wars and World War II. With a return to the more usual condition of military means unable to render a prompt decision, political factors may assume even greater importance. The contrast between the divergent political outcomes of Alexander's and Hannibal's victories could have relevance as could complexities of such events as the Thirty Years' War and the experiences of the conquests of the Romans, William the Conqueror, the Turks in Asia Minor, and Jenghiz Khan in Khwarizm. But political conditions could be more complicated than in the past. Literacy combined with the availability of books and newspapers and the electronic media have helped make all people more responsive to national and ideological motivations just as in the past they often responded to religious feeling and commitment.

Thus soldiers and political leaders, who had learned to draw their lessons if not from their own generation at least from the recent past, might have to consult more remote eras for guidance, particularly since the subsiding of the intensive persisting struggles of the European powers, which characterized the first half of the twentieth century, has given comparatively more prominence to the raiding strategy still representative of much of the rest of the world. Some of these conflicts have resembled the guerrilla warfare that typified much of the resistance to European expansion in the nineteenth century or those struggles waged against the persistent growth of the Roman Empire. Others seemed to have more in common with the raids of barbarians against whom the Romans developed a systematic defense. Accordingly, strategy recently has changed its emphasis but has still remained within the four compartments of the traditional matrix.

Further, raiding strategy in a slightly different form has gained prominence. Today's terrorism uses a type of raid to take hostages, kill people, or explode bombs, usually in an effort to extort political concessions. These terrorists exhibit the primacy of raiding on the offensive because they often have no identifiable base against which to conduct counterraids or a persisting offensive strategy. These terrorist raids have a different setting from similar occurrences in the past in that they often occur in cities. But cities, like forests, offer cover and concealment, facilitating the withdrawal of the terrorists and giving them the ready ability to retreat by rendering themselves indistinguishable from the city's population.

Strategy thus appears largely immutable, and there seems no discernible prospect of a revolution such as that of Napoleon's time. Nor, in spite of the proliferation of the means of transmitting and processing information, does the present state of logistics appear to augur any significant innovation in manpower organization or progress comparable to the nineteenth-century improvement in the staff. The new logistics of the motor age and armies' dependence on supply lines for fuel, ammunition, and spare parts look as if they will continue to dominate most operations, notwithstanding the constraints of geography. And tactics, which has responded so much to the influence of changes in articulation, seems to offer few prospects for any marked degree of alteration.

Because strategy is largely the dependent variable of tactics and logistics, and technology has had the greatest influence on tactics and logistics, one should naturally then examine technology as the source of future modifications in combat. Since the trend of the effect of technology on civil life is fairly clear, it may help first to look there for parallels to aid in gauging the prospective impact of technology on combat and logistics.

The agricultural, commercial, and industrial revolutions of the last two centuries have received much of their shape from, as well as helped foster, technological change. These revolutions have in turn profoundly modified the way people in the Western world live. Independent of the great advance in the standard of living made possible by the fall in the prices of food, services, and manufactured products and the better housing and education that this wealth has bought, a communication revolution has altered the opportunities available to mankind. As first the railroad and the steamer and then the automobile and the airplane gave people a mobility hitherto unknown, and the telegraph, telephone, wireless, motion pictures, radio, and television have added to the other dimensions of communication and enhanced ease, convenience, and recreation.

Yet these transformations have had a reduced effect on everyday life over time. All but one of these, television, flourished more than fifty years ago, and clearly the impact of technology is showing the consequences of the operation of the law of diminishing returns. The early progress in home-cooling, for example, from the hand-operated palm-leaf fan to the electric fan advanced comfort to a far greater degree than did the transition from the electric fan to air conditioning. One may find a more dramatic illustration of the decreasing impact of technology by comparing travel from London to Paris, which used to require the interruption of a change to sea transport and back again to land. In 1930 thirty-eight passengers in an airliner traveled at 100 miles an hour while dining on a sumptuous lunch. The jet aircraft has added comparatively little to the speed or convenience of such a journey when one reckons the time consumed traveling to and from the airports. Nothing more graphically exhibits the diminishing way technology has touched us than to notice that a 1985 trip taken in a 1935 automobile on an interstate highway or motorway fatigues the driver less than a 1935 trip on the two-lane roads of that period taken in a 1985 car.

In 1985 people drove on better roads in better automobiles playing better radios and were cooler in hot weather than in 1935, but, compared to the circumscribed access of waterways and the railroad and the limited speed and luxury of horse-drawn transport, far greater changes took place before 1935 than since. Equally, the 1985 dwelling with television, deep freezers, and home air conditioning differs less from the 1935 urban home with radio, refrigerator, and cooling by electric fans than the 1935 house varies from that of the age before central heat, indoor plumbing, home electrification, and the telephone. So technological change continues to alter production, but new and improved products have a diminishing effect on the manner of life. Power generation, including the use of nuclear power, for example, has changed markedly, but this has not modified use; the same 110 or 220 volts AC enters the home as before, and the application of this electric power has undergone progressively fewer alterations in the last five decades.

These same economic and technological revolutions affected warfare, changing logistics as they did commerical transportation and increasing the size and cost of armed forces by a measure proportional to the growth in economic productivity. But technology had its impact on tactics in a cyclical rather than in the linear way in which it altered civil life and logistics. First, the mid–nineteenth-century innovations in firearms abolished cavalry as a tactically useful weapon system, introducing a unique era when soldiers could have at their disposal only one weapon system, the rifle- or machine gun-armed infantrymen and their similar companions with artillery. Then, after a period, brief in comparison with the long history of warfare, technology restored by 1917, in new forms, the customary four weapon systems.

Since 1917 tactics have worked within the long tradition of heterogeneity of weapon systems as logistics has remained modern in its use of bases and motor transport on land and sea and in the air. Thus, though following a different course because of the tactical cycle from 1861 to 1917, the impact of technology on warfare also seems to exhibit the effect of diminishing returns, barring, of course, the use of strategic or tactical nuclear weapons.

So research and development since the World War II have altered aircraft and, particularly, tanks less than these weapons had changed between 1917 and 1945. The same is probably true of the antitank and antiaircraft systems; and artillery and small arms, older weapon systems, have undergone even fewer alterations. The portable voice radio used in World War II probably had more effect on tactical communications than any subsequent improvements. Thus military life in the last few decades seems to follow civil in the diminishing effect of technology and makes it easy to jump to the conclusion that it may not modify warfare in the future any more than it seems presently to be altering lifestyles. Transistors, for example, have improved radios and television sets without affecting the auditor or viewer very much, and computers have reduced the cost of office work and manufacturing without in any degree transforming the product. Accordingly, one may conclude that warfare may follow the same course, with tactics and logistics as little influenced by the transitor and computer as civil life. Soldiers will have to learn new tasks and discard old skills, as have civilians, but the end product will not differ much. Since nothing comparable to the breech-loading rifle or the tank seems on the horizon and the fundamentals of logistics have not altered, strategy, almost immutable in any case and to a large degree the dependent variable of tactics and logistics, also seems unlikely to change. Therefore the outlook for a major modification in the manner of combat has no more promise than that for civilian life.

If the past provides a reliable guide, the most dramatic effect technological change could have would be to eliminate or merge one or more of the four classes of weapon systems. The most likely prospect, a weapon system equally effective against tanks and aircraft, still eludes the weapons developers, even though, because both employ projectiles, the task seems more feasible now than it would have in the Middle Ages when the crossbow and the long pike differed so much.

So tactics, in spite of altogether different weapons, displays a significant consistency with the past. With terrain still restraining the nature of combat and with weapon systems still having a diversity and capabilities relatively comparable to those in ancient and medieval times, continuity looks as if it overmatches change. Today, combination of arms provides the motif just as it did in the days of Alexander, the Byzantines, William the Conqueror, the Crusaders, and Gustavus Adolphus.

But another form of technological influence on tactics seems discernible in the continued rapid advancement in electronics and rockets. Since the middle of the nineteenth century, the rate of fire has increased markedly, somewhat overshadowing the progress in the accuracy of small arms. In artillery, however, the augmentation in range and accuracy had more significance than the advance in the rate of fire. The steady improvements in electronics since the introduction of radar and the comparable development of the guided missile have continued the trend that artillery began more than a century ago.

Together these promise to alter tactics in a momentous way by revolutionizing the ability to see targets and to provide hitherto undreamed of accuracy of fire. Observers of these developments could readily, and with good reason, contend that the analogy of the diminishing returns of the effect of technology

on civil life breaks down here and that the changes in intelligence, target acquisition, range, and accuracy together amount to a difference in kind that will
profoundly alter tactics whether or not weapon systems remain in the traditional
four categories.

The soldiers of today have a vision of combining complete electronic intelligence of the enemy with weapons guided with perfect accuracy to create a
revolution in combat. They envisage a battle conducted at depths similar to
those introduced by tactical aviation in World War II and with an accuracy of
fire against distant targets far exceeding that attained by the best fire of calibrated
guns in World War I.

Combat at such great distances would tend to make flanks and rear, the
traditional weak points, irrelevant. If soldiers are visible by means of sensing
heat radiated as well as by sight and radar and are vulnerable from above, and
countermeasures do not defeat this variety of sensors, traditional concealment
and cover lose much of their merit, and combat may come closely to approximate
Lanchester's model of every weapon system being able to fire at every other.
This kind of warfare at a distance would deprive the defender of many of his
usual benefits, though, in the absence of nuclear weapons, he could have useful
assistance from modern fortifications such as the Maginot line. Even tactical
nuclear weapons might lose much of their defensive value if the great range of
weapons made the conventional concentration of force unnecessary.

Nevertheless, each of the four weapon systems retains its distinctive capabilities. But, with some of the customary advantages of the defense largely
abrogated, the stronger army might more easily attain primacy instead of a
deadlock. Though electronic intelligence and guided weapons are still far from
perfected, in two decades—the same period of time required to perfect the design
and reliability of the tank and military aircraft—such warfare might come close
to reality.

Yet just as electronic countermeasures and even so old-fashioned a denizen
of the military environment as smoke may thwart intelligence gathering and
missile guidance and so cause a departure from the model of complete intelligence and perfect accuracy, so also may the progress of the battle deform the
model. Combat may possibly deplete the adversaries' missiles and damage their
electronic equipment and diminish its capabilities. And like the elite, largely
mounted forces of the Byzantine Empire, these new armies in Europe would
have few replacements in men and equipment.

But unlike the experience of the destruction of the Byzantine army at Manzikert, which left the empire almost without an army, the combat envisioned
could likely revert to an earlier period in the history of weapon systems. As the
battle progressed, the hostile forces might witness a transition back to World
War II and even World War I combat conditions until replacement equipment
began to make possible a partial return to the initial conditions of the battle.
Thus some of the episodes in the recent history of tactics may well recur in
combat between these small, mounted, and elaborately equipped armies.

What strategic consequences would such a tactical transformation have? Clearly, the trend to small, capital-intensive armies would continue, as complex weapons and expensive ammunition absorbed the resources of the industrial powers that early in this century sufficed to equip millions of men. Would such armies resemble the mounted Parthians, supreme on their level terrain but unable to cope with the mountains of Armenia or the forests of Syria? Rather, in view of the integration of surface and air weapon systems and their use of comparable missiles and electronic intelligence, such armies would surely be at least somewhat less inhibited by forests and mountains than the mounted forces of old.

Yet such armies would exist primarily to fight each other. Accordingly, against an enemy armed with weapons characteristic of the first half of the twentieth century, they might often find themselves in the embarrassing and probably self-defeating situation of the missile costing more than the target. Thus, major parts of these armies might resemble the elite heavy cavalry of the Middle Ages: they could usually dominate wherever they went but depended on infantry for the sieges and garrisons necessary to control the country.

Perhaps their necessarily small size would eliminate the continuous front so typical of World Wars I and II and the conflicts between the Arabs and Israelis. In this respect these operations might also resemble North Africa's first modern combat between essentially mounted forces. Further, the reduction in the size of armies might impose an important restriction on their strategic significance, for such forces, with much equipment and comparatively few men would have a limited ability to control conquered territory. With the shrinking of armies, the traditional limitations on strategic results imposed by a low ratio of force to space would return. And the dependence of such forces on lines of supply would make them more vulnerable than the horse-mounted armies of old, which lived on the country and had no extravagant requirements for ammunition.

True, such a powerful but small army that found its supply lines interrupted by guerrillas could supply itself by air, but this would not remedy its small size in relation to the country it sought to dominate. In a large, politically hostile country its movements might have no more effect than Hannibal's after his victories against the Romans in Italy. Only by a Mongolian strategy of terror and extermination could such an army subdue a determined opponent, and for this task it would find its complex missile weapons and their expensive ammunition ill adapted.

It seems, then, that this expensive, predominantly electronic and guided missile warfare could exist only as a special case among many instances of universal human combat. Such diversity existed three centuries ago when Europeans began to accelerate their global expansion. And the partial worldwide synthesis found at the beginning of this century has already begun to dissolve in the face of the geographical obstacles to the new mounted ways of war. In forests, mountains, and cities the nineteenth-century warfare of rifles and artillery has of necessity flourished, in spite of some infusion of tanks and aircraft. It seems likely that economic constraints will also limit the use of the new electronic and missile weapons and the warfare contemplated in Europe will become more and more distinct from that practiced or planned in many other regions. Accordingly, the world seems headed back to diversity, with warfare varying to suit the economic resources and the political and geographical circumstances of the combatants. Thus, the world military situation may well resemble that of medieval Europe, with each region having methods that meet its specialized needs. Since this resurgence of heterogeneity and regionalism in warfare has the same roots as that in the past, there seems little reason to expect that it will not characterize warfare yet to come.

The foregoing attempt to glimpse what lies ahead, like most such efforts, does no more than extrapolate from some very obvious, recent trends. To do the same for other apparent tendencies would doubtless present other visions of tomorrow. No more than any other discipline can history predict the future. It can extend the line of extrapolation farther back in the past in the hope that, if done properly, it will plot a more accurate course ahead. It can also attempt the same task by seeking in the past analogies of potential value for understanding present changes and the possible course of events. More important, history should raise its own questions to ask of the present and to provide hypotheses for subsequent developments. If the themes in this work and the consistencies many of them exhibit aid readers in raising such questions and forming hypotheses and selecting parallels, then this book will have done its duty by the future.

NOTES

Chapter 1, "Ancient Warfare"

1. J. K. Anderson, *Military Theory and Practice in the Age of Xenophon* (Berkeley, 1970), 174.

2. Xenophon, *Hellenica*, VII, 4, 8, as cited in *The Greek Historians*, ed. Francis R. B. Godolphin and trans. Henry G. Dakyns, 2 vols. (New York, 1942), 2:216. All subsequent citations from Greek historians are from Godolphin's two-volume edition; therefore his name is not repeated, and only the name of the appropriate translator is given.

3. Sir Frank Adcock, *Greek and Macedonian Art of War* (Berkeley, 1957), 49.

4. Herodotus, *The Persian Wars*, IX, 22, as cited in *The Greek Historians*, trans. George Rawlinson, 1:526.

5. Herodotus, *Persian Wars*, IX, 49, as cited in *Greek Historians*, 1:537.

6. Herodotus, *Persian Wars*, IX, 61, 62, as cited in *Greek Historians*, 1:541, 542.

7. Thucydides, *The Peloponnesian War*, III, 97, 98, as cited in *The Greek Historians*, trans. Benjamin Jowett, 1:728.

8. Xenophon, *Hellenica*, IV, 4, as cited in *Greek Historians*, 2:100-101.

9. Xenophon, *Hellenica*, IV, 5.9-5.17, as cited in *Greek Historians*, 2:104-5.

10. Arrian, *Anabasis of Alexander*, I, 15, as cited in *The Greek Historians*, trans. Edward J. Chinnock, 2:420-21.

11. Arrian, *Anabasis*, III, 15; I, 16, as cited in *Greek Historians*, 2:480, 421-22.

12. Arrian, *Anabasis*, II, 10, as cited in *Greek Historians*, 2:448.

13. Arrian, *Anabasis*, II, 10, as cited in *Greek Historians*, 2:449.

14. Plutarch, *Plutarch's Lives of Illustrious Men*, ed. A. H. Clough (Boston, 1901), 488.

15. Arrian, *Anabasis*, III, 14, as cited in *Greek Historians*, 2:480; Plutarch, *Lives*, 488.

16. Polybius, *The Histories*, VI, 23.2-23.16, as cited in Polybius, *Histories*, trans. W. R. Paton, 6 vols. (Cambridge, Mass., 1966), 3:319, 321.

17. Polybius, *Histories*, VI, 22.4-23.11, as cited in Paton's translation, 3:319-21.

18. Polybius, *Histories*, XV, 9.7-9.9, as cited in Paton's translation, 4:485, 487.

19. Polybius, *Histories*, XV, 12.1-12.5, as cited in Paton's translation, 4:491, 493.

20. Polybius, *Histories*, XV, 14.2-14.3, as cited in Paton's translation, 4:497.

21. Polybius, *Histories*, XVIII, 30.910, as cited in Paton's translation, 5:153.

22. Polybius, *Histories*, XV, 15.7, as cited in Paton's translation, 4:499.

23. Polybius, *Histories*, XVIII, 31.5-31.6, as cited in Paton's translation, 5:153.

24. Polybius, *Histories*, XVIII, 32.2-32.5, as cited in Paton's translation, 5:153-57.

25. Plutarch, *Lives*, 391.

26. Ibid., 393.

27. Ibid., 394.

28. Ibid.

29. Dio, *Roman History*, XL, 22.4, as cited in *Dio's Roman History*, trans. Earnest Cary, 9 vols. (Cambridge, Mass., 1914), 3:439.

30. Plutarch, *Lives*, 395; Dio, *Roman History*, XL, 22.2-3, as cited in Cary's translation, 3:437.

31. Dio, *Roman History*, XL, 24.1, as cited in Cary's translation, 3:441.

32. Dio, *Roman History*, XL, 15.4–5, 29.1–3, as cited in Cary's translation, 3:427, 449.

33. I am indebted to Lt. Col. E. W. Gale for this paragraph explaining the unsuitability of the horse for the defense.

34. Caesar, *Civil Wars*, III, 93, as cited in Caesar, *The Civil Wars*, trans. A. G. Peskett (London, 1914), 329.

35. Arrian, *Anabasis*, VI, 24, as cited in *Greek Historians*, 2:583.

36. Arrian, *Anabasis*, VI, 25, as cited in *Greek Historians*, 2:583, 584.

37. Arrian, *Anabasis*, VI, 25, as cited in *Greek Historians*, 2:584.

38. Polybius, *Histories*, XVIII, 31.8, as cited in Paton's translation, 5:155.

39. Herodotus, *Persian Wars*, IX, 39, 41, as cited in *Greek Historians*, 1:533, 534.

40. Herodotus, *Persian Wars*, IX, 50, as cited in *Greek Historians*, 1:537.

41. Arrian, *Anabasis*, I, 12.7, as cited in *Greek Historians*, 2:418.

42. Arrian, *Anabasis*, I, 18, as cited in *Greek Historians*, 2:425.

43. Arrian, *Anabasis*, I, 20, as cited in *Greek Historians*, 2:427.

44. Plutarch, *Lives*, 487.

45. Carl von Clausewitz, *On War*, ed. and trans. Michael Howard and Peter Paret (Princeton, N.J., 1976), 77.

46. Arrian, *Anabasis*, IV, 5, as cited in *Greek Historians*, 2:505.

47. Arrian, *Anabasis*, IV, 17, as cited in *Greek Historians*, 2:518.

48. Arrian, *Anabasis*, IV, 16, as cited in *Greek Historians*, 2:517.

49. Arrian, *Anabasis*, IV, 19, as cited in *Greek Historians*, 2:520; Curtius, *History of Alexander*, VIII, 4.25, as cited in Curtius, *History of Alexander*, trans. John C. Rolfe, 2 vols. (Cambridge, Mass., 1956), 2:271.

50. Polybius, *Histories*, III, 90, as cited in Paton's translation, 2:223.

51. Polybius, *Histories*, III, 86.9–10, 87.1, 89.1–2, as cited in Paton's translation, 2:213, 217–19.

52. Polybius, *Histories*, III, 90.9, 90.1, 90.2–4, as cited in Paton's translation, 2:221, 219.

53. Polybius, *Histories*, III, 90.11, 90.2, as cited in Paton's translation, 2:223, 221.

54. Plutarch, *Lives*, 511.

55. Caesar, *Gallic Wars and Other Writings*, trans. Moses Hadas (New York, 1957), 159–60.

56. Ibid., 45.

57. Ibid., 189, 161.

58. Ibid., 194.

59. Ibid., 195.

60. Ibid., 145.

61. Caesar, *Civil Wars*, I, 43, as cited in Peskett's translation, 71.

62. Caesar, *Civil Wars*, I, 63, 64, as cited in Peskett's translation, 87, 89.

63. Caesar, *Civil Wars*, I, 65, 66, as cited in Peskett's translation, 91, 93.

64. Caesar, *Civil Wars*, I, 69, 70, as cited in Peskett's translation, 95, 97.

65. Caesar, *Civil Wars*, I, 84, as cited in Peskett's translation, 115.

66. Herodotus, *Persian Wars*, IX, 13, as cited in *Greek Historians*, 1:522.

67. Plutarch, *Lives*, 520.

68. Adcock, *Greek and Macedonian Art of War*, 76–77; Frontinus, *The Strategems*, IV, 7.1, as cited in Frontinus, *The Strategems and the Aqueducts of Rome*, trans. Charles E. Bennett (Cambridge, Mass., 1925), 309.

69. Livius, *The History of Rome*, XXVIII, 9.13, as cited in *Livy*, trans. F. G. Moore, 14 vols. (Cambridge, Mass. 1919–59), 8:41.

Chapter 2, "The Diversity of the Medieval Ways of War"

1. Hans Delbrück, *History of the Art of War within the Framework of Political History*, vol. 2, *The Germans*, trans. Walter J. Renfroe, Jr. (Westport, Conn., 1980), 263.

2. Sir Charles Oman, *A History of the Art of War in the Middle Ages*, 2 vols. (New York, 1924), 1:206.

3. Procopius, *The Gothic War*, VIII, 24.15–17, 19–20, as cited in *Procopius*, trans. H. B. Dewing, 7 vols. (Cambridge, Mass., 1961–62), 5:357, 359.

4. Oman, *Art of War*, 1:52.

5. Procopius, *The Persian War*, I, 18.18–21, as cited in Dewing's translation, 1:165, 167.

6. Alfred Friendly, *The Dreadful Day: The Battle of Manzikert, 1071* (London, 1981), 125.

7. Ibid., 190.

8. Ibid., 191.

9. Ibid., 128, 134.

10. Oman, *Art of War*, 1:204–5.

11. Ibid., 2:118–19.

12. Ibid., 1:164.

13. The foregoing is adapted, by permission of the Association of the United States Army, from Oliver L. Spaulding, Hoffman Nickerson, and John W. Wright, *Warfare* (Washington, D.C., 1937), 312–17.

14. Oman, *Art of War*, 1:448.

15. Ibid., 390.

16. Ibid., 438.

17. John Beeler, *Warfare in England, 1066–1189* (Ithaca, N.Y., 1966), 214.

18. Ibid., 138.

19. Ibid., 139–40.

20. Oman, *Art of War*, 1:275.

21. Ibid., 272.

22. Ibid., 329.

23. Ibid., 308.

24. Ibid., 309–10.

25. Ibid., 309.

26. Michael Prawdin, *The Mongol Empire: Its Rise and Legacy*, trans. Eden and Cedar Paul (London, 1967), 191.

27. Ibid., 192.

28. Ibid., 195.

29. Philippe Contamine, *War in the Middle Ages*, trans. Michael Jones (London, 1984), 220.

30. Dio, *Roman History*, LXVII, 5.6, as cited in *Dio's Roman History*, trans. Earnest Cary, 9 vols. (Cambridge, Mass., 1914), 8:327–29.

Chapter 3, "The Emergence of a New Combined-Arms Tactical Synthesis"

1. Oliver L. Spaulding, Hoffman Nickerson, and John W. Wright, *Warfare* (Washington, D.C., 1937), 371.

2. Sir Charles Oman, *A History of the Art of War in the Middle Ages*, 2 vols. (New York, 1924), 2:95.

3. Ibid., 105.

4. Ibid., 99.

5. Alfred H. Burne, *The Crécy War: A Military History of the Hundred Years' War from 1337 to the Peace of Brétigny, 1360* (Westport, Conn., 1955), 50.

6. Oman, *Art of War*, 2:142.

7. Ibid., 173.

8. Alfred H. Burne, *The Agincourt War: A Military History of the Latter Part of the Hundred Years' War from 1369 to 1453* (London, 1956), 82.

9. Sir Charles Oman, *A History of the Art of War in the Sixteenth Century* (New York, 1937), 146.

10. Ibid., 184.

11. Hans Delbrück, *History of the Art of War within the Framework of Political History*, vol. 4, The Modern Era, trans. Walter J. Renfroe, Jr. (Westport, Conn., 1985), 43.

12. Geoffrey Parker, *The Army of Flanders and the Spanish Road: The Logistics of Spanish Victory and Defeat in the Low Countries' Wars* (Cambridge, 1972), 173.

13. Ibid., 46.

14. Ibid., 30, 27.

15. Ibid., 176.

16. Oman, *Art of War in the Sixteenth Century*, 219.

17. Parker, *Army of Flanders*, 20.

18. Oman, *Art of War in the Sixteenth Century*, 221.

19. Parker, *Army of Flanders*, 10, 12.

20. Oman, *Art of War in the Sixteenth Century*, 517.

Chapter 4, "The New Tactical Synthesis in Transition"

1. Fritz Redlich, *De Praeda Militari: Looting and Booty, 1500–1815* (Wiesbaden, 1956), 61.

2. Fritz Redlich, *The German Military Enterpriser and His Work Force: A Study in European Economic and Social History*, 2 vols. (Wiesbaden, 1964), 1:473.

3. Ibid., 524–25.

4. Ibid., 475, 507–8.

5. Ibid., 512.

6. Michael Roberts, *Gustavus Adolphus: A History of Sweden, 1611–1632*, 2 vols. (London, 1958), 2:261.

7. Ibid., 200.

8. Ibid., 446.

9. Geoffrey Parker, *The Army of Flanders and the Spanish Road: The Logistics of Spanish Victory and Defeat in the Low Countries' Wars* (Cambridge, 1972), 19.

10. Roberts, *Gustavus Adolphus*, 2:520.

11. Ibid., 534, 537.

12. Hans Delbrück, *History of the Art of War within the Framework of Political History*, vol. 4, *The Modern Era*, trans. Walter J. Renfroe, Jr. (Westport, Conn., 1985), 175–76.

13. Roberts, *Gustavus Adolphus*, 2:556.

14. Theodore A. Dodge, *Gustavus Adolphus* (Boston, 1896), 475.

15. Martin van Creveld, *Supplying War: Logistics from Wallenstein to Patton* (Cambridge, 1977), 14; Redlich, *De Praeda Militari*, 17; J. Mitchell, *The Life of Wallenstein, Duke of Friedland* (New York, 1968), 240.

16. Delbrück, *Modern Era*, 251–52.

17. Ibid., 253.

18. van Creveld, *Supplying War*, 17.

19. Carl J. Ekberg, "The Great Captain's Greatest Mistake: Turenne's German Campaign of 1673," *Military Affairs* 41 (Oct. 1977):116.

20. Ibid., 115.

21. Redlich, *De Praeda Militari*, 62.

22. David Chandler, *The Art of Warfare in the Age of Marlborough* (New York, 1976), 111.

Chapter 5, "The Primacy of the Line of Bayonetted Muskets"

1. David Chandler, *The Art of Warfare in the Age of Marlborough* (New York, 1976), 82.

2. Ibid., 104.

3. Christopher Duffy, *The Army of Frederick the Great* (New York, 1974), 88, 89.

4. Chandler, *Art of Warfare in the Age of Marlborough*, 107.

5. Martin van Creveld, *Supplying War: Logistics from Wallenstein to Patton* (Cambridge, 1977), 30.

6. Hans Delbrück, *History of the Art of War within the Framework of Political History*, vol. 4, *The Modern Era*, trans. Walter J. Renfroe, Jr. (Westport, Conn., 1985), 302.

7. David Chandler, *Marlborough as Military Commander* (New York, 1973), 145.

8. Chandler, *Art of Warfare in the Age of Marlborough*, 54.

9. Chandler, *Marlborough as Military Commander*, 179.

10. Ibid.

11. Chandler, *Art of Warfare in the Age of Marlborough*, 261–62.

12. Nicholas Henderson, *Prince Eugene of Savoy* (New York, 1965), 119.

13. Ibid., 119, 121.

14. Ibid., 129.

15. Ibid., 131.

16. Christopher Duffy, *The Army of Maria Theresa: The Armed Forces of Imperial Austria, 1740–1780* (New York, 1977), 149.

17. Duffy, *Army of Frederick the Great*, 161.

18. Jay Luvaas, "Frederick's Campaign in Silesia, 1744–45," *Essays in Some Dimensions of Military History*, vol. 4, ed. B. F. Cooling III (Carlisle Barracks, Pa., 1976), 20.

19. Ibid., 21.

20. Duffy, *The Army of Frederick the Great*, 172.

21. Ibid., 174.

22. Christopher Duffy, *Russia's Military Way to the West: Origins and Nature of Russian Military Power, 1700–1800* (London, 1981), 87–89.

23. Duffy, *Army of Frederick the Great*, 183.

24. Delbrück, *Modern Era*, 358–59.

25. Duffy, *Army of Frederick the Great*, 195.

26. Ibid., 199.

27. Duffy, *Army of Maria Theresa*, 189.

28. Delbrück, *Modern Era*, 313.

29. Gaston Bodart, *Militär-historisches Kriegs-Lexikon (1618–1905)* (Wien and Leipzig, 1908).

30. Duffy, *Army of Maria Theresa*, 144.

31. Robert S. Quimby, *The Background of Napoleonic Warfare: The Theory of Military Tactics in Eighteenth-Century France* (New York, 1957), 296.

32. Ibid., 159, 168.

33. Ibid., 159–60.

34. Ibid., 168.

Chapter 6, "Tactical and Strategic Transformation in the Era of the French Revolution and Napoleon"

1. Ramsay Weston Phipps, *The Armies of the First French Republic and the Rise of the Marshals of Napoleon I*, 5 vols. (Oxford, 1926–39), 1:238.

2. John Lynn, *Bayonets of the Republic: Motivation and Tactics in the Army of Revolutionary France* (Urbana, Ill., 1984), 171.

3. Phipps, *Armies of the First French Republic*, 1:303; Lynn, *Bayonets of the Republic*, 276.

4. Phipps, *Armies of the First French Republic*, 1:306; Lynn, *Bayonets of the Republic*, 276.

5. Hans Delbrück, *History of the Art of War within the Framework of Political History*, vol. 4, *The Modern Era*, trans. Walter J. Renfroe, Jr. (Westport, Conn., 1985), 281.

6. *A Military History and Atlas of the Napoleonic Wars* (New York, 1964), map 3.

7. David G. Chandler, *The Campaigns of Napoleon* (New York, 1966), 74.

8. Ibid., 199.

9. Ibid., 279, 280.

10. Data from Martin van Creveld, *Supplying War: Logistics from Wallenstein to Patton* (Cambridge, 1977), 54.

11. Chandler, *Campaigns of Napoleon*, 396.

12. Ibid., 402.

13. The foregoing is based on F. W. Lanchester, *Aircraft in Warfare: The Dawn of the Fourth Arm* (London, 1916), 39–53.

14. Chandler, *Campaigns of Napoleon*, 687.

15. Gunther E. Rothenberg, *The Art of Warfare in the Age of Napoleon* (Bloomington, Ind., 1978), 210.

16. Chandler, *Campaigns of Napoleon*, 912.

17. Don W. Alexander, *Rod of Iron: French Counterinsurgency Policy in Aragon during the Peninsula War* (Wilmington, Del., 1985), 23.

18. Ibid., 39.

19. Ibid., 218.

20. [Antoine Henri] Jomini, *The Art of War*, trans. G. H. Mendel and W. P. Craighill (Philadelphia, 1862 ([1971 reprint]), 31–33.

21. Lynn, *Bayonets of the Republic*, 113–14.

22. Ibid.

23. Ibid., 115.

24. Delbrück, *Modern Era*, 410.

25. Based, with some variations, on B. P. Hughes, *Firepower: Weapons Effectiveness on the Battlefield, 1630–1850* (New York, 1974), 115–27.

26. Lanchester explicitly applied his ideas to the Battle of Trafalgar. See his *Aircraft in Warfare*, 62–66.

Chapter 7, "Technological Change and Doctrinal Stability"

1. Michael Howard, *The Franco-Prussian War: The German Invasion of France, 1870–1871* (New York, 1962), 111.

2. J. Colin, *The Transformations of War*, trans. L. H. R. Pope-Hennessy (London, 1912), 33.

3. Howard, *Franco-Prussian War*, 133.

4. Ibid., 168, 167.

5. Ibid., 170, 172.

6. *The War of the Rebellion: A Compilation of the Official Records of the Union and Confederate Armies*, 128 vols. (Washington, D.C., 1880–1901), series 1, 45, part 1, 1218.

7. F. N. Maude, *The Evolution of Modern Strategy* (London, 1905), 126.

8. Charles Moran, "Twenty Thousand Leagues over the Seas: The Odyssey of Admiral Rozhdestvenski," *United States Naval Institute Proceedings* (May 1955):570.

Chapter 8, "The Apogee of the Defense"

1. John Keegan, *Opening Moves: August, 1914* (New York, 1971), 136.

2. G. C. Wynne, *If Germany Attacks: The Battle in Depth in the West* (London, 1940), 198, 199.

3. B. H. Liddell Hart, *The Real War, 1914–1918* (Boston, 1930), 232.

4. Wynne, *If Germany Attacks*, 118.

5. Liddell Hart, *Real War*, 340.

6. Ibid., 343.

7. Wynne, *If Germany Attacks*, 55.

8. Timothy T. Lupfer, *The Dynamics of Doctrine: The Changes in German Tactical Doctrine during the First World War*, Combat Studies Institute, U.S. Army Command and General Staff College (Fort Leavenworth, Kans., 1981), 40.

9. B. H. Liddell Hart, *Through the Fog of War* (New York, 1938), 221, 224.

10. Liddell Hart, *Real War*, 368.

Chapter 9, "Prelude to Renewed Conflict"

1. Antony Thrall Sullivan, *Thomas-Robert Bugeaud, France, and Algeria, 1784–1849: Politics, Power, and the Good Society* (Hamden, Conn., 1983), 125.

2. Ibid., 127.

Chapter 10, "The Climax of Modern Warfare"

1. Robert Allan Doughty, *The Seeds of Disaster: The Development of French Army Doctrine, 1919–1939* (Hamden, Conn., 1985), 109.

2. John Lynn, *Bayonets of the Republic: Motivation and Tactics in the Army of Revolutionary France* (Urbana, Ill., 1984), 170.

3. Doughty, *Seeds of Disaster*, 32.

Chapter 12, "Continuity and Change"

1. Hans Delbrück, *History of the Art of War within the Framework of Political History*, vol. 4, *The Modern Era*, trans. Walter J. Renfroe, Jr. (Westport, Conn., 1985), 428.

2. Ibid., 371.

3. Herodotus, *The Persian Wars*, IV, 127, as cited in *The Greek Historians*, ed. Francis R. B. Godolphin and trans. George Rawlinson, 2 vols. (New York, 1942), 1:269.

INDEX

Bruix, Etienne Eustache, French admiral, 381–82

Brunswick, Karl Wilhelm Ferdinand, duke of, field marshal, 321

Bucquoi, count of, Imperial general, 214

Budenny, Simeon Mikhailovich, marshal, 552

Buell, Don Carlos, general, 410

Bugeaud de la Piconnerie, Thomas-Robert, marshal: strategy of, in Algeria, 497–98; strategy of compared, 662, 687, 690, 701

Bull Run, campaign of, second battle, 413, 415

Burgundy, Charles the Rash, duke of, fights the Swiss, 177–78, 182

Byng, Sir Julian H. G., general, 476

Byzantine Empire:

—army and doctrine of: 95–100, 623; compared, 119–20, 149, 599, 602, 606, 619, 629, 696, 713, 714

—defense of, against raiders, 99–100; compared, 132, 266, 618, 681–82, 694

Caesar, Gaius Julius: operations of, 35, 36, 43–44, 72–75; attributes of, 72; quoted, 82, 650; compared, 93, 122, 208, 350; Belgae campaign compared, 650, 706

Calais, siege of, 165

Calder, Sir Robert, admiral: 384; compared, 430

Camperdown: battle of, 378; battle compared, 379

Cannae: battle of, 29–30, 68; battle compared, 42, 44, 93, 160, 250, 345, 368, 407, 501–2, 637, 639, 642, 656

Canrobert, François Certain, marshal, 402

Cape Artemesium, battle of, 87, 88

Cape Matapan, battle of, 587–88

Cape St. Vincent, battle of, 378, 381

Caracole (cavalry fire tactic with pistols), 196–97

Caravaggio, siege of, 180–81

Carnot, Lazare Nicolas Marguerite, member of Committee of Public Safety, quoted, 370

Carrhae: battle of, 36–38; battle compared, 96, 496, 649, 699, 708, 709

Carrhae, second battle of, 137–38

Carthage: army of, 29–32; final destruction of, 690

Casilinum: battle of, 99; battle compared, 177, 709

Cassano, battle of, 280

Castiglione, battle of, 335–36, 349, 351, 353

Catinat, Nicolas de, marshal, 283–84

Cavalry: and tactical primacy of infantry, 9; Alexander's Companions, 21, 23–24, 505–6; as offensive troops, 30–31, 82, 203, 250, 481–83; cost, 41, 156; dismounted, 98,

105–6, 144, 159–60, 164, 170, 174, 413, 416, 481–83; and the stirrup, 103–4; and terrain, 135, 143

—heavy: defeated heavy infantry, 21–23, 137, 149; lost to heavy infantry, 43–44, 98, 158–59, 164, 175, 176, 177–78, 189–90; lost to light cavalry, 100, 107, 135; defeated light cavalry, 108, 134–35, 136; tanks as, 484, 502

—light: assailed heavy infantry, 17, 18, 19, 36–38, 63; lost to light infantry, 17, 135, 174; strategic role of, 58, 77–80, 184–85, 290–91, 295–97, 360; defeated heavy cavalry, 100–101, 107, 135; lost to heavy cavalry, 108, 134; not prominent in Europe, 144, 173, 182; compared, 192; aircraft as, 484–85, 501, 619–20

—reiter: 197–98, 234, 243–44, 249–52, 268–70, 297, 374, 375, 401, 416, 422

—*See also* Aircraft; Chariots; Elephants; Offensive troops; Tanks

Ceresole, battle of, 192

Cerignola, battle of, 184–85

Chappe, Claude, and Ignace Urbain Jean, telegraph of, 354, 395, 673

Chariots, 14, 25, 103

Charles I, the Great, or Charlemagne, emperor, 102, 145

Charles I, king of Naples, at Benevento and Tagliacozzo, 121

Charles III, claimant to throne of Spain, later Charles VI, Holy Roman emperor, 279

Charles V, king of France, 167–68

Charles V, Holy Roman emperor: 190; compared, 699

Charles VII, king of France, victorious over English, 171–73

Charles VIII, king of France; invaded Italy, 182–84; compared, 372

Charles Albert, king of Sardinia, campaigns of, 387–89

Charles of Lorraine. See Lorraine

Charles Louis, archduke, field marshal; abilities of, 354; 1809 campaign of, 355; mentioned, 322, 326, 356

Charles the Rash. See Burgundy, duke of

Chemin des Dames, German attack at, 477

Chester, Hugh, the Fat, of Avranches, earl of, 129, 685

Chiari, battle of, 284

Chotusitz, battle of, 295

Civilians: instances of their fighting soldiers, 59–60, 142, 207, 217–18, 219, 235, 238, 262, 333, 358–67, 417, 553; significance of their hostility, 83, 656–57; instances of their effective hostility, 258, 295, 321, 355, 358, 359, 369–70, 417, 551–52

NOTE ON THE AUTHOR

Archer Jones is profesor emeritus of history and a former dean at North Dakota State University. He is the author of *Confederate Strategy from Shiloh to Vicksburg* and joint author of *Politics of Command: Factions and Ideas in Confederate Strategy*, *How the North Won: A Military History of the Civil War*, and *Why the South Lost the Civil War*. He has served as Morrison Professor of History at the U.S. Army Command and General Staff College, member of the Department of the Army Historical Advisory Committee, and trustee of the American Military Institute.